second edition

COGNITIVE PSYCHOLOGY

Ken Gilhooly, Fiona Lyddy, Frank Pollick and Sandra Buratti

second edition

COGNITIVE PSYCHOLOGY

Ken Gilhooly, Fiona Lyddy, Frank Pollick and Sandra Buratti

London Boston Burr Ridge, IL Dubuque, IA Madison, WI New York San Francisco
St. Louis Bangkok Bogotá Caracas Kuala Lumpur Lisbon Madrid Mexico City
Milan Montreal New Delhi Santiago Seoul Singapore Sydney Taipei Toronto

Cognitive Psychology, Second Edition
Ken Gilhooly, Fiona Lyddy, Frank Pollick and Sandra Buratti
ISBN-13 9781526848277
ISBN-10 1526848279

Published by McGraw Hill
338 Euston Road, 8th Floor
London
NW1 3BH
Telephone: +44 (0) 203 429 3400
Website: www.mheducation.co.uk

British Library Cataloguing in Publication Data
A catalogue record for this book is available from the British Library

Library of Congress Cataloguing in Publication Data
The Library of Congress data for this book has been applied for from the Library of Congress

Portfolio Managers: Rosie Churchill and Isabel Berwick
Content Developer: Georgia Martin
Production Manager, EMEA: Ben King
Marketing Manager: Vee Suchak

Text design by Kamae Design
Cover design by Adam Renvoize
Printed and bound in Great Britain by Ashford Colour Press

First edition published in 2014 by McGraw-Hill Education

Published by McGraw Hill (UK) Limited, an imprint of McGraw Hill, 1325 Avenue of the Americas, 5th Floor, New York, NY 10019. Copyright © 2022 by McGraw Hill (UK) Limited. All rights reserved. No part of this publication may be reproduced or distributed in any form or by any means, or stored in a database or retrieval system, without the prior written consent of McGraw Hill (UK), including, but not limited to, in any network or other electronic storage or transmission, or broadcast for distance learning.

Fictitious names of companies, products, people, characters and/or data that may be used herein (in case studies or in examples) are not intended to represent any real individual, company, product or event.

ISBN-13 9781526848277
ISBN-10 1526848279
eISBN-13 9781526848284
eISBN-10 1526848287

© 2022. Exclusive rights by McGraw Hill for manufacture and export. This book cannot be re-exported from the country to which it is sold by McGraw Hill.

Dedications

To Mary

KG

With love to Laura and Josh

FP

With love to my son Gabriel and my husband Johan

SB

Brief Table of Contents

	Preface	xi
	About the authors	xiii
	Acknowledgements	xiv
	Guided tour	xv
1	Introduction	2
2	Perception	34
3	Motor Cognition	82
4	Attention	114
5	Consciousness	150
6	Sensory, Short-term and Working Memory	176
7	Long-term Memory	218
8	Learning and Forgetting	258
9	Concepts and Imagery	294
10	Language Production	324
11	Language Comprehension	374
12	Problem Solving	422
13	Decision Making	466
14	Reasoning	508
15	Cognition and Emotion	548
	Glossary	585
	References	594
	Name Index	644
	Subject Index	658

Detailed Table of Contents

Preface xi
About the authors xiii
Acknowledgements xiv
Guided tour xv

Chapter 1: Introduction 2
Preview Questions 3
What Is Cognitive Psychology? 4
   Box 1.1 Practical Application: The UK postcode and cognitive psychology 4
This Book 5
History and Approaches 6
   Box 1.2 Practical Application: How to train your memory 6
   Associationism 8
   Introspectionism 8
   Box 1.3 Research Close Up: Is this a dream? Experience sampling of qualities of waking and dreaming thoughts 10
   Behaviourism 11
   Box 1.4 Research Close Up: Cognitive maps 12
   Information Processing: The Cognitive Revolution 14
Cognitive Neuroscience 18
   Brain Basics 18
   Box 1.5 When Things Go Wrong: Using neuroscientific methods to detect awareness in 'vegetative states' 29
Summary 31
Review Questions 32
Discussion Questions 32
Further Reading 32

Chapter 2: Perception 34
Preview Questions 35
Introduction 36
   Box 2.1 Practical Application: Cognitive robotics and human–robot interaction 37
Fundamental Concepts
   From Physical World to Perceptual Representation 38
   Principles and Theories of Perception 39
   The Body and Perception 43
Human Perceptual Systems 44
   Visual System 46
   Box 2.2 Research Close Up: Discovery of feature detectors in primary visual cortex 49
   Auditory System 51
   Box 2.3 Practical Application: Cochlear implants 54
   Somatoperception System 55
   Multisensory Integration 57
   Box 2.4 When Things Go Wrong: Motion sickness and cybersickness 59
   Box 2.5 Practical Application: Multisensory warning signals for handover between autonomous and manual driving 60
Recognition 62
   Objects 63
   Scenes 69
   Events 71
Social Perception 72
   Box 2.6 When Things Go Wrong: Capgras syndrome 73
   Faces 73
   Box 2.7 Practical Application: Forensics – eyewitness testimony and super recognizers 76
   Voices 78
   Biological Motion 78
Summary 80
Review Questions 81
Discussion Questions 81
Further Reading 81

Chapter 3: Motor Cognition 82
Preview Questions 83
Introduction 84
Motor Control 84
   Box 3.1 Practical Application: Designing machines to help us move 85
   Theories of Movement Planning 86
   Box 3.2 Research Close Up: Tit-for-tat and force escalation 90
Producing Complex Actions 93
   Action Sequences 93
   Hierarchical Models of Action Production 94
   Brain Damage and Action Production 97
   Box 3.3 Practical Application: Cognitive rehabilitation for apraxia and action disorganization syndrome 99
Action Representation and Perception 100
   Theories of Action Representation 100
   Box 3.4 Research Close Up: Using dance expertise to study action representation 105
   Embodied Cognition 107
   Agency 110
   Box 3.5 When Things Go Wrong: Alien hand syndrome 111
Summary 112
Review Questions 112
Discussion Questions 113
Further Reading 113

Chapter 4: Attention 114
Preview Questions 115
Introduction 116
   Box 4.1 Practical Application: Robot attention 116
A Taxonomy of Attention 118
The Attention System of the Human Brain 119
Theories of Attention 120
   Filter Theory 121
   Resource Theory 122
   Evaluation 126
   Box 4.2 Practical Application: Video game play in enhancing cognition and attention 127
Visual Attention: Search, Inhibition of Return and Attentional Blink 128
   Box 4.3 When Things Go Wrong: Errors in the interpretation of medical images 129
   Box 4.4 Research Close Up: Using the attentional blink to examine emotion perception 134
Attentional Mechanisms in Perception and Working Memory 137
   Box 4.5 Research Close Up: Using a dual task to examine attention and working memory 140
Attentional Mechanisms in Controlling Actions 142

Failures of Attention	143
Box 4.6 Practical Application: Attention and continuity editing in movies	145
Box 4.7 When Things Go Wrong: Attention, misdirection and magic	146
Summary	148
Review Questions	149
Discussion Questions	149
Further Reading	149
Answer to Chapter Problem	149

Chapter 5: Consciousness — 150

Preview Questions	151
Introduction	152
Box 5.1 When Things Go Wrong: Sleepwalking and the law	154
Functions of Consciousness	155
Self-Awareness and Integration	155
Box 5.2 Practical Application: The effects of general anaesthesia on consciousness	156
The Case Against Consciousness	157
Unconscious Processing	157
Box 5.3 Research Close Up: Promoting healthy eating with supraliminal primes	159
Consciousness and the Brain	160
Neuropsychology	161
Neural Correlates of Consciousness (NCC)	162
Global Workspace Approaches	162
Box 5.4 Research Close Up: Consciousness and brain networks	163
Attention and Consciousness	167
Agency, Volition and Consciousness	168
Box 5.5 When Things Go Wrong: Out-of-body experience	171
Metacognition and Higher-Order Theories of Consciousness	172
Summary	174
Review Questions	174
Discussion Questions	175
Further Reading	175

Chapter 6: Sensory, Short-term and Working Memory — 176

Preview Questions	177
Introduction	178
Sensory Memory	179
Iconic Memory	180
Box 6.1 When Things Go Wrong: Synaesthesia and sensory memory	182
Echoic Memory	184
Haptic and Tactile Memory	186
Short-term Memory	187
A Double Dissociation of Function?	190
Box 6.2 Practical Application: Cognitive lockup – working memory, attention and human error	192
Working Memory	194
Box 6.3 Practical Application: Fatal distraction? Working memory and driving performance	196
Baddeley's Working Memory Model	197
Box 6.4 Practical Application: Understanding the effects of background noise	201
Box 6.5 Research Close Up: Working memory and mind wandering	207
Box 6.6 When Things Go Wrong: Case E.V.R.	211
Box 6.7 Research Close Up: Self-efficacy and working memory	214
Summary	216
Review Questions	217
Discussion Questions	217
Further Reading	217

Chapter 7: Long-Term Memory — 218

Preview Questions	219
Introduction	220
Box 7.1 When Things Go Wrong: The case of H.M.	220
Memory and Amnesia	223
The Structure of LTM	226
Multiple Memory Systems Model	226
Non-Declarative Memory	228
Skill Learning	229
Habit Learning	229
Repetition Priming	230
Declarative Memory	232
Episodic Memory	232
Box 7.2 Research Close Up: The role of schemas in memory	233
Prospective Memory and Imagining Future Events	237
Box 7.3 Practical Application: Improving prospective memory	238
Box 7.4 Research Close Up: Does a prospective memory deficit underlie checking compulsions?	239
Autobiographical Memory	241
Box 7.5 Research Close Up: Remembering traumatic events – does perspective matter?	242
Box 7.6 When Things Go Wrong: Experiencing involuntary traumatic recollections – suffering from PTSD	244
Box 7.7 Research Close Up: Reasons for withdrawing beliefs in autobiographical memories	247
Semantic Memory	249
Box 7.8 Research Close Up: Do we know what we don't know?	250
Box 7.9 Practical Application: Measuring everyday memory	254
Summary	256
Review Questions	257
Discussion Questions	257
Further Reading	257

Chapter 8: Learning and Forgetting — 258

Preview Questions	259
Introduction	260
Learning: Encoding, Storage and Retrieval	261
Levels of Processing	261
Box 8.1 Research Close Up: Levels of processing	261
Mnemonics	263
Box 8.2 Practical Application: Exceptionally good memories – nature or nurture?	264
Encoding Specificity	266
Context-dependent Retrieval	266
Spaced Versus Massed Trials	267
Forgetting	268
Interference	269
Decay and Consolidation	271
Box 8.3 Research Close Up: Wakeful rest improves long-term memory	272
Box 8.4 When Things Go Wrong: Consolidation, retroactive interference and amnesia	278
The Reconsolidation of Memories	279
Functional Approaches to Forgetting	280
Box 8.5 When Things Go Wrong: The recovered memories controversy	282
Everyday/Real-world Memory	283
Flashbulb Memories	284
Eyewitness Testimony	285
Box 8.6 Practical Application: The cognitive interview	287

Effective Studying	288
Box 8.7 Research Close Up: Does drawing facilitate the learning of terms and their definitions?	290
Summary	**291**
Review Questions	**292**
Discussion Questions	**293**
Further Reading	**293**

Chapter 9: Concepts and Imagery — 294

Preview Questions	**295**
Introduction	**296**
Theories of Conceptual Representation	**296**
Definitional Approach	297
Box 9.1 Practical Application: Cakes versus biscuits	297
Prototype Approaches	299
Box 9.2 Practical Application: Goal-derived ad hoc categories and consumer goods	302
Exemplar-based Approaches	303
Theory/Knowledge-based Approaches	304
Essentialism	305
Box 9.3 When Things Go Wrong: Category-specific deficits and pathologies	306
Grounded Representations Versus Amodal Representations	307
Box 9.4 Research Close Up: Testing grounded theory of concepts using dual task methods in working memory for action words	310
Concepts Connected: Network Models	311
Concepts in the Brain: The Hub-and-Spoke Model	311
Imagery and Concepts	**312**
Imagery and Visuo-spatial Processing: Overlaps?	313
Image Scanning and Comparing	314
Box 9.5 Research Close Up: Mental rotation	315
Ambiguity of Images	318
Neuropsychology/Neuroscience of Imagery	319
Box 9.6 When Things Go Wrong: Spontaneous vivid imagery – Charles Bonnet syndrome	319
Summary	**321**
Review Questions	**323**
Discussion Questions	**323**
Further Reading	**323**

Chapter 10: Language Production — 324

Preview Questions	**325**
Introduction	**326**
Language and Cognition	**328**
Language and Communication	**330**
Language Universals	330
Box 10.1 Research Close Up: Symbolic communication in non-human animals – vervet monkey alarm calls	334
Components of Language	336
Speech Errors	**343**
Hesitation and Pauses	343
Box 10.2 Practical Application: Using speech cues to detect deception	344
Slips of the Tongue	346
The Tip-of-The-Tongue State	348
Box 10.3 Research Close Up: Proper name retrieval in youth and mid-life	349
Theories of Speech Production	**350**
Modular Theories of Speech Production	351
Interactive Theories of Speech Production	355
Neuroscience of Language Production	**357**
Lateralization of Function	357
Box 10.4 When Things Go Wrong: The split brain	359
The Left Hemisphere and Language	**360**
Box 10.5 When Things Go Wrong: Use of verbal fluency tasks in the clinical setting	361

Evidence from the Typical Population	363
Evidence From Aphasia	364
Box 10.6 Practical Application: Should lecture notes be typed or handwritten?	370
Summary	**372**
Review Questions	**372**
Discussion Questions	**372**
Further Reading	**373**

Chapter 11: Language Comprehension — 374

Preview Questions	**375**
Introduction	**376**
Understanding Speech	**377**
Invariance	378
Segmentation of Speech	379
Cues to Word Boundaries	381
Slips of the Ear	382
Categorical Perception	383
The Right Ear Advantage for Speech Sounds	385
Box 11.1 When Things Go Wrong: Language comprehension in aphasia	386
Top-down Influences: The Role of Context	**387**
Box 11.2 Practical Application: The effect of leading questions on memory	388
Visual Cues: The Mcgurk Effect	390
Models of Speech Perception	**391**
The Cohort Model	391
Trace	393
Understanding Words and Sentences	**395**
Lexical Access	395
Box 11.3 Practical Application: Language ambiguity and accident prevention	399
Syntax and Semantics	400
The Brain and Language Comprehension	**403**
Neuropsychology of Speech Comprehension	403
Reading	**404**
Writing Systems	405
Box 11.4 When Things Go Wrong: Cross-language manifestation of dyslexia	407
Context Effects on Visual Word Recognition	410
Box 11.5 Research Close Up: The Stroop effect	411
Eye Movements	412
Box 11.6 Research Close Up: Reading sentences containing emoji	413
The Dual Route Model of Reading	415
Neuropsychology of Reading	416
Electrophysiological Data	417
Summary	**419**
Review Questions	**419**
Discussion Questions	**419**
Further Reading	**420**

Chapter 12: Problem Solving — 422

Preview Questions	**423**
Introduction	**424**
Problems and Problem Types	**424**
Brief History and Background	**425**
Gestalt Approach	426
Box 12.1 Practical Application: Life-or-death problem solving	426
Information Processing Approach	429
Box 12.2 Research Close Up: Travelling salesperson problems	436
Box 12.3 When Things Go Wrong: Right prefrontal cortex damage and real-world planning	438
Insight Revisited	**439**
Comparing Insight and Non-Insight Problem Solving	440
Information Processing Theories of Insight	443

    Box 12.4 Research Close Up: It's magic!
Use of magic tricks to generate insight — 446
Knowledge-rich (or Expert) Problem Solving — **448**
  Expertise Acquisition — 448
  Nature of Expertise — 450
Creative Problem Solving — **452**
  Personal Accounts — 453
  Wallas's Stage Analysis — 454
  Incubation Research — 454
  Information Processing Theory of Creative Processes — 456
  Increasing Idea Production — 457
    Box 12.5 Practical Application: The Generic Parts Technique — 460
    Box 12.6 When Things Go Wrong: Psychopathology and creativity — 461
Summary — **462**
Review Questions — **463**
Discussion Questions — **463**
Further Reading — **463**
Answers to Chapter Problems — **464**

Chapter 13: Decision Making — 466

Preview Questions — **467**
Introduction — **468**
Expected Value Theory — **469**
Utility and Prospect Theory — **471**
    Box 13.1 When Things Go Wrong: 'Bad things come to those who do not wait . . .' — 474
Subjective Probability and Prospect Theory — **475**
  Framing and Prospect Theory — 476
Making Probability Judgements — **477**
  Availability — 478
  Representativeness — 479
  Base Rates — 482
Decision Processes for Multi-attribute Alternatives — **483**
  Multi-Attribute Utility Theory — 483
  Elimination by Aspects — 484
  Satisficing — 484
  Testing Multi-Attribute Decision Models — 484
Two-system Approaches to Decision Making — **487**
    Box 13.2 Practical Application: Two system theory and 'nudge' — 488
    Box 13.3 Research Close Up: Unconscious thought effect on decisions — 490
Fast-and-Frugal Heuristics: The Adaptive Toolbox — **491**
  Heuristics and Consequentialism — 493
    Box 13.4 Practical Application: Resisting effective but forced policies — 496
    Box 13.5 Research Close Up: Your morals depend on language — 498
Naturalistic Decision Making — **499**
  Real-Life Choices — 500
    Box 13.6 Practical Application: Applying Social Judgement Theory methods to the detection of financial abuse of elderly people — 502
Neuroscience Approaches to Decision Making — **504**
Summary — **506**
Review Questions — **507**
Discussion Questions — **507**
Further Reading — **507**

Chapter 14: Reasoning — 508

Preview Questions — **509**
Introduction — **510**
Deductive Reasoning — **511**
  Propositional Reasoning — 511
    Box 14.1 When Things Go Wrong: The case of mental illness and reasoning — 517
  Syllogistic Reasoning — 518
    Box 14.2 Research Close Up: Reasoning and dyslexia — 525
    Box 14.3 Research Close Up: Do ideological beliefs affect reasoning? — 528
    Box 14.4 Practical Application: The psychological model of legal reasoning — 529
Inductive Reasoning: Testing and Generating Hypotheses — **530**
    Box 14.5 Practical Application: Training in reasoning – Lipman's *Philosophy for Children* programme — 531
  Testing Hypotheses: The Four-Card Selection Task — 532
  Generating and Testing Hypotheses — 540
    Box 14.6 Research Close Up: Does logical reasoning predict police recruits' abilities to generate investigative hypotheses? — 542
    Box 14.7 Practical Application: Real scientific research environments — 543
    Box 14.8 When Things Go Wrong: Catching the right perpetrator – the case of the Madrid bombings — 545
Summary — **546**
Review Questions — **547**
Discussion Questions — **547**
Further Reading — **547**
Answers to Chapter Problem — **547**

Chapter 15: Cognition and Emotion — 548

Preview Questions — **549**
Introduction — **550**
What is an Emotion? — **550**
    Box 15.1 When Things Go Wrong: Emotional processing after frontal lobe injury — 552
  Core Emotions — 555
    Box 15.2 When Things Go Wrong: Can those with psychopathic traits recognize emotion in facial expressions? — 555
    Box 15.3 Practical Application: Detecting deceit through microexpressions — 556
  The 'Core' of Emotion — 558
Theories of Emotion and Cognition — **560**
  Early Theories and their Influence — 561
  Two-Factor Theory — 564
  Affective-Primacy: Zajonc's Theory — 565
  Cognitive Primacy: Lazarus's Theory — 567
    Box 15.4 Research Close Up: When and why we try to regulate our emotions during daily life — 568
  The Theory of Constructed Emotions — 570
The Influence of Affect on Cognition — **570**
  Affect and Attention — 571
  Affect and Perception — 572
  Affect and Memory — 573
    Box 15.5 Practical Application: Cognitive behavioural therapy for depression — 577
  Affect and Decision Making — 579
    Box 15.6 Research Close Up: Do graphic warning labels influence risk perception and quit intentions in smokers? — 580
    Box 15.7 When Things Go Wrong: Brain damage and decision making – the role of 'somatic markers' and interoception — 582
Summary — **583**
Review Questions — **584**
Discussion Questions — **584**
Further Reading — **584**

Glossary — 585
References — 594
Name Index — 644
Subject Index — 658

Preface

During a typical day we all handle a vast amount of information, mostly smoothly and effortlessly. In fact, the running of our complex technological societies depends on the reliable way in which people doing safety-critical jobs, such as air traffic controllers, nuclear power workers, surgeons and train drivers, to name a few, correctly perceive situations and efficiently decide on suitable actions. Most of the time, the cognitive processes underlying complex behaviours, in both safety-critical and less hazardous conditions, run very effectively. However, sometimes, things do go wrong, as when we misperceive the outside world, fail to notice important pieces of information, forget previous correct representations of what has happened, make faulty predictions about what will happen next or make poor decisions, even when all the needed information is in front of us. As the good or bad consequences of our behaviour are dependent on accurately dealing with information, it is important to understand not only how we (mostly) do so, but also how errors can arise. This is the subject matter of cognitive psychology – one of the most dynamic areas of psychology.

Much research in cognitive psychology is laboratory based and uses pared-down situations to uncover basic processes, such as using word lists in carefully controlled studies to examine whether forgetting involves simple decaying away of memories or whether it is more a matter of later memories interfering with earlier memories and thus making them hard to remember. The use of laboratory situations in studying cognition can make it seem lacking connection with the real world. This book aims to overcome that apparent gap between real life and laboratory studies by providing an accessible account of the key cognitive topics through not only theory and pure research, but also through applications. Our approach is that relevance to the real world can make all the difference in understanding something, and engaging examples will bring the subject to life.

As will become apparent to readers, cognitive psychology is relatively young as a scientific endeavour. There is not always agreement on how each process should be understood or what methods of investigation are best. This is in the nature of a developing science but we believe that the bases for assessing explanations, in terms of clarity, logic and evidence, emerge and become clear as we progress through the chapters.

We've done our best to ensure that this text offers a student-friendly, integrated and up-to-date introduction to cognition. Naturally, the historical progression of theories and research is included as this is the basis for modern research, but the newer contributions of information processing approaches and cognitive neuroscience are also integrated throughout to provide a multidisciplinary approach.

The order of the chapters reflects the flow of information through the mind and thus, after a general introduction (Chapter 1), we deal with topics in the following order: perception (Chapter 2, motor cognition (Chapter 3), attention (Chapter 4), consciousness (Chapter 5), sensory, short-term and working memory (Chapter 6) and long-term memory (Chapter 7), learning and forgetting (Chapter 8), concepts and imagery (Chapter 9), language production and comprehension (Chapters 10 and 11), problem solving (Chapter 12), decision making (Chapter 13), reasoning (Chapter 14), and cognition and emotion (Chapter 15). This sequence of topics covers all the key areas of cognition and, for UK readers, has the benefit of meeting the British Psychological Society (BPS) requirements for cognitive psychology teaching in BPS-accredited Psychology degrees in the UK.

PEDAGOGY

A key component of the content is the integration of well-structured pedagogic features throughout each chapter, with a focus on research and application.

Preview and Review Questions – Each chapter opens with a set of preview questions highlighting the key coverage for that chapter and intended as a more interactive version of learning objectives. The review questions at the end of each chapter link back to these and challenge student understanding, application and evaluation.

Research Close Ups – Going back to real research is always important to understand methodology and theories. In these features, we take notable experiments that are relevant to the topics and provide an overview of the original research in a format and style similar to real papers. This helps to provide an emphasis on methodology and its importance to the subject, but also familiarizes students with reading real research.

Practical Applications – Whilst pure research is key to the development of the field, applications of key research and theories can help to provide relevance and context for topics. Cognitive psychology is crucial for our understanding of how we perceive, interpret and act upon the world; it has real benefit to the world at large and research doesn't simply stop in the lab. Discoveries can be applied in the real world to help us improve the way things work. For example, we can use research on attention and memory to determine whether it is safe to drive while using a mobile phone.

When Things Go Wrong – A lot of what we know about the mind comes not from research into how things work well but into investigation of what happens when things go wrong. This has been a key approach in cognitive psychology and one that continues to provide insight through behavioural and brain imaging studies. These features focus on what we have learned about a topic by considering things that have gone wrong and what this tells us about the mind. For example, in language we discuss loss of language abilities (aphasia) brought about by brain damage and how studies of aphasia help to identify the different functions and brain areas involved in speech production.

AND FINALLY...

We hope that this book will stimulate your curiosity about the cognitive workings of the mind and that some of you may go on to contribute to the field yourselves as cognitive psychologists of the future!

Ken Gilhooly, Fiona Lyddy, Frank Pollick and Sandra Buratti

About the authors

PROFESSOR KEN GILHOOLY is based at the University of Hertfordshire, where he is Emeritus Professor of Psychology. Having completed undergraduate studies at the University of Edinburgh and postgraduate studies at the University of Stirling, he went on to work at the University of Aberdeen before taking a Chair at Brunel University London, followed by another at University of the West of Scotland. Ken then moved to a Chair at Hertfordshire in 2004. He has served as the Chair of the Cognitive Section of the British Psychological Society (BPS) and continues to serve on a number of Research Council panels and boards. He is a Fellow of the BPS and the Academy of Social Sciences. Ken's research has focused on thinking and problem solving, and he has published numerous research papers in this area and held a number of Research Council and major charity grants.

PROFESSOR FIONA LYDDY is based at Maynooth University. She completed her undergraduate and postgraduate studies at University College Cork and lectured at University College Cork and University of Wales Institute Cardiff before joining Maynooth University in 2001. She has served as Head of the Department of Psychology and Dean of the Faculty of Science and Engineering at Maynooth University. She is a Fellow of the Psychological Society of Ireland and was Founding Chair of the Psychological Society of Ireland's Division of Teachers and Researchers in Psychology. Her research focuses on language and communication.

PROFESSOR FRANK POLLICK is a professor at the University of Glasgow. He completed undergraduate studies in Physics and Biology at MIT, and master's studies in Biomedical Engineering at Case Western Reserve University before obtaining his PhD in Cognitive Sciences from the University of California, Irvine. He then moved to Kyoto, Japan, where he worked at the Advanced Telecommunication Research Institute (ATR) as a researcher in the Human Information Processing laboratory. Since 1997 he has been at the University of Glasgow.

Dr SANDRA BURATTI is a senior lecturer in Psychology and serves as the Deputy Head of the Department of Psychology at the University of Gothenburg, Sweden. She is also a licensed clinical psychologist who has worked in primary care settings. Sandra completed her undergraduate and master's studies at the University of Lund, Sweden. She obtained her PhD from the University of Gothenburg. Her research focuses on judgement and decision making, metacognition and memory.

Acknowledgements

AUTHOR ACKNOWLEDGEMENTS

First, we would like to thank our students, whose curiosity into how the mind works, provides a constant inspiration for developing these materials. We would also like to thank the anonymous reviewers for their constructive comments throughout the process, which have helped to shape our writing.

We are grateful to colleagues at the University of Hertfordshire, Maynooth University, the University of Glasgow, and the University of Gothenburg for providing a supportive intellectual environment to work on this project. Helpful advice from Karl Ask, Pär Bjälkebring, Derek Brown, Mike Burton, Julia Christensen, Sang Chul Chong, Aurelio Cortese, Frank Durgin, Peter Hampson, Stefan Hansen, Mitsuo Kawato, Jonathan Keefe, Keith Laws, Scott Love, Pascal Mamassian, Mike Page, Richard Roche, Anne Ryan, Gert van Tonder, Stefan Winblad, and Stefan Vogt has been greatly appreciated.

Finally, great thanks go to Alice Aldous, Isabel Berwick, Rosie Churchill, Ben King and Georgia Martin at McGraw-Hill, whose insight and constructive criticism helped to guide this project.

PUBLISHER'S ACKNOWLEDGEMENTS

Our thanks go to the following reviewers for their comments at various stages in the text's development:

Magnus Blystad, Institute of Behavioral Science	Stuart McGregor, University of South Wales
Michael Capalbo, Maastricht University	Gerry Markopoulos, Bath Spa
Neil Dagnall, MMU	Aspa Paltoglou, MMU
Søren Staugaard, Aarhus University	Liam Cross, Buckingham University

We would like to thank Roy de Kleijn for his work on the Instructor Manuals, Seminar Materials and PowerPoints. Our continued thanks goes to Eamon Fulcher for his contributions to the digital materials, as well as the subject matter experts who have updated Connect materials for the new edition.

We would also like to thank Lynn Brown and Ben King for their work on the text during production.

Finally, we would like to thank the following people for permission to reproduce materials:

APA	Dirk Bernhardt-Walther
Elsevier	Instituto Italiano di Tecnologia
Laura Taverna	Mike Burton

Every effort has been made to trace and acknowledge ownership of copyright and to clear permission for material reproduced in this book. The publishers will be pleased to make suitable arrangements to clear permission with any copyright holders whom it has not been possible to contact.

Guided tour

Preview Questions

1. What is the function of perception?
2. Are there general principles of perception across the different senses?
3. How is our physical body involved in perception?
4. How is perceptual information integrated across our different senses?
5. How do we recognize objects and why is general object recognition difficult to achieve?
6. Our social interactions are guided by what perceptual information?

Preview Questions Linked to the end of chapter Review Questions, these questions provide clear learning objectives to guide you through each chapter.

Perception our sensory experience of the world.

Perception is the remarkable set of processes that organize sensory experience into an understanding of our surrounding world. The study of perception gives us insight into how properties of the physical world are transformed into our mental world, and informs our understanding of behaviours like navigation and recogni... cated set of directions in a dimly lit a... cannot find your destination, it is pos... erly hear the directions, (2) did not s... incapable of understanding and exe... examines these first two points of he... understanding of what information ab...

Key Terms These are highlighted and defined in the relevant chapters, providing ease of reference. All definitions can also be found in the Glossary at the end of the book.

Chapter 1, pxx

The essential problem of perception is that the physical world is 'out there' and our mental world has its home base inside our head. To address this problem we will emphasize an information-processing approach that looks at how the senses provide information about the world and how this information is transformed into understanding (for an introduction to the information processing approach, see Chapter 1). A primary question is whether enough information comes in thr... rately and completely represent the physical world, and if not... to this question is 'no', for the reason that our sensory org... Dogs provide an illustration of this since they can hear in ra... However, there is a deeper information-processing issue kno...

Chapter links highlight topic connections in the book. Chapter and page number are provided in the margin for quick cross-referencing.

 Box 2.1 Practical Application: Cognitive robotics and human–robot interaction

In the past, the field of robotics was largely concerned with industrial robots confined to repetitive tasks in predictable environments. However, cognitive robotics (Vernon et al., 2010) and human–robot interaction (Goodrich & Schultz, 2007; Sheridan, 2016) are two new fields of robotics that are defining the move of robots from these restricted environments to everyday scenes. One basis for the advancement in robotics has been an explosion in the availability of high-performance sensors, actuators, computers and power systems, which make it possible to develop and control incre... cated mechanisms (Siciliano & Khatib, 2019). However, to realize the potential of t... needs to know how to make a system that can sense and adapt to its environment a...

Practical Application boxes bring research, theories and concepts to real-world, practical situations.

Box 2.2 Research Close Up: Discovery of feature detectors in primary visual cortex

Source: Hubel & Wiesel (1959).

INTRODUCTION

Although conducted more than 50 years ago, the 1959 study by... fundamental advance in visual science that is still relevant toda... 2009). The body of work associated with this finding resulted in... Wiesel. Here, we will emphasize how this study gave a critical st... tures the visual system uses to represent incoming information.

Research Close Up boxes introduce you to the format of real research in cognitive psychology. Each box summarizes an important research paper, explaining the methods the authors used, the results they obtained and a discussion to help you think critically about the significance of the study.

Box 2.4 When Things Go Wrong: Motion sickness and cybersickness

Typically, the combination of sensory information aids our interpretation of the world by adding and corroborating different sources of information. However, this combination of the senses does not [go] smoothly. Ancient texts report motion sickness from those who would travel by sea and [...] report wave-like motion as a cause of the distress (Huppert et al., 2017). As travel technolog[y has diver]sified to include planes, trains and automobiles, motion sickness has remained a consiste[nt issue for] those affected (Zhang et al., 2016). In addition, with the recent rapid development of commercially available virtual reality (VR), it is now possible to get a variant of motion sickness, known as cybersickness (Rebenitsch & Owen, 2016) in the comfort of one's own home. The presumed cause of motion sickness and cybersickness, and common to both, is being present in a sensory environment where there is a mismatch between the sensory signals of vision and vestibular aspects of somatoperception

virtual realit[y...] a three-dime[nsional] environment [...] computer th[at is] presented t[o a user] typically thro[ugh] display equip[ment]

When Things Go Wrong boxes investigate what can happen when our brains don't function as we'd like, and what we can learn from this. With topics ranging from everyday occurrences to severe brain dysfunction, find out what these instances reveal about the mind.

Summary

Perception is an important topic in the study of cognition since it provides insight into the mechanisms that inform us about the external world. Although there is a vast literature on the detailed workings of perceptual capabilities, perception can be thought of as simply the early stages of an information processing system. The first section of this chapter described fundamental concepts in perception and pursued the view that perception can be described as information processing. A great b[enefit of this] approach is that it allows us to define concepts of perception that apply generally to man[y systems and] other organisms. The second section of the chapter examined human perceptual system[s as a special] case and provided examples of how perceptual systems are implemented in the human b[rain. We also] explored the relationship between brain and perception, and how damage to the brain alte[rs perception.]

The different perceptual systems of vision, audition and somatoperception were exam[ined and we] discussed how different perceptual inputs might optimally be combined to form a unita[ry percept of] objects and events. An important achievement of perception is our ability to recognize ob[jects...]

Chapter Summary

This briefly reviews and reinforces the main topics you will have covered in each chapter to ensure you have acquired a solid understanding of them.

Review Questions

1. What is perception used for, and how is it possible to compare perception in man and machine?
2. What properties are common to the processing of audio, video and touch information?
3. How does predictive coding change our understanding of bottom-up and top-down processing in the context of interpreting sensory information?
4. Contrast the differences between the modality appropriate hypothesis with the maxim[um likelihood] approach to multisensory processing.
5. What makes recognition a difficult problem to solve?
6. What types of social perception are common across different modes of perception?
7. If you were designing a perceptual system for a robot, how important would it be to take [into account] the physical properties of the robot?

Review Questions

Each chapter is followed by a range of questions to check your understanding of the material and challenge you to think critically.

Discussion Questions

1. What would be the advantages and disadvantages of defining rigid boundaries between sensation, perception and cognition?
2. What are the differences between perceiving objects and perceiving people?
3. Artificial deep neural networks can reach human-like performance on many tasks like [object recogni]tion. How can we exploit this capability to better understand human perception?

Discussion Questions

Each chapter concludes with a set of reflective questions to encourage discussion on topics raised in the chapter.

Further Reading

Bregman, A. S. (1990). *Auditory scene analysis: The perceptual organization of sound*. MIT Press.
Calvo, P., & Gomila, T. (Eds.). (2008). *Handbook of cognitive science: An embodied approach*. Elsevier Science.
Hoffman, D. (2019). *The case against reality: Why evolution hid the truth from our eyes*. W. W. Norton & Company.
Johnson, K., & Shiffrar, M. (Eds.). (2012). *People watching: Social, perceptual, and neurophysiological studies of body perception*. Oxford University Press.
Levitin, D. (2006). *This is your brain on music: Understanding [...]*
Marr, D. (1982). *Vision: A computational investigation into th[e human representation and processing of] visual information*. W. H. Freeman.
Palmer, S. E. (1999). *Vision science: Photons to phenomenology*[...]
Sacks, O. (2014). *The man who mistook his wife for a hat*. Picado[r...]

Further Reading

A selection of further reading suggestions are provided, which are designed to act as a springboard into further or more detailed study.

Transform learning with Connect®

Boost grades, stimulate engagement and deliver an amazing course

Connect® is an online platform that integrates the science of learning with award-winning adaptive technology, to offer students and teachers a more effective teaching and learning experience.

> Connect increases my students' knowledge and has made my teaching more effective.
>
> **University of Birmingham Business School, UK**

The Three Pillars of Connect®

Flexible and high quality content tailored to your course

Use a combination of your content with McGraw-Hill and OER resources to customise your course with the support of our dedicated academic and implementation consultants.

Detailed reporting and analytics

Monitor progress and improve efficiency with detailed Connect® reports. Students and teachers can use real-time performance measurement tools to monitor learning and focus on the gaps that require more attention.

Ease of set-up and continuous support

McGraw-Hill offers comprehensive service, support and training - face-to-face, online or over the phone, throughout every phase of working with us to ensure easy set-up and access to the platform.

Bring theory to life **within Connect®**

Students can **test and apply their knowledge** with our engaging excercises and activities within Connect®.

Discover the features on offer for your discipline on the next page!

Connect® for Psychology

We have a wide selection of activities on hand to help students gain valuable practice during their course. By applying what they have learned to real world scenarios, these exercises help test their knowledge and skills in preparation for their next steps in Psychology.

Application-Based Activities (ABAs)

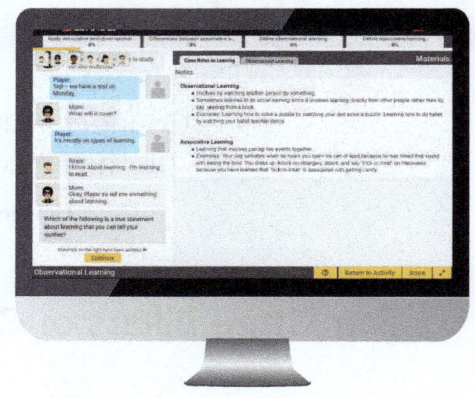

Provide students with valuable practice, using problem solving skills to apply their knowledge to realistic scenarios. Students progress from understanding basic concepts to using their knowledge to analyse complex scenarios and solve problems.

Each activity has been created to align with higher order thinking skills, from Bloom's Taxonomy to ensure students are developing from simple memorisation, to concept application. They are also categorised by difficulty to cater to each student's abilities.

Interactivities

Engage students with content through experiential activities. Students develop critical thinking skills and apply the concepts they have learned in these game like activities.

Videos and Concept Clips

Promote engagement and student understanding, offering content in a fresh format and reinforcing key concepts. They help students break down key themes and difficult concepts in psychology by using easy-to-understand analogies, visual cues, and colorful animation.

Power of Process

Moving students toward advanced critical thinking skills, Power of Process offers a hands-on tool for reviewing and analysing journal articles. Students are able to develop essential academic skills, such as understanding, analysing and synthesizing.

Smarter studying with

 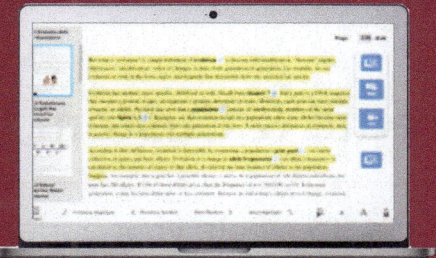

The **Smartbook 2.0®** tool integrated within Connect® maximises learning by helping students study more efficiently, highlighting the most important points in the chapter, asking verification questions and indicating additional resources.

More Personalised

Smartbook 2.0® constantly adapts to students' needs, creating a personalised learning experience.

More Productive

Smartbook 2.0® creates an extremely productive learning experience, focusing students' attention on the concepts they need to learn.

More Prepared

Smartbook 2.0® helps students prepare for lessons, allowing you to use class time more dynamically.

> I liked the idea of continuous assessment online as it helped me to keep track of student performance while it freed up my time spent marking and meant I could focus on my research.
>
> **Alejandra Ramos, Trinity College Dublin, Ireland**

The ReadAnywhere App

To help you study anywhere, anytime! Gain mobile freedom to access your eBook anywhere, even offline, on your smartphone or tablet.

You can:
- Read offline and data-free by downloading the entire text or only the chapters you need.
- Never lose an assignment, a note, or your place. ReadAnywhere includes the same functionality as the eBook offered in Connect® with auto-sync across both platforms.
- Start studying anytime, anywhere.

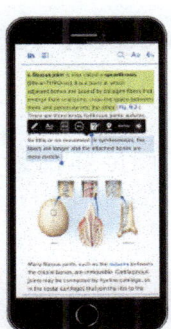

Available on:

Create & Custom Publishing

It's easy to create your perfect customised reader

At McGraw-Hill it's easy to create a bespoke reading resource for our students right from the comfort of your desk.

Using our tool Create you can browse and select material from our extensive library of texts and collections and if desired, you can even include your own materials, which can be organised in the order in which you'd like your students to work from them.

Available in both print and eBook format, you can offer your students a learning solution that works best for them, in addition you can add digital materials to go alongside your reader too.

What are the benefits of having a custom reader?

- You have one **tailor-made** learning resource
- **McGraw-Hill are here to support you** throughout your custom journey
- Students get **value for money**; they only need to purchase & read the required course material
- **Convenient** and students can easily find resources **all in one place**
- Students are **more prepared** for class

How do I Get Started?

1 **Find** and **Select** your content in **Create**

2 **Arrange** and **Integrate** your own content

3 **Personalise** your design and **Choose** the format

Learn more
https://www.mheducation.co.uk/higher-education/services/creating-custom-publishing

Contact the Team
marketing.emea@mheducation.com

Improve your Study, Research & Writing Skills

Clear and accessible guides on improving your reading, writing and researching skills. From undergraduate level to career researcher, we have a book to help you with your study and academic progression.

Our Study Skills books are packed with practical advice and tips that are easy to put into practice and will really improve the way you study.

- Develop your study skills
- Learn how to undertake a research project
- Enhance your academic writing and avoid plagiarism
- Learn effective ways to prep for exams
- Improve time management
- Increase your grades
- Get the job you want!

Special Offer!

As a valued customer, buy online and receive **20% off** any of our Study Skills books by entering the above promo code.

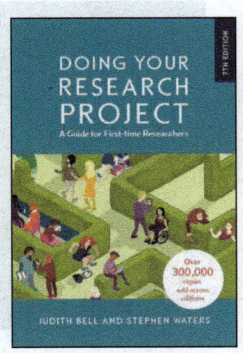

Learn more
https://www.mheducation.co.uk/open-university-press/study-skills

Contact the Team
marketing.emea@mheducation.com

INTRODUCTION

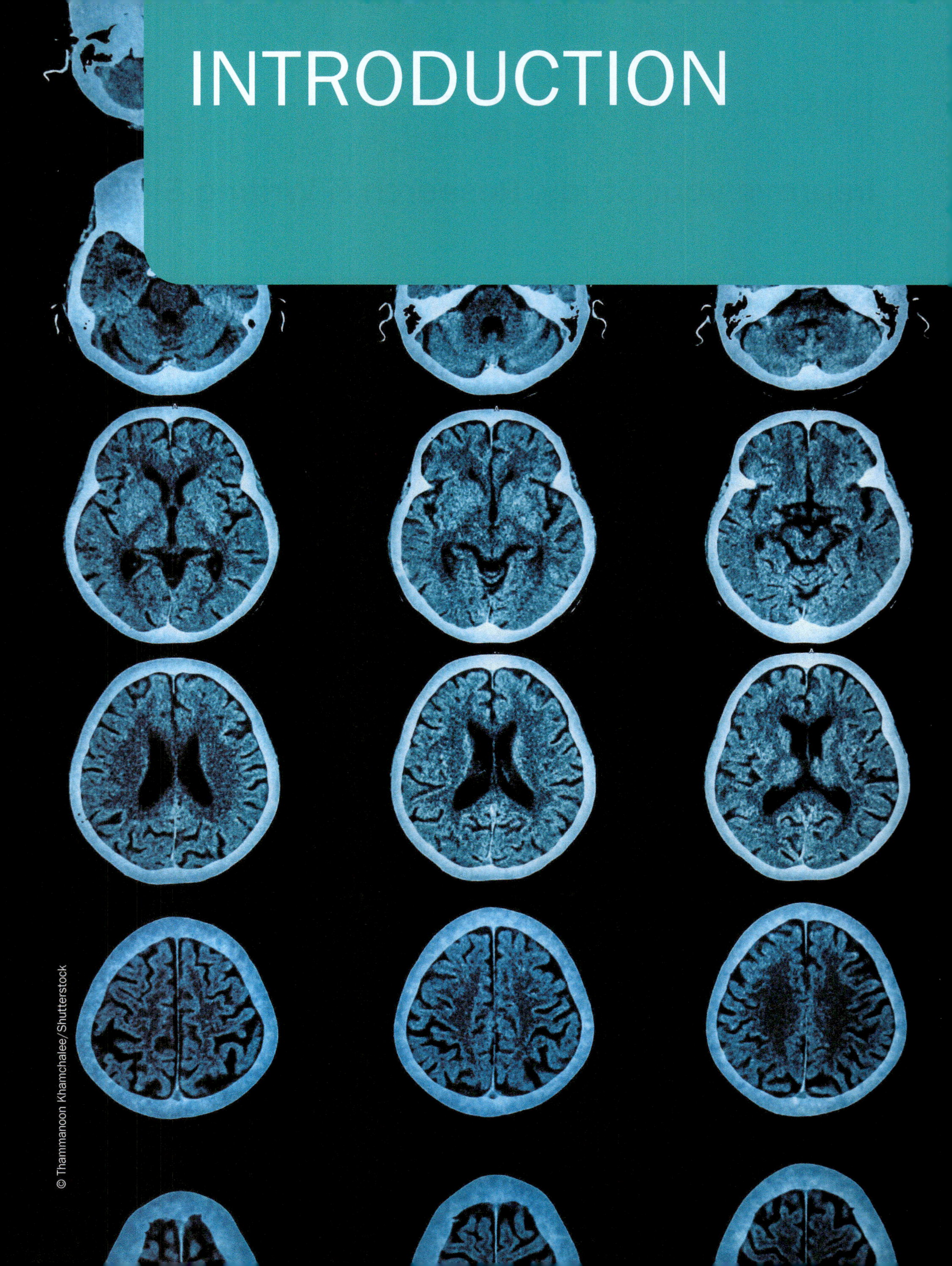

© Thammanoon Khamchalee/Shutterstock

1

PREVIEW QUESTIONS
WHAT IS COGNITIVE PSYCHOLOGY?
　　Box 1.1 **Practical Application:** The UK postcode and cognitive psychology
THIS BOOK
HISTORY AND APPROACHES
　　Box 1.2 **Practical Application:** How to train your memory
　ASSOCIATIONISM
　INTROSPECTIONISM
　　Box 1.3 **Research Close Up:** Is this a dream? Experience sampling of qualities of waking and dreaming thoughts
　BEHAVIOURISM
　　Box 1.4 **Research Close Up:** Cognitive maps
　INFORMATION PROCESSING: THE COGNITIVE REVOLUTION
COGNITIVE NEUROSCIENCE
　BRAIN BASICS
　　Box 1.5 **When Things Go Wrong:** Using neuroscientific methods to detect awareness in 'vegetative states'
SUMMARY
REVIEW QUESTIONS
DISCUSSION QUESTIONS
FURTHER READING

Preview Questions

1. What topic areas does cognitive psychology deal with?
2. What are the main approaches to cognitive psychology?
3. What is distinctive about the cognitive approach?
4. What can studies of brain injury tell us about how we think, remember and forget?
5. What can we learn from neuroimaging studies of brain function?
6. Is it really possible to communicate with 'locked in' vegetative-state patients via brain scans?

WHAT IS COGNITIVE PSYCHOLOGY?

Each day, we carry out a range of cognitive functions without great effort, allowing us to focus on matters of current importance. Think about an imaginary day you might experience as a student. On waking, you might look out of your window and see that it is raining and looks set to continue all day. This representation of the world can be later retrieved from memory and used to decide whether to carry an umbrella or not when you go out. You may then remember that you have a statistics tutorial at noon and decide to solve problems from the set book before going out. You begin attending to the first problem. You read the set question carefully but do not understand it and go back to your lecture notes for an explanation. Alternatively, you may forget that you have a statistics tutorial and reason that it would be best to focus on your essay due tomorrow. As the day goes on you are constantly dealing with information from many sources, from memory, and also from the environment, from other people via speech and reading and from assorted media. How do you deal with all this information?

> **Cognitive psychology**
> the scientific study of how people and animals process information.

Cognitive psychology seeks to answer that broad question and is the study of how humans (and other animals):

- acquire information
- store information in memory
- retrieve information
- work with information to reach goals.

> **Mental representations**
> inner representations such as an image or a verbal concept of some external reality.

In all these cases, we are dealing with internal or **mental representations**. How such representations are formed, stored and used is the essential business of cognitive psychology.

As an example of how cognitive psychology can be applied for practical purposes see Box 1.1 where we discuss cognitive aspects of designing a user-friendly system for coding postal addresses.

 Box 1.1 Practical Application: The UK postcode and cognitive psychology

Source: Baddeley (2019).

If you are a resident in the UK you will almost certainly know the postcode attached to your street address, which is needed to ensure correct delivery of letters and packets by post. You may well know other postcodes, such as SW1A 1AA (Buckingham Palace) or W1A 1AA (BBC Broadcasting House). Note that the codes are a mixture of letters and numbers – that is, an alphanumeric system. Curiously, the UK is one of only seven postal coding systems in the world that uses an alphanumeric system. The US zip code system, for example, is purely numeric and involves nine digits (e.g., 10011 4211).

Cognitive psychology played a part in determining whether the UK postcode was purely numeric or alphanumeric. As the leading memory researcher Alan Baddeley, who was involved in the design of the postcode in the 1950s, has explained (Baddeley, 2019), the limits of human memory were taken into account in deciding on the system. Immediate memory span, or the number of items a person can recall immediately after a brief exposure, is about six or seven items and so the length of the code was restricted to six. Further research showed that a mixture of letters and numbers was more easily recalled than just numbers or letters alone. Additionally, the use of initial letters relating to the location of the address made them more memorable. So, addresses in York have postcodes beginning YO, in

Glasgow beginning G, and so on. Additional research also indicated that the string was best remembered if the letters and numbers were in a mixed pattern – 'letter letter number number letter letter'.

Overall, the UK postcode was designed to be user friendly as well as versatile enough to allow the large number of possible codes needed for automated sorting and delivery purposes. Unsurprisingly perhaps, it was found in 2016 that 92 per cent of Britons reported that their postcode was easier to remember than a range of personal information, such as debit card PIN numbers or online banking passwords.

THIS BOOK

This textbook examines aspects of how representations are formed, retained and used, and covers topics such as perception and attention (Chapters 2 and 4), consciousness (Chapter 5), short-term (Chapter 6) and long-term memory (Chapter 7), learning and forgetting (Chapter 8), concepts and imagery (Chapter 9), complex motor skills (Chapter 3), problem solving (Chapter 12), decision making (Chapter 13), reasoning (Chapter 14), language understanding and production (Chapters 10 and 11), and emotional cognition (Chapter 15). To sum up: this book is about the systematic, scientific study of the cognitive processes that handle mental representations.

The order of topics in this book reflects the flow of information through the mind. Information is taken in through perceiving what is attended to, and is stored initially in short-term or working memory. Then, selected items are retained in long-term memory through learning processes and form knowledge that can be represented in a variety of ways. Later, stored information may be retrieved if it has been retained, or it may turn out to have been forgotten. Perceived and recalled information shapes skilled actions on the environment and enters into problem solving, reasoning and decision processes. Information can be shared with others via language and frequently involves an emotional aspect.

As will become apparent, cognitive psychology is relatively young as a scientific endeavour. There is not always agreement on how each process should be understood or what methods of investigation are best. This is in the nature of a developing science and we hope that the bases for assessing explanations, in terms of clarity, logic and evidence, will emerge and become clear as we progress through the chapters.

In the remainder of this introductory chapter, we will set out briefly the historical context for the discipline. Today's cognitive psychology deals with questions that have surely been raised since before written history began, when people first began to wonder about questions such as:

- Why do we sometimes remember things very clearly and sometimes not?
- Why do we remember faces better than names?
- Why do we find some decisions and problems easy and others hard?
- Why do our senses sometimes deceive us (e.g., when we fall for visual illusions)?

First, we will review the main historical approaches, which are those of the eighteenth-century associationist philosophers, the nineteenth-century introspectionists, the early twentieth-century behaviourists and the still dominant mid-twentieth and early twenty-first-century information processing theorists.

Finally, in this chapter, we also introduce the increasingly prominent neuroscientific approach to understanding cognition.

HISTORY AND APPROACHES

Wondering about cognition leads to theorizing about the processes involved, and such theorizing started at least as far back as the Greek philosophers, Plato and Aristotle, more than two and a half thousand years ago (Murray, 1988). Plato compared memory for information to writing on a wax tablet, which if not rubbed smooth by time could be read from, as in recall. Forgetting was the equivalent of the wax tablet becoming illegible. Alternatively, he suggested that memory was like an aviary in which the birds flying about correspond to specific memories, and remembering was like catching a particular bird. Often, we recall a memory that is nearly right, but not quite, just as we might grab a nearby bird but miss the target bird among a flock of birds flying in an aviary.

The ancient world was much concerned with the art of rhetoric (that is, persuasive speaking) and during that time a very practical way of remembering long lists of facts or points to make in a speech was developed. This is known as the method of loci (or places) by which vivid images are formed linking the objects to be remembered to a sequence of familiar places such as rooms in your house. See Box 1.2 and Chapter 8 for more on **mnemonics** or methods of boosting memory. The method of loci and variations are still used today. For example, a student learning a timeline of scientific discoveries, might picture a path through their house from their front door to the bedroom, with a sequence of images recreating the list. The student might visualize planets revolving around the sun at the front door (Copernican Heliocentric Theory), then an apple falling from a tree on their stairs (Universal Law of Gravitation), and the familiar face of Albert Einstein at the top of the stairs. Intermediate events could then be added along the timeline. Other date-based lists, such as lists of prime ministers or laws, might be remembered in the same way. A similar method is used by competitors in memory contests. Journalist Joshua Foer's book *Moonwalking with Einstein* recounts how he trained from scratch to become a US Memory Champion in a contest that included remembering the order of playing cards in a number of merged packs after one exposure, and up to 500 random words in sequence (Foer, 2012). Some further examples are discussed in Box 1.2.

Chapter 8, p263

Mnemonic
a learning device used to aid memory.

Box 1.2 Practical Application: How to train your memory

In modern life, much memory work is handled by external devices; we note family birthdays on a calendar; we store telephone numbers in our mobile phones; we record travel directions and routes in our satellite navigation systems. The use of such tools may lead us to underestimate the capabilities of our memories. In 2005, a science journalist named Joshua Foer visited the US Memory Championship as part of his preparation for an article on 'savant memory'. He returned and won the championship a year later, setting a new record for the 'speed cards' event in the process, by memorizing the order of 52 cards in 1 minute and 40 seconds. Foer's year-long quest to develop his memory is charted in his book *Moonwalking with Einstein: The Art and Science of Remembering Everything* (Foer, 2012), and he recounts a number of the techniques he used to expand his memory capabilities (see Figure 1.1 for example).

Many such mnemonic (or memory facilitating) techniques rely on the use of mental imagery and spatial memory. The *method of loci* relies on associating a visual image with the object to be remembered, and placing these images in a familiar location or along a familiar route. Let's say, for example, that you want to remember 10 items on a shopping list. You visualize a familiar route, such as from your bedroom to the front door of your house, and you place each object on your list at a location along that path. So, you might 'see' a loaf of bread on your bed, a jar of coffee hanging on your bedroom door, an apple at the top of your stairs, and so on. Remembering the list then simply involves working your way along the route, mentally, and seeing what object is at each location. This method is also useful for remembering items in a particular order, such as lists of historical figures.

Another approach, the *keyword method,* is used when learning foreign language (second language or L2) vocabulary and has been shown to be effective, albeit under some circumstances (see De Groot & Van Hell, 2005). The learner makes an association between the unfamiliar L2 word and a familiar word in

Figure 1.1 How to memorize names.
To remember the name Edward Bedford (1), we might picture the man lying on a truck bed (2), or see him fording a river on a bed (3). Adding an image of Edward Scissorhands provides a link to the man's first name (4).

Source: Foer (2011).

the native language (L1) that sounds like the L2 word. For example, to remember the French word *église* (church), an English speaker might use the keyword 'egg', and then picture a church carved out of an egg to remember the English translation. The use of an interactive visual image underlies the mnemonic effect. Imagery can be a useful mnemonic device. For example, say you need to remember someone's name. If you are shown a photograph of a man and told his names is 'Baker', memory for that association is poorer than if you were told he is a 'baker'. The occupation 'baker' is embedded in a network of other associations in memory – bread, tall white hat, hot ovens – and provides a richer memory for retrieval. The name Baker on the other hand is linked only to the photograph, and does not carry such a rich network of associations. Mnemonists make use of this paradox, using imagery to make names more memorable (see Figure 1.1).

Another system, called the *story mnemonic,* aids memory for lists of unrelated words by combining the words into a story. For example, unrelated words such as *orange, church, tower, singer, camera, farmer* and *insect* might be combined as follows: 'An *orange* fell from a *church tower* and hit a *singer* below who was posing for the *camera* of a *farmer* being buzzed by an *insect*.' Bower and Clark (1969) found this mnemonic to be very effective, with over 90 per cent recall of 12 lists of 10 words with the story method compared to 13 per cent recall for controls.

Hu and colleagues (2009) examined use of a story mnemonic by a memory champion, Chao Lu, who held the record for remembering and reciting *pi* to 67,890 decimal places. Lu was readily able to apply the story mnemonic to lists of 40 words with 100 per cent correct recall and a study time per word of 9–10 seconds. Further, he could apply the method to lists of 300 digits by associating each two-digit pair with a unique image and then combining the images into a story. In this way, Lu achieved near perfect recall of long digit lists. In a subsequent study, Ericsson et al. (2017) found similar mnemonic

> methods were used by another World Memory Champion, Feng Wang, who won by recalling 300 digits presented at a rate of one per second.
>
> The use of spatial learning strategies seems to be of particular importance for mnemonic techniques. Maguire et al. (2003), using neuropsychological tests and brain imaging, tested eight memory experts who had been placed highly at the World Memory Championships. They found that their superior memory did not seem to be related to superior intellect or structural differences in the brain; rather, the participants' use of a spatial learning strategy seemed to underlie their memory advantage. Such studies highlight the role of learning and experience, as opposed to innate abilities, in superior memory.
>
> Mnemonic techniques such as those described above allow us to create associations between unrelated pieces of information (such as items on your shopping list, or strings of digits) but, as Ericsson (2003) notes, they are less likely to help us complete meaningful and task specific memory tasks, and correspondingly World Memory Champions do not show superior performance on everyday memory tasks. Despite superior memory for vast sequences of playing cards or number strings, they may still forget their mother's birthday or where they have left their keys!

Turning from Classical times, to a more recent period, from the seventeenth until the early nineteenth century, the dominant approach to cognition was that of associationism, which we will now outline.

Associationism

Empiricism
the philosophical school which holds that all knowledge comes from experience.

Association
a linkage between mental contents such that activation of one content activates linked content, e.g. table → chair.

Empiricist philosophers, such as John Locke (1632–1704), David Hume (1711–1776) and John Stuart Mill (1806–1873), held that all knowledge came from experience and that ideas and memories were linked by **associations**. Locke (1690), for instance, pointed out that two unrelated ideas could become associated if they were often actively considered close together in time. So, if a bell is always followed by dinner, soon the idea of 'bell' will tend to arouse the idea of 'dinner'. Closeness (proximity) in space as well as in time also fosters associations. Thus, roof and chimney tend to be found close together and those ideas would become associated. Relationships of similarity will also cause associations to be formed. By that route, cup and mug will tend to be associated as they are very similar objects in general shape and function.

Locke, Hume and the other associationists relied on their own intuitions and introspections to guide their theorizing and did no experiments on others; the use of experiments had to wait until 1879 with the founding of the first psychology laboratory by Wilhelm Wundt (1832–1920) in Leipzig, Germany. Wundt was the leading proponent of the introspectionist approach, which we turn to next.

Introspectionism

Phenomenology
the view that the study of immediate experience should be the basis of psychology.

Wundt and his associates in the second half of the nineteenth century focused on the nature of conscious experience (**phenomenology**) and sought to break down complex experiences into elementary sensations. The approach might be described as a form of 'mental chemistry'. Just as chemists in the nineteenth century were analysing compounds into chemical elements, Wundt tried to analyse normal perceptions (e.g., of a table) into simpler sensations (brownness, straight lines, textures), which combined to give the perception.

The method favoured was 'Classical Introspection' (or 'Self-Observation') in which specially trained participants gave a verbal account of their sensations in terms of *mode* (visual, auditory, tactile, etc.), *quality* (colour, shape, texture, etc.), *intensity, duration* and *feeling* (positive, negative, relaxed, tense). Introspective reports were generally backed up by reaction times or other behavioural measures.

The method was of limited application as extensive training was required (*c*. 10,000 trials were judged just sufficient to master the technique) and clearly could not be used by some groups of interest, including children and people with reduced capacity or mental illness. It could not be applied to study cognition in non-human animals. So, data could be gathered on only a very limited population. Introspection could be applied to only some mental processes. It is reasonable to assume that a trained observer might be able to recount something useful regarding his or her problem-solving progress, but it is unlikely that an account of how he or she perceives visual illusions could be generated. Introspectionism was also problematic because the process of introspection might well confound the cognitive process of interest. If you are engaged in a mathematics problem, and you are required to give an account of your progress in solving the problem, does its additional cognitive demand alter the nature of processing of the primary task (i.e., solving a maths problem)? It may well do.

In addition, differences in results between laboratories were difficult to resolve. For example, Wundt's doctoral students, Edward Titchener (1867–1927) at Cornell, and Oswald Kulpe (1862–1915) at Wurzburg, after establishing their own laboratories, clashed over imageless thought. Titchener reported that faint imagery was always present in verbal tasks such as in answering general knowledge questions (e.g., 'What is the capital of France?'), while Kulpe's laboratory at Wurzburg supported the existence of thought without images (Miller, 1962).

More recently, Hurlburt and colleagues (Hurlburt et al., 2017; Hurlburt & Heavey, 2001; see also, McKelvie, 2019) have developed and explored new methods for obtaining and analysing descriptions of conscious experience. This work has involved a method known as **Descriptive Experience Sampling (DES)** in which participants are cued at random intervals by a beeper and are instructed to pay immediate attention to their ongoing experience at the moment they heard the beep. They then write down the characteristics of that moment in a notebook. Within 24 hours the participants are interviewed to describe the characteristics in more detail. The interviews aim to answer the question 'What was occurring in your inner experience at the moment of the beep?'

Descriptive Experience Sampling (DES)
a method of obtaining descriptions of inner experience, including thoughts, feelings, perceptions, sensations, by cuing self reports with randomly spaced beeps.

Heavey and Hurlburt (2008) found that participants' reports from DES could mostly be reliably classed into five types: *Inner speech; Inner seeing* (imagery); *Feeling* (affective experiences such as anxiety, joy, etc.); *Sensory awareness* (e.g., cold, tickles); and *Unsymbolized* thinking (meaningful thought but without words, images or symbols – 'imageless thought'). Over a sample of participants the five types were of roughly even frequency, with Inner seeing most common (34 per cent), and Sensory awareness and Unsymbolized thinking least frequent at 22 per cent each. However, within participants, one type of experience or other was more typical and for 70 per cent of participants one type accounted for more than 50 per cent of their reports – but the dominant type varied over participants, so that for some Inner speech was dominant and for others Inner seeing predominated. In a further study, different patterns of inner experience were reported for different clinical groups with schizophrenia, depression, anxiety and hypomania, Asperger's syndrome and bulimia (Heavey et al., 2010). These findings indicate that the DES method has some validity and so taps in to real differences between individuals and groups.

Similar methods to Hurlburt's DES have been used to look at possible differences and similarities between types of conscious thought while awake and while dreaming (see Box 1.3).

> **Box 1.3 Research Close Up: Is this a dream? Experience sampling of qualities of waking and dreaming thoughts**
>
> *Source:* Gross et al. (2020).
>
> ## INTRODUCTION
>
> Much of our conscious mental activity is taken up with *stimulus-independent thoughts* (SITs) – that is, mental activity that is independent of our immediate external environment. While awake, examples of SITs might be thinking in a goal-directed way about an upcoming career decision while riding in a bus, or remembering past events as one memory triggers another, but with no particular goal being pursued. When asleep, dreams are a form of SIT and are generally believed to be quite different from waking thoughts.
>
> In contrast to SITs, *stimulus-dependent thoughts* (SDTs) are waking thoughts closely tied to the current environment, such as thoughts involved in putting together some flat-pack furniture, or in driving a car through an unfamiliar environment.
>
> ## METHODS
>
> Gross and colleagues (2020) examined how SDTs and SITs may be similar and different in people's experience, by using an experience sampling procedure. Over seven days, 131 participants were intermittently cued day and night by a mobile phone app to indicate whether their thoughts were SITs or SDTs. They then rated the quality of their thoughts on a range of scales, including *novelty, meaningfulness, bizarreness, goal-directedness, emotionality, spontaneity* and *temporal orientation* (*present, past or future*).
>
> ## RESULTS
>
> For the daytime probes of waking thoughts, 35 per cent were SITs and 65 per cent were SDTs.
>
> Daytime SITs compared to daytime SDTs were:
>
> - more goal-directed (35 per cent vs. 27 per cent)
> - more spontaneous (50 per cent vs. 32 per cent)
> - more emotional (37 per cent vs. 22 per cent)
> - more future oriented (31 per cent vs. 14 per cent).
>
> Night-time probes of thoughts during dreams were classed as SITs and compared to waking SITs.
>
> Dream thoughts (dream SITs) compared to waking thoughts (waking SITs) were:
>
> - more novel (45 per cent vs. 33 per cent)
> - more fluid (79 per cent vs. 71 per cent)
> - more bizarre (20 per cent vs. 16 per cent)
> - more spontaneous (65 per cent vs. 50 per cent).

> **DISCUSSION**
>
> Overall, although there were considerable overlaps and similarities between the three types of thoughts, some clear differences emerged between SITs as against SDTs (e.g., SITs were more future oriented than SDTs), and between waking and dream thoughts (e.g., dream thoughts were more fluid and more bizarre than waking thoughts). Both SITs and dreams were more likely to be about the future than were SDTs. Dreams tended to be more novel and bizarre than SITs, indicating that, although both dreams and SITs may function to simulate the future, dreams allow less constrained simulations and are not limited to the logical, familiar or relevant. As Barrett (2015) put it, 'dreams are simply thoughts in a different biochemical state'. The biochemical state of the brain during dreams provides a different novel angle towards the same ideas, concerns and goals that fill much waking thought.

Behaviourism

Partly in reaction to the drawbacks and limitations of introspectionism, John Watson (1913), Edward Thorndike (1898) and others, mainly in the USA, developed the behaviourist approach. This abandoned the attempt to look inside the mind and took only observable behaviour and stimuli as its data. This approach essentially aimed to be a psychology without reference to internal cognitive processes. The focus was on learning, particularly about how behavioural responses could be predicted from knowing the history of rewards and punishments following behaviour in response to particular stimuli. Much of the research in this tradition was carried out with animals, particularly the laboratory rat and pigeon, as it was assumed that learning processes were the same in animals and humans.

Watson (1913, p. 158) stated the behaviourist manifesto very starkly as follows:

> *Psychology as the behaviorist views it is a purely objective natural science. Its theoretical goal is the prediction and control of behavior. Introspection forms no essential part of its methods, nor is the scientific value of its data dependent on the readiness with which they lend themselves to interpretation in terms of consciousness. The behaviorist, in his efforts to get a unitary scheme of animal response, recognizes no dividing line between man and brute. The behavior of man, with all its refinement and complexity, forms only a part of the behaviorist's total scheme of investigation.*

Watson proposed that all apparently mental phenomena could be traced to behavioural activity. So, for example, he argued that 'thinking' was actually slight movements of muscles in the tongue and larynx. On this view, thinking was behaviour. However, an unusual experiment by Smith and colleagues (1947) showed that this was not the case. They examined the cerebral effects of curare, a plant-derived poison that had been used for centuries by Amazonian tribes when hunting. In this study, a single participant (the first author of the paper, Smith) was injected with curare and his speech muscles were paralysed temporarily as a result. During the period of paralysis, various questions were asked and on the use of his muscles returning, Smith could report the answers to the questions in order and that he was aware of inner speech during paralysis. This study thus showed that movement of the speech muscles is not necessary for inner speech or thought. Such findings suggested that psychology needed an alternative to the behaviourist approach to thinking. However, Watson may not have been altogether wrong. A more recent study by Oppenheim and Dell (2010), for example, showed that inner speech differs when it is articulated compared to when it is not, and so while inner speech *can* occur without any movement of the speech musculature, it is not entirely independent of the movements that would be used if that thought were uttered.

> Chapter 3, p107
>
> Chapter 9, p307

Interestingly, Watson's idea that thought and behaviour overlap has been partially revived in 'embodied' approaches to mental representation (Barsalou, 2008), which propose that motor areas of the brain are involved even in abstract concepts (see Chapters 3 and 9 for more on embodied approaches). Continuing in the behavioural tradition, Watson's work was expanded on by B. F. Skinner, who brought to the fore the importance of consequences (that is, rewards or punishments) for behaviour (e.g., Skinner, 1938).

> **Mental maps**
> mental representations of a spatial layout.

Other behaviourists, such as Tolman, were less extreme than Watson on the status of mental activity and allowed that rats and other animals could be usefully seen as having goals and mental representations, or **mental maps**, that aided in learning the layout of mazes containing food rewards (see Box 1.4.).

Box 1.4 Research Close Up: Cognitive maps

Source: Tolman (1948).

INTRODUCTION

Although the behaviourist approach had many successes in accounting for basic animal learning, some studies raised the possibility that animals could be usefully seen as having goals and using some form of mental representations, or 'mental maps'. Edward C. Tolman made a significant contribution to our understanding of learning and motivation by showing that learning could occur in the absence of an obvious source of reinforcement, supporting the notion of a 'cognitive map' or abstract mental representation underlying performance. Tolman's studies involved maze-running in rats.

METHOD AND RESULTS

In one set of studies, three groups of rats were exposed to a maze task once a day for 22 days. The maze was a 14-unit T maze (see Figure 1.2). The food-deprived rats had to run from the starting unit to the end unit, where, in some cases, a food reward was waiting. Rats in Group A found a food reward when they got to the end of the maze each day. This group quickly learned the location of the food, and the number of errors made (wrong turns taken) decreased steadily over the duration of the experiment. Group B rats were placed in the maze but received no food

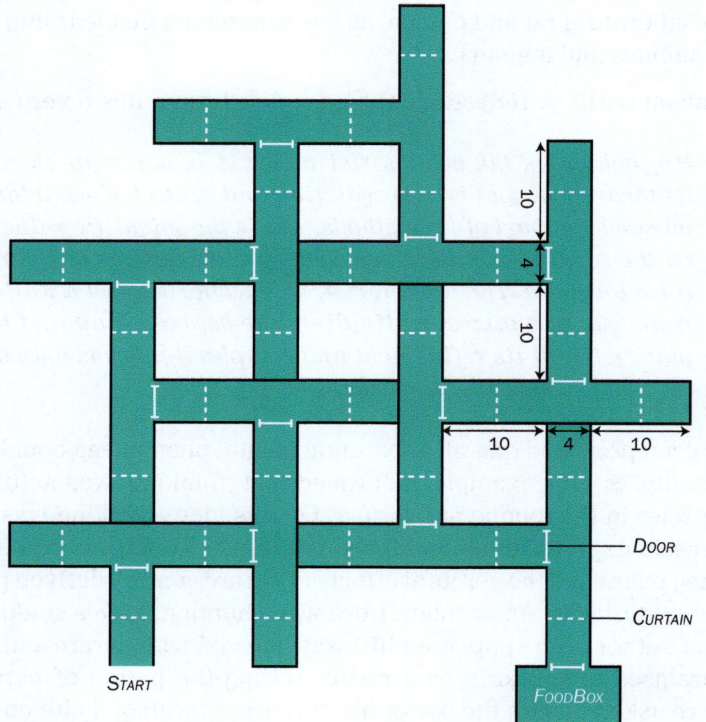

Figure 1.2 Tolman's 14-unit T maze.
The 14-unit alley maze used by Tolman contains a number of T-junctions leading to true path segments or blind alleys, which the rat must navigate in order to find the food.

Source: Tolman (1948). APA.

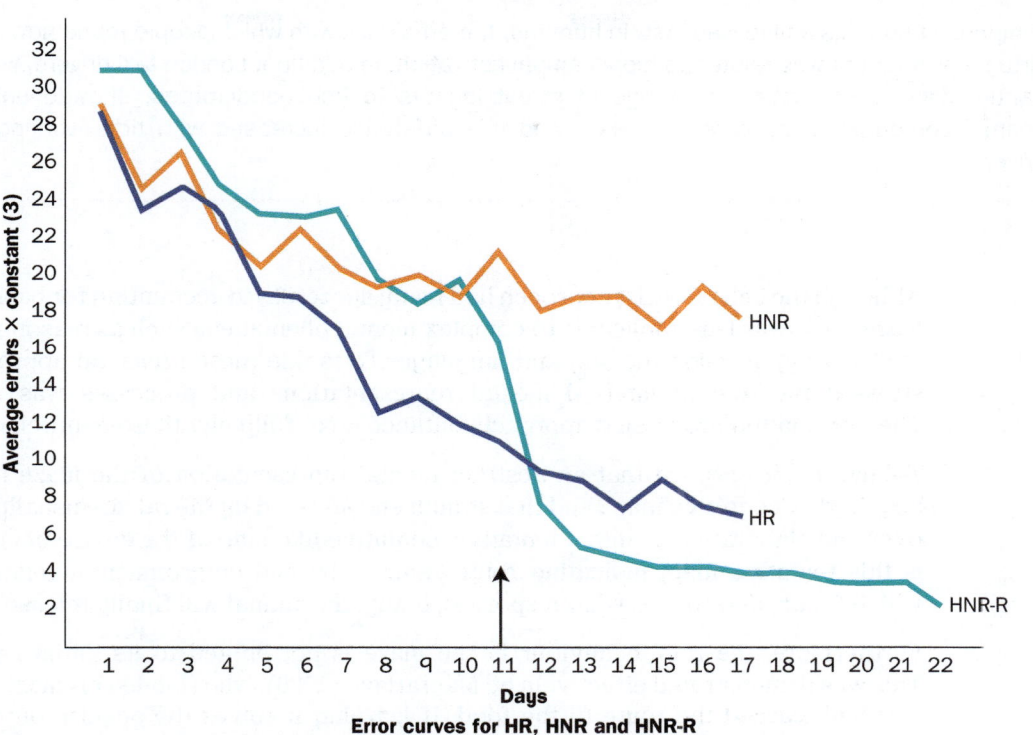

Figure 1.3 Error curves for Group A (HR: Hungry, reward), Group B (HNR: Hungry, no reward), Group C (HNR-R: Hungry, no reward until day 11).

The experiment used two control groups: a group that never found food in the maze (HNR) and a group that found food throughout (HR). The experimental group (HNR-R) found food on reaching the end of the maze from day 11 onwards.

Source: Tolman (1948). APA.

reward. This group showed relatively little change in the number of 'errors' made for the duration of the experiment. Group C received no reward for the first ten days, but on day 11, food was placed at the end of the maze. Rats in this group performed similarly to Group B for the first ten days, but showed a sudden decrease in errors once the food reward was introduced. Group C's errors dropped quickly such that their performance matched that of Group A, who had received the food reward all along (see Figure 1.3).

DISCUSSION

These data suggested that learning had occurred in Group C, but that this learning was not apparent until the food reward was provided. The term latent learning is used to describe a situation where learning occurs but is not immediately demonstrated in performance. The fact that learning had occurred became evident only when the reward was introduced.

Following Tolman's pioneering studies, further research, focusing on the neural bases of spatial learning and memory by O'Keefe (2014) and colleagues, has indicated a strong role for the **hippocampus** in acquiring and storing cognitive maps in the brain (see Figure 1.8 for location of the hippocampus in the brain). Specialized 'place' cells in the hippocampus were shown to encode spatial position in rats, and when rats who had learned to swim to a hidden platform in a **water maze** were given lesions

Hippocampus
a small curved formation in the brain involved in the formation of new memories and in processing spatial information.

Water maze
usually a circular container of milky water in which there is a submerged platform to which rats learn to swim from any starting point.

> to the hippocampus this ability was lost. In humans, the efficiency with which people found new routes in a virtual environment was related to hippocampal activation. In addition, London taxi drivers, who are constantly using their spatial knowledge of street layouts to find good routes, showed enlarged hippocampi compared to suitable controls – and this difference increased with time working as a taxi driver.

Although the behaviourist approach had many successes in accounting for basic animal learning, it was less applicable to complex mental phenomena such as reasoning, problem solving, decision making and language. To tackle these areas, an approach that stressed the role of internal mental representations and processes was required. The information processing approach, outlined next, fully met these requirements.

Tolman (1948) argued that an abstract mental representation of the maze had been acquired, a 'cognitive map', and that stimuli encountered by the rat 'are usually worked over and elaborated . . . into a tentative, cognitive-like map of the environment. And it is this tentative map, indicating routes and paths and environmental relationships, which finally determines what responses, if any, the animal will finally release' (p. 193).

Furthermore, the rats' behaviour in the maze is not limited to its initial responses. This was demonstrated effectively by Macfarlane (1930), who flooded his maze once the rats had learned the route to the food. If learning involves the acquisition of motor responses, then rats that had learned to run the maze should show a performance decrement when they were now required to swim the maze. Macfarlane showed that this was not the case; rats swam to the food instead of running to it. This supported the idea that they had acquired an abstract mental representation of some kind that was independent of the specific movements that allowed them to complete the maze (Rosenbaum, 2006).

Tolman's work pre-dated the cognitive revolution by several decades, but shows how cognitive factors, and issues of mental representation, were already being considered within psychology, even if his findings were not entirely inconsistent with the behavioural principles suggested by B. F. Skinner.

Information Processing: The Cognitive Revolution

Information processing approach
a metaphor for understanding mental activity, based on computing.

The **information processing approach**, which brought mental representations back to centre stage, was inspired by the development of programmable digital computers that began to appear in the mid-1940s. It was quickly realized that computers could be programmed to carry out any kind of symbol manipulation that could be specified in detail. The obvious problems and procedures that computers could carry out were numerical, such as calculating trajectories of missiles or working out payrolls. More interestingly for cognitive psychology, computers could also be programmed to tackle non-numerical problems such as playing chess, suggesting medical diagnoses given symptoms and (although still not perfectly) automatic translation between natural languages. Computer programs to solve suitable problems could be seen as comparable to **strategies** that humans might use to solve the same problems. In both cases there are definite steps to be carried out, decisions to be made, storage of new information and retrieval of old information from memory. For example, to solve an anagram problem ('What word can be made from PECNOCT?') a human strategy might be to pick two letters as possible

Strategies
systematic ways to carry out a cognitive task such as solving a problem.

starting letters, then search long-term memory for words that have those two starting letters and check each retrieved word in turn, to see if it matches the letters in the anagram; when a complete match is found the problem is solved. A computer with a list of all English words stored in memory could be readily programmed to follow the same strategy (Answer: Concept). Thus, a well-specified theory or model for how people tackle some task or set of tasks could be expressed as a program.

> Chapter 12, p429

A program that expresses a model of human thinking would be labelled a *simulation* program and should be distinguished from an *artificial intelligence* program, which seeks to solve the problem as effectively as possible without any attempt at mimicking human strategies. Despite this distinction, many ideas developed in artificial intelligence research have been adopted in the information processing approach to human cognition (particularly in the area of problem solving, as we will see in Chapter 12).

Simulation involves programming computers to solve problems in a similar way to humans.
Artificial intelligence the attempt to program computers to carry out complex tasks such as medical diagnosis, planning and using natural language.
Internal representations mental representations of external objects and events.
Mental operations inner actions manipulating mental representations.

The information processing approach has been dominant in cognitive psychology since the early 1960s and is still the major framework in the area. Theorists attempt to explain performance in cognitive tasks by using concepts of *internal representations*, which are transformed by *mental operations* using both long-term and working (short-term) memory (see Chapters 6 and 7). The theories are usually stated in verbal terms or with the aid of 'box and arrow' diagrams that illustrate the flow of information and the kind of operations being carried out. The chapters that follow this one contain many examples of such theories or models. One example is Baddeley's analysis of short-term working memory into separate stores for phonological and visuo-spatial information in which information is preserved by rehearsal (e.g., Baddeley, 2007; see Chapter 6). This model has been explored and tested by experimental methods, for example by having participants perform tasks that load one or other memory system and observing the effects, rather than by computer simulation. This reflects a general fact that although the information processing approach was inspired by computers, most work in the field does not involve computer modelling but progresses through experimental testing of model predictions. At times, however, the approach might be accused of reducing cognition to information flow, whereas people process information, of enormous variety, in a complex and at times unpredictable environment.

> Chapter 6, p176, p197

> Chapter 7, p218

Although, as we shall see in later chapters, most work in cognitive psychology does not involve computer modelling, information processing modelling often made use of computer models. For example, initially, the main examples of progress in the field involved simulation models such as Newell et al.'s (1958) General Problem Solver, which could tackle problems such as logic tasks and simple games in ways similar to humans, by breaking them down into goals and subgoals. A more recent example is that of Anderson's ACT-R model (2004), which can be applied to a wide range of laboratory tasks in memory and problem solving (see Chapter 12's discussion of the Tower of Hanoi). ACT-R is built up from simple if–then rules that check a working memory to see if their condition is met, in which case they fire and replace the contents of working memory. For example, '*if* goal is to solve anagram, *then* pick two letters from anagram and place in working memory'; '*if* goal is to solve anagram *and* two letters in working memory, *then* retrieve word from long-term memory that starts with the two letters'; and so on.

> Chapter 12, p443

Connectionism an approach to cognition in terms of networks of simple neuron-like units that pass activation and inhibition through receptor, hidden and output units.

An alternative style of information processing modelling that can be explored through simulation is known as *connectionism* (Rumelhart & McClelland, 1982). Connectionist models simulate basic learning and perceptual phenomena by means of a large network of simple units organized into input, output and internal (also known as 'hidden') units. The units are connected by excitatory or inhibitory links of varying strengths through which activation flows. Link strengths are modified through learning rules such as **backwards propagation**. These models are arguably more 'brain like' and utilize parallel distributed processing rather than the strictly serial processing of traditional symbolic models. However, although brain like, the units in such models are much simpler in their properties and functioning than the real neural units or neurons that constitute the brain (Figure 1.4) and so the similarity of a connectionist network to real neural networks is limited.

> **Backwards propagation**
> a way of modifying weights on the links between units in a connectionist network, in response to errors, to obtain the desired output.

The basic components of a connectionist network are:

- a set of processing units
- weighted connections between units
- a learning strategy.

The processing units can be input, output or hidden units (between input and output). The network's architecture is determined by the way in which the units are connected. In a feedforward network, input units are connected to output units such that information flows in one direction from input to hidden to output layers (see Figure 1.4 for example). In a recurrent network, some of the connections feed back to earlier layers. For example, some of the output units might send information back to the input layer, in order to take account of the previous output when processing the next input. Input units take in information as an input pattern from outside the network or from other parts of the network. Hidden units communicate with input and output units but are cut off from the external environment. They do the computational work of the network and pass activation to the output units. The output units produce the response that can be characterized as the 'behaviour' of the network.

All units have some level of activity, denoted by their activation value. This determines how much activation or output a unit passes on to connected units. Often, activation values are expressed in the range from 0 to +1, where 0 is 'off' and +1 is 'on'. Units affect each other by excitation or inhibition, that is a unit can act to cause a neighbouring unit to 'fire' or it can act to subdue the neighbouring unit's activation so that it is less likely to fire.

> **Deep network**
> a connectionist network with multiple layers of hidden units between the input and output units.

Deep networks

Deep networks have many layers of hidden units and have shown spectacular learning abilities. For example, Google's Deep Mind Project, known as Alpha Go Zero, by means of suitable learning algorithms applied to millions of games against itself has been capable of dramatic gains in performance in both chess and Go-moku, from complete beginner performance to world champion level in about 40 days (Silver et al., 2017). The mastery of Go is particularly impressive as Go is a game with an even larger problem space than chess. The game is played on a 19 × 19 board where players take turns to put down a white or a black counter (stone) and aim to encircle each other's stones to take stones and enclose territory on the board. The game had been thought to be beyond current computer technology and due to remain a domain of human dominance for many more years. However, the Alpha Go Zero program was superior to an earlier version (Alpha Go) that had defeated the human world champion, Ke Jie, the year before. Expert human analysts describe the style of play of the Alpha Go systems as amazing, strange and

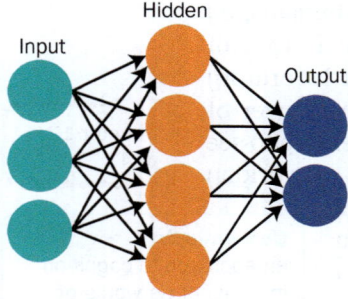

Figure 1.4
A connectionist network.
A simple three-layer feedforward connectionist network showing input, hidden and output layers and the connections between them.

alien (!). The systems tend to fight several small battles at once, hopping around the board, while human players tend to see through one battle at a time; they make more centre moves than human players and produce very unusual opening moves that defy the understanding of human analysts (Chan, 2017).

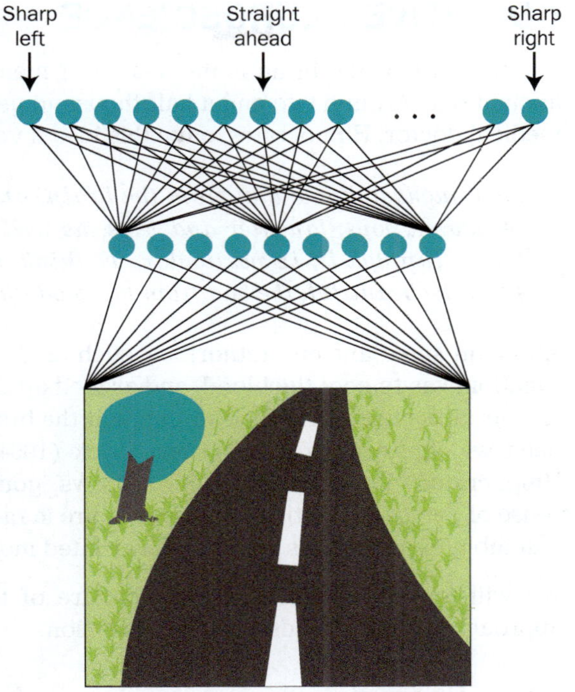

The functional level of analysis

Overall, the information processing approach can be said to focus on our 'mental software'. It asks 'What strategies are followed in processing information? How is information encoded during perception, stored in memory during learning and retrieved by remembering for further processing in thinking?' Essentially, these questions are about *functions* and *functional properties* and can be answered without referring to any underlying hardware, just as we can describe a computer program in terms of its processing steps without needing to say anything about the computer hardware that the programs run on. Some cognitive theorists are indifferent to the hardware of the brain, in which human strategies are executed, saying that, for them, the brain may as well be made of porridge – which is an interesting choice of word, as the English word 'brain' seems likely to be derived from the same root as 'bran', which the brain resembles in appearance (Liberman, 2009)! On the functionalist view, the nature of the brain and the details of underlying neural processes are of no concern for analyses at the cognitive level (Turing, 1950). Fodor (1999), for example, has an entertaining paper entitled 'Let your brain alone', in which he argues against the relevance of brain science for psychology and writes, 'If the mind happens in space at all, it happens somewhere north of the neck. What exactly turns on knowing how far north?'

However, despite such scepticism among functionalists (see also Page, 2006), there has been a growing trend within cognitive psychology that pays attention to the findings of neuroscience and considers the underlying brain hardware that allows cognition. We will now outline and discuss some key aspects of neuroscience being considered by cognitive psychologists.

Figure 1.5 A connectionist network for navigation.
An example of a simple three-layer feedforward connectionist network showing input, hidden and output layers and the connections between them. In this example, input is in the form of a visual scene presented to the input units. The network learns to steer left, right or straight ahead, over a series of trials.

Source: Pomerleau (1990).

Figure 1.6 Example of a completed Go game.

© Saran Poroong/Alamy Stock Photo

COGNITIVE NEUROSCIENCE

The notion that the brain is the source of mental activities and experience is a very ancient one. Around two and a half thousand years ago, the Greek thinker and pioneer medical doctor, Hippocrates, gave this idea a very clear statement:

> *Men ought to know that from the brain, and from the brain alone, arises our pleasures, joys, laughter and jests, as well as our sorrows, pains, griefs and tears. Through it, in particular, we think, see, hear, and distinguish the ugly from the beautiful, the bad from the good, the pleasant from the unpleasant.*

Although some ancient authorities, such as Aristotle, proposed that the brain's main function was to cool the blood, and argued against the brain as the seat of the mind in favour of the heart, the basic notion that the brain is necessary for mental life has long been widely accepted. As Francis Crick (1994, p. 3) put it in terms reminiscent of Hippocrates: 'You, your joys and sorrows, your memories and your ambitions, your sense of personal identity and free will, are in fact no more than the behaviour of a vast assembly of nerve cells and their associated molecules.'

We will now try to give a broad picture of the brain before discussing particular approaches and methods in the next section.

Brain Basics

The brain is the central part of the body's nervous system; the peripheral parts of the nervous system feed sensory information from external and internal sources into the brain, which in turn sends motor signals to the muscles in order to cause actions, from walking to talking. The inside front and back covers of this book show schematic views of the brain that you may find it useful to consult as brain areas are referred to in most chapters.

If the brain is removed from the skull it does look rather porridge-like, as has often been remarked. However, unlike a bowl of porridge, it is actually highly structured into distinct parts and subparts. At a very broad level, it is clearly divided into left and right hemispheres (connected by the **corpus callosum**). As you can see in Figure 1.7, four main sections (lobes) are apparent in the outer layer (the cerebral cortex) in both hemispheres: the frontal lobes, the parietal lobes, the occipital lobes and the temporal lobes.

> **Corpus callosum**
> the thick band of nerve fibres that connects the left and right cerebral hemispheres.

Deeper inside the brain are distinct structures such as the *thalamus* (from Greek: inner room), *hippocampus* (from Greek: seahorse) and *amygdala* (from Latin and Greek: almond). At the base of the brain is the *cerebellum* (from Latin: little brain), which is important in movement control. The names reflect the shapes of the structures (see Figure 1.8).

Finally, the following terms are often used to indicate locations in the brain: *dorsal* meaning towards the top (Latin: back); *ventral* meaning towards the bottom (Latin: belly); *anterior* meaning towards the front (Latin: before); *posterior* meaning towards the back (Latin: coming after); *lateral* meaning at the side (Latin: a side) and *medial* meaning in the middle (Latin: middle).

> **Neurons**
> the basic units of the nervous system, principally consisting of a cell, axon and dendrites.

All these structures in the brain are composed of the same building blocks – that is, the **neurons**. These are specialized cells that exchange information by transmitting electrical impulses. Neurons are somewhat varied but typically have a soma or cell body, dendrites, which receive signals, and an

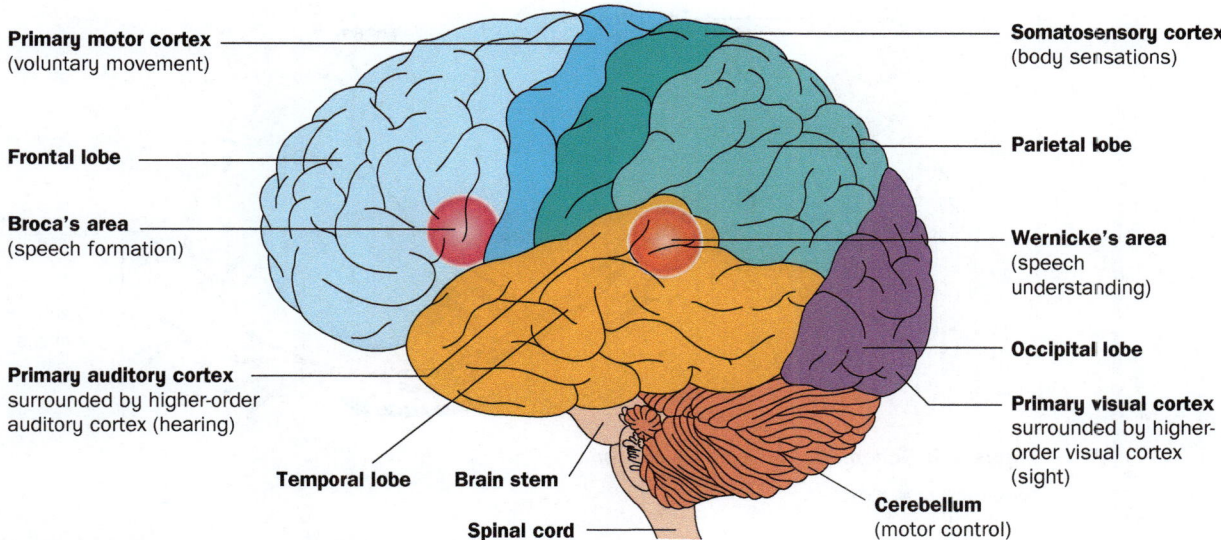

Figure 1.7 Lobes of the brain.
The four lobes of the brain are shown, along with some key areas for vision, hearing, language and motor function. The frontal lobes are shown in blue, temporal in yellow, occipital in purple and parietal in green.

Source: Adapted from Holt et al. (2012).

axon, which transmits signals to other neurons by chemical transmission across synaptic gaps. (See Figure 1.9, overleaf, for a typical neuron structure.)

In addition to the neurons there are also large numbers of support cells (**glia**) involved in tissue repair and the formation of myelin.

> **Glia**
> support cells of the nervous system that take part in tissue repair and in the formation of myelin.

The average human brain has a volume of about 1,400 cubic centimetres and weighs around 1,500 grams. But how many neurons are in the human brain?

It is not easy to determine the number of neurons by traditional slicing methods – and von Bartheld et al. (2016) reported that a wide range of estimates had been reported over the years, from three billion (Donaldson, 1895) to one trillion (i.e., one million billion) by Kandel and Schwartz (1985).

Suzana Herculano-Houzel (2009) pioneered a 'brain soup' method in which brains are homogenized and dissolved in a special solvent so that the nuclei are preserved in the resulting 'soup' (which looks like unfiltered apple juice). Samples are then taken from the 'soup', the nuclei in the samples are counted and the resulting sample numbers can be scaled up, leading to a best estimate of around *86 billion neurons* in the average human brain. The number of glial cells is also estimated at around 86 billion by the 'brain soup' method, although previous methods had led to estimates 10 times larger. See also

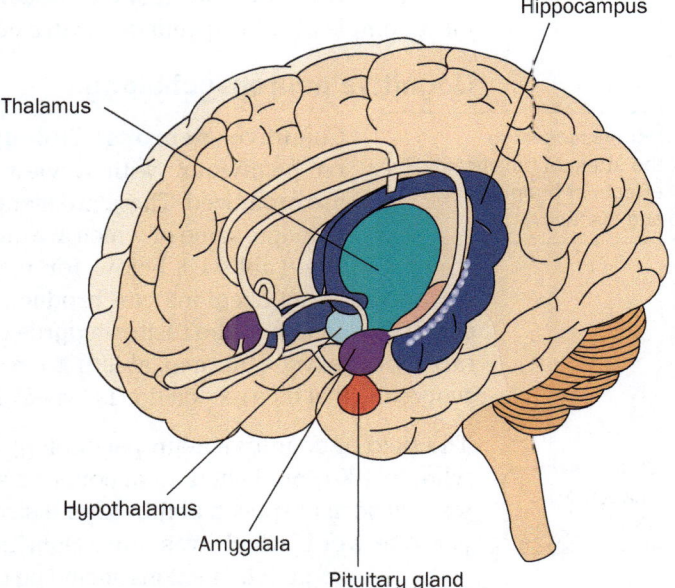

Figure 1.8 Key subcortical structures of the human brain.
The thalamus, hypothalamus, amygdala, pituitary gland and the hippocampus are shown.

Source: Adapted from Holt et al. (2012).

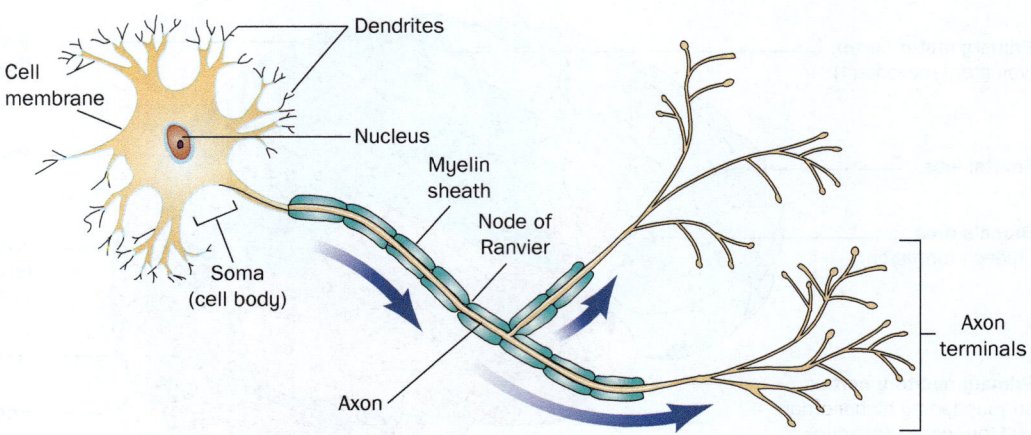

Figure 1.9 Schematic outline of a neuron.
Source: Holt et al. (2012).

Isotropic fractionator method
a method of dissolving brain tissue into a liquid form, preserving the nuclei of the neurons, which can then be counted in a sample and the count scaled up for a whole-brain estimate of numbers of neurons.

Herculano-Houzel (2016) for more on the 'brain soup' method – officially known as the **isotropic fractionator** method.

Thus, the human brain is a fantastically complex structure composed of approximately 86 billion neurons, each of which may connect with up to 10,000 other neurons. Therefore, the theoretical number of possible patterns of connections is of the order of 100 trillion different patterns. This huge number of possible patterns of connections underlies the brain's ability to encode an essentially indefinite range of knowledge. The question then arises – how can we possibly understand such a complex system as our own brains?

We will now look at two main approaches to gaining some understanding of how the ultra-complex brain system generates cognitive activity.

Cognitive neuropsychology

Neuropsychology
the study of psychological effects of brain damage and disease.

Cognitive **neuropsychology** examines the effects of *brain damage* on behaviour, with a view to identifying how psychological functions are organized. There are many naturally occurring causes or sources of brain damage, some of which are quite focused and some more diffuse (Ward, 2015). See Table 1.1 below for major sources of brain damage. Brain damage confined to small regions can produce informative breakdowns in performance; for example, damage to the fusiform gyrus can lead to a loss of ability to recognize familiar faces but leave a normal ability to recognize familiar objects (Grüter et al., 2008), suggesting that face recognition is a special function distinct from general object recognition.

Chapter 10, p357

The field of cognitive neuropsychology can be traced back to the work of Paul Broca, who, in 1861, published an account of a 51-year-old patient called Leborgne who had lost his normal speech ability after a stroke many years before and was left able to say just one word, which was 'tan'. Only the patient's speech was affected and all other cognitive functions, including understanding spoken language, were unaffected. At a post-mortem examination of the preserved brain, 30 years after the stroke, Broca (1861) found that there was a small area of damage or lesion in the inferior part of the left frontal gyrus. This region, now named **Broca's area**, is vital for speech production (see Figure 1.7, and Chapter 10 for more detail).

Broca's area
an area located in the left temporal lobe, damage to which is associated with aphasia (speech deficits).

Table 1.1 Main Sources of Brain Damage Studied in Neuropsychological Research

Source	Example damage
Surgery	• Focal removal of source area of epilepsy in brain • Split brain procedure, cutting the fibres of the corpus callosum, which connects the right and left brain hemispheres • Prefrontal lobotomy, cutting connections between prefrontal cortex and other areas; formerly used for a range of psychiatric disorders
Strokes (cerebro-vascular accidents: CVAs) causing death of neurons	• Haemorrhages (artery ruptures) • Embolism (fatty clot enters and blocks narrow blood vessel) • Thrombosis (clot enlarges to block blood vessel)
Closed traumatic head injuries (skull intact)	• Widespread damage effects, due to, e.g., boxing, repeatedly heading heavy balls, accidents
Open traumatic head injuries (skull fractured)	• Localized injuries, due to, e.g., gunshot wounds, knife wounds, accidents
Tumours	• These occur in supporting cells, such as meninges and glia rather than in neurons • Pressure from tumour damages neurons
Viral infections	• Herpes simplex encephalitis (HSE) • Human immunodeficiency virus (HIV) • Creutzfeldt–Jakob disease (CJD) • 'Mad cow disease' (bovine spongiform encephalitis: BSE)
Neurodegenerative disorders	• Dementia of the Alzheimer's type (DAT) • Parkinson's disease • Huntingdon's disease • Pick's disease • Multi-infarct dementia

For more on this topic see Ward (2015).

Since Broca's finding, it has become well established that in more than 90 per cent of right-handed people, and 70 per cent of left-handed people, language functions are strongly **localized** in the left hemisphere.

Broca's study exemplifies the basic ideas of neuropsychology, which are that most, if not all, functions are linked closely to the healthy working of specific brain areas and that impairments following localized damage can indicate which areas are important for which functions and can be informative about how broad functions are organized into narrower functions. Thus, Broca's patient showed that the broad language function could be split into spoken language production and language perception as separate abilities (because the patient could understand speech but could not himself speak). The notion of localization had been developed earlier by Franz Joseph Gall (1758–1828) and the **phrenological** school ('phren' being Greek for 'mind') which had tried to tie a host of very complex functions and personality characteristics, such as 'prudence', 'acquisitiveness', 'destructiveness', 'sense of justice', and so on, to particular underlying brain areas (see Figure 1.10, overleaf).

Phrenologists such as Gall sought to infer from bumps in the skull how well developed the underlying brain areas had become, and suggested for example, that a large bump

> **Localization**
> the view that specific mental functions are tied to specific brain areas; this also appears as the modularity hypothesis and may be contrasted with the distributed view, that functions are realized by joint action of many areas.
>
> **Phrenology**
> an early form of localization that attempted, unsuccessfully, to link psychological functions to bumps in the skull taken to reflect growth of the brain in specific areas.

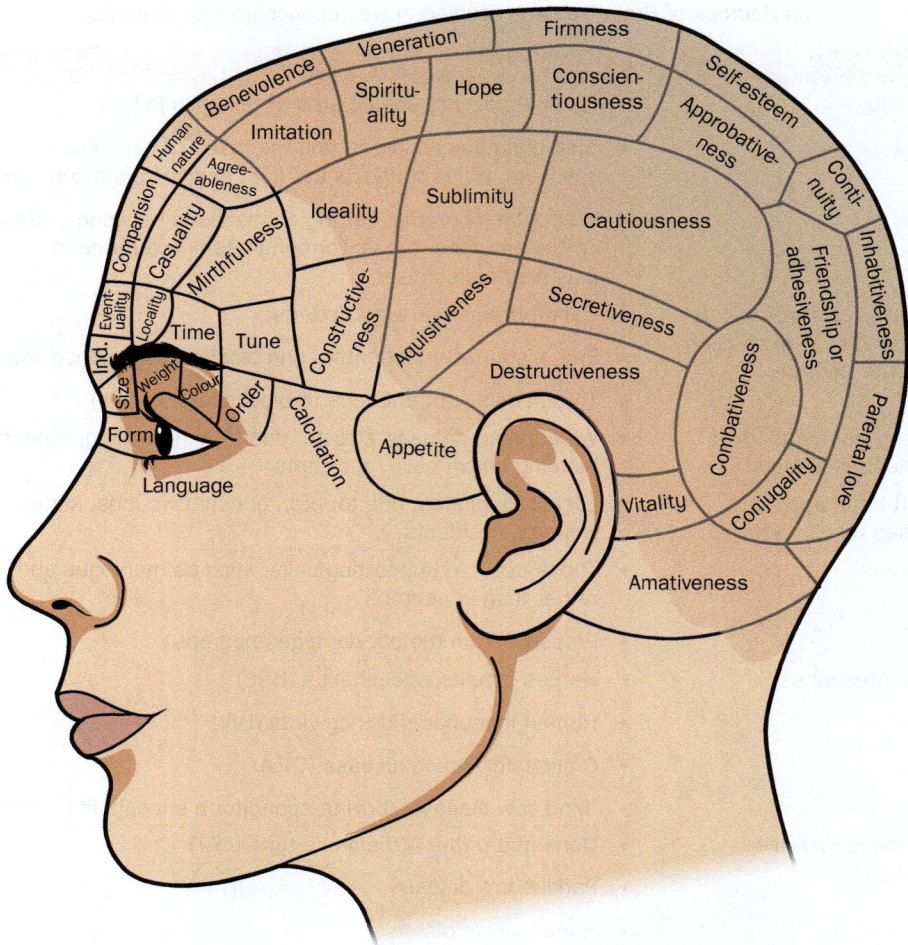

Figure 1.10 Phrenological map.
This phrenological map shows brain areas purported to be where various complex functions were localized. Growth of the brain in a given area would, it was thought, cause a corresponding bump in the skull. So, for example, a very destructive person would have a marked bump in the skull just above the left ear, and such a bump could be used to diagnose destructiveness.

Source: https://publicdomainvectors.org/en/free-clipart/Phrenology-chart/63360.html.

just above the left ear indicated destructive tendencies. Recently, it has become possible to examine phrenological claims with data from 5,724 brain scans that included detailed skull measurements and a range of lifestyle measures (Parker-Jones et al., 2018). This study found absolutely no connection between skull bump measures and any lifestyle scores. For example, there was no connection between the supposed 'amativeness' bump and reported lifetime sexual partners, or between the 'educability' bump and years of full-time education. Although the detailed project of phrenology failed, in that skull bumps were not in fact linked to the complex functions as hypothesized, the notion of localization of function has persisted strongly. Since the time of the phrenologists, the idea of localization has become labelled as '**modularity**' (Barrett & Kurzban, 2006; Fodor, 1983). The modularity view proposes that cognition involves a large number of independent processing units that work separately from each other and apply to fairly narrow domains (e.g., face processing, shape perception, perceiving word meanings, speech generation, and so on).

> **Modularity**
> the view that cognition involves many separate independent modules or processors specialized for different types of processing.

The opposite perspective to modularity is that mental functions, especially complex functions, are not localized but are distributed through the brain. On this view, impairments of mental functions due to brain damage depend on the quantity of tissue destroyed (Law of Mass Action, Lashley, 1929) and not on the specific site of the damage. Experimental studies on the effects of the amount of brain tissue removed on animal learning lent support to the distributed, or Mass Action, hypothesis (Lashley, 1929). Interestingly, the famous case of Phineas Gage (Harlow, 1848), who suffered the passage through his left frontal lobe of a metre-long, three-and-a-half-pound weighted iron bar, in an explosive industrial accident, was initially taken to support Mass Action, as he showed no intellectual impairment. However, the personality changes in Gage that became evident soon after the accident, from a conscientious, careful railroad worker to an impulsive individual who lacked perseverance, were later interpreted as indicating localization of executive, controlling functions in the frontal lobes. After a further period of time there seems to have been some recovery of executive controlling functions, indicating a degree of brain plasticity. (For more on the Gage case, see Chapter 15, Box 15.1.)

> **Law of Mass Action** states that the efficiency of any complex function of the cortical areas of the brain is reduced proportionately to the amount of damage the cortex as a whole has suffered but not to damage of any particular cortical area.

> Chapter 15, p552

Overall, human cognitive neuropsychology has found the localization assumption useful in interpreting effects of brain damage, and the general notion of localization underlies much neuropsychological research.

Double dissociation

Of particular interest for neuropsychology are cases of double dissociation, in which patients can be found with opposite patterns of impairment in two functions. For example, one case may have impaired short-term memory but normal long-term memory, while another may have the opposite pattern. This would suggest that long-term and short-term memory are indeed separate functions and not just aspects of a unitary single memory system. Simple dissociations, where patients show an impairment in one function but not in other functions, can also be informative, particularly regarding localization (this was the position with Broca's famous case, discussed above).

Brain stimulation methods

Information about brain functioning can also be derived from looking at the effects on behaviour of electrical or magnetic stimulation of the brain. The principal methods of brain stimulation are:

- point electrical stimulation of exposed brains during surgery
- transcranial magnetic stimulation (TMS)
- transcranial direct current stimulation (tDCS).

Point electrical stimulation

From 1928 to 1947 American-Canadian neurosurgeon, Wilder Penfield, applied point electrical stimulation directly to the exposed brains of more than 400 conscious patients during surgery for epilepsy under a local anaesthetic, to allow the skull to be opened painlessly. During these operations, he obtained hundreds of self-reports of what the patients experienced when stimulated and also records of motor responses when these occurred. Stimulation was applied by means of a thin wire electrode and current was initially set low at .5 volts. The current would be increased in small steps if no reports of experiences or signs of bodily movements were detected until a limit was reached or effects were obtained. The reports depended on the

> **Double dissociation** arises when, following brain injury, some people do well on one task, 'A', and poorly on a second task, 'B', while others with different brain injuries show the opposite pattern. In such cases the two tasks are said to be doubly dissociated.
>
> **Point electrical stimulation** a technique for directly stimulating points on the cortex exposed during surgery using a thin electrode and low-voltage current; body movements and verbal reports are combined with records of electrode placements to provide maps of cortical involvement with different experiences and body movements.
>
> **Transcranial magnetic stimulation (TMS)** a non-invasive method of temporarily exciting or inhibiting cortical areas by means of magnetic stimulation.
>
> **Transcranial direct current stimulation (tDCS)** a non-invasive method of stimulating the brain by passing a weak direct current through the brain.

> **Neurological homunculus**
> a representation of the areas of cortex involved in sensory and motor functions by a model human figure (Latin: homunculus = little man) in which the body parts are scaled to reflect the size of the cortical areas that involve those parts. Thus, hands and fingers of the homunculus are much larger than the trunk. The homunculus can be sensory or motor, and although both are similar they are not identical.

exact areas stimulated. For example, a patient stimulated on the occipital lobe reported 'A star came down towards my nose', while a patient stimulated on the temporal lobe reported, 'I heard music . . . like the radio.'

Penfield and Boldrey (1937) plotted the points on the cortex that led to head, shoulder or arm movements when stimulated; these points are shown in Figure 1.11. A similar plotting of sensory reports revealed that the extent of neural representation of sensory information was very large for the tongue, mouth and hands, but quite restricted for large areas such as the skin over the back. These data can also be memorably represented by a **neurological homunculus** where body parts are scaled to reflect their representations in the cortex (Figure 1.13), so that the hands, tongue and face are huge, and the trunk and legs are small.

For more on Penfield see Catani (2017) and this YouTube video: https://www.youtube.com/watch?v=68MiW2KK1us

Transcranial magnetic stimulation (TMS)

TMS is a non-invasive magnetic stimulation of the brain caused by rapidly changing electrical current in a coil held over the scalp. This procedure typically produces a 'virtual lesion' by which small cortical areas are temporarily disabled.

Transcranial direct current stimulation (tDCS)

Transcranial direct current stimulation (tDCS) involves sending a low direct current (around 1–2 mA) through the brain by connecting electrodes to the sides of the head. The procedure is completely painless and the current flow leads to alterations in brain function. Current flow can be *anodal* (from anode to cathode) or *cathodal* (from cathode to anode). Anodal flow generally boosts performance, while cathodal flow tends to disrupt performance in a way similar to a virtual lesion in TMS (Kadosh, 2013).

As an example study, we note that anodal tDCS through the parietal lobe appears to affect performance on mathematics tasks (Kadosh et al., 2010).

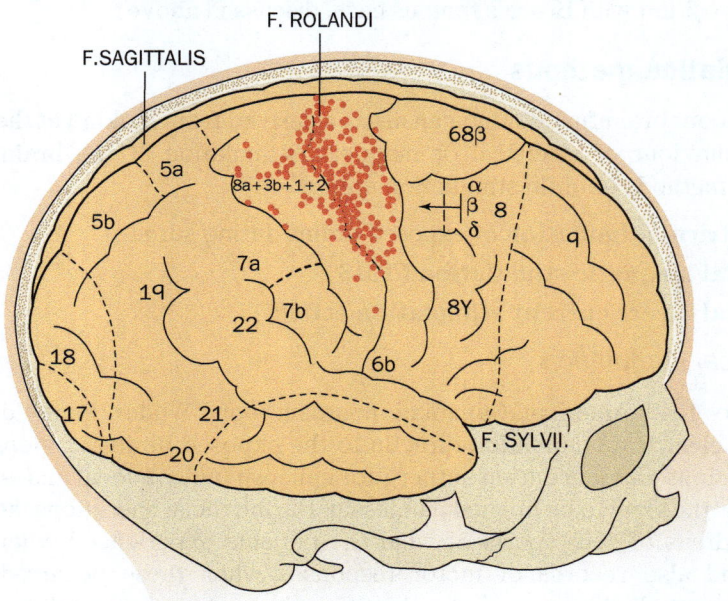

Figure 1.11 Point stimulation map of cortex showing where stimulation elicited movements of hand, shoulder and arm.

Source: Penfield & Boldrey (1937).

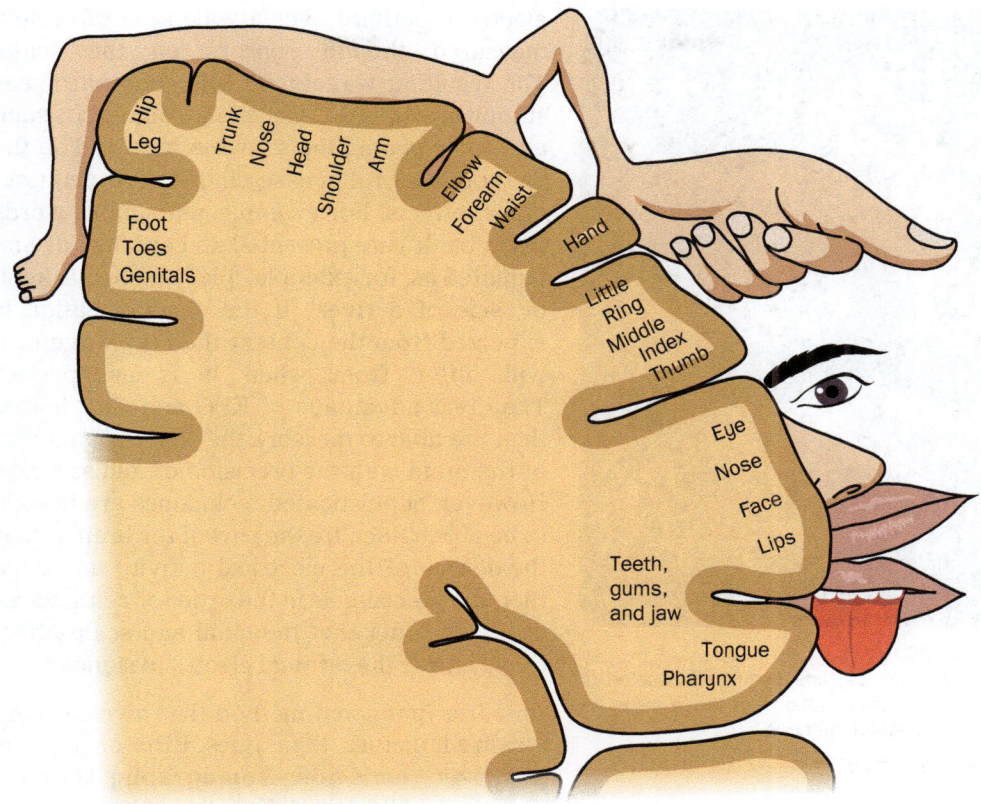

Figure 1.12 Motor cortex areas relating to movement of body parts.
This pattern of cortical area sizes reflecting fineness of movement control by those areas was revealed by point stimulation (Penfield & Rasmussen, 1950).

Recently, neuropsychology has benefited from the development of imaging or scanning techniques that enable researchers to see and accurately measure the location and extent of damage in living patients (rather than having to rely on information gleaned at autopsy). We will now outline some of the main imaging methods.

Brain imaging

Broadly there are two main categories of brain scanning or imaging. These are (1) **structural imaging**, which shows the static anatomy of the brain, and (2) **functional imaging**, which represents brain activity over time.

Over recent years, a number of structural imaging methods have been developed, such as X-ray computed tomography and computerized axial tomography (CAT) scans, which require highly focused X-ray beams to be passed through the body. **Magnetic resonance imaging (MRI)** is the dominant method currently and provides high-resolution anatomical images. This technique does not involve possibly damaging radiation, but uses radio waves and a strong magnetic field that surrounds the person being scanned as he or she lies in a narrow tunnel-like apparatus.

Turning to functional methods, **electroencephalography (EEG)** and **event-related potentials (ERP)** give a record of function as a summary of

> **Structural imaging**
> structural imaging methods show brain anatomy.
> **Functional imaging**
> functional imaging methods detect brain activity.
> **Magnetic resonance imaging**
> a high-definition method for structural imaging using strong magnetic fields.
> **Electroencephalography (EEG)**
> a functional brain imaging method showing waves of electrical activity from scalp recorders.
> **Event-related potentials (ERP)**
> a functional brain imaging method recording electrical activity during repeated stimulus presentations.

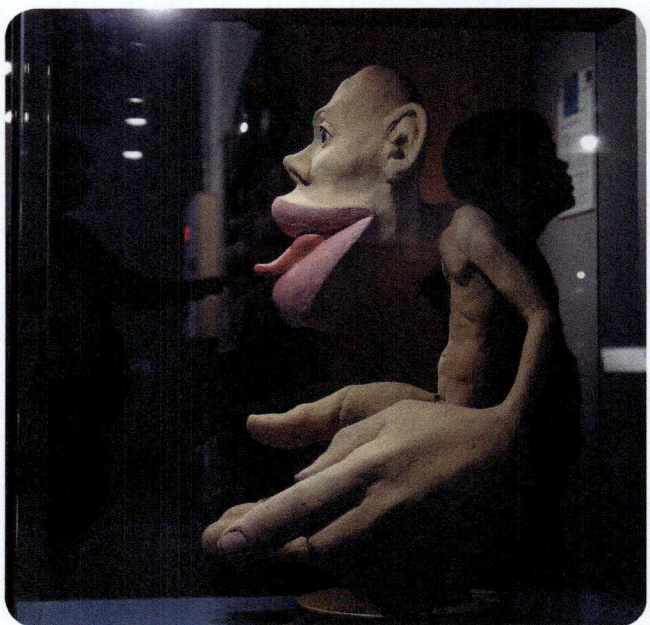

Figure 1.13 Sensory homunculus.
This model 'little man', or homunculus, has body parts scaled to reflect the sizes of the cortical representations of those parts as revealed by Penfield's point stimulation methods.

© ITAR-TASS News Agency/Alamy Stock Photo

> **Positron emission tomography (PET)**
> a functional imaging method that uses positron emissions from radioactive glucose to indicate areas of increased blood flow in the brain.

electrical activity over a wide area of cortex, measured though sensors on the scalp. The resulting waveforms following particular stimuli are different, depending on factors such as how expected the stimulus was, and so the method is useful in assessing expectancy (and other) effects. For example, ambiguous words (e.g., 'bank') are presented and are then disambiguated as, for example, 'place money is kept' or 'side of a river'. If the disambiguation is expected from the context then the waveform will differ from when it is unexpected. The great advantage of EEG and ERP is that they are able to measure the electrical activity of the brain with the precision of milliseconds. However, sophisticated techniques are needed to be able to localize the part of the brain that is the source of the electrical activity and even then the precision is in the order of centimetres due to the fact that the skull and scalp effectively smear the original electrical signal.

An early functional method that gives a more localized picture than does ERP or EEG is **positron emission tomography (PET)**. This requires injection of a radioactive compound into the bloodstream. The scans then measure the blood flow to different regions of the brain. Interpretation is based on the finding that when a brain area is active, more blood flows into it and thus there is increased chemical activity involving the radioactive compound. Interestingly, a nineteenth-century Italian physiologist, Angelo Mosso, first reported this fact, long ago, in the 1870s, from studies of patients whose skulls had been opened up by accidents, so that the cerebral arteries had been exposed to view and the increased blood flow could be seen, as it happened (Legrenzi & Umilta, 2011, p. 12).

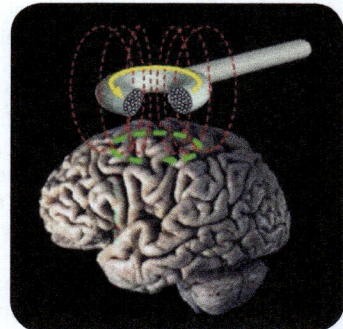

Figure 1.14 Transcranial magnetic stimulation (TMS).
This image shows how specific cortical areas are stimulated by transcranial magnetic stimulation (TMS).

Source: Wassermann (2013).

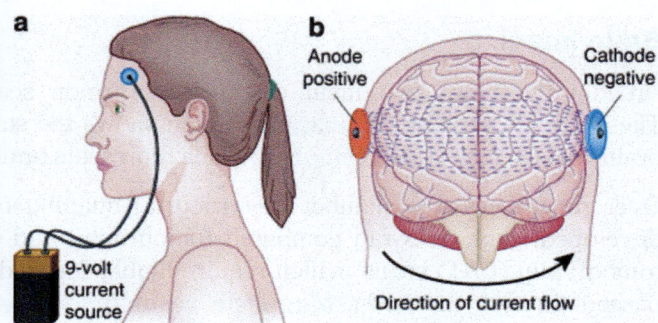

Figure 1.15 Transcranial Direct Current Stimulation (tDCS).
The images show how transcranial direct current stimulation is applied to the brain by passing a weak current through the brain.

Source: George & Aston-Jones (2010).

Although useful, PET scans only show activity averaged over about 90 seconds or longer, thus giving a very crude picture of the sequence of activity. This along with the need for an invasive injection of a radioactive material has discouraged the widespread use of PET for general experimental purposes.

The currently favoured technique for functional imaging is **functional Magnetic Resonance Imaging (fMRI)**. This method does not require injection of radioactive substances and measures the degree to which oxygen in the blood flow is depleted in many areas simultaneously. The more the activity, the more oxygen is taken from the blood by the neurons. What is measured in fMRI is known as the BOLD, or blood-oxygen-level-dependent contrast signal. It can show effects over quite a short timescale (1–3 seconds) relative to what is possible with PET and in small areas (approximately 3 cubic mm) known as 'voxels'. (However, it should be noted that many cognitive processes as measured by reaction times, seem to take 300–400 milliseconds and so are much faster than the 1–3 seconds required for BOLD signal changes; and a single voxel contains hundreds of thousands of neurons, so the temporal and spatial resolution of fMRI is not yet as high as would be wished.)

> **Functional Magnetic Resonance Imaging (fMRI)**
> a method of imaging brain activity that uses oxygenation levels of blood flow, and has good temporal and spatial resolution.

In recent years, results from fMRI brain scans have frequently been reported (or, some would say, misreported!) in the media. In such reports, typically a brain outline is shown on which red blobs are superimposed, reflecting areas of high activation, and sometimes blue blobs to indicate deactivation. In newspapers, magazines and websites, we are told that such blobs show centres for altruism, criminal tendencies, love, wisdom and religion, among many other complex functions (Vrecko, 2010), including, according to one claim, actual true romantic love for iPhones (Lindstrom, 2011). An internet search with a key phrase such as 'Brain scans show . . .' will yield many more examples for the curious reader. However, to really understand fMRI results, it is important to be aware of how these images arise. They are not simple snapshots of brain activity but rather are highly computed images based on many assumptions.

The images are frequently arrived at by a task subtraction method in which the brain activity of all the voxels in the control condition (measured by BOLD signal) are statistically compared to the brain activity in the corresponding voxels in the experimental condition. If the activity is greater in the experimental condition than the control condition then it is common to call this an 'activation'. Some of the complexity of dealing with fMRI data is shown in Figure 1.16 (overleaf), which shows the probability that a given brain voxel will be more active when a participant listens to a human voice than when they listen to other sounds (see also Chapter 2). While there is a relatively small region where the majority of listeners will show a difference in activation, this region is surrounded by an extensive area where some listeners will show a difference. Why there is this large region where some participants will show an activation remains an open challenge for fMRI. It has been suggested that the reliability of repeated scans is not high (Kong et al., 2007). There has also been debate over some commonly used statistical procedures, which have been criticized as overstating the significance of obtained differences by Vul et al. (2009), who pointed to the risks of capitalizing on chance. A typical brain volume obtained with fMRI involves tens of thousands of voxels and when activity in these voxels is compared between experimental and contrast conditions many differences will prove significant by chance alone. Even when conventional methods of dealing with multiple comparisons are applied, a tendency to report the mean effect sizes for the voxels above threshold significance will lead to spuriously high effects being reported.

> Chapter 2, p34

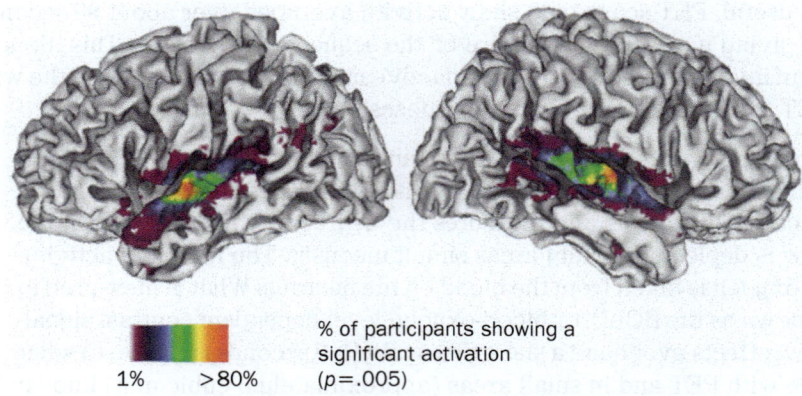

Figure 1.16 Probabilistic map of fMRI activity for a listening task.
An 'activation' is defined as greater activation for the experimental condition (human voice) than the control conditions (other sounds). From performing the experiment on many participants one develops a model of the probability that a voxel will show an activation.

Source: Reprinted from Chartrand et al. (2008), with permission from Elsevier.

Some further difficulties with generalizing fMRI results arise from the fact that the environment in which the measurements are carried out is very specific and highly unusual. Lying flat on one's back, while keeping perfectly still, in the claustrophobic noisy tunnel typical of fMRI machines, may well affect how tasks are tackled as compared to typical laboratory or real-life situations. There is evidence that posture affects problem solving; for instance, Lipnicki and Byrne (2005) found that being supine – that is, lying on one's back – facilitated anagram solving but hindered mental arithmetic compared to upright postures, so results from supine participants as in fMRI studies could well be specific to that posture.

What might imaging studies tell us about cognitive processes?

Despite all the difficulties just outlined, fMRI is now a much used method, and it is hoped that consistent results will emerge over laboratories as studies accumulate and the implications become clearer. Suppose I had devised a new spatial reasoning task and wondered if people might use verbal reasoning to solve it. I might make an argument from scans to processes along the following lines:

1. Broca's area is known to be activated in tasks independently classed as involving implicit speech.
2. Broca's area is activated in my new spatial reasoning task.
3. Therefore, my new spatial task involves implicit speech.

Here is a real example, which takes things a few steps further (Ferris et al., 2005):

1. The striatum is activated when animals receive pleasure through rewards.
2. The striatum is activated when rats suckle their young.
3. Therefore, suckling is pleasurable to rats.
4. The striatum is activated less by cocaine injection than by suckling in rats.
5. Therefore, suckling is more pleasure inducing in rats than is cocaine.

In these arguments we have examples of 'reverse inference' (Poldrack, 2006) – that is, going from 'If a task involves cognitive function F1 then brain area Y is active' *and* 'In task B, brain area Y is active' to 'In task B, function F1 is involved'. In strict deductive logic this is not a valid argument. It is the equivalent of saying, 'If it's Friday, then Smith eats fish at noon' and 'Smith is eating fish at noon today', 'Therefore, today is Friday'. But perhaps Smith eats fish at noon on Tuesdays and Wednesdays as well as on Fridays. The conclusion that today is Friday is not necessarily true. Similarly, brain area Y may be active when many different cognitive functions are involved. The reverse inference only works when the 'if' means 'if and only if'. This inference pattern is known in logic as 'affirming the consequent' and is an invalid argument or 'fallacy', which we will discuss more fully in Chapter 14. However, although reverse inference arguments are not conclusive or *necessarily* correct, they can be seen as generating plausible hypotheses for later testing, and this is a useful role that imaging results can play. In our mini example, if brain area Y is active, then function F1 cannot be ruled out, but further independent evidence would be needed to conclude that function F1 is indeed involved in task B (the negative case, in which brain area Y is not active would support the valid inference that function F1 is not involved in task B). Overall, then, imaging results often suggest hypotheses for further research rather than being decisive in particular cases. However, for cases when there is controversy over which cognitive model might more accurately reflect human capabilities, it is sometimes possible to design an fMRI experiment to critically evaluate these theories. Furthermore, for specific cases, such as retinotopy, fMRI data has been fairly decisive in mapping out the visual field in the visual cortex.

Chapter 14, p511

Imaging methods can also make practical contributions, as is indicated in Box 1.5 on the use of imaging in identifying patients in **persistent vegetative states**, who may well be conscious although unable to respond overtly to stimuli.

Persistent vegetative state a clinical condition involving 'wakefulness without awareness' – patients may open their eyes, move spontaneously, exhibit sleep and waking cycles, but be unresponsive to external stimulation and are assumed to lack any awareness.

Box 1.5 When Things Go Wrong: Using neuroscientific methods to detect awareness in 'vegetative states'

Following severe brain injuries, some patients emerge from a coma and appear to be awake but show no signs of awareness and no signs of purposeful behaviour in response to external stimulation. In circumstances such as this, there is no guarantee that the patient is not actually aware and just unable to respond normally. Given the application of imaging methods to see specific responses in the brain, these techniques are being investigated as a way of communicating with patients unable to respond in any other way. For example, Owen and colleagues (Owen et al., 2006) used fMRI methods with a female patient who met all the criteria for the diagnosis of being in a vegetative state. While being scanned, the patient and normal control participants were asked to imagine (a) playing tennis and (b) visiting all the rooms in their houses starting from their front door. The results were striking, as shown in Figure 1.17 (overleaf). The patient and normal controls showed essentially identical patterns of activation (compared to resting periods) to the two instructions. Imagining playing tennis activated the supplementary motor area and imagining visiting all rooms at home activated parahippocampal gyrus, posterior parietal lobe and lateral premotor cortex to similar extents in both the patient and controls. Owen and colleagues concluded that the patient did have awareness of instructions and could demonstrate this by her neural response.

The study attracted some criticism in that the patient's response could have been automatically cued by the words 'tennis' and 'house' (Greenberg, 2007; Nachev & Husain, 2007). However, Owen et al. (2007) were able to show that simply presenting the words without the instruction to imagine the activities did not produce any significant response. The results were confirmed in a larger follow-up with 54 patients and 16 healthy controls (Monti et al., 2010). This follow up study found that 17 per cent of patients who appeared behaviourally to be vegetative were conscious and could reliably produce

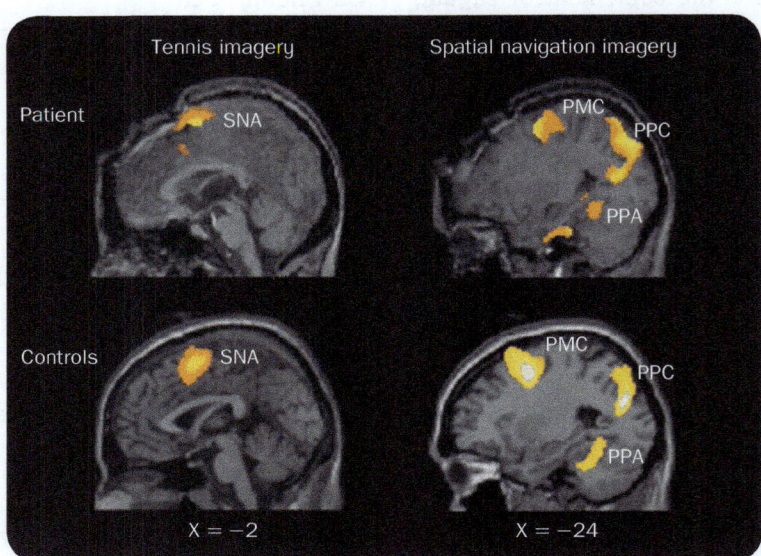

Figure 1.17 fMRI scans of patient in vegetative state and normal controls when undertaking imagery tasks.
SMA = supplementary motor area; PPA = parahippocampal gyrus; PPC = posterior parietal lobe; PMC = lateral premotor cortex.

Source: Owen et al. (2006). Reprinted with permission from AAAS.

meaningful responses via an fMRI scanner. One patient who had been diagnosed as vegetative for five years was able to answer correctly biographical questions (such as whether he had siblings and the last place he had visited before his traumatic accident) by imagining playing tennis for 'yes' and walking round his house for 'no'.

The basic finding of covert awareness in around 20 per cent of patients who appear to be completely vegetative has been confirmed in a review of some 37 published studies involving 1,041 patients (Kondziella et al., 2016).

Owen and colleagues (in Cruse et al., 2011) have found similar evidence for awareness in some patients in a vegetative state using the more portable (and more affordable) EEG methods. This work could lead to ways of communicating with patients who can respond to instructions. Patients could be asked to imagine wiggling their right thumb to signal 'yes' and their right big toe to signal 'no', and then answer yes/no questions. This method generates distinctive EEG traces in both patients and healthy controls. Thus, a questioner could read off their yes/no answers from the EEG trace. Another application might be to control machines modified to accept such binary thought signals.

As Owen (2019) has pointed out in a review of this field, sole use of behavioural indicators without brain activation indicators can be seriously misleading regarding awareness in apparently vegetative patients. In light of the findings reviewed here, the diagnostic criteria are being re-examined by the relevant professional bodies such as the Royal College of Physicians in the UK and the American Academy of Neurology in the USA, to include brain activation indicators of responsiveness. A major application of this work would be to involve apparently vegetative patients in giving their consent, or not, to proposed care and management options.

Networks and functional integration

> **Functional integration**
> the way in which brain regions communicate and act together.

Paying more heed to *networked* as against highly localized activity may yield useful results (Dobbs, 2005; Petersen & Sporns, 2015) and is sometimes referred to as the study of **functional integration**, as against the earlier study of functional localization. For example, it has become apparent from imaging studies that in a resting state many brain areas are active in a correlated way. Furthermore, the use of 'resting' states as control or contrast conditions yielded the unexpected finding of 'deactivation' across a range of brain areas when active tasks were worked on. Subtracting the resting activation levels from the task activation levels often produced negative patterns – that is, large areas of the brain were more active during 'rest' than when a focused task was undertaken. From these results, it was inferred that there is a **default mode network (DMN)** reflecting internal tasks such as daydreaming, envisioning the future and retrieving memories (Buckner et al., 2008). Activity in the DMN is negatively correlated with activity in other brain systems when people focus on external visual signals. In the infant brain, there is limited evidence of the default network, but default network activity is more consistently found in children aged 9–12 years, suggesting that the default network undergoes developmental change (Raichle & Snyder, 2007).

> **Default mode network (DMN)**
> a network of brain regions that is active when a person is not focused on the external environment.

Other networks have been identified by assessing correlations of activity in brain areas – areas of correlated activity can be regarded as forming networks (Menon, 2010). Principal among the identified networks are a *central executive network* (linking the dorsolateral prefrontal cortex and posterior parietal cortex) involved in higher-order and attentional control; and a *salience network* (linking the anterior insula and anterior cingulate cortex), involved in monitoring the salience or goal relevance of external inputs and internal brain events.

Summary

In this chapter we have indicated the main areas that cognitive psychology deals with: perception, motor action, attention, learning, memory and forgetting, language, decision making, reasoning, problem solving and emotional aspects of cognition. These topics all involve the processing of information and cognitive psychology can be seen as the study of how we and other animals acquire, store, retrieve and use information. These functions are carried out ultimately by brain processes and so neuroscience studies of the brain, involving functional and structural imaging and case studies of brain damage are relevant to cognitive psychology.

A number of approaches to understanding cognition have been explored over the centuries including associationism, introspectionism and behaviourism.

The associationists were philosophers who observed their own experiences and set out to specify laws by which ideas became associated with each other. One such law is the Law of Similarity by which similar ideas evoke each other, for example, "cup" and "mug". Other laws involve closeness in space or time, so that ideas that are often evoked close together in space ("cup" and "saucer") or time (for example, "clouds" and "rain") become associated.

The introspectionists were early empirical psychologists who sought to analyse complex experiences into component sensations using very artificial reports by trained participants. The introspectionist method could not be used with children, animals, people with psychiatric conditions or anyone not extensively trained in the method and so was of limited use. Moreover, disagreements about reports of thought without imagery could not be readily resolved. The focus on analysing experience continues to the present day using experience sampling methods and ratings of experiences on dimensions such as "goal-relatedness", "realistic v.bizarre", or degree of "visual imagery" and so on.

The behaviourist school aimed to overcome problems with introspectionism by focusing on objectively observable behaviour and especially on learning in animals.

The dominant approach today is the information processing approach which derives from analogies with computers and computer programs (particularly with artificial intelligence programs). In this analogy the brain is the hardware on which the cognitive software runs. The emphasis in this approach was typically on thinking and problem solving in the earlier period but more recently a considerable body of work has developed on learning using connectionist models.

> A direct focus on the brain and neural processes has grown in the form of cognitive neuropsychology (which focusses on effects of brain damage) and cognitive neuroscience (which focuses on scanning of intact brains performing live in laboratory tasks and on temporary interventions that can affect short term functioning.) A wide range of methods for scanning e.g., EEGs and fMRI are available. Intervention methods that temporarily boost or depress functions e.g., direct current stimulation and trans-magnetic stimulation are discussed. Finally, we note a very useful application in which fMRI traces can be used to tell whether apparently vegetative patients are aware and can be used by patients to communicate their preferences even although they cannot control any muscles in their bodies and so cannot communicate by speech or by gestures of any kind.

Review Questions

1. What topics are the focus of cognitive psychology?
2. Compare and contrast the strengths and weaknesses of the behaviourist and information processing approaches.
3. What is meant by a functional level of analysis?
4. What can brain imaging methods tell us about cognitive processes?
5. To what extent can we draw conclusions from brain stimulation studies about cognitive processes?
6. What can studies of people with brain injuries tell us about cognitive functions?

Discussion Questions

1. Does artificial intelligence need to build on what we know about human cognition?
2. Does cognitive neuroscience need cognitive psychology?
3. Could all the varied approaches to cognition outlined in this chapter be valid?

Further Reading

Baddeley, A. D. (2019). *Working memories: Postmen, divers and the cognitive revolution*. Routledge.
Foer, J. (2012). *Moonwalking with Einstein: The art and science of remembering everything*. Penguin Books.
Ward, J. (2015) *The students' guide to cognitive neuroscience* (3rd ed.). Psychology Press.

PERCEPTION

2

PREVIEW QUESTIONS
INTRODUCTION
    Box 2.1 Practical Application: Cognitive robotics and human–robot interaction
FUNDAMENTAL CONCEPTS
    FROM PHYSICAL WORLD TO PERCEPTUAL REPRESENTATION
    PRINCIPLES AND THEORIES OF PERCEPTION
    THE BODY AND PERCEPTION
HUMAN PERCEPTUAL SYSTEMS
    VISUAL SYSTEM
    Box 2.2 Research Close Up: Discovery of feature detectors in primary visual cortex
    AUDITORY SYSTEM
    Box 2.3 Practical Application: Cochlear implants
    SOMATOPERCEPTION SYSTEM
    MULTISENSORY INTEGRATION
    Box 2.4 When Things Go Wrong: Motion sickness and cybersickness
    Box 2.5 Practical Application: Multisensory warning signals for handover between autonomous and manual driving
RECOGNITION
    OBJECTS
    SCENES
    EVENTS
SOCIAL PERCEPTION
    Box 2.6 When Things Go Wrong: Capgras syndrome
    FACES
    Box 2.7 Practical Application: Forensics – eyewitness testimony and super recognizers
    VOICES
    BIOLOGICAL MOTION
SUMMARY
REVIEW QUESTIONS
DISCUSSION QUESTIONS
FURTHER READING

Preview Questions

1. What is the function of perception?
2. Are there general principles of perception across the different senses?
3. How is our physical body involved in perception?
4. How is perceptual information integrated across our different senses?
5. How do we recognize objects and why is general object recognition difficult to achieve?
6. Our social interactions are guided by what perceptual information?

INTRODUCTION

> **Perception**
> our sensory experience of the world.

Perception is the remarkable set of processes that organize sensory experience into an understanding of our surrounding world. The study of perception gives us insight into how properties of the physical world are transformed into our mental world, and informs our understanding of behaviours like navigation and recognition. For example, consider being given a complicated set of directions in a dimly lit and noisy environment like a nightclub. If later you cannot find your destination, it is possible that you failed because you (1) did not properly hear the directions, (2) did not see the relevant landmarks, or (3) were somehow incapable of understanding and executing the directions. The study of perception examines these first two points of hearing and seeing the world. It provides us with an understanding of what information about the world is available to our cognitive systems.

> **Sensation**
> entails the processes by which physical properties are converted to neural signals.

We can view perception standing in the continuum between **sensation** – where physical energy is transformed into brain signals, and cognition – where mental representations of the world and our goals are used to reason and plan behaviour. The study of perception emphasizes how physical properties of the world are represented mentally and, although it does not have sharp, distinct boundaries with either sensation or cognition, it forms a unique field of study. Perceptual information can come in many forms – sight, sound and bodily perception will be considered in this chapter. This perceptual information is essential to inform us about our surroundings, and guide our interactions with the physical and social world. If all relevant information about the physical world were captured in our perceptual representations, then the study of perception might be extremely straightforward. However, visual illusions (Figure 2.1) provide clear evidence that our perceptual systems do not always faithfully represent the physical world.

> **Somatic**
> perception of the body through touch and sensing the orientation of limbs in space.

In addition, rules of perceptual organization such as those advanced by the Gestalt psychologists in the early twentieth century illustrate that even for simple line drawings our perception appears to follow consistent rules to guide interpretation (Figure 2.2, opposite) that go past just the image content. The Gestalt psychologists are famous for their observation that the whole is greater than the sum of its parts and this observation motivates our efforts to explain perception not simply as the collection of sensory activities.

This chapter is organized into four sections. The first describes basic principles and theory that would be relevant to any perceptual system. The second section outlines the capabilities of visual, auditory and **somatic** perceptual processes, and how basic principles shape perceptual experience. The remaining two sections of the chapter describe how perception leads to recognition. In the third section we consider general recognition of objects, scenes and events, while in the final section we consider the case of social perception, where faces, voices and bodies are recognized. The understanding of perceptual processes is increasingly finding applications in new areas of technology, and we discuss one such advance in Box 2.1.

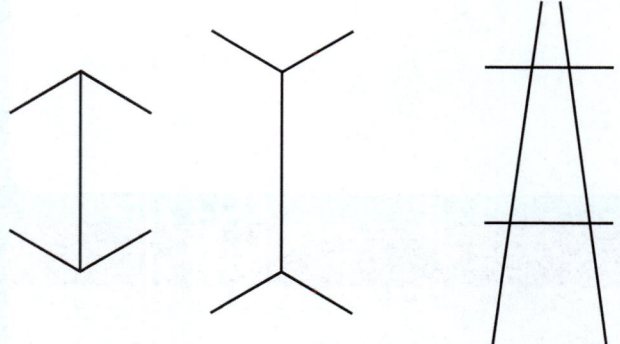

Figure 2.1 Illusions show perception is not always accurate.
To the left is an example of the Muller-Lyer illusion, where the two vertical lines are the same length but are not perceived to be identical. A similar effect is seen to the right in the Ponzo illusion, where the horizontal lines are the same physical length but not perceived as such. These and other illusions illustrate the fact that perception is not always accurate.

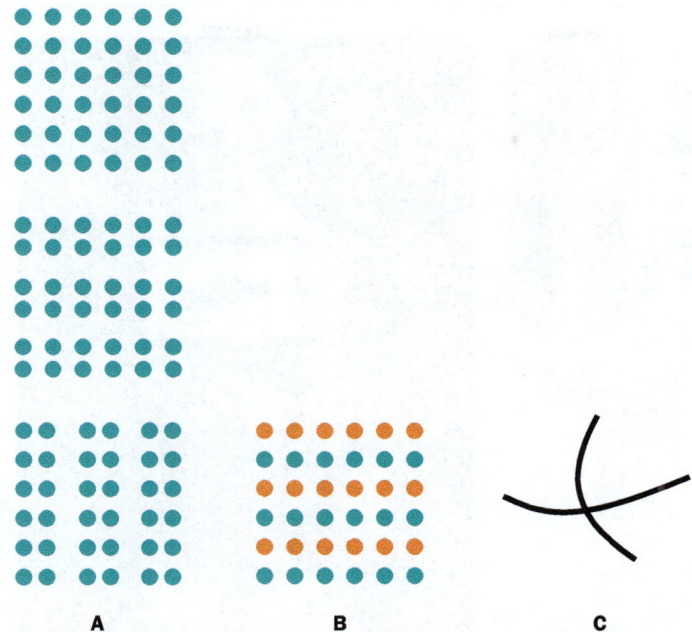

Figure 2.2 Examples of Gestalt laws of perceptual organization.
(A) Proximity between elements determines whether the figure is seen as rows or columns. (B) Similarity among elements determines that the figure will be seen as rows. (C) Good continuation determines that the figure will be seen as two lines crossing rather than two v-shaped figures.

> **Box 2.1 Practical Application: Cognitive robotics and human–robot interaction**
>
> In the past, the field of robotics was largely concerned with industrial robots confined to repetitive tasks in predictable environments. However, cognitive robotics (Vernon et al., 2010) and human–robot interaction (Goodrich & Schultz, 2007; Sheridan, 2016) are two new fields of robotics that are defining the move of robots from these restricted environments to everyday scenes. One basis for the advancement in robotics has been an explosion in the availability of high-performance sensors, actuators, computers and power systems, which make it possible to develop and control increasingly sophisticated mechanisms (Siciliano & Khatib, 2019). However, to realize the potential of these devices one needs to know how to make a system that can sense and adapt to its environment and cooperate with other agents in the world. Given that biological systems – in particular humans – excel in their ability to perceive information about their environment and to adapt, they have become models for the development of robot systems at many levels. This has provided an important link between the results of past decades of research into perception and cognitive science and the development of new robots.
>
> Among the goals of these new robots is the ability to achieve tasks in an unstructured environment and to be able to interact with humans efficiently so that task goals can be effectively communicated and controlled. Within this framework a variety of robots have been developed. At one end of robot design are basic robots such as Roomba, which faces the challenge of navigating an unpredictable and unstructured environment to make your home tidy. At another end are robot designs that mimic the form and function of humans and animals. Early examples were the dog Aibo from Sony and Asimo from Honda, while more recent examples include iCub, Nao and Pepper (Figure 2.3, overleaf). One motivation for mimicking human form is that if these robots are going to help us in our own environment then they should be able to navigate these environments, by, for example, having legs to climb stairs. Moreover, if we want to be able to teach the robot by example of our own actions then it is convenient for robot and human to share the same structure (Billard et al., 2016).

Figure 2.3 Nao (left) and Pepper (right).

Source: Shutterstock. Photos by Tinxi and Arnold O. A. Pinto.

This chapter includes many connections with current robotics research, which will be useful to reflect upon as you read through it. For example, we discuss fundamental concepts in perception and cognition, and the most fundamental concepts are those that apply to both human and robot perception (Bülthoff et al., 2016). We discuss human perceptual systems; these are useful for providing an existence proof that there is sufficient information in the perceptual world for the task to be achieved. Moreover, robots that mimic human form and structure make a fascinating test bed for exploring ever more complex theories of perception. Finally, we discuss recognition and social perception, and while reaching human levels of performance is still far in the future, progress is being made (Sciutti & Sandini, 2017; Senft et al., 2019), and even rudimentary skills could aid the performance of robots placed in care situations (Langer et al., 2019).

FUNDAMENTAL CONCEPTS

From Physical World to Perceptual Representation

Chapter 1, p14

The essential problem of perception is that the physical world is 'out there' and our mental world has its home base inside our head. To address this problem we will emphasize an information-processing approach that looks at how the senses provide information about the world and how this information is transformed into understanding (for an introduction to the information processing approach, see Chapter 1). A primary question is whether enough information comes in through our senses to accurately and completely represent the physical world, and if not, why? One simple answer to this question is 'no', for the reason that our sensory organs have limited ranges. Dogs provide an illustration of this since they can hear in ranges that humans cannot. However, there is a deeper information-processing issue known as the inverse-problem

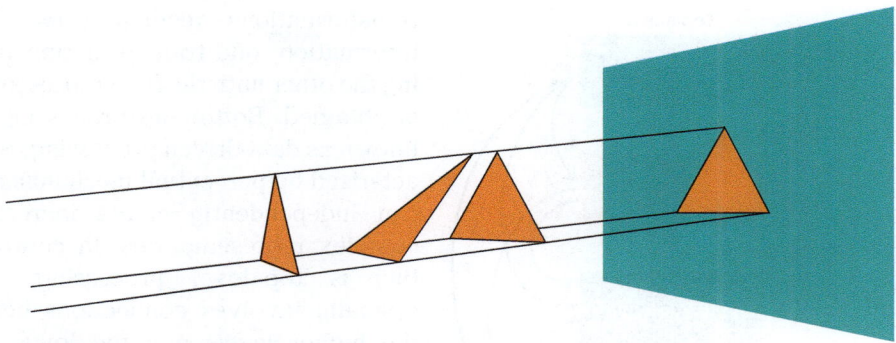

Figure 2.4 Different shapes in the world can produce the same image.
The image of a triangle with sides of equal length can be created by an infinite number of possible triangles in the world provided we orient them in a particular way. This demonstrates the inverse-problem: the image on the eye has lost information and the brain must somehow recover this information.

that describes why even for the best sensory organs perception cannot typically guarantee a faithful representation of the physical world (Fleming & Storrs, 2019; Pizlo, 2001) The nature of the inverse-problem can be illustrated with an example from vision. The world is three-dimensional, and this three-dimensional world is projected onto our eyes to become two-dimensional images. The inverse-problem is that typically these two-dimensional images do not have enough information to specify the exact three-dimensional world that created them. The images have lost a dimension and there is no way, given just the images and nothing more, to invert the image creation process from the two-dimensional images back to a unique three-dimensional scene (Figure 2.4). The crucial realization here is that there are fundamental ways that information is lost in the sensory encoding of the physical world. Thus, the fidelity of our mental representations of the physical world cannot wholly depend upon the incoming information. Crucially, it must depend upon the ability of perceptual processes to use assumptions about the structure of the world to analyse incoming sensory information in a way that we can overcome the inverse-problem to build plausible interpretations of what is out there.

The previous paragraph asserted that perception does not guarantee us a faithful representation of the physical world, due to the inverse-problem and the intrinsic loss of information as the physical world is transformed into a mental representation. However, the fact that most of us succeed with the great majority of our interactions with the physical world demonstrates that our perceptual systems have evolved effective principles to overcome theoretical limitations to the processing of perceptual information. We will discuss these general principles in the coming sections.

Principles and Theories of Perception

The inverse problem suggests that the solution to how we perceive the world will not be simple, however it does not prescribe any particular solution. To tackle this problem we will focus on how best to characterize the flow of information in the fully developed perceptual system and what principles might be at work to organize this information.

The flow of information: bottom-up and top-down processing

A fundamental distinction in perceptual processing is whether we achieve an understanding of the world through bottom-up or top-down mechanisms. In bottom-up processing, the original sensory input is transformed in an uninterrupted cascade of

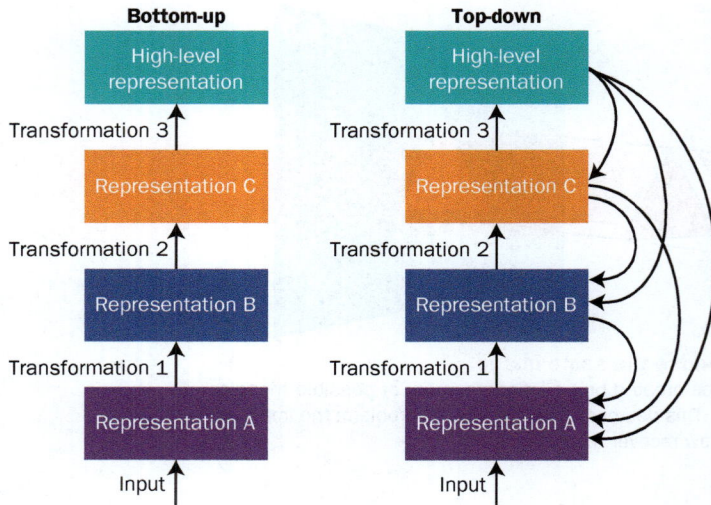

Figure 2.5 The flow of information in purely bottom-up and top-down processing.
(Left) In a bottom-up (data-driven) system, the answer bubbles up through a series of transformations that are not affected by factors such as expectancies. (Right) In a top-down system, the rising flow of information is filtered by the influence of information held higher in the processing hierarchy.

transformations feeding forward the information, one transformation following the other until the final representation is obtained. Bottom-up processing, also known as data-driven processing, is characterized by perceptual mechanisms that can independently create increasingly complex representations. In contrast to this is top-down processing, which crucially involves connections between the higher levels and the lower ones. Instead of an uninterrupted cascade of feed-forward transformations there are feedback connections that mediate the transformations with higher-level information. These two styles of information processing are shown in Figure 2.5.

An example of the distinction between the two styles of information can be given in recognizing an orange. In bottom-up processing the individual surface dimples would organize into a texture that could be combined with perception of the spherical shape and the orange colour, and from these separate processes the orange could be recognized. In top-down processing, it is critical that we start out with some expectation of what we are looking for, and this knowledge exerts influence on lower-level processes that will interact with the processing of colour, shape and texture. At the extremes, bottom-up processing holds that what we experience is an inevitable consequence of what sensation strikes our eyes, ears or skin, and top-down processing holds that this perception will be meaningfully influenced by what we expect to experience.

Evaluation

The bottom-up and top-down processing approaches provide contrasting views of theoretical principles behind how we process incoming sensory information. It is possible to debate whether bottom-up or top-down processing predominates. For example, that bottom-up processing would dominate for unambiguous perceptual input and top-down processing would dominate for situations where the perceptual input is ambiguous. However, for many situations the two can be seen to work together, as demonstrated by research that measured the response of visual neurons in monkeys and found that information about the emotional expression of a face could be encoded and transmitted faster than other information (Sugase et al., 1999). The research further proposed that an initial facial representation could be rapidly transmitted to centres that would begin to determine emotion. This emotional judgement could then be used to refine the further processing of information. Such a system might be important for quickly identifying friend or foe (happy or angry), and using this to shape the interpretation of the incoming information for deciding about other factors such as identity (Figure 2.6). This example used faces and emotion to illustrate the interplay of

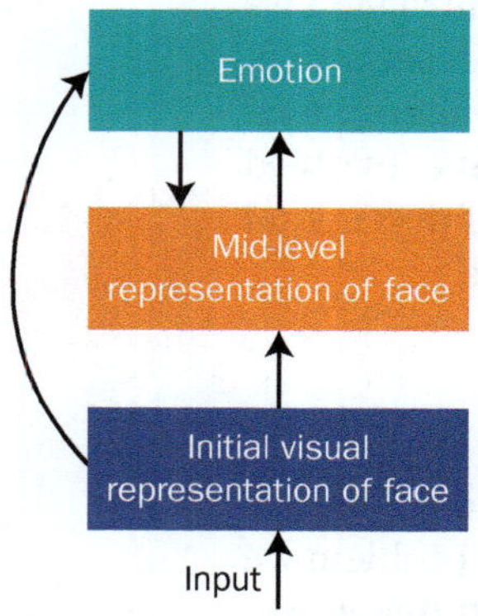

Figure 2.6 Example of top-down processing of faces.
In this example based on neurophysiology, data informative about facial emotion is transmitted ahead in the processing stream so that emotional information can be used to influence mid-level processing of facial information.

bottom-up and top-down processing and we will further discuss faces later in this chapter, and emotions in Chapter 15.

> Chapter 15, p550

One particular view of how bottom-up and top-down processing might interact is known as **predictive coding** (Friston, 2018; Rao & Ballard, 1999; Serences, 2008). In predictive coding, top-down information contains predictions of what is expected and predictions are compared with the input. If there is a large mismatch between prediction and incoming signal then a large prediction error signal will be produced. Because this error signal can then subsequently be considered a bottom-up signal, the simple dichotomy between bottom-up and top-down becomes necessarily more complex (Rauss & Pourtois, 2013). One notable property of predictive coding is that if the input matches the prediction then little energy is expended to send this signal.

Perceptual organization: likelihood principle

The direction of information flow is one aspect of information processing; another is how the incoming data are transformed. An important concept to discuss in this regard is the **likelihood principle** (Pomerantz & Kubovy, 1986).

> **Predictive coding** principle for encoding sensory information wherein the perceptual input is compared to the expected perceptual input, and this difference between expectation and input is what is encoded.
> **Likelihood principle** states that the preferred organization of a perceptual object or event will be the one that is most likely.

The likelihood principle states that the likelihood that an object or event will occur is important for the perceptual processing of that object/event. Indeed, it proposes that we will perceive the object/event that was most likely to have occurred, and this idea historically goes back to discussions of Helmholtz in the 1800s about unconscious inference (Helmholtz & Southall, 1962). The importance of the principle can be seen in light of the fundamental problem discussed earlier that perceptual input is typically not sufficiently rich in information to uniquely specify what will be perceived. Thus, something additional is necessary for us to infer the properties of the world. The likelihood principle suggests a statistical view is appropriate for evaluating our perceptual input to determine what we are experiencing. One statistical approach to perception is provided by a computational theory called Bayesian Decision Theory (Geisler & Kersten, 2002; Jazayeri & Shadlen, 2010; Mamassian & Landy, 2010; Mamassian et al., 2002). Other views of Bayesian approaches are given in Chapter 3.

> Chapter 3, p86

From a Bayesian point of view, perception is an inference problem: what is the most likely event responsible for my perception? For vision this becomes: given the image on my retina, what is the most likely scene to have caused it? In Bayesian Decision Theory there are three components involved in answering this question. First, there is the *likelihood*, which represents all the uncertainty in the image. The larger the number of scenes consistent with the image, the larger the uncertainty. The second component is the *prior* and this represents the knowledge one has about the scene before even looking at the image. The stronger the prior, the less one is subject to the uncertainty of the likelihood. Finally, the third component is the *decision rule*. Depending on the task and the objectives of the observer, one might be interested in finding the most likely interpretation given all the information available (from the likelihood and prior), or instead explore randomly one of the possible interpretations every time the same image is presented. The decision rule thus adds flexibility to the general framework to model behaviour.

For example, let us assume we have built a cat detector to look for photos of cats on the internet. Our (hypothetical) cat detector examines each input image to look for something fluffy with pointy ears. However, the ears of the cat may not always be visible in the image and to get the likelihood we need to know how many other photos might get our cat detector to fire in a similar way. The likelihood thus represents how uncertain we are that our detector is actually viewing a cat. The prior is the chances of seeing a picture of a cat on the internet, and might change depending on where we are browsing. If we are on a random web page then the prior is just the probability of seeing a cat on the internet – the number of cat pictures on the internet divided by the total number of photos on the internet. However, if we are on a super-cute cat picture website then, even if the image has a small likelihood of being a cat, the large prior would guide us to see a cat. Finally, the decision rule lets us take into account various other factors. For example, if we desperately need a picture of a cat and we were on a website with fuzzy and ambiguous photos (low likelihood) of many kinds of animals (low prior), we would change to a website with clear photos of only cats (high likelihood and high prior). However, if we were relaxed and seeking entertainment or a novel view we might explore further on the low likelihood and low prior website.

Information processing approach

In his book, *Vision,* David Marr (1982) proposed an information processing approach to perceptual processing in vision. This built upon earlier work led by the ecological psychologist Gibson (1979). Ecological psychology holds that perception works in a largely bottom-up fashion by exploiting regularities in the visual world that are termed **invariants**. By studying how perception works in the actual environment (not the lab) and uncovering these invariants we can understand how the perceptual system directly transforms perception into an interpretation of the world. This process was termed **direct perception**. Marr questioned how 'direct' this process could be and tried to understand the fundamental nature of information processing necessary for transforming perceptual input into an interpretation of the world. He suggested that, for any information-processing device to be completely understood, it must be understood at three different levels. The first level is the computational theory to understand the purpose of the computation and to demonstrate its appropriateness for the task at hand. The second level is the choice of representation for the input and output, and the algorithm to achieve the transformation between input and output. The third level is how to realize these computations – for example, in a human or a digital computer. The generality of this three-level approach was influential in opening boundaries between researchers working in computer vision, visual psychology and the physiology of vision.

> **Invariants**
> in vision, these are properties of the three-dimensional object being viewed that can be derived from any two-dimensional image of the object.
>
> **Direct perception**
> also termed event perception and ecological perception, this refers to the bottom-up process by which objects and their function are recognized.

First level: computational theory

At the first level, the question is what is the purpose of a computation and why does it do what it does? In the broadest sense, the purpose of the perceptual processes of vision, hearing and touch are to keep us aware of our external world and support our adaptability to the changing world. Why these processes exist can take on a more philosophical perspective, but as a matter of practical significance they exist to ensure our survival. Marr used the example of theorizing about a cash register to illustrate computational theory. At the computational level what a cash register does is add and why it does it is that this is appropriate for the task of summing a total. While this might seem overly simplistic, it has been noted that approaches based in physiology or psychology sometimes missed this basic consideration or did not keep it distinct from other details.

Second level: choice of representation

The second level is the choice of representation for the input and output, and the algorithm to achieve the transformation between input and output. To explain this level we can continue with the cash register example. With the cash register we can represent numbers using the Hindu Arabic system where four is represented as '4', or with the

Roman system where four is represented as 'IV'. Moreover, our choice of representation will motivate the use of different algorithms to achieve addition. This second level is an essential aspect of cognitive science. Light energy hits the eye, or energy from air vibrations hits the ear, or mechanical energy is applied to the skin. This input is transformed to an output; so with light we consider the transformation from light to output representations such as colour, edges and motion, while for sound we consider the transformation of air pressure into representations of pitch and volume. Although these transformations are in one sense transformations of physical energy from one form to another, a fundamental view of cognitive science is to consider them as transformations from one information state to another. With this perspective we will model human behaviour, and experience of the world, as the result of algorithms operating on representations of information.

Third level: achieving the computations

The earlier discussion about how faces might be processed in the monkey visual system raises the final point in Marr's hierarchy. Namely, the final level to discuss is the actual way in which the computations are achieved, whether by man, machine, monkey or banana slug. Every organism or machine will have its own limitations imposed by the device performing the computations, whether a brain or a computer chip. These limitations introduce practical considerations on the second level of what representation and type of algorithm is optimal to use, but they will not impact the first-level computational theory of what is the goal of the computation. Thus, keeping this choice of device as a separate consideration allows us to discuss perception in terms of transforming incoming stimulus energy into appropriate representation of information without worrying about the specific implementation. To return to our example, a cash register, an electronic calculator and an abacus can all be seen to solve the computational problem of adding the value of items. However, the particular hardware we choose to do the calculation can motivate different representations and different algorithms to solve the identical problem.

The approach of Marr to emphasize computational theory and keep the three levels of description distinct has enabled perceptual scientists in psychology, neurophysiology, computer science and engineering to communicate with one another, and has facilitated a cross-fertilization of research ideas.

The Body and Perception

Up to now in this chapter we have conceived of perception as providing us with an internal mental representation of the physical world. In a traditional view of cognitive science this representation would effectively be symbolic and the goal of cognition would be to appropriately manipulate the symbols. However, such a view leaves out how our own physical body and the actions it produces might influence perception. As a way to incorporate consideration of these physical and environmental factors, one can take an **embodied view of cognition** (Barsalou, 1999; Gomila & Calvo, 2008; Wilson & Golonka, 2013). Such a view of how perception and cognition interact draws upon, among others, the theories of Gibson and the ecological psychologists that to understand a cognitive system we need to take as the unit of analysis the 'system' embedded into its surrounding environment. Crucial to the embodied view of perception is that what one perceptually experiences of the world is related not only to the perceptual input but also to one's purpose, physiological state and emotions. For example, when wearing a heavy backpack it has been reported that hills

> **Embodied view of cognition** holds that cognition is about the experiences arising from a perceptual system tightly linked to an action system rather than the manipulations of abstract representations.

appear steeper and their distances appear greater (Proffitt, 2006). The claim is that perceiving spatial layout combines the geometry of the world with behavioural goals and the costs associated with achieving these goals. However, this claim remains controversial (Philbeck & Witt, 2015). In some cases, effects previously attributed to embodied perception have, under closer experimental scrutiny, been shown to depend on participants' spontaneous beliefs about the goals of the experimenter (e.g., Durgin et al., 2009, 2012; Shaffer et al., 2013) or on instructions that lead participants to consider non-visual information relevant to their reports (Woods et al., 2009).

The embodied view of cognition, that states of the body influence states of mind, has philosophical implications for our understanding of cognition (Clark, 1997; Haugeland, 1998; Hurley, 1998; Noë, 2004; Shapiro, 2019) that are beyond the scope of the current chapter. However, it is relevant to review six claims that form a basis for embodied cognition (Wilson, 2002):

1 Cognition is situated – it takes place in the real world and inherently involves perception and action.
2 Cognition is time-pressured – we need to evaluate our situation in the environment as quickly as it changes and this is essential to consider.
3 We offload cognitive work onto the environment – whether counting on our fingers or organizing a hand of cards in poker, we actively change our environment to reduce cognitive workload.
4 The environment is part of the cognitive system – given the continuous dense flow of perception and action it is not meaningful to study the mind alone.
5 Cognition is for action – perception and memory must be considered in terms of how they contribute to action.
6 Offline cognition is body based – even when the mind can be separated from the environment it is grounded in mechanisms involving perception and action, such as using metaphor based on physical relations.

These six claims are still relevant in forming a basis for embodied cognition (Gomila & Calvo, 2008; Núñez et al., 2019; Ostarek & Huettig, 2019), and while there has been criticism of the embodied approach (Goldinger et al., 2016), the six claims provide a basis for considering the essential role of perception (and action) in cognition. In the next section we discuss perceptual systems and include evidence, consistent with an embodied approach, that vision incorporates special systems designed for integrating perception with action. Related discussions of embodied cognition are provided in Chapters 3 and 9.

Chapter 3, p107 and 9, p307

HUMAN PERCEPTUAL SYSTEMS

In this section we briefly review some of the perceptual systems that mediate the transformation from physical energy to higher-order cognitive representations. Our emphasis will be on the forms of perception that are responsible for producing perceptual features like orientation, shape, colour, motion, timbre, pitch and felt pressure. Such features are important since models of perception and cognition rely on the existence of appropriate features to represent objects and events. For example, the shape of an object might be key to recognizing the object, or the tonal variation of a voice might signal aspects of the emotion of a speaker. Before proceeding, it is worth reminding ourselves that, consistent with Marr's three levels of information processing, the human brain is just one particular implementation of an information-processing device.

However, the human system provides a good starting point for understanding other organisms as well as for the design of biologically inspired machines.

We will organize our discussion of human perception around the auditory, somatoperception and visual systems, and will first consider the systems as separate and independent modules before covering multisensory perception, where the different modules can interact. One motivation for discussing the systems separately is that the human brain exhibits a large degree of modularity in its arrangement of sensory processing areas for audio, video and somatosensory processing (Figure 2.7). Our goal behind considering a few perceptual systems is that by distilling out what is common to all systems and examining how the different systems might interact we can obtain a general view of how perception works.

Before discussing the individual perceptual systems it is useful to preview that there is a degree of functional similarity across the visual, auditory and somatoperceptual systems. Their basic organization is a hierarchy going from specialized sensory receptors, through dedicated neural pathways to centres in the brain with patterns of organization that are specialized for the incoming modality. These centres in the brain can either be found in the cortex for information requiring elaborate processing and conscious awareness or in lower subcortical brain areas if the perceptual information is needed for immediate monitoring without conscious awareness. Table 2.1 provides a broad overview of the visual, auditory and somatoperceptual systems and provides terms useful for further study of perception. From the table it can be seen that the visual, auditory and also the touch component of somatoperception share many properties in going from specialized receptors to a systematically organized cortical structure. Note that we include **proprioception** and **vestibular sensation** within somatoperception since typically we not only need to know that a particular body part is being touched but also the orientation of that body part relative to the rest of the body (proprioception) and the orientation of the body in space (vestibular sense). Vision can also strongly contribute to a sense of the orientation of the body and limbs in space.

> **Proprioception**
> the sense of how our limbs are positioned in space.
> **Vestibular sensation**
> the sense of balance and orientation in space.

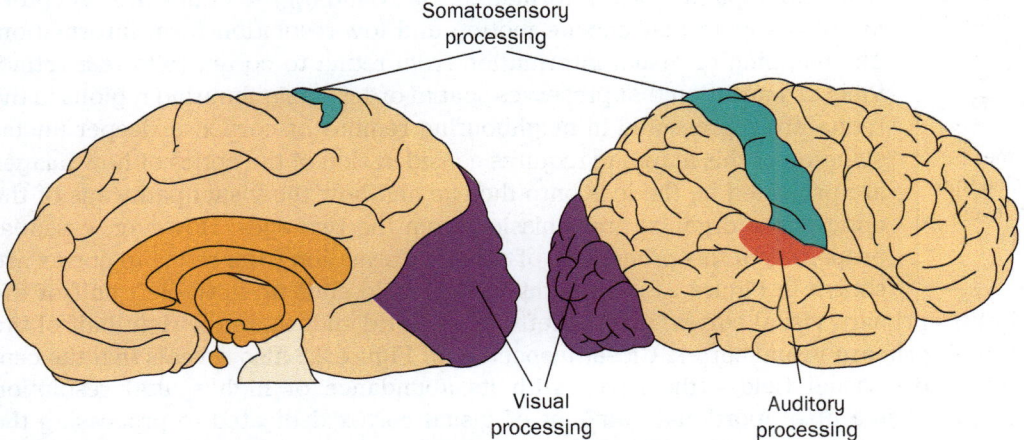

Figure 2.7 Primary sensory areas for sight, hearing and touch in the human brain.
Processing of vision, audition and somatoperception is supported by cortical areas that are largely dedicated to each single sensory modality. Loss of any of these primary sensory areas results in a profound loss of sensory awareness in that modality.

Table 2.1 Basic Organization of Perceptual Systems

	Vision	Audition
Location of receptors	Eyes	Ears
Receptors	Cones, rods in retina	Inner hair cells, outer hair cells in organ of Corti on basilar membrane
Pathway from receptor to cortex	Optic nerve → thalamus → cortex	Auditory nerve → thalamus → cortex
Primary cortical receiving area/organization	Visual cortex/retinotopic	Auditory cortex/tonotopic
Perceptual features	Colour, form, motion, orientation, distance/depth	Loudness, pitch, timbre, distance

This table illustrates the properties common to all the perceptual systems and provides a pointer to the vast literature on each component of the table. The row and column headings are the primary focus of our discussion, while the entries within the table provide terms to enable further study.

We will use the framework presented in Table 2.1 to present the visual, auditory and somatoperception systems. For each system we will discuss the flow of information from receptor to primary receiving area in cortex, further processing in related secondary sensory areas, and how damage to particular brain regions may lead to systematic changes in behaviour.

Visual System

The encoding of visual information begins in the retinas of the two eyes and is transmitted from there to the primary visual cortex. This process follows the basic pattern of using specialized receptors to transform light energy to a neural signal that is sent to specific brain regions with a unique functional organization (Figure 2.8). Towards the centre of each retina is a region known as the fovea, which contains an abundance of receptors known as **cones** that encode colour and high-resolution spatial form information. Surrounding the cones are receptors known as **rods** that encode motion and low-resolution form information. The mapping of visual information from retina to cortex follows a retinotopic organization that preserves spatial order – neighbouring regions in the retina are represented in neighbouring regions of cortex. A deeper understanding of this mapping requires consideration of the optics of how images are projected by the lens onto the eye and how the visual pathways of the optic nerve organize transmission from the two eyes. However, essential properties of this processing of visual information from retina to cortex are shown in Figure 2.8. The right visual world ends up in the left half of the brain's primary visual cortex, and the left visual world ends up in the right half of the brain's primary visual cortex. Closer inspection of Figure 2.8 also reveals that the centre of the visual field – the fovea with its abundance of high spatial resolution cones – has a disproportionate amount of visual cortex dedicated to processing the incoming visual information. This fact explains why, when we want to obtain maximal information about visual form, we move our eyes so that the region of interest projects onto the fovea. In Box 2.2 we further explore the function of primary visual cortex in describing a classic study involving the discovery of feature detectors for orientation in primary visual cortex.

> **Cones**
> special neurons in the retina that are sensitive to different-coloured light, and densely packed to resolve fine image detail.
>
> **Rods**
> special neurons in the periphery of the retina that are effective in low levels of light and to sense motion.

Somatoperception		
Touch	Proprioception	Vestibular
Skin	Tendons, muscles	Semicircular canals of ears
Meissner, Merkel, Ruffini and Pacinian receptors in skin	Golgi tendon organs, muscle spindles	Hair cells in otolith organ
Nerve fibres → spinal cord → thalamus → cortex	Nerve fibres → spinal cord → cerebellum → cortex	Nerve fibres → brainstem nuclei
Primary somatosensory cortex (Brodmann Areas 1, 2, 3a and 3b)/somatotopic	Brodmann Areas 2 and 3a of somatosensory cortex	No dedicated area
Pressure, vibration	Force of muscles, joint angles	Body movement and body orientation

From primary visual cortex there are two primary pathways for further visual processing (Ungerleider & Mishkin, 1982); these are shown in Figure 2.9 along with functions associated to these pathways. One pathway leads from visual cortex to the temporal lobe; it is specialized for determining what objects are in the visual world and is called by neuroanatomic convention the **ventral stream**. The other pathway, known as the **dorsal stream**, leads from visual cortex towards parietal cortex and is specialized for determining where objects are in the visual world. The characterization of the ventral and dorsal streams as supporting what and where was augmented by Goodale and Milner (1992) to include the distinction of separate visual systems for perception and action. In this two visual system model the ventral stream is responsible for processes that provide conscious awareness of what an object is, while the dorsal stream is responsible for processes that enable us to perform actions on an object. For example, if we were in a garden admiring the style of flower arrangements, the ventral stream would be involved in perceiving detailed shapes and colours and recognizing flowers, but if a wasp were about to land on our arm the dorsal stream would be involved to swat it away.

Ventral stream
the visual pathway from occipital cortex to temporal cortex that is involved in recognition of the object being viewed.

Dorsal stream
the visual pathway from occipital cortex to parietal cortex that is involved in locating and guiding how to use an object.

Evaluation

The idea that two independent visual streams from visual cortex form the basis of our further visual information processing for perception and action has met with some controversy. One question is whether there are examples of behaviour in typical individuals which provide evidence that these two streams are independent. Evidence consistent with the view that the streams are independent came from experiments suggesting that viewing a particular object might be influenced by a visual illusion but that directing an action towards the object will not be influenced by the illusion (Aglioti et al., 1995; Carey, 2001). However, subsequent experiments examining motor behaviour towards visual illusions yielded somewhat mixed results that the vision and action systems are independent (Brenner & Smeets, 1996; Bruno, 2001; Franz, 2001). An additional complication to the two-stream approach is that Glover (2004) suggested that a more complete understanding is available if we divide the dorsal, action stream into two separate components of planning and control. Planning was modelled to take place in the inferior parietal lobe and control

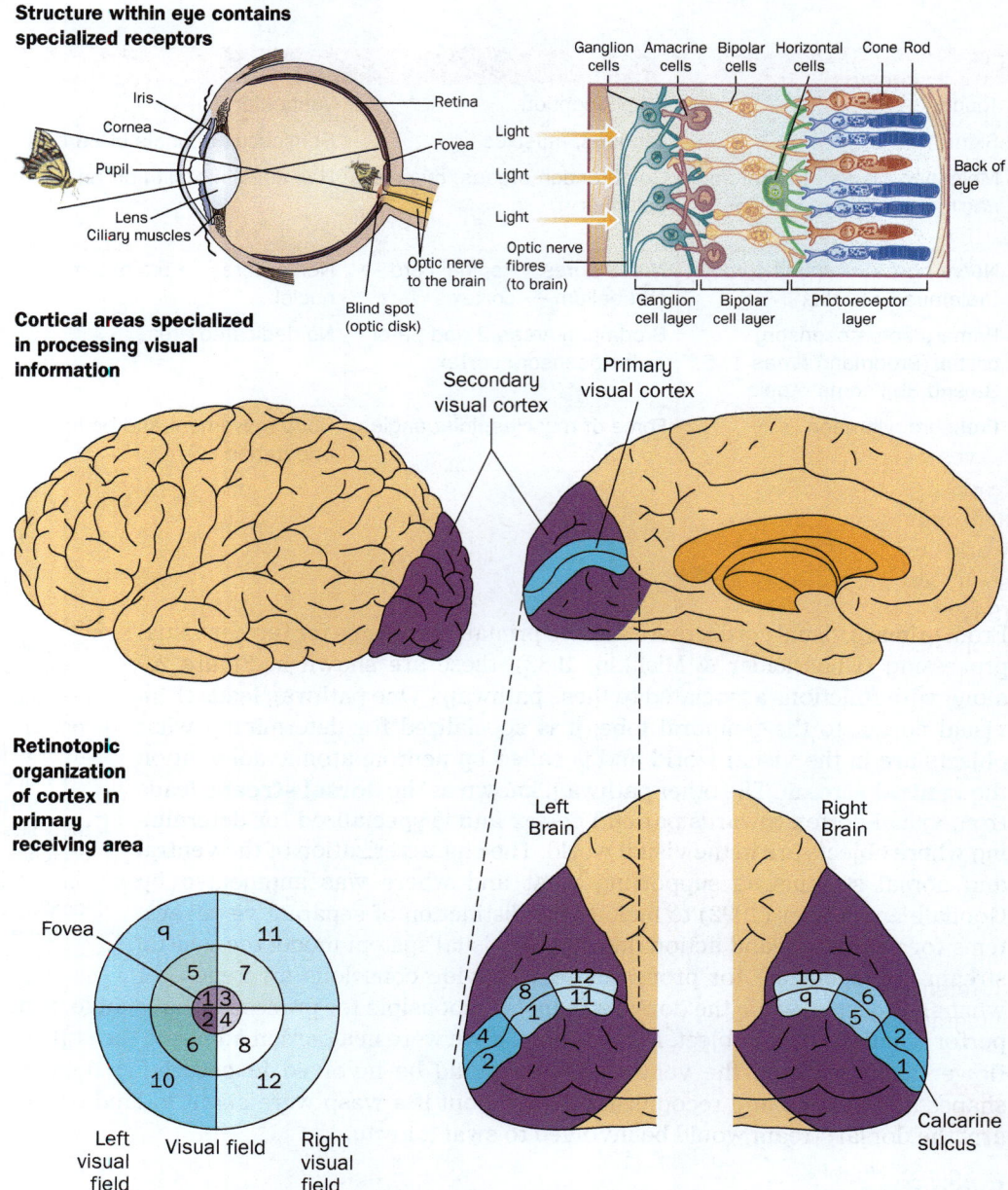

Figure 2.8 Information is sent from specialized receptors in the eye to the primary visual cortex.
The eye contains specialized receptors that transduce light energy into neural signals and these neural signals make their way to the primary visual cortex. Primary visual cortex is organized in a retinotopic fashion with specific parts of the visual world represented in specific parts of the brain. Surrounding the primary visual cortex are further secondary areas that are specialized for processing visual information.

Source: Adapted from Holt et al. (2012).

in the superior parietal lobe. Debate on these issues continues, with resolution complicated by the inherent complexity in modelling large networks of brain areas, and in conducting experiments that involve both perception and action.

Consistent with modularity of function as an organizing principle, it is possible to localize brain areas within the ventral and dorsal streams that are responsible for representing particular visual features. For example, a brain region in the dorsal stream located in the middle temporal cortex near the border with visual cortex has been shown to be responsible for seeing motion. Specific damage to this region leaves an individual capable of seeing aspects of the world such as colour and shape but not motion (Zeki, 1991; Zihl & Heywood, 2015); pouring tea into a cup becomes impossible because the fluid vanishes (Cooper et al., 2012; Otsuka-Hirota et al., 2014). Another brain region, this time from the ventral stream of visual cortex (Bouvier & Engel, 2006), is responsible for seeing colour. Damage to this region leaves one without colour vision and leads to a condition known as cerebral achromotopsia where the colours of the world are replaced with shades of grey such as in a black-and-white movie (Sacks, 1997), though different material properties, such as the milkiness of tea,

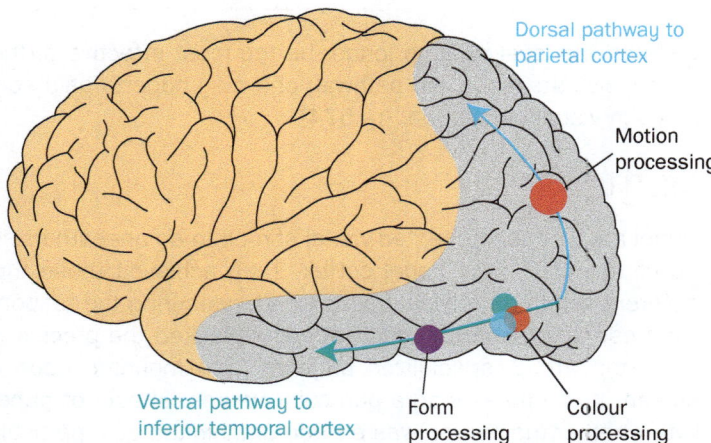

Figure 2.9 Two pathways out of primary visual cortex.
The dorsal stream travels to parietal cortex and specializes in motion processing as well as being important for visually guided action. The ventral stream travels towards temporal cortex and specializes in processing of colour and form. The processing of depth is distributed across these two pathways. Due to their different functions the dorsal pathway is sometimes referred to as the 'where' or 'how' pathway and the ventral stream as the 'what' pathway.

can be perceived (Chadwick et al., 2019). However, some perceptual features, like depth, are not precisely localized in the brain and thus our impression of depth must come from a combination of depth cues. This is due to the variety of ways in which information in an image could signal depth. For example, depth cues include (1) pictorial cues such as interposition where we see depth because one object obstructs the view of an object behind, (2) motion parallax where we see a faster-moving surface as closer than a slower-moving surface (for example, out the window of a moving vehicle where distant objects move slowly compared to those nearby), and (3) stereo depth where the difference in position of the two eyes yields differences in the two images that carry depth information (an effect exploited to create 3D movies). How we see depth thus raises the issue of how different sources of depth information are combined, and later when we cover multisensory integration we will discuss how different sources of sensory information are combined.

 Box 2.2 Research Close Up: Discovery of feature detectors in primary visual cortex

Source: Hubel & Wiesel (1959).

INTRODUCTION

Although conducted more than 50 years ago, the 1959 study by Hubel and Wiesel (1959) marks a fundamental advance in visual science that is still relevant today (Gunnars & Bruck, 2020; Wurtz, 2009). The body of work associated with this finding resulted in the 1981 Nobel Prize for Hubel and Wiesel. Here, we will emphasize how this study gave a critical starting point for explaining what features the visual system uses to represent incoming information. Although much was known about vision by 1959, physiological evidence was lacking as to how visual information is initially represented and subsequently transformed in primary visual cortex (also known as striate cortex). Hubel and Wiesel's study changed this, as the introduction to their paper makes clear: 'In the central nervous system the visual pathway from retina to striate cortex provides an opportunity to observe and compare single unit responses at several distinct levels. Patterns of light stimuli most effective in influencing units at one level may no longer be the most effective at the next. From differences in responses at successive stages in the pathway one may hope to gain some understanding of the part each stage plays in visual perception' (p. 574).

METHODS

Hubel and Wiesel presented visual stimuli to an anaesthetized cat while measuring the electrical activity of neurons in its visual cortex. They achieved these measurements by placing an electrode at different locations of visual cortex and measuring the response properties of neurons. Their methods for presenting stimuli, though effective, lacked the precise computer control of visual stimuli that is now standard. A specialized projector was mounted upon an adjustable tripod and shone upon a screen. When measuring a particular neuron, sheets of paper were affixed to the screen and marked with whether the neuron was excited or inhibited by a particular pattern of light placed at that location. In this way it was possible to map out the response properties of the neuron, and the sheets of paper formed the experimental record. Hundreds of neurons were mapped out in this way, each taking two to nine hours, and the results of 45 were presented in the paper.

RESULTS

An example from the study of a mapping with a very small diameter disk of light is shown in Figure 2.10. The results use 'x' to mark regions where the neuron was excited by the light and triangles to mark where the neuron was inhibited by the light. It can be seen that the overall pattern is consistent with an optimal response by a vertically aligned bar. The results of testing this same neuron with bars of different orientation are shown in two columns to the right, with the bar's orientation shown in the left column and the neuron response in the right column. As can be seen in how the number of spikes in the right column changes with orientation, this particular neuron is maximally stimulated by vertical lines. This example showed a neuron sensitive to vertical lines and examination of other neurons revealed some sensitive to other orientations.

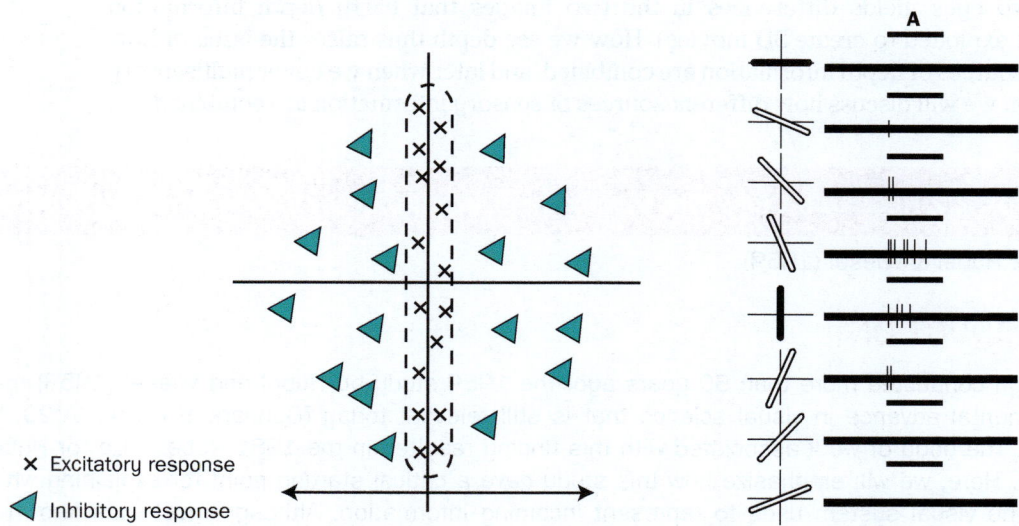

× Excitatory response
◀ Inhibitory response

Figure 2.10 Orientation specificity in response of a neuron in visual cortex.
(Left) An example of a mapping of the receptive field indicates that this neuron is optimally responsive to a vertical bar. (Right) An example of this orientation tuning. When a bar approaches vertical the firing of the neuron is greatest, as shown by the large number of spikes in the trace in the right column. When the bar is horizontal, the neuron does not fire.

Source: Hubel & Wiesel (1959).

▶ DISCUSSION

The significance of these findings is that they suggest short oriented line segments as primary visual features. This motivated a view of the visual system as taking a picture of the world and transforming it into a line drawing for subsequent analysis. An important further development of this finding involved considering how these line detectors could be created from basic neural mechanisms. At the time it was already known that neurons earlier in the visual pathway, in the retina and thalamus, had shown sensitivity only for spots of light (not oriented lines) in a manner known as a centre-surround receptive field. In this centre-surround design either a bright spot surrounded by a dark annulus or a dark spot surrounded by a light annulus is the best visual arrangement to stimulate a neuron. An insight of Hubel and Wiesel was that, theoretically, one could wire together arrays of these earlier centre-surround receptive fields as input to produce a neuron that was sensitive to an oriented line (see Figure 2.11). Moreover, it was possible to wire together these oriented line detectors to explain more sophisticated neural responses. Thus, this result launched an understanding of feature detectors in vision that were built upon increasingly complex arrangements of basic feature detectors.

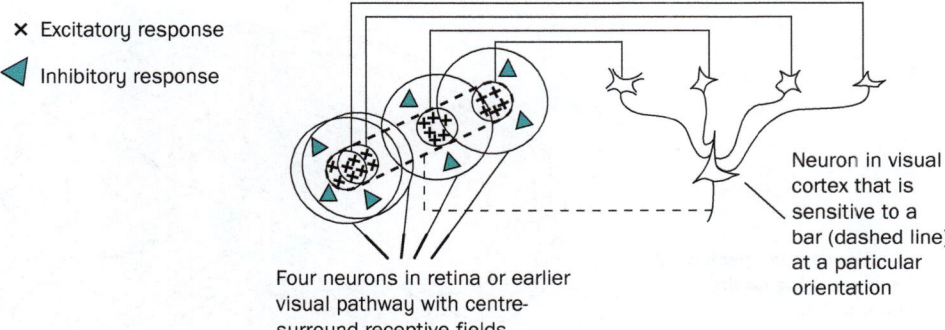

Figure 2.11 Simple detectors can be combined to make more complex feature detectors.
From Hubel and Wiesel (1962) we can see how four centre-surround circular receptive fields can be wired together in cortex to form a feature detector that is sensitive to an oriented bar. Four such centre-surround receptive fields are shown, with each being excited by light shone on the centre and inhibited by light shone in the annulus surrounding the centre. Combination of these receptive fields by a neuron in visual cortex produces a neuron that is sensitive to a bar at a particular orientation.

Source: Hubel & Wiesel (1962).

A wealth of both experimental and theoretical studies followed on from the 1959 experiment. For example, it was shown by Hubel and Wiesel that development of these feature detectors depends upon having an adequately rich visual experience. This result was of great practical significance in demonstrating that there are sensitive periods in the development of sensory processing, and resulted in more insightful treatment of infants and young children with sensory deficits.

Auditory System

The encoding of auditory information begins within a special structure in the ear known as the cochlea and is transmitted from there to a part of the brain known as primary auditory cortex (Figure 2.12, overleaf). The cochlea contains a band of nervous tissue known as the **basilar membrane** on which hair cells are located, and these hair cells move in

Basilar membrane
a stiff structural element located in the inner ear, which contains specialized fluids as well as the hair cells that are key in transducing sound energy into neural impulses.

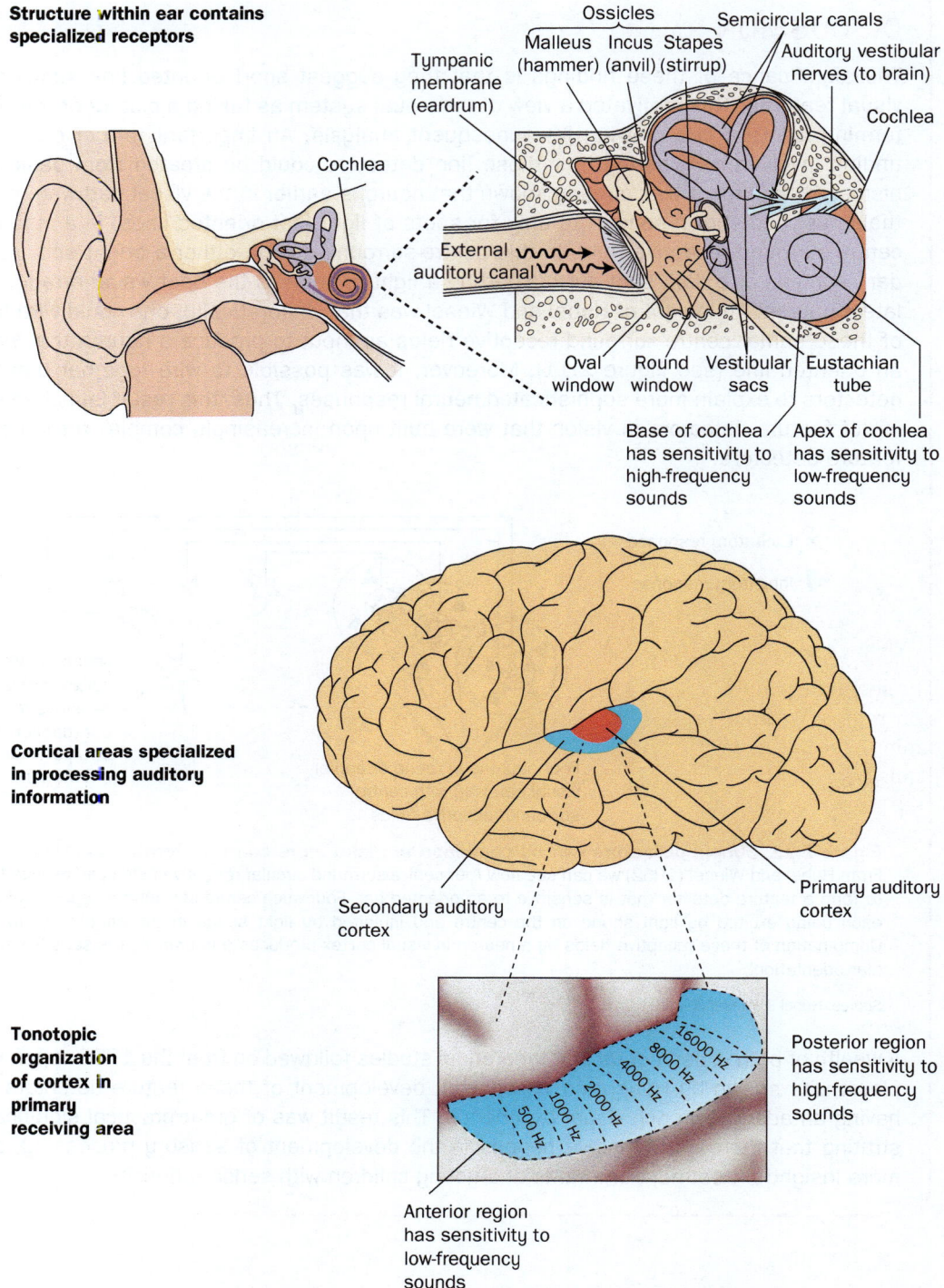

Figure 2.12 Information is sent from specialized receptors in the basilar membrane to the primary auditory cortex.
The ear contains specialized receptors that transduce sound waves into neural signals and these signals make their way to the primary auditory cortex. The primary auditory cortex is organized in a tonotopic fashion, with specific frequencies of sound represented in specific parts of the brain. Adjacent to the primary auditory cortex is the secondary auditory cortex, which is also involved in processing sound information.

Sources: Adapted from Holt et al. (2012); Kandel et al. (2000).

response to sound pressure to transduce vibration into a nervous signal to be sent along the auditory nerve. The perceived pitch of a sound depends in a complex way on the frequency of the sound pressure vibrations. One way that pitch is encoded, known as the **place model**, is that different sections of the basilar membrane are sensitive to different pitches of sound. Aspects of the basilar membrane near to the base of the cochlea encode high-frequency sound, while aspects at the apex of the cochlea encode low frequency. For example, if we listen to a choir we can imagine the voices of the sopranos being encoded at the base and the voices of the bass singers being encoded at the apex. Another way that pitch is encoded by the basilar membrane, known as the **rate model**, exploits the fact that **firing rates** in the auditory nerve can vary, with higher-pitch sounds creating higher-frequency firing rates. Firing rates have also been found to vary with perceived loudness, with greater firing rates corresponding to increased loudness. This knowledge of the functions of the cochlea has been applied to the design of cochlear implants (Box 2.3), which work to restore some hearing in individuals who have damage to the structures of their ear but an intact auditory nerve. From the cochlea, the output of the basilar membrane is carried via the auditory nerve to the primary auditory cortex, where pitches of similar frequencies are to be found neighbouring one another. This arrangement in auditory cortex, known as a **tonotopic map**, is similar to that found in vision, where there is a retinotopic mapping of visual space onto visual cortex.

The secondary auditory cortex, which includes the important speech perception region Wernicke's area, has been found to be sensitive to patterns of timing (see Chapter 11 for further discussion of Wernicke's area). Timing information is particularly important as most sounds we hear contain a complex mixture of sound amplitudes and frequencies, and decoding this information requires precise timing. Indeed, the critical property of sound known as timbre is the psychological correlate of the complex patterns of amplitude and frequency. An example of timbre is that both a clarinet and a piano can play a tone of the same pitch but they obviously sound different, and these differences in sound can be attributed to the timbre of the different instruments.

Damage to the auditory cortex and surrounding regions can lead to a variety of deficits, such as receptive aphasia and amusia. Aphasia is the inability to use either verbal or written language, and is discussed in Chapters 10 and 11. Amusia, commonly known as tone deafness, is characterized by a deficit in detecting fine-grained pitch changes in melodies (Ayotte et al., 2000; Ayotte et al., 2002). Individuals with amusia can thus find music to be an unorganized arrangement of sounds that is even unpleasant to hear. In some cases, amusia is a transient effect of a stroke, however it can sometimes persist for an extended period (Sarkamo et al., 2009). Amusia has also been reported to arise from abnormal development (Ayotte et al., 2002). Recent examination of the brain areas implicated in amusia has implicated a variety of other brain regions and thus it appears to not involve simply abnormal pitch encoding (Stewart et al., 2006). The involvement of other brain regions such as parietal cortex has been implicated in other deficits in processing sound such as phonagnosia (Vanlancker et al., 1989). In phonagnosia individuals cannot recognize the sound of familiar voices although they can discriminate a variety of other sounds. These individuals suffer particularly in not being able to recognize the identity of a speaker when talking on the phone.

Place model
a model of sound perception where the perceived pitch of a sound is determined by the location (place) on the basilar membrane that is stimulated.

Rate model
a model of sound perception where the perceived pitch of a sound is determined by the way the basilar membrane encodes the frequencies contained in the sound.

Firing rates
a term from neurophysiology where the activity of a single cell or group of cells is recorded. A high firing rate indicates great activity of the cell due to sensitivity to the incoming information.

Tonotopic map
where the auditory processing of different tones is arranged in an orderly layout in cortex.

Chapter 11, p403

Chapter 10, p364, and 11, p379

Box 2.3 Practical Application: Cochlear implants

Cochlear implants are devices that provide the profoundly deaf with the ability to hear and understand speech and other sounds (Wilson, 2015). Cochlear implants rely upon electrical stimulation of the auditory nerve, and efforts to use electrical stimulation to produce a sensation of hearing go back hundreds of years. However, producing successful designs required advancements in engineering (electronics, computer technology and compatible materials for implantation) as well as advances in understanding the relationship between the physiology of the ear and the psychology of hearing and speech perception. Modern research into cochlear implants started in the 1950s with the first devices implanted in the 1980s, and research to improve performance is ongoing. While their use has become widespread, there are still significant challenges regarding the psychology of their use, such as being able to predict individual differences in success of use, and the best ways to train people to hear using the cochlear implant (Pisoni et al., 2017).

A cochlear implant has two essential components (Figure 2.13). One is external and includes a microphone, sound processor and a transmitter system. The other is an implanted receiver and an electrode array system to transmit signals to the auditory nerve. The implantation procedure requires special surgery to secure the receiver and to place the electrode array along the winding length of the cochlea. From the perspective of psychology, the two most relevant aspects are the external sound processor and the internal electrode array. Together, the sound processor and electrode array must act to replace the complex acoustics of the inner ear and the complex transduction properties of the receptors in producing a signal to be sent along the auditory nerve that the brain can decode.

The sound processors have the job of taking as input the full audio signal and reducing this to the critical acoustic information for a user to function in the world. An example of a simple sound processor is the telephone, which takes our voice and transmits only the sound frequencies from around 400 to 3400 Hz (the full range of human hearing for a typical adult is around 15 to 15,000 Hz), which is why voices sound different on the telephone. Limiting the amount of information transmitted is an important design constraint as the sound processor has limited computing power and there are only a small number of electrodes to stimulate the auditory nerve. (There are tens of electrodes in a cochlear implant and this is small compared to the thousands of receptors along the basilar membrane in the

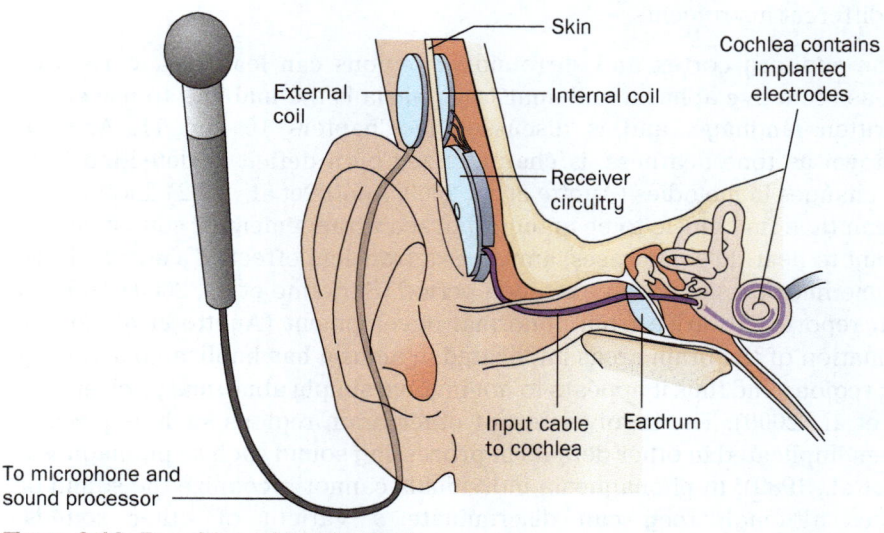

Figure 2.13 Ear with cochlear implant.
Source: Holt et al. (2019).

healthy ear.) The electrodes are spaced along the length of the cochlea to take advantage of the place encoding of pitch, and the sound processor can also exploit firing rate encoding of sound by varying the frequency of the stimulation.

In some cases cochlear implants are given to children and they develop with this experience of sound. Adults who receive cochlear implants typically require an extended period of time before the sound experience can organize itself into a useful signal. However, once this is achieved they are typically able to clearly understand speech in a relatively quiet environment, though if there is noise then performance at understanding speech can diminish. In particular, it has been noted that background music can produce a background noise that makes it difficult to understand speech. Indeed, there are complaints among adults that listening to music becomes unpleasant after a cochlear implant (Gfeller et al., 2003; McDermott, 2004). At least part of this results from the fact that while cochlear implants seem to enable the perception of rhythm, they cannot fully reproduce properties such as the timbre of a sound. Thus, one might be able to detect different pitches of a sound but not appreciate the difference between a piccolo and a violin playing the same pitch. Given the prevalence of music in everyday life this has formed a challenge for the field to appropriately advance the technology to enable music appreciation (Limb & Roy, 2014). It has also opened opportunities for using music as an aid to train hearing in individuals with cochlear implants (Looi et al., 2012; Torppa & Huotilainen, 2019).

Somatoperception System

The **somatoperception** system as revealed by Table 2.1 is a combination of several different subsystems, including proprioception, vestibular sensation and touch. Proprioception and vestibular sensation give us a sense of the position of our limbs relative to our body and our body in space. Both of these are important factors for producing and controlling action (Chapter 3). Touch is used to obtain information about objects in the world and in this way functions similarly to vision to enable us to recognize objects.

The processing of touch begins in specialized receptors in the skin, which project pathways of neurons to the brain. These pathways terminate in a portion of the brain called the primary somatosensory cortex, also known as SI, which is located next to the **central sulcus** (Figure 2.14, overleaf). The organization of this region is somatotopic, with local regions of cortex dedicated to specific body parts. The somatosensory homunculus ('little human') is a representation of the amount of somatosensory cortex dedicated to different body parts. It shows body size proportional to size of cortical representation and is a convenient way to visualize the allocation of somatosensory processing over the body (Figure 2.14). As can be seen, body areas like the lips and fingers, which are highly sensitive to touch, are large in the homunculus. A further organizing principle of the somatosensory system is the subdivision of processing specialization that runs in strips along the length of the primary somatosensory cortex. These different strips can be identified by the anatomic convention of brain areas defined by **Brodmann areas** (Figure 2.14). This division includes area 3A, which involves proprioception, and area 3B, which involves simple representations of touch. Areas 1 and 2 show sensitivity to more complex features, such as particular directions of skin stimulation in area 1 and particular shapes in area 2. Brain regions adjacent to the primary somatosensory cortex, such as the secondary somatosensory area (SII) and posterior parietal cortex, have been shown to be involved in further elaboration of somatosensory representations.

> **Somatoperception**
> perception related to the body itself, including the location of the body in space, the body's relationship to contact with external objects, and the perception of internal states of the body.
>
> **Central sulcus**
> a major anatomical landmark on the brain that forms the boundary between parietal cortex and frontal cortex.

> Chapter 3, p84

> **Brodmann areas**
> developed in 1909 by Korbinian Brodmann, a German neurologist, who divided the brain into approximately 50 regions distinguished by the structural properties of the neuronal architecture.

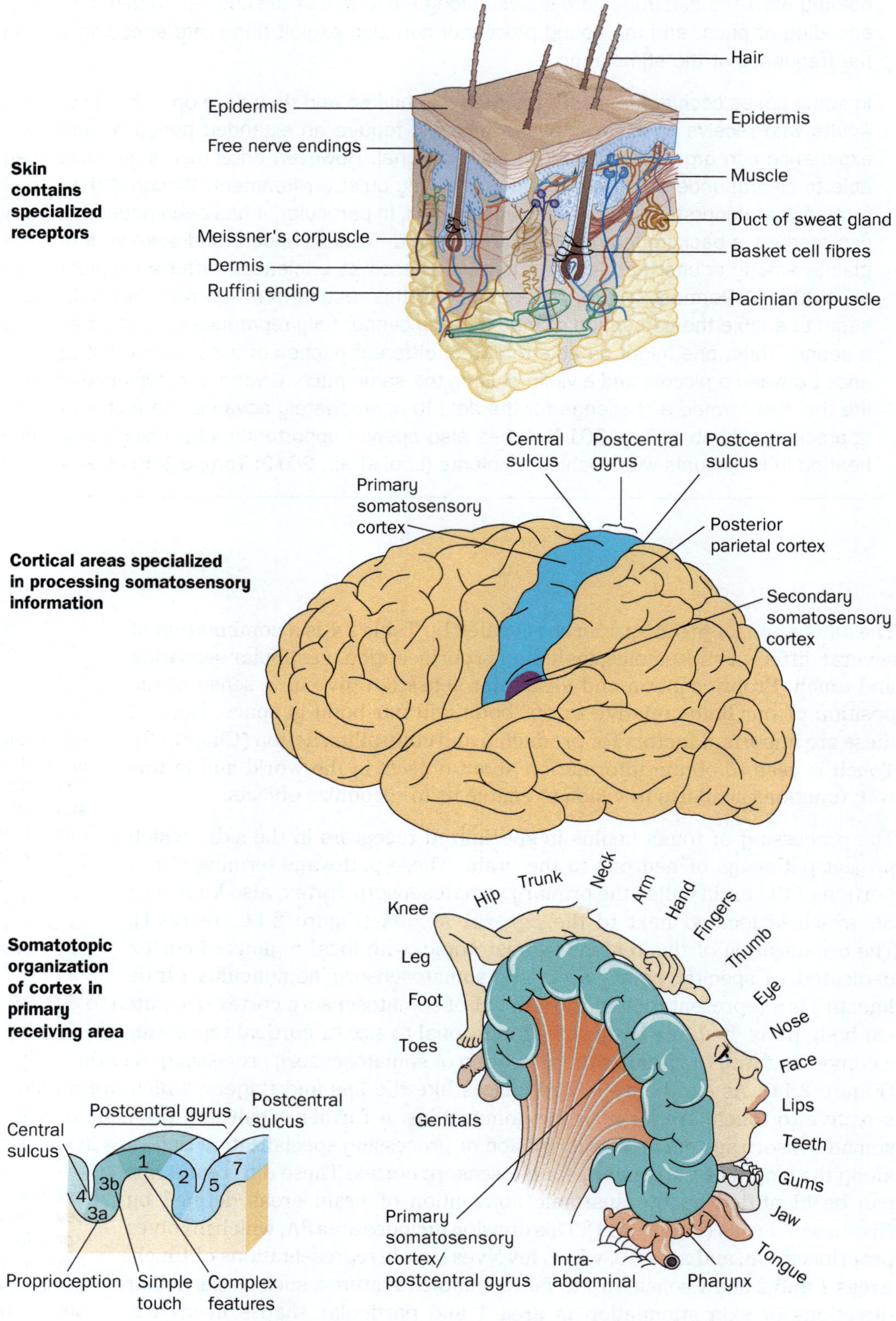

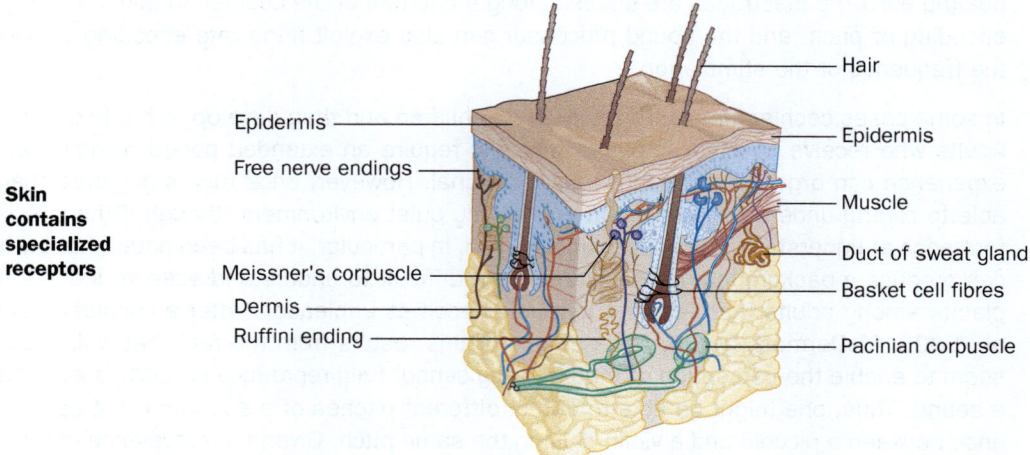

Skin contains specialized receptors
- Hair
- Epidermis
- Epidermis
- Free nerve endings
- Muscle
- Duct of sweat gland
- Meissner's corpuscle
- Basket cell fibres
- Dermis
- Ruffini ending
- Pacinian corpuscle

Cortical areas specialized in processing somatosensory information
- Central sulcus
- Postcentral gyrus
- Postcentral sulcus
- Primary somatosensory cortex
- Posterior parietal cortex
- Secondary somatosensory cortex

Somatotopic organization of cortex in primary receiving area

Knee, Hip, Trunk, Neck, Arm, Hand, Fingers, Thumb, Eye, Nose, Face, Lips, Teeth, Gums, Jaw, Tongue, Pharynx, Intra-abdominal, Genitals, Toes, Foot, Leg

Central sulcus — Postcentral gyrus — Postcentral sulcus
4, 3b, 3a, 1, 2, 5, 7
Proprioception — Simple touch — Complex features
Primary somatosensory cortex / postcentral gyrus

Figure 2.14 Information is sent from specialized receptors in the skin to the primary somatosensory cortex.
The skin contains specialized receptors that transduce mechanical energy into neural signals, which make their way to the somatosensory cortex. The somatosensory cortex is organized in a somatotopic fashion, with different parts of the body represented along its length. The homunculus shows how this representation of body surface is distributed in the brain, with greater brain area dedicated to body parts like the tongue and hand. Another organizational principle in the somatosensory cortex is found along its width, with simple representation of touch in Brodmann area 3 and more fine-tuned processing in Brodmann areas 1 and 2. Adjacent areas in the secondary somatosensory cortex and parietal cortex are also engaged in processing somatosensory information.

Sources: Adapted from Holt et al. (2012); Kandel et al. (2000).

Damage to the somatosensory cortex typically results in a loss of proprioception and fine touch. This can lead to deficits in the ability to know where on the body one is being touched or to be aware of being touched at all (Head & Holmes, 1911; Longo et al., 2010). However, one of the more profound examples of dysfunction of the somatosensory system arises from phantom limbs, which can occur when an individual loses a limb. Here, it is not damage to the cortex itself but to the body that creates unique perceptual experiences. Individuals with phantom limbs can report a clear perceptual awareness of their missing limb (Longo et al., 2012; Melzack, 1990, 1992) even though they are aware that the limb is missing. The primary issue is that the perceptual apparatus of the brain to represent the lost part of the body still exists and the resulting activity appears to override any cognitive awareness that the limb is missing. Individuals with phantom limbs can still experience pain in these limbs, and debate still surrounds the cause of this pain (Andoh et al., 2018; Kuffler, 2018). However, the primary hypothesis is that this pain is a result of cortical plasticity that arises as the adult cortex remaps the regions of somatosensory cortex that are no longer represented (Jutzeler et al., 2015; Ramachandran & Hirstein, 1998).

Multisensory Integration

We have so far discussed the senses and their processing channels separately. However, we do not experience the world as a collection of independent pieces of information but rather as a coherent whole. How we combine information within and across senses is thus an important problem in perception. The best explanation of why information should be combined is simply that each different source of information about the world has its own particular strengths and weaknesses, and thus combining the information should provide benefit. This is true regardless of whether information is combined within a sensory modality like vision, where motion, stereo and pictorial cues might all be incorporated to judge the shape and depth of an object, or whether visual and auditory information might both be used to indicate the location of an object. Combining sensory information has practical benefits for the construction of multisensory interfaces, as is later described in Box 2.5.

Before proceeding with typical examples of multisensory processing we introduce synaesthesia (Cytowic, 2003; Hubbard & Ramachandran, 2005; Simner, 2012; Ward, 2008) as a fascinating topic that does not fit squarely within either the study of multisensory processing or of individual sensory processing. Individuals with synaesthesia appear to combine the senses in a way that crosses over expected boundaries. For example, when a person with colour-grapheme synaesthesia views a grapheme (e.g., a letter of the alphabet), they not only see the letter but also experience a colour or other vivid visual pattern. For one synaesthete the letter 'A' might be red and for

Synaesthesia
an uncommon condition where stimulation of one perceptual modality results in experiencing a percept in a typically unrelated modality (e.g., tasting a sound).

another blue, but what is common is that their experience of written form includes a colour experience. Synaesthesia can appear in a multitude of ways and can work across sensory modalities such as chromesthesia, where individuals experience particular colours when hearing sounds. These sounds can be environmental or musical notes. At present there is no all-encompassing explanation of synaesthesia, though general ideas of cross-talk between brain regions (Grossenbacher & Lovelace, 2001) and neural models of specific synaesthetic experience (Ramachandran et al., 2019; Rouw & Scholte, 2007) have been put forward.

Returning to more standard topics in multisensory perception, two examples from audiovisual perception can be used to demonstrate how sights and sounds are typically integrated. The McGurk effect (McGurk & MacDonald, 1976) demonstrates that combination of sensory information can lead to a perception that is different from that produced by the independent sources. This effect is discussed in Chapter 11 and involves showing the lip movements of someone saying 'ga' while the sound 'ba' is played synchronously with the lip movement. The result from combining this visual 'ga' and auditory 'ba' is the experience of the sound 'da'. This is a clear example that combination occurs since the vivid impression of 'da' cannot be explained by either the visual or auditory component. The next example, the ventriloquist effect (Brun, 2019), demonstrates that the combination of sight and sound can lead to improved intelligibility. Acts of ventriloquism go back thousands of years (Connor, 2000) and are the related phenomena of misattributing the location of a sound source. This is a powerful effect and Driver (1996) showed that even when the visual and sound sources of a person speaking were presented at different locations speech intelligibility increased when participants mistakenly fused together the sight and sound to come from a common origin. This increase in intelligibility when sight and sound are fused together illustrates how integrating sensory information can lead to an advantage in understanding the world (Chen & Vroomen, 2013; Recanzone, 2009).

> Chapter 11, p390

Early research into multisensory perception provided several possible theoretical explanations of how the perceptual system might combine information. One of these is the modality appropriate hypothesis (Welch & Warren, 1980; Welch et al., 1986) which holds that for each physical property of the environment there is a particular sensory modality that has a higher acuity for estimating this property than the other senses; this modality will *always* dominate bimodal estimates of the property. Evidence for the modality appropriate hypothesis comes from experiments that show vision dominating on spatial tasks (Bertelson & Radeau, 1981; Warren et al., 1981; Welch & Warren, 1980) and audition dominating on temporal tasks (Gebhard & Mowbray, 1959; Recanzone, 2003; Shipley, 1964; Welch et al., 1986). An example, where vision dominates in a spatial localization task, is when a flash and sound are presented simultaneously at different locations, and the location of the sound is attributed to the position of the visual flash (Bertelson & Radeau, 1981; Warren et al., 1981). Vision has also been found to dominate a visual-somatoperception estimate of the straightness of lines (Easton & Moran, 1978; Hay et al., 1965). If distorting glasses are worn that make a straight object look curved, then when participants touch the straight object, despite it being straight, they feel/experience it as curved. These examples of vision dominating other senses are termed 'visual capture'. Hay et al. (1965) reported a large influence of vision on the other sense involved but very little, if any, influence of the other senses on vision. There is, however, evidence of an auditory corollary to 'visual capture', auditory driving. Whereas evidence for 'visual capture' comes from spatial tasks, evidence for auditory driving comes from cases where the rate of a visual stimulus is distorted by the rate of an auditory stimulus (Gebhard & Mowbray, 1959; Recanzone, 2003; Shipley, 1964; Welch et al., 1986). For example, using tempo discrimination experiments Recanzone (2003) showed conclusively that, even when asked to discriminate tempo solely on the basis of a visual cue (e.g., flashing light), the presence of a discrepant auditory cue (e.g., beeping tone) has a profound biasing influence on visual estimates of tempo; there was 'no measurable influence' from discrepant visual cues on auditory estimates of tempo.

Recent multisensory research, however, suggests that the idea of the modality appropriate hypothesis (i.e., the modality with the highest acuity for the corresponding physical property will *always* dominate bimodal estimates) is incomplete. For example, Ernst and Banks (2002) found that, depending on information quality, either visual or somatosensory information could dominate a visual-somatoperception bimodal estimate of location. Alais and Burr (2004) also showed that, despite vision under normal circumstances having a higher acuity for spatial estimates than audition, an auditory click can dominate a bimodal audiovisual location estimate ('an inverse ventriloquist effect'). These results have been described in terms of a maximum-likelihood estimation model (Clark & Yuille, 1990; Ernst & Banks, 2002; Landy et al., 1995). In this model the more reliable perceptual information for location is weighted more heavily than the less reliable perceptual information (see Box 2.4). In this way the perceptual system actively monitors the reliability of the incoming information and attaches more significance to the reliable input. In addition to using cue reliability for combining multisensory information, it is also possible to incorporate ideas of **causality** using an approach known as causal Bayesian inference (Körding et al., 2007; Macaluso et al., 2016; Shams & Beierholm, 2010). The causal Bayesian inference model behaves in such a way that if two events are close to each other in space, time and structure, a single underlying cause will be perceived, otherwise two independent causes will be perceived.

> **Causality**
> the relationship between cause and effect; the way in which one process or state produces another process or state.

Box 2.4 When Things Go Wrong: Motion sickness and cybersickness

Typically, the combination of sensory information aids our interpretation of the world by adding and corroborating different sources of information. However, this combination of the senses does not always go smoothly. Ancient texts report motion sickness from those who would travel by sea and consistently report wave-like motion as a cause of the distress (Huppert et al., 2017). As travel technology has diversified to include planes, trains and automobiles, motion sickness has remained a consistent problem for those affected (Zhang et al., 2016). In addition, with the recent rapid development of commercially available **virtual reality (VR)**, it is now possible to get a variant of motion sickness, known as cybersickness (Rebenitsch & Owen, 2016) in the comfort of one's own home. The presumed cause of motion sickness and cybersickness, and common to both, is being present in a sensory environment where there is a mismatch between the sensory signals of vision and vestibular aspects of somatoperception (Reason, 1978).

> **Virtual reality (VR)**
> a three-dimensional environment created by a computer that can be presented to an observer, typically through special display equipment such as a head mounted display.

Although sensory mismatch is the predominant explanation for motion sickness and cybersickness, details of the precise mechanisms behind these phenomena are not known. There are several reasons why our knowledge remains incomplete. One issue is that symptoms of the resulting sickness vary from general malaise to serious nausea, and can include dizziness, headaches and a variety of other symptoms. Explanation of these symptoms has brought an abundance of physiological effects to consider (Cohen et al., 2019), as well as drugs that alleviate the symptoms, but this knowledge has not revealed the basic mechanism. Another issue is that, for cybersickness, the visual phenomena of

Vection
the perception of one's body moving in space due to visual stimulation.

vection provides a sense of movement in space and it is not clear how critical this factor is in motion sickness (Koohestani et al., 2019). Third, while there are a wealth of studies exploring motion sickness and cybersickness, the data are sometimes inconsistent. One example is the common claim that females are more susceptible than males to motion sickness (Matchock et al., 2008). However, recent research has suggested that this effect derives from women experiencing menstrual pain and thus the claimed effect of gender might better be explained as resulting from pain sensitivity (Hemmerich et al., 2019). Finally, some people are variable in their susceptibility to motion sickness and this evidence has pointed towards an essential role for motivational aspects (Dobie, 2019; Mittelstädt et al., 2019).

Notwithstanding these complexities, recent work on multisensory perception has addressed how visual and vestibular information are combined to produce cybersickness (Gallagher & Ferrè, 2018). For example, Weech and Troje (2017) have used a technique called galvanic vestibular stimulation (GVS) to explore the perception of vection when vestibular information is made unreliable. GVS is frequently used in vestibular research (Dlugaiczyk et al., 2019) and uses a small electrical current applied to a location behind the ear to transmit a signal to the vestibular nerve. By using an electrical current that contained noise with a mean of zero Weech and Troje were able to inject a noise signal into the vestibular system. When this noisy signal was applied, the perception of vection was facilitated. Their explanation for this effect was that because the noise to the vestibular nerve will decrease the reliability of the vestibular signal the brain will down-weight the vestibular information and thus the visual information, in this case vection, will be up-weighted and the perception of vection enhanced. Whether such a technique can be further developed as a tool to rebalance the combination of sensory information to mitigate cybersickness remains to be seen.

Evaluation

The maximum likelihood model of cue integration explains that the cues will be combined in accordance with their reliability, and that this weighting can respond dynamically to environmental conditions. The extension of this model to the causal Bayesian inference model helps to deal with situations when there are multiple sources of sensory information by allowing segregation of these sources. These models do not necessarily contradict the previous modality-appropriate hypothesis, but instead add a dynamic aspect to what had been considered a static view of how cues would combine. However, recent work is beginning to address how these dynamic aspects of multisensory processing are achieved (Kilian-Hütten et al., 2017; Sheppard et al., 2013). Relatively little is known about the particular mechanisms that monitor reliability and how responsive they can be in changing cue weights. This points out the issue that as one moves from static to dynamic theories of perception and cognition there is a challenge to understand these dynamics.

Box 2.5 Practical Application: Multisensory warning signals for handover between autonomous and manual driving

Modern vehicles are a showcase for the delivery of advanced technology to improve safety and driving experience. With all these advances in safety technology, the driver is increasingly seen as a weak link in the system. Reasons for this, besides occasional poor judgement, include that a driver must contend with a potential overload of sensory information within the vehicle (Sivak, 1996) and further opportunity for distraction outside the vehicle. For example, in a naturalistic driving study (Klauer et al., 2006) it was found that 78 per cent of all crashes and 65 per cent of all near-misses involved the driver looking away from the forward roadway in the moments just prior to the incident. Thus, provided that technology can produce autonomous capabilities that are safe, there is a case for developing technology for autonomous driving where everyone in the vehicle would be a passenger.

While fully autonomous capabilities are not yet available, semi-autonomous driving is increasingly available and might ultimately be the prevalent driving scenario. It should be noted that, currently, semi-autonomous modes of driving are done under instructions for continuous human oversight, and failure to follow this advice can have tragic consequences (NTSB, 2016). With the semi-autonomous driving mode comes the issue that scenarios arise where the vehicle would require to communicate handover control back to the driver (Burnett et al., 2019; McCall et al., 2019). Techniques of cognitive psychology can be used to investigate what kind of warning signals would best communicate handover to a driver. Previous research has established that multisensory signals (audio-tactile) produce faster reactions than single sensory (audio, tactile) warnings for collision avoidance (Ho et al., 2007). It has also been shown that for an elderly group of drivers (mean age 71 years, ranging from 65–90 years) multisensory warning signals brought reaction times to be equivalent to those of younger drivers (mean age 28 years, ranging from 18–38 years), while responses of elderly drivers to unisensory warnings were 15 per cent slower (Laurienti et al., 2006).

Based on these results, recent research using a simulated autonomous driving task measured the time for drivers to respond to a warning that the vehicle had to switch out of autonomous mode and to hand over control back to the driver (Politis et al., 2019). The warning came as drivers were engaged in using a computer tablet, such as would be the case if the driver were checking their phone while in autonomous driving mode. The results of the time it took to react and the amount of lane deviation that occurred in response to the different warnings are shown in Figure 2.15 for each single modality (audio, visual, tactile) and their combinations. These average results showed that audiovisual warnings appeared to have the fastest reaction time with the smallest lane deviation, while visual-only warnings had the slowest responses and highest number of lane deviations. As a single cue, auditory appeared the most effective and was slightly still more effective when paired with another cue. These findings highlight a critical property of handover that some forms of warning clearly do not provide a timely and effective driver response. Reaction to the visual warning was very slow and even when it did occur there was substantial lane deviation. However, even for the quickest reaction time of around one second there is the question of whether that speed of reaction would be adequate for some critical events.

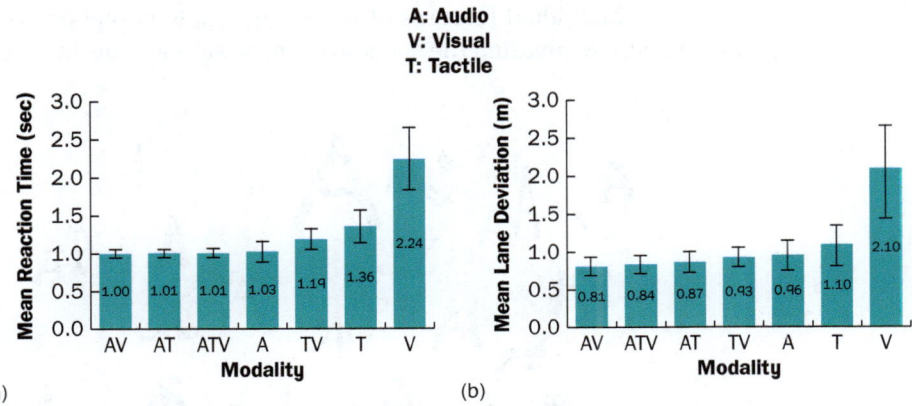

Figure 2.15 Reaction times and lane deviation produced by audio, visual and tactile warning signals, and their combinations.

Participants were in a simulated autonomous driving task while interacting with a tablet computer when they were given a warning signal that they must take back control over the vehicle. Plotted in the left panel are the times it took for participants to react to the warning and take back vehicle control, and in the right panel the amount of lane deviation that took place as they regained control.

Source: Data from Politis et al. (2019).

RECOGNITION

A straightforward view of how recognition works is that general perceptual processes produce an object representation that can be compared to a stored internal representation. If the perceptual representation matches an internally stored representation in memory then the object is recognized. While many potential recognition schemes have been examined, it has turned out to be a difficult problem to capture the essence of human recognition capabilities. The key capability in which human recognition excels is the robust way in which it can evaluate many different perceptual inputs and recognize these different inputs as the same thing. For example, take a moment to imagine all the ways a simple letter 'A' can be written and you can begin to appreciate the issue. If you include all the possible ways to transform these different versions of 'A', such as rotation and scaling (shrinking or enlarging), and an 'A' is still recognized then the capability becomes all the more impressive (Figure 2.16). Moreover, this recognition capability is not isolated to vision and in Chapter 11, when covering speech understanding, we will see there is the equivalent capability to recognize the sound of a letter despite the many ways it is produced by different voices. This robustness of our perceptual systems to such variability shows that we cannot be using a simple template matching system where, like the children's toy, the round peg goes in the round hole and the square peg in the square hole.

Chapter 11, p378

One property of effective recognition systems is that they are able to represent the information in a way that preserves the essence of the object upon different transformations. To examine this property further we return to our example of recognizing an 'A', with the goal of finding a representation that preserves the essential information upon transformation. One approach, known as a feature analysis, involves deconstructing an object into a set of component features that can be compared to a library. Inside this library each object is described by a unique set of features. The list of features could include the number of line segments and their patterns of connectivity, such as the types of angles between the different segments. The difficulty with such an approach is coming up with a unique feature list that could capture all the different versions of an 'A'. One way to overcome such challenges was the Pandemonium model proposed by Selfridge (1958). Taking the case of recognizing letters, in this model so-called demons are arranged in a hierarchy, with lower-level demons assigned to evaluate the utility of individual features of letters and higher-level demons, one for each letter, assigned with evaluating the success of these sub-demons in recognizing a letter.

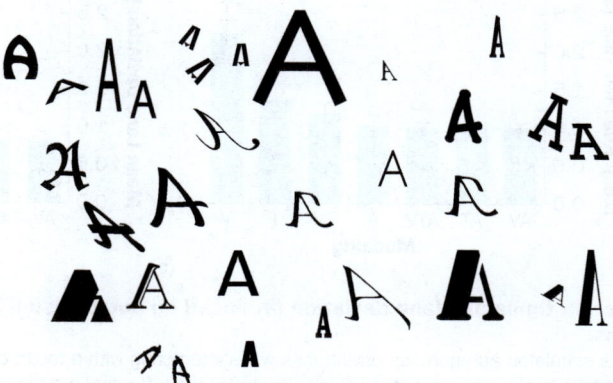

Figure 2.16 Many different shapes can have the same identity.
All these figures represent the letter 'A', however it is difficult to quantify the essential, invariant property of the figures that allows them all to be recognized as an 'A'.

At the next level up in the Pandemonium hierarchy, a demon is assigned to the final decision of which letter is perceived. This hierarchy could be extended to include demons for recognition of words, and higher still to assign meaning to the words in context.

We have been using the example of an 'A' to motivate our explanation of recognition. One essential issue discussed was that there is a large variety of shapes we might call an 'A' and this posed the challenge of how to come up with a distinct feature list that would capture the essence of an object. Another approach to solving this challenge is provided by prototype theory (Rosch, 1973), where the goal is to find what member of a category is the best example of that category (see also Chapter 9). For example, although all of the letters in Figure 2.15 can be seen as an 'A', some are rarer and more exotic examples of an 'A' while others are more typical or central to the category. Determining which members of a category are more central than others allows a more graded response to distinguish across the members of a category. For example, if we take the features of a bird to include (1) having a beak, (2) having feathers, and (3) able to fly, we see that a robin is a more typical exemplar of the category of birds than a penguin. A further notion of prototype theory is that of basic-level categorization, which is defined as the response that is most likely to be produced when asked to categorize an object. Thus, when presented with a photo of a basset hound and asked what you see, most people will respond with the answer 'dog', and this provides the basic level of categorization. While the response 'mammal' is clearly valid, this level is superordinate to the basic level of categorization; 'basset hound' is valid at a subordinate level of categorization. The boundaries between different category labels (superordinate, basic, subordinate) are not fixed since we are dynamically taking on new information that might cause us to rearrange our category boundaries. However, an essential assumption is that categorization works to come up with basic-level categories that maximize the difference between other basic level categories and minimize the variability within elements of the same basic level category. Such an approach leads to maximally informative categories, and while we can expect these to be largely similar among a population, differences would be predicted. For example, an expert dog breeder when shown the photo of the basset hound is likely to respond 'basset hound' rather than 'dog'. A reason for this is that within their rich knowledge of dog breeds they possess subordinate categories to distinguish between the Basset Artesian Normand and the Basset Bleu de Gascogne. Thus, 'basset hound' becomes their basic-level response.

Chapter 9, p299

Objects

We are going to discuss two cases of object recognition, the first involving the visual system and the second the somatoperception system. Although different in many ways, both illustrate the selection of features used for recognition. Defining the features used, and how they can be obtained and computed, is an essential aspect of object recognition research.

Visual object recognition

Most objects in the natural world are three-dimensional; this is problematic for vision since it faces the task of recognizing a three-dimensional object with only the two-dimensional information on the retina. An influential paper from Binford (1981) provided a series of assumptions about how to relate lines in an image or line drawing to the possible three-dimensional configurations that could have caused them to occur. For example, consider Figure 2.17 (overleaf) and the following statement made about it: 'If a true edge e of a solid is truncated by a visible surface S, the result is a vertex whose image is an arrow junction or Y junction.' This observation is critical in that it tells

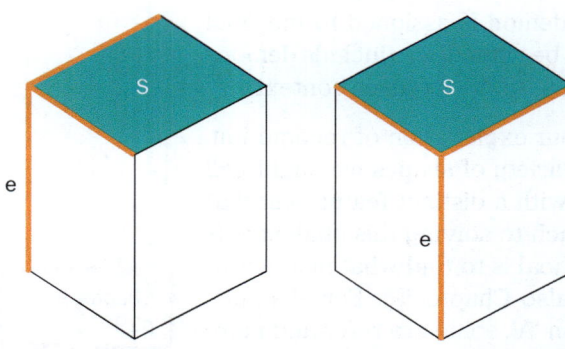

Figure 2.17 Truncating an edge with a surface creates a 'Y' junction that is viewpoint invariant.
Binford (1981) demonstrated that if an edge 'e' were truncated by a surface 'S', then the image would contain a 'Y' junction. This is demonstrated in the diagram by showing two different views of the edge 'e' truncated by 'S'.

Source: Adapted from Binford (1981).

> **Viewpoint invariant relationship**
> any aspect of an object that is preserved no matter the direction from which we view the object.
> **Geons**
> the elements of a set of volumetric primitives or shapes that can be recognized from any viewpoint, proposed by Biederman in his recognition by components (RBC) theory.

us that from whichever viewpoint we observe the object, when the world is projected onto our retina and the depth dimension lost, the Y junction will be formed. Thus the Y junction is known as a **viewpoint invariant relationship**. Following on from this logic, numerous other viewpoint invariant relations were derived and their significance to human object recognition explored (Jacobs, 2003; Pomerantz & Kubovy, 1986).

One way to exploit these viewpoint invariant relations for object recognition is to create a set of volumetric primitives that have unique combinations of viewpoint invariant relations. These volumetric primitives can serve as the letters of an alphabet do to generate words. If we can model objects as created by a set of volumetric primitives then we can recognize an object from arbitrary viewpoints since each part of the object is recognizable by its unique collection of viewpoint invariant properties. An example of such a volumetric primitive is a brick (Figure 2.18a), which is specified by its arrangement of arrows and Y junctions as well as parallel lines. The use of viewpoint invariant features for recognition was further advanced by Biederman (1987), who named his volumetric primitives '**geons**'. At the heart of his recognition by components (RBC) approach was that objects could be thought of as composed of a collection of geons. Since every individual geon in an object could be recovered by its unique collection of viewpoint invariant properties, this allowed the entire object to be recognized (Figure 2.18b).

This RBC approach was demonstrated to reflect human performance on a variety of object recognition experiments. One such experiment used systematic deletion of particular parts of a line drawing to demonstrate that geon recovery was crucial for recognition. Line drawings were made and then subsequent versions created that were either deleted at regions containing viewpoint invariant regions or elsewhere. It was found that performance suffered substantially when the regions containing viewpoint invariant information were removed (Figure 2.19a). Observers were much quicker to identify objects in drawings that contained the viewpoint invariant properties. This and other experiments were influential in demonstrating the importance of viewpoint invariant relationships and how RBC could account for viewpoint independent recognition of objects from line drawings. However, there has been some criticism of its ability to perform on images generated from the real world and doubts that it could be flexibly extended to model subordinate-level categorization. For example, RBC is clearly adequate to explain how a schematic model of a bird can be created for recognizing birds independent of viewpoint, but extending RBC to account for the ability to distinguish between the shape of a robin, a wren and a raven becomes more complicated.

One theory of object recognition, known as multiple views theory, rose to challenge the RBC approach, asserting that recognition is fundamentally image based (Tarr & Bulthoff, 1998). It argued that object recognition could be achieved by storing representations of a few select views of the object that had been learned. From these select views, sophisticated mechanisms could fill in representations of the intermediate views. Thus, when one observed a novel view of an object it could be recognized by mechanisms that matched the viewed image to the select and intermediate filled-in versions.

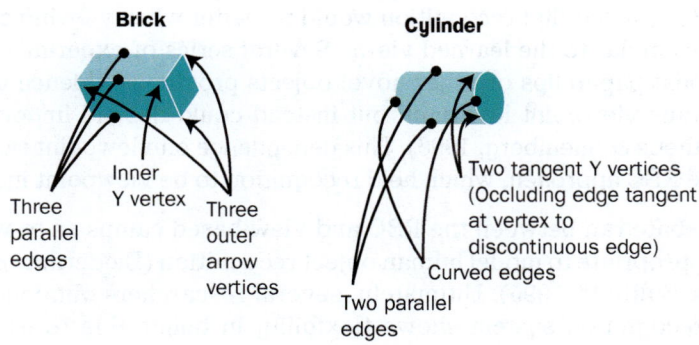

Figure 2.18 Geon properties and objects composed of geons.
(a) Viewpoint invariant properties of two different geons. (b) These and other geons are used to make a number of different objects.

Sources: (a) Biederman (1987b). APA; reproduced with permission. (b) Adapted from Gobet et al. (2011).

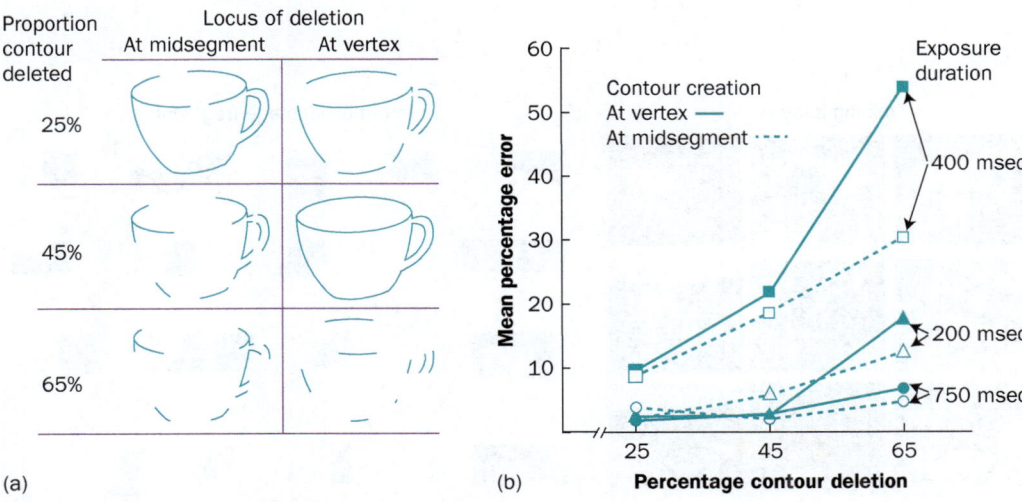

Figure 2.19 Visual stimuli and contour deletion.
(a) Portions of line drawings were removed either at a midsegment location or at a vertex location to impair recovery of the geon structure of the object. (b) Results show that removal of vertices has a greater impact on object recognition than at midsegment, particularly for short exposure to objects with extensive contour deletion.

Source: Biederman (1987b). APA; reproduced with permission.

This method predicted that recognition would be better when viewing objects from directions more similar to the learned views. Several series of experiments using stimuli containing bent paperclips or other novel objects provided evidence that recognition was not always viewpoint invariant, but instead could depend importantly on viewpoint (Logothetis & Sheinberg, 1996). This dependence on viewpoint ran counter to the claims of the RBC approach, which held recognition to be viewpoint independent.

A spirited debate ran between the RBC and view-based camps as to which approach was more appropriate to model human object recognition (Biederman & Gerhardstein, 1995; Tarr & Bulthoff, 1995). Ultimately, several researchers obtained evidence that the object recognition system shows flexibility in being able to utilize both view-dependent and view-independent properties to recognize objects (Foster & Gilson, 2002; Hayward, 2003). In addition, variants of these two approaches were developed. For example, an approach by Ullman and colleagues (2002) used information theory to show that patches of images with intermediate complexity were optimal to encode a set of images for subsequent recognition tasks (Figure 2.20). This approach shares with RBC the use of a set of informative image features but does not require them to be informative about three-dimensional structure, only that they optimally describe the objects to be recognized.

One question you might have considered already is whether object recognition also relies upon factors such as colour, or does shape dominate? Clearly, for tasks such as picking ripe fruit, colour is critical. However, it appears that, for human object recognition, colour comes into play only when shape is ambiguous, though long-term colour knowledge can play a role in top-down mechanisms (Mapelli & Behrmann, 1997). It is remarkable that shape alone is so influential, and that even simple line drawings can convey rich information about the object depicted. Possibly this can be explained by the human visual system's generous allocation of brain resources to the representation of spatial properties of the visual world.

Finally, a new perspective on object recognition has arisen from recent activity in a field known as deep learning that exploits the connectionism approach we described in

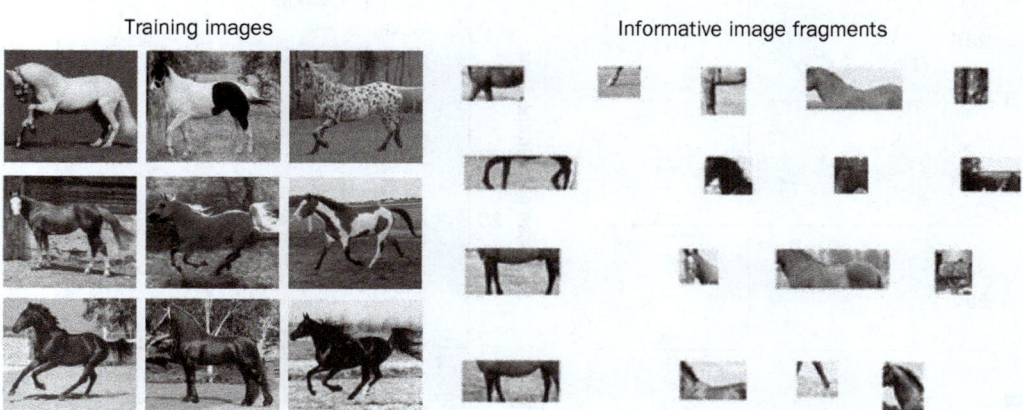

Figure 2.20 Learning features for recognition.
Ullman and colleagues (2002) developed a system that used the most informative image fragments to obtain recognition. Here we show on the left a set of horse images that the system was trained to recognize. The most informative image fragments are shown to the right and recognition of an image was obtained on the basis of how it matched this set of informative fragments.

Source: Adapted from Ullman et al. (2002).

Chapter 1. In the connectionism approach networks are trained to learn to match an input such as an image with an output such as the object category of the object in the image. For example, one such deep neural network, called AlexNet (Krizhevsky et al., 2012), has more than half a million nodes and more than 600 million connections distributed across its eight layers. The layers close to the input represent low-level image features and as one goes to higher layers of the network more abstract properties appear to be represented. By training AlexNet using a massive library of millions of labelled images and thousands of categories, known as ImageNet (Deng et al., 2009), it was possible for AlexNet to be given a new, unseen input image and to report the object category of that input image with high accuracy. Subsequent studies investigating these deep learning networks have been able to show that, after training, the different layers of the artificial network are similar to the different stages of human visual processing, with complexity of representation increasing as one goes from layer 1 to 5 in the deep neural network and from primary visual cortex, down the ventral stream to inferior temporal cortex in the human (Cichy et al., 2016; Guclu & van Gerven, 2015).

> Chapter 1, p14

Evaluation

By looking over the different approaches to object recognition, it can be seen that there is no simple consensus. There is strong evidence that we can recognize objects from different viewpoints, so that gives support to the idea that the features represented are viewpoint invariant. However, for the most successful systems – the deep neural networks – it is difficult to systematically generalize the features they use. While this issue of explainability is common in the use of deep neural networks (Akata et al., 2018; Gunning & Aha, 2019) it presents a challenge to informing our understanding of previous decades of psychological research into the features used for object recognition. However, this previous research can inform what we might look for when trying to validate any artificial object recognition system. Moreover, the deep neural network approach is opening new opportunities for the computational study of how complex neural systems can achieve tasks like object recognition (Kar et al., 2019; Richards et al., 2019)

Somatoperceptive object recognition

The second case of object recognition we will discuss is how the somatoperception system is used to recognize objects. Free exploration of an object, for example with the hands, will engage subsystems of the somatoperceptual system that involve estimating the weight and texture of an object as well as the position of the body parts touching the object. Collectively these subsystems contribute to what is called **haptic perception** (Lederman & Klatzky, 2009; Woods & Newell, 2004). When trying to identify an object using haptics it has been shown that frequently a single grasp is sufficient to recognize the object (Klatzky et al., 1985). However, when more detailed aspects are required, the hand engages in stereotypical 'exploratory procedures', as shown in Figure 2.21 (overleaf) along with a table providing the hypothesized functions of these different procedures (Lederman & Klatzky, 1986). These exploratory procedures have been adapted into robotic systems (Bartolozzi et al., 2016) and in guiding experiments in understanding how humans recognize surfaces. For example, it has been shown that a single hand sweep over a surface enables detection of roughness independent of the complexity of the surface (Plaisier et al., 2008). Exploratory procedures have also been shown to vary with surface type, with people using a smaller contact force and a lower scanning velocity when scanning rough compared to smooth surfaces (Tanaka et al., 2014). What appears crucial for these exploratory procedures is that the hand actively engages

> **Haptic perception**
> the combination of abilities that allow us to represent the material characteristics of objects and surfaces for recognition.

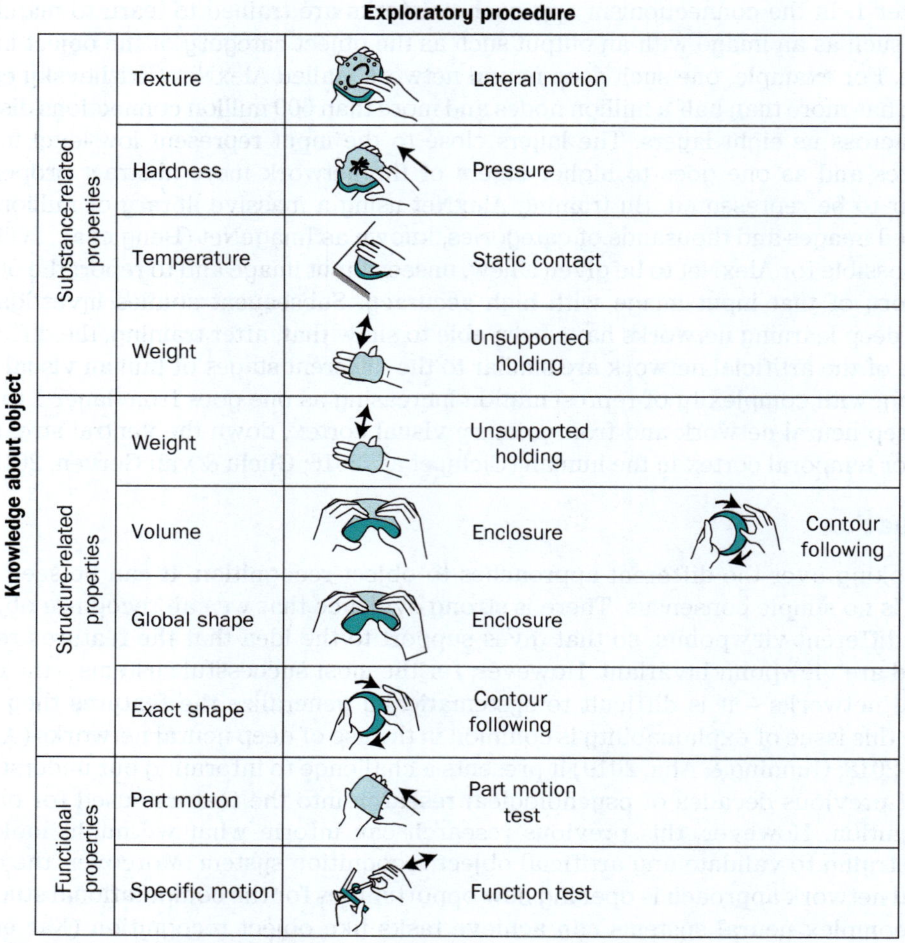

Knowledge about object		Exploratory procedure		
Substance-related properties	Texture		Lateral motion	
	Hardness		Pressure	
	Temperature		Static contact	
	Weight		Unsupported holding	
Structure-related properties	Weight		Unsupported holding	
	Volume		Enclosure	Contour following
	Global shape		Enclosure	
	Exact shape		Contour following	
Functional properties	Part motion		Part motion test	
	Specific motion		Function test	

Figure 2.21 Exploratory procedures used in haptic recognition.
Exploratory procedures describe the way we manipulate and move our hands over an object to determine its properties and function. For each of the three different categories of object properties (substance-related, structure-related and functional) there are exploratory procedures that provide specific information. For example, lateral motion over the surface provides texture information, which is a substance-related object property,

Source: Adapted from Lederman & Klatzky (1987).

with the surface. The importance of active engagement could be predicted by ecological psychologists. They argued that touch movements made by an active observer provide the phenomenal experience of *touching* an object, while when the observer is passive and the object is moved over the body to recreate the same physical pattern of contact the observer has an experience of *being touched* (Gibson, 1962). However, one note to take into account from the comparison of active and passive touch comes from physiological experiments that have shown that, when the body is moving, sensory transmission of touch is diminished. When this factor is taken into account, substantial differences between active and passive touch are not necessarily revealed (Chapman, 1994).

Visual agnosia

In our discussion of the visual system we mentioned how particular lesions of the brain in occipital cortex and along its border with temporal cortex could destroy one's sense of colour vision or motion perception. Lesions can also occur in the inferior region of temporal cortex that selectively impact the ability to recognize objects (Konen et al., 2011).

This condition is known as visual agnosia, and what sets it apart from a condition like blindness is that patients with visual agnosia appear able to extract a reasonably intact perception of what they see but are unable to assign any meaning to this percept (Farah, 1990; Humphreys & Riddoch, 1987). The evidence that visual agnosia is restricted to assigning meaning to vision is striking when observing an interviewer interact with a patient. For example, if we were to interview a patient about recognizing a spoon we could expect the following: we would expect a visual agnosic to be able to pick it up while blindfolded and correctly identify that it is a spoon by using haptic perception. Similarly, if we asked them to tell us what a spoon was, they could provide a rich description of its shape and uses. In addition, if we showed them a metal spoon they would be able to describe its basic visual features – shiny, rounded at one end, etc. However, if we show them a spoon and ask them what it is we will get a confused response that reveals a profound inability to recognize visual objects.

Scenes

The recognition of scenes provides a natural extension of studies in object recognition. In object recognition one typically studies how a single, precisely displayed object in isolation is recognized. Scene recognition involves perception of an environment and includes not only perception of individual objects but also the nature of all the objects taken together. For example, a typical scene of a city is different from a typical scene in a forest and, as we describe in Chapter 4, making this discrimination does not necessarily rely on the recognition of any specific object. Scene recognition is important for understanding how recognition works in the typical cluttered scenes we view when outside of perception labs.

Chapter 4, p116

Early research into recognition of a sequence of photographs of complex scenes indicated that presentation times of 250 milliseconds or less were adequate for participants to accurately judge whether or not they had seen a photo in the rapidly presented sequence (Potter & Levy, 1969). More recent studies examining recognition of whether or not an animal was present in a scene presented for 20 milliseconds (Figure 2.22) showed that manual key responses were produced in approximately 400 milliseconds. However, EEG data showed distinctive patterns of electrical activity that indicated correct recognition was obtained in under 150 milliseconds from stimulus presentation (Thorpe et al., 1996). These and other results (Kirchner & Thorpe, 2006; Van Rullen & Thorpe, 2001) confirm that humans are very good at rapidly processing visual scenes.

When we discussed the visual system we stated that an abundance of cortical area was dedicated to processing the fovea (the centre of the retina). For this extra processing power to be effective the eye must place the centre of the retina at the point of interest and keep it fixed to this location. The eyes change where they fixate approximately every third of a second and are poor at capturing information when they are not fixated. Figure 2.23 (overleaf)

Figure 2.22 Recognizing whether an animal is present can be done rapidly.
Various scenes and animals of the type used in the experiments by Thorpe and colleagues demonstrated that humans could encode whether an animal was present within 150 milliseconds of presentation.

Source: Reprinted from Kirchner & Thorpe (2006), with permission from Elsevier

shows an example of a pattern of fixations to a natural scene. What becomes evident is that the pattern of eye movement is complex and that not every part of the scene will be fixated (Henderson & Hollingworth, 1999; Tatler et al., 2010; Yarbus, 1967). An important question then is when presented with a random photo, why do we look where we do? What is driving our eye movements? The two basic possibilities are the familiar bottom-up and top-down explanations. The bottom-up explanation is that novel image properties such as brightness, colour or distinctive shape make particular image locations salient and this image salience is capturing our eye movements. Evidence that this is true comes from biologically inspired models of image salience, which use novelty to successfully predict image salience (Itti & Koch, 2001); we explore this further in Chapter 4. The top-down explanation is that our goals and expectations are at work to direct the eye movements (Rao et al., 2002; Torralba et al., 2006). One example of such high-level effects on eye movements comes from a study using a mobile eye tracker and video recorder to measure eye movements to scenes recorded from walking pedestrians (Foulsham et al., 2011). Comparison of what a person looked at when walking to what they viewed when reviewing a video of the recorded journey in the lab showed differences. For example, when another person became visible, for the first three seconds there was no difference in views to this person, however in the final three seconds there was a difference, with fewer views in the walking condition. This finding is consistent with social norms of avoiding eye contact with strangers that would be disinhibited when viewing a movie.

> Chapter 4, p116

Because eye movements are driven by both complicated information processing and brain circuits (Veale et al., 2017), they offer a novel window into an individual's cognitive and psychological status. While the inherent complexity of eye movement data has previously held back progress in using eye movements in any sophisticated diagnostic capacity, this has started to change. Medical devices are receiving approval in the use of eye movements for the diagnosis of concussion (Akhand et al., 2019; Voelker, 2019) and there is promise that eye movements towards complex, dynamic natural scenes might one day form part of diagnostic procedures for conditions such as autism and other neuropsychiatric conditions (Itti, 2015; Wang et al., 2015).

Vision is not alone in providing valuable information about the layout of a scene. Audition provides information about the distance, location and number of objects in a scene, as well as the general openness of the space. Although amplitude of the sound wave is one obvious cue to distance, the timbre of the incoming sound wave contains distance information. Much as the atmosphere absorbs and scatters light to make distant scenes hazy and thus appear distant, the atmosphere filters sound waves so the high frequencies are attenuated, and this change in the distribution of sound frequencies also signals distance. Similarly, what we hear is a combination of both the sound wave taking a direct path to our ear as well as all the reflections (echoes) of that sound wave. Comparison of the direct and the reflected waves is especially relevant indoors, where walls provide multiple reflecting surfaces. Thus, with our

Figure 2.23 Eye scan path of an observer as they view an image of a scene for 10 seconds.
The circles represent points where the eye fixed on a visual location and the diameter of a circle is proportional to the time spent looking at that point (fixating). The lines represent the eye movements (saccades) as the eye scans the image. If you are curious about what a scan path might look like for one of your own images, visit https://www.3m.com/3M/en_US/visual-attention-software-us/.

Image courtesy of Jeff B. Pelz, Carlson Center for Imaging Science, Rochester Institute of Technology.
Photo credit: Madeline Pelz (photograph taken at Prospect Park Dog Run, Brooklyn, NY, USA).

eyes closed, the sound quality of our footsteps can inform us whether we are walking in a small or large room. Proof of the richness of sound information is provided by bats' abilities to use echolocation to navigate, and there is even evidence from some blind humans that similar strategies can provide valuable information about the layout of an auditory scene (Rosenblum et al., 2000; Schenkman & Nilsson, 2010).

One critical property of auditory scene analysis is the ability to segregate incoming sound into different streams (Bregman, 1990). For example, there is evidence that properties such as frequency (O'Sullivan et al., 2015; Sussman et al., 2007) and distance between sound sources (Shiell et al., 2018) can be used in a bottom-up fashion to segregate different sound streams. However, top-down effects allow what we expect to shape what we hear. For example, if we are listening to a speaker in a noisy environment we do not hear just a bland mixture of all the sound but our knowledge of the speaker (language, voice pitch and tempo), as well as the context of what we expect to hear, guides our abilities to segregate voice from the background noise so that we can discern the meaning of the speaker. A recent study using invasive measures of brain activity from primary and secondary auditory cortex in neurosurgical patients has informed our understanding of how the brain encodes the voices of a mixture of multiple speakers (O'Sullivan et al., 2019). Results showed that neural sites in the primary auditory cortex responded to individual speakers in the mixture and were relatively unchanged by attention. In contrast, neural sites in secondary auditory cortex selectively represented the attended speaker. (See Chapter 11 for more on the topic of listening to speech.)

Chapter 11, p376

Events

So far, our presentation of the visual recognition of objects and scenes has treated the visual world as static and unchanging. However, motion and change are everywhere. A classic example of how actions unfolding over time are perceived comes from studying how observers interpret the interactions of physical objects. Studies conducted by Albert Éduard Michotte examined simple displays in which one geometric object approached another one that then itself began moving (Michotte, 1946, 1963; Michotte et al., 1990). The nature of the contact between the two objects, and subsequent direction and speed of motion of the two objects was studied, and Michotte characterized a range of conditions in which a sequence gives rise to the impression that one object has launched the other into motion (Figure 2.24). Critical variables to see a launching event include the object's proximity when the second object begins moving, the timing of the

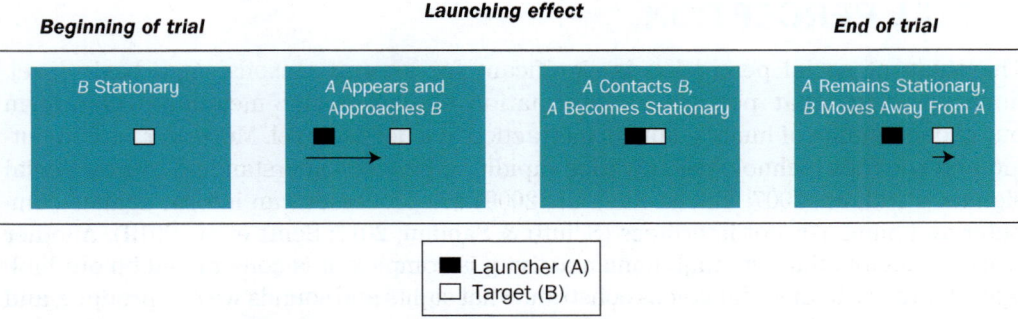

Figure 2.24 Launching phenomenon explored by Michotte.
When a moving launcher (object A) contacts a stationary target (object B) it is perceived as A launching B if the time between contact and object B moving is short enough and the speed of object A is sufficiently greater than the velocity of B.

Source: Hubbard & Favretto (2003).

motion change, and the relative velocities of the object's motions (Scholl & Tremoulet, 2000). Related work on perceiving objects in motion showed that even very simple displays composed of geometric objects could, when animated correctly, evoke the perception of complex narratives of social interactions (Heider & Simmel, 1944). The motion properties that make a display be seen as animate or alive include speed changes, direction changes and the relative non-rigid motion of different parts of an object (Schlottmann et al., 2006; Schultz & Bülthoff, 2013; Tremoulet & Feldman, 2000). Recent results suggest, however, that when the number of objects increases past three, the perception of animate motion decreases (Wick et al., 2019). An example of an inanimate object appearing animate is the plastic bag scene from the movie *American Beauty* (Mendes, 1999) where the motion of a plastic bag blowing in the wind is described as 'dancing with me. Like a little kid begging me to play with it.'

The term event perception has been defined in ecological psychology as changes in layout, changes in surface existence, or changes in colour and texture (Gibson, 1979). Another definition holds that an event is 'a segment of time at a given location that is conceived by an observer to have a beginning and end' (Zacks & Tversky, 2001, pp. 4–5). This deconstruction of ongoing activity into discrete events with a beginning and end has been argued to be compatible with known brain mechanisms (Richmond & Zacks, 2017) and can be used to organize our perception of the world. Furthermore, Shipley (2008) observed that the two definitions of events can be related to each other within the context of the perceptual cycle (Neisser, 1976). The perceptual cycle is defined as the cyclic process comprising the following steps: (1) memory in the form of **schema** drives exploration, which (2) leads to information pick-up of the kind described by ecological psychology, which (3) leads to potential modification of schema and subsequent repetition of the steps of this cycle. The important situation arises when the happenings of the world do not unfold to match expectations (i.e., our schema do not produce reliable predictions about what happens next). The time that these expectations are not met can be used to define the time of the boundary of one event finishing and the next one beginning (Richmond et al., 2017; Zacks et al., 2007). The importance of predictability resonates with earlier experiments by Newtson (1973), who investigated how observers divided action streams into events when they contained different numbers of occurrences where prediction failed. Results showed that action streams with more frequent occurrence of failed prediction were divided into more events than action streams where prediction was more successful.

> **Schema**
> a framework that represents a plan or a theory, supporting the organization of knowledge.

SOCIAL PERCEPTION

The study of social perception is significant for several reasons. At a basic level, understanding what perceptual information signals social meaning will inform our understanding of human–human interaction at a deeper level. Moreover, as computing and robotics technologies advance rapidly, a precise understanding of how social signals (Pentland, 2007; Vinciarelli et al., 2009) are processed can inform human–computer and human–robot interfaces (Sciutti & Sandini, 2017; Senft et al., 2019). Another reason is simply that although human activity is complex, it is constrained by our biology. Our faces, bodies and voices constrain what sights and sounds we can produce, and how these constraints can be applied to processing these complex signals informs understanding of our basic cognitive capabilities. Finally, there is the unique link between perceiving others, and our social and emotional responses. For example, following the suggestion of Marr (1982) we can ask, what is the computational theory behind social perception? In other words, what is social perception used for, and why does it do what it does? An answer to this is that social perception informs us about the thoughts, emotions and internal states of others and this is useful information to help us navigate our social world (Frith & Frith, 2003). Following on from this, and consistent with Marr's second level, we can view an important aspect of social perception as the transformation from social signals to representation of emotion. Emotion and cognition are covered in Chapter 15 when we discuss decision making, and extensively in Chapter 13, but the importance of emotional evaluation to social perception is illustrated when we discuss Capgras syndrome in Box 2.6.

Chapter 15, p550

Chapter 13, p468

> **Box 2.6 When Things Go Wrong: Capgras syndrome**
>
> An example of the complexity of human recognition within a social context is given by a condition known as Capgras syndrome. Capgras syndrome is a relatively rare condition where the sufferer believes that people, or in some instances things, have been replaced with duplicates (Ellis et al., 1994). Typically the people who the sufferer believes to be duplicates are close family members. These duplicates are rationally accepted to be identical in physical properties but the irrational belief is held that the 'true' entity has been replaced with something else. Some sufferers of Capgras syndrome have even claimed that the duplicate is a robot. Ellis and Lewis (2001) describe the situation of a man who after a car accident believed that his wife had died in the accident, and the woman he currently lived with (his wife) was a duplicate. Naturally, he found this situation to be uncomfortable. Similarly Hirstein and Ramachandran (1997) reported a man who after an automobile accident believed that his parents were imposters. Interestingly, this delusion was limited to the visual modality since when speaking on the phone he always thought that he was speaking to his true parents.
>
> While on the surface the Capgras delusion might seem to be a very special case of prosopagnosia, there is evidence that it is in fact quite different from prosopagnosia (Young & Ellis, 1989). The explanation for this begins with the fact that some prosopagnosia patients demonstrate an emotional response to familiar faces that they say they cannot recognize. The psychophysiological evidence for this emotional recognition is from skin conductance measures similar to those of lie detectors (Bauer, 1984). Thus, it is thought that when we see a face there are at least two processes occurring. One is overt recognition, and it corresponds to our ability to name and recall conscious properties related to the face. The other process is a covert emotional response and corresponds to visual information being sent to brain areas that are involved in emotions. Ellis and Lewis (2001) argue that Capgras syndrome arises from an intact system for overt recognition coupled with a damaged system for covert emotional recognition. It is argued that this leads to a conflict arising from knowing the identity of the person you see but failing to connect any emotional response to this identity. Resolution to the conflict of recognizing a family member but not having any emotional indication of emotional familiarity leads to the delusion that the person is some sort of impostor.
>
> Finally, Capgras syndrome can be considered a **double dissociation** with prosopagnosia since with Capgras syndrome an individual can recognize a person but does not feel they know them, while an individual with prosopagnosia cannot recognize a person but can sometimes feel that they know them.
>
> **Double dissociation** arises when, following brain injury, some people do well on one Task 'A' and poorly on a second Task 'B', while others with different brain injuries show the opposite pattern. Then the two tasks are said to be doubly dissociated.

Faces

Faces are important sources of social information that we use to recognize person properties such as emotion, gender, age, attractiveness and identity. Indeed, with the common use of photo IDs our face can become our identity. What makes recognizing

Figure 2.25 Face matching demonstrates the difficulty of recognizing unfamiliar faces.
The appearance of a face varies with lighting, viewpoint, expression and other changeable aspects of facial appearance. For familiar faces, we appear robust in identifying a face regardless of this variability. However, as these pairs of images show for unfamiliar faces, images taken from different identities (right) can appear as similar as images taken from the same identity (left).

Source: Phillips et al. (2018).

faces challenging is that although properties of the face, such as its shape, remain stable over years, any particular view of a face will be affected by lighting, viewpoint, make-up, health, expression, etc., which can drastically alter its appearance moment by moment (Figure 2.25). However, despite this multitude of complicating factors, recognition of faces can be surprisingly accurate. The literature on how we recognize faces is vast and reflects several decades of intense interest. From this, we can uncover some general properties of face recognition. First, humans are exquisitely tuned to recognize *familiar* faces and can do so under many adverse conditions (Johnston & Edmonds, 2009; Sinha et al., 2006). Until recently (Lu & Tang, 2015; Phillips & O'Toole, 2014), humans' levels of performance were above those of the best automatic computer recognition systems, but this is changing and face recognition technology is now a growing industry. Second, recognition of *unfamiliar* faces typically tells a different story, and except for a class of people known as 'super recognizers' (Russell et al., 2009), performance for typical people on the recognition of unfamiliar faces can be surprisingly poor (Hancock et al., 2000). How well humans can perform, and what influences their performance at face recognition has critical implications in the forensic domain and we discuss this in Box 2.7. Third, there are specialized brain areas and networks for facial recognition (Allison et al., 1994; Grill-Spector et al., 2017; Haxby et al., 2000; Kanwisher et al., 1997). Finally, the mechanisms of facial recognition are holistic, meaning that the particular way a configuration of facial features makes up a face is important in its own right, and one cannot deconstruct facial recognition into any simple collection of how individual facial features are recognized (Oruc et al., 2019).

An early cognitive model of face recognition (Bruce & Young, 1986), which has come to be known as the Bruce and Young model, set a framework for many of the subsequent studies in face perception. It outlined how the primary encoding of faces must feed into processes of recognition (*I know this person*), identification (*I know who this person is*), analysis of emotion through facial expression and the combination of additional information such as voice to augment facial processing. The Bruce and Young model predicts that recognition of identity and expression should be independent of each other and, although this is largely supported by behavioural data, the separation is not complete (Calder & Young, 2005). The influence of the Bruce and Young model was widespread because it considered both basic mechanisms of facial processing as well as the important social questions such as, Is the person with me familiar? Who are they? and What is their emotion?

To complement this cognitive model of Bruce and Young, a neural model of human face recognition was provided by Haxby and colleagues (2000) and comprised multiple regions spread throughout the brain (Figure 2.26). The organization of this distributed system emphasizes a distinction between the representation of invariant and changeable aspects of faces. The representation of invariant aspects of faces is responsible for the recognition of individuals, whereas the representation of changeable aspects of faces, such as eye gaze, expression and lip movement, facilitate social communication. The model divides facial processing into a core system and an extended system. In the core system, primary face processing occurs in the inferior occipital gyrus and representation of invariant aspects is mediated by face-responsive

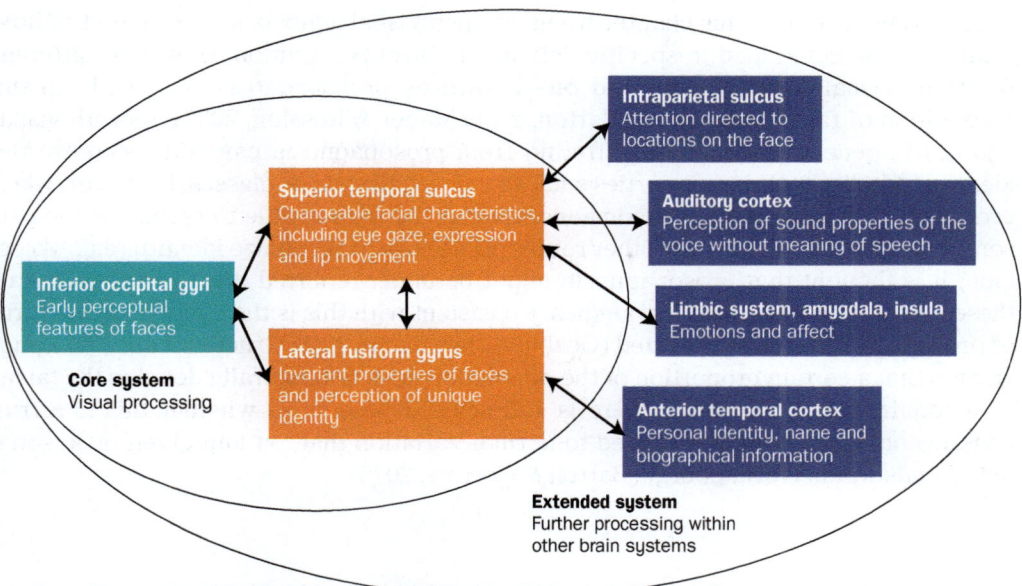

Figure 2.26 A neural model of face recognition.
Haxby and colleagues proposed a hierarchical model of face perception. The model incorporates a core system involving three brain regions for visual analysis and an extended system that complements these visual functions.

Source: Reprinted from Haxby et al. (2000)

neurons in the fusiform gyrus, whereas the representation of changeable aspects is mediated by face-responsive neurons in the superior temporal sulcus (Figure 2.26). The extended system includes other brain areas that aid face processing with functions of attention, emotion and identification as well as providing supplementary information from speech processing.

In the time since Haxby and colleagues proposed their model (2000) there has been much critical evaluation of the model (Atkinson & Adolphs, 2011). One particular component of the model, the fusiform face area (FFA) located in the lateral fusiform gyrus has attracted particular scrutiny. The FFA was identified as a face selective area using fMRI by comparing the brain response to faces with the response to other objects (Kanwisher et al., 1997). One criticism of this result was that the activity found in FFA is also consistent with a general-purpose recognition mechanism involving subordinate-level classification. This is to say that faces are just one particular example of an object category upon which we can recognize subordinate elements (Gauthier et al., 2000). With this view, FFA activity reflects perceptual expertise in subordinate classification rather than a face-specific mechanism, and there is still active debate on this issue. Another dimension to understanding the role of the FFA in face recognition has been raised by Weiner and Grill-Spector (2012), who argue that more sophisticated analyses of brain anatomy and function reveal that FFA is not a single cluster sensitive to faces, but instead appears to have a more complex structural organization. It has also been suggested by Duchaine and Yovel (2015) that there are additional face-selective areas that should be considered part of the core system, including face-selective areas in the anterior temporal lobe, the anterior superior temporal sulcus and in prefrontal brain regions. They further suggested that the FFA was also sensitive to changeable aspects of the face such as expression. Another recent development has involved using deep neural networks to model the functional neuroanatomy of the network of brain areas involved in face recognition (Grill-Spector et al., 2018).

In an earlier section in this chapter we mentioned visual agnosia in the context of how brain damage could lead to specific deficits in object recognition. However, different forms of visual agnosia exist and one known as prosopagnosia is specific to the recognition of faces (Albonico & Barton, 2019; Mayer & Rossion, 2007). As with visual agnosia in general, individuals suffering from prosopagnosia can still recognize the identity of individuals by properties such as voice, hairstyle or glasses. However, when presented with just the face of someone familiar they are unable to recognize the person. Since there are numerous other routes people use to recognize identity (e.g., voice, hair) it is thought that prosopagnosia might be under-reported due to the success of these alternative recognition strategies. Consistent with this is the claim that one form of prosopagnosia can be inherited (Geskin & Behrmann, 2018; Grueter et al., 2007), suggesting that a certain proportion of the population does not naturally develop the talent to recognize faces. However, there is still some debate as to whether this is a true genetic condition or simply related to normal variation that, on any given task, some individuals will perform poorly (Barton & Corrow, 2016).

Box 2.7 Practical Application: Forensics – eyewitness testimony and super recognizers

Face research continues to be a rich source for evidence-based practice in the field of forensics. Here we present two case studies, on eyewitness testimony and super recognizers.

EYEWITNESS IDENTIFICATION

Eyewitness identification of an individual during a trial can have a great impact on a jury. Given the importance of being able to correctly identify the perpetrator of a crime, and the dire consequences of making an error, the topic of eyewitness identification has seen considerable research to understand the conditions in which it can and cannot produce reliable results (for reviews see Albright, 2017; Fitzgerald et al., 2018; Lindsay et al., 2011; Loftus, 2019). The impact of this research can be seen in how it has influenced the policies and procedures of various governments around the world, such as in the UK (Police and Criminal Evidence Act 1984, Code D, 2010) and the USA (Technical Working Group for Eyewitness Evidence, 1999). Elsewhere in this book we will cover topics in eyewitness performance that are related to memory (Chapters 6 and 7), as well as the emotional state of the eyewitness (Chapter 15).

Chapter 6, p178, and 7, p220

Chapter 15, p573

While it might seem straightforward that an observer would recognize a face they have seen, recall that while our ability to recognize familiar faces is remarkably robust, our ability to recognize *unfamiliar* individuals can be surprisingly poor. Thus, if an eyewitness to a crime saw someone unfamiliar it is not certain how reliable they will be in making an identification. Numerous factors have been studied to see how they influence the reliability of eyewitness testimony; these factors fall into two categories:

1. Situational factors that are beyond the scope of what can be controlled by the legal system, including the duration for which the eyewitness observed the event, the race of the individuals involved and the state of the eyewitness at the time.
2. System factors that are under the control of the legal system, such as what instruction is provided to the witness, and the process of identification from photos, composites or line-ups.

We will now illustrate one factor from each of these categories.

The situational factor we will discuss is race. An individual is more likely to correctly identify, and less likely to incorrectly identify, a person of the same race than a person of a different race (Brigham et al., 2007; Meissner & Brigham, 2001). This is called the cross-race effect and has been found to be consistent across different ethnicities (Brigham, 2002). For example, Hispanics were found to be better at recognizing other Hispanics compared to black people across different encoding and decoding times, as well as arousal and attentional demands (MacLin et al., 2001).

The system factor we will discuss is the manner in which a potential suspect is identified. The standard procedure of a police line-up has been to present one or more suspects, along with other individuals who serve as foils, and have the eyewitness indicate whether any of the individuals is the one they saw. However, line-up identification appears to be sensitive to subtle aspects of the line-up process and has proven to be a substantial source of wrongful conviction in cases where DNA evidence has exonerated innocent people (Connors et al., 1996; Innocence Project, 2020). Wells and Turtle in 1986 compared target-present and target-absent line-ups and found that eyewitnesses have a high probability of selecting an individual from a line-up without a target. A recent review of actual police line-ups indicated that the rate of choosing a suspect when no target is present is as high as 37 per cent (Steblay, 2018). Probability of selection is also increased for a member of the line-up who stands out, and thus care is needed to ensure that the suspect does not stand out on the basis of the witness description. Finally, effects of investigator bias have shown that when the investigator knows which line-up member is a suspect there is a higher chance of that member of the line-up being chosen (Phillips et al., 1999). For this reason it is recommended that a line-up is administered by an individual who does not know the suspect (Lindsay & Wells, 1985).

SUPER RECOGNIZERS

Super recognizers are individuals who show high levels of performance on standard face recognition tasks (Russell et al., 2009). Given their apparent superior face recognition capabilities they have been used in face-related tasks (e.g., review of surveillance footage to identify a suspect), and in forensic services such as the London Metropolitan Police Force (Robertson et al., 2016) and other locations (Bobak et al., 2016).

There is little debate that people who are good at face recognition should be recruited to perform tasks involving faces, and that researchers and practitioners should collaborate to advance a theoretical and applied understanding. However, several issues have arisen in evaluating the efficacy of super recognizer use. A fundamental issue is that there is no clear objective or mechanistic definition of face recognition expertise (Young & Burton, 2018). Thus, it is possible that simply by natural statistical variation of test performance some people score low and are called developmental prosopagnosics and some score high and are called super recognizers. In this view there is nothing fundamentally missing in the prosopagnosics or extra in the super recognizers (Young & Noyes, 2019). To further complicate matters, there is no unique test to measure performance, most tests were developed for typical or low performance, and when different face recognition tests are given, the results can be variable with not every super recognizer performing excellently on every task (Ramon et al., 2019). Moreover, it is not clear that the lab-based tests appropriately tap into the particular face recognition skill that would be needed for a particular forensic task (Lander et al., 2018; Robertson & Bindemann, 2019).

While super recognizers are increasingly viewed as a viable approach to obtaining the highest levels of human performance on face-matching tasks, there is considerable scope for how this might occur in practice (Moreton et al., 2019). For example, there is evidence to show that a super recognizer teamed with a face recognition algorithm based on a deep neural network provides even better results (Phillips et al., 2018) than either the super recognizer alone or the deep neural network alone.

Voices

Like faces, the voice provides another important cue to our social environment. In this section we will discuss the voice, removed from any language content, as simply a sound cue that carries social information. For example, imagine staying in a hotel room where the walls are thin enough to hear the voices of your neighbours, but not so thin that you can understand any words. From just the sound of the voices we can make out the nature of their social interaction, whether our neighbours are fighting or having a party. Similarly, if you overhear two people speaking a language you do not understand, although you do not understand the language you will, without looking, be able to guess at the gender, age and size of the speakers (Ko et al., 2006; Latinus & Belin, 2011). Of course the voice also produces language, and this important property of voice is covered in Chapter 10. One way that voice carries information independent of linguistic content is found in the fact that the emotional content of an utterance can be carried in the **prosody** of the speech. For example, depending on prosody, even just the way one says 'hello' can inform our social evaluation of a speaker, such as whether they are trustworthy or not (McAleer et al., 2014; Ponsot et al., 2018). This aspect of voice has some similarities with music, and an extensive comparison of how emotion is perceived from music and voice showed that both use largely the same patterns of auditory information to convey specific emotions (Juslin & Laukka, 2003).

> Chapter 10, p326

> **Prosody**
> the rhythm, intonation and stress patterns in speech.

The sound quality of a voice is constrained by the combination of the folds of the larynx, which provide a sound source, and the vocal tract including the tongue, nasal cavity and lips that filter the sound. The resulting sound of each individual's voice is made unique by not only the size and shape of these physical structures but also the manner in which individuals form and articulate their vocal tract. Thus, voice contains an important source of identity information (Bachorowski & Owren, 1999; Baumann & Belin, 2010). As discussed earlier in the chapter, loss of the ability to recognize identity from voice is known as phonagnosia (Vanlancker et al., 1989). In phonagnosia individuals can understand the content of speech but are unable to identify the speaker.

Studies using fMRI in humans have found distinctive regions outside the primary auditory cortex, in the upper bank of the superior temporal sulcus (STS) that appear sensitive to human voice (Belin et al., 2000, 2004; Binder et al., 2000) (see Figure 2.27). This temporal voice area has been found to more actively respond to human voice sounds than to a variety of other sounds, including animal vocalizations and assorted non-vocal sounds. In addition, results from an fMRI experiment that examined training effects in learning prototypical voices has shown that a distributed system exists for independently representing acoustics and identity from voice (Andics et al., 2010).

Biological Motion

Observing the actions of others, like faces and voices can also be socially informative (Johnson & Shiffrar, 2013). For example, looking at the activity of a group of people in the distance gives us an idea of what they are doing, whether they are angry or sad and if possibly we know them. A variety of studies have indicated the ability of observers to use displays of human action to recognize identity (Cutting & Kozlowski, 1977), gender (Kozlowski & Cutting, 1977; Troje, 2002), emotion (Dittrich et al., 1996; Pollick et al., 2001), the action being carried out (Dittrich, 1993) and even whether a person appears vulnerable to attack (Gunns et al., 2002). It has been shown that even when there is little information available in a visual display, people are very efficient at using the limited information present to form judgements of social properties like gender (Pollick et al., 2005).

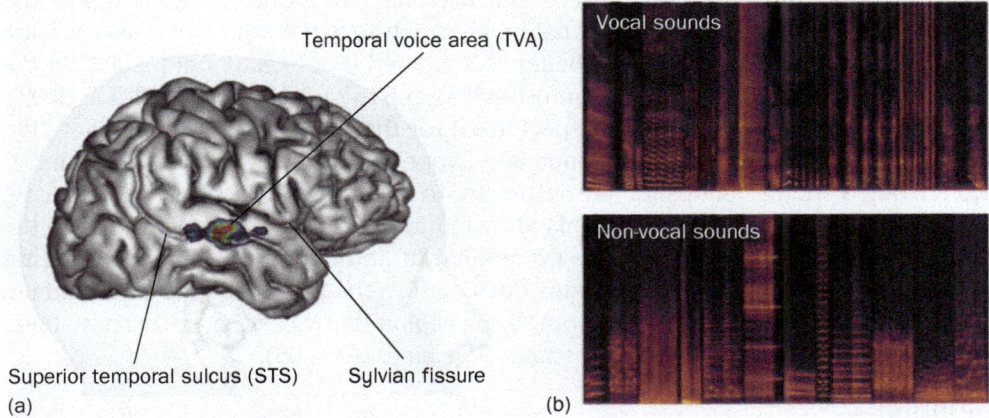

Figure 2.27 Voice-sensitive brain regions revealed by comparison of vocal and non-vocal sounds.
(a) Specific regions in temporal cortex known as the temporal voice area are more active when listening to speech sounds. (b) Frequency-time spectrograms of the vocal (top) and non-vocal (bottom) sounds used in an fMRI experiment to reveal brain regions involved in voice processing.

Source: Reprinted from Latinus & Belin (2011), with permission from Elsevier.

An important issue in the experimental study of body movement is how to isolate it from other person properties. This is important since facial attractiveness, clothes, haircut and body shape all add some extra information about the person being viewed, and if you are interested in just the effect of body motion then these other factors need to be eliminated. A solution to this problem was introduced into the psychology literature by Gunnar Johansson (1973), who filmed actors in dark rooms with points of light attached to their joints. He subsequently showed films of these actions where the contrast was adjusted so only the points of light could be seen. Rather than seeing this as a cloud of unorganized points, observers were able to vividly see a human form in action. The ability to perceptually organize these point-light displays into the percept of a specific human action has been termed biological motion perception. The utility of point-light displays is illustrated in Figure 2.28, which shows two frames from a point-light display of a man pushing an object. These individual frames (as well as all the frames together) provide little information about the actor or the action when viewed singly. However, when viewed in animation the action is vividly seen.

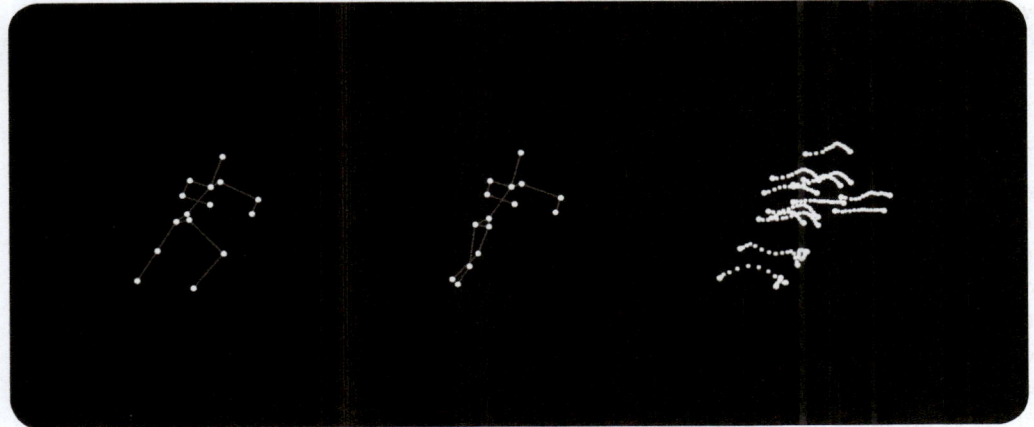

Figure 2.28 Point-light display of human movement.
Point-light displays depict a human as a collection of lights located at the main joints. The left and middle images show individual frames of a point-light display of an individual pushing a heavy weight. The links between joints are shown in grey but are not shown in actual experiments. To the right is a set of overlaid frames which when viewed sequentially give a vivid impression of the action being performed.

How we can effortlessly process these sparse displays into a rich perception of action is still under debate. One theory holds that body-structure and body-motion information are processed independently before being recombined (Giese & Poggio, 2003) in the posterior region of the superior temporal sulcus (pSTS) (Grossman & Blake, 2002). In this theory the pSTS is a key area specialized for the perception of human activity. A somewhat opposing theory from Lange and Lappe (2006) holds that structural information from a single 'snapshot' is sufficient to inform the recognition of many properties of point-light displays. In this view motion is still important to enhance the perception of human activity, but the processing of static information is a vital first step. Consistent with neural mechanisms dedicated to the processing of static human form is the finding of an occipitotemporal brain region known as the extrastriate body area (EBA), which represents body postures (Peelen et al., 2006).

Evaluation

In this section on social perception, as well as elsewhere in the book, we have attributed function to particular brain areas. The cases of pSTS and EBA provide a useful example that in some cases these attributions of function to specific brain location can still be considered work in progress. The current standard view is that while the EBA is involved in processing static images of bodies, the pSTS is the key region for biological motion perception due to being at the convergence of body-structure and body-motion information. However, increasingly there is awareness that the extended EBA region is sensitive to motion information (Ferri et al., 2013; Jastorff & Orban, 2009; McKay et al., 2012; Thompson & Baccus, 2012). Thus, while there seems little doubt that the pSTS is involved with converging information of social relevance (Allison et al., 2000) there is increasing interest in how body-form and body-motion information might be combined prior to arriving at pSTS (Vangeneugden et al., 2009).

Summary

Perception is an important topic in the study of cognition since it provides insight into the mechanisms that inform us about the external world. Although there is a vast literature on the detailed workings of perceptual capabilities, perception can be thought of as simply the early stages of an information processing system. The first section of this chapter described fundamental concepts in perception and pursued the view that perception can be described as information processing. A great benefit of this approach is that it allows us to define concepts of perception that apply generally to man, machine and other organisms. The second section of the chapter examined human perceptual systems as a special case and provided examples of how perceptual systems are implemented in the human brain. We also explored the relationship between brain and perception, and how damage to the brain alters perception.

The different perceptual systems of vision, audition and somatoperception were examined and we discussed how different perceptual inputs might optimally be combined to form a unitary percept of objects and events. An important achievement of perception is our ability to recognize objects, and the process of recognition was explored in the third section of the chapter. Recognition allows us to relate perceptual properties to mental categories and thus provides a powerful means for organizing our perceptual world. Key for recognition is the ability to efficiently represent objects and events in a flexible manner such that the essence of an object or event can be understood across different conditions: for example, the identity of an object when seen from different viewpoints or the sound of a word spoken by different speakers. In the final section of the chapter we investigated how faces, voices and body movements inform social perception. Social perception is an important talent for a social species like humans where fluent interactions are guided by our abilities to perceive social cues.

Review Questions

1. What is perception used for, and how is it possible to compare perception in man and machine?
2. What properties are common to the processing of audio, video and touch information?
3. How does predictive coding change our understanding of bottom-up and top-down processing in the context of interpreting sensory information?
4. Contrast the differences between the modality appropriate hypothesis with the maximum likelihood approach to multisensory processing.
5. What makes recognition a difficult problem to solve?
6. What types of social perception are common across different modes of perception?
7. If you were designing a perceptual system for a robot, how important would it be to take into account the physical properties of the robot?

Discussion Questions

1. What would be the advantages and disadvantages of defining rigid boundaries between sensation, perception and cognition?
2. What are the differences between perceiving objects and perceiving people?
3. Artificial deep neural networks can reach human-like performance on many tasks like face recognition. How can we exploit this capability to better understand human perception?

Further Reading

Bregman, A. S. (1990). *Auditory scene analysis: The perceptual organization of sound*. MIT Press.

Calvo, P., & Gomila, T. (Eds.). (2008). *Handbook of cognitive science: An embodied approach*. Elsevier Science.

Hoffman, D. (2019). *The case against reality: Why evolution hid the truth from our eyes*. W. W. Norton & Company.

Johnson, K., & Shiffrar, M. (Eds.). (2012). *People watching: Social, perceptual, and neurophysiological studies of body perception*. Oxford University Press.

Levitin, D. (2006). *This is your brain on music: Understanding a human obsession*. Dutton Adult.

Marr, D. (1982). *Vision: A computational investigation into the human representation and processing of visual information*. W. H. Freeman.

Palmer, S. E. (1999). *Vision science: Photons to phenomenology*. MIT Press.

Sacks, O. (2014). *The man who mistook his wife for a hat*. Picador Classic (Vol. 19). Pan Macmillan.

MOTOR COGNITION

3

PREVIEW QUESTIONS

INTRODUCTION

MOTOR CONTROL
- Box 3.1 Practical Application: Designing machines to help us move
- THEORIES OF MOVEMENT PLANNING
- Box 3.2 Research Close Up: Tit-for-tat and force escalation

PRODUCING COMPLEX ACTIONS
- ACTION SEQUENCES
- HIERARCHICAL MODELS OF ACTION PRODUCTION
- BRAIN DAMAGE AND ACTION PRODUCTION
- Box 3.3 Practical Application: Cognitive rehabilitation for apraxia and action disorganization syndrome

ACTION REPRESENTATION AND PERCEPTION
- THEORIES OF ACTION REPRESENTATION
- Box 3.4 Research Close Up: Using dance expertise to study action representation
- EMBODIED COGNITION
- AGENCY
- Box 3.5 When Things Go Wrong: Alien hand syndrome

SUMMARY

REVIEW QUESTIONS

DISCUSSION QUESTIONS

FURTHER READING

Preview Questions

1. How do we produce our movements?
2. Does the body shape cognition?
3. How is a sequence of actions planned and represented in the brain?
4. What evidence is there that representations of perception and action overlap?
5. Can gesture be thought of as visualized thought?
6. How do we determine that an action we sense is due to our own movement?

INTRODUCTION

Motor cognition explains how we move our body to achieve our goals. In its entirety this includes a vast range of activities such as kissing, blinking, singing, walking, hammering a nail, focusing your eye on a target, and any other human activity that requires a body part to move. You can appreciate that since all these actions are planned in the brain and performed by the body they must share something in common, but certainly the precise mechanisms for kissing are different from hammering a nail. The goal of this chapter is to step away from aspects specific to any one action and to present general principles that provide insight into what is common to how we move our body and form plans of action. To achieve this we break description of motor cognition into three parts. The first section describes how we use our **motor system** to produce movements. No matter what the motor activity, it is being coordinated by the nervous system and implemented by muscles. By adopting a common framework for describing how movements are planned and performed we enable a means to talk about general properties of movement control. However, such a framework for movement control is difficult to generalize for description of how we achieve complex action sequences. Thus, in the next section we move to a higher level of description that takes for granted that details of movement generation will be achieved and strives to understand how units of motor behaviour can be strung together. In the final section we discuss how the motor system interconnects with other psychological functions such as cognition and perception. This discussion includes how representations of action are shared between producing and perceiving actions, and how this supports views of embodied cognition. We conclude with the special nature of perceiving our own actions and how this leads to a sense of our own agency.

> **Motor system** includes the components of the central and peripheral nervous systems along with the muscles, joints and bones that enable movement.

MOTOR CONTROL

Motor control is the study of how body movements are planned by the brain and performed by the body. The modern study of motor control goes back for over a century to the studies of Woodworth (1899), who proposed different stages for the planning and control of movement. In a classic study, he examined how people perform the task of sliding a pencil back and forth between targets. Data from this experiment revealed that movement between targets could be described with a two-component process of motor control. The impulse phase initiated the movement and was planned in advance of the start of the movement. In essence, the brain would calculate in advance what limbs to move and how they should move, and this plan – in the form of a motor command – would be sent from the brain out to the body. The impulse phase was followed by a control phase where vision was used in controlling the accuracy of the final endpoint position. While details such as the estimate of time needed to incorporate visual information have been revised (Elliott et al., 2001), the basic question of how to produce a movement that is efficient and incorporates sensory information in a timely manner remains relevant today.

Following Woodworth, studies in the early twentieth century explored the motor control problem from primarily a physiological perspective (Latash & Zatsiorsky, 2001). A basic formulation of the problem was simply how to get the body from one posture to another, and research over the past century has revealed many fundamental problems the brain and body must solve to get from one point to another. One of the early pioneers of the twentieth century in studying motor control was the Russian scientist Nikolai Bernstein (1967). Like Woodworth, he also emphasized that the coordination of motor structures with sensory information was key to understanding motor control. However, a major contribution of Bernstein was to recognize that producing a movement plan requires overcoming what is known as the degrees of freedom problem. This **degrees of freedom** problem refers to the issue that the structure of joints and muscles in the body provides a redundant system. This means that when performing a goal-directed action there is not a single unique pattern of joint motions to achieve the goal. Instead, there are multiple combinations of how the joints can move to achieve the task. A demonstration of redundancy comes from when we get injured and even though we cannot perform a particular joint motion, we can still achieve many of the same tasks we did before the injury. This redundancy clearly provides us with great versatility in performing actions in changing situations. However, for a motor control system trying to formulate a movement plan, this redundancy poses a serious computational problem that we will discuss in the following paragraph.

> **Degrees of freedom** of a joint are the number of ways it can move – for example, the shoulder has three (up–down, forwards–backwards, rotate along axis of bone).

This computational problem of how to plan a movement out of the multitude of alternatives is reminiscent to what we encountered in vision (see Chapter 2) with the so-called **inverse problem**, where out of the multitude of possible interpretations of a visual scene, a unique one is perceived. To illustrate the situation faced by our motor planning system, consider standing in front of a lift, with your hand in front of you, having the goal of pressing the call button so you can ride the lift. You could move your hand along any number of paths, and for any particular path your speed along the path could vary (e.g., start fast and finish slow or start slow and finish fast). In addition, the joints you recruit to do the movement could differ (e.g., both the shoulder and elbow move and their contribution could vary), and your muscle activations could change (e.g., muscles relaxed or tense while achieving the same path). Given all the possible factors for achieving this simple goal, we can see that the motor planning system is confronted with a difficult task to plan what body parts will move with what motion. However, we don't stand on the ground floor frozen with confusion about how to press the call button. We simply act on achieving our goal and the effortless way in which this occurs shows that our brain has worked out an efficient strategy for producing movements. (While a more impressive example of motor expertise might be how an Olympic gymnast dismounts from the uneven bars, even the simplest movement reveals tremendous sophistication.) In the following we will review some of the proposals that have been put forth to describe how movements are planned and produced. However, before proceeding we will illustrate how developments in understanding motor control are being used to create new devices that provide help for those requiring assistance with their movement (Box 3.1).

> Chapter 2, p38

> **Inverse problem** in vision, where there is more than one interpretation of the 3D world given the 2D image information.

 Box 3.1 Practical Application: Designing machines to help us move

Tremendous progress has been made in creating robots that can locomote on their own. Examples of this include the many impressive recent robots from Boston Dynamics (www.youtube.com/user/BostonDynamics) that somersault, walk and run over complicated terrain and obstacles. For a sense of how far things have advanced in the past 30 years, one can view the early versions of these robots (Raibert, 1986). The development of these robots has been based on how humans move and, thus, these advances can be related to ways to provide mobility assistance for individuals who cannot move on their own (Chen et al., 2016; Gassert & Dietz, 2018). These mobility assistance devices generally strap to the body in the form of a robotic exoskeleton, and include a set of mechanical linkages with motors at the joints integrated with on-board computers and motion sensors that provide assistance for an individual to move. These systems are increasingly available commercially and used for rehabilitation and locomotion assistance for individuals who have experienced a spinal cord injury (Gorgey, 2018), a stroke or otherwise have weakness in their legs (Mekki et al., 2018). Special designs are available even to enhance strength.

In order to work, these systems must enable the intentions of the user to be transferred to the device. Currently this is generally achieved via instrumented crutches, or body posture sensors that make it possible to initiate movement with a predetermined signal, like leaning forward. Such a signal can trigger the device to perform a movement, from sitting to standing, or walking forward in a straight line. This capability can restore lost function for individuals with spinal cord injury or can be programmed to provide assistance to the degree needed for individuals in rehabilitation. In the context of rehabilitation, a further benefit of these systems is the ability to monitor the progress of rehabilitation by analysis of the resulting movement properties and the amount of assistance provided by the device.

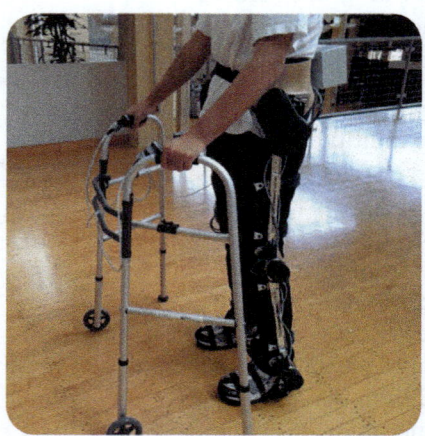

Figure 3.1 Robot assistive device to aid walking.
CYBERDYNE's Robot Suit HAL (Hybrid Assistive Limb) is connected to the body and has sophisticated electronics to sense intended motor activity, as well as algorithms to compute robot movement. Thus, it provides an assistive force to help those too weak to walk unaided.

© NCBI/National Center for Biotechnology Information

A vision for the future of these devices addresses the issue of how to more richly transfer the intentions from the user to the device. The measurement of bio-electrical signals in the brain, along nerve pathways and in the muscle, provides a window into the intentions. However, decoding these measurements into intentions is challenging, and few systems incorporate this capacity (Suzuki et al., 2007; Wall et al., 2015). Solving this challenge will require both technological breakthroughs and advances in understanding motor cognition (Ruiz Garate et al., 2017). If the intention was somehow not decoded properly then the commands from the on-board computers to the robot motors would not conform to the brain signals being sent to the muscles, and this could bring unintended consequences and harm to the user.

Theories of Movement Planning

How the brain plans and executes movements is still a hotly debated topic. The three approaches we will explain were developed independently, and each emphasizes a different aspect of how movements are planned and controlled.

> **Equilibrium point hypothesis** a theory of motor control that emphasizes how the problem of control can be simplified by taking into account muscle properties.

The first theoretical approach, known as **equilibrium point hypothesis**, emphasizes the special relationship between the brain and the muscles (Feldman, 1966, 1986; Feldman & Latash, 2005). This approach is sometimes termed a mass-spring model since it reflects an important intuition that our muscles, like springs, exert different forces depending on how much they are stretched. The model can effectively explain how we can begin a movement with our body in one stable posture and end in another stable posture. The crucial observation of the equilibrium point hypothesis is that any stable posture requires the setting of various control parameters for muscle activation to achieve stability. Thus, moving from one posture to another can be achieved by simply resetting these parameters so that the spring-like properties of the muscle move you into the next posture. This planning exploits the spring-like properties of the muscles to simplify what the brain must control to move the body. The problem of planning is simplified since one needs only to have a stable starting posture and know the parameters that are necessary to stabilize the body in the desired end posture. From this plan the movement can emerge from the inherent muscle properties. While this is an attractive theory in showing how incorporating knowledge of muscle properties can simplify motor planning there have been some criticisms. For example, it has been argued that it would be a successful strategy only for certain ranges of movements and muscle properties (Katayama & Kawato, 1993; Kawato, 1999; Kawato & Gomi, 1992). Outside of this range it was argued that planning using principles of the equilibrium point hypothesis became much more complex. However, there is debate over this point and arguments for the general utility of the approach (Ostry & Feldman, 2003).

The second theoretical approach, known as **dynamical systems** theory, is related to ecological theories of psychology (Gibson, 1979) and emphasizes motor control as a process of self-organization between an animal and its environment. In the simplest terms, dynamical systems is a branch of mathematics that includes rules that describe the evolution of the state of a system over time. For example, it can explain how the swinging motion of a pendulum will evolve over time. Of course, the human body and human movement are more complex than a pendulum, but dynamical systems are effective in explaining complex systems interacting with the environment (Kelso, 1995; Turvey, 1990). Models of behaviour that use dynamical systems have provided elegant descriptions of motor behaviours. For example, in locomotion, walking and running are distinct motor patterns and there isn't an in-between state. This situation can be modelled as a dynamical system with walking and running as different stable states and a transition occurring between them determined by speed. Another example of a state transition arises from the observation that when we move two limbs together there is a tendency for them to exhibit mirror symmetric movements (Schmidt et al., 1990; Swinnen, 2002), meaning that if we held a mirror between the limbs then the reflection of one of the limbs would match what the other limb was doing. Even if we try to move our fingers in an antisymmetric manner, we will spontaneously change to a symmetric manner at a particular frequency of movement (Haken et al., 1985; Kelso, 1984). This result is illustrated in Figure 3.2 and you can perform this

> **Dynamical systems** approach to motor control that emphasizes interaction between the body and the environment, and uses special mathematics that describe how a system's behaviour changes over time.

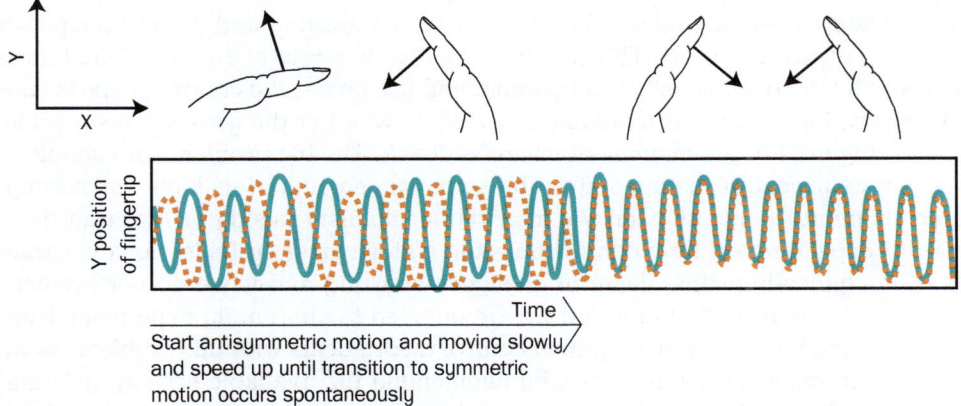

Figure 3.2 Example of dynamical systems theory.
Start with your two fingers moving in alternate directions – one moving towards the body and the other away – and steadily increase the frequency of these movements. At some point when the fingers begin to move more rapidly there is a transition from the original antisymmetric motion to a symmetric pattern. This transition is predicted by dynamical systems theory.

Source: Adapted from Haken et al. (1985).

experiment for yourself right now. Place your two hands in front of your body with palms facing each other. Now begin slowly with moving your fingers back and forth in an antisymmetric manner – one finger moving towards the body while the other is moving away in an alternating fashion. Once you have achieved a stable pattern of movement then start slowly increasing the frequency of these back-and-forth finger motions. At some point as you increase the frequency you will find that both fingers are moving in a symmetric manner – both are moving towards and away from the body at the same time. This transition from antisymmetric to symmetric is neatly described in dynamical systems by a state transition of the motor system that is controlling the finger movements. Strengths of the dynamical systems approach have been to draw upon parallels with the behaviour of physical objects and to offer a rigorous theory that enables detailed modelling and prediction of rhythmic behaviour. However, it is an open area how to apply this approach to discrete movements.

> **Optimal control theory** of motor control provides a framework for implementing principles that produce movements that optimally satisfy some criterion.

The next approach we will consider is known as **optimal control theory** (Diedrichsen et al., 2010; Scott, 2004; Wolpert & Ghahramani, 2000; Wolpert & Kawato, 1998). Optimal control does not focus on particular constraints of the body, but instead views motor control as the evolutionary or developmental result of a nervous system that tries to optimize organizational principles (Schaal et al., 2007). Optimal control has been influential in the field of robotics. In optimal control, the problem of planning a movement is solved by using an optimization principle to define the best movement. Optimization principles that have been explored include planning a movement to be the smoothest motion between two points (Flash & Hogan, 1985), planning the least amount of **torque** – change at the joints (Uno et al., 1989) – or planning the least amount of spatial errors in task achievement (Harris & Wolpert, 1998). The characteristics of coordination are therefore determined by the movement structure imposed by the optimization principle used. Optimal control theory arose from early engineering models for control of robots and has been actively used in developments in cognitive robotics, where engineers were faced with the difficult process of designing robot controllers that could mimic human actions (Atkeson et al., 2000; Fitzpatrick et al., 2016).

> **Torque** a measure from physics that measures rotational force such as when muscles apply a force for a limb to rotate about a joint centre.

Optimal control theory is an advanced form of a simple feedback mechanism. The classic example of simple feedback is a heating thermostat where you set the desired temperature. In this system the existing temperature is compared to the desired temperature and, depending on the difference between existing and desired temperature, the heat is turned on or off. This notion of feedback is related to the original ideas of Woodworth (1899), where after the original impulse phase, the control phase is entered and sensory information is available to evaluate whether the goal has been achieved and suitably modify the movement using feedback. The big problem with simple feedback is reminiscent of the uncomfortable experience many of us have had setting the water temperature in a shower. We alter the mechanism raising or lowering the temperature depending on how comfortable the water currently feels, however there is typically a time delay in changes occurring and if we do not predict this delay as part of our plan we are doomed to alternately experience freezing and burning water. Optimal control theory deals with this problem, as we do in adjusting temperature, by augmenting the available sensory information with predictions of the sensory information obtained from a **forward model** (Jordan & Rumelhart, 1992; Kawato, 1999). The forward model obtains these predictions from simulating the effects of our commands. Mental access to the prediction of a motor command is necessary because we need to be able to move quickly in complex ways, and predictions of the sensory consequences

> **Forward models** used to predict the relationship between actions and their consequences. Given a motor command the forward model predicts the resulting behaviour of the body and the world.

of our motor commands are available faster than the sensory feedback resulting from the motor commands. For example, early studies of typing on a keyboard showed that there does not seem to be time enough for feedback to be involved in this highly skilled activity (Rumelhart & Norman, 1982). Think about how quickly you can move your hands and fingers in a single second to achieve a complex interaction with the world, and consider further that visual information takes time to process and planning movements will also take some fixed amount of time. The challenge for the motor system is to deal with the world as it is *now* based on sensory information that is a tenth of a second old and with motor commands that will take effect in muscles a tenth of a second in the future.

A diagram illustrating optimal control theory is shown in Figure 3.3. As can be seen in Figure 3.3 the process of optimal control theory is cyclical, with motor commands being sent out of a control policy and the result of the motor command coming back to the control policy in the form of an estimate of the state that reflects how the motor command has changed things. To better understand the process we will describe this cycle starting with the control policy and going clockwise.

- *Control policy:* the control policy takes as input the current state estimate and outputs a motor command. The control policy is the most complex aspect of optimal control theory. It provides a set of rules that determine what to do given a particular goal and state estimate. The control policy can take into account the importance of the goal to be achieved, the confidence in both the incoming sensory information and the outgoing motor commands as well as other factors.
- *Motor command:* the motor command is output from the control policy and contains the information about how the body is supposed to move.
- *Noise:* physiological noise is introduced into the motor command due to imperfect neural transmission along the pathway from brain to body.
- *Forward model:* the forward model takes as input the motor command and outputs a prediction of the sensory consequences of the motor command.
- *Body and the world:* the body takes as input the motor command that has been degraded by noise, and produces an action that changes the state of the body and typically also the world; this creates new sensory information.

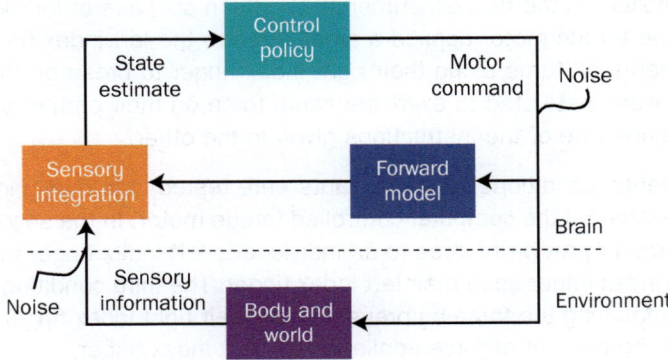

Figure 3.3 Optimal control theory.
A motor command is sent from the control policy to the body and this results in a change in the world that is sensed. This sensed change in the world, along with the prediction of the change provided by a forward model are combined to estimate the current state of the body in the world. Noise can arise in transmitting information in the nervous system, just as noise can arise in a telephone line, and this can affect both the transmission of the motor command from the brain to the body and the transmission of sensory information from the sense organs to the brain.

- *Sensory information:* the changes to the body and world create sensory information (e.g., visual information of an object being moved, auditory information of an impact sound, proprioceptive information of the limbs changing position).
- *Noise:* just like the motor command, the sensory information is also corrupted by physiological noise arising from imperfect sensing and neural transmission. This noise will lead to uncertainty in estimating the state of the body and the world.
- *Sensory integration:* sensory integration takes as input all the sensory information as well as the prediction of the forward model and outputs an estimate of the current state of the system.
- *State estimate:* the state estimate provides an internal representation of what is the current state of the body and world, and this is input to the control policy.

Optimal control theory is applicable to a broad range of topics and in Box 3.2 we explain how it can account for errors we make in judging the force of our actions.

Box 3.2 Research Close Up: Tit-for-tat and force escalation

Source: Wolpert et al. (2003).

INTRODUCTION

This research, conducted by Daniel Wolpert and colleagues, began with the observation that whenever two children play tit-for-tat it quickly ends in tears with one complaining they had unfairly been hit very, very hard (Wolpert et al., 2003). Since the goal of a game of tit-for-tat is to hit the other person as hard as you have been hit it should not inevitably end with claims of unreasonable force escalation. However, since it is known that forces can be mis-estimated Wolpert hypothesized that we reliably underestimate the forces we produce and thus we would always hit harder than we thought we did. To test this hypothesis Wolpert and colleagues explored how forces were exchanged under different experimental conditions.

METHOD

Three different experimental conditions were explored using specially designed equipment that included force transducers to measure the forces being applied and computer-controlled torque motors that allowed specific forces to be applied. In the first experimental condition six pairs of individuals participated. A session began when the torque motor applied a small force to the left index finger of one of the participants. Participants then took turns using their right index finger to press on their partner's left index finger. Both partners were instructed to exert the same force on their partner that they had just experienced, but they were unaware of the instructions given to the other.

In the second and third experimental conditions 12 participants were tested individually in their ability to match a range of forces generated by the computer-controlled torque motor. In the second condition the computer-controlled torque motor provided forces to an individual's left index finger that they then matched by pressing their right index finger upon their left index finger. The third condition was like the second, except that instead of matching the force by pressing with their right index finger they manipulated a joystick that controlled the amount of force applied to the left index finger.

RESULTS

The results of the first experimental condition (Figure 3.4a) showed that when trading touches partners quickly escalated forces by approximately 38 per cent per turn. If individuals had been accurate then there would have been a flat line showing no increase in forces as the original small force would have been obtained for all turns of force exchange. The results of the additional conditions are shown in Figure 3.4b, which plots the matched force against the presented force. When individuals matched the presented force by using finger presses then they consistently produced more force than had originally been applied to them by the computer-controlled torque motor. To appreciate the amount of force over-estimation one should compare the experimental results to the dashed diagonal line that represents correct performance (matched force equals presented force). In the third condition when individuals matched force by use of the joystick then performance was much more accurate, with the matched forces nearly overlapping the diagonal line of correct performance.

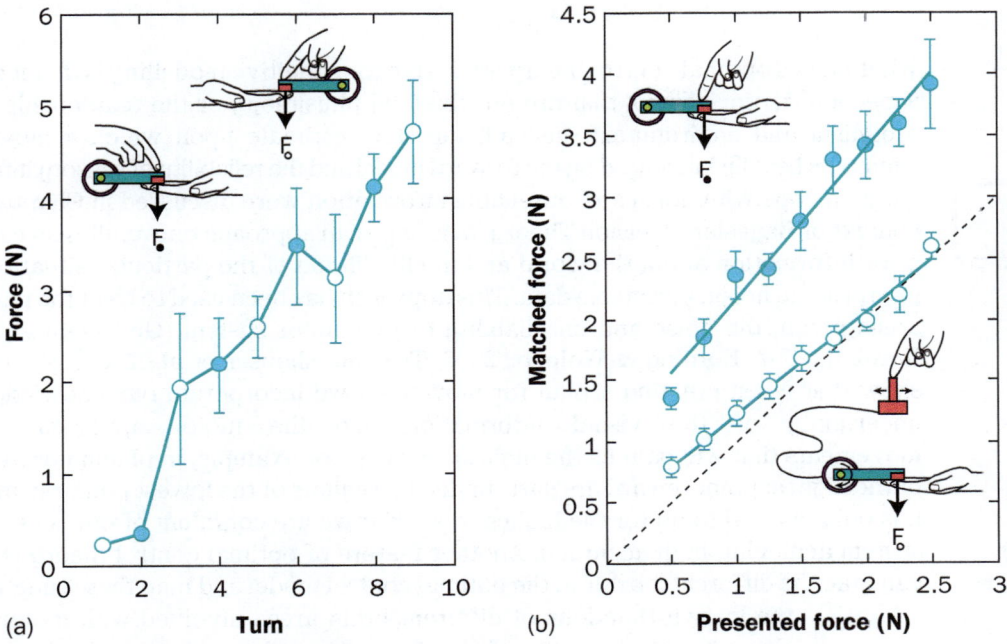

Figure 3.4 We underestimate the application of our own force.
(a) In a tit-for-tat game of exchanging touches there is a consistent escalation of force between partners as the number of turns increase. (b) When we match a computer-generated force with a force directly generated by our finger then we consistently overestimate forces (filled-in circles). However, when we match a presented force by using a joystick we are more accurate (open circles).

Source: Wolpert et al. (2003). Reprinted with permission from AAAS.

DISCUSSION

The results of this series of experiments demonstrate that although we can accurately match forces when mediated by an external device like a joystick, we are greatly inaccurate when we match forces generated by our own body. When asked to create a force that matches a received touch we greatly overestimate the force applied to others and even to ourselves. While this suggests that next time we want to touch someone gently we should touch them very, very lightly it also provides an opportunity to see how optimal control theory can be used to explain why this happens. The forces we generate ourselves also inform a forward model and the predictions of this forward model will be combined with the perceived sensory consequences of our self-generated actions. A consequence of this combination seems to be that perception of our own actions has a special status that leads to substantial underestimation of force. One possible reason for this is that for interactions with the environment, it is useful to attenuate the effect of the forces we generate ourselves, as a means to become more sensitive to forces we receive from external sources.

> The question of why internally generated forces might be mis-estimated was explored in a follow-up experiment that investigated schizophrenia (Shergill et al., 2005). Because schizophrenics can report self-generated actions as being of alien origin (Frith, 2012) it was hypothesized they would have less of a tendency to create excessive matching forces when using finger presses. Experimental results confirmed this hypothesis, with schizophrenics being more accurate than controls in generating matching forces. This illustrates the significance of mechanisms that treat our own actions as special. Moreover, interpretation of the results highlights that one important function of the forward model could be to diminish the effects of our own actions as a means to aid our sensory system in separating the effects of ourselves from the effects of the world.

What makes optimal control theory attractive for cognitive modelling is that it describes aspects of motor control that are not fixed by physiology or the relationship between organism and environment. Instead, the state estimate upon which a movement is planned is heavily influenced by the forward model and the reliability of sensory information. Ways to cope with noisy and unreliable information were discussed in Chapter 2 in the context of Bayesian Decision Theory. In a Bayesian approach one applies an estimate of prior information about the world and the likelihood of the particular situation to best interpret the noisy, unreliable data. This approach has been used to treat the uncertainty arising from the noise and unreliability of our motor system (Gepshtein et al., 2007; Kording, 2007; Kording & Wolpert, 2006; Trommershauser et al., 2006). These studies show that when creating a plan for movement we incorporate our knowledge of the uncertainty of the visual information and the motor apparatus to plan movements that will gain us the highest reward. For example, in playing darts, regions of the highest point reward are surrounded by regions of the lowest point reward and so it is only optimal to go for the highest reward if we are confident of our sensory-motor system achieving high accuracy. Another feature of optimal control theory is that one can take the different 'boxes' in the optimal control model and map these functions onto the known functions of different brain areas involved with motor control. For example, aspects of the forward model appear to be based in the **cerebellum**, aspects of sensory integration appear to be based in parietal cortex, and aspects of the control policy appear to be based in the **basal ganglia** (Shadmehr & Krakauer, 2008).

Chapter 2, p41

Cerebellum
brain structure located behind and underneath the larger cerebrum. Although traditionally known for its contribution to producing movement, it is also important for cognitive function.

Basal ganglia
a group of neurons in the base of the forebrain that are connected to cortex and involved in action selection. Disorders of the basal ganglia are related to movement disorders such as Parkinson's disease.

Evaluation

We have briefly reviewed three theories of motor control and these ideas provide us with insight into the fundamental building blocks of how movements are produced. Each theory highlighted an important consideration of how to solve this complex problem. The equilibrium point hypothesis showed that the complexity of forming a plan can be simplified by cleverly exploiting the properties of how muscles operate. Dynamical systems illustrated that theories of how a system evolves over time can, for repetitive rhythmic movements, successfully explain transitions between different action states. Finally, optimal control theory provided a framework to implement optimal organizational principles within the loop of planning, producing and sensing our actions. Resolving debate as to which is the most appropriate theory to explain what happens in the human brain has proven daunting. The issue is that each theory has a compelling description of some aspect of behaviour and theory; development past the 'sweet spot' of any one theory has led to more complicated versions, which by their complexity lose some of the compelling simplicity and parsimony of the original theory. An example of this is elegant work by Sternad and colleagues (2000) exploring dynamical systems that showed, for a special case of movement, how control of rhythmic movements (the 'sweet spot' for dynamical theory) could be tuned to produce single discrete movements.

PRODUCING COMPLEX ACTIONS

In the previous section we discussed how the motor system produces movements of the body. This discussion included concepts of how the brain, body and environment act together to produce movements. However, the goals of these movements were kept simple to emphasize the processes involved in planning individual body movements. In this section, we move from the problem of how individual movements are produced to focus on movement goals and how these lead to complex sequences of actions. In switching focus from achieving individual movements to achieving goals through sequences of movements we are moving into an area that is more tightly interwoven with other cognitive processes. It has been observed that cognitive theories of movement production are scarce (Rosenbaum, 2005; Rosenbaum & Feghhi, 2019). Though one exception to this has been the study of grasp, which is not surprising given the significance of hand actions in performing complex actions to achieve goals (Jeannerod, 1984; Jeannerod et al., 1995; Rosenbaum et al., 2001; Smeets et al., 2019). Even so, these models do not provide a seamless continuum of explanation from how we grasp a single raisin on a table to how we get up, go to the shop, buy the package of raisins and get them back home. Bridging this gap to describe how we produce complex sequences of actions is an ongoing challenge for theories of action production.

Action Sequences

Lashley (1951) observed in his seminal work that humans are continually active and this activity has a complex temporal structure that appears only in animals with a highly developed brain. Lashley went on to criticize the predominant explanation of the day – associative chain theory – as inadequate to completely explain how we produce a sequence of actions. **Associative chain theory** states that the end of one particular action is associated with stimulating the start of the next action in the sequence. This can be an effective method for simple and limited sequences but it has difficulty with general sequences such as when an element of the sequence repeats. For example, if the actions comprising the sequence are run-jump-spin-walk-turn then we can take the end of jumping to signal the start of spinning. However, if we are given the additional sequence of run-jump-spin-jump-turn then 'jump' becomes problematic since the end of jump now has to signal the beginning of both spinning and turning.

> **Associative chain theory** a behaviourist theory that explains how sequences of action arise from linking together associations between individual action components.

There are, of course, ways to fix this problem with associative models by creating new basic elements that include the preceding and following action (Wickelgren, 1969). Thus when jump is preceded by run and followed by spin we can code this as the triple: run-jump-spin. Likewise when jump is preceded by spin and followed by turn we can use the triple: spin-jump-turn. Though this solution is effective it generates the issue that the movement triples obscure the elemental nature of the individual movements; it would seem that a jump is a jump, regardless of the movements surrounding it. This example of a sequence of actions (run, jump, spin, walk, turn) is somewhat contrived, and the full force of Lashley's arguments was directed at language where behaviourist models of language production held that the words in a sentence were chained together

> Chapter 10 p326
>
> Chapter 11 p376

by associative links. There is extensive coverage of language in Chapters 10 and 11, and Lashley's own words are persuasive in relating language to general behaviour (1951, p. 121):

> *the problems raised by the organization of language seem to me to be characteristic of almost all other cerebral activity. There is a series of hierarchies of organization; the order of vocal movements in pronouncing the word, the order of words in the sentence, the order of sentences in the paragraph, the rational order of paragraphs in a discourse. Not only speech, but all skilled acts seem to involve the same problems of serial ordering, even down to the temporal coordination of muscular contractions in such a movement as reaching and grasping.*

There were two key ideas from speech production that were used to advance cognitive models of serial planning. These two ideas are the pattern of errors we make when we speak and how the production of different speech sounds is coordinated to produce fluent speech. A simple error that everybody makes at one time is a slip of the tongue, where words are switched about in a sentence. For example, Lashley points out the example 'Let us always remember that waste makes haste' where the words waste and haste are switched. These errors suggest that rather than a sentence being produced sequentially one word after another, it seems as if before the sentence begins all the words are somehow available and ready to take a particular grammatical structure. Errors occur by misplacing words in the structure rather than in purely sequential errors of what goes after what. Lashley also pointed out that the production of speech involves several interrelated but somewhat independent neurological systems. Moreover, different articulators of the vocal tract (e.g., lip, tongue) are critical at some times of an utterance and not critical at other times. When an articulator is not critical it is able to prepare for upcoming sounds to be produced as long as it does not interfere with the intelligibility of the current sound being produced. This leads to a phenomenon known as **co-articulation** where the target sound is being articulated at the same time that future sounds are being prepared (see Chapter 11). From these results, Lashley concluded that control of speech articulators are best modelled as arising from the interaction of separate mechanisms governed within a hierarchy of constraints. The question then becomes what mechanisms and what overarching constraints? Our discussion of motor control provides many choices of what mechanisms might be involved in producing movement. What we lack is description of what form the overarching constraints might take, and this is covered in the next section.

> **Co-articulation**
> the tendency for a speech sound to be influenced by sounds preceding or following it.

> Chapter 11, p378

Hierarchical Models of Action Production

What Lashley encouraged was a study of action sequences that was not dominated by the way one element related to its direct neighbours. Since different mechanisms could work simultaneously in **parallel** to create sequences it was important to consider how these mechanisms could be organized to produce sequences of actions. A first attempt at such a model of sequence production was provided by Miller et al. (1960), who developed what they called a test-operate-test-exit (TOTE) unit. Once selected, a TOTE unit would continuously test whether a condition was met and then exit once the condition was satisfied. For example, if we had one sock in our hand and a pile of socks on the floor and we wanted a matching pair then we would first 'test' to confirm we only had one sock. Next we would 'operate' to pick up a sock and 'test' to see if it matched. If it didn't we would 'operate' to pick up and check another until we found a match and could 'exit'. This architecture also allowed TOTE units to call other TOTE units, thus

> **Parallel processing**
> the ability to divide the process of solving a problem into multiple parts and to work simultaneously on each part.

permitting a hierarchical structure to be used in producing a sequence of actions. For example, the TOTE unit to find matching socks could be embedded within a larger structure to get dressed that contained additional TOTE units for finding your pants, finding your shoes and finding your shirt.

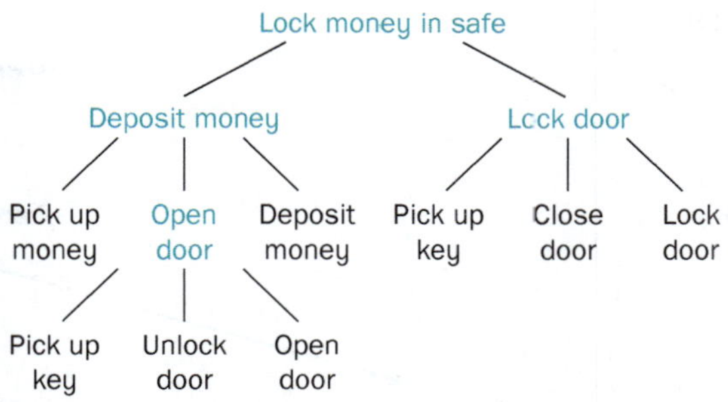

These ideas were further advanced by Estes (1972), who proposed hierarchies of control elements that activated other control elements at the levels below. An example of such a hierarchy is shown in Figure 3.5 for accomplishing the action of locking money in a safe. As can be seen in Figure 3.5 each node of the hierarchy corresponds to a particular action schema. In this example, the action schemas and their position in the hierarchy map directly onto the sequence of actions that need to take place for the action to be achieved. This way of representing the action hierarchy is straightforward and has an intuitive appeal to representing how accomplishing a goal can be achieved by a hierarchical arrangement of schema. However, it is not the only way to represent an action and it has been shown that another possible structure is to represent the correlational relationship of the different actions within the hierarchy (Botvinick, 2008; Botvinick & Plaut, 2002). For instance, picking up the key is more likely to occur with both locking and unlocking the door and thus forms a stronger correlational relationship than does picking up the key with picking up the money.

Figure 3.5 Hierarchical representation of an action sequence for locking money in a safe.
The action sequence is divided into the two main nodes of 'deposit money' and 'lock door'; however, a sub-node occurs on 'open door', which is the branch point for a further hierarchy.

Source: Reprinted from Botvinick (2008), with permission from Elsevier.

The example presented for locking money in a safe illustrates much of the essence of a hierarchical structure of an action sequence. However, what is not seen in this static figure is a sense of how the temporal structure of an action is achieved. To produce an action sequence it must be possible to traverse the hierarchy in a manner that activates currently desired units while suppressing currently undesired units. Models of how hierarchical structures can be used to produce sequences have developed from theories of **recurrent networks** (Elman, 1990; Jordan, 1986, 1997). Recurrent networks are a type of artificial neural network that can be designed to control the timing of operations. They have been used to demonstrate sequential behaviour resembling that of humans in a variety of domains. For example, Cooper and Shallice (2000) designed a network to produce a sequence of actions and used it to inform a theoretical understanding of how errors occurred when producing sequences. An example of the network demonstrating the making of instant coffee is shown in Figure 3.6a (overleaf). Within this hierarchy, patterns of activation and inhibition work in a manner of **interactive activation** (McClelland & Rumelhart, 1981; Rumelhart & McClelland, 1982) to produce a sequence. One operating characteristic of interactive activation is that when one unit of a hierarchy is selected for activation, other units at the same level of hierarchy are inhibited. This facilitates the selected action schema to complete. For example, when the schema for putting milk into coffee was activated the units for putting sugar and grinds into the coffee were suppressed. The temporal ordering of the activations of nodes in the schema is shown in Figure 3.6b (overleaf) for the hierarchy producing a proper sequence for making a cup of coffee.

Recurrent network
a type of artificial neural network with connections between units arranged so as to obtain a cycle of activation. This design allows a temporal context to be designed into the computation.

Interactive activation
used to describe the pattern of network activity generated by excitatory and inhibitory interactions of feature detectors and object representations.

As can be seen from the hierarchical model of a simple action such as making instant coffee, there are many ways producing an action can go wrong. Looking at the

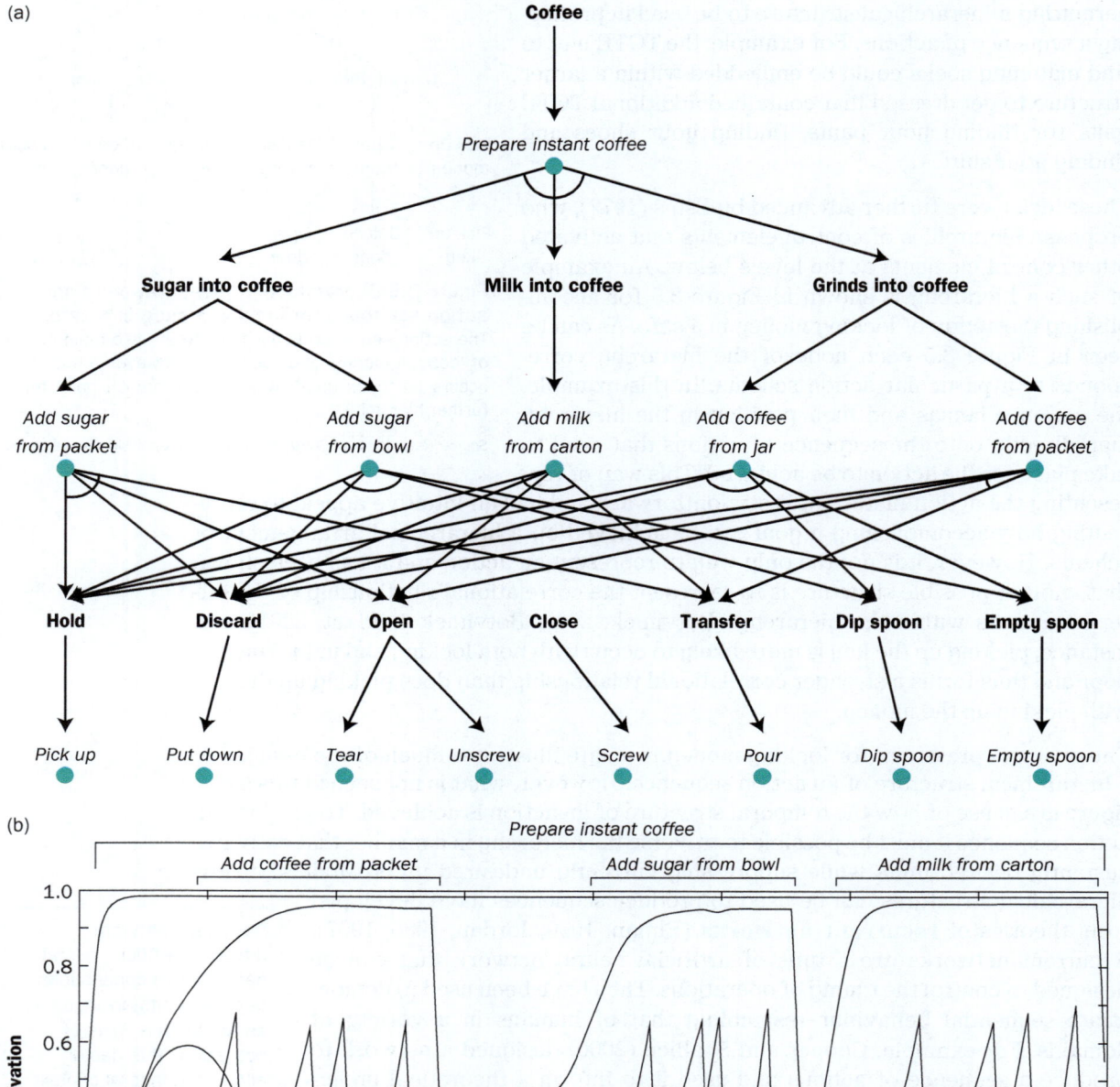

Figure 3.6 Cooper and Shallice's recurrent network (2000) for making instant coffee.
The hierarchical structure reflected in part (a) contains all the action elements necessary to make the coffee, with the three main divisions of the sequence 'sugar into coffee', 'milk into coffee' and 'grinds into coffee'. To make the coffee in the proper sequence, it is necessary to properly activate the different nodes. The timecourse of activation of nodes for successful coffee-making is illustrated in part (b).

Source: Cooper and Shallice (2000). Taylor and Francis (http://www.informaworld.com).

phenomenon of choking can illustrate ways in which complex actions might go wrong (Beilock, 2010; Belletier et al., 2019). Interviews with elite athletes who had catastrophic performance failures (Edwards et al., 2002) revealed that several factors influenced reductions in performance, including: self-confidence/control, anxiety/arousal and perceived effort. The effects of self-confidence and control occur following an athlete making an initial error that leads to a rapid decrease in self-confidence and feelings of control. This happens even if self-confidence and feelings of control had been high at the start of the performance. Anxiety and arousal are useful to discuss together since anxiety can be divided into a cognitive component and a somatic component that is similar to physiological arousal. Cognitive anxiety is demonstrated by expressing an upcoming event as difficult and that one feels nervous. Somatic anxiety and arousal are demonstrated by physical symptoms of feeling tension in the body, and other bodily feelings and autonomic body responses such as speeding up of the heart. Finally, effort is the response of an athlete to address the level of challenge. If an action is challenging, then increasing effort can work to compensate for difficulty. One theory that explains how performance degrades is known as the conscious processing hypothesis (CPH, Masters, 1992). In CPH, performance is modelled to decrease because increasing anxiety leads to a disruption of automatic processing. To compensate for the disruption of automatic processing, skilled performers are hypothesized to switch to a style of performance that, like novices, involves conscious awareness of individual components of an action. Thus, instead of performing actions automatically as a whole they begin to analyse and attend to their actions part by part, and this results in less fluency and effectiveness. Similar decreases in performance can be accomplished simply by asking experts to focus on a particular part of their performance.

> **Choking**
> the occurrence of inferior performance despite striving and incentives for superior performance.

Evaluation

Using the material presented so far in the chapter, such as the theories of motor control and sequential action production, we can hypothesize where the issues might arise in choking and why we sometimes perform worse under psychological pressure. For instance, the breakdown of smooth continuous performance could be modelled within hierarchical models of action production such as the one we presented for making instant coffee. The process described in CPH of breaking down a fluid action sequence to focus on particular components can be described as focusing on subnodes of a hierarchy and this is consistent with reducing top-down control, which leads to action production becoming disorganized. Considering the effect of arousal and somatic anxiety we can see that they have an effect on general motor activity, as reflected in the tension reported by athletes preceding their choking. Relating this to the model of optimal control theory (Figure 3.3), we can see that if this general arousal was not accurately accounted for in the forward model or if it contributed to internal noise in the nervous system then the predicted consequences of the motor command would not be accurate and this would lead to disrupted movement. Similarly, if the control policy didn't accurately reflect confidence in the probability that a particular movement could be achieved then movements would be attempted that were not optimal. These considerations illustrate how the theories presented in this chapter can be applied to explain how even highly trained movements can go wrong under pressure.

Brain Damage and Action Production

Not only was the model of Cooper and Shallice (2000) able to produce meaningful action sequences but the model could be 'damaged' to obtain the types of error associated with brain damage in the frontal cortex. The frontal cortex is responsible for action planning and it is thought that, as shown in Figure 3.7, the coordination of action is set in an organized manner across the anatomy of the frontal cortex. This organization can be seen as a hierarchy with high-level control of planning performed in anterior portions of the frontal cortex, and as one goes from anterior frontal cortex towards motor cortex the brain areas are involved in increasingly elemental aspects of control (Koechlin, 2008; Rouault & Koechlin, 2018). Damage to the frontal cortex is often diffuse across several regions of frontal cortex and leads to conditions such as dysexecutive syndrome (Chapter 6) and action disorganization syndrome (Humphreys & Forde, 1998; Schwartz, 2006; Schwartz et al., 1991), where patients make frequent errors in producing action sequences. These errors include such slips of action as insertions (entering a room and turning on the light even though it is daylight), confusions (putting shaving cream on a toothbrush), perseveration (repeatedly picking up and putting down a toothbrush) or omissions (leaving a key ingredient out when preparing a food and not noticing until ready to eat). These slips are not unique to individuals with brain damage and through the analysis of action diaries Reason (1979), where individuals recorded their own actions that did not go as intended, it was found that action slips are common in typical individuals. Moreover, similar errors in language production, known as slips of the tongue, are described further in Chapter 10. Cooper and Shallice (2000) were able to get their model of action production to increase the production of slips of action by specially adjusting a parameter of their model. This adjustment could be thought of as equivalent to a brain lesion or other such brain damage. The parameter they changed controlled whether a schema required a top-down signal to trigger the action or whether it could be triggered merely with presentation of the proper environmental conditions. They found that when the top-down signal was weakened and environmental conditions were sufficient to trigger a schema then the model performed perseveration errors such as repeatedly picking up and putting down the spoon or the sugar packet. With extreme weakening of the top-down signal the action sequence became profoundly disorganized.

Chapter 6 p176

Chapter 10 p346

Apraxia
a neurological condition typically resulting from brain damage, where a person loses the ability to perform activities that they are physically able and willing to do.

Action disorganization syndrome fits into a broader family of movement disorders known by the general term **apraxia**, which can arise from patterns of

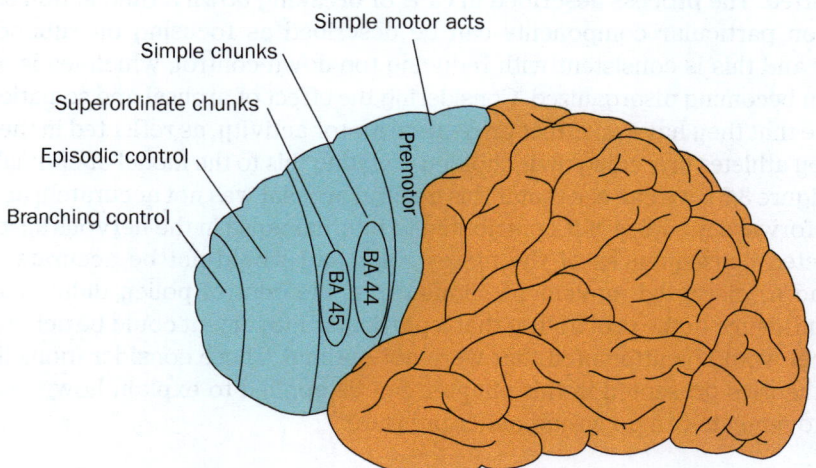

Figure 3.7 Brain imaging studies have shown that the anatomy of the frontal cortex reflects a hierarchical structure of action planning.
If we consider a tree diagram, then the final nodes of the tree are represented in premotor cortex, which would contain the motor primitives for simple motor acts. As one moves towards the tip of the frontal cortex, known as the prefrontal cortex, one encounters regions that are higher nodes in the planning hierarchy.

brain damage to the frontal and parietal cortex, basal ganglia and the nerve fibres connecting these regions (Cooper et al., 2005; Gross & Grossman, 2008; Wheaton & Hallett, 2007). The distinguishing characteristic of apraxia is the inability to successfully carry out skilled motor acts despite preserved sensory and motor systems as well as an ability to comprehend and cooperate. The most widely recognized type of apraxia is ideomotor apraxia and it is demonstrated by an inability to pantomime tool use and gesture when verbally instructed to do so. While there is a tendency that the same actions can be performed naturally during daily living, they can become slow, deliberate and error-prone (e.g., holding a comb upside down). However, this striking difference of capabilities between verbal instruction and natural performance cannot be attributed to a language deficit as patients with ideomotor apraxia can demonstrate that they know what they have been instructed to do. A typical cause of apraxia is stroke, where the blood supply to the brain malfunctions resulting in damage to brain tissue. Given the unfortunately common occurrence of stroke there is motivation to better understand specifically what brain damage leads to apraxia and how to rehabilitate individuals to best recover function. In Box 3.3 we discuss how technology and cognitive science are combining to tackle this problem of rehabilitation.

Box 3.3 Practical Application: Cognitive rehabilitation for apraxia and action disorganization syndrome

Brain damage can lead to a variety of deficits in the execution of multi-step actions that are associated with action disorganization syndrome and apraxia. A common feature of patients with these disorders is that they are impaired in performing tasks of daily living such as making a hot drink, preparing a meal, or self-care tasks like washing and dressing. These deficits reflect cognitive difficulties in performing a complex action sequence and are not attributable to physical weakness. Thus, it is cognition that needs rehabilitation rather than the physical body. Given the importance of tasks of daily living in maintaining independence from high levels of care, there have been efforts to develop effective means of cognitive rehabilitation (Sohlberg & Mateer, 2017). Research has shown that patients with apraxia and action disorganization syndrome do respond to therapy if visual or verbal prompts (cues) are given to guide the patient through successive steps in the required sequence of actions. However, this is labour intensive for the therapist and it is not clear whether short-term gains are maintained when a patient goes home and the cueing is no longer present.

Two approaches have been pursued to provide new types of therapies for apraxia and action disorganization syndrome that go past extensive training on specific activities of daily life (Worthington, 2016, 2017). One approach uses **metacognition** to develop strategies that can be used across different actions. Consistent with metacognition as a means for an individual to assess their own thoughts, the goal of this training is for individuals to derive strategies that generalize to a range of activities rather than heavily training on single actions. The other approach to cognitive rehabilitation is to use cognitive principles in partnership with principles of engineering and computer science to develop novel rehabilitation methods that incorporate advanced sensing and communication technology. This approach is in its infancy and relies upon creating an environment with **ambient intelligence** that can sense the state of the inhabitant and evaluate their actions in terms of how the environment can react to improve action outcomes. Components of the smart environment include physical sensors (e.g., cameras, microphones, force sensors) and smart devices to pick up information about the activities of the inhabitant. These components are

> **Metacognition**
> awareness of one's own thoughts and cognitive processes.

> **Ambient intelligence**
> an environment that senses our presence using advanced sensors and computing technology in a way that allows the environment to respond to the needs of people.

> linked to computers and software to determine how to assist and rehabilitate the inhabitant to perform everyday tasks. For example, if an individual with action disorganization syndrome were to go to the kitchen to make a cup of instant coffee then this would be sensed and the activity monitored so that prompts could be given to keep the process on track.

One additional condition to consider on the topic of complex movements is that of dyspraxia, which is defined by the presence of movements that are not as precise as in typical individuals (Zwicker et al., 2012). It is often considered to arise in childhood and currently is commonly known as developmental coordination disorder (DCD), with a reported prevalence of 6 per cent in children aged 6–11 (Mandich & Polatajko, 2003). A diagnosis of dyspraxia is based upon behaviour, and evidence of poor coordination in gross motor skills like riding a bike or fine motor skills like drawing and using cutlery can contribute to a diagnosis. However, to date there is no well-defined neural or physiological impairment associated with dyspraxia or its development. For example, while many brain regions have been suggested (Biotteau et al., 2016) there is no evidence that one particular region is associated with this condition. There are contrasting theoretical approaches to understanding DCD that are based in the theoretical approaches discussed earlier in this chapter. One account, based on the information processing approach of optimal control theory is that DCD results from a defective forward model. In effect the forward model of an individual with DCD makes poor predictions about the outcome of a motor command and this leads to lack of coordination (Adams et al., 2014). Another account emanates from the dynamical systems approach to argue that DCD arises from issues with perception–action coupling. In effect we need to consider task demands in concert with a person's understanding of their own capabilities to conceptualize the condition (Wade & Kazek, 2018).

ACTION REPRESENTATION AND PERCEPTION

Theories of Action Representation

> **Cognitive sandwich**
> the view that perception and action are like slices of bread that surround cognition as the filling of a sandwich.

The term **cognitive sandwich** is used to describe the view that cognition is like the filling of a sandwich: surrounded on one side by a slice of perception and on the other by a slice of action. Our discussions of motor control and sequence planning were largely consistent with such a sandwich model since it emphasized motor processes in isolation. In this section we place the sandwich in a blender by taking the view that cognitive representations of action intermingle with representations of both perception and action. These theories of action representation are becoming increasingly important to guide investigation in domains where the body plays a central role, such as sport, dance and rehabilitation.

Historical perspectives

> **Ideomotor theory**
> relates how thinking about the results of an action can give rise to producing the action.

There is a long tradition known as **ideomotor theory** that intimately connects perception to action. Ideomotor theory arose from the philosophical question of how could the mind, which apparently has no direct access to (neuro) physiological mechanisms, control the body to achieve its goals. The answer proposed was that human actions can arise from ideas of the sensory consequences they produce. For instance, a particular action is associated with the sensory outcomes of that action, and by thinking about these sensory outcomes one can produce the action. This effectively equates action planning with thoughts of what the sensory consequences of that movement would be. The history of ideomotor theories has been extensively reviewed (Shin et al., 2010; Stock & Stock, 2004). Ideomotor theory developed in the nineteenth century in Germany with the scholars Hebart, Lotze and Harless, and in Britain with the scholars Laycock and Carpenter; it was later incorporated by William James (1890) in his influential *The Principles of Psychology*. Ideomotor theory was largely ignored in the behaviourist approach to psychology since it was difficult to empirically verify. A factor contributing to this was that technical limitations of the early twentieth century made it difficult to measure the physical properties of movements with much precision and this held back the study of how motor intentions could be related to producing action. In contrast, during the same period research into perception advanced since it was possible to relate measures of physical stimuli to both their subjective experience and neural mechanisms (Haggard, 2001). However, this situation has changed dramatically in recent decades as the means to precisely measure human actions has greatly advanced and sophisticated models of action representation have developed.

Common codes for action perception and production

Concepts associated with ideomotor theory came to the fore again in the 1990s within the framework of **common coding** (Hommel, 2019; Hommel et al., 2001; Prinz, 1997). Common coding addressed the problem of how sensory codes can be internally related to motor codes. For example, if we are told that we have to press a button with our left hand when we see a green light and press a button with our right hand when we see a red light, then we need somehow to relate the colour seen to the hand used to press the button. To obtain this relationship, the cognitive sandwich approach holds that sensory codes are translated to motor codes by cognitive mechanisms. Common coding holds that instead of a translation mechanism between sensory and motor codes there is a layer of representation that includes event codes and action codes (Figure 3.8). In this extra layer, aspects of event coding overlap with those of action coding. One intuitive way to think of the situation is to imagine that the sensory codes are in Spanish and the motor codes are in English and the problem is to get the two to work together. One way to achieve this would be to obtain formal translations to send

> **Common coding**
> a theory of perception and action production which holds that both production and perception share certain representations of actions in the world.

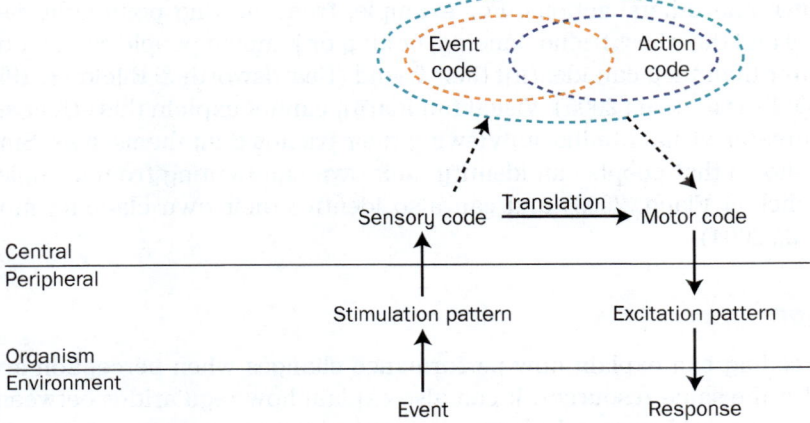

Figure 3.8 Common coding and the relationship between perception and action.
Events in the world are transformed into sensory codes which must activate motor codes to form a response. Common coding, shown by dashed lines, allows late representations of event codes and early representations of response codes to share the same codes.

Source: Prinz (1997). Taylor and Francis (http://www.informaworld.com).

between sensory and motor codes, and this is the cognitive sandwich approach. Another way would be to add an event/action manager that spoke Spanglish to mediate communication and this is the common coding approach.

One predicted consequence of common coding is that, because the common code is a resource for both perceiving and producing actions, there would be interference between perception and production when they both tried to access the same resource at the same time. Evidence for interference was shown in a number of studies using reaction times, which showed both that perception impaired action planning and that action planning impaired perception (for a review see Heyes, 2011; Vogt & Thomaschke, 2007). Another predicted consequence of common coding is that there will be properties of action that are common to both perception and production. One example is the 1/3 power law of drawing, which influences not only how we draw a motion but also how we visually perceive the drawing movement (Viviani & Stucchi, 1992). From the perspective of action production this law describes how, when drawing a shape on a flat surface, the hand will slow down for the highly curved parts and speed up for the straight parts in a way that follows a precise mathematical formulation (Lacquaniti et al., 1983; Viviani & Cenzato, 1985). From the perspective of visual perception, the law describes how uniform motion is perceived of a point moving along a curved path when the way speed changes along the path is according to the same formulation found for action production. Thus, the same regularity between speed and path geometry captures both motor and visual processes (Flash & Handzel, 2007; Handzel & Flash, 1999; Pollick & Sapiro, 1997). Brain imaging investigations of the 1/3 power law by Dayan and colleagues (2007) have shown results consistent with common coding. This fMRI study compared brain activity when viewing motion of targets that did and did not conform to a 1/3 power law. Results showed that when viewing a target that obeyed the power law there was extensive brain activation not only in visual areas, but also areas related to motor production.

A final result from common coding comes from the hypothesis that if the observed action of another is similar to how an observer would perform the action themselves, then there will be greater overlap of the common codes. Thus, viewing your own performance of an action would lead to a more effective activation of a common code and this would lead to individuals excelling at identifying their own actions. This prediction has been tested successfully in several experiments where people viewed recordings of their own and others' actions. For example, from viewing point-light displays of themselves and their best friend dancing, boxing or jumping people can identify themselves better than they can identify their friend (Beardsworth & Buckner, 1981; Loula et al., 2005; Prasad et al., 2005). Visual familiarity cannot explain this effect since people have greater visual familiarity viewing their friends than themselves. Similarly, it has been shown that people can identify their own handwriting from a single moving dot (Knoblich & Flach, 2003) and can also identify their own clapping movements (Flach et al., 2004).

Evaluation

Common coding can explain how performance changes when perception and action compete for the same resources. It can also explain how regularities between perception and action would exist and why we can recognize our own actions better than those of another. While these are significant theoretical accomplishments on their own, it is important to consider the wider implications of such a model for the cognitive sandwich approach. The pervasive separation of perception from action that exists under the cognitive sandwich approach has often created a research context where the motor system appears to simply serve perceptual and cognitive processes. Common coding can be seen to raise the status of motor processes in cognition. One aspect of common coding not discussed so far is what neural mechanism might support this function. In the next section we describe mirror neurons, which provide evidence of single neurons that represent both perceived and executed actions.

Mirror mechanisms and action observation

A neural mechanism to unite perception and action was provided by the discovery of so-called **mirror neurons** in the macaque monkey in a region of the frontal lobe known as the ventral premotor cortex (Dipellegrino et al., 1992; Gallese et al., 1996). These neurons displayed the remarkable property of being sensitive to an action being performed, say picking up a raisin, whether the monkey itself or the experimenter performed the act (Figure 3.9). Such neurons thus appear to represent both performing an action and viewing the same action performed by another. This representation unites perception and action in a single neuron and, it has been argued, provides a basis for understanding the goals of others (Rizzolatti & Sinigaglia, 2010; 2016). What is new in this mirror mechanism is that understanding of actions is not gained by mapping viewed actions onto abstract concepts built up from visual representations but instead by mapping them directly onto representations of action production (Rizzolatti et al., 2001).

> **Mirror neurons**
> neurons with the special property that they represent both the sensory aspects of perceiving actions as well as motor aspects of how to produce the action.

From the discovery of mirror neurons in the premotor cortex of the macaque monkey in the early 1990s neuroscience research proceeded in two directions. The first was to further explore the monkey brain for other evidence of mirror neurons. This resulted in mirror neurons being found in the parietal cortex that responded to both doing and seeing an action (Fogassi et al., 2005), as well as in the premotor cortex that responded to both doing and hearing an action such as cracking open a nut (Kohler et al., 2002). These results support the existence of a fronto-parietal mirror network in the monkey. The significance of this is twofold. First, the monkey data involve measuring from single neurons and thus provide direct evidence that a single neuron is encoding information relevant to perception and production. Second, the fact that mirror neurons were found in two regions of the brain and involved in the coding of two forms of sensory information (sight and sound) suggests that this is a general information processing strategy, rather than a mechanism with limited scope. The other major research direction was to

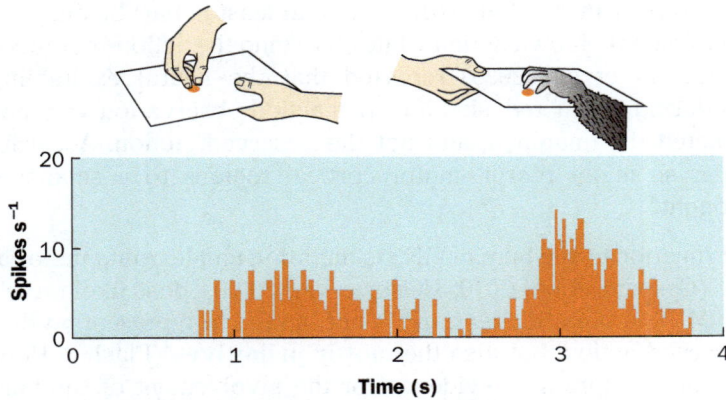

Figure 3.9 Example of the activity of a mirror neuron in monkey premotor cortex.
Mirror neurons found in area F5 of monkey cortex have the special property that they become active whether the monkey is observing the experimenter grasping a piece of food or if they grasp the food themselves.

Source: Reprinted from Rizzolatti et al. (1996), with permission from Elsevier.

explore whether mirror neurons would also be present in the human brain. Given the ethical difficulties in measuring properties of individual neurons in the human brain (Mukamel et al., 2010) this research primarily employed brain imaging methods to identify brain areas that would demonstrate mirror properties consistent with dual representations of perception and action. A diversity of tasks and types of analyses were performed to explore mirroring mechanisms in humans, and a variety of brain regions were put forward. For example, Kilner et al. (2009, see also Kilner & Lemon, 2013) used a **repetition suppression** paradigm with fMRI to probe adaptation of discrete neuronal populations in the human brain. Indeed, the authors found adaptation between specific executed and observed actions in the inferior frontal gyrus. However, agreement on a common definition of mirror areas in humans has proven elusive. One consequence of this is the proposal that the core human mirror neuron system (MNS) contains only the inferior frontal gyrus and the inferior parietal lobule, which are **homologous** to regions found in the monkey (Rizzolatti & Sinigaglia, 2010, 2016). Additional networks (e.g., for auditory working memory) become recruited according to specific task demands, such as imitation of rhythms or spatial sequences (Sakreida et al., 2018).

> **Repetition suppression**
> used in fMRI experiments; with repeated presentation of the same stimulus there is a decrease in activity that is not seen when stimulation is varied.
>
> **Homologous**
> in biology means to have the corresponding position, structure and possibly function. It is common to consider across species what anatomical parts are homologous. For brain regions this is important for using data obtained in, say, monkeys to predict relations in the human brain.

Central to debate over the anatomical extent of a human MNS, and interpretation of brain imaging experiments in humans, is a theoretical understanding of what functional capabilities mirror neurons provide for the interpretation of a movement. If we look at any movement there is the interpretation on the surface of a complex sequence of limb movements, but underlying this complex motion pattern there is frequently a simple goal that the movement is trying to achieve (Byrne & Russon, 1998). It is argued that the crucial function mirror neurons provide is access to the goal of the movement (Cattaneo et al., 2010). Thus, when we view somebody performing an action, mirror neurons act to simulate the viewed action in a way that gives us access to the goal of the viewed action. However, much intense debate remains about the role of the MNS regarding its role in action recognition and conceptual processing (Caramazza et al., 2014; Gallese et al., 2011; Hickok & Hauser, 2010; Kalenine et al., 2010; Kilner, 2011). A further issue with the existing studies on the neural correlates of action observation is that researchers rarely controlled for the involvement of motor imagery processes during action observation (Vogt et al., 2013). Thus, the overlap between areas activated during action observation on the one hand, and those activated during motor imagery and execution on the other hand (Hardwick et al., 2018), might at least in part be due to participants' strategy of imagining their own action while observing the actions of others. In support of this view, Meers et al. (2020) reported that the neural excitability of motor cortical areas during instructed, simultaneous action observation and motor imagery primarily reflected the imagined, and not the observed, action. Accordingly, action observation per se might recruit motor cortical regions to a smaller extent than previously thought.

One proposed function of the human MNS is imitation and learning motor actions from visual models (Caspers et al., 2010; Heiser et al., 2003). Most likely, the function of the MNS in imitation learning is not limited to representing the goal of the observed action, but also the **motor primitives** (Flash & Hochner, 2005). The most impressive evidence for the involvement of the human MNS in imitation learning comes from a series of fMRI studies where participants were asked to imitate guitar chords in the scanner (Buccino et al., 2004; Higuchi et al., 2012; Vogt et al., 2007). The beauty of this task is that participants are not restricted to action observation, but can also perform the

> **Motor primitives**
> the basis set of elemental movements that serve as building blocks for an animal's repertoire of movements.

to-be-learned actions in the scanner. Vogt et al. (2007) found that the MNS was activated more strongly during observation of non-practised actions compared to practised actions, and that passive observation induced weaker activations than observation in order to imitate (Buccino et al., 2004). In addition to the MNS, the prefrontal cortex was also activated during action observation and motor preparation (Buccino et al., 2004; Vogt et al., 2007). This implies that a (mirroring) mechanism of automatic perception–action matching alone is insufficient to account for imitation learning; instead higher-order supervisory operations associated with the prefrontal cortex are involved, which most likely subserve the manipulation and restructuring of the elementary motor representations provided by the MNS.

Evaluation

Does the existence of mirroring mechanisms mean that we can learn novel motor skills also by pure observation, from the couch? Certainly, a number of behavioural studies indicate the effectiveness of learning by observing and the likely involvement of motor encoding (e.g., Mattar & Gribble, 2005; Vogt, 1995). However, behavioural work on learning sequences of actions indicates limitations of observational practice (Shea et al., 2011). Higuchi et al. (2012) used the guitar chord task of Vogt and colleagues to study the brain mechanisms of learning by observing. They found evidence for the involvement of both the MNS and prefrontal cortex in pure learning by observing, thus confirming the validity of their model of imitation learning also for observational practice. However, chords learned by observation were executed less proficiently than chords learned by observation-imitation, and this was reflected in reduced neural efficiency effects for the observationally practised chords in cortical as well as subcortical regions, particularly the basal ganglia. These results, too, caution against the all-too-simple idea that, since motor structures are engaged during action observation, we can lean back and learn novel actions just by watching others do the work. See Box 3.4 for more on the topic of action observation in a research focus on watching dance.

 Box 3.4 Research Close Up: Using dance expertise to study action representation

Source: Christensen et al. (2016).

INTRODUCTION

Dance has proven to be a useful area to study how representations of action are influenced by experience (Bläsing et al., 2018). For example, consistent with ideas about the presence of mirror neurons in humans, it has been shown that the brains of experienced dancers process watching dance in ways that include brain systems that are normally involved in producing the movements yourself (Calvo-Merino et al., 2006; Cross et al., 2006). Although these results point to how experience relates to basic movement representations, little is known about whether these experience effects extend to the perception of social properties of movement, such as emotion and affect. Such questions are important since affect is part of the higher-level goals and intentions of movement and it is not clear whether enhanced perception of surface action properties would extend to higher-level representations of movement. Research by Christensen et al. (2016) addressed this question of whether dancers, who by training have experience in producing emotional dance movements, would perform better than novices in recognizing emotional dance movements. They did this by examining both subjective judgements of emotion and psychophysiological responses in novices and ballet dancers when presented with clips of emotional ballet dance.

METHOD

The study used 48 brief video clips of ballet as stimuli. To create control stimuli that contained the same amount and type of movement, but were different from what the dancers would have been exposed to in their training, the same 48 video clips were played backwards. For each participant, behavioural responses of felt emotion along with psychophysiological measures of the electrical conduction of skin, known as **galvanic skin response** (GSR) were collected. The advantage of using both measures is that one is a subjective measure of response, while the other is psychophysiological and not as susceptible to cognitive strategies. Participants included 20 female ballet dancers who were training or working professionally, along with 24 novices who were naive to ballet dance. The video clips of a single dancer were randomly presented on a black background with a fixation cross presented before (1,500 ms) and after (1,000 ms) each video clip, which lasted for 5 to 6 s. Participants performed the behavioural rating task after each video clip, in which they were asked to rate how sad or happy the movements made them feel (Christensen et al., 2014; Lang et al., 1998). Responses were collected using a continuous visual analogical scale (VAS) presented at the bottom of the screen, ranging from 0 (very sad) to 100 (very happy); 50 was neutral (Figure 3.10). The labels 'Sad' (left) and 'Happy' (right) were displayed on either side of the VAS, with the indication 'Emotion?' displayed in the centre of the screen. Throughout the experiment, GSR was recorded from the index and ring fingers of the participant's non-dominant hand.

> **Galvanic skin response** the electrical characteristics of the skin are known to change due to the activity of sweat glands, which can be linked to psychological arousal. This measure of galvanic skin response is often taken as an indication of emotional response.

Figure 3.10 Example of an experimental trial to recognize emotion in the study by Christensen et al. (2016).

Source: Christensen et al. (2016)

RESULTS

Results showed that for the subjective ratings of emotion, both the dancers and the novices rated the happy movements as more happy than the sad movements, whether played forwards or backwards. A closer analysis of the data revealed that the dancers had a greater difference than novices in their ratings between happy and sad movements, suggesting greater sensitivity in recognizing the emotion. What is more, dancers were sensitive to the forward–backward presentation of the movements, in that their ratings showed a significant difference between the two conditions: forward dances were rated more happy than the backward movements. Regarding the psychophysiological measures of GSR, novices had the same level of GSR to happy and sad movements, irrespective of movement direction, whereas dancers' GSR was sensitive to both emotion and movement direction: they had increased GSR to happy compared with sad movements, specifically only for movements presented in their forward presentation – that is, how they had learned the movements. Finally, a correlation analysis showed that subjective behavioural responses correlated with psychophysiological responses only in the expert group, and again this was specific when rating movements in their forward direction. In summary, the findings generally showed that expertise in dance indeed augmented psychophysiological sensitivity to observed affective body movements.

DISCUSSION

Results showed that experience with performing dance enhanced the recognition of emotion depicted in dance. Determining the precise mechanism from this study is not possible, however it does raise the possibility that the advantage was due to simulation of emotion in the dancer group. One interesting aspect of the study was that expertise was operationalized both between the groups (dancers versus novices) as well as with the movement pattern (forward video play versus backward). Psychophysiological differences between emotions were found only in the forward direction, indicating that this recognition of emotion is tuned for specific action features that are available only in movements in their canonical order (how they were learned). The findings suggest that experience in performing dance modulates intrapersonal as well as interpersonal emotional processes.

Finally, as with any experiment that compares novice versus expert groups, there is the question of training and whether the differences come about from training or from some form of self-selection. For example, would the people who become expert dancers already have the properties found? Another possibility might be that dance training enhances perceptual awareness of the body in general, and this also impacts the individual's ability to recognize and understand social gestures such as emotional body movements. Perceptual awareness of our own body is obtained through the sense of interoception.

Research has shown that the higher the interoceptive accuracy of a person, the higher their emotion recognition ability (Craig, 2002, 2003; Critchley et al., 2004). This is because our sensitivity to our own bodies (interoceptive ability) has been found to be linked to our sensitivity to others' bodies (Pollatos et al., 2007; Shah et al., 2016). Interoceptive accuracy is low in the general population, however it has been found that dancers, singers and musicians have a high interoceptive accuracy, and this accuracy correlated with years of training, suggesting a training effect and not a self-selection bias (Christensen et al., 2018; Schirmer-Mokwa et al., 2015). Future longitudinal or cohort studies examining the development of motor expertise, emotional expertise, and how these two relate to biopsychological mechanisms such as interoception, could reveal the basis of how dancers show higher performance in recognizing emotions.

Embodied Cognition

We discuss embodied cognition in Chapter 2 in the context of perception and in Chapter 9 for the embodiment of concepts, so it is useful now to turn to this topic to discuss how embodied cognition relates to motor control and action representation. In the embodied view of cognition, perception and action are intimately connected. In fact, in the most radical views of embodiment, the connection between perception and action is so tight and connected with the environment, there is little need for the kinds of abstract symbolic representations often used to explain cognition (Barsalou, 1999). Less radical views of embodiment hold that for simple actions, motor information is incorporated directly into representations; however, for complex actions both perceptual and motor information are combined in a flexible manner (Borghi, 2005).

Chapter 2 p34

Chapter 9 p294

Connections between perception and action that demonstrate embodiment are present in common coding and mirror neurons. Both illustrate that perceptual representations of the world are connected to representations of action. While mirror neurons, by definition, are restricted to observing other living beings, the theory of common coding has been shown by Tucker and Ellis (1998) to extend to interactions with inanimate objects.

These experiments by Tucker and Ellis had participants view photographs of objects and judge whether the objects were upright or inverted. The objects included such items as frying pans, teapots and knives, which afforded grasps by their handles. The photos were arranged so that some showed the object graspable with the left hand and some with the right. Response times were measured with both the right and left hands. What was found was that response times were quicker when the upright/inverted decision was produced with the hand that could produce the grasp. Further evidence that visual representation is not independent of the action response comes from experiments on categorizing objects (Borghi, 2005) as well as human brain imaging experiments which showed that just viewing tools activated brain regions involved in producing actions with the tools (Beauchamp & Martin, 2007; Grafton et al., 1997).

There are several consequences of work on embodied cognition (Shapiro, 2007, 2019; Gallagher, 2017). One of these has been to elevate our appreciation of the importance of the body in cognition, and to include it as an important component to understanding cognitive performance. For example, the importance of brain and body relations can be seen in the equilibrium point hypothesis, described earlier. In this theory the unique structure of the body – and in this case the spring-like properties of the limbs – is essential to how the brain plans the control of movement. Further examples of the importance of the body are described by Chiel and Beer (1997), who argue that it is the structure of the body that provides both constraints and opportunities for neural control. Such constraints have been demonstrated by showing that anatomical structure shapes functional brain networks (Kerkman et al., 2018). The link between brain and body can be extended even further to theoretically describe the brain as a system that actively minimizes the decay of our sensory and physical states (Badcock et al., 2019). Another consequence of work on embodied cognition has been to recognize the importance of the environment in cognition. Although it is debatable whether it should truly be considered cognition, it has been pointed out by Clark (1997) that we organize our environment to reduce cognitive load. From placing our TV remote control always at the same place to buying distinctive luggage that is easily recognizable at the baggage carousel, we actively put structure into the world that gives us advantage in solving everyday problems.

The final consequence of embodied cognition we will discuss is how the body plays a central role in metaphor. Metaphor provides us with a scaffolding upon which we can understand one thing in terms of another. When told that 'you are a star', you don't think that you are being called a luminous ball of hot burning gases, instead metaphorical reasoning provides you with the understanding that you are bright and high up above others. Lakoff and Johnson (2008) propose that basic spatial relations like up, down, front, back, etc., form the basis of this scaffolding and are interpreted in relation to our body. In this way 'up' is understood intrinsically as it relates to my body with my head corresponding to 'up' and my feet to 'down'. Thus, the communication of complex information relies on an embodied representation of the concepts we wish to express.

Gesture

An important topic that illustrates how the body and action are related to cognitive processes is gesture. It is a broad topic that crosses the boundaries of perception, action and cognition (Kendon, 2004; McNeill, 1992, 2005). Theories of gesture typically incorporate description of how gesture relates to the linguistic component of speech (de Ruiter, 2000; Goldin-Meadow, 2003; Kita & Ozyurek, 2003; Krauss et al., 2000; McNeill, 1992, 2005; McNeill & Duncan, 2000) as well as to speech prosody (Pouw et al., 2017) (see Chapters 10 and 11). However, it is clear that, even alone, gesture can con-

Chapter 10, p326

Chapter 11, p376

vey clear messages. In this section we will focus on how gestures make cognition visible and reveal embodied processes.

There are a variety of different types of gesture. Deictic gestures are pointing movements done in order to draw attention to a location or thing in the world. Beat gestures are baton-like movements that do not appear to have a direct meaning, but instead are used in tight synchrony with speech to accent important aspects of the information being conveyed. Metaphoric gestures (Cienki & Müller, 2008; Littlemore, 2009) exploit the structure of a metaphor to understand one thing in terms of another by using the spatial structure and timing of a movement to relate to concepts being communicated. Iconic gestures depict physical properties of the object of reference. For example, making the motion of putting on a hat to complement the words 'I put on a hat' or drawing a circle when saying 'doughnut'. These definitions of gestures are not exclusive since a single gesture might have a component of several different types of gesture. For example, in a study of academic lectures (Sweetser, 1998) one prevalent gesture was to use the index finger of the dominant gesture hand to point successively to fingers of the other hand. Here the individual fingers of the other hand could be considered to be icons representing various ideas represented as objects and the motion of the index finger could be a metaphor for the succession of ideas. Another example of a gesture was rotating the hand in circles starting outwards from the body as would be accompanied by the words *and so on* or *etcetera*. Iconically this gesture represents ideas travelling outwards from the speaker and metaphorically it can be seen as representing reasoning as motion through space.

Hostetter and Alibali (2008, 2019) have emphasized the embodied nature of gesture by considering gesture as simulated action. They theorize that gestures result because ideas are being simulated in terms of perceptual and motor properties, regardless of whether the idea is about something physically spatial or only metaphorically spatial. For example, when experimental participants describe a viewed cartoon where they saw a cat climb a drainpipe they will form the iconic gesture of moving hand over hand as if climbing since the action being discussed is activating a motor simulation that is part of the embodied representation. Similarly, it is argued that metaphoric gestures arise from the spatial representations upon which the metaphor is based. For example, describing fairness with the two palms facing up and arms moving up and down in alternating fashion represents the act of balancing two separate entities and this leads to the use of gesture to present this simulated action. It is acknowledged that we do not always gesture, even when possible, and the explanation for this is that context and other influences interact to form a dynamic threshold that controls the likelihood of a gesture. An example of the importance of context in setting a threshold can be seen in an experiment where people were told that their videotaped explanations of how to use survival items would be viewed by either first-year college students in a dormitory bonding exercise or by campers actively preparing for a winter excursion (Kelly et al., 2011). Results showed that the explanations to the campers, where the stakes were high, produced three times as many gestures containing semantic information, and three times as much time was spent gesturing.

A possible objection to the idea that our ideas are embodied in physical actions such as gestures can be offered by the proposition that ideas like those in the physical sciences and mathematics are abstract and have little connection to physical experience. However, at least for teaching physical sciences and mathematics, there is evidence that gesture can play a role. For example, Roth (2000) found that students who lack adequate domain knowledge to talk about a science topic can still use gestures to correctly explain these topics. Similarly, Núñez (2004) describes how professors of mathematics use gesture to explain concepts such as oscillation of a mathematical sequence by horizontal back-and-forth motion of the hand. Moreover, it has been shown that inhibiting gesture when explaining a maths task requires cognitive resources (Goldin-Meadow et al., 2001). While these examples do not eliminate a role of purely symbolic processing in scientific and mathematical reasoning, they add to an increasing literature of embodied views which hold that depicting (Tversky, 2011) and processing abstract information (Landy & Goldstone, 2007) is effectively grounded in physical relations that can be depicted by gesture.

Agency

> Chapter 5, p152

Agency is an important aspect of motor cognition that has relevance to our everyday experience of actions, and is closely related to topics such as consciousness (see Chapter 5). While agency has a range of definitions across psychology and the social sciences, in motor cognition agency refers to the phenomenon that we typically experience our own actions as being under our control and acting upon the external world to make things happen (Gallagher, 2012; Haggard, 2017). While most of the time this might seem trivial and obvious, the fact that we monitor our agency is evidenced by the occasional event where we might be interacting with something and after an unexpected response, we ask ourselves 'Did I do that?' A sense of agency is critical for distinguishing, in a world of activity, our own actions from those of other agents and the actions that occur from inanimate objects reacting to physical forces.

One aspect of motor cognition frequently associated with agency is the phenomenon of body ownership. However, while ownership of a body part is related to agency the sense of agency goes beyond mere ownership of our body parts (Braun et al., 2018). For example, if we consider the rubber hand illusion as a phenomenon demonstrating effects of body ownership (Botvinick & Cohen, 1998), we can see that it does not involve the sense of control of actions upon the external world. In the rubber hand illusion, an observer views a rubber hand in a plausible orientation placed next to their own hand, which is occluded from view. After a period of seeing the rubber hand stroked, while their own unseen hand is stroked in synchrony, the observer has an illusory feeling that the rubber hand is their own. Evidence supporting this subjective illusory feeling is that when asked to close their eyes and localize their hand, observers tend to mislocalize towards the rubber hand, a phenomenon known as proprioceptive drift.

The critical property of agency is that of assigning responsibility of our actions to ourselves. One explanation of how agency comes about relates back to optimal control theory (Blakemore et al., 2002). Recall that in optimal control theory the motor command is sent both to an internal model, known as the forward model, and to muscles to perform actions in the world. From this the sensory consequences of the action can be compared to the predictions of the forward model. If the sensory consequences match the predictions then agency can be assigned to these actions, otherwise not. While this so-called comparator model of agency provides a useful explanation of agency there are other factors that have been found to influence the sense of agency that are not necessarily described by the model. For example, actions that participants feel are easy to perform evoke a stronger sense of agency (Wenke et al., 2010). In addition a phenomenon known as intentional binding reveals that there is a subjective experience of a compression of time between a voluntary action (e.g., press a button) and its external sensory consequences (e.g., a sound) only when the action is voluntary, but not when it is involuntary (Haggard et al., 2002).

While research into the neural basis of agency has yet to reveal a definitive explanation of agency, existing results point to the importance of two brain areas: the angular gyrus and the insula (Farrer & Frith, 2002). The involvement of these areas was supported by a **meta-analysis** of many brain imaging studies of agency, which supported that these regions appeared sensitive to changes in agency (Sperduti et al., 2011). The angular gyrus is a brain region in the parietal cortex on the border with the temporal cortex. The angular gyrus appears as a sort of non-agency detection, showing activation that increases proportionately as the sense of agency decreases (Quesque & Brass, 2019). In distinction, the insula has been found to increase in activity with increasing agency. which is consistent with the suggested role of this brain region in evaluating the personal significance of sensory information (Craig, 2009). Further evidence of the role different brain areas play in determining agency can be seen in the phenomenon of alien hand syndrome (Box 3.5).

> **Meta-analysis**
> examination of a set of independent studies on the same topic done to provide a view of the what is revealed by the overall results.

Box 3.5 When Things Go Wrong: Alien hand syndrome

With alien hand syndrome one arm remains under control but the other arm is described as it 'doesn't do what it is supposed to do', that it 'has a mind of its own' and that it 'acts up'. These complaints reach the point that one sufferer from alien hand syndrome admitted that 'I talk about it like it's an entity of its own' (Bundick & Spinella, 2000). More complex observations about the behaviour of the alien hand exist as well. One individual claimed that their right hand anticipated future actions and performed movements prior to the patient actually intending them (Feinberg et al., 1991). The difficulty and frustration of living with this condition can be seen in a compelling video report published by Debray and Demeestere (2018) where we see the two hands wrestling to take control of a tissue. The phenomenon of alien hand was first noted more than 100 years ago and remains a perplexing disorder today, although the past 30 years have seen many advances as we gain a better understanding of the neural basis of motor cognition.

Alien hand syndrome arises from several kinds of brain damage, including stroke, and there has long been an issue with identifying a unique region responsible for the condition (Trojano et al., 1993). At present, there are three major classifications of alien hand syndrome that correspond to the three major sites where brain damage is found (Graff-Radford, et al., 2013; Sarva et al., 2014; Scepkowski & Cronin-Golomb, 2003). Two of these sites are in the front of the brain and include medial aspects of the frontal cortex as well as the corpus callosum, which is the fibre bundle connecting the two sides of the brain. The third site is in the posterior of the brain, in parietal cortex.

When alien hand arises from damage to the corpus callosum it is often seen that the two hands are in conflict with each other. Because a healthy corpus callosum communicates between the two sides of the brain and one side is typically dominant for motor control, the alien hand can be seen to arise from a lack of awareness of the commands being sent to the alien hand. When alien hand arises from damage to the parietal cortex then a frequent sign is the afflicted hand moving purposelessly – for example, raising up in what is termed levitation. With parietal damage there can also be a sensation of strangeness to the limb. Whether this posterior variant of alien hand syndrome might be related to mechanisms involving the angular gyrus for determination of agency deserves further investigation. Because brain damage is typically not isolated to precise locations, and is unique to every individual, it has been complex to map individual patients onto theoretical predictions of agency. However, what alien hand syndrome clearly demonstrates is that our sense of agency and body ownership is something that can be lost.

Summary

In this chapter, we divided the problem of motor control and action into three topics: (1) motor control; (2) producing complex actions; and (3) action representations and perception. Although each of these three topics has an independent research tradition, there are increasing efforts to investigate phenomena that span these traditional boundaries. The need to span the boundaries is prompted by applications such as robotics, where aspects of all three topics need to be integrated to realize a working system, and rehabilitation, where recovering motor function is intertwined with cognitive abilities.

The first section, on motor control, strived to provide an explanation of how we control our body to perform simple, basic actions. Achieving such an explanation has the potential to provide us with primitive mechanisms that can be used as building blocks for understanding ever more complex actions. There is, however, no theoretically defined motor primitive that has yet achieved universal acceptance as the essential building block. The three theories of motor control introduced – equilibrium point hypothesis, dynamic systems theory and optimal control theory – each has its relative strengths for explaining certain phenomena and future research is certain to see efforts to come up with a theory of motor planning that provides a broadly confirmed motor primitive.

In the second section, on producing complex actions, we essentially assumed that the problem of producing elements of a complex action was solved. With this assumption it was possible to make progress on understanding how extended sequences of action could be achieved. This led to the primary claim that complex action sequences are the result of hierarchical plans. Whether producing language or making a cup of instant coffee, we can construct action hierarchies that enable goals to be achieved by the interactions among the nodes of the hierarchy. Confirmation of this hierarchy came from models that could both produce action sequences in typical individuals as well as reproduce the types of errors in action planning found in individuals with brain damage to their frontal cortex.

In the final section we considered evidence that representations of action production are related to perceptual representations. While this conceptual duality of shared representations for perception and action has a long history in ideomotor theories, recent evidence from neuroscience has brought it back to the fore. The neuroscientific evidence includes the discovery of mirror neurons that have been shown to be active both when an action is performed and when the same action is perceived. Although the specific function of mirror neurons remains controversial it has helped to further inspire embodied theories of perception that tightly link our sensory perception of the world with the actions we produce. One example of embodiment we explored was gesture, where we saw how actions make our thoughts visible. We concluded our discussion of the relationship between produced and perceived actions by addressing the special topic of perceiving our own movements. Perceiving our own actions and their consequences provides us with a sense of agency, which can contribute to our sense of self-awareness.

Review Questions

1. Describe different models of human motor control.
2. How do hierarchical representations account for the production of action sequences, and how is this hierarchy represented in the brain?
3. What are the implications of action representations that include aspects of both producing and perceiving actions?
4. How does gesture make thought visible?
5. What is the basis of embodied theories of cognition?
6. How can a sense of agency be achieved?

Discussion Questions

1. What is the relationship between the brain, the senses, the body and the environment, and how does it differ between theories of motor cognition?
2. Why is there controversy about mirror neurons in humans?
3. What is the relationship between a sense of agency and self-awareness?

 Further Reading

Goldin-Meadow, S. (2003). *Hearing gesture: How our hands help us think*. Belknap Press of Harvard University Press.

Haggard, P., & Eitam, B. (Eds.). (2015). *The sense of agency*. Oxford University Press.

Hickok, G. (2014). *The myth of mirror neurons: The real neuroscience of communication and cognition*. W.W. Norton & Company.

Jeannerod, M. (2006). *Motor cognition: What actions tell the self*. Oxford University Press.

Jordan, M. I. (1997). Serial order: A parallel distributed processing approach. In J. W. Donahoe & V. Packard Dorsel (Eds.), *Neural-network models of cognition* (pp. 471–495). Elsevier Science.

Keysers, C. (2011). *The empathic brain: How the discovery of mirror neurons changes our understanding of human nature*. Lulu.com.

Lashley, K. S. (1951). The problem of serial order in behavior. In L. A. Jeffress (Ed.), *Cerebral mechanisms in behavior*. Wiley.

McNamee, D., & Wolpert, D. M. (2019). Internal models in biological control. *Annual Review of Control, Robotics, and Autonomous Aystems, 2*, 339–364.

Rosenbaum, D. A. (2010). *Human motor control*. Academic Press.

ATTENTION

4

PREVIEW QUESTIONS

INTRODUCTION
- Box 4.1 **Practical Application:** Robot attention

A TAXONOMY OF ATTENTION

THE ATTENTION SYSTEM OF THE HUMAN BRAIN

THEORIES OF ATTENTION
- FILTER THEORY
- RESOURCE THEORY
- EVALUATION
- Box 4.2 **Practical Application:** Video game play in enhancing cognition and attention
- VISUAL ATTENTION: SEARCH, INHIBITION OF RETURN AND ATTENTIONAL BLINK
- Box 4.3 **When Things Go Wrong:** Errors in the interpretation of medical images
- Box 4.4 **Research Close Up:** Using the attentional blink to examine emotion perception
- ATTENTIONAL MECHANISMS IN PERCEPTION AND WORKING MEMORY
- Box 4.5 **Research Close Up:** Using a dual task to examine attention and working memory
- ATTENTIONAL MECHANISMS IN CONTROLLING ACTIONS
- FAILURES OF ATTENTION
- Box 4.6 **Practical Application:** Attention and continuity editing in movies
- Box 4.7 **When Things Go Wrong:** Attention, misdirection and magic

SUMMARY

ANSWER TO CHAPTER PROBLEM

REVIEW QUESTIONS

DISCUSSION QUESTIONS

FURTHER READING

Preview Questions

1. Of the multitude of events happening in the world, how does attention select particular items?
2. How much of the objects and events around us can we attend to, and what happens to that to which we don't attend?
3. Are there particular regions of the brain dedicated to attention, or is attentional processing more widespread?
4. What are important theories and experimental methods of attention research?
5. What does attention have in common with other cognitive processes such as eye movements and working memory?
6. What are the practical and theoretical implications of understanding failures of attention?

INTRODUCTION

Attention is a topic that is relevant to understanding almost all forms of human perceptual, cognitive and physical activity. This ubiquitous nature of attention makes it difficult to provide a single precise definition. However, an idea that is common to nearly every model of attention is that attention is a limited resource that is deployed to facilitate the processing of critical information. This idea was, in the words of William James in his *Principles of Psychology* more than 120 years ago, 'Every one knows what attention is. It is the taking possession by the mind, in clear and vivid form, of one out of what seem several simultaneously possible objects or trains of thought. Focalization, concentration, of consciousness are of its essence. It implies withdrawal from some things in order to deal effectively with others' (pp. 403–404). This is a useful description of attention that will encompass all that is presented in this chapter. Attention is key to addressing the problem that at any given time there are more activities going on in the external world, and potential thoughts in our internal world, than we could cope with. Attention allows us to stay on task and to select relevant information. Besides selection, attention can focus our energies on relevant aspects of the world. This final aspect of attention makes it important for understanding the boundaries of human performance.

Since the time that James wrote the words 'Every one knows what attention is', there have been thousands of experiments exploring attention. However, it is difficult to distil this century of progress in attention research to a short and precise definition. It turns out that research into attention has produced numerous varieties of attention that defy a common explanation. There are several possible reasons for this state of affairs. One is that attention is pervasive and can be invoked in description of nearly every cognitive and perceptual process. Thus, how it exists as an independent topic rather than something bolted on to other cognitive and perceptual theories is not always clear. However, attention is clearly a critically important topic for explaining human performance, and the number of accidents in the world that can be attributed to lack of attention show that it is of great practical importance. Moreover, as we develop artificial systems to independently interact with the world it is proving useful to provide them with attentional mechanisms (see Box 4.1).

Our presentation of attention first provides an overview of the scope of attention research and this provides a framework to structure our understanding of attention in the widest sense. We next present a neuroscientific view of attention by discussing the different brain areas that are organized into the attention system of the human brain. Following this, we discuss theories of attention including how they vary in the where and when of attention and how they have developed over time. Examination of these theories leads to further discussion of methods that have proven important to the study visual attention. We next address the topics of how mechanisms of attention relate to perception, working memory and movement control. These topics help to illustrate the breadth of attention as a concept central to cognition. Finally, we discuss failures of attention, which emphasize that, although we might think we take in all the relevant and important information in our environment, what we can miss is really quite striking.

 Box 4.1 Practical Application: Robot attention

Traditionally, robots spent all their time on the factory floor doing repetitive tasks and could be programmed specifically for those tasks alone. Such a single purpose of their existence did not typically require them to deal with changes in goal states or changes in environment. However, modern robots are leaving the factory floor to take their place in less restrictive environments and this is creating the need for attention systems to be developed so that, when presented with changing environments, these robots can dynamically acquire essential information and change their goals. Here we discuss a specific case of human–robot social interaction (Chevalier et al., 2020; Cross et al., 2019) to demonstrate how principles of attention can be used in practice to design a robot system that appears socially engaging.

The case we will consider is described by Kroos and colleagues, and follows their efforts to model an attentional system within a robot controller (Kroos et al., 2011) that can be used to enhance social engagement with the robot. This attention system, although inspired by studies of human attention, should not be taken as an exact model of human attention. However, it does give us an idea of how attention can be designed into a physical system. Their system is called the Articulated Head and includes a highly realistic animation of a talking head attached to a large robot arm, along with various sensors such as a camera, microphone and motion sensor (Figure 4.1a). The robot system was built to inhabit a physical space with humans and was deployed in a public space at the Powerhouse Museum in Sydney, Australia.

In the Articulated Head project, attention was modelled as a mediator between perception and action control. This mediation includes selecting perceptual information relevant for action execution and limiting the potential actions based on the perceived context (Bachiller et al., 2008). This design principle of attention as a mediator between perception and action can be seen in Figure 4.1b, which provides

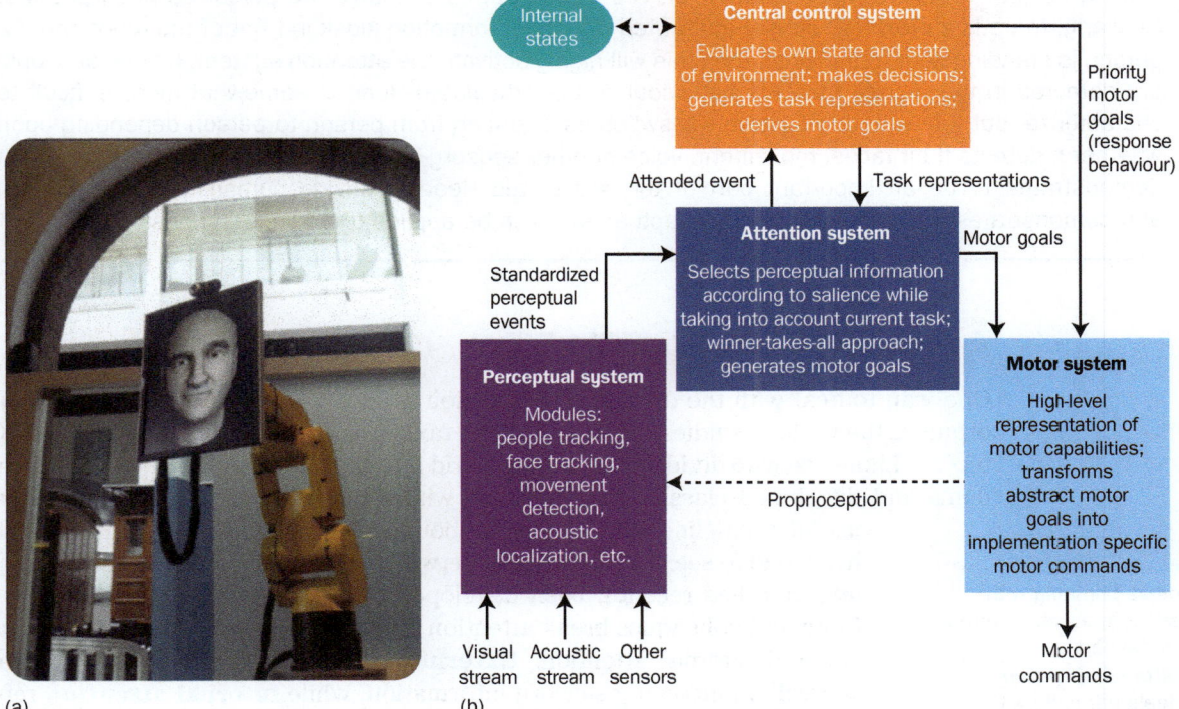

(a) (b)

Figure 4.1 An attention module enhances engagement between humans and a robot-activated head.
(a) The facial animation presented on a flat screen is attached to a large industrial robot that allows for dynamic patterns of motion of the face and the robot to engage people in a science museum setting. (b) A schematic of the robot control system includes an attentional module at the heart of the design to coordinate the activities of the perceptual, motor and central control modules.

Source: Kroos et al. (2011).

a schematic of the system design for the Articulated Head. It can be observed from the diagram that from all the information being sensed and perceived, the central control system 'sees' only the information that has been selected by attention. In coming sections of this chapter we will see how such actions can be described as a filter, a spotlight or a processing bottleneck. In the Articulated Head the attention system is tuned so that the robot behaviour gives an indication that it is aware of current human actions in its vicinity. Of course, although the Articulated Head is made of state-of-the-art sensors and computers, its awareness of the physical environment is limited. However, it is adequate to provide behaviours that appear to be neither random nor fully determined by the physical environment, thus generating a feeling within observers that it exhibits **agency** (see Chapter 3 for more about agency).

> Chapter 3, p110

Agency
ability of an entity, biological or physical, to independently act upon the world to create change in order to achieve goals

The attention system was designed as an essential component to drive the behaviour of the robot. If there is no environmental activity strong enough to attract attention, then the Articulated Head performs random scanning motions. If stimulation is not found then it goes into a sleep mode that includes increasing sensitivity to auditory events so that it is possible to awaken with a noise. Sleep mode is programmed to eventually end and if the attention system is not activated then the Articulated Head does some stretching movements. When awake, if there is a single person in the visual field, then the attention system will follow the movements of this person, but if the person stands still and does not make a sound attention will fade. However, if the face-detection software registers a face to confirm that the person is looking at the robot then it will speak a phrase from its repertoire of opening lines ('I am looking at you!', 'Did we meet before?' or 'Are you happy?') or mimic the perceived head posture. Similarly, there is a proximity sensor integrated into the information kiosk in front of the robot and if a person is standing near to the kiosk then this will highly activate the attention system. If several people are detected in the vicinity then the behaviour of the Articulated Head is somewhat more difficult to characterize, but the attention system will switch its attention from person to person depending upon whether it detects their faces, movement, voice or other sensory input. The attention system has been demonstrated to be an important part of the Articulated Head in driving human–robot interaction, and demonstrates how attention at a conceptual level can be applied to engineering design.

A TAXONOMY OF ATTENTION

One way to deal with the diversity of attention research is to develop a taxonomy to organize the various studies. An example of a taxonomy is the classic work in the 1700s by Carl Linnaeus, who divided the natural world into the plant, animal and mineral kingdoms and developed classification systems within these kingdoms. Taxonomies are useful for delineating the major boundaries within a large structure that helps one to see the relationship between different elements. A taxonomy of attention has recently been developed by Chun et al. (2011) (Figure 4.2). Chun and colleagues break attention down to two basic categories of external and internal attention. **External attention** refers to selecting and controlling incoming sensory information, while **internal attention** refers to selecting control strategies and maintaining internally generated information such as task rules, responses, long-term memory and working memory. Internal attention involves regulating our internal mental life so we can achieve our goals. For example, if we go to the shop to buy milk and a newspaper it is internal attention that keeps us on task so we do not return hours later with no money, milk or newspaper (see Chapter 6 for related discussion of the central executive). Internal attention is crucial for jobs such as being a guard, where vigilance

External attention
deals primarily with sensory events external to the body.
Internal attention
deals primarily with our internally generated thoughts, desires and motivations.

> Chapter 6, p205

is essential. External attention is influenced both by goal-directed processes, where we are searching for particular sensory information, as well as stimulus-driven processes, where sensory events such as loud noises and bright lights draw in our attention. For example, if we have seen the friend we are to meet across a busy street with many cars and people, then external attention makes us aware of the changing traffic signals to cross safely and enables us to keep sight of our friend in the crowd.

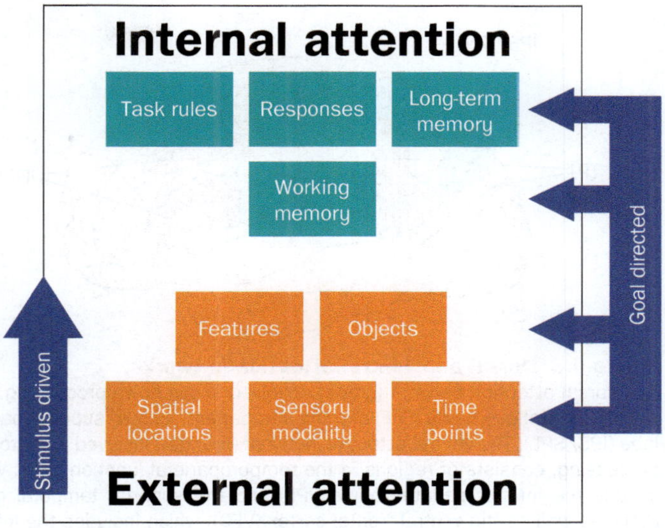

In the presentation of attention in the current chapter we do not cover all the areas of the taxonomy. We emphasize external attention, with a concentration on the modality of vision. Our discussion of internal attention is more limited, though we do discuss proposed relationships between attention and working memory. Working memory is covered more extensively in Chapter 6 and we discuss it here only in relation to attention.

Figure 4.2 A taxonomy of attention.
This taxonomy of attention was proposed by Chun and colleagues in 2011 and has two major divisions of attention: external and internal. External attention includes factors such as how things in the environment capture our attention, while internal attention is much more about keeping focus on internal states. Both external and internal attention are influenced by our goals. The boxes denote specific aspects of attention and many of them are covered in this chapter.

Source: Adapted from Chun et al. (2011).

THE ATTENTION SYSTEM OF THE HUMAN BRAIN

The taxonomy of attention had its major division between internal and external attention and thus it is not surprising that similar division is found in the most influential model of the **attention system** in the human brain (Petersen & Posner, 2012; Posner & Petersen, 1990). This framework, originally proposed by Michael Posner and colleagues, has been developed extensively over the past 30 years and holds that the attention system can be seen as independent from processing systems and that it utilizes a network of brain areas that carry out functions that are specified in cognitive terms. The model has the three basic components of alerting, orienting and executive function, whose functions are partitioned into specific brain areas. Orienting can be considered to be a type of external attention and executive function to be a type of internal attention. We will now discuss these components in more detail.

> Chapter 6, p176

> **Attention system**
> a framework of the human brain containing three different systems for alerting, orienting and the executive function.

The alerting system comprises brain areas in the **brainstem** and frontal cortex that are responsible for achieving a state of general arousal. Arousal promotes our ability to maintain alertness so that we can respond more quickly to a signal. For example, if a warning signal cues us to be alert then we will respond more quickly to a signal when it arrives. Thus, we can think of the alerting system as a kind of 'on' switch that prepares us for upcoming events.

> **Brainstem**
> the region in the posterior part of the brain that serves to connect the cortex to the spinal cord. Its functions include basic physiological processes, as well as the communication of sensory and motor information between brain and body.

The orienting system originally emphasized the role of the parietal cortex (Posner & Petersen, 1990), however as more became known, this expanded to include brain areas in frontal and parietal cortex (Petersen & Posner, 2012). In particular, an influential review of the literature by Corbetta and Shulman (2002) divided this orienting system into two networks (Figure 4.3, overleaf)

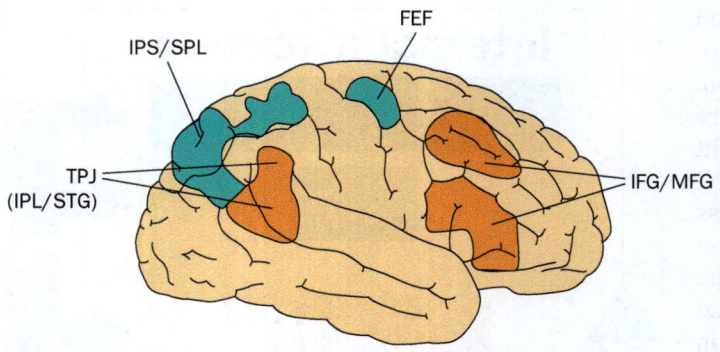

Figure 4.3 Dorsal and ventral attention networks.
The dorsal attention network (green), involved in top down processing, consists of frontal eye fields (FEF) and the intraparietal sulcus/superior parietal lobe (IPS/SPL). The ventral attention network (orange), involved in bottom up processing, consists of regions in the temporoparietal junction (TPJ), which include the inferior parietal lobule (IPL) and the superior temporal gyrus (STG) as well as the ventral frontal cortex (VFC), which includes the inferior frontal gyrus (IFG) and middle frontal gyrus (MFG).

Source: https://www.ncbi.nlm.nih.gov/pmc/articles/PMC3972460/pdf/fpsyg-05-00183.pdf

> **Top down**
> or conceptually driven processes reflect the influence of higher-order cognitive processes such as thoughts, beliefs and expectations.
>
> **Frontal eye fields**
> found in the frontal cortex and involved with the generation and control of eye movements.
>
> **Bottom up**
> stimulus-driven processing of incoming sensory information that produces increasingly elaborate and meaningful representations of the input.
>
> **Default mode network (DMN)**
> a network of brain regions that is active when a person is not focused on the external environment.

that take on different roles in directing attention to events in the external world. One network involves **top down** processing, including the selection of stimulus properties consistent with our goals. This network has come to be known as the dorsal attention network (DAN) and includes parts of the intraparietal cortex and the **frontal eye fields** found in the superior frontal cortex. The other network involves **bottom up** processing that is specialized to detect behaviourally relevant stimuli that are unexpected. This network has come to be known as the ventral attention network (VAN) and includes parts of the temporoparietal cortex and ventral frontal cortex, including the inferior frontal gyrus (IFG) and middle frontal gyrus (MFG). The ventral attention network has the important property of being able to break through processing of the task-based dorsal attention network, so that one can reorientate attention to unexpected but relevant aspects of the world. Brain imaging data support the idea that these two networks interact with each other in a collaborative manner in a way that changes with task demands (Vossel et al., 2014). One critical aspect of this interaction between ventral and dorsal networks is that while it is advantageous to reorientate to relevant stimuli, it can hurt performance to reorientate to irrelevant stimuli. As such, it has been proposed (Aboitiz et al., 2014) that overactivity in the ventral attention network might be a contributing factor to the complex condition of attention deficit and hyperactivity disorder (ADHD).

The executive system is related to internal attention since it is critical for control of starting tasks and sustained maintenance of performing a task. It originally included the anterior cingulate cortex and regions along the medial frontal cortex and this has been expanded to include parietal cortex and additional regions in frontal cortex. Taken together, these brain regions are often more recently referred to as the frontoparietal control network (Marek & Dosenbach, 2018) and are responsible for cognitive control. Evidence for this cognitive control comes from research (Dixon et al., 2018; Spreng et al., 2010, 2013) into how the frontoparietal control network interacts with the dorsal attention network that is active while someone is performing a task (external attention) and the **default network** that is active when someone is not performing a task and their mind is wandering (internal attention). These results showed that the frontoparietal control network acts to mediate goal-directed cognition by dynamically modulating the balance between the default and attention networks.

THEORIES OF ATTENTION

The concept of attention – that we have the ability to select and focus our mental energies – goes back millennia, and William James was writing about it at the end of the nineteenth century. However, there was a lull in attention research during the period that behaviourism held sway. One reason for this is that the more abstract nature of attention did not fit easily into the behaviourist traditions that emphasize the measurements of stimulus and response and minimize consideration of internal mental states. However, renewed interest in attention began with a series of experiments by Cherry (1953) using a task known as dichotic listening, which showed interesting properties of how we attend when different messages are simultaneously presented to different ears. When two messages were presented to both ears then participants had difficulty tracking any one message when asked to shadow it by speaking it aloud. However, when one message went to one ear and the other message to the other ear then participants were near perfect at shadowing the one message but were ignorant of the other message to the point they could not even report when it spoke a foreign language. This impressive skill, to tune in to one speaker against a noisy background, is known as the **cocktail party problem** as it is like when we are at a noisy party and can still hold a conversation. Interestingly, however, our ability to tune in to one speaker can be broken by certain sounds. For example, hearing our own name mentioned is something to which we are acutely sensitive (Moray, 1959). Efforts to use attention to explain these curious aspects of dichotic listening started with filter theory.

> **Cocktail party problem** describes how we successfully focus on one speaker in a background of noise and other conversations.

Filter Theory

Filter theory (Broadbent, 1958, 1971, 1982) addressed issues raised by experiments in dichotic listening and can be considered the first cognitive theory of attention. The research had a direct application to issues of the day surrounding how many pilots a single air traffic controller could effectively communicate with at the same time. As discussed, a core finding was that when a listener is presented with a different message to each ear, interference between the two messages can be avoided when the listener is instructed as to which message is not relevant. This established the idea that a filter is used to block irrelevant information so that only the important message would reach a central channel for further processing. Filter theory used the metaphor of radio communication where the goal is to get the important information on a piece of wire so it can be transmitted to a receiver. In this case the receiver was considered to be our conscious awareness and the issue was what information should attention select to put on the wire. Prior to accessing the central channel was a buffer that contained unprocessed information such as the pitch and other physical properties of the incoming sound. However, only one signal was let through the filter and all the other information in the buffer was flushed away.

This aspect of the model, that only one signal was let through and all the other information discarded, was termed **early selection** and proved controversial. Research by Deutsch and Deutsch (1963) proposed a model of **late selection** where more extensive processing was performed, leading to all stimuli being identified, but only those attended to given access to further processing. In a similar vein, Treisman (1964) suggested modifications to the filter theory of Broadbent, replacing the total filtering of irrelevant information with filtering where the intensity of the irrelevant information was diminished but not totally eliminated. In this way, the diminished information might still be detected if it was of high priority to an individual. This modification helps to explain why we can hear our name being said even if we are attending to another stream of speech, since it is of great personal relevance to know when we are being talked about.

> **Early selection** when the filter for attention occurs early in the stream of information processing.
> **Late selection** when the filter for attention occurs late in the stream of information processing. Thus the filter eliminates some information that has already been processed.

Within the context of filter theory, despite extensive efforts there was never a definitive resolution about early versus late selection. The question, however, is of general relevance since there are trade-offs between early and late selection. For example, if attention is allocated early then although there is a greater risk we might select the wrong information, the information being selected will receive the maximum effect of attention and minimum cognitive resources will be expended on irrelevant information. If attention is allocated late then we will decrease the chance that attention is allocated incorrectly but we will necessarily expend cognitive resources on irrelevant information. A framework for dealing with this trade-off in predicting the level of processing for unattended stimuli was provided by Lavie (2005) in **load theory**. The core idea of load theory is that the amount of processing an unattended stimulus will receive depends upon how difficult it is to process the attended target. If the principal target is easy to process, then attention resources will overflow to irrelevant factors and these will be identified, indicative of late selection (Lavie, 1995). However, if the principal target is difficult to process then the irrelevant factors will not appear processed, indicative of early selection.

> **Load theory**
> how the amount of processing an unattended stimulus will receive depends upon how difficult it is to process the attended target.

A final point to make is that regardless of whether attentional selection is early or late, filter theory imposes an important constraint on how attention functions. This constraint is that there is effectively only one channel of output to further processing and thus attention forms a bottleneck for information processing. For this reason filter theory is also known as bottleneck theory. While filter theory focused on where in attention the bottleneck occurred, the theory we will discuss next, resource theory, focused on the size of the bottleneck.

Resource Theory

A new theory of attention was proposed by Kahneman (1973) that also held attention to be limited; however, instead of the limit being the information capacity of a single central channel, attention was treated as a limited resource to distribute appropriately. The idea of a limited resource was motivated from the metaphor of the brain as a computer where various resources are available within the computing system and attention acts to get the right information to the **central processing unit (CPU)**. Such a formulation allowed more flexible modelling of how attention could be allocated across single and multiple input channels. The model also incorporated aspects such as the arousal of the individual and how different tasks influenced attention. In the following paragraphs we will discuss how different research based on resource theory approached the allocation of attention across space and the challenges this presented for the theory.

> **Central processing unit (CPU)**
> in computing, the central processing unit is the part of a computer that controls operations and executes commands.

The idea of attention as a resource is evident in research into vision that used the metaphor of a **spotlight** to describe how the resources of visual attention were distributed over space (Laberge, 1983; Laberge & Brown, 1987). Just like a spotlight can be shone on the location of a scene we want to observe, it was argued that the resources of attention can be shone on specific visual locations of interest. It is important to note that this spotlight of attention was shown to be able to move around the visual scene even when the eyes do not move. Movement of the eyes towards a subject signal an overt shift of attention, while moving attention when keeping the eyes fixed and attention moves is a covert shift of attention. This ability to move the spotlight of attention around is useful in certain kinds of social situations where we are interested in watching somebody but it would be awkward to look directly at them. One obvious

> **Spotlight**
> the metaphor of attention where we can think of attention as a spotlight that illuminates locations of interest.

question about a spotlight model is how large is the spotlight and whether, and at what cost, the size of the spotlight can be changed. This question was addressed by Eriksen and colleagues (Eriksen & St. James, 1986; Eriksen & Yeh, 1985), who proposed the zoom lens model. Here, the intuition is that, just as a zoom lens on a camera will change how much of the scene is contained in the image, we could effectively have a zoom function for attention that zooms in and out to cover different amounts of the scene. Since attention is a limited resource the amount of attention at any one location in the spotlight will decrease as we zoom out and attention must cover a larger area. The opposite will occur if we zoom in to the scene.

Both the spotlight and zoom lens models treat attention as a resource spreading across visual space without consideration of the objects that inhabit that space. However, it turns out that there is evidence that attention can be characterized as being applied to objects, rather than simply the spatial location that an object occupies. This evidence comes from experiments by Egly et al. (1994), which had participants attend to the end of one of two rectangles by brightening the end of the rectangle to cue the location for 100 milliseconds (Figure 4.4). The brightness was then reduced back to the original shade and then after 200 milliseconds the target appeared. Participants were asked to detect the onset of the target. The target could appear either at the cued location, the other end of the rectangle that had been cued, or a location on the other rectangle that was equal in distance to the length of the rectangle. Participants were faster to detect the target when it appeared at the other end of the cued rectangle than on the uncued rectangle. The important point is that the two uncued locations were equidistant from the cue and thus the results show enhanced processing of the entire rectangle. These findings support object-based attention.

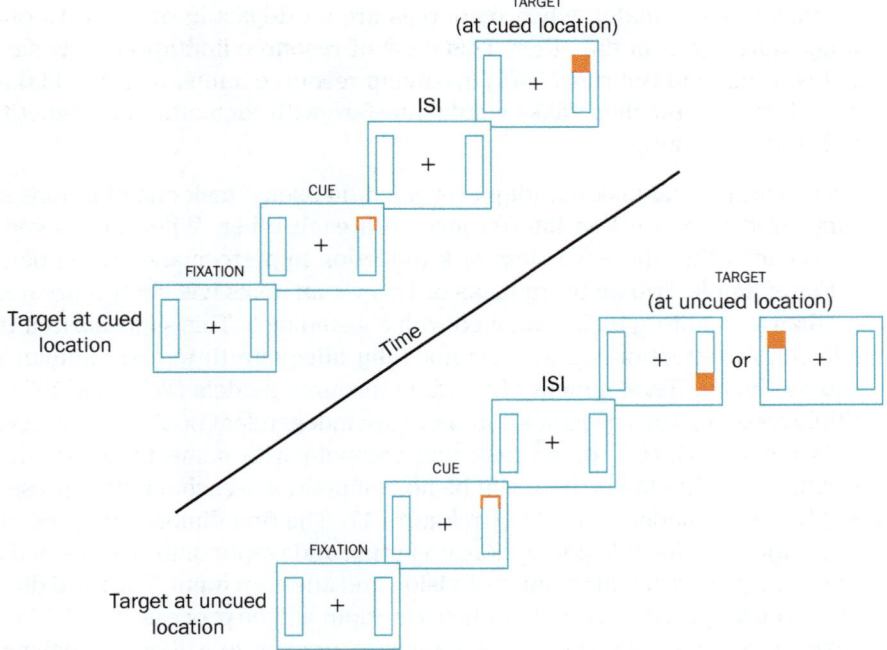

Figure 4.4 Attention can be attached to objects.
In 1994, Egly and colleagues showed that attention can be bound to objects. After fixation, participants are cued to a particular location on one of the objects, in this case the top of the right bar. After a delay the target comes up either at the cued location, on the other end of the same object or an equal distance away on the other object. Participants were faster to detect the target when it was on the same object than when it was an equal distance away on the other object.

Source: Adapted from Egly et al. (1994).

The fact that the objects inhabiting visual space would influence attention makes sense from the perspective of our interactions with the world. For example, as we are navigating through the environment the spatial positions of all the objects in the world are constantly changing and thus attaching attention to the object rather than the location would be an advantage for sustaining attention. Further explorations into object-based attention investigated whether once attention is attached to an object it is attached to the entire object, or perhaps only the parts of the object that are relevant. The results are mixed, with some studies revealing that there is a tendency for all the features of the object to undergo obligatory processing by attention (Duncan, 1984; O'Craven et al., 1999; Vecera & Farah, 1994). However, some more recent evidence suggests that only object features that are relevant for the task to be performed are processed (Woodman & Vogel, 2008).

Consideration of both the spotlight of attention and object-based attention raises the question of how the limited resource of attention is allocated. This interest in how we can distribute attention gave rise to dual-task studies of how attention is used to perform two tasks simultaneously (later in the chapter, in Box 4.3 we will show how a dual-task paradigm can be used to further explore attention). With a **dual-task paradigm**, task performance is measured individually for each task alone and for when both tasks are performed simultaneously. Typically performance is lower when performing both tasks simultaneously. Moreover, when performing both tasks simultaneously and asked to invest a greater percentage of effort in one of the tasks, participants are able to do so relative to the other task. These results are consistent with the notion that attention is a limited resource that is shared between tasks. When tasks are performed simultaneously, resources are split between the tasks and performance goes down due to decreased resources available for the individual tasks. Additionally, when resources are strategically diverted to one task, performance goes down in the other. This view of resource limitations was shared by theories of Norman and Bobrow (1975) involving resource limits, which held that once the resource limit was reached, tasks would interfere with each other in competition for the limited central resources.

> **Dual-task paradigm** arises when one measures performance on two tasks independently and together. If performance when performed independently and together is equal, then the two tasks do not compete for resources.

Experiments using a dual-task paradigm revealed that some task combinations systematically appeared to cause less interference with each other. When tasks were more dissimilar to each other there was less of a reduction in performance when performed together. For example, two auditory tasks or two visual tasks will show a greater negative effect than an auditory task combined with a visual task. This suggests that the idea of a single central attention resource is not fully adequate to explain human performance and motivated development of multiple resource models (Wickens, 1991, 2002). With multiple resources one assumes that there are independent pools of resources, each of which is limited. Thus, a given task will compete with some tasks for the same resources but with other tasks there will be no competition. A schematic representation illustrating Wickens' model is provided in Figure 4.5. The first dimension of the model is processing stages that include perception, cognition and responding. The second dimension includes the processing modalities of vision and auditory input. The third dimension includes the codes, spatial or verbal, for how the input will be processed and this separation is carried through to the response stage where a response will be manual/spatial or vocal/verbal. Our ability to do multiple tasks will depend on how far apart they are on the relevant dimensions. Being close along any one dimension implies competition for resources and a necessary reduction in performance. Although it has proven difficult to precisely specify the basis of the different resources, such models have been very influential in the applied area of designing man–machine interfaces as they provide a means for predicting how different interfaces will affect human performance.

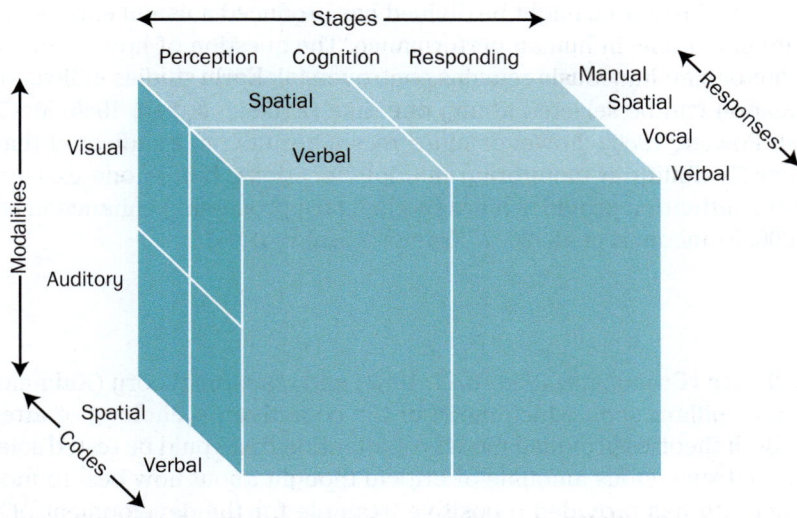

Figure 4.5 A diagram indicating how different attentional resources interact.
Wickens' model creates a space spanned by types of inputs, types of responses and processing stages to represent schematically how different tasks interfere with each other for attentional resources. If two tasks are close to each other in this space they will interfere greatly; if they are far apart they will interfere less. For example, a visuo-spatial task leading to a manual response will not compete so much with an audio-verbal task leading to a verbal response – you can talk while doing a simple jigsaw puzzle.

Source: Adapted from Wickens (2002).

Driving a vehicle is a common man–machine interface and we can use it to illustrate how Wickens' model depicts which dual tasks will be taxing. For a first task let us consider driving on a familiar road with a quiet passenger and with no radio or music playing. When driving, we need to navigate while obeying traffic signals, and this requires us to continuously be running a loop of perception, cognition and response. For the proposed condition of quietly driving a familiar route, we perceive a visual world and transform it into appropriate manual commands with little cognition. If for our second task we are shown a map that is upside down and asked to point the direction to an unknown landmark then we can see that this task will compete with both vision and manual response, as well as tax cognition, and thus would cause a large decrease in driving performance. If instead our second task were to respond to our passenger about what we thought of the weather today, then this would require verbal processing and a verbal response requiring little cognitive load, so would not be taxing since it didn't compete with driving. As a final point, we can add that the great majority of evidence shows a decrease when performing two tasks simultaneously and the question is more whether or not the decrease will be severe rather than whether it exists or not.

Although resource theory promoted a rich body of research considering how attention could be distributed across space and modality it has one theoretical drawback. This drawback is the problem of circularity regarding mechanisms of how attention is allocated (Allport, 1980; Navon, 1984; Navon & Miller, 2002). Namely, to maximize efficiency attention should be allocated to the most important events, but how can attention 'know' what the important sensory events are in all cases? If we give attention too much capability in evaluating the incoming stimuli then it no longer seems like attention. Moreover, studies of resource allocation generally examined how the resources were allocated across different tasks and the criticism was raised that it is possible that when performing dual tasks, participants could somehow rapidly alternate all of their attention between the tasks. A conclusive experiment to show that this rapid switching does or does not occur has proven elusive. Despite these issues, experiments studying how a limited attentional resource might be divided has produced a useful empirical literature to illuminate limitations in human performance. The question of how many sites attention can monitor simultaneously remains controversial. Early studies indicated that only a single location can be selected at any one time (Eriksen & Yeh, 1985; McCormick & Klein, 1990; Posner, 1980), however more recent results have indicated that viewers have greater flexibility in monitoring multiple locations, but as one expands from a single location attention provides more rudimentary processing enhancements (Awh & Pashler, 2000; Franconeri et al., 2007; Kramer & Hahn, 1995).

Evaluation

Both filter theory (Broadbent, 1958, 1971, 1982) and resource theory (Kahneman, 1973) can be seen as pillars upon which much of the cognitive psychology of attention has been built. Both theories provided models of attention that could be tested scientifically and generated tremendous amounts of critical thought about how best to model attention. This activity has provided a positive example for the development of theory in cognitive psychology by demonstrating how concepts can be developed by consecutive iterations of testing theoretical claims and revising theory. A potential byproduct of this intense scientific activity is that attention research has at times clustered around particular controversies or experimental paradigms rather than around a general theory of attention (Sutherland, 1998). However, despite any drawbacks of fads and controversies, it is acknowledged that this activity has generated progress in our understanding of attention (Logan, 2004).

Of course there are some criticisms of these theories of attention. One criticism is the use of metaphors to conceptualize attention. For example, it is mentioned by Di Lollo (2018) that the use of metaphors (e.g., the radio metaphor for filter theory, the computer metaphor for resource theory or the metaphor of attention as a spotlight) helps to promote ambiguity and provides a cover-up of precise definitions. Though in defence of this use of metaphors, it has been proposed that they have been crucial in assisting the science of attention to progress (Fernandez-Duque & Johnson, 2001). Related to this point, it was argued by Posner (1982) that the metaphors of attention were helpful in advancing attention research by placing discussion in a common context of information processing.

Another criticism of theories of attention is that there are too many different phenomena that all go under the same term of attention (Hommel et al., 2019). While this multiplicity of phenomena is clearly a factor that needs to be acknowledged, the issue can be addressed by the taxonomy of attention (Chun et al., 2011), which, by organizing the diversity of possible attentional viewpoints, provides a systematic way forward for future research. It can be noted that other integrative accounts of attention are available from different viewpoints. For example, using a clinical neuropsychological perspective, Cohen (2014) has combined the basic cognitive theories and behavioural aspects of attention with what is known of the brain systems of attention to produce a neurobehavioural model of attention. This model views attention as the by-product of four related but distinct neurobehavioural sets of processes that enable (1) sensory selection; (2) executive control; (3) focusing of resources relative to capacity limits; and (4) sustained attention, vigilance and persistence of response.

This section has focused on theory and we end with a presentation of how these theoretical advances might be put to use in understanding and advancing human performance. In particular, how video game play and other technological means might be used to enhance attention (see Box 4.2).

> **Box 4.2 Practical Application: Video game play in enhancing cognition and attention**

© Gorodenkoff/Shutterstock

Over the past decades video games for entertainment have become a global phenomenon, generating widespread use and billions of dollars of revenue. During this time, research has demonstrated that video games are capable of engaging human cognitive, emotional, physical and social processing systems (Anguera & Gazzaley, 2015). In particular, action video games such as *God of War*, *Halo*, *Grand Theft Auto*, *Call of Duty* and *League of Legends* have been consistently related to a number of cognitive abilities including perception, attention, multitasking and spatial cognition. Answering the question of whether video game use leads to improved performance in cognition and attention has required the development of strict experimental methods (Bisoglio et al., 2014). Results of this research indicate that regular playing of action video games appears to develop enhanced attention that enables individuals to perform faster without loss of accuracy (Castel et al., 2005; Greenfield et al., 1994; Large et al., 2019). Most importantly, this advantage is not isolated to only the video game in which they have become expert, but transfers to general attention tasks. Enhanced performance reported in game players includes improved spatial attention (Green & Bavelier, 2006a, 2007) as well as the number of objects that can be attended to simultaneously (Green & Bavelier, 2003, 2006b). While there is still limited evidence as to the mechanisms involved, a recent review suggests that peripheral vision and the dorsal attention network appear to receive the greatest enhancement from video game play and that it takes at least 20 hours of play for any changes to be seen (Chopin et al., 2019).

Besides action video games for entertainment, there is the serious gaming community that is interested in using video game technologies and approaches to address real-world problems. One of the domains of interest to serious gaming is training in medicine (Gentry et al., 2019).

One study (Schlickum et al., 2009) explored how game play influenced the ability of medical students to perform a simulated surgery using endoscopy. Three groups of medical students were involved: one played a 3D first-person shooter game, another played a 2D non-first-person shooter game and the remaining group played no video games. The experiment went on for five weeks and the video game participants had to play for between 30 and 60 minutes, five days a week. Although both gaming groups performed better on one virtual endoscopy task, only the 3D first-person shooter group also performed better on a second virtual endoscopy task. These kinds of results show the potential for gaming to enhance performance on a real-world task.

Related research investigating baggage screening (Hubal et al., 2010; Pavlas et al., 2008) has addressed the problem of how to maintain vigilance in face of the fact that the majority of bags being screened are harmless (McCarley et al., 2004). One approach to alleviating this problem is what is called threat image projection (TIP), where a 'dummy' weapon is virtually projected into the baggage. This serves the purpose of both keeping up the amount of threats presented to the screener to help maintain vigilance, as well as being used to assess and provide feedback to the screener (Buser et al., 2020; Cutler & Paddock, 2009; Hofer & Schwaninger, 2005). The technology behind virtually placing threat items and the psychology of how best to develop and maintain vigilance is an active area of research in training baggage screeners (Kramer et al., 2019; Mendes et al., 2011).

Visual Attention: Search, Inhibition of Return and Attentional Blink

Both the filter theory of Broadbent (1958) and the resource theory of Kahneman (1973) were overarching theories that provided a general model of the function of attention. However, as interest in attention intensified in the 1980s the diversity of approaches and results has made it difficult to conceptualize the function of attention under a single model. Two general trends are evident since this time. The first is an emphasis on vision as a primary modality to explore models of attention. This has been led by recent developments in vision research that have provided an extensive set of features (colour, size, location, shape, etc.) to explore and enabled study of how attention is distributed in space and time. The second trend is the rich development of experimental approaches like 'visual search', 'dual task interference', 'inhibition of return' and 'attentional blink' which started in single studies to later become general concepts with related experimental paradigms. In this section we discuss a selection of these approaches.

Visual search

Research into visual search addresses the problem of how we use attention to search for a target in a visual display (Eckstein, 2011). Search has important applications in the real world, as it can be a critically important task in some domains, where errors can have serious repercussions (see Box 4.3). An influential approach to this problem, known as feature integration theory (FIT), was introduced by Treisman and Gelade (1980) (see Figure 4.6). They considered that both the target being searched for and the distractor objects would be composed of visual features such as shape, size and colour.

> **Preattentive visual processes** can simultaneously analyse the entire scene and detect the presence of unique features.

Recognition of a target was modelled to be determined by two processes. The first process, termed **preattentive**, was capable of simultaneously searching the entire visual array. This preattentive process could independently examine features such as colour and form, and if the item could be identified by a simple primary feature then this preattentive stage alone could lead to recognition. For example, if we are searching for a green target in a field of red distractors then we can immediately identify the green target using preattentive mechanisms. If, however, recognition depends on combining multiple features then a process of focused attention is needed to combine the features. This use of attention to 'glue' together the different features helps to solve what is

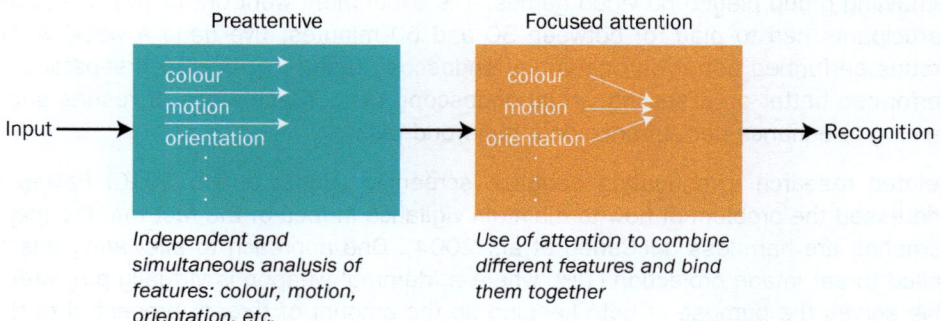

Figure 4.6 Schematic of feature integration theory (FIT) used to drive visual search.
Visual input first goes to independent feature analysers that analyse the entire visual field and then pass information to a focused attention stage. With focused attention the features are joined together and passed to a recognition stage.

Source: Adapted from Treisman & Schmidt (1982).

known as the **binding problem**. Namely, that from neurophysiology we know that different image features of an object such as colour and shape are not necessarily processed together, even though our subjective experience is that all these features are bound together into a unitary experience.

> **Binding problem**
> describes the issue that although perception works via analysis of separate perceptual features our subjective experience has all these features bound together.

Further insight into the role of focused search was provided by research into how the process of combining features could go wrong in what was termed illusory conjunctions (Treisman & Schmidt, 1982). These illusory conjunctions come about when attention is diverted or overloaded, and appear as confusions between features of objects. For example, if a red square and a green triangle are presented while attention is diverted then an observer might report seeing a green square or a red triangle. This provides evidence that the features have been processed but due to the lack of attention they have not been correctly bound together.

 Box 4.3 When Things Go Wrong: Errors in the interpretation of medical images

In fields of medicine such as radiology, a medical specialist with years of training has the visual search task of analysing an image to identify and interpret any regions of concern. Accuracy in the interpretation of these medical images is a complex topic both from a cognitive processing standpoint (Waite et al., 2019) and a medico-legal standpoint. From the medico-legal standpoint there exists a blurry line between errors and malpractice (Berlin, 2007b). However, it seems that the existence of errors is an expected occurrence and their presence does not necessarily indicate negligence. While this might seem surprising at first, it is consistent with data across many decades of monitoring errors across a variety of medical image formats, which show that errors appear consistently (Berlin, 2007a; Brady, 2017). Errors occur at a rate of approximately 4 per cent per day, or 30 per cent retrospectively (Berlin, 2014; Lee et al., 2013). This means that for a typical mixture of cases across a single day, 4 per cent of diagnoses will be incorrect, but if only anomalous scans are provided for review then 30 per cent of them will be incorrect. Applying a 4 per cent error rate to the 1 billion radiologic studies performed worldwide every year equates to about 40 million errors per year (Bruno et al., 2015). From this perspective, a quote taken from a Wisconsin (USA) appeals court (Berlin, 2007; Brady, 2017) can be understood:

> *In determining whether a physician was negligent, the question is not whether a reasonable physician, or an average physician, should have detected the abnormalities, but whether the physician used the degree of skill and care that a reasonable physician, or an average physician, would use in the same or similar circumstances . . . A radiologist may review an x-ray using the degree of care of a reasonable radiologist, but fail to detect an abnormality that, on average, would have been found . . . Radiologists simply cannot detect all abnormalities on all x-rays . . .*

Given the critical importance of getting diagnoses done correctly, research has looked into how these errors occur. One particular study (Kim & Mansfield, 2014) investigated 656 cases where diagnosis had been delayed due to errors and examined the source of the 1,269 errors that had arisen. From this they distilled 12 reasons for errors. Three reasons that can be attributed to visual search accounted for 71 per cent of the total and are summarized in Table 4.1. None of the other nine reasons individually accounted for more than 9 per cent of the errors. This value of 71 per cent is consistent with other quoted estimates of what are termed 'perceptual' errors in the literature (Berlin, 2014; Bruno et al., 2015), which range from 60 to 80 per cent. The term 'perceptual' arises from the dual process model of reasoning in clinical cognition (Croskerry, 2009), which classifies decisions (and errors) as either Type 1 (**heuristic**, fast and automatic) or Type 2 (analytical, slow and deliberate), where Type 1 and Type 2 can be referred to as perceptual and cognitive respectively.

> **Heuristic**
> a problem-solving method that often finds a low-effort solution but is not guaranteed to solve.

Table 4.1 Types of Error in Reading Medical Images That Can Be Attributed to Visual Search

Cause of error	Explanation	Occurrence (%)
Location	A finding is missed because of the location of a lesion outside the area of interest on an image	7
Satisfaction of search	A finding is missed because of failure to continue to search for additional abnormalities after the first abnormality was found	22
Underreading	A finding is present on the image but is missed	42

Source: Adapted from Kim & Mansfield (2014).

The most common type of error, at 42 per cent, was termed underreading, which means that the finding was present in the image but was not reported. This can be thought of as simply a failure of visual search. The second most common error, at 22 per cent, is 'satisfaction of search' where search terminates after the identification of one abnormality and does not continue to find additional abnormalities. This can possibly be considered a cognitive bias (Busby et al., 2018) and highlights the ways in which low-level image feature processing and high-level aspects of knowledge and motivation interact for visual search to complete properly.

Addressing these issues in visual search is complicated as reading the scan is considered to be the outcome of years of practice to develop automatic processes of visual search. However, research addressing how to reduce errors exists and covers a range of factors. At a very practical level it has been noted that fatigue of eye-focusing muscles, which might be more prevalent at the end of a shift (Lee et al., 2013) can diminish performance and this can be addressed with additional rests. In relation to visual search several ideas have been proposed. These include schemes to systematically explore an image to ensure that all regions are observed (Kok et al., 2016), computerized systems to facilitate **perceptual learning** (Krasne et al., 2013) and machine learning techniques of artificial intelligence to develop new tools to assist humans in their visual search (Kahn, 2017; Syeda-Mahmood, 2018).

Perceptual learning a type of learning that occurs at a low level of processing and includes the development of enhanced sensory processing abilities.

Further research into visual search has led to a new and evolving model known as Guided Search (Wolfe, 1994; Wolfe et al., 2011). A diagram of the model is shown in Figure 4.7, in which we can see similarities to and differences from FIT. The main similarity is that what Treisman and Gelade (1980) termed focused attention can be found in the selective pathway and, just like with FIT, it is important for binding features for recognition. Differences with feature integration theory include that although the pre-attentive stage still exists in the form of early visual processing, emphasis is given to how this analysis forms an abstract representation where particular features can be used to guide attention at the point of the attentional bottleneck. Another difference is the addition of a non-selective pathway, which analyses collective aspects of the visual input to guide attention. The problem of guiding attention is reminiscent of resource theory, where attentional resources were managed. However, resource theory models ran into issues with circular reasoning since efficient management seemed to require knowing what was being attended to before allocating the resources. To avoid this issue of circularity, the guidance information is not sufficient for recognition of complex scenes or objects but can be used to facilitate processing at the attentional bottleneck. For example, the guidance arising from early visual processing can highlight the utility of a particular feature, such as colour. Similarly, the non-selective pathway has access to information about the image that is insufficient for recognition but can inform

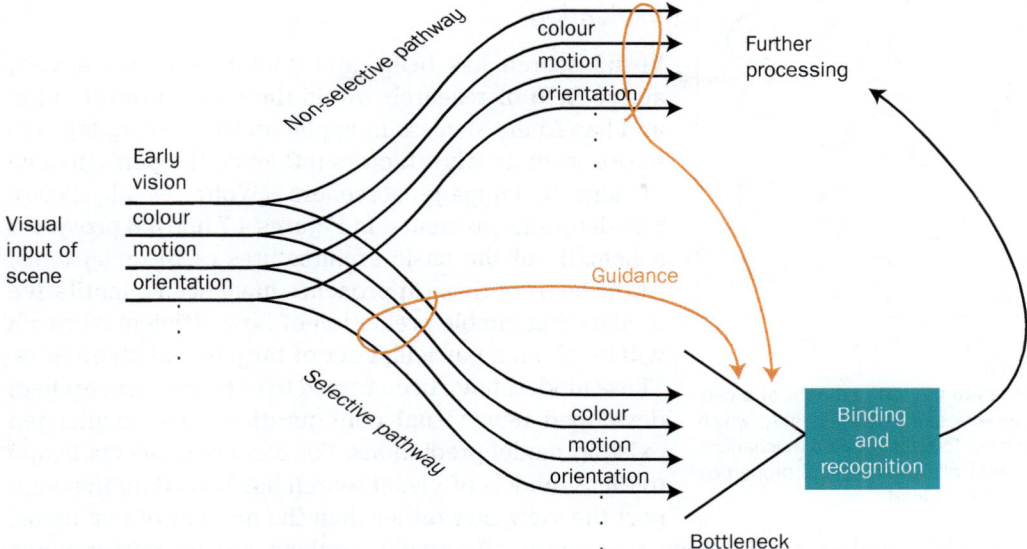

Figure 4.7 Schematic of Guided Search.
Guided Search comprises a selective pathway and a non-selective pathway that arise from early visual processing. The selective pathway leads to an attentional bottleneck that precedes the binding of features and recognition. Processing at the bottleneck is informed by guiding information based on an abstract representation of features such as colour. The non-selective pathway leads to processing of collective properties of the visual information, which can also provide guidance at the attentional bottleneck.

Source: Adapted from Wolfe et al. (2011).

the likelihood of what scene is being viewed. For example, this information might be sufficient to indicate that you are in a forest, rather than in a city (Biederman et al., 1974; Oliva & Torralba, 2001), but insufficient to tell you any other details. This capability has been termed 'obtaining the gist of a scene'.

One of the defining characteristics of the non-selective pathway is that it uses **distributed attention** (Treisman, 2006). Distributed attention is in many ways similar to what was previously considered preattentive processing as it allows a rapid evaluation of the entire image. It is proposed that distributed attention works by extracting statistical properties of the objects and features present in the image. These statistics enable one to perceive the overall layout and structure of the image but are insufficient to enable recognition of particular objects. It is important to note that distributed attention acts not simply by considering the image information at a coarser scale than focused attention but rather provides a relational analysis of the whole image. Research has explored which visual features are accessible to rapid statistical assessment for use in distributed attention. These features include orientation (Dakin & Watt, 1997), contrast texture (Chubb et al., 2007) and size (Chong & Treisman, 2003), as well as velocity and direction of motion (Atchley & Andersen, 1995). An example of this ability to perceive statistical properties of an image is shown in Figure 4.8 (overleaf) for the perception of size. In these experiments, observers were shown two groups of circles to the left and right of a central fixation and were asked to judge which side had the larger average size. Observers performed this task rapidly, demonstrating that they were able to use distributed attention to find the average size of the two groups of circles. How this averaging can be accomplished has been addressed in a computational model of distributed attention averaging that was able to account well for human performance at judging average size (Baek & Chong, 2020).

> **Distributed attention** is reminiscent of preattentive vision and allows rapid statistical analysis of the entire scene.

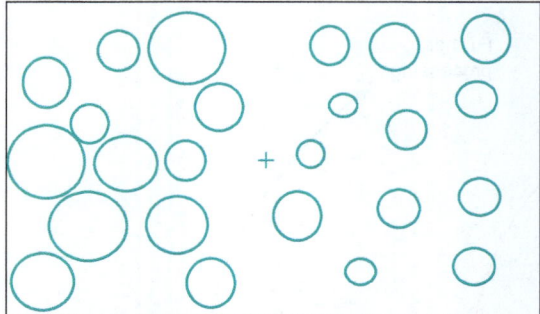

Figure 4.8 Distributed attention can rapidly determine average size.
Given two groups of circles to the left and right of a central fixation cross, observers can rapidly identify which side has larger average size. This occurs via a mechanism of distributed attention that allows statistical properties of the entire image to be determined.

Evaluation

Visual search has been, and continues to be, a very active field of research within the domain of attention and has found success in applications to everyday scenarios such as what factors influence the performance of airport baggage screeners (Wolfe et al., 2005). The diagrams presented in Figures 4.7 and 4.8 provide a schematic of the basic architectures of these systems. At the heart of these approaches have been quantitative models that enable prediction of how efficient a search will be given a particular set of targets and distractors. These models have been forced to evolve as researchers developed new visual configurations that challenged existing model predictions. For example, one challenge to these models of visual search has been data that support the view that rather than the number of test items, it is the number of fixations that more effectively predicts search performance (Hulleman & Olivers, 2017). Another challenge to the early models of visual search was that testing precise model predictions has often relied on the use of tightly controlled visual displays that are inherently artificial. However, this issue has been addressed by the study of search in natural scenes (Koehler & Eckstein, 2017) to advance our understanding of search. Moreover, research into the role of attention in visual search is being used to study attention in foraging behaviour, like for example finding the proper coins to pay a cashier at the checkout, where there are multiple targets of different types in potentially complex environments (Kristjánsson et al., 2020).

Inhibition of return

If attention is attracted to an event in the visual field there will be facilitation of processing around this location. However, after attention moves away, this location suffers from delayed responding to events (Klein, 1988, 2000). This phenomenon was first described by Posner and Cohen (1984) and named inhibition of return (Satel et al., 2019). As the name suggests, the mechanism promotes searching novel locations rather than returning to one that has already been examined. It has been proposed that inhibition of return is used in foraging behaviour to help the searcher not return to locations that have already been explored. Inhibition of return begins around 250–300 milliseconds after attention has been directed to a location and this inhibition appears to have a duration of around three seconds (Samuel & Kat, 2003). It was originally shown to exist with locations in space but it has also been shown to exist on attention directed to objects (Tipper et al., 1991). The original experiments of Posner and Cohen (1984) also showed that inhibition of return was coded in environmental coordinates rather than being fixed to the eye's retinal coordinates. They showed this by demonstrating that eye movements could be included during the inhibitory period and the effect was still observed.

Inhibition of return has been combined with the idea of saliency maps in computer vision to search an image (Itti & Koch, 2001; Krasovskaya & MacInnes, 2019). Image salience indicates which parts of the image are going to draw in attention based on purely the visual features. An influential description of how bottom-up attention based on saliency might work was provided by Koch and Ullman (1985). They discussed how different visual features (size, colour, etc.) might combine to form a single map of conspicuity based on which parts of the image were most different from their surrounds. These conspicuous or salient parts of the image are those that are most likely

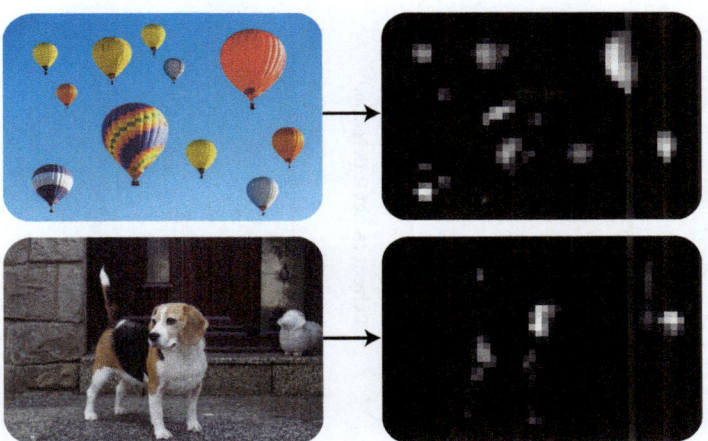

Figure 4.9 Examples of saliency calculated from input images.
Orientation, colour and other image properties are combined in a computer algorithm to find the image locations that are most conspicuous. These conspicuous regions are indicated in the right column with the brighter shades of white indicating the more conspicuous image regions.

Source: (TopL) © Image Source/Westend61/Carmen Steiner, (BottomL) © Frank Pollick (R); Saliency maps provided by Dirk Bernhardt-Walther. © Dirk Bernhardt-Walther.

to draw the attention of an observer (Figure 4.9). However, since the most conspicuous part of an image isn't necessarily the target we are looking for, inhibition of return provides a mechanism to disregard conspicuous locations for the remainder of the search as one explores less salient locations. Research into the how the brain might represent saliency maps has found neurons in the frontal eye fields (FEFs) that keep track of items that have previously been fixated (Mirpour et al., 2019) and it has been proposed that these neurons, together with neurons in the parietal cortex (Bisley & Mirpour, 2019), act to drive attention.

Attentional blink

If we are watching a sequence of rapidly presented visual displays (6–20 items per second), the second of two targets cannot be identified when its presentation is close in time to that of a first target. This phenomenon is known as attentional blink. For example, if we are given the task of identifying two letters within a sequence of rapidly presented numbers, then detection will be impaired on the second letter if it is presented close in time to the presentation of the first letter. Although the phenomenon had been noted earlier (Broadbent & Broadbent, 1987), it was described as the 'attentional blink' by Raymond et al. (1992). This notion of a blink captures the intuition that after attention has obtained the first target, it 'blinks' and thus does not see the second. The basic paradigm and results of this study are shown in Figure 4.10 (overleaf). A sequence of visual stimuli is presented in rapid succession and if participants are instructed to identify just a single target then the proportion of correct responses is nearly identical regardless of where in the sequence it is shown. However, when instructed to identify two targets, there is a substantial reduction in performance in identifying the second target, with recognition performance below 60 per cent, from 80 to 450 milliseconds after presentation of the first target. The attentional blink paradigm has been used extensively to study the availability of attention across time. It demonstrates a clear limitation of attention in showing that the best way to make a second target go unnoticed is to show it a short time after showing the first target. It is worth pointing out, though, that the lowest performance does not occur immediately after the first target (Figure 4.10b, overleaf). In Box 4.4 we see how the attentional blink can be used to study the processing of emotional faces.

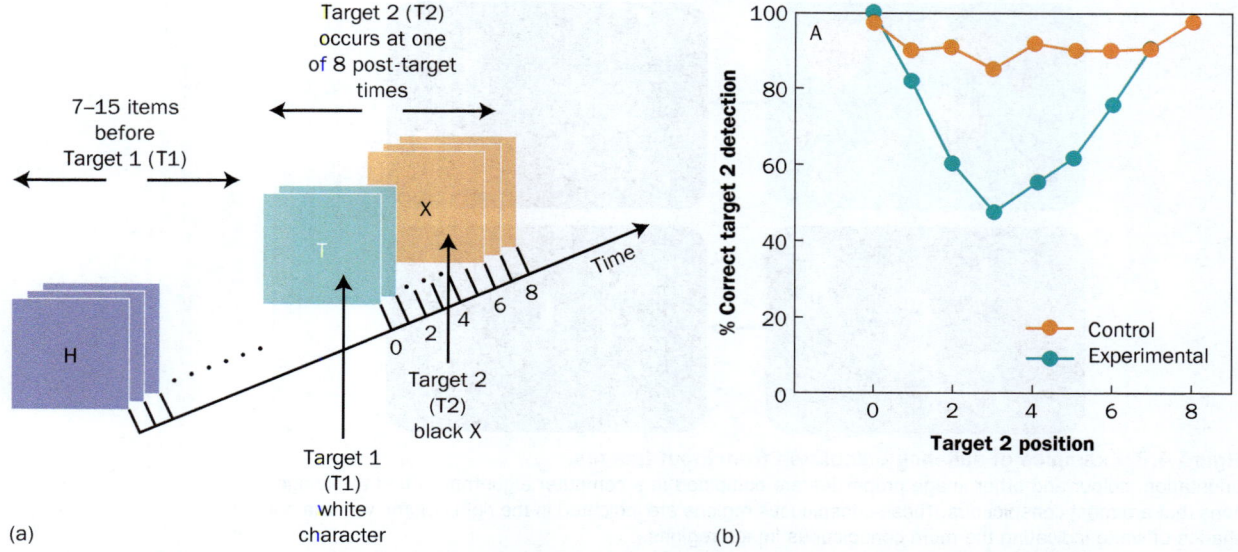

Figure 4.10 Attentional blink shows that attention temporarily decreases immediately after being used at a location.
(a) Example of a single trial of an attentional blink experiment. After a first target (T1) is attended to, a second target (T2) is shown at the same location at different times afterwards. The closer in time T2 is to T1, the lower the chances of correct identification. (b) Results of an attentional blink experiment show that in the control condition when only one target is shown there is no change in correct identification. However, in the experimental condition results show that when T2 is shown after T1 there is a decrease in ability to correctly identify the target.

Source: Adapted from Raymond et al. (1992).

Box 4.4 Research Close Up: Using the attentional blink to examine emotion perception

Source: Keefe et al. (2019).

INTRODUCTION

Detecting emotions is important for succeeding in the social world, and this has motivated study of how affective and emotional events engage attentional mechanisms (Pessoa, 2019). To study how emotions engage attention, the attentional blink has been adapted to show what is known as an emotional attentional blink (McHugo et al., 2013). Similar to the attentional blink (AB), the emotional attentional blink (EAB) refers to a temporary impairment of ability to identify a target when it is preceded by another stimulus, in this case an emotional stimulus. The EAB is thought to occur due to the salience of the emotional stimulus engaging attention for a brief duration that interferes with identification of subsequent targets.

For emotional stimuli, the experiment by Keefe and colleagues used erotic images of mixed-sex couples. Previous research has shown that erotic images induce a larger EAB than aversive images (Ciesielski et al., 2010; Most et al., 2007) and that arousal appears key to generating attentional capture. The neutral images included scenes involving one or more people in portrait or performing everyday activities.

The primary question addressed by the research was whether mechanisms of the EAB were identical to the AB. To examine this, the researchers took as a starting point the results of a previous AB study using a dual task paradigm, which showed that when participants performed a concurrent secondary task of monitoring stimuli in the periphery, the AB was diminished (Wierda et al., 2010). This means that participants do better at identifying the second target when given the extra task of monitoring the periphery. The explanation for this somewhat surprising result is that the second task draws resources away from attention to the first target so that there is not an over-investment in the first target (Olivers & Nieuwenhuis, 2006). This lack of over-investment leads to improvement in identifying subsequent targets. The experiment involved both a dual task and an AB aspect in its design so it is useful to keep two facts in mind: (1) in dual task experiments the crucial comparison is between performance at the single task and performance at the dual task; (2) in AB experiments the crucial comparison is performance at detecting the second target dependent on its temporal proximity to the first target. This experiment measured identification of the target image at either two time steps (lag 2) or eight time steps (lag 8) after presentation of the neutral or emotional distractor image. The experiment further included two types of images, neutral and emotional, so that comparison could be made between the EAB for both images. Figure 4.11 illustrates the predicted single task performance and various possibilities for the dual task performance of the neutral and emotional conditions.

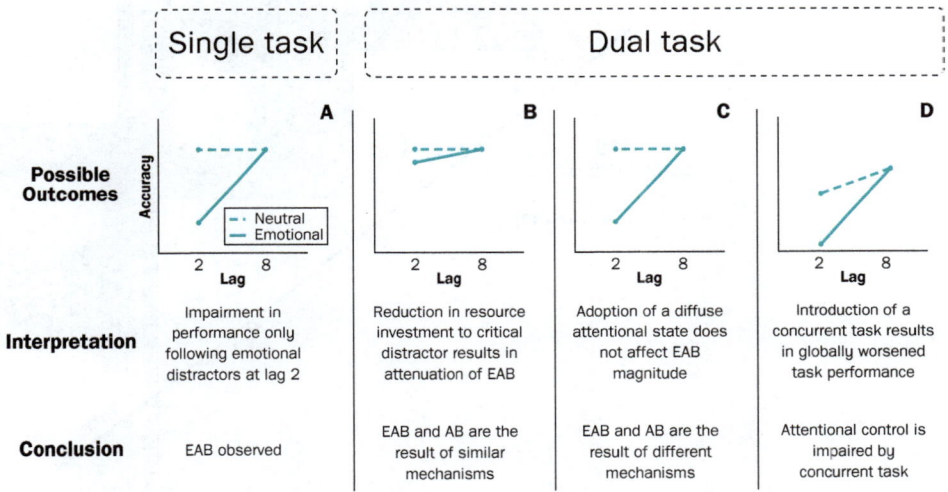

Figure 4.11 Predicted single task performance and possible outcomes for dual task performance.
Schematic of the possible outcomes of the experiment, and the interpretation and resulting conclusions. From the results of Wierda et al. (2010) we predict that if the emotional attentional blink (EAB) was similar to the attentional blink (AB) then in the dual task condition performance at lag 2 would improve compared to the single task (panel B). If, on the other hand, dual task performance was similar to single task performance then this would argue for different mechanisms between the attentional blink and emotional attentional blink (panel C). If the second task caused a general impairment of attentional control then performance would drop for all conditions (panel D).

METHOD

A total of 19 participants (11 female, 8 male) were recruited for the study, with one participant being excluded for not following instructions. After being informed of the nature of the visual stimuli and agreeing to proceed, each participant performed a single session of about one hour.

Across tasks, every trial involved the presentation of both rapid serial visual presentation (RSVP) images and a peripheral dot stimulus. Participants were instructed to keep their eyes fixed on a fixation cross at the centre of the screen throughout each experimental trial. A space bar press initiated an RSVP of 17 images presented at fixation for 93.33 ms each; an example is shown in Figure 4.12 (overleaf). All images on a given trial consisted of different upright landscape/architectural photographs, except for two: the distractor and the target stimulus. The distractor was displayed as either the fourth or sixth stimulus in the stream, and was either a neutral image of everyday interactions of people or an emotionally

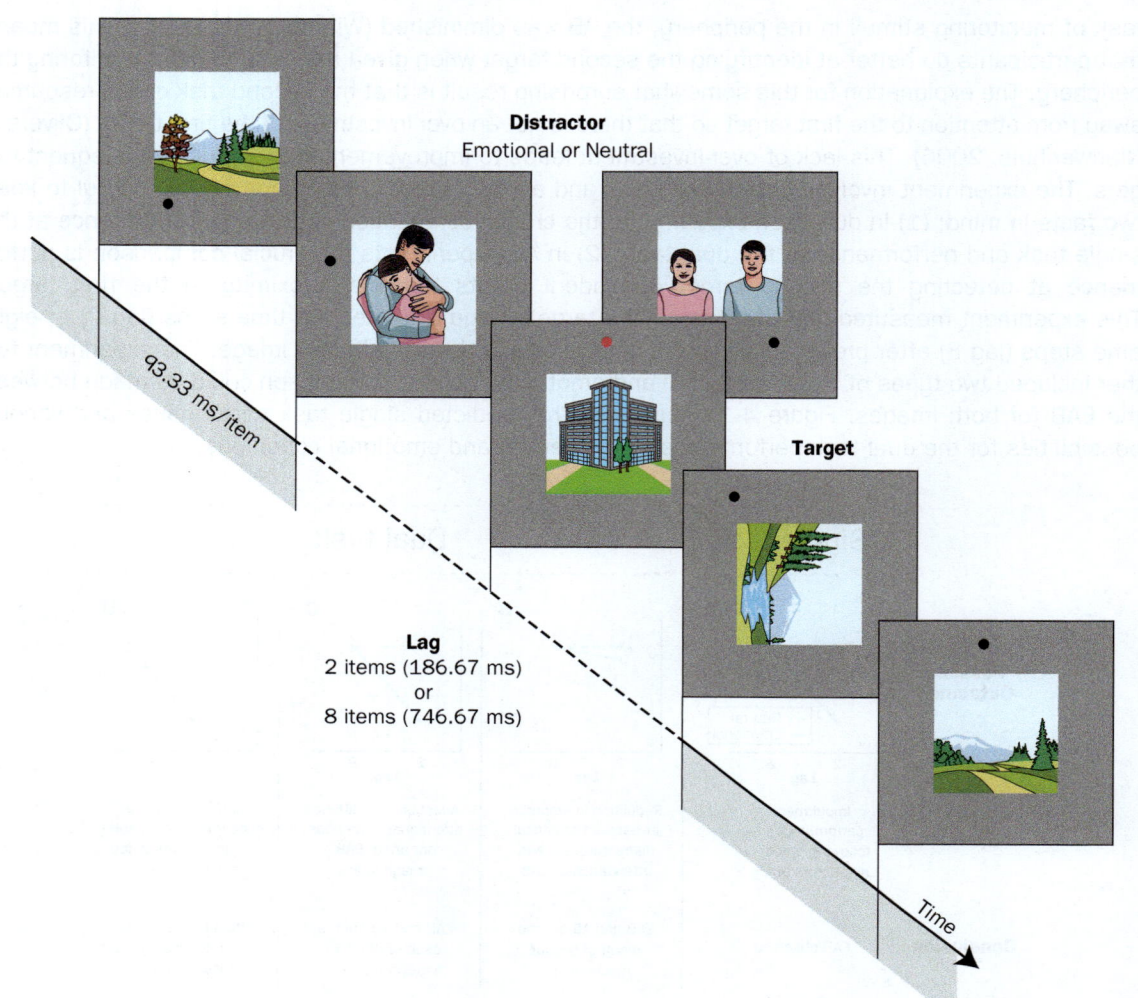

Figure 4.12 Trial design for emotional attentional blink (EAB).
Participants were shown a rapid serial visual presentation (RSVP) of upright landscape/architectural images and had the task of identifying a clockwise or counterclockwise rotation of the target landscape/architectural image. An irrelevant emotional (erotic) or neutral distractor preceded the target by either two or eight frames. In separate experimental blocks, attention to the RSVP stream was manipulated on the basis of task instructions to ignore or also attend to the peripherally presented dots.

Source: Keefe et al. (2019).

salient image of a couple engaged in erotic acts, presented with equal probabilities within each experimental block. The target was presented at a lag of either two or eight images after the distractor (186.67 or 746.67 ms) and consisted of a landscape/ architectural scene rotated 90° clockwise or counterclockwise from vertical. Concurrent with each image presentation, a dot was presented at 9° eccentricity from fixation. The location of the dot changed with each new RSVP image to one of 39 locations with equal probabilities, excluding the preceding location. In 80 per cent of the trials, all dots in that trial were black. In 20 per cent of the trials, one of the dots appeared red rather than black for one 93.33 ms image frame. The red dot could appear at any time during the RSVP stream, excluding the time of the first, second or final image. In the single task condition participants had only to identify the direction in which an image was rotated. In the dual task condition participants had to both identify the image rotation and whether a red dot had appeared. Trials when the dot appeared red were not included in analysis as these would have included extra processing of the colour change. Some additional aspects of the experiment, including a rating of vividness of the target and a condition where the location of the red dot was cued, are not presented in this summary of the experiment.

RESULTS

Results are shown in Figure 4.13. For the single task, when the distractor was emotional, there was a decrease in performance at lag 2 but not lag 8, indicating the expected EAB. When the distractor was neutral there was a high level of performance regardless of the timing of the distractor (lag 2 or 8). For the dual task, there was an EAB for both the emotional and neutral distractors, though it was less for neutral images.

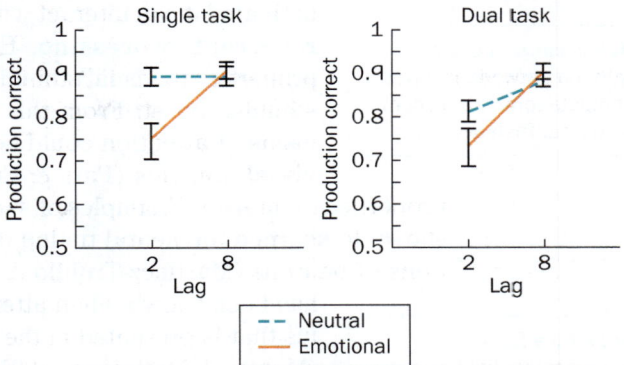

Figure 4.13 Results showing performance on the single task and dual task EAB.
Results for the single and dual task conditions are shown as the proportion of trials correct for both the neutral and emotional conditions at the two different lags.

DISCUSSION

Results in the single task replicated previous results and demonstrated a clear EAB. The prediction that, like the AB, the EAB would diminish when there was a second task was not obtained. This result indicates difference between the EAB and AB, indicating that the over-investment (Olivers & Nieuwenhuis, 2006) explanation does not apply to the EAB. This further demonstrates that once an emotional distractor begins to be processed, regardless of instructions to distribute attention to a concurrent task, visual attention does not quickly disengage, thus leading to a blink in subsequent target detection. The finding that increased attentional load in the dual task condition resulted in an apparent EAB for neutral images was surprising. One possible explanation is that it resulted from a general decrease in performance with increased load (Akyürek & Hommel, 2005). Another point is that even the neutral images have some salience to attract attention, as faces are known to attract increased attentional processing (Langton et al., 2008), with positive faces being reported to require fewer attentional resources (Ray et al., 2020).

Attentional Mechanisms in Perception and Working Memory

In our presentation of theories of attention, we discussed attention as something separate from other perceptual and cognitive functions. It is however possible to embed attentional mechanisms within other functions, in this section we cover two such examples. The first discusses how to achieve effects of attention within mechanisms of low-level vision, while the second describes similarities between attention and working memory.

A neural mechanism of attention in primary visual cortex

As an introduction we will review the time course of neural activity in the brain associated with seeing a stimulus. The first component of activity is known as the **feedforward** sweep (Lamme, 2003; Lamme & Roelfsema, 2000), which describes how incoming sensory information travels across the brain. The primary visual cortex responds 40 milliseconds after a stimulus onset, by 80 milliseconds most secondary visual areas are activated and

> **Feedforward**
> feedforward processing describes a bottom-up process where lower levels of a network progressively stimulate higher levels of the network.

by 120 milliseconds activations can be found throughout the cortex. Once an area is activated it can interact with both higher and lower brain areas in a mode of **recurrent processing**. However, it has been found that neural tuning properties to visual stimuli are quite sophisticated even at short times after stimulus onset. From this consideration, it is evident that neural mechanisms of attention could be effective in the very first stages of encoding a visual stimulus (Parr & Friston, 2019) by tuning neurons to best encode properties of interest. Examples of such a phenomenon include that attention has been shown to sharpen the neural tuning of single neurons (Spitzer et al., 1988) or populations of neurons (Martinez-Trujillo & Treue, 2004), and reduction in neural responses has been shown when attention is directed towards a non-preferred stimulus that is presented in the same **receptive field** with a preferred stimulus (Moran & Desimone, 1985; Reynolds & Desimone, 2003). Various neural models have been proposed to explain how attention can selectively amplify the visual response of neurons (Li & Basso, 2008; McAdams & Maunsell, 1999; Williford & Maunsell, 2006). Recently, a unifying model has been proposed by Reynolds and Heeger (2009) that incorporates the capabilities of many of the previous theories and explains a variety of experimental results regarding how attention operates at very early levels of the neural encoding of visual information.

> **Recurrent processing**
> within a network, involves computations that occur in a cyclical fashion.

> **Receptive field**
> the receptive field of a neuron indicates the physical space that stimulates the neuron. In vision it is the region of visual field to which that neuron is sensitive if stimulated with light.

The model of Reynolds and Heeger, called the Normalization Model of Attention, focuses on two functions of attention: (1) the capacity to increase sensitivity to faint stimuli presented alone, and (2) the capacity to reduce the impact of task irrelevant distractors when multiple stimuli are presented. To achieve this they developed a computational model of early stages of image processing in the visual cortex. In the model, the input, which is termed the Stimulus Drive, is multiplied by an Attention Field and divided by a Suppressive Drive to obtain the effect of attention on perception. The Suppressive Drive includes the interaction of all the attended and non-attended elements of the visual input. An example of how the model works is shown in Figure 4.14 for the case of observing two sets of vertical lines, one set to the left of fixation that is not attended and one to the right of fixation that is attended. The Normalization Model represents the Stimulus Drive and subsequent stages as a 'neural image' (Robson, 1980) in which the brightness at every spot of an image corresponds to the response of one neuron. In this example, the brightness of the Stimulus Drive corresponds to the sensitivity of a neuron to line orientation. The Stimulus Drive is the neural image of how orientation in the image is represented if there were no effects of attention. Thus, the two light bands on the left and right of the Stimulus Drive correspond to the two targets shown to the left and right of the centre fixation dot and are identical. In the Attention Field, a grey colour indicates no effect of attention and white indicates attention being applied. We can see that the Attention Field in this case is sensitive to the position of the stimulus but not the orientation, and its width reflects the size of the red circle around the vertical lines that denote the area to which attention is directed. It is apparent from the figure that attention is being applied to the target on the right of fixation. The result of multiplying the Attention Field by the Stimulus Drive gives the Suppressive Drive, which is more broadly tuned than the original Stimulus Drive. This Suppressive Drive is then used to divide the Stimulus Drive to obtain the Population Response. This process of division is known as normalization since it takes the original input and changes it according to the surrounding context. The final result of the Population Response shows that the attended target is enhanced while the other target receives a diminished response.

Since it was introduced in 2009 the Normalization Model of Attention has proven to be able to capture a wide variety of phenomena about how attention can be used to

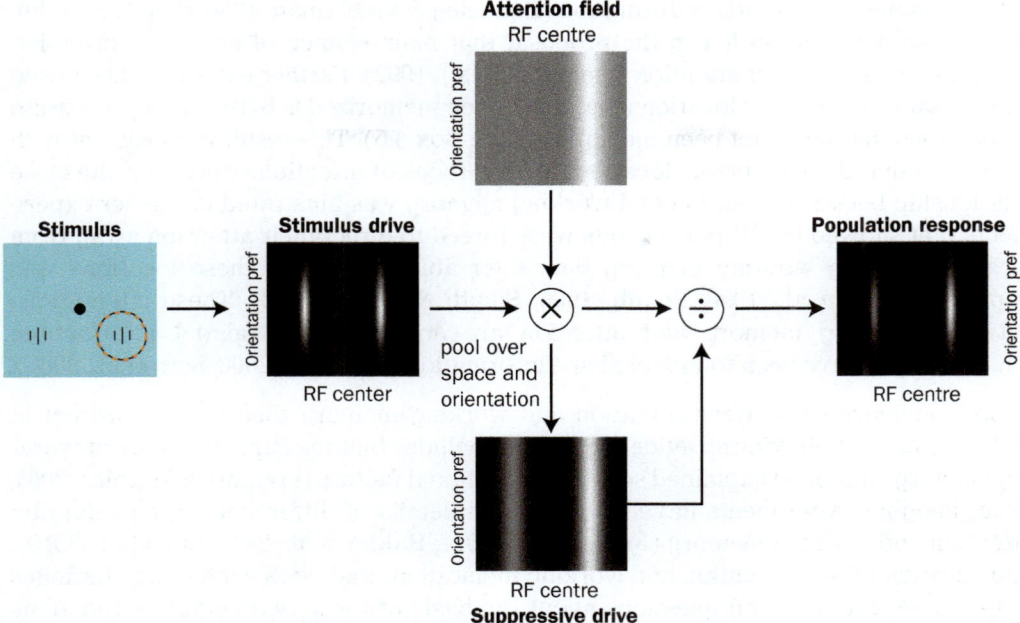

Figure 4.14 The Normalization Model of Attention.
The model shows how attention can modulate the response of neurons in primary visual cortex. Details of the process are described in the text. In this example, we show an input of oriented bars with the task of attending to the three bars on the right. The area of attention is denoted by the orange circle in the far-left box. In the box on the right-hand side, labelled population response, the output of the system shows enhanced processing of the target on the right, as illustrated by the brighter and larger response.

Source: Reprinted from Reynolds & Heeger (2009).

modulate the activity of neurons in visual cortex. The concept of normalization has been applied to understand the dynamics of integrating sensory signals (Ohshiro et al., 2011), and neurophysiological mechanisms for obtaining normalization of signals have been proposed (Ferguson & Cardin, 2020; Lee et al., 2012). One limitation of the model is that it is effectively a static model and this has been addressed to obtain a model that is dynamic and can respond to input stimuli that change over time (Heeger & Zemlianova, 2020).

Attention and working memory

We will discuss working memory in more detail in Chapter 6, but here we would like to discuss similarities that have been discovered between attention and working memory. To appreciate the connection between attention and working memory we need first to give a brief preview of working memory. Working memory is a central cognitive mechanism coupled with separate stores for visuo-spatial and phonological information. Just like attention, the capacity of working memory is limited. One utility of working memory is that the perceptual world is constantly changing and events can be fleeting. To cope with this, working memory allows relevant perceptual information to be maintained over time and serves as an interface between perceptual input and internal representations (Awh et al., 2006; Chun, 2011; Gazzaley & Nobre, 2012). Thus, it is not surprising that attention to particular information would have impact in working memory.

Research into possible interactions between attention and working memory began with experiments which showed that eye movements and arm movements could interfere with maintenance of spatial information (Baddeley & Lieberman, 1980; Smyth & Pelky, 1992). This observation led to the proposal that maintenance of spatial information involves covert shifts of attention (Smyth & Pelky, 1992). Further experiments showed that visual processing at locations that have been memorized is better than processing at locations that have not been memorized (see Box 4.5). This result is consistent with the notion that the memorized locations are the focus of attention. Moreover, the close relationship between attention and working memory was illustrated in further experiments that showed that if participants were forced to direct their attention away from locations held in working memory then their ability to recall these locations was impaired (Awh et al., 1998; Smyth, 1996; Smyth & Pelky, 1992). These interactions between working memory and attention are not limited to spatial information. Similar effects have been found for shape information (Downing, 2000; Soto et al., 2005).

Despite similarities between attention and working memory they remain distinct in their operation. Behavioural evidence for this includes that the capacity limits of working memory cannot be explained solely by attentional factors (Fougnie & Marois, 2006). Brain imaging experiments have also revealed details of differences in encoding by attention and working memory (Fusser et al., 2011; Hakim et al., 2019; Silk et al., 2010). The question of how attention and working memory interact with each other continues to give rise to interesting questions about the basis of these two cognitive functions (Kiyonaga & Egner, 2013; Oberauer, 2019).

Box 4.5 Research Close Up: Using a dual task to examine attention and working memory

Source: Awh et al. (1998).

INTRODUCTION

To test the claim that spatial selective attention could be directed towards a location stored in working memory Awh and colleagues (Awh & Jonides, 2001; Awh et al., 1998) performed a seminal dual task experiment. Their prediction was that improved efficiency in visual processing would be obtained at locations stored in working memory. In particular they tested whether impairing the ability of participants to direct attention towards locations in working memory would result in a corresponding decrease in memory accuracy.

METHOD

The basic set-up of the experiment is shown in Figure 4.15a. For the dual task conditions individuals performed both a spatial memory and a colour discrimination task. At the beginning of the experiment participants would be presented with a cue at a particular spatial location and given the task of keeping in memory the location of this cue. They would next perform a colour classification task to a target that was either a small disk that required a shift in attention or a large disk that did not require a shift in attention since it was large enough to cover all the potential memorized locations. The colour classification task involved judging the colour from a possibility of red versus pink or blue versus purple. Finally, a probe would be presented and participants had the second task to decide whether the probe was or was not at the same location as the cue. For the single task conditions, the experimental conditions were identical except that more colours were used and importantly no classification of the colour was required. Thus, observers first saw a cue and were asked to keep the location in memory,

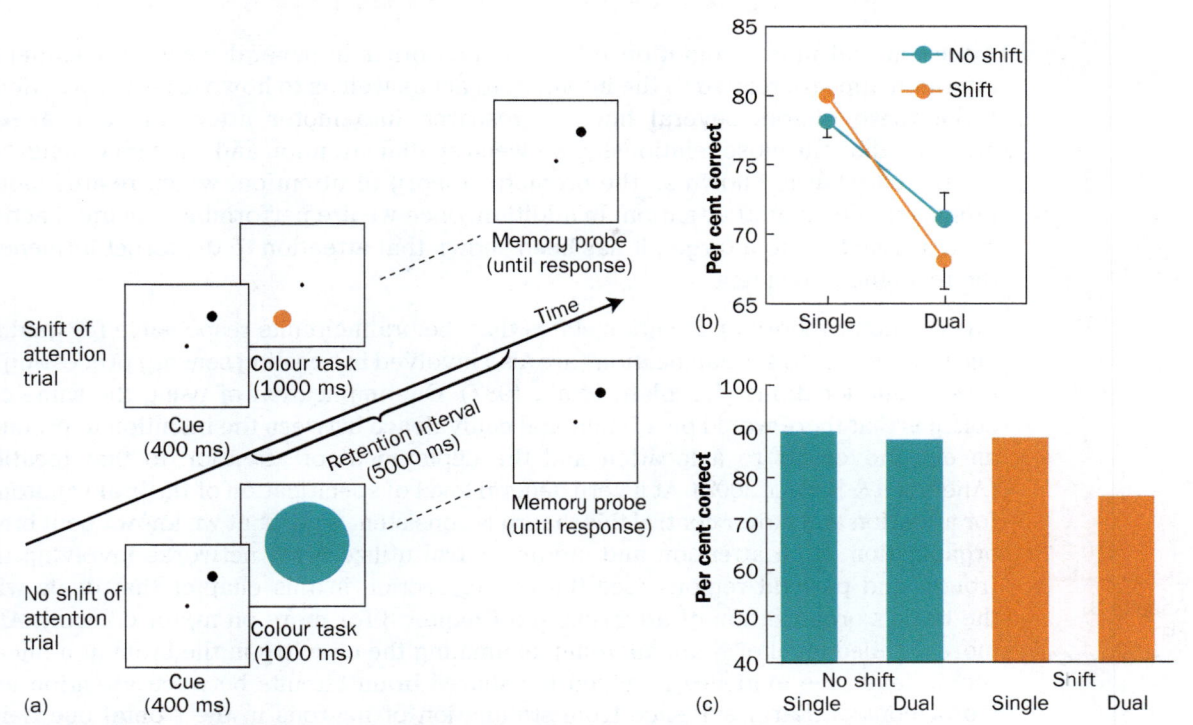

Figure 4.15 Experiment showing similarity between spatial attention and working memory.
(a) Schematic of the task that participants performed during the experiment. First, a cue provided a spatial location for people to remember. Next, while maintaining fixation, they were presented with either a small colour disk that required shifting attention to identify the colour (top) or a large disk that did not require shifting attention (bottom) (in control conditions participants didn't identify colour). Finally they were given a memory probe at either the same or a different location and asked to indicate if it was the same as the cue. (b) Percentage of correct responses in identifying location. (c) The percentage of correct responses in identifying colour.

Sources: (a) and (c) adapted from Awh & Jonides (2001); (b) Adapted from Awh et al. (1998).

second saw a small or large disk, and then *only* gave a memory judgement of whether the probe was in the same location as the cue.

RESULTS

The two important results to examine are performance on the spatial memory task (Figure 4.15b) and performance on the colour discrimination task (Figure 4.15c). Performance on the spatial memory task showed decreased performance for the dual task, and in particular accuracy was worse when the small disk was used, which required a shift in attention. This result shows that taking attention away from a location in working memory causes a decrement in memory performance. Performance on the colour discrimination task showed a decrement in performance for the shifting condition. This result indicates that there was interference between the colour discrimination task and maintaining the location of the cue in spatial working memory. These results are crucial in demonstrating that spatial attention plays a beneficial role in the active maintenance of location information.

DISCUSSION

In the taxonomy of attention presented at the beginning of the chapter, working memory was located within internal attention, while attention to spatial locations was located within external attention. However, the results of this experiment helped to establish that, due to the interaction between spatial attention and working memory, the boundary between internal and external attention is not distinct.

Attentional Mechanisms in Controlling Actions

Attention and motor cognition relate to each other in several ways. For example, attention appears related to the intention to act as well as to how we perform actions. From these factors several lines of research into motor attention have arisen. Most notably, the close relationship between spatial attention and eye movements has motivated what is known as the premotor theory of attention, which relates motor preparation to spatial attention. In addition, once we are performing a manual action such as reaching to a target, it has been shown that attention to the target influences the reaching movement.

The premotor theory of attention states that the brain circuits responsible for guiding eye movements to spatial locations are also involved in boosting sensory processing to these same locations (Rizzolatti et al., 1987). One implication of using the same circuitry is that there would be a functional equivalence between the intention to produce an eye movement to a location and the deployment of attention to that location (Andersen & Buneo, 2002). At a very general level of specification of the brain anatomy for attention and motor control this theory is consistent with what we know about brain organization. Both attention and motor control utilize brain networks involving the frontal and parietal regions (see the earlier section in this chapter that deals with the brain's organization of attention and Chapter 3 for more on motor control). At a more detailed level of brain anatomy, examining the circuitry in the brain at a microscopic level, the evidence is mixed for shared brain circuits between attention and motor control. Early evidence from stimulation of neurons in the frontal eye fields (FEFs) of the frontal cortex showed that stimulation of locations in the FEFs can produce both saccades and attention-like behaviour (Armstrong et al., 2006; Moore & Armstrong 2003; Moore & Fallah 2001). However, subsequent evidence suggesting that within the FEF this stimulation was activating multiple neuronal systems has weakened the empirical support for common brain circuitry (Smith & Schenk 2012; Thompson et al., 2005). Despite difficulty in proving shared circuitry, it still appears that, consistent with premotor theory, there are functional links between eye movements and attention-related increases in sensory processing (Fiebelkorn & Kastner, 2020). Thus there is ongoing research into premotor theory regarding functional equivalences between motor control and attention. For example, evidence has been provided that small eye movements towards a stimulus are required for attentional modulation of neuronal activity (Lowet et al., 2018).

Chapter 3, p97

Similar to the way it has been found that sensory processing of that location is facilitated when an eye movement is planned to a location, moving a limb to the vicinity of a target changes the allocation of attention to the target (Perry & Fallah, 2017). For example, it has been found that placing one's hand near a target, even when there is no reason or advantage for the hand to be in that location, changes the processing of a target (Abrams et al., 2008; Reed et al., 2006). These findings suggest that the presence of the hand results in attention being deployed to the region near the hand. Going beyond just the presence of a static hand, similar changes to attentional processing are found when planning and performing reaching and grasping movements (Pratt & Abrams, 1994; Rizzolati et al., 1994; Tipper et al., 1992). In fact it is even found that properties of the movement trajectory are influenced by the salience of the target and distractor objects (Howard & Tipper, 1997; Moher et al., 2015). Moreover, these effects appear to be modulated by task demands and it has been argued that the experiments exploring attention in action production demonstrate such a high degree of interconnectedness between movement intention, target selection and attention that it motivates a need to reconceptualize attention (Hommel et al., 2019).

Failures of Attention

Change blindness

Although we are very good at understanding the gist of a scene, we are not always so impressive in our capability to apprehend details of a scene. Convincing evidence of this comes from a phenomenon known as change blindness (Rensink, 2002; Rensink et al., 1997). Demonstrations of change blindness involve showing two nearly identical photos to an observer, each for 240 milliseconds, separated by a masking image of 80 milliseconds, and asking them to say what has changed in the image. The mask is necessary so that motion is not seen in the region around where the photos have been retouched. Observers are poor at spotting the change even though the cycle of photos is shown for up to 60 seconds, and as can be seen from the example in Figure 4.16 the change is extensive. These change blindness displays are prime examples that large changes can go unnoticed. Change blindness is related to a family of experimental results that have investigated how attention is related to whether or not we are able to report all aspects of what we see. In change blindness observers can freely search an image to detect the change, and thus a variety of factors related to how we search and remember image properties might be at work. In the next section we will see that even under conditions when eye movements and search are not required, the responses of observers are striking in terms of what they fail to report seeing.

> **Change blindness**
> the phenomenon where substantial differences between two nearly identical scenes are not noticed when presented sequentially.

Inattentional blindness

The term inattentional blindness was coined by Mack and Rock (1998) to describe the rather surprising visual phenomenon that we can be looking directly at a target but will report that we do not see it if attention is not allocated. The key experimental design is shown in Figure 4.17 (overleaf), which shows examples of what occurred for what Mack and Rock called non-critical and critical trials. By contrasting the difference between non-critical and critical trials we can see the effect of inattentional blindness. On both critical trials and non-critical trials a viewer's task was to first fixate on a central target and then,

> **Inattentional blindness**
> the failure to notice a clearly visible target due to attention being diverted from the target.

Figure 4.16 Change blindness.
Can you spot the difference? In a change blindness test, the images are shown one after another in sequence and observers are asked to spot the change. Very large changes go unnoticed and are difficult to detect even when both pictures are shown together. If you could not see the difference between images, the answer is given at the end of the chapter.

Source: © Ronald Rensink, available as a video file, along with other examples of change blindness at http://www.cs.ubc.ca/~rensink/flicker/download/index.html.

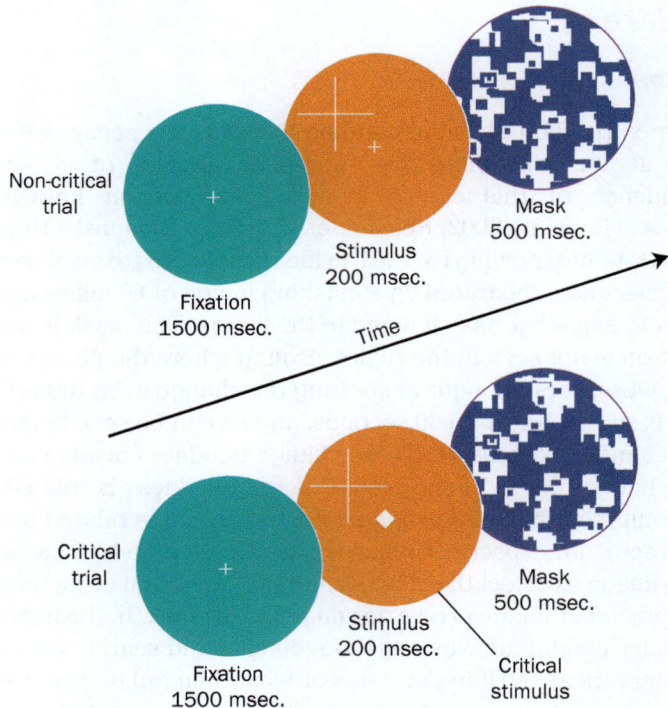

Figure 4.17 Demonstration of inattentional blindness.
Participants were instructed to fixate on a central cross and, after 1,500 milliseconds, a large cross appeared off fixation with different lengths of horizontal and vertical arms. Participants had to keep fixation while attending to the large cross and making their judgement of which arm of the cross was longer. On a small percentage of trials, termed critical trials, a small diamond unexpectedly appeared at fixation. At the end of the trials participants were asked if they saw anything different during the experiment, and 60–80 per cent of observers reported never seeing the small diamond figure appear at fixation.

Source: Adapted from Mack & Rock (1998).

when a large cross became visible, they were to examine it without moving their eyes to judge whether the horizontal or vertical arm of the cross was larger. Then a visual mask appeared to eliminate any **afterimage** and they reported which arm was longer. On the non-critical trials nothing happened at the fixation point and on the critical trials a small, unexpected figure appeared at fixation. It would seem common sense that on these critical trials people would experience seeing this small figure, however on 60–80 per cent of trials viewers failed to detect it even though it was at fixation in the centre of their view. These unexpected results from simple stimuli in a laboratory setting clearly demonstrate that although we go through life with the feeling that we are experiencing nearly all of what is appearing before our eyes, we are systematically able to miss events that are clearly presented to us if our attention is drawn away towards something else.

> **Afterimage**
> occurs when vision of an object remains after presentation has ceased – for example, after staring at a bright light.

The findings of Mack and Rock (1998) demonstrated that in the lab we can miss seeing a small diamond if our attention is diverted. While one could think that this result is just a peculiar curiosity of the psychology lab, subsequent research has shown that we can miss odd and otherwise startling visuals when our attention is directed elsewhere. These studies of inattentional blindness when viewing human activity began with the work of Dan Simons and colleagues. The work built upon earlier studies (Neisser & Becklen, 1975), which demonstrated that when people view two overlapping movies and are asked to attend to the activities of one movie they can miss striking changes in the other. For example, if a movie of people passing a basketball was overlapped with a movie of people slapping hands and people were asked to attend to the basketball movie they could miss when the hand-slapping game changed to handshaking. This task was modified by Simons and colleagues (e.g., Simons & Chabris, 1999) so that a single movie was shown. In this movie there were three players in white shirts who passed the ball among themselves along with three players in black shirts who passed among themselves. The task of observers was to count the number of passes of either the white or black team. Results showed that if an unexpected event happened during the movie, such as a person in a gorilla suit walked through the crowd, only approximately half of the viewers would notice this. Further research into how observers piece together a visual world from an edited movie was conducted by Levin and Simons (1997, 2000). They showed films with substantial differences between shots that were not detected. Examples of changes between shots include scarves appearing and disappearing as well as plates changing colour. Even though these changes are obvious once informed they go virtually unnoticed during natural viewing of the film, even when viewers are asked to watch carefully. Such errors in the continuity of a scene from one shot to the next occur even in high-budget films, as an internet search for continuity errors will reveal. See Box 4.6 for a discussion of psychological research into **continuity editing**.

> **Continuity editing**
> a film-making technique to produce a smooth continuous experience across changes in camera shot.

 Box 4.6 Practical Application: Attention and continuity editing in movies

As we watch a movie, different camera shots are constantly changing our view of a scene in a way that would never happen in real life. However, we typically do not find this disturbing and cheerfully pay to see the next movie. It would be satisfying if we could state the exact scientific principles behind how this seamless viewing experience is achieved, but it turns out that it is not known. Talented editors and film-makers are in effect applied psychologists with expertise in guiding our attention through a movie. It has even been argued that the evolution of film-making has led to timings of shot structures that best match the human attention system (Cutting, 2016; Cutting et al., 2010).

Work by Tim Smith has discussed how attention is manipulated in cuts from one shot to the next to obtain a continuous experience (Smith, 2010). As he points out, the explanation from the early days of film-making about why continuity editing worked was that we do not find cuts obtrusive since we can make the cut follow the expectation of the viewer (Münsterberg, 1916). For example, if one shot ends with someone turning their head to look at a particular object, then the next shot can show that object so as to guide attention from one shot to the next. This simple trick of initiating movement before a cut enables viewers to more quickly orient to the content of the new shot and to be less aware of the editing. This phenomenon was explored by Smith and Henderson (2008) in a study that used feature films to examine how different types of edit cuts affected perception. They compared four types of edit cuts for viewers' awareness that a cut had taken place. These four types of cuts were (1) cuts between scenes, (2) cuts within a scene, (3) cuts that matched action and (4) cuts that matched gaze (Figure 4.18, overleaf). Results showed that within scene and match action cuts had, respectively, 25 per cent and 32 per cent of cuts missed, while between scene and gaze match cuts had around 10 per cent of cuts missed. These results were consistent with the intuition used in continuity editing of film; that cuts which guide attention as well as provide a viewer with changing and optimum views of the action add interest to the viewer and engage them with the narrative. Engagement of the viewer with the narrative promotes inattentional blindness and this also helps to explain why these edit cuts are most invisible to an observer.

An interesting aspect of this research application is that the practical art of telling stories by moving images has become so advanced that most of the issues psychologists study aren't currently major

Figure 4.18 How a cut is made influences whether a viewer will be aware it was made.
Viewers watched excerpts from seven feature films for five minutes each and were asked to press a button every time they saw an edit. The data were analysed for four types of editing cuts: between scenes, within scenes, match action and gaze match. Results showed that within scene and match action cuts were most invisible. This is consistent with the fact that these guide attention and induce inattentional blindness.

Source: © Dr Tim Smith, Smith & Henderson (2008, p. 6). Stills from *Blade Runner* (dir. Ridley Scott, 1982).

practical problems since effective tools of the trade to present a visual narrative have evolved through a century of development. Nonetheless, film-making is a dynamic industry, and both film-makers and scientists are interested in how future practice can be shaped through a richer understanding of why current techniques are successful. In particular, research examining visual narratives (Loschky et al., 2020) is beginning to be able to describe how basic visual processes systematically combine to aid understanding of the depicted story. These findings might ultimately help us to better understand how the visual narrative interacts with the processing of film edits.

A real-world activity in which inattentional blindness has been reported to occur is driving, and it can contribute to serious accidents (National Safety Council, 2010; Qin et al., 2019). When driving is combined with any other task, the scene is set for dual task effects to decrease performance in driving due to attentional resources being consumed by the non-driving task. For example, individuals have reported driving through red lights without stopping while apparently looking directly at a traffic-light signal. Even though they could 'see' that the light was red, their attention was diverted to another activity like speaking on a mobile phone and this compromised their ability to attend to the driving environment. Our susceptibility to miss important aspects of the world has been revealed by the scientific study of magic. Box 4.7 discusses this further.

Box 4.7 When Things Go Wrong: Attention, misdirection and magic

In many ways, magic is a field unto itself. When young children try to explain how a trick worked, they often resort to supernatural explanations that take magic at face value and report simply that magic was the method used to perform the trick (Olson et al., 2015). However, a more critical view from the perspective of cognitive psychology suggests that magic works by capitalizing on human cognitive limitations. As such, it has been suggested that the scientific study of magic holds potential benefits for both magic and cognitive psychology (Kuhn & Tatler, 2005; Kuhn et al., 2008; Macknik et al., 2008; Lamont et al., 2010). Magic captivates an audience because the perceived effects of the magic trick have no obvious explanation from the methods experienced while viewing the trick. This dissociation between what happened and how it was achieved often relies on obfuscating the methods by use of a misdirection.

Misdirection in magic is a complex topic that involves explaining how a magician can direct an observer away from understanding the methods used to achieve a magical result. It is argued that misdirection can act at many different psychological levels, including perception, memory and reasoning. Here we will focus on the role attention can play to enable misdirection. In their discussion of a psychologically motivated taxonomy of misdirection, Kuhn and colleagues (2014) outline a detailed framework for how attention can contribute to misdirection (Figure 4.19). The three main factors of attentional misdirection include the focus of attention (where attention is deployed), the timing of attention (when attention is deployed) and the resources given (how much attention is deployed). While in practice these three factors might be hard to separate in any magic trick, we will discuss them individually now.

The focus of attention can be manipulated through either external or internal means. With external events there are, of course, loud noises or light flashes that would distract a person from seeing the method. However, these are generally frowned upon due to their somewhat obvious nature. Instead, it is preferred to organize presentation of the trick so that the critical aspects of the method would be shown in areas of low interest, while regions of little importance would be presented in regions with high interest. Performing magic is social and thus external attention can be manipulated through social influence, such as bringing someone from the audience on stage who will attract attention (Smith, 2015) or by the magician gazing in a certain direction, which will also attract attention to that region (Tatler & Kuhn, 2007). Similarly, if a trick requires a particular sleight of hand, it is important that this sleight action looks natural so it does not draw attention (Phillips et al., 2015). With manipulations of internal attention, the goal is to lead someone's expectations and interests away from elements that would reveal the critical method. Giving instructions such as shuffling a deck of cards or writing down information will guide a person to direct their attention to a task that is irrelevant to the procedure being conducted. Similarly, surprise can be used. For example, in a trick where participants are told that a coin will disappear on the third strike of the wand, this will draw attention to the coin and away from the wand, thus creating an opportunity to make the wand disappear. It is also important that the audience remain engaged and motivated by the activity of the magician, because it is thought that without

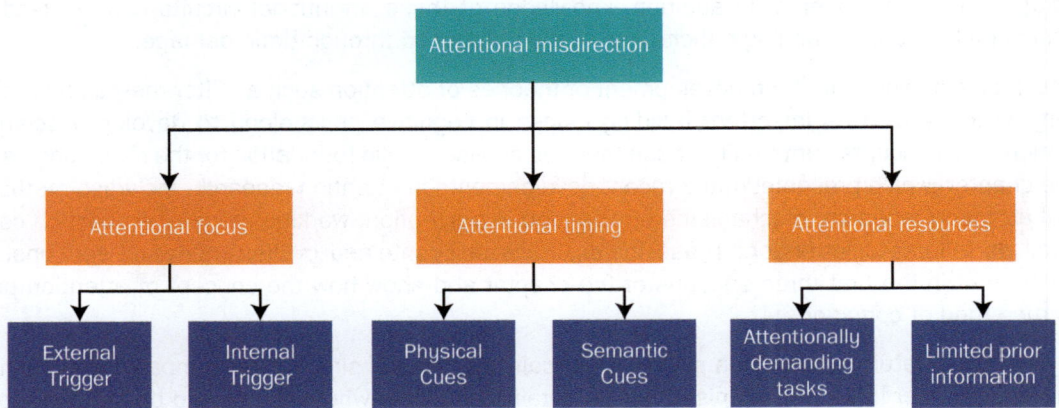

Figure 4.19 A schematic of attentional misdirection.
The three factors involved in attentional misdirection (Kuhn et al., 2014) and the mechanisms that underlie these factors.

the motivation for trying to follow or understand the trick, it is more likely that an unmotivated observer will attend to things that the magician does not want them to see (Lamont & Wiseman, 1999).

Misdirection through attentional timing is achieved through either physical or semantic means. Physical interventions include controlling the tension of the audience members through aspects of the performance such as posture, sound or light, to increase or decrease the overall attention of the audience. By modulating the vigilance of the audience so that it runs counter to times when critical methods are performed, the chance of detection can be decreased. Semantic means of obtaining misdirection involve the narrative structure of the performance – for example, individuals are less likely to be looking for key aspects of the method early in performing a trick or just as some other important event has occurred.

Misdirection through attentional resources is achieved through either increasing attentional demands or limiting prior exposure. Increasing the attentional demands – for example, by asking the audience to keep track of the colour of cards in a card trick – enables the magician to attract attentional resources to a distraction that might otherwise have been available to catch the method behind the trick. Similarly, if exposure to the trick is limited then more attention will be required when viewing it. This is because when an event is repeated an observer can gain fluency in processing the stream of events and this familiarity is associated with less demand on attentional resources.

In conclusion, a key feature of the success of magic is the failure of attention to detect the methods underlying the tricks. Evidence from research into failures of attention indicates that our moment-to-moment experience of the world is incomplete. However, intuitively, we seem to believe that our perception is complete, and this belief is undermined to create a world of magic.

Summary

Attention is a broad field that encompasses an enormous empirical literature and is of practical importance when understanding how we process information in increasingly complex, technology-driven environments. At the beginning of the chapter, we presented a taxonomy of attention, which provided a general framework to organize our thoughts about attention.

Following this, we described regions of the human brain that have been implicated as working together to form attentional networks. This knowledge provides basic ideas about how attention is organized and gives further evidence that rather than being one system, attention arises from the coordinated activity of different systems. In addition, knowledge of these attentional circuits can be used as a starting point for understanding deficits in attention produced through brain damage.

We next gave an account of the development of theories of attention such as filter theory and resource theory, which served as important building blocks in cognitive psychology to develop a science of attention. The concepts surrounding these theories provide a solid foundation for the remaining aspects of the chapter, which presented more recent developments in attention research, including methods of visual attention research, mechanisms of attention in perception, working memory and action control, as well as failures of attention. These topics, while self-contained in their individual sections, draw upon content in the first three sections of the chapter and show how the concept of attention permeates the study of cognition.

The ubiquitous nature of attention makes it difficult to provide a single all-encompassing definition of attention. Whether in the future this might be obtained, or even whether it should be set as a goal, is an open question. However, what is clear is that the many ways that attention provides the ability to process some elements more quickly and to greater depth than others is a critical capability.

Review Questions

1. What are the implications of attention being a limited resource?
2. How do filter theory and resource theory compare to each other and the so-called bottleneck of attention?
3. Is visual attention directed towards objects or locations in space?
4. What can a dual task experimental paradigm reveal about attention?
5. What is the relationship between the dorsal attention network and the ventral attention network?
6. How do change blindness and inattentional blindness compare to each other?

 Discussion Questions

1. Given the diversity of phenomena that can be described as attention, is this still a useful concept to advance cognitive psychology?
2. The distinction between internal and external attention made in the taxonomy of attention (Chun et al., 2011) has been criticized by Oberauer (2019) because 'The memory of a tree is not more internal than the perception of a tree: Both are internal representations of external objects.' What are the two sides to this disagreement?
3. What happens to information that we do not attend to?
4. How will attention influence behaviour directed at search and foraging?

Further Reading

Chun, M. M., Golomb, J. D., & Turk-Browne, N. B. (2011). A taxonomy of external and internal attention. *Annual Review of Psychology, 62,* 73–101.

Cohen, R. A. (2014). *The neuropsychology of attention.* Springer.

Gazzaley, A., & Rosen, L. D. (2016). *The distracted mind: Ancient brains in a high-tech world.* MIT Press.

Hommel, B., Chapman, C. S., Cisek, P., Neyedli, H. F., Song, J. H., & Welsh, T. N. (2019). No one knows what attention is. *Attention, Perception, & Psychophysics, 81*(7), 2288–2303.

Kahneman, D. (1973). *Attention and effort* (Vol. 1063). Prentice-Hall.

Kuhn, G. (2019). *Experiencing the impossible: The science of magic.* MIT Press.

Pashler, H. E. (1998). *The psychology of attention.* MIT Press.

Posner, M. I. (2012). *Cognitive neuroscience of attention* (2nd ed.). New York: Guilford Press.

Styles, E. A. (2006). *The psychology of attention* (2nd ed.). Psychology Press.

Wickens, C. D., & McCarley, J. S. (2008). *Applied attention theory.* CRC Press.

Wu, W. (2014). *Attention.* Routledge.

Answer to Chapter Problem

In Figure 4.16, the change is in the trees above the statue's back.

CONSCIOUSNESS

5

PREVIEW QUESTIONS

INTRODUCTION
  ! **Box 5.1 When Things Go Wrong:** Sleepwalking and the law

FUNCTIONS OF CONSCIOUSNESS
  SELF-AWARENESS AND INTEGRATION
  Box 5.2 Practical Application: The effects of general anaesthesia on consciousness
  THE CASE AGAINST CONSCIOUSNESS
  UNCONSCIOUS PROCESSING
  Box 5.3 Research Close Up: Promoting healthy eating with supraliminal primes

CONSCIOUSNESS AND THE BRAIN
  NEUROPSYCHOLOGY
  NEURAL CORRELATES OF CONSCIOUSNESS (NCC)
  GLOBAL WORKSPACE APPROACHES
  Box 5.4 Research Close Up: Consciousness and brain networks
  ATTENTION AND CONSCIOUSNESS
  AGENCY, VOLITION AND CONSCIOUSNESS
  ! **Box 5.5 When Things Go Wrong:** Out-of-body experience
  METACOGNITION AND HIGHER-ORDER THEORIES OF CONSCIOUSNESS

SUMMARY

REVIEW QUESTIONS

DISCUSSION QUESTIONS

FURTHER READING

Preview Questions

1. Why is consciousness a difficult topic for scientific inquiry?
2. What is the function of consciousness? Why do we have it?
3. How much can unconscious processing change our behaviour?
4. Do we know what principles the brain uses to obtain consciousness?
5. What is the relationship between attention and consciousness?
6. Is there experimental evidence to show that we have free will?

INTRODUCTION

Consciousness is a complex concept that has been contemplated over thousands of years in multiple ways, and stands at the crossroads of psychological, philosophical, cultural and spiritual explanations of our most fundamental experiences. Its complexity, along with the multiple forms of description used to explain it has made consciousness difficult to study from a purely scientific approach. Indeed, it is only recently that consciousness has found itself presented in any detail in textbooks such as this one. Advocates for the scientific study of consciousness, such as the Nobel laureate Francis Crick (1995), have pointed out that while consciousness is challenging for science to explain, it is too important a topic for science to ignore. Evidence for the practical importance of understanding consciousness comes from domains such as medicine and law, where **operational definitions** are required to make crucial life and death decisions. For example, in Chapter 1 we discussed how brain imaging has been used to determine whether someone appearing to be in a vegetative state can demonstrate consciousness (see Box 1.5), and in Box 5.1 we discuss how a neuropsychological understanding of consciousness during sleep informs legal decisions about crimes committed while sleepwalking. In light of these important applications, we can see the significance of gaining a greater scientific understanding of consciousness.

> **Operational definition**
> a description involving the actions, procedures or processes that can be used to evidence how a phenomenon is observed and measured.

> Chapter 1, p18

Interest in consciousness within cognitive psychology goes back to the early days in the writings of another Nobel laureate Roger Sperry and his interest in the mind–brain problem of how to identify brain activity related to consciousness (Sperry, 1952). This interest helped lead to his seminal work on split-brain patients, described in Box 10.4, which questioned whether consciousness could possibly be separable between the two halves of the brain. Since that time, there has been continued interest in finding aspects of consciousness that are open to scientific explanation. For example, different states of consciousness such as wakefulness versus sleep can be distinguished based on measures of electrical activity in the brain as reflected in measures of **EEG** (Zeman, 2006). Wakefulness, except in cases of severe brain damage, is what we commonly would consider to be consciousness. While the term awareness is often used interchangeably with consciousness, in a more technical sense it can be considered to be the contents of consciousness. Somewhat remarkably, our awareness spans a broad range of psychological capacities, including perceptions, thoughts, memories and emotions. Because we can report on our awareness and this awareness can be assessed using objective means, cognitive psychology has made great strides in detailing process and function in awareness.

> **Electroencephalography (EEG)**
> a functional brain imaging method showing waves of electrical activity from scalp recorders.

Going past understanding awareness as the contents of consciousness to a definitive understanding of consciousness has proven difficult. This difficulty is illustrated by an argument in philosophy that treats understanding the process and function of awareness as the easy problem of consciousness, while understanding consciousness itself is the hard problem (Chalmers, 1995; 1996; 2017). In this view, finding the brain activity correlated to general and specific conscious states is the easy problem(s). The hard problem(s) is to understand why that neural state has an associated conscious state at all and why it is associated with that particular conscious state; or more generally understanding why any neural (or physical) state has any associated conscious state.

One way to see the potential limitation of solving the easy problem can be illustrated with the thought experiment of 'Mary's Room' (Jackson, 1982). Imagine Mary to be a brilliant colour scientist who, somewhat cruelly, has been born and raised in a totally black-and-white environment. As a scientist, she knows all the physics, biology, psychology and neuroscience related to seeing the colour yellow. In other words, science provides her with a thorough knowledge about what it means to see yellow. The question arises if she is allowed to leave her black-and-white room and see yellow for the first time. Will her experience of seeing yellow be entirely predictable to Mary from her previous objective knowledge, or will the subjective experience of seeing yellow be something different? Will this subjective experience of yellow, termed qualia, have something that goes beyond what is available from the wealth of objective description?

> **Qualia**
> qualities of experience, most typically perceptual experience.

Another way of looking at this question of whether science can adequately explain consciousness can be by considering the following definition of consciousness: *that to be conscious is to be aware of one's own existence as evidenced by thoughts and perception of one's surroundings*. While this appears a sensible and adequate definition, deeper consideration reveals that it relies upon subjective, first-person experience of 'one's own existence' rather than the sort of objective, third-person perspective we expect from science. To further illustrate this, contemplate the existence and importance of your own consciousness while considering the following two claims:

1 I believe that my consciousness exists and that while both myself and the computer I use are made of physical stuff that process information, there is something about my mental life that sets me apart from the computer.

2 I cannot absolutely convince myself that others who read these words are conscious, nor do I think that I can absolutely convince others that I am conscious.

The purpose of this exercise is to clear the air that no matter whether you do or do not believe in consciousness or its importance, there currently is no unique, watertight, logical argument that can confirm or disconfirm these beliefs. The hard problem of consciousness is indeed hard. Calling what science can currently explain the easy problem should not trivialize what science can contribute, but rather should help us to focus on the challenges ahead. Certainly, the limits of what science can explain about consciousness are not yet known and there is hope that further illumination of the scientific basis of consciousness will bring practical benefits.

Our presentation of consciousness first addresses the question of why we have consciousness and what functions it might serve. From there, we move on to the issue that not all information that we process appears to enter our conscious awareness. How this unconscious processing might alter our behaviour is a long-standing issue in psychology and helps to guide us in understanding what is significant about the boundary between conscious and unconscious processing. Next, we address the important question of how brain activity correlates with consciousness, and relate this brain activity to different theories of consciousness. Exploration of brain activity correlated with consciousness addresses the essential issue of how consciousness comes to be. In the final three sections of the chapter we further explore the neural basis of consciousness while relating the areas of attention, agency, volition and metacognition to consciousness. These areas are all tightly intertwined with consciousness, and their study helps to illuminate how advances in research into consciousness have influenced and been influenced by other domains of psychology.

Box 5.1 When Things Go Wrong: Sleepwalking and the law

Sleepwalking occurs in 2–3 per cent of adults, with 0.4 per cent of adults having a weekly sleepwalk episode; in children it is even more common, with a prevalence of around 15 per cent in 5–12 year olds (Plazzi et al., 2005; Provini et al., 2011). In most cases the sleepwalk will begin in the first hours of sleep, and the sleepwalker will move about with their eyes open but displaying a low level of arousal and awareness, before returning to bed in 15–30 minutes (Provini et al., 2011). However, in some cases, complex behaviour is exhibited during a sleepwalk and extreme cases illustrate the challenging area where science and the law intersect. There is the well-known case of a man in Ontario, Canada, who after falling asleep on his living room couch got up, drove 23 kilometres, took a tyre iron and a hatchet out of the boot of his car, entered his wife's parents' house, went to their bedroom, assaulted his father-in-law and killed his mother-in-law. He then drove to a nearby police station and with a somewhat confused confession turned himself in to the police. Although it was clear what he had done, he was later acquitted of both assault and murder. To understand how this decision could have been reached, we will first consider the mental states associated with sleepwalking and then how these relate to the law.

> **Rapid eye movement (REM) sleep**
> during REM sleep the eyes move rapidly from side to side behind closed eyelids. Brain wave activity becomes closer to that seen in wakefulness, dreaming often occurs, and arm and leg muscles become temporarily paralysed.
>
> **Non-rapid eye movement (NREM) sleep**
> non-rapid eye movement (NREM) sleep has three stages, including the deep sleep you need to feel refreshed in the morning. During NREM sleep, muscles relax, dreaming is rare and brain waves have distinct characteristics.

Sleepwalking is a complicated phenomenon that can be understood in terms of the basic properties of sleep. When we sleep, there are the two basic states that include rapid eye movement (**REM**) sleep and non-rapid eye movement (**NREM**) sleep. Typically, during one night, we go through several cycles characterized by progressively deeper levels of NREM sleep punctuated with REM sleep. REM sleep brings about vivid dreaming that leads to a lighter level of NREM sleep and the beginning of another cycle. It turns out that sleepwalking occurs at the deepest level of NREM sleep. A general property of sleep is that by entering into the sleep cycle we are forming a disconnection between executive function in frontal cortex and the remainder of the brain (Braun et al., 1997). In other words, the evaluative and critical aspects that monitor our behaviour are not online. Intuitive evidence that this might be so is demonstrated by how uncritically we respond to some actually very bizarre events of our dreams. You might think that if the sleepwalker could move, then their frontal cortex and executive function would be engaged. However, brain imaging data from a single sleepwalker indicates that although the motor systems of the brain are working, the disconnect with executive function is still in place and the mind continues to be asleep (Bassetti et al., 2000). It thus appears that sleepwalkers are in a complex state between wakefulness, deep sleep and dreaming; importantly, they do not have control over their behaviour, which includes critical evaluation of their acts.

Returning to the case of the Canadian sleepwalking killer, we begin with the fact that he could not be deemed legally insane since sleepwalking is considered a sleep disorder and not a mental illness (Glancy et al., 2002). Next it is important to consider the properties required by many legal systems to establish guilt; these include that a person's mental state in regard to the criminal act is purposeful, knowing, reckless or negligent (Hirstein & Sifferd, 2011). Thus, for his acquittal, there must have been evidence that his actions weren't purposeful, knowing, reckless or negligent. We can dismiss negligence as a first step since, although he had a long history of sleepwalking, there was no reason for him to ever imagine a sleepwalk could go so wrong. To dismiss the other three conditions it is necessary to consider whether one can be purposeful, knowing, negligent or indeed conscious without the functions of executive control afforded by our frontal cortex integrated into our brain activity. Moreover, without executive function it is impossible to see how actions can be purposeful, knowing or reckless. In this way we can reach a verdict that agrees with the Canadian legal system.

FUNCTIONS OF CONSCIOUSNESS

In Chapter 2 we discussed a proposal by Marr (1982) that to understand any information processing system we must do so at a computational level. That is to say we need to know what it achieves and why it does what it does. Here, we relate Marr's proposal to consciousness and address the question of what is the function of consciousness.

> Chapter 2, p34

Self-Awareness and Integration

The subjective nature of consciousness suggests that it is tightly bound to awareness of our own self, and this **reflexive** connection provides a window into understanding our own thoughts and actions. This aspect of consciousness is special as it demonstrates a self-referential capability for the cognitive system to monitor itself. Consciousness of our self can provide us with an understanding of our own mental status, and it is thought that this understanding of our own status can be transferred to understand the status of others (Humphrey, 2002). This understanding of others provides us with a theory of mind (Baron-Cohen, 1997; Frith & Frith, 1999) that helps to guide us in social interactions. Self-consciousness of our mental world extends into an understanding of our physical body. Self-consciousness of our body is modelled to arise from an integration of two major sources of sensory information: **interoceptive** signals such as those that indicate heartbeat, and external sensory information such as vision or audition (Park & Blanke, 2019). This experience of self is a critical aspect of meditation, which in recent decades has gained increased interest in its scientific study (Vieten et al., 2018). Some reports of meditation practitioners indicate anomalous and seemingly bizarre states of self-consciousness, but these are highly controversial. There is, however, increasing evidence that a variant of meditation known as mindfulness is able to employ exercises in self-consciousness to improve well-being (Bartlett et al., 2019; Tang & Braver, 2020). A critical element of mindfulness is to develop greater awareness of our thoughts and body, and their relationship with one another. While at present our understanding is incomplete, it appears that self-consciousness can function to improve our health and well-being.

> **Reflexive**
> self-referential.

> **Interoception**
> sensitivity to internal bodily stimuli.

Another function proposed for consciousness is that it provides us with an executive summary of our current situation (Koch, 2004). Even with attention to limit input there is still a constant inflow of information from the world and any of a large number of personal desires we might wish to satisfy at any one time. The executive summary produced by consciousness might primarily serve to integrate this vast amount of information. This idea of consciousness performing an integrative function is similar to that proposed by **global workspace theory** (Baars, 1988, 2002), where consciousness facilitates flexible context-driven behaviour. An implication of consciousness performing an integrative function is that consciousness would work across extensive brain networks with the task of creating a joint summary for these networks. These integrative aspects of consciousness have been proposed to involve acting over both the role of attention in providing feelings of pain, colour, etc., as well as providing interpretive capabilities in constructing past and present events. Consideration of what is integrated and how the process of integration might influence the effects of general anaesthesia on consciousness is discussed in Box 5.2.

> **Global workspace theory**
> proposes that consciousness requires interactions across a broad range of brain areas.
>
> **Access consciousness**
> includes representations that are broadcast for use in reasoning and control of action and can be reported.
>
> **Phenomenal consciousness**
> includes the experiential properties of sensations, feelings and perceptions.

The importance of the integrative aspect of consciousness is also evident in one distinction made in in the field of consciousness between the concepts of '**access consciousness**' and '**phenomenal consciousness**' (Block, 1995). Access consciousness refers to conscious information that is accessible to numerous cognitive processors, such as those mediating working memory, verbal report or motor behaviour. Phenomenal consciousness refers to an idealized situation of pure subjective experience (also called qualia) without further associated information processing. One example of phenomenal consciousness is when we hear a noise like the refrigerator switching off – we can feel that we have heard it all along, but without noticing it until it turns off.

>
> ### Box 5.2 Practical Application: The effects of general anaesthesia on consciousness
>
> It is possibly stating the obvious that consciousness is a central consideration of general anaesthesia during major surgery. During surgery it is necessary to keep a person still and unresponsive to what would typically be tremendously painful. Although there is little question of the effectiveness of anaesthesia in enabling surgery, there are many questions as to how anaesthesia works and the state(s) of consciousness induced by anaesthesia. One roadblock to answering these questions comes from the fact that anaesthesia commonly induces amnesia. Thus, even if there was a rich conscious experience during surgery, it will not be remembered. Of concern though is the possibility of negative experience during surgery that could lead to the formation of **implicit memories** that might have detrimental psychological effects, even if there would be no explicit recall. These concerns and how they might be addressed scientifically have drawn together researchers in the fields of both consciousness and anaesthesia (Bonhomme et al., 2019; Sanders et al., 2012).
>
> > **Non-declarative or implicit memory**
> > memory that is not accessed consciously and that we are not able to report verbally. It includes memory which benefits from previous experience but without our awareness of that experience.
>
> Research into anaesthesia and consciousness defines three types of consciousness: unconsciousness, connected consciousness and disconnected consciousness. With unconsciousness, there is no external or internal awareness and this could typically be thought of as the goal of anaesthesia. In connected consciousness there is both external and internal awareness. It is thought that at least 5 per cent of patients might undergo a transient event of connected consciousness during surgery (Sanders et al., 2016), though they will not recall this incident afterwards. In disconnected consciousness, like a dream state, there is no external awareness but there is internal awareness. In fact, one study provided evidence that dreams occur during anaesthesia (Radek et al., 2018).
>
> One observation about these three states of consciousness is that they do not lie on a single-track continuum from light anaesthesia to heavy anaesthesia. Consistent with this, a review of the states of consciousness associated with different drugs and their hypothesized impact on brain activity suggests there is no common pathway towards effective anaesthesia (Bonhomme et al., 2019). Instead, it seems anaesthesia works by several different mechanisms that alter balance in the brain between the integration and segregation of information (Mashour, 2018). Studies investigating brain activity under anaesthesia do indicate disruption of the function of large-scale networks (Banks et al., 2020; Li et al., 2019; Vlisides et al., 2019). Relating these findings about anaesthesia and brains to consciousness, it has been suggested that anaesthesia works by fragmenting the self (Sleigh et al., 2018). In this view, anaesthesia is seen to fragment the typical hierarchy of components of the self, such as awareness of existence (core self), embodied self (sentience), executive self (agency/volition) and various other higher-order cognitive processes that normally interact with one another. States of disconnected consciousness arise as the core self is fragmented from these other aspects, until at the deepest level of anaesthesia there is only a disembodied core self that remains.

The Case Against Consciousness

Up to now, and for most of this chapter, we present a case for the importance of consciousness. Here, we pause to mention some critical views of consciousness that argue against its importance. The first, conscious inessentialism, claims that consciousness is simply not necessary. A basis of this argument is that we can take any behaviour and internal function performed by a conscious agent and have it performed by something that is not conscious. Descriptions of how this might come about typically invoke what philosophers of mind call 'zombies', which can perform the same actions without being conscious (Moody, 1994). While the assertion that consciousness is not essential might not seem correct, particularly with respect to our own feelings of consciousness, it is hard to thoroughly disprove. Moreover, cases appear where the argument has a ring of truth. For example, you might not be able to report anything that happened while driving on a long highway journey, and thus your zombie replacement would seem equally qualified.

The second view, epiphenomenalism, does not reject the existence of consciousness but holds that it has no function. T.H. Huxley likened consciousness to the whistle on a locomotive engine that makes a noise but is not involved at all in the primary mechanism of moving the train (Huxley, 1896). Like conscious inessentialism, such a view is hard to disprove. However, one idea for how such a situation might have arisen is that consciousness is an evolutionary **spandrel**, that it occurred as the by-product of adaptive selection of some other characteristic (Robinson et al., 2015). For further details of the philosophical basis of consciousness see the work of Dennett (Dennett, 1991; Schneider, 2017). Finally, **illusionism** is another term for these views against the requirement that consciousness explain anything of a special nature of experience (Frankish, 2016).

> **Spandrel**
> something that occurs as a by-product of the evolution of some other characteristic, rather than being a direct product of adaptive selection.
>
> **Illusionism**
> the view that consciousness is an introspective illusion caused by introspection creating the misrepresentation that experiences have special properties.
>
> **Subliminal perception**
> the case where a stimulus is presented below threshold (e.g., too fast or too dim) but its effects on behaviour can still be measured.

Unconscious Processing

Unconscious processing has long held a place in the study of consciousness. Starting with the work on **subliminal perception** (Pierce & Jastrow, 1884) the question has been asked whether it is possible to obtain a change in behaviour after being exposed to a stimulus that does not reach awareness (for example, an image shown very briefly). On the one hand it would seem that almost by definition such a thing could not occur. However, given the complex and distributed nature of cognitive structures it seems probable that we would internally possess information of which we have no awareness (Erdelyi, 1974), and thus it does not seem beyond question that this unconscious processing could change our behaviour.

A matter of terminology is useful to make here at the start of this section. The term unconscious is often used interchangeably with the term nonconscious. A primary difference between the two is that the term unconscious can mean when a person is asleep or has suffered a head injury. In the case of subliminal perception a person is awake and some researchers have adopted the term nonconscious to help make this distinction. Here we choose to use the term unconscious to avoid adopting another term, and alert the reader to this choice.

A subliminal stimulus, which is below the threshold of perception, can be contrasted with a supraliminal stimulus, which is above the threshold of perception. Critical for this division between subliminal and supraliminal stimuli is the perceptual threshold that defines the stimulus intensity below which (subliminal) the stimulus is not perceived and above which (supraliminal) the stimulus is perceived. One inherent complexity in the study of subliminal perception comes from how thresholds are measured and defined. In fact, the difficulty in experimentally obtaining meaningful and stable threshold measurements in the face of biased and sometimes unreliable human judgements has motivated development of the entire field of **psychophysics** since its origin by Gustav Fechner in the 1800s (Kingdom & Prins, 2016). Even with care in obtaining a threshold we still have the situation that thresholds are often defined as probabilities. For example, the loudness at which 50 per cent of the time an observer would report hearing a certain tone and 50 per cent of the time wouldn't report hearing the same tone can be thought of as the threshold for hearing the tone. An issue with this is that a tone that can be recognized 20 per cent of the time is certainly subliminal by a technical definition, but is still of sufficient intensity to be reported 20 per cent of the time. Thus, when performing experiments with subliminal stimuli there is always the risk that results can be driven by the percentage of experimental trials when we can expect that the subliminal stimulus did reach awareness. To avoid this issue in the interpretation of subliminal stimuli it is necessary to obtain some form of verification on a trial-by-trial basis that the stimulus did not enter awareness.

> **Psychophysics**
> a branch of psychology that examines the relationship between physical properties of stimuli and the resulting sensations and psychological events produced by these stimuli.

Obtaining evidence from the use of subliminal stimuli to experimentally verify an influence of unconscious processing on behaviour has proven to be a controversial and challenging area of research (Merikle & Daneman, 1998; Stein et al., 2020). We can illustrate the challenge by describing one kind of experimental design used in vision to explore unconscious processing (a similar design is described in Chapter 7). This design consists of showing participants two visual stimuli: one stimulus is called the **prime** and the other is called the target (Reingold & Merikle, 1988). The goal of the experiment is to find evidence that unconscious processing of the prime influences how the target is processed. In other words, a participant cannot be aware of the stimulus used as a prime, but its presence must be shown to influence how the target is perceived. To be able to verify that there was no awareness of the prime it is essential that experimenters solve the difficult problem of creating an effective way to monitor awareness of the prime. When evidence of unconscious processing is found it is useful to characterize the depth of this processing. Does it occur at a shallow, perceptual level (e.g., the prime produces a change in perceived lightness of the target) or does it occur at a deeper level involving meaning and semantics? A review of these results (Kouider & Faivre, 2017) suggests that unconscious processing of subliminal stimuli, which do not reach awareness, does indeed occur and can include processing of semantics. However, these effects are weak and comparable to non-specific properties that also influence the formation of behaviour.

> Chapter 7, p230

> **Prime**
> name for the stimulus used to affect subsequent response in an experiment.

In contrast to research in subliminal perception, researchers in social cognition have shown that unconscious processing of information can also be explored using supraliminal stimuli as primes (Bargh, 2016). Just as with experiments using subliminal stimuli as primes it is necessary for participants to not be aware of the prime when it is presented supraliminally. While supraliminal primes might seem contradictory, the key factor with priming in such instances is that although the prime is physically above the perceptual threshold, there is an aspect of the prime that is hidden and not obvious. Thus, when participants are asked at the completion of the experiment what they thought about the prime, they should rarely even mention it and if they do they should not be able to report anything meaningful. If they do happen to report understanding of the purpose of the prime then they can be removed from the data. However, just as with subliminal priming, confirmation that the prime was not processed consciously can be methodologically difficult (Shanks, 2017). An example of an experiment using unconscious priming is given in Box 5.3, which describes an experiment that investigated how a positive health prime, in the form of a free recipe flyer, was used to obtain healthier shopping habits in overweight grocery shoppers (Papies et al., 2014). The phenomenon of unconscious priming has many similarities with a form of behaviour engineering known by the term **nudge** (Thaler & Sunstein, 2009). While in principle using nudges to guide behaviour can appear better than more heavy-handed approaches, there are clearly ethical issues around the intention to guide the behaviour of individuals without their conscious awareness (Hansen & Jespersen, 2013).

> **Nudge**
> colloquially, a nudge is a gentle push; in the field of behaviour engineering it is the concept of unconsciously promoting one path of behaviour while not being restrictive about the availability or reward of other paths of behaviour.

 Box 5.3 Research Close Up: Promoting healthy eating with supraliminal primes

Source: Papies et al. (2014).

INTRODUCTION

This study used supraliminal primes in a **field study** to examine whether primes for healthy eating could change shopping behaviour by reducing the purchase of snack food. A motivation for the study was that in many places in the world there is an abundance of opportunities to consume food, particularly high-calorie snacks, and this has contributed to large numbers of people who are overweight and obese. Thus, providing a means to reduce consumption of snack food would be helpful in promoting better health. In particular, an approach using primes that would be effective in a real-world scenario could provide a helpful addition to existing ways of promoting healthy behaviour.

> **Field study**
> the collection of raw data outside of the laboratory in a natural environment.

The study chose to focus on high-calorie snacks due to the fact that overweight and obese individuals consume more of these food items than do typical individuals (Forslund et al., 2005). In addition, it targeted grocery shopping, since this event could potentially influence eating behaviour for several days and for an entire household. When considering the possible effectiveness of the prime it was noted that previous literature on priming has indicated that it is effective mostly when the prime is consistent with the goal state of the person receiving the prime (Custers & Aarts, 2010). Thus, it was predicted that the prime should work primarily on individuals who are overweight and obese as they are more likely to have the goal of healthy eating (Bish et al., 2005).

METHODS

A single experiment was performed in the field and employed a 2 × 2 between participant design. One experimental factor involved the weight status of the participant (overweight/obese versus normal weight) and the other factor involved the healthy eating prime manipulation (health prime versus control). Both the health prime and the control condition contained a simple low-calorie recipe accompanied by a picture. However, in the healthy eating prime around the main text were included words such as 'healthy', 'good for your figure' and the amount of calories, while the control condition was accompanied by neutral text such as 'new recipe', 'try it out'. Both conditions were supraliminal, but the health prime contained a message that could interact with the goal state of wanting to lose weight. Ninety-nine customers (5 men and 94 women, with a mean age of approximately 54 years) of a local supermarket agreed to participate in the experiment. They were met at the entrance of the supermarket and asked if they were willing to participate in a study on the way they do their grocery shopping. They were given a recipe flyer that contained either the health prime or the control condition. After completing their shopping and paying for their groceries, participants were met by a second experimenter,

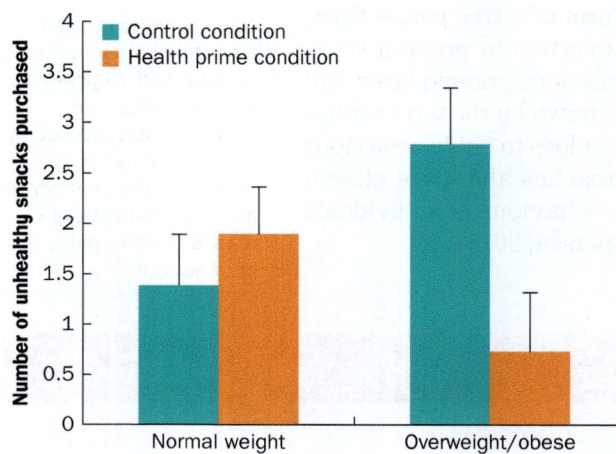

Figure 5.1 Results of a health prime on shopping behaviour in normal-weight and overweight/obese shoppers.

A prime for healthy eating influenced the shopping behaviour to purchase less snack food, but only for overweight and obese shoppers. Error bars indicate standard error of the mean.

Source: Papies et al. (2014).

who asked their weight and height and took a digital photo of their receipt so that contents of their shopping could be evaluated for purchase of unhealthy snack foods. Participants also provided demographic information and completed a brief questionnaire that assessed their attention to the flyer. They were also presented with a suspicion check that asked if they had noticed anything special about the recipe and what they thought was the purpose of the experiment.

RESULTS

Results showed that while the normal-weight group showed no effect of the health prime, for overweight/obese participants the health prime reduced snack purchases compared to the control condition (Figure 5.1). The effect of the health prime on the overweight and obese participants was that they bought almost 75 per cent fewer snacks than when not primed. Additional analyses performed with answers to the questionnaire assessing attention to the flyer indicated that the prime worked only when customers paid initial attention to the flyer that contained the health prime and did not require awareness during shopping. The suspicion check confirmed that no participants guessed the hypothesis of the experiment, though six participants in the health prime condition noted the recipe was low in calories or diet related, and one participant mentioned a belief that the experiment was examining buying behaviour related to the recipe.

DISCUSSION

This field study showed that when overweight/obese customers are primed for healthy eating, they considerably reduce their purchase of snacks. The healthy eating prime was simply a flyer handed to customers on entry to the supermarket. Analysis of the results confirmed that the effect was obtained without conscious awareness of the prime while shopping. However, customers did need to pay attention to the prime when it was given to them. The effect was found only for overweight/obese participants, and this is consistent with previous findings (Bish et al., 2005) that priming is more effective when the prime is consistent with the existing goal states of an individual. These results demonstrate priming as a potentially valuable tool for promoting healthy eating that can be easily achieved.

CONSCIOUSNESS AND THE BRAIN

Through the ages, philosophical investigations of consciousness have drawn from science to frame their questions, but there has traditionally been little direct, scientific testing of these questions. When it did occur, scientific study of consciousness was typically restricted to the field of neuropsychology and cases of individuals with brain damage. In such rare cases the task was to explain how the altered states of consciousness resulting from the brain damage could be related to the known functions of these brain areas (Cooney & Gazzaniga, 2003). However, in recent decades, there has been a sharp increase in the scientific study of consciousness. Using techniques such as brain imaging, these studies are investigating typical individuals for aspects of consciousness that can be related to brain function. In this section we will first review results from neuropsychology before moving on to consider how consciousness can be related to brain function in typical individuals.

Neuropsychology

It is basic neurophysiology that the brain is composed of two hemispheres connected by a structure known as the corpus callosum. Our knowledge of how these two halves of the brain specialize and interact with each other was greatly enriched by the activities of Roger Sperry and colleagues in studying consciousness in individuals who had the corpus callosum severed as a last-resort medical procedure to control epilepsy (Gazzaniga, 2005; Gazzaniga et al., 1965). Early observations suggested that these patients with split brains showed little effect of having a split brain, as they were able to perform under natural conditions without evidence of deficit. However, when tested under controlled lab conditions, fascinating differences emerged and it was for this research that Sperry received the 1981 Nobel Prize (Gazzaniga, 1981).

One experiment examined split-brain patients to see whether there was still a unity of consciousness between the two hemispheres. In particular, how the left hemisphere, which had language, and the right hemisphere, which did not have language, would behave when visual information was presented to only one hemisphere (see Chapter 10, Box 10.4). The left hemisphere could talk about what it was shown and thus report awareness. The right hemisphere could not talk about what it was shown but it could indicate awareness by directing the left hand under its control to act appropriately with the object. These results led to questions about how consciousness might be distributed across these differently specialized hemispheres. However, a limitation to interpreting these results is that even with the corpus callosum severed, the two hemispheres are still connected by indirect subcortical connections that can pass information between hemispheres (Corballis, 1994). Nonetheless, the study of split-brain patients helped immensely in understanding how the different parts of the brain interacted and how to go about scientifically addressing questions of consciousness.

> Chapter 10, p359

Blindsight is another form of damage to the brain that has revealed insight into the complex relations between perception, attention and consciousness (Sahraie et al., 2006; Weiskrantz et al., 1974). Anatomically, the condition arises from damage to the primary visual cortex and can be restricted to just a portion of the visual field with damage to only part of one hemisphere, or extensive over the entire visual field due to damage in both hemispheres. The defining characteristic of blindsight is that an individual cannot provide a conscious report about what they see but they can still respond in various ways to stimuli presented in this damaged visual field. In Type 1 blindsight there is denial of any awareness of the affected portion of the visual field, but in Type 2 blindsight individuals are able to report some attributes or feelings of knowing for stimuli such as movement or flashes. What is striking is that when an individual with blindsight is tested in their 'blind' field they can reliably discriminate factors like the orientation of lines when presented as forced yes/no types of question. However, at the completion of testing, when asked what they saw, they will indicate that they did not see a thing and were only guessing.

> **Blindsight**
> a phenomenon typically arising from brain damage to visual cortex where afflicted individuals report that they do not see certain visual targets, but when asked to report properties of these targets they do so better than chance.

The phenomenon of blindsight was not immediately accepted and early criticism raised a wealth of objections that have been examined empirically without refuting the basic claim of its existence. An explanation for how it is possible is that not all projections from the eye are sent to primary visual cortex. It turns out that alternative pathways bring visual information to other cortical structures. Thus, blindsight individuals can even report emotional expressions as there are alternative pathways to the brain centres important for emotion recognition (De Gelder et al., 1999; Gerbella et al., 2019). While the delivery of visual information to other brain regions explains how blindsight is possible, it does not address the substantial issue of why individuals are not able to show conscious awareness of this information in any form of verbal report. Indeed, research has even shown that attention can have an effect in the blind field (Kentridge et al., 1999) and that training of attention in the blind field can aid recovery of the ability to discriminate motion direction in the blind field (Cavanaugh et al., 2019). However, whether rehabilitation can restore conscious awareness of vision in the damaged visual field is an open question (Melnick et al., 2016).

Neural Correlates of Consciousness (NCC)

Neural correlates of consciousness defined by Christof Koch as the minimal set of neuronal events and mechanisms jointly sufficient for a specific conscious percept.

The term **neural correlates of consciousness (NCC)** was popularized by Christof Koch (Koch, 2004; Tononi & Koch, 2008) in empirical investigations of consciousness that arose from his collaboration with Francis Crick (Crick & Koch, 2003). The term is meant not so much to be prescriptive of a particular way to conduct empirical research, but more to make the empirical NCC approach distinct from previous philosophical approaches. The essence of the approach is to examine how brain activity changes when, everything else being as equal as possible, a stimulus is or is not experienced consciously. From comparison of the brain activity between the two situations, conscious versus non-conscious, one can infer brain mechanisms related to consciousness. The goal of the NCC approach is to find the minimal neuronal mechanisms that are jointly sufficient for a conscious percept to be obtained. Implicit in this approach is an appreciation that experiments involving different stimuli might indicate different brain areas that are involved in conscious processing. While this potentially could lead to a complicated situation with conflicting results, the belief is that ultimately the results will converge upon a basis for understanding how brain activity leads to consciousness.

A clear demonstration of the NCC research approach used single cell recordings in various brain areas of monkeys while they viewed different images presented to each eye (Leopold & Logothetis, 1996; Logothetis, 1998). This experimental technique is known as **binocular rivalry** and previous research has shown that monkeys, like humans, when presented a different image in each eye report that only one is visible at a time (Figure 5.2). The visible image dominates the invisible one in awareness, though both are clearly activating primary visual cortex. The results showed that in primary visual cortex only a small number of cells weakly modulated their activity based on which image was in visual awareness. However, further into visual processing, in the inferior temporal cortex, cells were found whose activity correlated with the image of which the monkey was currently aware. Research subsequent to these investigations explored how human primary visual cortex is related to consciousness. These studies have shown that activity in primary visual cortex is necessary for consciousness to occur, but is not sufficient on its own (Haynes & Rees, 2005; Chou et al., 2007).

Binocular rivalry arises when different images are presented simultaneously to the two eyes and results in experiencing seeing one image and then the other alternately.

Global Workspace Approaches

Much research into NCC has been motivated by the approach of the cognitive Global Workspace Theory (Baars, 1988, 2002). A core concept of Global Workspace Theory is

Figure 5.2 Binocular rivalry demonstrates neural correlates of consciousness.
In this binocular rivalry experiment, the top row (a) illustrates the training session where a monkey is first taught to press one lever when it sees the geometric figure and another lever when it sees a face, and to press no lever if it sees both simultaneously. Next, in the actual experiment illustrated in the bottom row (b), lever presses and recordings of brain activity at different brain sites were recorded when the two pictures were presented simultaneously, one to the left and the other to the right eye. Brain activity in the inferior temporal cortex (IT) was related to the lever presses, suggesting it as a neural correlate of consciousness.

Source: Logothetis (1998), by permission of The Royal Society.

that consciousness arises from the interaction of many processes, such as memory, attention, and so on. By enabling fleeting access between these otherwise separate processes, consciousness acts in an integrative capacity to create a global workspace. The nature of this integration is an area of much research. Because the brain is a highly complex structure, with a multitude of processes, there are many ways for integration to be achieved. An example of this complexity is discussed in Box 5.4 in a study that relates brain functional connectivity with states of consciousness. This complexity of brain function and the general nature of the global workspace has spawned various approaches to explain consciousness. We will discuss these different global workspace approaches in the following paragraphs.

 Box 5.4 Research Close Up: Consciousness and brain networks

Source: Demertzi et al. (2019). See Figure 1 in this cited paper for a visual representation of results.

INTRODUCTION

An essential aspect of global workspace theories relates to how different brain regions communicate with one another. One way that communication in the brain has been studied is by using fMRI to explore how activity in the brain is organized into different functional networks, and how these networks connect within themselves and with one another. It is important to emphasize that functional networks of connectivity do not need to follow the static anatomic connection between brain areas. Instead, functional connectivity reflects the dynamic nature of the brain as it reconfigures information processing for different tasks. In effect, anatomic connectivity provides us with the structure of roads, while functional connectivity reflects where the traffic is going on these roads. Functional network structure was obtained by Demertzi and colleagues (2019) for three groups of participants: healthy controls (HC), patients in a minimally conscious state (MCS) and patients in a vegetative state/unresponsive wakefulness syndrome (UWS). Patients in a MCS can show some complex behaviours that are consistent with awareness, such as visual pursuit, orientation to pain or non-systematic command following, yet remain unable to communicate their thoughts and feelings. Patients in UWS open their eyes but exhibit only reflexive movements, with no indication of preserved awareness. The goal of the research was to identify the predominant states of brain connectivity for all three groups and identify how that connectivity correlated to the different states of consciousness.

METHODS

A total of 159 participants (47 healthy controls and 112 patients with disorders of consciousness) underwent fMRI scanning at four independent sites in Europe and North America. The disorders of consciousness included MCS and UWS. After the fMRI scanning of around 10 minutes, data were pre-processed as preparation for analysis of functional connectivity. Analysis of functional connectivity was provided by measurement of coherence between 41 brain areas. These 41 brain areas were chosen on the basis of being representative of six different large-scale brain networks commonly found in healthy brains. These large-scale functional brain networks included the following networks: auditory (AUD), **default mode network** (DMN), frontoparietal (FP), motor (MOT), **salience** (SAL) and visual (VIS). The 41 brain areas can be viewed as a matrix of connectivity that is 41 × 41, containing 820 possible pairwise connections. The measure of connectivity between a pair of brain areas was sensitive to how connectivity changed over time and an analysis was performed to find which patterns of connectivity for the entire matrix were most typical across the data.

Default mode network (DMN)
a network of brain regions that is active when a person is not focused on the external environment.

Salience network
involved in monitoring the external and internal environments to allow detection of salient stimuli.

In addition to the computation of the most typical patterns of connectivity, measurements were made to help address the research question of how connectivity relates to consciousness. One such measure was obtained by placing individuals under general anaesthesia so that the pattern of connectivity associated with anaesthesia could be obtained. This measure could then be compared to the patterns of connectivity without anaesthesia. In addition, a measure was performed to predict what the pattern of connectivity would look like if functional connectivity was driven strictly by anatomical connections.

RESULTS

The results of the connectivity analysis revealed that there were four basic patterns of brain organization for these 41 regions. Pattern 1 showed a complex pattern, with some networks being highly correlated with one another and other networks being anti-correlated with one another. Pattern 2 showed a clear pattern of correlation within areas comprising the visual system and anti-correlation of the visual system with other brain areas. Pattern 3 showed a high degree of correlation among all brain areas. Pattern 4 showed a homogeneous lack of correlation between any brain areas and networks. Patterns 2 and 3 appeared possibly to be transition states and it was not possible to give a clear interpretation of these patterns. However, Patterns 1 and 4 provided insight into the relationship between connectivity and consciousness. Examination of the rate of the pattern occurrence between groups showed that Pattern 1 was most common in healthy controls while Pattern 4 was most common in UWS patients. Moreover, additional results showed that placing individuals under anaesthesia increased the chances of Pattern 4 being obtained. Pattern 4 was also similar to the pattern obtained if connectivity would be driven strictly by anatomical connectivity. Finally, it was noted that Pattern 4 was also found periodically even in healthy controls. (For a visual representation of these results, readers are directed to the paper cited at the beginning of the box.)

> ### DISCUSSION
>
> This research found patterns of brain connectivity associated with disorders of consciousness. This was achieved by using fMRI to examine patterns of brain connectivity in healthy controls (HC), patients in a minimally conscious state (MCS) and patients in a vegetative state/unresponsive wakefulness syndrome (UWS). Analysis of functional brain connectivity revealed four basic patterns of brain activity, termed Patterns 1–4. Pattern 1 was most common in healthy controls while Pattern 4 was most common in UWS. Further investigation of Pattern 4 indicated that it was most similar both to patients under general anaesthesia as well as the connectivity that would be predicted based on just anatomic connectivity. These findings draw parallels between the neural basis of (un)consciousness in UWS and general anaesthesia, and further suggest that this pattern of connectivity is driven mostly by anatomical connectivity. In distinction, healthy controls show distinct patterns of correlated and anti-correlated functional connectivity. These results advance our understanding of the neural correlates of consciousness by revealing functional brain connectivity in the presence and absence of consciousness. They also reveal some intriguing findings – for example, that even in healthy controls there appear times when their brain activity is in Pattern 4. Given the association of Pattern 4 with lack of conscious awareness, one can speculate that Pattern 4 occurring in healthy controls is an indication of mind blanking (Ward & Wegner, 2013).

Recurrent Processing Theory (Lamme, 2010) is consistent with Global Workspace Theory and provides a view of integrative brain activity that could lead to consciousness. It relies on the concepts of **feedforward** and **recurrent** brain activity, which we discussed in Chapter 4. As described by Lamme, the feedforward sweep entails the progression of activity from sensory input areas of the brain to brain areas involving higher-order sensory processing and thought. This feedforward sweep corresponds to the unconscious where information is processed but we do not have access to these representations in awareness. Recurrent processing involves cyclic processing between brain areas such that the activities at both areas are dependent on each other. In this case the feedforward sweep will activate increasingly higher brain areas that will feed back their results to lower levels, which in turn modifies activity at lower levels and the ongoing information is swept forward. Consistent with ideas from global workspace and NCC, Recurrent Processing Theory hypothesizes that consciousness is correlated with widespread recurrent interactions across the brain. Without these recurrent interactions a stimulus would not enter awareness.

Another view of consciousness arising from Global Workspace Theory is provided by the Global Neuronal Workspace (GNW) Hypothesis (Dehaene et al., 1998; Mashour et al., 2020). A schematic of GNW is provided in Figure 5.3 (overleaf), which shows the basic architecture of different functional processors sharing a common global workspace. If the global workspace becomes active then it enables communication among the different processors. In order for the global workspace to become involved there needs to be what has been termed 'ignition'. The act of ignition involves widespread brain activation such as described in recurrent processing. As an example, if we see a glass of water on the table in front of us, this visual sensation might fade away and not reach awareness if it was somehow occurring only in visual cortex. However, if this activation became widespread due to activation in higher brain levels and recurrent processing, then the visual information will enter the global workspace and get broadcast to other processors. Because of this ignition, we can talk about the glass of water, evaluate its relevance and reach out for it. Research into GNW has revealed that areas of prefrontal cortex as

> **Feedforward**
> feedforward processing describes a bottom-up process where lower levels of a network progressively stimulate higher levels of the network.

> Chapter 4, p128

> **Recurrent networks**
> a type of artificial neural network with connections between units arranged so to obtain a cycle of activation. This design allows a temporal context to be designed into the computation.

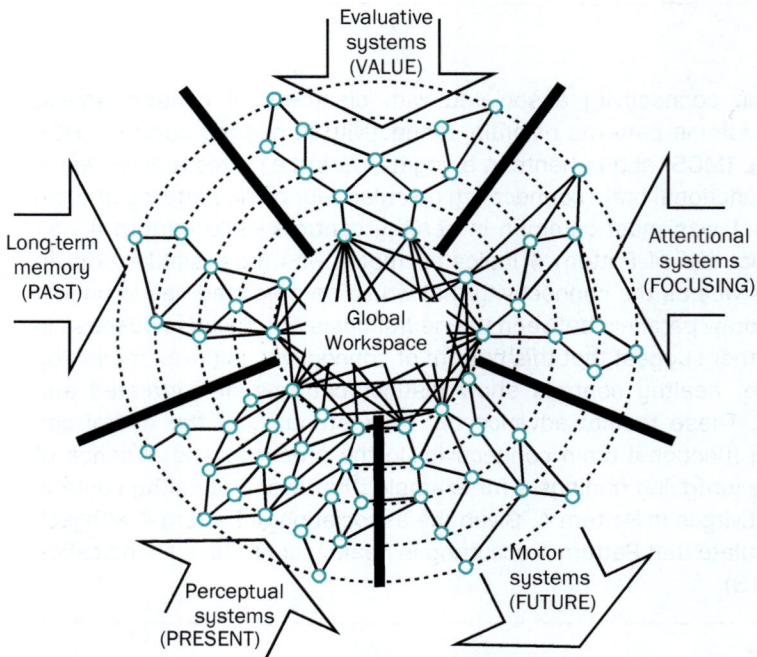

Figure 5.3 Schematic of the Global Neuronal Workspace Hypothesis.
Example of five local, specialized (attention, motor, perception, memory, evaluation) cortical processors that are centrally connected by a core set of highly interconnected areas. This core can at any moment select a piece of information within one or several processors, amplify it and broadcast it to all other processors, thus rendering it consciously accessible and available for verbal report.

well as parietal cortex are thought to be key regions for ignition to occur. In particular, direct recordings of neural activity in awake monkeys showed that the ability of the monkey to report a microstimulation of visual neurons in primary visual cortex correlated to activity in prefrontal neurons resembling an 'ignition' event (Van Vugt et al., 2018).

A final theory of consciousness, Integrated Information Theory (IIT), also relates to Global Workspace Theory by its use of integration as a fundamental property of consciousness (Tononi, 2008, 2017; Tononi et al., 2016). IIT works through **axioms** that identify aspects of experience that are essential for consciousness and **postulates** that characterize the physical systems that can produce consciousness. According to IIT, conscious experience is highly informative because it represents one particular experience out of a huge collection of experiences; it is also highly unified because conscious experience cannot be deconstructed into independently perceived sub-experiences. Conscious experience becomes possible in systems if there is a large repertoire of possible states to the system and there is integration within the system in the form of strong dependencies between components of the system. This idea is formalized in IIT by the definition of a conceptual structure that is specified by a complex of units in a state. The intrinsic irreducibility of the entire conceptual structure, a quantity theoretically defined as the quantity Φ^{max}, can be used to measure *how much* consciousness there is in a system. This measure can be used to assess consciousness of any system. However, in practice its computation requires detailed knowledge of all components of a system and does not seem currently practical to compute, except for fairly simple systems (Oizumi et al., 2014). Even if Φ^{max} cannot be fully calculated, the principles can still be useful to understand limits of consciousness and to make predictions. For example, although the cerebellum has more neurons than cortex and is densely connected to cortex, it is composed of small modules that process inputs and produce outputs largely independent of one another and this does not satisfy the condition of strong dependencies between components. Thus we can explain why lesions of the cerebellum do not influence consciousness (Lemon & Edgly, 2010; Tononi, 2017).

Although both GNW and IIT treat integration as a fundamental part of consciousness, and both can be related to the cognitive theory of global workspace (Baars, 1988, 2002), debates between the two have arisen in their development. One involves consciousness and the relative importance of prefrontal cortex and more posterior regions of the brain (Boly et al., 2017; Odegaard et al., 2017). In GNW the prefrontal cortex plays an important

---

Axiom
a statement that is taken to be self-evident as true, it serves as a starting point for further reasoning. In Integrated Information Theory (IIT) axioms describe regularities in conscious experience.

Postulate
suggested as true to form the basis for further reasoning. In Integrated Information Theory (IIT), properties required of a conscious physical substrate are called postulates, since the existence of the physical substrate is itself only postulated.

Φ
in Integrated Information Theory (IIT), the quantity Φ provides a measure of the amount of consciousness in a system defined by its conceptual structure. The quantity Φ^{max} is the intrinsic irreducibility of the entire conceptual structure.

causal role in consciousness and can be related to the idea of ignition, where sensory processing triggers consciousness and information becomes available across the global workspace. This key role for prefrontal cortex in GNW does not resonate with ideas from IIT where there is not the concept of ignition, and interaction among posterior brain regions are thought to be important for consciousness. Comparison of IIT and GNW is taking on an important role in the scientific study of consciousness. Both theories provide testable hypotheses and their comparison is leading to tractable studies exploring consciousness (Noel et al., 2019; Reardon, 2019).

A final note about the study of consciousness and the brain is that these brain studies could be seen to reduce consciousness to the study of mechanisms running in biological hardware. This begs the question of whether a successful theory of consciousness could be put into a machine so that the machine would be conscious (Dehaene et al., 2017). Both attention schema theory (Graziano & Webb, 2014), which we cover in the next section, and IIT (Tononi et al., 2016) take a mechanistic view of consciousness that in principle would allow it to be artificially constructed. While the possibility of consciousness in machines has yet to be achieved, it is a topic of discussion (Aleksander, 2017; Waskan, 2018) as advances in computing and artificial intelligence continually push the frontier of what is technically possible.

Attention and Consciousness

Attention is an important topic in the study of consciousness and the two areas have evolved together since the early days of cognitive psychology. Classic models of attention such as the filter theory of Broadbent (1958) left little room for anything but the subject of attention to enter our conscious awareness. However, regardless of any particular model of either attention or consciousness, there are many similarities between the two. For example, attention and consciousness share the property of involving selection of particular information above other information. In attention, the selected information receives deeper processing while in consciousness the selected information receives privileged access to our awareness. Moreover, in both models of attention and consciousness there is concern over the fate of the non-selected information as both unattended and nonconscious information have been found to still be able to influence behaviour.

Given the similarities between attention and consciousness it took some time for a clear relationship of the differences between the two to develop. Development of this relationship was spurred on by research (see Chapter 4) into **inattentional blindness** (Mack & Rock, 1998) and **change blindness** (Rensink, 2002; Rensink et al., 1997), which explored the effect of attention on conscious awareness (Lamme, 2003). In the case of inattentional blindness, participants are looking at a central target while attending to a peripheral location and because attention is at the peripheral, rather than the central, target they do not report conscious awareness of a change in the central target. In change blindness participants see two images separated by a visual discontinuity (blank screen of long duration) and cannot detect a difference between the images unless it is properly attended. These two phenomena show the importance of attention for participants to be able to report awareness. However, it is crucial to point out that attention does not guarantee the ability of conscious report. For example, we have already discussed earlier in this chapter the case of blindsight, where effects of attention have been shown in the region of blindsight (Cavanaugh et al., 2019). In addition, it has been found with unconscious priming that manipulations of attention can change the strength of the priming effect, even though the stimulus never reaches awareness (Naccache et al., 2002). The resulting

Inattentional blindness the failure to notice a clearly visible target due to attention being diverted from the target.
Change blindness the phenomenon where substantial differences between two nearly identical scenes are not noticed when presented sequentially.

Chapter 4, p143

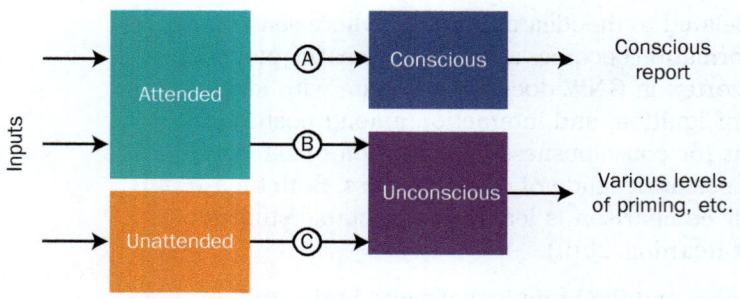

Figure 5.4 A model of the relationship between attention and consciousness.
Perceptual input is either attended or unattended. (A) If the input is attended then it potentially can be available for conscious report. (B) However, even if it is attended then it isn't guaranteed to be available for conscious report and might end up being processed unconsciously, as happens in experiments that use priming. (C) Finally, the input might not be attended and then it will always fail to be available for conscious report.

Source: Adapted from Cohen et al. (2012).

relationship between attention and consciousness implied by these results is shown in Figure 5.4.

The theory of consciousness known as Attentional Schema Theory (AST) (Graziano, 2013, 2016; Graziano et al., 2019) provides another view of how attention and consciousness might relate to each other. This theory draws upon concepts of optimal control theory discussed in Chapter 3 that describe how the brain controls the body to produce movement. However, with AST, in place of the brain using a model of the body to control the body we have the brain using a model of attention to control attention. This model is termed the attention schema and can be used to monitor changes in attentional state, make predictions of the effects of attention and can monitor the consequences of attention. Within AST, the model of attention can be considered awareness and from this follows how attention and conscious awareness relate to each other. As with any reasonable model, there is general alignment between the model (conscious awareness) and the subject of the model (attention). Thus, awareness and attention would generally be the same. However, because no model is perfect we can expect the model of attention (conscious awareness) to occasionally be misaligned from attention itself, leading to situations where attention does not lead to conscious awareness. This effect of misalignment between the model of attention and attention itself is consistent with the relationship between attention and consciousness presented in Figure 5.4. A final comment about AST is that it has been noted that its specific design makes it applicable to social cognition because improved modelling of one's own attention is likely to lead to better prediction of attention in others, which could lead to a better theory of mind (Graziano, 2013; Graziano & Kastner, 2011).

Agency, Volition and Consciousness

Agency and volition are two important aspects of how our actions reveal conscious awareness. Agency, discussed in Chapter 3, describes how actions happening in the world get assigned to be caused by ourselves rather than external forces. This is an essential part of shaping consciousness of a self that is separate from others and the world. Further to this ability to ascribe actions to ourselves is understanding how we generate these movements. The generation of these movements relates to the concepts of free will and volition. The topics are interrelated, but can be separated. While agency addresses the question of whether we have caused an action, it does not address the question of what process generated the action.

Agency

Experiencing the self as an agent involves the existence of interactive processes between the organism and the environment (Christoff et al., 2011). These processes can be thought to create a boundary between the self and the non-self that enables consciousness of the self to develop. It is postulated that these processes require multisensory brain mechanisms that can integrate information across the body (Blanke et al., 2015).

From this a sense of the self is localized in a body that is felt as one's own and occupies a given location in space. However, in some rare situations the sense is not stably present in the body; we discuss this in Box 5.5.

One interactive process we have already discussed, in Chapter 3, was the comparator model of agency (Blakemore et al., 2002). In this model, the motor system, along with a **forward model** produces a prediction of what planned movements should achieve. These predictions can be checked against the perceived actions. If there is a match then this provides evidence of agency. If the action is novel and there is not yet a model for it then it has been shown that movement regularity can contribute to detection of agency (Wen & Haggard, 2020). Regardless, one important theoretical point to make about the comparator model is that it makes a post hoc decision that the action belongs to the self. That is to say that it isn't until the movement is performed and the consequences measured that the judgement of agency can be made. This is crucial because such a judgement of agency cannot inform us about what initiated the movement. We next discuss this problem of how and when we become conscious of the initiation of a movement.

> Chapter 3, p110

> **Forward models** are used to predict the relationship between actions and their consequences. Given a motor command the forward model predicts the resulting behaviour of the body and the world.

Volition

Volition is defined as our ability to make conscious choices and demonstrate free will. It is a topic of interest to philosophers and neuroscientists (Roskies, 2010). Three features of volition have been outlined (Haggard, 2019). These are that volition: (1) demonstrates generation of an action; (2) is associated with consciousness – we are aware of voluntary actions; and (3) has a goal-directed nature. One commonly assumed function of consciousness is that it is related to our ability to choose which action to perform. For example, if we are asked in class to raise our arm when we know the answer to a question, then when we know the answer we decide to raise our arm and, *voila*, our arm moves. Introspectively it appears that there is a close causal link between our conscious experience and our actions. It turns out however that an experiment performed in the 1980s called into question this simple example of volition.

In a classic, but still controversial, experiment, Libet and colleagues (1983, 1985) explored the relationship between brain activity and the intention to move. In the experiment they instructed participants to start with their arm resting and, whenever they were ready, to flex their finger. Libet measured two aspects of participants' performance in moving their finger. First, with EEG he measured what is known as the readiness potential, indicating brain activity reflecting the initiation of preparing a movement. The readiness potential is a well-known signal in the EEG waveform that reliably precedes movements. Second, by asking participants to report the position of a dot rotating on a clockface when they first had awareness of their intent to move, he could find the time of this conscious awareness. What he found was that the readiness potential preceded the time of conscious awareness by around half a second. The fact that the readiness potential preceded conscious awareness of the intent to move violates our intuition that our conscious decisions always precede our actions. One clear interpretation of the data is that it appears that our actions are actually initiated by unconscious brain activity, a view that argues against the existence of free will. This in turn has been used to support various claims such as that our sense of volition is merely an illusion created as we observe our own actions and assign meaning to them (Wegner, 2003; Wegner & Wheatley, 1999).

Evaluation

Given the provocative nature of the results, numerous studies have more closely examined the original studies by Libet and colleagues (1983, 1985). Some 20 years after the original experiments, an entire issue of the journal *Consciousness and Cognition* was devoted to the topic (Banks, 2002). Around 40 years later and there are still publications, often critical, examining detailed aspects of the experiment and the interpretation that unconscious brain processes precede the moment we become aware of the intent to move (Dominik et al., 2017; Sanford et al., 2020). Before briefly summarizing these subsequent studies, it is important to point out that the experimental finding of the readiness potential occurring before reports of awareness is robust and can be replicated (Haggard, 2005; Haggard & Eimer, 1999). Thus, the results cannot be dismissed by some error of measurement. However, three points dampen a strong interpretation of the results as clearly demonstrating a lack of free will. First, the task required of participants is minimal – simply to raise a finger when they feel the urge. This action has no real goal and is far more simple than any number of actions we perform on a typical day. Thus, until similar results can be shown for a more complex action it would be prudent not to generalize the findings of the Libet experiment to all of free will; efforts have been made to develop more ecologically valid tasks to study intention (Verbaarscho et al., 2019). Second, the task of marking the time of awareness, by noting position on a clock, is perceptually and cognitively demanding, and is performed simultaneously when waiting for awareness of the urge to move. Thus, it is possible that the judgement of awareness is being interfered with by other irrelevant factors. Consistent with this, effects have been found for the speed of the rotating dot, showing that timing estimates of the conscious decision to move one's finger will change with rotation speed (Danquah et al., 2008; Pockett & Miller, 2007). Third, and somewhat related to the second point, is that measurement of the readiness potential has been shown to be influenced by other cognitive processes. For example, the process of monitoring the clock has been shown to influence the EEG signal used to obtain the readiness potential (Miller et al., 2011). This calls into question whether the readiness potential is the most reliable indicator, and has generated close examination of the causes of the readiness potential (Schurger et al., 2012; Travers et al., 2020), as well as development of improved measures (Khalighinejad et al., 2019; Vinding et al., 2014).

Reaction to the studies by Libet and colleagues illustrates a rich interaction between philosophy, science and the media. While Libet himself did not argue strongly against free will on the basis of his results, the results were striking in the way they called into question theoretical and common-sense ideas about volition and free will. They were seized upon by many as opposing the existence of free will. Moreover, many media articles reported that the experiments undermined the existence of free will without presenting details of the experiments (Racine et al., 2017). The situation has led to strong statements by neuroscientists and philosophers. The neuroscientist Libet (2002, p. 292) noted that: 'It is interesting that most of the negative criticism of our findings and their implications have come from philosophers and others with no significant experience in experimental neuroscience and the brain.' One cause for this is that individuals combine the experimental results with apparently reasonable assumptions to derive conclusions that generalize past what the data support. While such 'thought experiments' are useful they are not a replacement for actual experimental verification. The philosopher Searle argued that the effect of the clock (Trevena & Miller, 2010) invalidated interpretation of the Libet experiment, stating (Searle, 2013, p. 10346):

> *I believe the history of the readiness potential is an unfortunate chapter in recent scientific history and it raises the question: Why were people so eager to believe these implausible conclusions? The answer I think is that they wanted to discredit consciousness. Consciousness has typically been an embarrassment to the natural sciences, and, in these cases, it looks like we have scientific proof that consciousness does not really matter very much for our behavior.*

Box 5.5 When Things Go Wrong: Out-of-body experience

An out-of-body experience (OBE) provides a person with the unique perspective that their awareness has become detached from their body. They can view the world, including their body, from a disembodied, third-person perspective. This phenomenon raises the subjective nature of experience to new levels and challenges a view of consciousness that the self and sense of agency are contained within the body. There are three properties that characterize an OBE: disembodiment (location of the self outside one's body); impression of seeing the world from a distant and elevated visual perspective; and the impression of seeing one's own body from this elevated perspective (Figure 5.5). A description of the experience by one person was: 'I was in bed and about to fall asleep when I had the distinct impression that 'I' was at the ceiling level looking down at my body in the bed. I was very startled and frightened; immediately [afterwards] I felt that, I was consciously back in the bed again' (cited in Blanke & Arzy, 2005, p. 16; Irwin, 1985).

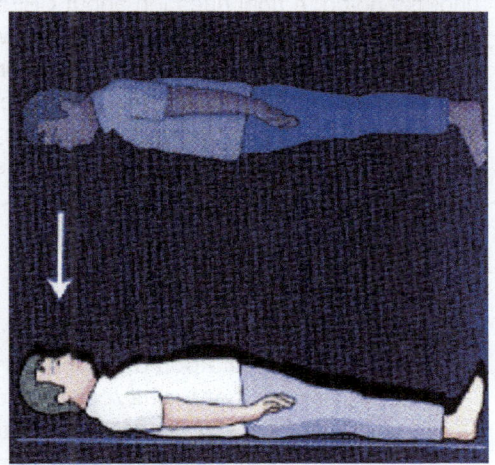

Figure 5.5 Example of an out-of-body experience.
During an out-of-body experience a person will have the experience of seeing the world from a vantage point not fixed to their own eyes. Frequently they have the sensation of themselves looking down at the world and their own body.

The bizarre and distinctive nature of OBE has attracted broad interest, particularly in relation to more extreme cases like near-death experiences (Peinkhofer et al., 2019). However, the psychological phenomenon of seeing oneself in ways that defy physical interpretation has a long history in medicine going back hundreds of years (Anzellotti et al., 2011). The condition has most often been reported in patients with epilepsy and migraine (Blanke & Arzy, 2005), which is consistent with a neurological origin. It has also been reported in childbirth, particularly during difficult births. In one study that examined 328 births, a feeling of floating above the scene occurred in 4.6 per cent of them (Zambaldi et al., 2011). Related to this, OBE has been examined as a contributing factor to women who experience post-traumatic stress disorder (PTSD) from childbirth (Bateman et al., 2017). In recent decades, the neuroscientific study of OBE has advanced hand in hand with research into neural correlates of consciousness.

Neuroscientific investigations of OBE have converged upon one brain region known as the temporo-parietal junction (TPJ), which appears crucial for the OBE. The TPJ is a multisensory (proprioceptive, tactile, visual) processing area that plays a role in providing a sense of agency in motor control (Zito et al., 2020). Activation of this region leads to a decreased sense of agency. Direct evidence of the role of the TPJ in OBE comes from a study done with an epilepsy patient who, in the course of preparation for surgery, had an array of electrodes attached to their brain. When the right TPJ was stimulated, the patient reported an out-of-body experience (Blanke et al., 2002). Another study examined individuals with brain lesions who had a history of OBE, and compared the sites of the lesions. It was found that the overlap of these lesions was at the TPJ (Blanke et al., 2004). These results point towards the view that OBEs are the result of temporary disturbances at the TPJ.

The phenomenon of OBE challenges the idea that self-awareness is contained in our own body and thus has provided an important case to consider. That it can be explained by brain dysfunction at the TPJ advances our scientific understanding but raises other questions. One such is why a brain dysfunction would bring about a phenomenon like an OBE. There is speculation that the mechanisms that go wrong in an OBE are related to those we use when we take the visual perspective of others, which also involve the TPJ (Kessler & Braithwaite, 2016). Visual perspective-taking explains how when sitting at a table with a friend we have an idea of what they can see. Given our earlier discussion that theory of mind can arise from consciousness of the self it is possible to see how exploration of this speculation might advance our understanding. A final question about OBEs is how its existence informs us more generally of bodily consciousness (Blanke et al., 2015), and how we will respond when using virtual-reality (VR) technologies that increasingly enable individuals to be immersed in disembodied experiences (Metzinger, 2018). In VR the relationship between a person and their avatar in the virtual world is up to the imagination. What are the limits and opportunities of this possibility for producing transformative experiences? An experiment using VR to produce a virtual OBE has been shown to reduce fear of death (Bourdin et al., 2017).

Metacognition and Higher-Order Theories of Consciousness

Higher-order theories of consciousness involve adding higher layers of representation that act upon the lower levels to obtain conscious awareness. The theories of consciousness that we have discussed thus far in this chapter are examples of first-order theories of consciousness. They did not call upon any higher-order representation for consciousness to arise. Take for example Global Workspace Theory – a key idea was that consciousness arose from communication broadly across the workspace. There was no hierarchy in this workspace, consciousness came from interactions of a single, first level. In this section we discuss higher-order theories of consciousness and present empirical evidence that support this theory. To better understand higher-order systems, we first provide an example of higher order cognition known as metacognition, which has proven to be a useful tool in exploring higher-order theories of consciousness.

Metacognition

Metacognition
awareness of one's own thoughts and cognitive processes.

Feeling-of-knowing
a subjective sense of knowing that we know a word; an example of metamemory – our knowledge about the contents of our memories.

Chapter 10, p348

Metacognition (Flavell, 1979) is most succinctly described as cognition about cognition. More formally, metacognition refers to higher-order thinking that involves active control over, and assessment of, the cognitive processes involved in learning and storing information. A guiding framework of metacognition was provided by Nelson and Narens (1990), which divided metacognition into two processes: monitoring and control. Monitoring includes the processes by which people self-reflect on their own cognitive and memory processes. One monitoring process discussed in Chapter 10 regarding language production is known as **feeling-of-knowing**. It describes the scenario when an individual indicates that they cannot currently answer a question but can provide a judgement (for instance, confidence) about whether they could potentially recall the answer in the future. The control process of metacognition refers to how people put their metaknowledge to use in regulating their information processing and behaviour. Control processes are often studied in education research where there is interest in how much awareness a learner has of their own learning progress and strategies (Norman et al., 2019). For example, after you finish reading this chapter will you think you understand it adequately or will you need to reread parts, and what strategy will you use to decide which parts?

To apply metacognition to the study of consciousness it is useful to make some observations. One important observation about metacognition is that it does not necessarily rely upon conscious processes (Koriat, 2007). When a metacognitive judgment such as feeling-of-knowing or confidence is provided, the judgement might be based on previous knowledge that is conscious or from some sort of heuristic that is unconscious. Regardless of its basis, the metacognitive judgement is something that reaches conscious awareness (Rosenthal, 2000). However, because metacognition does not typically permit reporting of the subjective state of consciousness it should not be taken to be identical to higher-order consciousness (Rosenthal, 2019). A second observation is that metacognition provides a unique window to study the relationship between task performance and metacognitive judgements of task performance. This is because task performance can be related to first-order cognitive processes and metacognition can be related to higher-order processes. One would predict that if measures of performance, like proportion of correct trials, were high then measures of metacognitive accuracy, like feeling-of-knowing or confidence, would also be high. This logic has been used in studies of consciousness using perceptual stimuli to explore for possible dissociations between first-order and higher-order theories of consciousness.

Higher-order theories of consciousness

The core idea of higher-order theories (HOT) is that consciousness requires a reflexive process whereby to make a first-order mental state conscious there needs to be a higher-order mental state that represents that one is now in that mental state. In other words, conscious awareness crucially depends on higher-order mental representations that represent oneself as being in particular mental states. That consciousness requires some kind of inner awareness. Higher-order theories come in many varieties and there is debate about the pros and cons of different theories as well as whether indeed first-order theories would be sufficient (Brown et al., 2019; Lau & Brown, 2019; Lau & Rosenthal, 2011). However, a pair of empirical studies (Lau & Passingham, 2006; Rounis et al., 2010) provide evidence from behaviour and neuroimaging to support higher-order theories of consciousness in humans.

The two studies (Lau & Passingham, 2006; Rounis et al., 2010) have many similarities. Both used a visual task and included objective measures of visual performance along with subjective or metacognitive measures. Both hypothesized that there would be a dissociation between visual perceptual performance and subjective/metacognitive performance. Finally, both support the idea that the **dorsolateral prefrontal cortex** (DLPFC), could act as a brain region for higher-order representation of consciousness. The first study, by Lau and Passingham (2006), used carefully controlled stimuli to demonstrate in healthy observers a situation akin to blindsight. Participants' subjective reports of visual experience (did you see the stimulus, or did you just guess what it was?) were more negatively influenced than their perceptual performance (was the stimulus a square or a diamond?). The experiment included examination of fMRI brain imaging while doing the task. These fMRI results revealed that visual consciousness was specifically related to activity in the DLPFC. A follow-up study by Rounis et al. (2010) found that when **transcranial magnetic stimulation** was directed at the DLPFC to temporarily disrupt its functioning there was a significant impact on people's metacognitive judgements of visual awareness (was the stimulus clear or unclear?), but their perceptual performance (was the stimulus a square or a diamond?) was not impaired. Taken together, these results show a dissociation between first-order visual processing and higher-order processing in the DLPFC involving subjective awareness. This dissociation is consistent with what would be predicted from a view that the DLPFC is a key region of higher-order consciousness.

> **Dorsolateral prefrontal cortex** the dorsolateral prefrontal cortex (DLPFC) is a brain region in the frontal cortex that has been implicated in cognition for functions such as working memory, executive function and metacognition.
>
> **Transcranial magnetic stimulation (TMS)** a non-invasive method of temporarily exciting or inhibiting cortical areas by means of magnetic stimulation.

These results, taken together with those presented earlier in the chapter, on consciousness and the brain, show that there is currently empirical support for both first-order and higher-order theories of consciousness. The question of which type of theory will ultimately be best supported by empirical data is unknown. Currently it is an open and exciting question of whether it is even possible to devise experiments to robustly answer this question.

Summary

The scientific study of consciousness is currently flourishing. As a field, it has many challenges. Foremost, it applies a reductionist approach to a phenomenon that through millennia has resisted reduction. It also must do this while navigating through concepts and terminology influenced by numerous other domains. We started our presentation of consciousness with a brief discussion of ideas from philosophy to demonstrate how some of these can put psychological research into perspective. However, consciousness has a central position in psychology, particularly regarding awareness of the self. From a psychological perspective, self-awareness is an essential element of our existence that deserves greater understanding.

Moving into the empirical science of consciousness, we first discussed unconscious processing. This is an important issue to understand as it appears that we do process information unconsciously, and we need to know where the boundary is between conscious and unconscious processing. Unconscious processing is also a complex problem to address due to difficulty in reliably verifying by behavioural report that processing is unconscious. This limitation in behavioural report provides an excellent opportunity for brain imaging techniques to examine both conscious and unconscious processing in an effort to identify neural correlates of consciousness. Many brain theories of consciousness hold integration to be a key concept, and this focus on integration makes a unique contribution to understanding how multiple, specific processes must combine in the brain.

The remaining sections of the chapter demonstrated how a deeper understanding of psychological concepts like attention, agency, volition or metacognition can be obtained when considered in the context of consciousness and its neural correlates. For example, the distinction between attention and consciousness, which has long been a question, is now becoming more clear, with advances of research into consciousness. Similarly, the controversial result by Libet suggesting that unconscious brain processes reliably precede conscious awareness of performing an action has driven a raft of experiments critical of this result that has benefited our knowledge of consciousness.

There is much yet to discover about consciousness and it is not clear how quickly research will be able to advance our basic understanding of the topic. However, consciousness research is already helping in practical areas such as understanding how anaesthesia achieves an unconscious state. In addition, the previously mysterious phenomenon of out-of-body experience has gained a scientific explanation through consciousness research.

Review Questions

1. What are the functions of consciousness?
2. How can priming be used to study unconscious processing?
3. What brain regions and processes appear crucial for consciousness?
4. How do the phenomena of inattentional blindness and change blindness shape our understanding of consciousness?
5. Why can the comparator model be used for determining agency but not volition?
6. Why is metacognition useful for the of study higher-order consciousness?

Discussion Questions

1. Why is the hard problem of consciousness hard?
2. The results of the classic experiment by Libet argue against free will. Assuming there is free will, why has it been difficult to refute this study?
3. Why is the concept of integration crucial to many theories of consciousness?

 Further Reading

Blackmore, S. (2017). *Consciousness: A very short introduction.* Oxford University Press.

Dennett, D. C. (1991). *Consciousness explained.* Little, Brown & Company.

Koch, C. (2012). *Consciousness: Confessions of a romantic reductionist.* MIT Press.

Rose, D. (2006). *Consciousness: Philosophical, psychological, and neural theories.* Oxford University Press.

Schneider, S., & Velmans, M. (Eds.) (2017). *The Blackwell companion to consciousness.* John Wiley & Sons.

Velmans, M. (2017). *Towards a deeper understanding of consciousness: Selected works of Max Velmans.* Taylor & Francis.

Zalta, E. N., Nodelman, U., Allen, C., & Anderson, R. L. (2005). *Stanford encyclopedia of philosophy.* Stanford University.

SENSORY, SHORT-TERM AND WORKING MEMORY

6

PREVIEW QUESTIONS
INTRODUCTION
SENSORY MEMORY
    ICONIC MEMORY
    ❗ **Box 6.1 When Things Go Wrong:** *Synaesthesia and sensory memory*
    ECHOIC MEMORY
    HAPTIC AND TACTILE MEMORY
SHORT-TERM MEMORY
    🧠 **Box 6.2 Practical Application:** *Cognitive lockup – working memory, attention and human error*
WORKING MEMORY
    🧠 **Box 6.3 Practical Application:** *Fatal distraction? Working memory and driving performance*
    BADDELEY'S WORKING MEMORY MODEL
    🧠 **Box 6.4 Practical Application:** *Understanding the effects of background noise*
    🔍 **Box 6.5 Research Close Up:** *Working memory and mind wandering*
    ❗ **Box 6.6 When Things Go Wrong:** *Case E.V.R.*
    🔍 **Box 6.7 Research Close Up:** *Self-efficacy and working memory*
SUMMARY
REVIEW QUESTIONS
DISCUSSION QUESTIONS
FURTHER READING

Preview Questions

1. How does short-term memory differ from long-term memory?
2. What are the characteristics of *sensory* memory?
3. What is *iconic* memory?
4. How does *working memory* support cognition?
5. What is 'cognitive lockup' and how might it be avoided?

Encoding
the function by which information is coded in a form that allows it to be stored in memory.

Storage
the function by which information is retained in memory.

Retrieval
the function by which information is recollected as needed.

Short-term memory
the store where information is temporarily held in an accessible state.

Long-term memory
the system where information is held for longer periods, and can be accessed when needed.

Recollection
the act of recalling something to mind.

Working memory
the system in which information is held and manipulated in order to perform a task.

Secondary memory
the term introduced by William James (1890) to refer to memory proper, which we now think of as long-term memory; for James it was '*the knowledge of an event, or fact,* of which meantime we have not been thinking, *with the additional consciousness that we have thought or experienced it before*'(p. 649).

Primary memory
the term introduced by William James (1890) to describe memory 'belonging to the rearward portion of the present space of time', now referred to as short-term memory.

Sensory memory
a temporary sensory register that allows input from the sensory modalities to be prolonged.

INTRODUCTION

Think of the last time you were standing on a street speaking with a friend. Try to remember the scene. What time of day was it? What was the weather like? What was your friend wearing? What did you speak about? Who and what else did you see? Now imagine you are told that a serious crime took place that day, on that street, around that time. You are asked to recall anything you saw or heard that might help with the investigation. You are asked whether you saw anything unusual. How confident would you be that you could recall a potentially significant detail?

Over the course of any one day, we encounter a vast array of sights, sounds, smells, tastes and experiences. It is important that we are able to remember the useful details without retaining every piece of information that meets the senses. In Chapter 2, we saw how the cognitive system makes sense of the complex array of information that meets the senses through perception. In this chapter and the next, we look at how memory allows us to code, hold, recover and use relevant information – that is, how we encode, store and retrieve information (see Figure 6.1).

The traditional view of memory makes a distinction between short-term memory (STM) and long-term memory (LTM). LTM allows you to answer questions such as: What is the capital city of Italy? What does the word 'esoteric' mean? What colour are bananas? What is your home address? Is a bat a bird? How did you celebrate your last birthday? It involves recollection of information. It also allows you to use memory to perform actions – to ride a bicycle, drive a car and sign your name. STM, on the other hand, allows a small amount of information to be held in mind, so that it is immediately accessible and can be used. For example, if you hear a string of digits and have to repeat them back aloud, you rely on STM to maintain that information in mind. The term working memory (WM) has been used in a number of different ways, but generally refers to memory that allows us to manipulate active information – to perform mental arithmetic, for example. As we will see, there is substantial overlap between the terms short-term memory and working memory, and there has been considerable debate about how they are best characterized.

The distinction between the hypothetical LTM and STM stores is long established. William James (1890), in *The Principles of Psychology,* described secondary memory as 'memory proper', while primary memory was, according to James, memory for the psychological present. This latter type of memory is the focus of the current chapter. According to the traditional view, before a piece of information enters short-term memory, its sensory aspects are stored temporarily in a very short-lived store called sensory memory. Sensory memory involves memory for stimuli as opposed to memory for ideas (Cowan, 2008), and there is good evidence in particular for a visual type of sensory memory, which allows a large amount of information from the eye to be held, but only for a very short period of time.

The traditional approach has viewed memory as a series of stages (Figure 6.2). Take for example your memory for the street scene described at the beginning of this chapter. The visual information that reaches the retina of the eye is processed by the brain and forms a visual percept (see Chapter 2). This is held in an initial visual memory store that forms part of sensory memory. Information is held for a short time in the sensory store. Information that needs to be acted on or

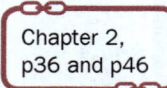
Chapter 2, p36 and p46

that will be retained is transferred to the short-term memory store and if it is to be retained long term it is transferred to long-term memory. Whether you can recall a particular event from the day you met your friend on the street will depend on whether it was successfully processed and stored in long-term memory. While the process is often conceptualized as a series of feed-forward stages, there is also considerable **top-down** influence on all stages of memory.

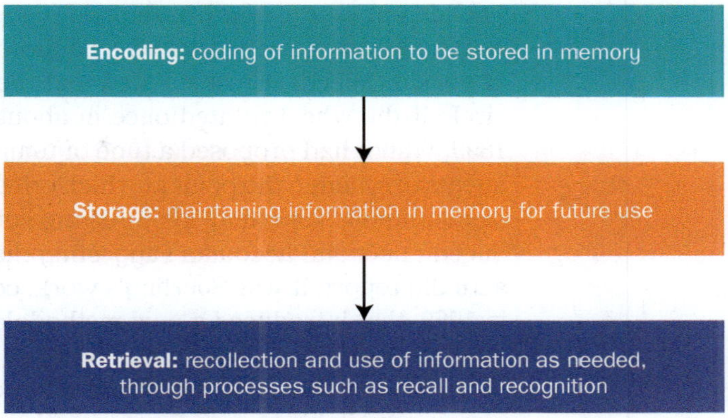

SENSORY MEMORY

It is a common experience for the mind to wander during a conversation (see Box 6.5). When this happens, it is often the case that, although we have not been paying attention, we can recall the last few words said and can continue the conversation without the other person noticing our lapse in attention. This ability reflects one aspect of sensory memory.

Sensory memory occurs at the border of perception and memory, a boundary that is not easily identified (Roediger et al., 2017). It involves the recollection of perceptual types of how a stimulus looks, sounds, feels, tastes and so on (Cowan, 2009), and as such is assumed to be pre-categorical in nature. Sensory memory allows input from the sensory modalities (vision, hearing, etc.) to be prolonged briefly in order for us to process relevant aspects of that input. It is essentially a temporary sensory register, which has a large capacity, but fades rapidly. Models of sensory memory assume a number of modality-specific sub-stores dealing with different types of input such as visual, auditory, haptic (that is, related to the sense of touch) and olfactory (related to smell) stimuli, with close links between the sensory memory store and the corresponding sensory modality.

As yet, relatively little is known about the neurobiological basis of sensory memory. The neurotransmitter **glutamate** plays a key role in the stability of sensory memory (Beste et al., 2008) and more rapid decay of sensory memory has been shown in individuals as a function of genetic variations in glutamatergic neural transmission (Arning et al., 2014). Animal studies have also shown that drugs that facilitate glutamatergic transmission enhance memory encoding (e.g., Staubli et al., 1994).

Figure 6.1 Three key processes of memory.
The three key processes involved in memory are encoding, storage and retrieval.

Encoding: coding of information to be stored in memory

Storage: maintaining information in memory for future use

Retrieval: recollection and use of information as needed, through processes such as recall and recognition

Top down
or conceptually driven processes reflect the influence of higher-order cognitive processes such as thoughts, beliefs and expectations.

Glutamate
an excitatory neurotransmitter that acts on both central and peripheral divisions of the nervous system and plays a key role in sensory processing.

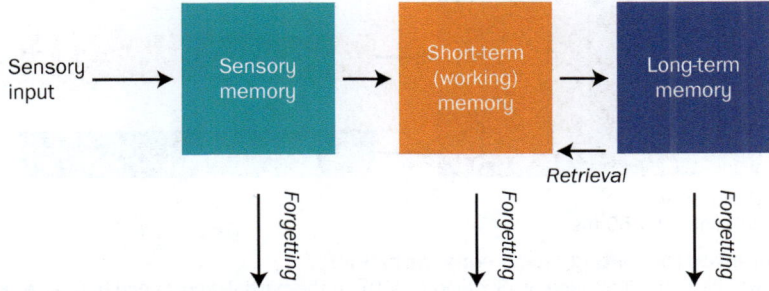

Figure 6.2 The three-stage model of memory.
The stage model of memory conceptualizes incoming sensory information as moving through a series of stores, from sensory memory to short-term and then long-term memory. See for example, Atkinson and Shiffrin (1968).

The idea of a brief sensory register dates back centuries. In 1740, a German physicist, Johann Andreas Segner, attached a glowing coal to a cartwheel and rotated the wheel at various speeds. He calculated that the glowing coal was perceived as a continuous circle if the wheel rotated once in about 100 milliseconds (Cowan, 2008). As early as 1899, Wundt had proposed a type of temporary visual store, based on data from experiments examining the point at which brief flashes of light would be perceived as distinct or continuous (Sperling, 1960). Many subsequent experiments on visual memory produced anecdotal accounts suggesting that people saw far more items than they could actually report. It was Sperling's work, conducted for his doctoral thesis and published in 1960, that introduced a new methodology to this area of research, and proved what anecdotal accounts had long suggested: that people initially store a large amount of visual information but this information decays rapidly, such that only a portion of it remains available to consciousness (Sperling, 1960).

Sensory memory consists of a number of modality-specific stores: the term iconic memory refers to the brief storage of *visual* stimuli; the term echoic memory refers to *auditory* stimuli. Other stimulus types may also be stored, such as *haptic* sensory memory for touch-related stimuli. The sensory stores prolong sensory information so that we can attend to important parts of it; aspects that are not attended to fade away. There is considerable evidence for an iconic memory store in particular.

Iconic Memory

> **Iconic store**
> the sensory memory store for visual stimuli.

The **iconic store** (which was so named by Neisser, 1967) was investigated in a series of experiments by Sperling (1960). Sperling started out with a typical memory span experiment in which participants were presented with a visual array showing, for example, three rows of four letters (see Figure 6.3). This was presented for a brief duration of 50 milliseconds. In a 'whole report' condition, participants were asked to recall as many items as they could. They could typically recall about four or five items. However, verbal reports suggested that the participant had seen more items than could be reported. Sperling introduced a 'partial report' condition, in which participants were asked to recall from only part of the array. Immediately *after* presentation of the array (that is, on stimulus offset), a tone was sounded to indicate which line the participants were to report from (see Figure 6.3). A high tone signalled that they should report what they had seen within the top line of the array. A medium tone meant they should report from the middle line of the array. A low tone meant they should report from the bottom line of the array. Participants had no way of knowing in advance which line would be probed. Using the

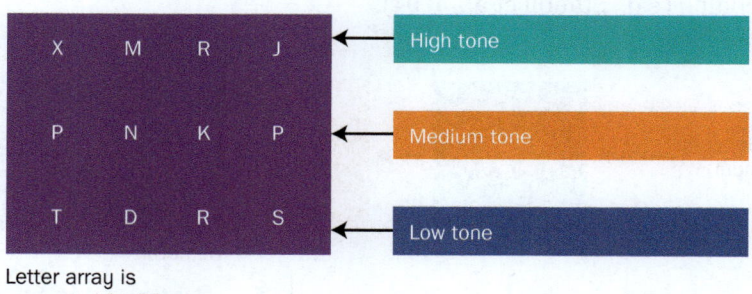

Letter array is presented for 50 ms

Figure 6.3 An array for testing visual sensory memory.
This figure shows the procedure used by Sperling (1960). In the partial-report condition, after a visual array is presented, a tone indicates which line participants are to report from. In the full report condition, there is no auditory cue; participants report whatever they can.

partial-report procedure, Sperling found that participants could typically recall about three items from each line; this meant that a much larger amount of information was available to participants than was suggested by the data from the whole-report condition (see Figure 6.4). This 'partial report' methodology has been used in many studies since to replicate the effect (see for example Box 6.1).

Sperling varied the size of the stimulus array that participants saw, and found that as array size increased, so did the amount of information available in the partial report condition. These results confirmed that, for a short time at least, participants can potentially register a large amount of information. In a subsequent experiment, Sperling investigated the speed of decay from the store, by manipulating the length of the delay between the offset of the stimulus array and the presentation of the tone. The results showed that the partial report advantage disappears after a delay of about half a second. Sperling's data supported the idea that there was a brief memory of a visual image, which is potentially very large in capacity but which rapidly fades away; this is iconic memory. Sperling's findings were confirmed by a number of subsequent studies; for example, Averbach and Coriell (1961) reported similar data using a version of the task that used a visual cue instead of an auditory tone.

Iconic memory allows visual input to be prolonged, which means that our visual experience is not an exact reflection of reality. For example, it allows us to see a series of still images as moving picture sequences in motion pictures and in animation. A motion picture presents images at a rate of 24 frames per second, but in order to ensure that we perceive a flicker-free, smooth moving picture, each frame is presented two or three times. The human visual system is sensitive enough to detect flicker at 24 frames per second (24 Hz) but by presenting the image twice and increasing the rate to 48 frames per second (48 Hz), the flicker will not be detected (Galifret, 2006). Other animals have greater sensitivity to flicker. Birds of prey fly at great speeds to intercept their quarry and can redirect their trajectory in order to do so – a task requiring keen visual perception. A bird of prey has sensitivity to flicker detection in excess of 100 Hz (Winkler, 2005) and bees' sensitivity may be as high as 300 Hz

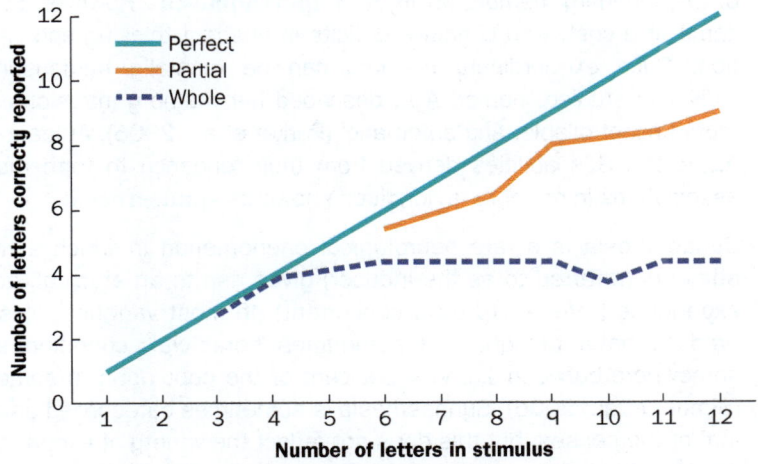

Figure 6.4 Results from the partial and whole report testing.
This figure shows the results from Sperling's (1960) first experiment. The number of letters that can be reported is limited in the whole report condition, while the partial report condition shows that a much larger amount of information is potentially available. The straight line shows the hypothetical perfect performance for comparison.

Source: Adapted from *Sperling (1960)*.

(Lea & Dittrich, 2000). Such sensitivity produces greater control over responses to visual stimuli at speed. Humans achieve such speeds only when driving a car, an activity for which the evolution of the visual system has left us underprepared.

The prolonging of visual sensory input is also evident in the way people perceive a lightning bolt as continuous although it consists of a number of separate strokes, which can be separated by as much as 40–50 milliseconds (Uman, 1986). Similarly, we are unaware of the flicker of fluorescent lights (which flicker at a rate of about 100 Hz). Flicker perception in humans, while less sensitive than that of some animals, is among the faster processes conducted by the visual system (see Chapter 2).

Chapter 2, p46

Evaluation

Some researchers questioned whether Sperling's data might reflect use of a guessing strategy in the partial report condition (e.g., Holding, 1970). Converging evidence soon emerged that supported Sperling's notion of a temporary visual register. Haber and Standing (1969) used a task in which participants saw a series of successive circles, which were presented for 10 milliseconds each and separated by brief intervals. They varied the duration of the interval and asked participants to report if the preceding circle had disappeared before the subsequent one was presented. They found that at intervals of less than a quarter of a second, participants reported no gap between presentation of the circles, whereas at longer intervals participants saw the first circle disappear before the second one appeared. These findings support Sperling's account and lend further support to the idea of stimulus persistence lasting about half a second. Research is beginning to uncover the neuronal basis for visual sensory and working memory, and to examine the role top-down processes play in the modulation of activity in the visual cortex (e.g., see van Kerkoerle et al., 2017).

Box 6.1 When Things Go Wrong: Synaesthesia and sensory memory

Sometimes when things 'go wrong', a pattern of advantages can be seen as well as disadvantages in some domains. Luria (1968) described the case known in literature as S., which has become the seminal case of extraordinary memory ability or '**hyperthymesia**'. However, S.'s ability came at a cost, with cognitive deficits in abstract thinking and categorization. Such extraordinary memory can be mentally burdensome; one individual studied, named A.J., described her memory intrusions as 'non-stop, uncontrollable, and automatic' (Parker et al., 2006). At least some of A.J.'s and S.'s abilities derived from their tendency to form multimodal associations in memory, a condition known as **synaesthesia**.

Hyperthymesia
'hypermemory' or highly superior autobiographical memory (HSAM), evident in some individuals.

Synaesthesia
an uncommon condition where stimulation of one perceptual modality results in experiencing a percept in a typically unrelated modality (e.g., tasting a sound).

Synaesthete
a person with synaesthesia.

Synaesthesia is a rare neurological phenomenon in which a triggering stimulus (referred to as the inducer) gives rise to an atypical, additional experience (referred to as a concurrent). In most varieties, it is considered to be a benign, and sometimes beneficial, condition affecting somewhere between 1 and 4 per cent of the population to some degree (Simner et al., 2006). Synaesthesia is sometimes categorized as a 'blending' of the senses, but this does not reflect the variety of experiences that can fall within the condition. Many different inducer–concurrent pairings can occur, and they can fall within or across sensory modalities or cognitive streams (see Auvray & Deroy, 2015; Lunke & Meier, 2018). The **synaesthete** may reliably associate a sound with a taste, or a shape with a colour; for example, hearing a doorbell may give rise to an experience of tasting custard, or seeing a number 3 shape may evoke the colour yellow. This latter variety, one of the most common forms of synaesthesia, is known as

▶ **grapheme–colour synaesthesia,** and in such cases seeing a letter or number evokes a colour. This happens spontaneously and involuntarily; the synaesthete has no control over the concurrent experience. Importantly, the relationship between the inducer and the concurrent is consistent; a given letter reliably evokes the same colour on each occasion. Neuroimaging studies confirm spontaneous activation of the brain areas associated with both the inducer and concurrent experiences (Paulesu et al., 1995).

> **Grapheme–colour synaesthesia**
> one of the more common types of synaesthesia in which a written letter or number is spontaneously associated with a colour.

Synaesthesia has been associated with a number of advantages in long-term memory (see Rothen et al., 2012) and creativity (Ward et al., 2008), linked to the richer memory traces laid down by activation of multiple sensory experiences. However, it has recently been shown that this advantage extends to sensory memory, which may well be the basis for the long-term memory advantage. Gosavi and Hubbard (2019) replicated Sperling's (1960) partial report paradigm (described above) using letters and non-alphanumeric symbols (such as # and &) as stimuli. Participants were grapheme–colour synaesthetes and a group of non-synaesthetic age- and sex-matched controls. The letters would be expected to evoke colours in the synaesthesia group, while the non-alphanumeric symbols would not, allowing a comparison to be made between the groups.

Participants were presented with an array of either 3 × 3 or 4 × 3 black letters or symbols on a white background. After a short delay of either 0, 150, 300, 500 or 1000 ms, they then heard a low, medium or high-pitched tone. As in Sperling's study, a low tone signalled that participants should report the bottom row, a medium tone indicated that they should report from the middle row, and a high tone that they should report from the top row. Participants could not tell which row would be probed until they heard the tone. They then had 2000 ms to recall as many letters or symbols as they could from the appropriate row.

As found in Sperling's study, longer delays were associated with decreasing performance overall. The results showed an advantage for the synaesthete group, who demonstrated a larger iconic memory capacity compared to the controls across both the 3 × 3 and 4 × 3 array sizes. This was evident only when the stimuli were letters; when the stimuli were non-alphanumeric symbols the advantage disappeared. The synaesthete advantage for the letter arrays was more prominent for the large 4 × 3 arrays. Gosavi and Hubbard (2019) concluded that the memory advantages of synaesthesia extend to the earliest stages of memory, and they suggested that the advantages that are evident in the later stages of memory may in fact arise from these earlier advantages in sensory memory.

This sensory memory advantage of synaesthetes may depend on attentional processes. Rothen et al. (2018) used a different type of partial-report task to explore the point at which the synaesthete advantage emerged. In their task, eight black letters were arranged on a circle around a fixation point on a grey background. The letters disappeared, and following a variable delay of 0, 50, 100, 250, 500 or 1000 ms, a red asterisk appeared to signal the position of the letter the participants was required to report. Black asterisks replaced the non-target letter positions. (This use of colour cues may well be problematic.) After participants gave their response they also rated the subjective clarity of the target letter, on a scale ranging from 'no experience of the letter at all/guessing' to 'clear experience of the letter'.

Participants were grapheme–colour synaesthetes, and age- and sex-matched controls. The experiment manipulated three additional factors: the length of the inter-stimulus delay, the target letter and the target position. Again, as in Sperling's study, longer delays were associated with decreasing performance. The results showed that while sensory memory was not generally enhanced in the synaesthetes compared to the controls, the synaesthetes showed a performance advantage when subjective clarity of the target was high. ▶

▶ This suggests that the effect is not pre-attentive but depends on participants' awareness of the inducer stimulus. However, an additional factor also emerged in the study that complicates matters. The results showed that the level of synaesthetic consistency was an important predictor of sensory memory performance. The group of synaesthetes showed a range of synaesthetic ability; some showed a high level of consistency in the experience; others less so. A general memory performance advantage would have emerged for the synaesthetes relative to the controls had the study included only the highly consistent synaesthetes. This points to the importance of strict inclusion criteria for studies involving synaesthetic participants, as the extent of synaesthetic experience may vary considerably, affecting the results of studies on memory. Furthermore, it has been shown that the memory advantage differs by *type* of synaesthesia (e.g., Lunke & Meier, 2018), giving another important variable to consider and underlining the diversity of experience within the synaesthetic population.

Echoic Memory

Echoic memory
sensory memory specific to auditory stimuli.

Echoic memory is the auditory equivalent of iconic memory; it is sensory memory for heard information. Sperling's partial-report technique was applied to auditory stimuli initially by Moray et al. (1965), and their procedure was extended by Darwin et al. (1972). Darwin et al.'s experimental set-up is illustrated in Figure 6.5.

The Darwin et al. study involved presenting auditory stimuli independently to each ear, or to both ears, using stereo headphones, such that the sounds would be heard from three spatial positions: from the left or right, or from the 'middle' (i.e., in stereo). Nine letters and nine digits were used to form sequences; three items were presented to the left channel, three to the right, and three were presented simultaneously in stereo. They were presented such that the first item of each group was heard simultaneously;

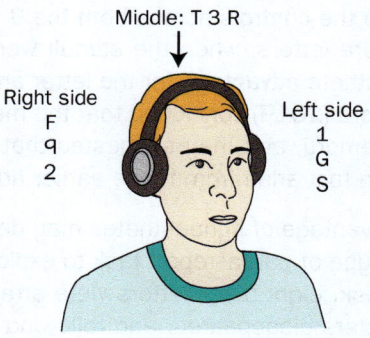

Participant wears stereo headphones
1. Present nine stimuli: left   1 G S
                         middle T 3 R
                         right   F 9 2
2. Following last letters variable delay interval, 0–4,000 milliseconds.
3. Signal bar presented on a screen. Bar is left of, in front of or to right of participant.
4. Participant attempts to report stimuli signalled by bar.

Figure 6.5 The procedure used by Darwin et al. (1972).
The illustration shows the procedure used by Darwin et al. (1972). The participant hears letters and numbers presented simultaneously to one or other ear, or to both, via the headphones. A visual cue signals which location to report from.

Source: Adapted from Loftus & Loftus (1976).

similarly, the second items were presented simultaneously, and then the third. In the example shown in Figure 6.5, participants would hear 1, T and F, simultaneously, then G, 3, 9 and finally S, R, 2.

Following Sperling's procedure, the auditory stimuli were presented and, after a delay that varied from 0 to 4 seconds, a cue indicated from which set the participants were to report. In this case, a visual cue (e.g., a signal bar appearing on screen) was presented to the left, middle or right, and the participants reported what they had heard from the corresponding location. Consistent with Sperling's findings on iconic memory, Darwin and colleagues found that performance in the partial-report condition suggested a large initial memory of auditory information, which decayed rapidly. At zero delay participants could report about five of the nine items. After a delay of 4 seconds, performance had dropped to 4.25 items on average, the same number as would be expected in a whole-report condition. This suggested that there was a sensory store for auditory information that was similar in some ways to iconic memory; this became know as the echoic store (another term coined by Neisser, 1967). The echoic store provides an acoustic register, allowing auditorily presented information to be prolonged so that some aspects of the input can be retained for processing.

The auditory partial report data are broadly consistent with findings using the shadowing technique, in which participants must 'shadow' or repeat back a message presented to one ear or the other. For example, Glucksberg and Cowan (1970) had participants shadow a passage of prose that was presented in one ear while another prose passage was presented to the other, 'unattended' ear. Participants were to ignore the second passage, but were warned that digits would occur in that text from time to time, and that when a light flashed, they were to report the last digit heard in the unattended message. The duration between the presentation of the digit and the light cue was manipulated. Performance on the task deteriorated at about 4 seconds. Similarly, Treisman (1964) found that if participants shadowed a message while a second unattended message was presented, they only recognized that the two messages were the same if they occurred within about 2 seconds of each other. More recent research has confirmed that echoic memory provides a brief register of auditory input, and is highly sensitive both to decay and to interference (for example, see Kinukawa et al., 2019).

> **Shadowing**
> a technique that involves repeating back an auditorily presented message.

Evaluation

From Darwin et al.'s data, the span of echoic memory seemed to be less than that of the iconic store and its duration longer, but this may reflect a limitation of the procedure used. While Sperling could present the visual stimuli all at once without affecting the spatial relationships between the stimuli, in an auditory version of the task, all the sounds could not be presented simultaneously; three sets of temporally distinct sounds were presented. This produces some clear differences between their two procedures and may have led to an over-estimation of the duration of storage in the echoic register. Efron (1970a, 1970b, 1970c) had participants adjust the onset of a light to coincide with the offset of an auditory tone. The duration of the tone was varied and it was found that, for very short tones (e.g., 60 milliseconds), participants adjusted the light to come on 150 milliseconds after the onset of the tone. In other words, short tones were prolonged in echoic memory so that they were perceived by participants as lasting longer than they actually were. This supports the idea of a modality-specific store that prolongs auditory stimuli, and provides an estimation of echoic persistence that is more accurate and more consistent with other estimates (e.g., Massaro, 1975, estimated 250 milliseconds).

What can be done with the information stored in sensory memory? Another of Sperling's experiments used an array that contained both letters and digits, and introduced a second partial report condition, in addition to the whole and partial report conditions described above. In the new partial report condition, participants were instructed to report only the letters or only the digits within the array; a tone cued which type they were to report (letters or digits). In this partial report condition, no advantage over the whole report condition was evident. Participants could report only about four to five items. This gives us a clue as to the nature of the representation of the stimuli in the iconic store; it appears that participants have access to a visual stimulus but cannot yet categorize it or access its meaning. As Cowan (2008, p. 25) put it, 'we can think of sensory memory as the memory for the knowledge-free, sensation-based characteristics of stimuli that resemble what a newborn would perceive'. Sperling's letter/digit experiment demonstrated that information held in the sensory register is not yet in a form that the cognitive system can effectively utilize and manipulate. For this, further processing and transfer to short-term memory is needed.

> **Masking**
> reduced perception of a visual stimulus when another stimulus is presented in spatial or temporal proximity to it.
>
> **Stimulus onset asynchrony**
> the time between the onset of a stimulus and the presentation of a mask.

Sensory memory is fragile and can easily be disrupted before stimuli can be transferred into short-term memory (STM). Backward **masking** procedures involve the presentation of a 'masking' stimulus immediately after the target stimulus; for example, a briefly presented visual stimulus (e.g., a letter) might be followed by a row of hash marks (####). The participant is subsequently required to identify the letter in a recognition test. Recognition increases as the duration between the presentation of the target stimulus and the masking stimulus (the **stimulus onset asynchrony**, or SOA) increases, to about 250 milliseconds. Data from backward masking also support a shorter duration to echoic memory than the partial report data outlined above (see Cowan, 2008, for an overview).

Cowan (e.g., 1984, 1988) suggested that there are two stages to sensory memory in each of the modalities (see also Massaro, 1976). The first phase is a short, pre-perceptual phase lasting about 250 milliseconds, while the second is longer, lasting several seconds, and involving more substantial processing and access to memory. The modality-specific differences in the partial-report data outlined above came about because Sperling's visual array data involve the first of these sensory phases, while Darwin's auditory data involve the second (see Cowan, 2008).

Haptic and Tactile Memory

It is likely that there are also sensory memory stores serving other modalities. Support for a haptic (related to touch) sensory store was provided in a study by Bliss et al. (1966), who used a tactile version of Sperling's partial report procedure. Their participants were trained to associate a letter of the alphabet with three sections on each of four fingers of one hand. Participants then placed their hand in a device that administered a puff of air to some of these regions, and had to report which regions had been stimulated by giving the associated letter. In the partial report condition, a visual stimulus cued whether participants were to report stimulation presented to the upper, middle or lower sections of the fingers. A small advantage for the partial-report condition was found, as long as the visual cue appeared within 800 milliseconds of termination of the tactile stimulation.

Similarly, Gallace et al. (2008) used the partial report procedure to investigate whether information regarding the number of tactile stimuli presented across the body (rather than just to the fingers as in the Bliss et al. study). Across a series of experiments, they found a partial report advantage similar to that seen in iconic memory, with participants able to report, on average, five items, compared to three items in the whole report condition. Their data suggest that a maximum of five items can be stored in tactile sensory memory. The data also show that the capacity of tactile sensory memory is far smaller than that of its visual counterpart, iconic memory, and that it decays rapidly. These data support a temporary register for tactile input and are consistent with data demonstrating **change blindness** (see Chapter 4) in the tactile modality (e.g., Gallace et al., 2006; Gallace et al., 2006; Gallace & Spence, 2014).

> Chapter 4, p143

While sensory memory provides a temporary register that is rich in sensory detail, such memory is short-lived and cannot be manipulated. In order for effective processing to occur, information must be held in short-term memory. It is to this aspect of memory that we now turn.

> **Change blindness**
> the phenomenon where substantial differences between two nearly identical scenes are not noticed when presented sequentially.

SHORT-TERM MEMORY

Short-term memory (STM) holds information in consciousness; it provides temporary storage for active information. STM has a limited capacity, and information can be lost from it relatively easily. If someone gives you their telephone number, but you forget it as you try to enter it on your phone, you will be aware of the capacity limitations affecting STM. STM allows us to complete the many daily tasks that involve active use of information, from understanding a conversation or a passage of text, to calculating a tip in a restaurant, to imagining an alternate route home when you find your usual route blocked. This last example illustrates that STM is not limited to verbal information; similarly, if you are asked how many windows there are on the front of your house, the visual image you create to address this question is also inspected in STM. Much of the information that we process in STM is not retained, and is quickly purged from STM, allowing our attention to move on to the next task. This is important for the efficiency of STM. As Bjork (1972) noted: 'We overhear conversations, we see things in newspapers and store windows, we add up numbers, we dial telephone numbers, we pay attention to advertisements, and so on – nearly all of which we have no use for beyond the point at which we attend to them' (p. 218).

William James's (1890) description of short-term memory as primary memory equated it with the psychological present, the information that is available in consciousness. Hebb (1949) also made the distinction between short-term and long-term memory, and a number of models in the 1950s and 1960s supported the distinction between stores of different types (e.g., Broadbent, 1958; Neisser, 1967; Waugh & Norman, 1965). Atkinson and Shiffrin (1968) introduced a model of memory that became known as the *modal model* ('modal' because it was similar to various other models at the time; see Norman, 1970; Waugh & Norman, 1965). It proposed three memory stores, and made the distinction between a long-term store (LTS, or also LTM) and a short-term store (STS, or STM). The model was heavily influenced by the growing use of the **computer metaphor** in cognitive psychology, and made a distinction between permanent, structural aspects of memory and flexible control processes, which could vary depending on task requirements, analogous to the distinction between hard drive storage and active (RAM) memory in a computer.

> **Computer metaphor**
> in cognitive psychology, an analogy drawn between human cognitive processing and information processing in a computer, which provides a tool for thinking about how the mind operates.
>
> **Rehearsal**
> a set of processes by which we can act on currently active information.

According to the Atkinson–Shiffrin model, information is first registered in the sensory store, and salient information is transferred to STM. A number of control processes are supported by STM and the type of processing carried out will determine whether information will be stored in LTM. **Rehearsal**

> **Maintenance rehearsal**
> retains information in STM.
>
> **Elaborative rehearsal**
> organizes the information so that it can be integrated into LTM.
>
> **Decay**
> a process by which information is lost from STM over time.
>
> **Displacement**
> a process by which information coming into STM causes information already held there to be lost.

involves recycling the information (such as repeating it to yourself to keep the information refreshed in memory; **maintenance rehearsal**), encoding involves the extraction of some information in order to transfer to LTM (**elaborative rehearsal**), and retrieval strategies allow access to LTM. Information is lost from STM through **decay**, a time-based limitation, and **displacement**, a capacity-based limitation by which incoming information gains precedence over previously active information (Atkinson & Shiffrin, 1968).

The basic assumptions of the modal model were that:

- there are separate short-term and long-term stores
- processing in the short-term store determines memory storage in the long-term store, and
- short-term memory is a limited-capacity store.

> **Digit span**
> the number of digits that can be held in memory and is used as a measure of STM.

There was general agreement that STM had a limited capacity. Attempts to measure its capacity made use of tasks involving digit span and the recency effect in free recall (described below). **Digit span** tasks present participants with digit strings of increasing lengths; participants have to repeat them back in the order they were presented. The task becomes more difficult as the length of the string increases, and the point at which errors begin to occur indicates the limits of the participant's STM. Miller (1956) is often cited as quantifying the functional limit of STM as 7 ± 2 items (the so-called 'magical number seven'), suggesting that, on average, people will be able to report about seven items (plus or minus 2), whether those items are individual letters or digits, or larger 'chunks' of information. For example, the digit strings on a credit card could be read as individual digits or as chunks: for example, 1010 2543 6754 2194. Taken as individual digits there are 16 digits, but read as four sets of four numbers there are four 'chunks'. Therefore more than seven individual digits might be recalled in this case. **Chunking** increases the capacity of STM; as Miller (1956, p. 95) noted: 'the span of immediate memory imposes severe limitations on the amount of information that we are able to receive, process and remember. By organizing the stimulus input simultaneously into several dimensions and successively into a sequence of chunks, we manage to break (or at least stretch) this informational bottleneck.'

> **Chunking**
> a strategy to improve memory by grouping smaller units together into a larger unit, or 'chunk'.

> Chapter 1, p6

Information from LTM can be used to facilitate chunking (see Chapter 1 for some examples used by world memory champions). The string FBICIAMI5 is easier to recall if we break it into more meaningful components FBI CIA MI5. The larger the chunks, the more memory is required, however, and fewer will be recalled. Chunking is seen as a key contribution of the Miller paper (Cowan, 2015).

Miller's estimation of seven items, give or take two, was approximate and, given the humorous tone of his highly cited article, it may have been meant as a rhetorical device (see Cowan, 2015, for an interesting discussion on this point). Various sources have proposed a limit that is closer to four (e.g., Broadbent, 1975; Henderson, 1972; Mandler, 1967; see Cowan, 2001, for a review). Cowan et al. (2007) noted that Sperling's research, described above, showed that, of a large amount of information in sensory memory, only a small number of items make it through to STM; when participants are shown 12 characters at once, they can typically only report around four items. A number of other sources suggest that it is the capacity of STM, rather than the decay rate of sensory memory, that is reflected in these four items (Cowan, 2010).

> **Recency effect**
> the tendency, given a list of items to remember, to recall those from the end of the list more readily than items from the middle.

The **recency effect** in free recall refers to the fact that people recall more items from the end of a presented list than from the middle of the list.

This pattern was first reported in the 1920s (Welch & Burnett, 1924), but it was only in the 1960s that it was interpreted in light of differences between STM and LTM. In the task graphed in Figure 6.6, participants hear a list of 12 unrelated words. They are then required to report the words in any order. The performance of participants is then graphed as shown in Figure 6.6 to give the **serial position curve**, with the word's position in the list graphed along the x-axis, and probability of recall shown on the y-axis. The typical serial position curve shows an advantage for more recently presented items (the recency effect). Performance is also relatively good for items at the start of the list (the **primacy effect**). Compared to words at the end and at the start of the list, recall is relatively poor for items that are presented in the middle of the list.

> **Serial position curve**
> used to plot recall of a word list such that performance is examined as a function of a word's position in a list.
>
> **Primacy effect**
> enhanced recall of items at the start of a list compared to those in the middle.

The recency effect reflects items held in STM. The primacy effect reflects items that have already been transferred to LTM; as more items are added to the list, there is less time to transfer them to LTM, and so some items are not successfully transferred to LTM and are displaced from STM. If the recency effect reflects items stored in STM, then it should be relatively straightforward to disrupt it without affecting the primacy effect, which reflects another aspect of memory (LTM). Studies have attempted to support this distinction between STM and LTM by examining the effects of distraction on the primacy and recency effects. For example, participants might be required to count backwards in threes immediately after presentation of the list: this should interfere with the information that was being held in STM by preventing the participant from rehearsing it. But the counting task should not affect recall of the items that have already been successfully transferred to LTM. In other words, the counting task should affect the recency effect but not the primacy effect. This is precisely what is found in such studies.

The capacity of STM should therefore be reflected in the number of items in the recency effect, but this has proved rather difficult to estimate, as it varies depending on the nature of the information to be recalled. Glanzer and Razel (1974) conducted a series of free recall experiments and initially estimated the size of the recency effect as being 2.2 words. When they used proverbs in the recall task, they found recall of 2.2 proverbs, but

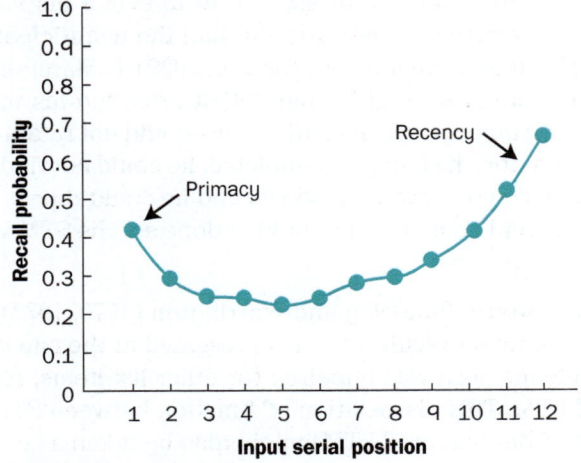

Figure 6.6 The serial position curve.
The serial position curve shows the probability of free recall of a word as a function of the position in which it was presented in a word list. Items at the end of the list show increased recall, a pattern called the recency effect. Items at the start of the list also show better recall than those in the middle, a pattern referred to as the primacy effect.

Source: Adapted from Parkin (2000).

for unfamiliar sentences performance dropped to 1.5 sentences. Cowan (2001), assessing the available evidence, identified a capacity limit of on average four chunks and outlined the task conditions under which this estimate might be predicted to differ.

> **Negative recency effect**
> the tendency for recall of items from the end of a list to be poorer than for those from the start or middle of the list in a final, cumulative recall task.

The **negative recency effect** provides further support for separate short-term and long-term stores. Craik (1970) had participants immediately recall 19 lists of 15 words. He later had participants report any words they could remember from any of the lists in a final free recall task. If the recency effect reflects items in STM, we would expect to see a recency effect in the immediate recall task but no such effect in the final free recall task, as this task required reporting from LTM. Craik's data showed that not only was this the case, but in fact performance for list-end items was poorer than mid-list items in the final free recall task; this is the negative recency effect. This pattern supports the idea of separate short-term and long-term memory stores. In the immediate recall task, participants held the list-end items in STM and did not transfer them to LTM. This meant those items were at a disadvantage in the final recall task.

A Double Dissociation of Function?

> Chapter 7, p223

If recency reflects storage in STM, we might expect to find it spared in individuals who have had a brain injury affecting LTM, but leaving STM intact. Individuals with **amnesia** (see Chapter 7) show this pattern of memory impairment. In the next chapter, we look at long-term memory and a pattern of memory impairment called the **amnesic syndrome**. The amnesic syndrome is characterized by impairments in long-term memory function, particularly affecting the person's knowledge of their own life events, while short-term memory is spared. The affected individual may be able to hold a conversation with a visiting friend, for example, but as soon as the friend leaves their presence the information is lost; they may not even recall the visit.

> **Amnesia**
> a pattern of memory loss affecting elements of long-term memory, while short-term memory remains intact.
> **Amnesic syndrome**
> a pattern of memory loss characterized by impaired long-term memory and spared short-term memory.

In Chapter 7, we will look in detail at one of the most cited cases of amnesia in neuropsychology, that of H.M. As a young man, H.M. underwent an experimental surgical procedure in an attempt to alleviate his medically intractable epilepsy. The surgery reduced his seizures, but had the unanticipated consequence of severely damaging his long-term memory (Squire, 2009). H.M. retained some childhood memories, but he had a severe and lasting deficit affecting his memory for ongoing events. He did not remember people he had met; he could not retain his doctors' names; he could not recall activities he had just completed; he could not find his way around the hospital. However, he could answer questions, and he could repeat back a sequence of digits, though he later had no memory of having done so. His STM was intact, while his LTM was defective.

Consistent with this pattern, Baddeley and Warrington (1970, 1973) found that individuals with amnesia had intact recall for items presented at the end of the list (a normal recency effect) while memory was impaired for other list items, reflecting the impairment of LTM. This dissociation of function between STM and LTM (that is, intact STM but impaired LTM) might also be taken as evidence for separate stores; however a **double dissociation of function** would provide more persuasive evidence.

> **Double dissociation of function**
> contrasting patterns of deficit in two patients or patient groups; provides evidence for functionally independent systems.

A double dissociation of function provides evidence of a functional dissociation between two tasks or cognitive processes. It was first described by Teuber (1955, p. 283) and has become a key pattern in cognitive neuropsychology. As Shallice (1979, p. 260) noted, 'strong neuropsychological evidence for the existence of neurologically distinct functional systems depends on double dissociation of function'. A dissociation occurs when a brain lesion causes impaired performance on one task (Task A), while performance on a second task (Task B) is unaffected. This provides, at best, weak evidence that the two tasks are controlled by different brain regions only one of which has been damaged by the lesion. After all, it could be the case that task B is simply easier than task A and less taxing for the individual with a brain injury. The site of the brain injury might not be directly relevant to the task. However, if the reverse pattern is also found, in a different patient, this provides stronger evidence, as it cannot be the case that the 'harder' task can be completed but not the 'easier' task. Such evidence would suggest that two different lesion sites are associated with the performance in Task A and Task B – the double dissociation shows that the two tasks are differentially localized (Jones, 1983).

If human memory is a unitary system, a double dissociation of function between LTM and STM would not be predicted. We have seen that in the amnesic syndrome there is a dissociation between STM and LTM, with STM being intact while (much of) LTM is deficient. While the reverse pattern – that is, impaired STM with intact LTM – is rare, such cases have been reported. The first reported case was that of K.F. (Shallice & Warrington, 1970), a man who sustained severe damage to the left parieto-occipital region of his brain in a motorcycle accident. In addition to language problems (a pronounced aphasia affecting speech, reading and spelling; for more on aphasia see Chapter 10), K.F. had impaired STM, as measured by digit span and recency. However, K.F. had relatively intact LTM. He had a digit span of just 2 (an average of 1.8 on letters, 2.3 on words and digits) and yet performed normally on a paired-associate task (requiring LTM). Warrington and Shallice (1972) found that K.F.'s STM deficit was more pronounced in auditory memory than in visual memory, and his long-term memory processes were normal (Warrington & Shallice, 1969). Shallice and Warrington (1974) found that K.F.'s problems were further limited to verbal stimuli such as words and digits, while his immediate recall of other sounds (e.g., cats meowing, a ringing telephone) was unimpaired. Since K.F., a number of similar cases have been reported involving impaired STM as measured by span-type tasks and intact LTM function (e.g., Saffran & Marin, 1975; Shallice & Butterworth, 1977; Warrington et al., 1972).

> **Aphasia**
> the term given to a group of language disorders that occur following brain injury.

> Chapter 10, p357

The case of P.V., an Italian woman with similar deficits to K.F., has been studied over many years. She showed a stable pattern of selective STM impairment (as measured by digit span and other such measures) with spared LTM after a left hemisphere stroke (Basso et al., 1982; Vallar, 2019). P.V.'s performance on a non-word repetition (span) task showed that she performed reliably only when repeating back single disyllabic items. When the non-words had three syllables, a 20 per cent error rate was seen. Her error rate rose to 100 per cent for four- and five-syllable non-words. By contrast, she showed normal long-term learning when presented with meaningful material; compared to a control group her scores fell within the normal range, albeit towards the lower end of that range (for these data see Baddeley et al., 1988). While such cases tend to be rare, and differ from one another due to the nature and sites of brain injury, this contrasting pattern of impaired STM and intact LTM processes has now been documented on many occasions. Reviews by Logie (2019) and by Shallice and Papagno (2019) show that there are now around 20 such cases in the literature, providing good evidence for separate short-term and long-term stores and for the fractionation of short-term memory. Such cases have played an essential role in the development of models of working memory, a topic we will look at in the following section.

Evaluation

The double dissociation of function in LTM and STM was an important development for theories of memory. The Atkinson and Shiffrin model suggested that information passes through a unitary STM in order to enter LTM. The characterization of STM as a unitary store did not explain the pattern of function seen in individuals such as K.F., who have impaired STM function, but whose LTM is relatively unimpaired. If STM is compromised, how is information getting access to long-term memory? It would seem that STM is not a single, unitary store. The early models focused on the verbal aspects of STM, but are there other kinds of STM? Furthermore, short-term memory allows us to hold information in an accessible state so that we can act on it, but there is also a range of processes we can apply to allow us to manipulate and use the information so as to set and achieve goals. What is the relationship between these processes and STM? The idea of a unitary STM store was abandoned, and replaced with a concept called **working memory**.

> **Working memory**
> the system in which information is held and manipulated in order to perform a task.

Miller et al. (1960) introduced the term 'working memory' to refer to memory that allows us to make plans and to keep track of goals. The concept of working memory overlaps substantially with that of short-term memory, and includes storage and processing components. Miller and colleagues described working memory only very briefly and they did not provide any detail on its components. They wrote that when a plan is being executed it has 'special access to consciousness and special ways of being remembered. . . . We should like to speak of the memory we use for the execution of our plans as a kind of quick-access, "working memory"' (p. 65). This leaves the term 'working memory' open to interpretation so that it has come to mean different things to different theorists. The most influential account of working memory was developed and empirically tested in a series of studies, beginning with Baddeley and Hitch (1974). Working memory has become one of the most important and debated concepts in cognitive psychology, and it is to this concept that we now turn.

Box 6.2 Practical Application: Cognitive lockup – working memory, attention and human error

> Chapter 4, p114

In Chapter 4, we looked at attention and the central role it plays in cognition. Attention is closely related to working memory – that is, the memory that supports the cognitive operations currently in mind, whether that is reading a textbook or solving a puzzle. When attention fails, various cognitive errors can result. One such error is **cognitive lockup**. Cognitive lockup refers to a pattern of cognitive error that results from the human tendency to detect and deal with faults sequentially. It leads to a delay in responding to consecutive failures and is one of a number of cognitive error-producing mechanisms that has serious real-world practical applications. It is particularly troubling in automation contexts, which often require attending to, and switching attention across, multiple variables.

> **Cognitive lockup**
> a type of cognitive error that results from the human tendency to detect and deal with faults sequentially.

The term 'cognitive lockup' was introduced by Moray and Rotenberg (1989) in a study that examined the behaviours of student participants acting as operators during a fault-detection task. The task involved controlling set points for temperature, level and flow rate in a simulated thermal hydraulic system. Various disturbances were applied to the system, and participants had to respond to and deal with the failures as they arose. The participants' eye movements were recorded as an index of their locus of attention, along with their behavioural responses to the failures (key presses on a computer). The behavioural and eye movement data revealed a preference for serial fault management and a tendency for the participants to examine faulty subsystems more frequently. This led to a failure to switch attention appropriately and delayed action on other subsystems.

A real-world example of cognitive lockup resulted in the Eastern Air Lines Flight 401 crash of 1972. Flight 401 was a scheduled flight from New York to Miami, which crashed into the Florida Everglades, killing 101 people; 75 passengers and crew survived. An experienced crew flying a new aircraft had an unremarkable flight until coming towards landing. On approach to Miami airport, the crew lowered the landing gear. The nose landing gear indicator light failed to engage. Not knowing whether this was due to a faulty bulb or a failure of the nose gear, the captain requested clearance to circle and climbed to 2000 feet. The crew then investigated the faulty bulb. One member removed the bulb casing and attempted to replace it. Another crew member climbed out of the cockpit to get a view of the landing gear in order to confirm it had engaged. At some point, the captain inadvertently nudged the control wheel, disengaging the autopilot and causing the plane's nose to tilt downwards. This went unnoticed by the crew, as did an auditory alarm signalling a drop in altitude. While the crew were still focused on the landing gear light, the aircraft dropped to 900 feet. By the time the crew noticed, it was too late. The aircraft lost too much altitude and crashed. The accident report released by the National Transportation Safety Board noted that the likely cause was the failure of the crew to monitor the flight instruments during the final four minutes of flight and to detect the unexpected descent in time to correct for it. They were preoccupied with the malfunctioning landing gear light and did not switch attention appropriately to deal with the drop in altitude.

Such incidents are referred to as 'loss of control' incidents and are, unfortunately, not uncommon. The Air France AF447 crash of 2009 resulted from a similar loss of control, when the autopilot disengaged and the aircraft stalled, leading to the loss of the aircraft and all 228 passengers and crew on board. As in Flight 401, the catastrophic failure in cognition occurred over just four minutes of an otherwise competent and uneventful flight (Oliver et al., 2017).

Human error is often not the only factor at work in loss of control incidents. In the case of Flight 401, a safety feature of the aircraft allowed the autopilot to be disengaged easily by nudging the control wheel. An unintended consequence of this was that it became too easy to disengage the autopilot inadvertently. Scheduled civilian air travel is statistically 'ultra-safe' – that is, the risk of disastrous accident is below one accident per million events. As technology has advanced to control more systems, a paradox has arisen, referred to as 'the paradox of almost totally safe systems' (Amalberti, 2001). In the case of aviation, technology has improved safety by controlling and providing information on many of the aircraft's systems, reducing the complexity of the environment in which the crew is operating. However, in doing so, it has also reduced a pilot's situational awareness in that he or she spends much of their time monitoring digital indicators (the 'glass cockpit') and not so much time actually flying the airplane. This means that when an unexpected occurrence arises, the cognitive system may be less prepared to deal with the novel event, leading to errors. The paradox means that ultra-safe systems behave differently than less safe systems, and therefore require a different approach to detect and prevent errors (Amalberti, 2001; Oliver et al., 2017). A complex web of factors rather than one single cause tends to account for disastrous errors in such cases, with issues around machine–human handover requiring particular attention (for further examples from aviation see Dismukes et al., 2007).

Recent research has shown that individuals with better working memory and sustained attention have an advantage when detecting these kinds of failures, and that this advantage is particularly evident in situations involving consecutive failures. A study by Jipp (2016) examined individual differences in the memory factors underlying cognitive lockup. Participants were required to monitor automated aircraft functions. An initial automation failure was applied to the system. It occurred alone or was followed by a consecutive failure. Participants' reaction times to respond to the failures were recorded and standardized tests were used to assess their working memory capacity and sustained attention.

> The results showed that participants' reaction times were slower for consecutive failures compared to initial failures. However, this effect was stronger for those with poorer working memory and sustained attention scores. Participants who performed strongly on the tests of working memory and sustained attention showed a small advantage over those with poorer working memory and attention when responding to initial failures. This advantage was seen to increase, however, when consecutive failures occurred. The study has implications for both the selection and training of personnel in tasks where cognitive lockup might be predicted or where it might have serious consequences.
>
> Research is beginning to explore the interactions between working memory and attention that might allow an operator to avoid cognitive lockup. Unsworth and Robison (2019) have proposed a *cognitive-energetic* account of individual differences in working memory capacity and sustained attention that relates to differences in intrinsic alertness, whereby participants who are lower in working memory capacity are less skilled at controlling the intensity of attention compared to individuals who have high working memory capacity. Such accounts may be useful in understanding loss of control incidents and avoiding disastrous consequences. They are also relevant to individual differences in mind wandering, a topic explored in Box 6.5.

WORKING MEMORY

As previously discussed, if LTM is dependent on STM processes, then findings from patients such as K.F. and P.V. cannot be explained if we retain the assumption that STM is a unitary store. K.F. had severely deficient STM, as measured by digit span and the recency effect, and yet he showed intact long-term memory, and performed normally on tasks requiring information to be transferred to LTM, such as the paired-associate task. This finding suggests that different subsystems must underlie tasks such as digit span and word list learning. For K.F., and individuals with a similar pattern of performance after brain injury, the subsystem of STM underlying digit span is impaired, but some components of STM remain intact and allow relatively spared performance on tests of LTM. In other words, K.F. must have some intact short-term memory in order to demonstrate the pattern of performance he does on memory tasks. The concept of working memory (WM) has been helpful in understanding the pattern of ability in such neuropsychological case studies as well as in other real-world scenarios such as that illustrated in Box 6.3.

Working memory has been described as the 'workbench' of human cognition (Klatzky, 1980). It is 'the collection of mental processes that permit information to be held temporarily in an accessible state, in the service of some mental task' (Cowan, 1998, p. 77). It can be thought of as 'the small amount of information held in a readily accessible state, available to help in the completion of cognitive tasks' (Cowan, 2010, p. 447). Miyake and Shah (1999, p. 450) proposed a comprehensive definition of working memory that can be applied across the various models:

> *working memory is those mechanisms or processes that are involved in the control, regulation, and active maintenance of task-relevant information in the service of complex cognition, including novel as well as familiar, skilled tasks. It consists of a set of processes and mechanisms and is not a fixed "place" or "box" in the cognitive architecture. It is not a completely unitary system in the sense that it involves multiple representational codes and/or different subsystems. Its capacity limits reflect multiple factors and may even be an emergent property of the multiple processes and mechanisms involved. Working memory*

is closely linked to LTM, and its contents consist primarily of currently activated LTM representations, but can also extend to LTM representations that are closely linked to activated retrieval cues and, hence, can be quickly activated.

Miyake and Shah's (1999) definition emerged from a small conference on working memory in which presenters were each asked to give their definition of working memory; no two definitions agreed (Cowan, 2010). The term working memory means different things to different people, with researchers using the term in at least three ways (see Beaman, 2010; Cowan, 1998). Researchers may view working memory as:

- the focus of attention, consistent with James's (1890) view of primary memory (e.g., Engle, 2002)
- the information that is temporarily activated in the system, including information about our current goals and plans, consistent with Miller et al.'s (1960) original use of the term working memory
- a sensory-specific multicomponent storage system for short-term storage and processing of information (e.g., Baddeley & Hitch, 1974).

Accounts of working memory also vary in their approach to the relationship between working memory and long-term memory. Cowan's embedded processes model (e.g., 1995a, 1999) presents WM as consisting of a capacity-limited focus of attention and a temporarily activated subset of long-term memory (see Figure 6.7). This account places emphasis on the interaction of attention and memory, and considers WM in the context of LTM. Thus, by this account, three components contribute to WM: temporarily activated information that is not yet accessible to conscious awareness; memory within the focus of attention; and information stored in LTM, which is currently inactive but could be retrieved/activated if relevant to the task (Cowan, 1999; see also Oberauer's (2002) three-embedded-components model). The model proposes that these key components contribute to WM as embedded processes, with the current focus of attention being a subset of active memory and active memory presented as a subset of LTM (see Figure 6.7). By this account, information is lost from WM through processes of both decay and displacement. The focus of attention is capacity limited and information can

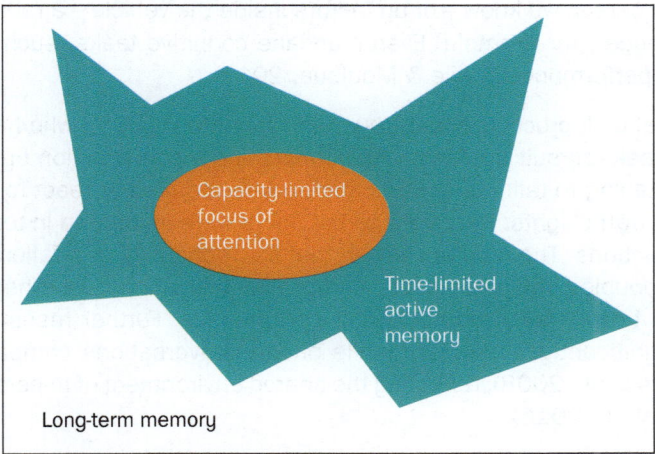

Figure 6.7 Cowan's embedded processes model.
The embedded processes model presents WM as three components: temporarily activated information that is not yet accessible to conscious awareness; memory within the focus of attention; and information stored in LTM, which is currently inactive but could be retrieved/activated if relevant to the task.

Source: Reprinted from Cowan (1998), with permission from Elsevier.

easily be displaced from it, while the activated memory is time limited, and information can decay if not rehearsed. In contrast to the multiple component model discussed below, in Cowan's model, the nature of the representation may vary in WM but it does so within a single structure that has fixed properties (see also Engle & Oransky, 1999), thus 'the distinctness and non-interchangeability of phonetic and spatial information occurs because different types of features are being activated, not because of distinctly different storage modules' (Cowan, 1995a, p. 36).

On the other hand, multiple component models of WM propose that WM can be fractionated into component parts. This approach sees the principal function of WM as the coordination of resources, and focuses on identifying and examining the nature of the structures that carry out this function (Baddeley, 1986; 1992a, 1992b). WM consists of both storage and processing components (Baddeley, 1986) and might be defined as 'the simultaneous processing and storage of information' (Salthouse, 1990, p. 104). Towse and Hitch (2007, p. 110) see WM as a 'multicomponent, limited-capacity system responsible for retaining as well as transforming fragile representations'. For Baddeley (1992b), the term working memory 'refers to a brain system that provides temporary storage and manipulation of the information necessary for such complex tasks as language comprehension, learning and reasoning' (p. 556). Baddeley and Hitch's (1974) working memory model (and its subsequent versions) has been the most influential of such accounts, and it is to this model that we now turn.

 Box 6.3 Practical Application: Fatal distraction? Working memory and driving performance

The ability to multi-task is a key component of safe driving. As the task requirements increase, so too does the working memory load, and performance on one or other task will begin to suffer. Working memory (and in particular the central executive, a component we will learn about shortly) plays a central role in controlling the allocation of resources across competing tasks. Many of the difficulties facing drivers involve what are essentially dual-task demands: paying attention to, or avoiding being distracted by, features of the environment that may not be central to the primary task of safely navigating and controlling a motor vehicle. We can be distracted by factors external to the vehicle – a dog running onto the road, seeing a person we know – or by factors inside the vehicle – a radio commentary or a conversation with a passenger, for example. Even mundane cognitive tasks, such as recalling a grocery list, can impair driving performance (Louie & Mouloua, 2019).

This was demonstrated in a dual task procedure by Strayer and Johnston (2001), who had participants complete a driving-analogous task (pursuit tracking) while conducting a conversation by mobile phone (hand-held or hands-free) or listening to talk radio. Participants were required to react to red and green lights, simulating responses to traffic lights. Reactions to the lights were measured in terms of failures to detect lights and delayed reactions. The results showed that the probability of a failure to detect the light and react appropriately doubled for participants using a mobile phone, whether hand-held or hands-free. Passively listening to talk radio did not affect performance. Further research has shown that driving performance is significantly worse for mobile phone conversations compared to driver–passenger conversations (Drews et al., 2008), reflecting the shared environment of in-person exchanges (see also Oviedo-Trespalacios et al., 2016).

A secondary task may even be advantageous in some conditions. Traffic conditions are a clear determinant of working-memory load. A study by Nijboer et al. (2016) used a simulated multi-lane driving task in which participants were assigned to one of two scenarios. One scenario required the driver to navigate a quiet road, with no traffic. The second scenario required driving in traffic and overtaking

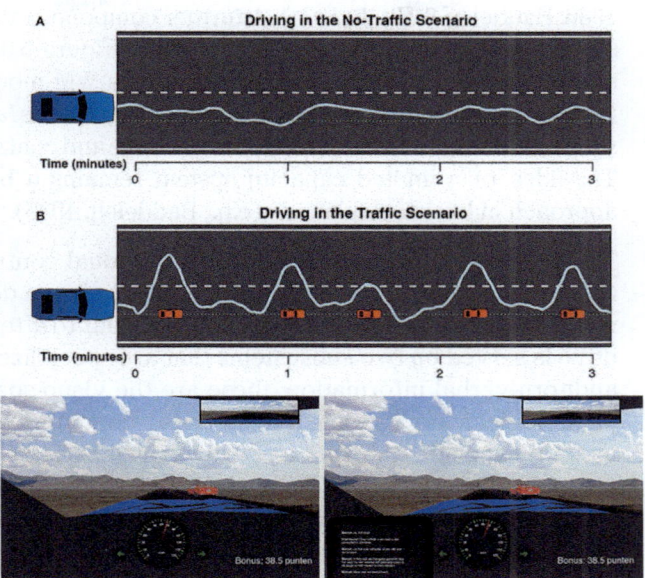

Figure 6.8 Nijboer et al.'s driving task.
The top panel shows two examples of driving paths in the (A) No-Traffic and (B) Traffic scenarios. The blue line shows the path taken by the participant, while the green dotted line shows the middle of the lane, and the white dashed line shows the boundary of the two lanes. The red cars represent slow moving traffic which must be overtaken by participants. The bottom panel shows the simulated driving environment used by Nijboer et al. (2016); left, the view as seen during the single, passive listening and radio-quiz conditions and, right, as seen during the tablet-quiz condition. *(Note that the study was conducted in a country with right-lane driving and the materials reflect this.)*

Source: Nijboer et al. (2016).

vehicles when necessary. Four different secondary task conditions were then applied: no secondary task; listening to a radio talk programme; listening to and giving responses to a radio quiz show using a button press response; and reading and giving responses to quiz items using a tablet device. Measures included driving speed, deviations from lane, overtake distance, direction changes and collisions.

In both driving scenarios (traffic and no traffic), performance was the worst in the tablet quiz condition, which resulted in dangerous driving. This is to be expected given the increased working memory load and the overlap with the task requirements of the primary driving task. It is also consistent with studies examining the effects of texting (e.g., Bayer & Campbell, 2012) and of social media use (e.g., George et al., 2018; Hashash et al., 2019) while driving.

Interestingly, however, Nijboer et al. (2016) found that the best driving performance was associated with passively listening to the radio or answering the radio quiz questions, rather than driving without any secondary task. In the traffic scenario, passively listening to the radio produced the best performance. These results suggest that listening to the radio might be advantageous in monotonous driving conditions and that the nature of the secondary task and the overall driving context are key factors.

Baddeley's Working Memory Model

According to Baddeley (1986), 'the essence of the concept of working memory lies in its implication that memory processes play an important role in non-memory tasks' (p. 246). WM is not just a store for maintaining information in consciousness – it plays an integral role in ongoing or 'online' cognitive processing. Baddeley and colleagues' multi-component working memory model proposed three main components to working memory: the **central executive**,

> **Central executive**
> the component of working memory proposed to control and coordinate the activity of the other components, including the phonological loop and the visuo-spatial sketchpad.

> **Visuo-spatial sketchpad**
> the component of working memory proposed for the temporary storage and manipulation of visual and spatial information.
>
> **Phonological loop**
> the component of working memory proposed for the temporary storage and manipulation of sound or phonological information. It comprises a short-term phonological store for auditory memory traces and an articulatory rehearsal component to reactivate memory traces.
>
> **Episodic buffer**
> the component of working memory proposed for the temporary storage of information integrated from the phonological loop, the visuo-spatial sketchpad and long-term memory into single structures or episodes.

the visuo-spatial sketchpad and the phonological loop (e.g., Baddeley, 1986; Baddeley & Hitch, 1974). A further component, the episodic buffer, was subsequently added (see Baddeley, 2000). Figure 6.9 illustrates the relationships between the main components of this WM model. Baddeley and Hitch (1974, p. 76) described the core of the WM system as 'a limited capacity "work space" which can be divided between storage and control processing demands'. This idea of a limited capacity system remains a basic assumption of the approach in later formulations (e.g., Baddeley, 1986).

The central executive provides the attentional control of working memory (Baddeley, 1996a). It is modality-free, in that it can deal with input from any modality (visual, auditory, etc.), and is similar to attention. The central executive is served by two subsystems that are specialized for visual-spatial and auditory-verbal information; these are the visuo-spatial sketchpad and the phonological loop, respectively. These components hold and manipulate modality-specific information, the visuo-spatial sketchpad dealing with visual information and the phonological loop dealing with speech-based information. The pattern of deficit described in the case of K.F., encountered above, suggests damage to the verbal aspect of working memory, while the other components remain unaffected by the brain injury, thus allowing access to long-term memory and effective long-term memory functioning. While Baddeley's model focuses on visuo-spatial and verbal-auditory input, research is beginning to explore modalities other than these (see Lawson et al., 2015, for a discussion of tactile and haptic working memory). We will first look at the component of WM that has received the most scrutiny: the phonological loop.

The phonological loop

The phonological loop is specialized for speech-based information. This component of WM is closest to earlier notions of a short-term memory store (e.g., Atkinson and Shiffrin, 1968), and is implicated in tasks involving verbal materials, such as digit span and serial position tasks (see Figure 6.11). While Baddeley and Hitch (1974) initially called this component the 'articulatory loop', the term 'phonological loop' replaced it, to reflect the more central processing involved in subvocal articulation; the 'inner voice' does not rely on the speech musculature, and is retained in individuals who have brain damage affecting overt articulation (conditions such as anarthria for example; see Baddeley & Wilson, 1985).

> **Anarthria**
> a disorder affecting the motor function underlying speech.

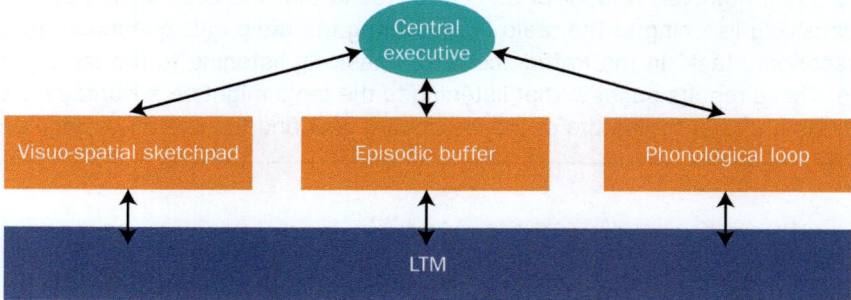

Figure 6.9 The working memory model showing the interaction with long-term memory structures and the episodic buffer.
The three main components of working memory – the central executive, phonological loop and visuo-spatial sketchpad – interact with structures in long-term memory.

Source: Adapted from Baddeley (2000).

Baddeley et al. (1975) proposed that the phonological loop has a limited capacity restricted by temporal duration, and that it holds as many verbal items (words, letters, etc.) as a person can say in about two seconds.

The WM model proposes that the phonological loop has two subcomponents: a phonological store, which holds speech-based information for a period of about two to three seconds (unless the information is rehearsed), and an articulatory control process, which allows the maintenance of information in the store and converts visual information (such as a written word) to a speech-based form. The articulatory control process uses subvocal rehearsal to fulfil these functions, a process that can be likened to '**inner speech**' (Baddeley, 1986, 1992). Auditory presentation of phonological (speech-based) information gains direct access to the loop, while visually presented information gains access via subvocal articulation by the articulatory control process. **Rehearsal**, which refers to a number of processes by which content being held in working memory is refreshed, is assumed to play a key role in verbal working memory in particular (the nature of that role continues to be debated; see for example Oberauer, 2019). Evidence for the phonological loop comes from four main sources or benchmark findings (e.g., see Baddeley, 2012), which we will now examine.

> **Inner speech**
> the subjective experience of hearing our thoughts, as if 'spoken' by an inner voice, when reading silently for example.
>
> **Rehearsal**
> a set of processes by which we can act on currently active information.
>
> **Word length effect**
> the recall advantage for shorter words compared to longer words when immediate serial recall is tested.

1. The word length effect

If participants can hold in memory as many words as they can say in two seconds, then one might reason that the shorter the words are, the more of them that will be remembered. The **word length effect** refers to the advantage found for recall of lists of short words (e.g., car, lake, pen, chair) compared to longer words (e.g., television, university, candlestick, hippopotamus). The duration it takes to articulate the word is the crucial factor, not the number of syllables (Baddeley et al., 1975). The words 'ticket' and 'harpoon' both contain two syllables, but 'harpoon' takes longer to say than 'ticket'. The longer the word, the more time it takes to refresh the word in the phonological store by subvocal articulation, therefore fewer long words can be accommodated in the store. This difference in rehearsal underlying the word length effect is supported by the finding that the effect is eliminated by subvocal rehearsal; if a participant has to repeat an irrelevant string (e.g., saying 'the' over and over) while learning the list, the advantage for shorter words disappears (Baddeley et al., 1975).

While the word length effect is well established, there have been some contradictory findings. The difference in effect for words with the same number of syllables but different articulation speeds ('ticket' versus 'harpoon') has not always been replicated using different word sets (for a discussion see Mattys et al., 2018). Furthermore, some studies have shown that the word length effect may be affected by orthographic neighbourhood size – that is, number of words that differ from the target word by one letter (e.g., *plant* and *plank*). Shorter words tend to have more neighbours, and while the words used in experimental word lists are carefully controlled for factors such as concreteness and imageability, neighbourhood size had not been controlled in demonstrations of the word length effect. A confounding variable had therefore been introduced into such studies. Jalbert et al. (2011) identified this issue, and found that the word length effect disappeared when short (one syllable) and long (three syllable) words were controlled for neighbourhood size (see also Derraugh et al., 2017). This suggests that linguistic properties other than word length are also of relevance and points to a role for LTM in WM tasks (information about the properties of words is stored in LTM). However, Guitard et al. (2018) failed to replicate the effect, and found a large and reliable word length effect after controlling for neighbourhood size.

We might predict cross-linguistic differences in memory span that reflect variation in word length across languages. This has been demonstrated in a number of languages, with estimated spans of 9.9 in Chinese (Hoosain, 1984), for example, compared to 5.7 in Arabic (Naveh-Benjamin & Ayres, 1986). Mattys et al. (2018) reported a digit span of 8.8 for Chinese compared to 6.9 for English speakers, and a word span difference of 7.1 for Chinese and 5.2 for English. Chen et al. (2009) found that the mean digit span of a sample of English speakers was equivalent to the lowest individual score of their Mandarin-speaking sample (see also Mattys et al., 2018). The relatively larger digit span of Chinese speakers has been argued to reflect faster articulation rates for Chinese digits, a finding demonstrated both with Mandarin (Hoosain, 1984; Hoosain & Salili, 1988; Mattys et al., 2018) and Cantonese (Stigler et al., 1986). Ellis and Hennelly (1980) reported a shorter digit span in Welsh compared to in English, reflecting longer articulation times for Welsh words and the smaller number of Welsh words that could be articulated in two seconds. **Coarticulation effects** of words (see Chapter 10) have also been shown to be an important factors in the Welsh–English difference however (Murray & Jones, 2002). Such data provide further evidence for a speech-based store with temporal limits. The cross-linguistic data concur with developmental data showing that span increases through childhood (from about the age of 4 years) as speech rate increases (e.g., Hulme et al., 1984). It is important to understand such cross-linguistic differences, not least because digit span measures form the basis of many neuropsychological and educational test batteries (e.g., see López et al., 2016).

> Chapter 10, p343

> **Coarticulation effects** the modification that occurs to any given speech sound due to the sounds that occur before or after it in the speech chain.

2. The effects of articulatory suppression

As observed above, the ability to rehearse subvocally can be disrupted if we require a participant to rehearse a string that is not relevant to the current task. For example, the participant might be required to repeat the word 'the' or to count to three over and again, a process referred to as articulatory suppression (Murray, 1965). **Articulatory suppression** reduces memory span (Peterson & Johnson, 1971) and eliminates the word length effect (Baddeley et al., 1975). It also disrupts transfer of visually presented material to the phonological store, leading to poorer memory (Baddeley et al., 1984). This difference between visual and auditory material has been interpreted as reflecting direct access to the store for auditory information (e.g., spoken words), while visually presented information (e.g., written words) requires sub-vocalization for access (e.g., Baddeley, 2012). The repetition of an irrelevant word or string uses the capacity of the articulatory control process, and prevents information in the phonological store from being refreshed, leading to a detriment in performance. Articulatory suppression does not eliminate phonological recoding completely, but does reduce it considerably. For example, Norris et al. (2018) were able to induce a dramatic deficit in their participants across a variety of tasks, with degraded performance analogous to patients with a phonological STM deficit.

> **Articulatory suppression** the interference that occurs when participants are required to repeat (non-relevant) verbal material while engaged in a primary task drawing on the same modality.

3. The irrelevant speech effect

Recall of visually presented verbal material is poorer when irrelevant speech is presented during learning (e.g., Larsen & Baddeley, 2003). One does not need to understand what is being said in order for the speech to disrupt processing – even hearing irrelevant speech in an unfamiliar language (Colle & Welsh, 1976) or nonsense words (Salame & Baddeley, 1986) produces the effect. Any speech gains access to the phonological store and therefore irrelevant speech uses some of the available capacity, reducing performance on the target task. Initially it appeared that non-speech sounds did not elicit the effect; Colle and Welsh (1976) found no effect for white noise, for example.

But in fact some non-speech sounds, particularly changing-state sounds, do disrupt STM. Jones and Macken (1993) showed that a stream of fluctuating tones disrupted recall of visually presented material in the same way as speech. Box 6.4 examines a number of other ways in which extraneous sound can affect working memory.

> **Box 6.4 Practical Application: Understanding the effects of background noise**
>
> Many people work or study in open-plan office settings, relying on working memory to reduce the influence of distracting stimuli and to allow resources to be allocated to the task at hand. However, it is not always easy to dismiss the distracting influence of background noise. Banbury and Berry (2005) found that 99 per cent of workers in open-plan offices reported impaired concentration caused by various office noises; the sound of telephones ringing at unattended desks and background speech sounds were particularly distracting. Banbury et al. (2001) noted that the distraction effect is rooted in the changing nature of the acoustic signal, which gains our attention; repetitive sounds or tones are not as disruptive and the sound level itself would also seem to be relatively unimportant. If reducing the sound level does not eradicate the ill effects on cognition, how might workplace design compensate for the effect?
>
> One way to reduce the effect on cognitive performance is to mask the office sounds by adding a continuous noise signal. It may seem paradoxical to address the problem by adding more sound, but the continuous signal is designed to reduce the perception of acoustic change, which is the basis of the distraction. A study by Schlittmeier and Hellbrück (2009) examined the use of background music compared to continuous noise for masking office sounds. Their participants completed a serial recall task while office noise was played at 55 dB, a typical sound level in open-plan offices. The office noise was presented alone, or was overlaid with legato music, staccato music or continuous noise. A silence condition was also included. While the participants reported preferring the music to the continuous sound, memory performance was better only in the continuous noise condition. That is, office noise affected serial recall performance negatively, in comparison to silence, whether it was presented alone or overlaid with music. Only the office noise with continuous noise produced similar performance to the silence condition. So, while the subjective ratings did not favour continuous noise, cognitive ill effects were minimized only in that condition.
>
> The type of noise and the interaction of noise type and task type are also of relevance. Schlittmeier et al. (2015) examined the effects of different levels of road traffic noise within a moderate range of 50–70 dB(A) on cognitive performance. Four traffic noise conditions were compared with background speech and a silence (control) condition. The tasks used varied in terms of reliance on attention or storage functions of working memory. Three experiments allowed comparison of performance on the Stroop task, which relies on attention, a mental arithmetic task, which makes use of both sustained attention and short-term storage, and a verbal serial recall task, which relies on WM storage functions.
>
> The results showed that road traffic noise disrupted performance in tasks that require attentional control, namely the Stroop test and the mental arithmetic task. However, consistent with the irrelevant sound effect, none of the road traffic noise conditions had an effect on serial recall. Performance in the serial recall task was disrupted however by background speech. Performance on the mental arithmetic task was also found to be disrupted by background speech. These results demonstrate the effect of temporal-spectral variability in background speech on WM storage functions; the traffic noise, lacking this variability, had no effect. Similar effects can be seen for aircraft noise, with working memory seen to be largely immune from the detrimental effects evident in long-term memory tasks (Molesworth et al., 2017; see also Hygge, 2003; Sörqvist, 2010). In addition, easier tasks may be more affected by noise level, while difficult tasks are more sensitive to the type of noise (Golmohammadi et al., 2020).

4. The phonological similarity effect

> **Phonological similarity effect**
> the finding that recall is poorer for an ordered list of verbal items when the items sound alike, compared to performance on lists of items that do not sound alike.

Recall is poorer for an ordered list of verbal items when the items sound alike, relative to performance on lists of items that do not sound alike. This is referred to as the **phonological similarity effect**. Items that are similar in meaning (as opposed to sound) do not show this effect. For example, the sequence 'pit, day, cow, pen, rig' is easier to recall than the sequence 'man, cap, can, map, mad' (Baddeley, 1992b). The second list contains items that sound more alike than the first list. Similarly, recall of lists of similar-sounding letters (e.g., c, b, d, v) is poorer than for lists of dissimilar letters, (e.g., c, r, m, k) (Conrad, 1964). If we assume that the phonological store uses a speech-based or phonological code, then refreshing the items in the store makes use of phonological fragments within the items; confusion arises as the number of shared fragments increases. The phonological similarity effect disappears under conditions of articulatory suppression, supporting the use of a basic phonological code (Richardson & Baddeley, 1975). However, when information from LTM comes into play, the phonological similarity effect may be diminished or absent. Nursery rhymes and song lyrics commonly utilize words with shared sounds, and memory for such sequences may well be improved (e.g., Copeland & Radvansky, 2001). Under some conditions, a phonological similarity *facilitation* effect can even be observed in working memory span tasks (Chow et al., 2016).

Functions of the phonological loop

Given that the phonological loop holds and manipulates speech-based information, we could expect to see a substantial and obvious role for this WM structure in language and related cognitive processing. However, in adults, the role is not as obvious as one might expect. As Baddeley (1992b) notes, individuals who have a brain injury affecting phonological loop functioning show relatively few signs of general cognitive impairment. For example, the case of P.V. (discussed above) described by Baddeley et al. (1988), involved a severely reduced digit span (of one or two items) following a left hemisphere stroke, yet her day-to-day life was relatively unaffected. She ran a shop successfully and she raised a family. Her intelligence and short-term *visual* memory were normal and her language function was relatively intact, with normal language comprehension for all but the most convoluted of embedded sentences (sentences that require you to hold the beginning of the sentence in mind until you get to the end, with a number of intervening clauses). The case of P.V. and other single case studies in neuropsychology have been tremendously important in the development of the concept of the phonological loop (Baddeley & Hitch, 2019).

What, then, are the functions of the phonological loop? The phonological loop is known to play a key role in the acquisition of new vocabulary, not just in the person's native language but also in a second language (Service, 1992). Baddeley et al. (1988) found that P.V., who had intact long-term memory as measured by performance on a paired-associate task, showed a severely reduced ability to learn words in Russian, a language with which P.V. was not familiar. The loop's precise role in other aspects of adult language processing, such as complex speech comprehension, remains controversial (see Caplan & Waters, 1999; Engle & Conway, 1998; Was & Woltz, 2007). In children, poor performance on measures of phonological loop function is associated with poor vocabulary learning (e.g., Gathercole & Baddeley, 1989; Gathercole et al., 1997; Service, 1992), and very poor phonological loop skills are associated with developmental disorders such as specific language impairment (SLI; see Gathercole & Baddeley, 1990). The phonological loop would also seem to play an important role in learning to read (for an overview see Baddeley & Hitch, 2019). There is evidence that the phonological loop is involved in the temporary storage of part solutions during mental arithmetic, while the central executive performs the more demanding manipulations. For example, Logie et al. (1994) found effects of both articulatory suppression and irrelevant speech on an addition task using a series of two-digit numbers (e.g., 12 + 43 + 18 + 26 + 35 = ?). Such data suggest a specific role for the phonological loop in mental arithmetic, although a more substantive role is performed by the central executive (Adams & Hitch, 1998). The phonological loop may also have a role in action control (see Baddeley et al., 2001).

The visuo-spatial sketchpad

Suppose you are asked to say how many windows there are on the front of your house. To answer this question, you will most likely construct a mental image of your house and inspect that image in order to count the number of windows. Or suppose you are asked to describe the Sydney Opera House. Again, it is likely that you will try to visualize the building in your mind's eye, and try to describe what it looks like based on the visual image. The ability to manipulate visual images relies on visual short-term memory, and Baddeley and Hitch's model proposed that this type of memory is provided by a separate component, the visuo-spatial sketchpad (VSSP).

We saw above how neuropsychological case studies of individuals with very short verbal memory spans have been used to support the existence of the phonological loop component of working memory. There are fewer cases of selective impairments affecting visuo-spatial working memory, but some cases have been reported that support a WM component specialized for visuo-spatial processing. Hanley et al. (1991) described the case of E.L.D., who reported difficulties learning to recognize new faces and routes after a right-hemisphere brain injury. E.L.D. had moved to a new part of the city, and reported difficulty in forming a mental picture of routes she had taken; instead she found herself having to rely on landmarks to find her way around. Her verbal memory span was similar to that of controls, and visual perception was normal, but she performed extremely poorly on tasks that required the temporary storage of visual and/or spatial information (see also Hanley & Young, 2019). Studies showing activation of the same inferior temporal areas during visuo-spatial, but not verbal, working memory tasks further support the fractionation of WM (e.g., Hamamé et al., 2012).

While the phonological loop is specialized for speech-based information, the VSSP is specialized for dealing with visual and spatial information. The VSSP, like the phonological loop, has a limited capacity, of about three or four objects according to Baddeley (e.g., 2003). Logie (1995) suggested that two components comprise the VSSP. A **visual cache** stores information relating to visual form and an **inner scribe** allows spatial processing. Evidence supports the notion of separate but strongly interconnected components for visual and spatial information. Logie (1995) proposed that the VSSP is analogous in structure to the phonological loop. By this account, the visual cache is similar to the phonological store, in that it is a passive store that holds information, while the inner scribe (similar to the articulatory control process) maintains information in the store through a type of rehearsal process. Logie's account (e.g., 1995) sees long-term memory involvement as central to VSSP functioning.

> **Visual cache**
> the component of the visuo-spatial sketchpad, within working memory, that stores visual information.
>
> **Inner scribe**
> the component of the visuo-spatial sketchpad, within working memory, that allows spatial processing.

VSSP processing is evident in performance on the Brooks matrix task. Brooks (1967) devised a matrix task in which participants were presented with sentences to commit to memory; the sentences were either easy to visualize or could not be visualized (see Figure 6.10, overleaf). In a 'spatial condition', the sentences were accompanied by a 4 × 4 matrix, which could be used to aid memory, as the sentences could be visualized. Sentences such as 'in the starting square put a 1', 'in the next square to the right put a 2',

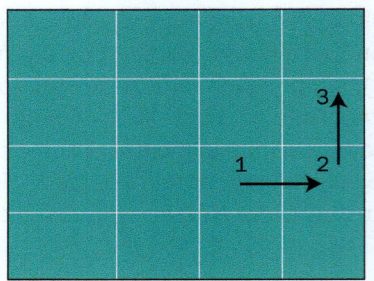

Figure 6.10 Depiction of the Brooks matrix task.
In the Brooks matrix task, instructions are either easy to visualize using a 4 × 4 grid matrix or they cannot be visualized using the matrix. Memory for the sentences is then tested.

Visualizable/spatial instructions
in the starting square put a 1
in the next square to the right put a 2
in the next square up put a 3

Non-visualizable/nonsense instructions
in the starting square put a 1
in the next square to the quick put a 2
in the next square to the good put a 3

'in the next square up put a 3', were used in the spatial condition. In a 'verbal condition', the adjectives 'up-down' and 'left-right' in the sentences were replaced with the non-spatial adjectives 'good-bad' and 'quick-slow'. This produced sentences that could not be readily visualized using the matrix (e.g., 'in the starting square put a 1', 'in the next square to the quick put a 2', 'in the next square to the good put a 3'). Memorizing these sentences required verbal coding, using the verbal component of WM, the phonological loop. Participants were required to recall the sentences. In the spatial condition, they typically recalled about eight sentences compared to six in the verbal condition. Brooks then compared auditory and visual presentation of the sentences and found that for the spatial task auditory presentation was best, but for the verbal task visual presentation produced better performance. Auditory presentation in the spatial condition frees up the VSSP for the primary task, while visual presentation in the verbal task frees up the phonological loop for the primary task.

A neuropsychological case study reported by Hanley and Young (2019) showed a contrasting pattern of performance on the Brooks matrix task. While the typical pattern is superior recall of sentences in the spatial imagery condition compared to the 'nonsense' condition, E.L.D. showed significantly better performance in the nonsense condition, producing four times as many errors in the spatial condition (Hanley et al., 1991, p. 105). This pattern of performance is consistent with an account suggesting selective damage to the VSSP.

Baddeley et al. (1975) developed a task designed to interfere with performance on the Brooks task. In their pursuit rotor task, participants were required to track a moving target using a hand-held stylus (requiring visuo-spatial involvement) while sentences were presented auditorily. This dual-task requirement interfered with performance in the spatial condition, but not in the verbal condition (see Figure 6.11), providing further support for the involvement of the VSSP in the task. Baddeley and Lieberman (1980) later tried to separate out the effects of the visual and spatial components of this task using two secondary task conditions. In one condition, participants made brightness judgements, a task requiring visual but not spatial processing. In a second condition, blindfolded participants were required to track a moving pendulum with a torch. The pendulum contained a photosensitive cell that, when in contact with light from the torch, caused an auditory tone to be emitted. Sentences were again presented auditorily. The researchers found greater disruption of performance in the spatial condition, relative to the brightness judgement condition.

Data from dual-task performance shows selective interference of visual and spatial working memory tasks (e.g., Della Sala et al., 1999). Further evidence supporting the distinction between the visual cache and the inner scribe comes from neuropsychological

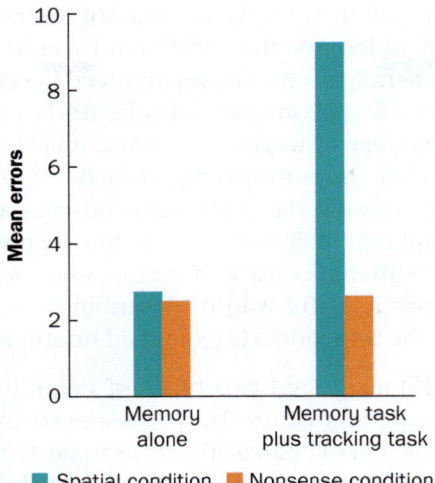

Figure 6.11 The effect of concurrent tracking on memory for visualizable (spatial) and non-visualizable (nonsense) sentences in Baddeley et al's., (1975) task.
Disruption of performance (mean errors per participant) is evident in the spatial condition, compared to the verbal condition. Data from Baddeley et al. (1975).

Source: Gathercole & Baddeley (1993).

case studies. Farah et al. (1988a) studied a patient, L.H., who sustained bilateral damage to the occipito-temporal regions of the brain in a traffic accident, while his parietal lobes were unharmed. L.H. performed well on tasks that involved manipulation of spatial imagery. He performed well on the Brooks task and on mental rotation tasks. He could point out locations on a map and he could also describe routes he was familiar with in the city where he lived. However, he showed impairments on visual tasks that required him to make judgements about relative size, colour and form. L.H.'s pattern of deficit suggested an impaired visual cache but an intact inner scribe, and his performance on spatial and visual imagery tasks supported Farah and colleagues' distinction between visual mental imagery and spatial imagery.

A second patient, R.T., showed the reverse pattern (Farah & Hammond, 1988). Following a stroke, R.T. had lesions affecting the right parietal lobe and part of his right temporal lobe. He had impaired spatial manipulation abilities, with poor performance on mental rotation tasks, for example, but reading and object recognition were intact. A further case (M.G.) reported by Morton and Morris (1995) presents a similar profile of spared visual imagery despite impaired spatial imagery. Luzzatti et al.'s (1998) case, E.P., demonstrated a similar impairment of spatial imagery while her ability to represent objects visually remained intact. Neuroimaging data support this dissociation, with separate brain areas for visual and spatial processing identified within the occipital, parietal and frontal lobes (e.g., Jonides et al., 1993; Sack & Schuhmann, 2012) consistent with the visual dual-pathway model (see Chapter 2).

Chapter 2, p46

The central executive

The central executive has been described as 'the workhorse and mastermind of human cognition' (Caplan & Waters, 1999, p. 77). It is the most important component of working memory – it is also the least well understood. Baddeley and Hitch's original model presented the central executive as a general processing mechanism that handled the more complex types of short-term memory task that were not delegated to the phonological loop or the VSSP. It was presented as a supervisory system that played a key role in controlling and regulating working memory function. It coordinated the activities of the phonological loop or the VSSP, and focused and switched attention. The central executive is generally seen as being involved in controlling active information, but not in storage per se (e.g., Baddeley & Logie, 1999), and it is useful to separate the storage and control functions of working memory. It is likely that the central executive consists of a number of subsystems, which have yet to be identified. Later versions of the model present the central executive as an attentional controller, similar to Norman and Shallice's (1986) concept of the supervisory activating system (SAS) in their model of attentional control of action, and Baddeley (1986) suggested that the SAS model provides a useful way of describing the functions of the central executive. For this reason the SAS model is examined briefly here.

Norman and Shallice (1986) suggested two types of cognitive control reflecting the distinction between automatic and controlled processes (Schneider & Shiffrin, 1977). The automatic system of control allows us to perform routine and well-practised actions through the selection of learned habits and **schemas** without the need for deliberate cognitive control. We can perform quite complex sequences of actions through this mode of operation, using a system Norman and Shallice refer to as the contention scheduling system. Our actions are directed by relevant schemas, activated by triggers in the environment. For example, we can drive home along a familiar route without fully concentrating on the route; we may even make it all the way home without being fully aware of key stages along our route ('Were the traffic lights green?'; 'What car was ahead of me?'). A second type of process makes use of an attentional control mechanism (the supervisory activating system, or SAS), which can interrupt automatic processing, select an alternative schema and allow attention to be directed towards a goal. Staying with the example of driving, if you go abroad and are required to drive on the opposite side of the road than you normally would, you have to exert more effort and deliberate control over what might otherwise be highly automated actions. It is important that routine actions do not dominate on such occasions. These two qualitatively distinct control systems allow three levels of functioning, according to the Norman and Shallice model:

> **Schema**
> a framework that represents a plan or a theory, supporting the organization of knowledge.

1. a fully automatic mode for routine actions
2. an intermediate, partially automatic mode, which allows attentional control of actions, and
3. the deliberate control of action for non-habitual or novel tasks.

> Chapter 11, p411

Thus, according to this approach, 'contention scheduling – the system responsible for routine selection of action – was held to operate in the intact adult human modulated by a second system – the supervisory system – held to be responsible for the organization of non-routine (novel) behaviours' (Cooper & Shallice, 2000, p. 303).

> **Capture errors**
> involve a failure to override a routine set of actions; a routine or well-practised action is performed when another action was intended.
> **Stroop task**
> used to demonstrate the Stroop effect, whereby the naming of colours shows interference when the colour of the word and meaning of the word are incongruent.

Evidence for two separate control systems, one governing performance of routine actions and the other allowing control of non-routine action comes from studies of individuals with frontal lobe damage. Patients with damage to the prefrontal cortex experience problems completing tasks that require SAS-type attentional control and their errors often reflect intact contention scheduling (Shallice, 2002). For example, 'capture errors' are associated with prefrontal damage. **Capture errors** involve a failure to override a routine set of actions; for example, we might leave the house on a Saturday and drive to work or to college instead of to our intended destination. William James (1890) recounted an occasion when he went upstairs with the intention of changing his clothes, but instead went to bed. In the **Stroop task** (see Chapter 11) the automatic reading of a word when the task requires us to simply name the colour provides another example of a capture error.

Baddeley and Wilson (1988) used the term **dysexecutive syndrome** to refer to the type of impairment that specifically involves deficits in executive function, and which is often associated with dorsolateral prefrontal damage. Affected individuals may demonstrate 'disturbed attention, increased distractibility, a difficulty in grasping the whole of a complicated state of affairs . . . [they are] well able to work along old routine lines. But they cannot learn to master new types of task' (Rylander, 1939, p. 20). Dysexecutive syndrome is characterized by an inability to exert control over one's behaviours and it may involve difficulties initiating, ceasing, suppressing or modifying actions as environmental cues change. For example, some individuals demonstrate **perseveration**, the inappropriate repetition of an action. On the **Wisconsin Card Sorting Test**, a test of frontal lobe function, the participant is required to alter his or her card selection as a 'rule' supplied by the examiner changes (Milner, 1963). A number of trials follow one rule (for example, 'sort the cards according to colour'), then the rule changes (to, for example, 'sort the cards according to pattern'). Individuals with frontal lobe damage often show perseveration in continuing to respond with the old rule even though the rule has now changed. Patients are aware that the rule has changed and are often aware that they are making errors – despite this they continue to apply the inappropriate rule.

> **Dysexecutive syndrome**
> a range of deficits reflecting problems with executive function and control, and often associated with injury to the frontal areas of the brain.
> **Perseveration**
> the inappropriate repetition of an action.
> **Wisconsin Card Sorting Test**
> a standardized neuropsychological test that assesses set-shifting, an aspect of executive functioning that allows us to change cognitive strategy as the demands of a task require.

The central executive also allows us to maintain focus and to keep our attention on the task at hand, ignoring competing input from the environment; individual differences in working memory capacity, for example, predict the likelihood that one's mind will wander while engaged in a task requiring concentration (see Box 6.5 for further discussion of 'mind wandering'). A patient may show spontaneous and apparently uncontrollable imitation of a doctor, for example, or a compulsion to interact with objects (such as picking up and miming the use of an object, when not asked to do so), a tendency referred to as **utilization behaviour**. The ability to control responses to environmental cues is compromised: 'in the absence of control from the SAS, the patient simply responds to any cues of opportunities afforded by the environment (Baddeley, 2009, p. 54). The case of E.V.R. (Box 6.6) illustrates such a pattern of deficit.

> **Utilization behaviour**
> dysfunctional automatic reaching for and use of objects in the environment.

Baddeley (2012) notes four key functions of the executive: focusing attention; dividing attention; switching between tasks; and interfacing with LTM. The variety of executive deficits seen in such patients suggests that the central executive is further fractionated into subsystems or subprocesses, maybe suggesting a 'series of parallel but equal processes, an executive "committee" perhaps' (Baddeley, 1996a, p. 13,471). Shah and Miyake (1996) suggest visual and verbal subcomponents, but, as yet, the executive has not been refined into subcomponents in the way that the phonological loop and visuo-spatial sketchpad have been.

Box 6.5 Research Close Up: Working memory and mind wandering

Source: Kane et al. (2017).

INTRODUCTION

A significant proportion of our waking day is spent engaged in task-unrelated thoughts (TUTs) and can be considered to constitute 'mind wandering'. While sometimes associated with cognitive error, mind wandering often occurs without negative consequences, as a natural shift in attention from external to internal focus. This type of spontaneous thought, far from being a cognitive weakness, may reflect fundamental properties of the architecture of the mind, helping us to consolidate memory, and to integrate and categorize experiences throughout the day (Christoff et al., 2008). If this is the case, we might expect to see an association between aspects of working memory capacity (WMC) and mind wandering. As it turns out, this relationship is not uncomplicated and varies with the nature of the task and its complexity, as well as many individual difference variables including WMC.

A study by Kane et al. (2007) examined daily life mind wandering, using an experience-sampling approach, a technique in which participants are required, at various times during a day, to report on their current thoughts, and to categorize those thoughts as being 'on task' or 'off task'. That study produced three notable findings. Participants reported that their minds had wandered off-task on almost a third of occasions on average, with considerable individual differences observed. Context was important: participants were less likely to report their minds wandering when they felt happy and competent, were concentrating or when enjoying their current activity. WMC predicted mind wandering only as a function of the cognitive demands of the task. Participants with higher WMC were less likely to report their minds wandering while engaged in tasks for which concentration was required. However, when engaged in tasks requiring little concentration, individuals with high WMC were significantly *more* likely to mind-wander compared to participants with lower WMC. Participants with lower WMC reported more incidents of mind wandering as the challenge and effort involved in their current task increased (see Figure 6.12). Kane et al. (2017) replicated and extended their earlier study with a larger sample, measuring WMC more broadly and comparing reports of mind wandering probed during laboratory tasks and daily life contexts.

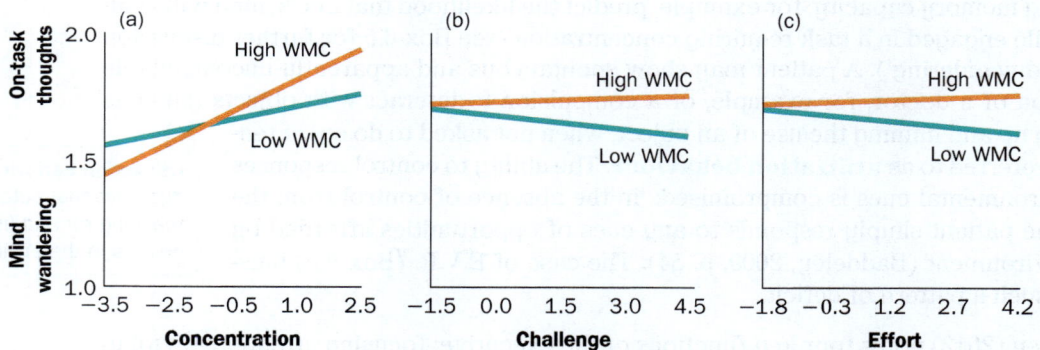

Figure 6.12 Differences in working memory capacity (WMC) reflect differences in mind wandering during a cognition task.
The lines show the means for participants in two groups, the top and bottom quartiles of the working memory scores. The y-axis shows whether the participant was on task; a lower score indicates mind wandering. The x-axis shows self-ratings indicating whether the participants found the task to require concentration, whether they found it challenging and whether they rated it as requiring effort.

Source: Adapted from Kane et al. (2007).

METHOD

Kane et al. (2017) used the experience-sampling methodology to collect data on mind wandering in participants' daily lives but they also probed mind wandering during a series of experimental tasks completed in the laboratory. Thought probes appeared at unpredictable intervals during a series of computer-based experimental tasks, including the Sustained Attention to Response Task (SART) and the Number Stroop task. These are tasks requiring attentional control. The SART required participants to press a key when animal names were presented and not to respond when vegetable names were presented. In the Number Stroop task, a row of two to four digits was presented on each trial. Participants were required to press the key corresponding to the number of digits present, while ignoring the meaning (for example, given '4 4 4' respond by pressing key 3. Trials could be congruent ('2 2' respond 2) or incongruent (e.g., '3 3 3 3' respond 4) (for more on the Stroop task, see Chapter 11).

> Chapter 11, p404

At each probe, subjects indicated which of eight presented options was closest to the content of their immediately preceding thoughts (for example, 'everyday things', 'current state of being', 'personal worries', 'daydreams'). Outside of the laboratory tasks, participants completed eight questionnaires per day over seven days, when prompted at various points by a mobile device alert. WMC was measured through a series of complex span tasks including reading span.

RESULTS

Participants reported that their mind had wandered, on average, for 32 per cent of the probes, with considerable individual differences (SD = 17 per cent, range = 2–97 per cent). This is consistent with previous estimates that participants' thoughts are off-task on a third of probes (Kane et al., 2007).

The results showed that participants tended to be aware of daily life TUTs and that the content of such thoughts was often focused on everyday plans and goals. Participants tended to remain mentally on task when concentrating. Mind wandering was associated with negative affect (feeling anxious, sad, irritable or confused), tiredness or boredom. The interaction effect reported by Kane et al. (2007) between WMC and task demand was replicated and extended, as WMC only predicted mind wandering as a function of participants' concentration level. When participants reported concentrating, those with higher WMC were more likely to have remained on task compared to those with lower WMC. In tasks requiring less concentration, participants with higher WMC were more likely to report their mind had wandered. Furthermore, participants' scores on WMC and attention correlated with TUTs in the lab, but not in daily life and, interestingly, the laboratory TUT rate did not significantly predict daily life mind wandering, the effect falling just outside statistical significance ($p = .07$).

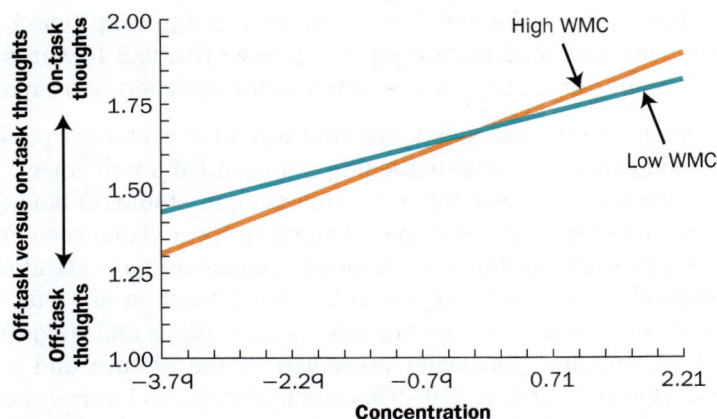

Figure 6.13 **The relationship between daily-life mind wandering and working memory capacity (WMC) as a function of self-reported concentration.**
The y-axis shows whether the participant was on task; a lower score indicates mind wandering. The x-axis shows self-ratings indicating whether the participants found the task to require concentration.

Source: Kane et al. (2017, Figure 1, panel 1).

DISCUSSION

Kane and colleagues' study shows the importance of considering individual differences such as WMC, but also the context of the task, and the cognitive demands posed by it. It also highlights important differences between measurements taken in laboratory studies and those sampled in daily life. Laboratory mind wandering did not significantly predict daily-life mind wandering, the correlation falling just outside significance. Before concluding that there is no relationship between these measures, however, the reliability of the self-report method would have to be questioned. Self-report methods of thought sampling can be *self-caught* (the participant reports when they notice that their mind has wandered) or *probe-caught* (a probe occurs at various points), as in the Kane et al. studies, and the participant reports whether their mind had wandered at that point in time. The latter method provides an estimate of the proportion of the time the person was in a mind-wandering state. It does however require a level of insight and relies on self-report accuracy and therefore some have questioned whether better methods are needed (e.g., see Voss et al., 2018).

Recent research has pointed towards mind-wandering as a heterogeneous set of processes, some beneficial and some detrimental, with some theorists advocating for a 'family-resemblances' approach to the study of mind-wandering, recognizing the variety of experience that can fall within that construct (Seli et al., 2018). Research has also differentiated between spontaneous and deliberate mind wandering (e.g., Vannucci & Chiorri, 2018), and is beginning to examine the relationship between mind wandering and mindfulness, which might be seen, in some aspects, as an opposing construct (Ju & Lien, 2018; Mrazek et al., 2012).

The episodic buffer

Baddeley's working memory model (e.g., Baddeley, 1996b) originally considered the role of the central executive in focusing, dividing and switching attention, and in linking WM to LTM, but it did not seem to have a storage component of its own (Baddeley, 2012). But some verbal learning tasks involve a larger storage capacity than is supported by data on the phonological loop, suggesting that working memory can make use of additional storage capacity. For example, when unrelated words are presented in a span task, a limit of about five or six items is typically found, but if the words are presented in a sentence, memory span increases to about 15 words (Brener, 1940). If the loop holds only seven or so items, where is the extra storage capacity coming from?

Furthermore, performance is facilitated when the sentences presented are grammatical, yet judgements of grammaticality require LTM involvement. LTM access has also been shown to affect VSSP function. For example, studies of boundary extension errors show that participants' visuo-spatial memory for a visual scene can be distorted (see Figure 6.14), such that the scene is often remembered as extending beyond the boundary originally presented (e.g., Intraub, 1997; Intraub et al., 1998; Intraub et al., 1996). Such errors occur after even very brief presentations and suggest 'a seamless integration of information physically presented in the picture and information that was inferred' (Intraub, 1997, p. 219). This would depend on information in the VSSP making contact with relevant information stored in LTM (Radvansky, 2006). The original WM model of Baddeley and Hitch did not suggest how this might occur, but other accounts speculated on the interaction of these memory systems. For example, Ericsson and Kintsch (1995) proposed a 'long-term working memory', whereby information from long-term memory can be used to compensate for the limited capacity (short-term) working memory.

The need to explain how WM interacts with LTM and how WM can sometimes involve a larger storage capacity led to a proposed further component within WM. Baddeley's (2000) WM model differs in two ways from the earlier model. First, it shows that the WM modality-specific subsystems (phonological loop and visuo-spatial sketchpad) link to

Figure 6.14 Viewers tend to remember seeing the area of a scene as extending beyond the boundary of the original photograph.
Panels a and b show similar scenes; panel b had a wider, broader frame than panel a. When asked to draw what they had seen, participants tend to extend beyond the actual boundary. Panel c shows a participant's recall of seeing panel a, and panel d shows a participant's recall of seeing panel b. The drawing in panel d shows the roof of a house and an outline of a tree that were not in the original photograph (panel b).

Source: Reprinted from Intraub (1997), with permission from Elsevier.

LTM, and, second, the episodic buffer was introduced, which can be accessed by the central executive or by the modality-specific subsystems, and which links to LTM (see Figure 6.8). The buffer is 'a crucial feature of the capacity of working memory to act as a global workspace that is accessed by conscious awareness' (Baddeley, 2003, p. 836). The episodic buffer is a temporary storage structure of limited capacity (it can hold about four chunks of information; Baddeley, 2009) that is controlled by the central executive and allows information from different sources (visuo-spatial sketchpad, phonological loop, LTM) to be integrated, essentially providing a means of interface between the modality-specific systems of WM and LTM. It can be considered to be the storage component of the central executive (Baddeley, 2003) and it 'is episodic in the sense that it holds episodes whereby information is integrated across space and potentially extended across time . . . it is assumed to be a temporary store . . . [and is] assumed to play an important role in feeding information into and retrieving information from episodic LTM' (Baddeley, 2000, p. 421). Baddeley (2012) provides a useful overview of the development of the various components of the WM model.

Box 6.6 When Things Go Wrong: Case E.V.R.

Executive function is crucial for effective planning and goal-directed behaviour. What happens when brain injury affects this function? Eslinger and Damasio (1985) described the case of E.V.R., an accountant, who at the age of 35 had a brain tumour – a large orbitofrontal meningioma that had been compressing both frontal lobes – removed, leading to bilateral damage to the ventro-medial frontal areas. His intellectual abilities remained largely intact. He had above average intelligence, scoring in the top 1–2 percentile, with a verbal IQ of 132 and a performance IQ of 135. Before his illness he was responsible, hard-working and had been promoted at his job. He was sociable and active in his community.

But, after his surgery, E.V.R. could not keep a job, his planning of activities both immediate and into the future was severely impaired, and even minor decisions (what to wear, where to eat out) took an inordinate amount of consideration. He could no longer plan his finances and his business ventures ended in bankruptcy. His altered social behaviour and personality profile led Damasio (1994) to suggest that E.V.R. presented a case of 'acquired sociopathy' (see also Damasio et al., 1992). While E.V.R.'s intellectual capacity remained largely unaffected by his illness, he lacked the emotional or social intelligence to be able to flexibly alter his behaviour or predict the consequences of his actions. As Damasio put it, 'we might summarize [his] predicament as to know but not to feel' (1994, p. 45). This case illustrates the important role that emotion plays in cognition, an issue we will return to in Chapter 15.

Chapter 15, p550

Abnormal performance on everyday tasks despite apparently intact intellectual functioning is a commonly reported feature of frontal lobe damage. Shallice and Burgess (1991) had three people who had frontal brain damage attempt a real-world task called the multiple errands task. The test required the participants to complete a number of tasks within an unfamiliar shopping centre. The tasks varied in complexity (e.g., buy a postage stamp or find out the euro–sterling exchange rate) and there were a number of rules the participants had to follow (e.g., 'do not go into a shop except to buy something that's on the list'). All three participants scored normally on tests of language and intellectual ability, yet all three performed poorly on the multiple errands task, having deviated from the rules (e.g., gone into shops when they were not supposed to) or failed to complete tasks. A number of socially inappropriate behaviours occurred (see Burgess et al., 2007). One participant left a shop without paying for the goods, while another offered sexual favours in lieu of payment, an unusual and socially inappropriate offer.

Such cases demonstrate the key role played by executive functioning in everyday planning and goal-directed behaviour. It is important to note however that a range of outcomes is possible following frontal lobe damage and that even very severe injuries can be associated with good recovery of function. The classic case of Phineas Gage, reported by Harlow (1848), is one of the earliest reports of executive dysfunction after a frontal lobe injury (see Chapter 15, Box 15.1). Gage suffered a severe frontal lobe injury while blasting through rocks during his on the railroads. Gage is one of the most cited cases in cognitive neuropsychology, and is generally presented as showing severe personality change and executive dysfunction after frontal lobe damage. It is now generally accepted that Gage must have shown some recovery, as he spent many years subsequently working as a stagecoach driver. This would have been a demanding job in terms of executive functioning, requiring interaction with passengers, taking payments, loading luggage, remembering routes and caring for the horses (see Macmillan, 2000, pp. 104–106). A modern case described by Mataró et al. (2001) also suggests some recovery of function.

Chapter 15, p552

Evaluation

Baddeley's working memory model was proposed as a replacement for the concept of a unitary short-term store, and the concept of working memory has provided a useful description of a flexible, adaptable, yet capacity-limited system. It introduced a number of subsystems and showed how WM structures are involved not just in memory functions but in complex cognitive tasks more generally, such as learning and reasoning (Baddeley, 1996a, 2000). The model explained how, following brain injury, impaired STM (as measured by digit span) could accompany normal LTM, and it explained selective deficits in verbal or visuo-spatial processing evident in other case studies. The model detailed a number of components, the activities of which can be tested, through dual task experiments for example. The addition of the episodic buffer went some way towards considering how LTM interacts with WM (although the model does not detail how this interaction occurs) and provided a general multi-modal storage capacity to WM, but other models (e.g., Cowan, 1988) have dealt with LTM involvement more explicitly.

The most successful component of the model is the phonological loop, although there continues to be much debate around the detail of the component. Various accounts continue to debate whether forgetting is best characterized as occurring through time-based decay or interference, a debate that has been ongoing since the 1960s (see Baddeley, 2012). Baddeley's model assumed that information is lost from memory through decay unless it is refreshed. Interference accounts argue that forgetting is due to interference among items in memory (e.g., see Farrell et al., 2016). While most models of working memory assume a crucial role for rehearsal processes, some experimental studies and computational models have called into question the causal relationship between rehearsal and memory (Oberauer, 2019; Souza & Oberauer, 2018).

Furthermore, there remain some data that do not fit with the WM model (e.g., see Ward, 2001) and findings such as the word length effect and the effect of articulatory suppression, which seem to point to a key role of rehearsal processes, may not be quite as reliable as once believed (Oberauer, 2019). On balance, however, the introduction of the phonological loop has been an extremely useful concept for understanding verbal short-term memory and its limits, and has led to many new directions in research.

The central executive, clearly a pivotal component in the WM model, is as yet not fully understood, and further research will be required in order to determine whether it is a single component of WM or actually consists of a number of high-level processes, involving many interacting brain areas. Donald (1991) described the central executive as presented in working memory models as 'a hypothetical entity that sits atop the mountain of working memory and attention like some gigantic Buddha, an inscrutable, immaterial, omnipresent homunculus, at whose busy desk the buck stops every time memory and attention theorists run out of alternatives' (p. 327). This is a weakness common to many models of short-term memory: the central executive as a concept invokes the idea of an executive controller, a 'ghost in the machine' or 'homunculus' that controls the system. And this gives rise to the homunculus problem: if there is an executive controller then who or what controls that controller? There must be another executive controller overseeing the processing of the first executive controller. And then who controls the second controller? Who is deciding what information to act on and how it should be processed? This creates an infinite regress or succession of homunculi, and detracts from the explanatory value of the model. Baddeley (2012) suggests that rather than being a weakness, the homunculus concept can be a useful marker of issues that require explanation (p. 14). Baddeley's model of working memory attempted to avoid the homunculus problem by fractionating working memory into component parts and, as noted by Logie (2016), Baddeley anticipated the issue by treating the central executive as a 'conceptual ragbag' or umbrella term which over time would be elucidated by additional data (Baddeley, 1996). Unpacking the functions of each subsystem reduces the need for a central executive. We may soon arrive at the point where the central executive concept might be given a 'dignified retirement' (Logie, 2016), although as Hopkins (2017, p. 2) points out, what will be left following its retirement is rather unclear.

Alternative accounts of working memory share this weakness, and there remains a need to specify the mechanisms that control working memory and the conditions under which they operate. The relationships between working memory, attention and consciousness are poorly understood, and it remains unclear as to whether working memory is the basis of conscious experience, or whether it arises from consciousness

Chapter 5, p152

(see Chapter 5); WM is closely associated with conscious experience, but they are not one and the same (Baars, 1997). Neuroscientific research is beginning to unpack the complex relationship between memory and attention (e.g., Lewis-Peacock et al., 2012).

Research looking at how to improve working memory, and the role of **self-efficacy** (see Box 6.7) and other individual differences, is also providing new insights into memory functioning (see, for example, Hoffman, 2010; Hoffman & Schraw, 2009; Kingston & Lyddy, 2013).

> **Self-efficacy**
> a person's sense of their own competence to complete a certain task or achieve a goal.

Baddeley's WM model is arguably at its best when factors relating to LTM are minimized (Cowan, 1995b), and links to LTM are considered to a greater extent in other models of working memory (e.g., Cowan, 1995a; Ericsson and Kintsch, 1995; see also Oberauer, 2002). In practice, it is difficult to separate the processes of LTM and WM in everyday cognition, and research has begun to focus on the interactions between WM and LTM (e.g., see Burgess & Hitch, 2005, for an overview). On balance, however, and despite its detractors, Baddeley's multi-component WM model remains remarkably robust to criticism, having survived coming up to 50 years of scientific scrutiny, retaining much of its predictive and explanatory power in the process (Logie & D'Esposito, 2007). It counts as one of the most influential works in the field of cognitive psychology (see Logie & Cowan, 2015), along with the Atkinson–Shiffrin predecessor (Malmberg et al., 2019).

 Box 6.7 Research Close Up: Self-efficacy and working memory

Source: Autin & Croizet (2012).

INTRODUCTION

We often think of working memory capacity as if it were fixed. But, in fact, the performance of our working memory can be affected by situational factors, by aspects of the task and by factors such as stress or emotion. But does self-efficacy affect working memory? Self-efficacy refers to a person's sense of their own competence to complete a certain task or achieve a particular goal. A study by Autin and Croizet (2012) examined this, across three experiments with 11-year-old children; their first two studies will be considered here.

METHOD AND RESULTS
Study 1

In their first study, Autin and Croizet randomly allocated children to three groups. Two groups of children completed an anagram task before their working memory task. The anagrams were so difficult that they could not be solved within the time allocated. One group of children, in the 'reframing' condition, were told that having difficulty with the task was normal and in fact showed that learning was occurring. The second group who did the anagrams did not get this reframing information. A third control group were not exposed to the anagram task, but went directly to the working memory task. All participants performed a listening span test. In the listening span task, participants listen to a series of sentences. After each sentence is presented the participant has to report whether the sentence makes sense or not, and also repeat back the last word in the sentence. At the end of the series, participants have to repeat back as many last words as possible, in the same order as they were presented. The series of sentences vary from two to five sentences, so participants have to remember up to five sentence-final words. The results showed that children allocated to the reframing condition had a greater working memory span than either of the two other groups (see Figure 6.15).

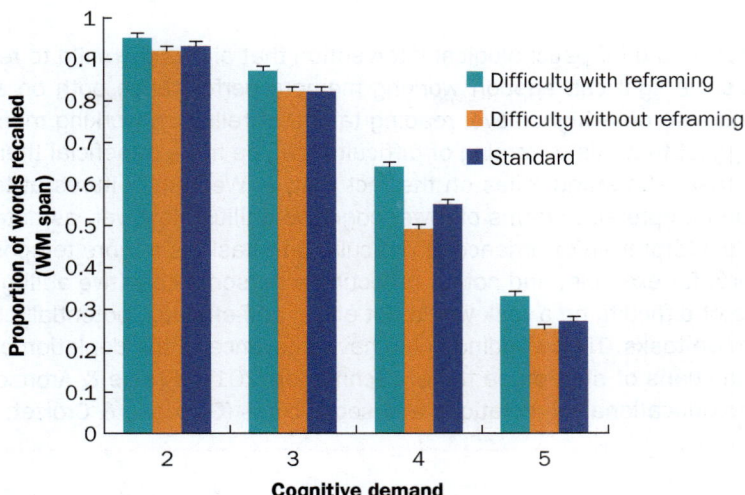

Figure 6.15 Working memory (WM) span as a function of the experimental condition in Study 1.
Having a difficult task but reframing it; having a difficult task without the opportunity to reframe it; and the standard control condition. Cognitive demand of the WM test (two, three, four or five words to remember) is shown along the x-axis. Error bars represent standard errors.

Source: Autin & Croizet (2012). APA; reprinted with permission.

Study 2

In the second study, Autin and Croizet examined whether this effect would extend to higher-level processing that relies on working memory span, in this case reading comprehension. The three conditions from the first study were replicated with a new sample of 11 year olds, with one further condition added. In a 'success' condition, children did easier anagrams and got them right. A difficult reading test followed, instead of the working memory test used in Study 1. The results were consistent with those of Study 1. Children in the reframing condition showed better reading comprehension than the other three groups, which did not differ significantly from one another (see Figure 6.16).

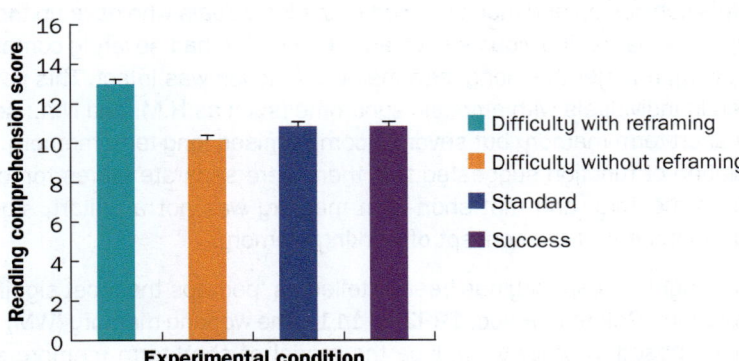

Figure 6.16 Reading comprehension score as a function of experimental condition.
Having a difficult task but reframing it; having a difficult task without the opportunity to reframe it; the standard control condition; and an additional 'success' condition. The maximum score was 18. Error bars represent standard errors.

Source: Autin & Croizet (2012). APA; reprinted with permission.

DISCUSSION

These data suggest that a brief psychological intervention that allows the child to reinterpret difficulty with a task in a positive light can support working memory performance both on a standard test of working memory and also on a higher-level reading task that relies on working memory. The findings of Study 2 even suggest that this reframing of difficulty may be more beneficial than an experience of success on a prior task. The study relies on the fact that, in Western cultures at least, experiencing difficulty tends to be interpreted in terms of lower cognitive ability. However, as noted by the authors, some cultures would interpret an experience of difficulty on a task as a more temporary issue, reflecting a lack of mastery, for example, and not as reflecting a person's cognitive ability. In such cultures, a child's experience of difficulty on a task would not affect self-efficacy, potentially bringing an advantage on some cognitive tasks. These findings also have relevance to the depletion of working memory resources under conditions of stereotype threat (Schmader, 2010; Steele & Aronson, 1995), as well as biases relating to educational expectations and social class (Goudeau & Croizet, 2017).

Summary

In this chapter we have considered how information is held and manipulated in memory. Early models of memory, such as Atkinson and Shiffrin's (1968) model proposed three stores: sensory, short-term and long-term stores. We saw that the sensory memory stores are large-capacity stores that hold information for a very short duration, serving to prolong rapidly presented input for processing in the short-term store. Sensory memory contains subsystems specialized for visual, auditory and other types of sensory input. The sensory stores hold information but do not code it in a form that allows categorization or processing of meaning. In order for the meaning of a stimulus to be appreciated, the information must be transferred to short-term memory. Sensory stores are modality-specific and there is now good evidence for separate visual (iconic), auditory (echoic) and haptic/tactile (touch related) stores.

The short-term memory store as proposed by the multi-store account (such as that of Atkinson and Shiffrin) was a unitary store that had a limited capacity of about 7 ± 2 pieces of information. Information had to flow through this store in order to access long-term memory. This, as it turns out, is an over-simplification of the short-term system, which must involve a number of relatively independent processes. Neuropsychological case studies of individuals with left-hemisphere brain injury were extremely useful in coming to this conclusion and much is owed to the individuals who gave up their time to take part in testing, often over many years. Individuals such as K.F. and P.V. had severely compromised short-term memory after brain injury, and yet their long-term memory function was intact. This pattern of deficit contrasted with that seen in individuals with amnesic syndrome (such as H.M. and N.A.; see also Chapter 7), who showed normal short-term memory but severely compromised long-term memory. This double dissociation of function suggested that there were separate stores for long-term and short-term memory, and that short-term memory was not a unitary store. This led to the development of the concept of working memory.

Chapter 7, p223

Working memory as a cognitive capacity has been extolled as 'perhaps the most significant achievement of human mental evolution' (Goldman-Rakic, 1992, p. 111). The working memory (WM) model of Baddeley and colleagues was proposed in order to replace the model of short-term memory as a unitary store. The WM model suggested three components to WM: a central executive, like internal attention (see Chapter 4), which oversees the activities of two modality-specific systems – the visuo-spatial sketchpad for storing and manipulating visual and spatial information, and the phonological loop for storing and manipulating speech-based

Chapter 4, p114

information. Later, an additional component, the episodic buffer, was added to explain the additional storage capacity of the central executive and to link the components of WM and LTM. Other theories of WM have taken a different approach; for example Cowan's account focuses on WM as embedded systems for attentional control with activation of stored knowledge from LTM playing a central role in WM processing. The central executive, a key concept in working memory, remains to be adequately specified, and while various models of working memory have been proposed, no full explanation of executive functioning has as yet been forthcoming. Research has begun to address the relationship between long-term memory and working memory, examining whether they are structurally separate systems and the means by which they interact. The Baddeley and Hitch (1974) model (with later versions) has proved to be a landmark contribution in the history of cognitive psychology, and has spawned what is approaching 50 years of progressively illuminating research.

Review Questions

1. What is meant by working memory?
2. What are the components of the phonological loop?
3. How might we best measure the capacity of short-term memory?
4. What is sensory memory and what is its function?
5. What evidence is there supporting the main components of Baddeley's working memory model?

Discussion Questions

1. How essential has evidence from brain injury – and particularly single cases – been to our understanding of short-term memory?
2. What is the relationship between short-term and working memory? Do these two terms mean the same thing?
3. What is the relationship between working memory and attention?

Further Reading

Baddeley, A. D. (2003). Working memory: Looking back and looking forward. *Nature Reviews Neuroscience*, 4(10): 829–839.

Baddeley, A. D., & Hitch, G. J. (2019). The phonological loop as a buffer store: An update. *Cortex, 112*, 91–106.

Cowan, N. (2010). The magical mystery four: How is working memory capacity limited, and why? *Current Directions in Psychological Science, 19*, 51–57.

Miller, G. A. (1956). The magical number seven, plus or minus two: Some limits on our capacity for processing information. *Psychological Review, 63*, 81–97.

Roediger III, H. L., Zaromb, F. M., & Lin, W. (2017). A typology of memory terms. In R. Menzel (Ed.), *Learning theory and behavior*, Vol. 1 of Byrne, J. H. (Ed.), *Learning and memory: A comprehensive reference* (2nd ed.) (pp. 7–19). Academic Press.

7

PREVIEW QUESTIONS
INTRODUCTION
 ❗ **Box 7.1 When Things Go Wrong:** The case of H.M.
MEMORY AND AMNESIA
THE STRUCTURE OF LTM
  MULTIPLE MEMORY SYSTEMS MODEL
NON-DECLARATIVE MEMORY
  SKILL LEARNING
  HABIT LEARNING
  REPETITION PRIMING
DECLARATIVE MEMORY
 🔍 **Box 7.2 Research Close Up:** The role of schemas in memory
  PROSPECTIVE MEMORY AND IMAGINING FUTURE EVENTS
 🧠 **Box 7.3 Practical Application:** Improving prospective memory
 🔍 **Box 7.4 Research Close Up:** Does a prospective memory deficit underlie checking compulsions?
  AUTOBIOGRAPHICAL MEMORY
 🔍 **Box 7.5 Research Close Up:** Remembering traumatic events – does perspective matter?
 ❗ **Box 7.6 When Things Go Wrong:** Experiencing involuntary traumatic recollections – suffering from PTSD
 🔍 **Box 7.7 Research Close Up:** Reasons for withdrawing beliefs in autobiographical memories?
  SEMANTIC MEMORY
 🔍 **Box 7.8 Research Close Up:** Do we know what we don't know?
 🧠 **Box 7.9 Practical Application:** Measuring everyday memory
SUMMARY
REVIEW QUESTIONS
DISCUSSION QUESTIONS
FURTHER READING

Preview Questions

1. What can we learn about normal memory from the study of memory disorders?
2. How is the long-term memory system organized?
3. How does long-term memory differ from short-term memory?
4. What are declarative and non-declarative memories?
5. What is prospective memory?
6. What is autobiographical memory and which functions does it serve?

INTRODUCTION

> Chapter 6, p190

In Chapter 6, we briefly mentioned one of the more famous cases in neuroscientific literature, that of H.M. In 1953, at the age of 27, he underwent an experimental surgical procedure that aimed to alleviate his medically intractable epilepsy. H.M. had temporal-lobe surgery that involved removing the amygdala, the anterior two-thirds of the hippocampus, adjacent hippocampal gyrus and the parahippocampal gyrus (Squire, 2009). Following his operation, H.M.'s seizures were dramatically reduced. However, the reduction in seizure activity came at an enormous and unanticipated cost: H.M. was left with a profound and pervasive memory impairment, a pattern of memory deficit known as **amnesia**. H.M. retained his childhood memories, but he had a severe and lasting deficit affecting his memory for ongoing events. He did not remember people he had met; he could not retain his doctors' names; he could not recall activities he had just completed; he could not find his way around the hospital. However, his short-term memory was relatively intact – he could answer questions, for example, and repeat back a sequence of digits – but these experiences were not subsequently retained. His personality, intellect and ability to use language remained largely intact.

> **Amnesia**
> a pattern of memory loss affecting elements of long-term memory, while short-term memory remains intact.

H.M.'s case, one of the most cited cases in neuropsychology, demonstrates three important aspects of long-term memory (LTM) processes (see Corkin, 2002). First, long-term memory processes are not distributed throughout the brain as had been previously thought; damage to particular areas within the temporal lobes will cause profound long-term memory loss. Before H.M., the standard view of long-term memory within psychology, influenced by Karl Lashley's work, was the idea that memory functions were widely distributed over the brain. Lashley performed experiments on rats, systematically removing particular areas of the cortex and examining the effects on the rats' learning. On the basis of his experiments, he could not locate any particular brain region that was necessary for memory, and so he concluded that it was the size of the cortical areas and not its location that was the important factor (the principle of mass action; Lashley, 1929). H.M.'s case (see Box 7.1) showed that particular brain regions are responsible for long-term memory function, and that disruption to these regions has devastating effects. Second, long-term memory encompasses a number of different abilities and some learning may be possible after damage to the system. H.M. was able to learn some new skills, but he could not remember new facts. Third, H.M.'s case showed that memory is separable from language, perceptual and other cognitive functions (Squire, 2009). These were relatively unaffected in H.M.'s case, despite his profound memory impairment.

! Box 7.1 When Things Go Wrong: The case of H.M.

'Every day is alone in itself, whatever enjoyment I've had, and whatever sorrow I've had' (H.M. in Milner et al., 1968, p. 217).

The severe memory impairment that H.M. developed following brain surgery changed the way that cognitive psychology approaches the subject of LTM. An only child, H.M. was born in Hartford, Connecticut, in 1926. When he was 7 years old, he was knocked down by a cyclist; the accident left him unconscious for several minutes (Scoville & Milner, 1957). By the age of 10 years, H.M. was experiencing minor seizures. Whether this was related to the accident is unclear; epilepsy was also noted in H.M.'s family history (Corkin, 2002). By the age of 16, H.M.'s condition had deteriorated. He experienced general convulsions, without warning and on a regular basis, with tongue-biting, urinary incontinence, loss of consciousness and subsequent drowsiness (Scoville & Milner, 1957). The frequency and severity of the seizures increased over time and the condition was unresponsive to medication. By his twenties, H.M.'s condition was so severe that he could not work and his quality of life was severely compromised.

In 1953, at the age of 27, H.M. underwent an experimental surgical procedure that aimed to alleviate his symptoms. Neurosurgeon William Beecher Scoville resected H.M.'s medial temporal lobes (see Figure 7.1 and 7.2), removing the amygdala, the anterior two-thirds of the hippocampus, adjacent hippocampal gyrus and the parahippocampal gyrus (Squire, 2009). Following his operation, H.M.'s seizures were dramatically reduced, but he was left with a profound and pervasive memory impairment, a pattern of memory deficit known as the amnesic syndrome.

H.M.'s most striking impairment was a profound anterograde amnesia – he was unable to retain information encountered after his surgery. He did not recognize the researchers who worked with him regularly over five decades. He was unable to learn new words or the names of public figures he first encountered after the surgery. Half an hour after he ate lunch, he could not remember if, and what, he had eaten. It seemed that once the information left his consciousness, it was forgotten. However, as we will see, not all of his memory was affected; studies soon showed that he had some preserved function.

H.M. also showed some retrograde amnesia, which is loss of memory for information encountered before the onset of the amnesia. Scoville and Milner (1957) noted a retrograde loss spanning three years prior to the surgery. Later studies showed that H.M.'s retrograde amnesia extended to a period of 11 years prior to the onset of amnesia (Corkin, 2002). Retrograde amnesia tends to affect memory such that a temporal gradient is apparent: newer memories are more susceptible to disruption than

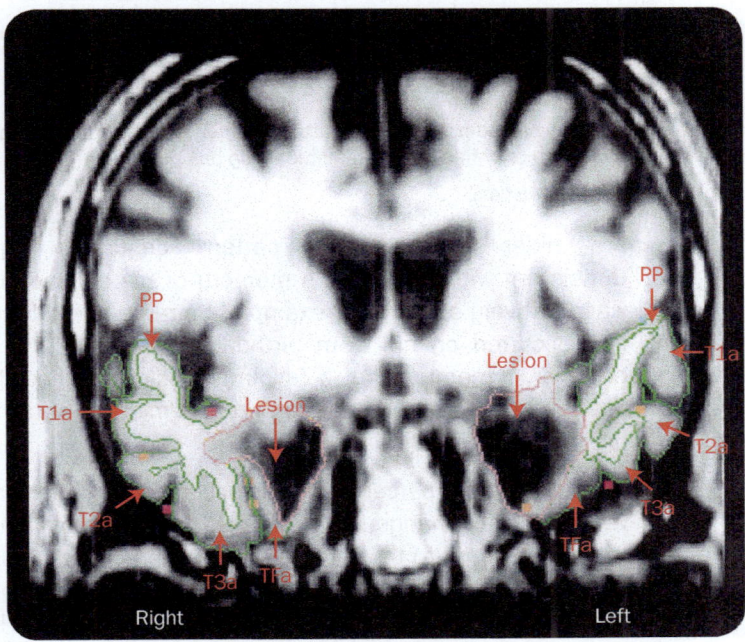

Figure 7.1 H.M.'s bilateral medial temporal lobe lesion.
Left temporal-lobe white matter is more severely damaged than the right. (Coloured squares identify key sulci.) PP, planum polare; T1a, superior temporal gyrus, anterior; T2a, middle temporal gyrus, anterior; T3a, inferior temporal gyrus, anterior; Tfa, temporal fusiform, anterior.

Source: Kensinger et al. (2001).

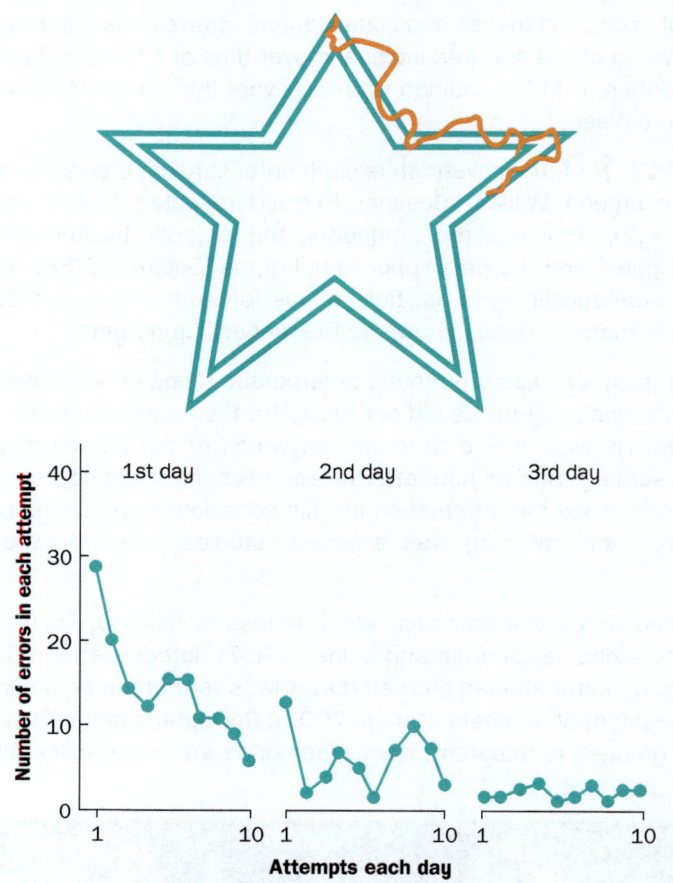

Figure 7.2 H.M.'s performance on the mirror-drawing task.
The upper panel shows the double-star outline and a typical early attempt to remain within the boundaries of the two stars. By day three, H.M.'s performance is close to error-free, showing that learning has occurred.

Source: Eichenbaum (2011). Data from Milner et al. (1968).

Ribot's Law (1881)
Ribot's Law of retrograde amnesia states that recently formed memories are more susceptible to impairment than are older memories.

Wechsler Memory Scale
a widely used neurocognitive assessment that measures visual memory, auditory memory and working memory.

Chapter 6, p176

are older memories, a pattern described by **Ribot's Law**. Consistent with this, H.M.'s memory of his childhood and adolescence was relatively spared. For example, he remembered that his first seizure had occurred on his 16th birthday (Hilts, 1995, p. 87). He did not, however, remember that a favourite uncle had died three years before his operation, nor did he recognize the medical staff he had met before his surgery (Shimamura, 1992).

H.M. had intact perception, intellect and language, and his personality was largely unchanged. He retained his sense of humour. When asked 'What do you do to try to remember?', he replied, 'Well, that I don't know 'cause I don't remember what I tried.' (Corkin, 2002, p. 158). This quote also illustrates H.M.'s insight into his own condition. H.M.'s IQ remained in the normal range, and even increased slightly after the surgery, presumably due to the reduction in seizure activity (Kalat, 2007). By comparison, his performance on the **Wechsler Memory Scale** was far lower than would be expected given his intellectual capacity (Scoville & Milner, 1957). His short-term memory was intact and his digit span (see Chapter 6) was normal – he could carry out a conversation and retain information as long as he could rehearse it in short-term memory. He showed good sustained attention – he could, for example, retain a three-digit number for up to 15 minutes if he was allowed to continually rehearse it. But as soon as his attention shifted from the task at hand, the information was lost.

Studies of H.M.'s memory showed that he retained some preserved learning. Milner et al. (1968) used a mirror drawing task to demonstrate this preserved ability. In the mirror drawing task (see Figure 7.2), the participant is presented with a star-shaped pattern consisting of one star outline inside another. The task is to draw a line between the outer and inner stars – however, the participants can see their hand, the pencil and the stars only through a mirror (with left and right reversed). This is a tricky task, and participants generally require a few attempts before they can complete it. If H.M. could not form any new memories, then we would expect practice on the task to have no effect on his performance. But, as is evident from the graph shown in Figure 7.2, H.M.'s performance improved with practice. The time required to complete the task and the numbers of errors made decreased with practice. By the third day, H.M.'s performance was almost error-free.

These data provided the first experimental demonstration of preserved learning in amnesia; other preserved domains of learning also became apparent (see Corkin, 2002, for an overview). For example, five years after his operation, H.M. moved with his parents to live in a bungalow near Hartford, Connecticut. Tested a few years later, he was able to draw an accurate floor plan of his house.

In December 2008, H.M. died at the nursing home where he had lived for 28 years, and his real name, Henry Gustav Molaison, was released. While he could not have fully appreciated his contribution to the scientific understanding of memory processes, he did seem to appreciate that the research would be of use. Speaking about his neurosurgeon, he once remarked, 'What he learned about me helped others, and I'm glad about that' (Corkin, 2002, p. 159).

In the previous chapter, we looked at memory for currently active information. In this chapter, we consider long-term memory, the vast store of memories for events, facts and know-how that we accumulate over a lifetime and make use of every waking moment. By examining which aspects of memory are preserved and which are not in cases like H.M., much has been learned about the structure of long-term memory and its relationship to short-term memory. Before we consider long-term memory in normal cognition, we will look at memory function in amnesia and how the study of this condition has contributed to our understanding of long-term memory.

Chapter 6, p176

MEMORY AND AMNESIA

The term 'amnesia' as used in cognitive psychology and neuropsychology generally refers to a condition known as the **amnesic syndrome**. This is a permanent and pervasive disorder of memory, affecting many memory functions. While individuals with amnesia differ considerably from one another, depending on the site, extent and cause of their brain damage, there are a number of general characteristics of amnesia, as outlined by Parkin (1997):

- Short-term memory, as measured by digit span for example, is intact.
- Memory for language, and concepts, is largely intact.
- There is a severe and lasting **anterograde amnesia** – memory for events after the onset of the amnesia will be impaired.

Amnesic syndrome
a pattern of memory loss characterized by impaired long-term memory and spared short-term memory.

Anterograde amnesia
impairment of memory for events that occurred after the onset of amnesia.

> **Retrograde amnesia**
> impairment of memory for events that occurred before the onset of amnesia.

- There will be a **retrograde amnesia**, of variable extent – the patient will have loss of memory for events prior to the onset of amnesia.
- Skill learning, conditioning and priming will be unaffected. The patient will also be able to engage in skills acquired prior to the onset of amnesia (e.g., play a musical instrument).

The brain areas involved in long-term memory are shown in Figure 7.3, and some of the implications for functioning with the amnesic syndrome are outlined in Box 7.1, which considers the case that was introduced briefly at the opening of this chapter, that of H.M.

Causes of amnesia include effects of brain surgery (as in H.M.'s case), infections such as herpes simplex encephalitis, head injuries or stroke, or conditions such as Korsakoff's syndrome (Markowitsch & Staniloiu, 2012; Parkin & Leng, 1993). Korsakoff's syndrome (or Wernicke-Korsakoff syndrome) describes a type of brain damage related to thiamine (vitamin B1) deficiency. It generally occurs following prolonged alcohol abuse in predisposed individuals, although it has been reported in other groups affected by inadequate nutrition. This reaction to thiamine deficiency often goes undiagnosed, and the opportunity to reduce some of its effects by administering thiamine is lost. Often, alcohol-misusing patients present with non-specific symptoms or with symptoms that mirror those of alcohol intoxication, and therefore the illness can cause severe damage before it is diagnosed (Kopelman et al., 2009). Korsakoff's syndrome is associated with damage to thalamic, mammillary body and frontal brain areas (Colchester et al., 2001; Kopelman et al., 2001).

Amnesia can also follow injury, as in the case of N.A., a man who, at the age of 22 years, sustained a stab wound to the brain when a colleague accidentally thrust a miniature fencing foil up his nostril (Milner et al., 1968; Squire & Slater, 1978), causing damage to the left dorsal thalamus and adjacent structures (Squire & Moore, 1979).

Infections such as herpes simplex encephalitis, a viral infection of the brain, can also cause amnesia. This illness can cause extensive brain damage to the temporal areas within a very short time from onset of symptoms. The case of Clive Wearing, a classical musician and scholar who developed herpes simplex encephalitis after a sudden illness demonstrates the degree of memory loss that can result. His retrograde memory loss extended back for many years, affecting both episodic and semantic memories. However, his musical ability was relatively unaffected; he retained the ability to sight read music (although he avoided the more complex scores) and he could still play the piano. Although Wearing could play the piano, he was not *aware* that he could do so – when asked whether he could play, he could not affirm it. This case demonstrates the intact skill performance that occurs in amnesia in the absence of conscious recollection (Sacks, 2007).

In patients with amnesia, language and concepts are generally intact – the person can answer a question and can understand what a particular object is, and what it does. However, most of our knowledge about the world and about language is laid down early in life. Is this kind of memory spared because it is different from our recollections of past events? Or is it spared because it is learned early on in life? What happens to new words that patients with amnesia will have encountered only recently? One of the problems with testing patients with amnesia is being sure that the information was stored in memory in the first place – 'we must never underestimate one of the most obvious reasons for forgetting, namely that the information was never stored in memory in the first place' (Loftus, 1980, p. 74). Butters (1984) describes the case of P.Z., a college professor who developed amnesia as a result of Korsakoff's syndrome. He wrote an autobiography before his illness began, and so researchers had an accurate record

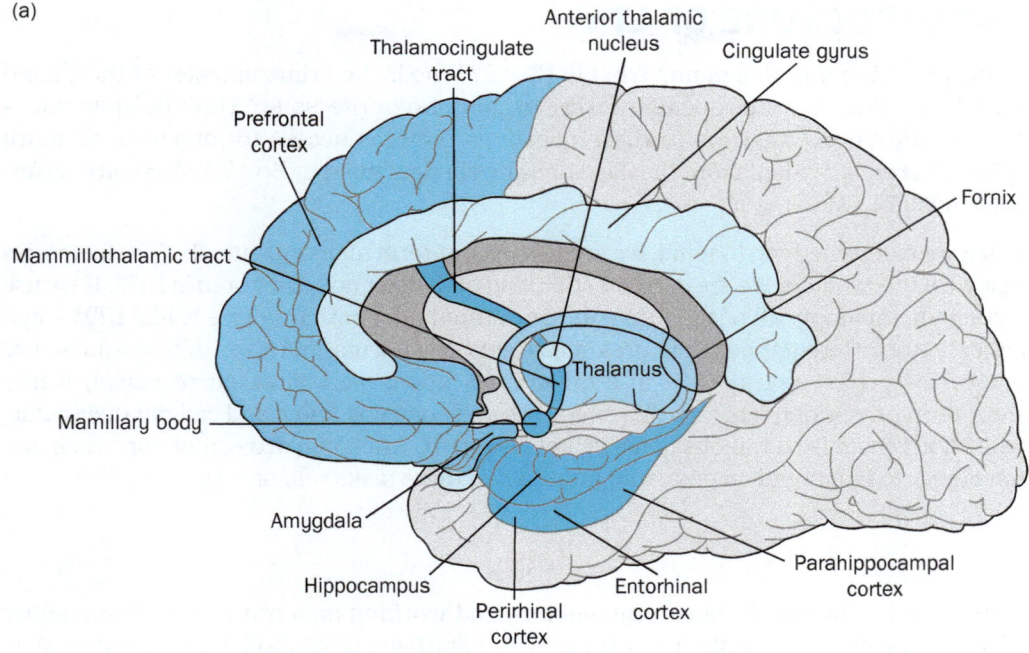

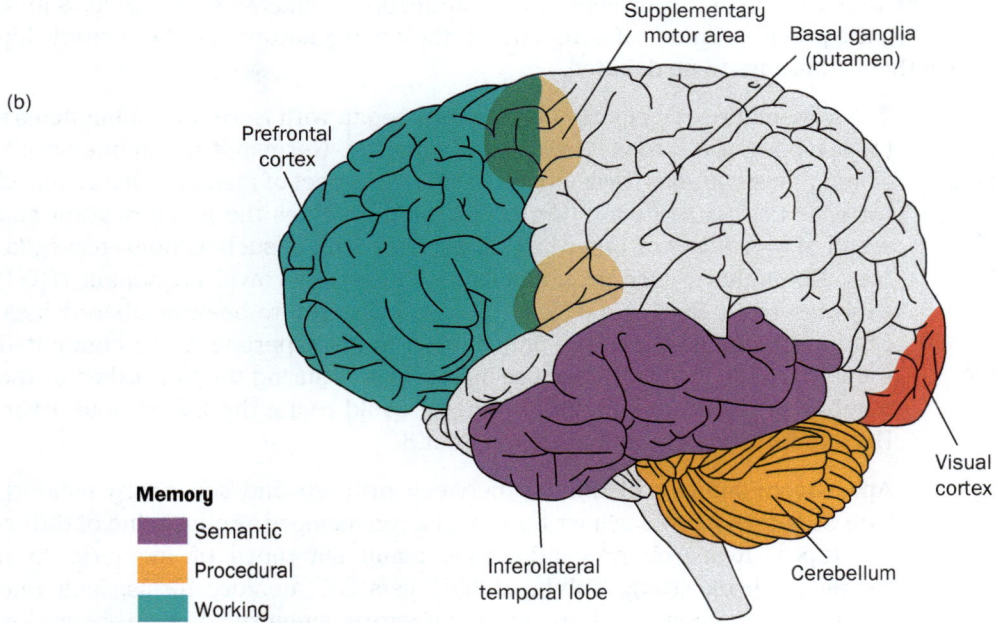

Figure 7.3 The brain areas involved in long-term memory.
(a) A midline view of the areas involved in episodic memory, highlighting the medial temporal lobes including the hippocampus and parahippocampus. (b) A lateral view of the brain highlighting the areas involved in semantic, procedural and working memory.

Source: Adapted from Budson & Price (2005).

both of personal events and concepts (e.g., new terms and theories in his field of expertise). He showed a similar retrograde amnesia for both life events and knowledge of scientific terms, whereby any terms encountered early in his career were intact but those acquired later were lost. We turn to these different types of long-term memories in the next section.

THE STRUCTURE OF LTM

Is an apple bigger than a plum? What is 16 × 2? Who is the prime minister of the United Kingdom? What are the opening lyrics to your favourite song? How do you ride a bicycle? Providing answers to these questions requires access to long-term memory (LTM), but as is evident from the case of amnesia described in Box 7.1, there are different kinds of LTM.

When we call something to mind, we are using short-term memory, but all of the memories that we have, whether we are currently thinking of them or not, are stored in LTM. If we use a computer analogy, all of the files you have stored on your hard drive is like LTM – you have files of different types – pictures, music, text documents, and so on. If you want to use one of these files, you open it in a given application; the equivalent of calling it into short-term or working memory. When you see someone you know and call out their name, when you recognize a famous name in a news report, when you drive your car, when you remember to buy bread on your way home, all of these tasks rely on LTM.

Multiple Memory Systems Model

As we saw in Chapter 6, short-term memory and working memory consist of a number of independent components. The Atkinson and Shiffrin (1968) model presented LTM as a single store. However, as is the case for short-term memory, there is general agreement that LTM consists of separate components (Schacter et al., 2000; Squire et al., 2004); the precise number of components, their exact nature and the relationship between them continues to be debated.

> Chapter 6, p176

Verbal learning
the area of experimental psychology concerned with how we learn and remember language-based items such as word lists.

Non-declarative or implicit memory
memory that is not accessed consciously and that we are not able to report verbally. It includes memory which benefits from previous experience but without our awareness of that experience.

Declarative or explicit memory
involves conscious recollection of memories such as events, facts, people and places.

The systematic investigation of memory began with Hermann Ebbinghaus's (1885) book *Über das Gedächtnis* (which is German for 'on memory'). Ebbinghaus's studies focused on a particular aspect of memory, that required for rote **verbal learning**. Verbal learning involves the memorization and recall of word lists or other language-based stimuli such as nonsense syllables. Ebbinghaus used pronounceable consonant–vowel–consonant (CVC) trigrams (e.g., ROG, VAM, ZIG) as the basis for to-be-remembered lists. Ebbinghaus himself was the only subject in his experiments; he committed to memory long lists of nonsense syllables, measuring the time taken or the number of repetitions required until he could recite the list without error. His experiments are outlined in Chapter 8.

Apart from James's distinction between primary and secondary memory (see Chapter 6), few early writers considered memory as consisting of different types. Research now addresses many sub-types of memory. In a tongue-in-cheek essay, Tulving (2007) lists 256 memory terms, including intentional memory, gist memory, olfactory memory, object-recognition memory, non-conscious memory, flashbulb memory and generic memory. The use of so many terms for various kinds of memory reflects the breadth of tasks and skills that need to be considered. As Roediger and colleagues (2002, p. 1) note, memory 'is a single term, but refers to a multitude of human capacities'. One way to approach this multitude of memory types is to group them according to whether they require conscious recollection.

> Chapter 8, p268

> Chapter 6, p178

It is generally agreed that there is a distinction in LTM between **non-declarative** (or **implicit**) **memory** and **declarative** (or **explicit**) **memory**. In a seminal example, Ryle (1949) describes this distinction as 'knowing that' as opposed to 'knowing how'.

We know that a bicycle has two wheels (declarative) and we know how to ride a bicycle (non-declarative). Declarative memory involves conscious recollection of information, whereas non-declarative memory is evident when performance that does not require conscious recollection is facilitated by prior learning – such as practising to ride a bicycle (Graf & Schacter, 1985, 1987; Schacter, 1987; Squire & Dede, 2015). For example, when an experienced driver drives a car, automatic processes guide behaviour; the driver does not have to consciously think about each step involved in driving and can often think about entirely unrelated matters while driving. However, past experience of driving is guiding current performance, even though the driver is not consciously dwelling on that past experience.

Some tests of memory rely on explicit recollection of information; others measure implicit memory. Methods such as **free recall** (e.g., What is the capital of France), **cued recall** (e.g., What word beginning with P is the capital of France?) and **recognition** (e.g., Is Paris the capital of France?) require conscious recollection, whereas other methods, such as word association or word fragment completion (more on this below), do not.

> **Free recall**
> when participants in a task recall the information in any order, without hints or clues to recall.
> **Cued recall**
> when a hint or cue is given to task participants to aid recall.
> **Recognition**
> when a task participant must verify if an item is a target.

The case of H.M., described at the beginning of this chapter, provides an example of this difference. H.M.'s amnesia led to a loss of declarative memory but non-declarative memory was relatively intact. H.M. could, for example, learn some new skills, such as mirror drawing. It has since become apparent that learning in amnesia can extend to a wide range of types of task; what these tasks have in common is that they do not require explicit memory – that is, they do not require retrieval of the original learning episode (Baddeley, 2004). Subsequently, cases of amnesia have provided clear evidence for a dissociation between declarative and non-declarative memory. Spiers et al. (2001) reviewed 147 cases of amnesia; in all cases, difficulties with declarative memory were noted, while non-declarative memory was intact.

Endel Tulving (1972) proposed a tri-partite (three part) model of LTM. He made a distinction within declarative memory between **episodic memory**, memory for personally experienced events and episodes, including autobiographical memory, and **semantic memory**, memory for facts about the world, including concepts and language. These different aspects of memory will be outlined in later sections of this chapter. Episodic memory relies on temporal context for recall; semantic memory does not.

> **Episodic memory**
> memory for events, experiences and episodes.
> **Semantic memory**
> memory for facts and knowledge about the world.

For example, let us say that you volunteer to take part in a memory experiment. On day one you are presented with a list of words, and on day two you are given another list of words, some of which you saw on day one and some of which you did not see. Your task is to identify the words that were presented on day one. This task is a test of your episodic memory – if you fail to remember one of the words, it is not the case that you have forgotten the word entirely, rather you have failed to recall that the word was presented in the context of the task on day one. Tulving (1972) makes the distinction between remembering and knowing; remembering that you saw the word is different from knowing the word (see Table 7.1, overleaf).

However, not everyone agrees that there is a clear-cut distinction between episodic and semantic memory. Cohen and Squire (1981) pointed out that not all information can be reliably classified as either episodic or semantic. For example, if you are asked if you are a good writer, and you agree that you are, are you recalling a specific event, say a good grade on a recent assignment (episodic memory), or are you using your knowledge about yourself and your own abilities (semantic memory) to answer the question?

Table 7.1 Some Key Differences between Episodic and Semantic Memory (see Tulving, 1972)

Episodic	Semantic
Memory for events, experiences and situations	Memory for facts and language
Time-dependent	Not time-dependent
Experiential	Symbolic
More vulnerable to interference	Less vulnerable to interference
Reflects questions such as When? Where?	Reflects questions such as What?
Reflects statements such as: 'I remember . . .' '"Dog" was in the word list presented during the experiment.' 'I had carrot soup for lunch.'	Reflects statements such as: 'I Know . . .' 'My teacher's name was Mr Brown.' 'Paris is the capital city of France.'

(See also Baddeley, 1984; Ratcliff & McKoon, 1986.) The distinction also blurs when we consider autobiographical memory (discussed later in this chapter). Squire (1986, 1993, 2004) proposed that LTM should be conceptualized as distinguishing between declarative (explicit) and non-declarative (implicit) memory, where declarative memory includes both episodic and semantic memory (see Figure 7.4).

Whether semantic and episodic memory involve separate or interacting stores continues to be debated. The evidence supporting a dissociation between non-declarative and declarative memory is far clearer, however.

NON-DECLARATIVE MEMORY

When we think of remembering, we generally think of the conscious recall of an event, experience or fact. If someone asks you what you did last Saturday evening, you would make an explicit recall attempt when trying to answer the question. However, much use of memory occurs without our conscious awareness. When you play a musical instrument, read a letter string, drive a car, you are not consciously

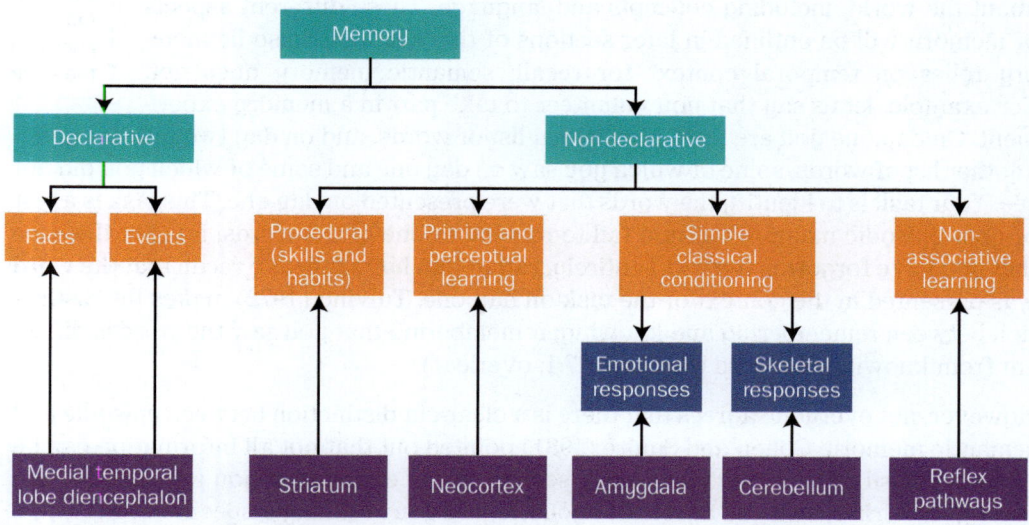

Figure 7.4 Squire's taxonomy of long-term memory.
The types of memory and related brain structures involved in aspects of declarative and non-declarative memory.

Source: Reprinted from Squire (2004), with permission from Elsevier.

trying to recall how to perform these actions from memory. Yet, memory plays a vital role in you to be able to perform these tasks, since they require that you at one time learned *how* to perform them.

Non-declarative memory is demonstrated on a wide range of tasks, including classical conditioning, motor skill learning (see Chapter 3) and priming, which will be discussed later in this chapter (see Figure 7.4). While there are likely to be differences between these subcategories of non-declarative memory, it makes sense to group them as memories that do not require conscious recollection. Tulving (1985, 1999) proposed that this type of memory, unlike declarative memory, is found in all animals and that it is, in evolutionary terms, the oldest of the LTM systems.

> Chapter 3, p84

Skill Learning

One example of non-declarative memories is **procedural memory**, which includes knowledge of skills such as driving, tying your shoelaces, writing your signature, playing a musical instrument or the motor skills involved in playing a sport. Procedural memory is closely associated with motor performance, but cognitive skills (such as being able to subtract two numbers, for example) and some perceptual learning skills are also aspects of procedural memory. Such knowledge is generally acquired over time through practice and can become automatic; in fact, sometimes when we concentrate our thoughts on a skill we can disrupt the processes involved and performance can suffer, an effect sometimes referred to by sports psychologists as 'paralysis by analysis' (for an overview of how cognitive psychology has informed sports psychology see Moran, 2012).

> **Procedural memory**
> a type of non-declarative memory involving memory for how to perform skills and actions.

As noted earlier, procedural memory is generally preserved in patients with amnesia, and as we have seen Clive Wearing, a musician who developed severe amnesia following a viral illness, also had intact procedural memory. His declarative memory was severely impaired, with a profound anterograde loss in addition to an extreme retrograde loss. However, his musical ability remained relatively unaffected by the illness; he retained the ability to sight read (although he avoided the more complex scores) and could still play the piano (see Sacks, 2007).

Habit Learning

Habit learning refers to memory acquired over time through repeated associations between stimuli and responses. This type of memory has been studied extensively in experimental animals but it remains poorly understood in humans because of the difficulty in eliminating the influence of conscious (declarative) memory on the learning situation (Bayley et al., 2005; Knowlton et al., 1994). One set of tasks that has been used to investigate habit learning in the absence of input from declarative memory involves **probabilistic classification learning**. In such tasks, participants are required to learn a set of associations. The associations are not obvious, and they cannot readily be memorized, because of the probabilistic nature of the associations between stimulus and response. The participant has to use information gleaned across many trials to complete the task successfully (Knowlton et al., 1994). In one such study, Squire and Zola (1996) had participants complete a weather prediction task. On each trial, participants had to predict a weather outcome (rain or sunshine) based on one, two or three cues (out of a total of four possible cues) that were presented

> **Probabilistic classification learning**
> involves learning a set of associations that cannot readily be memorized; information from across many trials must be used to complete the task.

(see Figure 7.5). Cues consisted of cards featuring squares, triangles, circles and diamonds. Each cue was associated with a weather outcome with a fixed probability, with associations of 75 per cent, 57 per cent, 43 per cent or 25 per cent. When more than one cue was presented on a trial, outcome was predicted by conjoint probabilities. Participants responded by pressing a key to select a weather outcome, and they were given immediate feedback as to whether their response was correct or incorrect. Participants could not rely on memory for previous trials to learn the task, because the same configuration of cues had the potential to generate different outcomes, and so this ensured that declarative memory was not involved in the task. Typically on this task, participants' performance improves from guessing (50 per cent) to about 70 per cent correct. Patients with amnesia typically learn the task at about the same rate as controls, with similar response accuracy (about 65 per cent) after training over a 50-trial block (Squire, 2008; Squire & Zola, 1996). Patients with amnesia, while able to perform almost as well as controls on the task, remain unable to report factual details about the training episode, however (Squire & Zola, 1996). In recent years habit learning has been further explored within the research field of drug addiction. Studies have suggested that drug addiction develops from recreational drug-taking to compulsive drug-seeking habits (for a review, see Everitt & Robbins, 2016).

> **Priming**
> an implicit memory effect whereby exposure to a stimulus affects a subsequent response.
>
> **Category exemplar tasks**
> tasks where participants are given category names one by one and are asked to generate exemplars for each. Some categories will have been encountered during an earlier stage.

Repetition Priming

The term **priming** refers to the facilitatory effect of previous exposure to a stimulus on the subsequent processing of that stimulus or a related stimulus. For example, performance may be faster, accuracy may be improved or there may be a bias towards a particular stimulus. In a typical repetition priming study, a set of stimuli are presented during a study phase; then, in the test stage, these (or related) stimuli are presented alongside new stimuli, and processing differences are examined. Priming can be conceptual or perceptual, depending on whether it is the stimulus form or the stimulus meaning that is salient (e.g., Roediger et al., 1989). Examples of perceptual priming tasks include word fragment completion, word stem completion, and identification of degraded stimuli or stimuli presented at the visible threshold. Conceptual priming tasks include **category exemplar tasks** and word association. Most repetition priming tasks do not require declarative memory processes and performance is unimpaired in patients with amnesia (Graf et al., 1984; Vaidya et al., 1995).

An example of a priming task is provided by Tulving et al. (1982). Their participants learned a list of low-frequency words (e.g., toboggan, theorem, pendulum). The words were presented singly on a screen at a rate of one every five seconds. Participants were instructed to look at each word and they were told to 'Do the best you can to learn each of the words as they appear, as you will be tested later for your memory of them.' Participants were tested after one hour and again after one week. There were two types of test, a yes–no recognition test (declarative memory) and a fragment completion test (non-declarative memory). In the fragment completion test, participants were given incomplete word fragments, with dashes indicating the position of missing letters (e.g., _ob_gg_ _) and were asked to complete the word by replacing the dashes with letters. Half were words from the target list, and half had not been seen during the learning phase. The results showed that performance was facilitated for fragments of words that had been presented during the learning phase. Tulving and colleagues also compared performance on the fragment completion task with that on the recognition task, thereby comparing implicit and explicit memory. They noted that recognition was not better for fragments that had been successfully identified compared to those that had not been identified, supporting the notion that fragment completion requires non-declarative, but not declarative, memory.

Squire (1987) used a similar task to demonstrate intact repetition priming in the absence of declarative memory in amnesic patients. A word stem completion task was used in this case. Participants studied a list of words. Then, in the test phase, the initial part of the word, the stem, was presented and the participants had to complete the word. For example, the word 'element' might have appeared in the study list. During testing, the stem ele___ would be presented. Note that there are several plausible responses to this stem; 'element' has been seen on the study list, but 'elephant' would also complete the stem. Squire used three test conditions. In the free recall task, participants had to report as many words from the list as they could. In a cued recall task, participants were presented with stems and were asked to recall words from the list that would complete the word. In the completion task, participants were asked to complete the stem – no mention was made of recalling words from the previous list. As is clear from Figure 7.5, patients with amnesia performed as well as controls on the fragment tasks, supporting the idea that the task relies on non-declarative, implicit memory. However, those with amnesia showed the usual deficit in performance on the declarative memory recall tasks, compared to controls.

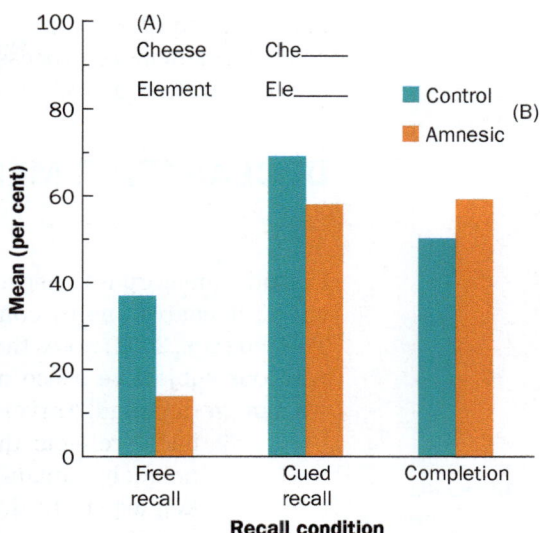

Figure 7.5 Word stem completion task from Graf et al. (1984).
Patients with amnesia and controls saw common words and then had to recall them (free recall), or recall them given the first three letters (cued recall). (A) Two examples of study items. (B) Performance of the patients with amnesia and controls differs depending on the test used.

Source: Adapted from Squire (1987).

The priming effect can occur in very brief intervals, but how long they last still needs to be determined. Two separate studies have found priming effects that lasted 17 years (Mitchell, 2006; Mitchell et al., 2018). In both studies, the participants were presented with a perceptual priming task consisting of fragmented pictures that they were asked to identify. Some of the participants had seen these images during a laboratory study 17 years earlier, while others, who functioned as the control group, had never seen them before. The participants who had previously seen the pictures were better at identifying them than the participants in the control group. Furthermore, the participants who had no recollection of participating in the laboratory testing performed just as well as those who did. However no such results were found for category-based priming (Mitchell et al., 2018).

Evaluation

These data support a dissociation between declarative and non-declarative memory, but it is important to appreciate that there is considerable interaction between the memory systems, and they are often bound together in terms of everyday experience. To use Squire's (2009) example, a frightening childhood event, such as being knocked over by a big dog, could provide a lasting conscious memory for the event, but it may also result in the person developing a fear of dogs.

The relationship between declarative and non-declarative memory may go even further. Some cognitive psychologists have argued that there is some procedural involvement in many tests of declarative or episodic memory (Kolers & Roediger, 1984).

Similarly, studies examining memory consolidation have shown declarative and procedural memory processing to interact (e.g., Brown & Robertson, 2007). We turn to this, declarative, aspect of memory next.

DECLARATIVE MEMORY

Episodic Memory

Episodic memory is the system within LTM that allows us to remember our past experiences; it enables us to consciously re-experience past events (Tulving, 1983, 2002). Tulving (e.g., 2002) notes three key properties of episodic memory. First, it is associated with our subjective sense of time that allows use to engage in 'mental time travel' – we can, in the mind, 'travel back' to remember past events. The phrase 'that takes me back' reflects this property of episodic memory and is, Tulving argues, uniquely human. Second, there is a connection to the self. Self-reflection is a key aspect to this kind of memory; as Tulving (2002) puts it, 'mental time travel requires a traveller' (p. 2). Third, mental time travel is associated with a special kind of conscious awareness called **autonoetic (self-knowing) consciousness**. This type of consciousness allows us to imagine ourselves in the future, and to plan ahead and set goals. It allows us to recall a past incident and imagine how we might have behaved differently. It lets us put ourselves in another's shoes and answer hypothetical questions such as 'If you were the juror how might you have voted?' Tulving (2002, p. 5) proposes that episodic memory:

> **Autonoetic ('self-knowing') consciousness**
> allows humans to use memory to relive past events and imagine ourselves in the future, from a self-perspective. It is a distinctive aspect of episodic memory.

- evolved recently
- develops late
- deteriorates early
- is vulnerable to disruption by brain damage
- is unique to humans
- evolved from semantic memory.

Episodic memory might be thought of as the pinnacle of human memory, and its loss in amnesia is devastating. But episodic memory is not simply a record of past experiences; memories are constructed anew when they are called to mind, and can differ from the original event and with each recall of the event. In other words, memory is a constructive process.

Memory as a (re)constructive process

The concept of 'mental time travel' neatly describes the experience of remembering or of reminiscing. We have all experienced how vivid and well defined past memories can be. However, it is important to appreciate that episodic memory is not an exact copy, it is not like watching a replay of an event or situation. Memory is constructive and when we recall our past experiences, we reconstruct the event in our minds, using information gained before, after and at the time of the event or episode itself.

Bartlett's (1932) pioneering research opposed the view that memory is based on 'unalterable traces', a notion typically identified with Freud's account of memory (e.g., 1900/1976). Bartlett showed that memory is reconstructive and not a passively recalled record of events. He wrote (1932, pp. 204–205):

> *The first notion to get rid of is that memory is primarily or literally reduplicative, or reproductive. In a world of constantly changing environment, literal*

recall is extraordinarily unimportant. If we consider evidence rather than supposition, memory appears to be far more decisively an affair of construction rather than one of mere reproduction.

This is not to suggest that recall is necessarily inaccurate, only that it is not an exact replica of past experience – it can be open to modification and error. It becomes important, then, to identify the conditions under which memory might be trusted as accurate and those that might lend themselves to inaccurate recollection.

Bartlett focused on the role of the schema (plural: schemata or schemas) in remembering past events. He defined the schema as 'an active organization of past reactions, or of past experiences' (Bartlett, 1932, p. 201). Recall involved 'condensation, elaboration and invention . . . and these all very often involve the mingling of materials belonging originally to different "schemata"' (p. 205). Schemas are organized memory structures that allow us to apply past experience to novel situations so as to guide behaviour. As such, they demonstrate the interaction between semantic and episodic memory. Schemas produce expectations that reduce the ambiguity of new situations, however these expectations can sometimes lead to erroneous judgements. For example, Brewer and Treyens (1981) found that participants in a memory task often reported items they had expected to see, based on context, but which had in fact not been present (see Box 7.2). The influence of schemas is also seen in boundary extension errors, whereby people remember more of a visual scene than was originally presented (see Chapter 6).

Chapter 6, p176

Box 7.2 Research Close Up: The role of schemas in memory

Source: Brewer & Treyens (1981).

INTRODUCTION

As we encounter new information, schemas can guide our memories so that we are more likely to remember some objects or events than others (schema-consistent items) and we may even mistakenly 'remember' items that were not present. This schema-expectancy effect was demonstrated by Brewer and Treyens (1981). Their study set out to examine five hypotheses (p. 207):

1 that schemas determine which objects are encoded into memory
2 that schemas act as frameworks for episodic information, so that schema-consistent information is more likely to be recalled
3 that information from schemas is integrated with episodic information, so that schema-consistent items might be recalled in error
4 that retrieval is guided by schemas, and
5 that schemas influence what is communicated when retrieving information from memory.

METHOD

Brewer and Treyens set up a room so that it looked like the office of a graduate student. The objects within the room were carefully selected, and had been coded for saliency and schema-expectancy. The saliency rating was essentially an index of how noticeable the object was within the room.

Figure 7.6 The room used in Brewer and Treyens' study, showing the typical (e.g., chair) and less typical (e.g., skull) objects that might be recalled.

Source: Reprinted from Brewer & Treyens (1981), with permission from Elsevier.

The schema-expectancy rating was an index of how consistent an object was with the 'office schema'. The room contained a typewriter (it was the early 1980s after all) and typical desk items. There was a table with coffee-making facilities. Another table held a Skinner box (an essential piece of kit for the 1980s graduate student) as well as electronic parts and some tools. There was shelving on one wall, with box files, and the other walls contained a bulletin board and a calendar, among other items (see Figure 7.6, above). There were a few items that would not be expected: a skull and a toy top, for example. Some items that would be expected were missing; there were no books in the office, for example, nor was there a telephone.

The participants ($n = 86$) were brought into this room, individually, and asked to wait there until they were called to take part in an experiment. After a delay of 35 seconds, the researcher returned and asked the participant to follow them to a nearby room. After a further minute, the participant was then told the real purpose of the experiment: to test their memory for the room they had just been in. Thirty participants completed a written recall task, 29 completed drawing recall (an outline drawing of the room was provided) and 27 were tested using verbal recognition only. Participants had a minimum of 15 minutes to complete the retrieval task, and could continue up to 30 minutes.

RESULTS

Objects reported by participants were classified as objects that were present, inferred objects that had not been present, or room frame objects (that is objects that were part of the room structure, such as the door, frame, doorknob, light switch, etc.). In total, 88 items were reported by one or more participants: seven were room frame objects, 62 objects had been present and 19 were inferred objects. The inferred objects tended to be schema-consistent items. For example, 30 per cent of participants reported that there were books in the office; in fact there had been none. For objects that had been present, recall was better for items that were consistent with the office schema.

In the verbal recognition condition, participants were presented with 131 object names; 61 of the named objects had been present in the office, 70 had not. Thirteen objects that had not been in the room, but that were consistent with the office schema, were mistakenly identified as having been present. Saliency was positively associated with memory performance in all three retrieval conditions: the more noticeable an object the more likely the participant would recall it and the less chance that an error would occur.

DISCUSSION

The Brewer and Treyens study made a number of important contributions to our understanding of schemas in memory. First, it brought a measure of ecological validity to a laboratory task, while at the same time controlling variables such as duration of exposure and testing time. Second, the study showed that information from schemas is integrated with episodic information, such that the resulting memory is a combination of schema and stimulus information. Third, the need to separate saliency from schema consistency is apparent. Salient objects, such as the skull, were likely to be recalled; they stand out as being distinctive. Some schema-consistent objects may be more salient than others. Furthermore, the participants, as students, would have been more familiar with a graduate student's office than they might have been with a novel location.

The study also showed how information from schemas affects retrieval, and that correct identification of objects, and erroneous recall of non-present objects, could be predicted by schema consistency. More recent studies have found similar effects of schema influence during retrieval of memories for scenes (Webb & Dennis, 2019) as well as in eyewitness memories (e.g., Tuckey & Brewer, 2003), a topic addressed in Chapter 8. Similar results have also been found when investigating memory in more naturalistic settings (e.g., Neuschatz et al., 2002).

> Chapter 8, p285

Bartlett (e.g., 1932) was interested in the way in which participants recalled stories and the influence that memory biases, such as are provided by schemas, might have on retrieval. His method involved presenting participants with a story and testing their recall using a repeated reproduction method. They subsequently wrote down what they recalled of the story and their recollection of the details of the story was tested at various time intervals. Bartlett also used a serial reproduction technique, whereby one participant communicated the story to the next, and so on, similar to the children's game. One story Bartlett used was a North American Indian folk tale called 'The War of the Ghosts'. This story, collected and translated by anthropologist Franz Boas, contains concepts that are quite unusual from a Western cultural perspective, with themes of supernatural entities and imperviousness to harm. The story is reproduced in Figure 7.7, overleaf.

As participants recounted the tale, they shortened the details considerably, remembering the gist rather than the complete story. However, they also made considerable changes to the detail of their abbreviated versions, changes that Bartlett characterized as 'transformation in the direction of the familiar' (p. 178). For example, Bartlett noted that the phrase 'something black came out of his mouth' was replaced by one participant as the more familiar 'foamed at the mouth' (p. 72), while another participant stated that 'his soul passed out from his mouth' (p. 127). Similarly, participants made inferences based on the limited information provided in the story. For example, in the story,

> One night two young men from Egulac went down to the river to hunt seals, and while they were there it became foggy and calm. Then they heard war cries, and they thought: "Maybe this is a war party." They escaped to the shore, and hid behind a log. Now canoes came up, and they heard the noise of paddles, and saw one canoe coming up to them. There were five men in the canoe, and they said: "What do you think? We wish to take you along. We are going up the river to make war on the people." One of the young men said: "I have no arrows." "Arrows are in the canoe," they said. "I will not go along. I might be killed. My relatives do not know where I have gone. But you," he said, turning to the other, "may go with them." So one of the young men went, but the other returned home. And the warriors went on up the river to a town on the other side of Kalama. The people came down to the water, and they began to fight, and many were killed. But presently the young man heard one of the warriors say: "Quick, let us go home: that Indian has been hit." Now he thought: "Oh, they are ghosts." He did not feel sick, but they said he had been shot. So the canoes went back to Egulac, and the young man went ashore to his house and made a fire. And he told everybody and said: "Behold, orphan accompanied the ghosts, and we went to a fight. Many of our fellows were killed, and many of those who attacked us were killed. They said I was hit and I did not feel sick." He told it all, and then he became quiet. When the sun rose he fell down. Something black came out of his mouth. His face became contorted. The people jumped up and cried. He was dead.

Figure 7.7 The story, 'The War of the Ghosts', illustrates how memory is influenced by prior knowledge.
Participants were told the story and had to re-tell it; they changed aspects of the story to fit their expectations.
Source: Bartlett (1932, p. 65).

one of the young men declines the offer to join the group, saying 'I will not go along. I might be killed. My relatives do not know where I have gone. But you,' he said, turning to the other, 'may go with them'. One participant recalled this as 'But you have no one to expect you' (p. 71), while another wrote 'You have no parents' (p. 20). In both cases, participants are making an inference that is plausible given the information in the story; but they are mistaken in thinking that the information was provided in the story. They are using information from memory schemas to adapt the story. Bartlett noted that the confidence with which the tale was recounted did not reflect its accuracy (p. 61), a problem that is discussed further in Chapter 8, when we look at the issue of eyewitness memory.

Bartlett was not himself immune to memory distortion. Brewer (1999) notes that Bartlett reported that one participant had replaced 'paddling' with 'rowing', but in fact the word 'paddling' does not appear in the story, which only mentions that the noise of paddles was heard.

Bartlett's study is often presented as demonstrating that memory is inherently inaccurate. However, this is an oversimplification of his findings. Bartlett was keen to use more ecologically valid tasks, but he himself noted that the types of story he used were likely to encourage abbreviation and transformation. He noted, for example, that the stories contained 'characters which would normally be expected to undergo much change in the course of transmission' (Bartlett, 1932, p. 119).

There are further issues that must be considered concerning Bartlett's methodology and his description of his results. It is also recognized that his quest for ecological validity was not entirely successful. As Roediger et al. (2000) point out, 'The War of the Ghosts' is 'about as similar to normal prose as . . . nonsense syllables are to words' (p. 117). That said, Bartlett's work was pivotal in showing that memory is a reconstructive process, a finding that has been confirmed many times since. We will have a further look at how memory may be distorted later on in the section concerning autobiographical memory, when we take a closer look at the susceptibility of human memory.

When we think of episodic memory, we tend to focus on the past, to think of it in terms of remembrance of past events. But the adaptive functions of memory also allow us to use past experiences in order to adapt our behaviour so as to deal more effectively with present and future events. For example, you may remember a past examination, and perhaps regret choosing to answer a particular question. Perhaps you got overly anxious and this affected your performance. Or perhaps you look back with satisfaction and note a good performance. The focus on past performance may serve a purpose in influencing future behaviour – that is, you can learn from the experience and apply it to a future examination or similar experience. Thus one of the adaptive functions of episodic memory lies in its potential for imagining future events (Suddendorf & Corballis, 2008). Memory that allows us to keep track of plans and carry out intended actions is called **prospective memory**; it allows us to remember to remember (Winograd, 1988).

> **Prospective memory** allows us to remember to perform certain actions. It has been described as the ability to 'remember to remember'.

Prospective Memory And Imagining Future Events

Tulving (2004) proposed that a key role of the episodic memory system is to allow people to mentally 'travel forward in time'. This use of memory is an essential component of forward planning – it allows us to, for example, imagine the future, to think about what career path we might like to take after completing our degrees, it allows us to plan a summer holiday, and it allows us to remember to buy bread on the way home from work. This latter type of planning involves a type of memory called prospective memory – that is, memory for intended actions, actions that are to be performed at some future time (see Einstein et al., 2005). Individuals with amnesia lose their prospective memory, and find it difficult to conceptualize a personal future (Klein & Loftus, 2002). We use this kind of memory every day – remembering to take medication at a certain time, remembering what we intended to buy when we get to the store, remembering to submit an essay before the deadline, for example, all require prospective memory.

The most common prospective memory failure involves neglecting to carry out an action at the appointed time (Ellis & Cohen, 2008) – forgetting that we intended to post a letter by 6 p.m., for example. Prospective memory lapses often involve a failure to interrupt habitual routines (e.g., going straight home instead of taking a detour to the post office to post the letter). They differ from **action slips**, errors within established or habitual routines, such as forgetting to brush your teeth before bed, or putting sugar into the teapot instead of into the cup (Morris, 1992, p. 199). Prospective memory is normally highly effective. Marsh and colleagues (1998) found that while about a quarter of people's plans for the forthcoming week remained uncompleted, this was normally for reasons other than forgetting, which accounted for only 3 per cent of failures. However, when prospective memory fails the results can be embarrassing, or even catastrophic (Dismukes, 2012). Einstein and McDaniel (2005, p. 286) describe a distressing, and unfortunately not unique, example:

> **Action slips** involve an action being completed when it was not intended.

> *After a change in his usual routine, an adoring father forgot to turn towards the daycare centre and instead drove his usual route to work at the university. Several hours later, his infant son, who had been quietly asleep in the back seat, was dead.*

In this case, a child was left to die in a hot car because of a failure to interrupt the normal routine.

Unlike other kinds of memory, prospective memory is not necessarily triggered or cued by an obvious external event, rather retrieval in prospective memory is self-initiated (Craik, 1986). This aspect of the process 'defines one of the challenges to explanations of prospective memory: What happens to allow recall to take place?' (Morris, 1992, p. 202).

We can distinguish between event-based and time-based prospective memory tasks. Event-based memory may be triggered by a particular cue – for example, seeing my friend John reminds me to pass on a message to him, or passing by the computer reminds me to send an email to a friend. Tests of this kind of prospective memory are said to be event-based or event-cued tests (Graf & Grondin, 2008). When an intention is time-cued, a specific time prompts action – for example, remembering to attend a meeting at 3 p.m. or remembering to take a meal out of the oven in 30 minutes. Ellis (1988) makes the distinction between two kinds of intention: **pulses** and **steps**. Pulses are intentions that must be carried out at a particular time (e.g., I must remember to go to a dentist appointment at 4 p.m.); steps are intentions that have a wider timeframe (e.g., I must telephone John some time this week). Ellis found that pulses are associated with better recall, and are more likely to be facilitated by means of a memory aid, such as making a note in a diary. In Box 7.3, we take a closer look at how prospective memory can be improved.

> **Pulses**
> involve intentions that are time-locked.
> **Steps**
> intentions that have a wider time frame in which they can occur.

Box 7.3 Practical Application: Improving prospective memory

As previously mentioned, failure to carry out tasks can have consequences that range from annoying to lethal (Dismukes, 2012). It is natural to wonder therefore if there are any strategies we may employ to improve our prospective memory. Using external aids such as calendars is useful for some types of task, such as remembering to go to the dentist, but for event-based tasks, like remembering to give a book to a friend when you see them next, external aids are often of little use. Event-based tasks demand that intentions must be retrieved when a particular external event occurs. Thus, when you see your friend (cue) you need to remember to give them the book (intention). One such well-researched technique is the so-called implementation intention (e.g., Chen et al., 2015; Gollwitzer, 1999). This planning strategy involves the following steps.

1. Decide on a specific time and place to initiate the intended action.
2. Link these specific situational cues (time and place) to the intended action.

Thus, if you need to remember to give your friend a book, you would decide on a specific time and place to do this. For example, you know that you and your friend are taking a class together and so you decide that you will give them the book at the lecture the following day. To link your action to these situational cues, you can imagine yourself giving your friend the book at the lecture, or you can make a verbal when–then statement of your intended actions: 'Tomorrow, when I meet my friend at the lecture, then I will give her the book.' The best way, however, is to combine the imagery exercise with the verbal statement (Chen et al., 2015). This strategy is effective not only for improving prospective memory in healthy individuals, but also in showing promising results for healthy habit formations such as ceasing to smoke (McWilliams et al., 2019).

Another newly investigated strategy for event-based tasks is enacted encoding, which entails physically performing the task on the imagined object (Pereira et al., 2015, 2018). So, if you were to remember to post a letter the next time you went outside, you would physically pretend to post the letter by raising your arm and performing the mailing movement.

Both the implementation intention and enacted encoding are suggested strategies to improve prospective memory via enhanced encoding of the intended action needing to be performed, thus making the retrieval more automatized (e.g., Cohen & Hicks, 2017; Pereira et al., 2018).

Wilkins and Baddeley (1978) carried out an early investigation of pulses or time-based prospective memory using a pill-taking analogue. This task simulated a real-life task – say, for example, you have to take antibiotics for a week, and you need to take pills at specified times each day. Wilkins and Baddeley's participants (31 women) were required to push a button at 8.30 a.m., 1 p.m., 5.30 p.m. and 10 p.m. for one week, and a device recorded the times at which the button was pressed. While the majority of responses occurred within five minutes of the required time, 30 per cent of participants forgot to push the button on at least one occasion during the week and they were unaware of this omission for as many as 36 per cent of the errors. However, in no case did a participant forget that she had already pushed the button and repeat the action. Wilkins and Baddeley also found that those with better scores on a free recall task performed *worse* on the time-based task. While there were a number of possible explanations in this case, Wilkins and Baddeley noted that better free recall was associated with a higher level of education, a result that 'seem[s] to support the myth that absent-minded persons tend to be those with higher educational level' (p. 33). However, Kvavilashvili (1987) found no correlation between participants' performance on retrospective and prospective memory tasks.

This is not to suggest that such results reflect the workings of two different components within memory; the task requirements are quite different in each case, and for a fair comparison to be made, more comparable tasks are needed. Such an example was provided by Hitch and Ferguson (1991). They had filmgoers recall films they had seen and report films they intended to see; they found a small but statistically significant correlation between retrieval of the seen and anticipated films. Furthermore, while memory for films already seen showed a recency effect, in that recall was better for those recently seen, retrieval of films to be seen in the future showed a proximity effect, with films to be seen sooner associated with better retrieval. Neuroscientific evidence also supports substantial overlap between brain areas engaged when thinking about the past and when imagining the future. Shared activity is evident in prefrontal cortex and medial temporal lobe regions, including the hippocampus and parahippocampal gyrus (see Schacter & Addis, 2007, for an overview).

It is only in the past two decades that prospective memory has begun to be studied systematically within cognitive psychology. For much of the history of memory research, the focus was on the past, on what was learned and remembered. Prospective memory is emerging as an interesting component of memory, and deficits in prospective memory have even been linked to clinical conditions such as compulsive behaviours, a topic we explore in Box 7.4.

Box 7.4 Research Close Up: Does a prospective memory deficit underlie checking compulsions?

Source: Cuttler & Graf (2007).

INTRODUCTION

Compulsive checking behaviours – repeatedly checking that a door is locked, for example, or that the oven has been switched off – are evident in more than 50 per cent of patients with obsessive-compulsive disorder (OCD) and are found at a subclinical level (i.e., below the threshold for determining a clinical condition) in about 15 per cent of the general population (Stein et al., 1997). Compulsive checking can affect a wide range of behaviours and in OCD occurs as a rigid pattern of behaviour that causes distress and impairs functioning. One prominent theory of compulsive checking, the memory deficit theory, proposes that a deficit in prospective memory underlies the condition: the person knows, or believes, that they have a poor prospective memory and therefore thinks that they will make an error; this underlies the need to check that an intended action has been completed. This possibility of a link between memory and compulsive behaviours was explored in a study by Cuttler and Graf (2007).

METHOD

Cuttler and Graf (2007) recruited 126 undergraduate students (40 men and 86 women) and divided them into three groups on the basis of reported frequency of checking behaviours as reported on a standardized self-report inventory; three groups – high, low and medium checkers – were formed. Participants completed one event-cued and one time-cued prospective memory task, and they completed two questionnaires measuring subjective (self-reported) prospective memory. Event-cued episodic prospective memory was measured using a modified version of the standardized belonging task. In this task, a personal item (such as a watch or a mobile phone) is taken from the participant at the start of the testing session and he or she is instructed to ask for its return at a later point, in this case when told later in the testing session 'we are now finished with all of the tests'. Participants rated how confident they were that they would remember to ask for the item back.

Time-cued episodic prospective memory was measured using the 'Phone-Call Reminder' task. Participants were told that the experimenter had to leave the room in exactly 30 minutes and that they should let the experimenter know when that 30 minutes had passed. Participants were allowed to check a stopwatch; they could look at it when and as often as they wished, but they were instructed to keep it facedown otherwise. Each stopwatch check was recorded, as was the time the participant gave the reminder.

RESULTS

The data showed that participants who reported more checking behaviours also reported more general prospective memory failures. Differences on the time-cued prospective memory task were not statistically significant, but those in the medium and high checking groups performed more poorly on the event-cued memory test (asking for their personal belonging back) compared to the low checkers: 56 per cent of the high checkers, 59 per cent of medium checkers and 80 per cent of low checkers requested the return of their belonging at the end of the task. There were also differences on the subjective measures of prospective memory, with reported frequency of prospective memory failure associated with checking behaviours, for example.

DISCUSSION

The Cuttler and Graf study supports the memory-deficit account of compulsive checking – that is, the view that checking occurs in response to memory failure – the person cannot remember whether they locked the door and so they have to check it. Cuttler and Graf's study extended work in this area by considering prospective memory in addition to retrospective memory. Further studies investigating prospective memory in clinically diagnosed OCD patients have also shown prospective memory deficits (Bhat et al., 2018; Harris et al., 2010; Racsmány et al., 2011; Yang et al., 2015). However, there exists a few studies that fail to show a link between prospective memory deficits and OCD. Moritz et al. (2006) found no differences using source memory and meta-memory tasks comparing OCD patients with and without checking compulsions with controls, and Jelinek et al. (2006) found no differences between patients with OCD and healthy controls on tests of verbal, non-verbal, and prospective memory. The relationship between memory failures and checking behaviours therefore remains to be established.

Autobiographical Memory

Most of the day-to-day events that we will remember over a short period of time disappear from memory quickly. If you are asked what you ate for lunch today, you will probably be able to recall the details easily. If you are asked this question in a week's time, those details are likely to have been lost. This makes sense, as it would not be useful for us to remember the banal details of everyday experience; we remember what is useful, salient or distinctive, and other details are lost. As Conway (2009) notes, episodic memories provide a record of short-term goals and the degree to which they have been met. When certain episodic memories become embedded in the broader conceptual system, along with semantic memories, **autobiographical memories** are formed. Thus, autobiographical memory involves personal experience (Linton, 1978) and it is closely associated with the self (Conway, 1992). It might be thought of as our life histories, the facts and events that we can consciously recollect in some detail and that are time-marked as belonging to a particular phase in our lives. It can be said to hold several dimensions, and we will next take a closer look at the four dimensions suggested by Williams et al. (2008):

> **Autobiographical memories**
> episodic memories for personally experienced events in a person's life.

1. Autobiographical memories may include **autonoetic memories**, which consist of personal episodic information such as personally experienced events, from everyday activities to once-in-a-lifetime experiences; for example, remembering our 10th birthday or remembering when we first bought a car (see Brewer, 1996). In contrast **noetic memories** consist of facts about ourselves, such as where we were born, or where we went to school, and are therefore classified as semantic memories.

> **Autonoetic memories**
> memories that are associated with a sense of self-awareness and that are relived during recollection.
> **noetic memory**
> memory for facts.

2. These memories can also differ in the degree to which they can be considered *generic* or *specific*. For example, you might have a specific memory of what you did last Christmas, such as which presents you received and with whom you celebrated the holiday, but you may also have generic memories concerning how you usually spend Christmas.

3. Autobiographical memories can also differ in the extent to which they are experienced as *copies* or *reconstructions* of the original events during recall. Memories that are recalled with a large amount of irrelevant detail and with vividness are often experienced as copies, however, and this will be discussed in more detail later on in this chapter; even these memories are susceptible to bias.

4. During recollection of these memories they can either be recalled from a **field perspective** or an **observer perspective**. If a person recalls a memory from a field perspective they recall it from a first-person vantage point. However, there are also reports of people recalling an event as if they are observing it from the outside – that is, from a third-person perspective. Recalling from a field perspective has been associated with the recollection of newer memories and also with more vivid memories, in contrast to observer memories, which more often are associated with older and, at least partially, reconstructed memories (see Nigro & Neisser, 1983). In Box 7.5, we take a closer look at whether type of perspective is associated with different types of subjective experience when recalling traumatic events.

> **Field perspective**
> when a person recalls a memory from a first-person perspective. They are experiencing the event.
> **Observer perspective**
> when a person remembers a memory from a third-person perspective. They are observing the event from the outside.

Box 7.5 Research Close Up: Remembering traumatic events – does perspective matter?

Source: Mooren et al. (2019).

INTRODUCTION

Witnessing a traumatic event can often result in **intrusions**, which are intrusive memories where people involuntary re-experience the distressing event. It has long been theorized that the perspective a person takes during recollection might influence the subjective experience of remembering the event. Taking the observer perspective, in contrast to the field perspective, could be a strategy that makes the person distance themselves from the traumatic memory, and may in turn lead to less anxiety and fewer intrusions, at least in the short term. This possible association was investigated in a study by Mooren et al. (2019).

> **Intrusions**
> involuntary mental pictures with very detailed sensory impressions of the witnessed event, such as sights, sounds, feelings and bodily sensations.

METHODS

The participants in the study listened to an audiotape of an eyewitness report of a real-life road traffic accident. The report contained, among other things, descriptions of the scene and the injured victims, as well as the emotional distress of the narrator (a journalist played by an actress).

The participants were then divided into three groups and asked to recall their most distressing scene. Those in the first group were told to recall the scene from an observer perspective – as if they were watching themselves take part in the scene. The second group were told to recall it from a field perspective – as if they were experiencing the situation themselves. Those in the last group, which was a control group, were told to recall a neutral memory (having dinner last night), but from an observer perspective, to account for the strain involved in taking an observer perspective.

The participants rated their mood and their level of anxiety before and after listening to the report from the traumatic event, as well as after recall. They were also told to keep a diary on the number of intrusions they might experience during the following week.

RESULTS

The level of negative mood and anxiety was higher for all groups directly after listening to the traumatic event, however there was no difference in level of mood and anxiety between the groups. The difference arose after the participants were asked to recall from different perspectives. The group that was asked to remember from a field perspective experienced higher levels of anxiety and negative mood than both the observer and control groups. They also reported a higher number of intrusions during the follow-up week than did the other two groups.

© ESB Professional/Shutterstock

DISCUSSION

The results suggest that experiencing a distressing event from a field perspective is associated

> with more negative mood and higher levels of anxiety, as well as more intrusions. The results are in line with findings from McIsaac and Eich (2004), who investigated the association between perspectives and emotional distress during recall of a traumatic event in persons suffering from post-traumatic stress disorder (PTSD), a clinical disorder that may develop in those who have experienced or witnessed a life-threatening event. The condition is characterized by vivid and intrusive recollections of the traumatic event, as well as nightmares. However, it should be noted that there are studies that have failed to find a similar association between vantage perspective and emotional distress (e.g., Robinaugh & McNally, 2010), thus further research is needed to thoroughly understand the association.

Remembering personal past experiences

Research literature has long focused on *how well* we remember events and only over the past decade has the focus turned more towards *why* we remember. Which functions does recalling specific events of our life serve? Although many different functions of autobiographical memory have been identified, these can broadly be classified into three main subsets: social, self and directive functions (Bluck, 2003; Pillemer, 1992).

Even though there is something of a debate concerning which functions are considered the most fundamental, several researchers point to the social function as one of the more prominent (see Nelson, 1993). Alea and Bluck (2003) note that the social function of sharing memories of personal events may serve many different purposes. First, it might be done in order to facilitate intimacy or a social bond between persons, but memories can also be shared to teach or inform the person with whom they are shared. A possible example of the latter is when a parent shares the story of a past experience with their child, in the hope that it will advise the child on a certain matter. However, a memory may also be shared to elicit or provide empathy. For example, we might share a memory with a friend of when we made a silly mistake, so the friend feels better about their own recently made error.

A person's **self-concept** is, by and large, construed from remembered events that have had significance for them (see Conway, 2005). For example, a person who views themselves as highly conscientious probably has recollections of specific past events where they displayed this trait. The relationship between identity and autobiographical memory is however reciprocal – our self-concept is formed by what we remember – but how we view ourselves makes us more prone to remember certain events that are consistent with our self-concept. As noted by Fivush (2011), it is particularly **self-continuity** that has a strong association with autobiographical memory.

Self-concept
the beliefs a person holds about themselves regarding behaviours, traits and abilities.

Self-continuity
the view of oneself as being the same person over time.

Autobiographical memory may also serve a directive function. That is, it may help us to solve problems, and guide our current and future behaviour (see Pillemer, 2003). For example, if you are nervous about an upcoming challenging exam, you might search your memory for a specific event where you were in a similar situation that ended well. You could then use the successful behaviour from that event to guide you during your study. It should be noted that it is a specific event that serves as a guide in this case and not a general memory or a script of 'how to study for an exam'. As a further example of how memory can have a directive function, Pillemer (2003) points to the change in behaviour of many Americans following the 2001 terror attack on the World Trade Center. He proposes that one of the main reasons why Americans started to avoid public spaces and flying on airplanes was because of the horrifying images of the attack.

It should however be noted that these three broad functions may often overlap in real-world scenarios (see Pillemer, 2003). For example, a person who has lived through a traumatic event may have specific memories that serve a self-function, in that the recollection identifies them as a survivor of the trauma. But the narrative may also contain directive functions of which places to avoid, as well as also serving a social function in bringing people who experienced similar events closer together by sharing similar narratives.

> **Involuntary memories**
> the unintentional recollection of past personal experiences.

When we think about memories of the past, we often think about intended recollections of specific events. However, many people report the occurrence of **involuntary memories** during their everyday lives (e.g., Berntsen, 2012). These involuntary memories can be cued by either elements in the present surroundings – such as when the smell of ginger and spices brings back a memory of a past Christmas experience – or by a thought one is currently holding in mind, which may bring about an unintentional recollection. An example of the latter could be that when you are planning to study for an examination, another earlier exam, which you failed miserably, pops into your mind. Studies show that involuntary memories seems to be experienced at least as frequently as voluntary memories (e.g., Rasmussen & Berntsen, 2011; Rasmussen et al., 2015). Furthermore the involuntary memories are more associated with moments of boredom, daydreaming or having nothing to think about, and thus seem to come about during moments of unfocused attention, whereas voluntary memories are more associated with directive functions, such as problem solving and decision making.

Involuntary memories are also commonly experienced by individuals suffering from conditions such as schizophrenia, depression or anxiety disorders (Brewin et al., 2010). These so-called intrusions are often experienced as vivid, with anxiety-provoking content, and are one of the key symptoms in PTSD, which we will take a closer look at in Box 7.6.

Box 7.6 When Things Go Wrong: Experiencing involuntary traumatic recollections – suffering from PTSD

Post-traumatic stress disorder (PTSD) is a psychiatric condition that can develop in survivors of different types of trauma (DSM-IV). For a person to develop PTSD, they or someone close to them needs to have experienced an actual death or life-threatening situation such as war, rape, abuse or natural disaster. Thus, PTSD commonly develops in soldiers but also in many survivors of abuse. The disorder may also develop in those that have not experienced a traumatic event themselves, but have a close relative or friend who has.

One of the key symptoms of the disorder is intrusive memories, as well as dreams about the traumatic event. These memories occur involuntarily, and are often triggered by something in the surroundings which brings the traumatic event to mind. A former soldier may be triggered by the sound of fireworks, making them suddenly remember a scene from their deployment involving gunfire. In severe forms of PTSD, these memories become so vivid that the patient experiences flashbacks transporting them back to the event, making them feel as if they are partially, or completely, reliving the experience. These flashbacks seem to be a specific indicator of PTSD (Bryant et al., 2011) and are often considered to be quite different from other autobiographical memories (e.g., Hellawell & Brewin, 2002). During these episodes, a person can lose complete awareness of their surroundings, as time distortion can occur, making them feel as though the memory is happening in the present. The flashbacks often focus on the most distressing periods of the traumatic event, called 'hotspots' – periods signalling when the trauma was about to start or when a situation was becoming even more alarming. To avoid having to re-experience these distressing memories, the patient starts to avoid situations, people or other types of stimuli that might remind them of the event and trigger the memories.

Fortunately, a number of evidence-based treatments for PTSD exist (for a review see Schnyder et al., 2015). One common feature of these treatments is for patients to be exposed to the environments or stimuli that trigger the traumatic memory until their fear and anxiety decline. This is done repeatedly until the patient no longer feels the same amount of anxiety when encountering the situation. The best treatment outcomes, however, seem to be achieved when people are exposed to specific content in their flashbacks (e.g., Nijdam et al., 2013), which is not always easily achieved after the traumatic experience has passed. One technique to accomplish this is the use of so called imaginal exposure. The patient is guided by a therapist to think back and re-experience in a safe environment a situation that is the focus of a frequent flashback. The person thinks of the situation until their anxiety begins to subside and, together with the therapist, the patient also has the opportunity to explore the traumatic experience, perhaps leading to new insights. For example, the patient might remember details that change their perception of their own involvement. They might suddenly remember seeing a knife in their attacker's back pocket, making the action of not crying for help seem highly adequate, since they were afraid for their life.

The susceptibility of human memory

Even highly personal memories are not free from bias, however. Memory is a reconstructive process and, when we recall life events, we reconstruct or interpret the memory 'record' rather than play it back passively.

Neisser (1981) provided an account of the potential susceptibility of autobiographical memory to bias and change. John Dean was the former counsel to US President Richard Nixon and a key witness during the Watergate hearings in the 1970s. Dean provided a detailed account of various conversations he took part in, including those with Nixon. His accounts were so detailed and expressed with such confidence as to be very convincing. However, the conversations with the President conducted in the Oval Office had been recorded, as was standard practice, and when the transcripts of these recordings were released and compared with Dean's testimony, it became apparent that his memories were somewhat distorted. His recollection of particular conversations had been affected by subsequent events and by his beliefs about his own role in events. As Neisser remarked, Dean was basically correct with regards to the existence of a 'cover-up' and the roles played by the particular individuals involved, but his account of the conversations was affected by memory distortions that involved, among other factors, confusion of single events with repeated episodes, and biases reflecting his own self-image and his perception of his role in the events. Dean's account of events might be characterized as 'systematic distortion at one level of analysis combined with basic accuracy at another' (Neisser, 1981, p. 102).

Dean's distortions that favoured his self-image mirror those reported in other contexts. For example, Bahrick and colleagues (1996) asked college students to recall their high school grades. The students accurately remembered A grades on 89 per cent of occasions, but D grades were remembered only 29 per cent of the time. In fact, 79 of the 99 participants inflated their grades and reported them as being higher than they actually were.

> **False memories**
> inaccurate recollections of events that did not occur, or distortions of events that did occur.

An experimental demonstration of such '**false memories**' was provided by Loftus (1993, 1997). Her procedure was designed to increase the probability with which participants would report a fictional event as having occurred, in essence to plant a false memory that was 'at least mildly traumatic, had the experience actually happened' (Loftus, 1997, p. 71). Loftus had her participants recall childhood events, some of which had been provided by close family members, who acted as confederates in the experiment. Three of the events had actually happened, one had not, but was a reasonably plausible childhood event – a shopping trip when the participant was five years old during which he/she had become separated from family members. The 'lost-in-the-mall' scenario contained elements that were plausible: the child was separated from family and lost for an extended period of time; he or she was upset and crying; an older woman helped the child; and he or she was subsequently reunited with the family (Loftus, 1997). Participants were invited to provide as much detail as they could about the four events.

Immediately after the presentation of the scenarios, participants recalled, on average, 68 per cent of the true events. But close to a third of participants reported remembering the false event, and a quarter of participants continued to report recollection of the false event during two follow-up interviews.

> **Imagination inflation**
> the strengthening of a false memory through repeated retrieval.
>
> **Demand characteristics**
> the aspects of a research study that convey the hypotheses or aims to the participants and may thereby shape performance.

Why would participants' false memories have persisted over time? Research has shown that imagining false events increases the likelihood that they will be 'recalled', an effect referred to as **imagination inflation**. Hyman and Pentland (1996), using a similar procedure to Loftus, had participants consider true and false events. In one condition, participants were instructed to imagine the event so as to aid their memory of it. The false event in this case was a scenario in which the participant, aged 5, while playing with other children at a wedding, knocked over a punch bowl onto the parents of the bride. Those who imagined this scenario were more likely to report false memories of the event, although Hyman and Pentland note that **demand characteristics** may have played a role.

It remains a possibility that, unbeknown to family members, the participant had experienced something like the false event described. Mazzoni and Mamon (2003) conducted an experiment using a false event that, while plausible, was not possible. They had their British participants consider two events; one was relatively common (having a dentist extract a tooth); the other described a medical test that is not conducted in the United Kingdom (having a nurse remove a skin sample from the little finger). They found that imagining the false event increased the number of reported memories and belief that the event had taken place.

Anecdotal accounts of false memories for autobiographical episodes within families have been commonly reported. In such cases, a disputed memory arises between twins or siblings who are close in age, whereby the ownership of the memory is uncertain. Each member thinks that they are the protagonist in the event but the memory of one person has actually been appropriated by the other as their own. In such cases, visual imagery is often vivid, leading to confidence in the veracity of the memory. Sheen and colleagues (2001) found disputed memories to occur relatively frequently among twins, and that the content of disputed memories was not different to that of non-disputed memories, nor were disputed memories of more personal significance. In one case reported by Sheen et al., each of a pair of twins claimed that the other had been the protagonist in a 'running away from home' memory. The researchers found that the details of the disputed memories were harder to recall.

Converse to the contested memories reported by Sheen et al. (2001), people sometimes stop believing their memories (for a review, see Scoboria et al., 2014). Considering that during a life course we become more aware of the malleability of human memory, it is not surprising that we may also start questioning some of our recollections. Research shows that people might even go so far as to withdraw their belief in a memory for an event they once believed had occurred. The most common reason is due to social feedback – for example, a close friend or relative says that the event could never have taken place. These and other reasons for why people decide to withdraw their belief in memory are more closely investigated in Box 7.7.

Box 7.7 Research Close Up: Reasons for withdrawing beliefs in autobiographical memories

Source: Scoboria et al. (2015).

INTRODUCTION

Much research has been concerned with the development of false memory. However, the research concerning the converse, when we reevaluate our autobiographical memories and decide to stop believing in them, has been scarce. In a study by Scoboria et al. (2015), the authors investigate the reasons people gave for not believing in a particular autobiographical memory.

METHODS

The participants were selected from a large university-based participant pool by answering yes to the following question: 'Do you have an event you stopped believing happened to you, but you have not stopped remembering?' They were then asked to describe the memory for the event, when it took place and how old they were. They were also asked to provide reasons for why they stopped believing in the memory. A qualitative data analysis was employed to identify categories of reasons for withdrawal from the participant reports.

RESULTS

Eight major categories for withdrawing beliefs in autobiographical memories emerged. The most important ones were social feedback, event plausibility, alternative attributions, and general beliefs regarding memory and memory ability. The categories and examples can be found in Table 7.2, overleaf.

CONCLUSIONS

The results from the study suggest that people engage in systematic reasoning in order to explain why they do not believe in a vivid autobiographical memory. This reasoning may be the consequence of trying to reduce the dissonance of having a very vivid memory of an event, which is contradicted by, for example, other information sources. It should be noted, however, that the study focuses on the subjective appraisal of the events and because the memories are real-life recollections the objective accuracy of the memories can not be established.

Table 7.2 Reasons Provided for Choosing to Withdraw Belief in the Memory

Category	Description	Brief example
Social feedback	Another person provided information that contradicted the event or no one could corroborate that the event had taken place.	'Nobody else remembers it' '. . . told me it didn't happen'
Event plausibility	The event was judged as being subjectively implausible (this can not have happened), illogical or scientifically implausible.	'It's impossible for a car to flip like that' 'In my memory I am flying'
Alternative attributions	The source of the event was not attributed to real-life experiences but rather to other types of sources and mental states.	'It was all just a dream' 'I was really drunk'
General beliefs regarding memory and memory ability	General beliefs as to how memory functions, as well as beliefs about childhood memories or beliefs about the reconstructive nature of memory made the person question the memory.	'Children have wild imaginations' 'If that did happened I would remember it better'
Internal features of event representations	Some features of the internal representations, such as objects, people, vividness, led them to the question the memory.	'i can't remember the details and it seems blurry'
External evidence	They had found or had been confronted with disconfirming evidence of the validity of the memory.	'I found a group photo and I wasn't even in it' 'If I had injured myself I would have a scar.'
Notions of self/others	The event seemed incompatible with their view of themselves or others.	'I am a neat freak so there is no way' 'My mother would never lie about that'
Personal motivation	The person expressed a desire to not remember the event and had thus been successful in altering the belief in the memory.	'I convinced myself it wasn''t real' 'I am just unsure about it'

Source: Adapted from Scoboria et al. (2015).

Approximately 21–25 per cent of people report having these so called 'non-believed memories' and they are experienced in a similar way to believed autobiographical memories, in terms of vividness of perceptual detail, richness of emotional content and experience of mental time travel (e.g., Mazzoni et al., 2010). We next turn to another type of memory anomaly, namely déjà vu, which bears some similarities to non-believed memories in that it involves a sense of the recollection of events that can not have occurred.

Déjà vu is a type of illusion of autobiographical memory; it might be described as the 'knowledge that a situation could not have been experienced, combined with the feeling that it has' (Thompson et al., 2004, p. 906). The term is applied to visual experience in particular. If you have visited a new place, a place you know you've never been to before, and yet the scene looks familiar – the layout of the environment, the people present – then you are among the estimated two-thirds of the population that have experienced déjà vu (Brown, 2003, 2004a, 2004b).

Brown and Marsh (2010) propose three possible mechanisms for déjà vu. The first is split perception – we get a brief glimpse of a visual scene before becoming fully aware of it. A second mechanism is implicit memory; we have already experienced the scene or part thereof but it has been stored such that only a feeling of familiarity is elicited when we re-encounter it. The third mechanism involves the notion of Gestalt familiarity, that overall configuration of the present scene closely resembles a scene that we have encountered in the past, though the specifics are different. We therefore experience a sense of familiarity without being able to put our finger on why.

Research has established some consistent features of déjà vu (see Brown, 2003, 2004a, 2004b). As noted above, around two-thirds of people will experience déjà vu at some stage in their lives, and most will experience it more than once. Déjà vu is reported in equal frequency by men and women and it decreases with age. There is a positive relationship between déjà vu and both education and socioeconomic class, and frequency of travel is positively related to déjà vu experiences. Déjà vu is more likely to occur when the person is under stress or tired – it has, for example, been noted in increased frequency in soldiers on active duty (e.g., Linn, 1954). Déjà vu is most commonly reported for novel places or physical contexts, but something similar also occurs when new people are met and in novel conversations (Kusumi, 2006). The déjà vu experience typically lasts no longer than 30 seconds (Brown, 2004a), and it may be related to a number of other experiences including *déjà vecu* (the feeling that one has lived through a moment before), *jamais vu* (when something familiar momentarily seems unfamiliar) and *presque vu* (the feeling that we are about to experience a moment of insight). It is a normal aspect of memory but also occurs in pathological conditions (e.g., Brázdil et al., 2012).

As we have seen, autobiographical memory is mainly thought of as being about our experiences, recollections of events and episodes in our lives, but our knowledge of facts about ourselves (our names, where we were born, the name of our school) is an attribute of semantic memory, and it is to this aspect of declarative memory that we now turn.

Semantic Memory

Semantic memory is our store of general knowledge about the world and the people in it, as well as facts about ourselves. It includes our knowledge of facts, language and concepts (see Chapter 9). It contains all the knowledge we need in order to use language. It is a 'mental thesaurus, organized knowledge a person possesses about words and other verbal symbols, their meaning and referents, about relations among them, and about rules, formulas and algorithms for the manipulation of these symbols, concepts, and relations' (Tulving, 1972, p. 386). It contains knowledge we acquired at school and at university, as well as words we acquired as young children, and all the information that might be termed 'general knowledge'.

Chapter 9, p296

While episodic memory is personal and differs considerably from individual to individual (even people who have shared the same experience will have somewhat different memories of the event), people who share the same language and culture have much in common in terms of semantic memory. For example, people share common concepts and categorization structures. If you are asked to describe a dog, the description is likely to be similar to that provided by a friend. You might both mention features such as 'has a tail', 'barks', 'likes to chase a ball', and so on. Of course semantic memory also contains individual knowledge; a particular dog's name, for example, or the passcode for your bank card.

> **Metamemory**
> the ability to monitor and control the content of memory. It allows us to know whether we know something.

Semantic memory differs from episodic memory in a number of other ways. For example, metamemory, our ability to monitor and control the content of our memory (see Box 7.8 for an example), would seem to differ for semantic and episodic memory, and the neural correlates of episodic and semantic metamemory would seem to differ in some respects (e.g., Reggev et al., 2011). Metamemory is not memory per se, rather our knowledge about what we have stored in memory and how readily it might be accessed. Feeling-of-knowing judgements, for example, allow us to rate the likelihood that we know something that we cannot currently recall.

Chapter 9, p294

In Chapter 9, we will look at how concepts and knowledge are represented in semantic memory. Here, we focus on the durability of semantic memory and its relationship to other kinds of memory: how long term is semantic memory?

Box 7.8 Research Close Up: Do we know what we don't know?

Source: Hampton et al. (2012).

INTRODUCTION

> *[T]here are known knowns; there are things we know that we know. There are known unknowns; that is to say there are things that, we now know we don't know. But there are also unknown unknowns – there are things we do not know we don't know.*
>
> United States Secretary of Defence, Donald Rumsfeld, 2002

The term metamemory refers to people's judgements about the contents of their own memories (Metcalfe & Dunlosky, 2008). There are things we know we know, and there are things we know we don't know. Hampton et al. (2012) examined whether these things we know we don't know, 'known unknowns', are restricted to particular types of memory, asking whether people are aware of the reliability of their judgements and whether this varies for different categories of knowledge. They examined the consistency of this knowledge over two time points. They predicted that the response options provided would affect performance depending on the kind of memory involved; a three-response condition (yes, no, unsure) should show more consistency than a two-response (true/false) condition for general knowledge. They hypothesized that, if long-term memory contains a set of stable known facts, then better consistency over the two time points would be evident for the three-response condition, since participants have the option of saying that they are unsure.

METHOD AND RESULTS

Experiments 1 and 2

In Hampton et al.'s first experiment, 32 students saw 150 statements: 50 general knowledge, 50 category membership and 50 autobiographical memory (see Table 7.3). Within each set, 15 statements were clearly true, 15 were clearly false and 20 items were likely to create uncertainty.

The statements either appeared with a True/False response option or with three response options ('100 per cent sure it's true', 'Not 100 per cent sure either way', and '100 per cent sure it's false'). Participants were instructed to only use the sure options if they were 100 per cent certain either way. The statements were presented in random order, and presented again one week later. The results showed that the general knowledge statements showed more consistency over the two tests when the

Table 7.3 Examples of the Types of Statements used in Each Category

	Uncertainty	True	False
General knowledge	The internet was originally developed for military reasons.	Some boats have motors, others have sails.	The Earth is flat.
Autobiographical	Growing up, I was often ill.	I have stayed in a hotel.	I am a certified pilot.
Category	Olive [fruit] Doormat [furniture]	Apple [fruit] Shelf [furniture]	Onion [fruit] Suitcase [furniture]

third response option (Don't know) was included, but there was no difference for the autobiographical or category statements. Participants were far more likely to be unsure about general knowledge statements than about the other types of statement. In Experiment 2, the categorization condition of Experiment 1 was replicated on a larger scale and confirmed the results.

Experiment 3

In Experiment 3, information of a more personal nature was examined by including statements about beliefs and aspirations. Forty-four students saw 90 statements: 30 general knowledge statements (see Table 7.3), 30 belief statements (e.g., 'A father figure is important in a child's life') and 30 aspirations (e.g., 'It is my ambition to own a house one day'). Response options were as in Experiment 1. Consistency across tests was not greater for statements about personal aspirations or beliefs, but the pattern for general knowledge questions was as in Experiment 1 – that is, general knowledge statements showed more consistency over the two tests when the third response option (Don't know) was included. Participants were far more likely to be unsure about general knowledge statements than about the other categories.

Experiment 4

This experiment extended the procedure to consider another type of personally related information: hedonic statements, likes and dislikes. Forty students saw statements on general knowledge, categorization, and likes and dislikes (e.g., 'I like pizza', 'I like watching tennis'). The previous results were again confirmed. For general knowledge alone, consistency was facilitated by the additional response option.

DISCUSSION

Across the four experiments, knowledge statements showed greater consistency when participants were allowed to use an 'unsure' response option, whereas for statements about personal beliefs and aspirations (Experiment 3) or likes and dislikes (Experiment 4), there was no such effect. These data illustrate an important difference in our metamemory for personal semantic information (such as aspirations, or what we like and don't like) and general knowledge. If we are unsure about a general knowledge statement, we are open to the possibility that it is accurate, or that we might have encountered the information but are unable to recall it, we are willing to use the 'unsure' response option. But, if we cannot recollect an autobiographical event, we are more likely to dismiss the event as not having ever occurred.

As Hampton et al. (p. 350) note, '[f]ailure to find traces in autobiographical memory will be taken as evidence that a statement is false, whereas failure to find information about a general knowledge

> statement does not give any reason to believe that it is false'. In the same way, eyewitnesses can fail to recall an event that occurred, or be quite certain that they remember an event or recognize an individual, and yet confidence is not a good predictor of accuracy in the context of eyewitness testimony (see, for example, Wells & Loftus, 2003) and eyewitnesses can express high confidence in incorrectly recalled items (e.g., Buratti et al., 2014). This is an issue we will return to in Chapter 8.

Chapter 8, p285

We know from studies of amnesia that much of semantic memory remains intact and available even after a brain injury affecting memory. Our knowledge about language and concepts about the world tends to be formed early on in life and to be used throughout life. What about knowledge learned at school or at university? Does this remain? Despite the popular belief that much of the information is lost, research shows that after a period of initial forgetting, much knowledge remains over a very long retention period.

Bahrick (1984) examined memory for Spanish learned at school in a large sample ($n = 773$) with an up to 50-year retention period. A total of 146 participants were still at school or college and learning Spanish at the time of testing; 587 participants had left school or college, and ceased formal language instruction, between 1 and 50 years previously. Forty participants who had never learned Spanish were also included. This group was included as a baseline measure to establish how much Spanish one might pick up without ever having had formal instruction, incidentally – through popular media, for example. Participants formed eight groups, depending on the time that had elapsed since their last course was taken in Spanish.

Participants were tested on measures of recall, recognition and comprehension. The data showed an initial sharp decline in retention over a six-year period, following which the remaining memories became stable and there was no further loss of knowledge until up to 25 years later. Some further forgetting occurred beyond the 30-year period (see Figure 7.8). Once knowledge has stabilized in semantic memory, it remains resistant to forgetting over potentially a very long period; this long-lasting store of knowledge was referred to by Bahrick (1984) as the **permastore**.

Permastore involves the long-term retention of content that has been acquired and relearned over a period of time, even if rarely used thereafter.

Such findings have been repeated for other knowledge areas such as mathematics, cognitive psychology or memory for novels (see Conway et al., 1992, for a review) as well as basic science knowledge (Custers & ten Cate, 2011).

Similar findings pointing to very long-term retention have been noted for personal semantic memory. Bahrick et al. (1975) tested 392 high school graduates. The time since graduation varied from 2 weeks to 57 years across nine age cohorts. Tests were constructed using individual participants' high school year books, with a random selection of names and faces from the participants' graduating class included. Several measures were taken. In a free recall task, participants were asked to list as many names of people in their graduating class as they could. In the picture recognition test, participants were required to identify which of a set of pictures appeared in their year book and which did not. In a name recognition test, participants were required to identify which of a list of names were graduates in their class. A matching test required participants to match pictures to names and names to pictures. In the picture cueing task, participants were shown pictures and their recall of the name was tested.

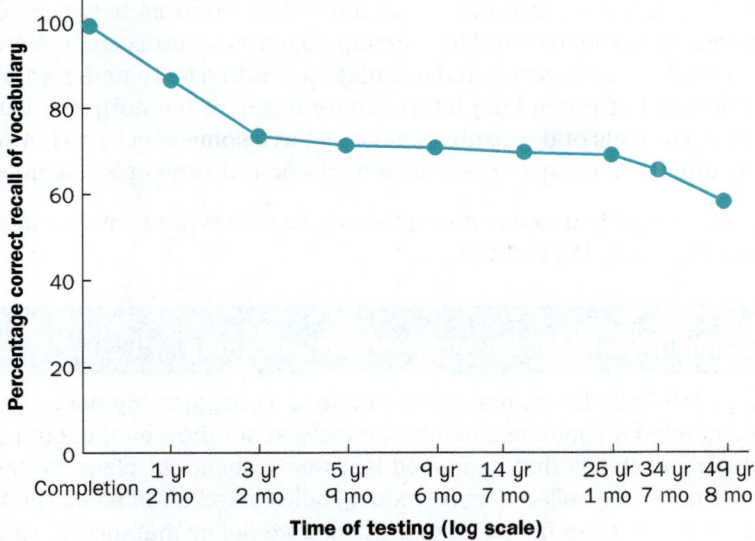

Figure 7.8 Memory for Spanish learned at high school.
Memory for a foreign language learned at school undergoes some initial forgetting, but much knowledge of the language is retained even after a significant period of time has passed. The diagram shows the average recall of Spanish vocabulary for participants up to 50 years out of school, based on a sample of 773 participants.

Source: Bahrick (1984).

Bahrick et al. found that their participants could identify approximately 90 per cent of the names and faces of those in their graduating classes. Visual memory was retained for at least 35 years, while verbal memory was found to decline after 15 years. The ability to match names with faces is similarly long lasting. At graduation, participants could match 90 per cent of the names and pictures, and this level of retrieval showed little decline over the following 15 years. Performance on the free recall and picture cued recall tasks was poorer than on the matching and identification tasks and greater declines over time occured on these tasks. After 48 years, free recall had decreased by about 60 per cent of initial performance, while cued recall declined by over 70 per cent.

As Bahrick et al. note, these data demonstrate far less decline in memory over time than is typically reported in laboratory investigations using material that lends itself less to real-life comparison.

Evaluation

It is clear that we can draw a general distinction, within declarative and non-declarative memory and, within declarative memory, between semantic and episodic memory. However, the degree of separation or overlap between these systems continues to be explored and they may function more as a continuum, with a number of intermediate memory states that require study. Autobiographical memory – part episodic recollections and part semantic memory for the self – demonstrates the overlap of the two systems. This latter aspect of autobiographical memory, the area of personal semantics, is only beginning to be explored in depth. Personal semantics is highly personal but is not linked to any particular episode that can be recollected. It is in some ways like episodic memory and in other ways like semantic.

As Renoult et al. (2012) note, 'Although drawing a stark contrast between episodic and semantic memory has proved useful in spurring cognitive neuroscience research, these systems have largely been investigated in isolation, leading to an under-appreciation of their interactions and of potentially intermediate forms of memory' (p. 550). It would seem that existing models of declarative memory have some way to go before they can fully describe, and predict, capacities realized by semantic and episodic memory.

We close this section with an opportunity for you to assess your own memory. Box 7.9 looks at measuring everyday memory.

Box 7.9 Practical Application: Measuring everyday memory

In seminal work, Schacter (e.g., 1999; 2013) points out that there is a duality to memory – on the one hand, we are capable of remembering an immense number of facts about the world, about people we know, about childhood events, about things that happened last week, about our plans for the future. These pieces of information are generally called to mind readily, quickly and effortlessly. On the other hand, there will be times when our memories fail us, and, assuming we notice that failure, such lapses hint at the complexity of the underlying processes. Schacter (1999) suggests seven categories of memory failure that he refers to as the 'seven sins of memory' – but, rather than seeing these as design flaws, he suggests that they are 'more usefully conceptualized as by-products of otherwise desirable features of human memory' (p. 183). You have encountered many of these 'sins' already in this chapter:

1. **Transience**: a type of forgetting, decreasing accessibility of memories over time.
2. **Absent-mindedness**: a type of forgetting that reflects shallow processing, or attention failure.
3. **Blocking**: forgetting caused by a temporary access failure, as in the case of the tip of the tongue effect (see Chapter 10). [Chapter 10, p348]
4. **Misattribution**: a source error, whereby we misattribute a memory to the wrong source.
5. **Suggestibility**: openness to false memory, as in the 'lost in the shopping mall' scenario, described earlier in the chapter.
6. **Bias**: distortions based on beliefs or prior knowledge – for example, re-interpreting the past in line with self-image.
7. **Persistence**: the tendency for some memories to be remembered even when we don't want to remember them, as occurs in obsessive thoughts or in some cases of memory following psychological trauma (post-traumatic stress).

You can get an idea of the extent of your own memory failures using the 'Everyday Memory Questionnaire' (EMQ), which was developed by Sunderland and colleagues (1983). The EMQ asks 28 questions about common lapses in memory. For each statement, you rate the frequency of each lapse using a scale from 1 to 9 (see below). Some of the types of lapse are more commonly experienced than others. See if you can identify how each lapse fits within Schacter's seven categories.

Scale
1 = Not at all in the last six months
2 = About once in the last six months
3 = More than once in the last six months
4 = About once a month
5 = More than once a month, but less than once a week
6 = About once a week

7 = More than once a week, but less than once a day
8 = About once a day
9 = More than once a day

1. Forgetting where you have put something. Losing things around your house.
2. Failing to recognize places that you are told you have often been to before.
3. Finding a television story difficult to follow.
4. Not remembering a change in your daily routine, such as a change in the place where something is kept, or a change in the time something happens. Following your old routine by mistake.
5. Having to go back and check whether you've done something that you meant to do.
6. Forgetting when something happened; for example, forgetting whether something had happened yesterday or last week.
7. Completely forgetting to take things with you, or leaving things behind, or having to go back and fetch them.
8. Forgetting that you were told something yesterday or a few days ago, and maybe having to be reminded about it.
9. Starting to read something (a book or a newspaper or magazine article) without realizing you have already read it before.
10. Letting yourself ramble on to speak about unimportant or irrelevant things.
11. Failing to recognize, by sight, close relatives or friends that you meet frequently.
12. Having difficulty picking up a new skill: for example, having difficulty in learning a new game or in working some new gadget after you have practised once or twice.
13. Finding that a word is 'on the tip of your tongue'. You know it, but cannot quite find the word.
14. Completely forgetting to do things you said you would do, and planned to do.
15. Forgetting important details of what you did or what happened to you yesterday.
16. When talking to someone, forgetting what you have just said.
17. When reading a newspaper or magazine, being unable to follow the thread of a story; losing track of what it is about.
18. Forgetting to tell someone something important. Perhaps forgetting to pass on a message or remind someone of something.
19. Forgetting important details about yourself, e.g., your birthday or where you live.
20. Getting the details of what someone had told you mixed up and confused.
21. Telling someone a story or joke you have told them once already.
22. Forgetting details of things you do regularly, whether at home or at work. For example, forgetting details of what to do, or at what time to do it.
23. Finding that faces of famous people, seen on television or in photographs, look unfamiliar.
24. Forgetting where things are normally kept or looking for them in the wrong place.
25. Getting lost or turning in the wrong direction on a journey, a walk, or in a building where you have *often* been before.
26. Getting lost or turning in the wrong direction on a journey, a walk, or in a building where you have been *only once or twice before.*
27. Doing some routine thing twice by mistake. For example, going to brush/comb your hair, or putting two lots of tea in the pot, when you have just done so.

> **28.** Repeating to someone what you have just told them or asking them the same question twice.
>
> **Scoring:** A total score of between 28–57 is good; 58–116 is average; 117–252 is below average (Baddeley, 1999). However, as Baddeley (1999) notes, having a 'below average' performance does not necessarily indicate that you have a poor memory – it could just mean that you lead a busy life and encounter more situations and opportunities for a lapse to occur in the first place!
>
> *Source:* Sunderland et al. (1983).

Summary

This chapter examined long-term memory. Cases such as that of H.M. have shown that LTM processes are not distributed throughout the brain; damage to particular areas within the temporal lobes will cause profound LTM loss. H.M. and other cases with the characteristic deficits of amnesia show that memory consists of a number of different systems, some of which are unaffected by amnesia. Amnesia is associated with intact short-term memory, as measured by digit span, for example; memory for language, and concepts, is relatively unaffected; but there is severe amnesia for events that occur after the onset of the illness/injury. Skill learning, conditioning and priming will be unaffected. The patient will also be able to engage in skills acquired prior to the onset of amnesia (e.g., play a musical instrument).

It is generally agreed that there is a distinction in LTM between implicit or non-declarative memory and explicit or declarative memory, a distinction described as 'knowing that' as opposed to 'knowing how'. Explicit memory involves conscious recollection of information, whereas implicit memory is evident when performance that does not require conscious recollection is facilitated by prior learning. Some tests of memory rely on explicit recollection of information; others measure implicit memory. Methods such as free recall, cued recall and recognition require conscious recollection, whereas other methods, such as word association or word fragment completion, do not.

Declarative memory includes episodic and semantic memory. Episodic memory is memory for events and episodes we have experienced. Memory is constructive and when we recall our past experiences we do not call to mind an exact copy of events as they occurred. When certain episodic and semantic memories become embedded in the broader conceptual system, autobiographical memories are formed.

Autobiographical memory involves personal experience and it is closely associated with the self. It might be thought of as our life histories, the facts and events that we can consciously recollect with some detail, which are time-marked as belonging to a particular phase in our lives. Autobiographical memories facilitate interaction between persons through the sharing of memories, as well as being important for our sense of self. It has also been suggested that they have a directive function, whereby they guides our current and future behaviour and help us with problem solving.

Memory that allows us to keep track of and carry out intended actions is called prospective memory. Prospective memory is normally highly effective and only a small percentage of failure to carry out planned tasks during a week is due to memory failure.

Semantic memory is our store of general knowledge about the world. It includes our knowledge of facts, language and concepts, and, after a period of initial forgetting, much knowledge remains over a very long retention period.

Metamemory refers to people's judgements about the contents and accuracy of their own memories. It can also refer to judgements about how easily something can be remembered.

Review Questions

1. What can we learn about memory from amnesia?
2. What is the difference between declarative and procedural memory?
3. How do episodic memories differ from semantic memories?
4. What kinds of tasks require the use of prospective memory?
5. What are the dimensions of autobiographical memories?

Discussion Questions

1. Amnesia is one way of gaining insights into how our memory works – however, can you see any difficulties with using this method?
2. Is the Multiple Memory Systems Model valid – are there any components unaccounted for or could LTM be modelled in another way?
3. In this chapter, a wide array of memory errors and deficits have been covered – do any of these deficits cause graver consequences than others? Why?

Further Reading

Cohen, G., & Conway, M. A. (Ed.) (2008). *Memory in the real world* (3rd ed.). Psychology Press.

Einstein, O., & McDaniel, M. (2005). Prospective memory: Multiple retrieval processes. *Current Directions in Psychological Science, 14,* 286–290.

Fivush, R. (2011). The development of autobiographical memory. *Annual Review of Psychology, 62,* 559–582.

Graf, P., Squire, L. R., & Mandler, G. (1984). The information that amnesic patients do not forget. *Journal of Experimental Psychology: Learning. Memory, and Cognition, 10,* 164–178.

Scoboria, A., Jackson, D. L., Talarico, J., Hanczakowski, M., Wysman, L., & Mazzoni, G. (2014). The role of belief in occurrence within autobiographical memory. *Journal of Experimental Psychology: General, 143*(3), 1242–1258.

Squire, L. R., & Dede, A. J. (2015). Conscious and unconscious memory systems. *Cold Spring Harbor Perspectives in Biology, 7*(3), a021667.

LEARNING AND FORGETTING

8

- **PREVIEW QUESTIONS**
- **INTRODUCTION**
- **LEARNING: ENCODING, STORAGE AND RETRIEVAL**
  - LEVELS OF PROCESSING
    - Box 8.1 Research Close Up: Levels of processing
  - MNEMONICS
    - Box 8.2 Practical Application: Exceptionally good memories – nature or nurture?
  - ENCODING SPECIFICITY
  - CONTEXT DEPENDENT RETRIEVAL
  - SPACED VERSUS MASSED TRIALS
- **FORGETTING**
  - INTERFERENCE
  - DECAY AND CONSOLIDATION
    - Box 8.3 Research Close Up: Wakeful rest improves long-term memory
    - Box 8.4 When Things Go Wrong: Consolidation, retroactive interference and amnesia
  - THE RECONSOLIDATION OF MEMORIES
  - FUNCTIONAL APPROACHES TO FORGETTING
    - Box 8.5 When Things Go Wrong: The recovered memories controversy
- **EVERYDAY/REAL WORLD MEMORY**
  - FLASHBULB MEMORIES
  - EYEWITNESS TESTIMONY
    - Box 8.6 Practical Application: The cognitive interview
  - EFFECTIVE STUDYING
    - Box 8.7 Research Close Up: Does drawing facilitate the learning of terms and their definitions?
- **SUMMARY**
- **REVIEW QUESTIONS**
- **DISCUSSION QUESTIONS**
- **FURTHER READING**

Preview Questions

1. What is learning?
2. How do we learn?
3. Are there ways in which we can learn more effectively?
4. What causes forgetting?
5. Are memories for surprising, dramatic events (flashbulb memories) really accurate and complete, compared to memories for ordinary events?
6. Can we reduce or encourage loss of particular memories?
7. Is extraordinary memory an innate ability or a developed skill?
8. Which studying techniques are the most effective?

INTRODUCTION

As a student you are very much concerned with learning and with remembering learned information when required during examinations or in tutorials. If you have hastily read Chapter 1 you may have trouble remembering whether Wundt was a Gestalt psychologist, an introspectionist or a behaviourist; and was his first name Karl or Wilhelm? On the other hand, if you had gone over the chapter at intervals and tested yourself as you finished each study session you will most likely remember these details (see the final section of this chapter on effective studying). In everyday life, we often struggle to remember some kinds of material (such as new computer passwords) but readily remember some other types of material (such as where we first heard of the sudden death of a famous celebrity). As we shall see, there have been many suggested models for memory that try to explain its strengths and weaknesses. One popular idea is that memory is like a storeroom. A version of this view is put forward by the fictional detective Sherlock Holmes, in the following narrative:

> 'You see,' he explained, 'I consider that a man's brain originally is like a little empty attic, and you have to stock it with such furniture as you choose. A fool takes in all the lumber of every sort that he comes across, so that the knowledge which might be useful to him gets crowded out, or at best is jumbled up with a lot of other things so that he has a difficulty in laying his hands upon it. Now the skilful workman is very careful indeed as to what he takes into his brain-attic. He will have nothing but the tools which may help him in doing his work, but of these he has a large assortment, and all in the most perfect order. It is a mistake to think that that little room has elastic walls and can distend to any extent. Depend upon it there comes a time when for every addition of knowledge you forget something that you knew before. It is of the highest importance, therefore, not to have useless facts elbowing out the useful ones.'
>
> From *A Study in Scarlet*, A. Conan Doyle (1887)

Learning
processes of acquiring information for mental storage and later use.

Forgetting
processes leading to a loss of ability to retrieve previously learned information.

In the course of this chapter we will present psychologists' ideas about **learning** and **forgetting**, some of which are similar and some different to Sherlock Holmes's view that memory is like an attic in the brain. As we will see as we progress through this chapter, the overall picture of memory, learning and forgetting that emerges from more than 100 years of research is much more complex and intriguing than the simple 'attic' model suggests.

For the cognitive psychologist, learning is the process of acquiring knowledge which, if all goes well, can be retrieved later to help us meet our goals. Thus, we will review the factors that help or hinder learning, and the factors that can lead to forgetting – that is, failure to retrieve previously acquired knowledge when needed. We will look at the retention (or otherwise) of learned information over time periods of at least several minutes extending to weeks, months and years. We will focus on storage and retrieval from long-term memory (see Chapter 7) rather than short-term or working memory (see Chapter 6). Chapter 7 focused on the different kinds of information (e.g., semantic, episodic, procedural, prospective) stored in long-term memory; this chapter concentrates on the processes by which information becomes stored in (i.e., learned) and retrieved (i.e., remembered) from long-term memory, and how information may fail to be retrieved (forgotten) when needed.

Cognitive analysis suggests that *encoding, storage* and *retrieval* (see Chapter 6 for an introduction to these topics) are the three main stages involved in learning and in remembering (or forgetting), and we will consider these stages in the following sections.

> Chapter 6, p176

LEARNING: ENCODING, STORAGE AND RETRIEVAL

The first step in learning new information is to encode that information in an internal representation in working memory (see also Chapter 6). The initial representation then needs to be processed further to develop a **memory trace**, or record, in long-term memory (LTM). Processes, such as rehearsal in which the basic representation is repeated, are presumed to strengthen the trace. With meaningful materials, other processes of encoding can elaborate the traces and link the traces to already stored information.

> **Memory trace**
> a mental representation of stored information.

Levels of Processing

Craik and Lockhart (1972) stressed the importance of encoding in their **levels of processing** theory. On this view, 'shallow' or surface encoding of materials leads to poor retention, but 'deep', more meaningful encoding leads to improved retention and remembering. Simple repetitive rehearsal on this account does not help memory but deeper processing does. Further, on this view, learning need not be intentional. **Incidental learning** in which learning is a by-product of attending to the material in some way could be strong if the material is processed deeply. An early test of the levels of processing theory (Craik & Tulving, 1975) is described in Box 8.1.

> **Levels of processing**
> a theory that better learning results from deeper semantic processing, which produces stronger, more elaborated memory traces than superficial-level processing.
>
> **Incidental learning**
> learning that takes place without any intention to learn.

 Box 8.1 Research Close Up: Levels of processing

Source: Craik & Tulving (1975).

INTRODUCTION

To test the idea of the levels of processing theory that more elaborate ('deeper') processing of the items to be learned would benefit learning and recall, Craik and Tulving (1975) ran the following study.

METHOD

Participants were presented with words printed in capitals or in lower case and, for each word, were asked to carry out one of three operations, which were as follows: (1) to say whether the word (e.g., CHAIR) was printed in capital letters or not; (2) to decide whether the word rhymed with another word (e.g., Does this word rhyme with mat? DOG) and (3) to decide if the word fitted a given sentence or not (e.g., Does the word field fit into this sentence? 'The horse lived in a —.'). Note that some items should be answered 'Yes' and some 'No'.

The three types of task vary in depth of processing required from shallow (1) to deep (3). It is worth noting that the participants were not instructed to learn the words – that is, the study was one of incidental learning. Thus, after the operations had been carried out on the words, participants were unexpectedly shown a mixture of words, 50 per cent of which had previously been used in the task and 50 per cent of which had not been previously used in the task. The participants were to say which words they had seen in the first part of the task and the percentage recognized correctly indicated how well the words were remembered.

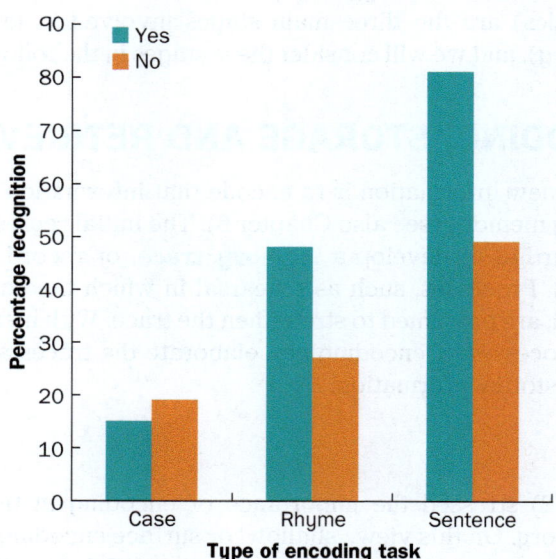

Figure 8.1 Effects of type of encoding task on recognition memory.
This figure shows recognition memory separately for words that were judged 'Yes' and 'No' on the encoding decision.
Source: Adapted from Craik & Tulving (1975).

RESULTS

From the results in Figure 8.1 it can be seen that as expected on the theory, a surprise memory test found that best recognition of the words occurred after the deeper, semantic processing required by the decision as to whether the word fitted a sentence and the poorest recognition was after the shallower surface processing of the print case reporting task, with the rhyme judging task being intermediate in its effects.

DISCUSSION

Although the results were in line with the levels of processing theory, this initial study was open to an alternative interpretation in that the times needed to make the three word judgements varied, with the semantic task taking longer than the other two, so that the semantically judged words were seen for longer, which might explain their better retention. However, when the exposure time factor was controlled, in subsequent studies in the same paper, the same results were found.

A large number of studies have been carried out to test the levels of processing theory. In a recent study, Baddeley and Hitch (2017) tested if the theory could be extended to include learning of visual stimuli. In a series of tests, they compared the level of processing effects for visual tasks with those for different verbal tasks. They found that deeper processing led to better retrieval both for visual and verbal tasks. However, the effects on the visual task were modest, while the effects on the verbal task differed substantially in magnitude between tasks. The largest effects were found for learning familiar animals and household items, while the effects for remembering unfamiliar animals and people's names were only modest. Baddeley and Hitch suggest that these results might be explained by the concept of affordance, 'whereby the object provides, or "affords", the opportunity to perform an action' (p. 10). Familiar animals and household items, therefore, can be associated with a wide number of different representations, which results in deeper encoding. For example, a chair can be represented as an object to sit on, but also as an object to reach a high shelf. Such richness in representations will not be available for unfamiliar animals that we know very little about.

Similar levels-of-processing results to those reported by Craik and Tulving (1975) were also found when non-verbal items were to be learned. Bower and Karlin (1974) used faces as the stimuli and found that memory was better for faces that had been judged for 'honesty' rather than simply classed as 'male' or 'female'.

An incidental finding was that in semantic judgement tasks (Is the word an 'animal'? Is the word a 'plant'?), words that were responded to positively ('Yes') were better remembered than those given a negative response. Craik (2002) suggested this showed a role for elaboration of encoding as well as depth of coding. Positive trial encodings strengthen pre-existing links between the stimulus word ('Dog', say) and the category ('Animal'), but this does not happen in the negative trials (e.g., 'Cat' does not have a pre-existing link to the test category 'Plant' to be strengthened).

Despite the strong empirical data showing effects in line with the levels-of-processing approach, the theory has been criticized as basically circular in that there is no independent measure of depth of processing. There is the risk of saying that processing was deeper because retention was better and that retention was better because processing was deeper (Baddeley, 1978; Eysenck, 1978).

Mnemonics

Various strategies of encoding can enhance memory performance markedly. Such strategies to boost memory are known as mnemonics and many can be traced back to antiquity when orators had to rely on memory when making long speeches. (See Chapter 1 for more on mnemonics.)

> Chapter 1, p2

One key mnemonic principle is **categorization**. This principle is that items grouped or organized into categories will be better recalled than unorganized lists of items (see Chapter 9 for more on categorization). Bousfield (1953) found that if lists of words were drawn from a few categories (such as animals, vegetables, professions, names) then even when 60 words were given in scrambled order, participants tended to recall them in groups or clusters by category. Mandler and Pearlstone (1966) asked participants to group 52 words into categories repeatedly until they produced reliable groupings. After this exercise in organizing the words, participants were unexpectedly tested on their ability to recall the words. Memory for the words was very strongly positively related to the number of categories (which ranged from two to seven) in the participants' groupings. It was also found that the basic result was not due to differences in study time during the organizing stage of the study. The key factor was the degree of organization that the participants had imposed on the materials. Bower et al. (1969) found further that hierarchically structured categorizations were particularly beneficial for retention. For example, if a list of words included specific animal words and car names it would be helpful to group the animals into, say, domestic and wild animals and the cars into, say, saloon cars, trucks, sports cars, and so on. This is as Sherlock Holmes would have expected from his 'little attic' model of memory; material is best retrieved if it is stored in an organized way.

> Chapter 9, p296

In addition to organizing material into meaningful structures, use of images in encoding is an important aspect of many mnemonics, such as the **method of loci**, the **method of interacting images** and the **pegword method**.

In the method of loci, which some trace back to *c.* 500 BC (Paivio, 1971), a familiar sequence of places is imagined and in each place along the sequence is an object to be remembered. For example, if you needed to remember a

Categorization
a mnemonic strategy involving the grouping of items into familiar categories.
Method of loci
a mnemonic strategy in which a familiar route is imagined and images of the items to be recalled are linked to landmarks on the route.
Method of interacting images
a mnemonic strategy in which vivid and bizarre images are formed of the items to be recalled, interacting in some way.
Pegword method
a mnemonic strategy in which items to be recalled are linked by imagery to an already learned sequence list of imageable words.

shopping list (cheese, butter, milk, bread, tomatoes), using the method of loci you might imagine going around your home and seeing a giant cheese on the carpet in the first room, a pack of butter on a table in the second room, a bottle of milk in the third room, and so on. To retrieve the items, you would re-imagine the tour of your home and, if the method works, you will 'see' the to-be-remembered items in your 'mind's eye'. Ross and Lawrence (1968) found that people trained in using the method of loci could recall 95 per cent of 40-item lists after a single presentation. The method works best when the images are seen as interacting. Bower (1970) found that recall of arbitrary pairs of nouns was greatly enhanced when participants were instructed to form images of the nouns interacting rather than just side by side. For example, imaging a dog driving a car rather than a dog beside a car would facilitate recall of the dog–car pair.

The pegword method is similar to the method of loci, but uses a sequence of highly imageable nouns linked by rhymes to the number sequence. The standard example is 'One is a bun, two is a shoe, three is a tree, four is a door, five is a hive, six is sticks, seven is heaven, eight is a gate, nine is wine and ten is a hen.' To recall up to 10 items in sequence, using the pegword method, you would image the first item interacting with a bun, the second interacting with a shoe, and so on. Bugelski et al. (1968) found near perfect one trial learning of lists of 10 words using the 'One is a bun' pegword mnemonic with quite fast presentation rates of one new word per four seconds. A follow-up study (Bugelski, 1968) found that people could readily learn many successive lists using the same 'One is a bun' system, with little or no interference between lists. Thus this mnemonic is a robust and easily learned method.

> **Dual-coding hypothesis**
> proposes that concrete words can be encoded both verbally and by means of images representing their meaning; in contrast, abstract words can only be coded verbally. Dual coding is one explanation of why concrete words are easier to remember.

How might the benefits of these mnemonic methods be explained? Paivio (1969, 1971, 1983) and Yuille (1983) applied a **dual-coding hypothesis** according to which concrete words can be coded in two different ways: in a verbal code and in an imagery code. Abstract words can only easily be coded in one way: verbal. Thus, concrete words have two internal codes and so two ways of being remembered. Paivio (1965) found in a study using noun pairs representing the four possible combinations of abstract and concrete words that concreteness, especially of the first word of a pair, greatly facilitated recall of the pairs. The first word, it was argued, serves as a conceptual peg to which the second is linked.

Thus, mnemonics using imagery show the benefits predicted by the dual-coding hypothesis.

Although specific mnemonics can be learned, is it possible to improve our memory abilities by training? This question is addressed in Box 8.2, which discusses exceptional memory and whether it can be acquired.

Box 8.2 Practical Application: Exceptionally good memories – nature or nurture?

Memory failures are a common experience and most people would probably say that they wished their memory was better. This box concerns the practical question of whether we could improve our memory ability by training, or whether good memory is essentially innate and not open to improvement by training. See Box 1.2 for a discussion on exactly how we train our memory.

Some rare individuals have the opposite complaint – that their memory is too good! The best-known case of truly exceptional general memory ability is that of a Russian journalist, Solomon V. Shereshevskii. He was tested extensively by A. R. Luria (1968) and was found able to recall a huge variety of complex materials after very brief study periods, such as lists of more than 100 numbers, poems in foreign languages, technical diagrams and scientific formulae; moreover, he could recall such materials perfectly after gaps of many years and recall the materials in reverse order if asked.

The basis of Shereshevskii's remarkable ability was a strong capability to generate visual and other images, which in turn seems to have built on synaesthesia (see Chapter 2). This is a tendency for stimuli from one sensory modality to evoke images in another modality. Thus musical tones would elicit strong coloured images and taste images for Shereshevskii. He also had particular images for numbers, so that '1' was a well-built man and '2' a high-spirited woman! Sometimes, he complained, the vivid and complex imagery evoked by the sound of the voice when someone spoke to him made it hard to focus on the meaning of what was said.

> Chapter 2, p34

A more recent case of unusual memory has been reported by Parker and colleagues (2006), regarding a 41-year-old woman known as A.J., who can recall extraordinary details of every day of her life from her teens onwards. She reports that her remembering is automatic and effortless, and is like a constantly running movie that never stops. A.J. likens the experience to having a split screen in awareness on which memories are constantly being replayed while she tries to attend to present tasks and interactions. At times she says that her condition is a burden and, along with the Shereshevskii case, these real-life examples suggest that having a normally forgetful memory is not so bad as we sometimes feel.

Most examples of exceptional memory ability, as are found in memory experts, or mnemonists, are unlike Shereshevskii or A.J., in that the exceptional memory ability is highly domain specific and has been acquired by extensive practice using suitable mnemonic methods, rather than being an effortless innate condition.

Practice effects in expanding short-term memory were demonstrated by Ericsson and Chase (1982). They repeatedly tested the digit span of one participant and his measured span grew from the typical seven items level to a span of around 80 digits after practising for an hour per day, three to five days a week, for 20 months. This remarkable result was achieved through the use of a special mnemonic based on the participant's strong interest and knowledge of running times for various distances. Thus, 3 4 9 2 would be recoded as '3 mins 49.2 secs, near record for mile'. Sequences not suitable as running times were recoded as dates or ages, so 1 9 4 4 becomes the year 1944, 'near end of WW2', 8 9 2 becomes 89.2 years, 'a good age'. Ericsson and Chase were able to teach the method to another participant with an interest in running and he also increased his digit span from 7 to 75 with extensive practice.

Some individuals deliberately practise memory skills for specific domains, such as memorizing packs of playing cards, number sequences, faces and names in order to compete effectively in memory championships. Maguire et al. (2003) in a brain imaging study of competitors in the World Memory Championships found that during memorizing the mnemonists showed more activity than controls in brain areas used in navigation and spatial memory. This result is consistent with the high level of self-reports of using mnemonics of the method of loci type (discussed earlier).

A striking case of superior acquired memory is provided by Rajan Mahadevan, who shows a high level of ability to remember numbers. He held the world record for reciting the digits of *pi* to 31,811 places for a number of years. On being tested he was found to have a digit span of about 60 (Thompson et al., 1993). However, Ericsson et al. (2004) carried out further tests with Mahadevan and gathered evidence that his exceptional digit span was based on mnemonic methods that he had developed over the years as a mnemonist, rather than being due to an exceptional basic innate short-term or working memory capacity. His span for symbols such as !, *, &, @, and so on, was in the normal range, as was his memory for word lists and stories. It was noted that he did expand his symbol span after a number of trials by recoding the symbols into digits to which he could apply his practised mnemonics.

Overall, it appears safe to conclude that, with a very few exceptions such as Shereshevskii and A.J., exceptional memory performance results from extensive practice with suitable mnemonics and is very specific to the domains in which practice has taken place.

Encoding Specificity

> **Encoding specificity principle**
> if the context at recall is similar to the context at encoding then memory will be enhanced.

The **encoding specificity principle** (Thomson & Tulving, 1970) looks forward from the cues used at the encoding stage or study stage to the cues present during the test period. It will be helpful for retrieval at test, on this view, if the same cues are present at test as were available in the study period.

Thomson and Tulving (1970) tested the principle in the following study. They had participants study pairs of words in which the to-be-remembered words, or 'targets', were printed in capitals. Alongside the 'targets' were words in lower case. These lower-case words were either strong cues of the target (e.g., black–WHITE) or were weak cues, not related to the target words (e.g., table–WHITE). At recall, the participants were then shown cue words and had to recall the targets. Sometimes the cue words at recall were the same as at study (weak or strong) and sometimes the cue words were different (strong at recall if weak at study, and vice versa). Recall was best if the same cues were present at study and at recall. The participants were greatly aided by the weak cues at recall if the cues had been present at study. This result showed that the presence of the same cues at test and at study was beneficial and indicated that people formed associations that encoded links between the weak cues and the target items during the study period. So, in the example above, it seems that people sought out associations of 'WHITE' to 'table', perhaps by imaging a white painted table, and so the cue 'table' became effective at retrieval.

The encoding specificity principle in essence says that recall will be best if the cues available at the time of testing match the context that was present in the study period.

Context-dependent Retrieval

> **Context effects**
> occur if memory is better when the external environment at testing is the same as at learning.

It has also been found in a number of studies that reinstating the general context in which learning took place can assist later recall (e.g., Isarida & Isarida, 2014; Smith & Vela, 2001). A striking example of such **context effects** was provided by Godden and Baddeley's (1975) study of scuba divers who learned lists either under water or on dry land, and were then tested either 20 feet under water or on land. It was found that lists learned under water were better recalled under water than on land, and the lists learned on dry land were better recalled on land than under water. Overall, recall in the same context as study was some 50 per cent better. It may be noted that recognition memory did not show the same context effects in later studies of divers (Godden & Baddeley, 1980) with high recognition irrespective of context. This difference between recall and recognition may well be due to the reduced need to encode cues for recognition tests in which the test itself supplies the needed cues. (See Chapter 7 for more on recognition versus recall.)

Chapter 7, p218

> **State-dependent learning effect**
> occurs if memory is better when internal physiological conditions at learning are reinstated at testing.
>
> **Mood-dependent memory effect**
> means that memory is better when mood at learning is reinstated at testing.

Similar results have also been found for what we might call 'internal contexts' in the form of physiological states brought about by psychoactive agents (**state-dependent learning effect**) or in the form of moods (**mood-dependent memory effect**). Eich (1980) found that materials learned while participants were in an altered physiological state due to alcohol or marijuana were recalled better when the state was recreated. As with the (external) context effect, the state-dependent learning effect was found for recall but not for recognition (Roediger & Guynn, 1996). Bower (1981) and Eich (1995) have reported mood manipulation studies in which happy/sad moods were induced at study and test, and it was found that being in the same mood state at study and test was beneficial for recall. Mood-dependent effects are generally stronger for positive moods, perhaps because positive moods are more easily maintained (Ucros, 1989). As with other context effects, mood-dependent effects are generally stronger for tasks involving recall as against recognition (Kenealy, 1997). See Chapter 15 for more discussion of mood and emotion effects on memory.

> Chapter 15, p573

Spaced Versus Massed Trials

The **spacing effect** is that people remember material better when it is studied on a number of different occasions (possibly briefly) over a long period of time ('spaced presentation'), rather than studied in one long period ('massed presentation'), even when the total study time is equal.

> **Spacing effect** occurs when material studied on many separate occasions is better learned than material studied in one continuous session even if total study times are equal.

The spacing effect was first identified in experimental studies by Ebbinghaus and reported in his 1885 book *Memory: A Contribution to Experimental Psychology*. This phenomenon has been reported many times since, in a range of memory tasks such as free recall, recognition and cued recall (Crowder, 1976; Greene, 1989). For example, Jost (1897) found that the recall of a list of nonsense syllables was three times better when 24 repetitions of the material were distributed across 12 days (two repetitions per day) as against when the same number of repetitions was spread over three days (eight repetitions per day). Similar results have been found for foreign vocabulary items (e.g., Bloom & Shuell, 1981) and on educational material such as spelling lists and multiplication facts (Rea & Modigliani, 1985), and even for lectures on statistics (Smith & Rothkopf, 1984). The practical benefits of distributed practice were also established by Baddeley and Longman (1978) in the setting of a post office, where workers had to learn to use typing machines to add postcodes to letters for automatic sorting.

In practical terms, the spacing effect suggests that 'cramming' the night before an examination is not likely to be as effective as studying at intervals over a much longer span of time. Indeed, numerous studies have shown that spacing is important to promote student learning in educational settings in general (for a review, see Carpenter et al., 2012) and therefore spacing is becoming formally applied in school learning situations (Willingham, 2002) so that physical activity breaks are inserted at frequent intervals during a class period and the same short lesson is repeated a number of times after each break.

Several possible explanations of the spacing effect have been offered. According to the **deficient processing** view, massed presentation leads to deficient processing of the second presentation – we simply do not pay much attention to the later presentations (Hintzman, 1974). According to the **encoding variability** view, spaced repetition is likely to cause some variability in representation; under massed presentations, on the other hand, the corresponding memory representations are similar and relatively indiscriminable (Glenberg, 1977; Ross & Landauer, 1978). Thus the spacing effect can be linked to encoding specificity in that some of the wide range of cues associated with items at study are more likely to recur at test with spaced as against massed learning conditions.

> **Deficient processing** the view that massed repetitions lead to deficient processing of the second presentation.
> **Encoding variability** encoding varies with the context at the study period.

Evaluation

In this section we have been focusing on learning, particularly of verbal material. The role of encoding at time of study is important according to the main approaches reviewed here: the levels of processing and the encoding specificity theories. Levels of processing theory drew support from studies of encoding using imagery mnemonics, such as the one-is-a-bun, etc., method. Despite the strong empirical data showing effects in line with the levels of processing approach, the theory has been criticized as basically circular in that there is no independent measure of depth of processing. There is a risk of saying that processing was deeper because retention was better and that retention was better because processing was deeper (Baddeley, 1978; Eysenck, 1978).

The theory of encoding specificity received strong experimental support for its idea that reinstating cues present at study aids later retrieval. This approach explains the dependency of recall on context, whether external and environmental, or internal and involving moods or pharmaceutically induced states.

Further evidence in favour of encoding specificity arose from findings that study sessions spaced out over time are more effective than massed study sessions involving 'cramming' over a shorter period. This type of finding fits well with ideas of encoding specificity in that some of the wide range of cues associated with items at study are more likely to also be present at test with spaced as against massed learning.

The encoding specificity approach is not without its critics. In particular, Nairne (2002, 2010) has criticized the encoding specificity principle as in need of further refinement. He proposed that successful memory retrieval is brought about by cue distinctiveness rather than simple overlap. For example, on the distinctiveness view, a driver returning to a parking area would find it easier to recall where he or she had parked in an unfamiliar parking area than in a familiar one. Why? Because the familiar parking area is associated with many past parking memories but the new parking area is associated only with one. The two situations differ in distinctiveness of cues but not in overlap. Some experimental support has been found for Nairne's proposal (Goh & Lu, 2012), which is essentially a refinement of the encoding specificity principle rather than a completely distinct theory.

FORGETTING

Forgetting is said to occur when someone cannot retrieve information that had been previously available from memory. Forgetting has been a key topic from the earliest days of experimental psychology when Ebbinghaus (1885) undertook extensive studies of learning and forgetting with himself as the sole participant. He pioneered the use of lists of 'nonsense syllables' as the experimental materials to be learned and remembered. Nonsense syllables are three letter consonant–vowel–consonant strings that do not form words (e.g., CUV, LEL, ZIR). These materials were devised with the intention of ruling out any effects of meaning by making all the materials equally free of meaning. This proved difficult as nonsense syllables vary in resemblance to real words and can be scored for 'meaningfulness' in terms of the number of associations they elicit (Glaze, 1928; Hull, 1933); however, in Ebbinghaus's studies, he discarded syllables that were too reminiscent of words in his judgement and otherwise learning materials were drawn at random so that meaningfulness differences between conditions can be taken to have had no effect on his basic findings. Later researchers moved away from the nonsense syllable technique to study meaningful learning, but for many years the nonsense syllable was the preferred type of item in the study of learning.

> **Savings**
> a way of assessing forgetting by comparing trials needed for relearning as against trials required for original learning. If fewer trials are needed for relearning then savings have been demonstrated.

It is estimated that over a period of years, Ebbinghaus devoted some 830 hours to studying 6,600 lists totalling 85,000 syllables. Among other results, these studies revealed the classic forgetting curve (see Figure 8.2). The graph in Figure 8.2 measures forgetting in terms of the **savings** in relearning a list after various amounts of time. So, with near immediate relearning, a saving of close to 100 per cent is achieved compared to initial learning time; even after a delay of 31 days, some savings are still made (20 per cent), indicating that at least some memory of the list is retained even after a month's retention interval. In general, the typical forgetting curve shows steep forgetting at first followed by a gradual levelling off. The rate of forgetting is not constant but diminishes over time. Similar curves have been found repeatedly in experimental studies (e.g., Averell & Heathcote, 2011; Rubin & Wenzel, 1996) and with real-life materials, as in Bahrick's (1983) studies of recall for street names after retention intervals of up to 46 years.

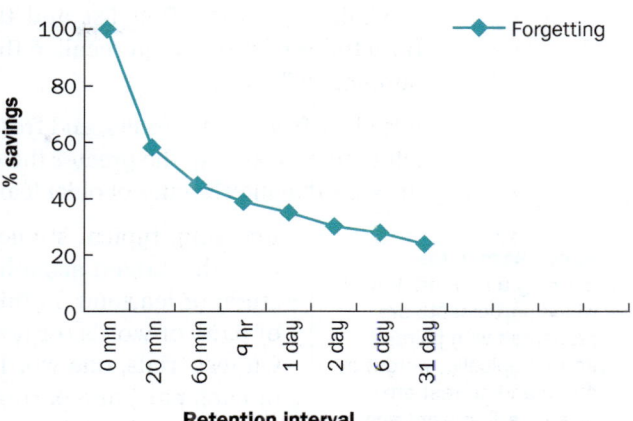

Figure 8.2 Ebbinghaus's (1885) forgetting curve.
This curve plots amount retained (percentage savings on re-learning) against retention interval.

Why does forgetting happen? As with short-term memory (see Chapter 6), decay of relevant traces is conceivable, but until recently most theorists proposed that **interference** from other related memories, rather than decay, was the principal explanation for forgetting.

> **Interference** occurs when remembering is disrupted by related memories.

Accordingly, in the next section we will review the major findings regarding interference and its role in forgetting.

> Chapter 6, p176

Interference

Two types of interference are typically distinguished; these are **proactive** and **retroactive interference**.

> **Proactive interference** occurs when previous learning impairs later learning.
> **Retroactive interference** occurs when later learning impairs memory for earlier learning.

Proactive interference involves prior learning impairing later learning and retrieval; in retroactive interference, later learning interferes with retention and retrieval of earlier learning. This is the kind of interference that Sherlock Holmes proposed in his 'little attic' model when he said 'there comes a time when for every addition of knowledge you forget something that you knew before'.

The simplest experimental design to examine retroactive interference would be as laid out in Table 8.1.

The two groups learn the same material (A) to the same criterion of learning and both remember as much as they can of material A after different interpolated activities. The experimental group engages in a second learning task and the control group has some non-demanding filler activity, such as describing photographs or reading materials unrelated to the original learning task.

An early study by McGeoch and McDonald (1931) involved a number of groups initially learning lists of adjectives; the experimental groups then learned new lists that varied

Table 8.1 Design for study of retroactive interference

	Experimental group	Control group
Time 1	Learn A	Learn A
Time 2	Learn B	Filler activity C
Time 3	Remember A	Remember A

in similarity to the first list and the control groups read jokes as a filler activity. Both types of group then recalled the initial training list of adjectives. Their results are outlined in Table 8.2.

It is clear from these results, and from many subsequent studies, that the more similar the intervening learning, the greater the degree of forgetting of the original learning; this fits the view that interference of older learning by newer learning is a major factor in forgetting.

> **Paired associates learning** a memory task in which participants are presented with pairs of items (typically, words) at study and on test are given the first word and asked to recall the second word in each pair.

Recently, typical studies of interference in long-term remembering have used the **paired associates learning** paradigm, which is often used in the study of learning. In this method, people are presented with lists made up of pairs of words (or nonsense syllables in early studies) on learning trials. On test trials, one word of each pair is presented (typically, the first word of each pair) and participants attempt to recall the other word. The experimental designs for examining proactive and retroactive interference using paired associates are shown in Table 8.3.

Underwood (1957) pooled data from 14 experiments using paired associates and the proactive design and found a marked effect, such that the more previous trials of the A-B type, the more proactive interference on tests of A-C learning. Similarly, retroactive interference has been regularly demonstrated (Postman et al., 1969) in laboratory studies of paired associates learning.

Anderson and Neely (1996) explained interference in terms of cues becoming associated to competing responses in the interference conditions but not in the control conditions. They give the everyday example of people remembering where they have parked their cars in a supermarket parking area. The more times the same store has been visited the harder it becomes to remember where the car is parked, because the cue, asking oneself where the car is, becomes associated with many different locations (there is more about this here).

Table 8.2 McGeoch and McDonald's (1931) results on retroactive interference

Interpolated activity	Adjectives recalled (%)
Reading jokes (control)	45
Learning three-digit numbers	37
Learning nonsense syllables	26
Learning adjectives unrelated to originals	22
Learning adjectives of opposite meaning to originals	18
Learning adjectives of similar meaning to originals	12

Table 8.3 Experimental designs for testing for proactive and retroactive interference using paired associates

Stage	Experimental group	Control group
Proactive interference		
1	Learn List A-B	Unrelated activity
2	Learn List A-C	Learn List A-C
Test	List A-C	List A-C
Retroactive interference		
1	Learn List A-B	Learn List A-B
2	Learn List A-C	Unrelated activity
Test	List A-B	List A-B

Decay and Consolidation

If interference could be eliminated, would forgetting still occur? If so, then trace decay – that is, weakening of memories due solely to the passage of time (see also Chapter 6) – would be implicated as a possible cause of forgetting. However, it is impossible to examine the effects of pure passage of time without any possibility of interfering interpolated activity. Sleep has been explored as, at least, a state of reduced activity; given this we can compare the rate of forgetting following sleep with the rates measured following activity in an alert stage. An early study by Jenkins and Dallenbach (1924) had two student participants who underwent a wide range of tests involving learning and later recall of lists of 10 nonsense syllables. In the waking conditions the list was learned in the morning to one perfect recall and then recalled after varied periods of normal awake activity. In the sleep conditions, the participants learned the lists at night just before going to bed and were then woken to recall the lists after different time periods. For both sleeping and awake conditions, the retention intervals were one, two, four and eight hours. The results were as shown in Table 8.4.

Chapter 6, p176

Recall after varying retention intervals, when awake, showed the typical forgetting curve in that there was a steep early decline followed by a slower decline. After retention intervals filled with sleep, there was a small initial drop with no further loss after two hours. These results indicated that decay alone cannot explain the usual forgetting curve. However, interference could be the explanation, as interference would be much less during sleep as against when awake, hence the difference between the forgetting curves after waking and sleeping periods. The small drop in recall in the sleeping condition after one to two hours could be due to interfering effects of the small amounts of conscious activity before sleep and on waking before testing. Overall, Jenkins and Dallenbach (1924, p. 615) concluded that 'forgetting is not so much a matter of the decay of old impressions and associations as it is a matter of interference, inhibition, or obliteration of the old by the new'. This conclusion is rather similar to the memory theory of Sherlock Holmes, in which new memories displace old memories, with which we started this chapter!

An influential study by Minami and Dallenbach (1946), using unusual participants (cockroaches), provided further support for the consolidation theory of learning. It had been found that these insects would spontaneously squeeze into narrow boxes lined ever more thickly with tissue paper until they were held fast and so were immobilized. This tendency provided an opportunity to reduce post-learning activity to a minimum and thus reduce the chance of interference greatly.

Minami and Dallenbach had cockroaches learn to avoid the dark path of a T maze in which an electric shock awaited and then had one group (controls) placed in their normal holding pens, which allowed exploratory activity for varying times before returning to the T maze. Experimental group cockroaches were held immobilized in narrow cardboard boxes lined with tissue paper, for varying times after learning and before re-testing. Furthermore, the immobile insects were kept in dark conditions to minimize stimulation.

Table 8.4 Recall scores (max. = 10) as a function of retention period and sleep vs. waking in jenkins and dallenbach's (1924) study

	Number of hours since learning				
	0	1	2	4	8
After sleeping	10	7.0	5.4	5.5	5.6
After waking	10	4.6	3.1	2.2	0.9

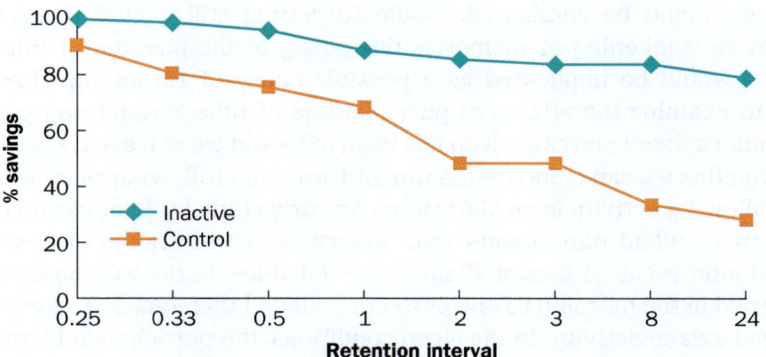

Figure 8.3 Savings scores.
Savings scores on re-testing of cockroaches after retention periods of 0.25–24 hours for normally active control versus inactive experimental conditions.

Source: Based on data reported by Minami & Dallenbach (1946).

The results on re-testing showed considerable savings for the immobilized inactive cockroaches as against the normally active control cockroaches, over time periods from 15 minutes to 24 hours (see Figure 8.3).

The results of this study with cockroaches lend support to the consolidation theory of forgetting (Wixted, 2004, 2010). According to this theory, memories when first formed are fragile and a period of consolidation is required to strengthen memory traces; retroactive interference interrupts the consolidation process and that is why forgetting occurs after interpolated learning activities. Sleep or inactivity allows consolidation to take place without interference from new memories. However, recent studies have shown that wakeful rest is also associated with better recall (e.g., Craig et al., 2014; Dewar et al., 2012). A study by Dewar et al. (2014) investigated whether this improvement could be due to the consolidation process or the possibility of intentional rehearsal during the resting period. We will take a closer look at this study in Box. 8.3.

Box 8.3 Research Close Up: Wakeful rest improves long-term memory

Source: Dewar et al. (2014).

INTRODUCTION

Studies have shown that wakeful rest periods after learning seem to boost long-term memory recall in both young and senior adults, compared to periods with high sensory stimulation (e.g., Craig et al., 2014; Dewar et al., 2012). However, the explanations for these results could be, at least, twofold. Either the recall performance is boosted due to the possibility of intentional rehearsal during the resting period, or the improved retention could be due to consolidation processes. Dewar et al. (2014) set out to investigate this issue in two experiments.

EXPERIMENT 1: METHOD

The aim of Experiment 1 was to test whether the effects of earlier experiments could be replicated and whether the boost in performance also was evident on recognition tests. The participants consisted of healthy senior adults. They were orally presented with a list of 15 common nouns and were instructed to remember as many words as possible. After the presentation of the list, they were subjected to an an immediate recall test, which was followed by a 10-minute period of either high-sensory stimulation or low-sensory stimulation. Participants in the high-sensory stimulation group did a visual spot-the-difference task, which served two functions. First, it presented the group with new cognitive information, thus hindering the possibility of consolidation of the word list. Second, due to the visual nature of the task, the retrieval interference with the word list was minimized. The participants in the low-sensory stimulation group were told to rest in a dark room. They were then asked to recall the 15 words both 15 minutes and seven days later. At the seven-day follow up, a recognition test was also administered.

EXPERIMENT 1: RESULTS

The results showed a boosted recall effect for the low-sensory stimulation group, both at the 15-minute delayed recall and the seven-days delayed recall. This boost was also evident in the recognition test.

EXPERIMENT 2: METHOD

The aim of the second experiment was to investigate whether consolidation alone could explain the boosting effect. However, to prevent the intentional rehearsal of the stimuli in the experiment, non-recallable pseudowords (for example, 'toijcunn' instead of 'junction') needed to be used. Also, in order to test the retention of the non-words, a recognition test needed to be administered. The procedure was very similar to Experiment 1, with the major difference being that the words used in Experiment 1 were scrambled to create non-words.

EXPERIMENT 2: RESULTS

The results showed a boosted effect for the participants in the low-sensory stimulation group on the recognition test both at the 15-minute delay as well as at the seven-day delay.

CONCLUSIONS

The study supports the view that consolidation is enough to cause improvements in long-term memory after wakeful rest periods and that intentional rehearsal is not necessary.

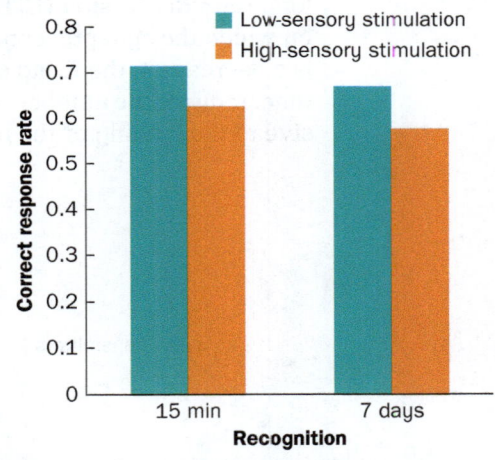

Figure 8.4 Correct response rate.
Correct response rate on recognition test for non-words.

The consolidation view incorporates the idea of decay (traces decay unless consolidated) and an idea of interference as operating by preventing consolidation. The approach to memory and forgetting in terms of consolidation is the dominant approach in neuroscience and neuropsychology, and this is something will turn to now.

The neuropsychological mechanism of learning and forgetting

Within neuropsychology, the phenomenon of consolidation and decay can be connected to the mechanism of long-term potentiation (LTP) and long-term depression (LTD), which occurs in the hippocampal area of the

> **Long-term potentiation (LTP)** the long-lasting improvement in signal transmission between two neurons that results from stimulating them at the same time.
> **Long-term depression (LTD)** the long-lasting reduction in the effectiveness of the signal transmission between two neurons.

Chapter 1, p18

brain (Cooke & Bliss, 2006). To understand these mechanisms we turn to what we referred to in Chapter 1 as the building blocks of the brain, namely neurons.

The communication between neurons takes place at the synapse, which is the junction between the axon terminals (which transmit signals) and dendrites (which receive signals). The communication occurs via electrical pulses called 'action potentials', which cause the sending neuron (presynaptic neuron) to release chemical neurotransmitters into the synaptic cleft, which binds to the receptors in the receiving (postsynaptic) neuron. During learning, there is a strengthening of the synaptic connection where these transmissions take place, namely LTP. To illustrate this further, we take a closer look at the process in Figure 8.5.

Action potentials that arrive at the presynaptic terminal cause the neurotransmitter to be released into the synaptic cleft. The neurotransmitters bind to the receptor in the postsynaptic terminal. During learning, the synapse is repeatedly stimulated by action potentials, causing more receptors to evolve. The neurotransmitters, therefore, have more receptors to bind to, making the synaptic communication more efficient. However, the effects of LTP are not limited to changes in existing neurons. Long-term memory formation is also associated with the development of new synaptic connections during the later phases of LTP, whereas short-term memory formation is associated with changes to already existing synaptic connections (Kandel, 2004).

The neuropsychological mechanism through which forgetting takes place is called long-term depression (LTD); it can be considered the opposite of LTP. It is the process by which the synaptic connections are weakened (Figure 8.5). During forgetting, there is a decrease in the firing of action potentials from the presynaptic neuron, which, with time, reduces the number of receptors in the postsynaptic neuron, making it less responsive to the binding of the neurotransmitter.

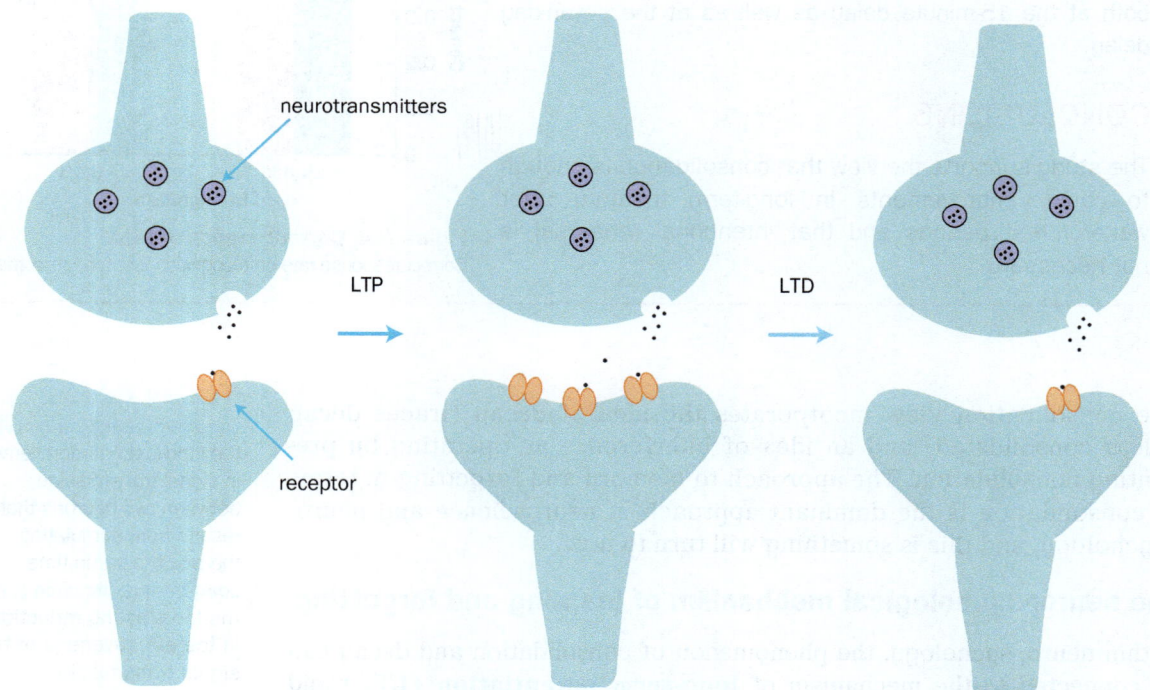

Figure 8.5 Long-term potentiation (LTP) and long-term depression (LTD).

Thus the approach to memory and forgetting in terms of consolidation is the dominant approach in neuroscience and neuropsychology, but has been rather ignored until recently in cognitive psychology, where the interference-based theories largely deriving from laboratory studies of paired associate learning have been the norm. However, the two approaches are not incompatible and both might apply (e.g., Hardt et al., 2013). A number of recent studies have addressed the effects of sleep on forgetting, to test out ideas about the role of consolidation and we will now discuss some highlights of this work.

Effects of sleep on memory

As we have seen from Jenkins and Dallenbach's (1924) classic study, it has long been established that a list of words is better remembered if it is followed by a retention interval where the learner sleeps than if the learning is followed by the same retention interval filled by normal daily activity. It is generally assumed that sleep protects memory from interference (e.g., Ellenbogen et al., 2006), and it has been suggested that this reflects active consolidation processes that occur during sleep (e.g., Born et al., 2006). In support of a consolidation view, the protective benefits of sleep are particularly pronounced if it occurs right after study. For example, Ekstrand (1972) showed that retention after a 24-hour period that included eight hours of sleep was better if subjects slept right after study (81 per cent recall) than if they slept right before the test (66 per cent recall). The beneficial effect of a period of sleep or inactivity is sometimes labelled **retrograde facilitation** (Wixted, 2004, 2010).

> **Retrograde facilitation**
> the beneficial effect on memory that can be the result of a period of sleep or inactivity following a study period, or even the result of taking certain drugs.

Neuroscience accounts of sleep effects on consolidation

We now consider the neuroscience approaches to sleep effects on learning and forgetting, which stress the notion of long-term potentiation (LTP), which we discussed earlier.

It seems that different phases of sleep may have different effects on memory. Sleep periods with rapid eye movement (REM), associated with dreaming, have different effects from non-REM sleep. It seems that non-REM sleep blocks the induction of hippocampal LTP (Jones Leonard et al., 1987) without disrupting the maintenance of previously induced LTP (Bramham & Srebo, 1989); these experiments, which were performed on sleeping rats, showed that while LTP can be induced during REM sleep (possibly accounting for the fact that we can sometimes remember our dreams), it cannot be induced during non-REM sleep (possibly accounting for the fact that we cannot remember any mental activity that takes place during that stage of sleep). As a result, it might be hypothesized that, during non-REM sleep, recent memories that have begun to be consolidated through LTP are protected from interference that would occur if new memories began to be laid down by LTP.

Ekstrand and colleagues (1972; Yaroush et al., 1971) examined effects of non-REM and REM sleep on human verbal learning. These researchers used the fact that non-REM sleep typically precedes REM sleep. Some participants in this experiment learned a word list, went to sleep immediately and were awakened four hours later for a test of recall. Others slept for four hours, were awakened to learn the list, slept for another four hours and then took a recall test. The control (i.e., awake) participants learned the list during the day and were tested for recall four hours later. The participants all learned the initial list

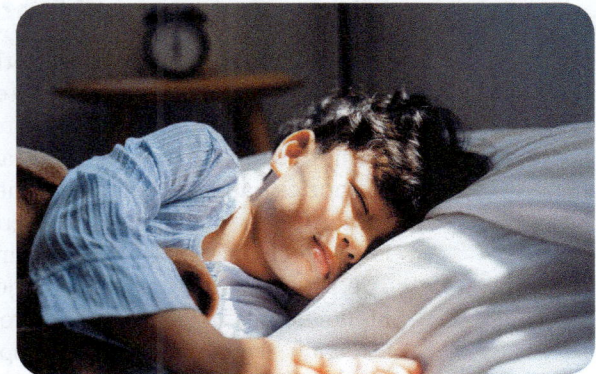
© theshots.co/Shutterstock

to the same degree, but the results showed that four hours of mostly non-REM sleep facilitated delayed recall relative to the other two conditions, which did not differ from each other (i.e., REM sleep did not facilitate memory). These results have been replicated in studies by Plihal and Born (1997, 1999) and fit with the finding that many antidepressant drugs, which greatly reduce REM sleep, do not seem to cause memory problems (Vertes & Eastman, 2000).

Overall, it seems that consolidation processes are important in explaining the effects of non-REM and REM sleep. It seems likely that consolidation problems also underlie patterns of forgetting in amnesia, and we will now outline some recent research exploring this idea.

Retrograde amnesia

Chapter 7, p218

As discussed in Chapter 7, clinical findings over more than 100 years have indicated that brain damage leading to anterograde amnesia (i.e., to the inability to lay down new memory records) is also associated with temporally graded retrograde amnesia (Ribot, 1882) in which memories formed prior to brain damage are impaired, but the effect depends on the age of the memory trace at the time the damage occurs, with more recently formed memories suffering the most (Ribot's Law). In support of Ribot's Law, Brown (2002) reported a meta-analysis of 247 outcomes from 61 articles, which supported the view that the impairment gradually and continuously reduces as memories become increasingly temporally distant from the trauma.

It is accepted in neuroscience that the medial temporal lobes, which include the hippocampus and adjacent cortex, play a critical role in the formation of new memories. When patient H.M. (see also Chapter 7) had those areas removed to control his epileptic seizures, it soon became clear that his ability to form new memories was severely and permanently impaired (Scoville & Milner, 1957). Studies have found that temporally graded retrograde amnesia is very likely to be observed if the brain damage in question involves the hippocampal region (e.g., Manns et al., 2003). A review of 13 precisely controlled prospective animal studies, in which memory loss was examined over time following surgical lesions, supports the existence of temporally graded retrograde amnesia and its association with hippocampal lesions (Squire et al., 2001).

The temporal gradient of retrograde amnesia provides strong evidence that memories consolidate over time and that the hippocampal formation plays an important role in that process. On this view, if the hippocampal formation is damaged before the consolidation process is complete, recently formed memories that are still undergoing the consolidation process will be impaired. Older, consolidated memories will be retained, but more recent memories that have not completely consolidated are likely to be lost.

Effects of alcohol and benzodiazepines

As indicated above, damage to the medial temporal lobes induces permanent anterograde amnesia. Temporary anterograde amnesia can be induced by certain drugs which, strange to say, can also produce retrograde facilitation. That is, recently formed memories are retained better than they otherwise would have been, even though new memories cannot easily be formed while in the drugged state. This phenomenon reinforces the view that memories consolidate over time and that much of what we forget is lost because of retroactive interference arising from ordinary mental activities. The argument is that certain agents (such as alcohol and benzodiazepines) close the hippocampus to new input, thereby inducing temporary anterograde amnesia, without affecting the ability of the hippocampus to consolidate previously formed memories (Bruce & Pihl, 1997). Because new input is prevented, recently formed (and, therefore, incompletely consolidated) memories are protected from the retroactive interference that they would otherwise encounter. As such, these drugs act in the same way that sleep does, even though the individual remains conscious while intoxicated.

The anterograde amnesic effects of alcohol consumed prior to the learning of new material are well established (Lister et al., 1987). The extreme version of this effect is the alcoholic 'blackout', which involves a complete loss of memory for events occurring while the individual was conscious and (very) intoxicated with a blood alcohol concentration of around 0.20 per cent (White, 2004). It is generally accepted that blackouts are not the result of state-dependent learning but instead reflect a failure to encode or consolidate new information (Lisman, 1974). In spite of its effects on the formation of new memories, alcoholic intoxication generally does not affect retrieval of old memories after intoxication (Birnbaum et al., 1978). Whereas alcohol consumption induces a certain degree of anterograde amnesia for material studied under the influence of the drug, many studies have reported that it actually results in improved memory for material studied just prior to consumption (Bruce & Pihl, 1997; Lamberty et al., 1990; Mann et al., 1984; Parker et al., 1980, 1981). This phenomenon is referred to as retrograde facilitation or retrograde enhancement, and its existence makes alcohol-induced amnesia unlike the amnesia produced by damage to the medial temporal lobes.

How might the curious phenomenon of drug-induced retrograde facilitation be explained? Recent evidence suggests one very plausible explanation is that alcohol facilitates recently established memories because it prevents the formation of new memories that would otherwise cause retroactive interference (Mueller et al., 1983). Drinking alcohol does not protect memories that are years old (and fully consolidated). Instead, it is the recently formed memories that benefit most because, theoretically, those are the ones most vulnerable to the effects of retroactive interference.

Retrograde facilitation has also been observed with another class of amnesia-inducing drug, namely benzodiazepines. The basic experimental paradigm is the same as that used with alcohol. Participants typically study one list of words before taking the drug and then study another list following drug administration. Memory for both lists is tested some time later (usually while the participants are still under the influence of the drug), and performance is compared to that of a placebo control group. Typically, the drug group exhibits impaired recall for the list learned under the influence of the drug (thereby confirming its amnesia-inducing properties) and enhanced recall for the list learned prior to taking the drug (Coenen & Van Luijtelaar, 1997; Fillmore et al., 2001; Hinrichs et al., 1984; Weingartner et al., 1995). Coenen and Van Luijtelaar (1997) argued that the effects of benzodiazepines on memory were analogous to the beneficial effects of sleep. In both cases, information learned prior to being sedated is remembered better than it otherwise would have been, because retroactive interference is reduced due to the reduced rate of information uptake while sedated (or asleep).

This explanation is consistent with the idea that ordinary forgetting is a retroactive effect of subsequent memory formation that accompanies ordinary mental activity. If mental activity is reduced by sleep or if memory formation associated with mental activity is reduced by alcohol or a benzodiazepine drug, prior recently formed memories are protected from the effects of retroactive interference. To summarize, sleep, alcohol and benzodiazepines all result in retrograde enhancement of memory, and the reason seems to be that a reduced rate of memory formation during the altered state protects recently formed memories from the interference that would otherwise take place.

It seems that, in normal participants, memory is adversely affected if consolidation is impaired by interfering later activities. Might people suffering from amnesia be especially liable to disruption of consolidation? This possibility is addressed in work reported in Box 8.4 (overleaf).

> **Box 8.4 When Things Go Wrong: Consolidation, retroactive interference and amnesia**

Much of amnesic patients' difficulties in remembering new information (anterograde amnesia) may be due to extreme susceptibility to interference from incoming information disrupting consolidation of earlier acquired information. This theory draws support from observations such as those of Scoville and Milner (1957), who reported that all their patients with severe amnesia, including the famous amnesiac H.M. (see also Chapter 7), 'were able to retain a three-figure number or a pair of unrelated words for several minutes, if care was taken not to distract them in the interval. However, they forgot the instant attention was diverted to a new topic' (p. 15).

Chapter 7, p218

Cowan et al. (2004) examined the hypothesis that amnesia is often due to an extreme susceptibility to interference effects in a study inspired by Minami and Dallenbach's (1946) experiment with cockroaches (which we discussed earlier, in Box 8.3). They sought to determine whether amnesic patients would retain material better if the training period was followed by an unfilled interval, resting alone in a quiet darkened room as against an interval filled with further cognitive tests. The material consisted of 15 words, and patients and suitable control participants were tested immediately after presentation and again after 10 minutes, which were either filled or unfilled. The results are shown in Figure 8.6 and clearly indicate better retention after unfilled intervals than after filled intervals, both for the patients and the controls.

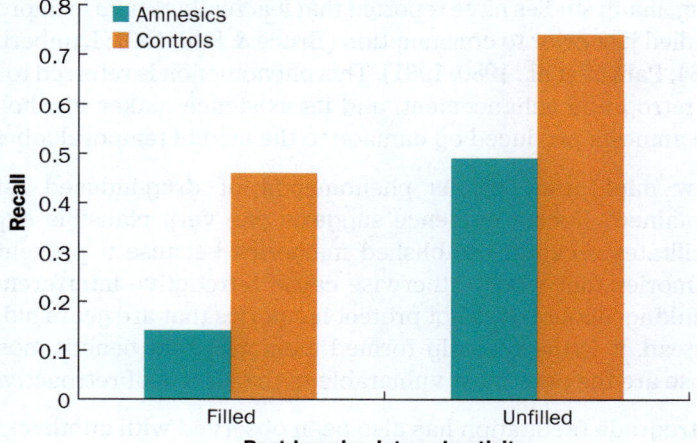

Figure 8.6 Proportion of list of words recalled.
These data are after 10 minutes of filled or unfilled intervals for amnesic patients and healthy controls.

Source: Adapted from Cowan et al. (2004).

Research on normal participants (Dudai, 2004) had found that new memory traces are relatively susceptible to interference, and Dewar et al. (2009) examined this effect in amnesic patients by inserting the interfering activity at different points (early or late) in the retention interval. Amnesic and control participants were presented with 15 word lists and, after immediate recall, had a nine-minute retention interval before delayed recall. During the retention interval a three-minute picture naming task was inserted immediately after the first recall test or after three or six minutes; there was also an unfilled nine-minute retention interval. The results, shown in Figure 8.7, clearly indicate that the amnesic patients were particularly susceptible to early occurring interference.

Dewar and colleagues interpret these results as showing that new memory traces can become consolidated in amnesic patients, but

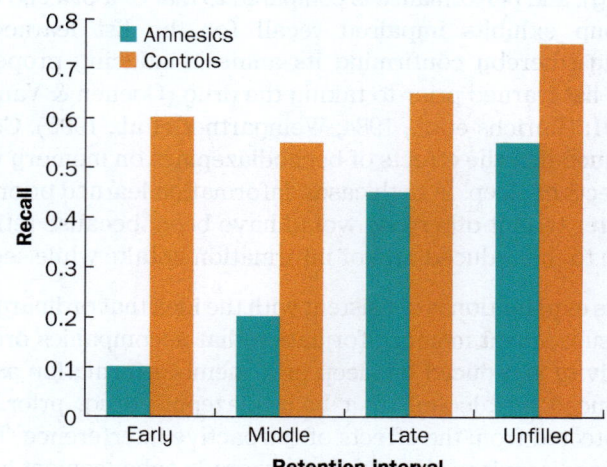

Figure 8.7 Proportion of list of words recalled.
Data after nine-minute retention interval with interfering activity after varying time periods for amnesic patients and healthy controls.

Source: Adapted from Dewar et al. (2009).

that post-learning interference disrupts this process substantially. As found in previous literature, this interruption is most detrimental when the interference occurs directly following new learning – that is, when the new memory trace has not yet had a chance to consolidate, but decreases with delay in interference. The results were expanded in a further study showing that minimizing interference for amnesic patients may lead to a memory performance boost that is evident up to seven days after the learning session (Alber et al., 2014).

In a follow-up study by Dewar et al. (2010) it was shown that even when the interfering task (detecting notes in a piano recital) was quite dissimilar to the main memory task (memory for stories) strong retroactive interference was found for amnesic patients (see Figure 8.8).

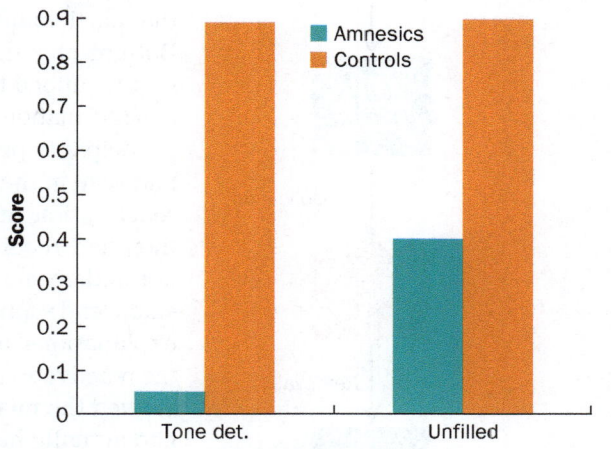

Figure 8.8 Proportion of correct answers.
Data are correct answers for the story after a 10-minute retention interval with or without interfering activity (tone detection) for amnesic patients and healthy controls.

Source: Adapted from Dewar et al. (2010).

Evaluation

Overall, the studies outlined here strongly support the view that an important factor in anterograde amnesia is a heightened susceptibility to retroactive interference preventing consolidation. It appears that consolidation is hindered by any mentally demanding activity and not just activity involving materials similar to the to-be-remembered information. Dewar et al. (2007) distinguish similarity-based retroactive interference, which affects retrieval, and diversionary retroactive interference, which affects consolidation. This distinction of two types of interference was actually made by early researchers on interference such as Muller and Pilzecker (1900) and Skaggs (1925, 1933), but was subsequently ignored, with emphasis being placed on similarity-based interference (Anderson, 2003; McGeoch & Nolen, 1933).

The Reconsolidation of Memories

During the past few decades, a new avenue of research has emerged, concerning the updating of memories (e.g., Alberini & LeDoux, 2013; Lee et al., 2017). When already consolidated memories are retrieved, they may undergo a destabilization phase, which reactivates them, and thus makes them fragile and susceptible to modifications. As a consequence of this phase, the memory may be altered and stored in a new, updated version. This process is referred to as **reconsolidation** (see Figure 8.9, overleaf).

Reconsolidation
the process by which old memories become destabilized during retrieval and therefore susceptible to modifications.

Several studies lend support to the idea of this process (e.g., Elsey et al., 2018; Lee et al., 2017). For example, episodic memory can be impaired if amnesic treatments such as electroconvulsive shock are given after a memory has been reactivated (Kroes et al., 2014).

In a study by Chan and LaPaglia (2013) participants watched an episode of the TV series 24. In the memory reactivation group, the participants performed a recall test

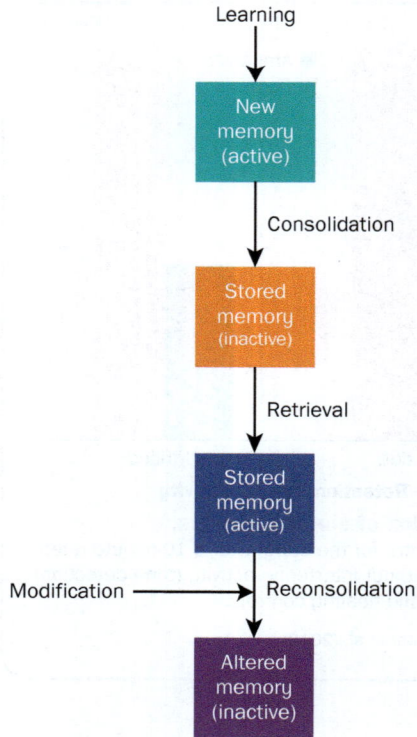

Figure 8.9 The consolidation and reconsolidation process.
When the memory is learned it is in an active phase. Consolidation stores the memory and makes it inactive. The retrieval of the stored memory may return the memory to an active phase during which the activated memory can be modified. The phase when the retrieved activated memory is returned to an inactive phase is referred to as reconsolidation.

Intrusive memories
persistent unwanted memories (e.g., of traumatic events) that frequently come to mind.

Chapter 7, p244

Retrieval-induced forgetting (RIF)
an impaired ability to recall some items caused by earlier retrieval of related items.

with questions concerning the TV series, while in the control group the participants played the video game Tetris (no-activation). Both groups then listened to an eight-minute long audio narrative that recapped the episode they had watched, however it contained misinformation concerning eight details from the episode. Finally, all participants performed a recognition test concerning details they had seen in the episode. Results showed that the participants in the reactivation group were more susceptible to the misinformation they had received in the narrative than the participants that had not undergone a memory reactivation. Although the results of this study lend support to the idea of a reconsolidation process, alternative explanations are also plausible. For example, it could be that the reactivation increased attention to the misinformation or that they viewed the misinformation as corrective feedback regarding what had actually happened in the video (Rindal et al., 2016).

It is easily recognizable that the reconsolidation process should hold promise for the treatment of clinical disorders such as anxiety disorders (e.g., PTSD) or addiction (Schwabe et al., 2014). The findings within clinical applications have, however, been mixed, with some studies showing an improvement in treatment when memory reactivation has been combined with other treatment features, while others have not (e.g., Elsey et al., 2018).

Functional Approaches to Forgetting

Although forgetting is typically regarded in a negative light, as causing us problems in retrieving information when it is needed, there are times when we wish to forget things (e.g., Bluck, 2017). When you change town it is useful to forget your old phone number and when a computer password has to be changed it is helpful if the old one is forgotten. In more dramatic cases, people are sometimes plagued with **intrusive memories** of traumatic events that they would rather not remember (Brewin, 2001). For more of these intrusive memories see Box 7.6 in Chapter 7 regarding PTSD.

How selective forgetting might be brought about has been investigated using three main paradigms: retrieval-induced forgetting (Anderson et al., 1994); directed forgetting (Bjork et al., 1998) and the think/no-think method (Anderson & Green, 2001). We will now discuss in turn these approaches to bringing about forgetting.

Retrieval-induced forgetting (RIF)

The **RIF** paradigm was developed by Anderson et al. (1994; Anderson, 2005) and deals with the forgetting of memories apparently caused by retrieval of related memories. For example, if you focus on retrieving memories of what went well on a holiday this is likely to reduce memory for what went wrong.

In the laboratory, RIF is generally studied by having participants learn category-item pairs such as 'fruit-apple', 'fruit-banana', 'furniture-chair', 'furniture-table'. After the learning phase, participants are given repeated retrieval trials with the same category and retrieval cue each time, such as 'fruit-a?'. In the example, participants repeatedly retrieve 'apple'. Finally, participants are asked to recall all the examples for each category. Typically, people are less likely to retrieve 'banana' than 'apple' or 'chair' or 'table'; this is known as the RIF effect, whereby retrieval practice impairs recall of unpractised category members. It is explained on the assumption that the category cue 'fruit-a?' activates 'banana' to some extent and so successful retrieval of 'apple' requires inhibition of the competing response 'banana' (Bjork et al., 1998). The inhibition interpretation gains support from the finding that the effect persists even when novel cues are used, such as 'monkey-b?' which would cue 'banana' (Anderson & Bell, 2001; Saunders & MacLeod, 2006) and from impaired recognition memory (Hicks & Starns, 2004) and reduced lexical decision speed (Veling & Van Knippenberg, 2004) for the unpractised target category member.

Directed forgetting (DF)

In the **DF** paradigm participants are instructed to forget some items but remember others. A real-life example is provided by short-order cooks who must try to forget previous orders and retain only the current order until it is in turn supplanted by the next order (Bjork, 1970).

> **Directed forgetting (DF)**
> memory impairment brought about by instructions to forget some items.

There are two variants of DF, which are the *item-based* form of DF and the *list-based* method of DF. In the item-based method, participants are shown items to remember one at a time and, after each item, are told whether that item should be forgotten or retained. After the complete list, participants are tested on memory for all the items. Basden and Basden (1996) found markedly impaired recall for to-be-forgotten items than for to-be-remembered items, and the effect held for words and pictures. DF effects for the item-based approach were also found on tests of recognition memory (Basden et al., 1993) in which participants only have to indicate whether each item was seen previously rather than recall items. It seems likely that participants carry out extra encoding of the to-be-remembered items when the 'remember' instruction is given and stop rehearsing the to-be-forgotten items when the instruction is received to 'forget'.

In the list method of DF, the participants are given two lists (both initially to be memorized) and are only told to forget the first list after it has been presented and before going on to memorize the second list. Finally, participants are asked to remember both lists. Typically, participants given the 'forget' instruction remember less of the first list than control participants and recall the second list *better than controls*. Thus there is reduced proactive interference from the first list after instructions to forget it have been given. Unlike item-based DF, recognition of the to-be-forgotten items seems to hold up (Bjork et al., 1998). List-based DF seems to affect accessibility rather than availability. Accessibility refers to the ease with which a stored memory can be retrieved and is measured by ease of recall; availability refers to whether the trace is stored at all or not, and is indicated by whether the item is recognized or not.

Think/no-think (TNT)

The **TNT** paradigm is a relatively new type of task that reflects situations where a person wants to not retrieve a memory when confronted with a strong cue for that memory. For example, if you had been in a car crash at a set of traffic lights on your way to work or school, you might not want to remember the event every time you pass those lights. It has so far been explored using verbal materials rather than real-life traumatic stimuli.

> **Think/no-think (TNT)**
> a memory manipulation in which participants are instructed not to retrieve a memory even when a strong cue is present.

In the TNT method, participants study cue-target pairs, such as 'ordeal-roach' so that they can reliably recall the second word when given the first word as a cue. In the next stage, participants see the cue words and in most cases have to recall the target response word, but on some trials the cue words are printed in red and participants are instructed not to retrieve the response when the cue is red. The instructions are not only to not say the word, but also to keep the response from entering consciousness. After many trials with TNT instructions, there is a final test of people's ability to recall all the response words. Levy and Anderson (2008) found the expected effect with about 95 per cent of 'think' words recalled as against about 75 per cent of 'no-think' words. A neuroimaging study (Anderson et al., 2004) found that on no-think trials people showed reduced activation in the hippocampal area relative to think trials. Hippocampal activation had been shown to be related to subjective reports of retrieval (Squire, 1992) and so the finding helps validate the method by indicating that no-think trials probably did indeed involve absence of retrieval, and also suggests that people can deliberately regulate hippocampal activation.

Although the TNT paradigm still can be considered fairly new, the evidence for a rather robust TNT effect for words has been accumulating (e.g., De Vito & Fenske, 2017). The effect has not only been found for words but also for the suppression of visual objects (e.g., Gagnepain et al., 2014). However, a failure to replicate the effect over three experiments that closely followed Anderson and Green's (2001) procedure was reported by Bulevich et al. (2006). A study by Hertel and Calcaterra (2005) showed that the TNT effect depends on the participants' strategies; in their studies, the TNT effect was found only when participants used the strategy of thinking of a different word in the 'no-think' conditions, whether spontaneously or as a result of strategy instructions.

Research concerning retrieval inhibition of unwanted memories such as the TNT method are sometimes used as support for the phenomenon known as repression, which also has been the object of one of the largest controversies in modern psychology (e.g., Otgaar et al., 2019). We take a closer look at the debate concerning this phenomenon in Box 8.5.

Box 8.5 When Things Go Wrong: The recovered memories controversy

Do people have the ability to suppress highly painful memories so they no longer have a conscious recollection of these experiences? And can these memories be recovered after decades of no available recollections?

The idea that this was possible originated from Freud, who claimed that traumatic memory could be repressed so that the person who experienced the trauma could no longer recall it. This defence mechanism was named repression. During the 1990s, the belief in repression among psychoanalytically trained clinical psychologists was highly common (e.g., Otgaar et al., 2019). It was not an uncommon practice that therapists suggested the possibility of repressed memories as the reason behind various disorders, such as anxiety, personality disorder, depression and eating disorder. Patients that, before treatment, had no recollections of any traumatic events were suggested to have these unconscious memories. During treatment, suggestive techniques such as hypnosis, guided imagery and diary methods were often used to help patients recover these so-called repressed memories. This often resulted in patients suddenly remembering different types of abuse, often sexual, that they claimed had occurred during childhood. Some of these recovered memories cases even led to lawsuits against the alleged perpetrators (e.g., Loftus, 1994). The veracity of the recovered memories was questioned by many memory researchers, since the phenomenon of repression contradicted the evidence found from clinical practice, where victims of trauma rather had difficulties in forgetting the event and suffered from intrusive recollections (see Box 7.6). The results from the false memory paradigm (see Chapter 7) also suggested that the recovered memories may be the product of incorporated misinformation (Loftus, 1994).

Chapter 7, p245

> McNally and Geraerts (2009) offered another possibility as to why some people may report recovered memories, in particular of childhood abuse. In a study, Clancy and McNally (2005/2006) found that when interviewing 27 adults who reported having recovered memories of childhood abuse, only two of them remembered experiencing the event as traumatic and terrifying when it took place. The vast majority remembered the experience as confusing or uncomfortable. It was rather when recalling the experience as an adult that they grasped the significance of what had taken place and the event was reappraised as a trauma. Thus forgetting the abuse could be a consequence of not having experienced the event as traumatic when it unfolded. While offering an explanation as to why some memories may be recovered, this lends no support to the need of a psychological defence mechanism such as repression. Instead, the explanation put forward by McNally and Geraerts points to normal memory processes.
>
> Although repression has been highly questioned by many cognitive scholars, and the scientific evidence of the phenomenon is extremely scarce, belief in repression by both lay people as well as professionals remains strong (Otgaar et al., 2019).

Evaluation

In this section, we have discussed forgetting – the loss of the ability to retrieve information that had been learned. Early studies used material intended to be meaningless, particularly nonsense syllables, in an attempt to understand pure learning without the complications of meaningful materials. However, nonsense syllables themselves proved to vary in their meaningfulness to participants and later studies used meaningful words, although often in lists rather than in meaningful text. The strong roles of interference from earlier learning on later learning (proactive interference) and of interference from later learning on remembering earlier learning (retroactive interference) was shown early in the study of memory. The importance of consolidation of memories was shown in studies of sleep versus waking activities following learning, and from work with cockroaches that were immobilized or not after maze learning. Consolidation approaches furthermore explain the counterintuitive benefits on later recall of alcohol and some other drugs following a study period. These findings may explain the common student habit of study by day followed by drinking in the evenings! The symptoms of people suffering from anterograde amnesia after trauma can be explained quite well by difficulties with consolidation of new memories in that they seem especially badly affected by retroactive interference following study.

EVERYDAY/REAL-WORLD MEMORY

The research on learning and forgetting that we have been discussing so far has largely been driven by theoretical concerns, such as is forgetting due to decay, interference or consolidation problems? The resulting laboratory studies that use artificial materials with tightly controlled learning and recall conditions can seem far removed from everyday memory. In 1978, Ulric Neisser expressed some exasperation with laboratory-based research in a keynote speech at an international conference on practical aspects of memory, when he said, 'If X is an interesting or socially significant aspect of memory, then psychologists have hardly ever studied X' (1978, p. 4).

These remarks provoked considerable controversy (e.g., Baddeley, 1993; Banaji & Crowder, 1989; Koriat & Goldsmith, 1996; Kvavilashvili & Ellis, 2004) and seem to have influenced many researchers towards studying memory phenomena drawn from everyday life (such as eyewitness testimony, face recognition, autobiographical memory and

> **Ecological validity**
> the degree to which the results of a laboratory study can be applied to a real life situation.
>
> **Representativeness**
> increases with the realism and naturalness of the study's materials and tasks.
>
> **Generalizability**
> the degree to which results are broadly applicable to a wide range of situations.

flashbulb memories) and to using more naturalistic methods and materials. The thrust of the everyday memory movement is often said to be a search for **ecological validity** in research. A study has ecological validity to the extent that its findings are applicable to everyday or real-life settings. Two aspects of ecological validity have been distinguished by Kvavilashvili and Ellis (2004) in their thorough review of the history of the everyday memory movement; these are **representativeness** and **generalizability**. Representativeness increases with the realism and naturalness of the study's materials and tasks. So, a study of different strategies employed by fast and slow learners of statistical computing methods (as in Green & Gilhooly, 1990) would be relatively high on representativeness of, in this case, classroom learning. Generalizability refers to the degree to which results are broadly applicable. Ebbinghaus's (1885) original studies of spaced versus massed learning using nonsense syllables may have been low in representativeness but the basic result has proven highly generalizable to many real-world learning situations. Kvavilashvili and Ellis (2004) argued strongly that generalizability is the more important aspect of ecological validity since the more widely a finding can be applied, the better.

© Phil Boorman/Shutterstock

Over the years, the controversy as to how to best study different aspects of memory has faded. Even by 1988, at the second International Conference on Practical Aspects of Memory, Neisser had modified his position and said: 'If X is an interesting or socially important memory phenomenon, the chances are good – though not 100 per cent – that quite a few people are trying to study it' (Neisser, 1988, p. 546). A concern with everyday aspects of memory is that it has become mainstream and everyday memory research typically uses laboratory methods to reach generalizable conclusions, and theory-driven researchers look for connections with everyday memory issues to show that their work has practical relevance. Thus, the two approaches are largely reconciled.

> Chapter 7, p218

Some of the typical topics of everyday memory research, such as autobiographical memory and prospective memory, are discussed in Chapter 7, which deals with long-term memory. Next in this chapter, we will turn to work on flashbulb memories as a good example of research that derives from a phenomenon in everyday life but that uses methods derived from laboratory studies.

Flashbulb Memories

> **Flashbulb memory**
> a vivid memory of a dramatic event and of the circumstances in which the event was experienced or heard about.

Most people feel that they have exceptionally detailed and vivid memories for the circumstances in which they first learned of dramatic and highly significant events such as the attacks on the World Trade Center on 11 September 2001, the London transport system attacks of 7 July 2005, the death of Princess Diana on 31 August 1997 and, for older readers, the assassination of John F. Kennedy, on 23 November 1963. Brown and Kulik (1977) examined memories for the Kennedy assassination and labelled such memories **flashbulb memories**. They proposed that dramatic, surprising events that were important for the individual, caused a special memory mechanism to activate and record in a permanent form information about the event and surrounding contextual information, such as who gave the information, where the news was learned, and what the individual did after learning the news.

Neisser (1982) suggested that the apparent permanence of flashbulb memories was due to the well-established mechanism of rehearsal rather than to a special, specifically 'flashbulb' mechanism. In this view, people are much more likely to discuss the news with others and that includes rehearsing the circumstances under which the news was heard. Important and dramatic public events are also repeated extensively in the news media not only on the initial occasion and for days afterwards, but also on anniversaries, and so memories of the flashbulb events are cued and retrieved relatively often as compared to other events. Consistent with the rehearsal explanation, Bonhannon (1988) in a study with 686 participants, found that memory for the Challenger space shuttle disaster after eight months was more detailed in participants who reported more re-tellings of the event during the retention period.

Although it was initially proposed that flashbulb memories were unusually accurate, it turns out that major inaccuracies are not uncommon in flashbulb memories. For example, Pezdek (2003) found that 73 per cent of respondents agreed that they had seen video records on television of the first plane striking the first tower of the World Trade Center on 11 September 2001. However, there were no such video records available. Presumably, participants were confused by the recordings of the second plane which were available. Perhaps more striking is the report by Ost et al. (2002) that a substantial number of UK respondents agreed that they had seen a film of Princess Diana's car crash; but this film does not exist. Granhag et al. (2003) found that as many as 55 per cent of their participants claimed to have seen non-existent film footage of the MS *Estonia* ferry disaster in 1994, when 852 people lost their lives as the ferry was crossing the Baltic Sea from Tallinn, Estonia, to Stockholm in Sweden. It seems, then, that flashbulb memories are open to effects of leading questions, as has also been demonstrated in studies of eyewitness testimony based on normal memory situations (Loftus, 1975). See the following section for more on the effects of leading questions.

Weaver (1993) examined changes over time in recall of ordinary memories (for a meeting with a friend or roommate) and of flashbulb memories (for the first President Bush announcing the beginning of the first Gulf War on television) over a total of one year. Memories were elicited on three occasions: within two days, after three months and after 12 months. Weaver found that accuracy, as indicated by consistency, fell off quite markedly after three months but thereafter was stable, for both flashbulb and non-flashbulb memories. Both types of memory were equally accurate (consistent with first-recall records). The main difference that emerged was that participants were more confident about the flashbulb memories but this did not translate into increased accuracy.

Overall, it appears that flashbulb memories are susceptible to similar forms of forgetting and distortion as normal memories. Advantages for memories of 'flashbulb' events may be attributed to their distinctiveness, which reduces interference from similar memories, and to rehearsal effects (Bonhannon, 1988). The possible role of emotion in flashbulb memories is considered in Chapter 15.

Chapter 15, p548

Eyewitness Testimony

An important real-life area in which considerable reliance is placed on memory is the legal system, where witnesses are questioned about what they remember of events around a crime (e.g., Granhag et al., 2014; Loftus, 2019). A number of factors, however, suggest that eyewitness testimony should be treated with caution. Some witnesses may not have attended very much to the events they are asked to report. For example, if you are walking down the street and a man steps briskly out of a bank as you are passing, jumps into a waiting car and is driven off, you may not attend much at the time, but later be asked to give a detailed report of the man's height, hair colour, clothes, and the make, colour and registration plate of the car, if it turns out that you had witnessed a getaway from a bank robbery. Witnesses inside the bank probably would realize that a robbery was happening but their recalls would probably be adversely affected by stress and anxiety. Indeed, Deffenbacher et al. (2004), in a meta-analytic review, found clear impairing effects of stress and anxiety on recall of faces and of details in crime scenes compared with low anxiety and stress conditions. Thus a number of conditions may affect how a person remembers a witnessed event.

Further, if the crime involves a weapon, witnesses focus their attention on that, and are impaired in reporting non-weapon details (Tollestrup et al., 1994). A recent meta-analytic review confirmed that a witness's ability to accurately recall the details of the event, and ability to identify a perpetrator, was affected by the presence of a weapon (Fawcett et al., 2013). See also Chapter 15 for more detailed discussion of the role of emotion in memory.

When judging the credibility of an eyewitness report many people attend to the level of confidence the eyewitness expresses in their report, and the level of detail of the report, as clues to the veracity of the testimony (e.g., Magnusson et al., 2010). However, as also noted in Chapter 7 with the results from Bartlett's test subjects, the level of confidence that a person has in their memory does not necessarily correspond with the accuracy of the report. Just as memory is susceptible to influence so are confidence levels, as is evident in the the case of Ronald Cotton (e.g., Garrett, 2011; Wixted & Wells, 2017). In 1984, Jennifer Thompson was raped during an apartment break-in. After being interviewed by the police she was called in for a photo line-up, where she hesitantly and with low-confidence, picked out a man, Ronald Cotton, as her attacker. During the course of the investigation Jennifer's confidence in her memory grew as a consequence of receiving confirmatory feedback from the police that suggested she had identified the correct person. Thus Ronald Cotton was eventually convicted of the rape of Jennifer Thompson, a conviction that rested on the highly confident testimony of Jennifer. Thus it came as a shock to her when Ronald Cotton was exonerated by DNA testing after serving approximately 10 years in prison.

Even though there is need for caution when attending to the confidence level a eyewitness expresses, it should be noted that research suggests that the confidence–accuracy relationship can be rather reliable under certain conditions (Wixted & Wells, 2017). First, it is important that the level of confidence is assessed early in the investigation. Second, measures should be taken so that line-ups are conducted fairly, and caution should be exercised when interviewing eyewitnesses so that the influence of the questioning in itself is minimized. We next turn to the important issue of interviewing eyewitnesses.

Interviewing eyewitnesses

The different ways in which witnesses are questioned during a police investigation and in court may affect recall. In a classic study, Loftus and Zanni (1975) showed participants a film of a multi-car accident. For Group A, a broken headlight was seen in the film; for Group B, no broken headlight was seen in the film. Later, participants were asked either 'Did you see A broken headlight?' or 'Did you see THE broken headlight?'

It was found that Group A showed no difference as a result of the wording but, in Group B, 15 per cent of those asked a question about 'THE' broken headlight responded 'yes' compared to 7 per cent who were asked about 'A' broken headlight. The small change from the word 'a' to the word 'the' doubled the false reporting of a broken headlight. See also Box 13.4 for a rather similar finding by Loftus and Palmer (1974).

Not just the words in questions, even small ones like 'the' and 'a', but also the gestures that accompany the questions, can influence recall by eyewitnesses. Gurney et al. (2013) interviewed 90 people about the contents of a video they had watched. During the interviews, the researchers deliberately performed misleading hand gestures to suggest inaccurate information about the detail in the video. These hand gestures included chin stroking to suggest someone had a beard, although the man in the video did not have a beard. It was found that the witnesses were three times more likely to recall seeing a beard when one was gestured to them, than those interviewees who were not gestured to. Other hand gestures used in the research included touching a ring finger (to suggest a ring), grasping a wrist (to suggest a watch) and pretending to pull on gloves. All of these gestures implied details that did not actually appear in the video, and the results were similar to those with the misinformation about the beard.

From these and related studies, such as Loftus's study of implanting false autobiographical memories (discussed in Chapter 7), it seems that post-event questions and cues can change memory for the event. These effects can be seen as examples of *retroactive interference*, as we have discussed earlier in this chapter, in which later information impairs and distorts recall of earlier learned material. These findings fit well with the view that memory is changeable and reconstructive rather than fixed and simply reproductive of what was initially perceived, as Bartlett (1932), Neisser (1967) and others have long proposed (see also Chapter 7).

> Chapter 7, p218

To effectively interview witnesses, many interview protocols have been developed (e.g., Fisher & Schreiber, 2017). One of the best-known protocols is the cognitive interview, which is based on empirical findings from memory research and is discussed further in Box 8.6.

Box 8.6 Practical Application: The cognitive interview

We have seen in Chapters 7 and 8 how memory can be influenced by questioning. The cognitive interview is one of the most effective ways of reducing the bias that might be introduced when questioning eyewitnesses. It was developed by psychologists Ed Geiselman and Ron Fisher and has been shown to substantially increase the number of correct details that witnesses provide, with a small increase typically also found, however, for the number of incorrect details (for a recent review, see Fisher & Geiselman, 2018). The cognitive interview is based on Tulving's (1983) idea of encoding specificity – that is, the idea that memory is facilitated when there is overlap between the conditions at encoding and those at retrieval. The greater the match between the cues available during retrieval and the details encoded during the initial event, the better memory will be. The goal of the cognitive interview is to reinstate aspects of the event during questioning to act as cues for the witness to effectively recall the event. The cognitive interview originally used four techniques designed to aid participants' recall (Geiselman et al., 1984):

1 Reinstating the context
2 Reporting everything
3 Recalling the events in different orders
4 Changing perspectives.

Geiselman et al. (1984) showed 89 participants films of (simulated) violent crimes. Each film lasted approximately four minutes, and at least one individual in the film was shot and killed. The films, designed for police training purposes, were realistic and emotion-inducing, and scenarios included a bank robbery, an armed robbery at a store, a family dispute and a warehouse search. Participants were questioned individually, 48 hours after viewing the film, by experienced interviewers. Compared to a standard (control) police interview, a greater number of correct items were produced using the cognitive interview.

Subsequent studies have supported the effectiveness of the cognitive interview (e.g., Memon et al., 2010). In a meta-analysis of studies conducted over the previous 25 years, Memon et al. (2010) found that the cognitive interview produced better recall compared to structured interviews, while a small increase in the recall of incorrect details was also noted. They also noted particular gains for older adults using the procedure, with correct details enhanced without observed differences for incorrect details. Memon and colleagues suggest that this effect is consistent with the environmental support hypothesis, which predicts that older adults rely more on external cues when retrieving information, as opposed to internally generated retrieval strategies, compared to young adults. A recent study showed that not only did the cognitive interview elicit more perpetrator descriptor cues than a standard police interview, but that it also increased the rate of identifying the perpetrator by 30 per cent (Satin & Fisher, 2019).

Effective Studying

Student readers are faced with the major real-life task of learning large volumes of information and then recalling and using it in examinations. Although most examiners do not want to see verbatim regurgitation of their lectures or of chunks of set text, nevertheless students must retain learned material and recall accurately what is important, in order to answer possibly challenging questions. Does the cognitive psychology of learning and forgetting offer any useful advice for student learning?

Earlier in this chapter we saw that laboratory studies have shown that the deep processing of unconnected items (as in word lists) promotes memory as against superficial processing. Similar results have been found in real-life learning of meaningful material at university level. Much of this work has involved comparing effects of learning strategies. Three main strategies of learning have been identified through questionnaire studies (Biggs et al., 2001); these are:

- *Surface learning:* in which students try to learn texts by heart without seeking understanding.
- *Deep learning:* in which students make a determined effort to understand the material and make it meaningful to them.
- *Strategic learning:* in which students put effort into finding out what topics and types of questions are likely in their examinations and devise strategies to cover the minimum number of topics required.

It has been found that deep learning produces better examination results than surface learning (Entwhistle, 1987). In a study of medical students those combining deep and strategic learning did especially well in examinations (McManus et al., 1998). Thus, overall, as in the laboratory, deeper processing is more effective in real life than superficial processing; deeper processing focused on likely examination topics is especially effective, at least for medical students.

Promoting deep learning is therefore an important goal when studying. Many different types of studying techniques exist which may enable deep learning. One important technique is quizzing yourself after reading material, whether that is notes from lectures or material in textbooks. Testing requires recall, as do examinations, and so testing can indicate which material you need to study further (Roediger et al., 2011). Simply rereading texts and notes can give one an illusion of knowing the material because it becomes familiar, but it may not be well enough learned for recall.

A number of experiments have shown that testing in itself, even without feedback about the correct answers, can be effective. For example, Roediger and Karpicke (2006a) ran two experiments in which students studied texts covering scientific topics. Some experimental groups took one or three immediate free-recall tests, without feedback, or restudied the material one or three times without the tests. Finally, all students then took a retention test, which occurred five minutes, two days or one week later. When the final test was given after five minutes, repeated studying improved recall as compared to repeated testing. However, on the delayed tests, more testing produced much greater retention than studying, even though repeated studying increased students' confidence in their ability to remember the material. It seems that testing is an effective means of improving learning, not just of assessing it.

Overall, Roediger and Karpicke argue that the use of testing during learning may improve performance in educational settings at all levels, from primary through to university level, at least in very factual subjects (Roediger & Karpicke, 2006b). Frequent testing leads students to space their study efforts (and spacing is known to boost learning, as discussed earlier in this chapter), and this permits them and their instructors to assess their knowledge on an ongoing basis, so that re-studying can focus on problem areas.

One may of course wonder if frequent testing enhances the memorization of only the particular material being studied or whether the learning effects can generalize to other knowledge domains? Butler (2010) investigated this issue by having undergraduates study knowledge concerning mammals. One group of students was repeatedly tested on the material while the other group was only told to re-study the material. The students who were repeatedly tested during the study phase outperformed the re-study student group, not only on tests that concerned facts and concepts concerning mammals, but also on tests containing inferential questions – that is, questions for which answers could be inferred from the originally studied material. More interestingly, however, is that Butler also found that students who were repeatedly tested during the study phase also performed better on inferential questions concerning other knowledge domains, which in turn support the idea that testing effects may transfer.

Another important technique that promotes deep learning is generating explanations for the material during studying (e.g., Dunlosky et al., 2013; Roediger & Pyc, 2012). By asking questions such as 'Why is this true?', 'Why does it makes sense?', the student is prompted to generate an explanation that facilitates learning. This technique is known as **elaborative interrogation** and allows the student to integrate new knowledge with already acquired knowledge. The technique also promotes the processing of similarities and dissimilarities among facts and concepts, which helps the learner to discriminate further between learned concepts. Although generating explanations seems to be very advantageous for learning general patterns and overarching principles in materials, it seems to come at a cost when learning details (see, e.g., Williams & Lombrozo, 2010).

> **Elaborative interrogation**
> a learning technique where the learner prompts her- or himself to generate explanations for facts.

Two common studying techniques employed by many students while reading textbooks are either to highlight key phrases or to make summaries of the chapters. However, the utility of these techniques is low (for a review see Dunlosky et al., 2013). Although highlighting can help performance in instances where the text studied is highly complex, students often tend to underline too much information which, in turn, makes it difficult to separate the main points from repetitious information. There is, however, some support for the highlighting technique and that it can be improved if the students receive feedback on their performance (e.g., Hayati & Shariatifar, 2009). Regarding the writing of a summary, it needs to capture the main points of a chapter to be effective, therefore, similar to highlighting, the technique may require extensive training if the students are to acquire the skill of adequately making their own summaries. Also, the technique in itself can be really time-consuming and therefore reduce valuable study time that could otherwise make use of better-supported study techniques. Luckily, though, many textbooks already provide written summaries that contain the main points of the chapters.

We have now reviewed several techniques for facilitating learning but, considering the effects of visual imagery, which we discussed in the mnemonics section, can drawing facilitate learning? A study examining this issue is addressed in Box 8.7.

Box 8.7 Research Close Up: Does drawing facilitate the learning of terms and their definitions?

Source: Wammes et al. (2017).

INTRODUCTION

Studying often involves learning a multitude of new terms and their definitions. Given that the creation of images for material often leads to better recall (Van Meter & Garner, 2005), it is reasonable to assume that the effect might also generalize to the learning of key concepts in an educational setting. This issue was explored in several experiments by Wammes et al. (2017).

EXPERIMENT 1: METHODS AND RESULTS

In Experiment 1, participants (undergraduates) were prompted to either copy by writing or to draw the terms and their definitions, which were presented on a screen. The terms came from a vast number of different subjects, such as astronomy, biology, engineering and psychology. The participants then continued to a filler task where they classified different tones as either low, medium or high pitched. During the recall phase of the test concepts, which had been drawn, their definitions were recalled better than those that were only copied, even when controlling for familiarity.

EXPERIMENT 2: METHODS AND RESULTS

The set-up in Experiment 2 mimicked that of Experiment 1, with the difference being that the concepts and definitions used were fictitious, thereby ruling out the role of familiarity, which may have occurred had students studied the subjects used in Experiment 1. Results from Experiment 2 confirmed the earlier results; the nonsense concepts that were drawn were better recalled than those that were merely copied. However, the effect was more modest than in the earlier trial.

EXPERIMENT 3: METHODS AND RESULTS

The set-up in Experiment 3 was similar to that in Experiment 1, with the difference here being that the participants, after the writing prompts, were told to paraphrase the terms and their definitions. Thus they were to rewrite in their own words the definitions of the terms, instead of merely copying the definitions. The results of this experiment did not show any difference in recall between the concepts that were drawn during encoding and the concepts that were paraphrased.

> ### DISCUSSION
> The study lends support to the idea that drawing concepts facilitates learning, compared to only copying the text by writing it. It could be that drawing activates a number of different retrieval cues, such as pictorial information. However, when compared with paraphrasing the definitions, there was no gain by drawing. This suggests that the underlying mechanism could be a deeper level of processing, which also may be achieved by having the students paraphrase the concepts to be learned.

Evaluation

Early studies that focused on learning lists of nonsense syllables were very removed from real-life learning and forgetting. More recent research has tried to remedy this gap between laboratory and everyday learning by studying more ecologically valid situations.

Flashbulb memories for dramatic and highly significant events, such as the World Trade Center attacks, have been compared with memory for more routine events; it appears that these memories can be explained in terms of features that usually benefit memories, such as distinctiveness and frequency of rehearsal. A special kind of memory does not seem to be needed to explain flashbulb memories.

Eyewitness testimony is an important real-world activity based on personal memories and recall processes. However, research has shown that the knowledge judges and jurors have concerning eyewitness memory is limited. Eyewitness confidence and detail in testimony may be used as reliability cues, which can lead all too readily to false convictions based on what is actually mistaken eyewitness identification. Research has shown how memories can be affected by misleading questions and by retroactive interference from events after the crucial incidents of the crime.

Finally, we discussed effective study methods to boost efficiency of learning and recall for meaningful material as found in university courses. This brought us round again to the importance of deep processing (for meaning) as against superficial processing (for rote recall without understanding). Elaborative interrogation, by which the learner generates explanations for the facts or concepts, is one technique that may facilitate learning through deeper processing. Frequent self-testing was also found to be useful to monitor the progress of learning and to avoid false confidence that one knows something merely because it has become familiar through reading over and over. In an examination, material needs to be recalled, not recognized, and so effective study will practise recall and assess progress in being able to recall what is needed when it is needed.

Summary

This chapter has covered the acquisition of knowledge (learning), its retrieval successes (remembering) and failures (forgetting).

What happens at encoding is important for later remembering. Levels of processing theory stresses the role of deep (meaning based) versus shallow (surface based) encoding. Tests of incidental memory support the approach in that 'deep' orienting tasks lead to better memory than 'shallow' tasks. The theory has been criticized for its possible circularity.

Mnemonic methods using interacting imagery at encoding (methods of loci and pegwords) have a long history, and experiments support their value for memory.

A few very rare individuals display superior memory in general and seem to have underlying neural functioning differences from the normal. Shereshevskii, for example, had extremely strong synaesthesia, which automatically generated vivid multisensory images. However, most people who display exceptional memory abilities do so in limited domains, such as number sequences, names and faces, the order of playing cards taken from a number of packs shuffled together, and extensive practice with suitable mnemonics can be shown to underlie their skills.

The encoding specificity theory points to the importance of having the same cues available at test as were present at encoding. Context-dependent retrieval, whereby materials are best recalled in the same environmental (or internal) state as at learning, further supports the encoding specificity theory.

Spacing of learning trials is a way of boosting later memory and this too is linked to encoding specificity in that spaced trials give more encoding variability, which gives more chance of some cues overlapping at test and learning.

Forgetting occurs when we cannot retrieve information that had been available from memory in the past. Early studies using nonsense syllables established the form of the forgetting curve (steep initial decline and then gradually reducing rate of decline), which has been found to hold over many types of materials.

The main theoretical ideas about forgetting are that it may be due to: decay of traces with time, proactive and retroactive interference with other memories, or lack of consolidation of memories (which are fragile initially, but strengthen with consolidation). Early studies minimizing activity during the retention (storage) stage, through sleep or other methods, found that rates of forgetting were markedly greater after retention periods filled with activity, and attributed these results to greater retroactive interference from new memories formed during the active periods than during the inactive periods. Neuroscience-based studies stress the role of consolidation as recall of material learned shortly before sleep or ingesting alcohol or benzodiazapines is enhanced. A marked susceptibility of amnesiacs to consolidation failure when any intervening activity occurs between acquisition and test has been found.

Reconsolidation is a process where already consolidated memories are retrieved and undergo a destabilization phase that reactivates them and thus makes them susceptible to modification. As a consequence of this phase, the memory may be altered and stored in a new, updated version.

Functional approaches to forgetting stress the benefits of normal forgetting and have examined how selective forgetting may be brought about deliberately.

A movement to increase the real-life relevance, or ecological validity, of memory research has been influential since Neisser deplored the artificiality of much laboratory research. As an example of real-world memory, we discussed flashbulb memories for dramatic events. Overall, such memories seem explicable in terms of established memory phenomena (such as vividness, distinctiveness and rehearsal effects) and do not seem to require special processes. Research on eyewitness testimony uncovered problems in such testimony caused by misleading questions and post-event information as well as by anxiety and stress. Finally, effective study methods have been devised that stress deep processing and frequent testing to check progress. Simple re-studying without testing boosts confidence but is less effective than studying with repeated testing. Asking questions regarding the material being studied, such as 'Why is this true?' or 'Why does this makes sense?', prompts the generation of explanations that facilitate learning.

Review Questions

1 What are the main factors that affect efficiency of learning?
2 To what extent is forgetting due to decay, to interference and to consolidation failures?

3 Are flashbulb memories special?
4 Can we deliberately forget information?
5 Could practice produce exceptional memory abilities?
6 How well does Sherlock Holmes's 'little attic' model for learning and forgetting hold up in the face of the evidence?
7 Which study methods are especially effective, and why?

Discussion Questions

1 Is forgetting always a bad thing? What different beneficial functions may it serve?
2 Which criticism(s) can be directed towards the reconsolidation theory?
3 Consider studying situations – can you think of any other factors that may affect your learning, other than those mentioned in this chapter?

Further Reading

Baddeley, A. D., Eysenck, M. W., & Anderson, M. C. (2009). *Memory*. Psychology Press.

Dunlosky, J., Rawson, K. A., Marsh, E. J., Nathan, M. J., & Willingham, D. T. (2013). Improving students' learning with effective learning techniques: Promising directions from cognitive and educational psychology. *Psychological Science in the Public Interest, 14*(1), 4–58.

Ericsson, K. A. (2003). Exceptional memorizers: Made, not born. *Trends in Cognitive Sciences, 7*, 233–235.

Granhag, P. A., Ask, K., & Giolla, E. M. (2014). Eyewitness recall: An overview of estimator-based research. In D. S. Lindsay & T. J. Perfect (Eds.), *The SAGE handbook of applied memory* (pp. 541–558). SAGE Publications.

Lee, J. L., Nader, K., & Schiller, D. (2017). An update on memory reconsolidation updating. *Trends in Cognitive Sciences, 21*(7), 531–545.

Loftus, E. F. (2019). Eyewitness testimony. *Applied Cognitive Psychology, 33*(4), 498–503.

Putnam, A. L., Sungkhasettee, V. W., & Roediger III, H. L. (2016). Optimizing learning in college: Tips from cognitive psychology. *Perspectives on Psychological Science, 11*(5), 652–660.

Wixted, J. T. (2004). The psychology and neuroscience of forgetting. *Annual Review of Psychology, 55*, 235–269.

CONCEPTS AND IMAGERY

9

PREVIEW QUESTIONS
INTRODUCTION
THEORIES OF CONCEPTUAL REPRESENTATION
    DEFINITIONAL APPROACH
        Box 9.1 Practical Application: Cakes versus biscuits
    PROTOTYPE APPROACHES
        Box 9.2 Practical Application: Goal-derived ad hoc categories and consumer goods
    EXEMPLAR-BASED APPROACHES
    THEORY/KNOWLEDGE-BASED APPROACHES
    ESSENTIALISM
        Box 9.3 When Things Go Wrong: Category-specific deficits and pathologies
    GROUNDED REPRESENTATIONS VERSUS AMODAL REPRESENTATIONS
        Box 9.4 Research Close Up: Testing grounded theory of concepts using dual task methods in working memory for action words
    CONCEPTS CONNECTED: NETWORK MODELS
    CONCEPTS IN THE BRAIN: THE HUB-AND-SPOKE MODEL
IMAGERY AND CONCEPTS
    IMAGERY AND VISUO-SPATIAL PROCESSING: OVERLAPS?
    IMAGE SCANNING AND COMPARING
        Box 9.5 Research Close Up: Mental rotation
    AMBIGUITY OF IMAGES
    NEUROPSYCHOLOGY/NEUROSCIENCE OF IMAGERY
        Box 9.6 When Things Go Wrong: Spontaneous vivid imagery – Charles Bonnet syndrome
SUMMARY
REVIEW QUESTIONS
DISCUSSION QUESTIONS
FURTHER READING

Preview Questions

1. What are concepts? And what are they for?
2. What advantages and disadvantages might there be to using concepts?
3. Can you clearly define Cake as against Biscuit?
4. Are some birds more 'bird-like' than others?
5. In what way is imagining a chair similar to seeing and using an actual chair?
6. Thinking of one concept quickly leads to thinking of others that are very different from the starting one. How might this be useful?
7. How might mental concepts be represented in the physical brain?

INTRODUCTION

Although the world is full of unique objects and events, it is very useful to treat many distinct objects as if they were the same. So, new cups, tables and dogs are usually treated as if they are essentially the same as previously experienced cups, tables and dogs. When we treat distinct objects as the same as other distinct objects, we are using **concepts** to represent all the distinct objects that make up the categories concerned. Thus, concepts are mental representations of broad classes or categories of things, actions and relationships.

> **Concepts**
> mental representations of classes of items such as 'cats', 'even numbers', and so on.

Dealing in concepts rather than in distinct individual objects is clearly an efficient way to work and emerges as an inevitable result of how the brain responds to stimulation, in that similar stimuli evoke similar activation patterns and, by association, will arouse similar memories and action tendencies. So, if something that looks like a previously encountered tiger comes round the corner, this will activate thoughts of tigers and their properties, one of which is that they are dangerous to humans and the action tendency to flee will become very strong, very rapidly. Concepts allow us to organize information in long-term semantic memory very efficiently into hierarchical structures. Thus, if we have 'tiger' linked to the higher-order concept 'mammal' we do not need to explicitly store the fact that tigers suckle their offspring; if required, that can be deduced from the knowledge that 'all tigers are mammals' and that 'mammals suckle their offspring'.

Overall, our long-term knowledge about the world is based on concepts and relations among concepts. Also, representations of current situations are in terms of concepts. So, for example, faced with the problem of a car that will not start we will draw on concepts of 'car batteries', 'ignition systems' and 'electrical leads' to represent the situation and invoke rules such as, 'If the car battery is flat, then the car will not start', to help us towards a solution.

> Chapters 12, p424
> Chapters 13, p468
> Chapters 14, p510

As we shall see, all higher-level mental activity, such as problem solving, reasoning and decision making, discussed in Chapters 12, 13 and 14, involves imagining possible actions, choices and inferences, in terms of concepts. Clearly, then, the study of concepts is a key area of cognitive psychology, essential to understanding how we represent knowledge, and consequently has attracted a great deal of research interest over the years.

In the first main section of this chapter, we will discuss theories about what concepts are and how they are used. The second main section will deal with the fact that, when people work with concepts of concrete things such as 'cats', 'cups' or 'cars', they often experience images of the objects. Such images are like pictures but are purely mental. Visual images convey information as to what an object looks like, and the image associated with a concept would seem likely to be important in using that concept. We will discuss whether images do play an important role and, if so, how? For example, do images help people to solve problems and make good decisions? Thus, the second main section of this chapter will discuss what we know about images and **imagery**.

> **Imagery**
> the mental representation of sensory properties of objects, experienced like perceiving the object but with less vividness than in reality.

THEORIES OF CONCEPTUAL REPRESENTATION

Despite the pervasive role of concepts in cognition, there is no universal agreement on the best way to define concepts as a whole. It is more useful to think in terms of different types of concepts; in the following sections we will consider a number of alternative approaches to 'concepts' that have been put forward, and explore the extent to which any of these approaches can cover all the data or if they apply to some but not all concepts. The approaches we will consider are those in terms of definitions, prototypes, exemplars, theory, essentialism and grounded representations.

Definitional Approach

Think of arm chairs and reading chairs and dining room chairs, and kitchen chairs, chairs that pass into benches, chairs that cross the boundary and become settees, dentist's chairs, thrones, opera stalls, seats of all sorts, those miraculous fungoid growths that cumber the floor of arts and crafts exhibitions, and you will perceive what a lax bundle in fact is this simple straightforward term. In cooperation with an intelligent joiner I would undertake to defeat any definition of chair or chairishness that you gave me.

(H.G. Wells, 1908)

Some concepts are well defined, and clear black-and-white definitions can be given. Well-defined concepts are the essence of formal subjects such as mathematics and are sought throughout the sciences. So, for example, the well-defined concept of an 'even number' is of 'a number that is divisible by itself and by 2 without remainder'. An 'odd number' is simply 'any number that is not-even'. Some everyday concepts are similarly well defined, such as the concept of 'bachelor' as an adult, unmarried male. Note that concepts are typically formed from combinations of features that are themselves concepts. So, in the bachelor case, the definition uses concepts of 'adult', 'male' and 'unmarried'. Each of these requires its own definition and within a given legal system each would have its own clear criteria. So, to be adult, one would have to be above a certain age, currently 18 years in the UK; to be unmarried, one would have to have not entered into a legally binding state of wedlock; to be classed as male is normally unproblematic, but even this feature or concept has difficult cases, such as intersexed individuals – where a person has genital features characteristic of both sexes.

Many, and perhaps most, everyday concepts are not so well defined and exhibit a degree of fuzziness. So, for example, as pointed out in the quote above from H.G. Wells, there is no agreed formal definition of a chair (as against a stool, say) or of a cup (as against a mug). The lack of clear definitions can have important real-life consequences. For example, a famous legal case in the UK hinged on the definition of 'cake' versus 'biscuit'. You can see some of the details of this and similar cases in Box 9.1.

 Box 9.1 Practical Application: Cakes versus biscuits

You might briefly consider what you feel are the defining features of cakes as against biscuits (or cookies in the USA). This is not an easy matter. A food manufacturer in the UK produced a product that was sold as 'Jaffa Cakes' from 1927 onwards. These were orange flavoured, of a size typical of biscuits and covered in chocolate, but of a consistency typical of cakes (i.e., soft) rather than the consistency typical of biscuits (hard). Figure 9.1 (overleaf). shows a cross-section of a Jaffa Cake.

This product belatedly attracted the attention of the tax authorities in 1991 because chocolate-coated biscuits, but not chocolate-coated cakes, were liable to a purchase tax, known as Value Added Tax (VAT).

Figure 9.1 The outside and inside of a 'Jaffa Cake'.
Source: © CKP1001/Shutterstock.

The tax authorities argued that Jaffa Cakes were instances of the concept 'biscuit' and being chocolate coated should be taxed at 17.5 per cent. The manufacturers fought the matter in court, asserting that Jaffa Cakes were actually instances of the concept 'cake' and so should be liable for 0 per cent tax. As a result of this dispute, many of the country's finest legal brains tussled over the issue, 'Was the so called Jaffa "Cake" an example of the concept "cake" or of the concept "biscuit"?'

The judge noted that the Jaffa Cake had some features typical of a biscuit – size, placement in shops with biscuits, eaten like a biscuit – and features typical of a cake – ingredients, texture and sponge content. Eventually a ruling* was reached that the product should indeed be classed as 'cake' because of a key feature that when it went stale it became harder (as did clear-cut, agreed, examples of cakes), while clear-cut, agreed, examples of biscuits went soft when stale.

The Irish tax authorities, in a similar case, also agreed that the Jaffa Cake was indeed a cake rather than a biscuit, largely on the grounds that its moisture content was less than 12 per cent.

A recent case similar to that of the Jaffa Cake has recently tackled the question of whether a health food brownie (the Pulsin' Raw Choc Brownie), containing dates and brown rice, should be considered an example of the concept 'cake', and so be exempt from VAT, or as an example of the concept 'confectionery' and so be liable for VAT.

The judge decided that although the brownies concerned were sweet enough to be possible items of confectionery, the ingredients, the manufacturing method, their taste and texture were all consistent with those of cake and so, overall, these brownies were indeed cakes (Butler, 2019).

*United Biscuits (UK) Ltd. No. 2 (LON/91/160).

Although clear-cut definitions of concepts are often desirable and can be found in formal subjects and sciences, such as mathematics, it appears that most everyday concepts are not well defined. McCloskey and Glucksberg (1978) showed this for a range of everyday categories in a study in which people were asked to put items such as 'chair' and 'bookends' into everyday categories, such as 'furniture' or 'ornaments'. Everyone put 'chair' into the 'furniture' category, but unusual items such as 'bookends' caused considerable disagreement between participants and inconsistency within participants over time. If the furniture concept was well defined such results would not be found because everyone would agree what was furniture and what was not, just as everyone would agree that '3' is an odd number and '4' is an even number.

Although some important concepts are well defined and can be worked with using rules (Smith et al., 1992), most concepts that we work with in everyday life are not well defined. Accordingly, a major part of this area of study concerns alternative ways in which ill-defined concepts might be represented and used. This is the topic we will now go on to discuss.

Prototype Approaches

Consider for example the proceedings that we call 'games'. I mean board-games, card-games, ball-games, Olympic-games, and so on. What is common to them all? Don't say: 'There must be something common, or they would not be called "games"' – but look and see whether there is anything common to all. For if you look at them you will not see something that is common to all, but similarities, relationships, and a whole series of them at that.

I can think of no better expression to characterize these similarities than 'family resemblances'; for the various resemblances between members of a family: build, features, colour of eyes, gait, temperament, etc. etc. overlap and criss-cross in the same way. – And I shall say 'games' form a family.

(Wittgenstein, 1953, pp. 66–67)

Introducing prototypes

One point that emerges from the Jaffa Cake saga is that everyday categories have members that vary markedly in how typical they are. The Jaffa Cake is not a typical cake, being biscuit-like in shape and size, but it is not a typical biscuit either, and so lies in a border area. If all concepts were purely definitional and well defined then all examples would be equally representative and decisions about category membership would be clear cut. So, the number '7' and the number '13' are equally good examples of odd numbers. However, Rosch and colleagues (Rosch, 1973; Rosch & Mervis, 1975) found that over many everyday categories, people reliably judged some examples as more typical of the category than others. So, a robin is judged more typical of the 'Bird' category than is an emu. Both are agreed to be birds and on a simple definitional view should thus be equally typical, but they are clearly not seen as equally typical by most people.

A number of aspects of performance with concepts are affected by **typicality**. So, in sentence verification tasks (that is, judging whether a sentence is true or false), people were faster to respond 'True' to 'A robin is a bird' than to respond 'True' to 'A chicken is a bird' (McCloskey & Glucksberg, 1978; Rosch, 1973). In the study of semantic memory, as discussed in Chapter 7, an often used task is one of listing examples of category members (e.g., list as many birds as you can). As you would expect, in such tasks, highly typical instances are produced more often than non-typical instances (Rosch et al., 1976).

> **Typicality**
> the extent to which an object is representative of a category.

> Chapter 7, p218

People generally find it quite easy to make typicality judgements. The typicality rating task asks participants to rate on a seven-point scale how good an example is (e.g., a robin) of a given category (e.g., 'Bird') but the question arises of how are typicality judgements made? Rosch and Mervis (1975) obtained evidence on this question by asking participants to list all the attributes or properties that they could for 20 examples of six different categories (Furniture, Fruit, Vehicle, Vegetable, Weapons & Clothing). The examples varied widely in rated typicality – for example, in the Furniture category from the most typical, Chair, to the least typical, Telephone. It was found that very few properties were shared by all instances of a given category (contrary to the Definitional approach) but rather some properties were shared more or less widely among group members. Rosch and Mervis proposed that the members of a category shared a **family resemblance** to one another and that members could be given scores for

> **Family resemblance**
> the tendency for members of a category to be similar to one another but without having any one characteristic common to all of them.

how much they resembled other members of the group. So, if an item had say three attributes and the first attribute was also found in 16 other members, the second in 10 other members and the third in two other members, it was given a family resemblance score of 16 + 10 + 2 = 28. It was found that the family resemblance scores for the items in the six categories correlated very highly with the ratings of the items' typicalities on a seven-point scale So, the more an item had a family resemblance to other items in the category, the more typical it was rated to be. From this it could be argued that typicality judgements could be based on how closely the item resembled all other category members. For example, a robin has more shared features with other birds than does a penguin, and is regarded as a more typical bird than is a penguin.

> **Prototype**
> an ideal example that best represents a category.

The item in a category that has the highest overall family resemblance to the other category members could be said to be a **prototype** of that category. However, most prototype theories do not propose that the prototype needs to be an actual instance but rather that the prototype is a statistically average member of the category. Just as the average family with 2.2 children does not actually exist, so also the prototype may not actually exist. In support of this idea, it has been found that people can form a prototype without experiencing it directly. Studies of category learning have presented participants with examples derived by modifying an unseen prototype and, after learning, participants correctly classified the prototype on its first presentation more quickly and reliably than other new instances. This has been found with a wide range of stimuli, from dot patterns (Posner & Keele, 1970) to written character descriptions (Reed & Friedman, 1973) and schematic faces (Reed, 1972). The mental prototype seems to build up as an average picture of the category members even though the average is never actually experienced.

Levels of categories and prototypes

Categories and concepts typically form into hierarchies, such as Animal, Dog, Pekingese, and so on (see Figure 9.2).

In a conceptual hierarchy, lower-level categories are nested within higher-level categories.

When we deal with objects, there is thus often a choice of level of categorization. For example, if we have to name a picture (of a particular saw) as quickly as possible, will we tend to give a high-level superordinate category label (e.g. Tool) a low-level subordinate category label (Cross-cutting handsaw) or an intermediate level label (Saw)? In practice, the mid-level concepts seem to be most readily evoked and used. Rosch et al. (1976)

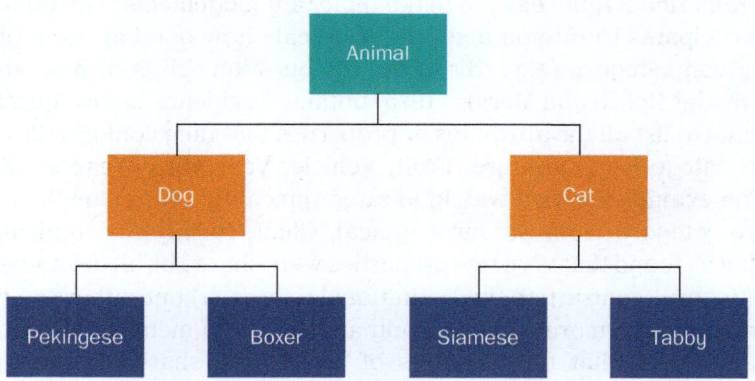

Figure 9.2 Example conceptual hierarchy of dogs and cats.
Animals form natural hierarchies of species and breeds.

argued that the mid-level is the fundamental one and called it the **basic level of categorization**. At this level the members of the categories are highly similar to one another but the category concepts are quite distinct. So Hammers and Saws are distinct from each other (few features in common) while types of saws are similar to one another, as are types of hammers. The superordinate category, Tools, consists of exemplars that have little in common. Another way of thinking about basic levels is to say that a basic level categorization is most informative for communication purposes. As Fodor (1998) commented, "'It's a car" tells you a lot about a vehicle; but that it's a sports car doesn't add a lot to what "it's a car" already told you' (p. 91); and we could add that saying 'It's a vehicle' or, worse, 'It's an artefact', is not as informative as 'It's a car'.

> **Basic level categories** categories formed of items that are highly similar and at an intermediate level in a concept hierarchy, between superordinate and subordinate levels.

Developmental studies of early language (Rosch et al., 1976) support the primacy of basic level concepts in that early acquired and early used words are labels for basic level concepts ('Dog' rather than the superordinate 'Animal' or the subordinate 'Alsatian'). Clerkin et al. (2017) found that basic level categories were most frequently encountered by infants acquiring their first nouns.

Evaluation

Although the prototype approach has been usefully applied to a range of conceptual tasks such as category-exemplar generation and has led to fruitful theoretical ideas such as typicality, family resemblance and basic level concepts, some limitations have been pointed out.

First, can simple similarity to a prototype be the whole basis of categorization? It seems not. For example, a small dog, such as a Pekingese, may be more similar to a cat than to other much larger dogs, due to its appearance (Komatsu, 1992) yet it is readily categorized as a dog.

© Oksana Valiukevic/Shutterstock

This type of finding is difficult for the prototype approach, which stresses similarity to prototypes as the sole basis of categorization. If that were the case, we would have more difficulty with separating small dogs from cats than we do.

Second, not all concepts have prototypes. For example, very abstract concepts, such as 'rules', 'beliefs' and 'instincts', were found by Hampton (1981) to lack prototypes.

Third, the linkage between typicality and family resemblance scores seems to break down for goal-derived or **ad hoc categories** that are generated for specific goals. Examples of goal-derived categories would be 'things to rescue from a burning house', 'ways to escape from a hitman' and 'things to take to a picnic in the rain'. Barsalou (1985) found that the correlation of typicality and family resemblance score was near zero for members of goal-derived categories but was over +0.7 for established common categories of the type used by Rosch and colleagues. The items that make up goal-derived categories have little in the way of common features although all, in their own way, contribute to the goal. (A practical application of the notion of ad hoc or goal-derived categories to consumer behaviour is given in Box 9.2.)

> **Ad hoc categories** categories formed of items that meet a given goal – e.g., the category of 'items to take on a picnic' is ad hoc.

Fourth, if a concept is represented only by a single prototype, then it is hard to account for people's knowledge of variability within the concept – for example, that coins of a set value do not vary in size (low variability) while pizzas vary greatly in size (high variability). This aspect of knowledge is dealt with better by exemplar theories (Rips & Collins, 1993), which will be discussed in the next section.

Fifth, people bring to bear knowledge about likely relations between features and category membership (Malt & Smith, 1982). For example, in dealing with types of birds, seeing a single instance of a small blue bird on a tropical island being labelled a 'warrum' is enough to make people reliably judge subsequent small blue birds as 'warrums'. However, if a local heavily built tropical islander is labelled as a member of the 'klaatu' tribe, we are unlikely to class the next heavily built islander we see as a 'klaatu'. Knowledge about variability of features and their usefulness as cues affects judgements in ways not predicted by prototype approaches. Such knowledge allows rapid learning of some concepts, even from single examples, as in the case of the 'warrum' bird, which goes against the gradual build-up of prototypes over many examples. In addition, prior knowledge that some features 'go together', such as that small birds tend to sing and large birds tend to squawk, make it easier to learn concepts of new birds that match expectations as opposed to those that do not (Malt & Smith, 1982). Knowledge-based approaches to concepts, discussed in a later section, address these issues, which are not dealt with by the prototype approach.

Overall, prototype approaches have dealt well with some aspects of concept learning and the categorization of new examples, particularly when concrete concepts are involved. Limitations arise in dealing with abstract and ad hoc concepts, knowledge of concept boundaries, and of variability and relations among features. Problems with prototype approaches led to the development of exemplar and knowledge-based approaches, to which we now turn.

Box 9.2 Practical Application: Goal-derived ad hoc categories and consumer goods

Ratneshwar et al. (2001) applied the ideas of goal-derived or ad hoc categories to the concepts that people use to represent consumer goods.

We might initially imagine that people would represent, say, nutritional goods as a hierarchy with Food and Drink at the top level. Drink might then be subdivided into Alcoholic versus NonAlcoholic and NonAlcoholic then subdivided further into Natural versus Artificial. Natural drinks could be further classified as Water versus Juice, and so on. Food could similarly be subdivided into lower and lower level categories.

© Juan Carlos Nunez Mena/Shutterstock

Ratneshwar and colleagues emphasized a more top-down perspective and examined categories that consumers might construct ad hoc depending on current goals. Specifically, they investigated how different goals affected category representations and participants' similarity judgements of food products.

The food products involved were: granola bars, chocolate bars, fruit yoghurt, frozen yoghurt, ice cream, plain popcorn, an apple, an orange, a doughnut, a chicken sandwich, a turkey sandwich and a cheese pizza.

> Participants rated the similarity of pairs of foods on a 10-point scale, either in a general context of 'things people might eat' or in a more specific context of 'things people might carry along to eat in their cars'. In the general context of 'things people might eat', apples and doughnuts were rated as quite dissimilar to each other (mean rating = 1.72) but in the specific context of 'things that people might carry along to eat in their cars', apples and doughnuts seemed much more similar (mean rating = 6.2).
>
> In a separate manipulation, participants were divided into those for whom healthy eating was a prominent personal goal and those for whom this goal was of low importance. In the general eating context, people with a strong healthy eating goal, regarded granola bars and chocolate bars as quite dissimilar (mean similarity rating, 4.4) but those without a strong healthy eating goal regarded chocolate and granola bars as pretty similar (mean rating = 6.45). Presumably people with a low healthy eating interest see both bars as acceptable snacks, while people with a strong healthy eating goal see granola bars as healthy food (which is how they are marketed) and chocolate bars as anything but healthy! Conversely, health-conscious eaters saw frozen yoghurt and plain popcorn as more similar (mean rating = 4.6) than did non-health-conscious eaters (mean similarity rating = 2.7).

Exemplar-based Approaches

In view of the difficulties outlined above with prototype theory, other approaches have been explored. A popular theoretical alternative to the prototype approach can be found in the form of **exemplar** approaches, which we will now discuss. Exemplar theories assume that concepts are represented by stored examples alone; no prototype is assumed. How might this work? Suppose the task is to decide whether a new creature (a 'Wug') is a bird or not. The Wug's representation is compared with examples or instances of 'birds' already stored in long-term memory; if the Wug's similarity to previous birds is above a particular threshold, we decide it is also a 'bird'. The Wug would now be one of the examples available if the concept of 'bird' is considered in future. Different specific exemplar models propose that all examples (Reed, 1972) are stored and used, or that only selected, most typical examples are stored and used (Rosch, 1975). (Where typical examples are those that are highly similar to most other instances – e.g., a robin as against a penguin in the Bird category.)

Exemplar theories propose that categories are represented purely by stored examples or instances, and each example is linked to the category name.

Exemplar models were initially applied to data from experiments in which people learned artificial categories, such as categories of dot patterns or of schematic faces; while prototype models were mainly tested using natural pre-existing concepts and categories. Storms et al. (2000; also see Storms, 2004) sought to compare exemplar and prototype approaches in two studies that took four different measures of categorization performance (Category naming, Exemplar generalization, Typicality ratings and Speeded categorization) using natural categories. Eight everyday categories (fruit, vehicles, birds, and so on) were used, with 25 exemplars and six non-exemplars for each category. The exemplars and non-exemplars were scored for similarity to each other exemplar (instance similarity) and to prototypes for each category derived by Rosch and Mervis's (1975) family resemblance method and by Hampton's (1979) method in which prototype properties are directly listed by participants. It was found that instance similarity measures were better predictors of categorization performance than either Rosch and Mervis's family resemblance or Hampton's similarity-to-prototype measure, thus supporting the exemplar approach.

Evaluation

An advantage of the exemplar approach is that it readily represents variability within a category which prototypes do not. For example, Rips and Collins (1993) invited participants to decide if an unseen object was a ruler or a pizza, based only on the information that the object was 19 inches. Pizza was the overwhelming choice even though prototypical rulers and pizzas are 12 inches, but pizzas are much more variable and so instances of 19-inch pizzas could be retrieved but instances of 19-inch rulers could not.

Although there are data supporting the exemplar approach, outstanding problems remain, such as how to deal with hierarchical structuring of concepts (Murphy, 2004), and how to incorporate the role of knowledge, and particularly the role of causal knowledge in forming categories. Shared causes are important for many concepts that cover very varied examples, such as concepts of 'drunken actions' or of 'tropical diseases'. The role of knowledge is considered explicitly in the theory- and knowledge-based accounts that we will deal with in the next section.

Theory/Knowledge-based Approaches

Prototype and exemplar approaches are based on notions of similarity or feature sharing between instances or between instances and prototypes. However, not all categories exhibit much superficial similarity or feature sharing. Goal-driven or ad hoc categories (Barsalou, 1983), as we have seen, generally consist of very disparate objects. So, the category of 'things you would rescue from a burning house' might include, babies, pets, money, jewellery, house deeds, insurance papers – all of which lack shared features and belong in the category only because they serve the purpose of the goal behind the category (which is to rescue things valuable to you).

Other categories may also have very diverse appearances – for example, the category of 'drunken actions' or that of 'things you would keep in your backpack'.

In the case of 'drunken actions', Murphy and Medin (1985) argue that there is an underlying theory or knowledge that intoxication leads to unusual and reckless behaviour because of the effects of alcohol on the brain, and this knowledge is important in classifying individuals as intoxicated from instances of their behaviour (such as jumping into a swimming pool while fully clothed or throwing television sets out of hotel windows).

A study carried out by Rips (1989) indicated that categorization can be driven by knowledge, rather than by similarity. He told participants to think of a pizza and a 25 cent coin (a quarter) and to estimate the largest and smallest size these might be. Then they were told that a third object was larger than the largest estimated quarter size and smaller than the smallest estimated pizza size. Two judgements were then asked for. First, was the new object more likely to be a pizza or a quarter? Answers favoured it being a pizza. The second question was whether the new object was more similar to a quarter than to a pizza. This time, the object was judged to be most similar to a quarter. In other words, category membership was assigned on grounds other than similarity, and was presumably based on knowledge of variability of pizzas versus quarters in size. Similar dissociations between categorization and similarity have also been found by Rips and Collins (1993) and Roberson et al. (1999). Such findings indicate that similarity to a prototype or to other instances is not the sole basis for deciding category membership.

The role of causal knowledge in forming concepts was demonstrated in a study by Ahn et al. (2000). A category was presented such that its members tended to have blurred vision, headaches and insomnia. Further, participants were told that blurred vision caused headaches and headaches caused insomnia. New items with missing pieces of information were presented and the items that were missing blurred vision were far less likely to be judged members of the group than were items in which insomnia was missing but the other features were present. Causal knowledge played a clear role in these judgements of category membership.

Theories in the form of prior knowledge about a domain are also recruited in order to account for externally given categorizations, and one mechanism for this appears to be the process of subjects trying to form explanations for the observations (Williams & Lombrozo, 2013; Williams et al., 2013). Williams and Lombrozo (2013) presented participants with examples of two classes of imaginary robots labelled either 'Indoor vs. Outdoor' or 'Drents vs. Glorps'. Correct classifications could be made on the basis of either foot shape or antennae type. Participants were asked to try to explain the classification or not. It was found that the requirement to explain produced higher solutions in terms of foot shape especially when the category label was meaningful (Indoor vs. Outdoor) as foot shape was relevant to operating indoors or outdoors.

Evaluation

In the theory-based view, concepts are thought to include information about their relations to one another and about the relations (particularly, causal relations) among the features displayed by their examples. This approach helps deal with points that were difficult for the prototype view, such as the role of knowledge of variability and how features typically relate to one another.

The theory-based view gives insights into how concepts can cover extremely varied examples, such as 'drunken behaviour' or 'healthy foods' on the basis of shared causation rather than shared surface features or characteristics. However, the approach leaves open the question of whether and how explanatory knowledge might affect judgements about similarity and typicality.

Essentialism

As we have seen, most categories allow considerable variability among their members. So, the basic level category 'dog' includes examples from Pekingese to Great Danes. These vary markedly in appearance but do they share some essence of 'dogness'? An ability to cross-breed with each other might be a candidate 'essence' although it is not a simple feature. Many people seem to believe that objects do contain some 'essence', which may be hard to define but makes them what they are, whether they are cats, dogs or toasters. **Essentialism** can be seen as a special case of the theory approach and is the view that people tend to believe that category members share some essential properties and that, although appearances may be useful guides to category membership, it is the essential properties that are critical (Medin, 1989; Medin & Ortony, 1989). A bird with its feathers removed is still seen as a bird; the essential properties may be seen as residing in the creature's DNA. In a developmental study, Gelman and Wellman (1991) found that young children, of 4–5 years of age, believed that the insides of objects were more critical or essential than the outsides. Children felt that dogs would cease to be dogs if their insides were removed, but would still be dogs if their outsides were removed.

> **Essentialism**
> the view that all members of a given category share some key property.

Barton and Komatsu (1989) argued that there are different types of concepts that may have different forms of essential properties. They distinguished three broad types of concepts, which can be labelled as *nominal, natural kind* and *artefact* concepts. Nominal concepts have clear definitions (e.g., 'Triangles are three-sided closed figures') and so fit the classic definitional approach. Natural kind concepts are those commonly identified as naturally occurring, such as cats, dogs, rainy days, and so on. Artefact concepts relate to designed and human-made objects that are generally defined in terms of their functions, such as television receivers, laptop computers, cars, and so on.

Barton and Komatsu (1989) asked participants to consider different transformations of natural kind and artefact categories. Three types of transformation were compared. These were functional transformations (a she goat that did not produce milk; a television that did not show a picture), physical feature transformations (a striped goat or a pencil that was not cylindrical) and molecular transformations (water not composed of H_2O, a mirror not made of glass). It was found that natural kind concepts were most affected by molecular transformations but artefact concepts were most sensitive to functional changes. This indicates that the essential properties of artefacts are their functions; it does not matter what materials the television set is made from, it remains a television as long as it functions as a television should. On the other hand, the essential properties of natural kind categories are their physical make-up; so a goat made out of silicon ceases to be a goat even if it behaves like a goat.

> **Box 9.3 When Things Go Wrong: Category-specific deficits and pathologies**
>
> From a variety of studies it seems that functional features or properties (what does the item do) are especially important in categorizing man-made objects and perceptual features (what does the item look, sound, smell like) are more important when categorizing living things.
>
> This difference in the bases of concepts about living and non-living things is reflected in results of brain damage, in that many people with brain damage show category-specific deficits – that is, they have difficulties with some categories of things but not with others. An early study by Warrington and McCarthy (1983) examined a global aphasic patient (known as V.E.R.) who had sustained a major left-hemisphere infarction; such patients are aphasic because they have partially or totally lost the ability to articulate themselves either in written or spoken form as a result of an injury (see also Chapters 1 and 12 for more on aphasia). They found that V.E.R. showed a selective preservation of knowledge about foods, animals and flowers, and a selective impairment of knowledge about non-living objects. Later Warrington and Shallice (1984) identified a case (known as J.B.R.) who was very poor at naming pictures of living things (6 per cent correct) as against non-living things (90 per cent correct). Thus, a double dissociation was identified, suggesting that the neural basis of knowledge about categories of living things is separable from the neural basis of knowledge about non-living objects. The same double dissociation showed up in a more recent study by Laws et al. (2006), who found category-specific deficits among a group of 55 individuals with schizophrenia, with some showing impairments in living thing categories and some in non-living thing categories.
>
> [Chapter 1, p2]
>
> [Chapter 12, p422]
>
> Warrington and Shallice (1984) proposed the *sensory-functional distinction,* meaning that for some categories perceptual features were critical and for others functional characteristics were critical. The most common pattern of deficit is for patients to have problems with living things but not with non-living things. Martin and Caramazza (2003) found this pattern to be four times more common than the reverse pattern of spared knowledge of living things and impaired knowledge of non-living things. Gainotti (2000) found that the common pattern was associated with temporal lobe damage and the less common pattern was associated with fronto-parietal damage. Silveri et al. (2018) also found supporting evidence for loss of knowledge of living versus man-made things associated with damage to the temporal lobes. Interestingly, some yet more specific dissociations have been reported of patients with category-specific impairments in their knowledge of fruit and vegetables but preserved knowledge of animals and man-made objects (Samson & Pillon, 2003). Further, specific brain damage in Alzheimer's

> patients has been associated with selective loss of knowledge of raw food and living things (occipital cortices), and with selective loss of knowledge of processed food and non-living things (middle temporal gyrus) in a study by Vignandoet al. (2019). As the occipital areas are involved in sensory information processing and the temporal areas are involved in processing functional properties, it was concluded that these results support the sensory-functional distinction of Warrington and Shallice (1984).

On the essentialist view, experts in different domains (such as zoologists, botanists, chemists) identify the true essences of the concepts they deal with and lay people tend to defer to expert judgements. So, lay people accept that a platypus is a 'mammal', even if a highly untypical one, as that is the expert view. Malt (1990) gave participants objects that they were instructed were 'Halfway' between categories (such as a tree halfway between an oak and a maple, or a sea vessel halfway between a ship and a boat). The participants were given a choice between 'asking an expert', 'calling it whatever you want' and indicating that they could tell which it was if they thought long enough. If the pairs were natural categories, the expert option was strongly favoured, but for artefacts the preference was strongly for 'calling it whichever one liked'. Thus, people seem to be more essentialist regarding natural categories than for artefact categories. Further evidence counter to the purely essentialist view was reported by Malt (1994). In this study it was found that although participants considered it essential that a liquid consist of H_2O molecules to be water, their judgements of what counted as water were influenced by other factors. So, pond water was judged to be water although its H_2O content was judged to be around 79 per cent; but tears were judged to be not water although believed to contain 89 per cent H_2O. Thus, source, location and function of a liquid also seemed to play a role in making judgements of whether a liquid counted as 'water' or not, as well as H_2O content.

In a related study Tobia et al. (2020) explored 'Twin Earth' **thought experiments** (originally devised by philosopher Hilary Putnam, 1975), which ask participants to imagine that on another planet much like Earth there is a liquid that has all the superficial properties of water (clear, drinkable, freezes into ice, boils into steam, etc.), has entirely different deeper causal properties (i.e., a different essence) and is composed of new elements XYZ rather than H_2O. Participants reported that the new liquid was in a sense *not* water but in another sense *was* water. It is proposed that people tend to have two distinct criteria for membership of natural categories – one based on deeper causal properties (essence) and one based on superficial observable properties. The general conclusion that both types of criteria are used in natural kind judgements was also supported by similar studies by Haukioja et al. (2020).

> **Thought experiment**
> use imagined situations to work out the implications of a theory.

Grounded Representations Versus Amodal Representations

The approaches to concepts discussed so far have not specified the degree to which concepts are purely abstract as opposed to involving sensory or motor processes. In typical information processing approaches to knowledge it has been assumed that conceptual knowledge is represented by abstract symbols (e.g., Newell, 1980; Pylyshyn, 1984; Vera & Simon, 1993) and so the various models could be simulated in computer programs using abstract symbols to represent sensory and motor features such as 'red', 'graspable' or 'rough feeling'.

Recently, however, a number of theorists, of whom Lawrence Barsalou (1999, 2003, 2008; Matheson & Barsalou, 2018) is the most prominent, have argued for a more embodied view of concepts as grounded in modality-specific systems for perception (e.g., vision, audition), action (e.g., movement, proprioception) and introspection (e.g., mental states, affect), with no need for **amodal** abstract symbols. Barsalou stresses the role of **simulation** in cognition, where simulation is the **re-enactment** of motor and introspective states acquired during experience of the world. So, when we interact with a chair the brain takes on states representing what it looks like, the action of sitting on it, resulting feelings of relaxation, and so on. When we encounter a new chair those states are re-activated to simulate the previous experience. Imagery is an example of mental simulation that can play a role in problem solving. For example, given the task of finding new uses for a brick, participants often imagine a brick and seem to read off properties from the image that can then support different uses (Gilhooly et al., 2007).

> **Amodal representations** are abstract and do not involve any sensory codes.
> **Simulation** involves programming computers to solve problems in a similar way to humans.
> **Re-enactment** the partial repetition of the internal processes involved in previous perceptions or actions.

Evidence for a role for bodily states in conceptual processing has come from a number of studies. Klatzky et al. (1989) found that seeing an object, such as a car key, activates the appropriate hand shape – in this case, a precision grip for grasping and turning. Glenberg and Kaschak (2004) showed further evidence that object concepts activate arm movements. When participants were to indicate whether sentences made sense by a pulling movement, they were faster to verify 'Open the drawer' than when a pushing movement was to indicate acceptability of the sentence. In a study by Wit et al. (2010), volunteers had to name tools or animals shown in pictures as fast as possible while squeezing a foam ball in one hand. Volunteers were slower and less accurate in naming tools when the tool's handle was on the same side as the squeezing hand than when the ball was in the other hand or when they were naming animal pictures. Squeezing the ball may have impaired tool naming by interfering with the motor simulation of grasping the tool with that hand, suggesting that motor simulation may play a functional role in tool identification.

Simulation also appears to play a role in the conceptual task of property verification. In this task, participants are given a word (say, horse) and then a property word, which may or may not apply to the object (has mane or has horns, say). Solomon and Barsalou (2004) found that the larger the property mentioned the slower the verification responses and the greater the number of errors. This mirrors findings from studies where the objects and properties were perceptually available (Morrison & Tversky, 1997) and supports the simulation view. In related studies, Solomon and Barsalou (2001) found a modality switching effect such that verifying *loud* for 'blender' was faster after verifying *rustling* for 'leaves' than after verifying *tart* for 'cranberries'. Switching from one modality to another slows verification, and property sizes also affect verification. The abstract amodal view of concepts would not predict these findings.

Grounded theory also sees a role for simulation in consumer experience and choices (Papies et al., 2017). For example, the grounded concept of 'wine' will contain information about sensory effects of wine, affective experiences, actions involving wine, resulting bodily states, and so on. Previous experiences and actions are simulated on presentations of wine stimuli, and affect subsequent experience motivation and behaviour. In a typical study in this area (Elder & Krishna, 2012) it was found that presenting a picture of a bowl of yoghurt with the spoon facing participants' dominant hands led to more spontaneous eating simulations and higher purchase intentions than when the spoon was not present. This result indicates that external cues facilitate related simulations and the simulations incline participants to overt actions.

Neuropsychological evidence has been invoked in favour of the grounded approach. For example, lesions to brain areas dealing with different modalities affect different types of conceptual knowledge. Damage to visual areas particularly increases likelihood of impaired performance with animal categories, which are presumed to be processed visually; and damage to motor areas particularly affects tool concepts because motor processing is the main modality for such concepts (Barsalou, 2008; Pulvermuller, 2013; Simmons & Barsalou, 2003).

Neuroimaging evidence also indicates that when conceptual knowledge about objects is activated through object names being presented, brain areas that represent the object's properties in perception become active. So, processing artefacts stimulates motor areas while processing animals activates visual areas (Keither, 2005). Processing food terms causes activation of taste areas, and processing names of smelly items stimulates smell areas (Gonzales et al., 2006). In the property verification task (Solomon & Barsalou, 2004), areas related to the properties being tested become active, including brain areas for shape, sound, action and touch (Goldberg et al., 2006). *Carota et al. (2012)* found that cortical regions involved in mouth and face movements were activated by presentation of food words, and hand-related cortical areas were activated by tool words as would be expected from the actions related to the named objects. Further, they noted that tool words activated specifically the right cerebellum while food words activated the left orbito-frontal and fusiform areas.

Evaluation

Overall, a strong evidence base is emerging that supports the idea of embodied or grounded modality specific aspects of conceptual representation. However, whether abstract concepts such as 'truth' and 'justice' can be wholly explained in terms of simulated or re-enacted experience is highly controversial. Barsalou (2008) points to the widespread use of physical metaphors when dealing with abstract concepts, as indicating a role for grounded representations in dealing with abstract concepts. So, happiness is associated with 'up' and 'high', and sadness with 'down' and 'low'; time is seen in Western culture as flowing from front to back, with us facing forwards, and so meetings that are brought forward are then closer than they had been, in our typical spatial model of time (Boroditsky & Ramscar, 2002). For more on physical metaphors and time concepts see the discussion in Chapter 3. The area of abstract concepts as a whole has hitherto been relatively little studied by either the traditional amodal approach or the grounded approach. However, a recent study by Harpaintner et al. (2019) has addressed the issue. Using fMRI, this study compared brain activations to abstract concepts related to motor domains with activations to abstract concepts related to visual domains. For example, the concept 'fitness' is motor related and 'beauty' is visually related. Responding to motor abstract words activated frontal and parietal areas, whereas visual abstract words activated temporo-occipital visual areas. This pattern of differential activation was similar to that observed between hand movements and object perception activity. Overall, the results suggested that, similarly to concrete concepts, abstract concepts relating to action and vision are grounded in modality-specific brain systems typically activated in actual perception and action.

Chapters 3, p82

> **Box 9.4 Research Close Up: Testing grounded theory of concepts using dual task methods in working memory for action words**

Source: Shebani & Pulvermuller (2013).

INTRODUCTION

Language and action systems of the human brain are functionally intertwined. As predicted on the grounded theory of concepts, speaking about actions and understanding action-related speech activates the motor system of the human brain and, conversely, motor system activation has an influence on the comprehension of action words and sentences. Although earlier research had shown that motor systems *become active* when we understand language, a major question still remained as to whether these motor system activations *are necessary for* processing action words. Shebani and Pulvermuller reported the following relevant study.

METHOD

Fifteen monolingual, native speakers of English took part in the experiment.

The word stimuli used in the experiment consisted of 72 words, 36 arm-related action verbs (e.g., *clap, braid, grab*) and 36 leg-related action verbs (e.g., *step, kick, hop*).

There were two specific interference conditions in the experiment in which hand or foot motor movements were required. A control condition, during which no movement had to be performed (rest), was added to provide information about verbal working memory performance without motor interference, and, in addition, an articulatory suppression condition was run. In each of the four conditions (control/rest, hand movement, foot movement, articulation), a fixation point was presented alone in the centre of the screen for 3 sec. The fixation point was then replaced with four words presented serially. The words in each trial were either all arm-related action words or all leg-related action words. Each word was presented for 100 msec. Stimulus presentation was followed by a 6 sec memory period during which subjects were required to retain the four words in memory in the order in which they were presented. After this delay, a beep prompted subjects to repeat the words they saw on screen.

RESULTS

The main result, directly addressing the key hypothesis motivating this study, from a 2 × 2 analysis (Word Type × Moving Body Part) revealed that when participants engaged in performing a rhythmic motor pattern with either their hands or feet, errors in memory performance increased and a significant interaction effect was found, as shown in Figure 9.3.

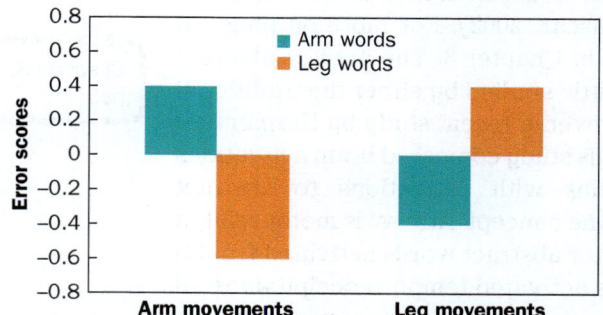

Figure 9.3 Short-term memory errors with dual tasking. Errors in short-term memory for 'arm' words (e.g., throw) and 'leg' words (e.g., walk) as affected by concurrent leg and arm movements in a dual-task study.

Source: Shebani & Pulvermuller (2013).

DISCUSSION

The rhythmic movements of either the hands or the feet lead to a differential *impairment* of working memory for concordant arm- and leg-related action words, with hand/arm movements predominantly impairing working memory for words used to speak about arm actions and foot/leg movements primarily impairing leg-related word memory. The resulting cross-over

> double dissociation demonstrates that body-part-specific and meaning-related processing resources in specific cortical motor systems are shared between overt movements and working memory for action-related words, thus documenting a genuine motor locus of semantic meaning.
>
> It should be noted that this finding has recently been replicated in Montero-Melis et al. (2019).

Concepts Connected: Network Models

Concepts are connected with one another to varying degrees and this has long been a noted feature of conceptual knowledge. As the early associationist theorist Thomas Hobbes noted in around 1650, thoughts of concepts can quickly move, in a few associative steps, from a starting point such as 'war', to an apparently unrelated concept, such as 'Roman penny' via intermediate associations – e.g., War ->Treason->Betrayal->Christ's betrayal->30 pieces of silver->Roman pennies. In this way, apparently unrelated concepts can be brought together and, as we shall see in Chapter 12, this ability is useful for creative thinking. Collins and Loftus (1975) gave an early example of such a network, as shown in Figure 9.4.

Chapters 12, p452

Recently, attempts have been made to represent conceptual or semantic networks more precisely (e.g., Baronchelli et al., 2013) using measures from the mathematical theory of networks, which can be applied very widely to all kinds of systems where nodes are connected by links, such as transport networks, social networks and energy distribution systems, as well as conceptual knowledge. Schilling (2005), Marupaka et al. (2013) and Kennet (2018) have found from word association and other data that the conceptual network displays 'small world' properties. In small world networks, concepts are tightly linked into clusters and there are sparse but sufficient links between clusters so that apparently unrelated concepts can be reached from one another by a small number of steps along network links. There is an analogy here with social networks and the finding that the average number of steps along connecting links of 'knows' between random individuals in a large society is quite small and usually numbers around six links (Milgram, 1967). As a personal example of a small world effect, I (K.G.) know my previous boss, who knows my University President, who knows the UK Minister of Education, who knows the Prime Minister of the UK, who knows the President of the USA; thus, I am only five steps from Donald Trump! In a similar way, apparently unrelated concepts can be linked through a small number of intermediate links.

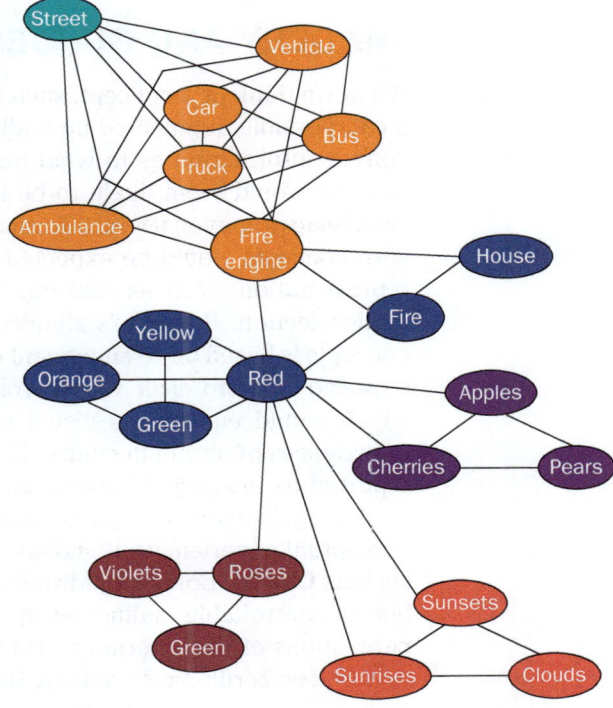

Figure 9.4 Example semantic network of concepts.
Source: Collins & Loftus (1975).

Concepts in the Brain: The Hub-and-Spoke Model

How does the brain encode conceptual representations? A widely accepted view, which can be traced back to the pioneers of neuropsychology such as Wernicke (1874), is that individual concepts are not highly localized as unitary representations in a specific brain region, but rather involve mass action of many modality-specific sources of information, each coded in different regions of the cortex (Lambon Ralph, 2014). In addition to the widely distributed featural information, there are many grounds for proposing some central representation that connects up the many features that contribute to a single concept. Thus, it is proposed in the influential hub-and-spoke model that information about what a 'cat' looks like, feels like, sounds like, etc., is integrated by a 'hub' that connects the disparate features together (Rogers et al., 2004).

> **Semantic dementia**
> a progressive neurological disorder exhibiting gradual impairment of semantic memory functions.

> **Transcranial magnetic stimulation**
> a non-invasive method of temporarily exciting or inhibiting cortical areas.

Studies of patients exhibiting semantic dementia, a progressive disorder exhibiting gradually increasing impairments of semantic memory, often exhibit lesions in the anterior temporal lobe. Such patients have been shown to have particular problems with atypical category members, such as deciding that 'emus' are 'birds' (Mayberry et al., 2011). Consistently with these observations, it is proposed in the hub-and-spoke model that conceptual hubs are located in the anterior temporal lobe. A supporting study by Pobric et al. (2010) found that application of transcranial magnetic stimulation (TMS) to the anterior temporal lobe in normal participants impaired performance on naming pictures of living things, objects that could be manipulated and objects that could not be manipulated. Thus, TMS had affected the 'hub' area. The 'spokes' in the model are the connections to feature information and TMS applied to the inferior parietal lobule (involved in processing action information) specifically affected naming only of the manipulable objects but not of living things or non-manipulable objects.

Overall, the hub-and-spoke model of how conceptual information is represented and structured in the brain fits well with much observed data from both normal participants and patents with semantic dementia. (See Lambon Ralph, 2014, for a very detailed account.)

IMAGERY AND CONCEPTS

When we think of a concept, such as 'cat', most of us will experience a visual image of a cat, possibly augmented by auditory imagery of purring or meowing. Visual images convey information as to what an object looks like and the image associated with a concept would seem likely to be important in using that concept. To what extent do such images convey useful information and how do we use images? Imagery associated with concepts would be expected to be important on embodied views of knowledge representation, such as that put forward by Barsalou (2008), and introduced in an earlier section. Barsalou's simulation view of concepts proposes that knowledge of concepts is based on re-enactment of previous experiences with category members and so seeing the word 'chair' would evoke re-enactments of previous chair-related experiences, which would encompass visual experience and possibly motor and haptic (touch) experiences of sitting in chairs. These re-enactments or simulations could normally be reported as imagery. Imagery partially replicates actual experience, but can usually be distinguished as being less vivid and more under the person's control than actual perceptual experiences. It should be noted that there are rare pathological conditions, such as Charles Bonnet syndrome (see Box 9.6) in which people have extremely vivid but uncontrollable hallucinatory images that are visually indistinguishable from perceptions of the external world (Plummer et al., 2007; Santhouse et al., 2000). For a review, see Zerilli-Zavgorodni & Bisighini (2014).

Although imagery can be found in all sensori-motor domains, most research on imagery has focused on visual imagery as vision is, for most of us, the dominant perceptual channel and so we will focus on visual imagery. Images may be regarded as representing the appearance of objects, and such knowledge of what members of common categories look like is an important part of our conceptual knowledge. We will now review findings on imagery, including: the relationship between imaging and perceiving; scanning images; mental rotation; ambiguity in images, and neuroscience approaches to imagery.

Imagery and Visuo-spatial Processing: Overlaps?

We start with the question of the extent to which imagining an object uses the same processes as actually perceiving it. Regarding visual imagery, this is often discussed in the literature in terms of the degree to which imagery and **visuo-spatial processing** overlap. We all have the experience that closing our eyes helps when we try to imagine an object; this everyday observation is consistent with the idea that the same mental machinery is involved in seeing as in imagining. A number of experimental studies have reported interference between imagery tasks and simultaneous visuo-spatial processing, which supports the idea that imagery and perception draw on the same mental and neural resources. This type of result was first reported by Brooks (1968) in a series of studies that have now become classics in the field (see also Chapter 6 for more on dual tasking, working memory and the Brooks task). Brooks asked participants to imagine a capital letter 'F' and then had them imagine going round the letter clockwise from a starting corner and indicate whether each corner was at the extreme top or bottom of the letter (see Figure 9.5).

Visuo-spatial processing the mental manipulation of visual or spatial information.

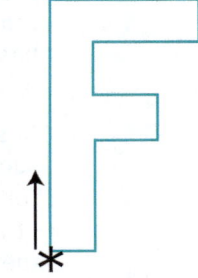

Going round the figure F, is each corner encountered at extreme top or bottom or neither? Beginning at the bottom left corner of the 'F', the answers should be 'yes, yes, yes, no, no, no, no, no, no, yes'. Participants were asked to either say their responses or point to a Y or N on a sheet of paper with Ys and Ns in rows in an irregular pattern. It was found that making a spatial response (pointing) slowed down performance compared to a verbal response. The reverse pattern was found when the main task was verbal – that is, remembering a sentence such as 'A bird in the hand is not in the bush' and indicating for each word whether it was a noun or not. These patterns of interference are consistent with the visual imagery task drawing on visuo-spatial resources.

Figure 9.5 Brooks' imagery task.

Chapter 6, p176

A similar conclusion can be drawn from Baddeley and Andrade's (2000) study of reported vividness of imagery when imaging was combined with a range of dual tasks (see Figure 9.6). Participants were asked to imagine the appearance of various familiar objects while carrying out tapping in a pattern (visuo-spatial task) or counting aloud from 1–10 repeatedly (a verbal task). Participants were also asked to rate the vividness of their images on a 0–10 point scale where 0 meant 'No image at all' and 10 meant 'Image as clear and vivid as normal vision/hearing'. For visual images, self-reported vividness of the images was reduced by a tapping task but not by the counting task. When participants were given the task of generating auditory images of familiar sounds, such as the ringing of a telephone, reported vividness of auditory images was reduced by counting but not by spatial tapping. In terms of the Baddeley and Hitch model of working memory (see Chapter 6

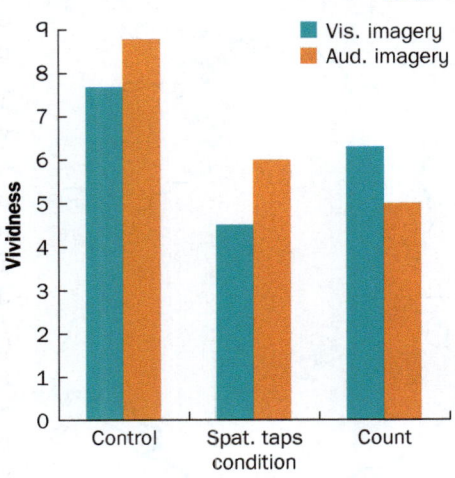

Figure 9.6 Baddeley and Andrade's (2000) result.
Vividness of visual and auditory imagery as affected by Spatial (tapping) and Auditory (counting) dual tasks.

Source: Adapted from Baddeley & Andrade (2000).

for more details), this result indicates that visual imagery uses the visuo-spatial sketchpad part of working memory, while auditory imagery involves the phonological loop component of working memory.

In related studies, Keogh and Pearson (2014, 2011) found that participants with more vivid mental imagery performed better in visual working memory tasks but not in verbal working memory tasks. Also, participants with vivid imagery were negatively affected during visual working memory storage by bright background luminance but not during verbal working memory storage.

Image Scanning and Comparing

Images are usually generated for a practical purpose. For example, you might have to move a large wardrobe out of a room. Will it be too wide to go through the door? Using imagery, you could try to compare the dimensions of the wardrobe with the height and width of the doorway to 'see' whether the wardrobe could go through. Or you may have bought a complicated electrical item that needs several electrical outlets to plug into. Are there enough outlets in your bedroom? Using imagery you might try to scan an image of your bedroom to find and count electrical outlets. A number of studies have examined such image scanning and comparing, focusing largely on the question of whether image scanning and comparing are like picture scanning and comparing.

In a typical experiment, Kosslyn (1973) asked participants to study pictures of objects such as a plane, a submarine and a clock tower. The participants were then asked to form an image of one of the objects and to focus on one part such as the left or the top of the object in the image. Next, they were asked to look for a particular part such as the flag on the bell tower and indicate when they found that part. Times to report finding the target part of the image varied in accordance with how far the target was from the starting point in the image. So, parts of the pictures that were separated in space were also separated to a corresponding degree in the image. These results support the idea that images are like pictures in the mind.

Similar results emerged from a map-scanning study (Kosslyn et al., 1978). Participants first studied a map of a fictitious island containing seven landmark objects (see Figure 9.7).

The participants first studied the map, then imagined the map and were asked to focus on one object, and next to scan the map image to find a second named object. Time to report finding the second object showed a very strong linear correlation (r = 0.97) with the physical distance between the objects on the map (see Figure 9.8). These results again support the view that images encode relative distances with some accuracy.

Other studies have asked people to compare images. For example, Finke (1989) asked participants 'Which is larger, a pineapple or a coconut?' and concluded that such comparisons were imagery based. Moyer (1973) found that such size questions were answered more rapidly the larger the difference between the objects in real life. Paivio (1975) had also found the same pattern when real objects were presented. So people are quicker to agree that a whale is larger than a cat, than that a cat is larger than a toaster, suggesting that the relevant images encode size in a picture-like way. The basic finding that difference judgements between symbolically

Figure 9.7 Map for the scanning task.
Participants studied the map before the scanning task.

Source: Kosslyn et al. (1978). APA; reprinted with permission.

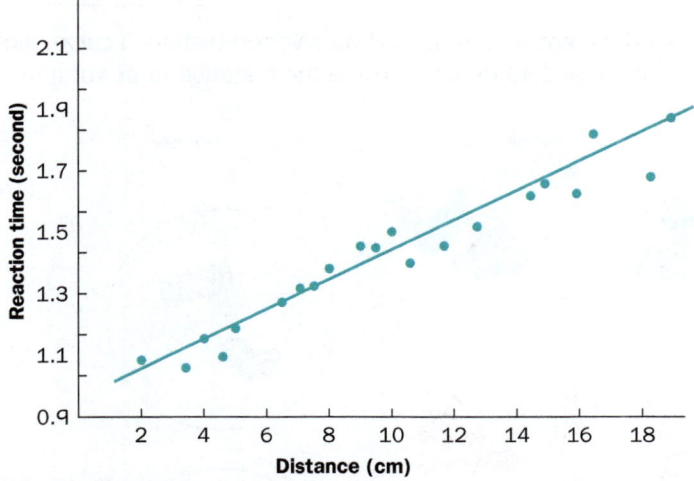

Figure 9.8 Scanning distance and reaction times.
The longer the distance to be mentally scanned the longer the time to scan between two points.

Source: Kosslyn et al. (1978). APA; reprinted with permission.

presented items are made more easily for objects that are indeed widely different in reality is known as the *symbolic distance effect*. Again, the studies of image comparison tasks have been taken to support the view that images are picture-like representations that are examined by the mind's eye just as pictures are processed through the brain's eye. Similar conclusions can be drawn from studies of our ability to carry out mental rotation of images of three-dimensional objects, as described in Box 9.5.

Box 9.5 Research Close Up: Mental rotation

Source: Shepard & Metzler (1971).

INTRODUCTION

In addition to being able to create, scan and compare images, people can also transform images, and in particular can undertake mental rotation. Is mentally rotating the representation of a three-dimensional object similar to physically rotating an actual object, in terms of time taken and accuracy with which it can be done? In a series of classic studies, Shepard and Metzler (1971) investigated this issue.

METHOD

Shepard and Metzler gave people pairs of pictures which were perspective drawings of three-dimensional objects (see Figure 9.9, overleaf).

The pairs of drawings were either of the same object rotated in different ways or one object was the mirror image of the other and so not identical. Participants had to say whether the two drawings were of the same object.

RESULTS

Times to make correct 'Same' and 'Different' judgements showed a very strong relationship with the angle of rotation between the two pictured objects such that the more rotation needed to match, the longer the time taken to make a judgement. This results in an inverted U-shaped curve, plotting rotation angle against time taken, with a peak at 180 degrees where the distance to be rotated is at its maximum (see Figure 9.10).

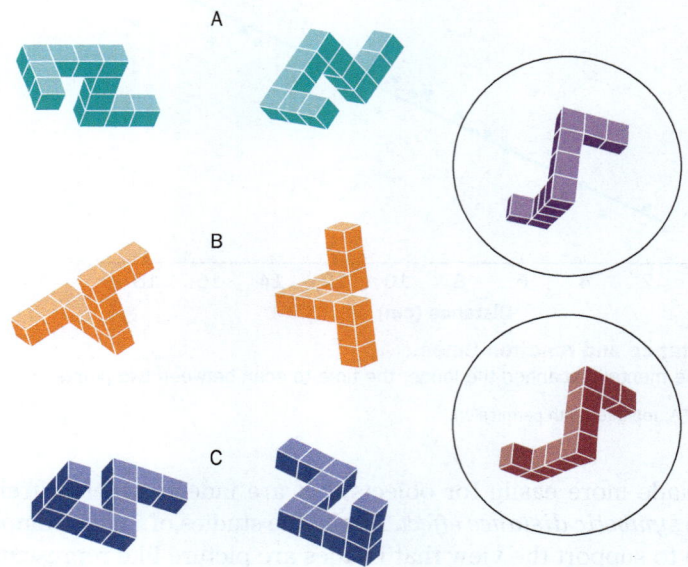

Figure 9.9 Mental rotation stimuli.
Are the left and right figures A, B and C the same or different? Are the two circled figures the same or different?

Source: Based on Shepard & Metzler (1971). Reprinted with permission from AAAS.

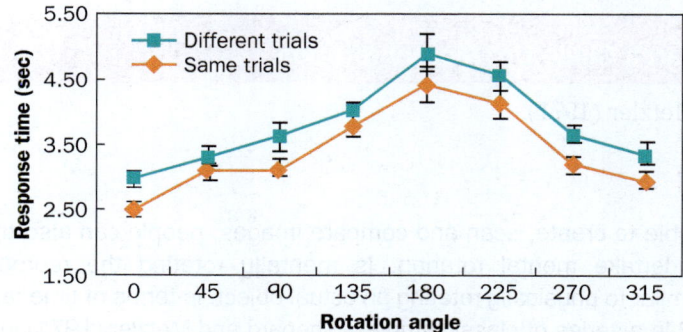

Figure 9.10 Time to make 'Same' and 'Different' judgements as function of angle between shapes.

Source: Based on Shepard & Metzler (1971). Reprinted with permission from AAAS.

DISCUSSION

The results are consistent with the view that participants imaged one object and rotated the image until it either matched the other object or not. Other analyses indicated that participants would rotate either clockwise or anticlockwise depending on which direction would yield the smaller angular separation. Advance information on the object and the degree and direction of rotation given before the comparison stimulus was shown eliminated the angle size effect. This suggests that with advance information participants carried out the mental rotation before the comparison stimulus appeared. Overall, the results of the mental rotation studies indicated that visual images represented three dimensions and that mental rotation of three-dimensional images was similar in many respects to physical rotation of objects.

> Later studies, e.g., Logie et al. (2011), show different solving strategies in mental rotation tasks for participants varying in their vividness of imagery. People with relatively weak imagery perform more poorly on mental rotations although drawing conclusions with similar speeds as those with strong imagery. Logie et al. (2011) proposed a poorer strategy of trying to imagine oneself going around the objects as against rotating the objects being used by participants with weak imagery as compared to participants with strong imagery abilities. Age differences were also found in strategies used by younger and older participants, especially with more complex objects. Younger participants adopted a piece-by-piece approach to rotating complex objects, but older participants tried rotating the whole object, and were slower and more error-prone (Zhao et al., 2019).

Critical views of imagery research and theory

Despite the results on scanning, comparing and rotating of images, which are consistent with the idea that images operate like pictures in the head, some researchers, particularly Pylyshyn (see below), have raised objections to that view and we will now discuss these criticisms.

Pylyshyn (1981) proposed that the image scanning results of Kosslyn et al. (1978) could reflect participants' beliefs or tacit knowledge about what should happen in such tasks. Participants would tend to know that it takes longer to scan a longer distance and respond accordingly by inserting a pause as suits the distance involved.

Pylyshyn (1981) tested participants using island materials similar to Kosslyn et al. (1978). He replicated the original results when the scanning task was given. However, when participants were asked to say what direction was one landmark from another (North-west? Directly south?) the distance between the landmarks did not affect response time. So, if scanning was explicitly requested, participants produced scanning-like results. However, if the task does not explicitly request scanning, participants do not produce results consistent with image scanning. Further support for a possible role for task demand and experimenter effects came from a study by Intons-Peterson (1983) in which experimenters were given different expectations about how image scanning experiments might work out. In a map-scanning task based on Kosslyn et al. (1978), half the experimenters were told that scanning an image of the map would be faster than perceptually scanning the actual map and half were told the reverse. The results obtained reflected the experimenters' expectations. When perceptual scanning was expected to be faster, it was significantly faster than imagery scanning by 230 milliseconds. When imagery was expected to be faster, the gap between the imagery and perceptual conditions was reduced to a non-significant 41 milliseconds (and the imagery speed was increased by a significant 201 milliseconds over the condition with the opposite expectation). Presumably, the expectations were subtly picked up by participants from small unconscious cues given by the experimenters, and affected how participants responded.

Pylyshyn (1973) criticized the image-as-picture metaphor (also known as the **depictive representation theory**) on theoretical grounds. He pointed out that pictures can be arbitrarily damaged (e.g., cut in half or torn up into small pieces) but images can be transformed only in terms of meaningful components being added or removed. Also, we can perceive pictures without advance warning of their contents but images have to be intentionally constructed and are based on our knowledge of the objects being imaged. Thus, two people may form an image of the same chess position, but the

Depictive representation theory in a depictive representation, each part of the representation corresponds to a part of the represented object, as in a photograph.

expert player will 'see' relationships of attack and defence in the image that the non-player or the beginner will not 'see', because the expert has the requisite underlying knowledge.

Pearson et al. (2015) have argued in favour of the depictive view, both from the earlier results on scanning and rotation but also from studies supporting the similarity of effects of imagery and of weak external stimuli. For example, Winawer et al. (2010) found that prolonged imaging of motion of a pattern in one direction produced an illusion of movement in the other direction when a real static version of the imaged pattern was presented – a motion after-effect as found with external stimuli. Similarly, Laeng and Sulutvedt (2014) found that the pupil of the eye adjusts to imaginary light. In their study, imaging a bright stimulus had a reliable and predictable effect on pupil constriction just as real stimuli varying in brightness would have had during perception.

Ambiguity of Images

The well-known Necker cube and the duck–rabbit figure (Jastrow, 1899) are good examples of ambiguous reversible figures that typically generate alternative and indeed alternating structures. In the Necker cube, perception alternates between a cube with the leading face to the right or left and in the duck–rabbit, perception alternates between a duck facing one way and a rabbit facing the other (see Figures 9.11 and 9.12). The Gestalt theory of perception proposed that ambiguous figures caused unstable representations that resolved themselves into alternating representations.

Figure 9.11 Jastrow's duck–rabbit ambiguous (reversible) figure.

If images are like percepts, then images of figures like the duck–rabbit should also be ambiguous and reversible. To investigate this possibility, Chambers and Reisberg (1985) showed their participants a line drawing version of the duck–rabbit figure for five seconds and told them to image it for a later drawing task. Participants all indicated either seeing it as a duck or as a rabbit (but not both). They were then shown other ambiguous figures and how these reversed as one changed one's focus of attention. Participants were next asked to imagine the duck–rabbit figure and seek alternative interpretations of their image. Finally, they drew the duck–rabbit figure and reported their impressions of the drawing. It was found that although participants could easily reinterpret their drawings – that is, come to see a rabbit they had *drawn* turning into a duck, and vice versa – they could not reverse the mental image of either a duck (into a rabbit) or a rabbit (into a duck), that they had constructed at the beginning of the experiment. This supports the view that images are not exactly like pictures but rather always have some fixed interpretation on which they are based. Similar findings were also reported later by Chambers and Reisberg (1992). In this second study, participants were told the duck–rabbit figure was either a duck or a rabbit and then imaged the figure. On being tested with comparison figures that differed minutely from the original, participants who were told the figure was a duck were more sensitive to differences in the bill/ears part of the picture than to changes in the nose/back of duck head. The reverse

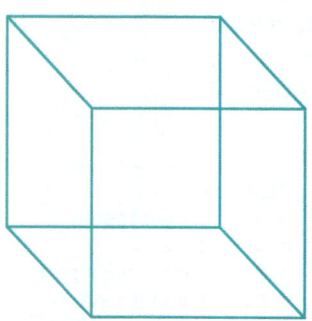

Figure 9.12 The Necker cube: an ambiguous (reversible) figure.

pattern held for those participants who had been told the picture was of a rabbit. Chambers and Reisberg (1992) argued that, in interpreting a picture and in forming an image of a creature, people attend mainly to the face and for the duck interpretation the face is to the left (bill) and for the rabbit the face is to the right. Similar results showing difficulty in reinterpreting images have also been reported by Pylyshyn (2002). However, in some circumstances, when plentiful hints and cues were provided, Mast and Kosslyn (2002) did find image reversal with a stimulus that looked like a young woman in one orientation and an old woman if rotated 90 degrees. It seems, then, that image reversal is sometimes possible, but generally very difficult.

Neuropsychology/Neuroscience of Imagery

If imagery is a re-enactment of perception then it would be expected that brain areas known to be involved in perception would also be involved in imagery. A number of studies have examined this issue. Roland and Friberg (1985) found large activation effects in the occipital lobe (which is heavily involved in visual perception), as indexed by blood flow measures, when participants carried out visual imagery tasks as compared with tasks of similar difficulty levels that did not involve visual imagery (such as mental arithmetic). Farah et al. (1988b) found similar results for visual imaging with a range of neuroscience measures including event-related potentials. Zatorre et al. (1996) found similar effects with auditory imagery. Forming and using auditory images of songs had an activating effect in the secondary auditory cortex, which was similar to but weaker than the activation obtained when listening to the songs.

In related studies, Kosslyn et al. (1995) had participants form images of varying size, and not only found increased occipital activation but also that the specific occipital area activated depended on the size of the image being formed. Ganis et al. (2004) compared fMRI results when people imaged figures and actually perceived the figures. This fine-grain comparison indicated that although similar brain areas were involved in the imagery and perceptual versions of the tasks, the areas most activated in imagery (occipital and temporal regions) were a reduced set of those activated during perception. This is consistent with the fact that people rarely confuse images with percepts, except in certain pathologies (see Box 9.6).

> **Box 9.6 When Things Go Wrong: Spontaneous vivid imagery – Charles Bonnet syndrome**
>
> Being able to generate appropriate mental images when remembering or problem solving is a useful ability. However, in some clinical conditions very vivid spontaneous images can occur uncontrollably that are as detailed as real perceptions but frequently rather bizarre.
>
> The first attempt to study and record such hallucinatory imagery began in 1760, when a Swiss naturalist, Charles Bonnet, became concerned when his grandfather Charles Lullin, who had severe cataracts, began to experience 'amusing and magical visions'. The 89-year-old Lullin had visions of people, birds, carriages and buildings, all of which were invisible to everyone but him. These vivid images appeared spontaneously and were superimposed upon such vision as he still had.
>
> Bonnet recorded his grandfather's reports and the condition he described is now known as *Charles Bonnet syndrome*. People with this syndrome see non-existent patterns such as brickwork or tiles, or phantom objects in great detail, including people, animals and buildings. The images are very vivid and

often fit in with the surroundings – for example, a non-existent man in full Highland dress might be seen in the sufferer's favourite arm chair. These images last for a variable range of times, from seconds to hours. The hallucinations are purely visual and are not accompanied by imaginary sounds or smells.

Floating, disembodied faces are often reported that appear at random times. These faces often have wide, unblinking eyes and prominent teeth, rather like gargoyles. The visions are sometimes life-sized, but often the hallucinations appear in miniature, an effect called 'Lilliput hallucinations', after the small Lilliputian people from *Gulliver's Travels.*

Charles Bonnet syndrome is most common in people at the early stages of sight loss, and the hallucinations usually begin while their vision is still present but slowly diminishing. The most common factor is *macular degeneration,* where cells in the retina malfunction and cause a slowly spreading blind spot in the centre of vision. Glaucoma and cataracts can also cause symptoms.

The prevalence of Charles Bonnet syndrome is difficult to assess as patients are often reluctant to seek medical attention for fear of being labelled as psychiatric cases (Zerilli-Zavgorodni & Bisighini, 2014). However, incidence in visually impaired patients has been estimated as ranging from 10 to 38 per cent (Jackson & Ferencz, 2008).

The cause of Charles Bonnet syndrome is not definitively known, but it seems likely that the brain is attempting to compensate for a shortage of visual stimuli. Because the visual system is active without constraining retinal inputs the syndrome is also sometimes referred to as 'visual release syndrome' (Kaufman & Milstein, 2013).

Plummer et al. (2007) and Santhouse et al. (2000) suggest a specific mechanism. The most plausible hypothesis, they argue, is that neurons in the visual pathway going from the retina to the cortex become hyper-excitable, due to the loss of light receptors. It is as if the pattern-recognition regions of the cortex are trying to interpret the reduced light patterns that are coming into the eye, and are trying out hypotheses to explain the noisy input. The end result is a sequence of cortical guesses based on the degraded stream of incoming visual information. These guesses are experienced as vivid hallucinations – for example, of little men in top hats and tails dancing on the kitchen table.

In terms of treatment, improving the patient's vision with spectacles, improved lighting or other visual aids, and with cataract surgery, has been found to reduce Charles Bonnet hallucinations (Zerilli-Zavgorodni & Bisighini, 2014).

Overall, a large number of early studies, reviewed by Kosslyn and Thompson (2003), have typically found involvement of the early visual cortex in imagery tasks, especially when finely detailed images and tasks involving object shape as against motion are involved.

Lee et al. (2012) further examined differences and similarities in brain activation patterns in imagery and perception. In this study 11 participants were shown pictures of 10 familiar objects (bag, car, chair, clock, jet, lamp, necklace, pen, umbrella and violin) and an auditory input of the object name, or were asked to form visual images of the objects given the spoken name. On the basis of fMRI recordings it emerged that visual perception led to relatively greater activation in the early visual cortex than in the later visual cortex, but that pattern was reversed when participants were imaging. The results indicated that while imagery and perception have similar neural bases they involve different network dynamics, probably resulting from the removal of bottom-up input during imagery. Similar conclusions emerged from a recent extensive literature review by Dijkstra et al. (2019), who argued that while both imagery and perception share high-level processing the early bottom-up processing characterizing perception is absent during imagery.

Despite the wealth of neuroscience evidence that imagery and perception share brain mechanisms as re-enactment theory proposes, some neuropsychological studies have found cases of brain-damaged individuals who have intact visual perception but imagery impairments and others who have intact imagery with visual perceptual deficits (Bartolomeo, 2002). These cases of double dissociation support the view that although brain areas for perception and imagery overlap they are not identical (Bartolomeo, 2008).

Evaluation

Processing of images seems to involve the same mental and neural resources as processing the objects represented. Brooks showed this in visual image processing and similar results have been found with auditory images. Scanning and comparing images shows temporal characteristics similar to scanning and comparing objects. Similarly, mental rotation of images to compare images for identity shows similar characteristics to actual object rotation.

An area in which images show clear differences lies in the detection of ambiguity in images. This is relatively easy with real pictures such as the duck–rabbit, but much harder and rarely possible with images.

Finally, we note that neuropsychology and neuroscience studies tend to support the view that visual imagery involves a subset of the brain regions active in visual perception. These results are difficult to explain in terms of demand characteristics and implicit knowledge.

Summary

This chapter has concerned two important aspects of mental representation. First, how do we represent general ideas or concepts? And, second, how do we represent information about sensory characteristics of objects in imagery?

We need concepts to deal with members of the same class or category as if they were identical. Although all cats are unique and even the same cat on two different occasions has changed even if slightly, it is not economical of mental resources to treat each unique object as if it were completely novel. Hence, we have developed everyday concepts of cats, dogs, tables, chairs and many other things.

The *definitional* theory is that concepts are represented by clear-cut rules stating necessary and sufficient features for an item to belong to the concept. Formal or nominal concepts fit this view, so 'triangles are three-sided two-dimensional closed figures' or bachelors are 'never married, adult males'. However, few everyday concepts are so readily defined. It is not easy to provide hard-and-fast rules to decide what is a chair as against a stool, say, or what is a cake versus a biscuit.

An alternative to the definitional approach is that concepts are defined by resemblance to a prototypical member of the category. So, a blackbird may be seen as the prototypical bird and new possible bird objects are compared with the prototype and those sufficiently similar to the prototype are accepted as birds. This *prototype* view is associated with Rosch and her colleagues, who have reported studies showing that typicality is a good predictor of many concept processing tasks such as making membership judgements and attribute listing. Some difficulties with this view are that similarity can be a poor guide to category judgements; for example, a small dog may resemble a cat more than a typical dog, but still be readily categorized as a dog; not all concepts, particularly abstract concepts, have prototypes, and goal-derived categories (e.g., 'things to take from a burning house') do not show the link between typicality and degree of resemblance to other items in the category.

Exemplar approaches propose that concepts are represented by stored instances without any one prototype. Exemplar models have generally been tested by having participants learn new artificial categories such as dot patterns, and have shown good fits to such data. It has also been shown that exemplar models can be applied to natural everyday categories. Difficulties for this approach include dealing with hierarchical structuring of concepts and explaining the role of knowledge in using concepts.

Knowledge-based approaches and *essentialist* approaches focus on relevance of prior beliefs about why categories have their characteristics. For example, the category of 'drunken behaviours' includes reckless behaviours in pursuit of immediate goals ignoring important distant goals. The category 'makes sense' through some understanding of the effects of alcohol on the brain's frontal lobes, which are involved in inhibition. Essentialism argues that people tend to assume there is a hidden 'essence' that scientists may uncover that makes, for example, a cat a 'cat', or water 'water'. Children do show strong beliefs that the 'insides' of animals are what make them the animals they are. However, source, location and function of liquids seemed to influence judgements of whether a liquid was water more than did percentage of H_2O – the essence of water.

The *grounded* (or *embodied*) approach to concepts, associated with Barsalou and colleagues, proposes that when we think of a 'chair', previous experiences with chairs are re-enacted or simulated and guide suitable naming and using actions. In line with this approach, seeing tools have been shown to activate appropriate anticipatory finger and hand movements. Neuropsychological and neuroscience studies also report conceptual processing involving the same brain regions as processing the objects themselves; for example, thinking of smelly objects activates olfactory regions. How this approach can deal with abstract concepts is less clear, although studies have indicated frequent use of physical metaphors in dealing with abstract concepts, such as regarding time as flowing from one's front to one's back.

Concepts interrelate to one another via associative links, and can be seen as forming a vast network. Studies indicate that the conceptual network has 'small world' properties in that apparently unrelated concepts can be connected in a few associative steps.

In terms of the neural basis of conceptual knowledge, a widely accepted current approach is the *hub-and-spoke model* (Lambon Ralph, 2014; Rogers et al., 2004). This approach is consistent with the embodied approach of Barsalou, but adds the idea of conceptual hubs to tie together the sensory-motor features of concepts that will be widely distributed across the cortex. The hubs appear to be located in the anterior temporal lobes, which tend to show marked lesioning in cases of semantic dementia. Overall, the hub-and-spoke model of how conceptual information is represented and structured in the brain fits well with much observed data from both normal participants and patients with semantic dementia.

In regard to imagery, scanning, rotating and comparing images show temporal characteristics similar to scanning and comparing objects, which supports interpretations of images as 'pictures-in-the-head'. However, implicit knowledge and effects of demand characteristics might also be involved in producing such results. An area in which images show clear differences from pictures lies in the detection of ambiguity in images. This is found to be easy with real pictures such as the duck–rabbit, but much harder with images. Overall, neuropsychology and neuroscience studies indicate that visual imagery involves a subset of brain regions active in visual perception.

Review Questions

1. What is wrong with the 'definitional' approach to conceptual knowledge?
2. What are the strengths and weaknesses of the prototype and exemplar approaches?
3. How promising do you find the embodied, grounded, approach of Barsalou and colleagues?
4. Are images just like pictures?
5. What do you think neuropsychological and neuroscience studies have added to our understanding of concepts and images?

 Discussion Questions

1. Devise possible experiments to test the exemplar approach vs. the prototype approach.
2. Make as many predictions as you can from the view that 'imagery has the same effects as weak perceptions'.
3. Could all the varied approaches to conceptual representation outlined in this chapter be valid?

Further Reading

Barsalou, L. W. (2010). Grounded cognition: Past, present and future. *Topics in Cognitive Science, 2,* 716–724.

Goldstone, R. L., Kersten, A., & Carvalho, P. F. (2018). Concepts and categorization. In *Stevens' handbook of psychology* (3rd ed.), Vol. 3 (pp. 275–317). John Wiley & Sons.

Kosslyn, S. M. (2005). Mental images and the brain. *Cognitive Neuropsychology, 22,* 333–347.

Lambon Ralph, M. A. (2014). Neurocognitive insights on conceptual knowledge and its breakdown. *Philosophical Transactions of the Royal Society B, 369,* 20120392. http://dx.doi.org/10.1098/rstb.2012.0392

LANGUAGE PRODUCTION

10

- **PREVIEW QUESTIONS**
- **INTRODUCTION**
- **LANGUAGE AND COGNITION**
- **LANGUAGE AND COMMUNICATION**
    - LANGUAGE UNIVERSALS
        - 🔍 **Box 10.1 Research Close Up:** Symbolic communication in non-human animals – vervet monkey alarm calls
    - COMPONENTS OF LANGUAGE
- **SPEECH ERRORS**
    - HESITATION AND PAUSES
        - 🧠 **Box 10.2 Practical Application:** Using speech cues to detect deception
    - SLIPS OF THE TONGUE
    - THE TIP-OF-THE-TONGUE STATE
        - 🔍 **Box 10.3 Research Close Up:** Proper name retrieval in youth and mid-life
- **THEORIES OF SPEECH PRODUCTION**
    - MODULAR THEORIES OF SPEECH PRODUCTION
    - INTERACTIVE THEORIES OF SPEECH PRODUCTION
- **NEUROSCIENCE OF LANGUAGE PRODUCTION**
    - LATERALIZATION OF FUNCTION
        - ❗ **Box 10.4 When Things Go Wrong:** The split brain
- **THE LEFT HEMISPHERE AND LANGUAGE**
    - ❗ **Box 10.5 When Things Go Wrong:** Use of verbal fluency tasks in the clinical setting
    - EVIDENCE FROM THE TYPICAL POPULATION
    - EVIDENCE FROM APHASIA
        - 🧠 **Box 10.6 Practical Application:** Should lecture notes be typed or handwritten?
- **SUMMARY**
- **REVIEW QUESTIONS**
- **DISCUSSION QUESTIONS**
- **FURTHER READING**

Preview Questions

1. How does human language differ from animal communication systems?
2. How might we define 'language'?
3. What do slips of the tongue tell us about the processes involved in speech production?
4. How does damage to the left hemisphere of the brain affect speech production?
5. What information remains available in the tip-of-the-tongue state?

INTRODUCTION

In 1970 in California, a case of child abuse was discovered that was to have a profound impact on our understanding of language development. A girl, named in the literature as 'Genie', had been isolated from the age of 20 months until she came to the attention of social services at the age of 13 years and 7 months. When found, Genie was undersized and severely malnourished. She had painful calluses from being physically restrained over long periods. Throughout her years of isolation, Genie had not been spoken to and she had been beaten when she made a noise. She had not been exposed to language – she had spent many years locked in a room at the back of the family home, where she was not able to overhear her family's conversations, and where she was not exposed to language sounds from radio, television or other sources (Curtiss, 1977).

When Genie was found, she did not speak and seemed to understand no more than a few words (Rymer, 1992). Once she was taken into care and was exposed to language, in some ways her language development appeared to proceed as it would for a younger child who had had typical exposure to language (Curtiss, 1977). She progressed from single words to two-word and then three-word combinations, and she rapidly acquired vocabulary. However, her language development showed some significant deviations from the normal pattern. Genie had a vocabulary of more than 200 words before she began to combine them, whereas children typically combine words earlier. The word types evident in her early vocabulary also differed from the normal pattern. For example, while most children's early vocabulary consists of basic class words (e.g., 'dog', 'cat'), Genie's vocabulary development showed an emphasis on colours and numbers, shape and size terms, and basic (e.g., 'dog'), superordinate (e.g., 'animal') and subordinate (e.g., 'Labrador') category words (Curtiss, 1981; Fromkin et al., 1974). Genie seemed to seek out words that would allow her to differentiate between similar objects (e.g., pen versus pencil) rather than acquiring labels for a category of object. By contrast, a typically developing child might initially use 'pen' for pens, pencils, crayons and other objects of similar shape, a pattern referred to as **over-extension**.

> **Over-extension**
> a normal pattern of error in language development whereby children use the same word for a wider class of objects than is appropriate, for example using the term 'bird' for all flying things.
>
> **Syntax**
> the rules governing the ways words can be combined to create meaningful sentences.
>
> **Content words**
> words that provide meaning to the sentence; these contrast with function words, which do the grammatical work of the sentence.

The most striking feature of Genie's language reflected problems in the development of **syntax** or grammar (see Table 10.1), and was evident in the ways she combined words. Curtiss (1981) described Genie's sentences as 'the stringing together of **content words**, often with rich and clear meaning but with little grammatical structure' (p. 21). Some examples of Genie's utterances illustrate this aspect of her language: 'I like hear music ice cream truck'; 'Think about Mama love Genie'; 'Dentist say drink water'; 'Applesauce buy store' (Curtiss, 1977). Despite significant instruction, Genie remained unable to differentiate between sentences such as 'place the bowl behind the cup' and 'place the cup behind the bowl' (Curtiss, 1981). Her gestural signs also showed some anomalies, with a preference for middle finger over index finger pointing (Looney & Maier, 2014). It is not clear whether Genie's language would have progressed with continued instruction and support; following a move to a series of foster homes, her language is known to have regressed (Jones, 1995). It is also difficult to disentangle the effects of deprivation and abuse from those of language isolation; in other cases, language development has been more successful post-isolation (e.g., see Brown & Jones, 2014). However, other studies suggest a similar pattern of lasting grammar deficits in late language learners. Mayberry et al. (2018) described the case of a deaf man whose linguistic experience began in young adulthood. While he acquired sign language and used it daily over three decades, his signs remained atypical, syntactically limited and sometimes ill-formed, making them difficult to interpret out of

Table 10.1 Levels of Linguistic Analysis

Level	Concerned with:
Semantics	Meaning in language
Syntax	The rules by which words are combined to make meaningful sentences
Morphology	The rules by which words are constructed and modified
Phonology	The systems of sounds in a language

context. Other studies of sign language also point to the importance of robust early language experience for normal language development (e.g., Twomey et al., 2020).

Genie's case reflects three key issues in language acquisition. First, her failure to fully acquire language suggests that there may be a critical or sensitive period for language acquisition, and particularly for grammar development; if the child is not exposed to language in a social context within this period, normal development is constrained (see Lenneberg, 1967). Second, her language reflects the dissociation between the acquisition of vocabulary and the flexible use of this vocabulary to form novel sentences. Third, her case suggests that language acquisition, like many cognitive functions, relies on interplay between input from the environment (nurture) and biological make-up (nature).

This chapter examines the nature of language and the cognitive processes involved in **language production**, with a focus on speech production. In practice, language production and comprehension go together and do not neatly delineate in the manner suggested by two separate chapters. Language occurs in a conversation, with a natural back-and-forth between speaker and listener. Many of the topics in this chapter will be relevant to aspects of the next chapter and vice versa.

> **Language production**
> a number of processes by which we convert a thought into language output, in the form of speech, sign language or writing.
>
> **Social cognition**
> the ways in which people make sense of themselves and of others in order to function effectively in a social world.

Language is a quintessentially human ability and the ability to communicate our thoughts to others through language is fundamental for **social cognition**. Language also shapes mental representation and thinking and, once acquired, is 'fundamental to all distinctly human thought and consciousness' (Donald, 1999, p. 139). It is therefore important for cognitive psychology to study the processes involved in language production and comprehension, and to try to understand how a thought is turned into spoken words and how our understanding of language affects cognition.

Two basic stages in speech production have long been recognized: the formulation of a thought and its conversion into speech (e.g., James, 1890). However, cognitive psychology remains relatively poorly informed as to the precise nature of the processes underlying language production. As we will see in the next chapter, greater progress has been made towards understanding language comprehension, while less research has addressed the processes underlying production (MacNeilage, 1999). Methodological constraints provide one reason for this bias: it is difficult to control experimental stimuli in order to study language production. When examining language comprehension, we can manipulate the words, sentences or other stimuli that are presented to research participants and measure the effect on comprehension. Comprehension follows on the presentation of the stimuli. But production proceeds from cognition to motor output, and it is a far more difficult task to control or inspect the content of someone's thoughts. Speech production proceeds in a top-down manner – that is, it is **conceptually driven** (see Chapter 2).

> Chapter 2, p34

> **Concepts**
> are mental representations of classes of items such as 'cats', 'even numbers', and so on.

In spite of the methodological challenges, our understanding of speech production has seen substantial development in recent decades. Knowledge of speech production derives from a number of sources, involving, for example, experimental methods, computational modelling, neuroscientific methods and neuropsychological case studies. In much of the present chapter we focus on learning about language production by examining what happens when the system fails. Two types of system failure are considered. First, we consider speech errors. Slips of the tongue and other speech errors reveal much about the processes underlying speech. Errors can be induced experimentally or recorded from spontaneous speech. Second, the effects of physical damage to the areas of the brain responsible for language production will be examined.

This chapter focuses on spoken language and the processes involved in the production of speech. The following chapter will examine language comprehension. Let's start by exploring why the study of language is so important to our understanding of human cognition and by considering some properties of language.

LANGUAGE AND COGNITION

Language is a quintessentially human capacity. Language is used not only for communication, but for many aspects of mental processing and particularly higher cognitive processes such as decision making, reasoning and problem solving. We are aware of the role of language when we hear an inner voice as we engage in a task, but language can often affect thought without our awareness. We reshape our experiences using language, affecting memory for those experiences. In order to use language we must engage many cognitive processes: attention, visual and auditory perception, memory, motor cognition and reasoning, among others. Understanding language is therefore of fundamental importance to cognitive psychology.

A central debate within cognitive science is the nature of the relationship between language and cognition. While this debate has raised many questions over several decades, it can be distilled down to two key issues. First, is language special? Are language and thought related or are they distinct cognitive abilities? Is language a by-product of other cognitive abilities, does it emerge from general cognition, or does it reflect a separate and special set of processes? Is language the product of a dedicated set of modules that are independent of other cognitive processes? Is language a special and perhaps genetically hard-wired process, that develops readily given input?

By the age of 6 years, children have an almost complete grasp of grammar and an already impressive command of vocabulary. Bilingual children will have mastered the complexities of two languages. Yet, the 6 year old's thinking is far from fully formed and will continue to develop for many years. Furthermore, children who have cognitive difficulties can have strong language capability, a pattern that would not be predicted if we assume that language development follows on from cognitive milestones.

For example, children with a rare neurodevelopmental disorder called **William's syndrome** demonstrate a fractionation of language and other cognitive abilities, such that their language development is relatively spared (albeit delayed) while there are clearer deficiencies in their non-linguistic cognitive functioning. Children with William's syndrome have been observed to produce highly fluent language and are able to tell detailed stories. By contrast, their visuo-spatial functioning is very poor. These children can provide detailed verbal descriptions of an object, such as a bicycle for example, yet are unable to reproduce the object in a simple line drawing

> **William's syndrome**
> a neurodevelopmental disorder with a number of distinctive features, including a fractionation of linguistic and non-linguistic cognition.

(Bellugi & Wang, 1996). While it has been established that the language of children with William's syndrome is not normal as such, with anomalies in syntax and morphology (e.g., Clahsen & Almazan, 1998), their linguistic performance remains superior to that of children with both linguistic and non-linguistic cognitive deficits, such as children with **Down syndrome**. Language in William's syndrome is also sometimes contrasted with that of **specific language impairment** (SLI), a specific learning disability diagnosed (in the absence of genetic markers) when language development lags behind cognitive development without explanation. Suggestions of a double dissociation of function are overly simplistic, however; while language is a relative strength in William's syndrome, it remains below age-appropriate norms (D'Souza & Karmiloff-Smith, 2017).

The second strand of the language–thought debate addresses the degree to which language affects thought. Once we have acquired language, does it thereafter shape thought? In a strong form, a positive response to this question would carry significant implications. It would suggest that there is a qualitative difference between verbal and pre- or non-verbal thought. It would suggest that thought in the absence of language (such as following damage to the language areas of the brain) is qualitatively different. It would even suggest that speakers of different languages, lacking direct mapping of translations, think differently and perhaps have different capabilities in terms of capacity for higher cognition.

The proposal that language influences cognition is known as the **Sapir–Whorf hypothesis**, after linguists Edward Sapir and Benjamin Whorf and their work exploring how one's native language shapes thinking. A strong version of the proposal that language drives cognition, **linguistic determinism**, is not supported. Reasoning can be preserved despite language impairment following brain injury (Varley, 2014) and individuals who speak different languages do not demonstrate radically different cognitive capacities. However, a weaker version of the proposal, that language *influences* cognition, has found some support. This is known as the **linguistic relativity** hypothesis.

In a now classic experiment, Loftus and Palmer (1974) demonstrated the effect of language, specifically **leading questions**, on memory for an event. Participants in their study saw film clips of automobile accidents and subsequently answered questions about events depicted in the clips. The question that was asked of the participants varied across experimental conditions such that the verb used was experimentally manipulated. Participants were asked 'About how fast were the cars going when they _____ each other?' One of the following verbs was substituted: collided, bumped, contacted, hit or smashed into. Participants' speed estimates were found to vary as a function of the verb used. (This experiment is explored in detail in Chapter 11, Box 11.2).

In a similar vein, Boroditsky (2001) demonstrated that the differing metaphors used for time references in Mandarin and English (e.g., 'I am looking *forward* to the party') can shape thinking about time. The proposal that the language we speak profoundly affects the way we think, from perception to abstract reasoning (e.g., see Boroditsky, 2012), remains controversial, and there is a need for further replication and for consideration of the complex interplay between culture and language (e.g., Imai et al., 2016). On balance, cognitive psychology continues to treat language and thought as involving separable but highly interconnected processes (for an overview see Gage & Baers, 2018).

> **Down syndrome** or trisomy 21, is a genetic disorder characterized by the presence of a third copy of chromosome 21 and associated with mild to moderate intellectual disability.
>
> **Specific language impairment (SLI)** a specific learning disability wherein language development lags behind cognitive development without explanation.

> **Sapir–Whorf hypothesis** the proposal that language affects thought and, in a strong form, that the way we think is determined by the language we use.
>
> **Linguistic determinism** the proposal that language determines thought.
>
> **Linguistic relativity** the proposal that language affects thought.
>
> **Leading questions** questions that suggest or prompt a particular answer, and that can skew or bias the information provided, particularly in the context of witness questioning.

> Chapter 11, p388

LANGUAGE AND COMMUNICATION

> **Communication**
> any means by which information is shared.

Language is our principal means of communication and forms the basis of the majority of social interactions. Communication can be fairly readily defined as any means by which information is shared (e.g., Field, 2003) or as a process whereby 'a source encodes and transmits a signal, which is detected by a receiver and decoded into meaningful terms' (MacFarland, 1999, p. 387). Many definitions of language would include its use in communication as a core feature, but clearly language goes beyond communication. The information-sharing function of language may be a relatively minor role; Aitchison (1996, p. 25) suggests that language has been particularly important for human evolution because it promotes social bonds and social interaction, and because it provides an effective means of persuading others.

There are two ways in which we can use language to communicate. One is through writing. Written language is a new (and arguably humankind's greatest) invention; the earliest evidence of writing dates to about 5,000 years ago. Writing developed from a number of distinct systems originating in different parts of the world and this is reflected in considerable cross-language variation in scripts today (see Chapter 11). Writing involves converting thoughts or speech to print. In contemporary society, reading and writing are essential skills and anyone who fails to acquire them, for whatever reason, is at a considerable disadvantage. Writing also plays a vital role in language survival, by allowing a record of the language to be retained across generations: a language without writing is unlikely to survive. Writing is explored further in Box 10.6.

Chapter 11, p374

The principal way we use language is through speech or a related mode of output such as sign language. Speech has been a feature of human cognition for tens of thousands of years and is without parallel in the animal kingdom. Spoken language is found in all human groups and would seem to be qualitatively different from the communication systems of other species.

People also communicate non-verbally. Non-language vocalizations (such as grunts or groans) can convey information, and gestures can supplement or substitute for spoken language (see Jacobs & Garnham, 2007; McNeil, 1992). There are many speculative accounts of the origins of human speech. Some highlight the interaction between spoken language and gesture (e.g., Corballis, 2003; Rauschecker, 2018). Gesture is so closely tied to human language that we continue to gesture even when we cannot be seen; it is common for people to gesture as they communicate over the telephone, for example (Bavelas et al., 2008; see Chapter 3 for more on gesture and embodied cognition). Subtler non-verbal signals using body language and tone of voice also communicate to others, whether we are aware of this or not.

Chapter 3, p107

Languages vary on a number of dimensions, but also have features in common, an issue we explore next.

Language Universals

Estimates regarding the number of languages in use worldwide vary considerably, depending on the criteria used to count speech systems as distinct languages. Estimates place the figure at more than 6,000 languages (e.g., Amano et al., 2014; Comrie, 1989; Krauss, 1992; Moseley, 2007) and this number is decreasing. Many languages are close to extinction, with a very small number of speakers and insufficient intergenerational transmission with few or no child speakers. Just 4 per cent of the world's languages are spoken by 96 per cent of the world's population, placing many languages on the 'endangered' list (Crystal, 2000). Krauss (1992) counted 187 indigenous languages in North America, only 20 per cent of which were still being learned by children. Krauss (1992, p. 7) also estimated that as few as 10 per cent of the world's languages will remain in a hundred years, with minority languages facing increasing pressure from the dominant, majority languages (see also Crystal, 2000). Amano et al. (2014) identified 25 per cent of languages as being at risk of extinction because of a small geographical range, small speaker population and rapid speaker decline rates. Their analysis noted 'hotspots' of language decline in the tropics, the Himalayas, northern Australia, eastern Eurasia and northern Russia/Scandinavia, and northwestern North America.

Languages show considerable diversity in their features and vary in the number and types of sounds used, in basic word order, in the size of their vocabularies (reflecting the number of items in the lexicon) and in their rules for sentence construction (see Evans & Levinson, 2009). However, all languages are capable of expressing complex and new ideas: there are no 'primitive' languages. Though the precise way in which concepts are expressed may differ across languages (e.g., Boroditsky, 2001; see Chapter 11), the expression of complex ideas is evident in all languages and in all human groups.

> **Mental lexicon** our store of knowledge about words and their uses.

> Chapter 11, p374

Languages have some key features in common, though it proves to be a difficult task to identify a set of linguistic universals – that is, features that are shared by all languages. Aitchison (1996, p. 177) lists the following features as 'absolute universals':

> **Linguistic universals** are linguistic features said to be found in all languages.

- consonants and vowels
- combination of basic sounds into larger units
- nouns (words for people, places and objects – e.g., book)
- verbs (words that represent actions or 'doing' – e.g., to read)
- combination of words in meaningful ways
- expression of who did what to whom
- expression of sentences as negatives
- expression of sentences as questions
- structure-dependence – that is, use of a syntactic structure or grammar
- recursion – that is the use of a rule within itself, allowing, for example, embedded sentences.

There are, as Aitchison points out, immediate problems with this listing. Sign languages are language, though they do not use a system of vowels and consonants. Some languages do not reliably distinguish between classes of nouns and verbs. Some nouns can represent actions (e.g., 'destruction') and nouns can be used as verbs ('to text'). Table 10.2 provides a summary of the parts of speech, such as nouns and verbs (for a more detailed account see Huddleston & Pullum, 2002). While all spoken languages are based on combinations of vowel and consonant sounds, the precise set of sounds varies considerably across languages (see the section on phonology). MacNeilage (1999) identifies the syllable, that is a vowel and consonant combination, as a universal unit of speech. Some languages use other sounds in addition to vowels and consonants. For example, in tonal languages, altering the tone of expression communicates meaning. In English, and non-tonal languages generally, we can change the tone of the utterance for emphasis, or to convey emotion, but doing so does not alter the meaning of the word. In a tonal language, the tone carries meaning. In Mandarin, for example, a language with a relatively small number of syllables, 'ma' can mean 'mother', 'horse' or 'scold', if the tone is even, falls then rises, or falls, respectively (Ladefoged, 1993, p. 255).

> **Tonal languages** use changes in tone to alter the meaning of the word.

Table 10.2 The Lexical Categories (Word Classes, or 'Parts of Speech') with Examples in English

Category	Description
Verb	Words denoting actions (*run, jump*), states or experiences (*feel, think*)
Noun	Words denoting people, places, things or abstract ideas (*desk, absence, thought, London, Barack Obama*)
Pronouns	Words used to refer to nouns without naming them (*he, she, they*)
Determinative	Words used to specify definiteness or quantity (*the, a, some, all*)
Adjective	Words that modify or qualify the meaning of a noun (*red, happy, rainy*)
Adverb	Words that modify words other than nouns (*recently, soon, quite*)
Preposition	Words that indicate spatial or temporal relationships (*after, at, before*)
Conjunctions	Words used to link or mark clauses or phrases such as coordinators (*and, or, but*) and subordinators (*that, whether*)
Interjection	Expressions of emotion or sentiment rather than words per se (*yikes, ouch, woohoo*)

Even in languages with many features in common (e.g., German and English) the precise set of speech sounds varies. Some languages use unusual classes of consonant sounds, such as the 'click' phoneme sounds of the Khoisan language family and some other African languages (Huybregts, 2017; Knight et al., 2003). Sounds that are treated as meaningful differ substantially across languages.

Given this diversity, an approach to defining language based on broad 'design features' may prove more useful than identifying a strict set of universals. Even this task has proven problematic however. Charles Hockett's (1960) set of 16 design features for human language was formulated with the aim of identifying properties that are unique to human languages and differentiate them from other animal communication systems. The idea is that while animal communication systems share some of the features, only human language demonstrates the full set. While this approach provides a useful general description of aspects of language, and has had considerable influence within the fields of linguistics and psycholinguistics, it is far from a complete description of language. These features are summarized in Table 10.3.

These features are not independent, as Hockett noted. For example, semanticity and arbitrariness are related: words have meaning, they refer to something in the world (semanticity) and the relationship between the sound of the word and the thing it refers to is not (usually) physically direct (arbitrariness). So, for example, the word 'dog' refers to the canine animal, and the sounds of the word 'dog' do not relate directly to that animal; the word 'chien', 'hund' or 'madra' could be used to refer to the same entity.

This approach may provide a useful general way of differentiating animal communication systems from language, however there are limits to such an approach. The design features treat speech as the standard mode of expression and do not apply fully to sign languages, which, it is generally agreed, show similar linguistic properties to spoken language. The features do not apply fully to written language. Furthermore, some features, such as arbitrariness, do not always apply. While it is generally the case that there is an arbitrary relationship between words and sounds, some words show an iconic link to sounds. **Onomatopoeia**, the direct representation of sounds from nature, is the obvious example, but there are many more examples; this issue of **sound-symbolism** in language is increasingly being explored (see Lockwood & Dingemanse, 2015, for a review).

Onomatopoeia
words that sound like the thing to which they refer – for example, the bird name 'cuckoo' or the 'beep' of a car horn.

Sound-symbolism
the idea that the sounds of words can themselves carry meaning.

Table 10.3 Hockett's Design Features for Language

Feature	Description
1. Vocal–auditory communication channel	The sender vocalizes and the receiver hears the spoken signal
2. Broadcast transmission and directional reception	The speech signal is transmitted out from the source and is localized in space
3. Rapid fading	The spoken message fades after production
4. Interchangeability	The sender can also be a receiver, and vice versa
5. Feedback	The speaker has access to the message and can monitor its content
6. Specialization	The energy expended in producing the message does not alter the meaning of the message
7. Semanticity	Sounds within speech refer to objects and entities in the world: words have meaning
8. Arbitrariness	The relationship between the spoken word and its referent in the world is arbitrary
9. Discreteness	The speech signal is composed of discrete units
10. Displacement	Language can be used to refer to things that are displaced from the present situation, either in time or space
11. Productivity	Language allows us to create novel utterances; this is also called openness or generativity
12. Cultural transmission	A language is learned through interaction with more experienced users of the language within a verbal community
13. Duality of patterning	Meaningful elements are created by combining a small set of meaningless units
14. Prevarication	Language can be used to deceive and lie
15. Reflexiveness	Language can be used to communicate about language
16. Learnability	A language can be learned by a speaker of another language

A useful demonstration of this was provided by Ramachandran and Hubbard (2001). They presented participants with figures like the one shown in Figure 10.1 and asked 'One of these two figures is a 'bouba' and the other is a 'kiki'; which is which'? They found that 95 per cent of participants selected the spiky shape on the left as *kiki* and the rounded shape on the right as *bouba*, having never been exposed to these stimuli before. They explained this effect as reflecting a cross-modal correspondence between the angles of the visual stimulus and the inflection of the sound. The kiki–bouba effect has since been reliably demonstrated across a range of ages and languages. The effect can be elicited even when the link between the shapes and sounds is implicit and irrelevant to the task (Peiffer-Smadja & Cohen, 2019) and a haptic version of the effect has been demonstrated with blind participants (Graven & Desebrock, 2018). The role of the written (orthographic) form of the words in eliciting the effect in literate participants has been explored and may account for some of the findings (Cuskley et al., 2017).

Wacewicz and Żywiczyński (2015) note two further problems with Hockett's classification. First, the focus is on the medium of transmission at the expense of content.

Figure 10.1 The kiki–bouba stimuli.
Presented with these novel stimuli, participants reliably select the spiky shape on the left as 'kiki' and the rounded shape on the right as 'bouba' rather than vice versa.

Thus there is a bias towards spoken language, and other types of language, such as sign language, are excluded. Second, they argue, Hockett's system focuses on the code rather than the users of that code, and it is the cognitive abilities of the users that allow us to differentiate human language from what can be complex and impressive animal communication systems. For example, there is an element of semanticity in some animal calls. Vervet monkeys use a system of predator alarm calls, with distinct calls for snakes, eagles and leopards (Seyfarth et al., 1980). The calls are more likely to be made in the presence of other monkeys and, in particular, in the presence of kin (Cheney & Seyfarth, 2005). This use of specific calls by animals is referred to as **functional reference** and the information contained in the signal allows the signaller's **conspecifics** to react appropriately. However, there is little flexibility in the use of these calls. By contrast to human language, animal systems tend to be tied to the current context. In the vervet monkeys' signalling system, the issuing of an alarm call is triggered by the presence of a perceived threat, but the calls cannot be used flexibly outside of that context. As Harley (2010) noted, there is no way to communicate 'I saw that eagle earlier' or 'Bob says he saw a leopard'. This is explored further in Box 10.1.

> **Functional reference**
> the use by animals of a specific call to stand for a specific object or threat.
> **Conspecifics**
> members of the same species.

Hockett's system also gives little sense of an order of priority, which, again, a focus on the cognitive abilities of the user would provide. For example, Bickerton (2014) identifies displacement, rather than arbitrariness or semanticity, as 'the road into language' (p. 93) and others have also argued that displacement, and the 'mental time travel' it allows, is critical to language (Corballis, 2017).

  Box 10.1 Research Close Up: Symbolic communication in non-human animals – vervet monkey alarm calls

Source: Seyfarth et al. (1980).

INTRODUCTION

© Chad Wright Photography/Shutterstock

Alarm signalling is an important capability for social animals. Animal communication systems demonstrate a striking diversity in how information about threats can be communicated to others in the group. The alarm calls of vervet monkeys (*Chlorocebus pygerythrus*) have been studied for many decades as a classic example of semantic communication in non-human animals. In order to communicate about a threat, vervet monkeys give acoustically distinct calls for different predators. These sounds bear an arbitrary relationship to their referent – they are not, for example, a mimicking of the predator. When other members of the group hear the alarm call, their responses are appropriate to the predator referred to. Seyfarth et al. (1980) demonstrated that there are distinct calls for leopards, eagles and snakes, which can be readily distinguished and which produce appropriate reactions in other group members.

For example, monkeys hearing the alarm call for 'eagle' look upwards, while those hearing the call for 'snake' look down. These responses occur reliably even when the predator is not itself present.

METHODS

Seyfarth et al. conducted a detailed observational study over a period of 14 months with three groups of free-ranging vervet monkeys in Amboseli National Park in Kenya. The groups contained a mean of 4 adult males and 7.6 adult females, 6.2 juveniles and 6.5 infants. The researchers collected recordings of vocalizations over an extended period of time while observing the individual monkeys verbalizing in context. This resulted in field recordings of more than 100 alarm calls. These could be categorized into acoustically distinct patterns for various predators; three of the most used calls referred to leopards, eagles and snakes. The researchers observed an appropriate adaptive response associated with the distinctive calls. The recordings of alarm calls were then played back to the monkey groups in the absence of the predator to examine whether it was the call itself or the predator's presence that elicited the adaptive response. The recordings were played back on occasions when the monkeys were on the ground and in the trees. Issues such as amplitude and call length were controlled for.

RESULTS

The results showed that alarm calls elicited two types of response. After a recording was played back, male and female monkeys of all age groups looked towards the sound and scanned their surroundings. They also produced a distinct set of responses, with different behaviours for different predators and depending on whether they were on the ground or in the trees. For example, when the monkeys were on the ground, the 'leopard' call caused them to run into the trees and snake alarms caused them to look downwards. Analysis of the calls themselves showed that younger monkeys gave alarm calls for a wider variety of species including species that posed no threat. By adulthood, the monkeys produced alarm calls only for salient threats. Similarly, infants used the snake alarm call for snakes and long thin objects. By adulthood, the call was confined to snakes.

DISCUSSION

Seyfarth and colleagues' seminal study showed that vervet monkey alarm signalling demonstrated semanticity and arbitrariness, two features of symbolic communication. It also showed the development of calls over age groups, with error patterns reminiscent of the over-extension errors seen in human language development. A more recent study by Price et al. (2015) provided a detailed quantitative analysis of the acoustic structure of vervet alarm calls and confirmed that the calls are predator- and context-specific. These studies show that elements of language-like communication exist in other species. They also, however, demonstrate some key differences in the communication systems of humans and non-human animals.

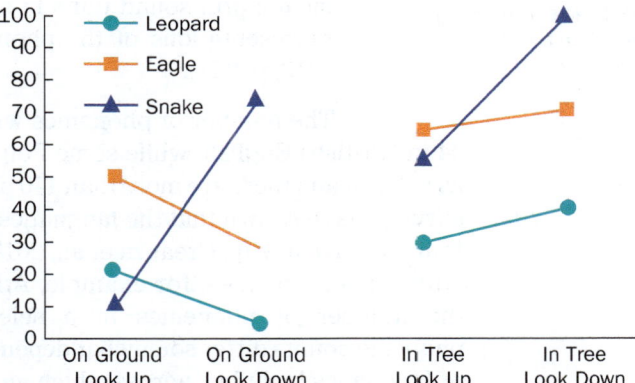

Figure 10.2 Reactions to vervet monkey alarm calls.
The graph shows the looking responses for monkeys to playbacks of alarm calls for leopards, eagles and snakes. Data show incidences when monkeys looked up or down when on the ground or in a tree. Data show the percentage of trials in which at least one individual showed a response for longer in the 10 seconds after playback than in the 10 seconds before.

Source: Data from Seyfarth et al. (1980), Table 1.

Many animal systems use vocalization as a means of communication. Non-vocal animal communication can also be incredibly sophisticated, rich in detail and sensitive to context. For example, the honey bee (*Apis mellifera*) uses a 'figure of eight' shaped dance, referred to as the 'waggle dance', to signal information about the location, distance and quality of a food source (Von Frisch, 1962). The dance can be adjusted to provide additional information. Bees that encountered danger or overcrowding at a food source can use a stop signal vibration to interrupt the 'waggle dancer', and cause her to terminate her dance and produce a distinctive freezing response. This warns the bees' nest mates and results in reduced foraging at the particular location (Kietzman & Visscher, 2015). The stop signal can even encode the level of threat. For example, Tan et al. (2016) found that stop signalling increased as the size of the predator, and therefore the threat level, increased, comparing attacks on the bees by large and small hornets. This demonstrates the complexity of alarm signalling in bee communication.

Components of Language

Language is a structured system that uses a finite set of sounds to construct words, sentences and ultimately conversations. The components of language, from the smallest to the largest parts, are phonemes, morphemes, syntax and discourse. In order to examine language processing, it is useful to consider these components independently. We will start with the sounds of language – phonemes.

Phonemes

> **Phonology**
> the system of sounds in language.
> **Phones**
> the basic speech sounds.
> **Phonetics**
> the study of speech sounds.
> **Phoneme**
> the smallest meaningful sound unit within a language.

Phonemes are the basic sounds that make up speech within a language and the term **phonology** refers to the system of sounds in a language. There are about 100 basic sound units, or **phones** (as listed in the International Phonetic Alphabet), that can be used to make up words. This represents the full set of available sounds; the study of these raw sounds is called **phonetics**. No one language uses all these sounds; instead, languages use a subset of phones. The sounds within a language are called **phonemes**. These are the smallest meaningful sound units in a language or, more precisely, 'abstract mental representations of the phonological units of a language' (Fromkin et al., 2018, p. 224).

The number of phonemes within a language varies considerably. There are 44 in (British) English, while some Polynesian languages (e.g., Hawaiian) have as few as a dozen and there are more than 140 phonemes in some African languages. Large-scale surveys have shown that the languages with the largest phoneme inventories are to be found in Africa (e.g., Creanza et al., 2015), an intriguing pattern from the perspective of language origins (see, for example, Atkinson, 2011; Fleming, 2017). Table 10.4 shows the number of phonemes in a selection of languages. The ranges show that phoneme counts differ somewhat depending on the data sources, sampling and varieties of languages included, across which an average can be calculated. For example, Swiss German has a higher phoneme count than standard German, and British English and Australian English have more phonemes than American English. A useful online database of phoneme inventory data has been made available by Moran and McCloy (2019) and illustrates the complexity involved in computing phoneme counts.

> **Aspirated**
> aspirated consonants are pronounced with a small puff of air, depending on their position in a word.

Basic vowel sounds occur in all languages, but consonants can be used differently and are perceived differently. For example, in English, there is no meaningful difference between the **aspirated** (i.e., said with a puff of air)

Table 10.4 The Estimated Number of Phonemes in a Sample of Languages

Language	Number of phonemes[1]	Range[2]
German	51	37–56
English	44	33–45
Dutch	39	26–58
French	36	32–42
Hawaiian	13	13–19

1. The number of phonemes is taken from Tambovtsev and Martindale, 2007, Table 1, with counts based on running texts of fictional prose.
2. The ranges of phoneme estimates are taken from the PHOIBLE database, which reports counts for language varieties including creoles.

/p/ sound in *pin* and the unaspirated /p/ in *spin*, but in Thai two distinct phonemes are created. (Note that by convention phonemes are shown between slashes, to differentiate the phoneme /p/ from the written letter p, for example.) Similarly, in English the /t/ sounds in *tea* and in *trip* are different phones, but these are treated as one phoneme; if you substitute the *t* sounds, the pronunciation may sound a little odd, but it is still the same word. Phonemes also change as a function of the surrounding sounds in words and in sentences, an effect referred to as **co-articulation**. Different phones that are treated as the same phoneme within a language are called **allophones**. Phonemes therefore do not correspond directly to physical sounds; rather they are 'abstract representations of the phonological units of a language, the units used to represent the forms of word in our mental lexicons' (Fromkin et al., 2003, p. 285). A phoneme is a rather subjective category that is recognized as meaningful by the speakers of a language, but is not necessarily constant as objectively measured (see Chapter 11).

Co-articulation the tendency for a speech sound to be influenced by sounds preceding or following it.
Allophones phonetic variants of the same phoneme.

The ability to perceive the difference between two allophones is evident at a very young age (Hohne & Jusczyk, 1994) and decreases with age (e.g., Iverson et al., 2003), suggesting a critical period beyond which the adult is 'tuned' to the sounds of his or her native language. While a child can discriminate between the full set of phones, an adult generally cannot. A child who is exposed to a second language can acquire native-like ability and accent, while the parents, if coming late to the language, may struggle to acquire it and never acquire a native-like accent (see Bongaerts et al., 1995; Dewaele, 2009; Singleton, 2001). For example, the difference between /l/ and /r/ sounds in English is not readily discriminated in Japanese, where /l/ and /r/ are treated as allophones (Ingram, 2007). While young children can appreciate the difference, by adulthood this ability is reduced. This reduction in discrimination with linguistic experience may serve to reduce the ambiguity in the incoming speech signal, facilitating language comprehension, an issue we return to in Chapter 11.

Chapter 11, p374

Chapter 11, p378

Phonological and **phonotactic rules** describe which sounds can go together in a given language. For example, in English, a /t/ sound does not follow a /b/ sound and [ng] can occur at the end of the word (as in 'king') but not at the beginning. These rules differ across languages so that sounds that are 'natural' and easy to produce and discriminate in one language may not be so easy for adult speakers of another language. Speech segmentation relies on knowledge of word boundaries using information about phonotactic probabilities in a language (see Chapter 11).

Phonotactic rules stipulate which combinations of sounds are 'permitted' in a language.

Changing a phoneme within a word, for example *bat* and *pat*, changes the meaning of that word. This is an example of a **minimal pair**, so called

Minimal pair a pair of words in a language that differ in just one sound.

because the words differ by just one phoneme. All spoken languages use vowels and consonants, but, as outlined above, the exact set used varies across languages. Maddieson (1984) examined a 300-language sample and found that the number of consonants varied from 6 to 95 sounds, with a mean of 23, while vowel sounds varied from 3 to 47, with a mean of 9.

Morphemes

> **Morphemes**
> the meaning units of language.
> **Morphology**
> the level of linguistic analysis concerned with morphemes and their role within words.
> **Syntax**
> the rules governing the ways words can be combined to create meaningful sentences.
> **Free morpheme**
> a morpheme that can stand alone as a word.
> **Bound morpheme**
> a morpheme that cannot form a word on its own, but forms a word when attached to a free morpheme.
> **Inflectional morpheme**
> serves a grammatical function, changing the case or tense of a word for example.
> **Derivational morphemes**
> create new words with new meaning when added to a stem.
> **Content words**
> words that provide meaning to the sentence; these contrast with function words, which do the grammatical work of the sentence.

Morphemes are the meaning units of a language. They are the building blocks of words. A single word may consist of several morphemes. The term **morphology** refers to the study of the rules in a language according to which words can be constructed. Morphology can be considered as a special case of **syntax** (see below).

In English, regular plural nouns are created by adding –s to the end of a word, for example, *one car* but *two cars*; *one horse, two horses*, etc. In these examples, there is one morpheme in the singular form (*car*) but two in the plural (*cars*), the stem or root word (car) and the plural suffix inflection (–s). The noun *car* is an example of a **free morpheme**, as it can occur on its own, whereas the plural form –s is a **bound morpheme**, because it does not carry meaning unless it is attached to a free morpheme. Here, the –s is an example of an **inflectional morpheme**; it serves a grammatical function but does not change the syntactic category of the word to which it is attached (*car* is still a noun when the –s is added to make *cars*). Similarly, the verb endings –ed and –ing are inflectional morphemes. Some bound morphemes, like –ify, –ish, –able and –ment, are **derivational morphemes**, as they create new words with new meaning when added to a stem. They can change the grammatical category of the word. For example, the verb *develop* becomes a noun when you add –ment to give *development*. Words can be altered by adding a morpheme to the start of the word (a prefix) or to the end (a suffix), and language-specific rules govern the ways in which words can be altered. The verb *depend* becomes *dependence* when we add the suffix –ence, meaning 'condition' or 'state'; adding the prefix –in, meaning 'not', yields *independence*, and so on.

Such alterations apply only to content words (e.g., nouns, adjectives and verbs); these are open class words that can be altered or invented as usage changes. In some languages, inflections on **content words** can be particularly informative. In Hungarian, for example, the morpheme at the end of the word indicates the word's role in the sentence, and codes whether it is a direct or indirect object. For example, consider these sentences in English and in Hungarian (example from Hoff, 2005):

The boy gave a book to the girl.

A fiú egy könyvet adott a lánynak. (The boy a book gave the girl.)

> **Direct object**
> in a sentence is the receiver of an action denoted by the verb.
> **Indirect object**
> in a sentence states to or for whom (or what) the action of the verb affected.

Here, 'book' is the **direct object** in the sentence (it is given), while girl is the **indirect object** (the book is given to the girl). While in English we tend to rely on word order, in most cases, to understand the role of the word in the sentence, in the Hungarian sentence above the morphemes *et* at the end of 'könyvet' and *nak* at the end of 'lánynak' give the role of the word. In this example, content words are altered to indicate the word's role in the sentence; in grammatical terms the inflections are accusative and dative case markers, respectively.

Function words, the words that do the grammatical work of a sentence, do not change (prepositions, for example; see Table 10.2) – they are a closed class of morphemes. As we will see, content words and function words are to some extent treated differently in language processing.

Semantics and the lexicon

Morphemes make up words, which in turn make up our vocabulary. Our knowledge of words and their meanings are stored in a kind of mental dictionary called the **mental lexicon**. The lexicon is a part of the **semantic memory** system (see Chapter 7). It holds our store of words and associated knowledge, and links words with our general knowledge about concepts and the world. From this store, we normally have immediate access to target words as we construct a sentence. Only occasionally will we experience difficulty in calling a target word to mind, a temporary failure referred to as the **tip-of-the-tongue** effect (more on this later in this chapter).

> **Function words**
> provide grammatical structure that shows how content words relate to each other within a sentence.
> **Mental lexicon**
> our store of knowledge about words and their uses.
> **Semantic memory**
> memory for facts and knowledge about the world.
> **Tip-of-the-tongue**
> a temporary inability to access a known word.

It is difficult to estimate the size of an adult's lexicon. Estimates vary depending on how a word is defined and what level of knowledge is required. What is the unit of measurement? Should we count words that a person recognizes as a word, even if they cannot define it or use it in a sentence? In addition, words within languages are constantly added to and used in new ways. At the time of writing, the COVID-19 pandemic has introduced to everyday use terms such as 'flatten the curve', 'social distancing', 'R-numbers', 'lockdown', 'self-isolating', 'cocooning', 'superspreaders', and even 'covidiots' and 'quarantinis'. Some studies suggest that adults know about 70,000 words (e.g., Nagy & Anderson, 1984), while other estimates put the figure closer to 20,000 word families, where a word family consists of a base word (**lemma**), and inflected and derived forms (e.g., Goulden et al., 1990). A large-scale crowdsourcing experiment by Brysbaert et al. (2016) estimated that the average 20-year-old native speaker of American English knows 42,000 lemmas, while the average 60 year old knows 48,200 lemmas.

> Chapter 7, p218

> **Lemma**
> an uninflected word from which inflected words can then be derived.
> **Word**
> the smallest unit of grammar that can be meaningfully produced on its own; it can consist of one or more morphemes.

Words are symbols; they are meaningful sounds and generally have a particular referent. A word might be defined as 'the smallest unit of grammar that can stand on its own as a complete utterance' (Crystal, 1997, p. 440); in writing, words are generally separated by spaces. People also use other meaningful sounds, though not all are words. For example, we might use a groan to signal disagreement or a yawn to signal boredom, but these are not words. A few words are not referential, that is they have no clear referent – greetings and social conventions (e.g., saying *hello*) for example.

The question of what words mean and how they relate to one another raises some complex issues. **Semantics** refers to the meaning of words and morphemes, and the relationship between the words we use and the objects they refer to in the world.

> **Semantics**
> the study of meaning.

Syntax

We construct novel sentences when we speak; we do not generally repeat back or 'parrot' previous productions. Imagine you are telling a story to some friends when another person joins the group and you have to start your story over. The chances are, though the meaning or gist of your story will not change, the exact sentences you use

> **Productivity of language**
> the ability to generate novel utterances.

> **Syntax**
> the rules governing the ways words can be combined to create meaningful sentences.
>
> **Phrase**
> a group of words referring to a particular idea.
>
> **Sentences**
> can be thought of as a linguistic representation of a complete thought, and in writing is marked with an end point punctuation mark such as a full stop, question mark or exclamation point.
>
> **Slang**
> an informal pattern of speech that is considered to be 'non-standard'.
>
> **Subject**
> of a sentence is the word or words that gives what the sentence is about or performs the action.
>
> **Object**
> of a sentence is the word or words that receives the action, or is acted on, by the subject of the sentence.
>
> **Homesign**
> a gestural language system that emerges through use by linguistically isolated deaf persons.
>
> **Recursion**
> the ability to extend sentences infinitely by embedding phrases within sentences.

will differ. This reflects the **productivity** of human language; we do not rely on rote or stock phrases, or on memory for practised utterances. Instead we create new sentences as and when we need them. This is evident from the earliest stages of syntactic development in young children.

Two aspects of the language system allow us to use language productively: syntax and morphology. The term **syntax** describes the rules that determine the construction of **phrases** and **sentences** in a language. Syntax relates to grammar, but is distinct from the notion of 'prescriptive' grammar. Prescriptive grammar reflects conventions for sentence construction and is based on tradition and language prestige rather than language use. For example, split infinitives ('*to boldly go* where no one has gone before') and end-of-sentence prepositions ('prepositions are not good words to end a sentence *with*') violate conventions of prescriptive grammar, but are often found in everyday speech, and would not be considered to be ungrammatical as such. Similarly, **slang** may not always meet with approval, but will follow rules of syntax. The study of syntax reflects descriptive grammar – that is, it reflects how language is used.

Sentences follow a hierarchical structure and are made up of two parts: a noun phrase (NP), which contains a noun, often the **subject** of the sentence, and a verb phrase (VP), which contains the verb and conveys the 'action' of the sentence. For example, in the sentence 'Sarah drank the coffee', Sarah (the subject of the sentence) is the NP and 'drank the coffee' is the VP. Languages such as English, French, Italian and German use a subject–verb–object or SVO word order – that is, in a declarative (active voice) sentence the subject (or agent of the sentence) comes first, followed by the verb and then the **object** of the sentence. In other languages, such as Irish, Welsh and Scottish Gaelic, the verb comes first (VSO). Some languages, such as Russian, have flexible words orders. The order in which the words occur determines the meaning of the sentence; to use Pinker's (1994) example, 'dog bites man' and 'man bites dog' have very different meanings, and one sentence is newsworthy where the other is not (p. 83). The most common word orders are SOV and SVO (Greenberg, 1963) and although there are examples of the six possible types (SOV, SVO, VSO, VOS, OVS, OSV), OVS and OSV are extremely rare (e.g., Dryer, 2005), giving rise to interesting theories of the word order of an ancestral proto-language (see Gell-Mann & Ruhlen, 2011). This agent-first bias in world languages is not restricted to spoken languages. It is also found in the **homesign** produced by deaf signers with hearing parents (Goldin et al., 1990). It also appears in second languages acquired without explicit instruction (Klein & Perdue, 1997).

One key property of syntax underlies the productivity of sentence construction. **Recursion** refers to the repeated application of a rule and, using recursion, the same rule can be applied again and again to create a novel utterance. Recursion has been argued to be an essential property of human language (e.g., Chomsky, 1986). Embedded sentences make use of this property, and sentences can in principle (though not in practice) be extended indefinitely. For example, the English language nursery rhyme 'The house that Jack built' is an example of a cumulative rhyme using recursion:

> *This is the house that Jack built.*
>
> *This is the malt that lay in the house that Jack built.*

This is the rat that ate the malt that lay in the house that Jack built.

This is the cat that killed the rat that ate the malt that lay in the house that Jack built.

This is the dog that worried the cat that killed the rat that ate the malt that lay in the house that Jack built . . .

Recursion would seem to be a resilient property of human language as even young children who have been deprived of language input retain the ability to use recursion (Goldin-Meadow, 1982; see also Oesch & Dunbar, 2017). The extent to which recursion is uniquely human has been challenged, however. For example, songbirds have been shown to be sensitive to recursion, and can classify novel patterns accordingly and reliably reject 'ungrammatical' patterns (Gentner et al., 2006).

Discourse

Discourse refers to multi-sentence speech and includes dialogue, conversation and narrative. At this 'higher' level of language function, the social conventions that affect language processing become increasingly relevant and people rely on **schemas** (see Chapters 7 and 9) in order to process language. **Pragmatics** refers to the understanding of the communicative functions of language and the conventions that govern language use. At the level of discourse, the function of language in communicating directly and indirectly comes to the fore. A distinction is made between linguistic competence, which refers to our ability to construct sentences, and communicative competence, which refers to our ability to communicate a message effectively (Hymes, 1972). Language can be perfectly well formed, but if we fail to appreciate the social conventions governing its use, we may not communicate as we intended.

> **Discourse**
> multi-sentence speech and includes dialogue, conversation and narrative.
> **Schema**
> a framework that represents a plan or a theory, supporting the organization of knowledge.
> **Pragmatics**
> the understanding of the communicative functions of language and the conventions that govern language use.

Effective discourse is based on a shared understanding between those engaging in a conversation. For example, if two people are conversing and one asks the other a question, there is an implicit agreement that the response will be related to the question. Similarly, participants in a conversation are expected to adhere to the topic of the conversation. If someone wishes to deviate from the topic or to change the subject, it is customary to signal this change of focus, by prefacing the utterance with 'by the way . . .', for example.

> Chapter 7, p218
>
> Chapter 9, p294

Conversations require turn-taking and cooperation, and participants follow a set of implicit social conventions. A variety of verbal and non-verbal signals serve to regulate the conversation by indicating who speaks when and for how long. These turn-taking cues act to minimize overlap between speakers, and reduce gaps or silences in conversation (see Beattie, 1982). Conversational turn-taking has several features (Sacks et al., 1974). One party speaks at a time; the person speaking changes. The duration of a turn is not predefined; the order of turns also varies. Transitions between turns are coordinated; overlap is minimized. These patterns hold in the absence of face-to-face information – for example, in telephone conversations (De Ruiter et al., 2006) and in online communication (e.g., Degand & van Bergen, 2016). Turn-taking is also evident in the group communication of social animals (e.g., Demartsev et al., 2018).

Despite the differences in linguistic features across languages, there are striking universals in conversational turn-taking patterns. For example, Stivers et al. (2009) examined the extent to which there are cultural differences in turn-taking in everyday conversations. They tested two opposing hypotheses. The 'universal system' hypothesis predicts little cross-linguistic variability and predicts that most languages will use a 'minimal-gap minimal-overlap' convention, as in found in English. On the other hand, the 'cultural variability' hypothesis, based on anthropological accounts, holds that turn-taking practices differ considerably across languages and cultures. Stivers and colleagues analysed video recordings of informal conversations in 10 languages from five continents. The languages varied in structural properties (e.g., word order, grammar) and were drawn from different cultures, ranging from hunter–gatherer groups to large-scale industrialized societies. All conversations were spontaneous, informal conversations, with two to six participants. Questions and responses were timed and coded for their form and function, and coders judged whether the responses were delayed. Striking similarities emerged across the languages supporting a 'minimal-gap minimal-overlap' norm. While there was some variation across languages, the mean response time for a turn transition was very similar across languages. Furthermore, the factors that predicted the speed of a response were identical across the languages. When visible responses were made (e.g., a shake of the head, a nod), they occurred faster than speech in all the languages. Confirmation responses were faster than disconfirmation responses. Questions accompanied by a gaze received faster responses than those without, and answer responses (e.g., 'yes') were significantly faster than non-answer responses (e.g., 'I don't recall'). These data (while limited to question–response sequences) support strong universals in turn-taking patterns across languages and a common pattern whereby the gaps between turns, and overlaps, are minimized.

These fast responses reflect what is a cognitively complex and challenging feat. Levinson (2016, p. 14) has proposed that turn-taking is 'the elite capacity of our species', which emerged prior to human language – a proposition supported by the universal nature of turn-taking in humans and the existence of turn-taking, in vocal or gestural channels, in primate (and many other) species. Turn-taking lies at the intersection of language production and comprehension, and is only beginning to attract significant attention within cognitive psychology.

What kind of implicit rules guide discourse? Grice (1957, 1975) identified four rules or maxims that describe effective conversations and reflect the expectations of listeners. Grice's four maxims are:

1 *Maxim of quantity:* The speaker should provide enough information in order to be understood, but not too much information.
2 *Maxim of quality:* The speaker should provide accurate information.
3 *Maxim of relevance:* The speaker should provide information that is relevant to the current topic of conversation.
4 *Maxim of manner:* Ambiguity and vagueness should be avoided.

If the maxims are violated, more cognitive processing is required to determine the response, or the participants may have to backtrack or repair the conversation. Of course, violation of these rules can also form the basis of humour – hyperbole, sarcasm and irony violate the maxim of quality.

Thus far, when we consider the meaning of words we have treated this as what the word *denotes*, that is its literal meaning; a word denotes its referent. We are also able to communicate indirectly, however. If you were sitting next to an open window and someone said to you 'It is cold', the utterance might be taken as meaning 'Can you close the window?' We must also consider the connotations that words evoke. Connotation refers to the non-literal aspects of word meaning, and reflects social and cultural factors that affect the literal processing of word meaning. Words can be perceived as having a positive or negative connotation (see Jay & Danks, 1977). If you hear someone say, 'Bob eats like a pig', it is of course literally true, in that the action of eating (the movements of the jaw, and so on) is similar in animals; however, it is likely that something else is meant. It is likely that Bob is being insulted and the connotation created by the phrase could mean that Bob is a messy eater or is greedy. Similarly, words can attract a positive value through use and this affects understanding of their literal meaning. The word 'natural' is much used in advertising, for example, and its use relies on the fact that people perceive 'natural' as having a value: 'natural' is equated with 'good'. The many natural but life threatening infectious diseases that assail humanity do not seem to be evoked by the term, nor do 'natural disasters' spring to mind. (See Box 11.2 for some further discussion on how language shapes thinking.)

> Chapter 11, p388

Having considered the constituents of language we now move on to examine how language is put together so that phonemes, morphemes and syntax become discourse. Much of what we know about this process is derived from the study of speech errors.

SPEECH ERRORS

Speech is produced at a rate of about 15 speech sounds and two to four words per second (Levelt, 1989), and for the most part is fluent and well formed. Slips and errors in spontaneous speech are quite rare, with some studies finding errors less than once per 500 uttered sentences (Dell et al., 1997; Garnham et al., 1981; see also Levelt, 2001). Error rates are low despite the rapid rate at which sounds must be selected from a production vocabulary of about 20,000 words (Groome et al., 1999). When errors are made, they tend to be detected by self-monitoring and repaired (see Nooteboom & Quené, 2020). While errors are rare, hesitations and pauses in spontaneous speech are common. It is estimated that about 6 per 100 words uttered contain a disfluency (a normal interruption in speech) such as a pause, correction or a filler such as 'um' or 'er' (Fox Tree, 1995).

Many of the theories of speech production (some are outlined later in this chapter) originate from analyses of speech errors. Data about errors come from several sources. The first source involves examining temporary breakdowns in the system's functioning, which occur from time to time, under normal conditions. Speech errors such as slips of the tongue and tip-of-the-tongue effects (when we cannot fully access a target word from the lexicon) are examples of this type of 'malfunction'. Second, errors can be induced in the laboratory, by having people articulate very quickly, for example. Third, the study of acquired brain injury has shown how damage to certain brain areas affects speech and language processing. **Aphasia** is the term used for acquired disorders of language, a topic we return to later in this chapter. First, we look at hesitation and pauses in normal speech.

Hesitation and Pauses

Disfluencies such as pauses are more common than actual errors and vary with the situation and the individual. They are a natural characteristic of fluent speech. Estimates suggest that about 6 in 100 words are affected by disfluency (Fox Tree, 1995). These pauses can be silent or filled (common fillers include *um*, *ah* or *er*; see Maclay & Osgood, 1959, for an early account of their use). Filled pauses occur with less frequency than silent pauses (O'Connell & Kowal, 2004) and may serve to announce a delay in speech (Clark & Fox Tree, 2002). During pauses, the speaker plans the articulation

Aphasia
the term given to a group of language disorders that occur following brain injury.
Disfluency
a hesitation or disruption to the normal fluency of speech. By contrast, the term 'dysfluency' is used to refer to an abnormal disruption to fluency, such as following brain damage. The use of the prefix 'dys-' signals 'abnormal'.

of their next words (Butterworth, 1980). Goldman-Eisler (1968) found that when participants were instructed to speak about a given topic, pause duration accounted for as much as half of the total time (although the method used to arrive at this estimate has been questioned; O'Connell & Kowal, 2004). The use of pauses varies with context, task demands and from individual to individual. Schachter et al. (1991) found that pauses in academic lectures varied with discipline, with science lecturers producing fewer pauses than humanities lecturers. This may reflect the more precise terminology employed by scientists; if there are fewer words to choose from, word choice is facilitated. This is consistent with research showing that science lectures and publications contain fewer different words compared to humanities sources (Schachter et al., 1994). Pauses within **clauses** and sentences would seem to reflect formulation of ideas and word selection (Velmans, 2009).

> **Clause**
> a part of a sentence containing a subject and verb.

Some disfluencies may facilitate comprehension. For example, Fox Tree (2001) found that hearing an 'uh' aided listeners' recognition of subsequent words, suggesting that some disfluencies may act as cues that direct listeners' attention towards a particular word. Hesitations and other cues have also been studied as potential cues to deception, as is explored in Box 10.2.

Box 10.2 Practical Application: Using speech cues to detect deception

There is a widespread misconception that a liar can be identified from his or her demeanour, that certain behavioural cues reliably indicate when someone is deceptive. In the criminal courts, jurors make this assumption every day. In fact, detection of deception is very challenging – the average person cannot detect lies reliably and often attends to the wrong cues when attempting to do so (for a review see DePaulo et al., 2003). Even people who might be considered to have considerable expertise are not always effective at lie detection. Ekman and O'Sullivan (1991) examined lie detection by a large sample of participants, including members of the US Secret Service, CIA, police, judges and non-experts. They showed participants a videotape of individuals who had been instructed to lie or tell the truth. Only the Secret Service personnel could detect lies at an above chance level, and the average accuracy of this group, at 64 per cent, was not as high as one might expect.

What can cognitive psychology tell us about how to detect lying? Research has examined the content of verbal statements (e.g., Vrij & Fisher, 2016) and the manner in which these statements are delivered. Someone who is lying, compared to someone telling the truth, tends to use a higher voice pitch, produces more hesitations and speech errors, speaks more slowly, uses fewer illustrators (e.g., hand gestures), and shows decreased hand, leg and foot movements (Vrij et al., 2001). The content of their speech also differs, with fewer details compared to a true account, for example (Vrij, 2004). These features are associated with the increased cognitive load involved in lying and are also observed when people engage in a cognitively complex or challenging task. Such findings suggest that cognitive techniques might give rise to useful applications in lie detection. However, developing ecologically valid tests of these methods has proved challenging.

Many studies of lie detection involve laboratory manipulations, with 'liars' instructed to deceive under various conditions. In real-life, lying presents differently, particularly when the stakes are high. Vrij and Mann (2001) analysed a series of videotaped police interviews with a man accused of murder. The man initially denied that he was involved in the murder, but subsequently confessed and was convicted. The videotaped interviews therefore allowed the researchers to examine the man's behaviour while lying (pre-confession) and telling the truth (during his confession). While lying, the man produced longer pauses, slower speech and had more speech disturbances than when telling the truth, features that are consistent with the heavier cognitive load associated with lying. In a second part to the study, police officers watched video fragments from the same interviews. Their accuracy rate was 64 per cent, which was significantly above chance; however, this resulted from good detection of truth rather than accurate detection of lies. In fact, accuracy of lie detection (at 57 per cent) was not above chance, and the individual differences in lie detection were striking.

Hesitations and pauses, however, are not always reliable indicators. A study by Whelan and colleagues (2014) examined a range of verbal and non-verbal cues in video footage of public appeals for help in finding missing persons. The video recordings were collected from news sites, and cases were selected for analysis if they met criteria consistent with overwhelming evidence of involvement in the death or disappearance of the victim. These criteria were selected from published sources and included scientific evidence (e.g., soil traces, pollen traces, clothing fibres, blood), DNA evidence, CCTV footage, knowledge of the crime, confessions and medical evidence. This initial analysis resulted in 32 recordings being selected for analysis, of which 16 were categorized as deceptive and 16 as honest.

Based on the literature, the researchers identified a number of verbal and non-verbal cues as the focus of the analysis; note than only some of these are reported here. Four types of verbal cue were selected. Equivocation was defined as words or phrases that conveyed uncertainty or vagueness; examples include 'kind of', 'possibly', 'maybe' and 'a little. Speech errors, including grammatical errors, and words and sentence fragments, were noted. Phrase repetitions were counted. Finally, filled pauses (speech sounds made as we construct the next sentence or part of a sentence), such as 'uh', 'um' and 'er', were recorded. The non-verbal cues included gaze aversion, head shaking and shrugging. A rater coded the recordings noting these cues, and a second rater analysed a sample to ensure interrater reliability. Raters were blind as to the condition (deceptive or honest).

The results revealed statistically significant differences between the deceptive and honest conditions in equivocation, gaze aversion and head shaking (Table 10.5). The difference in speech errors did not reach statistical significance in this case, which may reflect the combination of spontaneous and prepared statements made. The strongest effect was evident for gaze aversion, a finding that is out of line with the wider literature in this area (e.g., Mann et al., 2004) but may reflect the high-stake and real-world scenario here – participating in a public, televised, appeal about a missing person. The study points to the need to consider multiple cues, and the difficulties inherent in analysing naturalistic data, in the context of criminal deception.

Table 10.5 Percentage Means and Effect Sizes for Selected Verbal and Non-Verbal Cues

Cue type	Cue	Deceptive mean	Honest mean	Effect size (d)
Verbal	Equivocation*	4.69	2.03	0.77
	Speech errors	4.9	2.89	0.68
	Phrase repetition	4.84	4.72	0.03
	Filled pauses	1.47	1.10	0.22
Non-verbal	Gaze aversion*	59.35	23.53	1.32
	Head shaking*	25.26	11.04	0.73
	Shrugging	2.19	1.77	0.09

Note:* denotes a statistically significant difference between conditions.
Source: Data from Whelan et al. (2014), Table 2.

Slips of the Tongue

> **Parapraxes** are slips of the tongue or other actions originally thought to reflect unconscious motives.

In *The Psychopathology of Everyday Life*, Freud (1914) treated speech errors as a particular class of **parapraxes** (action slips). While his emphasis was on supposed underlying repressed thoughts, he recognized that errors could be informative as regards language processing, asking whether 'the mechanisms of this disturbance cannot also suggest the probable laws of the formation of speech' (p. 71). So-called 'Freudian slips' are errors based on a substitution of a semantically or phonologically similar word (see Table 10.6) and, most researchers now agree, they reflect the cognitive processes underlying sentence formulation rather than unconscious motivations or conflicts (e.g., see Norman, 1981; Reason, 1990, 2000). Speech errors can be classified by the level of speech (e.g., phoneme level, word level) and the mechanism of error (e.g., exchange, substitution; see Harley, 2006), as shown in Table 10.6.

Fromkin's (1971) analysis provided the first systematic account of error types. Fromkin showed that when errors occur they are not random; in fact they are systematic and are highly informative as to the nature of the underlying processing. The majority of speech errors are sound-based and errors tend to occur at one linguistic level (e.g., affecting phonemes or morphemes). Types of error are summarized in Table 10.6.

Analysis of speech errors points to the importance of the phrase as a unit of production, as errors rarely jump across phrase boundaries. The vast majority of morpheme exchanges occur within clauses (Garrett, 1975). Errors preserve the consonant–vowel distinction and phonological errors are in keeping with the phonological constraints of

Table 10.6 Examples of Types of Speech Error

Type	Description	Example(s)
Anticipation	Substitutions of a sound in anticipation of a sound that occurs later in the phrase; a full word can also be produced too early within a sentence	cuff of coffee [cup of coffee]
Perseveration	The repetition of a sound from a previous part of the utterance	proliperation [proliferation]
Transposition/exchange errors (also called metatheses or spoonerisms)	Transposition of two segments; exchange errors can also affect words, where two words swap places in the sentence	You hissed all my mystery lectures [missed all my history lectures] You have tasted a whole worm [wasted a whole term]
Blend	A non-word is made based on two semantically related words	mownly [mainly/mostly] swinged [switched/changed]
Additions	A sound is added in	similarily [similarly]
Deletions/omissions	A sound is omitted	slit second [split second]
Semantic substitutions including Freudian slips	Retrieval of an incorrect but semantically related target	This room is too hot [cold]
Phonological substitutions or malapropisms including Freudian slips	A phonologically similar word is selected in error; mixed errors, in which the target word and error share both semantic and phonological features, can also occur	projects [products] There's a pest in every class [pet] (this could be a deletion)

a given language (Fromkin, 1971). Exchange errors show a **lexical bias** in that they are more likely to result in a word than a non-word (Rapp & Goldrick, 2000) – for example, 'barn door' becoming 'darn bore' (Nooteboom & Quené, 2008). The frequency of lexical bias has been disputed; some researchers have argued that it is not common in spontaneous speech and is more likely to be induced experimentally (e.g., Garrett, 1980), but others argue that it also applies to natural speech (Dell & Reich, 1981). It would seem that the lexical bias effect reflects both immediate feedback between speech sounds and word forms (Dell, 1986) and monitoring of inner speech producing a real word bias (Levelt et al., 1999). In other words, non-word errors are more readily detected and repaired, while real word errors can 'slip through the net' and remain undetected before being uttered (Nooteboom, 2010).

> **Lexical bias**
> a tendency for phonological speech errors to result in real words.

Content words tend to exchange with content words and function words with other function words. Harley (2008) found no instances of content words and function words exchanging in a corpus of several thousand speech errors. Function words and bound morphemes (such as inflections) are generally left in place when a content word or morpheme moves, a pattern referred to as morpheme stranding. The following examples from Fromkin (1971) illustrate:

- nerve of a vergious breakdown [verge of a nervous breakdown]
- a weekend for maniacs [maniac for weekends].

Boomer and Laver (1968) found that stressed and unstressed syllables did not exchange with each other; errors were consistent with the stress pattern in the utterance. Furthermore, transpositions generally stay within the same syntactic or morphological class (Fromkin et al., 2010). These patterns of error suggest a systematic process whereby a sentence is constructed such that 'the word's skeleton or frame and its segmental content are independently generated' (Levelt, 1992, p. 10) and show that speech production is highly rule governed (Fromkin et al., 2010).

Transposition errors, or metatheses, have been noted for centuries, and have become associated, perhaps unfairly, with the Reverend William Archibald Spooner, who was warden of New College, Oxford, in the early 1900s. Many transposition errors were attributed to Spooner and this class of error has therefore become known as '**spoonerisms**'. Among the errors attributed to the Reverend Spooner (see also Table 10.6) are the following:

> **Spoonerisms**
> a type of speech error in which sound components of words are transposed during their utterance, resulting in a humorous error.

- you were fighting a liar in the quadrangle [target – lighting a fire]
- work is the curse of the drinking class [target – drink is the curse of the working class]
- the queer old dean [target – the dear old queen].

Many such Spoonerisms are apocryphal or exaggerated; if they were as frequently produced as some commentators have supposed it might suggest an underlying pathology (Potter, 1980).

Speech errors are generally collected from spontaneous speech, either by recording speech or having participants note their own errors in diaries, and large collections of speech errors can be accumulated in this way (e.g., Fromkin, 1971; Harley, 2008). An early example of such a **corpus** is provided by Meringer and Meyer's (1895) analysis based on a collection of an estimated 8,800 errors in German. Errors can also be induced experimentally, with various techniques developed to elicit errors. For example, the SLIP

> **Corpus**
> a collection or database of linguistic data, often nowadays held in electronic form.

(Spoonerisms of Laboratory-Induced Predisposition) technique introduced by Baars and Motley (1974) aims to force transposition errors in research participants within a controlled setting. A number of web-based tools are also now available for volunteers to log their own errors, making a large sample of speech errors, from different languages, available for future research (e.g., see Vitevitch et al., 2015).

The Tip-of-the-Tongue State

Another type of speech error that has been induced experimentally with some success is the tip-of-the-tongue state. The tip-of-the-tongue (TOT) state is a temporary inability to access a word from memory. William James (1890, p. 251) described the TOT state as 'a gap that is intensely active. A sort of wraith of the name is in it, beckoning us in a given direction, making us at moments tingle with the sense of our closeness and then letting us sink back without the longed-for term.'

> **Proper nouns**
> names for specific people and places, typically written with a capital letter, such as Ken, Sandra and London.

Proper nouns are often affected, and particularly acquaintances' names (Cohen & Faulkner, 1986). Low-frequency words elicit more TOTs than do high-frequency words (e.g., Navarrete et al., 2015). TOTs may also recur on particular words (D'Angelo & Humphreys, 2015). When we experience a TOT, we can generally say whether we know the word and we may have access to some information about the word, such as its initial letter (e.g., Brown et al., 2013), what it sounds like, or whether it is a long or short word. Gesture production during the TOT state suggests knowledge of word meaning (e.g., Theocharopoulou et al., 2015). Some studies have suggested increased TOT states for positively valenced compared to negatively valenced targets (e.g., Cleary, 2019) and when the speaker is being observed or evaluated (James et al., 2018). In languages in which the noun has gender, this information can be available in the TOT state, showing that access to syntactic category information is preserved, although access to the specific phonological word form is unavailable (e.g., Vigliocco et al., 1997). This has implications for models of speech production, as will be discussed below.

> **Feeling-of-knowing**
> a subjective sense of knowing that we know a word; an example of metamemory – our knowledge about the contents of our memories.
> **Metacognition**
> awareness of one's own thoughts and cognitive processes.

In the TOT state the target word is known to us, but we (temporarily) cannot access it. However, we have a **feeling-of-knowing** about the target – that is, we are aware that we know the word, yet we cannot produce it. As such it is a **metacognitive** state (see also Chapter 5), in that we are aware of our failure to retrieve the word. In an influential review of research on the TOT state, Brown (1991) noted that the TOT state:

- is universal
- occurs about once a week
- increases in frequency with age
- frequently affects recall of proper names

> Chapter 5, p172

- often involves an available initial letter
- is often accompanied by other words
- is resolved on almost half of occasions.

The TOT state is a universal phenomenon, but as it increases in frequency with age, it is a frequent source of cognitive complaint and concern in older age groups (see Box 10.3). Research is beginning to examine whether TOT data might be used to discriminate between cognitively unimpaired adults and those with mild cognitive impairment, and a decline in phonological access in TOT would seem to be a particularly useful measure (e.g., Campos-Magdaleno et al., 2020).

Brown and McNeill (1966) were the first to induce the TOT state experimentally. They read participants' definitions of rare words and asked them to produce the word to which they were referring. For example, they read the definition 'a navigational instrument used in measuring angular distances, especially the altitude of sun, moon and stars at sea'. The target word in this case was 'sextant'. The inability to access low-frequency targets induced a TOT state in some participants (9 of 56 participants for this particular definition). Analysis of the incorrect words produced by participants showed that some information is available and that lexical retrieval can involve partial activation. For example, in the case of the target *sextant*, some of the errors included *sexton, sextet, compass* and *protractor*; these are phonologically or semantically related targets.

Bilinguals would seem to be more prone to the TOT experience (e.g., Gollan & Acenas, 2004), a finding that also applies in bilinguals who speak one language and sign another (Pyers et al., 2009). This latter finding suggests that phonological competition is not the source of the effect; it may be that competing lexical (semantic) activation increases the likelihood of a TOT state in bilinguals or it may be an effect due to different frequency of use in the languages. Importantly, the small differences in reaction times observed in the laboratory do not carry profound implications for everyday functioning of bilinguals and do not detract from bilinguals' advantages in other domains.

 Box 10.3 Research Close Up: Proper name retrieval in youth and mid-life

Source: Kljajevic & Erramuzpe (2018).

INTRODUCTION

Studies of the tip-of-the tongue (TOT) state reveal a clear advantage for young people in word retrieval and particularly in recall of proper names. The TOT effect becomes more frequent with age and for older people experiencing a TOT state the additional information that gives rise to a 'feeling-of-knowing' the word may be absent. For example, the older participant may not have access to the initial letter of the word or may not be able to say what the word sounds like, although they will be confident that they know the word but are temporarily denied access to it (see Bredart et al., 2002). Many studies have examined the TOT effect in older adults, but as yet there are few studies comparing retrieval of proper names in middle age and young adulthood. A study by Kljajevic and Erramuzpe (2018) addressed this lacuna by examining the TOT experience in young and middle-aged adults, and investigating whether any observed age differences were associated with differences in the structural integrity of the cerebral cortex.

METHOD

The sample consisted of 115 cognitively healthy middle-aged participants (average age 50 years) and 68 young adults (average age 25 years). Participants completed a TOT task in which they were presented with 50 pictures of famous people (actors, musicians, politicians, etc.). Each picture was shown on a computer screen for 500 ms and the participants' task was to name the person. There were three possible responses: (1) participants could signal that they knew the response – that is, that they could retrieve the name; (2) they could signal that they did not know the name of the person; and (3) a third possible response signalled that the participant knew the person but could not retrieve the name – this was a TOT response. 'Know' responses were coded as correct or incorrect depending on the name produced. **MRI** data

> **Magnetic resonance imaging (MRI)**
> a high-definition method for structural imaging using strong magnetic fields.

were also collected, and cortical thickness maps were computed, adjusting for gender differences and total intercranial volume. In addition, a number of regions of interest were examined, based on previous findings linking these areas to proper noun retrieval. These areas were the left anterior temporal lobe, left insula, and left superior and middle temporal gyri.

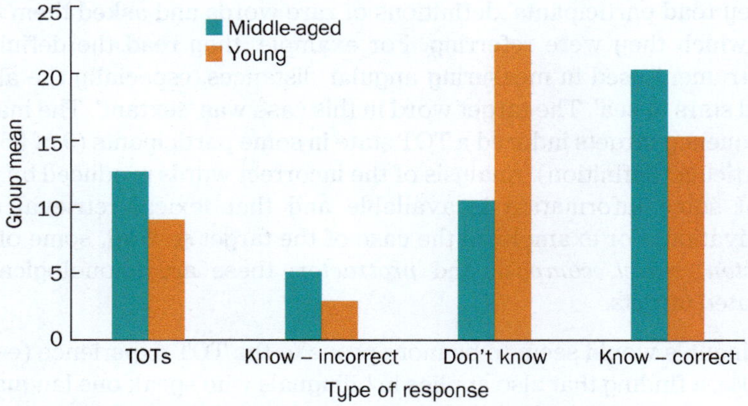

Figure 10.3 The groups' means for each type of response.
The mean responses for each of the four categories of response are shown. Data are derived from Kljajevic and Erramuzpe (2018), supplementary graph S, Figure 1.

RESULTS

The results from the TOT experiment showed statistically significant differences between the middle-aged group and the young group on all four recall response types (see Figure 10.3). The middle-aged participants experienced more TOT states, with on average 12.6, compared to an average of 9 for the younger participants. The middle-aged group produced more 'know – correct' responses but also more 'know – incorrect' responses. However, the younger group gave significantly more 'don't know' responses, with a mean of 22.1 compared to 10.5 for the middle-aged group, suggesting lower familiarity with the materials, but also lower likelihood of a TOT effect.

The neuroimaging data showed differences in structural integrity in a range of cortical areas, with the middle-aged group having lower grey matter density and thinner cortex relative to the younger group. However there were no associations between higher TOT scores in the middle-aged group and structural features of the brain regions previously identified as playing a role in proper noun retrieval. Instead, there were associations over a range of other areas.

DISCUSSION

Kljajevic and Erramuzpe's study showed that TOT states are more common in cognitively healthy middle-aged participants compared to the younger group. The older group also made more incorrect retrievals, while believing that they had produced the correct answer. In this study, while the younger participants had poorer knowledge of the famous persons shown in the test stimuli, and gave significantly more 'don't know' responses, they had better awareness of their lack of knowledge. The data show that while the younger group were less familiar with the materials used, they were also less likely to experience a TOT effect. This suggests that the decline in name retrieval evident in the TOT state is already under way by middle age. The imaging data point to the recruitment of a wide network during the naming task.

Several of the most influential theories of speech production have been based on analysis of speech errors. We will now look at three models of speech production: Garrett's and Dell's accounts, which are based on speech error data, and Levelt's account, which takes a different approach.

THEORIES OF SPEECH PRODUCTION

It is generally agreed that there are a number of stages to speech production (e.g., Levelt, 1989). The first, conceptualization, is a poorly understood process by which a thought forms and is prepared to be conveyed through language. The processes by which an abstract thought or idea becomes a verbal thought remain elusive (think, for example, of the stages before you say to yourself 'I wonder if I turned the oven off before leaving the house'). The second stage involves the formulation of a linguistic plan. The concept or proposition must be translated so that the thought becomes language and the sentence that we want to output is planned. Translating from concept to language also remains a mysterious process, and if the goal of such theories is, as Clark and Clark (1977, p. 10) suggested, 'to discover how speakers turn ideas into words', we are arguably no closer to the holy grail. Levelt (e.g.,1989) considers the formulation stage as comprising two substages. During the lexicalization substage, the words are selected from the mental lexicon. In order for this to occur the concept must connect with the abstract word form or **lemma**. The lemma contains semantic and syntactic information about the target word but does not yet specify its phonological form. Formulation also involves syntactic planning; during this substage the order in which the selected words will be output is decided. The third stage involves articulation of the plan. During this stage the sounds for the word are accessed, the **lexeme** is specified, giving the full phonological form of the word, and the motor programme for speech output is planned and articulated. In a final fourth stage, the output is monitored so that corrections can be made if necessary.

> **Lemma**
> an uninflected word from which inflected words can then be derived.
>
> **Lexeme**
> is the basic lexical unit that gives the word's morpho-phonological properties.

The theoretical approaches to understanding speech production have much in common. It is recognized that **clauses** seem to be an important structure for speech planning and that processing proceeds from the abstract concept to syntactical processing to precise phonological patterns. The various models of speech production differ in terms of the emphasis placed on these various components and in the extent to which they consider the processing stages to involve serial, parallel or interactive processing – that is, whether they favour a modular or interactive view of speech processing. Modular or serial theories posit a series of non-interacting stages, with different types of processing being completed at each stage (e.g., Fromkin, 1973; Garrett, 1980, 1982; Levelt et al., 1991). On the other hand, interactive or parallel theories (e.g., Dell, 1986; MacKay, 1987) propose a less constrained account, with multiple sources of information operating to influence speech output. The debate over which type of theory provides the more accurate account continues.

> **Clause**
> a part of a sentence containing a subject and verb.

Modular Theories of Speech Production

Garrett's model

Serial or modular theories propose that speech production progresses through a series of stages or levels, with different types of processing being completed at each level. According to Garrett's hierarchical model (e.g., 1980, 1982, 1992), speech is produced via a series of stages, proceeding in a top-down manner (see Chapter 2) so that processing at lower levels does not influence that at higher levels (see Figure 10.2). Garrett developed his model to address patterns of errors in speech production (see also Dell, 1986, described below).

> Chapter 2, p34

Figure 10.4 (overleaf) shows the various levels proposed by Garrett. At the inferential level, we conceptualize the message that we want to express. As noted previously, little is known about processing at this level or how the initial leap from thought to language-like representation might occur, particularly given that there may be a number of ways to express a thought. At the functional level, the syntactic and semantic framework of the sentence is constructed. At this stage, word exchanges would be predicted because the structure is present but the selected words, while activated, have not yet been

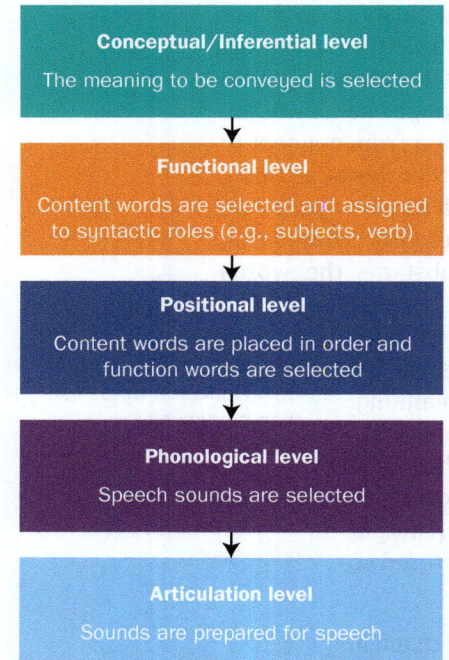

Figure 10.4 The stages of speech production proposed by Garrett (e.g., 1975).
At the inferential level, we conceptualize the message that we want to express. At the functional level, the syntactic and semantic framework of the sentence is constructed. At the phonological level the sounds for the content words are acquired.

> **Non-plan internal errors** occur when the intrusion is external to the planned content of the utterance.

allocated to their places within that structure or framework. Because the syntactic category of the word has already been determined, this model predicts that errors will not cross syntactic category (e.g., that nouns will swap with nouns but not nouns with verbs; verbs may swap with other verbs, though in reality verb exchanges are relatively rare). At the positional level, the words are allocated to positions within the syntactic frame. The function words are in place at this stage and so, where errors occur, bound morphemes tend to remain in their correct place (e.g., verb endings such as –ed and –ing). At the phonological level the sounds for the content words are acquired and sound errors can occur at this stage. In this model, the lexical bias effect described earlier in this chapter occurs during a later monitoring or editing stage where non-word errors are detected – word errors are more likely to 'slip through' undetected. The interactive models provide a rather different account of lexical bias, as we will see.

Evaluation

Garrett's model suggests that content and function words are treated differently, and this is supported by the data on errors. One might argue that the relative sparing of function words reflects their higher frequency in language use (e.g., see Stemberger, 1985), however bound morphemes have a lower frequency of use and yet are treated like function words in that they are retained in the syntactic frame of the sentence.

Garrett's model provides a good account of the speech error data. However, Garrett's stages operate independently of one another and therefore this model does not predict errors that occur 'across levels'. For example, a type of error called a **non-plan internal error** occurs when concepts from the message level intrude when articulating the sentence, specifying the words at the phonological level. For example, someone intending to say 'let's get a coffee' while standing outside the library might say 'let's get a book'. Some 'Freudian slips' fall into this category, as a suppressed thought might interfere with current output; by Freud's account this was always the case: 'A suppression of a previous intention to say something is the indispensable condition for the occurrence of a slip of the tongue' (Freud, 1922, p. 52). Such errors have led to more interactive accounts of the stages of processing, such as that of Dell and colleagues outlined later. Before we look at interactive models, however, another influential modular account is considered, Levelt's model.

Levelt's model

Levelt and colleagues (e.g., Bock & Levelt, 1994; Levelt, 1989; Levelt et al., 1999) have presented a number of computational models of speech production leading to the sequential system called Weaver++ (Weaver stands for Word-form Encoding by Activation and Verification). This model focuses on the production of single words rather than the construction and output of whole sentences – it considers, for example, how we access (and say) the word 'cat' when we see a picture of a cat. A series of stages follow sequentially, from conceptualization to articulation (see Figure 10.5). Levelt's theory is based mainly on latency data (e.g., reaction times to picture naming) rather than error patterns, in contrast to Dell's and Garrett's models.

The theory focuses on the lexical access aspects of speech production. In Weaver++, the first two stages of processing involve lexical selection. Three stages of form encoding follow, before articulation occurs. These two systems, for lexical selection and for form encoding, would seem to involve quite different processes and involve different areas of the brain (Levelt, 2001).

The first stage is conceptual preparation, which Levelt et al. (1999) define as 'the process leading up to the activation of a lexical concept' (p. 3). The second stage involves lexical selection: a lemma or abstract word is retrieved from the mental lexicon and its syntactic category is activated. A number of words might be primed based on meaning, with selection dependent on relative activation so that the more appropriate selection occurs. For example, if I am shown a picture of a horse and asked to name it, the concepts *horse* and *animal* might be activated. These concepts activate the corresponding lexical items in the lexicon. This is an abstract word or lemma, which is 'essentially the lexical item's syntactic description' (Levelt, 2001, p. 13464).

Levelt and colleagues' third stage involves morphological encoding. Once the lemma is selected, processing proceeds from the conceptual/syntactic domain to the phonological/articulatory domain; Levelt et al. recognize this as a crucial change. At this point, a TOT state can be produced – a lemma has been activated but the specific phonological form (lexeme) is not yet available. Because the lemma is a syntactic word, information about syntax is available, while the sound of the word is not yet accessed. This predicts the finding that in a TOT

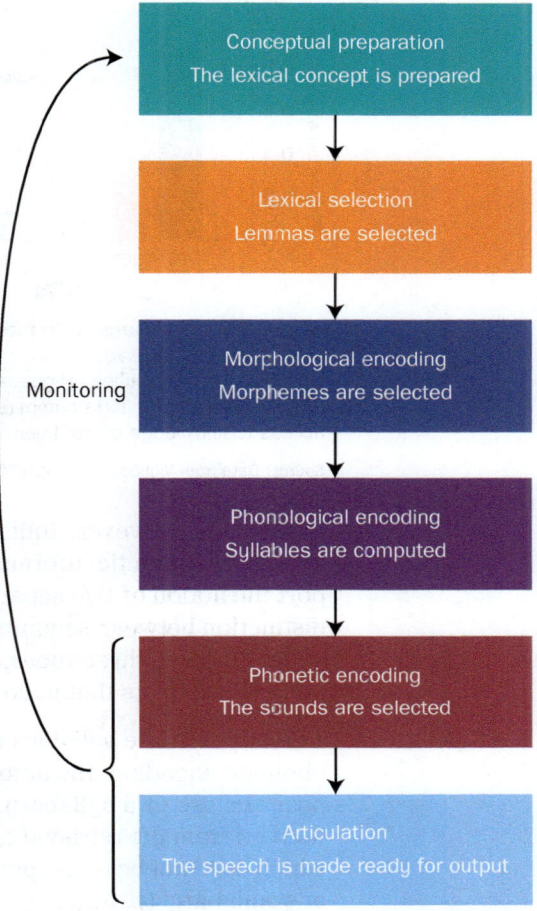

Figure 10.5 Levelt's model of speech production.
In parallel to the processing stages, output monitoring allows the speaker to detect and correct errors.

Source: Adapted from Levelt et al. (1999).

state a speaker has access to syntactic information, although they cannot produce the word. In many languages nouns have grammatical gender; this is unrelated to word meaning – that is, grammatical gender is a linguistic property unrelated to the conceptual properties of the referent. For example, in French *mouton* (sheep) is a masculine noun while *chèvre* (goat) is feminine. The word for 'milk' is masculine in French and Italian, and feminine in German, Dutch and Spanish. In languages with grammatical gender, information relating to noun gender can be activated in the TOT state, when the word itself is not accessible. Vigliocco et al. (1997) demonstrated this in Italian. Their participants were presented with definitions and asked to provide the corresponding word. Whenever a participant was unable to provide the word, they were asked to guess the gender of the noun (masculine/feminine), guess the number of syllables, give as many letters in the word as possible and state their position in the word, and report any other word that came to mind. Participants were subsequently shown the target word and asked whether it was the word they were thinking of. Vigliocco and colleagues found that noun gender was correctly reported 84 per cent of the time when participants were experiencing a TOT state (see Figure 10.6, overleaf). By contrast, when participants could not produce the word and later could not affirm that the provided word was the target, performance was at chance level (53 per cent).

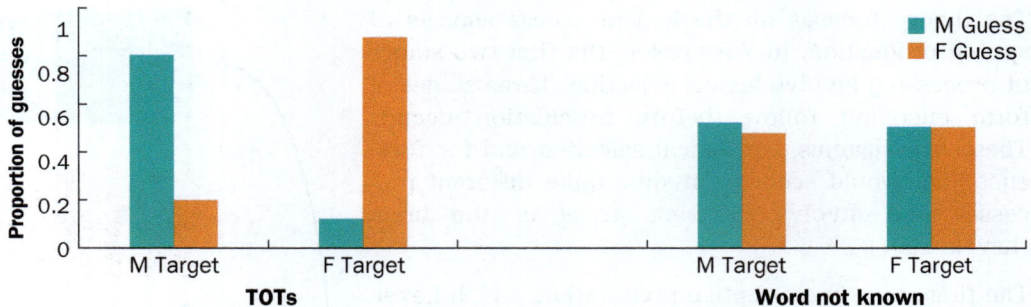

Figure 10.6 Responses to masculine and feminine target words for TOT words and words that could not be retrieved.
Distribution of masculine (M guess) and feminine (F guess) responses for masculine (M target) and feminine (F Target) words, for TOTs compared to words that were not retrieved (here labelled 'Word not known'), show access to knowledge of word gender for TOT words.

Source: Data from Vigliocco et al. (1997).

Sometimes, however, Italian speakers can access phonological information without accessing syntactic information (e.g., Miozzo & Caramazza, 1997), which does not support the notion of two separate stages for syntactic and phonological information – the distinction between semantic and phonological information remains. Processing at this stage involves three types of information: the word's morphology, its stress patterns and the segments that make up the word are activated.

At stage four the syllables that make up the word are computed. Stage five performs phonetic encoding: the actual speech sounds activate at this stage. Levelt et al. (1999) posit the use of a syllabary, with phonological information allowing word articulation derived from the retrieval of syllables. These are 'highly overlearned gestural patterns, which need not be recomputed time and again. Rather they are ready made in the speaker's syllabary' (p. 5).

The sixth and final stage is articulation. The phonological information is transferred to a motor plan, and executed by the articulatory system and speech musculature. The stages are presented in Figure 10.5.

The model considers the role of self-monitoring at multiple levels throughout the processing stages (Figure 10.5). This provides a mechanism for the detection of errors that allows us to repair speech, and involves the cognitive mechanisms involved in speech comprehension (see Chapter 11). Given the time course of corrections and repairs of speech errors, this monitoring process is likely to involve both internal and external channels (Wheeldon & Levelt, 1995; but see also Nozari et al., 2011). The precise means by which the mechanism operates and the attentional systems governing it are not elaborated.

Chapter 11, p374

Evaluation

Levelt's account shows how a series of specialized modules contribute to the process of speech production. It accounts for much data on speech production, including some patterns in bilingual speech. It also shows how speech might be monitored so that errors can be corrected, and there are interesting data supporting the contention that speech errors can be detected both through internal speech and external speech monitoring (e.g., Nooteboom & Quené, 2017, 2020). However, as a modular account, feedback between levels is limited. The retrieval of the word form occurs only after the lemma has been selected; there is no feedback from word form to lemma levels. However, some types of speech error suggest that feedback does occur. Sometimes, the target word and the error share both form and meaning information – for example, saying 'rat' when you meant 'cat' (Treiman et al., 2003). This suggests that there is interference from lower to higher levels; Levelt and colleagues explain such errors as resulting from a failure in the monitoring processes. However, interactive models account for these and some other types of speech errors more successfully. We now turn to one influential account of an interactive type.

Interactive Theories of Speech Production

Dell's model

The final model of speech production that we will consider is Dell's cascaded or spreading activation account (Dell, 1986, 1995; Dell & O'Seaghdha, 1991; Dell et al., 1997), which is based on connectionist principles (see Chapter 1). This model uses the concept of spreading activation in a lexical network to show how competing activation across different levels might predict speech errors. In this model, activation from one level can affect processing at other levels – that is, processing is interactive. Processing is also parallel such that information can be processed at the different levels at the same time. These features, interactive and parallel processing, differ from the features of the serial models such as Levelt's.

> Chapter 1, p2

There are four levels in Dell's model with processes corresponding to those described for Garrett's model above – that is, a semantic level, a syntactic level, a morphological (word) level and a phonological (sound) level. The semantic level is where we conceptualize what it is we want to say; at the syntactic level the structure of the sentence is devised; at the morphological level the morphemes that make up the target words are selected and at the phonological level the sounds that make up those words are activated.

Figure 10.7 illustrates the levels and connections. The connections between the layers allow bidirectional spreading of activation. That is, a word unit can activate the phonological units at the layer below (top-down spreading) and the semantic units at the layer above (bottom-up spreading; Dell & O'Seaghdha, 1991).

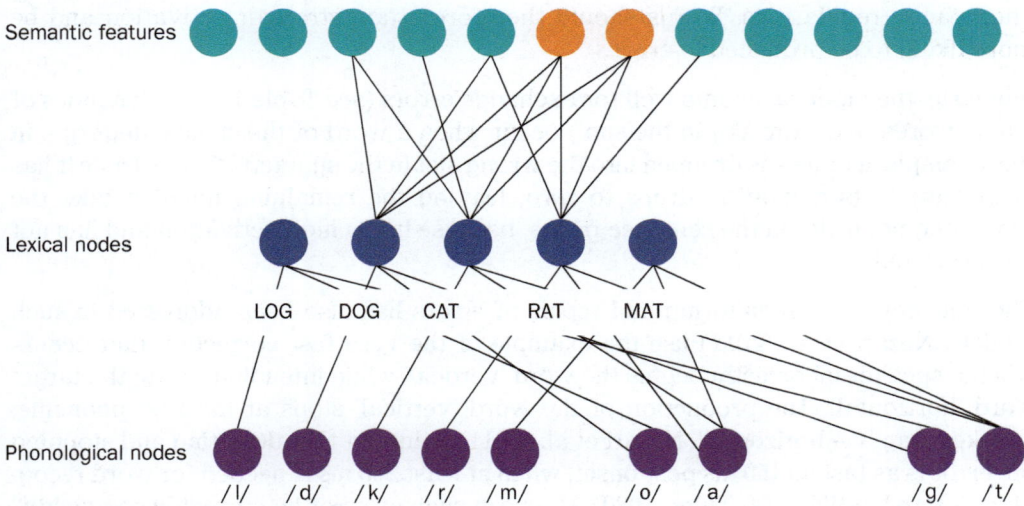

Figure 10.7 Dell's spreading activation model.
The nodes in the top layer represent the semantic features of the words. The words cat, rat and dog share semantic features and shared nodes are highlighted in orange. The nodes in the middle layer represent lemmas or words. The nodes in the bottom layer represent the sounds that make up the start of the word, the vowel in the middle of the word and the sound at the end of the word. Activation spreads throughout the network and the word that receives the most activation is the one that is selected (see also Levelt, 1999).

Source: Adapted from Dell & O'Seaghdha (1991).

According to this model, lexical access involves six steps:

1. The semantic units are activated by an external source (e.g., information from vision in a picture naming task, when you see a picture of the concept to be lexicalized or translated into words).
2. Activation spreads through the network.
3. The word unit with the highest level of activation is selected and linked to the syntactic frame for the sentence, in the appropriate slot. Once the word has been placed in the frame, its activation reduces to zero.
4. When the time is right, based on the slot in the syntactic frame the word is assigned to, the phonological information activates. If a single word is to be produced (e.g., in a picture naming task), selection of the word triggers the phonological information.
5. Activation continues to spread, but phonological units linked to the selected word become more highly activated.
6. The most active phonological units are selected, and these are linked to slots in a phonological frame for the word; this allows the correct phoneme to drop into the correct 'slot' in the word so that the sounds are output in the correct order (see Dell & O'Seaghdha, 1991, pp. 605–606).

During the planning stage, the various words selected for the sentence become active; activation drops off once the word is placed in the sentence. This is an interactive rather than sequential account and feedback can occur from later to earlier levels such that phonological level activation can inform processing at earlier stages. Like Levelt's model, Dell includes a monitoring process to account for self-corrections and repairs. Errors occur when activation for a non-target overrides that of the target morpheme, phoneme or word. So word substitutions occur because a semantically related, but incorrect, choice achieves a higher activation than the target word. The lexical bias effect is accounted for by a backward activation process. Because words have lexical entries, they are represented by nodes in the network; non-words do not have associated nodes, but may have activation associated with phonotactic regularities. Words should therefore attain stronger activation and be more likely to be produced in error.

Similarly, the model accounts well for exchange errors (see Table 10.6). Exchanges of whole words (e.g., 'the sky in the sun') occur when a word of the same category – in this example, a noun – is dropped into the wrong slot in the syntactic frame. Once it has been output, its activation drops to zero, leaving the remaining noun to take the remaining noun slot in the sentence frame, because it has high activation and has not been selected.

The time course of monitoring and repair of errors has also been addressed in such models. Nozari et al. (2011) use the example of the very fast correction that occurs when a speaker incorrectly begins the word 'vertical' while intending to say the target word 'horizontal'. The production of the word 'vertical' stops at the first phoneme; speakers say 'v – horizontal'. Nozari et al. (2011) point out that detecting and stopping the error is as fast as 150 ms post-onset, when at least 200 ms is needed for word recognition (Marslen-Wilson & Tyler, 1980). How can such as error be corrected so quickly? Nozari et al. (2011)propose an account based on response conflict during the production process itself rather than a monitoring task during comprehension as in Levelt's model to account for such quick repairs. This monitoring and repair stage of speech production is in itself beginning to attract significant attention within cognitive psychology (see Nooteboom & Quené, 2020 for an interesting discussion).

Evaluation

This model accounts well for many patterns of speech error, and some errors produced by people with aphasia are more in keeping with a parallel model than a serial model. For example, Blanken et al. (2002) reported a mixing of word selection and word form access in a German patient with aphasia, which supports an interactive account. Similarly, mixed errors, in which the target word and the error share both form and meaning information, suggest that feedback does occur.

The spreading activation model deals with data from speech errors rather well. It also contributed to our understanding of sentence production rather than focusing on single word production alone, as is the case in Levelt's model. However, the model does not address the semantic level in any detail, focusing instead on the construction of syntactic, morphological and phonological representations (Dell, 1986).

As yet there is no resolution to the debate between modular and interactive accounts of speech production, and a complete model may need to consider both modular and interactive aspects of the system. Dell and O'Seaghdha (1991) suggested that Levelt et al.'s (1991) data might be reconciled with spreading activation accounts by a 'characterization of the language production system as globally modular but locally interactive' (p. 604). The degree of informational encapsulation and interaction between components remains to be established in future research.

NEUROSCIENCE OF LANGUAGE PRODUCTION

Language involves a number of cognitive processes, interacting with systems for attention, memory, perception and motor function. Sociocultural knowledge informs the ways in which we use language with others. Therefore many areas of the brain must contribute to language processing. **Neurolinguistics** is the study of the relationship between brain areas and language functioning. Language involves a number of interacting brain areas, with many of the key language areas located within the left cerebral hemisphere in the majority of individuals.

> **Neurolinguistics**
> the study of the relationship of brain function to language processing.

Lateralization of Function

Sensory information coming into one side of the body is processed on the contralateral (opposite) side of the brain. Similarly, fine motor movements such as hand movements are controlled by the contralateral cortical hemisphere. Information presented to the left **visual field** is processed in the right hemisphere, while information presented to the right visual field goes to the left hemisphere. The right side of the brain controls the left hand and the left side of the brain controls the right hand. Information presented to each ear is processed in both hemispheres, but precedence is given to the contralateral side; stimuli presented to the right ear are processed in the left hemisphere.

Different functions are associated with the left and right cortical hemispheres. When a cognitive function is lateralized, one cortical hemisphere is dominant for that function; this is referred to as **lateralization of function**. Language is largely a left hemisphere function while the right hemisphere is specialized for functions related to spatial/holistic processing, such as face recognition (e.g., see Springer & Deutsch, 1981).

> **Visual field**
> the total area within which objects can be seen in central or peripheral vision; as such, each eye receives input from right and left visual fields to create binocular vision.
>
> **Lateralization of function**
> the asymmetric representation of cognitive function in the cerebral hemispheres of humans and higher primates.

Electrocortical stimulation of the surface of the cortex allows a surgeon to locate, and avoid damage to, brain regions associated with a particular cognitive function.

Wernicke–Geschwind model a simplified model of language function used as the basis for classifying aphasia disorders.

Wernicke's area a brain area in the lower posterior left Sylvian fissure that plays an important role in language comprehension and the production of meaningful speech.

Broca's area an area located in the left temporal lobe, damage to which is associated with aphasia (speech deficits).

Arcuate fasciculus the band of fibres connecting Broca's and Wernicke's areas.

Speech production results from the processing that occurs in a number of language areas located around the Sylvian fissure (or lateral sulcus) of the left hemisphere, an area referred to as the peri-Sylvian language region. Damage to any of these areas can affect the ability to produce speech or writing. Some of the key left-hemisphere language areas are shown in Figure 10.8. There is some variability in the functional localization of language, from person to person, however. In patients undergoing brain surgery that might affect language, **electrocortical stimulation** is carried out while the patient is awake to allow the surgeon to locate individual language areas and to reduce the risk of post-operative neurological deficits.

The **Wernicke–Geschwind model**, originally proposed by Karl Wernicke (1874), and also referred to as the Wernicke–Lichtheim–Geschwind model, notes a number of key areas for language (see Figure 10.8) and presents a simplified account of their role in language processing. The model proposes that we repeat a heard word by processing of the following sequence of brain areas. Following processing of the word in the auditory cortex, information about word meaning is processed in an area referred to as **Wernicke's area** and the output is sent to a more anterior region known as **Broca's area** via a band of connecting fibres called the **arcuate fasciculus** (see Figure 10.8). Broca's area prepares the speech output, and a motor programme for output is then articulated via the motor cortex. When we read a word out loud, a similar sequence is involved, with processing starting at the back of the brain in the primary visual cortex and continuing into Wernicke's area via the connections of the angular gyrus. While this model represents a simplification of the processing involved, it does provide a useful overview of the principal cortical brain areas for language and their functions.

Lateralization of function is particularly apparent when we consider the effects on cognitive processing of a set of conditions that gives rise to the

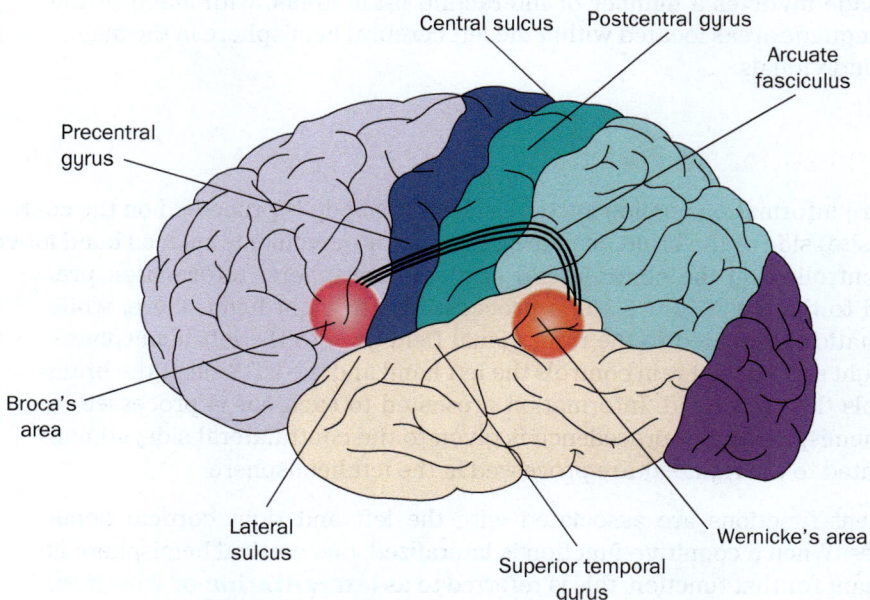

Figure 10.8 Key left hemisphere language areas described by the Wernicke–Geschwind model.

In fact, the precise location, and role, of the language areas continue to be debated, not least because of the considerable individual variability that is evident in the functional localization of language.

split brain phenomenon. When the band of fibres connecting the two hemispheres, the corpus callosum, is severed, the functions of the two hemispheres can be isolated and studied. In rare cases, these fibres are severed surgically, to treat epilepsy for example. In such cases, the difference in the hemispheres' functions becomes more visible. As Sperry (1974), a pioneering researcher in this field, and Nobel Prize winner in 1981, noted (p. 7):

> **Split brain**
> a set of disorders resulting from disconnection of the cerebral hemispheres by partial or complete severing of the corpus callosum.

Each hemisphere . . . has its own . . . private sensations, perceptions, thoughts and ideas all of which are cut off from the corresponding experiences in the opposite hemisphere . . . In many respects each disconnected hemisphere appears to have a separate 'mind of its own'.

The split brain is explored further in Box 10.4.

Box 10.4 When Things Go Wrong: The split brain

We are unaware of the division of labour between the left and right hemispheres of the brain because the two hemispheres communicate so effectively via a number of connecting bands of fibres, called commissures. The largest of these is the corpus callosum. This band of more than 200 million fibres is surgically severed in a *commissurotomy*, a rare surgical procedure that is performed, normally in adulthood, in order to reduce the effects of a type of intractable epilepsy that is unresponsive to drug therapy. After the procedure, the 'split-brain patient' behaves surprisingly normally, considering such a radical operation has been performed. However, on careful testing, it is apparent that the left and right hemispheres no longer communicate and are effectively working independently.

The left hemisphere is dominant for language in most people. The left hemisphere also controls, and gets input from, the right arm. If an object is placed in the right hand of a (blindfolded) split brain patient, he or she can name the object, as the information is relayed to the left hemisphere and it can make contact with the speech areas. However, if the object is placed in the left hand, the patient cannot name it. The patient can, however, pick a matching object from an array of objects, using the same hand. A picture that is presented to the right visual field can be named; a picture presented to the left visual field cannot, although again the object can be matched given an array of choices. Interestingly, when information is presented to the right hemisphere and cannot be named, the person reports not seeing it, suggesting a close alliance between language and subjective experience and consciousness (e.g., Cooney & Gazzaniga, 2003; Gazzaniga, 1980; Marinsek et al., 2016; Gazzaniga & Sperry, 1967). However, the patient can select a related picture using the left hand, but, unaware of what the right brain saw, he or she may invent a reason for the selection, a tendency referred to as **confabulation** (see Figure 10.9).

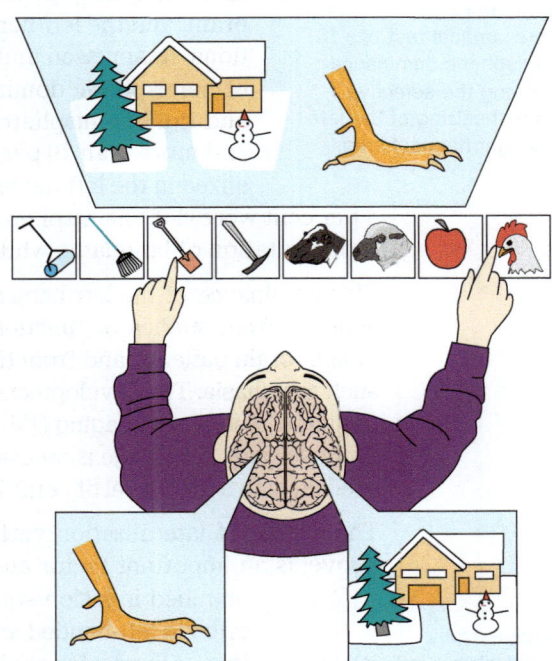

Figure 10.9 Demonstration of cognition in the split brain.

A picture of a chicken claw is presented briefly to the right visual field, and goes to the (speaking) left hemisphere, while a snow scene is shown to the (non-speaking) right hemisphere. Asked to point out what he saw from a set of pictures, the patient's left hand points to a snow shovel while his right hand points to a chicken. When asked why he picked those particular pictures, the patient said 'Oh, that's simple. The chicken claw goes with the chicken, and you need a shovel to clean out the chicken shed.'

Source: Gazzaniga et al. (1998).

> **Confabulation**
> the tendency for patients with memory, frontal lobe or other deficits to fill in gaps in their recollection with fabricated details; these can be plausible or fantastical in nature, the former type presenting a challenge for testing.

While a variety of effects can be demonstrated with split brain patients in the testing setting, in everyday life the person is relatively unaffected by the surgery, apart from the very positive outcome of alleviation of their seizures. While some problems have been reported by patients in the early stages after surgery, these are quickly compensated for. A common complaint involves inter-manual conflict, when the two hands should be working in tandem – when buttoning up a shirt or tying shoelaces, for example. One patient, Vicky, reported particular problems during her weekly grocery shop: 'I'd reach with my right [hand] for the thing I wanted, but the left would come in and they'd kind of fight . . . Almost like repelling magnets' (Wolman, 2012, p. 260).

The split brain patient quickly learns to coordinate the hands under the new circumstances of separate control by right and left hemispheres. The use of cross-cuing across modalities and hemispheres can be extensive and highly effective (see Volz & Gazzaniga, 2017). The implications for theories of consciousness continue to be debated (e.g., see de Haan et al., 2020; see also Chapter 5).

Chapter 5, p160

THE LEFT HEMISPHERE AND LANGUAGE

> **The Wada test**
> a pre-surgical test of hemispheric dominance involving the selective anaesthesizing of the left and right hemispheres.

In the majority of people, speech is lateralized in the left hemisphere of the brain, and the left hemisphere is dominant for the majority of language functions. Rasmussen and Milner (1977), using the **Wada test**, a pre-surgical test of hemispheric dominance involving the selective anaesthetizing of the left and right hemispheres, found that 96 per cent of their right-handed patients and more than 70 per cent of those who were left handed had language lateralized in the left hemisphere (see also Kemp et al., 2008). Of the right handers, 4 per cent were right hemisphere dominant. Of the left handers, 15 per cent had bilateral representation of language, while 15 per cent were right hemisphere dominant.

This dominance of the left hemisphere for language is evident in data from a number of sources: from studies of functional asymmetries in the typical population, from testing of split brain patients, and from the patterns of deficit seen in acquired language disorders such as aphasia. The development of non-invasive imaging technologies such as functional magnetic resonance imaging (fMRI) has aided pre-surgical assessment of patients awaiting brain surgery. Language is an essential cognitive function and it is important to be able to predict, with a high level of confidence, any language deficit that might result from surgery.

> **Ambidextrous**
> ambidextrous individuals show a reduced hand preference, and are typically able to use their right and left hands with equal ease.

The degree of lateralization varies in the general population. Handedness, as discussed above, is an important factor and recent studies using fMRI have confirmed the pattern obtained in lesion studies that atypical language lateralization is found more often in left-handed and **ambidextrous** individuals compared to right handers (e.g., Allendorfer et al., 2016; Szaflarski et al., 2012). Age differences are commonly reported, with left-hemispheric language lateralization increasing with age through childhood (e.g., Szaflarski et al., 2012), while language functions become less lateralized with increasing age in adulthood (e.g., Batouli et al., 2016). Increased right hemisphere activation is particularly evident in language tasks with an executive function component (e.g., Gertel et al., 2020).

Findings of sex differences in lateralization and in language function are less consistent (e.g., Fiske, 2010; Hyde, 2005, 2016; Wallentin, 2009). Wallentin's (2009) review of the literature on sex differences in brain structure and language function concluded that the evidence for sex differences in adult language processing was very weak, a finding that has been repeated for children's language processing (e.g., Etchell et al., 2018).

In a meta-analysis, Sato (2020) concluded that there was little evidence of sex differences in language proficiency and lateralization, or in underlying brain structures and functions, noting only subtle temporal differences on auditory processing tasks.

Bilingualism is associated with greater bilateral hemispheric activity during language processing compared to monolingualism, with further differences in lateralization between early and late bilinguals (Hull & Vaid, 2007). Połczyńska et al. (2017), comparing monolingual and bilingual patient groups, found that bilinguals had greater bilateral hemispheric involvement, while monolingualism was associated with stronger left hemisphere lateralization. However, they also noted some (12 per cent) atypical cases with different lateralization patterns in each of their languages. This finding underscores the need for careful mapping of each language in bilingual surgical candidates.

While the left hemisphere plays a key role in language function, the brain can be remarkably resilient in cases of early left hemisphere brain damage. Asaridou et al. (2020) reported a longitudinal case study of a child who was born without a left hemisphere, due to an extremely rare neurological condition. She went on to develop age-appropriate language skills and showed particularly good performance on tests involving phonology, speech repetition and decoding (reading) tasks, using the reorganized right hemisphere. Similarly, Mayberry et al. (2018) reported recruitment of the right hemisphere in an adult sign language user who acquired (syntactically limited) language for the first time in adulthood.

Various tasks are used to examine lateralization of language function. One such task, verbal fluency, is explored in Box 10.5.

> **Box 10.5 When Things Go Wrong: Use of verbal fluency tasks in the clinical setting**
>
> Tests of verbal fluency are widely used in neuropsychological and psychiatric contexts. There are two main varieties of such tests. In the semantic fluency task (or category task), participants are asked to produce as many words as they can within a particular category in a fixed period of time. For example, participants are asked to name as many animals as they can or to name as many types of fruit as they can. The time period is typically set at one or two minutes. In the letter (phonemic) fluency version of the task, participants are asked to produce as many words as they can, again within a fixed period of time, that begin with a given letter of the alphabet. A version of these tests is included in many neuropsychological test batteries with standard administration guidelines, and norms are available for many languages. For example, the F–A–S test requires participants to produce, in one minute each, as many words as they can that begin with F, then A and then S (e.g., Spreen & Strauss, 1998). The participant's score in each task is the number of unique words (excluding proper nouns) that are correctly generated. This simple task is quick to administer and does not require any special materials, yet it is surprisingly informative about a range of conditions.
>
> Verbal fluency tasks are commonly used in the assessment of language disorders, but also have wider utility. Patterns of performance in semantic and phonemic verbal fluency can indicate cognitive decline and the onset of dementia. Semantic fluency typically declines with age, more so than phonemic fluency, and an exaggerated pattern of this type is frequently found in early Alzheimer's disease (e.g., Henry et al., 2004). The tasks also prove useful in identifying older adults at risk of cognitive decline (Holtzer et al., 2020; Mueller et al., 2015). The phonological version of the task is thought to rely more heavily on executive control, and has been shown to be useful in the detection of cognitive deficits in pathologies with frontal involvement, such as the executive deficits seen in **Parkinson's disease** (e.g., Torralva et al., 2015). Performance on certain verbal fluency tasks differs in individuals with Parkinson's disease who are taking or not taking their (dopamine treatment) medication (Herrera et al., 2012).
>
> **Parkinson's disease**
> a progressive degenerative neurological disorder characterized by a distinctive pattern of motor and cognitive dysfunction.

There are also other versions of the task. The action fluency task requires participants to generate verbs (e.g., 'name things that people do'). It would seem to tap in to aspects of cognition additional to those involved in semantic and letter fluency (e.g., Ross et al., 2019), and has been used, for example, in research on high-functioning autism spectrum disorder (Inokuchi & Kamio, 2013). The ability to switch between one type of fluency task and another requires executive control and has been found to be compromised in conditions such as obsessive–compulsive disorder (e.g., Shin et al., 2016).

> **Perseverative errors** involve the inappropriate repetition of a previous response when that response is no longer appropriate.

Clustering is also informative; this refers to the selection of words within a subcategory – for example, naming a selection of zoo animals before moving on to farm animals during the semantic fluency task requiring naming of 'animals'. As well as examining the number of words produced, researchers can examine the semantic typicality of the words in order to explore how cognitive dysfunction may be affecting word retrieval. Individuals with schizophrenia, for example, may produce more **perseverative errors** during a verbal fluency task (Galaverna et al., 2016).

Verbal fluency tests are also useful in the cross-linguistic context. Ardila (2020) examined the semantic fluency ('name animals') task across 15 languages and concluded that linguistic factors, such as word length, did not significantly affect performance, supporting cross-language comparison. However, Ardila noted that age and education (but not sex) significantly affected results and furthermore that the effort expended in performing the test was an important, and often overlooked, factor.

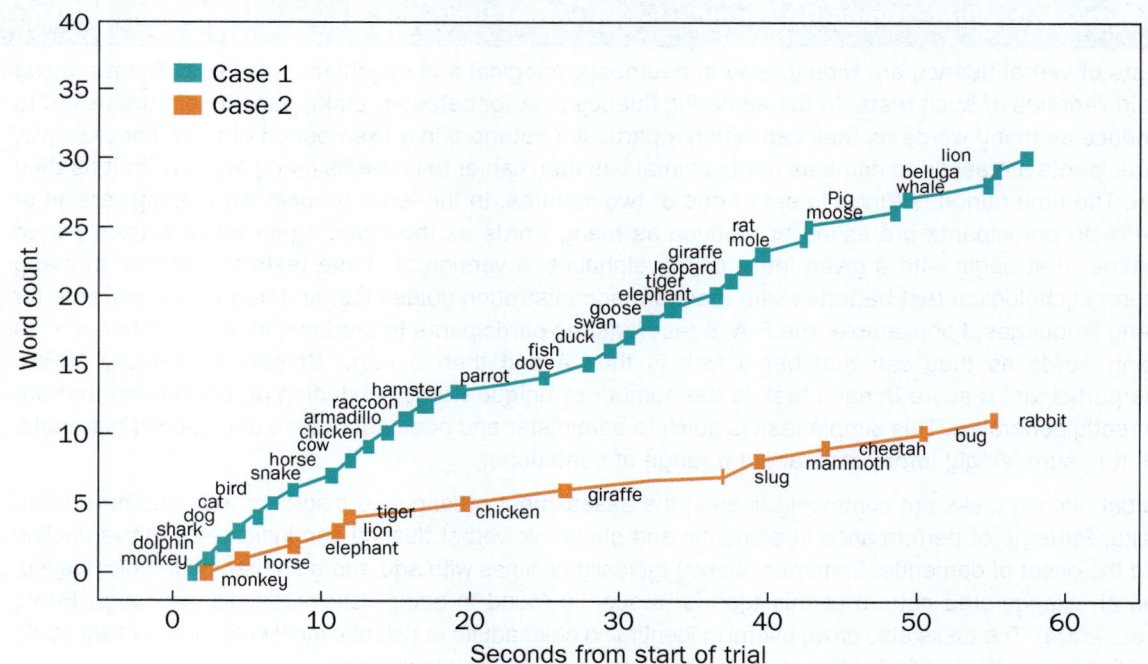

Figure 10.10 The temporal sequence of words produced by two participants.
Case 1 is a healthy volunteer who generated 31 words, and her performance is compared to Case 2, a (male) inpatient volunteer who produced 12 words in the one-minute period. Each individual word response is plotted on the x-axis from the start (i.e., '0') to the end of the one-minute trial (i.e., '60'). The lengths of the coloured boxes represent the duration of the respective onsets and offsets of the responses, and the vertical axis shows the word count. Periods with a fast succession of words result in a steeper trajectory.

Source: Holmlund et al. (2019), Figure 1, Panel A.

> New technology holds promise for more forensic examination of verbal fluency output. Holmlund et al. (2019) used automatic speech recognition to extract temporal and semantic information in a category fluency task. Their participants' responses on the 'animal naming' task were recorded. The recordings were transcribed and the words produced were timestamped. An index of semantic associations between the word pairs was then computed to quantify the degree of semantic association. Holmlund and colleagues compared the verbal fluency performance of healthy volunteers with an inpatient group of participants with a diagnosis of major depressive disorder (who also had a co-morbid substance use disorder). The results revealed a small but statistically significant difference between the groups' word fluency scores; healthy participants produced 25 words, with a range from 8 to 36, compared to 19 words on average and a range of 11–36 for the inpatient group. Holmlund et al.'s analysis of the temporal trajectories and semantic associations of the words allowed a new level of analysis (see Figure 10.10). Speed of speech output predicted the semantic coherence between successive words and longer pauses occurred between semantically dissimilar words. Differences between the two groups suggest a role for computational methods in moving verbal fluency tests beyond word counts; such an analysis might be applied to a range of disorders.

Evidence from the Typical Population

A number of tasks allow us to study the role of the left hemisphere in the typical population. The **dichotic listening task** (see also the section on attention in Chapter 4) involves the simultaneous presentation of stimuli to the left and right ear. While auditory processing involves both contralateral (opposite side) and ipsilateral (same side) connections from ear to brain, contralateral connections are dominant – that is, while stimuli presented to the right ear are received by the auditory cortex of both cerebral hemispheres, the dominant connections are contralateral and therefore verbal stimuli presented to the right ear are predominantly processed by the left hemisphere (Kimura, 1967). Tests using the dichotic listening task have shown that there is a right-ear advantage for verbal stimuli (see Chapter 11). Participants report more words (or speech sounds) that have been presented to the right ear compared to the left (Springer & Deutsch, 1981). This left hemisphere specialization seems to be in place at quite a young age, as children as young as two years of age show a right-ear advantage for speech sounds (Hiscock, 1988) and infants under 10 months show greater left hemisphere activity when brain waves are measured during presentation of speech (Molfese & Betz, 1988). Studies suggest that the right-ear advantage may be restricted to consonant sounds (Best, 1988). Consonants and vowels may be treated differently; many non-speech vocalizations, and even the calls of apes, are vowel-like. On the other hand, the rapid changes in consonant sounds evident in human speech are complex auditory patterns and require high-level sequential processing.

> **Dichotic listening task** a task where different stimuli are presented to each ear.

Another way in which we can examine language in the normal brain is through measuring **event-related potentials** (ERPs; see Chapter 1). ERPs provide high temporal resolution (meaning that very quick changes in brain activity, with timescales of milliseconds, can be detected) and are tied to a particular event, such as a stimulus presented to a research participant. Electrodes are placed on the scalp to measure changes in electrical activity in the cortex as stimuli are presented. The changes in the brain wave form are informative as regards the nature of language processing. Different areas within the left hemisphere process information relating to meaning and to syntax. Kutas and Hillyard (1980) compared brain waves as normal, semantically anomalous and physically anomalous sentences were presented (as written stimuli) to participants. Brain activity in response to semantically incongruous sentences differed from that seen when physically incongruous sentences were presented (see Chapter 11), supporting the notion that syntactic and

> **Event-related potentials (ERP)** a functional brain imaging method recording electrical activity during repeated stimulus presentations.

semantic information are treated differently and processed in different areas of the brain (see also Hagoort & Brown, 2000; Osterhout & Holcomb, 1992).

> **Transcranial magnetic stimulation (TMS)**
> a non-invasive method of temporarily exciting or inhibiting cortical areas by means of magnetic stimulation.

Language has also been studied in the normal brain using a method called **transcranial magnetic stimulation** (TMS). TMS is a non-invasive way of stimulating particular cortical areas such that processing is facilitated or inhibited. While the stimulation is short-lived and effects are largely temporary, in some circumstances TMS has been shown to alter the functioning of the brain beyond the initial period of stimulation, and therefore the method has possible applications in terms of therapeutic interventions. For example, Wirth et al. (2011) used TMS to enhance participants' performance on an overt picture naming task, and de Vries et al. (2010) used TMS to enhance grammar learning, specifically the ability to detect syntactic violations. De Vries et al. showed that Broca's area plays a crucial role in grammar processing. Such studies suggest potential applications to remedial intervention in cases of language disorder after brain injury.

> **Prosody**
> the rhythm, intonation and stress patterns in speech.

So far we have considered the left hemisphere as the site of language processing, but the right hemisphere also has a role to play, albeit a supporting one. The right hemisphere is involved in emotional aspects of speech, **prosody** and aspects of non-literal speech. People who have damage to the right side of the brain may have difficulty in appreciating the emotional tone of an utterance (Caplan, 1987), and in understanding non-literal speech such as sarcasm, figurative language and indirect requests (Weylman et al., 1988). Such patterns suggest a role for the right hemisphere in processing the pragmatic aspects of an utterance (see also Holtgraves, 2012). A right hemisphere advantage has been found for sarcasm-related words in a reading task (Briner et al., 2011) and for the processing of puns (Koleva et al., 2019). Similarly, studies of individuals with split brain syndrome show that the right hemisphere is limited when it comes to syntactic and phonological processing but it may be capable of other language functions, albeit not in the specialized way of the left hemisphere (e.g., Gazzaniga, 1983). While the right hemisphere is involved in the processing of tone in non-tonal languages (such as English), it is the left hemisphere that processes tone in tonal languages (such as Chinese) in which tone carries meaning (Gandour et al., 1992).

> **Aphasia**
> the term given to a group of language disorders that occur following brain injury.
> **Agraphia**
> the inability to produce written words as the result of a brain injury.
> **Alexia**
> the inability to understand written words as the result of a brain injury.
> **Apraxia**
> is a neurological condition typically resulting from brain damage, where a person loses the ability to perform activities that they are physically able and willing to do.
> **Anarthria**
> a disorder affecting the motor function underlying speech.
> **Crossed aphasia**
> language dysfunction following right hemisphere damage in a right-handed individual.

Evidence From Aphasia

Some of the key left-hemisphere language areas in the peri-Sylvian language region are shown in Figure 10.8. Damage to these areas affects language production and comprehension. We can learn much about speech processing in normal cognition by examining the ways in which language is affected by brain injury.

Aphasia (or dysphasia as it is sometimes called) is the term used to describe a deficit in language following brain injury. It generally refers to spoken language, with the terms **agraphia** and **alexia** used specifically for deficits in writing and reading, respectively. In aphasia, the internal processing of language has broken down; it is not that the person's muscles or motor control for producing language have been damaged (as may occur in conditions such as **apraxia** and **anarthria**, for example). Aphasia is generally associated with left hemisphere damage. A small percentage of people with aphasia have damage to the right hemisphere of the brain; aphasia following right hemisphere damage is referred to as **crossed aphasia**.

Aphasic disorders can be classified according to whether they are of fluent, non-fluent or pure type. In the pure disorders a particular facet of language (e.g., the ability to repeat back sentences) is affected, while other language functions remain relatively intact. The fluent disorders are characterized by fluent but empty speech. The affected individual may produce fluent sentences, but the content of the utterances is not as they intended. The non-fluent disorders are characterized by reduced speech output, slow or effortful speech. Generally, damage to the anterior regions (near the region marked as Broca's area in Figure 10.8) creates a non-fluent type of disorder, while more posterior damage (near Wernicke's area) can cause a fluent type of aphasia. However, the site of damage can vary somewhat from patient to patient, even with similar deficits, and it has proven difficult to establish the borders of the regions known as Broca's and Wernicke's areas (e.g., see Ardila et al., 2016; Federenko & Blank, 2020). Younger people tend to show a non-fluent pattern of deficit over various sites of damage, and fluent disorders have very rarely been reported in children (e.g., Murdoch, 2009). In what follows, we will describe in a general way the main deficits associated with each category of aphasia; in reality, people with aphasia show a range of individual differences in performance on language tasks and in terms of recovery of function.

Broca's aphasia

One of the first cortical areas involved in language production to be identified occupies the left inferior frontal gyrus and is known as Broca's area (see Figure 10.8). In 1861, a French doctor, Paul Broca, localized language to the left hemisphere, and attributed the production of speech to the area now named after him. (A paper by Marc Dax, dated to 1836, is now acknowledged as the first to identify the left hemisphere as the seat of language.) Broca's account was based on the aphasic disorder of a patient he encountered at the Bicêtre hospital in Paris. This man, named Leborgne, presented in his twenties with a severe reduction in speech output. Over the subsequent years he gradually lost the use of his right arm and leg, an impairment confirming left hemisphere damage, as limb movement is largely controlled by the contralateral cortical hemisphere. Broca (1861, cited in Dronkers et al., 2007, p. 1443) wrote of Leborgne:

> *He could no longer produce but a single syllable, which he usually repeated twice in succession; regardless of the question asked him, he always responded: tan, tan, combined with varied expressive gestures. This is why, throughout the hospital, he is known only by the name Tan.*

While it initially seemed that the problem was one of production and not comprehension, it is now recognized that there are some comprehension problems associated with the disorder that is now known as **Broca's aphasia**, and these problems are particularly apparent when test sentences move beyond simple syntax (e.g., passive voice constructions). It is also now clear that it is the abstract representation of speech that is impaired in Broca's aphasia and not just the output mechanisms of speech; in deaf signers with aphasia, the linguistic components of sign language are similarly affected (LeBrun & Leleux, 1986; Poizner et al., 1984), suggesting that similar neural systems underlie spoken and signed languages (Emmorey, 2015).

Broca's aphasia an acquired language disorder characterized by non-fluent speech, reduced speech output and problems with grammar processing.

After Leborgne's death, his brain was examined by autopsy and a large abscess was observed in the area now known as Broca's area. Broca concluded that this area of the brain was responsible for speech production. Leborgne's deficit was severe, leading some modern commentators to question whether he had a more **global aphasia**. Broca did not dissect the brain but preserved it and so his analysis of the damage was restricted to a surface inspection. Dronkers and colleagues (2007) were able to access Leborgne's preserved brain, and subject it to high-resolution MRI scanning. They found substantial lesions extending into medial

Global aphasia is an acquired language disorder involving extreme impairment of language function.

Figure 10.11 The Cookie Theft picture from the Boston Diagnostic Aphasia Examination.
The picture shows a number of characters and actions within a familiar scene (a stereotypical kitchen) and elicits predictable spoken descriptions involving nouns (boy, girl, cookie, stool, sink, water) and verbs (looking, taking, spilling, falling), as well as discourse around intentions (such as to take without being seen).

Source: Cookie Theft picture adapted from Goodglass et al. (2001). Copyright 2001 by PRO-ED, Inc. Reprinted (adapted) with permission.

regions of the brain, in addition to the surface lesions that Broca had reported, suggesting that global aphasia may be the more likely diagnosis.

Patients with Broca's aphasia show deficits ranging from severe mutism to dysfluency or laboured speech. Broca's aphasia is one of a number of disorders that can be categorized as **non-fluent**, expressive or productive aphasia. Speech output is reduced and non-fluent, but word selections tend to be meaningful. Function words (those that do the grammatical work in a sentence) rather than content words tend to be compromised. People with non-fluent aphasia are aware of their speech problems, which has implications for testing, as motivation may be an issue.

The following excerpt from Buckingham (1981) illustrates the marked dysfluency and reduced output associated with non-fluent aphasia. In this excerpt, B.L., a patient with Broca's aphasia, is trying to describe a picture from the Boston Diagnostic Aphasia Examination, called the Cookie Theft picture (see Figure 10.11). The Cookie Theft picture requires the description of a plot and a number of characters and actions, and tests access to vocabulary and syntactic ability as well as pragmatic function. The task has well-established norms and standardized scoring, and is quick to administer. While the scene it depicts may seem rather stereotypical or outdated, it has proven to be extremely useful in assessing language function over a range of age groups, language backgrounds and disorders, and it continues to be used widely (e.g., Berube et al., 2019; Cummings, 2019; de Lira et al., 2014; Keator et al., 2019).

> **Non-fluent aphasia**
> when the patient's speech output is reduced, laboured, or absent.

The description from Buckingham (1981) is as follows:

B.L.: Wife is dry dishes. Water down! Oh boy! Okay Awright. Okay . . . Cookie is down . . . fall, and girl, okay, girl . . . boy . . . um . . .

Examiner: What is the boy doing?

B.L.: Cookie is . . . um . . . catch

Examiner: Who is getting the cookies?

B.L.: Girl, girl

Examiner: Who is about to fall down?

B.L.: Boy . . . fall down!

> **Telegraphic speech**
> a pattern of speech characterized by reduction to basic content words; the term derives from the days when the sending of telegrams required payment per word, which led to the sending of short, efficient messages.

A number of features of Broca's aphasia are apparent from this excerpt. First, reduced output is apparent. This type of speech output is sometimes known as **telegraphic speech** because the sentences are reduced to the most basic units required to convey meaning – the content words such as nouns and verbs. The selection of content words is correct, showing that the patient can access the words from the lexicon. The function words are by comparison relatively sparse – inflections such as verb endings, conjunctions (e.g., and, but) and prepositions (to, under) are absent.

Goodglass and Geschwind (1976) defined Broca's aphasia as a condition 'marked by effortful, distorted articulation, reduced speech output, and agrammatic syntax but sparing of auditory comprehension' (p. 237). However, as mentioned above, while comprehension of simple sentences within everyday conversation may be relatively intact, people with Broca's aphasia have difficulties in understanding complex syntax. When comprehension depends on processing and understanding the syntactic structure of the sentence, it fails (Cornell et al., 1993). Grodzinsky and Santi (2008) provide a useful overview of the functions of Broca's area and reiterate a key role in syntactic processing.

Wernicke's aphasia

A few years after Broca's discovery, Carl Wernicke reported a contrasting pattern in two patients who, after brain injury, showed normal pace and intonation but jargon-like speech. **Wernicke's aphasia** is associated with damage further back in the brain than the region associated with Broca's aphasia, in the upper part of the left temporal lobe and extending to the angular gyrus, and the supramarginal gyrus, a region called the inferior parietal lobule. The exact location and extension of Wernicke's area has defied precise mapping and again, as with Broca's area, there is considerable inter-individual variability to take into account (e.g., Ardila et al., 2016).

> **Wernicke's aphasia**
> a fluent aphasia, characterized by fluent but meaningless output and repetition errors.

Wernicke's aphasia can be classified as a **fluent aphasia**. While speech output is fluent, it is 'empty' – that is, it is not meaningful. This condition was sometimes referred to as neologistic jargonaphasia, the word **neologism** referring to the patients' tendency to produce non-words, which may reflect partial activation of phonological information (Ellis et al., 1983). These patients are generally unaware of the problem with their speech output. An example from Goodglass and Kaplan (1983) illustrates some of the characteristic speech patterns of the disorder, again using the Cookie Theft picture (see Figure 10.11):

> **Fluent aphasia**
> when the patient's speech is fluent, but not meaningful.
> **Neologisms**
> in aphasia, neologisms are non-words that are produced in place of intended word targets and, if excessive, constitute what is referred to as jargon aphasia.

> *Well this is . . . mother is away here working her work out o'here to get her better, but when she's looking, the two boys looking in other part. One their small tile into her time here. She's working another time because she's getting, too.*

Another excerpt from Goodglass (1993, p. 86) shows similar features. In this case, the patient was responding to being asked 'How are you today?':

> *I feel very well. My hearing, writing been doing well. Things that I couldn't hear from. In other words, I used to be able to work cigarettes I didn't know how . . . Chesterfeela, for twenty years I can write it.*

People with Wernicke's aphasia are likely to produce phonemic **paraphasias** – that is, substitution errors in which a similar sounding word (or non-word) is produced instead of the target word (e.g. 'why' for 'wine'). There are made-up words or neologisms and overall there is a striking contrast to the pattern seen in Broca's aphasia. For example, several neologisms

> **Paraphasias**
> speech errors in aphasia whereby unintended phonemes, syllables or words are output.

are evident in the following excerpt, taken from Bose and Buchanan (2007), as patient F.F. describes the Cookie Theft picture:

> ... like the cold air the water is breaking out of the sink and it's going under this floor ... an um ... going up the floor when uh birchgo and ... and this kib ... is goboingbig is going pri on an ank ... can't see what this dates got a lot of pigyham and poirb ib ib ts but over is yub ya ... she is got her job ... and ... pigyburger ... she got dentalated and one pigbigger ...

Bose and Buchanan (2007, p. 728) note the appearance of a similar neologism (some version of '*pigyburger*') in several contexts by F.F., such as while talking about himself and when telling the Cinderella story. By contrast to the content, the function words and the grammatical structures of the sentences produced are relatively intact in Wernicke's aphasia. Wernicke (1874) speculated that while Broca's area was involved in motor programmes for speech output, the area now known as Wernicke's area was involved in processing sounds for meaning. He also speculated as to what would happen if the connections between the two areas were severed: the patient would have difficulty in repeating back what was said.

> **Arcuate fasciculus**
> the band of fibres connecting Broca's and Wernicke's areas.
>
> **Conduction aphasia**
> when the patient has a specific difficulty affecting the repetition of speech.

The **arcuate fasciculus** is the band of fibres that connects Broca's and Wernicke's areas (or Wernicke's and the motor/premotor frontal areas) and 'disconnection' of this band of fibres is associated with a specific deficit in repetition, a disorder known as **conduction aphasia**. Bartha and Benke (2003) outlined the main characteristics of conduction aphasia: severely impaired repetition, frequent phonemic paraphasias (saying unintended syllables or words – e.g., saying 'whine' instead of 'while'), repetitive self-corrections and word-finding difficulties. Repetition deficits are a key feature; spontaneous speech is generally fluent, although paraphasic, and comprehension is close to normal. Neuroimaging studies have revealed that the neurological bases of conduction aphasia are more complex than was originally thought. As Ardila (2010) notes, relatively few cases of conduction aphasia have a lesion limited to the arcuate fasciculus, and furthermore conduction aphasia can occur when damage is limited to the cortex, without subcortical lesions. The main symptoms of the different categories of aphasia are summarized in Table 10.7.

Anomic aphasia

Anomia is a word-finding disorder that has been likened to the TOT effect in normal speech. Relatively small lesions within the language areas can produce anomia, as can

Table 10.7 Summary of Language Deficits in Aphasia and Site of Damage

Type	Lesion site	Effect on speech output	Other deficits
Broca's aphasia	Anterior	Non-fluent output, reduced effortful speech	Repetition Naming
Wernicke's aphasia	Posterior	Fluent but 'empty' or meaningless speech	Comprehension Repetition Naming
Conduction aphasia	Arcuate fasciculus	Fluent	Repetition Naming
Anomic aphasia	Can occur anywhere in language region	Fluent but with word-finding difficulty	Naming
Global aphasia	Large area of damage	Extremely limited language function	Comprehension Repetition Naming

transient conditions that reduce blood supply to these areas (Obler & Gjerlow, 1999). For the individual with anomia, access to the word that he or she is searching for is denied, but the patient has not lost knowledge of the word or of its meaning. Allport and Funnell (1981, p. 405) illustrated one patient's word-finding problem with the following excerpt, again using the Cookie Theft picture in Figure 10.11 (the square brackets shows the researchers' guess as to what the patient was trying to say):

> *Well it's a . . . [kitchen] it's a place and it's a girl and a boy and they've got obviously something which is made . . . some . . . [biscuits], some . . . made . . . well . . . [the stool] it's just beginning to . . . [fall] go and be rather unpleasant . . . and . . . this is the [mother?] the woman, and she is [pouring?] putting some . . . [water] stuff . . .*

The same patient could select the correct name for an object when shown a picture and two written object names as long as the two words were not related in meaning. Therefore it is not that knowledge of words is impaired; rather the patient's ability to access the words is deficient. Allport (1983) suggests that this reflects a problem with translation between word forms and their conceptual representations. A similar pattern has been observed in developmental disorders of language such as **specific language impairment** (SLI). Constable et al. (1997, p. 507) reproduced the speech of a 7-year-old boy with word-finding difficulties as he tried to name a set of handcuffs presented in a picture naming task:

> **Specific language impairment (SLI)** a specific learning disability wherein language development lags behind cognitive development without explanation.

> *Key . . . oh what do you call them . . . oh yeah . . . you put . . . you put . . . with your . . . with your . . . oh . . . with your . . . when you . . . when someone's stole something . . . and . . . what do you call them . . . necklace? . . . no . . . I just don't know the word.*

Aside from the lexical impairment, individuals with anomic aphasia typically demonstrate fluent speech and largely correct use of syntax (e.g., Dronkers & Larsen, 2001) but some deficits in discourse have been uncovered, as a consequence of the primary lexical deficit. Andreetta et al. (2012) examined the storytelling skills of 10 individuals with anomic aphasia and compared their performance with that of healthy controls. They noted two problems with narrative for the anomic group, as consequences of the lexical deficit. The individuals with anomia tended to interrupt their own utterances, leading to reduced sentence completeness and cohesion in their stories. In addition, their use of strategies to overcome the lexical impairment (such as use of fillers and repetitions) again detracted from the overall coherence of their narratives (see also Andreeta & Marini, 2015).

Individual differences in aphasia

The descriptions above and the summary provided in Table 10.7 suggest that individuals with damage in similar areas of the brain demonstrate predictable patterns of language deficit. While this is a useful generalization, it is important to recognize that there are considerable individual differences in the manifestation of, and recovery from, aphasia. One importance source of individual variability is age. Individuals with Broca's and conduction aphasia tend to be significantly younger than those with Wernicke's and global aphasias (Ellis & Urban, 2016; Eslinger & Damasio, 1981). While there are isolated cases of fluent aphasia symptoms in children, these are very rare.

A second source of difference concerns the individual's language history. Bilingual and multilingual individuals with aphasia show a variety of deficits in their languages.

These deficits may affect each language equally, in parallel, or there may be quite different effects in each of the languages. Kuzmina et al. (2019) examined patterns of language dysfunction in a meta-analysis of bilingual aphasia and found better performance in L1 compared to L2. This pattern was moderated by premorbid language proficiency and frequency of use, while linguistic similarity did not affect the pattern of results. There is some evidence that bilingualism may be protective for individuals with aphasia (Dekhtyar et al., 2020).

Evaluation

Neuropsychological cases have contributed valuable data towards cognitive accounts of speech and language production. However, we must be cautious in interpreting data from such cases. As mentioned above, there is considerable variation between cases; individuals with the same pattern of deficit can have damage to different areas and those with similar damage can have differing language deficits. Lesions to Broca's area can occur without Broca's aphasia (Dronkers, 1996) and a Broca's-type aphasia can follow damage to areas outside Broca's area (Caplan & Hildebrandt, 1988). The precise functions of the language areas and the boundaries of the areas continue to be debated (Ardila et al., 2016; Binder, 2015, 2017). The main language areas have evaded consistent anatomical definition and the classic Wernicke–Lichtheim–Geschwind model has therefore been criticized as inherently limited (e.g., Tremblay & Dick, 2016).

For the purposes of understanding language processing, generalizations are often made; the reality is more complex. Deficits can be partial rather than complete. Particular types of aphasia are generally associated with a reduction in a particular behaviour (use of function words, for example) rather than a complete absence of such features (Kolk, 2007). These factors must be taken into account when considering aphasia syndromes as applied to models of normal language use. Furthermore, classifications of aphasia can differ. There are difficulties with a classification based on fluency, which can mask other patterns (e.g., see Clough & Gordon, 2020). Various other typologies have been proposed and observations may differ from a perspective other than a fluent/non-fluent categorization (see Ardila, 2010, for a review).

Box 10.6 Practical Application: Should lecture notes be typed or handwritten?

This chapter has focused on the production of speech. However, writing is also an important form of language, for the individual and for a culture. Written language provides a record that can be passed between generations, ensuring the continued health of a language. For a society, it allows a record to be shared over time and space. For the individual, it allows thoughts to be captured for communication or as an aid to cognition. The processes involved in writing are similar to those involved in speech production, but writing requires access to the **orthographic** written) form of a word rather than phonological output. Writing differs from speaking in that when we write we have more time to think about what it is we want to express and to 'translate' it into a written form. We can take our time over the construction of sentences, whereas speaking is time pressured. We can also monitor the output more easily; we can read the sentence we have written, inspect it and correct it if necessary. Unlike speech, writing is often a solitary activity; while a writer will have a reader in mind when writing, he or she lacks the immediate feedback that occurs during a spoken conversation. Another difference between discourse and writing is that writing makes fewer demands on memory and therefore more complex ideas can develop through writing.

Orthographic
the conventions used to represent a language in a writing system.

▶ Writing makes use of a number of left-hemisphere cortical and subcortical areas as well as motor areas (Planton et al., 2013). The act of writing down ideas can facilitate thinking and bring about a deeper understanding of the subject matter (Pijlaarsdam et al., 1996). Early handwriting experience has been shown to play an important role in children's developing letter recognition, facilitating symbol processing and linking visual processing with motor cognition (e.g., James, 2017). Is this facilitative effect due to the act of handwriting itself or is it due to the written form more generally? With the increasing use of laptop computers in workplaces and in colleges and schools, handwriting is being relegated to less substantial tasks. What effect might this change have on cognition?

Mueller and Oppenheimer (2014) compared the use of a laptop to handwriting for lecture note taking. Their college student participants listened to short talks of about 15 minutes' duration. They were invited to take notes using either a laptop or notebook and pen, depending on the condition. Laptops had full-size keyboards and were not connected to the internet, to reduce the possibility of distraction. In an initial experiment, participants were instructed to use their normal classroom note-taking strategy. In Experiment 2, participants were warned to 'Take notes in your own words and don't just write down word-for-word what the speaker is saying.' Following the lecture, participants engaged in some distractor tasks for a period of 30 minutes before they were tested on the lecture content. They were then presented with factual recall questions (e.g., 'Approximately how many years ago did the Indus civilization exist?') and conceptual-application questions (e.g., 'How do Japan and Sweden differ in their approaches to equality within their societies?') based on the content of the lectures they had seen. In the two experiments, laptop users performed more poorly than handwritten note takers on the conceptual questions.

In a third experiment, the researchers used a 2 (laptop, handwriting) × 2 (opportunity for study, no study) design to examine whether any disadvantage of laptop use might be compensated for by the increased volume of notes taken. On this occasion, testing took place a week after the lectures were seen. Participants in the 'study' conditions were allowed 10 minutes to look over their notes before the test. Participants in the 'no-study' conditions took the test without any opportunity to look over their notes. In the no-study conditions, there was no difference between the performance of laptop users and those who took handwritten notes; performance was poor in general after the week's delay. However, there was a clear advantage for handwritten note takers when participants were provided with an opportunity to study their notes, and this advantage applied to both factual content and conceptual understanding.

To summarize Mueller and Oppenheimer's results across the three experiments, the researchers found that use of a laptop was associated with shallower processing and poorer subsequent performance on tests of conceptual lecture content. While the use of laptops generated more notes (as typing is faster than writing by hand), those notes tended to be verbatim transcriptions of the lectures. By contrast, those taking written notes tended to take condensed notes, which required reframing the content in their own words. This may have resulted in better learning. These results and others (e.g., Manzi et al., 2017) support the case for the continued use of handwriting in educational and other contexts.

Writing processes differ with the orthographic properties of a given language (this will be explored in more detail in the section on reading in Chapter 11). It is therefore also important to consider differences in orthography (Bialystok et al., 2000; Kazi et al., 2012) and between L1 and L2 note taking (Asaly-Zetawi & Lipka, 2019). Cultural effects on motivation to write are a further factor of influence (Yeung et al., 2019).

Chapter 11, p374

Summary

In this chapter we have considered the nature and components of language and the cognitive processes involved in the production of speech. Language is our principal means of communication and seems to be uniquely human. While language shares properties with other animal communication systems, no animal system has all its features. Among the special features of language are productivity, displacement and duality of patterning.

The components of language are phonemes, morphemes, syntax and discourse. The basic sound units of a language are phonemes; its meaning units are morphemes. Sentences are composed of morphemes and are structured using syntax.

Speech production involves four main stages. The first stage, conceptualization, prepares a thought for conversion into language. The second stage involves the formulation of a linguistic plan. Formulation also involves syntactic planning; during this substage the order in which the selected words will be output is decided. The third stage involves the articulation of the plan. During this stage the sounds for the word are accessed and articulated. In a final fourth stage, the output is monitored so that corrections can be made if errors occur. Models of speech production differ in terms of the degree of modularity and interaction said to occur between processing levels.

This chapter examined speech errors and their contribution to our understanding of speech production. Speech errors occur in a number of types and are not random. They support the idea that the production of speech involves a number of distinct stages.

This chapter also examined the language deficits that follow brain injury in adults. The patterns of deficit in Broca's aphasia, Wernicke's aphasia and anomia suggest a dissociation between syntactic/output and semantic/comprehension processes in language processing.

Review Questions

1. What are the main features of human language?
2. What do the acquired disorders of language contribute to our understanding of normal speech production?
3. How does the analysis of speech errors contribute to our understanding of normal speech production?
4. What are the key differences between modular and interactive accounts of speech production?
5. What are the key differences in language production in the different types of aphasia?

Discussion Questions

1. Is animal communication language-like in any ways or is it fundamentally different from human language?
2. Is the dichotomous classification of aphasia syndromes by fluency useful or misleading?
3. Under what circumstances will handwriting notes give an advantage over laptop use?

Further Reading

Brown, R., & McNeill, D. (1966). The 'tip of the tongue phenomenon'. *Journal of Verbal Learning and Verbal Behavior, 5,* 325–337.

Brysbaert, M., Stevens, M., Mandera, P., & Keuleers, E. (2016). How many words do we know? Practical estimates of vocabulary size dependent on word definition, the degree of language input and the participant's age. *Frontiers in Psychology, 7,* 1116.

Dronkers, N. F., Plaisant, O., Iba-Zizen, M. T., & Cabanis, E. A. (2007). Paul Broca's historic cases: High resolution MR imaging of the brains of Leborgne and Lelong. *Brain, 130*(5), 1432–1441.

Hockett, C. F. (1960). The origin of speech. *Scientific American, 203,* 88–96.

LANGUAGE COMPREHENSION

11

PREVIEW QUESTIONS
INTRODUCTION
UNDERSTANDING SPEECH
    INVARIANCE
    SEGMENTATION OF SPEECH
    CUES TO WORD BOUNDARIES
    SLIPS OF THE EAR
    CATEGORICAL PERCEPTION
    THE RIGHT EAR ADVANTAGE FOR SPEECH SOUNDS
    ❗ **Box 11.1 When Things Go Wrong:** Language comprehension in aphasia
TOP-DOWN INFLUENCES: THE ROLE OF CONTEXT
    Box 11.2 Practical Application: The effect of leading questions on memory
    VISUAL CUES: THE MCGURK EFFECT
MODELS OF SPEECH PERCEPTION
    THE COHORT MODEL
    TRACE
UNDERSTANDING WORDS AND SENTENCES
LEXICAL ACCESS
    Box 11.3 Practical Application: Language ambiguity and accident prevention
    SYNTAX AND SEMANTICS
THE BRAIN AND LANGUAGE COMPREHENSION
    NEUROPSYCHOLOGY OF SPEECH COMPREHENSION
READING
    WRITING SYSTEMS
    ❗ **Box 11.4 When Things Go Wrong:** Cross-language manifestation of dyslexia
    CONTEXT EFFECTS ON VISUAL WORD RECOGNITION
    🔍 **Box 11.5 Research Close Up:** The Stroop effect
    EYE MOVEMENTS
    🔍 **Box 11.6 Research Close Up:** Reading sentences containing emoji
    THE DUAL ROUTE MODEL OF READING
    NEUROPSYCHOLOGY OF READING
    ELECTROPHYSIOLOGICAL DATA
SUMMARY
REVIEW QUESTIONS
DISCUSSION QUESTIONS
FURTHER READING

Preview Questions

1. How do we segment speech?
2. How does visual information influence speech perception?
3. What cues help us locate word boundaries?
4. What is known about the brain areas involved in speech comprehension?
5. How does reading differ across languages?
6. What is known about the brain areas involved in reading?

INTRODUCTION

Imagine you are a passenger in a car on a cold day. Your friend is driving. The driver's window is open. You say 'It is chilly today.' Your friend closes the window. This example illustrates some of the complexities involved in language comprehension. Your friend must detect speech sounds over background noise and decipher words within a string of sounds (itischillytoday) that correspond to 'It is chilly today.' The meaning of these words and the grammatical structure of the sentence must be analysed. And then, the intention of the utterance must be considered. Here, you are not merely commenting on the fact that it is cold; a request is implied – that your friend closes the window or asks if you would like it closed. The complexity of the task is evident in the programming required, and the frequent errors made, by artificial speech recognition systems, which often fail to detect verbal commands, across context, speakers and accents.

> Chapter 10, p336

The goal of language comprehension is understanding – to extract meaning from the language that we hear or read. This requires access to a very large store of words, the **lexicon** (see Chapter 10). It is estimated that an adult knows between 50,000 and 100,000 words (Clark, 2003) and that the average 20-year-old native speaker of English knows 42,000 **lemmas** (Brysbaert et al., 2016). Through adulthood, from the ages of 20 to 60 years, it is estimated that the average person learns 6,000 new lemmas, equating to about one new lemma every two days (Brysbaert et al., 2016). When we encounter a word, either by hearing it or reading it, the goal is to recognize and understand it. This is achieved quickly, accurately and automatically; it is only when the system breaks down that we become aware of its complexity (see, for example, Box 11.1).

> **Mental lexicon**
> our store of knowledge about words and their uses.
>
> **Lemma**
> an uninflected word from which inflected words can then be derived.

In this chapter, we will focus on how we understand speech and written language. The higher-level cognitive processes involved in these two comprehension tasks have much in common; whether we are listening to speech or reading text, understanding requires accessing semantic information and appreciating the meaning of the words, the intention of the utterance and sometimes the non-literal meaning (when we encounter figurative language, sarcasm and metaphor, for example). The objective when either listening to someone speak or when reading written text is to understand what is being communicated. At lower levels, however, the processes involved in **speech perception** and visual word recognition differ markedly. Speech presents us with a virtually continuous signal of sounds from which we must decipher words, phrases, sentences and, ultimately, meaning. It is a rapidly decaying signal and is often encountered in less than optimal conditions (requiring processing over background noise, for example). Furthermore, speech is not simply a string of easily identifiable **phonemes** (speech sounds; see Chapter 10). Sounds blend into one another and are affected by previous and subsequent sounds within utterances, as well as factors specific to the speaker. In other words, speech perception is not a simple matter of categorizing incoming sounds into classes of sounds used within a language. It is a far more complex process. Although the result of speech perception may well be to assign sounds to categories, it is not achieved via a serial bottom-up sound-by-sound process (see Chapter 2 on bottom-up processes in perception).

> **Speech perception**
> the process by which we convert a stream of speech into individual words and sentences.
>
> **Phoneme**
> the smallest meaningful sound unit within a language.

> Chapter 10, p324

> Chapter 2, p34

In addition to considering speech, the current chapter also examines comprehension of written language. When we read, we are presented with written text, a visual string of words, with boundaries indicated by spaces (between words) and punctuation marks (between phrases and sentences). In many scripts this written signal can be decoded into corresponding speech sounds. Some of the challenges involved in extracting meaning from text reflect related cross-linguistic differences in the representation of sounds in scripts.

We will begin by considering speech. Speech comprehension is a fast, accurate and automatic process – once we have acquired language, we readily understand a spoken utterance. The speed with which the task is achieved does not reflect the complexity of the process. We take speech perception for granted and underestimate the challenge posed by the speech signal. In English, we do not even have a specific word for the act of recognizing spoken words (McQueen & Cutler, 2001). The word 'read' refers to the act of recognizing written words, but there is no word for the process of word recognition in speech. Some languages, McQueen and Cutler point out, do have words for this purpose – such as '*verstaan*' in Dutch and '*kikitoru*' in Japanese.

As Pinker (1994, p. 15) remarked, 'simply by making noises with our mouths, we can reliably cause precise new combinations of ideas to arise in each other's minds'. This ability to convert 'noises' into thoughts begins with understanding speech.

UNDERSTANDING SPEECH

In Chapter 10, we encountered the sounds that make up speech within a language: phonemes. As we hear someone speak, we hear the sounds that make up words, and we gain other prosodic information from the sound signal, such as the rhythm and stress patterns of the language, intonation, speech rate, placement of pauses and emotional tone. **Prosody** might be defined as 'aspects of an utterance's sound that are not specific to the words themselves' (Ferreira, 2003, p. 762) and can serve as a cue to sentence comprehension (e.g., Kwan & Cutler, 2020). While we perceive a sequence of words within the stream of speech, the speech signal itself is not produced as discrete units. There are few clear boundaries between words in spontaneous speech, and sounds blend together as they are produced so that phonemes differ as a function of the other sounds used. Words in speech are not presented as distinct units as occurs when we read. Some commentators have questioned the importance of the word as a unit in early speech analysis; for example, Grosjean and Gee (1987) suggested that an over-reliance on the concept of a 'written dictionary' word is misapplied to speech perception. A key issue for those conducting research in the area of speech perception is: given the variation in incoming sounds, how does the system come to treat them as a small number of discrete phonemes making up particular words within a given language?

> Chapter 10, p324

> **Prosody**
> the rhythm, intonation and stress patterns in speech.

The speech sounds produced by a single speaker vary with context. There are further variations when we consider individual differences, differences in accent and indeed changes over time. Factors such as speech rate, the speaker's age and sex, as well as the amount and type of background noise affect the acoustic form of a spoken word. The sounds we produce change as we age (e.g., Hodge et al., 2001; Reubold & Harrington, 2017; Russell et al., 1995) and they change as societies change; sound patterns in old radio or television recordings seem archaic to modern listeners. In a fascinating longitudinal study, Harrington et al. (2000a, 2000b) analysed Queen Elizabeth II's annual Christmas broadcast recordings over a period of 40 years. They noted considerable change in the Queen's pronunciation of vowel sounds from the 1950s to the 1980s. These changes mirrored the changes in vowels within Standard Southern British English during the same period, while the distance between the Queen's language and the average speaker's vowels remained about the same. Changes in adult speech have a biological basis and a socio-phonetic basis (Reubold & Harrington, 2017), and cross-language effects are evident in bilingual speakers (e.g., de Leeuw, 2019).

A speaker may produce as many as 150 words per minute, with each word spoken in, on average, 400 milliseconds. When someone is speaking quickly, this rate can double to one word per 200 milliseconds (Levelt, 1989). Speech occurs at a rate of 10–15 phonemes per second, and can be understood at rates as fast as 50 phonemes per second for artificially speeded speech (Pinker, 1994). Syllables are produced every 200–400 milliseconds (Buonomano & Karmarkar, 2002). Recognition precedes completion of the heard word; some studies suggest that people can recognize a word on average just 275 milliseconds after the start of the word (Marslen-Wilson & Tyler, 1980). Speech perception requires rapid segmentation of this continuous signal. The problem of deciphering speech becomes apparent when we hear a foreign language that we do not understand. It is initially very difficult to work out where one word ends and the next begins, without knowledge of the structure of the language. As we will see, speech perception utilizes a number of cues in order to make sense of the incoming stream of sounds.

Massaro (2001, p. 14870) defined speech perception as the 'process of imposing a meaningful perceptual experience on an otherwise meaningless speech input', a process whereby a 'continuous input is transformed into more or less a meaningful sequence of discrete events'. Speech provides a continuous signal extended in time, where each segment cannot be taken on its own but instead depends on what went before and what follows. Blended sounds can occur at boundaries between words so that there is no 'gap' in the signal that would reliably indicate a word boundary. A spectrogram (see Figure 11.1) provides a visual representation of a speech waveform, by mapping the frequencies of sounds within an electrical signal generated from a recorded sound. It shows that the speech signal is continuous without clear boundaries between words. Low-amplitude gaps in the signal are not reliable indicators of word boundaries, but may simply reflect a closure of the airway during the production of a word; for example, in the word 'spoken', the airway closes as the lips are pursed to produce the /p/ sound. (As noted in Chapter 10, following convention, a letter between forward slashes, e.g. /p/, is used to denote a speech sound.) When we read text, gaps between words and punctuation marks denote word boundaries; there is no equivalent in the speech waveform. Furthermore, the same phoneme can vary depending on the other sounds being produced. For example, consonants are affected by the following vowel sound. The two major issues of speech perception can be conceptualized as the problems of segmentation and of invariance (see Miller & Jusczyk, 1989).

> Chapter 10, p324

Invariance

> **Invariance problem**
> the variation in the production of speech sounds across speech contexts.

The **invariance problem** refers to the lack of invariance in speech sounds and the challenge this poses for speech perception. We are probably aware of the differences in speech sounds of non-native speakers with a foreign accent, and it may take a moment to adjust to a strong-accented speaker. But a particular sound is not uttered in exactly the same way on each occasion even by the same speaker; its form is affected by other phonemes that precede or follow it. Contextual factors also affect the sound; think of someone speaking with a pen in their mouth or while eating, for example (e.g., Liu & Jaeger, 2018). Adaptation allows listeners to overcome variability between speakers (see Kleinschmidt & Jaeger, 2015; Liu & Jaeger, 2018; Weatherholtz & Jaeger, 2016), but there is also considerable within-speaker variability to be accommodated.

> **Co-articulation**
> the tendency for a speech sound to be influenced by sounds preceding or following it.

Co-articulation is one contributor to this problem, while also providing the basis for the ability to produce fast, articulate speech (Hardcastle & Hewlett, 1999). The articulatory and acoustic properties of a speech sound differ depending on the surrounding context of the speech signal. The position of the vocal apparatus from a previous sound, or its required position to produce the next sound, will affect the production of a given phoneme. Sounds blend together so that a continuous, fluent output of speech is produced. Therefore, a one-to-one correspondence between acoustic cues in the speech signal and our perception

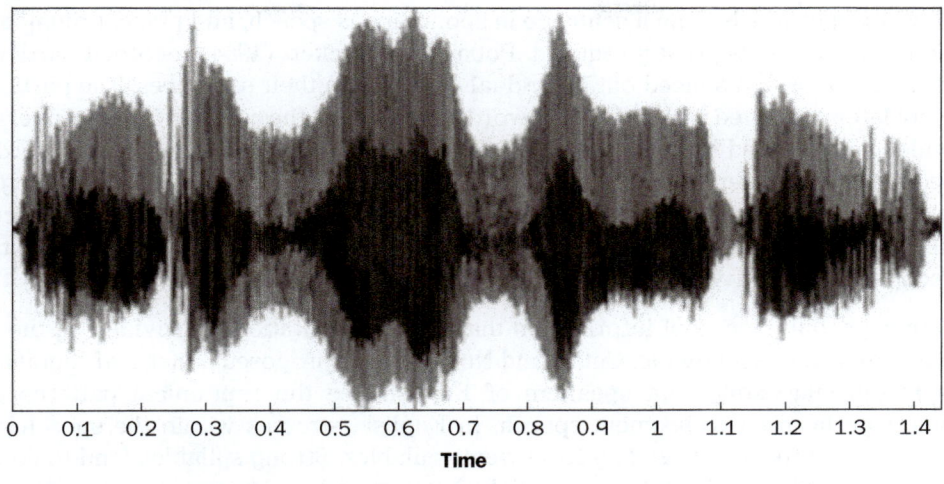
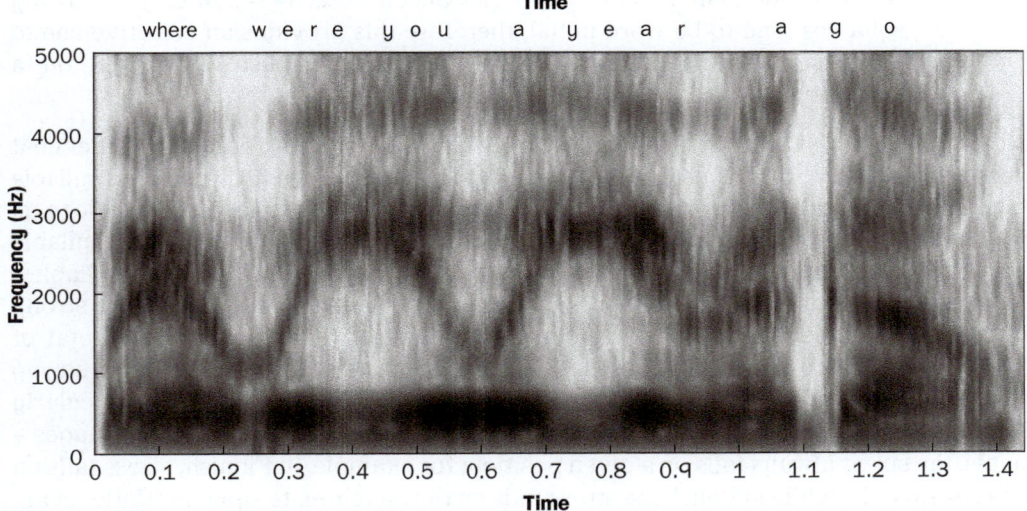

Figure 11.1 A waveform (top panel) and spectrogram (bottom panel) for the sentence 'Where were you a year ago?'
Note that there is not a straightforward correspondence between word boundaries and points of low acoustic energy.

Source: Byrd & Mintz (2010).

of the speech sounds that make up words is not provided, and the same word can be produced with slight variations as a function of surrounding words. This creates a complex cognitive task with competing requirements of flexibility and stability, in order to process speech with within- and between-speaker variability (Baese-Berk, 2018). The complexity of the process is most evident when we consider artificial speech recognition systems, which often struggle with such variations despite extensive programming and training samples. This complexity is also evident when the system breaks down following brain injury (see Box 11.1).

Segmentation of Speech

If spoken language forms a continuous signal, and if there are few reliable gaps in the signal that reflect word boundaries, how then do we segment speech so that we perceive discrete words? It is not as if each sound can be taken and analysed in and of itself.

If we extract words from a sentence in spontaneous speech, and present them in isolation, recognition is greatly reduced. Pollack and Pickett (1964) recorded participants' conversations and spliced out individual words from their sentences. The participants were later presented with individual words produced in the course of their conversation, which were played back to them out of context. Recognition of individual words was reduced to between 35 per cent and 62 per cent accuracy. For four-word segments played back to participants, recognition improved to between 70–100 per cent accuracy, depending on the speaker. This demonstrates the role of the surrounding context in the recognition of individual words.

One important source of information that aids segmentation is provided by the sound patterns within a language. Cutler and Norris (1988) proposed a metrical segmentation strategy, suggesting that speakers of English use the rhythmical patterns of the language in order to segment speech. In English, stresses within the speech stream differentiate strong from weak syllables. Strong syllables tend to contain a full vowel, while weak syllables have a reduced vowel, usually **schwa** – that is, the /ə/ sound in about or paper (McQueen et al., 1994). In English, strong syllables tend to be word initial, therefore this provides an effective cue to guide segmentation; most content words in English will begin on a strong syllable.

> **Schwa**
> an unstressed neutral vowel sound found in many English words.

In their analysis of 33,000 English words, Cutler and Carter (1987) found that 12 per cent were monosyllabic, 50 per cent were polysyllabic with the stress on the first syllable (e.g., 'cycle'), 11 per cent were polysyllabic with secondary stress on the first syllable (e.g., 'psychological'), and 27 per cent were polysyllabic with a weak initial syllable (e.g., 'illogical'). So 73 per cent of the words in their list had word-initial strong syllables. In the same study, an analysis of spontaneous speech showed that words with strong initial syllables accounted for more than 90 per cent of the words used (a total of 190,000 words were sampled). Therefore while it is not always the case that a strong syllable marks a word boundary in English, on a majority of occasions, particularly considering content words, this applies. Other languages are fixed stress languages – that is, the stress always falls on a given position; for example, in Finnish, stress falls on the first syllable, while in Polish the stress falls on the penultimate syllable (Cutler et al., 1997). Infants are highly sensitive to syllable-like structures in their native language long before they develop language (e.g., Räsänen et al., 2018).

Stress patterns, as well as factors such as prosody, provide an important cue to a speaker's accent, and accented prosody can produce predictable segmentation errors in listeners (Hawthorne et al., 2018). Brain injuries that affect the production of such patterns can lead to perception of a foreign accent, a condition referred to as '**foreign accent syndrome**'. Whitaker (1982, pp. 196–198) identified four characteristics to this disorder:

> **Foreign accent syndrome**
> a rare condition, resulting from brain injury, whereby an individual produces phonetic and prosodic errors in their speech, such that it sounds non-native like.

1. the accent sounds foreign to listeners and to the patient
2. the accent differs from the patient's speech before injury
3. the disorder results from brain damage (as opposed to a psychiatric condition, for example)
4. there is no history of the foreign language in the patient's background.

In one case, dating from 1941, a young Norwegian woman (Astrid L.) received a shrapnel injury to the left frontal brain area, initially causing a Broca's type aphasia (see Chapter 10). While her language difficulties became less pronounced over time, she was left with an odd manner of speech affecting prosody, which listeners perceived as a foreign accent. In many cases, her speech was mistaken as sounding 'German' and a threat in the context of the German occupation during the Second World War. She complained that shop assistants refused to serve her once they heard her speak (Monrad-Krohn, 1947, p. 410). She had never ventured abroad or learned a foreign language. Analysis of her speech patterns revealed alterations in pitch and prosody that might be interpreted as being non-native (Moen, 2004).

More recently, Miller et al. (2006) described the case of E.J.C., a retired shop assistant from Tyneside in the north of England. She had lived in the same locality for most of her life, had not spent much time abroad and did not speak a foreign language. Following a brain haemorrhage, E.J.C. was perceived as speaking with an accent that most listeners identified as Italian. Comparing a detailed analysis of E.J.C.'s speech to that of a native Italian speaker, Miller and colleagues concluded that 'E.J.C. did exhibit a number of changes typically associated with Italian speakers' (p. 402). E.J.C. also exhibited grammatical errors, which would have contributed to the perception of foreignness in her speech.

Scott et al. (2006) described the case of E.M., who, following a stroke, developed an accent described as sounding German, Polish or South African, and quite unlike her original Scottish accent. E.M. had a small left hemisphere lesion in the white matter underneath the precentral sulcus, dorsal and medial to the anterior insula, and ventral to the primary motor cortex (see Figure 11.2). This pattern of damage is found in several other cases of foreign accent syndrome in the literature, and suggests that the disorder reflects a disconnection between motor control and planning of articulation (Scott et al., 2006). However, the perceiver may be as important as the speaker in determining the interpretation (Miller et al., 2006). Listeners use their extant knowledge of the sounds of other languages to make a judgement about heard speech. They 'focus on salient elements in speech, and these are interpreted through their experiential and attitudinal filters' (Miller et al., 2006, p. 404). The various patterns of altered speech grouped together as foreign accent syndrome may tell us as much about listener perceptions than the speaker's underlying pathology.

> **Head turn preference procedure** (or the preferential looking paradigm) a method used to examine infants' and toddlers' sensitivity to changes in visual and auditory stimuli.

Cues to Word Boundaries

Infants exposed to English as their native language learn to use a stress-based strategy to segment speech. By the age of about 7 and a half months, English-learning infants can segment English words that conform to the dominant stress patterns of the language, treating strong syllables as markers of word onsets, while errors are made when the dominant stress pattern is violated (Jusczyk et al., 1999). This has been established using a method called the **head turn preference procedure**. The infant sits on the parent's lap, facing forwards. The parent wears headphones playing background noise, so that no subtle signals are unintentionally communicated to the child. There is a light in front of, to the left of and to the right of the infant, and each light has a loudspeaker next to it. The speakers and lights are controlled by the researcher who is watching the infant in an adjacent room through a one-way mirror. At the start of the experiment, the light in front begins to blink on and off. When the infant focuses on that

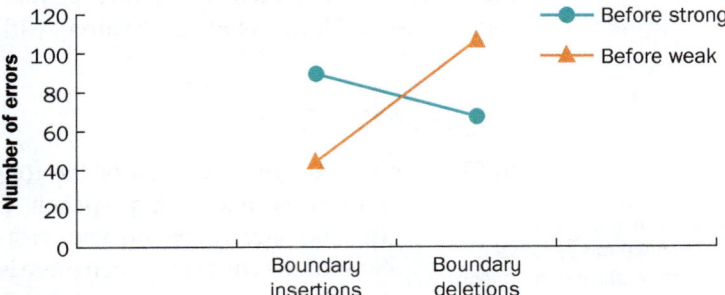

Figure 11.2 **The number of word boundary insertions and deletions before strong and weak syllables in spontaneous slips of the ear.**
In English, more boundary insertion errors occur before strong syllables, while boundary deletions tend to be more frequent before weak syllables.

Source: Data from Table 2 in Cutler & Butterfield (1992).

light, the light stops blinking, but a light to the left or to the right then begins to blink. When the child looks at the blinking light, a speech sample is played over the speakers. The speech sample continues to play as long as the child looks at the light. When the child looks away for more than two seconds, the sound stops and the light in front blinks again to direct the child's attention back before the next trial begins. Because the length of time for which the speech sample plays is dependent on the child's attention, this tells us something about the child's interest. For example, infants tend to show a preference for their native language over an unfamiliar language, or for familiar over unfamiliar voices; this is reflected in longer eye fixations and playing durations.

Jusczyk and Aslin (1995) used this method to examine the segmentation abilities of young infants. They familiarized infants for 30 seconds to word pairs such as *feet* and *bike*, or *cup* and *dog*. These words were subsequently embedded in fluent speech passages, which were played to the infants. If the infant recognizes the familiar word from among the embedded speech – that is, successfully segments the speech – this should be associated with longer gaze time. Such studies show that by around 7 and a half months, English-learning infants are able to segment words that conform to the predominant stress patterns of English words (Jusczyk, 1999). Initially, infants rely heavily on stress patterns, but they subsequently begin to appreciate other cues (such as those described next) so that by the age of 24 months the perception of word boundaries is at a level similar to that of native-speaking adults (Jusczyk, 1999). The reliability of the syllable for identifying word boundaries has also been demonstrated in languages with different stress patterns (e.g., Räsänen et al., 2018).

> **Phonotactic constraints**
> the language-specific sound groupings that occur in a language.
>
> **Onset**
> of a word is the initial phoneme or phonemes. The time follows the onset.
>
> **Rime**
> the remaining syllable that follows the onset in a word.

The development of word recognition requires the extraction of the regularities in a language that can be reliably used to distinguish word boundaries. **Phonotactic constraints**, 'permissible' patterns of sounds within a language, also serve as effective cues to segmentation. In English, for example, a word can end in 'rk' (e.g., 'work', 'dark') but words do not start with 'rk'. This is an example of an **onset** pattern; the onset of a word is the initial phoneme or phonemes (e.g., the initial /c/ sound in cat), while the **rime** follows the onset. In the word 'train' for example, /tr/ is the onset and the /ein/ sound is the rime. Cross-linguistic surveys of sound patterns (e.g., Greenberg, 1978) show clear preferences for some onset patterns over others. Onsets like the 'bl' in 'blip' are commonly used, while the onsets in 'bnip', 'bdip' and particularly 'lbip' are less so. English tolerates onsets like 'blip' only, while 'lbip' tends to be avoided in many languages, and is misperceived by speakers of English (as 'lebip'; see Berent et al., 2007). Through early exposure to our native language, we develop tacit knowledge about how sounds go together in a language. This knowledge then guides speech perception. Knowledge about sentence structure, provided by syntax, may also play a role in speech segmentation (Mattys et al., 2007) along with the overall context (Kim et al., 2012).

Slips of the Ear

In Chapter 10, we saw how slips of the tongue contribute to our understanding of the processes underlying speech production. In the same way, 'slips of the ear' are revealing with respect to the processes of speech perception. Slips of the ear occur when there is a misperception of a word boundary and the error reveals language-specific patterns affecting the segmentation process.

> **Slips of the ear**
> when we misperceive a word or phrase in speech.

Chapter 10, p346

These kinds of slips are sometimes referred to as 'mondegreens' after a mishearing of a line in the seventeenth-century Scottish ballad 'The Earl of Murray' reported by Wright (1954). One line of the ballad is 'They had slain the Earl of Murray and laid him on the green'. The latter part of the sentence was misheard as recounting the fate of the

Table 11.1 Examples of 'Slips of the Ear'

Input	Error
She's a must to avoid	She's a muscular boy
How big is it?	How bigoted?
Into opposing camps	Into a posing camp
I can't fit any more on	I can't fit any moron
The effective firing rate	The effect of firing rate
She'll officially	Sheila Fishley
The parade was illegal	The parade was an eagle
For an occasion	Fornication

Source: Cutler and Butterfield (1992).

unfortunate 'Lady Mondegreen' ('They had slain the Earl of Murray and Lady Mondegreen'; Wright, 1954; see also Pinker, 1994). Such errors are relatively common when we listen to poems and song lyrics, because the prosodic information that might guide segmentation may be reduced, context may not cue word selection, or archaic or unfamiliar language might be used. Many such errors have been noted in song lyrics (Beck et al., 2014; Beck Lidén et al., 2016).

These errors are typically word boundary errors and are consistent with the types of spontaneous errors reported in the research literature. For example, Bond and Garnes (1980) examined multiple word slips and found that 70 per cent involved errors in identifying the word boundary. They identified word boundary shifts ('an ice bucket' – 'a nice bucket'), word boundary deletions ('ten year party' – 'tenure party') and word boundary additions ('descriptive linguistics' – 'the script of linguistics'). Linell (2015) reported an analysis of 220 mishearings in Swedish conversations and noted that they are nearly always situation-appropriate, making use of relevant contextual assumptions. As such the role of **top-down** processing is central.

> **Top down**
> or conceptually driven processes reflect the influence of higher-order cognitive processes such as thoughts, beliefs and expectations.

Cutler and Butterfield (1992) collected examples of slips of the ear from spontaneous speech (see Table 11.1) and described four categories of slip: deletion of a boundary before a weak or strong syllable and insertion of a boundary before a weak or strong syllable. They reported errors of all four types among the 246 errors they collected. Based on the stress patterns of English described above, they predicted more insertion errors before strong syllables and more deletion errors before weak syllables. The data confirmed this hypothesis (see Figure 11.2), supporting the role of strong syllables in segmentation in English; people hear strong syllables in English as marking the onsets of lexical words (content words).

Such cues are language-specific, and just as the structure of one's native language will affect accent in a second language, segmentation of incoming speech is also biased towards the dominant patterns of the native language. Listeners use knowledge of the rhythmic structure in their native language in order to segment speech, leading to language-specific differences in segmentation (see Cutler et al., 1986, 1992; McQueen et al., 2001) and errors in segmentation when listening to a non-native language with a different rhythm (see Cutler et al., 1997, for a review).

Categorical Perception

While there is much variation in the way sounds are produced, we are rarely aware of this and we generally find speech perception to be unambiguous. This is because

> **Categorical perception**
> the perception of stimuli on a sensory continuum as falling into distinct categories.

the cognitive system tends to treat speech sounds as falling within discrete categories rather than as falling along a continuum. This tendency, called **categorical perception**, helps counteract the invariance problem. Categorical perception means we are more sensitive to differences in speech sounds *across* phonetic categories than *within* (Osterhout et al., 1997), although we are still able to detect differences and discriminate between speech sounds within a category (Massaro & Cohen, 1983). Categorical perception applies in particular to consonant sounds; vowel sounds are produced by unobstructed air leaving the larynx and are treated as continuous (see Studdert-Kennedy, 1974). Vowels carry information about stress, rhythm and prosody, but produce smaller categorical effects (Altmann et al., 2014), and a small or absent right ear advantage (see Studdert-Kennedy, 1975; see also Molfese et al., 1983, p. 32, Table 1), a pattern to be discussed in the next section. Neurophysiological evidence suggests that the time course of categorical perception maps to cortical responses present by ~175 ms after sound enters the ear (Bidelman et al., 2013).

Categorical perception was first demonstrated by Liberman et al. (1957). Using a speech synthesizer, they created an artificial continuum of sounds to test the perception of phonemes. Their study showed that, while the physical presentation of sounds may be continuous, perception is categorical – that is, a distinct phoneme will be perceived even for ambiguous points on the continuum. For example, the /b/ sound in 'bit' and the /p/ sound in 'pit' differ in just one feature – **voicing**. The /b/ sound is voiced – that is, the sound is produced while the vocal cords are vibrating; this is said to give a voice onset time of zero. Unvoiced sounds, such as /p/, are made without vibration of the vocal cords; there is a short delay between the closing of the vocal tract and the beginning of the vibration of the vocal cords (the difference actually reflects the duration before the voicing of the subsequent vowel sound; see Field, 2003). This delay may be as little as 80 milliseconds but this small difference allows us to make a /p/ sound or a /b/ sound. By artificially altering the voice onset time using synthesized sounds, a continuum from /b/ to /p/ can be created. While the mid-points along that continuum are objectively ambiguous, people will perceive a /p/ or /b/. For example, using a voice onset time of zero, participants will clearly perceive a /ba/ sound; at a voice onset time of 80 milliseconds, the sound will be a clear /pa/. The boundary at which a /p/ becomes a /b/ is determined by a number of factors, including the rate of speech and context, and can be altered through selective adaptation – by repeatedly presenting a /ba/ sound, the boundary can be moved towards the /p/ end of the continuum (Eimas & Corbit, 1973).

> **Voicing**
> when speech sounds are produced while the vocal cords are vibrating.

> **High amplitude sucking paradigm**
> a method used to study young infants up to 4 months old by reinforcing non-nutritive sucking responses with sound stimuli.

Categorical speech boundaries emerge at a young age. Eimas et al. (1971) devised the **high amplitude sucking paradigm** to test categorical perception in young infants. This technique relies on the fact that babies tend to suck on a soother at a fairly regular rate and this rate increases when the child's attention is drawn to a new stimulus, such as an unusual noise or other change in the environment. Eimas and colleagues played a sound to babies aged 4 months. The same sound was played repeatedly until the infants' sucking rate had settled into a steady rhythm. The sound was then changed. The assumption was that if the sucking rate increased, the child had detected a change in sound. The infants were played sounds along the /ba/–/pa/ continuum, and showed categorical perception by the age of 4 months. This ability has also been demonstrated in non-human species – for example, chinchillas (Kuhl & Miller, 1978).

Babies can distinguish between the speech sounds of many languages at a young age but this ability disappears as they acquire experience of the sounds of their native language (Kuhl, 1993). Phonemes come to sound like a prototype as categorical perception develops and distinctions not made in the native language are treated as belonging to the same category. For example, in Japanese the /l/ and /r/ sounds are assigned to the same category, but they are perceived as absolutely distinct by a native English speaker (see Massaro, 1994).

The Right Ear Advantage for Speech Sounds

In Chapter 10, we saw that, in the vast majority of individuals, the left hemisphere is dominant for language. In Box 10.4 we examined the 'split brain syndrome' and the advantage that occurs in such cases when objects are selected with the right hand, which is controlled by the left hemisphere and therefore gains access to the speech areas. By contrast, objects handled with the left hand have right hemisphere access and do not connect to speech. They therefore cannot be named. Such advantages are not restricted to motor function; other modalities also show a similar effect, including within the typical population.

> Chapter 10, p360

Connections between the ears and auditory cortex are mainly **contralateral**, such that the left hemisphere language areas are accessed more efficiently by stimuli presented to the right ear. This is reflected in the fact that adults show a **right ear advantage** for speech sounds over non-speech sounds (Kimura, 1961). Along with data from categorical perception, the right ear advantage has been taken as evidence for the special treatment of language by the brain. The advantage was initially demonstrated using **dichotic listening** tasks (see also Figure 6.5), in which different words are presented to the right and left ears simultaneously (e.g., see Hugdahl, 2011; Hugdahl & Westerhausen, 2016). Participants in such experiments report more verbal items presented to the right ear, an advantage that holds both for words and nonsense syllables. The advantage applies to consonant sounds in particular; Shankweiler and Studdert-Kennedy (1967) found no advantage for vowels but a large right ear advantage for stop consonants followed by a vowel (such as /pa/, /ga/, /ba/; see Molfese et al., 1983, p. 32, Table 1, for a summary of findings on this point). This right ear advantage reflects superior left hemisphere processing of language stimuli. While inconsistent results have been reported in studies of dichotic listening in tonal languages, this may reflect the nature of the stimuli used. A study that systematically manipulated the levels of speech and linguistic information provided to participants suggested a pattern of ear preference as linguistic information increased, with acoustic analysis of tones preferentially processed in the right hemisphere, and a left hemisphere bias emerging as phonological and lexical-semantic processes were recruited (Mei et al., 2020). However, as is the case with categorical perception, the right ear advantage is not restricted to humans and therefore may not be language specific. Sea lions, for example, show a right ear advantage for recognition of calls of **conspecifics** (see Böye et al., 2005) and macaque monkeys show a similar advantage (Petersen et al., 1978).

> **Contralateral** relating to the opposite side of the body.
> **Right ear advantage** for speech sounds refers to the finding that language sounds are processed more efficiently when presented to the right ear compared to the left.
> **Dichotic listening task** a task where differing stimuli are presented to each ear.

> Chapter 6, p184

> **Conspecifics** members of the same species.

A disruption of the right ear advantage in individuals with aphasia following brain injury has provided further insight into the lateralization of language comprehension, as is discussed in Box 11.1.

> **!** Box 11.1 When Things Go Wrong: Language comprehension in aphasia

Language comprehension, in our native languages, is a seemingly effortless and automatic process for adults. When a brain injury leads to difficulties in language comprehension, we can learn much about the complexity of the cognitive processes underlying the task.

Chapter 10, p364

In Chapter 10, we looked at Wernicke's aphasia and the speech problems associated with this type of aphasia following damage to the temporal region of the language dominant hemisphere (Wernicke, 1874). Speech is typically fluent but impaired, and peppered with phonological **paraphasias** and **neologisms** (Brown, 1981; Goodglass & Kaplan, 1983). Wernicke's aphasia is also associated with a significant deficit in comprehension; the affected individual has difficulties not only comprehending the speech of others, but monitoring and correcting their own speech. This monitoring problem causes significant problems with day-to-day conversations, with impaired comprehension even of single words and an inability to detect and correct verbal output. Even the simple task of repeating back a word may be problematic for the person with Wernicke's aphasia. The right-ear advantage for speech sounds, described above, has been found to be absent in individuals with Wernicke's aphasia (e.g., Crosson & Warren, 1981).

Paraphasias speech errors in aphasia whereby unintended phonemes, syllables or words are output.

Neologisms in aphasia, neologisms are non-words that are produced in place of intended word targets and, if excessive, constitute what is referred to as jargon aphasia.

Pure word deafness is deficit affecting the ability to recognize speech sounds, while comprehension of non-speech sounds remains intact.

There are a number of other very rare conditions that affect language comprehension selectively after brain injury. **Pure word deafness** (sometimes called auditory verbal agnosia) refers to an inability to process auditory speech after a brain injury. In its pure form, pure word deafness is restricted to speech sounds. Individuals with pure word deafness have intact speech, reading and writing, and can differentiate speech from non-speech sounds, but cannot repeat back a spoken word or understand speech. Hemphill and Stengel (1940, cited in Symonds, 1953) give the following description of one patient's experience of pure word deafness:

> *I can hear you dead plain, but I cannot get what you say. The noises are not quite natural. I hear your voice, but not the words. I can hear, but not understand. It does not pronounce itself.*

Maffei et al. (2017) reported a case of pure word deafness in an Italian-speaking woman, referred to as F.O., who after a left temporal stroke showed a selective impairment of auditory speech processing. At the onset of her condition, F.O. reported feeling like she 'had gone deaf', and that what she heard was 'garbled speech'. Her relatives reported that her language was fluent but that she initially had some grammatical problems with neologisms and paraphasias, with errors mostly of a phonemic type. Her speech gradually improved, and normal prosody and articulation were regained, but a speech comprehension deficit remained. By contrast to her speech processing problems, F.O.'s recognition of non-speech sounds was intact: she could recognize environmental noises (such as a doorbell, a police siren), voices and music. She also showed intact reading and writing and, after the initial period of recovery, speech.

Maffei et al. (2017) used a dichotic listening task of the type discussed in the section above to examine how F.O. was processing speech in the cerebral hemispheres. Three consonant–vowel (CV) syllables (/ba/, /da/ and /ga/) were recorded in a female voice and played simultaneously via headphones such that two CV syllables played at a time, one to each ear. The syllables were presented in various iterations for a total of 90 randomized trials and F.O. was asked to report the syllables she had heard on each trial. Her performance was compared to that of a control group of cognitively unimpaired participants. The control group produced the standard effect found in the dichotic listening task – that is, a right ear advantage for speech sounds, with more syllables reported from the right ear than from the left. But F.O.'s performance on the task showed an almost complete suppression of information presented to the right ear (see Figure 11.3). Maffei and colleagues then analysed the responses to right-ear and left-ear syllables separately. While F.O. could report fewer syllables presented to the right ear compared to controls, her performance matched the controls on the left-ear syllables.

Pure word deafness is usually associated with bilateral damage, but can also appear following damage to the dominant hemisphere and is usually explained as a disconnection of Wernicke's area from auditory input (Feinberg & Farah, 2004). In F.O.'s case, the pattern of damage revealed by brain imaging was not altogether supportive of a disconnection account, but pointed to a key role for the left posterior superior temporal gyrus in the processing of speech sounds (Maffei et al., 2017).

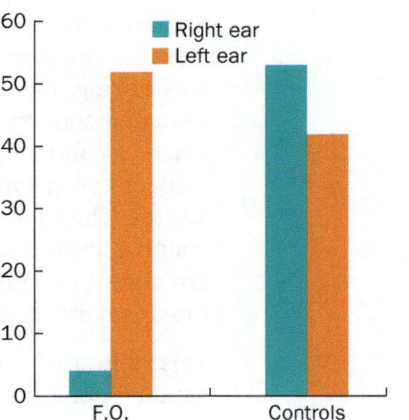

Figure 11.3 Performance of F.O. on the dichotic listening task compared to controls.
The control group shows the typical right-ear advantage. F.O. shows the reverse pattern, with an almost total suppression of stimuli presented to the right ear. Note that the difference between F.O. and the control group on the left-ear task is not statistically significant. Her performance is normal but not superior to the control group for left-ear stimuli.

Source: Data from Maffei et al. (2017), Figure 2.

While individuals with pure word deafness are unable to repeat back spoken words, in an even rarer disorder, called **pure word meaning deafness**, individuals can both hear and repeat words, yet do not know the meaning of a heard word (see Ellis & Young, 1988). Pure word meaning deafness appears to affect the ability to map a word's phonology to its meaning: the individual can listen to the spoken word and repeat it back, thereby showing access to the word's phonemes, yet remains unable to understand its meaning. Because the individual has access to phonology, they can spell the word they have heard and write it down, and then understand the word via its written form (Hall & Riddoch, 2010). There have even been a small number of reports of selective sparing for particular categories of auditorily presented words (e.g., Caño et al., 2008). Such single case studies have proven extremely valuable in the quest to understand how knowledge about language is represented and organized in the brain.

> **Pure word meaning deafness**
> when the patient can repeat back the word, but cannot understand it.

TOP-DOWN INFLUENCES: THE ROLE OF CONTEXT

Thus far, we have seen that a number of factors affect the perception of speech and that context, such as is provided by surrounding sounds, influences recognition. The effect of context can lead to the perception of absent speech sounds, so that perception is consistent with the sentence context. This may be an important property of the system controlling speech recognition, as much speech perception takes place against a backdrop of background noise, which might well obscure some phonemes. It is important that we can still understand what is being said when some of the sounds within the speech stream become inaudible. The **phoneme restoration effect** demonstrates this property of the cognitive system. Warren and Warren (1970) presented participants with recordings of spoken sentences in which a phoneme had been deleted and replaced with a non-speech sound (e.g., a cough or hiss of air). The deleted phoneme is indicated by the asterisk in the following sentences, with the critical sounds (*eel) produced in exactly the same way in each one:

> **Phoneme restoration effect**
> describes the tendency to hear a complete word even when a phoneme has been removed from the input.

- It was found that the *eel was on the axle.
- It was found that the *eel was on the shoe.
- It was found that the *eel was on the table.
- It was found that the *eel was on the orange.

Participants were unaware of the missing phoneme and instead reported a sentence that was consistent with the overall context; that is, for the above sentences, they reported the words 'wheel', 'heel', 'meal' and 'peel' respectively. Since the actual sound was always the same, perception was guided by top-down processing such that the sentence context dictated the meaning. In a similar study, Warren and Obusek (1971) placed a coughing sound in the middle of the sentence 'The state governors met with the respective legislatures convening in the capital city', replacing the last letter 's' in legislatures. Their participants restored the 's' to its correct location and estimated that the cough occurred at a boundary, and not in the middle of the word. Thus, phonemes that are absent can be restored in speech perception; however, whether the effect is a true top-down effect on perception or occurs after perception is debated (Samuel, 1997).

This ability of the cognitive system to restore distortions in speech suggests that a detailed auditory analysis is not always necessary for effective speech perception and it explains our ability to understand speech in poor conditions, such as over a poor telephone connection or above background noise. Saberi and Perrott (1999) partitioned a recorded sentence into short segments of about 50 milliseconds and then time-reversed each segment, before splicing them back together into their original order; the sentence was therefore 'globally contiguous but locally time-reversed' (p. 760). They found that participants had accurate comprehension of the sentences using segments of up to 5 milliseconds in length. Longer segments (100 milliseconds) were partially intelligible. Such data reflect the many sources of information operating to allow accurate speech perception. Some higher-level effects of context are explored in Box 11.2.

>
> ### Box 11.2 Practical Application: The effect of leading questions on memory
>
> **Chapter 6, p176**
>
> **Chapter 15, p548**
>
> **Chapter 10, p328**
>
> **Linguistic determinism**
> the proposal that language determines thought.
> **Linguistic relativity**
> the proposal that language affects thought.
> **Schema**
> a framework that represents a plan or a theory, supporting the organization of knowledge.
>
> In Chapter 6, we saw that memory is a reconstructive process; our long-term episodic memory for events consists of aspects of the events but also our interpretation or recall of those events. In Chapter 15, we examine the effect of emotion on memory. Highly emotional events can have an unpredictable effect on memory, sometimes facilitating and sometimes blocking memory for event details. When somebody is a victim or is a witness to a crime, it is important to be confident that the account given by that individual is accurate. Language comprehension plays a role in event memory, as language and the words used to describe an event can have an effect on memory for that event. In Chapter 10, we encountered the concept of linguistic determinism, the idea that language affects the way we think. The **linguistic determinism** hypothesis, associated with the work of Whorf (1956), proposed that the way in which we use language determines the way we think. In its strong form, the hypothesis lacks empirical support. However, a weaker version of the hypothesis has found some support. This idea of **linguistic relativity** suggests that language can shape or influence thought, to some degree.
>
> A classic demonstration of this, with implications for real-world witness memory, was provided by Loftus and Palmer (1974). Their study examined how the words used when a witness is questioned might influence memory for an event. The study made use of the fact that mental **schemas** affect the way we process information. Bartlett (1932) demonstrated that recall of a story is affected by schemas, which he described as 'an active organisation of past reactions, or of past experiences, which must always be supposed to be operating in any well-adapted organic response' (p. 201; see also Chapter 6). For example, if we

were to witness a car accident, we might expect to see broken glass from a smashed headlight or dented metal from the impact. These schema-consistent expectations may affect memory for the event. If language taps in to these expectations, accuracy of memory may be compromised.

In Loftus and Palmer's first experiment, participants saw short video films depicting a traffic accident and completed a set of questions about them. The critical question involved a judgement of the speed of the vehicles at the time of the collision. The verb was varied in the questions, so that participants were asked *one* of the following questions (the critical word is indicated by an underline):

1. About how fast were the cars going when they hit each other?
2. About how fast were the cars going when they smashed into each other?
3. About how fast were the cars going when they collided with each other?
4. About how fast were the cars going when they bumped into each other?
5. About how fast were the cars going when they contacted with each other?

The results showed that the participants' estimates of the cars' speed varied depending on the verb used during questioning, even though the cars' speed was always the same in the film. Speed estimates varied from 40.5 mph when the verb 'smashed' was used to 31.8 mph when the verb 'contacted' was used (see Table 11.2). While these differences in the estimates may seem quite small, they are statistically significant and in a real-world scenario might mean the difference between a law-abiding driver and a driver who broke the law.

In a second experiment, participants saw another short clip of a car accident. A third of the participants were asked 'About how fast were the cars going when they smashed into each other?' and a third were asked, 'About how fast were the cars going when they hit each other?' The final third of the participants were not questioned about the speed of the vehicles. A week later, all participants were asked 'Did you see any broken glass?' There was no broken glass in the film clip, but Loftus and Palmer hypothesized that, if the language used had affected the reconstructive process of memory, the participants who heard the verb 'smash' would be more likely to report having seen broken glass, since that would be consistent with the schema of a car 'smash'.

The results showed that participants who were questioned using the verb 'smash' estimated the vehicle speed as being significantly faster than those who heard 'hit'. Table 11.3 shows the distribution of responses to the question 'Did you see any broken glass?' The use of the verb 'smashed' was associated with more 'yes' responses to the presence of broken glass, as well as the higher speed estimates.

The findings of the first experiment, taken alone, could be due to a response bias; perhaps the participants were uncertain as to the actual speed of the vehicles and so they estimated in line with the expectation that seemed to be suggested by the wording of the question. The findings from the second

Table 11.2 Verbs Used and Mean Speed Estimates in Miles Per Hour as Reported by Participants

Verbs	Mean speed estimate (mph)
smashed	40.5
collided	39.3
bumped	38.1
hit	34.0
contacted	31.8

Source: Data from Loftus & Palmer (1974), Experiment 1.

Table 11.3 Distribution of Responses to the Question 'Did you see any broken glass?'

	Verb used in questioning		
Response	Smashed	Hit	Control (no question about speed)
Yes	16	7	6
No	34	43	44

Source: Data from Loftus & Palmer (1974), Experiment 2.

experiment, however, support a 'reconstructive hypothesis' – that is, that memory had been distorted by the verbal label. A week after the participants had viewed the film, those who were questioned using a biasing verb ('smash') reported aspects of the event that had not occurred (broken glass). These data suggest an influence of language comprehension on memory that persists over time.

Since these demonstrations by Loftus and Palmer, various effects of language comprehension have been demonstrated in criminal interrogations. Negative effects of cross-examination on the accuracy of eyewitness testimony have been demonstrated in both adults (e.g., Valentine & Maras, 2011) and in children (e.g., Zajac et al., 2018). Use of 'bait questions' – where a suspect is questioned about the existence of hypothetical evidence – can affect participants' memory such that they can come to believe that the hypothetical evidence really existed (Crozier et al., 2020; Luke et al., 2017). Susceptibility to leading questions increases with the level of perceptual load in a task – that is, the amount of information involved in processing task-relevant stimuli (see Murphy & Greene, 2016). For the suspect, leading questions asked during interrogation can lead to a false confession, even when interrogation tactics are not coercive (Paton et al. 2018; see also Gudjonsson, 2018; Kassin, 2017).

Understanding the factors that can influence memory for events, and that place individuals, witnesses, suspects or victims at a heightened risk of giving a confident but inaccurate account, or produce a false confession, is essential for the prevention of miscarriages of justice. The study of language comprehension has an important role to play in uncovering such factors.

Visual Cues: The McGurk Effect

Chapter 2, p34

McGurk effect
a perceptual illusion that illustrates the interplay of visual and auditory processing in speech perception.

We think of speech perception as a task of auditory perception, but cues from other modalities, notably vision, also play a role in accurate comprehension (see also the discussion of multisensory perception in Chapter 2). Face processing involves analyses conducted specifically to facilitate speech recognition, lip-reading being the most obvious example of a visual cue to speech content. Particularly in a noisy environment, we can use facial cues to aid understanding of speech. This influence of visual stimuli is well demonstrated by a phenomenon known as the **McGurk effect**. McGurk and MacDonald (1976) presented participants with conflicting visual and auditory cues. Participants heard a recording of the sound /ba/, but at the same time viewed a video recording of a person mouthing /ga/. The participants reported a blending of the visual and auditory cues, perceiving the sound as /da/. The boundary between sounds created by categorical perception can be manipulated via a conflicting visual stimulus. For example, Massaro and Cohen (1983) used a speech synthesizer to create a set of sounds along a continuum from /ba/ to /da/. As participants listened to these recordings, they saw a video of a person mouthing either /ba/ or /da/. When an ambiguous marginal version of a sound was played – for example, a marginal version of /da/ – participants were more likely to interpret it as /ba/ when the face seen in the video was saying /ba/.

The McGurk effect demonstrates the role of visual cues in disambiguating speech and facilitating speech perception. It has proven to be a robust effect, even holding across genders, where a male voice might be paired with a recording of a female face (Green et al., 1991). However, individual differences in the degree to which (and the conditions under which) the effect might be experienced have been reported (Basu Mallick et al., 2015; Shahin, 2019; see also Proverbio et al., 2018), suggesting that some people can override the effect better than others.

MODELS OF SPEECH PERCEPTION

Models of speech perception attempt to explain how information coming in from the continuous stream of speech that we hear makes contact with our stored knowledge about words. These models fall into two broad categories: those that consider the processes of speech perception to be modular and those that argue that interactive processing underlies speech perception. Modular theories propose a series of independently functioning modules that process information without being influenced by context; that is, at the lower level of speech processing, knowledge about words does not influence processing (e.g., Cutler & Norris, 1979). While the influence of top-down knowledge on initial processing continues to be debated, it is clear that our store of knowledge about words affects speech perception in some key ways (Treiman et al., 2003).

The degree of interactivity between **top-down** and **bottom-up** processes is explored in the second class of models. Interactive models propose that multiple sources of influence affect speech processing, and that top-down influences play a major role. Two influential models will be discussed here, both of which take an interactive approach, but consider interactivity of top-down and bottom-up processes to different extents: the cohort model proposed by Marslen-Wilson and Tyler (1980; see also the distributed cohort model, Gaskell & Marslen-Wilson, 1997) and the TRACE model of McClelland and Elman (1986).

> **Top down**
> or conceptually driven processes reflect the influence of higher-order cognitive processes such as thoughts, beliefs and expectations.
>
> **Bottom up**
> stimulus-driven processing of incoming sensory information that produces increasingly elaborate and meaningful representations of the input.

The Cohort Model

We do not have to wait until the whole word is uttered before it is processed; some words can be recognized based on partial information (although that is not to say that all words can be recognized before their acoustic offset; see Grosjean & Gee, 1987). Marslen-Wilson and Tyler's (1980) cohort model of speech recognition reflects the sequential nature of speech perception and assumes that incoming speech sounds have direct and parallel access to the store of words in the mental lexicon. The model proposes that we establish expectations regarding likely target words once we have heard the initial phonemes of a spoken word. The set of words that is consistent with the initial sounds is the 'word initial cohort'. As more phonemes follow as input, and therefore more information about the target word is provided, the set of available candidate words reduces, such that those which no longer fit the incoming pattern lower in activation and are dropped from the set while those remaining in the cohort become fewer, until only the target remains (see Figure 11.4). This is the *uniqueness point*, although of course the target may be recognized before this point, if few words share the acoustic sequence, for example.

The original model assumed that candidate items dropped out from the set once any inconsistent information was input. The autocomplete function of predictive texting and of some internet search engines follows a similar logic: candidate words are suggested, and the set alters as you continue to type. The original

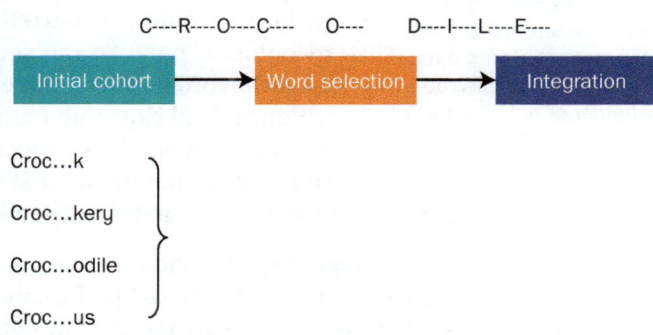

Figure 11.4 The cohort model of spoken word recognition.
Initially a large set of words forms the cohort based on the initial phonemes heard. As the speech input progresses the options decrease until only the target word is left. Here, the word 'crocodile' is recognized at 'od' as no other words in English compete thereafter.

Source: Adapted from Marslen-Wilson & Tyler (1980).

cohort model considered sentence context as a strong cue to word identity; the cohort can reduce down based on information such as context, so that unlikely selections will attract lower activation and drop from the set of candidate words. The original version of the cohort model proposed that the bottom-up processing of the acoustic signal and the top-down influence of sentence context would operate simultaneously. However, the revised model (e.g., Marslen-Wilson, 1990) has moved the role of context to a late point in processing; instead of affecting word selection early on, context plays a role only at the integration stage, at the point at which sentence meaning is decided. The revised model therefore places more emphasis on bottom-up processes. The revised theory has also reappraised the notion of activation of cohort words so that activation of items is a matter of degree rather than all-or-none. For example, words that are acoustically similar but not entirely consistent with the target can have some degree of activation associated with them. Similarly, there is more flexibility in the degree of match required from the first phoneme of the word. This revision has addressed some findings that were inconsistent with the original model (e.g., Frauenfelder et al., 2001).

The gating paradigm (Grosjean, 1980) has been used to identify a word's uniqueness point. A spoken word is presented as a 'left to right' sequence of sounds, in segments of increasing duration. For example, initially 40 milliseconds of the word might be presented, then 80 milliseconds, and so on until the word is presented in full. The participants must guess the word in each case and may also supply a confidence rating as to how sure they are that they have identified the correct target word (see Grosjean, 2008). This method allows one to determine how much of a word needs to be heard before it can be correctly isolated – the word's isolation point is the point at which the listener has a definite candidate word in mind, and this point occurs close to Marslen-Wilson and Tyler's uniqueness point. Grosjean (1985) uses the term total acceptance point for the moment, beyond the isolation point, when the selected word comes to be used in sentence interpretation; this is effectively the point of word recognition.

> **Event-related potentials (ERP)**
> a functional brain imaging method recording electrical activity during repeated stimulus presentations.
> **Lexical decision task**
> a task where participants are presented with a letter string and must decide whether or not it is a word.

Electrophysiological evidence for the model was provided by an **event-related potential (ERP)** study by O'Rourke and Holcomb (2002). They had participants perform a **lexical decision task** (that is, to decide whether a letter string is a word) while ERPs were measured. The stimuli were selected such that they differed in their recognition points – that is, for some words, the point at which no other words matched the acoustic sequence occurred early, for some it occurred late. For example, the word 'crocodile' has a recognition point at the second syllable (see Figure 11.4), since no other English words will complete the segment 'crocod . . .' (Taft & Hambly, 1986). O'Rourke and Holcomb found that the N400 ERP component (a wave linked to processes involved in word recognition; see Bentin et al., 1985; Holcomb, 1988) occurred sooner for words that had early recognition points, consistent with a faster response time in the lexical decision task.

Electrophysiological evidence also supports the facilitatory effect of context, and suggests that it plays an early role, consistent with the original cohort model but not the revised version. For example, Van Petten et al. (1999) recorded ERPs as participants heard consistent or incongruous words at the end of spoken sentences. They found that the N400 started 200 milliseconds before the words' isolation points, which supports the idea that word recognition can occur before the point at which the provided acoustic input is sufficient to be able to *uniquely* identify the word. Such a process is efficient as access to meaning can occur before the word is complete and multiple meanings are briefly activated within the cohort words (Marslen-Wilson, 1987).

Evaluation

Generally, tests of the cohort model have treated words as isolated within the speech stream. The cohort model itself proposed that the starting sounds of a word form the initial word cohort. However, the model does not address precisely how the start of a word is identified within a fluent and continuous stream of speech. The size of the cohort generated would also seem to be important, yet the model does not directly address the effect of cohort size on the speed of word recognition. Furthermore, some studies have shown that the recognition of a word within fluent speech can occur after subsequent words have been presented (e.g., Bard et al., 1988; see Dahan, 2010) – the cohort model suggests that a word is identified once other candidate words have been ruled out, and so it is not clear why such a delay in word recognition is sometimes experienced.

TRACE

The TRACE model of speech perception (McClelland & Elman, 1986; see also Elman & McClelland, 1988) presents an alternative to the modular view that lower-level phonemic processes are unaffected by processing that occurs at higher levels in the system. TRACE considers top-down effects as playing a key role in speech perception. TRACE is a connectionist model, the 'trace' referring to the entire network of units and the particular pattern of activation associated with it: 'the pattern of activation left by a spoken input is a trace of the analysis of the input at each of the three processing levels' (McClelland & Elman, 1986, pp. 66–67). The model has some similarities with the cohort model of Marslen-Wilson and Tyler (1980). The concepts of activation and competition are central, for example, but TRACE claimed to improve on the cohort model by considering top-down processes and the processing of suboptimal (noisy) input. Like the revised cohort model, TRACE takes a gradated approach to activation levels, in that words can acquire a level of activation as a function of shared features with other candidate words.

McClelland and Elman (1986) use as an example the sentence 'she received a valuable gift' – what contributes to the perception of the phoneme /g/ in 'gift'? A number of factors, including acoustic information, cues from other phonemes in the same word, as well as the syntactic and semantic context, contribute to speech perception. They recognized that a model must capture these multiple sources of information influencing speech perception. The model therefore addresses the fact that 'the perceptual system uses information from the context in which an utterance occurs to alter connections dynamically, thereby effectively allowing the context to retune the perceptual mechanism in the course of processing' (McClelland & Elman, 1986, p. 62). When conditions degrade (such as when encountering speech against a noisy background), more top-down processing comes into play, and semantic and syntactic cues may become more influential. The model's architecture is based on that of earlier models (e.g., HEARSAY; see Erman & Lesser, 1980) but it uses a dynamic, self-updating processing system in order to reflect the online and interactive nature of speech processing.

Processing units form three levels, dealing with features, phonemes and words. The three levels of units follow a **localist representation** – that is, particular units represent particular features, words etc., rather than activation being distributed across a set of units to represent features, as is typically the case in connectionist models. At the feature level, feature detectors process information about several sound properties, (sub-phoneme features, such as voicing and manner of articulation, for example). Phoneme detectors respond to each phoneme and at the word level detectors represent each word. Processing occurs in time slices to simulate the gradual build-up of information from the incoming speech stream (and to account for

> **Localist representation**
> where a single unit represents a particular concept.

effects such as co-articulation). TRACE does not make a word-by-word sequentiality assumption, however, unlike the cohort model (see also Grosjean & Gee, 1987). Activation can be bidirectional, with bottom-up connections from feature to phoneme to word, and top-down activation from word to phoneme to feature. Excitatory and inhibitory links within levels create a set of possible responses such that activation of a unit represents the 'combined evidence' for the presence of the particular linguistic unit (McClelland et al., 2006). Figure 11.5 shows the architecture of the TRACE model, with processing units at the feature level, phoneme level and word levels. As shown in Figure 11.5, excitation is bidirectional – that is, there are both bottom-up (features to phonemes to words) and top-down (words to phonemes to features) influences. Inhibitory connections within a level allow units to compete for activation; for example, units at the phoneme level represent different possible interpretations of the speech input at that moment, and so activation of one unit inhibits other units at that level, reducing ambiguity.

Evaluation

This interactive account of the processes involved in speech perception shows how a number of factors contribute to the perception of a particular phoneme, and accounts for categorical perception, co-articulation and lexicality effects. McClelland and Elman (1986) summarized TRACE's successes as:

- successfully identifying successive phonemes from overlapping speech input
- accounting for how word level information is used to supplement speech information in identifying phonemes
- accounting for phonotactic effects without explicit phonotactic rules being represented while also accounting for irregulars.

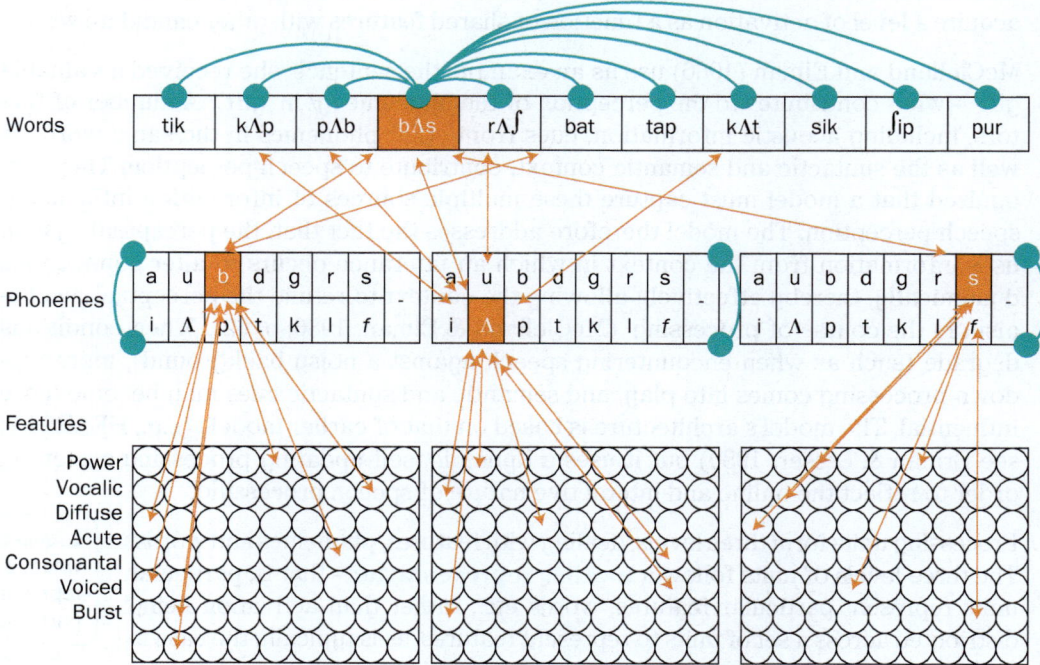

Figure 11.5 Architecture of the TRACE model.
Red lines indicate excitatory links and blue lines inhibitory links. Units within a layer compete through inhibitory connections – note that the full set is shown here for the lexical layer only, and for clarity only a schematic connection is shown at the phoneme level.

Source: Reprinted from McClelland et al. (2006), with permission from Elsevier.

However, TRACE arguably overestimates the role of top-down effects; given the acoustic information provided in the speech signal under normal conditions, will top-down processing always have a great deal of involvement, from the earliest stages, in speech perception? Given the information available in the speech signal it may be that the role of top-down processes is overplayed. Norris et al. (2000) suggest that such models 'run the risk of hallucinating' (p. 302); in the case of a mispronunciation, for example, empirical evidence suggests that such errors are noticed, and do affect performance.

Electrophysiological data has been used to demonstrate a direct effect of lexical context on sublexical processing, as predicted by interactive models such as TRACE (e.g., Noe & Fischer-Baum, 2020). While the balance of evidence arguably leans towards the interactive accounts, the precise extent of top-down influence on early perceptual processes continues to be debated.

UNDERSTANDING WORDS AND SENTENCES

Words do not occur in isolation; language comprehension generally involves understanding sequences of words and sentences. Levy (2008, p. 1127) suggested that any realistic theory of sentence comprehension must be able to account for:

- processing of input that is not perfectly formed
- how we resolve ambiguity
- how we make inferences on the basis of incomplete input, and
- how we overcome points of difficulty within a sentence (some grammatical structures, as we will see, pose difficulty for the system).

The ambiguity that we noted in the speech signal (see above) continues at the level of sentences. Words may have multiple meanings and there may be more than one way to interpret the grammatical properties of words as used in a sentence.

Lexical Access

Word recognition is a process of **lexical access**. This is the process by which we retrieve information about word meaning from the store of words called the lexicon, a component of semantic memory, so as to understand what is being communicated. There are two main types of model of lexical access. Serial search models or autonomous search models (e.g., Forster, 1979, 1989) propose a series of stages to word recognition, with orthographical access, phonological access and semantic/syntactic access occurring at three separate stages, only one of which is accessed at a given time. When a word is initially encountered, either by reading it or by hearing it, a perceptual analysis is carried out and the pattern is then analysed. Entries in each lexicon are arranged by frequency and are retrieved via a search process. Direct access models, such as Morton's (1970, 1979; Morton & Patterson, 1980) logogen model, propose parallel word access. Each word or morpheme within the lexicon is represented by a logogen (a unit that specifies the word's phonological, semantic, orthographic features) and retrieval occurs through activation rather than a search process. Information from orthographic, phonological and semantic representations can be processed in parallel. Similarities between stimuli will lead to activation and this, combined with thresholds on words, accounts for effects such as semantic priming. This model has influenced subsequent models of word recognition, particularly connectionist accounts.

> **Lexical access** is the process by which we access stored knowledge about words.

> **Lexical decision task**
> a task where participants are presented with a letter string and must decide whether or not it is a word.
>
> **Word naming tasks**
> require participants to name a word, while response time is measured.
>
> **Sentence verification tasks**
> present a sentence frame with a target word, and the participant must decide if the word fits in the frame.

Lexical access has been investigated using a number of experimental and neuroscientific methodologies. **Lexical decision tasks** present strings of letters to participants; some of these strings are words (e.g., clip) and some are non-words (e.g., plic). Participants must decide if the string is a word; accuracy and response times are measured. The assumption is that the duration it takes to respond reflects the amount of processing involved in the decision. **Word naming tasks** require participants to name a word, while response time is measured. Speed of access is inferred from speed of response. **Sentence verification tasks** present a sentence frame and a target word; the participant must decide if the word fits in the frame (e.g., 'The carrot grew in the . . .' LAKE). This requires access to word meaning. By manipulating the stimuli used in such tasks, we can investigate how the process of lexical access is achieved and the different stages involved. A number of important factors affecting lexical access have been identified. Here, we will look at the effects of frequency, semantic priming, syntactic context and lexical ambiguity.

Frequency effects

Although we have a large vocabulary (estimated at 40,000+ uninflected words), a large set of these words will be used rarely (low frequency words), while a smaller number of words will be used very often (high frequency words). The frequency with which a word is used in a language affects cognitive processing; the higher the frequency, the easier the word is to process, generally. Frequency effects apply to **open-class words** such as nouns, verbs and adjectives, while **closed-class words** (such as articles, conjunctions, prepositions) do not tend to produce such effects. Frequency is a particularly important factor in lexical decision (deciding whether a letter string is a word; Whaley, 1978). The magnitude of the effect of frequency differs depending on the task used (e.g., Balota & Chumbley, 1984), which has led researchers to try to develop a method that can capture performance *during* lexical access, as response time to experimental tasks may reflect lexical access or post-access decision making. **Eye tracking** provides one such method. Studies of eye movements when reading show that people fixate on low frequency words for about 40 milliseconds longer (Rayner et al., 2003). Because frequency has such an effect on performance, it is important that it is controlled in experiments using words as stimuli. Several lists of word frequency counts are available for that purpose, for example the Kucera–Francis (1967) written frequency norms, CELEX (Baayen et al., 1995), the Brown verbal frequencies (Brown, 1984) and the Thorndike–Lorge counts (Thorndike & Lorge, 1944). Eye-movement data is discussed in further detail below.

> **Open-class words**
> content words such as nouns, verbs and adjectives. New words can be added to this class of words.
>
> **Closed-class words**
> such as articles, conjunctions, prepositions, remain stable over time and are not added to.
>
> **Eye tracking**
> the measurement of people's eye movements while reading or inspecting a visual scene.
>
> **Priming**
> an implicit memory effect whereby exposure to a stimulus affects a subsequent response.
>
> **Semantic priming**
> the finding that responses to a target word are faster when it is preceded by a semantically associated word, the 'prime'.

Priming effects

Priming (see also Chapter 7) refers to a methodology used to examine the influence of task context on performance. The methods used to study priming effects measure responses to a target stimulus as a function of its relationship with a preceding stimulus, the prime, which provides a context for the target. When semantically related words are used in a lexical decision task, response time decreases, an effect known as **semantic priming**. This effect was first described by Cattell (1888). For example, if the target word *nurse* is preceded by the prime *hospital*, lexical decision is faster than when the target is preceded by a neutral word (*school*). The word *hospital* primes responses to *nurse*; through spreading

> Chapter 7, p218

activation, the related word becomes more likely to be selected (Meyer & Schvaneveldt, 1971). The closer the words are in meaning, the greater the semantic priming effect. Semantic priming speeds processing and allows context to be used in speech and visual word recognition. The priming stimuli that are studied generally have a facilitatory effect but an inhibitory effect can also be observed.

Another type of priming effect, related to frequency (see above) is **repetition priming**. Response times in a lexical decision task decrease with repeated exposure to a word (Scarborough et al., 1977). The effect of repetition on low frequency words is stronger than that on high frequency words, a finding known as the frequency attenuation effect (Forster & Davis, 1984).

> **Repetition priming** the finding that repeated exposure to a word leads to faster responses in a lexical decision task.

Syntactic context

The syntactic category of the word and sentence context have also been shown to affect lexical decision time. For example, Wright and Garrett (1984) presented participants with sentences such as:

a If your bicycle is stolen you must   FORMULATE
b If your bicycle is stolen you must   BATTERIES
c For now, the happy families live with   FORMULATE
d For now, the happy families live with   BATTERIES

The target word in each case is the last word, shown in capital letters above. Target words were matched for frequency and were semantically incongruous with the preceding sentence. In sentences (a) and (d), the nonsensical final word belongs to the correct syntactic category (a main verb to follow the modal verb 'must'). Participants were significantly faster in recognizing words when they occurred in sentences that provided the appropriate grammatical context than when not. For example, in the sentences above, the word 'batteries' is recognized faster when it occurs in sentence (d) compared to sentence (b). Targets belonging to the syntactic category appropriate to the context produce faster response times, an example of syntactic priming of the target word.

Mostly, research has considered syntactic priming in the context of speech production, and it is well documented that exposure to certain syntactic constructions increases the likelihood that they will subsequently be used (e.g., Bock, 1986). However, emerging data suggest a similar effect for comprehension. For example, Thothathiri and Snedeker (2008), using an eye movement paradigm, noted reliable effects of syntactic structure on ambiguity resolution in sentence processing.

Lexical ambiguity

Many words have multiple meanings. The word 'bank', for example, has more than one meaning. Its most frequent meaning refers to a financial institution, but it could also mean 'side' (as in 'riverbank'), or 'lean' or 'rely' (to bank on something). In the case of 'bank', the various meanings are associated with the same pronunciation. By contrast, **homographs** share spelling but have more than one pronunciation (e.g., *tear, row, lead*). Dominant meaning and context play key roles in resolving lexical ambiguity.

> **Homographs** are words with the same spelling, but more than one meaning and pronunciation.

Ambiguous words will have multiple representations in memory and therefore may be treated differently than unambiguous words. Foss (1969, 1970) demonstrated this difference using a phoneme monitoring task in which participants listened to sentences and responded when they detected a particular phoneme – for example, /r/.

Foss found that response times were slower when the phoneme followed an ambiguous word in a sentence compared to when it followed an unambiguous word. This is consistent with the view that when an ambiguous word is encountered, more than one meaning is initially activated, rather than just the one appropriate to the current context. Context subsequently influences processing, but initially multiple meanings are active.

To explore this effect, Swinney (1979) used a cross-modal priming technique in which participants performed a visual lexical decision task while at the same time listening to related sentences, such as:

> *The government building had been plagued with problems. The man was not surprised when he found several [spiders, roaches and other] bugs in the corner of his room.*

The disambiguating phrase [spiders, roaches and other] was included in some cases. The ambiguous word 'bug' has two meanings: a surveillance device and an insect. Presence of the phrase [spiders, roaches and other] suggests the latter meaning: 'insect'. A concurrent lexical decision task presented words visually; words such as 'ant', 'spy' or the neutral word 'sew' were presented visually and the time taken by participants to decide if the stimulus was a word was measured. If the context provided by the auditory phrase [spiders, roaches and other] primes the meaning of 'ant' but not 'spy', we could conclude that only one meaning of the word 'bug' was active. However, Swinney found that both meanings were initially active, as facilitation occurred for both 'ant' and 'spy' for target words presented closely following the ambiguous word. These and subsequent data suggest that, in general, context does not affect initial access to multiple meanings, although the nature of the task, the context and the word (meaning) frequency play important roles in activation of meanings (see Harley, 2008, for an overview).

Ambiguous words have also been used extensively in studies of bilingual lexical access. The use of cross-language or interlingual homographs has contributed to research in this area, as many languages share lexical items that have different meanings and pronunciations in the two languages. Examples include the French and English PAIN and COIN, the German and English GIFT and WAS, or the Dutch and English ANGEL and STEM or the Irish and English TEACH and FEAR. Evidence from such studies suggests that both languages are activated in bilinguals – that is, that initial access is language non-selective (e.g., Dijkstra, 2005; Kroll & Dussias, 2004).

> **Human factors**
> the multidisciplinary study of the interplay between human capabilities and failings and interactions with technology, machines and other aspects of the physical environment.
> **Linguistic relativity**
> the proposal that language affects thought.

Ambiguity at the sentence level has also been studied extensively in **human factors** research and particularly in relation to human error. The study of the contribution of language comprehension to accident prevention has a long history. The concept of **linguistic relativity** is explored in Box 11.2. An interesting application of this to accident prevention is illustrated by Whorf's (e.g., 1956) example of the 'empty' gasoline drums. Whorf worked for a company assessing insurance risk. He gave the example of a storage area in a factory where gasoline drums are placed when they are no longer in use. If this area is referred to as containing 'gasoline drums', we might predict cautious behaviour. However, if they are described as 'empty' drums, workers' behaviour might be more risky. Whorf argued that assumptions flow from different meanings of the use of the word 'empty'. The 'empty' drums are hazardous as they contain explosive vapour. But if the drums are thought of as empty, workers might be careless around them. At a time when workers might have carried a lit cigarette, and perhaps tossed the ends into an empty drum, a hazard would be created. A more recent example of how language comprehension might contribute to an accident is explored in Box 11.3.

Box 11.3 Practical Application: Language ambiguity and accident prevention

Language comprehension is generally an effortless and error-free process. When a miscommunication occurs in everyday conversation, we might not immediately recognize it, but we can generally correct it once it is recognized. In high stakes environments, however, an error in language can produce catastrophic results. One such environment is air traffic control.

As noted by Barshi and Farris (2016), experts who operate in such complex environments are not immune from comprehension errors, and the working memory requirements and language processes are the same as for non-experts. Air traffic control requires very

© Daniil Skoblov/Shutterstock

fast decision making, under high pressure. It requires use of a common vocabulary by speakers of many languages (see Estival et al., 2016), often in the presence of background noise and with many visual and auditory distractions. Language errors have been identified in a number of serious air traffic accidents, and analysis of these errors has proven essential for the avoidance of future accidents. Applied cognitive psychology has a critical role to play in accident prevention, because understanding language processing errors requires knowledge of many other facets of human cognition. One particularly stark example of a language problem leading to an air traffic accident has been the subject of extensive analysis.

In March 1977, two Boeing 747 passenger aircraft collided at Tenerife's Los Rodeos airport, killing 583 people. A number of factors contributed to the disaster, not least the fog engulfing the airport that day, diverted flights due to airport closures, and technical issues affecting radio communication between the control tower and the two aircraft. One key element that contributed to the disaster was miscommunication between the aircraft crew and air traffic control.

Cushing (1994) analysed the voice-recorder data from the accident and identified several points at which miscommunication contributed to the unfolding of events. One miscommunication stemmed from ambiguity in the segment transcribed below. The pilot of one of the airplanes stated, 'we are now at take-off', meaning 'we are now taking off'. But the tower controllers interpreted the phrase as 'we are now at the take-off point'. The dialogue from the tower recording illustrates the point of error (underlined) and the precise timestamp of each event shows how quickly events unfold (from Cushing, 1994):

> 1705:53.41 Tower: KLM eight seven zero five you are cleared to the Papa Beacon, climb to and maintain flight level nine zero, right turn after takeoff, proceed with heading four zero until intercepting the three two five radial from Las Palmas VOR (1706:08.09).
>
> 1706:09.61 KLM 4805: Ah – roger sir, we are cleared to the Papa Beacon, flight level nine zero until intercepting the three two five. <u>We are now at takeoff</u> (1706:17.79)
>
> 1706:18.19 Tower: OK . . . <u>Stand by for takeoff</u>, I will call you. (1706:21.79).

As Cushing notes, part of the confusion here comes from line 1705:53.41, because an instruction is given to the pilot concerning actions after take-off. This does not necessarily imply permission to take off. The pilot interpreted the instruction as permission to take off, however. The air traffic controller expected the pilot to be standing by for take-off and went on to direct the second airplane on to the runway and directly into the path of the (KLM) airplane, which had begun its take-off run. (1706:50: Collision occurs.) The pilot should have been alerted by the phrase 'Stand by for takeoff'. However, an

> engine squeal is heard at 1706:19.39, ending at 1706:22.06, and may have compromised that communication. The phrase 'We are now at takeoff' should not be ambiguous. It should be clear to each side what was meant, and yet it would seem that the tower controller thought that the pilot was awaiting further instruction.
>
> Note the timeline here. Like any conversation, the dialogue moves on quickly; the ambiguity goes undetected, with devastating consequences. The pilot began to take off, without having being cleared to do so and the plane collided with another airplane already on the runway. All 248 people on board the fully fuelled airplane that was taking off were killed. There were 335 fatalities and 61 survivors from the airplane that had been on the ground. As a result of the subsequent investigation, changes were introduced to standardize communication in the aviation sector, which has improved passenger safety (see Estival et al., 2016). However, while the meaning of phrases can be agreed, ambiguity at the sound level remains a significant problem, particularly in the presence of background noise.

Syntax and Semantics

Chapter 10, p330

The term syntax refers to the rules that govern language use; for example, most languages favour a particular word order, such as subject–verb–object in English (see Chapter 10). Several species can respond to 'words' or verbal labels, but only humans can use complex syntax. In Chapter 10, we saw that animal communication systems can have symbolic and arbitrary features. Vervet monkeys use different calls to warn their group members of imminent threats, and the sounds made are arbitrarily related to the predator. Other animals can also show a remarkable ability for word learning, with dogs proving particularly impressive. For example, Kaminski et al. (2004) demonstrated that Rico, a Border collie, could 'fast-map' – that is, infer the referent of a new word by exclusion learning. Rico knew the labels of more than 200 objects and, when presented with a new spoken word and a novel item among a set of familiar items, could reliably infer that the new word must belong with the novel item (see also Kaminski et al., 2009). Pilley (2013) extended this line of research by examining understanding of word order. He demonstrated comprehension in another Border collie, Chaser (who had a vocabulary of more than 1,000 nouns), of sentences consisting of three grammatical elements: a prepositional object, verb and direct object (e.g., *to Frisbee take ball* versus *to ball take Frisbee*). A key limitation is that of working memory; in order to be able to comprehend a sentence, one must hold the elements of the sentence in mind while processing is ongoing. This is a restriction for animals, and efforts to train syntax in animals have produced rather limited results compared to their word learning abilities (e.g., see Herman et al., 1984; Savage-Rumbaugh et al., 1998).

© xkunclova/Shutterstock

When we hear or read a sentence, we generally readily assign structure and meaning to it, although many sentences can be ambiguous, at least temporarily. The adage 'Time flies like an arrow' has almost 100 grammatically possible interpretations (Altmann, 1998), among them the interpretation attributed to Groucho Marx: 'Time flies like an arrow; fruit flies like a banana.' Despite this ambiguity, on hearing the sentence, we show a preference for one structure and interpretation; it is only when we realize that a mistake may have been made that we go back and look for other alternatives. The process by which we establish a mental representation of the syntactic structure of a sentence is called **parsing**. The psychological study of parsing has been heavily influenced by ideas from the field of linguistics. In fact, the study of the psychology of language is sometimes referred to as **psycholinguistics**, reflecting the influence of linguistics on psychological models of language generally. The influence of linguistics reflects a recognition that 'human minds feed on linguistic symbols' (Miller, 1968, p. 29).

> **Parsing**
> the process by which we assign a syntactic structure to a sentence.
>
> **Psycholinguistics**
> the branch of study concerned with the mental processes underlying language comprehension and production.

Cognitive psychology has been greatly influenced by the linguist Noam Chomsky (1957, 1965, 1980). Chomsky aimed to establish a set of rules, a grammar, that would describe the well-formed grammatical sentences in a language, but produce none that are ungrammatical. Chomsky made the distinction between a sentence's deep and surface structure (or, to avoid connotations raised by the terms 'deep' and 'surface', d-structure and s-structure). This influential idea suggests that superficially different sentences can have the same underlying structure and meaning, and that sentence components can maintain their role in a sentence even though their position in a sentence changes. Chomsky's work had the advantage of providing a framework that could be tested empirically by cognitive scientists.

For example, active and passive voice sentences have different surface structures but essentially have the same deep structure:

- Active voice: The boy ate the cake.
- Passive voice: The cake was eaten by the boy.

There may be a change in emphasis (the focus of the first sentence is on the boy while in the second it is on the cake), but in each case the boy is doing the eating and the cake is being eaten.

It might be predicted on this basis that passive voice sentences would take more time to process than their active voice counterparts. However, this is not always the case. Semantic information interacts with syntactic processing and can reduce processing load in cases where meaning can inform syntactic processing. For example, Slobin (1966) used a **sentence verification task** with reversible and irreversible passives. Sentences were presented along with a picture that in some cases matched the sentence and participants decided if the sentence described the picture. In a reversible passive, either noun could perform the action of the verb; its agent cannot be inferred from semantics. In an irreversible passive, there is only one feasible agent, for example:

> **Sentence verification tasks**
> tasks present a sentence frame with a target word, and the participant must decide if the word fits in the frame.

A The boy chased the dog; the dog was chased by the boy.
B The boy called the dog; the dog was called by the boy.

> Chapter 10, p324

Sentence A is reversible: taking the content words 'boy', 'dog' and 'chase', it could be that the dog is chasing the boy or the boy is chasing the dog. But in sentence B there is only one possible interpretation – the dog cannot be calling the boy.

Slobin (1966) found that irreversible passives did not require more processing time than an active voice sentence, whereas reversible passives did. Such data show the interaction of semantic and syntactic processing in sentence comprehension and are consistent with evidence from neuropsychology. Carramazza and Zurif (1976) found that people with **Broca's aphasia** (see Chapter 10) with impairments consistent with **agrammatism** could

> **Broca's aphasia**
> an acquired language disorder characterized by non-fluent speech, reduced speech output and problems with grammar processing.
>
> **Agrammatism**
> a pattern of syntactic deficit affecting speech production following brain injury.

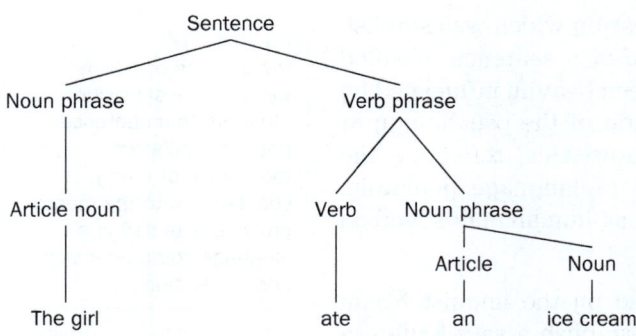

Figure 11.6 A phrase structure tree for the sentence 'The girl ate an ice cream.'

Wernicke's aphasia
a fluent aphasia, characterized by fluent but meaningless output and repetition errors.
Phrase structure tree
a graphic representation of the syntactic structure of a sentence.
Garden path sentence
a grammatically correct but ambiguous sentence that biases the reader's initial parsing.

match pictures to irreversible sentences but performed poorly when presented with reversible sentences. This difference suggests that they could use semantic information in irreversible sentences to compensate for the deficit in syntax processing. By contrast, patients with **Wernicke's aphasia** performed poorly on both types of task.

We conceptualize syntactic processing or mental parsing as building up a **phrase structure tree**, again reflecting the influence of linguistics. As a sentence is heard or read, the listener constructs a phrase structure that assigns incoming words to a grammatical category on a phrase structure tree (see Figure 11.6), showing the relationships between the words in the sentence.

We see the processes at work when we look at what happens when the system breaks down. Ambiguous sentences can be used to study parsing errors. Sentences of this type are sometimes referred to as **garden path sentences**, because we are led astray (or 'up the garden path') in our initial parsing of the sentence. Bever (1970) provided this much cited example:

The horse raced past the barn fell.

The sentence is essentially 'The horse (that was) raced past the barn fell'; the ambiguity arises at 'raced', which is initially parsed as past tense verb, but when we arrive at the verb 'fell', we realize an error has been made. Some other frequently cited examples include:

Fat people eat accumulates.

The man who hunts ducks out on weekends.

Minimal attachment
introduces new items into the phrase structure using as few syntactic nodes as possible.
Late closure
attaches incoming material to the phrase that is currently being processed.

In the first example, 'fat' is a noun not an adjective and in the second 'ducks' is a verb not a noun. The goal of parsing is to assign incoming words to the appropriate role in the sentence as simply and efficiently as possible. Two strategies used to accomplish this are summarized by Frazier (1987): minimal attachment and late closure. **Minimal attachment** allows us to create the simplest tree structure that is consistent with the grammar of the language by introducing new items into the phrase structure using as few syntactic nodes as possible. In Bever's (1970) example, 'the horse' is a noun phrase and 'raced' is the main verb in the past tense referring to the noun. We therefore parse 'raced' as the past tense and not the past participle (although there may be some differences across languages – e.g., in Spanish; Cuetos & Mitchell, 1988). **Late closure** attaches incoming material to the phrase that is currently being processed, as long as that is grammatically permissible, reducing the load on working memory (Frazier, 1987). In other words, the clause we are processing remains open as long as possible, and therefore incoming input is associated with the more recent clause (Altmann, 1998). For example, take the sentence:

John read the essay Mary wrote in the hospital.

Did the reading of the essay or the writing of the essay take place in the hospital? Late closure sees 'hospital' attached to 'wrote'.

Serial models such as that of Frazier (1979) propose that parsing is incremental in that we allocate a word to a syntactic role as the word is perceived. Parsing is seen as autonomous and modular in such accounts in that the syntactic analysis is independent of semantic and other factors (Frazier, 1989). The interactive view, by contrast, proposes that semantics can influence syntax, that there is interaction between the levels of language (e.g., Taraban & McClelland, 1988). Grodner et al. (2005) report a range of semantic and contextual influences on parsing. For example, in Bever's 'the horse raced...' sentence, lexical frequency affects parsing (see Trueswell, 1996): because 'raced' rarely occurs as a past participle, it is more likely to be parsed as a past tense main verb.

Garden path sentences require the person to revise their initial interpretation of the sentence, as new, conflicting, information is presented. However, this reanalysis does not always produce the 'ideal' sentence structure, and revision of the roles initially assigned to the word may not be consistent, suggesting that structures that are 'good enough', rather than ideal, suffice (Ferreira et al., 2001, p. 3; Slattery et al., 2013). Bilinguals may have an advantage in recovery from garden path sentences, reflecting superior cognitive control (Teubner-Rhodes et al., 2016).

The treatment of semantic and syntactic information by the brain is discussed next, and in the section on reading.

THE BRAIN AND LANGUAGE COMPREHENSION

Neuropsychology of Speech Comprehension

The brain area most associated with deficits in language comprehension is **Wernicke's area**. Affected patients have profound problems with comprehension of even relatively simple sentences (Goodglass, 1993), while Broca's aphasia (see Chapter 10) generally produces comprehension deficits only for sentences with more complex morphosyntactic structures (e.g., see Berndt & Caramazza, 1980). A number of other areas in the brain's left hemisphere that play key roles in language comprehension have been identified. Dronkers et al. (2004) evaluated 64 patients who had suffered left hemisphere strokes affecting language comprehension. Using subtests from a receptive language test, the Curtiss-Yamada Comprehensive Language Evaluation (CYCLE-R), they identified five left hemisphere areas that were associated with performance detriments on the test. These areas were the posterior middle temporal gyrus, anterior superior temporal gyrus, superior temporal sulcus and angular gyrus, and mid-frontal cortex in Brodmann's area 46 and area 47. The middle temporal gyrus was also identified as having a key role in language comprehension.

> **Wernicke's area**
> a brain area in the lower posterior left Sylvian fissure that plays an important role in language comprehension and the production of meaningful speech.
> **Anomia**
> a word finding disorder.

> Chapter 10, p324

The main types of aphasia are discussed in Chapter 10. Considering comprehension, cases of Wernicke's aphasia have been informative with regard to the distinction between syntactic and semantic processing. In Wernicke's aphasia, content words are problematic but the overall syntactic structure of the sentence, including function words and inflections, remains relatively intact, as does prosody, suggesting relatively independent processes within speech production. Comprehension is profoundly affected in Wernicke's aphasia, and word retrieval problems (anomia), use of made-up words (neologisms) and word substitutions (paraphasias) are com-

Chapter 10, p324

mon (see Chapter 10). The person with Wernicke's aphasia has difficulty understanding the language of others, and does not appreciate the errors in his or her own language.

A number of other 'pure' language disorders are of relevance here (see also Box 11.1). Pure word deafness is a deficit affecting the ability to recognize speech sounds, while comprehension of non-speech sounds remains intact. It is a 'pure' disorder in that other aspects of aphasia are absent – the patient can speak and read as normal – and perception of (most) non-speech sounds is intact. Patients have described the sounds they hear as being 'far away' or like words in a foreign language (Albert & Bear, 1974). In pure word meaning deafness, as described by Franklin et al. (1994) for example, the patient can repeat back the word, showing that he or she can access and represent the phonetic sequence in short-term memory, but cannot understand it. The patient may, however, be able to recognize the same word when it is written down. Ellis and Young (1996) suggest a three-route model for processing spoken words (see Figure 11.7), which provides a useful framework for understanding these disorders. A first route allows direct access to the phoneme level from initial auditory analysis; this route would allow us to repeat back a non-word or a foreign word that we do not know. The other two routes are for known words, and auditory analysis gives access to the auditory input lexicon where information regarding a known word is stored. We generally can access the semantic system from this point (Route 2) and will therefore understand the word and what it relates to. But we can sometimes bypass semantic access, such that the auditory input lexicon connects directly to speech output, without semantic access (Route 3). In pure word meaning deafness, the patient has access to the auditory input lexicon and can make a judgement that the stimulus is a word but they cannot understand it as there is no access to the semantic system: Route 3 is intact but Route 2 is compromised. By contrast in pure word deafness a problem affects phonemic processing, occurring before access to the auditory input lexicon: Route 1 is damaged. A third pattern predicted by the model suggests a distinction in the treatment of familiar and unfamiliar words. If Route 1 alone is damaged, one might predict a difficulty with repeating unfamiliar strings without a difficulty affecting known words. This pattern has been reported in cases of auditory phonological agnosia (e.g., see Ellis & Young, 1996).

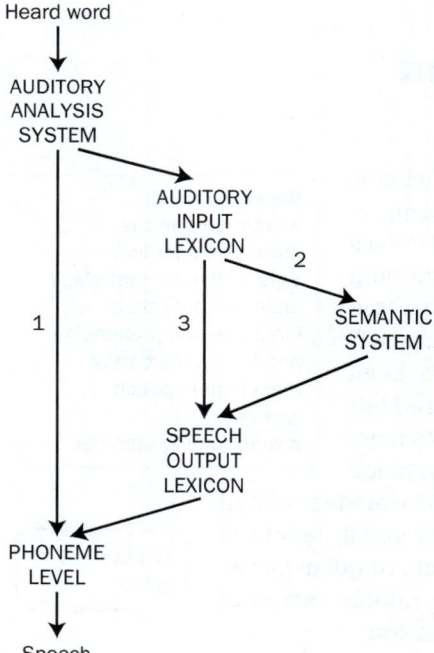

Figure 11.7 A three-route model for processing spoken words.

The first route allows direct access to the phoneme level from initial auditory analysis. The other two routes are for known words and auditory analysis gives access to the auditory input lexicon where information regarding a known word is stored.

Source: Adapted from Ellis & Young (1996).

READING

So far in this chapter we have been considering language comprehension as it applies to spoken language. However, much of the language we encounter day to day is written down, and it is important to be able to read and understand it. We understand written language through reading. It has been estimated that adults read at a rate of about 250 words per minute (wpm) and that any increase on this speed (through speed reading for example) will come with a comprehension cost (Rayner et al., 2016). In a comprehensive meta-analysis of English-language studies of reading, Brysbaert (2019) estimated that the average silent reading rate for adults is 238 wpm for non-fiction and 260 wpm for fiction; the difference between fiction and non-fiction is accounted for by longer word lengths in non-fiction sources (Brysbaert, 2019; see also Rayner et al., 2016).

Reading is a relatively new development in human history. The oldest ancient writing system dates to the late fourth millennium BCE (Comrie, 2005). It is only within the past century that widespread literacy has been attained in 'developed' countries, and literacy rates remain very low in many parts of the world. Speech is the natural form of language, while written language might be considered to be an 'optional accessory that must be painstakingly bolted on' (Pinker, 1997, p. ix). The process of learning to read contrasts with learning to speak; children acquire spoken language readily, requiring little by way of explicit instruction. Reading presents more of a challenge and its development differs as a function of features of the script used in the native language. There are vast differences in scripts, in terms of direction of reading, size of symbol repertoire required to read, and the symbolic representation of speech by writing.

Writing Systems

Scripts vary across languages in the extent and manner of representation of speech sounds. All spoken languages have phonemes or basic speech sounds that can be combined in various ways, but written scripts differ markedly in the extent to which, as well as the ways in which, this phonetic information is represented. Four main types of script are typically identified:

1. **Logographic scripts**, or ideographic scripts, represent morphemes or the units of meaning of words. For example, the Chinese symbol for 'sun' (ri) is 日; the symbol does not map on to the sound 'ri', it represents the meaning 'sun'. We use number words in the same way – the symbol '4' can be read as 'four', or as 'quatre' in French, or 'vier' in German. The symbol '4' is associated with a meaning and not a sound.
2. **Syllabic scripts** use a symbol to represent each syllable.
3. **Consonantal scripts** represent the consonants of the language.
4. **Alphabetic scripts** use letters to represent the phonemes or sounds in a language.

> **Logographic scripts** morphemes or the units of meaning of words.
> **Syllabic scripts** use a symbol to represent each syllable.
> **Consonantal scripts** the consonants of the language.
> **Alphabetic scripts** the phonemes or sounds in a language.

Some writing systems combine elements of these types; for example, Japanese uses both kana (syllabic) and kanji (logographic), and Devanagari, a South Asian language, uses a script with elements of both syllabic and alphabetic systems, an alpha-syllabic writing system (e.g., Vaid & Gupta, 2002).

Early writing systems were pictographic. There was a direct pictorial or iconic representation of the meaning of the word, which limited the script to depiction of concrete, highly imageable words. Logographic scripts developed from earlier pictographic forms, but the relationship between the symbol and referent became arbitrary (see Table 11.4 for example). Chinese, Korean hanja and Japanese kanji are examples of this type of script and although there may be some phonetic components to the scripts, the individual symbols are not pronounceable in the way that occurs in other scripts. The basic unit of representation in a logographic script is the morpheme.

In syllabic writing, each syllable is represented by a character, so that the precise pronunciation of each symbol is known. In a language with a relatively small number of syllables, this is effective. For example, Japanese has just 69 syllables that need to be represented in a syllabic script, kana (Harris & Coltheart, 1986). But such a script could not be used in English or in other languages with a large set of syllables. (In Japanese,

Table 11.4 The Word 'Dog' as Written in Several Scripts, Along with an Approximate Pronunciation in Alphabetic Script

Chinese	Japanese kanji	Japanese kana	Hebrew	Russian (Cyrillic alphabet)
狗	犬	イヌ	כלב	собака
gǒu	inu	inu	kelev	sobaka

it is supplemented with the morpheme-based kanji script because kana cannot represent homophones, different words with the same pronunciation; kana is used mainly for functional words; Chen et al., 2002). In consonantal scripts (e.g., Hebrew) letters represent consonants but not vowels, although in some such scripts the vowels might be represented using diacritics (e.g., in Arabic).

The alphabetic writing system is the most dominant across world languages (Comrie, 2005) and its basic unit of representation is the phoneme. Alphabets developed from the Greek system and later split into those based on the Roman script and those based on the Cyrillic script. The **grapheme** is the written representation of a phoneme. However, a grapheme can consist of more than one letter. In some languages, letters correspond to phonemes. These are said to be **transparent** or **shallow orthography** languages, because there is a one-to-one correspondence between the letters and sounds. In transparent languages a 'sounding out' strategy will always produce the correct pronunciation. In **opaque** or **orthographically deep languages**, by contrast, there is not a one-to-one grapheme-to-phoneme relationship; the same sound may be written in a number of ways and the same letter string might be associated with multiple pronunciations. Homophones (e.g., rain, reign) and homographs (e.g., tear – can rhyme with beer or bear; bow – can rhyme with low or cow) require the same sounds to be attached to different spellings or different sounds to be attached to the same spelling respectively. The orthographic depth of the writing system has implications for the models of reading discussed below. It also has implications for reading development; children learning to read a shallow orthography show advantages over those learning a deep orthography (e.g., Frost et al., 1987; Seymour et al., 2003; Spencer & Hanley, 2003). Table 11.5, based on Seymour et al. (2003), shows the orthographic depth of some European languages as a function of syllable complexity. The challenges to beginner readers of English reflect both a deep orthography and complex syllabic structure in the language.

How is reading achieved in orthographically consistent languages? In English, there may be more than 1,100 ways to represent the 44 or so phonemes in the language, while

> **Grapheme**
> the written representation of a phoneme.
> **Transparent or shallow orthography**
> uses a one-to-one correspondence between the letters and sounds.
> **Opaque or orthographically deep languages**
> those where the relationship between letters and sounds is more complex.

Table 11.5 Classification of Some European Languages According to Syllabic Complexity and Orthographic Depth

| | | Orthographic depth | | | |
		Shallow ⟶			Deep
Syllabic structure	Simple	Finnish	Greek Italian Spanish	Portuguese	French	
	Complex		German Norwegian Icelandic	Dutch Swedish	Danish	English

Source: Based on Seymour et al. (2003, p. 146).

consistent languages show far less ambiguity in the print–sound mappings. In Italian, for example, there are 25 ways to represent the 33 phonemes and in an intermediate language such as French there are 250+ ways to spell the 32 phonemes of the language (see Table 2.2. in Sousa, 2014). This means that very consistent languages provide a one-to-one correspondence from print to sound. Paulesu et al. (2000) used positron emission tomography (PET) to examine brain activity while English- or Italian-speaking students read high-frequency regular words in their native language or non-words. The Italian students were faster to read both words and non-words, an effect that was independent of articulation or naming rates. For both groups, reading of non-words was performed more slowly than reading of words. The PET data reported by Paulesu et al. (2000) identified a number of brain areas activated in common for the two languages: the inferior frontal and premotor cortex, the left hemisphere superior, middle and inferior temporal gyri and fusiform gyrus, and the right superior temporal gyrus. English speakers showed particularly strong activation in the left posterior inferior temporal area and in part of the inferior frontal gyrus, and particularly when reading non-words. The Italian readers showed greater activation of an auditory area associated with phonological processing, the planum temporale, while reading both words and non-words. These data support commonality in left hemisphere brain structures for reading in both orthographically deep and transparent scripts, with additional activation of specific brain regions that may be orthography-specific (see also Box 11.4).

Chinese provides an excellent test of this idea of a common network for reading, allowing comparison of two script types within a single language group. In Chinese a logographic script is used along with an alphabet, pinyin (meaning 'assembling sound'; Chen et al., 2002). Reading non-alphabetic Chinese characters makes little use of letter–sound assembly, while reading pinyin is a process of reading sound from letters. Chen et al. (2002) used fMRI to examine brain activity in Chinese readers exposed to the two types of Chinese script. They found that the alphabetic and non-alphabetic Chinese scripts activated a common brain network, while some script-specific differences were also evident, with activation of the inferior parietal cortex during reading of pinyin and of the fusiform gyrus for Chinese non-alphabetic characters.

> **Box 11.4 When Things Go Wrong: Cross-language manifestation of dyslexia**
>
> **Developmental dyslexia** is a prevalent and persistent neurodevelopmental disorder that affects the learning of reading and writing. It would seem to be moderately heritable, with several candidate genes now identified as playing a role in the complex aetiology of dyslexia. Comparisons of reading progression in **monozygotic** and **dizygotic** twins suggest that genetic influence accounts for, on average, about twice that of shared family environment (see Olsen et al., 2019, for a review). A comprehensive review by Peterson and Pennington (2015) noted that developmental dyslexia affects an estimated 7 per cent of children, with a small but significant predominance of boys, which may in part reflect a referral bias; boys with dyslexia, they note, present with higher rates of comorbid disorders, such as attention-deficit/hyperactivity disorder, which may affect the likelihood of referral and diagnosis (see also Krafnick & Evans, 2019).
>
> Developmental dyslexia cannot be accounted for by difficulties with vision or hearing, or by variations in intelligence, motivation or classroom
>
> > **Developmental dyslexia**
> > a prevalent and persistent neurodevelopmental disorder that affects the learning of reading and writing.
> > **Monozygotic**
> > identical twins that develop from a single zygote and share all of their genes.
> > **Dizygotic**
> > or fraternal, twins develop from two separate eggs and are not genetically identical.

instruction practices. There are many theories as to the nature of the core disability; a dominant approach posits an underlying phonological deficit. The phonological theory of dyslexia focuses on the ability to manipulate sound information, which is key to grasping the grapheme–phoneme correspondences in a language. Other theories focus on the role of automatization of reading skills, or on the visual and auditory mechanisms underlying the phonological deficits.

Developmental dyslexia is not a cognitively homogeneous condition; it exists on a continuum and there are different subtypes within an orthography. While much of the early research on dyslexia, and the theoretical accounts that drew on these data, were based on the English language experience, there is now a considerable bank of data from other languages which suggests that variations in writing systems affect reading outcomes for many children, including those with dyslexia.

In Table 11.5, we saw that orthographic depth is one aspect of writing systems that varies across languages. English has a particularly deep or opaque orthography, and has complex correspondences between grapheme and phoneme. The same sounds can be associated with different spellings (e.g., right, write, rite) and the same spelling can be associated with more than one pronunciation (e.g., bow, row, tear). Sounding the word out will not always yield the correct result and so the language is very challenging for the beginning reader. By contrast languages such as Italian, Finnish and Welsh have consistent relationships between orthography and phonology or print–sound correspondences, facilitating early reading. There are cross-language differences in the way that dyslexia manifests which suggest that the consistency of spelling in a language is an important factor (Goswami, 2002). While dyslexia is generally associated with slower word reading, particular problems with the mapping of graphemes to phonemes are seen in deep orthography languages such as English. Phonological awareness is a reliable predictor of reading ability in alphabetic languages, with a stronger effect in opaque than in shallow orthographies (for a review see Peterson & Pennington, 2015).

Functional Magnetic Resonance Imaging (fMRI)
a method of imaging brain activity that uses oxygenation levels of blood flow, and has good temporal and spatial resolution.

The neurobiological basis of developmental dyslexia is being uncovered using neuroscientific methods such as **functional magnetic resonance imaging (fMRI)**. Reading-related tasks are conducted while participants' brains are scanned. A pattern of functional brain abnormalities has emerged that suggests some commonalities in dyslexia across languages, as well as some differences. A meta-analysis by Martin et al. (2016) showed that participants with dyslexia demonstrated under-activation (compared to typically developing readers) in the left temporoparietal cortex, occipitotemporal cortex and inferior frontal gyrus, three key regions of the left hemisphere reading network. The temporoparietal region is believed to play a key role in phonological processing and grapheme to phoneme conversion, while the occipitotemporal region is implicated in whole-word recognition and includes an area referred to as the visual word form area (Peterson & Pennington, 2015). Reduced grey matter has also been observed in these brain areas. These alterations pre-date reading experience and have been found in pre-reading children with a family history of developmental dyslexia (Raschle et al., 2011).

The under-activation of these regions occurred for participants reading alphabetic scripts regardless of whether the language was opaque or shallow in orthography. However, the analysis by Martin et al. (2016) also showed a range of patterns of over- and under-activation, which differed for opaque and shallow orthographies. A review by Richlan (2020) provides an overview of the commonalities and differences across a range of languages, extending the analysis to non-alphabetic scripts. Again, there is consistent under-activation within the left occipitotemporal cortex for logographic scripts such as Chinese, with script-specific patterns additionally. For example, in the case of logographic Chinese writing, the left middle frontal gyrus would seem to play a key role, which Richlan (2020) suggests reflects the engagement of working memory processes for the recognition of the (visually complex) written logographic characters. This suggests a number of brain areas (see Figure 11.8) which act as

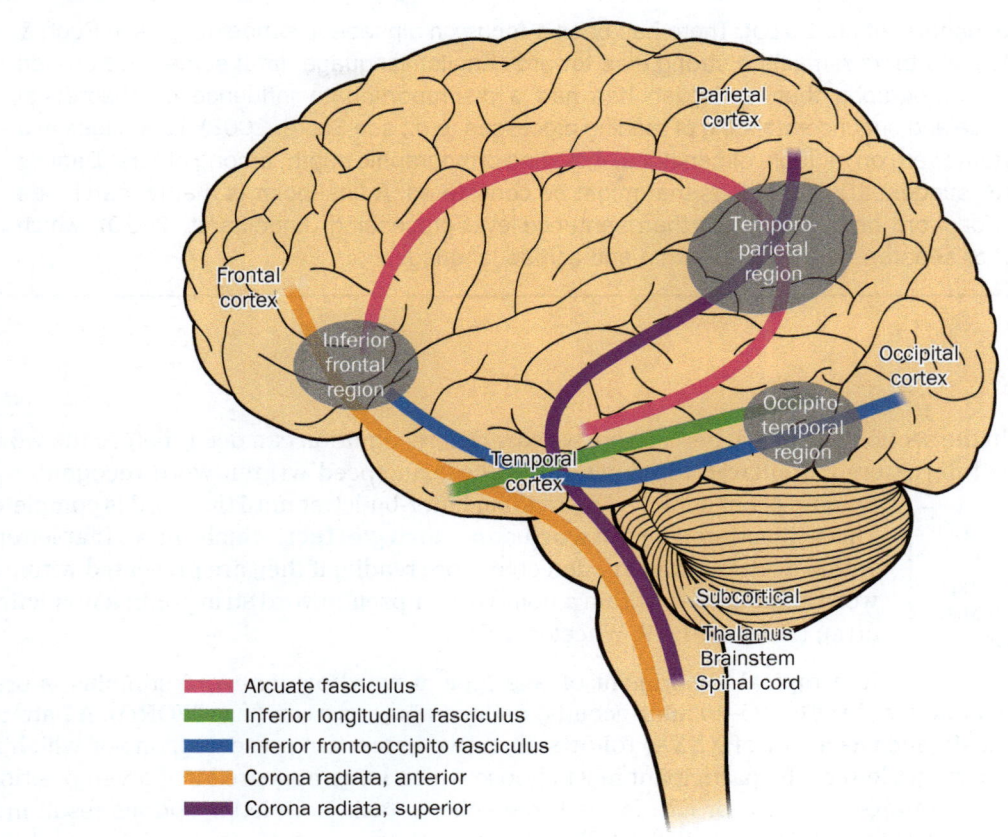

Figure 11.8 Grey and white matter regions of relevance to reading.
The image shows a number of regions and connections that are relevant to reading and dyslexia.

Source: Peterson & Pennington (2015), Figure 1.

the core network for reading across languages with additional areas tied to script-specific skills. Peterson and Pennington (2015, p. 294) sum up that the 'cross-cultural work suggests universality in the neurobiological and neurocognitive causes of dyslexia, but there is cross-cultural specificity in the manifestation of these underpinnings, with the same biological liability more likely to cause substantial impairment in some languages than in others'.

A number of other factors are worthy of note, bearing in mind that written language is a recent cultural invention and scripts vary considerably in how they represent the words of a language. Hadzibeganovic et al. (2010) point to two key problems that a universal theory of dyslexia would need to capture. The first is that the information-processing requirements of reading vary greatly across languages; the task of reading English differs from the task of reading Chinese or Arabic. Second, they point to the subtypes of dyslexia, which exist both within a single orthography and also manifest differently across languages (e.g., Sotiropoulos & Hanley, 2017). If two children with (different subtypes of) dyslexia demonstrate very different abilities, will a single theory capture the underlying processing deficits, with a common brain abnormality underlying all subtypes?

Furthermore, it can be difficult to draw conclusions from cross-language comparisons. Neuroimaging studies use various reading tasks; meta-analytic studies, such as that conducted by Martin et al. (2016), have been careful to include only studies with tasks that share key features. While care can be taken in matching tasks, the tasks will not be identical (nor can they be) across languages. There are also differences in sampling and diagnostic criteria, which hinder cross-language comparisons of dyslexia (Hadzibeganovic et al., 2010). There has been a focus on alphabetic scripts (e.g., see Pugh & Verhoeven, 2018) and there remains a strong bias towards English-language data; some have argued that the 'outlier' orthography that is English has had a disproportionate influence on theoretical accounts of dyslexia and our understanding of reading processes (e.g., see Share, 2008). Languages and their writing systems vary on multiple dimensions, including orthographic depth, among others; Daniels and Share (2018) suggest 10 dimensions that might be considered. A final point is that research has tended to focus on word decoding rather than sentence-level processing (Engelhardt, 2020), which raises a number of separate issues both within and across languages.

Context Effects on Visual Word Recognition

In the section on speech perception, we saw that recognition can occur before the word is fully uttered. Similarly, top-down influences can speed written word recognition – reading is not achieved by reading letter-by-letter until the word is complete. This is illustrated by the **word superiority effect**, which shows that letters within a letter string are detected more readily if they are presented within a word compared to within a non-word or pseudoword string or in a non-letter array (Reicher, 1969; Wheeler, 1970).

> **Word superiority effect** the finding that a target letter within a letter string is detected more readily when the string forms a word.

In a typical experiment of this type, a word or non-word stimulus is presented very briefly (25–40 milliseconds) on a computer screen (e.g., WORD). A pattern mask (such as a row of XXXX) follows; then two letters are presented, one of which is the target letter. The participant must choose which letter appeared in a given position (for example, _ _ _*: D or K?). In the forced-choice task, both letter options result in a real word (e.g., WORD or WORK). The effect is relatively unaffected by letter position (Rayner & Clifton, 2002), suggesting parallel processing of letter information rather than left-to-right, letter-by-letter reading. A pseudoword advantage over non-words has also been reported (e.g., Carr et al., 1978).

Context has a considerable influence on visual word recognition. Meyer and Schvaneveldt (1971) presented subjects with a lexical decision task that incorporated a semantic priming component. Participants had to decide as quickly as possible if a presented letter string was a word. The stimuli were primed by preceding them with a semantically related word in some cases. The semantic prime produced faster word recognition. For example, the word NURSE was recognized faster when primed by DOCTOR than when preceded by the semantically unrelated word BUTTER. Similarly, Zola (1984) examined participants' eye fixations while they read sentences such as:

A. Movie theatres must have buttered popcorn to serve their patrons.

B. Movie theatres must have adequate popcorn to serve their patrons.

Participants fixate on the word 'popcorn' for longer in sentence B compared to sentence A. They are primed in sentence A by the context provided by the word 'buttered'; this places limits on the (semantically congruous) possibilities for words that will come next, reducing processing effort. The link between the written word and its meaning is explored further in Box 11.5.

Box 11.5 Research Close Up: The Stroop effect

Source: Stroop (1935).

INTRODUCTION

In 1935, J. R. Stroop published a research article describing an effect that continues to form the basis for many diverse experiments today. Stroop's (1935) paper in the *Journal of Experimental Psychology* is one of the most cited publications in the history of experimental psychology, with at the time of writing 10,692 citations on the Scopus database, providing an approximate estimate of the paper's influence. A typical Stroop colour-naming task requires a participant to name the colour in which a word is printed, when the word is itself a colour term. When the word meaning agrees with the print colour (for example, the word **BLUE** printed in blue and requiring the response 'blue'), response times are faster than when naming a neutral colour block, a non-word or a neutral word (one that is not associated with a particular colour), an effect called 'Stroop facilitation'. When the word colour and meaning do not concur (e.g., the word **RED** written in blue ink requiring the response 'blue'), response times are slower than on the neutral condition, an effect known as 'Stroop interference'. Stroop's original experiments, which differ somewhat from the typical Stroop study today (see Table 11.6), are considered here. Stroop's original experiments did not employ a congruent colour word condition in a colour naming task. The first use of colour-congruent trials was by Dalrymple-Alford and Budayr (1966).

METHOD AND RESULTS

In Stroop's study, three experiments explored colour and word naming conditions. In Experiment 1 ($n = 70$), Stroop used five colour stimuli (red, blue, green, brown and purple) to examine the effect of colour on word reading, using a colour-incongruent and a neutral (words in black ink) condition. In this first experiment, no interference was found when reading words from the incongruent colours.

In a second experiment ($n = 100$), Stroop used a colour-naming task: rather than reading words, participants named the colours in which words were printed. Ink colours were incongruent with word meaning, and a neutral condition used solid colour squares. On this task, participants demonstrated a significant interference effect. Colour naming was significantly slower when the colour of the ink was incongruent with word meaning compared to the neutral condition, with a 74 per cent increase in response times. The contrast between the effects in Experiment 1 and Experiment 2 tells us that word reading is more automatic than colour naming (MacLeod & MacDonald, 2000). As MacLeod (1991) described it, 'the basic idea is that processing of one dimension requires much more attention than does processing of the other dimension. Thus, naming the ink color draws more heavily on attentional resources than does reading the irrelevant word. Moreover, reading the word is seen as obligatory, whereas naming the ink color is not. Presumably, this imbalance derives from our extensive history of reading words as opposed to naming ink colors' (p. 188).

Stroop's third experiment ($n = 32$) explored the effects of practice. Participants named ink colours of incongruent words (e.g., given **RED** in blue ink, respond 'blue') or read words in a series of sessions over eight days, while the colour squares were replaced with a symbol. Interference was found to decrease with practice. In addition, practice was found to interfere with word reading to an extent, an effect known as the reverse Stroop effect.

Table 11.6 Conditions Compared in a Typical Stroop Task

Congruent condition	Incongruent condition	Neutral condition
Red	Blue	■
Blue	Red	■

DISCUSSION

The Stroop interference effect itself is robust and has been replicated across dozens of studies, whether employing printed cards, as in Stroop's original work, or using computerized stimulus presentation with precise time recording, and varying colour stimulus and control conditions (see MacLeod, 1991, for a review). The exact basis of the effect continues to be explored. One interpretation of the Stroop effect is that it shows that, for proficient readers, word reading is mandatory: even though the participants' task is to name the colour, they cannot avoid reading the word – access to the conflicting meaning creates interference. The Stroop effect thus emerges with reading ability and provides a useful index of a reader's mastery of the orthographic code (Megherbi et al., 2018).

The Stroop task has been typically associated with activation of anterior cingulate and dorsolateral prefrontal cortex, as well as inferior frontal gyrus, inferior and superior parietal cortex and insula, areas associated with overcoming interference in a cognitive task (see, for example, Nee et al., 2007). A meta-analysis of fMRI studies of the Stroop interference effect by Huang et al. (2020) broke down the activation within a fronto-temporoparietal network. They found that the contrast of incongruent conditions and congruent conditions revealed seven significant clusters, including the right cingulate cortex, left dorsolateral prefrontal cortex, bilateral inferior frontal gyrus, right superior frontal gyrus and temporal cortex. In addition, the comparison of incongruent and neutral conditions activated a network including the right inferior frontal gyrus, left dorsolateral prefrontal cortex, bilateral medial frontal cortex, left insular cortex and bilateral inferior parietal lobule. A greater role for a broad network of frontal areas was evident for healthy younger participants.

The Stroop effect is also found in non-alphabetic scripts, but neuroimaging studies have shown differential activation in brain regions when reading different writing systems. For example, Coderre et al. (2008) found that the Stroop task activated an area in the left inferior parietal region when participants completed the task in Japanese kana script (syllable based), but the left inferior frontal gyrus was activated during the same task completed in kanji, a logographic writing system. Coderre and colleagues suggest that these data reflect differences in how the brain detects and resolves conflict in syllabic and logographic writing systems (see also Qiu et al., 2006).

Eye Movements

Saccades
fast movements of the eye made when reading or scanning an image.

Fixation
when the eye settles briefly on a region of interest in a visual scene.

Analysis of eye movements has provided much insight into the processes underlying reading. As we read a line of text, our eyes do not move smoothly from one letter to the next or from one word to the next. Instead, there are some fast movements of the eye, called **saccades**, with periods in between, called **fixations**, when the eyes are relatively still. The saccades are very fast, ballistic movements of about 20 to 60 milliseconds' duration, with a (relatively) still period of 200 to 250 milliseconds in between (Rayner, 1998). Saccades cover about seven to nine letter spaces (Rayner 1998), or fewer in a logographic writing system (Field, 2003).

The two most robust findings to come from eye movement research, according to Clifton et al. (2007), are, first, that fixation time on a word is reduced if the reader has managed to preview the word prior to fixating it, and, second, that fixation time is reduced for words that are readily identified. Evidence from eye movements shows that we do not just move 'forward' (left to right if reading English), reading each word, nor are all words treated equally (see Rayner, 1998, for a review; see also Rayner, 2009). Many saccades (about 10–15 per cent according to Rayner, 1998) are regressions. There may also be multiple fixations of the same word (re-fixations) or skipping of words. Content words are fixated more often than are function words (Carpenter & Just, 1983; Rayner & Duffy, 1988). As word length increases, the likelihood that it will be fixated increases (Rayner & McConkie, 1976). Context adds to the efficiency of the process, as a predictable word is more likely to be skipped than a less predictable word (Ehrlich & Rayner, 1981; O'Regan, 1979), with a similar effect for high frequency over low frequency words (e.g., Veldre et al., 2020). Text difficulty affects eye movement; as difficulty increases, the saccade length decreases and the number of regressions increases (e.g., Jacobson & Dodwell, 1979).

Seidenberg (2017, as summarized in Brysbaert, 2019, p. 3) gave the following estimates regarding the speed at which information can be extracted from text, suggesting a reading rate of about 280 words per minute:

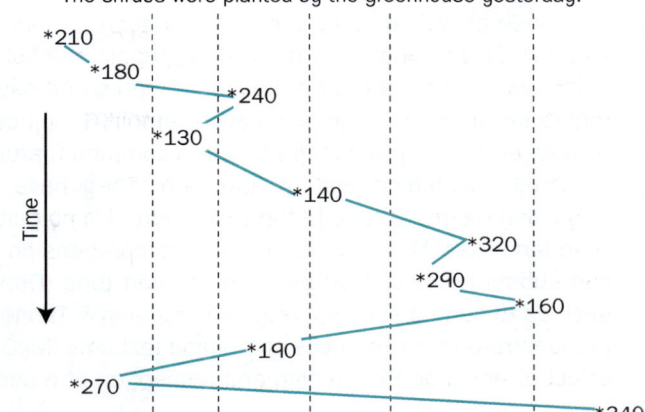

Figure 11.9 A hypothetical eye movement record of a participant reading the sentence 'The shrubs were planted by the greenhouse yesterday.'
Each fixation is represented by an asterisk, with the duration of fixation indicated by the number next to it. Time is shown going down the figure. A number of regressive fixations are evident.

Source: Reprinted from Liversedge & Findlay (2000).

- About seven to eight letters are read clearly on any given fixation.
- Fixation durations average around 200–250 ms (with four to five fixations per second).
- Words in most texts consist of five letters on average.
- Four fixations per second = 240 fixations per minute.
- 240 fixations × 7 letters per fixation = 1,680 letters per minute.
- 1,680 letters/6 (five letters per word plus a space) = 280 words per minute.

Eye movement data have also been informative with regard to processing at the sentence level. The eyes respond predictably to semantic and syntactic anomalies as well as to parsing errors such as those elicited by garden path sentences (as discussed earlier), although studies addressing the sentence level have produced more variable findings than those addressing word identification (see Clifton et al., 2007). Furthermore, while much research has been conducted using English language materials, studies of other languages are revealing effects of orthographic depth on eye movement patterns (e.g., Krieber et al., 2016). Box 11.6 examines eye tracking in a novel context, exploring the reading of sentences containing emoji characters.

Box 11.6 Research Close Up: Reading sentences containing emoji

Source: Robus et al. (2020).

INTRODUCTION

Communication, both written and verbal, has changed with advances in technology and the move to the online world. Communication that is conducted via an electronic device, be that a mobile phone or a computer, is referred to as computer mediated communication (CMC). CMC has become a leading means of communication, in particular for exchanging personal messages. Text and instant messaging make use of orthographic variants and abbreviations called 'textisms' (e.g., see Lyddy et al., 2014; Thurlow, 2003), and have introduced graphic symbols called 'emoticons'. Emoticons are constructed using punctuation and other keyboard marks and have largely been replaced by a rapidly developing repertoire of graphic symbols called 'emoji'. Emoji can represent facial expressions, body gestures, objects and concepts. Emoji are now a common feature of electronic-mediated communication, both in personal messaging and on the web. They have a role to play in managing the conversation (e.g., Sampietro, 2019), in the resolution of ambiguity (Kaye et al., 2017; Riordan, 2017; Walther & D'Addario, 2001) and in facilitating comprehension (Daniel & Camp, 2020). Emoji and emoticons can substitute or convey emotions or add tone (Dresner & Herring, 2010; Thompson et al., 2016), such as to denote sarcasm (e.g., Weissmann & Tanner, 2018). A processing cost for reading has been demonstrated for sentences containing textisms (McCausland et al., 2015; Perea et al., 2009), but the effect of emoji on the reading and perception of a sentence is less clear.

A study by Robus et al. (2020) examined emoji effects on reading behaviours. Their participants read neutral narrative sentences containing smiling or frowning emoji in sentence-initial or sentence-final positions. Participants' eye movements were recorded and they rated the perceived emotional valence of the sentence.

METHOD

Robus and colleagues used 2 × 2 within-subjects experimental design. Their first variable was the valence of the emoji, positive or negative, denoted by a smiling or frowning face emoji. The second variable was the position in the sentence where the emoji appeared (sentence-initial or sentence-final). The emoji were presented within neutral narrative sentences, and placed either before or after the sentence. Each sentence contained a five-letter target word, positioned towards the centre. The target words were carefully selected to reduce emotional context. The following are examples of the sentences used with the target word underlined:

When the guest returned to the hotel later there was nobody to be seen

The jury returned and told the judge their decision on the verdict

Michael turned on his digital radio to listen to the latest broadcast

Areas of interest in eye tracking research these provide detailed quantitative data on eye fixations and durations related to key sentence elements.

Robus and colleagues measured participants' responses to the sentences in several ways. They used eye tracking to examine the participants' eye movements while reading the sentences (see Figure 11.10), focusing their analysis on standard eye-tracking measures calculated from **areas of interest** (AOIs) on the emoji region and the target word region. These standard measures included: first fixation durations (the duration of the first fixation in an AOI); total fixation durations (the sum of all fixation durations in an AOI) and fixation counts (number of fixations in an AOI). They also measured the total sentence reading time. Participants rated the perceived emotional valence of the sentences using a 1–9 rating scale (from highly negative to highly positive).

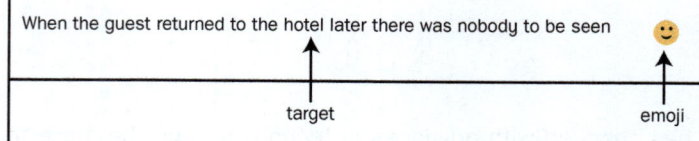

Figure 11.10 Example of a sentence used with a positive sentence-final emoji stimulus.
The text above the line is what participants saw. The lower line indicates the position of the target word and the emoji.

RESULTS

The AOIs chosen for analysis were the regions in which the emoji appeared – that is, at the start (sentence-initial) or end (sentence-final) of the sentence, and the mid-sentence region containing the target word (see Figure 11.11). The results showed that sentence-final emoji were associated with longer fixation times compared to sentence-initial emoji, with significant main effects of emoji position on first fixation durations and total fixation durations. When the emoji appeared in a sentence-final position, participants took longer to read the sentence and spent more time fixating on the target words. However, the number of fixations was higher for sentence-initial emoji. The valence of the emoji (positive or negative) did not affect fixation durations. There were no significant differences in the valence scores (on the 1–9 scale) for the four conditions of sentences.

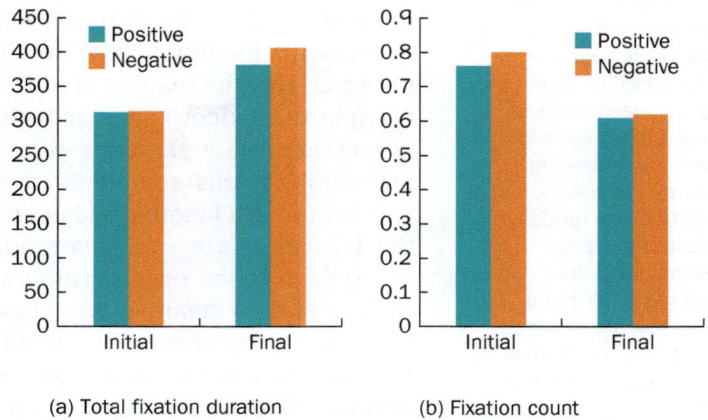

Figure 11.11 Total fixation duration and fixation count for the four sentence types.

Source: Data from Robus et al. (2020), Table 2.

DISCUSSION

Robus et al.'s study provides useful data on the reading of sentences containing emoji. Readers spent longer reading sentences and fixated longer on target words when emoji appeared at sentence-final position compared to the sentence-initial position. However, participants also produced more fixations on sentence-initial emoji compared to sentence-final emoji, despite the fact that initial fixations on the sentence-first emoji were not longer, even on the first pass through the sentence. This may reflect the fact that a sentence-initial emoji is an unusual occurrence, perhaps requiring more returns to that sentence position, or it may suggest that sentence-initial emoji make semantic integration more challenging for the reader, requiring further fixations on the initial emoji. It might also reflect an expectation effect created by a within subjects design, or the juxtaposition of emoji symbols in neutral statement-type sentences. The valence of the emoji did not have an effect when interpreting the neutral sentences; emotionally congruent sentences may have been treated differently by readers. Further research, with a wider range of emoji and sentences, would extend this research question.

The Dual Route Model of Reading

Most models of reading are based on studies in which the participants were reading English. Because of the differences in writing systems used around the world, models of reading that are based on a particular script or language may not generalize well to other systems. Written English is orthographically deep – that is, there is not a one-to-one correspondence between written symbols and the sounds represented. To be able to read English, we need to be able to: sound out new words and non-words; and retrieve the pronunciation for words that do not follow the 'rules' for sounding out words from the lexicon.

Words that follow the general rules for converting print to sound could be read either way, by sounding them out or by retrieving the relevant entry for the word in the mental lexicon. This distinction between print–sound rules and lexical entry look-up forms the basis for the dual route model of reading. One version of this is Coltheart et al.'s (2001) dual route cascaded model, which proposes two (or three) routes for reading (see Figure 11.12, overleaf). Route 1 allows the conversion of print to sounds, the

> **Grapheme-to-phoneme conversion (GPC) route** allows us to sound out words based on letter–sound correspondences.
> **Lexical or direct route** this route to reading involves the selection of a word from the lexicon.
> **Acquired dyslexia** reading difficulties following brain injury.
> **Non-semantic reading** a pattern of reading deficit whereby the patient can read an irregular word (which cannot be sounded out) and yet cannot access its meaning.

grapheme-to-phoneme conversion (GPC) route. This allows someone to sound out a word once they have analysed the letters, without necessarily having access to the word in the lexicon. This route is necessary for the reading of unfamiliar or new words (which will have no entry in the lexicon) and can be used to sound out regular words (that is, words that follow the print–sound rules) also. In a language with a deep orthography, this sounding-out strategy will produce errors, as many words in such a language do not follow GPC rules. A second, direct, route – the **lexical route** – allows reading via word recognition. The word is recognized based on its orthographic features, its entry is found in the lexicon and its meaning is accessed via the semantic system. Thereafter the sound properties of the word are accessed. In Figure 11.12, we also find a third route that bypasses the semantic system. This route accounts for occasions when an irregular word is read correctly when meaning is not available. This last route also accounts for a pattern of deficit observed in some types of **acquired dyslexia** called **non-semantic reading** (this is discussed below).

Much evidence for this model comes from data from neuropsychological case studies and these are discussed below. Alternative accounts propose that we do not need two routes for reading. Connectionist accounts such as that of Seidenberg and McClelland (1989) and Plaut et al. (1996), using a single network, produce what might be considered as 'rule based' or assembly responses, as well as dealing with exception words via access.

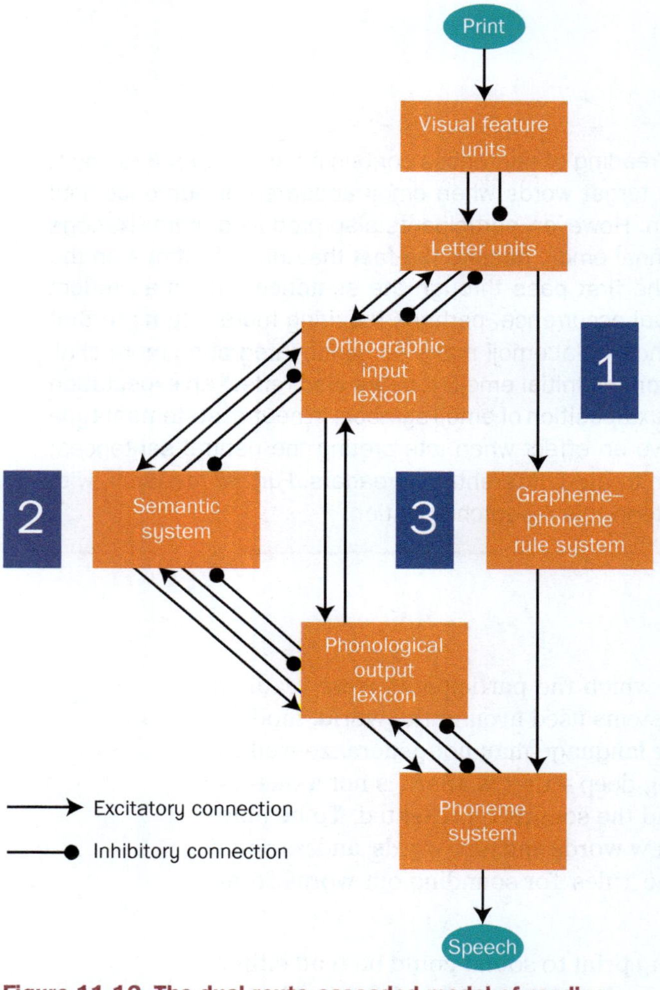

Neuropsychology of Reading

The cascaded dual-route model of reading proposes that there are two main routes involved in reading in English: an indirect route involving grapheme-to-phoneme conversion, and a direct lexical route in which pronunciation follows access to the word's entry in the lexicon and semantic system. A third route is also suggested, which bypasses the semantic system but looks up the written word in the lexicon. Support for these three routes has come from neuropsychological case studies of acquired dyslexia. This involves studying the deficits in reading following brain injury in adults who were able to read normally before the injury; however, the patterns of deficit seen in acquired dyslexia are rarely simple.

Based on the dual-route model, we might predict a **double dissociation of function** (see Chapter 1), between the two main routes – that is, between the indirect sound-based route and the direct lexical route. This is the pattern

Figure 11.12 The dual route cascaded model of reading.
Route 1 allows the conversion of print to sounds, the grapheme-to-phoneme conversion (GPC) route. A second, direct, route – the lexical route – allows reading via word recognition. A third route bypasses the semantic system.

Source: Coltheart et al. (2001), APA.

seen when we contrast **surface** and **phonological dyslexia**. Surface dyslexia is characterized by a deficit in the reading of irregular or exception words, while the reading of regular words is spared (e.g., Marshall & Newcombe, 1973). People with surface dyslexia tend to make over-regularization errors when they try to read exception words; that is, they will read them as they would sound if they followed the rules. For example, they might pronounce 'pretty' to rhyme with 'jetty'. This suggests that they are using their indirect, grapheme-to-phoneme route to read, due to damage to the lexical route. Since the lexical route is required to read exception words, regularization errors are made. Some individuals cannot access the meaning of words that they have not been able to pronounce correctly, supporting the model's prediction that phonology is accessed before meaning using the lexical (direct) route. While a dissociation between reading of regular and irregular words is evident here, a range of deficits occur in surface dyslexia, and so to say that this the pattern of error reflects reading in the absence of a lexical route may be an oversimplification (Patterson et al., 1985).

People with phonological dyslexia have problems pronouncing non-words or pseudowords but they can read real words (e.g., see Beauvois & Derouesné, 1979), whether regular or irregular. For example, they may be able to read 'rain' but cannot read 'rait'. Visual errors are common; the individual may read the non-word as if it were a real word. Given 'rait' they might read 'rail', 'rite' or 'rat', for example. This pattern suggests an intact lexical route but damaged grapheme-to-phoneme conversion. As Harley (2008) points out, these patterns of deficit are rarely complete, and conclusions regarding support of the dual route model must take this into account; no patients have been reported who have a complete inability to read non-words while words are completely intact, for example. Funnell (1983) reports the case of W.B., who could read no non-words, but he also had a deficit affecting word reading, with performance at about 85 per cent.

Neuropsychological data also support two stages to the lexical route: retrieval of the lemma (see Chapter 10), then access to phonology (Harley, 1995). Reilly (1999) reported an unusually well-documented case of temporary dyslexia. A radio presenter, R.H.R., experienced a progressive worsening of dyslexia symptoms when he suffered a seizure while making a live broadcast. He was reading from a script at the time, introducing the topic of the radio programme, and the broadcast continued for just over a minute before the editor cut to another presenter. R.H.R.'s reading errors fell into three broad classes (see Reilly, 1999):

1 errors at the orthographic stage prior to lexical access
2 disruption in lexical access
3 errors assembling the phonology.

Evidence for a third route from orthography to phonology via the lexicon but not the semantic system comes from a pattern of deficit called non-semantic reading. A few cases have been reported of people who can read irregular words without understanding them (e.g., Coslett, 1991). These cases generally involve dementia, and as access to semantic information is lost it would seem that ability to read the words is retained. As the patients can read irregular words they cannot understand, they must be using the lexical route, yet semantic access is not possible. This supports a third route bypassing semantics (see Figure 11.7).

Electrophysiological Data

Electrophysiological studies using **event-related potentials (ERPs)** provide an online view of how the brain treats language. ERPs are changes in

> Chapter 1, p2

> **Double dissociation of function** contrasting patterns of deficit in two patients or patient groups; provides evidence for functionally independent systems.
> **Surface dyslexia** is characterized by a deficit in the reading of irregular words, while the reading of regular words is spared.
> **Phonological dyslexia** affects non-word reading, but real words can be read.

> Chapter 10, p324

> **Event-related potentials (ERP)** a functional brain imaging method recording electrical activity during repeated stimulus presentations.

EEG brain activity that occur in response to a stimulus event. They are collected by means of electrodes placed on an individual's scalp. By time-locking EEG activity to stimulus presentation, we can see how the brain responds to particular stimuli. ERPs provide a non-invasive method of observing brain activity and the temporal resolution means that changes are recorded as they occur; this online measurement is a valuable addition to experimental methodologies which address an end process but often cannot provide an online account.

ERPs have been shown to contain a number of important waves or components. The N400 component is a negative-going potential that occurs approximately 400 milliseconds after the presentation of a triggering stimulus. It has been shown to be associated with the time-course of some aspects of word processing and with semantic processing in particular. Kutas and Hillyard (1980) were the first to show that the N400 is relatively larger when a semantically anomalous word is presented to participants (e.g., 'He spread the warm bread with socks'.) Kutas and Hillyard suggested that the N400 was an 'electrophysiological sign of the 'reprocessing' of semantically anomalous information' (p. 203). Subsequent accounts suggested that the N400 reflects increased processing effort when dealing with semantic information (e.g., Brown & Hagoort, 1993; Holcomb, 1993). The functional interpretation of the N400 continues to be debated (e.g., see Delogu et al., 2019). Osterhout et al. (1997) provided the following examples of sentences eliciting an N400 wave:

- 'The cats won't bake the food that Mary leaves them.'
- 'I take my coffee with cream and dog.'
- 'A hammer is a bird.'

By contrast the P600 wave occurs when syntactically anomalous words are presented (Osterhout & Holcomb, 1992) and has an onset around 500 milliseconds after presentation of the stimulus. Osterhout et al. (1997) provide the following examples of sentences eliciting a P600 wave:

- 'The cats won't eating the food that Mary leaves them.'
- 'The broker persuaded to sell the stock.'
- 'The elected officials hopes to succeed.'

The P600 was initially associated with resolution of syntactic anomalies but is now understood to play a broader role in conflict monitoring or in integration processes more generally (Brouwer et al., 2012; Delogu et al., 2019).

Figure 11.13, taken from from Osterhout et al. (1997), illustrates the N400 and P600 waves in semantically and syntactically anomalous sentence conditions (the negative ERP component is plotted on the upper part of the graph).

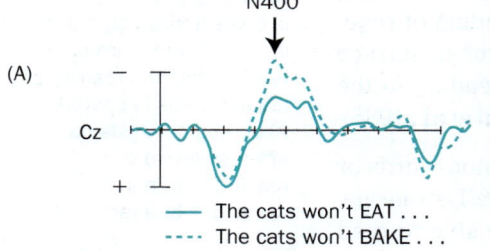
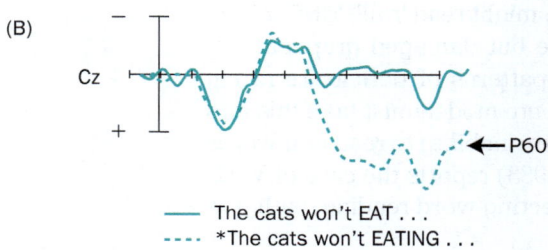
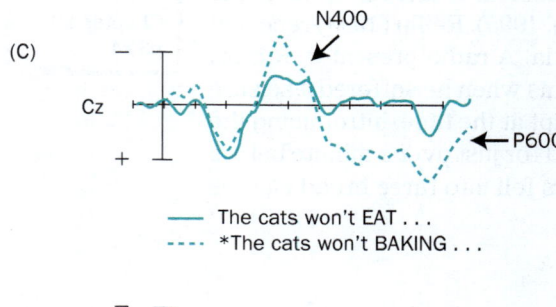
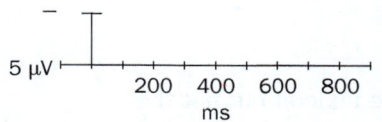

Figure 11.13 The N400 and P600 waves in semantically and syntactically anomalous sentence conditions.

The negative ERP component is plotted on the upper part of the graph. An asterisk next to a sentence indicates ungrammaticality. Panel A shows responses to a semantically anomalous word, B shows a syntactically anomalous word, and C shows a sentence containing both a semantic and syntactic anomaly, in each case compared to a non-anomalous sentence.

Source: Reprinted from Osterhout et al. (1997), with permission from Elsevier.

Summary

In this chapter we looked at language comprehension. The challenge of language comprehension begins with speech perception. Understanding speech requires us to perceive and interpret input from a continuous stream of speech sounds. The processes involved make use of top-down information (e.g., from context) as well as bottom-up information sources from the speech signal itself. These combine to allow fast and generally accurate perception. Occasional 'slips of the ear' reveal how the cognitive system detects word boundaries, using language-specific features to guide segmentation. We also saw how categorical perception and other properties of the system facilitate perception.

Understanding words and sentences requires lexical access, syntactic and semantic processing. We considered some of the main factors influencing lexical access, such as frequency, semantic context, syntactic context and word ambiguity. We also looked at the interaction of semantic and syntactic information during sentence processing.

Reading differs from speech in a number of key ways and differs across languages, particularly in the extent to which phonetic information is represented in the script. The dual route model proposes two (or possibly three) routes for reading: a direct route involving lexical access and an indirect route involving grapheme to phoneme correspondences. Evidence from neuropsychology and brain imaging was considered.

Finally, the brain areas involved in language comprehension were discussed, with data from neuropsychology, brain imaging and electrophysiology informing our knowledge in this area.

Review Questions

1. What can 'slips of the ear' tell us about the processes involved in speech perception?
2. How has evidence from acquired aphasia contributed to our understanding of language comprehension?
3. What do cross-language differences in brain activation during reading tell us about the common processes involved?
4. Does the evidence support a 'dual route' account of reading?
5. What differentiates orthographically 'deep' and 'transparent' languages?

Discussion Questions

1. What does the 'right ear advantage' reveal about language lateralization?
2. Is there evidence for a universal neurocognitive basis for developmental dyslexia?
3. How does orthographic depth affect reading processes?

Further Reading

Brysbaert, M. (2019). How many words do we read per minute? A review and meta-analysis of reading rate. *Journal of Memory and Language, 109,* 104047.

Loftus, E. F., & Palmer, J. C. (1974). Reconstruction of auto-mobile destruction: An example of the interaction between language and memory. *Journal of Verbal Learning and Verbal Behaviour, 13,* 585–589

MacLeod, C. M., & MacDonald, P. A. (2000). Inter-dimensional interference in the Stroop effect: Uncovering the cognitive and neural anatomy of attention. *Trends in Cognitive Sciences, 4,* 383–391.

Mattys, S. L., Melhorn, J. F., & White, L. (2007). Effects of syntactic expectations on speech segmentation. *Journal of Experimental Psychology: Human Perception and Performance, 33,* 960–977.

Rayner, K., Schotter, E. R., Masson, M. E., Potter, M. C., & Treiman, R. (2016). So much to read, so little time: How do we read, and can speed reading help? *Psychological Science in the Public Interest, 17*(1), 4–34.

PROBLEM SOLVING

12

PREVIEW QUESTIONS
INTRODUCTION
PROBLEMS AND PROBLEM TYPES
BRIEF HISTORY AND BACKGROUND
- Box 12.1 Practical Application: Life-or-death problem solving
- INFORMATION PROCESSING APPROACH
  - Box 12.2 Research Close Up: Travelling salesperson problems
  - Box 12.3 When Things Go Wrong: Right prefrontal cortex damage and real-world planning

INSIGHT REVISITED
- COMPARING INSIGHT AND NON-INSIGHT PROBLEM SOLVING
- INFORMATION PROCESSING THEORIES OF INSIGHT
  - Box 12.4 Research Close Up: It's magic! Use of magic tricks to generate insight

KNOWLEDGE-RICH (OR EXPERT) PROBLEM SOLVING
- EXPERTISE ACQUISITION
- NATURE OF EXPERTISE

CREATIVE PROBLEM SOLVING
- PERSONAL ACCOUNTS
- WALLAS'S STAGE ANALYSIS
- INCUBATION RESEARCH
- INFORMATION PROCESSING THEORY OF CREATIVE PROCESSES
- INCREASING IDEA PRODUCTION
  - Box 12.5 Practical Application: The Generic Parts Technique
  - Box 12.6 When Things Go Wrong: Psychopathology and creativity

SUMMARY
ANSWERS TO CHAPTER PROBLEMS
REVIEW QUESTIONS
DISCUSSION QUESTIONS
FURTHER READING

Preview Questions

1. We cannot observe thinking directly in others, so how can it be studied scientifically?
2. Problems come in all shapes and sizes. Can we sort them into types?
3. Can we explain how some problems are solved with a sudden flash of inspiration or 'insight'?
4. What can analogies with computer problem solving tell us about human problem solving?
5. How do experts differ from beginners in solving problems in their area of skill?
6. Can creativity be increased by training?
7. Are highly creative people likely to be mentally ill?

INTRODUCTION

Cognition involves the acquisition, storage, retrieval and use of information. In previous chapters the focus has been on acquisition of information in perception, its storage and retrieval in learning and memory. In this chapter we examine how we use information in problem solving, and then in later chapters go on to discuss using information in decision making and reasoning. First, what do we mean when we say we have a problem?

> **Problem**
> a situation in which you have a goal but do not know how to achieve it.

> **Thinking**
> a process of mental exploration of possible actions and states of the world.

Whenever we want something, but do not have an immediate way to get what we desire, there is a **problem**. For example, suppose you are studying at university far from home when a family emergency breaks out. You want to go home to help but there are vital exams that week and there are many possible ways to get home, varying in costs and speed. When can you leave campus and how should you travel? By train, bus, plane or by a mixture? This is a difficult problem, which calls for extensive **thinking**. Thinking involves exploring possibilities mentally, in imagination, so that good solutions can be reached in advance of physical action. In our example, by thinking, you might remember that there is a cheap coach home that would meet your needs, and so avoid impulsively buying an expensive plane ticket.

This chapter focuses on the kinds of thinking involved in problem solving. We begin by defining and explaining key terms such as 'thinking' and 'problem' more fully, and then briefly set the historical context of current research. We will discuss ideas about problem solving as a sort of search and then go on to current studies of 'insight' problem solving in which the solver has a strong 'Aha!' experience as a solution comes suddenly and surprisingly. The role of knowledge or expertise in problem solving will be discussed, and finally we will look at solving 'divergent' or 'creative' problems where many new solutions are sought rather than just a single solution. Problem solving is clearly an important cognitive process and is the basis for progress in every area of human activity. Technology provides many cases of effective problem solving, as in developing mobile phones, computers, space vehicles, and so on. The arts and sciences, as we shall see when discussing creativity, also involve extensive problem solving, as in developing better theories of the structure of matter, or devising new styles of music or genres of literature, for instance.

PROBLEMS AND PROBLEM TYPES

> Chapter 13, p466
>
> Chapter 14, p510

Although thinking may often be relatively free-floating and undirected, as in daydreaming, much thinking is directed towards achieving particular goals such as solving a problem, making a difficult decision (see Chapter 13 on decision making), drawing a logical conclusion (see Chapter 14 on reasoning) or producing a creative product.

Research on thinking has generally focused on goal-directed thinking in problem solving. This raises the question of what we mean by a 'problem'? Problems can be said to arise when a person or animal has a goal but does not have an immediately available way of reaching the goal. All problems have a goal, a starting situation in which the goal is not yet achieved, and a set of actions that can be selected from and combined to bring about the goal state. Problems come in a great many shapes and sizes but can be classified in terms of a few broad characteristics, such as degree of definition; whether an adversary is involved or not; whether extensive knowledge is needed or not; and whether the timescale of the problem is long or short.

There are a number of ways we classify problems based on these characteristics, which help us to group different types of problems together for understanding and research.

In general, we tend to refer to problems as either **well defined** or **ill defined** depending on the amount of information provided initially. We then determine whether specialized knowledge is required to solve a problem, making it either **knowledge rich** or **knowledge lean**. Finally, we consider whether the type of problem involves a rational opponent. All of these components help us to understand a problem more fully so that we can consider the different problem-solving techniques and strategies involved or required in each. It also means that research can be conducted on the same types of problems.

As indicated, some problems are well defined; this means that the nature of the initial state, goal state and possible methods to be used to solve are clearly laid out. In contrast many problems are ill defined in that one or more of the key components are not fully specified. Some examples are given in Table 12.1.

Problems may be classified as **non-adversary** or **adversary problems**. In adversary problems the solver is dealing with a thinking opponent who seeks to defeat the solver's goals (e.g., noughts and crosses (or tic tac toe), chess, poker, bridge). On the other hand, in non-adversary problem solving the problem material is inert and is not behaving with a view to frustrating the solver (e.g., anagram puzzle solving, computer programming.)

A further difference is that between knowledge-rich problems, which require a high degree of specialist knowledge (e.g., medical diagnosis, high-level chess), and knowledge-lean problems, which can be tackled by anyone without specialist knowledge (e.g., anagrams, simple logic tasks). Finally, some problems are *large scale* and require months or years of effort (e.g., designing power stations, writing epic novels) and some are *small scale* and can be tackled within minutes (e.g., crosswords, simple decision tasks).

> **Well-defined problem**
> a problem in which starting conditions, actions available and goals are all completely specified.
>
> **Ill-defined problem**
> a problem in which starting conditions, or actions available or goals are not completely specified.
>
> **Knowledge-rich problems**
> problems that require extensive specialist knowledge.
>
> **Knowledge-lean problems**
> problems such as puzzles that do not require specialist knowledge.
>
> **Non-adversary problems**
> problems in which the solver is dealing with inert problem materials with no rational opponent.
>
> **Adversary problems**
> problems in which the solver has to deal with a rational opponent, as in board games.

All these have been studied by psychologists, although research has generally been carried out using non-adversary, well-defined, small-scale, knowledge-lean puzzles. Such materials are good starting points for research as non-adversary problems avoid the complexity of anticipating a competitor's actions, well-defined problems are likely to be interpreted similarly by all participants, small-scale problems fit into the usual time available in a laboratory study and knowledge-lean problems can be tackled by most participants with a normal educational background.

BRIEF HISTORY AND BACKGROUND

Although the main historical approaches to cognitive psychology, as outlined in Chapter 1, have addressed the study of thinking and problem solving, only the *Gestalt* and *information processing* approaches are still influential in this area. We will now explain these two approaches, which have focused on different aspects of thinking and problem solving, and differ in methods of data gathering, as much recent research (discussed in later sections of this chapter) is based on these approaches and builds on the earlier research.

Chapter 1, p2

Table 12.1 Examples of Well- and Ill-Defined Problems

Well defined	Ill defined
Anagrams	Improve quality of life
Chess	Devise a fair tax system
Rubik cube	Invent a best-selling toy

Gestalt Approach

Chapter 9, p294

Restructuring
changing how one represents a problem.

The Gestalt psychologists saw problem solving as much like perceiving a new pattern in an ambiguous drawing (e.g., seeing first the duck then the rabbit in the duck–rabbit figure discussed in Chapter 9). The key process, they argued, was one of changing the way the problem was seen, or in other words of **restructuring** the way the problem was represented.

A frequently cited example of restructuring (Wertheimer, 1945) comes from a true story regarding the nineteenth-century mathematician Gauss (Hall, 1970). When Gauss was a 6-year-old schoolboy his class were given the task of adding all the numbers from 1 to 100. Within a very short time Gauss announced the answer: 5050. How had he done it? Not by super-fast addition of $1 + 2 + 3 + 4 + \ldots + 98 + 99 + 100$, but by noticing a structure in the number sequence. The numbers form into pairs (1, 100), (2, 99), (3, 98) all of which have the same sum (101) and there are 50 such pairs so answer is $101 \times 50 = 5050$. A restructuring that leads to a rapid solution is known as an **insight**.

Insight
a restructuring of a problem that makes the solution obvious and understandable.

Box 12.1 gives some real life examples of insight problem solving in which a Gestalt-style restructuring was life-saving.

Box 12.1 Practical Application: Life-or-death problem solving

1. FIREFIGHTERS' DILEMMA

On 5 August 1949, a group of 15 firefighters in Montana, USA, set out to tackle a forest fire in a steep-sided gulch, known as Mann Gulch (Lehrer, 2008). The side of the gulch that was alight was mainly pine trees and the side from which the men began their advance largely contained tall dry grass. At first the wind was blowing the flames away from the men. Suddenly the wind reversed and sparks started a fire in the tall grass on the men's side of the gulch, which was soon spreading extremely rapidly towards the men. The leading firefighter, 'Wag' Dodge, ordered the men to drop their gear and run up the side of the gulch to the ridge. Very soon it became clear that the fire could not be outrun. What to do?

Dodge stopped and with the flames less than 50 yards away did a surprising thing: he lit a match and started another fire in the grass in front of him! Why?

The flames of the fire he had started quickly moved up the slope leaving a large patch of burned ground in front. He then went into the middle of the burned out patch and lay down. The main fire then burned fiercely around the patch where he was lying, before sweeping on up the hill. When it had passed, Dodge emerged alive and well. Thirteen of his colleagues died because they did not have the crucial insight at the critical time that the fire could be deprived of fuel by burning the grass ahead of the flames and so creating a fire break. Dodge's method of creating an escape fire is now standard practice but had never been used previously by US forest service firefighters.

2. 'HOUSTON, WE'VE HAD A PROBLEM…'

The Apollo 13 mission to land on the Moon took off on 11 April 1970. All went well until, 55 hours and 55 minutes into the flight, an oxygen tank blew up, causing a second tank to also fail, some 200,000 miles from Earth. The Command Module lost its normal supply of power, light and water. The first novel aspect of the solution was to use the Lunar Module as a kind of lifeboat. The three crew squeezed into a space meant for two and eked out its power, water and oxygen supply to orbit the moon and get on the return trajectory for Earth. The removal of carbon dioxide produced by the breathing astronauts from the Lunar Module was a problem because the Module was not designed for use for so long and by an additional person. Extra canisters of lithium hydroxide, which removed carbon dioxide from the air, were present in the Command Module and had to be moved into the Lunar Module, where they did not quite fit the round openings used by the removal system in the Lunar Module. Mission Control managed to overcome functional fixity here, devising a way to attach the canisters using plastic bags, cardboard and tape.

With the flexible problem solving of the crew and Mission Control, all lives were saved in what had been an incredibly dangerous situation.

Source: www.nasa.gov, 'Apollo 13', 8 July 2009.

Interestingly, much of the early Gestalt work on problem solving was carried out with animals, particularly with apes (Kohler, 1925). If insight could be demonstrated with animals then its existence in humans would be hard to doubt. Kohler set apes manipulation problems in which they had to build towers from boxes to reach high-hanging fruit or use a short stick to retrieve an out-of-reach long stick, which could then be used to retrieve otherwise unreachable fruit. Kohler reported that the apes frequently solved such problems with little or no overt trial and error but quite suddenly after a period of apparently examining the problem situation.

Duncker (1945) sought to demonstrate insight and to find out how it is achieved in human participants by using a think aloud method to make the normally covert thought processes more observable. In this method participants simply report as much as they can in normal language. This think aloud method is widely used in the study of thinking (see Ericsson & Simon, 1993, for more details) and we will come across other examples later. In Duncker's (1945) study, participants with no specialist knowledge were shown a figure similar to that in Figure 12.1, representing a body with a tumour in the middle, and the goal was to find a way of destroying the tumour by radiation without destroying the healthy tissue around the tumour. Participants' think aloud records indicated that they restructured the goal into subgoals that, if achieved, would solve the problem, such as 'try avoiding contact between the rays and healthy tissue'. In turn, this subgoal could lead to a further subgoal of 'try to use the throat as a route for the rays to the tumour'. The key subgoal was 'to reduce the intensity of the rays on their way through healthy tissue' which in turn led to the insightful solution 'use a lens to focus a weak bundle of rays on the tumour' (see Figure 12.2). The insight was that the large effect desired could be achieved by adding together small effects at the target site. The kind of restructuring seen here, of the overall problem into subproblems is also addressed in the information processing approach, discussed later in this chapter.

> **Set**
> a tendency to persist with one approach to a problem.
> **Functional fixity**
> a difficulty in thinking of a novel use for a familiar object.

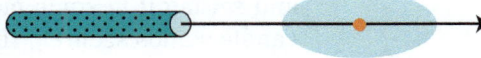

Figure 12.1 Duncker's X-ray problem.
Find a way to destroy a tumour in the centre of the body without destroying healthy tissue. Participants are told that someone has envisaged the problem as in the diagram.

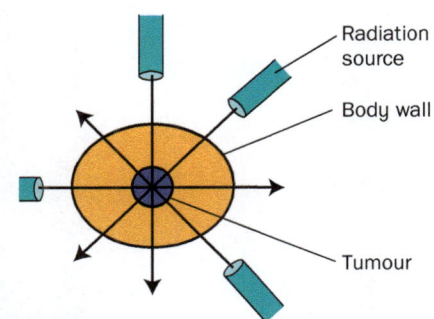

Figure 12.2 Solution to Duncker's X-ray problem.
The solution is reached by crossing weak rays so that the total effect adds up to enough strength at the site of the tumour.

Barriers to insight

The Gestalt psychologists identified two important barriers to insight, which were labelled **set** and **functional fixity**.

Set effects arise from a tendency to solve problems in one particular way, using a single approach, or being stuck in a rut in your thinking. A famous example is the nine-dot problem: connect the nine dots below with four connected straight lines without lifting your pencil from the page as you draw. See if you can solve it!

• • •

• • •

• • •

Most people confine their efforts to the lines that stay within the square shape. The layout induces a strong set effect and the problem cannot be solved until the self-imposed restriction of solutions to the square shape is overcome and the person 'thinks outside the box'. (The solution is given at the end of the chapter.)

Sets can also arise from extensive experience or training with particular types of problems. So, given a run of water jar problems in which three jars of different sizes have to be used to get target amounts of water, people will be greatly slowed down or fail altogether when a problem comes along in which only two out of the three jars must be used (Luchins, 1942) even when the 'set breaking' problem is very simple for people not exposed to the set inducing training.

Another block to insight is functional fixity (Maier, 1931), which refers to a tendency to use objects and concepts only in their customary way. An example problem that demonstrates fixity effects is Duncker's (1945) candle problem in which the task is to support a candle on a door using an assortment of materials such as a box of tacks and some matches (see Figure 12.3). The problem requires using the box in an unusual way. The box is emptied and the tray of the box is attached to the door by a tack. The tray can then serve as a platform on which the candle can be secured by lighting the candle and setting it in some molten wax dripped onto the tray. When the wax hardens the candle stands securely fixed to the door. Duncker found that this task became significantly easier if the box was presented empty with the tacks out already. Duncker argued that when the box was presented full, its container role was salient, making it harder to restructure the way participants represented its function.

Adults often find it difficult to think of novel uses for familiar objects, as in the candle problem. However, young children (of about 5) suffered less from functional fixity in

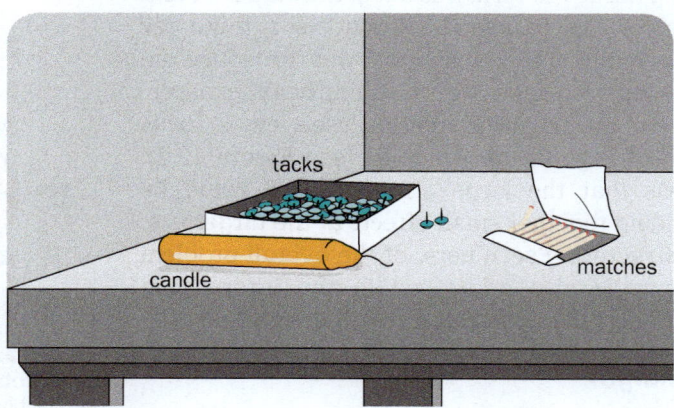

Figure 12.3 Duncker's candle problem.
The task is to use the items in the picture to fix a candle to the door so that it will burn securely.

tasks requiring unusual uses of familiar objects, presumably because they had less strongly fixed associations of how objects are used (Defeyter & German, 2003). Similarly, Amazonian Indians, unfamiliar with the tools to be used in a task, showed less functional fixity than Westerners for tasks requiring the tools to be used in unusual ways *until* the typical use was shown to them (German & Barrett, 2005) whereupon they also showed functional fixity at similar levels to Western participants.

Evaluation

The Gestalt approach stressed organization, insight and restructuring, showed how these processes could be investigated, and highlighted the roles of set and functional fixity as barriers to solving problems. These were major contributions. Many of the issues raised by the Gestaltists are still under active investigation (e.g., insight processes, which will be discussed again later in this chapter). However a major drawback with the approach was a lack of clarity in its explanations. How restructuring actually came about was always unclear. Also, the approach did not address how we solve problems that do not require restructuring or insight. The information processing approach, to be discussed next, offers a route to greater clarity of explanation and is more widely applicable to a range of problem types, while preserving some of the strengths of the Gestalt approach.

Information Processing Approach

The information processing approach was inspired by the development of programable digital computers, which began in the mid-1940s. As explained in Chapter 1, it was quickly realized that computers could be programmed to tackle many complex tasks, such as playing chess, suggesting medical diagnoses given the symptoms and (still not perfectly) automatic translation between natural languages. Computer programs to solve problems could be seen as comparable to *strategies* that humans might use to solve the same problems.

> Chapter 1, p2

The general information processing approach to cognition has been described by Thagard (2005) as a hypothesis that thinking and problem solving are performed by computational processes operating on mental representations. This **Computational-Representational Understanding of Mind (CRUM)** hypothesis assumes the mind has mental representations (as discussed in Chapter 9) similar to data structures in computing systems and computational procedures similar to algorithms. See also Rescorla (2020) for more background on the CRUM approach.

> Chapter 9, p296

Computational-Representational Understanding of Mind (CRUM) the general hypothesis that the mind has mental representations that are acted upon by mental computational processes.

On the CRUM approach it should be possible to develop computer programs to mimic human thinking. Such programs would be labelled simulation programs and should be distinguished from artificial intelligence programs, which seek to solve problems as effectively as possible without any attempt at mimicking human strategies. So, for example, an artificial intelligence program to play chess might explore millions of possible move sequences in seconds, which a human cannot do. A simulation program might build up a memory bank of opening move patterns through exposure to many games, which is a more human-like approach. Despite this distinction, many ideas developed in artificial intelligence research have been adopted in the information processing approach to human problem solving and modified as possible descriptions of human approaches.

Some key ideas of the information processing approach to problem solving will now be considered.

> **Problem space**
> an abstract representation of possible states of a problem.
>
> **State-action space**
> a representation of how problems can be transformed from starting state through intermediate states to the goal.
>
> **Goal-subgoal space**
> a representation of how an overall problem goal can be broken down into subgoals and sub-subgoals.

Problem space

A very important idea in the information processing approach to problem solving is that of **problem space**, which is a way of representing a problem as a graph, with points representing states of the problem and with lines connecting the points representing possible actions that lead from one state of the problem to other states. Problem spaces may be defined further into two subtypes – **state-action spaces** and **goal-subgoal spaces** – which we will now outline.

State-action spaces

In state-action space representations problems may be solved by searching through a series of operations that will transform the starting state into intermediate states that, in turn, are transformed into further intermediate states until ultimately the goal state is reached.

These operations may be represented in diagrams such as tree graphs which resemble an upside-down tree with the starting state at the top. A partial tree diagram is shown in Figure 12.4 for the familiar game of noughts and crosses (or tic tac toe). This is an adversary problem in which each player takes turns entering their symbol, an X or an O, and the first to get a row, column or diagonal in the grid filled with their symbol is the winner.

At the start of the noughts and crosses game the grid is empty. The first player puts an X in one of the empty cells. There are nine possible first moves. For reasons of space, Figure 12.4 shows only three of the possible first moves. To each possible first move there are eight places for the second player to put a circle. To show the whole tree just for the first and second moves we would need a diagram with 73 grids (i.e., 9 × 8 plus the starting empty grid). The whole tree representing all possible games, where the game stops when someone wins or a draw occurs, would have 10 levels and a total of 255,168 grids or states. So, even this fairly simple game generates a very large tree of possible states. Analysis of the whole tree confirms what you may have found from experience of playing, that if both players adopt a strategy of blocking their opponent from getting a line, then a draw will always result.

Consider also the eight-puzzle task shown in Figure 12.5. In this task you are presented with a square tray containing eight tiles numbered 1–8 and a space. The task is to

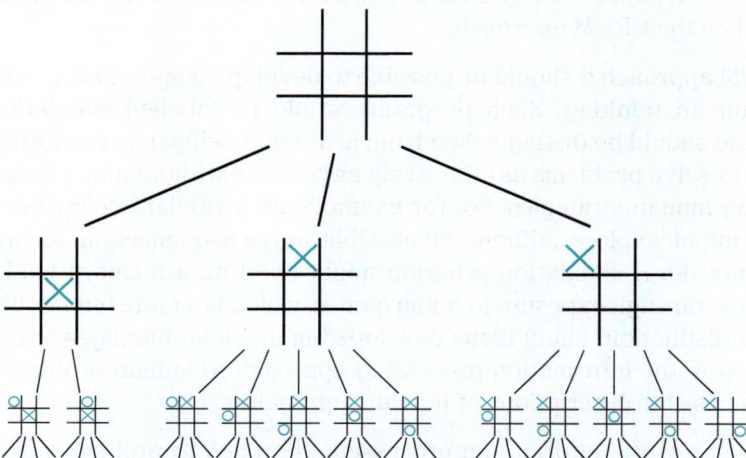

Figure 12.4 Part of a tree diagram for noughts and crosses.

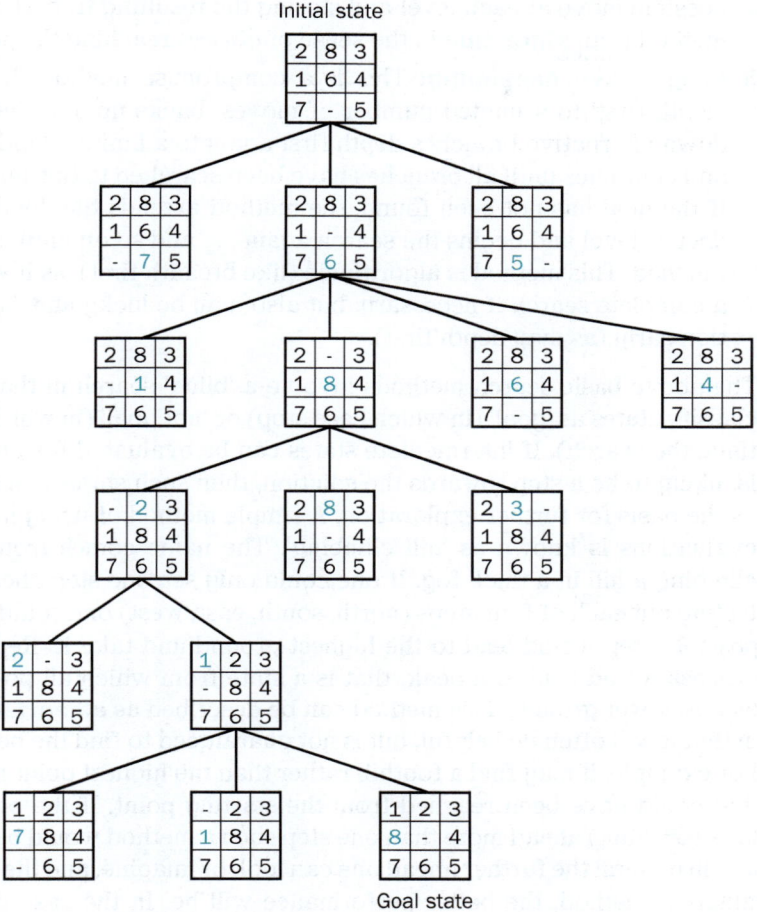

Figure 12.5 State-action tree for the eight-puzzle task.
Move one tile at a time into the empty space on the tray until the numbers are in order 1–8 starting at the top left.

Source: http://www.aspgod.com/project/ai/8-puzzle.html.

rearrange the tiles, moving one at a time into the empty space until a target arrangement is reached (usually having the numbers in order 1–8 as you read from left to right in the usual way). This is, in a way, simpler than the noughts and crosses situation, as there is no opponent to deal with.

As can be seen from Figure 12.5, as with noughts and crosses, the state-action tree grows rapidly. Even with just four possible moves at each state, by the fifth level of the tree some 1,024 ($= 4^5$) states would be generated. How might the goal state be found in large problem spaces?

Analysis of possible strategies indicates three main methods by which a state-action tree can be searched systematically.

1 **Depth first search**: This involves a light load on memory in that only one possible move at a time is considered. An example of depth first search would be to take the rightmost move at each choice point in the eight-puzzle tree. However, this may or may not find the goal and would not generally be guaranteed to find the best solution even if it did eventually solve.

2 **Breadth first search**: This generally involves a very heavy working memory load in that it generates the whole tree by considering each

Depth first search searching a state-action space by generating one state only from each intermediate state.
Breadth first search searching a state-action space by generating all possible states from each intermediate state.

> **Algorithm**
> a problem-solving method that is guaranteed to solve but may do so only with high mental load.
>
> **Progressive deepening**
> searching a state-action space by using depth first search to a limited depth. When depth limit is reached, search backs up to start and repeats, avoiding previously explored branches, and so on until the whole space has been searched up to the initial depth limit. If a solution is not found, increase depth limit and repeat until the goal is reached.

possible move at each level and storing the resulting tree. However, this method is an **algorithm** in the sense of *always* reaching the goal.

3 Progressive deepening: This is a compromise method that involves 'depth first' to a limited number of moves, backs up and then searches down alternative branches depth first again to a limited depth, backs up and continues until all branches have been searched to this limited depth. If the goal has not been found, the method extends the depth limit to a deeper level and begins the search again ... and so on until a solution is reached. This method is algorithmic (like breadth first), as it will execute a complete search if necessary, but also may be lucky and find the solution early (as may depth first).

The above basic search methods involve a 'blind' search in that they only classify states as 'goal' (in which case stop) or 'not goal' (in which case continue the search). If intermediate states can be evaluated for promise, that is, likely to be a step towards the solution, then such states can be selected as the basis for further exploration. A simple method of using intermediate evaluations is known as 'hill climbing'. The name comes from a way of climbing a hill in a thick fog. If one could only see one step ahead, then by testing out each of four steps (north, south, east, west) one could find which possible step would lead to the highest ground and take it. Repeating this process would lead to a peak, that is a state from which all possible steps lead to lower ground. This method can be described as a **heuristic** method, in that it will often be helpful, but is not guaranteed to find the best solution. For example, it may find a foothill rather than the highest point in the space that could have been reached from the starting point. If the person could look (or think) ahead more than one step such a method would be improved,

> **Heuristic**
> a problem-solving method that often finds a low-effort solution but is not guaranteed to solve.

and in general the further ahead one can look or imagine, and the more accurate the evaluation method, the better performance will be. In the case of the eight puzzle a possible evaluation procedure might be to count the number of tiles in their target positions or one might try counting the number of tiles that are in sequence. The development of more accurate evaluation functions has been one important factor in improvements in chess-playing programs over the years.

A number of studies have examined human search in problems that lend themselves to a state-action representation. An early example is Thomas's (1974) experiment on the Hobbits and Orcs task.

The task was based on the Hobbits and Orcs characters in *The Lord of the Rings* (Tolkien, 1966) and the goal is to get three Hobbits and three Orcs across a river. The only way to cross is by a boat and the boat can carry only one or two passengers at most. There must be at least one passenger in the boat for it to cross, and you have to avoid Orcs outnumbering Hobbits on the same side of river or the Hobbits will be eaten! The task was presented on a computer and participants could see only one state at a time.

Although the problem could be solved in a minimum of 11 moves, participants typically required more than 20 moves. Thomas (1974) found that states 5 and 8 presented most difficulty in terms of errors and times to make moves.

The difficulty at state 5 may be because there is a larger number of possible moves than usual at this state. The difficulty at state 8 may well be because people are engaging in a hill-climbing form of search, feel that they are making progress at that point (four creatures are on the target bank) and are reluctant to backtrack, which is necessary at this point in order to progress – the correct move involves going to a state with only two

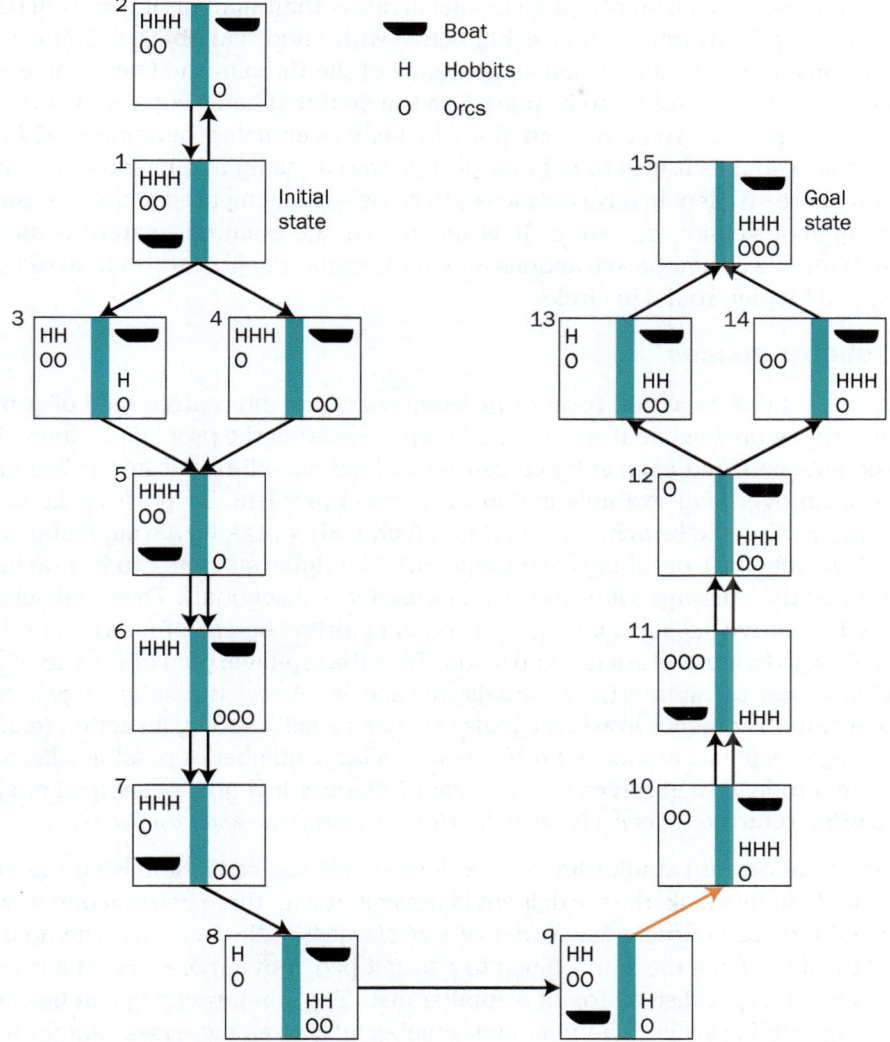

Figure 12.6 Hobbits and Orcs problem space.
All possible moves and states of the problem are shown in this diagram.

Source: Adapted from Thomas (1974).

creatures on the target bank. Problems such as this, which require a detour, are typically difficult (Wickelgren, 1974), presumably because of the prevalence of simple hill-climbing strategies.

Similar results favouring the use of simple hill climbing with a look (or think) ahead of only one step were found in detailed analyses of possible models for human search patterns in a range of water jar tasks and variants of the Hobbits and Orcs task (Atwood & Polson, 1976; Atwood et al., 1980; Jeffries et al., 1977). Hill-climbing has also been found in some insight problems, such as the nine-dot problem, which require back-tracking (MacGregor et al., 2001), and we will discuss these later in this chapter.

River crossing problems and interactivity

River crossing problems such as the Hobbits and Orcs task have generally been presented in quite abstract formats using pencil-and-paper or computerised displays, with the items in the task represented in symbol form (e.g., as Hs or Os). Since real-world problems must very often involve actual objects rather than symbols it may well be that problem solving is different and possibly better with vivid real objects. Guthrie et al. (2015) examined this question using an analogue of the Hobbits and Orcs problem, but with toy Chickens and Wolves to be taken in a toy boat that had a capacity for two animals across a painted river without the Chickens ever being outnumbered by the Wolves. In two studies it was found that groups who actually manipulated the toys to solve were more efficient in terms of moves to cross when compared to groups using an abstract symbol version on paper. It is likely that the concrete materials aided in imaging of effects of alternative actions and in remembering past states to avoid backtracking and looping round in circles.

Goal–subgoal spaces

In addition to the state-action form of problem space, an alternative type of problem space involves a goal-subgoal space. In this representation the problem is divided into goals and subgoals and each subgoal can be tackled by splitting it into subsubgoals, and so on. An everyday example is that of a travel problem. To go from London to Edinburgh (goal) could be achieved by flying (subgoal), or taking a train (subgoal), or taking a bus (subgoal), or taking a car (subgoal). The flying subgoal can be reached by contacting British Airways (subsubgoal), or easyJet (subsubgoal). These subsubgoals can yield alternative subsubsubgoals (e.g., contact airline by use of internet, or use of telephone, or go to a travel agent), and so on. Thus the top-level goal of the travel problem yields a tree of alternative subgoals at each level and the subgoal generation process eventually reaches low-level goals that can be achieved by an action (e.g., dial the travel agent's phone number). Problems with a large number of possible alternative actions seem to lend themselves to this form of hierarchical goal = subgoal analysis, which is often referred to as *problem reduction* or as *means–ends analysis*.

A number of laboratory studies have investigated problem reduction using the Tower of Hanoi task. In this task, the participant is presented with three pegs on one of which are stacked n discs in descending order of size (largest at the bottom). The goal is to move all the discs from the starting peg to a target peg, moving one disc at a time and never placing a larger disc on top of a smaller disc. The non-target peg can be used as a temporary holding place. The minimum number of moves increases rapidly with n according to the formula $2n - 1$. A three-disc example is shown in Figure 12.7 and requires a minimum of seven moves. A four-disc version would need 15 moves, a five-disc version 31 moves, and so on.

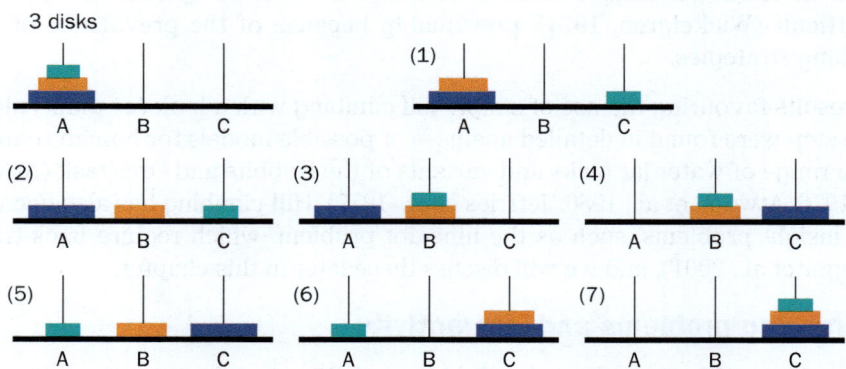

Figure 12.7 Tower of Hanoi.
The task is to move discs from the left peg to the right peg, never placing a larger disc on top of a smaller disc. The solution path of this three-disc problem is through states marked 1–7.

Anzai and Simon (1979) found that the strategies used in this task tended towards problem reduction as more experience was built up with the task. At first participants tried a state-action representation with forward search from the starting state, trying to work from the start to the end in a linear process. It was only with more experience that they came to the problem reduction strategy, which works back from the overall goal to generate subgoals and subsubgoals until action can be taken.

Tower of London tasks

In move problems, such as the Tower of Hanoi, planning ahead is clearly important in finding efficient solutions. Planning is generally taken to involve the prefrontal cortex, and studies of prefrontal patients have indeed found deficits in planning tasks (Ward, 2006). Studies with patients have generally used problems similar to the Tower of Hanoi, but simplified to be suitable for patients and to provide a more closely graded set of problems. Shallice (1982) developed the Tower of London task in which patients have to make a plan to move beads from one peg to another to reach a goal configuration.

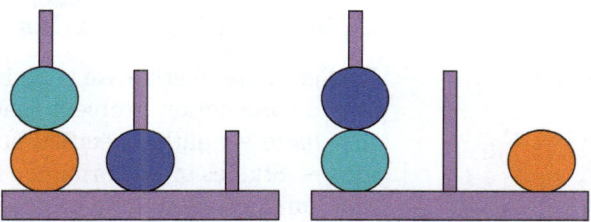

Figure 12.8 Shallice's (1982) three-ball Tower of London task example.
The left-hand side is the starting state and the right-hand side is the goal state to be reached in as few moves as possible by moving one ball at a time. Can you solve in the minimum four moves?

Source: Shallice (1982, Fig. 2, p. 204).

As expected, patients with frontal lobe damage take more moves than do controls. Further, fMRI studies find that dorsolateral prefrontal cortex activity increases with the number of moves needed to solve, consistent with a role for this region in manipulating information in working memory during planning (Rowe et al., 2001).

A further modification of the Tower of London task extended the number of beads or discs from three to five, which made the task more suitable for normal participants (Ward & Allport, 1997).

Gilhooly et al. (1999) investigated age differences in planning using the five-disc Tower of London task. Participants thought aloud while planning and it was found from analysis of the thinking aloud records that older participants (average age 67 years) developed significantly shorter plans (*c.* four moves ahead) than did younger participants (average age 21 years), whose plans averaged six moves ahead. Older participants' plans also were more error-prone. These differences were attributed to reduced working memory capacity in older participants, which impaired extended planning. Although the older and younger participants differed in effectiveness of planning ahead, both groups followed a similar 'goal selection' strategy in which a current goal was set of clearing that disc with the fewest obstructions between it and its target position and then moving the selected disc to its goal position. A possible alternative 'move selection' strategy of examining each possible move at each choice point and choosing the most promising was not followed. A follow-up study (Gilhooly et al., 2002) indicated a role for the visuo-spatial component of working memory in planning in this task.

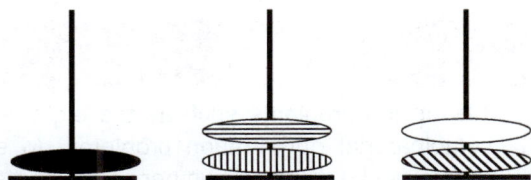

Figure 12.9 Five-disc Tower of London task.
The upper panel is the goal state and the lower panel is the starting state. The task is to move the discs one at a time to change the starting state into the goal state in as few moves as possible. Can you solve in the minimum four moves?

Source: Gilhooly et al. (1999).

Eight- and fifteen-puzzles

Earlier in this chapter we introduced the eight-puzzle (see Figure 12.5) as an example of how a state-action problem space can be generated readily for well-defined problems that have a tightly specified starting state, goal state and set of possible actions or moves. Studies of performance in the eight-puzzle by O'Hara and Payne (1998) indicate that human solvers tend to adopt a means–end approach rather than a forward search through the state-action space. Forward search would try to look ahead through possible paths up to some depth limit imposed by working memory limitations, and evaluate possible paths by how closely they would lead to states similar to the goal state. However, think aloud records reveal a predominance of means–ends approaches. One simple such approach is to try to reduce the overall problem goal into eight subgoals where each subgoal corresponds to getting each separate tile in its place. Typically participants address the subgoal of placing tile 1 first and seek to move obstructing tiles so that tile 1 can be slotted into position, and then move on to tile 2 with the constraint that tile 1 cannot be moved out of position. This method works only with the simpler puzzles and has to be adapted when 'detours' are needed, necessitating temporary movements of earlier goal tiles to allow later goal tiles to be placed in their spots. O'Hara and Payne found also that the depth of mental planning before physically moving pieces was greater when the 'costs' of physically moving tiles were increased (by making the move instructions on the computer presentation involve three keystrokes versus one). When move costs were low, participants tended to reduce effortful mental planning and engage in more simple trial and error.

Pizlo and Zheng (2005) examined performance on a range of tile-moving puzzles from the five-puzzle (using a 2 × 3 board), the eight-puzzle, the 15-puzzle (a 4 × 4 board) and the 35-puzzle (a 6 × 6 board). The size of the problem spaces corresponding to the five-, eight-, 15- and 35-puzzles goes up astronomically. It is 360 states for the five-puzzle, 181,440 states for the eight-puzzle, and for the 15-puzzle it is 10 to the power 13, which is greater than the number of neurons in the human brain (*c.* 10 to the power 10 – i.e., 100 billion). It was found that participants' times to solve went up linearly with the lengths of the solution paths rather than with the size of the problem spaces. Pizlo and Zheng thus concluded that participants applied fairly simple heuristic problem reduction or means–ends approaches, and as in O'Hara and Payne's study of the eight-puzzle, progressed one tile at a time without extensive forward search. They also found that people were poor at judging how far intermediate states were from the goal and this was consistent with participants *not* using a look-ahead through the state action space since that method depends on having a good evaluation function to choose moves that will lead to states closer to the goal.

Box 12.2 Research Close Up: Travelling salesperson problems

Tile-moving problems such as the eight- and 15-puzzles are examples of a general class known as combinatorial optimization problems. In such problems, the number of possible solutions grows exponentially with the number of elements in the problem, so generating and scanning all possible candidate solutions is not practicable – we saw this even with the 15-puzzle. An important real-world problem of this type is the travelling salesperson problem in which the best route is sought around a number of destinations. Interestingly, in 1962, the Procter & Gamble personal care products multinational company, which had a large army of travelling salespeople, ran a contest worth around $500,000 in today's money, to find the shortest round-trip route through 33 US cities, beginning and ending in Chicago. The number of possible round trips for *n* cities is $((n-1)!/2)$, which is 132 billion trillion trillion possible routes for Procter & Gamble's 33-city problem. Although there is no practicable algorithm to determine with certainty the best route, two winning solutions (later shown to be the best solutions)

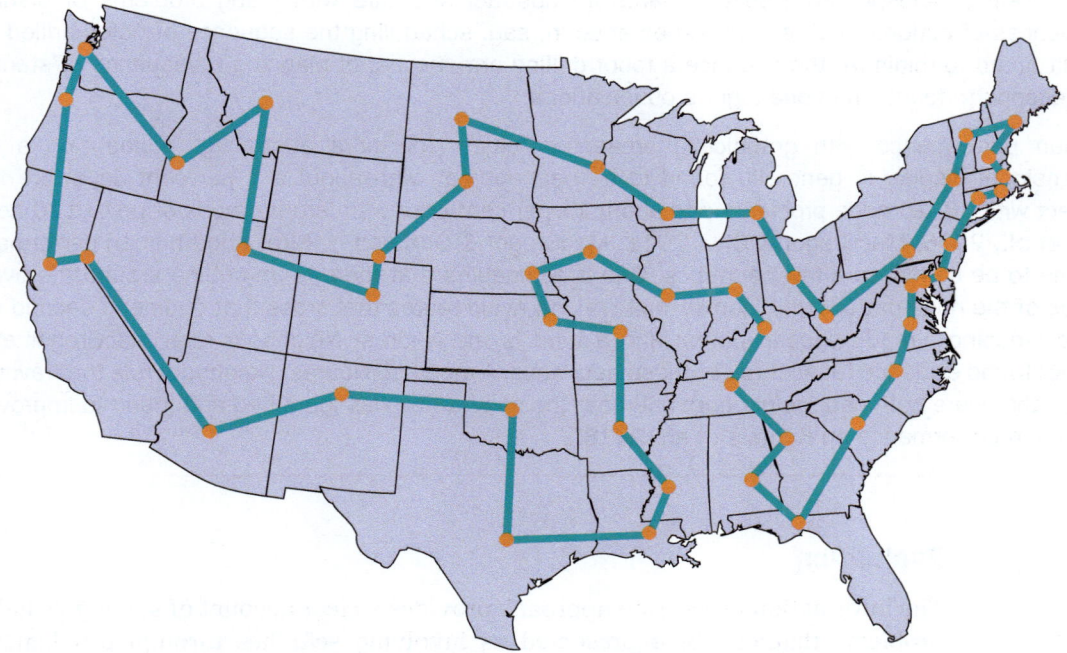

Figure 12.10 Solution to travelling salesperson problem of visiting all US state capitals.
Minimum distance for a road trip around US state capitals, 12,345 miles. Calculated 'by hand' by Dantzig et al. (1954).

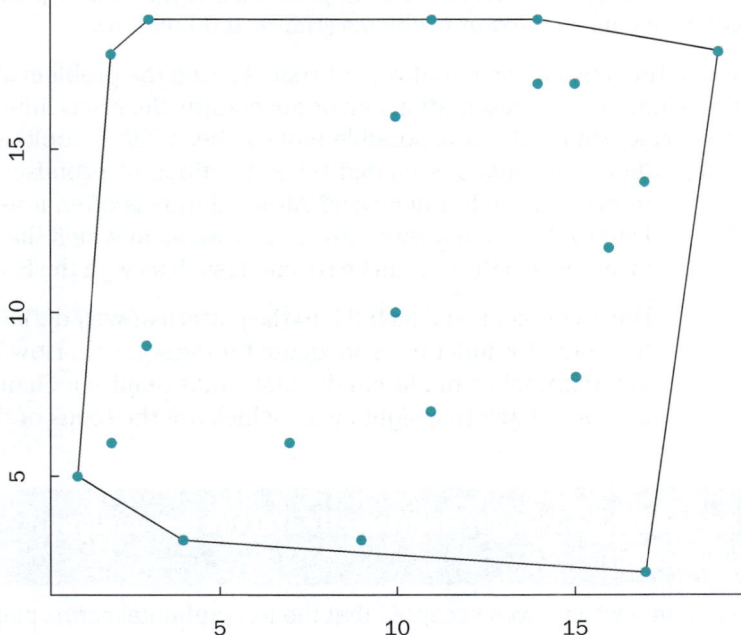

Figure 12.11 Example 'convex hull' around nodes in a travelling salesperson problem.
The 'convex hull' heuristic restricts paths considered to those within the convex hull enclosing the nodes.

Source: Kyritsis et al. (2018, Fig. 1).

tied, by using simple heuristics such as the Nearest Neighbour (NN) method. Applied to the Procter & Gamble problem, this method would start by going to the nearest city to Chicago then the nearest neighbour to that city, and so on (Applegate et al., 2006).

The travelling salesperson problem shares its abstract structure with many problems of planning sequences of actions, and related issues arise in, say, scheduling the sequence of holes drilled in a circuit board to minimize the distance a robot drilling arm moves; or planning a sequence of stars for a telescope to focus on in one night's observations.

Human performance with graphically presented 'cities' (or more abstractly 'nodes') on a two-dimensional display is generally found to be near-optimal, with about a 1 per cent departure from perfect with 10–20 node problems and about 11 per cent error with larger graphs of up to 120 nodes (Dry et al., 2006; MacGregor & Chu, 2011; MacGregor & Ormerod, 1996). Good human performance seems to be based on a few heuristics. One is to imagine that there is an outline around the overall shape of the node pattern (the 'convex hull') and to avoid routes that cross that outline; a second is to avoid crossing already chosen paths; and a third is the Nearest Neighbour rule. MacGregor et al. (2006) found evidence for all three of these heuristics. A modified Nearest Neighbour rule that favoured nodes that were both near neighbours and near the convex hull was identified and found to improve fit to human performance by Kyritsis et al. (2018).

Evaluation

The information processing approach provides a clear account of solving well-defined problems that can be represented as involving searches through problem spaces whether by searching forward through a state-action space or by problem reduction (also known as means–ends analysis or goal-subgoal analysis. The approach has been applied successfully to river-crossing problems, eight- and 15-puzzles, travelling salesperson problems and tower problems (Hanoi and London).

In well-defined tasks, the initial way of representing the problem allows a solution, and search within that representation can be successful. Search is limited by working memory to considering just a few possible moves ahead. Often looking ahead is limited to one step. Choice of moves is guided by evaluations of promise – does a move look to bring the solution closer? Although this is often a useful heuristic, it can lead to difficulties with **detour problems** in which the goal must be moved away from before it can be reached (such as with the Hobbits and Orcs task).

> **Detour problems**
> problems in which the hill-climbing method does not work well, as the solver has to move away from the goal at some stage.

However, not all tasks fall into the pattern of well-defined problems in which the initial formulation is adequate for the solution. How information processing approaches might handle tasks that require a change in representation brings us back to insight tasks, which are the focus of the next section.

Box 12.3 When Things Go Wrong: Right prefrontal cortex damage and real-world planning

Goel et al. (2013) noted that while it was accepted that the left prefrontal cortex plays a critical role in planning tasks the role of the right prefrontal cortex was less clear.

Previous studies had focused on artificial well-defined tasks such as the Tower of London or Tower of Hanoi. Goel et al. (2013) addressed the role of prefrontal structures in a real-world ill-defined task in which an initial stage is seen as seeking to define or constrain the task before examining specific action sequences.

The task was to plan a one-week trip to Italy for a middle-aged American couple, given their interests and a limited budget.

Four groups of participants were formed. One group had focal damage to the right prefrontal cortex (RPFC), one group had focal damage to the left prefrontal cortex (LPFC), one group had posterior lesions and a final group were healthy controls (NC).

Participants were instructed to think aloud while tackling the real-world planning task and all participants were able to comply with the thinking aloud requirement.

Analysis of the verbal records (protocols) indicated that the rated quality of plans was impaired for the RPFC group relative to controls but the other brain-damaged groups were not significantly impaired.

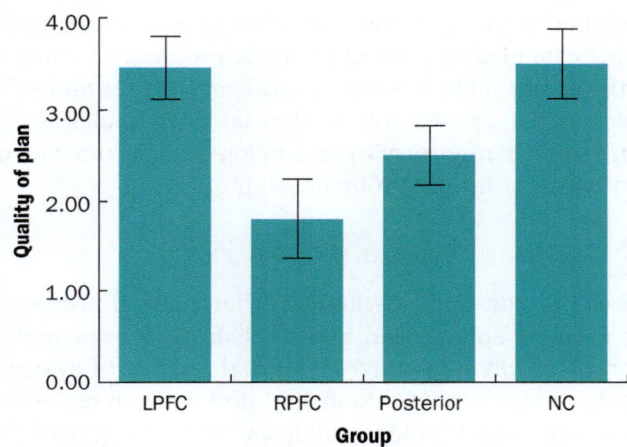

Figure 12.12 Planning scores for left prefrontal cortex, right prefrontal cortex, posterior and normal controls in Goel et al. (2013).
The right prefrontal cortex damage group were significantly impaired in planning in a real-world ill-defined task.

Closer analysis of the reported plans indicated that the RPFC group planned at a more concrete level more quickly than the other groups. For example, the RPFC participants would right away go to concrete details such as 'Start with two days in Pisa then three days in Venice'; the healthy normals would start at the more abstract level, such as 'We'll start with a few days in the north then the Rome region then the south', before specifying the exact order of cities and days per city.

Overall, it was concluded that successful real-world planning needs initial abstract representations, which are then refined into detailed plans, and that this process of initial abstract-level planning is specifically impaired by RPFC damage.

INSIGHT REVISITED

The information processing approach outlined in the previous section provided convincing analyses of processes involved in solving problems that can be tackled by searching within a particular representation, either by using state-action space search methods or goal-subgoal strategies. However, the understanding of how we solve problems that need a change in the way they are represented (i.e., insight problems) has lagged behind. More recently there has been a growing interest in explaining insight problems in information processing terms and we will look now at some of this work.

We previously introduced the X-ray problem and the nine-dot task as insight problems investigated by the Gestalt school; two further examples of insight problems are as follows:

1 The matchstick problem: how would you arrange six matches to form four equilateral triangles?
2 A man married 20 different women in one month. All the women are still alive and not divorced. No anti-polygamy law was broken. How can this be?

In both these examples the initial representation needs to be restructured. In Problem 1, there is a strong tendency to work in two dimensions but the solution requires the use of three dimensions to build a small pyramid so that the base is one triangle and the sides form three more triangles. In Problem 2, the word 'married' is usually interpreted as 'became married to' but needs to be re-interpreted as 'causes to become married', that is, the man is entitled to carry out marriage ceremonies.

'Insight problems' and insight solving processes

Earlier research tended to assume that problems could be cleanly divided into 'insight' problems that required re-structuring and 'non-insight' problems that did not (Gilhooly & Murphy, 2005; Weisberg, 1995). However, it turns out that many problems can be solved either by re-structuring or by search within an initial structuring so that all solutions of such problems should not be assumed to involve insight in the sense of 're-structuring'.

For example, a Remote Associates Test item, say 'What word connects Cottage, Swiss, Cake?' could be tackled by systematically trying out one associate to each word in turn until a solution is found; or it could be tackled by awaiting a sudden solution to come to mind ('It's "cheese"'). In view of the uncertain link between problem features and solution methods, a number of researchers (e.g., Bowden & Grunewald, 2018; Danek, 2018) now stress the value of considering solvers' reports of experiencing an 'Aha' moment of insightful re-structuring as the criterion for insight problem solving.

Comparing Insight and Non-Insight Problem Solving

A major line of research addresses the question of whether differences in processes between insight and non-insight problem solving can be established experimentally. The Gestalt view is that insight problem solving involves a special process of 'restructuring'. Weisberg (2006), on the other hand, argues that insight problem solving arises from normal ordinary processes of search and problem analysis, without any need for special or unusual processes.

One method for tackling the question of whether special processes are involved in insight tasks as against non-insight tasks uses ratings of feelings, specifically on how close the solver is to the solution and on how confident they feel about solving the problem when they first hear it (Metcalfe & Weibe, 1987). Metcalfe and Weibe compared insight versus non-insight tasks and found that 'Feeling of knowing one could solve' taken at the start was a better predictor (correlation with solution = 0.4) for non-insight than for insight tasks (correlation = 0.08). **'Feeling of warmth'** per 15 seconds during solving, shown in Figure 12.8 indicated a steady increase in feeling that one is near solution with non-insight tasks but no increase in warmth with insight tasks until solution was reported. This result supports the idea of sudden restructuring in insight tasks.

> **Feeling of warmth**
> a rating of how close the solver feels to problem solution, taken at intervals during the solving process.

Neuroscience approach to insight versus non-insight problem solving

The first major brain imaging study in this area used functional magnetic resonance imaging (fMRI) and electro-encephalogram (EEG) methods to determine whether the differences in brain activation patterns between insight and non-insight problem solving were measurable (Jung-Beeman et al., 2004). The study used 124 Remote Associate Test (RAT) items. In this task people have to find a word that is an associate of three test words – e.g., What word links 'boot', 'summer' and 'ground'?

To compare insight versus non-insight solving, the researchers had participants give self-reports after each item as to whether the solution arose from insight or not.

A self-reported insight solution was one in which participants reported an 'Aha' feeling coupled with certainty that the solution was correct. Non-insight solutions could arise from a systematic process of trying out one association after another on each item until an association was found that fitted all three items. The results indicated that fMRI showed increased activity in one particular brain area, the right anterior superior temporal gyrus, for insight solutions compared to non-insight solutions. EEG records also showed increases in activity in the same area shortly before solution. These findings suggest differences in neural processes between insight versus non-insight solving. The findings are consistent with a previous study (Bowden & Jung-Beeman, 2003), which found that priming words sent to the right hemisphere produced more insight solutions in RAT tasks than primes sent to the left hemisphere.

Similar results showing correlations between right anterior temporal activation and insight-based solutions have been reported in a number of other studies (Kounios & Beeman, 2014; Sprugnoli et al., 2017).

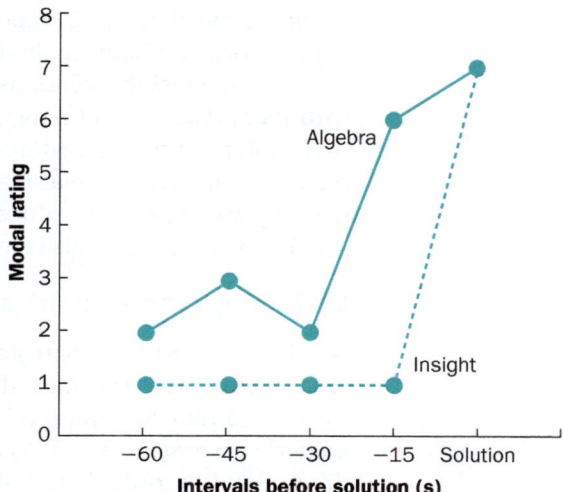

Figure 12.13 Warmth ratings for insight versus non-insight problems.
Indicates steady growth of 'warmth' for algebra but sudden leap in warmth for insight problem just before solution.
Source: Metcalfe & Weibe (1987).

Strong evidence for a causal connection between right temporal lobe activation and insight problem solving comes from a recent study by Salvi et al. (2020). In this study, transcranial direct current stimulation (TDCS) was applied to the right temporal lobe or the left frontopolar region while participants solved Compound Remote Associate (CRAT) items – before, during and after stimulation. It was found that participants solved a higher percentage of items overall and a higher percentage by self-declared insight when they received right anterior temporal lobe stimulation than in any of the other conditions. This result supports a causal role for the right anterior temporal lobe in solving the verbal insight CRAT problems. It is suggested that the right anterior temporal lobe contributes particularly to the recognition of distant (remote) semantic associations, which would benefit CRAT problem solving.

Overall, problem solving with insight shows objectively detectable differences in brain activity compared to solving by incremental step-by-step processes, thus supporting the reality of the insight vs. non-insight distinction.

Working memory in insight versus non-insight problem solving

Insight processes, as envisaged in representational change theory, are assumed to operate at an unconscious level and not to load working memory. Some support for this view derives from studies examining correlations between working memory measures and performance on insight as against non-insight tasks. If insight solving does not load working memory (which non-insight problems generally do load) then we would expect lower correlations between working memory and performance on insight than on non-insight tasks. Gilhooly and Webb (2018) reviewed this literature and on the basis of eight correlational studies with a combined N of 741 found a small average difference in the correlations in the direction predicted by the special process hypothesis. Another approach is to examine the effects of impairing working memory on solving insight as against non-insight problems. If insight does not involve working memory, such manipulations should have little impact on insight tasks. In one such manipulation study (Jarosz et al., 2012) reported that alcohol consumption, presumed to impair working memory, actually facilitated performance in RAT problems and raised the rate of self-reported insight solutions. Similarly, Reverberi et al. (2005) found that 35 patients with focal damage to the lateral frontal cortex (implicated in working memory function) solved difficult matchstick arithmetic problems at a significantly higher rate (82 per cent) than 23 matched controls (43 per cent). Overall, there is evidence that working memory has a reduced role in insight problem solving compared to non-insight problem solving, and this is in line with the special process view of insight solving.

Is the impasse–insight sequence necessary?

Weisberg (2018) has contested some aspects of the Representational Change model, and in particular the idea that there is an inevitable 'impasse–insight' sequencing. He argues that multiple paths to re-structuring are possible, including by conscious analytic processes as well as by automatic routes. Fleck and Weisberg (2004) analysed think aloud records from participants attempting insight tasks. They estimated that relatively few (6 per cent) showed the impasse to insight sequence assumed in the Representational Change approach. Sudden re-structuring sometimes occurred without a preceding impasse; and re-structuring was sometimes arrived at analytically by re-examining the problem statements. Similarly, Cranford and Moss (2012) took think aloud records while participants tackled RAT type problems – which, as noted in Jung-Beeman et al. (2004), can be solved either with sudden insight or through deliberate searching through item associations. They found insight (or 'Aha') solutions often occurred without a preceding impasse.

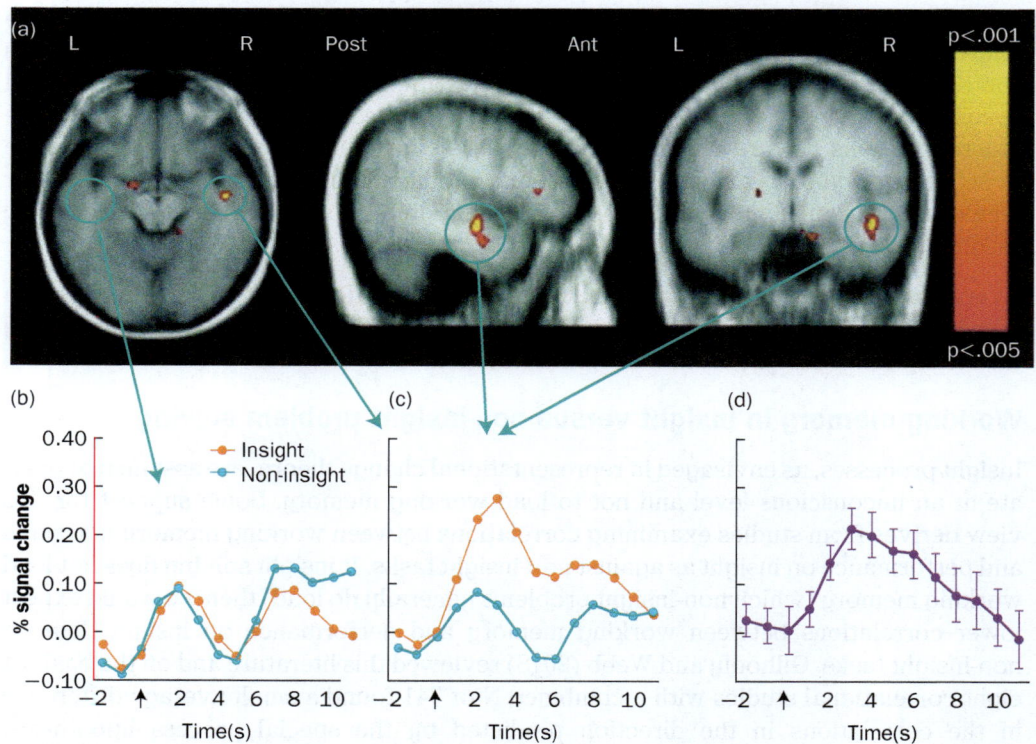

Figure 12.14 fMRI results for insight vs. non-insight problem solving.
Indicates increased activity in right anterior superior temporal gyrus just before solution reports in insight task.

Source: Jung-Beeman et al. (2004).

Information Processing Theories of Insight

From the results reviewed above, the empirical distinction between insight and non-insight problem solving seems to be well established. However, *how* to explain insight solving theoretically is still an active area. Two main approaches have been developed: *representational change* (initially developed by Ohlsson, 1992); and *progress monitoring* (MacGregor et al., 2001) – sometimes labelled 'the criterion for satisfactory progress theory'.

Representational change

As we mentioned earlier, the Gestalt accounts of insight processes such as re-structuring were vague. Ohlsson (2018) has developed a more fully specified, less vague, account of insight in information processing terms in his most recent version of representational change theory.

The main stages and processes in Ohlsson's representational change theory may be described as follows:

- *Problem perception.* Person encodes the problem.
- *Problem solving.* Heuristic search processes based on initial representation. These processes draw on possible actions or operators from long-term memory, which change the current state of the problem into new states.
- *Impasse.* With insight tasks, the initial representation is misleading and does not permit a solution. Hence, impasses arise in which the person experiences a blank mind and can think of no more actions to try.
- *Restructuring.* A new encoding is derived through elaboration, re-encoding, or constraint relaxation. Elaboration involves adding information to the initial representation by noticing previously ignored features. Re-encoding involves completely changing the encoding rather than just adding new features. For example, changing the interpretation of 'married' in the marrying man problem leads to a re-encoding of the problem. Constraint relaxation involves loosening constraints on what is required in the goal or what actions are permitted. Removing the constraint to work within the square shape in the nine-dot problem is an example of this process. Ohlsson proposes that these restructuring processes take place outside consciousness and involve automatic processes such as spreading activation.
- *Partial insight.* Retrieval of possible actions following restructuring breaks the impasse and leads to a sequence of steps that achieve solution.
- *Full insight.* Retrieval of possible actions following restructuring leads immediately to a solution state or to a state close enough to the solution so that the solution can be anticipated within a limited mental look-ahead.

Representational change theory has been investigated using matchstick algebra problems (Knoblich et al., 1999). In these tasks, an incorrect equation involving Roman numerals is presented and the participant's task is to reposition one match to make the equation correct (see Figure 12.15).

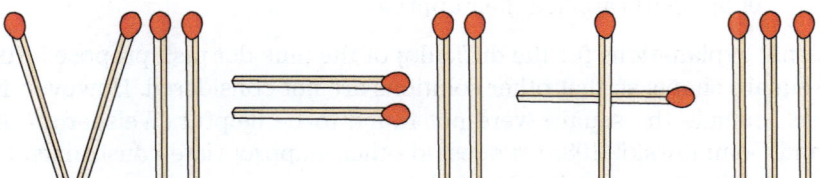

Figure 12.15 Matchstick algebra problem.
Reposition one match to make this equation correct.

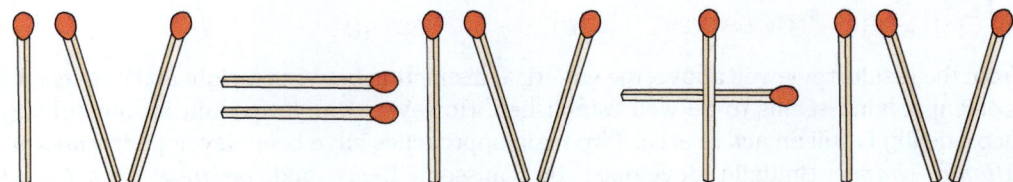

Figure 12.16 Matchstick algebra problem requiring constraint relaxation.
Reposition one match to make this equation correct.

Our usual experience of equations often involves changing numerical values but not changing operators (+, −, =). These problems require re-encoding in which groups of matches forming conceptual units or 'chunks' need to be broken up and reconfigured. More difficult problems also require relaxation of constraints on the form of equations (see Figure 12.16).

Knoblich and colleagues found that re-encoding chunks – e.g., changing VII to VI and II to III by moving one match in the first problem – was easier than relaxing the constraint on the typical form of equations – e.g., from IV = IV + IV to IV = IV = IV, in the second problem.

Overall, the matchstick algebra problem-solving studies lent support to representational change theory, but how well the theory would extend to a wide range of other problem areas remains to be determined by further research. So far, the theory has been extended to apply to magic understanding tasks, discussed in Box 12.4, the eight-coin problem (Figure 12.19) (Ollinger et al., 2013) and the classic nine-dot problem.

Previous studies of the nine-dot problem had found that the hint to take the line outside the box was not very effective. On the basis of representational change theory, Ollinger et al. (2014) suggested that the hint to go outside the box after impasse had been reached was too broad and did not narrow the search space of possible actions enough to facilitate solutions, and that more specific hints after impasse would be more helpful. Three hints were tested. The first suggested a possible route for the solution; the second additionally indicated the dot at which the lines meet on the solution path and the final hint provided non-dot locations along the solution path. All the hints led to more rapid representational change and more solutions than control conditions.

Progress monitoring

> **Progress monitoring theory**
> theory that, during problem solving, people track progress to the goal and switch approach if insufficient progress is detected.

MacGregor et al. (2001) developed an alternative to representational change theory that is known as **progress monitoring theory**. According to this approach, the main source of difficulty in insight tasks is the use of inappropriate heuristics (particularly hill-climbing methods). They propose that, as people search for actions that would help them to reach a solution, they monitor their progress against some criterion. Failure to meet a progress criterion triggers restructuring, rather than impasses. The theory can be explained through the example of the nine-dot problem to which MacGregor et al. (2001) applied their approach.

Traditional explanations for the difficulty of the nine-dot task propose a fixation (set) on the square shape, so that other solutions are not considered. However, instructions to search outside the square were not found to be helpful (Weisberg & Alba, 1981). Lung and Dominowski (1985) suggested other inappropriate constraints, for example assuming all lines begin and end with dots.

Progress monitoring theory proposed an alternative explanation involving two main points. These are (1) use of a *maximization heuristic* in which each move or decision

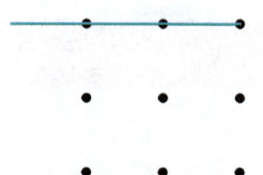

Figure 12.17 Modified nine-dot problem (version A).
A version of the nine-dot problem with a hint to go out of the box.

Source: Adapted from MacGregor et al. (2001).

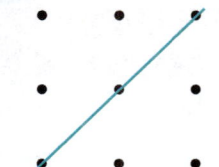

Figure 12.18 Further modified nine-dot problem (version B).
This includes a hint to use the diagonal.

Source: Adapted from MacGregor et al. (2001).

is an attempt to make as much headway as possible towards the goal and (2) use of *progress monitoring* in which the rate of progress is assessed constantly, and if it is deemed to be too slow and inefficient, then *criterion failure* occurs. An alternative strategy may then be sought.

Progress monitoring theory as applied to the nine-dot task suggests (1) the maximization heuristic would be for each move to cover as many new dots as possible and (2) that progress monitoring would involve the rate of progress being assessed against the number of dots required to be covered per line to solve, and if no move meets the criterion, *criterion failure* occurs. An alternative strategy may then be sought (e.g., extending lines).

MacGregor and colleagues explored the progress monitoring theory explanation of the nine-dot task by testing participants with two variants of the problem labelled version A and version B, shown in Figure 12.17.

If 'constraint relaxation' is all that is required to think 'outside the box', then participants should do better on version A than B since A shows a line going out of the box. However, if criterion failure is necessary, then participants will do better on version B, because they can cover fewer dots in the next two moves, and so will realize they are on the wrong path sooner. MacGregor et al. found that only 31 per cent of those given version A were successful but 53 per cent of those given B solved.

Further experiments on progress monitoring theory used coin manipulation problems such as the eight-coin problem shown in Figure 12.19 in which people have to move only two coins so that each coin is left touching exactly three others.

If the strategy employed simply seeks to achieve a short-term goal of bringing *one* particular coin to rest in contact with three others, then there is 'no move available' in the upper version of the problem, but 20 moves are available in the lower version. Thus, criterion failure will be reached much sooner in the upper version and so more solutions should result. In the lower version, a lot of effort would be wasted exploring what look to be promising moves which would not lead to solution. As predicted by the theory, 92 per cent solved the problem in the upper version compared with 67 per cent in the lower version. (The solution is shown in Figure 12.20.)

Figure 12.19 Two versions of the eight-coin problem.
Move only two coins to leave each coin touching three others.

Source: Adapted from Ormerod et al. (2002).

Figure 12.20 Solution to the eight-coin problem.

Source: Adapted from Ormerod et al. (2002).

Box 12.4 Research Close Up: It's magic! Use of magic tricks to generate insight

Source: Danek et al. (2014).

INTRODUCTION

Danek and colleagues have investigated the use of magic tricks as sources of genuine insight (Danek, 2018; Danek et al., 2014).

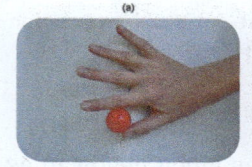
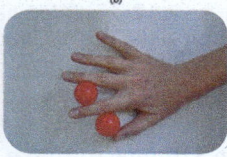

Ekroll, Sayim & Wagemans (2013)

They point out that magic tricks are very well suited to investigate representational changes yielding sudden insights into solution, because to gain insight into the hidden secret of a magic trick, participants must overcome implicit constraints or assumptions and change how they represent the situation.

For example, in the trick known as the 'Chicago multiplying billiard balls', the magician first shows his right hand empty, then takes a ball between his index finger and thumb, flicks his wrist and the ball apparently multiplies into a second ball and then a third. (A video of the trick can be seen at http://www.amorydanek.de/).

The hidden method or secret of the trick is that because the balls are only seen from one side, a false representation is created that the balls are solid; but, one of the balls is a hollow half ball containing another ball. The normal and very strong assumption that the balls are solid make it a hard trick to understand. As soon as that assumption is relaxed solution becomes very likely.

METHODS AND RESULTS

Danek and colleagues report two studies.

In Experiment 1, 50 participants saw 34 different magic tricks and were asked to explain how the tricks were done. After solving each trick, participants indicated whether they had solved with or without a feeling of insight. A feeling of insight was defined as 'a kind of 'Aha!' characterized by suddenness and obviousness, like an enlightenment. You are relatively confident that your solution is correct without having to check it,' In contrast, solving without an insight feeling was defined as occurring 'if the solution occurs to you slowly and stepwise, and if you need to check it by watching the clip once more' (Danek, 2018, p. 71).

Overall, insight was reported in 41 per cent of solutions and, compared to non-insight solutions, insight solutions were more likely to actually be correct, were reached faster and elicited higher confidence ratings.

In Experiment 2, the role of self-imposed constraints or assumptions was examined. A total of 62 participants were shown 12 magic tricks. One group were given verbal hints that were relevant to the solution but did not give the whole answer. The cues or hints related to the assumption or constraint that blocked understanding of how the trick was done. For example, in one trick, a faked throw from one hand to the other is carried out, guiding the participants' attention to the wrong hand and thus allowing a coin to seem to vanish and reappear under a napkin. Here, the main constraint to be relaxed is the fake throw that leads to the false representation that the coin has been moved from one hand to the other. In this case, the hint or cue was 'Transfer to the other hand', which suggested to participants that they should think more about the apparent transfer.

The experimental group, with the representational cues or hints, solved at a significantly higher rate (33 per cent) than the control group (21 per cent), indicating that constraints can be relaxed by cueing.

> **DISCUSSION**
>
> The task area of magic tricks gives clear contrasts between solutions achieved with and without insight, such that insight solutions were more accurate, reached faster and inspired more confidence in the solver. These results further strengthen the view that the insight vs. non-insight distinction is valid and informative. Also, the second study showed that magic tricks work by activating assumptions or constraints, and that these constraints can be overcome by suitable cues or hints about what constraints need to be relaxed. Overall, the results are consistent with representational change theory.

Jones (2003) sought to compare the representational change and progress monitoring theories, and to do so used car parking problems in which toy cars in a parking lot must be moved around to let a toy black taxi out of the parking lot. The problems varied so that some were simple and would not induce impasses, re-structuring or insight, while others were more difficult and did tend to produce impasses and insight. The main difficulty in the insight-inducing problem is to consider moving the taxi before the exit path has been cleared. Example problems are shown in Figures 12.21 and 12.22.

Jones's (2003) experiment involved three conditions: in the normal condition, four progressively harder problems that required ever more moves (but in which the taxi always moved last) were followed by an insight task in which the black taxi had to be moved as an intermediate step as well as at the end to get out. The rotated condition was the same as the normal condition except that, for the insight task, the display was rotated 90 degrees so the exit was to one side rather than at the foot of the picture; and in the easy condition, four easy problems were followed by an insight problem. A number of dependent variables were examined: moves; times per move; eye movement fixations and durations. Representational change theory predicted that impasses would occur before the taxi was moved and that the rotated and easy conditions would lead to better performance on the insight problem than the normal condition. Progressive monitoring theory predicted that there would be no difference between rotated and easy conditions, and that early impasses would be associated with better performance (because

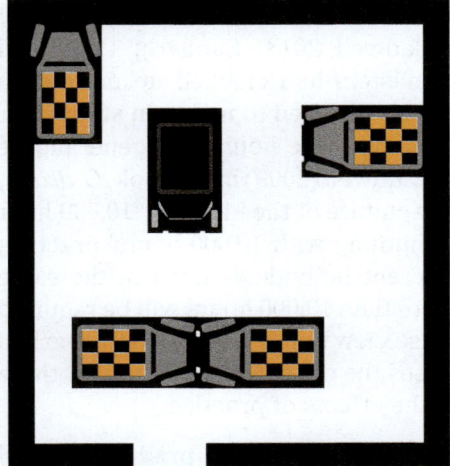

Figure 12.21 Taxi problem.
Move cars to let the black taxi out of the parking area.

Source: Jones, G. (2003).

Figure 12.22 More complex taxi problem.
Move cars to let the black taxi out.

Source: Jones, G. (2003).

looking ahead further would lead to the solver seeing the impasse before actually reaching it). Results indicated that impasses did tend to precede moving the taxi, and that rotated and easy conditions did involve earlier impasses and showed better performance than the normal condition.

It was concluded that both representational change and progress monitoring received some support. The results suggested that progress monitoring applies to the first stage of solving, leading to impasse, and that representational change applies to the breaking of the impasse and subsequent insight. Thus, it seems that both theories have support and we can conclude that the two theories can be seen as dealing with different stages of insight solving and so are complementary rather than contradictory.

Overall, the central claim of progress monitoring theory is that insight is most likely to occur when constraint relaxation follows criterion failure. There is good evidence for this from the above studies. So, the theory deals well with the motivation for changing strategy but is less clear about how new strategies are actually reached.

KNOWLEDGE-RICH (OR EXPERT) PROBLEM SOLVING

> **Expertise**
> the accumulated high-level knowledge that allows outstanding performance in complex problem areas.

So far, we have been considering largely knowledge-lean problems in which no specialized knowledge is required. Recent years have seen a growth of interest in the study of knowledge-rich problems in which domain **expertise** is required. We will now look at how expertise is acquired, what expert knowledge involves and how it affects problem solving.

Expertise Acquisition

Acquisition of domain expertise in many areas seems to require approximately 10 years of intensive study. Chess is a clear case in which we have objective performance ratings and good records of starting ages and lengths of time playing. From these data 10 years is the typical time of intensive study before reaching grandmaster level (the highest level) (Holding, 1985). Simon and Chase (1973) made a rough estimate of 10,000 to 50,000 hours of study being needed to reach grandmaster level in chess and other complex areas. Howard (2012) found a figure of 14,000 hours for a sample of chess grandmasters to reach that level and it may be noted that the Polgar sisters took more than 50,000 hours to reach grandmaster status (Gladwell, 2013). Similarly, Campitelli and Gobet (2011) found that international-level masters had clocked up more than 25,000 hours on average. Clearly, strong motivation is required to maintain study over many years even to achieve 10,000 hours – and many more hours will generally be needed. Although popular writers such as Malcolm Gladwell (2009) in his book, *Outliers*, have contributed to a widespread acceptance in the culture of the idea of a '10,000-hour rule' by which anyone can become an expert at anything with 10,000 hours' practice, there is a wide spread of hours required by different individuals even in the same domain (e.g., chess) and normally considerably more than 10,000 hours will be required for expertise in complex domains. The common-sense view that there are surely marked individual differences in the effects of practice raises the distinct possibility that there are individual differences in talent that will affect the effects of practice.

> **Deliberate practice**
> practice activity specifically designed to improve aspects of performance.

Ericsson (1999) has highlighted the view that **deliberate practice** of skill components, guided by a training schedule and by coaching, is needed to achieve expertise – not sheer unguided practice or experience with the activity. Consistent with this idea, Ericsson et al. (1993) found large differences in total hours of deliberate practice between professional and amateur musicians accumulated over many years, and found that these differences began to show from early ages. In this very influential paper, two studies are reported. In Study 1, four groups of violinists were recruited. One group comprised the 10 'best' students at the Music Academy of West Berlin, a second group were 10 'good' students at the same institution, while the third group was composed of 10 violin students at a teacher training college. The three groups were formed to differ in their level of violin-playing expertise. A fourth group of 10 middle-aged violinists from West Berlin symphony orchestras also took part to provide additional developmental data. Study 2 involved a group of 12 expert pianists who were advanced students in the West Berlin Music Academy and a group of 12 amateur pianists of similar ages (around 24 years) to the experts but not studying music. In Study 1 it was found that, by age 18 years, the best and the professional violinists had accumulated around 7,400 hours of practice but the good players had significantly fewer hours (*c.* 5,300) by age 18 years and the lowest-skill 'teacher' group had only 3,400 hours by age 18. There was a complete correspondence between the skill levels of the groups and their accumulated hours of practice. Very similar findings emerged from Study 2, with the expert pianists showing 7,600 hours and the amateurs 1,600 hours' practice by age 18 years.

Similar findings relating expertise level closely to total deliberate practice were reported by Campitelli and Gobet (2011), who found a correlation of more than .5 between total practice hours and chess skill rating; by Tuffiash et al. (2007), who found that, among tournament-level Scrabble players, the top players practised much more than average players and that total accumulated time in Scrabble practice was a good predictor of Scrabble skill level; and by Hambrick et al. (2014), who found correlations of .58 and .55 between amount of deliberate practice and skill levels in chess and musical performance, respectively.

Although there would be broad agreement that groups differing widely in expertise will differ in accumulated practice and that within individuals those who practice more will improve, there is less agreement that differences among elite experts can be explained simply by levels of deliberate practice. Gobet and Ereku (2014), in a paper provocatively titled 'Checkmate to deliberate practice', cite the case of the young Norwegian Magnus Carlsen who became World Chess Champion at age 22 in 2013. Using the 2014 chess rankings, Gobet and Ereku estimate that Carlsen had around 18 years' deliberate practice at chess, but the average of the next 10 players below Carlsen had around 24.6 years of practice – this result is of course the opposite of what would be expected on the assumption that skill depends purely on amount of deliberate practice. The most obvious explanation is to assume that some **talent** is present that enables some players to improve faster than others with similar degrees of training.

> **Talent**
> having a talent for a particular activity means having pre-existing capacities and abilities relevant to acquiring skill in that activity – often assumed to be innate.

Macnamara and Maitra (2019) sought to replicate Ericsson et al.'s (1993) seminal study of violin students. They drew very similar samples of students in the 'best', 'good' and 'less accomplished' categories from similar-level music academies to those used in the original study. As far as possible the same procedures

Figure 12.23 Magnus Carlsen, World Chess Champion at the age of 22.
Carlsen's early success supports a role for talent as well as deliberate practice.

© Carl Court/Getty

and measurements were followed, but the method was improved by following a double-blind procedure. Statistical analysis was also tightened up to avoid capitalizing on chance effects due to multiple comparisons. The main result was that Macnamara and Maitra did not find differences between the 'best' and the 'good' students in levels of accumulated practice by age 18, as had been found by Ericsson and colleagues. In fact the 'good' students had if anything more practice hours (average 9,844 hours) than the 'best' students (average 8,224 hours). However, both the more expert groups were significantly ahead of the less accomplished group (4,558 hours) in practice hours by age 18, as had been found in the original study.

Overall, deliberate practice is undoubtedly an important and necessary factor in determining expertise in a wide range of domains and although it seems to explain around 20–30 per cent of variance in performance, it leaves around 70–80 per cent to be explained by other factors. Other factors include 'talent', which for complex symbolic skills can probably be summed up as general intelligence which, as measured by standardized tests, correlates about .60 with complex job performance (Gottfredson, 1997). Intelligence tests scores were found to correlate .35 with chess skill ratings in a sample of 90 adult tournament chess players (Grabner et al., 2007) and the chess player group had a mean IQ score of 113 – i.e., just under one standard deviation above the population average of 100. Further support for the role of general intelligence emerged from a meta-analysis carried out by Burgoyne et al. (2016). This study merged the findings from 19 separate published reports involving a total of 1,779 participants. It was found that general fluid intelligence scores correlated on average .24 with chess skill ratings and the link was markedly stronger for younger players (.32) than for older players (.11). There is a hint here that extended practice may reduce initial benefits conveyed by higher general intelligence in developing chess skill.

In addition to talent and deliberate practice, motivation, family influences, and support from the social and community environment must also be important factors that can be expected to interact in complex ways with one another in determining expertise. As Gobet (2019) puts it, a 'spaghetti model' probably applies in which the environment affects practice, intelligence and performance, intelligence affects practice and performance, and practice and performance mutually affect each other, with better performance boosting motivation and increasing performance still further in a beneficial cycle.

Nature of Expertise

Expertise typically seems to involve extensive memory for familiar patterns that cue appropriate actions. This was shown initially in chess via the chess recall memory task. In this task participants are shown a chess board containing around 20 pieces for a short period (typically five seconds) and then attempt to reconstruct the seen position on a fresh board. Early studies found repeatedly that experts remembered realistic board patterns well after brief exposure but not random patterns, while novices were equally poor on both (Chase & Simon, 1973; De Groot, 1965). Further, this advantage is domain specific in that chess experts are no better than novices in non-chess memory tasks. The explanation for this domain-specific memory advantage was that experts have built up extensive long-term memory of familiar patterns, which helps them encode or chunk new (realistic) positions into familiar sub-patterns. Similar findings have been reported in numerous other domains, such as the Japanese game of Gomoku (Reitman, 1976), bridge (Charness, 1989) and programming (Adelson, 1981).

This neat picture of expert memory superiority for realistic material in the domain of expertise, but not for random material, had to be adjusted in the light of later research.

Fernand Gobet ran computer simulations of the chunking model of memory in chess and found that the model persistently predicted a small but real expert advantage even for random stimuli. Gobet and Simon (1996) examined previous findings more closely in a meta-analysis of 13 published studies involving 171 participants, and although no single study found a significant expert superiority with random chess positions, 12 out of the 13 studies did find results favouring the more expert groups. Overall, when the results were combined there was a significant advantage for the expert groups, who recalled correctly on average about 5 pieces out of 20, whereas the less expert groups correctly recalled 2.5 pieces on average. The explanation is that the experts are more likely to see randomly arising patterns than the less expert groups. Gobet and Waters (2003) replicated this finding of expert superiority in a study involving a greater degree of randomization. Previous studies had taken real positions from published games and randomized the position of the pieces. Truly randomized boards involved allowing each square to have a random piece or be empty. In such boards there could, for example, be three or more kings or no kings at all, which can never arise in a real game. Even with such highly randomized positions there was a small but significant correlation between skill level and recall score ($r = .34$), with the most expert players scoring 15 per cent correct and the weakest 12 per cent correct.

Sala and Gobet (2017) further extended the finding of expert superiority in memory even for randomized material to domains other than chess in a meta-analysis of 28 studies involving 903 participants. The domains included programming, music, sport, chemistry, card games, and board games other than chess. All studies but one were in the expected direction of an expert superiority effect even with randomized stimuli, but with only 15 results being individually significant. When the results were combined over the 28 studies, a significant correlation of .41 was found between expert skill level and recall of randomized material. So, as in chess, experts can detect patterns that occur by chance in randomized materials.

Experts represent or 'see' problem situations differently from novices as they draw on a more elaborate set of schemata. For example, in physics, Chi et al. (1982) used sorting tasks in which participants grouped problems into categories and the groupings indicated that experts would put together problems that required similar physical laws, while novices tended to group together problems that involved similar concrete objects. Thus, the experts 'saw' the problems in terms of underlying principles (e.g., laws of motion) while the novices 'saw' the problems in terms of more superficial characteristics such as the objects involved (e.g., slopes, pulleys, weights).

In terms of problem solving, Larkin (1978) found that experts in physics problem solving tend to spend more time analysing problems to fit them into familiar schemas before trying actions than do novices who lack ready-made schemas. Experts then tend to work forwards from the starting state to the goal using approaches they recognize as promising, while novices tend to work backwards in a more effortful search as they lack pre-existing schemas that can be readily applied. This pattern probably arises because experts have a large repertoire of familiar types of problem with which they can classify new problems and reapply old solutions, whereas novices have to work out problems from basic principles.

Although De Groot (1965) found few differences between more and less expert chess players in depth or breadth of search in deciding moves in chess, his study was small scale, with only five experts and five novices. Later studies using larger groups of participants and wider ranges of skill did find steady increases in depth, breadth and speed of search as skill level increased (Charness, 1989; Holding & Reynolds, 1982). So, it seems that experts can carry out wider, deeper and faster searches through possible sequences of chess moves than can novices. Campitelli and Gobet (2004) found much more extensive mental search through possible sequences of moves and counter-moves when the positions were unusually difficult. In such positions the grandmasters considered 13.8 possible moves and looked ahead up to 25 moves deep; in contrast, weaker players considered only 2.8 moves and looked ahead no more than 10 moves deep. Gobet (2019, p. 35) found expertise differences in use of progressive deepening when searching the space of possible actions. Experts tend to investigate to a certain depth and then immediately reinvestigate deeper, whereas novices tend to examine a number of options before reinvestigating the most promising avenue. Experts tend to continue to investigate lines that look positive and immediately abandon lines that look negative. This strategy is aided by more accurate evaluations of intermediate positions. Holding (1979) also found that experts were better able to evaluate possible moves in terms of how likely they were to lead to a winning position. Thus, experts in chess have developed more appropriate search processes as well as more useful representations of the tasks.

Evaluation

Overall, expertise research has extended the information processing approach to problems that require extensive background knowledge to tackle. In the case of expert problem solving, the emphasis is mainly on recognition of familiar problem patterns and application of previously acquired solutions as against extensive searching through possible action sequences. Thus, chess masters and expert diagnosticians in medicine can recognize many thousands of patterns (of board positions or of symptoms) and apply previously learned solutions or diagnoses. If need be, however, experts can engage in more extensive search. Acquisition of expertise requires extensive practice over roughly 10 years, a time that has been found to apply in many different areas. In addition to deliberate practice, which is necessary for expertise, talent, in the form of relevant abilities and capacities, plays a role in determining the benefits of practice.

CREATIVE PROBLEM SOLVING

So far, we have been looking at problems, whether insight or non-insight, knowledge-rich or knowledge-lean, that have one correct answer; these are often labelled 'convergent' problems. Problems that have many possible answers are labelled 'divergent' and it is often said that these require creative thinking because of the variety of solutions that could be considered. We will now review research on creative thinking, from early studies to more recent work on unconscious processes in creativity.

Creative
in the 'standard definition', this denotes a product novel to the producer of the product and valuable in some way; an alternative definition is that the product is novel and is intended to meet a goal (without necessarily succeeding in meeting a goal).

First, some definitional points should be addressed. What do we mean by '**creative**'? When is a solution creative? A definition commonly given as to what makes a solution creative, sometimes known as 'the standard definition', is 'Creativity requires both originality and effectiveness' (Runco & Jaeger, 2012, p. 92).

Regarding originality or novelty, Boden (2004) distinguishes the personally creative (novel for the individual) versus the historically creative (i.e., novel in the history of world). From the point of view of psychology, personal creativity is critical. Even if a particular solution has been found before, if it is new to the solver, it may be creative.

Weisberg (2006, 2018) disagrees with the inclusion of 'value' or 'effectiveness' in the usual definition, and suggests instead that a creative product is *novel*, and is also *intentional* – that is, designed to meet a goal. This is a useful proposal since it removes possible changes in the 'creative' status of a product whenever value judgements shift, as can happen, particularly in the arts. For example, Van Gogh's paintings were little valued in his lifetime but are now very highly regarded.

In discussing creativity it is also useful to distinguish between small 'c' creativity and big 'C' Creativity (Simonton, 2013). Small 'c' creativity is what we find in the everyday production of novel and useful solutions to minor problems. We are all creative in this small-c sense every time we speak a novel and useful sentence. Other everyday examples would be combining ingredients from the fridge that we have not previously put together to make a quick stir-fry meal; using chewing gum to secure a loose key on a laptop keyboard; or using a hand-held vacuum cleaner to remove a cloud of small flies that have settled on a ceiling. Small 'c' creativity is the subject of typical laboratory studies and psychometric tests in which, for example, participants generate novel uses for familiar objects or seek to combine familiar shapes into interesting new structures. Big 'C' Creativity refers to major productions of scientific, technological, social or artistic importance. Examples of big 'C' Creativity would include Darwin's theory of evolution; the invention of the printing press; Picasso's *Guernica* painting. Big C creativity is much harder to investigate than small 'c' creativity, and relevant research tends to look at personal accounts, historical and productivity data. However, it is assumed that there is some process overlap between big 'C' and small 'c' creativity.

The main approaches that have been followed in the study of the processes of creative thinking draw on personal accounts, and on theories and laboratory studies. We will now review these approaches.

Personal Accounts

Many famous scientists and artists have given personal accounts of their experiences of creative problem solving – often long after the events described – which leads to concerns about the accuracy of such long-delayed accounts. However, such accounts have been used as the bases of some models of creative problem solving, so two accounts will be given here.

Henri Poincaré

Poincaré (1908) was an important French mathematician in the nineteenth century and took a strong interest in the psychology of creative thinking. He provided the following report of his own experience in solving some difficult problems in mathematics:

> *For 15 days I strove to prove that there could not be any functions like those I have since called the Fuchsian Functions. Every day I seated myself at my work table – stayed an hour or two, tried a great number of combinations and reached no results.*
>
> *One evening, contrary to my custom, I drank black coffee and could not sleep.*
>
> *Ideas rose in crowds; I felt them collide until pairs interlocked, so to speak, making stable combination. By the next morning I had established the existence of a class of Fuchsian Functions; I had only to write out the results, which took but a few hours.*

Herman Helmholtz

Helmholtz (1898) was a major figure in nineteenth-century physiology and made important contributions to the study of colour vision, among other topics. At a dinner in his honour he made the following remarks about his views on creative work:

> *So far as my experience goes, happy thoughts never came to a fatigued brain and never at the writing desk. It was always necessary, first of all, that I should have*

turned my problem over on all sides to such an extent that I had all its angles and complexities in my head and could run through them freely without writing.

To bring the matter to that point is usually impossible without long preliminary labour.

Then after the fatigue resulting from that labour has passed away, there must come an hour of complete physical freshness and quiet well being, before the good ideas arrived. Often they would come in the morning as I awoke, but they especially liked to make their appearance while I was taking an easy walk over wooded hills in sunny weather.

Wallas's Stage Analysis

On the basis of reports such as those by Poincaré, Helmholtz and many others, Wallas (1926) proposed an influential analysis of creative problem solving into stages. There are four main stages – Preparation, Incubation, Illumination and Verification – and so the model is often referred to as the four-stage model. However, as Sadler-Smith (2015) pointed out, there is also a brief Intimation stage between Incubation and Illumination, and so it may more accurately be called the five-stage model. In more detail, the five stages proposed were:

1 Preparation
   - Person familiarizes themselves with problem
   - Involves conscious work
   - Rarely leads to solution
   - However – this stage is essential – without initial work no further progress would come about

2 Incubation
   - Problem 'set aside'
   - No conscious work – *relaxation*
   - Conscious work on another task – *distraction*

3 Intimation – a fleeting feeling that Illumination is about to occur

4 Illumination (or inspiration or insight)
   - Doesn't always lead to solution of problem
   - 'Great idea' might come to mind, but must be developed and verified

5 Verification
   - Conscious work must be done on ideas generated through illumination
   - Solutions can be tested and developed

Although the above order was intended to be typical, Wallas also suggested that not every problem goes through the stages from 1 to 5 in strict order, stating that: 'The stages constantly overlap each other as we explore different problems' and 'Even when exploring the same problem the mind may be unconsciously incubating on one aspect of it, while it is consciously employed in preparing for or verifying another aspect' (1926).

> **Incubation**
> a period in which a problem is set aside; it may be 'immediate', directly after presentation, or 'delayed', after a period of conscious work.

Incubation Research

As indicated in the previous section, Wallas (1926) proposed as beneficial an **'incubation'** stage in problem solving, during which the problem is set aside and not consciously addressed. In an extensive review, Dodds et al. (2012)

identified 39 relevant experiments since the 1930s of which 29 (i.e., 75 per cent) reported significant beneficial effects of incubation. Such studies have generally used a method in which participants in the incubation condition work for a pre-set time followed by a different (interpolated) activity for a fixed time (incubation period) and finally return to the target problem for a post-incubation period. A variation involves having participants work until an impasse is experienced (Ohlsson, 1992), following which an incubation period is provided. Performance of the incubation groups is contrasted with control data from groups working continuously.

Further support for the reality of incubation effects came from a quantitative meta-analysis of 117 experiments from 37 publications, carried out by Sio and Ormerod (2009). Around 73 per cent of experiments included in the analysis showed incubation effects, and the average effect size ($d = .29$) was significant and of medium magnitude, at around one-third of a standard deviation.

How might incubation work?

The three main hypotheses regarding incubation effects can be summarized as follows.

Intermittent conscious work: This suggests that although incubation is intended to be a period without conscious work on the target task, participants may nevertheless carry out intermittent conscious work (Seifert et al., 1995, p. 82). Any conscious work during the supposed incubation period would reduce the time required when the target problem was re-addressed – but would impair performance on the interpolated task. As a check against this possibility, performance on the interpolated task during the incubation period should be compared with performance of a control group working on the same interpolated task without being in an incubation condition. A deficit in the interpolated task on the part of the incubation group would be consistent with the hypothesis of some conscious work on the target task during incubation. Although this seems a rather basic methodological check, surprisingly it had not been routinely carried out in previous research (Dodds et al., 2003) until Gilhooly et al.'s (2012) study, which found no evidence of intermittent conscious work during incubation on a divergent task. See also Gilhooly et al. (2015).

Unconscious work: This approach argues that incubation effects occur through active but unconscious processing of the problem materials. Poincaré (1929) suggested that the 'subliminal self' unconsciously combined and recombined ideas until an interesting relevant combination was formed whereupon the valuable idea would become conscious (i.e., Wallas's inspiration stage). More recently, Dijksterhuis and Meurs (2006) have applied a theory of unconscious thought to incubation. On this view, unconscious thought, compared to conscious thought, has a large capacity, proceeds relatively slowly, tends to be bottom up, is good at integrating many sources of information, is relatively poor at following rules and tends to divergent rather than convergent thinking. Dijksterhuis and Nordgren (2006) report a number of studies in which better decisions were made and better creative thinking found when the tasks were not worked on consciously. However, their studies did not follow the classical method of incubation research in which the problem is set aside after an extended period of conscious work. Rather, Dijksterhuis and Meurs had the participants *immediately* put aside the problem for a period after the task was presented, and before any conscious work could be carried out. This manipulation made explanations of incubation in terms of reductions in set less likely as participants had not had time to develop misleading sets. They interpreted their results as favouring an explanation in terms of unconscious work. The results in favour of the immediate incubation group are striking in that the time available for conscious work is much less (one minute – i.e., the response generation period) in the incubation condition than in the conscious work condition (four minutes total – i.e., three minutes' conscious work without writing down responses plus one minute written response generation). This contrasts with standard incubation studies in which the amount of conscious work time is equal for incubation and continuous work conditions. Dijksterhuis and Meurs' basic result appears to be robust and we have replicated the main findings of a benefit from an incubation period immediately after the task instructions for divergent thinking in studies in our laboratory (Gilhooly et al., 2012). The notion of unconscious work seems to be supported for divergent tasks such as the brick uses problem.

Fresh look: This view proposes an important role for automatic reduction in idea strength or activation. The proposal is that misleading strategies, mistaken assumptions and related 'mental sets' weaken through forgetting, and thus a fresh start or 'set shifting' is facilitated when the problem is resumed. Simon (1966) specified this hypothesis further in terms of decay of irrelevant or misleading material in working memory (see Chapter 6 for more on working memory) when attention was shifted away from the problem while useful information accumulated in long-term memory over repeated attempts.

Information Processing Theory of Creative Processes

We have previously seen that information processing ideas of search through spaces of possible actions and working with goals and subgoals can explain much routine problem solving. Can such concepts be usefully applied to creative problem solving? Three example attempts addressing creative problem solving in information processing terms are those of Herbert Simon (1966), the blind-variation and selective-retention approach, and the Geneplore model (Finke et al., 1992).

Simon model

Simon (1966) applied standard information processing approaches to creative problem solving. He pointed out that, 'Creative advances are rare events' and any theory should be consistent with this rarity of occurrence. The information processing approach to problem solving proposes considerable search through vast numbers of alternative hypotheses. In this model, search is slowed by the limited capacity of working memory (see Chapter 6) and by the slow rate of transfer of information into long-term memory. On the other hand, search is aided by improved representation methods and by good heuristics; consistent with this view are the many scientific advances Simon noted that followed improvements in instruments that give better representations of very small objects (microscopes) or of very distant objects (telescopes). In this approach, incubation is analysed as familiarization with repeated attempts and selective forgetting in between attempts, allowing fresh approaches to be taken.

Blind Variation and Selective Retention model

Poincaré (1910) was convinced that unconscious processes of some sort have a role in problem solving. Thus, he proposed that the unconscious combines and recombines ideas in a quasi-random manner until an *interesting* combination is formed, which *then* becomes conscious. How might this happen? Poincaré imagined ideas to be like hooked atoms that hang on a wall until preparation work on a task sets the atoms loose and in motion. Moving atoms collide, and sometimes the hooks snag together and a new combination or compound is formed. If the atoms represent ideas then a new combination would be an original idea, which will sometimes be useful.

Ideas derived from Poincaré's notion of the quasi-random combination of ideas have been put forward by a number of other theorists regarding creative thinking, such as Donald T. Campbell. In an influential paper, Campbell (1960) developed his *Blind Variation and Selective Retention* model. Campbell argued that creative problem solving involves a quasi-random generation of associations between mental elements ('Blind Variation') to produce novel combinations of ideas, some of which may be useful and so be subject to Selective Retention. This approach draws an analogy with biological evolution in which random changes in genetic material lead to changes in organisms, some of which are useful and hence retained by natural selection. Similarly, it is argued that ideas are modified in creative problem solving in ways that are blind to the final solution and only by chance lead ultimately to modifications that solve the problem and are retained for future use. Campbell (1960) quoted extensively from Poincaré's (1910) account of creative thinking in mathematics, as involving extensive quasi-random search, although Campbell did not stress any special role for unconscious processing. His concern was very much with the role of blind trial-and-error, whether carried out at a conscious or an unconscious level.

Simonton (1995, 2003, 2018) developed Campbell's ideas further and used the notion of 'mental elements', which are similar to Poincaré's (1910) 'hooked atoms'. However, unlike Campbell, Simonton *did* stress the role of unconscious processes, which lead to new combinations, some of which are retained and selected to enter consciousness on the basis of their 'stability'; that is, some combinations fit together and are retained, whereas others do not and are not stored in long-term memory.

Geneplore model

Finke et al. (1992) developed the **Geneplore** model, whose name is derived from 'generate' and 'explore'. The proposal is that creative work involves an initial stage in which 'pre-inventive structures' are generated and are then interpreted during an exploratory phase.

The Geneplore model has been investigated using the **creative synthesis task** in which participants were given three shapes to combine to make 'interesting objects'. See Figure 12.24 for sample constructions in the creative synthesis task.

Finke and colleagues examined the effects of (a) giving broad target categories first (e.g., make a mode of transport or a piece of furniture) or (b) giving target categories *after* the object produced, and found that more highly rated 'creative' responses (33 per cent vs. 22 per cent) were produced when the category was given second. This result is thought to arise because the initial pre-inventive forms would be less constrained by preconceptions if no goal were given in advance and hence more unusual solutions would be forthcoming.

Increasing Idea Production

Setting a problem aside, or incubation, as discussed earlier, is a possible way of boosting creativity, but can we take deliberate steps to increase the flow of creative ideas? A large number of suggestions have been made over the years. One of these that you are very likely to hear about is *brainstorming*. We will now outline this method and the main research findings about it.

Geneplore
a model for creative thinking that stresses the role of a generative and exploratory phase.

Creative synthesis task
a task in which participants have to combine presented shapes to make novel interesting combinations.

Presented symbols

"Rectangle, triangle, rectangle, letter V, number 8"

Examples of legitimate patterns

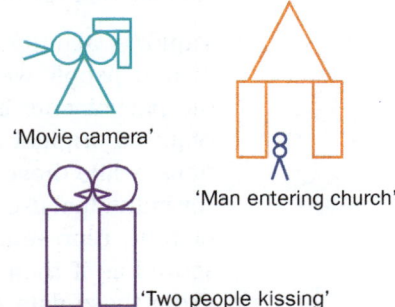

Figure 12.24 Example creative synthesis responses.
The task is to make interesting combinations of presented shapes.

Source: Finke et al. (1992). Examples of presented symbols and legitimate patterns. © 1992 Massachusetts Institute of Technology, by permission of the MIT Press.

Brainstorming

A practical businessman who worked in the advertising industry, Alex Osborn, became dissatisfied with conventional means of developing new ideas – which were constantly needed in advertising. In response to this need, Osborn (1958) developed the **brainstorming** method described in his book *Applied Imagination*. The method has subsequently been taken up very widely by a broad range of organizations. It was originally proposed as a method for problem-solving groups but can be readily adapted for individual use.

> **Brainstorming**
> a method that stimulates the production of unusual ideas, by stressing quantity as against quality, and deferring the evaluation of ideas.

Brainstorming aims to assist in the idea-generating stage of problem solving. It involves two main principles:

1. Deferment of judgement
2. Quantity breeds quality

and four rules:

1. Criticism is ruled out
2. Free-wheeling is welcomed
3. Quantity is wanted
4. Combination and improvement are sought.

The deferment of judgement principle means that the evaluation of ideas is postponed until after a fixed period of idea production. This counters the normal tendency to evaluate ideas as they are produced, which could inhibit developments from earlier ideas that could lead to later useful ideas. The quantity breeds quality principle stresses that the more ideas produced, the more likely at least one good idea will be produced. The rules suggest ways of generating ideas without evaluation and by freely associating with and modifying previously generated ideas.

Early studies indicated that brainstorming did result in more ideas and more high-quality ideas than were obtained with conventional methods for tasks that required novel ideas (Meadow et al., 1959; Parnes & Meadow, 1963; see also Goldenberg et al., 2013; Kerr & Murphy, 2004).

A practical issue that arises, however, is when we have a number of people, say 12, who could work on a brainstorming problem. Is it better to have one large group or three or four smaller groups, or even have people work individually?

Taylor et al. (1958) examined this issue in a study in which the results from 12 groups of four people were compared with the pooled results from 48 individuals, where all the participants had followed brainstorming instructions on suitable problems that required original thinking. The real groups followed standard brainstorming instructions, while those working individually followed brainstorming instructions modified for individual use. After idea production, the 48 individuals' ideas were put into 12 sets of four, representing nominal groups of four, and these nominal groups were then scored as if they were real groups – i.e., duplicated ideas were counted only once. From these data emerged what is known as the 'nominal group superiority effect'. In other words, the nominal groups outperformed the real groups. This effect has been found over a range of tasks and indeed has been shown to increase with group size (Bouchard & Hare, 1970; Dillon et al., 1972; Dunnette et al., 1963) so that the bigger the groups, the bigger the nominal groups' advantage. In practical terms, it seems, then, that use of nominal groups can be a good way of using a number of people to generate many possible solutions.

Why were nominal groups better for brainstorming than real groups? One suggestion was that being in a real group inhibited the free flow of ideas. Perhaps people feared implicit evaluation by other group members even if overt evaluation was allowed by the rules of brainstorming?

Another type of explanation of the nominal group superiority effect stresses the notion of 'production blocking' resulting from people in the group having to wait their turn to contribute an idea. This may result in people forgetting ideas and being distracted by others' suggestions (DeRosa et al., 2007; Nijstad et al., 2003). Interestingly, better performance has been found with electronic real groups as against electronic nominal groups, as with electronic groups there is no need to wait for a turn and so there is no response blocking (Kerr & Murthy, 2004; Vallacich et al., 1994). Moreover, even large electronic groups ($N > 9$) outperform nominal groups – in contrast to the general finding that greater group size leads to greater nominal group superiority in face-to-face groups (Vallacich et al., 1994). Overall, it does seem that brainstorming with real groups can be useful if production blocking can be overcome with the use of electronic groups. Specific training in face-to-face groups, to pay attention to all group members and encourage the reticent members to contribute and combine their ideas with those of others, has been found to help overcome response blocking (Harvey, 2014).

Brainstorming does not give specific guidance on how to go about generating new ideas. A number of detailed suggestions have been made over the years, including **Synectics** (Gordon, 1961, 1981) and **lateral thinking** (de Bono, 1967, 2015).

The word *synectics* is derived from the Greek word *synecticos* and means the joining together of previously unrelated elements. On the basis of his experience in business consulting, Gordon proposed that the use of four types of analogy could be helpful in making novel connections. The four types of analogy are personal, direct, symbolic and fantasy. In personal analogy, the solver is asked to consider what it would feel like to be a part of the problem. So if the problem was to deal with pollution of a river, how would you feel if you were the polluted river? In direct analogy one seeks some similar problem for which perhaps nature has a solution. If the problem was one of tunnelling, you could look at natural tunnelling by animals and insects. Symbolic analogies are sometimes called 'book titles' and try to summarize a problem in two or three words. If a problem involved a risky journey it might be described as 'On Thin Ice'. Fantasy analogies involve suspending the normal laws of nature or society. For example, to get water to the top of a hill, imagine if there were no gravity. Would that help?

> **Synectics**
> a set of methods developed by G. M. Prince and W. J. J.Gordon in the 1950s for combining different apparently irrelevant concepts to produce creative solutions.
>
> **Lateral thinking**
> a set of techniques developed by E. de Bono for solving problems creatively by using indirect approaches to find novel solutions.

Although Synectics has been and continues to be widely used in the business world (Nolan, 2003) there has been little academic evaluation of its utility, although some positive results have been reported in educational settings (Wilson et al., 1973; de Villiers Scheepers & Maree, 2015).

Lateral thinking was initially proposed by Edward de Bono in 1967 and has been widely used in education and a range of business settings. The basic idea is to change how the task is represented in order to find a better way of seeing the problem. Instead of digging a hole ever deeper (vertical thinking) it may well be better to start a new hole (lateral thinking).

An example lateral thinking tool is Random Input, where a word is picked at random from a dictionary and connections are sought between that word and the problem being dealt with. Another tool is Provocation, in which one thinks of a false, impossible or absurd statement about the problem and sees if that cues useful ideas.

Despite the popularity of de Bono's books there has been no real evaluation of the lateral thinking approach. Dingli (2008) found that reports in the literature were all case studies, anecdotes and personal experiences from practitioners, and there was a clear lack of any rigorous evaluation.

> **Generic Parts Technique**
> a method of overcoming functional fixity by analysing objects into parts and sub-parts.

One of the more recent suggestions for a specific method to increase creative problem solving is the **Generic Parts Technique** devised by McCaffrey (2012) and discussed in Box 12.5.

Box 12.5 Practical Application: The Generic Parts Technique

McCaffrey (2012) has proposed as an effective means of generating novel solution ideas and overcoming functional fixity his Generic Parts Technique (GPT).

The GPT instructs participants to explicitly list features of the problem materials, and this leads to noticing obscure features. Using obscure features is a common aspect of innovative solving. For example, consider the two rings problem in which the goal is to fasten two heavy steel rings using only a long candle, a match and a 2-inch cube of steel.

A control group tackled the problem in the normal way. A GPT group were instructed to describe the objects in the problem in terms of parts and parts of parts, and to form a generic-parts diagram that makes explicit the properties of the objects and their component parts, as in Figure 12.25, which shows how a candle could be de-constructed.

McCaffrey (2012) reported very marked benefits for the GPT method (c. 80 per cent solution rates vs. 50 per cent in controls) over eight insight problems, $p < .001$, as shown in Figure 12.26.

A similar method to GPT (Disassembly) was observed to be developed spontaneously by some participants generating novel uses for familiar objects in the Alternative Uses Task (Gilhooly et al., 2007), and use of a Disassembly strategy was associated with more creative unusual uses being put forward.

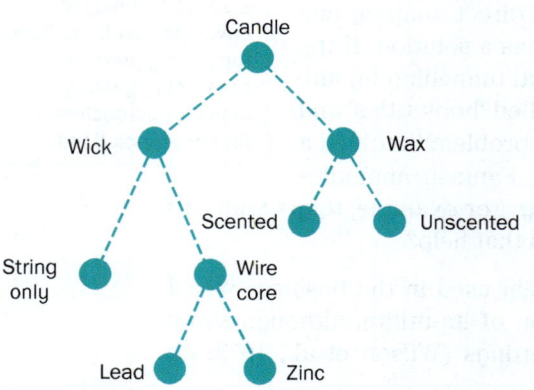

Figure 12.25 Generic Parts diagram breaking a candle into components.

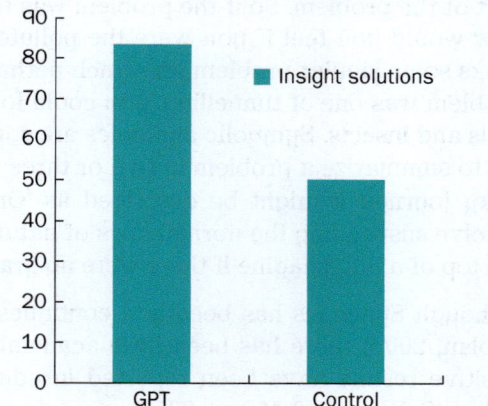

Figure 12.26 Solution percentages for Generic Parts Technique group vs. control group.

Evaluation

Working in face-to-face brainstorming groups with an emphasis on generating ideas as against evaluating ideas has some benefits compared to conventional working. However, merging the results of individuals (nominal groups) has been found to give better results than face-to-face group work. There are problems with real groups in the form of anxiety about implicit evaluation by group members and production blocking due to waiting for turn taking. Electronic versions of brainstorming overcome these problems and seem promising.

For individuals when the solution requires familiar objects to be used in new ways, explicitly noting the parts of the object and how those parts are made of sub-parts, and so on, can aid solutions by drawing attention to obscure aspects of the object.

Box 12.6 When Things Go Wrong: Psychopathology and creativity

Is there any truth in the popular idea that creative genius and madness are linked? There is some evidence that *manic depression* is especially frequent among writers and poets (Jamison, 1993). Manic states are characterized by a rapid flow of ideas and extreme confidence, and so may promote the development and expression of unusual ideas. Mood cycles would also provide contrasting perspectives that could feed in to creative work.

Weisberg (1994) analysed the work of composer Robert Schumann, who suffered bouts of mania and depression throughout his career. It turned out that Schumann was definitely more productive in the years when he was manic compared to the years when he was depressed. However, when the quality of the compositions was examined, by noting how many recordings were available for each piece, it was clear that there was no link between the quality of the work and whether Schumann was manic or depressed.

Note that the connections reported between mania and creativity are basically correlational, and it may be that being productive and creative leads to manic states (of euphoria) and not being productive leads to depression; the causal direction may not be from psychopathology to creativity but may be the reverse (Weisberg, 2006).

The investigation of connections between creativity and psychopathology has been put on a firmer footing by very large-scale studies that go well beyond single case studies.

Kyaga et al. (2011) examined Swedish national database records of 300,000 people with severe mental disorders and found that people with bipolar disorder (manic depression), or who were siblings of people with bipolar disorder or with schizophrenia, were over-represented in artistic professions such as visual artists, photographers, designers, composers, musicians and authors. People with schizophrenia were not over-represented in the artistic professions.

A link between manic depression and creativity was also found in a meta-analysis of 28 separate studies (Baas et al., 2016).

In a follow-up study to Kyaga et al. (2011), MacCabe et al. (2018) used Swedish national records to examine links between psychopathology and level of education in artistic subjects, in a study involving more than 4.4 million cases. It was found that people who had studied artistic subjects at tertiary level showed markedly higher rates of developing schizophrenia, manic depression and depression compared to the general population. It is suggested that people with susceptibility to schizophrenia and mood disorders may be inclined to artistic studies, but if schizophrenia develops they tend not to hold down artistic jobs (Kyaga et al., 2011) but rather are unemployed.

In a large study using an Icelandic population sample of 86,292, a Swedish sample of 8,893 and a Netherlands sample of 18,452 individuals, Power et al. (2015) found that higher genetic risk scores for both schizophrenia and bipolar disorder were associated with measures of creativity, including membership of artistic societies, being in a creative profession or high creative achievement scores. Creative achievement was measured using the well-established Creative Achievement Questionnaire

(CAQ) which sums achievement ratings over 10 distinct domains (Carson et al., 2005). Power and colleagues concluded that creativity and psychosis share genetic roots. This is consistent with Kyaga et al.'s (2011) finding that siblings of people with schizophrenia were more likely than average to be in creative occupations. As Carson (2019) concluded, inheriting part but not all of the schizophrenic genotype may benefit creativity.

A part of the schizophrenic spectrum that has been associated with creativity is schizotypy. People high in schizotypy are not necessarily mentally ill but display odd or eccentric beliefs and behaviours, and tend to be socially aloof. Schizotypy can be divided into *positive* (involving hallucinations and delusions) and *negative* (involving lack of pleasure or anhedonia in socializing and cognitive disorganization) (Mason & Claridge, 2006). A meta-analysis of 45 studies indicated a significant positive link ($r = .14$) between positive schizotypy and creativity, and a smaller but still significant inverse link ($r = -.09$) between creativity and negative schizotypy (Acar & Sen, 2013).

Overall, the build-up of evidence indicates that at high levels of creative achievement there are increased risks of bipolar disorder and schizotypy, and that these traits share some genetic components. Mild, subclinical versions of these disorders seem more beneficial than the full clinical variants for creativity (Carson, 2019). Subclinical schizotypy, for example, may aid in generating highly unusual combinations of ideas but unlike full schizophrenia may not be sufficient to lead to maladaptive hallucinations and delusions.

Summary

This chapter has concerned the kinds of thinking involved in problem solving and creative thinking.

'Thinking' was defined as involving changes in mental representations, usually in the service of goals. Although problems vary widely in content and in the degree to which they are well or ill defined, it can be said that problems, in general, arise when a person does not know how to reach a goal and must think through alternative possible actions and ways of representing the problem before solving.

The key approaches that were important historically and still inform the questions addressed in current research were outlined. These were the Gestalt and the, currently still dominant, information processing approaches. The key notions of problem structuring and re-structuring, insight, fixity, problem space, heuristics and problem reduction are set out.

Recent research on insight problem solving within the information processing approach was discussed. In particular, two main theories (representational change and progress monitoring) were presented and evaluated. Progress monitoring seems to account well for the initial stages of insight problem solving that lead to impasses that are then resolved through representational change. Recent evidence from neuroscientific studies is also discussed. A special role for right hemisphere representations in creativity tasks emerged from these studies.

The role of expert knowledge was considered in the light of research on skill in problem solving in chess and other areas that require extensive knowledge for effective performance. Expertise generally requires extensive study (10-year rule) to develop, and much expertise involves recognizing patterns that are not evident to the novice.

Creative problem solving was considered, with a discussion of evidence from self-reports by famous creative artists and scientists. Wallas's influential stage model (Preparation, Incubation, Intimation, Insight and Verification) was explained, and recent research on incubation effects and why they might occur discussed. Incubation seems to arise from a number of distinct processes including beneficial forgetting and unconscious work.

Recent information processing theories regarding creative thinking have been presented. Simon's model illuminates large historical trends, such as the relative rarity of creative advances in science due to large problem spaces and the importance of technological developments such as microscopes in improving problem representations. Campbell and Simonton's Blind Variation and Selective Retention approach emphasizes the role of extensive trial-and-error search, and the similarities between creative search and evolutionary processes.

The brainstorming technique was outlined. Its emphasis is on separating generation and evaluation. Working in real face-to-face groups proves inhibiting compared to nominal groups, which combine individuals' work. However, electronic groups do show some benefits.

Possible links between creativity and mental disorders, especially schizophrenia and bipolar disorders, were considered. Evidence suggests some link with subclinical conditions such as schizotypy and creativity.

Review Questions

1 In the light of work presented in this chapter, can human thinking be studied scientifically?
2 Evaluate the main historical approaches and their contemporary influence.
3 To what extent does research explain problem solving with insight?
4 How do experts differ from novices in problem solving?
5 Why might putting a problem aside for a while be helpful?
6 Is brainstorming worthwhile?
7 Are creativity and madness really linked?

Discussion Questions

1 Devise possible experiments to test the progress monitoring approach vs. the representational change approach to insight problem solving.
2 Make as many research predictions as you can from the view that anyone can be an expert at anything with 10 years' intensive practice.
3 Are all the varied approaches to incubation outlined in this chapter valid?

Further Reading

Abrahams, A. (2018). *The neuroscience of creativity*. Cambridge: Cambridge University Press.

Gilhooly, K. J. (2019). *Incubation in problem solving and creativity: Unconscious processes*. London: Routledge.

Gobet, F. (2018). *The psychology of chess*. London: Routledge.

Kaufman, J. C., & Sternberg, R. J. (Eds.). (2019). *The Cambridge handbook of creativity*. Cambridge: Cambridge University Press.

Weisberg, R. W. (2020). *Rethinking creativity*. Cambridge: Cambridge University Press.

Answers to Chapter Problems

1 Solution to the nine-dot problem:

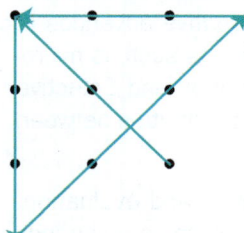

2 Solution to Tower of London task (Figure 12.8):

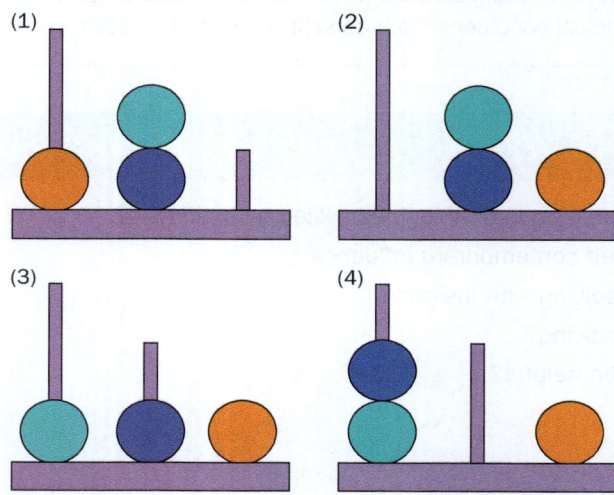

3 Solution to five-disc Tower of London task (Figure 12.9):

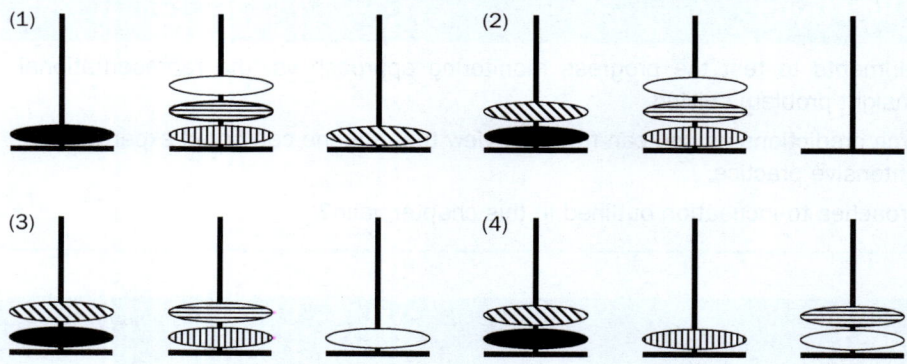

DECISION MAKING

13

- **PREVIEW QUESTIONS**
- **INTRODUCTION**
- **EXPECTED VALUE THEORY**
- **UTILITY AND PROSPECT THEORY**
  - **Box 13.1 When Things Go Wrong:** 'Bad things come to those who do not wait...'
- **SUBJECTIVE PROBABILITY AND PROSPECT THEORY**
  - FRAMING AND PROSPECT THEORY
- **MAKING PROBABILITY JUDGEMENTS**
  - AVAILABILITY
  - REPRESENTATIVENESS
  - BASE RATES
- **DECISION PROCESSES FOR MULTI-ATTRIBUTE ALTERNATIVES**
  - MULTI-ATTRIBUTE UTILITY THEORY
  - ELIMINATION BY ASPECTS
  - SATISFICING
  - TESTING MULTI-ATTRIBUTE DECISION MODELS
- **TWO-SYSTEM APPROACHES TO DECISION MAKING**
  - **Box 13.2 Practical Application:** Two system theory and 'nudge'
  - **Box 13.3 Research Close Up:** Unconscious thought effect on decisions
- **FAST-AND-FRUGAL HEURISTICS: THE ADAPTIVE TOOLBOX**
  - HEURISTICS AND CONSEQUENTIALISM
  - **Box 13.4 Practical Application:** Resisting effective but forced policies
  - **Box 13.5 Research Close Up:** Your morals depend on language
- **NATURALISTIC DECISION MAKING**
  - REAL-LIFE CHOICES
  - **Box 13.6 Practical Application:** Applying Social Judgement Theory methods to the detection of financial abuse of elderly people
- **NEUROSCIENCE APPROACHES TO DECISION MAKING**
- **SUMMARY**
- **REVIEW QUESTIONS**
- **FURTHER READING**

Preview Questions

1. How do we make decisions?
2. Why take out insurance when the insurance companies always win?
3. Why bet on lottery tickets when the lottery always wins?
4. When does deciding on the basis of 'gut feelings' help? When does it hinder?
5. Why are 'good resolution' decisions hard to stick with?
6. What affects decisions about sacrificing one life to save many?
7. How do experts make decisions in critical situations?
8. Can brain studies help explain how we decide?

INTRODUCTION

Decision making
the cognitive process of choosing between alternative possible actions.

In everyday life we face an endless stream of **decisions** ranging from the not very important, such as which socks to wear today, to the moderately important, such as where to go on holiday, to the very important, such as which university's offer of a study place to accept. We could say that decisions are a type of problem in which the alternatives are set out and the problem is to choose the best of the options available. This may be easy – for example, if the choice is between different amounts of money, most people most of the time would readily choose the larger amount. However, if the alternatives are complicated and have uncertain consequences – for example, deciding between job offers – the decision may be very difficult and have no clear correct solution. Typically, difficult decisions require a lot of thinking to figure out the possible results of different choices and so decision making is a major cognitive activity, which will draw on long-term knowledge, working memory and mental simulations to anticipate events.

© sebra/Shutterstock

How then do we make decisions, both great and small? Are there ideal ways to decide that would always deliver the best answer? For centuries, these questions have been of great interest to a wide range of researchers in different disciplines, including economists, philosophers and mathematicians, as well as more recently to psychologists. Economists, philosophers and mathematicians have focused on proposals for ideal ways to make decisions and, as we shall see, have come up with ways of making the best choices in small-scale, well-defined decision tasks, such as simple gambles. The search for good ways to make decisions is sometimes labelled the **normative** approach. Psychologists, in contrast, follow a **descriptive** approach of trying to understand what people actually do as against what they should, ideally, do. As we will see, normative approaches have supplied ideas that have then been used in descriptive theories. Economists are beginning to develop theories of behavioural economics that make more realistic assumptions about human thinking based on descriptive theories. So, there has been a lot of interaction between descriptive and normative approaches.

Normative approaches
attempt to establish ideal ways of deciding that will give the best decision possible. Economists have tended to develop normative models.

Descriptive approaches
aim to describe how decisions are actually taken as against how they should be made. Psychologists focus on the descriptive approach.

Risk
a decision involves risk if there is a probability that one of the options could lead to negative outcomes for the decision maker.

Riskless
riskless decisions involve choices where the outcomes of the choices are known with certainty.

Although all decision problems are similar in that they all involve choosing between alternatives, decision problems differ in a number of ways. One major difference is between problems that involve **risk** as against those that are **riskless**. If you decide to bet that a particular horse will win a race that is clearly a risky decision. The result of the bet is unknown when you make the decision. You may lose the money you bet or you may win a great deal. On the other hand, deciding between pairs of socks to wear is riskless. If you choose the red socks that is what you will be wearing.

The objects which you are choosing between may vary in only one way—for example, the socks may be identical except for colour or for type of material. Such choices are among **single-attribute** alternatives. In real life, **multi-attribute** alternatives are surely more common. For example, deciding between mobile phones that differ in terms of functions, size, weight, charging scheme, and many other aspects, represents a multi-attribute decision problem.

In the rest of this chapter we will explain in more detail about normative and descriptive approaches built on normative theories; discuss risky and risk-less choices; heuristic (short-cut) decision methods; naturalistic decision making out of the laboratory; and neuroscience approaches that are leading to the new field of neuroeconomics.

We will first consider normative approaches, which were developed early in the study of decision making and built on the idea of **expected value**, which will be explained in the next section.

EXPECTED VALUE THEORY

The earliest normative approach to risky decision making goes back to the seventeenth-century mathematicians Blaise Pascal (1623–62) and Pierre de Fermat (1601–65), who both had a strong interest in gambling and in the practical question of which gambles were good and which should be avoided (Hacking, 1975). They proposed that people should act to *maximize* the expected value of choices. What does this mean? The expected value of a risky choice is the average result you would get if you repeated the action many times over. For example, if a lottery ticket had an 85 per cent chance of winning £100, its expected value would be 0.85 × £100 – that is, £85 (an average). If you can continually take the same risk (i.e., your lottery ticket is valid every week with the same chance of winning), you would sometimes get nothing (15 per cent of the time) and you would get £100 the rest of the time (85 per cent of the time). So a long-term average over all the purchases is £85. Looking at this example using the expected value model, you should be willing to buy the lottery ticket for any price under £85 as it would mean you would profit overall (even if it is only a small profit). Even buying the ticket for £84.99 would be considered rational because you would make something, even if it is only 1p.

The expected value approach is an optimal way to deal with risky decisions in which we can put a money value on the possible outcomes and can say exactly what the probabilities of the possible outcomes are. Both of these conditions are met in many gambling situations in which the outcomes are monetary and the events have known properties of randomness (e.g., dice, coins, roulette wheels, lottery tickets).

Does the expected value model fit people's behaviour in real life? Research suggests not. With similar decisions to the lottery ticket case, Kahneman and Tversky (1984) found that people's choices showed marked departures from the expected value model predictions. For example, nearly all their participants would not bet $10 on a fair coin coming up heads if they would lose $10 for tails. The expected value of such a bet is zero (because you would win $10 as often as you would lose $10). As the experimenters increased the gain for heads while keeping the loss for tails constant, most people would not take the gamble until the gain for heads was $30 with the loss for tails fixed at $10. In this latter case, the expected value is (0.5 × $30 − 0.5 × $10) = $10. This means that many people passed up the opportunity of smaller but positive expected gains of up to $9.99. From the expected value point of view, people are acting against their own interests in not accepting bets with positive expected values, even if the expected values are quite small. To put it bluntly, the participants made choices that left most of them poorer; if they had all followed the expected value approach, most would have been richer at the end of the experiment than when they started.

© untitled/Shutterstock

> **Single-attribute**
> single-attribute decision problems involve alternatives that vary in only one dimension.
>
> **Multi-attribute decision problem**
> a decision task in which the alternatives vary in many dimensions or aspects.
>
> **Expected value**
> the long-term average value of a repeated decision that is determined by the probability and size of the outcome. So if the chance of winning £100 in a gamble is 0.5, then the expected value is £50.

Real life throws up other striking departures from what the expected value model would predict. For example, why do most of us take out insurance? The insurance companies, to stay in business, must give in claim payments less than they take through charges to customers. Thus, overall, the average customer must lose – that is, pay in more than he or she gets back. So from the expected value point of view people should not take out insurance. Why people take out insurance will be considered further when we discuss more recent theory.

Why do so many people engage in gambling at casinos, racetracks, street bookmakers and so on? Casinos set the odds on their games so that overall customers as a whole will lose. The expected value for the gambler of any casino bet is negative and so on the expected value model should not be taken.

Tens of millions of people buy national lottery tickets every week in many countries around the world. In such lotteries, typically there is a very large prize for correctly predicting which six out of 49 numbers will be drawn plus a range of smaller prizes for getting five, four or three correct. Usually, about half the total money staked on the lottery is returned to the players. This means that the expected value of a lottery ticket is around 50 per cent of its purchase price. On average you pay a pound and get back on average 50p. So, the expected return from buying a single ticket for £1 in the UK's weekly draw is *minus* 50p. In other words, when you buy a single £1 lottery ticket, an expected value theorist would say that you are basically throwing away 50p!

Overall, from all the examples we have just looked at, it seems very clear that the simple expected value model does not fit actual behaviour very well. (However, you might like to note that, if you sincerely want to be rich, it is certainly a defensible view that you should follow the expected value model whenever the outcomes are monetary and the probabilities can be accurately known. It's your decision!)

The departures in actual behaviour from expected value theory are intriguing, and subsequent theories stressing subjective probabilities and subjective measures of value (utility) have been developed to provide better explanations. We will consider these alternative ideas in the following sections.

Further difficulties for the expected value model as a descriptive model come from other experiments by Kahneman and Tversky (1984). They gave participants the following questions. Try to decide your answers as you read the questions.

1. 'Would you prefer $800 for certain, or an 85 per cent chance to win $1,000 (and so, a 15 per cent chance of winning nothing)?'
   What would you answer?
2. 'Would you prefer an 85 per cent chance of losing $1,000 (with a 15 per cent chance of losing nothing) or a sure loss of $800?'
   What would you prefer?

For question 1, Kahneman and Tversky found that most people preferred the certain option of $800 for sure. This finding is counter to the prediction of the expected value model. If we do the expected value calculation as follows then the gamble is worth $(0.85 \times \$1{,}000 + 0.15 \times 0) = \$850$.

> **Risk aversion**
> avoiding risky choices even when they have a higher expected value than riskless alternatives.

So, on the expected value model, since the gamble is worth $850 and the sure thing is only worth $800, the gamble should be preferred; but, as we have seen, the sure thing is generally preferred to the gamble, despite the gamble having a greater expected value. This preference may be said to reflect **risk aversion**.

In a similar study, Kahneman and Tversky (1984) asked participants question 2 above and found that most people preferred to take the gamble. However, once again the expected value model would predict the opposite pattern of choices to that found. This time the expected value calculation would be that the gamble was worth (0.85 × −$1,000) = −$850, while the sure loss would be worth −$800. So, on the expected value analysis, the sure loss is less bad than the gamble and thus the sure loss should be preferred. This preference can be labelled **risk seeking**.

The departures of results from those predicted by the expected value model may be due to people dealing not with objective money values or indeed with objective probabilities but rather with subjective value (or **utility**) and **subjective probabilities**.

> **Risk seeking**
> a preference for risky choices even when riskless alternatives of higher value are available.
> **Utility**
> the subjective value of an option.
> **Subjective probability**
> how likely a person believes an outcome to be irrespective of the objective probability.

UTILITY AND PROSPECT THEORY

The idea of utility as against objective value has a long history and goes back at least to the eighteenth-century mathematician, Bernoulli (1954). In the case of money, utility theory proposes that the subjective value or utility of a given additional amount of money decreases the more money you already have. Theoretically, a plot of utility against money will be a plot showing diminishing returns. The graph shown in Figure 13.1 captures our intuition that an extra £1 is worth more to a penniless person than it is to a billionaire. The poor person would cross a busy road to pick up a pound coin, while a rich person probably would not, because the utilities of the coin are very different for the two individuals.

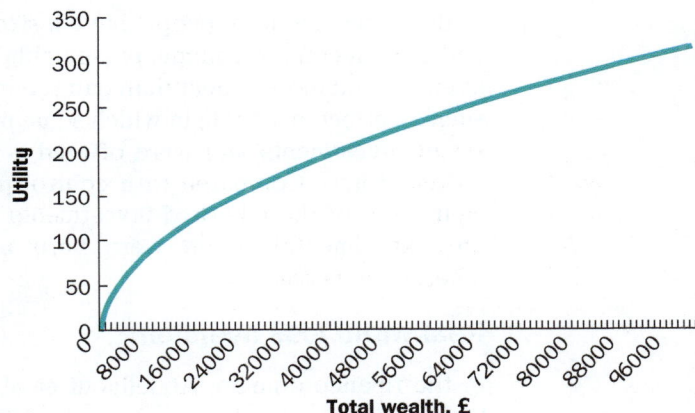

Figure 13.1 Plot of utility versus money.
This figure shows the diminishing growth of utility of extra wealth as wealth grows.

Kahneman and Tversky (1979, 1984; Kahneman, 2003; Tversky & Kahneman, 1992) developed **prospect theory** to overcome problems with the expected value approach. The theory deals with how people choose amongs gambles (or 'prospects') and importantly extended the utility plot into the area of losses. Kahneman and Tversky proposed that decisions about monetary gambles are about *gains and losses relative to one's current wealth*. A key insight of prospect theory is that losses are felt more keenly than corresponding gains – that is, a loss of £10 has greater negative utility than the gain of £10 has positive utility. The general finding that losses of any kind are weighted disproportionately to gains of the same amount is often labelled **loss aversion**. The resulting S-shaped utility function is shown in Figure 13.2. The S-shaped utility function with a steeper slope for losses than for gains explains risk aversion in the area of gains and risk seeking in the area of losses.

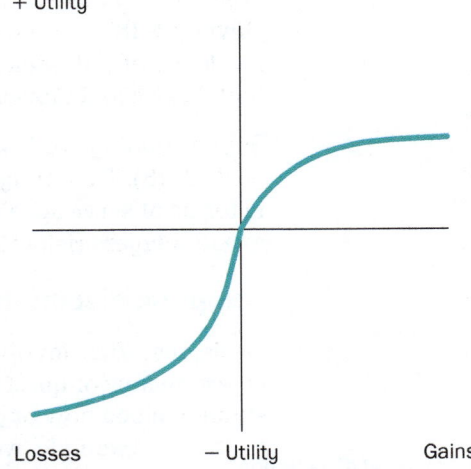

Figure 13.2 Schematic plot of gains and losses versus utility according to prospect theory.
The S-shaped curve shows a steep fall with losses and more gradual growth with gains.

> **Prospect theory**
> a decision theory stressing relative gains and losses.
>
> **Loss aversion**
> a key idea of prospect theory that there is a greater dislike of losing utility than liking for gaining the same degree of utility.
>
> **Endowment effect**
> a tendency to over-value a possessed object and to require more money to sell it than to buy it in the first place.
>
> **Status quo bias**
> a tendency to prefer the current state of affairs.

The notion of loss aversion is a key idea of prospect theory and its reality is supported by the real-world phenomena of the **endowment effect** and **status quo bias**, which prospect theory explains quite readily.

The endowment effect (Thaler, 1980) involves an unwillingness to give up some good, say a coffee mug, even for a sum greater than one would pay for it in the first place. A classic demonstration of the endowment effect was provided in a study by Kahneman et al. (1990) in which they gave some participants coffee mugs worth about $5. The participants were then asked for how much they would be willing to sell the mugs. A similar group of participants were shown the same mugs and asked how much they would pay for the mugs. The sellers tended to want about $7 to sell the mugs but the prospective buyers on average would offer only about $3. The sellers require more to compensate for the pain of losing something they already have, the mug, than the buyers are willing to pay for the pleasure of gaining the same mugs that they do not yet have.

In the status quo bias, people have a strong preference for the current state of affairs and are reluctant to change, presumably because of the risk of losses, which are more aversive and more salient than gains. Samuelson and Zeckhauser (1988) demonstrated such an effect in a study in which some participants were told that they had inherited a set of investments and were offered a set of alternative investments that could be switched into. Compared to a control group who were to imagine having the cash equivalent of the inherited investments and the same alternatives to select, those in the experimental group were very unlikely to move away from the original inherited investments.

Real-world loss aversion

In the finance domain, Abdellaoui et al. (2013) found that, in accord with prospect theory, finance professionals (private bankers and fund managers) showed loss aversion. In more detail, they were risk averse for gains and risk seeking for losses in a money-based task. Furthermore, their utility was concave for gains (showing reducing marginal utility for gains) and convex for losses (showing steeply increasing negative utility for losses) as prospect theory proposes. Similar patterns were also found by Oliver (2018) in a study involving health outcomes as well as monetary outcomes. Evidence of risk seeking in the area of losses was particularly strong in this study for both health and monetary outcomes.

Similar findings of loss aversion have also been found in professional tennis (Anbarci et al., 2018). This study found that, when behind, players put more effort into their serve in terms of serve speeds and challenging target locations of the ball than when they are ahead. Players risk-take more when behind, presumably to avoid losing.

Temporal discounting and utility

Decisions often involve options that involve different time delays, such as: smoke a cigarette now or quit for a long-term health benefit that may take years to be felt; enjoy staying in bed now or get up to make an appointment in two hours' time. In a monetary example, would you rather be given £10 right now or £12 in 12 months' time?

> **Temporal discounting**
> the decline in subjective value (utility) of an outcome with a time delay to its being received.

Typically, people exhibit some **temporal discounting** – that is, an option now is preferred to the same or a better option delayed. From an expected value perspective, this is rational when the options are cash amounts and positive interest rates are available for savings. If the savings interest rate were 5 per cent then one should indeed prefer £100 now to £104 in a year as the £100 now could be turned into £105 pounds if saved for a year.

However, the way people tend to discount future outcomes does not always fit the rational expectations of expected value theory.

Would you prefer £12 in 13 months to £10 in 12 months? Most people say 'yes' to the more delayed payment. But if the question is £10 now or £12 in one month, many opt for the immediate £10 – that is, there is a **preference reversal** (Newell et al., 2007). It appears that the rate of discounting is greater to begin with and reduces with time (so called hyperbolic discounting function). Such functions can allow reversals of valuations and so of preferences that straightforward fixed discounting rates do not allow.

> **Preference reversal**
> when an original preference switches – for example, as the decision maker moves closer in time to the choice alternatives being delivered.

Two other effects are those of magnitude and of sign. Outcomes of greater magnitude show a lower discounting rate than those of lesser magnitude and gains show more discounting than do losses. Chapman and Winquist (1998) had participants imagine they had won a lottery or received a speeding fine. They were then asked how much the amount given would have to be for the lottery win to be delayed three months. On average, participants wanted $2,100 to delay their winnings by three months – that is, they preferred $100 now to nearly $2,100 in three months' time (a huge 2,000 per cent annual discount rate). To defer paying a speeding fine of $100 they would accept a fine of $500 in three months' time – that is, they were indifferent between a loss of $500 in three months' time and an immediate loss of $100 (implying a discount rate of 400 per cent). With larger wins and fines, discount rates were clearly reduced (magnitude effect).

Bulley and Schacter (2020) have examined the role of **deliberation** in temporal decision making. Deliberation in turn involves **prospection** and **metacognition**.

> **Deliberation**
> a process by which decision makers consider their options, representing the options and outcomes as well as evaluating them.
> **Prospection**
> the capacity to represent the future.
> **Metacognition**
> awareness of one's own thoughts and cognitive processes.

Prospection allows the consideration of possible future states in one's personal future and has been labelled as episodic future thinking.

Metacognition allows people to represent beliefs about the future and assess the plausibility, possibility, probability, likelihood, and so on, of those beliefs. Metacognition would also include self-knowledge about one's own tendencies for say temporal discounting or ability to look very far ahead. Thus, a person may be metacognitively aware that a decision to give up smoking in the new year may well fail when temptation appears on new year's day, and to help maintain the initial decision, 'precommits' by destroying all their remaining cigarettes on new year's eve.

Interestingly, if people metacognitively anticipate the negative emotion of dread, this can lead to *not delaying* the dreaded experience and just 'getting it over with'. Equally, the metacognitive awareness of pleasurable anticipation of a positive outcome can lead people to *delay* the positive outcome. For example, when students were asked when (in theory) they would like to kiss their favourite film star, the average response was three days later, not immediately as might have been assumed (Loewenstein, 1987)!

Bulley et al. (2019) found that if participants were cued to imagine positive and negative future events in detail, this

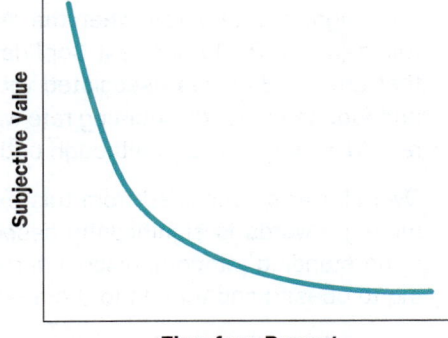

Figure 13.3 Temporal discounting curve.
The curve shows a drop in the subjective value (utility) of an outcome as it is placed further and further into the future. Thus a given amount of money, say £100, a year from now is subjectively valued as being of less worth than £100 now. The steeper the slope, the greater the temporal discounting rate.

Opportunity costs
the loss of potential gains from one alternative when another alternative is chosen.

markedly reduced temporal discounting, possibly because imaging increases attention given to the future possibilities. An aspect of choice options that may be overlooked with insufficient attention is that of **opportunity costs**. Typically, inter-temporal choice questions do not refer to the forgone alternatives implicit in each option. Thus, the question, 'Would you prefer £40 today or £55 in 62 days?' has implicit zero values that are explicit if the question is worded as follows: 'Would you prefer £40 today and £0 in 62 days *or* £55 in 62 days and £0 today?' This explicit 'zero framing' was found to reliably reduce delay discounting (Rung et al., 2019). This framing seems to draw attention to the opportunity cost of choosing the smaller, sooner reward – that is, the forgone opportunity to gain more later (Read et al., 2017).

The generally found magnitude effect whereby people discount large future rewards less steeply than small rewards may occur because people invest greater cognitive effort into more important choices. To test this idea, Ballard et al. (2017) had participants justify their choices in temporal decision problems, which require them to consider the reasons for choices. It was found that the magnitude effect was reduced – that is, the temporal discounting of smaller rewards became less steep when justifications were given for the choices made. Discounting of larger rewards was little affected as they presumably attracted more consideration already without special instructions.

Box 13.1 When Things Go Wrong: 'Bad things come to those who do not wait...'

Sources: Amlung et al. (2016); Kejic et al. (2020).

Temporal discounting may seem a rather abstract topic, but a considerable number of studies have examined links between *temporal discounting* rates and *health problems,* in particular obesity and overeating disorders such as binge eating.

Amlung et al. (2016) carried out a meta-analysis and identified 59 studies (total $N = 10,278$) which reported associations between obesity as measured by body mass index (BMI). These included studies with temporal discounting of food (e.g., choose between 2 pieces of chocolate now versus 10 pieces of chocolate in 5 hours) as well as temporal discounting of money amounts.

All 59 studies in the meta-analysis found a link in the predicted direction although not all were individually significant. Overall, when the results were combined, a highly significant medium size effect was found ($d = .43$, 95 per cent Confidence Interval = .40–.44; equivalent to a Pearson's $r = .21$) such that greater BMI was associated with steeper discounting rates. Interestingly, the link between BMI and food temporal discounting rate was stronger ($d = .74$, $r = .35$) than that with monetary discounting rate ($d = .41$, $r = .20$), although both were highly significant.

Overall it was concluded from this extensive meta-analysis that steep discounting of future food and money rewards is significantly associated with obesity to a moderate extent (medium effect sizes). Understanding temporal discounting processes may therefore help in understanding behaviours leading to obesity and feed in to therapeutic possibilities.

The tendency to act on immediate pleasure-driven desires resulting from temporal discounting of future benefits as against immediate rewards is associated with a number of substance abuse disorders. The study by Kejic et al. (2020) described here involved a large unselective sample ($N = 432$) and examined possible links between temporal discounting and compulsive overeating.

Participants carried out an online survey that included an 80-item test to assess rates of temporal discounting through binary choices between monetary amounts varying in amount (small or large) and

> delays (small or large). They also completed two eating disorder questionnaires and the DAss-21 questionnaire, which measures stress, anxiety and depression.
>
> Controlling for the possible confounding factors of age, gender, income, education level, depression, anxiety and stress, rates of temporal discounting in the monetary domain correlated significantly at around $r = -0.20$ level with frequency of compulsive overeating, with overeating psychopathology, food addiction measures and with BMI.
>
> It was concluded that higher rates of temporal discounting are possibly causally linked to overeating behaviour and its consequences, and so could be a target area for interventions to reduce temporal discounting and could help in the treatment of overeating disorders.

SUBJECTIVE PROBABILITY AND PROSPECT THEORY

Prospect theory also addresses the issue of probability. The expected value model assumed both objective values and known objective probabilities. Prospect theory, as we have seen, replaces objective values with subjective values or utilities. It also proposes that people's perceptions of probability systematically depart from objective values. In particular, Kahneman and Tversky (1979) proposed that objective probabilities are transformed into subjective probabilities, which they refer to as 'decision weights'. In general, people tend to *overweight* small probabilities and *underweight* large probabilities, as indicated in Figure 13.4.

The overweighting of small probabilities could explain why people are fairly willing to gamble on lotteries where the prize is large but very low probability and to take out insurance where the potential loss is large but very unlikely.

Kahneman and Tversky (1979) demonstrated the overweighting of small probabilities using the following two choice problems.

1. Would you prefer a .001 chance of gaining $5,000 or a certain $5?
2. Would you prefer a .001 chance of losing $5,000 or a certain loss of $5?

People strongly tended to choose the risky option (72 per cent) in the first choice and the non-risky sure option (83 per cent) in the second choice problem. Thus, with small probabilities, due to overweighting of those probabilities, people tend to take the risky option for gains and the sure option for losses, which reverses the usual pattern of risk avoiding in the area of gains and risk seeking for losses with medium to large probabilities.

Overall, prospect theory accounts well for the four-fold pattern of choices in gambles in the areas of gains and losses with small and medium probabilities (Newell, 2015). Table 13.1 (overleaf) provides more information on this.

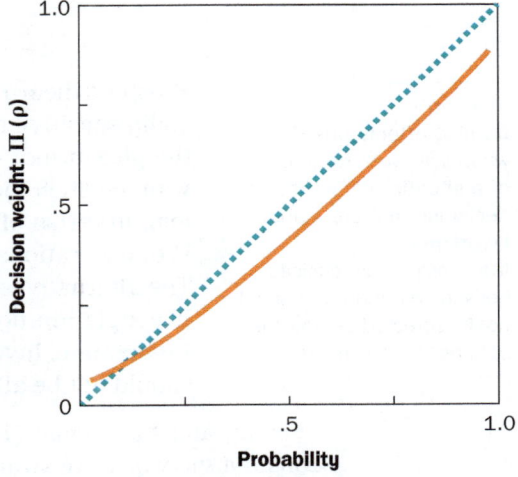

Figure 13.4 Decision weights versus probability. This figure shows that decision weights (the solid line) overweight low probabilities and underweight high probabilities. The dotted line shows what would happen if the decision weights equalled the objective probabilities.

Table 13.1 The Four-Fold Pattern of Choice Behaviour Accounted for by Prospect Theory

	Gains	Losses
Small probabilities	Risk seeking	Risk aversion
Medium and large probabilities	Risk aversion	Risk seeking

It is worth noting that the main results from early studies on prospect theory (Kahneman & Tversky, 1979), including the important reflection effect, have been replicated is a large-scale study involving 4,098 participants from 19 countries with 13 languages involved (Ruggeri et al., 2020).

Decisions from experience

Prospect theory was largely developed on the basis of studies that involved stated probabilities of the outcomes, as in the choices discussed in the previous section. Some research has looked into the effect of the probabilities of options being *learned from experience* as against being simply *stated* in the task presentation, and it seems that decisions based on experience differ from those based on statements (Schulze & Newell, 2018).

The problem of deciding between a sure 3,000 points and an 80 per cent chance of 4,000 can be presented in an 'experience' method by having participants try out two buttons – 'A' for a sure thing and 'B' for some chance of reward or loss – over trials, seeing the outcomes but not getting any rewards until a final 'choice' trial where participants choose 'A' or 'B'. In this experience-based set-up, the riskier option, B (an 80 per cent chance of 4,000 points), is preferred even although this choice goes against the usual pattern of risk aversion in the realm of gains. Similarly, if the final choice following experience is one whereby button 'A' delivers a sure loss of 3,000 points and the other an 80 per cent chance of losing 4,000 points, participants prefer the 'A' button, going against risk seeking in the area of losses (Camilleri & Newell, 2013; Hertwig & Erev, 2009). These results are probably due to the lower probability option occurring very rarely during the exploratory learning period and so the low probability being *underweighted* in the experience-based paradigm (Newell, 2015).

Framing and Prospect Theory

> **Framing**
> framing effects arise when irrelevant features of a situation affect the decisions that are made.
> **Invariance**
> the principle that choices between alternatives should not be affected by how the options are described.

Prospect theory includes the idea of loss aversion – that is, that we are especially sensitive to losses. The pain of losing £10 is more repellent to us than the pleasure of gaining £10 is attractive. This leads to predictions that the way in which the alternatives are presented (or **framed**) in a decision problem, in terms of gains or losses, will strongly influence the choices made. From a rational point of view, framing should not have any effect. The alternatives are the same whether described in terms of gains or losses. If people are not affected by framing then their choices are said to show **invariance**. Invariance requires that a person's choice between two options should not be affected by the way in which the options are described.

Tversky and Kahneman (1981) examined the degree to which participants showed a constant view or were swayed by framing (alternative presentation) when given a pair of problems (the *Asian disease problems*) that could be presented in terms of lives lost or lives saved. It was predicted from prospect theory that these different ways of presenting the alternatives would sway the choices made, so that a risky option would be preferred when the choices were among losses and a sure option would be preferred when the choices were among gains. The problems were as follows:

Problem 1: Imagine that the USA is preparing for the outbreak of an unusual Asian disease, which is expected to kill 600 people. Two alternative programmes to combat the disease have been proposed. Assume that the exact scientific estimates of the consequences of the programmes are as follows:

- If Programme A is adopted, 200 people will be saved.
- If Programme B is adopted, there is a one-third probability that 600 people will be saved and a two-thirds probability that no people will be saved.

Which programme, A or B, would you choose?

Now consider *Problem 2*. The same introduction is followed by a choice between two programmes, C and D.

- If Programme C is adopted, 400 people will die.
- If Programme D is adopted, there is a one-third probability that nobody will die and a two-thirds probability that 600 people will die.

Which of programmes C and D would you choose?

It was found that there was a strong preference for Programme A over Programme B (72 per cent vs. 28 per cent in a study with 152 participants). In a separate similarly large group of participants ($n = 155$) there was a strong preference for Programme D over Programme C (78 per cent vs. 22 per cent). The intriguing point of these results is that Programme A is completely equivalent to Programme C (in both, 200 live and 400 die) and Programmes B and D are also completely equivalent to each other (in both, there is a one-third chance that 600 will live and a two-thirds chance that 600 will die).

Tversky and Kahneman explain the pattern of results in these problems by saying that participants 'frame', or construe, the problems in different ways.

In Problem 1, participants are working in a positive 'gains' frame – i.e., in terms of lives saved. The majority choice of the sure option is typical of risk aversion in the domain of gains.

On the other hand, in Problem 2, participants are working in a 'losses' frame – i.e., in terms of lives lost. The majority choice of the risky option reflects typical risk-seeking behaviour in the domain of losses, as discussed earlier in the text.

Thus, Tversky and Kahneman induced participants to show a striking departure from one of the major assumptions of normative decision theory. Participants did not show invariance and were clearly affected by the way the problem was described.

Similar effects of framing have been demonstrated within individuals as well as between individuals, and over many areas of decision making (Maule & Villejoubert, 2007), such as business, finance, politics, management and medicine. In the case of medicine, Edwards et al. (2001) found that patients were much more likely to accept a surgical treatment when it was presented as having a 90 per cent survival rate as against a 10 per cent death rate. Thus, as in many areas of problem solving, how a decision problem is presented, and so internally represented, is extremely important.

MAKING PROBABILITY JUDGEMENTS

In order to choose effectively between options the decision maker often has to reach judgements about the probability of certain outcomes. For instance, a business traveller in Britain might have to decide whether to fly to Paris or take the Eurostar train.

> **Availability heuristic** involves judging frequency or probability of events by how easy it is to bring the events to mind.
>
> **Representativeness heuristic** involves judging frequency or probability of an event or object by how representative or typical it is of its category.

Which outcomes might be considered and the subjective probabilities ascribed to those outcomes will be critical in which decision is made. If a plane bound for Paris had recently crashed, this possible outcome will be salient and may deter the executive from the plane choice. Since the perceived probability of outcomes (as against the objective probability) is critical in decision making, much research has been aimed at unravelling some of the processes involved in probability judgements. Tversky and Kahneman (1974) have been particularly influential in this area and have proposed two major heuristics, **availability** and **representativeness**, which they argue are often used in making probability judgements.

Availability

Consider the following question:

If a word of three letters or more is sampled at random from an English text, is it more likely that the word starts with 'r' or has 'r' as its third letter?

What do you think? Using this word problem, Tversky and Kahneman (1974) found a very strong tendency for people to report that a word beginning with 'r' was more likely to be picked out by random sampling than a word with 'r' in the third position. However, in fact the reverse is true. Tversky and Kahneman suggest that people tackle this question by comparing how easy they find it to think of words beginning with 'r' as against words with 'r' as the third letter. Since starting letters usually provide the best cues for word retrieval, people are able to think of more words that start with 'r' than with 'r' in third place. That is, words beginning with 'r' come to mind more readily, are more available, than words with 'r' as the third letter. Differences in availability thus lead people to misjudge the relative frequency of the two types of words.

Reliance on availability of examples to judge frequency is actually a reasonable thing to do, since frequency does affect availability. However, since availability can also be affected by recency and emotional impact, among other factors, availability is not always a valid guide to objective frequency or probability. Thus a single, recent, vivid accident can deter possible travellers from flying across the Atlantic, say, because a recent well-publicized accident makes the highly unlikely outcome of another accident very available when the person contemplates travelling. Consistent with this view, Lichtenstein et al. (1978) showed that causes of death that receive more publicity (e.g., murder) are judged more likely than causes that receive less publicity (e.g., suicide), contrary to the true state of affairs.

The availability heuristic can lead to contradictions of basic laws of probability as well as to the simple inaccuracies indicated above. Tversky and Kahneman (1983) reported that when subjects were given 60 seconds to list seven-letter words of the form '- - - - ing', more words were reported than when subjects were given the same time to list seven-letter words of the form '- - - - - n -'. This result reflects a difference in availability since, of course, the set of '- - - - - n -' words includes the set of '- - - - ing' words, and so is considerably larger. Interestingly, Tversky and Kahneman also found that when subjects were asked to rate the frequencies (in a sample of 2,000 words from a novel) with which they would expect '- - - - ing' and '- - - - - n -' words to occur, they rated the former much more frequent than the latter. Comparable results were found in a comparison of frequency judgements for words of the forms '- - - - - ly' and '- - - - - l -'. Those judgements, based on availability, violate a fundamental law of probability, known as the 'extension rule'. If the extension of a set, A, includes the extension of a set, B, then the probability of A must be greater than or equal to the probability of B. For example, if I have a bag of mixed fruits (say some apples, bananas and pears), the probability of pulling a fruit out of the bag must be bigger than the probability of pulling out an apple.

So, use of the availability heuristic can lead to rather gross errors, which decision makers should strive to avoid.

Representativeness

A second heuristic which Tversky and Kahneman (1983) identified is that of representativeness. Representativeness is an assessment of the degree to which an example fits our idea of a typical member of the category (for more on representativeness see Chapter 9). It is well established (Rosch, 1978) that judgements of the representativeness of examples of categories can be made reliably and with high agreement among participants (e.g., that 'robins' are a representative or highly typical instances of 'birds' but 'penguins' are not). You might like to think how representative is a particular individual (say 'George Clooney' or 'Johnny Depp') of the category 'Hollywood actors' or how representative is a particular act (e.g., 'murder') of the behaviour of a category of people (e.g., 'police officers')? Tversky and Kahneman propose that representative or typical instances tend to be judged as more likely to occur than unrepresentative instances, and that such judgements can lead to error.

> Chapter 9, p294

Conjunction fallacy

A particular form of error attributed to the representativeness heuristic is that known as the **conjunction fallacy**. A classic task was used by Tversky and Kahneman to demonstrate the conjunction fallacy. They presented people first with information about an imaginary person (Linda) such that the information evoked the stereotype of a feminist. As Linda was very representative of the class of feminists, would that skew people's judgements about the likelihood of other possible characteristics of Linda? And in particular would the conjunction fallacy be strengthened by the stereotypical information?

> **Conjunction fallacy**
> the mistaken belief that the conjunction of two events (A and B) is more likely than either one of A or B.

The description of Linda in the problem was intended to be representative of a feminist (F) and unrepresentative of a bank teller (T). In Tversky and Kahneman's study, a group of 88 undergraduates then ranked eight further statements about Linda by 'the degree to which Linda resembles the typical member of that class'. The description given and the eight statements were as follows:

> *Linda is 31 years old, single, outspoken and very bright. She majored in philosophy. As a student, she was deeply concerned with issues of discrimination and social justice, and also participated in anti-nuclear demonstrations.*
>
> *Now rank the following statements according to how likely you think they are to be true of Linda.*
>
> 1. *Linda is a teacher in elementary school*
> 2. *Linda works in a bookstore and takes yoga classes*
> 3. *Linda is active in the feminist movement (F)*
> 4. *Linda is a psychiatric social worker*
> 5. *Linda is a member of the League of Women Voters*
> 6. *Linda is a bank teller (T)*
> 7. *Linda is an insurance salesperson*
> 8. *Linda is a bank teller and active in the feminist movement (T and F)*

The overwhelmingly chosen order of *typicalities* for the key statements ('Feminist', 'Teller' and 'Teller and Feminist') was, 'Feminist' most typical, then 'Teller and Feminist', then 'Teller'. Thus Linda was seen as highly typical of the class 'Feminist', moderately typical of the class 'Feminist bank tellers' and untypical of the class 'Bank tellers'. More surprising, and in violation of the extension law of probability, was that nearly all participants also ranked the conjunction 'Teller and Feminist' as *more probable* than either 'Teller' or 'Feminist' alone.

Since the set of Tellers includes the set 'Tellers and Feminists', the probability of Teller must be greater than the probability of 'Teller and Feminist'; similarly, the probability of Feminist must be greater than the probability of 'Teller and Feminist'. Thus, it seems that the representativeness heuristic has led to an error (violation of the extension law), just as did the availability heuristic when participants judged the probabilities of words ending 'ing' or '- n -'.

The conjunction fallacy has proved to be a very robust phenomenon and has been replicated under many variations of the task, described by Tversky and Kahneman (1983). For example, given a description of another individual, 'Bill', who fitted an 'Accountant' stereotype, the probability that he was a 'Jazz-playing Accountant' was rated more highly than the probability that he was an 'Accountant'.

Even medically trained participants were affected by the fallacy when given a brief case history and asked then to say whether the patient was more likely to develop one particular (unusual) symptom (B) or a combination of the unusual symptom (B) and a typical symptom (A). The experts overwhelmingly judged the conjunction A and B to be more likely than the single symptom B. Again, this judgement violates the extension law of probability.

Interestingly, if the task was stated in terms of frequencies rather than probabilities, this manipulation greatly reduced the fallacy. Consider the following:

> *A health survey was conducted on a sample of 100 adult males in British Columbia, of all ages and occupations. Please give your best estimate of the following values.*
> - *How many of the 100 participants have had one or more heart attacks?*
> - *How many of the 100 participants both are over 55 years old and have had one or more heart attacks?*

Only 25 per cent of 117 statistically naive participants gave a higher estimate for the conjunction question (Tversky & Kahneman, 1983). When 147 similar participants were given the same problem but asked to estimate percentages rather than absolute numbers, a clear majority gave higher estimates for the conjunction. Fiedler (1988) found the same facilitating effect in a frequency version of the Linda problem in which it was stated after the standard Linda description that 100 people fitted her description. Participants were asked to say how many of the 100 people fitting Linda's description are bank tellers and how many are bank tellers and active feminists; in this frequency version the rate of conjunction fallacies fell to 22 per cent from the 91 per cent in the original version. Gigerenzer et al. (1999) replicated this result almost exactly.

Overall, it seems that using frequencies rather than percentages facilitates correct thinking in conjunction tasks, probably by inducing a more concrete representation of the task.

Beyond representativeness: other explanations for the conjunction fallacy

The strength of the conjunction effect or fallacy is affected by many factors, and this variation in the effect has led to alternative theories beyond the representativeness explanation.

The effect is stronger when the added 'conjunct' (e.g., that Linda is a feminist activist) is *more probable* than the initial term ("bank teller"). Fisk and Pidgeon (1996) found rates of conjunction fallacy around 60 per cent, with likely and unlikely events being combined, as against around 30 per cent if both events were likely or both were unlikely.

Another important factor is that the effect is stronger when the two components are *causally linked*. For example, Tversky and Kahneman (1983) gave one group a problem with a causal link:

> *A health survey was conducted in a representative sample of adult males in British Columbia of all ages and occupations. Mr F was included in the sample. He was selected by chance from the list of participants.*
>
> *Which of the following statements is more probable? (check one)*
> *Mr F has had one or more heart attacks.*
> *Mr F has had one or more heart attacks and he is over 55 years old.*

A total of 58 per cent of participants ticked the conjunction as more likely thus exhibiting the conjunction effect.

A second group were given the following version.

> *A health survey was conducted in a representative sample of adult males in British Columbia of all ages and occupations. Mr F and Mr G were both included in the sample. They were unrelated and were selected by chance from the list of participants.*
>
> *Which of the following statements is more probable? (check one)*
> *Mr F has had one or more heart attacks.*
> *Mr F has had one or more heart attacks and Mr G is over 55 years old.*

A significantly lower proportion of participants (29 per cent) showed the conjunction effect in this version of the problem. The key difference here is that the two components are causally connected in the first version (a person's age has causal connections to heart health) but the two components are not connected causally in the second version (Mr G's age cannot affect Mr F's health).

The role of representativeness was cast in doubt by studies by Gavanski and Roskos-Ewoldsen (1991). In these studies conjunction effects were found for problems of the same form as the Linda problem but involving statements about aliens from outer space for whom no representativeness information was available (questions were about numbers of eyes and the hair colours of the aliens). The size of the effect was similar to that found with the Linda problem itself.

Tentori et al. (2013) argued that sheer probability of the conjunct was not explanatory of the conjunction effect. If the conjunction in the Linda task was '*Linda is a bank teller and owns a pair of black shoes*' the conjunct '*owns a pair of black shoes*' would be extremely likely to be true of any adult woman, and yet the conjunction effect they suggest would not be any greater than that for the conjunct '*active in the feminist movement*'. The difference between the two cases being that '*active in the feminist movement*' gains strongly in likelihood from the backstory, while '*owns a pair of black shoes*', although very likely, does not *gain* in likelihood from Linda's backstory.

Examining a range of scenarios, for example:

> *O has a degree in violin performance.*
> *Which of the following hypotheses do you think is the most probable?*
> *O is an expert mountaineer.*
> *O is an expert mountaineer and gives music lessons.*
> *O is an expert mountaineer and owns an umbrella.*

it was found that conjunctions that involved a possibility made more likely (supported) by the backstory (e.g., *gives music lessons*) were endorsed much more, as most likely, than those that contained a very likely possibility (e.g., *owns an umbrella*), which was not particularly supported by the backstory.

Base Rates

> **Base rate**
> the base rate of an event is the overall probability of the event in a population; so the base rate of 'engineers' in the UK is the probability that a randomly selected person in the UK will be an engineer.

In considering the extent to which evidence affects the probability of a hypothesis being true one should generally take into account the probability that the hypothesis is true when the evidence is not taken into account (i.e., the **base rate**). A number of studies have found a tendency to ignore base rates. However, as we shall see, whether base rates are used varies with task conditions. A striking example study is that of Casscells et al. (1978) using the Harvard Medical School problem presented below:

> *If a test to detect a disease whose prevalence is 1/1000 has a false positive rate of 5 per cent, what is the chance that a person found to have a positive result actually has the disease, assuming you know nothing about the person's symptoms or signs?*

If you are inclined to answer '95 per cent' to the problem, then you are in agreement with most of the medically trained participants in Casscells et al.'s study. However, the correct answer is 2 per cent. Most participants answer on the basis of the *false positive* rate and the inferred *true positive* rate of 95 per cent. However the base rate of the disease is very low and must be taken into account. The rationale of the correct approach is perhaps most clearly conveyed for the non-mathematically inclined by considering frequencies as follows. Of 1,000 patients only 1 will have the disease and 999 will not. Of the 999 healthy patients the test will report that *c.* 50 have the disease. So even assuming the test correctly diagnoses the one sufferer, it will misdiagnose 50 as ill who are not. Thus, of the 51 who are diagnosed ill only one will actually be ill, giving the probability that a person with a positive result is ill as 1/51 = 2 per cent. Of course this is an increase over the base rate of 0.01 per cent, but still quite a low probability in absolute terms.

As with the conjunction fallacy, a manipulation that reduces or even removes the base rate fallacy is to state the problems in terms of frequencies. For example, Cosmides and Tooby (1996) developed a frequency version of the Harvard Medical School problem, which reads as follows:

> *One out of 1000 Americans has disease X. A test has been developed to detect when a person has disease X. Every time the test is given to a person who has the disease, the test comes out positive. But sometimes the test also comes out positive*

when it is given to a person who is completely healthy. Specifically, out of every 1000 people who are perfectly healthy, 50 of them test positive for the disease. Imagine that we have assembled a random sample of 1000 Americans. They were selected by a lottery. Those who conducted the lottery had no information about the health status of any of these people. How many people who test positive for the disease will actually have the disease? _____ out of _____.

With this version the proportion of correct answers rises from 12 per cent with the original Casscells et al. (1978) wording to 76 per cent with the frequency wording. Thus, expressing base rate problems in frequency terms helps considerably (as was the case also with conjunction effect problems). Gigerenzer (1993, 2007) suggests that thinking in frequencies is developmentally (and evolutionarily) prior to thinking in probabilities or percentages, which requires specific training. Posing problems in terms of frequencies may evoke quite concrete representations of the situations described, and hence provide guidance for inferences and checks on erroneous inferences.

DECISION PROCESSES FOR MULTI-ATTRIBUTE ALTERNATIVES

Most real-life choices involve selecting among complex alternatives that vary in many ways. For example, in buying a new mobile phone, there are many functions a phone may have that differ in quality and ease of use. How good is the camera? How easy would it be to watch a video on the screen, or to read extended documents? How lightweight is the phone? How long does a battery charge last? What is the payment scheme? How long are you locked in to the contract? And so on. This is an example of deciding between alternatives that vary on many attributes. How can one balance out advantages on low costs, say, with disadvantages in terms of short battery life or less good photo quality? The phone purchasing problem is an example of the general problem of deciding between multi-attribute alternatives.

How should such decisions be made (the normative question)? And how do they actually seem to be made (the descriptive question)? We consider these questions in the following sections.

Multi-Attribute Utility Theory

Even when no risk is involved, making a choice among items that differ on many attributes can be demanding. A normative approach, known as **multi-attribute utility theory (MAUT)**, suggests that the decision maker should (1) identify the relevant dimensions or attributes, (2) decide on weights to be assigned to the attributes, (3) obtain a total utility for each object by summing the weighted attribute values and (4) choose the object with the highest weighted total (Wright, 1984). For example, if the decision maker has to choose between a number of houses, he or she might identify buying price, distance from work, number of rooms, garden size, privacy, and distance from services (shops, schools, etc.) as relevant attributes. Then the relative importance of the attributes would have to be considered. Is price a more important consideration than distance from services? Each alternative must then be scored on the attribute dimensions. The same scale length should be used for all attributes (e.g., from 0 to 100). So a given house may be assessed at '50' in terms of cost and '90' in terms of garden space, but '10' on distance from work. Clearly all the scales have to be used in such a

> **Multi-attribute utility theory (MAUT)** a procedure in which the utilities of the attributes of an option are aggregated to produce an overall utility for an option having many attributes.

way that a higher score is 'more desirable' than a lower score. Having obtained the scores on each house for each attribute, overall utilities for each house can be obtained and the 'best' chosen. Needless to say, there are difficulties with this approach in practice. The decision maker may not be certain what the relevant dimensions are, and the attribute weightings and scorings may suffer from unreliability over time.

MAUT is one possible model for how decisions might be made between complex alternatives. Some alternative possible strategies will now be outlined and then we will review relevant empirical studies to see which seem most useful.

Elimination by Aspects

> **Elimination by aspects (EBA)**
> a decision procedure for multi-attribute choices that considers attributes of alternatives in order of importance, eliminating alternatives that do not meet a minimum value on each attribute as the process continues.

A less demanding procedure than MAUT was described by Tversky (1972) as a possible strategy that individuals might use in order to reduce cognitive effort or processing load. This procedure is known as **elimination by aspects (EBA)**. In an EBA process, the chooser would first select an attribute and eliminate all options that did not meet some criterion level on that attribute. In the example of house purchasing, for instance, 'price' is usually a critical attribute. The chooser will often have determined a ceiling price and so all houses over that ceiling price could be eliminated from consideration (irrespective of their other desirable qualities). Then, 'distance from work' might be taken as the next important consideration and all houses more than a certain journey time from work could be eliminated. If the chooser continues in this way to eliminate alternatives, sooner or later only one option will be left and so the decision will effectively be made. EBA is clearly a less demanding procedure than that proposed by MAUT. Very different choices can arise depending on the order in which aspects are used to eliminate alternatives. Tversky suggests that the importance or weighting of attributes will influence the order of elimination.

Satisficing

> **Satisficing**
> a decision procedure for multi-attribute choices that sets minimum acceptable levels for each attribute and selects the first alternative that meets or satisfies those requirements.

A further simplifying technique that might be used in decision making, known as '**satisficing**', has been described by Simon (1956, 1978). The fundamental idea is that rather than expend time and effort in a bid to maximize utility, people are generally content to set a minimum acceptable level which will satisfy them but be short of the maximum. This may apply especially in the case of sequential decisions. For example, in buying a house, houses come on to the market continually and it would be difficult to establish that a given house was actually the optimum choice, since a better one might appear the next day. Thus, buyers may set acceptable levels, either for a total utility or on key aspects of the properties, and choose the first property that meets all their minimum requirements. Should the initial minimum requirements prove too ambitious, Simon (1978) suggests that the satisficing level is gradually adjusted in the light of the average values present in the market, so that the decision maker may become more realistic about his or her criteria in the light of experience.

Testing Multi-Attribute Decision Models

In order to determine which (if any) of the main models for multi-attribute decisions are reasonably descriptive of behaviour one needs to be able to infer how people process information during decision making. Payne (1976) pioneered a technique that has proven useful in the study of choice processes. In Payne's study, participants were presented with information, on cards, about aspects of a number of properties. Each card was face down and gave information about one aspect of one property (e.g., House B is in the suburbs). The cards were arranged in a property × attribute array so that participants could easily either obtain information property by property (i.e., examine all the attributes of Property A then all the attributes of Property B, and so on) or obtain information attribute by attribute (e.g., check properties first for 'number of rooms', then check for 'cost', and so on). Figure 13.5 shows an example display of the type Payne used as modified into a computerized version (Payne et al., 1993). Participants were free to examine the cards in any order they wished. Payne distinguished two classes of strategies. One class was labelled 'compensatory' and the other 'non-compensatory'. The MAUT approach, described above, is an example of a compensatory strategy in which an overall assessment is arrived at for each alternative by summing over all attribute values (a good rating on one attribute can compensate for a poor rating on another attribute). On this approach people would tend to scan all the attributes of a property before going on to the next property. EBA and satisficing are non-compensatory strategies and would lead to people going through each property in relation to a key attribute such as cost, before scanning properties for, say, location. On the basis of the information search patterns shown by his participants, Payne reported a variety of different compensatory and non-compensatory strategies. Interestingly, decision makers often used both within the same task, for example by using non-compensatory strategies to reduce the number of choices to a small number and then using a compensatory strategy to make the final choice. Payne also observed that non-compensatory strategies increased in frequency as task complexity was increased by manipulating the number of alternative apartments and the number of attributes per alternative.

Time pressure has also been found to shift preferred decision strategies. For example, Zakay (1985) reported that use of **lexicographic strategies** increased with time pressure. Payne et al. (1988) found that processing accelerated, focused on a narrower subset of information and became more attribute based (i.e., more non-compensatory) under severe time pressure.

> **Lexicographic strategies**
> a class of decision procedures that consider attributes in a fixed order – e.g., elimination by aspects (EBA).

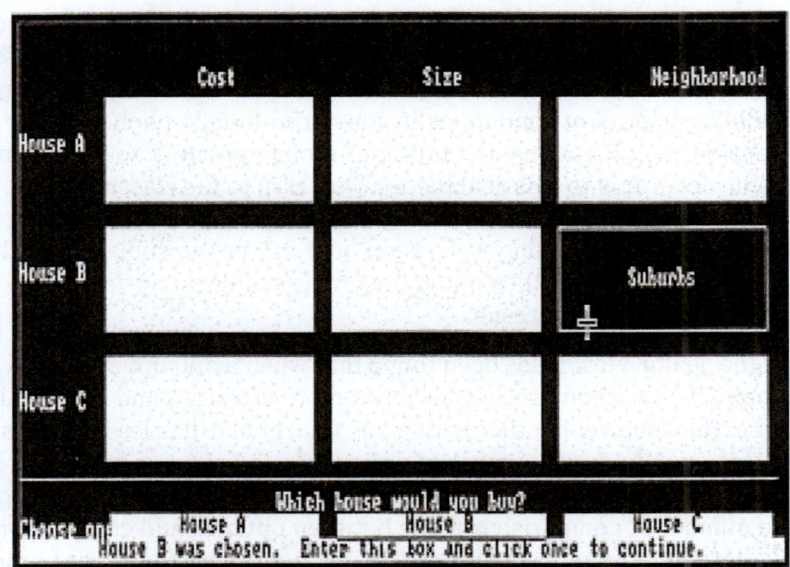

Figure 13.5 Information board of the type used by Payne (1976).
Participant chooses a card to reveal information about the property's standing on the attribute of interest. In this case, that House B is in the suburbs.
Source: Payne (1976).

In a related study, Fasolo et al. (2005) examined the effects of conflicts among the attributes of the alternatives on choice strategies. They pointed out that difficult decisions arise when alternatives that are attractive on one aspect (say, price) are less attractive on another (say, convenience), and vice versa. Participants were asked to recommend a digital camera to a friend, making a selection from five models described according to eight features (zoom, resolution, image capacity, and so on). Information about alternatives was displayed on a board, similar to the kind used by Payne et al. (1988), containing an 8 × 5 grid of boxes where the rows were attributes and the columns cameras. Fasolo et al. (2005) varied the amount of conflict among attributes and found that when conflict was high participants tended to use compensatory strategies (getting an overall evaluation of each alternative) before choosing, and when conflict was low participants preferred a non-compensatory strategy (e.g., eliminating all alternatives above a certain price) to simplify the problem. The results indicate that when choices are difficult people adopt a more demanding strategy to help ensure a good decision; with easier tasks less effortful strategies are seen to suffice and tend to be used.

Overall, then, studies indicate that no single decision strategy is always used in choosing between multi-attribute alternatives. Rather, it seems strategies are adopted that tend to compromise between minimizing cognitive load and maximizing the utility of the outcome chosen. Generally, cognitive load in decision making could be minimized by simply choosing at random but the resulting decisions would tend to be very poor. Quality of decision making would be maximized by assessing all alternatives on all relevant dimensions, integrating the resulting information for all alternatives and selecting the best, but the information processing required would be very demanding. Participants generally compromise between effort and quality of decisions and may change method during a task; for example, in Payne's (1976) study people used simple (non-compensatory) techniques to reduce the number of choices and then analysed the remaining few options more exhaustively using compensatory methods such as MAUT.

'Leaky' rationality

In classical expected utility theory, *how* decisions are arrived at was not regarded as having an impact on the utility of the chosen options. So whether an option was chosen following a thorough analysis of all the alternatives or by random choice should not affect the subjective value of the chosen option. For example, if you chose mobile phone X at random or if you chose mobile phone X after carefully considering all options, the utility of mobile phone X to you should be the same according to classical theory. Contrary to the classical view, Keys and Schwartz (2007), with their notion of **'leaky' rationality**, have argued that the process of reaching a decision *does* affect the subjective value of the chosen option or, as they put it, the process of deciding '*leaks*' into the experienced utility of the result.

> **'Leaky' rationality**
> the view that the process of deciding on a chosen option can affect the utility or satisfaction that the decision maker obtains from the chosen option.

In support of the 'leaky' view it has been found that when many options are available to choose amongst, the decision process becomes more effortful, and leads to less satisfaction with the final choice. In other words, the final choice has less utility (subjective value) when it is one of a large number of options. As the number of options increases beyond a low level, satisfaction with the final choice declines. Adding options increases the number of comparisons made between options, and comparisons tend to make every alternative seem worse as loss aversion gives more weight to the ways in which options are worse than the alternatives (Schwartz, 2004).

Consistent with the 'leaky' view, people who tend to adopt a 'maximizing' approach to real-life decision making, by considering many alternatives at choice points (e.g., when choosing a new phone, they would consider all mobile phone packages available to them) tend to be less satisfied with their final choices than 'satisficers', who settle for a good enough option when one is encountered (Schwartz, 2004). A questionnaire measure of maximizing tendencies is available and has good reported reliability and validity (Nenkov et al., 2008). Typical items are 'When I watch TV I channel surf, often scanning through the available options, even when attempting to watch one program'; 'I never settle for second best'; 'I often find it difficult to shop for a gift for a friend'.

Even when maximizing does produce objectively better decisions, 'maximizers' may well be less satisfied, and experience less utility, than 'satisficers' (Schwarz et al., 2002). In a related study, Iyengar et al. (2006) found that graduates looking for jobs who maximized did obtain jobs with higher starting salaries than did 'satisficers', but were less satisfied, both with the job obtained and the process of deciding, than were the 'satisficers'.

If it is rational to seek to maximize experienced utility or satisfaction, then as Keys and Schwartz (2007) suggest, satisficing can be a rational strategy, as it can lead to more overall satisfaction, even if the outcomes are less objectively valuable than those reached by maximizing.

Naturalistic choices?

The studies discussed so far on multi-attribute choices have used rather artificial presentations of the options in terms of experimenter-set dimensions and values. So, in an apartment choosing task, the options are described in terms of values on attributes such as number of rooms, monthly rent and distance from work. However, it can be argued that results from such artificial presentation methods may not generalize to real-world natural situations (Frederick et al., 2014).

Bhatia and Stewart (2018) examined choices of naturally presented familiar objects such as movies and food items. In the study participants, chose between pairs of movies such as *Star Wars* or *Toy Story*, drawn from a set of 100 movies, as possible movies to watch.

To assess different choice models such as MAUT or simpler alternatives, Bhatia and Stewart (2018) used novel computational techniques to identify underlying dimensions for the objects. These methods draw out underlying dimensions from frequencies of words used in texts about the class of objects. For example an 'Adult' dimension emerged for movies so that movies high on 'Adult' would have textual entries featuring words like 'murder', 'nudity', 'blood', 'violence', 'sex', 'death'. Another main dimension one might label 'Action', and would be high on mentions of 'martial arts', 'fist fight', 'shoot-out'. The method yielded a large number of dimensions, all of which could be used by the various models tested in this study. The fit of a range of choice models to the participants' data was assessed. The best-performing model (fit = 78 per cent accuracy) was a model similar to MAUT, and the poorest (fit = 55 per cent) was a model similar to satisficing (but it may be noted that both were better than random level of fit, 50 per cent). Similar results were found with a related study of food choices. Overall, this work suggests that naturalistic decision making between familiar items does involve effects of many dimensions in combination as against simpler heuristics often found in more artificial non-naturalistic decision making.

TWO-SYSTEM APPROACHES TO DECISION MAKING

Intuitively, you will probably feel that some of your decisions are made almost immediately, with little or no conscious work, while other decisions are reached only after extensive thought. Deciding between complex alternatives, such as job offers say, by using MAUT surely involves extensive conscious work, whereas decisions about less weighty matters, such as choices between posters for a bedroom wall, seem less effortful and more intuitive. Can psychology cast any light on these very different modes of decision making?

Two-system
the view that there are two modes of thought, System 1 and System 2.
System 1
a hypothetical system that carries out rapid intuitive thinking.
System 2
a hypothetical system that carries out slow, deliberate thinking.

The differences between the intuitive and more reflective forms of decision making have been highlighted recently in what are known as **two-system** approaches to thinking and decision making – for example, Evans (2003, 2008), Kahneman (2003), Sloman (1996), Stanovich and West (2000) and others. In these accounts two distinct cognitive systems are proposed. **System 1** is seen as automatic, implicit, fast, effortless and emotional, and as generating intuitive, immediate responses. This system is assumed to be relatively old in evolutionary terms and is very similar between humans and other animals. Only the final product of such processes is available to consciousness – that is, the person cannot explain why they made their decision. **System 2**, on the other hand, is seen as evolutionarily recent and is specific to humans. It permits abstract reasoning and hypothetical thinking, operates relatively slowly and sequentially, is unemotional, is limited by working memory capacity, and is highly correlated with general fluid intelligence and with performance on sequentially solvable problems. People can explain the bases of such decisions. The two systems are seen as interacting, and an important role for System 2 is to inhibit and override System 1 when appropriate – for example, when the costs of errors are high an immediate gut reaction probably is not a wise basis for action and should be checked. In the other direction, automatic System 1 processes markedly influence what information the person attends to and focuses on, and so what information System 2 works with (Evans, 2008) in reaching a decision.

In decision making both intuitive System 1 and reflective System 2 routes are possible. Overall, System 2 will be more involved in careful analytical decision making that seeks to combine many types of information in a rule-governed procedure. Normative procedures such as proposed by MAUT would be expected to require System 2 processing. System 1 will be more involved in decision making based on heuristics and biases (Tversky & Kahneman, 1974) and on 'gut feelings' (Gigerenzer, 2007).

Box 13.2 Practical Application: Two system theory and 'nudge'

As we have discussed, many of our decisions can be explained in terms of the operation of a fast automatic system (System 1) that comes to rapid conclusions by the low-effort use of heuristics and biases. To make slower, considered decisions that require cognitive load and effort, we draw on System 2 (Kahneman, 2011).

A practical application of the dual-system approach to understanding human decision making has been developed in the 'nudge' approach to influencing people's decisions about important real-world issues and consumer choices (Sunstein, 2015; Thaler & Sunstein, 2008).

In the area of public policy, such as increasing donation rates of bodily organs such as hearts, lungs, kidneys and so on, Thaler and Sunstein proposed that, rather than legal compulsion, people be offered a choice, but the choice be structured in such a way as to maximize the rate of choices desired by policy makers. This general approach of seeking public agreement to policy options is often referred to as *liberal paternalism*. People are free to not agree with the preferred policy (so, it is liberal), but the choice is presented in a way that inclines, or 'nudges', people to accept the policy makers' preferred option (which experts believe is best for the greater good, so it is a paternalistic approach). We may note that the way a choice is structured is sometimes referred to as the *choice architecture.*

How well policy goals regarding organ donation are achieved in different countries provides a good example of the role of choice architecture. In many countries when people apply for a driving licence they indicate whether they agree to donate their bodily organs should they die in an accident. Johnson and Goldstein (2003) noted that the rates of agreement for organ donation varied hugely between neighbouring and culturally similar European countries, and was 100 per cent in Austria but only 12 per cent in Germany, 86 per cent in Sweden but only 4 per cent in Denmark. These large differences were explained easily by differences in the choice architectures. In the high-donation countries the decision was indicated by ticking an opt-out box, but in the low-donor countries the decision was indicated by ticking an opt-in box. By doing nothing (omission bias) people were agreeing to donate in Austria and Sweden and not agreeing to donate in Germany and Denmark! The lesson for policy makers is to set the desired option as the default option, which holds if the respondent does nothing. As it is much easier to do nothing, System 1 prefers the default and the default will be the typical choice. You may have noticed that commercial organizations often use this feature of human decision making and include you on their emailing list unless you specifically opt out. Another example is Pichert and Katsikopoulos's (2008) finding that choice of a renewable energy option for electricity was much higher when it was the default choice.

The default approach has also been applied to pension policy in the UK. In order to increase low pension saving rates among private-sector workers the government introduced an automatic enrolment scheme in 2012, making pension saving the default for employees. As a result membership of private pension schemes increased markedly, from 2.7 million in 2012 to 7.7 million in 2016 (Chu, 2017).

Thaler and Benartzi (2004) developed a similar scheme in the USA called the 'Save more tomorrow' programme, which also involved use of a default sign-up but with an added feature of starting with very small contributions (overcoming loss aversion) and the contributions increasing (automatically, by default) only when wages increase. This has led to a very large take-up of private pension schemes.

Although when dealing with formal probability problems heuristics (such as availability) often lead to errors (as in the Linda problem), Gigerenzer (2007) has proposed that heuristics often have some validity in the real world. In a later section, we will look further at this idea that heuristics are adaptive and useful (and not just sources of error).

System 1 involvement would be expected if a decision task is set aside and not consciously addressed but the setting aside then leads to faster and better choices when the task is revisited. Intuitively, we probably all feel that setting a complex decision aside does help resolve the problem when it is revisited. In the next section we look at research on this topic.

Unconscious thought and decision making

In the previous chapter, on problem solving (Chapter 12), we saw that putting a problem aside (incubation) helped in reaching solutions. Does putting a decision problem aside similarly aid in decision-making problems? If so, why?

Chapter 12, p424

A key study on this issue was reported by Dijksterhuis et al. (2006). See Box 13.3 for more details.

> **Box 13.3 Research Close Up: Unconscious thought effect on decisions**

Source: Dijksterhuis et al. (2006).

INTRODUCTION

Putting problems aside is often helpful, as indicated by studies of incubation in problem solving, as discussed in Chapter 12, but does putting a decision problem aside similarly aid in decision making problems? If so, why?

A key study on this issue was reported by Dijksterhuis et al. (2006).

METHODS

This study involved participants choosing between fictional cars. Participants read information about four hypothetical cars. Each car was either described by four attributes (simple condition), or by twelve attributes (complex). Example attributes were mileage per gallon of fuel, boot size, servicing frequency, number of cupholders, colour choice, and so on. The attributes could have either positive or negative values. One of the four cars available was characterized by 75 per cent positive attributes, two had 50 per cent positive attributes and one had 25 per cent positive attributes.

The attributes were presented one by one in random order on a computer screen, with each attribute presented for eight seconds.

After seeing the information about the four cars, participants in the Conscious Thought condition were asked to think about the cars carefully for four minutes. During the thinking time the information about the cars was not available externally. After the thinking period, they chose the car they thought was best.

In the Immediate Incubation condition, after seeing the information about the four cars, participants were distracted for four minutes and were told that after the period of distraction they would be asked what the best car was. During the distraction period, participants solved anagrams.

> **Unconscious Thought Effect (UTE)**
> the beneficial effect on decision making of setting the decision aside immediately after the choice information is presented.

RESULTS

The results showed an interaction, $F(1,76) = 4.85$, $p < .04$), such that Immediate Incubation was beneficial for the more complex twelve-aspect choice but not for the simpler four-aspect choice problem.

DISCUSSION

The authors proposed that the Immediate Incubation condition involved unconscious thought and so labelled the result the **Unconscious Thought Effect** (UTE).

The UTE in decision making quickly proved both influential and controversial, with numerous non-replications but also replications of the basic effect among some 1,557 citations to the original paper in Google Scholar by early 2020.

The results showed an interaction such that Immediate Incubation was beneficial for the more complex choices but not for the simpler choice problems.

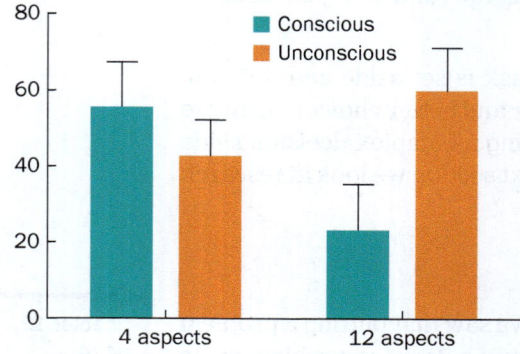

Figure 13.6 Percentage of participants who chose the most desirable car as a function of complexity of decision and presumed mode of thought ($n = 18$ to 22 in each condition).

Source: Dijksterhuis et al. (2006).

Following Dijksterhuis et al. (2006) further studies of the UTE in decision making reported both replications and non-replications of the basic effect and so, to clarify the overall picture, Strick et al. (2011) carried out a meta-analysis of 92 studies of UTE in decision making. This indicated a significant overall effect size ($g = .224, p < .01$) supporting a benefit for immediate incubation versus a conscious thought period. As well as an overall effect, Strick et al. (2011) identified certain conditions (moderators) that tended to lead to stronger or weaker effects. The moderator effects favouring UTE were task complexity (e.g., more attributes), more options, short presentation times and less demanding distraction tasks. All these conditions led to stronger UTE effects.

Alternative explanations for the apparent UTE have been suggested (e.g., Newell & Shanks, 2014). Could it be that decisions are actually made online as the information about alternatives is being presented and that UTE reflects an *impairing* effect of *further conscious thought* after presentation, rather than a benefit of unconscious thought?

Strick et al. (2011) examined the possible impairing effect of the conscious thought period in their meta-analysis and found a beneficial effect for Immediate Incubation vs. Immediate Deciding ($g = .272, p < .01$). This result goes against the idea of online deciding coupled with an impairing effect of conscious thought as an explanation for the UTE. Overall, the results seem consistent with the unconscious thought theory in that the UTE is more likely to appear when the task is too complex, and the time available is too short for conscious thought to work effectively.

FAST-AND-FRUGAL HEURISTICS: THE ADAPTIVE TOOLBOX

As we have seen, a number of heuristic methods have been proposed as ways of simplifying decision making, and a number of studies have supported the descriptive value of heuristics such as satisficing, EBA and so on. Gigerenzer and colleagues (Gigerenzer, 2007; Gigerenzer et al., 1999; Hoffrage et al., 2018) have developed the idea that as well as saving cognitive effort, many simple heuristics have considerable real-world validity and can do as well or even better than more complex methods that take into account more information. Gigerenzer and colleagues refer to these heuristics as fast and frugal, as they are simple and fast to execute as they require little effort; thus their use would involve System 1 rather than System 2. Together, Gigerenzer and colleagues argue that the heuristics form an 'adaptive toolbox' as the heuristics are generally valid for the real-life situations in which they have developed.

In an example study of fast-and-frugal heuristics, Goldstein and Gigerenzer (2002) asked American and German students, 'Which city has the larger population, Detroit or Milwaukee?' Although the German students had far less knowledge of American geography than the American students, they were nearly 100 per cent correct (Detroit) but the American students scored only 60 per cent correct. The German students used the *recognition heuristic* in which the option recognized is chosen as having the target attribute (largest). Many German students had not heard of Milwaukee and so only recognized Detroit, while all the American students recognized both and so could not apply the recognition heuristic as it would not distinguish between the two options for them. Ayton et al. (2011) found the same advantages of the recognition heuristic in a study comparing predictions by English and Turkish students of the outcomes of English Football Association matches in which famous football teams often play against less well-known teams (e.g., Manchester United vs. Shrewsbury Town). The Turkish students outperformed the English students by using the recognition heuristic.

Again, Ortmann et al. (2008) found that selections of stocks and shares by laypeople which were based on whether a company was recognized or not, outperformed selections made by financial experts. Thus, the recognition heuristic is often a good way to make decisions where recognizability is correlated with the criterion attribute for the groups of people being tested. Too much knowledge of the domain can make the heuristic unworkable. So knowledge of some US cities, some companies and some English football teams enables the recognition heuristic to be effective in the studies just outlined since larger cities, more successful companies and richer (more successful) football teams will be better known worldwide.

Gigerenzer and colleagues have also identified simple decision trees (fast-and-frugal trees) in areas such as medicine and law where one might expect a great deal of information to be integrated in reaching treatment or sentencing decisions. Only a few key attributes are considered in a priority order so that if the first attribute has the critical value a decision is made, otherwise the next most important value is considered. For example, around 19 medical measurements could be used to measure severity of a suspected heart attack. However, Breiman et al. (1993) found that very effective decisions can be made using just three cues, in order of priority (blood pressure >91, age >62.5, sinus tachycardia present). Smith and Gilhooly (2006) found similar use of fast-and-frugal decision trees by general practitioners making decisions about whether or not to prescribe antidepressants (see the decision tree for antidepressant prescription in Figure 13.7). More recently, Van Rooij et al. (2015) found that a four-question tree matched medical practice and was found useful by physicians in prescribing for pain medication when a choice was needed among morphine, codeine and non-prescription drugs. Woike et al. (2017) found further evidence supporting the utility of fast-and-frugal decision trees in a study covering 11 different medical datasets including alcoholism, diabetes, hepatitis and breast cancer. Fast-and-frugal trees using a few cues averaged around 75 per cent accuracy, which compared very well with a full Bayesian model using all available cue information (around 73 per cent average accuracy).

In the judicial area, Dhami and Ayton (2001; Dhami, 2003; Dhami & Belton, 2011) found that magistrates in the English court system very clearly tended to make decisions about whether to grant defendants bail or not on the basis of a small decision tree involving again just three cues, which were checked in priority order (Did prosecution oppose bail? Had a previous court opposed bail? Did the police hold the accused in custody?). If any of these cues were positive, bail was refused.

On the other side of the judicial process, Snook et al. (2011) found that burglars made decisions as to whether a target property was unoccupied (and so a target) or occupied, by using small fast-and-frugal trees, typically with two cues (e.g., Is there a vehicle parked outside? Are curtains closed at ground level?).

Evaluation

Overall, the heuristics identified and explored by Gigerenzer and colleagues generally work well because the bases of the decisions reflect some underlying reality in the environment which permits effective shortcut solutions. The use of shortcut, rules-of-thumb heuristics are experienced as intuitions or 'gut feelings' and can be assigned to the operations of System 1. The main difference between Gigerenzer's approach and that of

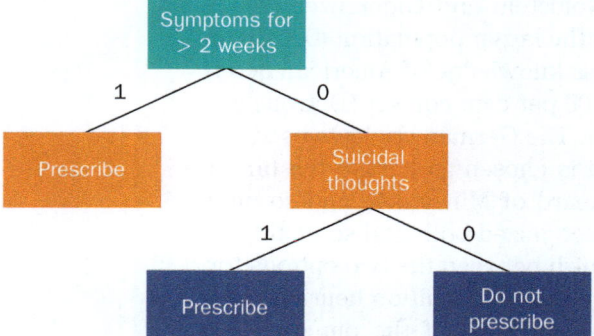

Figure 13.7 Example of a two-cue fast-and-frugal tree for prescribing antidepressants: 1 = Yes, 0 = No.
Source: Smith & Gilhooly (2006).

Kahneman and Tversky's heuristics-and-biases approach is that Gigerenzer stresses the validity and adaptive value of real-life heuristics while Kahneman and Tversky were more inclined to point out the errors that heuristics (such as availability) can lead to. As a broad generalization, heuristics seem to be most useful when dealing with common situations but tend to mislead when dealing with abstract problems that are best dealt with by explicit calculations following logical and mathematical rules.

Heuristics and Consequentialism

So far, we have largely been assuming that decisions are made on the basis of the *consequences* expected to follow from each of the choices available, a view known as **consequentialism**.

A prominent version of consequentialism in the history of ideas is the **utilitarianism** approach developed initially by the eighteenth-century British thinker Jeremy Bentham (Figure 13.8; Bentham, 1789; Liberal Democrat History Group, 2019). On the utilitarianism approach, decisions should be made so that the consequences of the decision maximize the happiness (or utility) of the decision maker. As Bentham (1789) put it in the first sentence of his Introduction to *The Principles of Morals and Legislation*, 'Nature has placed mankind under the governance of two sovereign masters, pain and pleasure. It is for them alone to point out what we ought to do . . .'. To decide between courses of action (including inaction) Bentham proposed a "felicific calculus" or "**hedonic calculus**" by which, for each possible action, people should add up the pleasures on one side and the pains on the other side, to decide which action would be most beneficial, the most beneficial action being the one that has the greatest excess of pleasure over pain. This hedonic calculus approach can be seen as an antecedent of multi-attribute utility theory in seeking an overall assessment of options that mix attractive and unattractive features or consequences. When a social or political policy decision affecting many people is needed, Bentham advocated seeking the option that contributes to 'the greatest happiness of the greatest number'.

In contrast to Bentham's utilitarianism is the view that decisions affecting others (i.e., moral or ethical decisions) should be based on principles or enduring rules of conduct, encompassing rights and obligations, irrespective of consequences. This is the **deontological approach** (from the Greek, *deon* = duty and *logos* = science or study) and would include prohibitions on killing humans no matter what the hedonic benefits that might result for others. Other possible deontological rules would be to avoid any harm to fellow humans ('Torture is always wrong, no matter what') or, more broadly, to other sentient creatures ('Killing animals to eat or use in other ways is always wrong'). The Ten Commandments of the Old Testament may also be seen as example deontological rules, in which consequences are not taken into account.

Consequentialist utilitarianism and deontological theories could be seen as essentially normative (i.e., proposing ways to make good decisions). From the psychological point of view we can

Consequentialism
the view that decisions between options are based on the expected results or consequences of selecting each option.

Utilitarianism
a theory of choice whereby choosers act so as to maximize their happiness or utility.

Hedonic calculus
a utilitarian proposal that an option be assessed in terms of the overall balance of pleasure as against pain that would result from choosing that option. The option having the greatest excess of pleasure over pain should be chosen on this view.

Deontological approach
the view that decisions affecting others (i.e., moral or ethical decisions) should be based on principles irrespective of consequences.

Figure 13.8 Jeremy Bentham – auto-icon.
On his death in 1832 at age 84, following instructions in his will, his skeleton and mummified head were dressed in his habitual clothes and hat and positioned in a case for viewing. Bentham saw this use of the actual body as an 'auto-icon' after death to be a good use for bodies. The head is now a wax replica but the auto-icon is still on public view at University College London.

Source: © World History Archive/Alamy Stock Photo

ask whether either has descriptive validity or could be modified to be more descriptive in the same way as normative expected value theory was modified into the more descriptive subjective expected utility theory or into prospect theory. Instances of non-consequentialist, deontological decision making can often be found in the areas of moral decision making, as we will see shortly. Baron (1994) suggested that simple deontological rules function as heuristics, which often do work well (i.e., match consequentialist recommendations) but fail in certain circumstances. Some example deontological heuristics would be: 'Do no harm', 'Avoid unfairness', 'Don't breach people's rights'. Such heuristics can be seen as further examples of fast-and-frugal heuristics of the type identified by Gigerenzer and colleagues that simplify decision making. So, if one simply applied a rule that "Stealing is always wrong", then an answer could be given immediately ("No") to the question of whether a starving person should steal food from a profitable supermarket if the only alternative was to die of hunger. Here, it is likely that most people would want to take account of the consequences. In other cases, such as the rules "Torture is always wrong" and "Capital punishment is always wrong", a consequentialist approach seems less likely to be universally accepted – especially probably in the case of capital punishment. In the following sections we will discuss research on when consequentialist and deontological approaches tend to be followed in behavioural tests.

Omission bias

Ritov and Baron (1990) asked people to make decisions about vaccinations, where omission (not giving vaccine) and commission (giving vaccine) were options. In one study, people were to imagine that their child had 10 chances in 10,000 of dying from flu in an epidemic if the child was not vaccinated. The vaccine would prevent flu but would itself kill a certain number of children. Participants were asked to state the maximum death rate due to the vaccine at which they would still give their child the vaccine. From the consequentialist point of view, a rate of vaccine-caused deaths up to 9 out of 10,000 should be acceptable as it is an improvement over the unvaccinated rate of 10 out of 10,000. The mean acceptable risk reported was considerably lower at 5 deaths per 10,000. People tended to state that they would feel more responsible for deaths caused by their action (of vaccinating) than by their omission (not vaccinating). This pattern of judging harms from *omissions* (inactions) as less serious or culpable than the same harms from *commisions* (actions) is known as **omission bias**.

> **Omission bias**
> the tendency to judge harms resulting from inactions (omissions) as less harmful or culpable than the same harms resulting from actions (commissions).

Very similar results arose from a study of 142 parents in the United Kingdom (Brown et al., 2010) in 2009 when there was an imminent epidemic of "swine flu" (official name: 2009 H1N1 influenza A). Despite the risks of this particular flu epidemic, around 50 per cent of parents planned to reject a vaccine against it. In this study it was found that the sample of parents of young children judged the same adverse outcomes (e.g., loss of appetite, fever, and so on) as less serious when due to a hypothetical disease as against when due to a vaccination. This tendency to regard possible adverse outcomes as less serious and so more acceptable when due to a disease than to vaccination was significant at $p < .01$ for 17 out of 22 possible adverse outcomes. These results suggest that any vaccine is at a disadvantage in many parents' beliefs, compared with the infection itself, and that minor adverse possibilities have a large negative effect on vaccine uptake. Brown et al.'s study indicated a marked level of omission bias that could underlie low levels of vaccine uptake generally – only around 20 per cent of high-risk individuals took up the "swine flu" vaccine. Similarly, whooping cough vaccinations fell to around 30 per cent in the UK in 1975 due to fears over unlikely adverse effects of vaccination despite the severity of the actual highly likely effects of the disease (Kardas-Nelson, 2019).

Other studies, outside the disease domain, have also found a tendency to judge consequences less bad when they are due to omissions rather than commissions. For example, Spranca et al. (1991) gave people scenarios in which one tennis player knowingly allows his rival to eat an allergy-producing substance before a match (omitting to warn him) or deliberately causes the rival to eat the allergen (commission). In terms of consequences, the omission and commission have the same effect, yet people tend to judge the commission worse.

Overall, there seems to be a bias to downplaying the negative consequences of omissions as against commissions that have the same effects. Allowing bad things to happen through inaction is seen as less wrong than causing such things to happen through one's own actions (and so breaching a "Do no harm" deontological rule.)

Punishment

From the consequentialist point of view, punishment of actions is valuable only if it has a deterrent effect and prevents the undesired acts being repeated by the perpetrator or others. However, it seems that many people feel that retribution, rather than deterrence, is the main function of punishment, and endorse punishment irrespective of the consequences of punishment. For example, Baron and Ritov (1993) had people assess penalties for makers of vaccines and birth control pills that had caused harm. In one scenario, participants were told that a high penalty would make the company try harder to make a safer product. In a contrasting case, people were told that a high penalty would make the company stop making the drug, leaving only more dangerous products on the market. Most participants, including a group of judges, gave the same high penalties in both cases, despite the very different consequences of the high penalties in the two situations. These results suggest a bias towards retribution in making decisions about punishment, following the deontological rule of retributive justice (Walen, 2016) that wrongful acts should be punished, even if punishing them would produce no other good over not punishing.

Resistance to coerced reform

Although people will often endorse certain reforms as having desirable consequences for society, or even the planet, the same people will often say that they would not vote for the consequentially desirable reforms. For example, most of Baron and Jurney's (1993) participants in the USA agreed that a 100 per cent tax on gasoline (petrol in the UK) would be a good measure on the whole (to reduce global warming) yet many of the same people would not vote for such a tax. The main reasons given for this inconsistency were (1) that the tax would be unfair and harm some more than others, (2) that harm would be caused to some and (3) that the tax would impair the right of people to choose for themselves.

In a more recent study, Huber et al. (2019) examined public attitudes in a sample of 2,034 Swiss citizens towards seven possible policies aimed at increasing the use of electric vehicles to reduce emissions from fossil-fuelled vehicles. Although the respondents viewed road pricing (i.e., charging per mile driven) as the most effective policy (i.e., the best consequentially) it was deemed unacceptable because it violated deontological norms of fairness and in the degree of coercion involved. See Box 13.4 for more details.

> **Box 13.4 Practical Application: Resisting effective but forced policies**
>
> *Source:* Huber et al. (2019).
>
> Huber and colleagues examined public attitudes in a sample of 2,034 Swiss citizens towards seven possible policies aimed at reducing emissions from fossil-fuelled vehicles by encouraging use of electric vehicles and so contributing to the reduction of global warming caused by vehicle emissions.
>
> Seven possible policies that should reduce total emissions were identified. These were:
>
> 1. Car taxes – to promote switching to electric cars
> 2. Financial purchase incentives – a price subsidy to promote switching to electric cars
> 3. Banning fossil-fuelled cars
> 4. Parking regulations – extra parking spaces for electric cars and reduced parking spaces for fossil-fuelled cars
> 5. Information campaigns on the benefits of electric cars and disadvantages of fossil-fuelled cars
> 6. Road pricing – charges for mileage driven with lower charges for electric cars
> 7. Energy labels – clearer labelling of cars as high- or low-emission vehicles.
>
> Policies were rated on perceived *effectiveness* (how capable a policy was believed to be of reaching its goal), perceived *intrusiveness* (degree of coercion the policy would involve) and perceived *fairness* (how fair the policy is seen to be for all groups in society). By presenting choice between policies, a measure of the *acceptability* of each policy was obtained.
>
> Although the respondents viewed road pricing (i.e., charging per mile driven with lower rates for electric vehicles) as the most effective policy (i.e., the *best consequentially*) it was found to be *less acceptable*, presumably because it was judged *less fair* and *more intrusive*, than favoured policies, such as subsidies for low-emission vehicles.
>
> Overall, the perceived best policy consequentially was not preferred, because it violated deontological norms regarding fairness and degree of coercion.

Similar results were found when the proposed reforms involved many other issues, such as abolition of television advertising during political campaigns, compulsory vaccination for a dangerous flu virus, compulsory treatment for a highly contagious disease and elimination of lawsuits against obstetricians. In all cases, consequentialism was breached as a result of the application of deontologically based, simple heuristic rules (Baron & Jurney, 1993).

Sacrifice dilemmas: utilitarianism vs. deontological rules

> **Sacrifice dilemmas**
> problems in which decisions are required about whether to cause the deaths of one or more people to save the lives of a greater number of people.

The starkest contrast between the prescriptions and predictions of consequentialist utilitarianism and deontological approaches based on moral rules, is found in the study of **sacrifice dilemmas**. In such problems people have to decide whether an individual person should be killed to save the lives of others. Three main forms of sacrifice dilemma have received considerable research attention and these are: the Transplant Dilemma, the Trolley Problem and the related Footbridge Problem. We may note that these sacrifice dilemmas originated as 'thought experiments', devised by moral philosophers (Phillipa Foot and Judith Thomson) to illustrate problems in moral philosophy, such as whether an action intended to be beneficial (e.g., easing pain with morphine) can be permissible when it has foreseen but unintended harmful side effects, such as the death of the patient – an example of the *problem of double effect*.

In the Transplant Dilemma (Foot, 1967) doctors have to decide about sacrificing the life of a man by surgically removing a gland that secretes a unique hormone capable of counteracting a deadly new strain of smallpox and so saving thousands of lives. Aguilar et al. (2013) had participants respond to the Transplant Dilemma in conditions where the **psychological distance** of the participant from the decision was manipulated. Psychological distance in this case indicates how closely the person is involved in the act. So a witness to a murder is more distant from the act than the person who carries out a killing; a bureaucrat who orders a killing (e.g., an assassination for reasons of state security) is closer than a witness but further than the killer from the act. It is often suggested that greater distance makes a utilitarian approach more likely. In Aguilar et al.'s studies participants indicated how sure they would have to be that the extracted hormone would work before agreeing that killing the donor was justified. Distance was manipulated either by varying the time between decision and operation from 48 hours to two years or by inducing a *Concrete* or an *Abstract* (i.e., more distant) mindset by a prior writing task. In both cases, a more distant (*Abstract*) mindset led participants to agree the operation with a lower chance of success, indicating a greater readiness to follow a consequentialist or utilitarian approach.

> **Psychological distance**
> the subjective experience of how close or far something or someone is from the self in the here and now.

In the Trolley Problem (Foot, 1967) (Figure 13.9), participants have to decide whether to divert a runaway trolley (called a "tram" in Europe) on a railway line to save the lives of five people on the line who cannot escape from the trolley – but, by diverting the trolley onto a side track, another person will be hit and killed. The Footbridge Problem (Thomson, 1976) is a variant in which the participant has to decide whether to push a fat person off a footbridge, killing the fat person but thereby stopping a runaway trolley that otherwise will hit and kill five people. Intuitively, you probably find it easier to agree to divert the trolley as against pushing someone into its path. Between 2001 and 2014 some 65 empirical studies on the Trolley and Footbridge Problems were reported (Bauman et al., 2014). Reviews of a number of studies of these types of problems (Enoch, 2013; Hauser, 2006) indicated that about 90 per cent of participants say they would divert the trolley, but only 10 per cent would agree to push the fat person on to the track, even though, consequentially, both actions lead to the same result of five lives saved at the cost of one life lost. Greene et al. (2001) in the earliest reported experimental study, suggested that the Trolley Problem is less emotionally engaging as the killing is less personal and this facilitates a more calculating utilitarian approach. They label the Trolley Problem a moral-impersonal problem, as against the Footbridge Problem, which is labelled a moral-personal problem.

As with the Transplant Dilemma, it seems that psychological distance enables utilitarian approaches to the Footbridge Problem. For example, presenting the Footbridge Problem in a second, foreign language increased the rate of utilitarian decisions (Costa et al., 2014). It is hypothesized that foreign language triggers emotional distance, which in turn prompts deliberative processing typical of System 2 in dual process theories of cognition and so leads to utilitarian calculations as against the more emotionally based deontological responses.

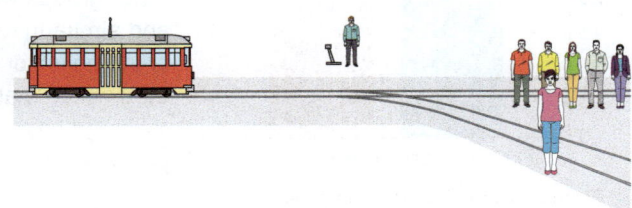

Figure 13.9 The Trolley Problem.
Unless the switch is thrown, the trolley (tram) will run over and kill five people. But if the switch is thrown, one person will die and five will be saved.

Sources: https://nymag.com/intelligencer/2016/08/trolley-problem-meme-tumblr-philosophy.html; Feldman (2016).

Box 13.5 Research Close Up: Your morals depend on language

Source: Costa et al. (2014).

INTRODUCTION

In deciding whether to sacrifice one life to save five, the answer should be independent of the language in which the issue is posed. However, there are grounds to suppose that presentation in a second, foreign language may boost the rate of utilitarian decisions to sacrifice one life for the sake of five. The authors of the study argued that material in a foreign language elicits less intense emotional reactions compared to native language presentations. Emotional factors seem to drive heuristic deontological decisions and so a less emotion-eliciting presentation should elicit more reasoned controlled thinking leading to utilitarian choices.

Figure 13.10 The Footbridge Problem.
Should you push the fat man to stop the runaway trolley (tram) before it kills the five people?

Source: Adapted from http://advocatusatheist.blogspot.com/2011/10/trolley-problem-thought.html.

METHOD

This study used the 'footbridge' version of the Trolley Problem. Participants imagine they are standing on a footbridge over a railway line. A small oncoming train is about to kill five people on the track and the only way to save them is to push a heavy man off the footbridge in front of the train. He will be killed but the other five will be saved.

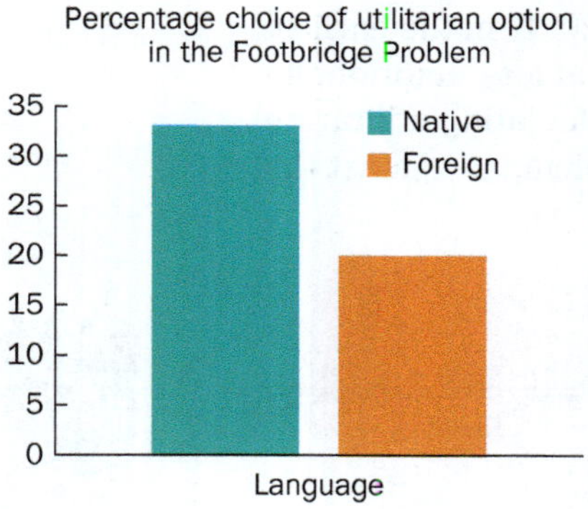

Three groups of English speakers received the problem either in English or in a second, foreign language (Spanish or French; other groups were native speakers of Korean, French or Spanish and similarly received the problem either in their native language or in English or Hebrew). In all cases participants indicate whether they would make the utilitarian choice or not.

Figure 13.11 Foreign language effect in the Footbridge Problem.
Choice of utilitarian option to sacrifice one life to save five is greater when the dilemma is presented in a language foreign to the participant.

Source: Graph based on Table 2 in Costa et al. (2014).

RESULTS

Across all groups ($N = 317$) more people chose the utilitarian option to kill one in order to save five when using a foreign language (33 per cent) than when using their native language (20 per cent).

This difference was statistically significant (Chi-square $(1,317) = 6.9$, $p < .01$, phi $= .15$).

> **DISCUSSION**
>
> The results support the hypothesis that the reduced emotional impact of a foreign language presentation inclines people to be less affected by any emotional aversion to pushing a man to his death and this allows them to make more utilitarian decisions.
>
> It should not matter to native English speakers who also know Spanish whether they are deciding about sacrificing 'the large man' or 'el hombre grande', but apparently it does!

An extensive review of 53 studies on sacrificial dilemmas, such as the Transplant Dilemma, and Trolley and Footbridge Problems, supported the role of System 2 involvement in utilitarian approaches. Klenk (2019) found that in situations promoting System 2 activation, such as abstract mode of thought, cognitive control, time delay in effects or psychological distance from the problem, there was an increased frequency of utilitarian judgements. Also, situations that would be expected to disrupt System 2, such as time pressure, stress and secondary task cognitive load, decreased utilitarian judgements. If emotion or affect was high, with System 1 presumably activated through situational factors such as emphasizing harm severity, there was a decrease in utilitarian judgements.

Overall, studies of the Trolley and Footbridge Problems indicate as Tremoliere et al. (2018) concluded, that deontic responses are intuitive, heuristic, System 1 responses, whereas the utilitarian responses are reflective of System 2 responses. This pattern is also supported, as we will see in a later section, by brain activation studies that link utilitarian decisions to brain areas implicated in System 2 processing.

NATURALISTIC DECISION MAKING

Although, as we have seen in earlier sections, there has been a long tradition of psychological research on decision making, this work has been dominated by carefully controlled artificial laboratory tasks in which specified alternatives are given to the participants to choose among. Such studies are aimed at testing general hypotheses about choosing or deciding, and are based on alternative theoretical approaches. This line of work was difficult to apply in settings such as aviation, military and emergency services, where important and often rapid decisions were required of personnel and typically the alternatives are not given but must be generated on the spot. A particular impetus to study real-life decision making directly came from the tragic incident in 1988 in which an Iranian airliner was mistakenly shot down by the US Navy ship, *Vincennes*. As Klein (2015) recounts, this terrible event led to a small conference in Ohio in 1989 involving a number of decision researchers to seek explanations for such events and to develop ways of improving training to prevent similar tragedies in future. A key step agreed at the conference was to directly investigate real-life expert decision making in time-pressured situations more extensively and intensively than had been done previously.

Following the 1989 Ohio conference, Klein (1998), Lipshitz et al. (2001), Phillips et al. (2004) and others (e.g., Schraagen, 2018) studied decision making by firemen, nurses, the police and military in real-life emergency settings. This work goes out of the laboratory settings typical of Kahneman and Tversky and even of Gigerenzer and his group, to analyse what happens in real situations. In such **naturalistic decision making** situations the decision maker may not be explicitly presented with options to decide amongst but rather has to generate

> **Naturalistic decision making**
> making real-life decisions in the field.

> **Critical incident analysis** gaining information about naturalistic decision making by analysing detailed recalls of recent important decisions.
>
> **Recognition primed decision making** expert knowledge-based decision making in which cues in the situation are recognized as indicating particular actions.

one or more possible actions. The method followed by Klein and his colleagues was that of **critical incident analysis** in which participants were asked to recall in as much detail as possible a recent case in which they had to make an important decision.

In a range of such enquiries it was found that **recognition primed decision making** was very common. For example, during a critical incident analysis a fire officer reported that recently he had been in a burning building and noticed a pattern of cracks developing in the walls (Klein, 1998). From the crack pattern he recognized that this was a situation of imminent collapse of the building and the associated decision of leaving the building as soon as possible came immediately to mind – and was acted on.

Typically, it was found that in many critical situations only a single action was mentally generated and it was then chosen to be executed. Klein et al., (2010) identified 156 decision points from interviews with fireground commanders and found that in 80 per cent of cases the commanders considered only *one* option. Generating two or more options for systematic evaluation was rare and if more than one option was considered the process stopped when the first satisfactory option was found – that is, a *satisficing* strategy was followed and if the first option was satisfactory (which was usually the case) the decision process terminated there and action was taken. The highly time pressured situation of dealing with fires did not permit effective generation and systematic evaluation of many options. As one officer said, 'Look, we don't have time for that kind of mental gymnastics out there. If you have to think about it, it's too late' (Klein et al., 2010, p. 578).

The basic finding that the initially produced possible actions by experts are often very appropriate has also been found in less time-pressured situations, and was replicated in a study of expert chess players (Klein et al., 1995). The players were asked to think aloud while deciding their moves to sample positions and it was found that the very first moves that came to mind were rated as high quality and much better than chance by independent expert judges. Although the first move generated was often good, Moxley et al., (2012) found that both experts and novice chess players benefited from extra deliberation in that moves chosen after deliberation were generally better than first generated moves. Nevertheless, experts did choose their first generated move as their final move some 50 per cent of the time, in line with recognition primed decision making.

Real-Life Choices

The relevance to real life of laboratory-based theories of decision making such as multi-attribute utility theory (MAUT) may seem questionable compared to the more field-based naturalistic decision making model. But are the decision processes typical in naturalistic decision making during emergency situations a better explanation of real life deciding when important choices must be made and people are acting *without extreme time pressures*?

In studies of real-life organizational decision making by *groups*, where time pressures were low, Nutt (1984) examined 78 decisions and found that the number of alternatives considered was typically very low. Active search for new options beyond the original set was rare (15 per cent of cases). In later studies of 400 decisions, Nutt (2005) found that only 30 per cent of decisions considered more than one alternative at all. The average number of alternatives considered was 1.8. Normative approaches to decision making would expect that the more alternatives considered, the better the final decision should be, and this was borne out in Nutt's (2005) study.

Results from five studies of real-life decision making in non-emergency situations, by *individuals*, were compared with laboratory and naturalistic decision making models by Galotti (2007). In these studies, participants reported on their experiences of tackling real-life decision problems covering areas such as choosing a college, choosing a major subject, choosing a birth attendant/helper and choosing a kindergarten. Participants consistently limited the amount of information they considered to relatively few options and to a somewhat larger set of criteria. Over time, the number of options considered shrank as the problem was pondered, but the number of criteria used did not. Participants gave subjective ratings for the importance of their criteria and for the value of each option on each criterion, and finally for the overall attractiveness of each option. Using these data, the fit of people's intuitive choices with the predictions of normative models (such as MAUT, using the subjective weights and values) was surprisingly good. In these non-expert decisions, without time pressure, people did indeed consider a number of options in contrast to the 'one-option' decisions often seen in time-pressured expert naturalistic decision making, which is generally based on recognition primed decision mechanisms (Klein, 1998).

Social Judgement Theory (SJT) and real-life choices

Social Judgement Theory (SJT) is an approach to analysing many real-life decisions and judgements as involving the combination of cues in the environment to reach an overall evaluation of alternatives. For example, in personnel selection, one might need to choose among a number of candidates for a salesperson job. Factors that might predict job performance could include extraversion/outgoingness, problem-solving skills (IQ), conscientiousness, openness to experience, age, gender, years of prior experience in similar jobs, strength of recommendations in reference letters, number of days sickness leave per year, numerical ability, and many others. SJT essentially treats decision makers or judges as being 'intuitive statisticians' who combine all the separate pieces of information in a way that can be modelled by a statistical regression equation. A regression equation takes the correlations between each cue and the outcome (job success – however measured) and finds that linear equation that best predicts the job success measure. So, in our example, it might turn out that only three factors or cues make significant contributions to the regression equation but it could predict well at, say, a correlation of .7 between predicted and obtained job success:

> **Social Judgement Theory (SJT)** an approach to modelling complex judgements as linear equations combining cue values to reach an overall judgement.

$$\text{Predicted job success} = .6 \times \text{IQ} + .2 \times \text{Extraversion} + .1 \times \text{Years' experience}$$

This approach derives from a perceptual theory developed in the 1940s and 1950s by Egon Brunswik, which was known as **probabilistic functionalism** (Brunswik, 1943, 1955). In Brunswik's approach, perceptual judgements, such as judgements about the distance of an object from an observer, result from combining cues correlated with actual distance, such as apparent size of object, clarity of the object image, the number of intervening objects, binocular disparity in retinal images of the object, and so on, to make a judgement of actual distance based on a linear combination of cue values. Brunswik's concepts were then developed by Hammond (1996, 2001) into Social Judgement Theory, which has subsequently been applied very widely in several hundred studies of real-life tasks (Dhami & Mumpower, 2018) in a wide range of domains such as medical decision making, personnel selection, judicial decision making, fraud detection, educational prediction, and so on.

> **Probabilistic functionalism** theory of perception (developed by Egon Brunswik) as involving the use of cues from the environment that can probabilistically predict some feature of the environment.

A meta-analysis by Kaufman et al. (2013) of 31 studies covering a range of domains (medicine, business, education, psychological assessments) found that the Social Judgment Theory model's predictions fitted responses well (correlation of actual and predicted responses = .85 over domains) and the average accuracy score of the participants was also high (correlation of responses with true values = .45 over domains).

These results are consistent with participants basing judgements of criteria values using linear combinations of cue values over a range of domain areas.

Although a large number of cues may be available to be *potentially* integrated in the judgement process, it is generally found that individual's patterns of judgements are fitted well by linear regressions with relatively few cues making a significant contribution to the overall judgement (Dhami, 2003). For example, Smith and Gilhooly (2006) found that medical practitioners' judgements about prescribing antidepressant drugs were well fitted by linear equations that used only three cues out of the eight cues presented per case to be judged.

Evaluation

Overall, it seems that many real-life 'decisions' by experts do not actually involve conscious decision making between alternatives. From Klein and colleagues' interviews, it seems that a heuristic identified by Gigerenzer (2007) as take-the-first-option can be, and is, usefully applied by experts in time-critical situations. The naturalistic decision making approach then strongly supports the use of fast-and-frugal heuristics, particularly those based on expert recognition, in real-life situations where immediate responses are required. Again, System 1 intuitive processes are strongly implicated in such time-pressured situations. However, when decisions are important but time pressure is low, people do tend to approximate to the more reflective, effortful decision processes indicated by MAUT, and these processes call on System 2.

Box 13.6 Practical Application: Applying Social Judgement Theory methods to the detection of financial abuse of elderly people

Source: Davies et al. (2013).

Elder financial abuse is defined as 'theft, fraud, exploitation, pressure in connection with wills, property or inheritance or financial transactions, or the misuse or misappropriation of property, possessions or benefits'. Research has shown that around 1 per cent of older people in the UK have experienced financial abuse by a close friend, relative or carer.

Given the access finance professionals have to customers' financial information, they play a key role in terms of identifying elder financial abuse at an early stage, thereby enabling action to be taken before money or assets are lost. Training to support the development of professional decision making in this domain of expertise needs to be underpinned by research in order for it to be evidence based.

This research aimed to identify which cues or factors had the greatest influence on decision making by finance professionals in cases of elder financial abuse.

Applying the methods of Social Judgement Theory, banking and finance professionals were shown a series of elder financial abuse case scenarios on a website developed for the project, and were asked to make judgements. The method measures the relationships between the cue information contained in the case scenarios and the judgements that are made, by examining how well regression equations based on the cue information predict responses.

▶ A typical scenario read:

> The case concerns an 86 year old female. A family member tells you that this older person's bank account is overdrawn and she does not know why. This older person has major physical health problems. She is extremely confused and forgetful and has a Lasting Power of Attorney managing her affairs.

The scenarios then have cue information on the case's *age* (66, 76, 86, 96); *gender* (male, female); *identifier of abuse* (you, family member, carer, other staff); *suspected problem* (relative due to inherit; third party manipulation; overseas transfers; overdrawn account; unusual cash withdrawal); *physical capacity* (no problems, minor problems, major problems); *mental capacity* (fully aware, slightly confused, extremely confused, forgetful; *in charge of money* (the older person, third party, person with Lasting Power of Attorney).

With these seven cues one can combine their possible values to create $(4 \times 2 \times 4 \times 5 \times 3 \times 3 \times 3) = 4{,}320$ possible cases. From this population of possible cases, 35 were selected in such a way that the cue values were uncorrelated within that set, which simplifies interpretation of multiple regression results.

A total of 70 banking and finance professionals took part.

Participants were asked to make two judgements in response to each scenario. These were level of certainty of financial abuse (scale ranging from 'certain abuse is not occurring' to 'certain abuse is occurring') and, second, the likelihood that they would take action (ranging from 'Unlikely to take action' to 'Likely to take action'). Both judgements were represented on a 0–100 scale.

Which factors explain banking and finance professionals' certainty that elder financial abuse is taking place?

Regression analysis was conducted at a group level using the scenario cue information to predict the average certainty of abuse for the banking and finance professionals.

The results showed a significant impact of 'type of financial problem suspected', as well as of 'who is in charge of the money', and of the older person's 'mental capacity'.

The cue 'Type of financial problem suspected' contributed the most to the variance predicted by the regression equation (78 per cent), the 'mental capacity' cue contributed 14 per cent and the cue 'Who is in charge of money' contributed 3 per cent, with the remaining cues not adding to the prediction of responses.

These significant cues in the regression equation were the same three cues that had been identified through prior *critical incident* interviews with independent groups of participants, thereby indicating that the critical incidents had been an effective method of eliciting key cues.

Cases involving winning an overseas cash prize had significantly higher certainty of abuse than other categories such as an out of the ordinary cash withdrawal or an overdrawn account. Financial problems where certainty of abuse was rated as significantly lower than others were those where the extent of financial losses was lower. For instance, a cash withdrawal that was out of the ordinary for the customer's routine would involve less financial loss than a fraudulent objection by a relative when the customer's house was being sold to cover care costs.

Professionals' attention to who is in charge of the older person's money may be expected given that where an individual is not in charge of their own finances, the opportunities for elder financial abuse are increased. This observation is supported by the fact that there was no significant difference between certainty of abuse where the individual was under a Lasting Power of Attorney in comparison ▶

> to a third-party signatory (i.e., someone in charge other than the individual themselves). In both instances, certainty of abuse (and likelihood of action) was higher than where the individual was in independent control of their finances.
>
> *Implications*
>
> The emphasis on the nature of the financial problem suspected has possible implications for the types of financial problem that finance professionals are most likely to identify. While it seems that professionals are attuned to certain types of financial problem, such as well-known scams, cases involving small amounts of money being taken over of a long period of time may be less likely to be identified.
>
> The case scenarios and the key cues identified in this work were then used in developing online training for finance professionals.

NEUROSCIENCE APPROACHES TO DECISION MAKING

Two key ideas from studies of human decision making are the notions of utility and the role of dual systems in reaching decisions. Recently, researchers have begun to apply tools of neuroscience such as brain imaging and neuropsychological analyses of effects of lesions to decision making, to uncover neural bases of deciding and so build up a new hybrid discipline of **neuroeconomics** (see Camerer, 2013; Nermend & Latuszynska, 2017).

> **Neuroeconomics**
> the study of neural processes underlying economic decisions.

When alternatives differ widely it seems natural to suppose that decisions between such alternatives must be made by assessing the alternatives on a common scale of subjective value or utility. Is there a neural basis for a common utility scale? A number of early animal studies indicated the existence of brain reward systems (Olds, 1956) localized in brain areas such that animals would take electric shocks, exert large effort and forgo food to have those areas stimulated electrically. Activity in such areas could serve to represent a common scale of pleasure or utility for a range of desirable inputs. An option that activated reward systems strongly (indicating a more desirable, higher utility option) would be preferred to one that activated reward systems more weakly. So, decisions would favour options that activate reward systems most strongly.

Recordings from dopamine neurons (Tobler et al., 2005) in the orbitofrontal cortex (Roesch & Olson, 2004; Tremblay & Schulz, 1999) and posterior cingulate cortex (McCoy et al., 2003) have shown neural responses that relate directly with reward size in primates, and similar results have also been reported in human studies, for example with monetary rewards (Elliot et al., 2003). Thus activity in dopamine neurons is linked to reward size and such activity is linked to choices as choices follow reward. An interesting fMRI study by McClure et al. (2003) found that people's stated preferences for Pepsi versus Coke were matched by responses in the ventromedial prefrontal cortex on tasting these drinks.

Neuroscientific studies have also supported the dual systems approaches to decision making discussed previously. For example, when people are asked to decide between, say, £10 today or £11 in one month, many people choose £10 today. However, if the choice is between £10 in a year and £11 in a year and one month, the delayed alternative is often preferred, even though the time gap between the two alternatives is still one month, just as it was when £10 was available immediately. It was hypothesized that short-run impatience is driven by the limbic system, which reflects System 1 activity and responds impulsively to immediate rewards. Choices of the delayed rewards are governed by the lateral prefrontal cortex, which reflects System 2 activity. In an fMRI study McClure et al. (2004) found indeed that there was relatively greater fronto-parietal activity (associated with deliberative processing) when participants chose delayed options and relatively greater activation of the limbic system (associated with emotional processing) when participants made choices of immediate options.

Similar results emerged from studies of the intriguing **Ultimatum Game** (Sanfey et al., 2003). In this game, the participant is told that a certain sum of money, say £10, is available and that the other unseen player can decide how the £10 should be split. However, if the participant does not agree with the split then neither player will receive any money. Typically, the game is to be played once and once only on a completely anonymous basis and no bargaining or discussion is allowed. From expected value or expected utility points of view, the participant should accept any split in which he or she gets something greater than zero, no matter how small. Typically, however, people will reject splits in which they would receive only small amounts. Low offers (say around £2 in our example) have about a 50 per cent chance of being rejected (see Roth, 1995) even though it is clearly better to have £2 than nothing. The rejection of low offers seems to be based on an emotional (System 1) response of anger to what is seen as an unfair offer (Pillutla & Murningham, 1996). A cooler System 2-based judgement would accept the low offer. Consistent with this view, Sanfey et al. (2003) in an fMRI study found that rejection of unfair offers was associated with relatively greater activation in the right anterior insula (related to negative emotions such as disgust) and acceptance of unfair offers was associated with relatively greater activation in the dorsolateral prefrontal cortex (related to controlled cognitive processing). See Figure 13.12.

> **Ultimatum Game**
> a bargaining game in which one player decides a split of money with a second player – if the second player does not accept the split, both get no money.

A related game to the Ultimatum Game is the **Dictator Game**.

In the Dictator Game, the experimenters give one player, the Dictator, a sum of money to split with a second player, the receiver. The receiver has no say and no choice but to accept whatever the Dictator decides. If people followed a pure monetary value expectancy, or simple, selfish, utilitarian approach

> **Dictator Game**
> a game in which one player, the Dictator, decides on a split of a money amount with a second player who has to accept the Dictator-decided split.

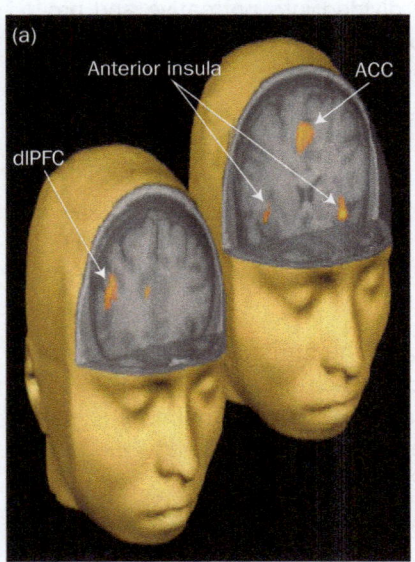 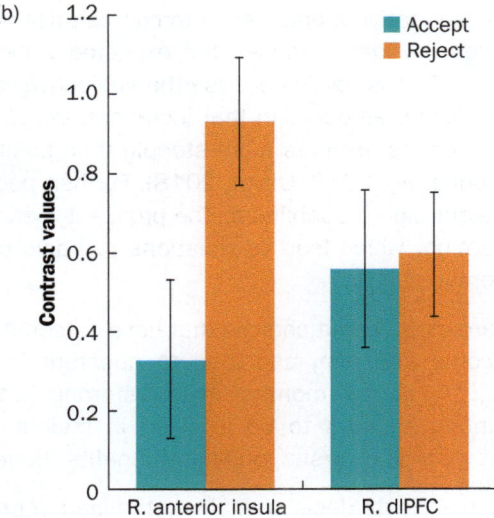

Figure 13.12 Deciding and fMRI.
Rejection of unfair offers was associated with relatively greater activation in the right anterior insula (related to negative emotions such as disgust) and acceptance of unfair offers was associated with relatively greater activation in the dorsolateral prefrontal cortex (dlPFC), related to controlled cognitive processing.
Source: Sanfey et al. (2003). Reprinted with permission from AAAS.

model, the Dictator would take 100 per cent of the available money and leave the recipient with nothing. Perhaps surprisingly, over many variations of the task, Dictators tend to give around 30 per cent to the receiver (Engel, 2011). This holds even when the Dictator has complete anonymity and there is no opportunity for an unfair split to be punished or reciprocated in later plays. This suggests a very strong tendency to cooperation and pro-sociality, which are lacking in simple models of rationality (Wills et al., 2020).

Dual process or dual system approaches have been proposed in which pro-social decisions in the Dictator Game and similar situations are driven by intuitive System 1 responding. The *social heuristics* view (Rand et al., 2014) is that pro-social responding is a useful heuristic and reflects System 1; on this view it is argued that 'deliberation only ever reduces co-operation in social dilemmas . . . or has no effect . . . but never increases social-dilemma co-operation' (Bear et al., 2017).

In line with the social heuristics view, fMRI studies found that greater dlPFC activity was associated with decisions that prioritized individual gain over another's pain, while reduced dlPFC activity was associated with more generosity in the Dictator Game, which suggests links between System 2 deliberation and self-interested (more utilitarian) decision making (Fermin et al., 2016).

Overall, results from the new area of neuroeconomics are encouragingly consistent with concepts previously developed through behavioural studies (e.g., utility and System 1 vs. System 2 based decision making).

Summary

In this chapter we have reviewed some of the major concepts and research findings in the area of decision making.

Decision problems were characterized in terms of whether they were risky versus riskless or single attribute versus multi-attribute. Approaches in decision making were divided into normative and process approaches. Normative models seek to characterize the behaviour of an ideally rational decision maker. The simplest normative model, the expected value maximization model, clearly does not fit individual behaviour. This is partly because the subjective value (utility) of money, say, is not a simple linear function of money amounts in that increases in utility for gains show diminishing returns and negative utility for losses declines more steeply than positive utility rises for gains – leading to loss aversion (Abdellaoui et al., 2013; Oliver, 2018). Further, people tend to overweight very small probabilities and underweight high probabilities. The prospect theory approach fits much of the data including the effects of framing, which lead to violations of basic principles of rationality such as invariance (Tversky & Kahneman, 1981).

When decisions are made about choices that have outcomes delayed into the future, effects of temporal discounting come into play and lead to apparent inconsistencies such as preferring £11 in 13 months to £10 in 13 months, but preferring £10 now to £11 in one month's time. Temporal discounting appears to be involved in maintaining overeating and other behaviour that overweights short-term gain versus long-term benefits (Bulley et al., 2019).

In the case of multi-attribute decision making, the load of processing differing attributes into an overall value measure leads to suboptimal but simple strategies such as elimination-by-aspects and satisficing. Use of elimination-by-aspects, at least as an initial stage in multi-attribute decision problems, has been shown by Payne (1976; Payne et al., 1993). Some support for a multi-attribute utility theory (MAUT) approach was found in realistic choices by Bhatia and Stewart (2018).

Since risky decisions require that decision makers take account of probabilities, the question of how people handle probability information has been tackled in a number of studies. Tversky and Kahneman (1974, 1983) have provided many demonstrations of how inappropriate usage of heuristics such as availability, representativeness and ignoring of base rates can lead to misjudgements of likelihood and to violations of laws of probability, such as the extension rule. However, it seems that if problems are posed in terms of frequencies rather than probabilities most responses are quite accurate.

Gigerenzer (1993, 2007) has stressed the generally beneficial aspects of real-life heuristics such as the recognition heuristic, which allow effective decision making with little effort (fast-and-frugal heuristics). Studies of real-life decision making using the naturalistic decision making approach (Klein, 2015) also support the real-life prevalence of fast-and-frugal heuristics, such as take the first option thought of in a given situation.

Studies of the neural bases of decision making indicate the frequent use of emotion-based heuristics and the involvement of System 2, deliberative processes in overriding impulsive, impatient and emotion-based choices (e.g., Fermin et al., 2016).

Review Questions

1. To what extent are people rational decision makers?
2. What are the relative roles of System 1 and System 2 processes in decision making?
3. Compare and contrast Tversky and Kahneman's heuristics and biases approach with Gigerenzer and colleagues' fast-and-frugal heuristics approach.
4. What problems do people have when dealing with probabilities?
5. Why does converting probability questions into frequency questions help people get the right answers?
6. What role do 'gut feelings' play in decision making?
7. Why do people typically find it difficult to make firm decisions about choices with outcomes in the future?
8. Do neuroscience approaches increase our understanding of decision making?

Discussion Questions

1. Devise possible experiments to test the deontological approach vs. the utilitarian approach as descriptions of decision making.
2. Make as many research predictions as you can from the view that decision making involves System 1 and System 2 processes.
3. Could all the varied approaches to decision making outlined in this chapter have some validity?

Further Reading

Fischoff, B., & Broomel, S. B. (2020). Judgment and decision making. *Annual Review of Psychology, 71,* 331–355.

Gigerenzer, G. (2015). *Simply rational: Decision making in the real world.* Oxford University Press.

Johnson, S. (2018). *Farsighted: How we make the decisions that matter the most.* John Murray.

REASONING

14

PREVIEW QUESTIONS
INTRODUCTION
DEDUCTIVE REASONING
   PROPOSITIONAL REASONING
     Box 14.1 When Things Go Wrong: The case of mental illness and reasoning
   SYLLOGISTIC REASONING
     Box 14.2 Research Close Up: Reasoning and dyslexia
     Box 14.3 Research Close Up: Do ideological beliefs affect reasoning?
     Box 14.4 Practical Application: The psychological model of legal reasoning
INDUCTIVE REASONING: TESTING AND GENERATING HYPOTHESES
     Box 14.5 Practical Application: Training in reasoning – Lipman's Philosophy for Children programme
   TESTING HYPOTHESES: THE FOUR-CARD SELECTION TASK
   GENERATING AND TESTING HYPOTHESES
     Box 14.6 Research Close Up: Does logical reasoning predict police recruits' ability to generate investigative hypotheses?
     Box 14.7 Practical Application: Real scientific research environments
     Box 14.8 When Things Go Wrong: Catching the right perpetrator – the case of the Madrid bombings
SUMMARY
REVIEW QUESTIONS
DISCUSSION QUESTIONS
FURTHER READING
ANSWERS TO CHAPTER PROBLEM

Preview Questions

1. Are people rational thinkers?
2. Why do we often leap to conclusions?
3. Why do apparently simple reasoning tasks lead to so many errors?
4. Has evolution programmed us to be very good at reasoning about social contracts and cheating?
5. Why is it hard to seek out and deal with evidence against our beliefs?
6. Do scientists show biases in their thinking in the same way as lay people?

INTRODUCTION

Reasoning
the cognitive process of deriving new information from old information.

Reasoning processes extract new information from already established pieces of knowledge and so are very useful in many areas of life. Reasoning is one of the ways in which information is used and so its study has become an important part of cognitive psychology. We will start introducing the topic with some examples of reasoning in action, before going on to more general points about reasoning and its study. First, a famous example of reasoning, featuring Sherlock Holmes:

> 'Is there any point to which you would wish to draw my attention?'
> 'To the curious incident of the dog in the night-time.'
> 'The dog did nothing in the night-time.'
> 'That was the curious incident,' remarked Sherlock Holmes.
>
> (A. C. Doyle, *Silver Blaze*, 1892)

In the *Silver Blaze* story, a racehorse of that name disappears from its Dartmoor stable one dark night, despite a guard dog being in the stable. Moreover, the horse's trainer is found dead not far away, on the moor. As a crucial step in solving the mystery, Holmes engages in reasoning, which we may reconstruct as follows:

> Someone entered the stable and led Silver Blaze away.
> If a stranger enters a place guarded by a guard dog, then the guard dog will bark.
> The guard dog in the stable did not bark.
> Therefore, whoever entered the stable and led Silver Blaze away was not a stranger.

This piece of reasoning reduced the number of suspects to one and the case was solved.

We do not have to be Sherlock Holmes to reason and, in fact, reasoning is pervasive in our thinking although in simple cases it may be so automatic as not to be recognized as such.

For example, suppose you are waiting for a friend who is arriving by train and has agreed to call you on arriving at the station. At the expected time she does not call. You conclude she has not yet arrived. The reasoning pattern would be similar to that of Holmes in the case of Silver Blaze:

> If my friend has arrived she will call.
> She has not called.
> Therefore, she has not arrived.

During the rest of this chapter we will be reviewing research and theory on how people derive new information from old information through reasoning. Why is this of interest? One reason is that people who can correctly derive new information by reasoning do well on tests of general ability or intelligence, and in turn do better in education and in the occupational world (Stanovich, 1999). So, understanding reasoning will help us understand an important individual difference. Second, reasoning processes, which serve to produce new knowledge from existing knowledge, are crucially involved in many real-world occupations, such as law, science (see Boxes 14.4 and 14.7) and detection (as in the Sherlock Holmes example above). So, the study of reasoning is relevant to many real-world occupations and activities.

DEDUCTIVE REASONING

The reasoning problems discussed in this chapter can be broadly classed as deductive and inductive tasks respectively. Inductive reasoning is concerned with establishing the likely truth or falsity of statements in the light of evidence. We will initially consider deductive tasks and explain inductive reasoning in later sections.

In deductive tasks, people are required to determine what conclusions, if any, *must* follow when they are given statements that are *assumed* to be true. For example, if we take it as true that 'All statistics lectures are extremely interesting' and that 'Today's 9 am lecture is a statistics lecture', it *must* be true that 'Today's 9 am lecture is extremely interesting'. The conclusion is true only if the assumptions (known as premises) are themselves true and the argument is valid. Deductive reasoning is of two types. The first is propositional reasoning, which deals with simple statements linked by logical relationships such as *if, and, not, or*. For example, 'If it's Tuesday then there's a psychology tutorial' and 'There is not a psychology tutorial today' leads with certainty to the conclusion 'Today is not Tuesday'. (Note that the pattern of reasoning here is the same as that used by Sherlock Holmes in the story of the dog that did not bark in the night.) The second type of deductive reasoning is syllogistic reasoning which deals with statements about groups related by terms such as *all* and *some*. For example, 'All apples are red things' and 'Some apples are sweet' leads to a conclusion through syllogistic reasoning that 'Some red things are sweet'.

> **Deductive reasoning** drawing logically necessary conclusions from given information.
> **Inductive reasoning** the process of inferring probable conclusions from given information.
> **Premises** statements assumed to be true, from which conclusions are drawn.
> **Valid** valid arguments are those in which the conclusions must be true if the premises are true.
> **Propositional reasoning** reasoning about statements connected by logical relations such as 'and', 'or', 'not', 'if'.
> **Syllogistic reasoning** reasoning about groups/sets using statements connected by logical relations of 'some', 'none', 'all' and 'some not'.

The topics of deductive and inductive reasoning are very closely related and both have been studied extensively in recent years. In the case of both deductive and inductive reasoning, clear normative theories of how these tasks should be tackled have been developed by logicians over the centuries and human performance can then be compared to these ideal benchmarks. As we shall see, there are frequent departures from the normative benchmarks when people tackle reasoning tasks, which leads to questions about the extent to which people are completely logical or rational in their thinking.

In the remainder of this chapter we will look both at research involving formal reasoning tasks and real-life reasoning as found in science, law and medicine. We start with deductive reasoning dealing with propositions, move on to syllogisms and then discuss inductive reasoning involving testing and generating hypotheses.

Propositional Reasoning

Propositional logic is a set of rules devised by logicians that enable valid arguments to be developed. This form of logic concerns arguments consisting of sequences of simple statements linked by logical relations such as *and, or, not* and *if . . . then* (also known as the *conditional rule*). For example, given 'If it's Wednesday, then I eat fish', and 'It's Wednesday', what follows? For most people it is obvious that 'I eat fish' follows. But if the second statement is 'I am not eating fish today', many people find the conclusion ('It's not Wednesday') harder to draw. A considerable research effort, which we review later in this chapter, has gone in to looking at how people handle propositional reasoning tasks and the extent to which human reasoning matches propositional logic, or doesn't.

> **Inference rule**
> a rule for reaching a conclusion given a particular pattern of propositions – for example, *modus ponens* (from the Latin for 'mode of affirming'), which states that, given 'If p then q' and 'not q', we can infer 'not p'.

Logicians have developed **inference rules** that can be used to derive correct conclusions from patterns of propositions, such that different patterns trigger different inference rules. Three examples of inference rules are as follows:

1 *Modus ponens* (from the Latin for 'mode of affirming') states that given 'If p then q' and given p is true, it follows that q is true. For example, 'If it's Saturday then I go to the cinema'; 'It's Saturday'; 'Therefore, I go to the cinema'.

2 *Modus tollens* (from the Latin for 'mode of denying') states that given 'If p then q' and given 'not q'; therefore, not p follows. For example, 'If it's Saturday then I go to the cinema'; 'I am not going to the cinema today'; 'Therefore, today is not Saturday'.

3 *Double negation:* not (not p); therefore, p. For example, 'It is not not Saturday'; 'Therefore, it's Saturday'.

The conditional ('if . . . then') rule has attracted much research in the psychological study of reasoning. As we have seen above, there are two valid inference patterns involving such rules (viz., *modus ponens* and *modus tollens*). On the other side of the coin, there are two main mistakes or fallacies when arguing from conditionals and these are:

1 *Affirming the consequent:* arguing from 'If p then q' and 'q' that 'p' is true. For example, 'If it's Saturday then Sue goes to the cinema'; 'Sue is going to the cinema'; 'Therefore, it's Saturday'. This is an invalid inference because the rule does not mean Sue only goes to the cinema on a Saturday.

2 *Denying the antecedent:* arguing from 'If p then q' and 'not p' that 'not q' is true. For example, 'If it's Saturday then Sue goes to the cinema'; 'It's not Saturday'; 'Therefore, Sue is not going to the cinema today'. This is an invalid inference because the rule does not mean Sue only goes to the cinema on a Saturday.

Now that we have reviewed some of the different inference rules and fallacies of propositional reasoning, let's check your understanding by completing Exercise 1.1.

Exercise 1.1 Which of the following inferences are correct and which are fallacies?

Rule	Inference	Is the inference correct?	Which type of inference rule or fallacy is this an example of?
1. If it rains then Mary puts on her raincoat	Mary puts on her raincoat, therefore it is raining		
2. If it is Sunday, then grandpa makes a roast	Grandpa is not making a roast, therefore it is not Sunday		
3. If Gabriel is sick, then he will call Susan	Gabriel is not sick, therefore he did not call Susan		
4. It is not not Wednesday	Therefore it is Wednesday		
5. If it is sunny on Sunday, then Harry will go out for a stroll	It is sunny on Sunday, therefore Harry goes out for a stroll		

Before going on to discuss results from studies of human reasoning, we should mention that the type of 'if...then' conditional discussed so far is known as *material implication* and that there is a different form of conditional – that is, the 'if and only if' rule of *equivalence* (also known as the *biconditional*). For example, 'A closed figure is a triangle if and only if it has exactly three sides' is an equivalence rule. In the case of equivalence, from 'q if and only if p', one can validly assert 'p' given 'q' (affirming the consequent) and 'not q' given 'not p' (denying the antecedent). That is, in the example, if a closed figure is a triangle, then it has three sides and if it does not have three sides it is not a triangle. Thus, affirming the consequent and denying the antecedent are valid arguments if the rule is one of equivalence but not if the rule is one of material implication. Misinterpretation of material implication as equivalence is a possible source of error in conditional reasoning.

Basic results

A number of studies have examined performance with conditionals involving both abstract materials (e.g., 'If there is an A then there is a 7') and concrete materials (e.g., 'If it is Wednesday then Mr Jones eats fish at 3 am'). Participants have been asked to say whether each of the four possible arguments – *modus tollens, modus ponens*, affirming the consequent and denying the antecedent – are valid. We can summarize results from a wide range of studies (e.g., Evans, 1977; Marcus and Rips, 1979; Markovits, 1988; Schroyens, 2010; Taplin, 1971) by saying that people typically perform with near 100 per cent accuracy in the case of *modus ponens*, and about 60 per cent accuracy on *modus tollens*. About a quarter of the time people correctly reject the two fallacies, affirming the consequent and denying the antecedent. Typical results are shown in Figure 14.1.

Suppression effects

It has been suggested that what are usually classed as fallacies in conditional reasoning could result from misinterpretations of the premises (Rumain et al., 1983). For example, given the premise, 'If there is a dog in the box, then there is an orange in the box', participants may assume this also means 'If there is not a dog in the box then there is not an orange in the box'. Interpreting the 'if...then' relationship as equivalence, conclusions that would be fallacies under the intended conditional interpretation now follow validly; so, 'there is not a dog' implies 'there not an orange' and 'there is an orange' implies 'there is a dog', on the equivalence interpretation. However, Rumain and colleagues found that giving participants additional antecedents, such as 'If there is a tiger in the box then there is an orange in the box', makes it clear that dogs are not required for there to be an orange in the box and so block equivalence interpretations and thus *suppress* the fallacies of affirming the consequent and denying the antecedent.

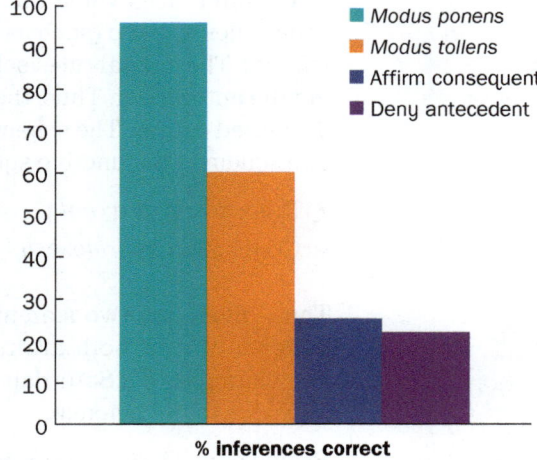

Figure 14.1 Typical percentage correct responses for the four main conditional arguments.
Good performance on *modus ponens,* fair performance on *modus tollens,* and high error rates on affirming consequent and denying antecedent.

Source: Adapted from Marcus & Rips (1979).

Later studies have found that some kinds of additional antecedents also block valid inferences on the bases of *modus ponens* and *modus tollens* (Byrne, 1989). To illustrate the findings, let us consider for example the following conditional statement:

- If she meets her friend then she will go to a play.

If you were told that 'She meets her friend', is the inference 'She went to a play' correct? Well, this is an example of a *modus ponens* so you probably quite easily judged this inference as correct. But, let us consider another example. You are now given two conditionals:

- If she meets her friend then she will go to a play.
- If she has enough money then she will go to a play.

You again are told that 'She meets her friend', but is the inference 'she went to a play' still correct under these conditionals? Actually, it is correct, but you probably felt quite unsure that it was. This is what Byrne (1989) also found when conducting her studies. In these studies, Byrne used pairs of conditional statements such as the example given above, where the second statement was an additional condition. When participants were given the above dual premises and were told that 'She meets her friend', they were unsure whether she had gone to the play, and the rate of correct *modus ponens* conclusions was far lower than with the single conditional premise ('If she meets her friend then she will go to a play'). Similarly, when given as true that 'She did not go to the play' the rate of valid *modus tollens* conclusions also dropped sharply. It seems that they are now unsure why she did not go to the play. It is as if the extra premises are interpreted as forming a conjunctive condition with the first premise (e.g., to make 'If she meets her friend *and* she has enough money, then she will go to the play'). In a study by Bonnefon and Hilton (2002), support was found for this interpretation, which is much in line with how one would interpret a conversation where these two conditionals were mentioned. Thus, the lack of confidence in whether Susan actually goes to the play, given that she meets her friend in the example above, is due to not knowing whether the second conditional is also met. These studies indicate the importance of premise interpretation, and how surrounding context can affect interpretations and so influence reasoning.

Mental logic approaches

David Braine proposed that people have mental logic rules that they can apply to solving reasoning problems. Braine et al. (1984) argued that people generally have available a set of mental inference rules (or *schemas* in their terminology) that permit direct inferences when the schema conditions are met. The schemas typically match some rules of logic (such as *modus ponens*) but may not include others (such as *modus tollens*). The mental rules/schemas may also include fallacious inferences, such as denying the antecedent. Thus, the schemas may or may not match the formal inference rules discussed earlier. The schemas take the form of 'Premises → Conclusion'. For example, one schema ('disjunctive syllogism') may be represented as:

- Premises: p *or* q; *not* p
- Conclusion: *therefore*, q.

Thus, given any two statements whatsoever, represented by p and q, if it is true that either p or q or both are true and not p is also true, it follows that q must be true. For example, 'It's Saturday or Sue goes to the cinema'; 'It's not Saturday'; 'Therefore, Sue goes to the cinema'.

Braine et al. (1984) proposed some 16 simple inference schemas on which people make few errors. When given problems that should directly evoke particular individual schemas they generally rate these schemas as being unproblematic. The proposal is that given information such as 'Either I will go out or I will study' and 'I will not go out' the appropriate schema (disjunctive syllogism) is evoked and, by applying it, the conclusion 'I will study' is reached.

In an experiment carried out to test and explore Braine et al.'s (1984) mental logic theory that people reason by applying rules in the form of schemas, participants were presented with premises on a computer monitor, one line at a time at a speed they determined, and finally they were shown a proposed possible conclusion which they had to judge as true or false. An example problem is as follows:

1 There is an L or a W.
2 If there is an L then there's not an E.
3 If there is a W then there's not an E.
4 There is an E or an O.

Is there is an O?

(Answer: 'Yes, there is an O'.)

As you can see, the tasks required application of more than one schema. From the first three lines above, it can be concluded that there is not an E. Using that conclusion, we can infer from line 4 that there is an O.

Braine and colleagues argued that participants' ratings of problem difficulty would depend on the length of the problem in words and on the difficulty of the schemas used in solving the problem. As expected, they found that problem length and rated schema difficulty did contribute separately to rated problem difficulty. Overall, Braine and colleagues' mental logic theory, that people reason using a limited number of schemas, met with a good measure of support from their experiments.

Mental models

In the **mental models approach** (Johnson-Laird, 2008; Johnson-Laird & Byrne, 1991; Johnson-Laird et al., 1992; Schaeken et al., 2013), the basic notion is that the meaning of connectives (*and, or, if,* etc.) can be represented by mental representations of possible states of the world, known as mental models. What is meant by mental models should become clear by considering a participant's report on how he had thought about the premise 'All the artists are beekeepers' (note: this is equivalent to '*if* people are artists, *then* they are beekeepers'). The participant reported, 'I thought of all the little artists in the room and imagined that they all had beekeepers' hats on' (Johnson-Laird & Steedman, 1978, p. 77). This self-report suggested to Johnson-Laird the hypothesis that a class of things (e.g., 'artists') can be represented by thinking of a few examples. So, to represent the above premise, the reasoner imagines a small number of artists (e.g., people with paintbrushes) and tags each of them as a beekeeper by adding a beekeeper's hat to each image of them. Since the sets of artists and beekeepers are not identical, the reasoner should add a few beekeepers without paintbrushes who are therefore not linked to artists in the representation.

> **Mental models approach** the view that people tackle logical reasoning problems by forming mental representations of possible states of the world and draw inferences from those representations.

Deductive propositional reasoning then begins, with the construction of one or more mental models that represent the first premise. One source of variation lies in how completely the models are developed to take all possibilities into account. For instance, '*if* a person is an artist *then* that person is a beekeeper' may be initially represented just as:

a Artist – beekeeper.

So, if we are now told that 'Smith is an artist', the conclusion 'Smith is a beekeeper' can be drawn (*modus ponens*). However, the simple one-model representation will mean we cannot draw a conclusion if told there is someone who is not a beekeeper. To draw a conclusion from 'denial of the consequent', the representation must include two models and would look like this:

a Artist – beekeeper.

b Not beekeeper – not artist.

As an argument is built up, premises are added and the set of models is modified until a conclusion is drawn from the final set of models. Mental models, it is argued, offer economical forms of representation that appear psychologically plausible. Johnson-Laird (1999, p. 116) proposed that models are built in accordance with the principle of truth, and wrote: 'Individuals minimise the load on working memory by tending to construct mental models that represent explicitly only what is true and not what is false.' Thus, mental model representations tend to be incomplete from the strictly logical point of view (since they tend not to represent what the logic of the premises rules out as not true) and this incompleteness is a source of error in dealing with reasoning tasks.

Incomplete mental models can explain the striking phenomenon of 'illusory inferences', which are seemingly compelling, but invalid, inferences. Consider the following situation:

Either Jane is kneeling by the fire and she is looking at the TV or else Mark is standing at the window and he is peering into the garden.

Jane is kneeling by the fire.

Does it follow that Jane is looking at the TV?

Did you say 'yes'? Most people do answer 'yes' to this question (Johnson-Laird, 2006; Legrenzi et al., 2003). However, the inference is not valid; it is an example of an illusory inference. Simply because Jane is kneeling by the fire, it does not follow that she is looking at the TV; she may be, but it is not *necessarily* the case.

Johnson-Laird argues that the principle of truth leads people to form models in which the possibility of it being false that she is both kneeling and watching TV is not represented, and this principle explains the illusory inference.

Johnson-Laird et al. (1992) applied his mental models theory to more than 60 problems used by Braine et al. (1984) and found that the number of mental models needed per problem correlated highly ($r = 0.73$) with rated problem difficulty reported by Braine et al. (1984). Thus, the results are consistent with the notion that the more models required for a correct deduction the harder the task will be.

Other tests of the theory have concerned the basic phenomena of '*if . . . then*' reasoning. The theory is consistent with the usual finding that *modus ponens* is easier than *modus tollens* for conditionals because *modus ponens* requires only one model while *modus tollens* requires three models.

Further data reported by Johnson-Laird et al. (1992), found that as predicted on the basis of the number of models involved, exclusive disjunctions (i.e., '*p or q, but not both*') were harder than conditionals and that *modus tollens* was easier with biconditionals (or equivalences) than with conditionals.

Evaluation of mental models versus mental logic

Johnson-Laird et al. (1992) stated that the mental models theory has the virtue of being falsifiable, which is a desirable property of any scientific theory. The mental models approach 'is in principle simple to refute: an easy deduction that depends on many models violates its principal prediction' (p. 436). In response, mental logic theorists

O'Brien et al. (1994) presented results from tasks that would appear to require many models, but that participants handled well. For example, consider the following problem:

If O or K or R or C then X

If E or F or G or H then Y

K

F

What follows?

In O'Brien et al.'s study 100 per cent of participants answered correctly, 'X and Y', although the problem involves 58 mental models. In response, Johnson-Laird et al. (1994) argued that participants would not blindly generate models unnecessarily but would realize that only a small part of the premises needs to be represented, which could be done with a manageable number of models. However, this means adding procedures to the model to enable participants to know when models are unnecessary, and makes the approach less straightforward than it initially seemed.

Although both mental logic and mental models approaches have had reasonable success in dealing with propositional reasoning, the mental models approach, as we shall see, also applies readily to the next type of reasoning, syllogistic reasoning, which we consider in the following section.

Box 14.1 When Things Go Wrong: The case of mental illness and reasoning

Obsessive-compulsive disorder, anxiety and depression are three common forms of mental illness. One view of these types of mental illnesses is that they are due to faulty reasoning either from invalid inferences or from false beliefs. This is the basis of Beck's (1976, 1991) influential cognitive-behavioural therapy (see also Box 15.5). An example of a typical invalid inference (affirming the consequent) that a depressed person might make without realizing that it is invalid, is: 'If you're worthless then you fail at everything'; 'I failed my exam'; 'So, I am worthless'.

In contrast to the cognitive-behavioural approach, Johnson-Laird et al. (2006) proposed that mental illnesses originated in overemotional reactions to situations (the hyper-emotion theory) and that reasoning errors were not a key factor in such mental illnesses. They argued that, if anything, patients should reason better about material related to their disorder than controls, because the patients tended to be very preoccupied with their condition and mulled over material related to their condition very often.

To test this idea, Johnson-Laird et al. (2006) tested three groups – controls, obsessive-compulsives and depressives – with materials relating to guilt or sadness or neutral topics. The tasks presented participants with a short background story followed by a proposition for which they were to list all possible states of affairs consistent with the proposition. An example would be the proposition:

The alarm rings or I feel tired or both.

Participants were to list possible combinations of being tired and the alarm ringing or not, given the proposition was true. The correct listing would be:

The alarm rings and I don't feel tired. The alarm does not ring and I feel tired. The alarm rings and I feel tired.

Participants were also asked to list what was impossible. In this case, that 'The alarm does not ring and I do not feel tired'.

The obsessive-compulsives, the depressives and the controls performed equally well with this neutral material.

Participants were also given the following short story:

> Suppose I am at my house with some friends. We decide to join some other friends in a bar. We leave the house joking among ourselves, but I forget to close the bathroom window.

Then, they were asked to list possibilities and impossibilities for either:

> The burglar alarm rings and I feel guilty.

or

> The burglar alarm rings and I feel depressed.

The results (see Figure 14.2) showed that the obsessive-compulsives did better (63 per cent correct) than depressives or controls on the 'guilt' test sentence (21 and 23 per cent respectively) but the depressives did better (66 per cent) than obsessive-compulsives (7 per cent) or controls (27 per cent) on the 'depression' test sentence. So it seems that, contrary to common sense and to Beck's (1991) theory, a tendency to a particular mental illness can enhance reasoning about matters related to that specific mental illness.

The results from the study have been replicated by Gangemi et al. (2013), who showed that depressed individuals and individuals with high levels of anxiety drew more valid conclusions concerning their illness than did healthy controls.

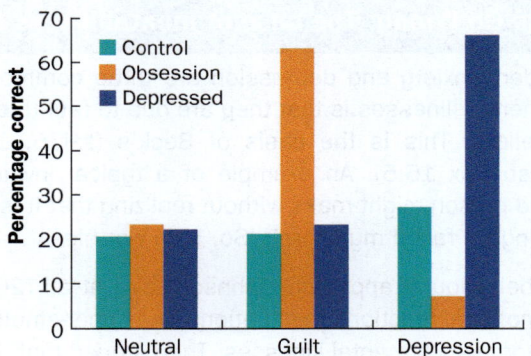

Figure 14.2 Pattern of per cent correct results in reasoning about neutral, guilt and depression-related materials by normal controls, obsessive-compulsive and depressed patients.
Depressives have advantage in reasoning about depression-related material and obsessive-compulsives have advantage in reasoning about guilt-related material.
Source: Adapted from Johnson-Laird et al. (2006).

Syllogistic Reasoning

Chapter 9, p296

Categorical syllogism
a deductive problem where one determines which inferences follow from the assumptions of category membership.

A fairly common type of deductive problem, even in everyday thinking, is to determine what conclusion, if any, follows from assumptions about category membership (for more on category membership see Chapter 9). Such problems are known as **categorical syllogisms** and represent the other main type of deductive reasoning, after propositional reasoning, discussed in the previous sections. For example, you have been told by your doctor to eat more fruit since fruit is high in vitamin C. As you go to the grocery store you therefore pick up pears and bananas since these are fruit and therefore contain vitamin C.

This everyday problem can be considered a categorical syllogism where you infer whether pears and bananas should contain vitamin C. Syllogisms have been frequently used in laboratory studies of reasoning and their main features may be conveyed by a few examples. Consider the following:

All dogs have whiskers

All terriers are dogs

Therefore, all terriers have whiskers.

In this problem we have to determine what conclusion, if any, follows from assumptions about categories of things, 'terriers', 'dogs' and properties such as 'having whiskers'. In this example about dogs, since the third statement (the conclusion) definitely follows necessarily from the first two (the premises) this is a *valid* syllogistic argument that leads to a true conclusion. Now, consider the following syllogism. Is it valid?

All cats are mammals

All dogs are mammals

Therefore, all dogs are cats.

In this case the conclusion plainly does not follow from the (true) premises and the form of the argument is *invalid*.

In addition to validity, syllogisms can be varied in many ways for experimental purposes. For example, they may be varied by changing the quantifiers ('some', 'all') used in the argument; the terms may be abstract or concrete; the premises and conclusion may be negative or affirmative; the propositions in the argument may be empirically true or false, and so on. Clearly, many features of the task can be readily manipulated. A number of variations are also possible in the response requirements. Participants can be asked to generate valid inferences from given premises; to judge a possible conclusion as valid or not; or to select a valid conclusion from a list of alternatives.

Basic findings from syllogistic reasoning studies

Some of the main factors associated with the difficulty of syllogisms, such as beneficial effects of concrete material as against abstract material, were established in very early studies (Wilkins, 1928). Consider the following argument about abstract letters. Is it valid?

All Cs are Ms

All Ds are Ms

Therefore, all Ds are Cs.

This abstract argument may well be accepted, even though it follows the same invalid pattern as a previous concrete example, which led from true premises to the conclusion that 'all dogs are cats'. Try substituting 'Cats' for Cs, 'Dogs' for Ds and 'Mammals' for Ms and the invalidity should be clear.

Wilkins found that although concrete premises led to better performance, even in the case of concrete syllogisms, participants accepted many invalid conclusions. Why might this be so? A controversial proposal is that there is an **atmosphere effect** that leads participants to accept invalid conclusions that are similar to the premises. For example, if both premises are of the form 'All . . . are . . .' people are inclined to accept a conclusion of the form 'All . . . are . . .'. We will now discuss the atmosphere effect.

Atmosphere effect
a tendency to draw conclusions in syllogisms that are over-influenced by the form of the premises rather than the logic of the argument.

The atmosphere effect

To account for common errors in syllogistic reasoning, Woodworth and Sells (1935) hypothesized an 'atmosphere' effect, which predicted that the form of the premises would influence people's expectations about the form of the conclusion. In particular, they proposed that if *both* premises involve 'all', people are disposed to accepting an 'all' conclusion. If any *one* premise involves 'some', people will be disposed to a 'some' conclusion. If any *one* premise involves 'not', people are disposed to accept a 'not' conclusion. The argument below is often accepted by participants as valid, as the atmosphere hypothesis would predict:

> All Cs are Ms
> All Ds are Ms
> Therefore, all Ds are Cs.

The above argument is invalid (substitute cats for Cs, dogs for Ds and mammals for Ms to make the invalidity clear). However, the abstract version is often accepted as valid by participants and so are many other invalid arguments (Sells & Koob, 1937; Woodworth & Sells, 1935).

Atmosphere versus conversion errors (illicit conversion) and probabilistic inference

An alternative to the atmosphere hypothesis was put forward by Chapman and Chapman (1959), who proposed that people applied heuristics that were not appropriate (known as 'conversion' and 'probabilistic inference'). These terms will be explained below, but first let us look at the Chapmans' results from giving participants a number of syllogisms that did not have any valid conclusions. For example:

> Some Ls are Ks
> Some Ks are Ms
> Therefore, (1) No Ms are Ls, (2) Some Ms are Ls, (3) Some Ms are not Ls, (4) None of these, (5) All Ms are Ls.
> (The correct conclusion is (4) 'None of these'.)

Participants tended to be wrong on these items and the kind of error that they made depended on the form of syllogism. The study used different types of syllogism and the atmosphere effect predicted the preferred errors on many of these; but it failed on syllogisms that involved premises of the following type:

> (A)
> Some X are Y
> No Y are Z
> and
> (B)
> Some X are not Y
> No Y are Z

The predicted response for both (on atmosphere) is 'Some Z are not X', but in fact participants tended to choose 'No Z are X', especially on (A), but split fairly evenly between the universal and the particular conclusions on (B). The Chapmans proposed that their results could be better explained by the operation of two reasoning errors called 'conversion' and 'probabilistic inference'. There are two conversion errors.

These are to assume (1) from 'All X are Y' that 'All Y are X' and (2) that 'Some As are not Bs' implies 'Some Bs are not As'. Using concrete versions makes the errors clear. 'All women are human' does not imply that 'All humans are women'. Again, 'Some humans are not politicians' does not imply that 'Some politicians are not humans'. The Chapmans argued that participants tend to make conversions unless they have information to the contrary (which they do not have with abstract material). Probabilistic inference involved 'plausible reasoning' that is not valid in deductive logic, so people will tend to argue that 'Some cloudy days are wet', 'Some wet days are unpleasant', and so 'Some cloudy days are unpleasant'. The conclusion could be true but it does not necessarily follow even if the premises are true. The Chapmans reported that these two errors accounted better for their data than did the atmosphere hypothesis.

In 1969, Begg and Denny re-examined the atmosphere versus illicit conversion issue with new experimental results and reported that atmosphere predicted the data very well. They also re-analysed the data from earlier studies (Chapman & Chapman, 1959; Sells, 1936) and found that there was considerable consistency among the various data sets and that, overall, the atmosphere predictions were more often upheld than the conversion and probabilistic inference predictions. Begg and Denny (1969) emphasized that although their results do support the use of the atmosphere 'formula' as a convenient predictor of error patterns, their study was not decisive about the underlying processes that lead people into error.

Wason and Johnson-Laird (1972) made other observations which suggested that the atmosphere hypothesis cannot be the complete explanation of syllogistic reasoning. For example, from Sells' data, when participants are given:

All B are A
All C are B

they accept the correct conclusion 'All C are A', *twice* as often as the incorrect conclusion 'All A are C' although both are equally predicted by the atmosphere hypothesis. Again, Wilkins' (1928) data show that the atmosphere effect is weaker with familiar as opposed to abstract or unfamiliar material, and the atmosphere hypothesis does not explain this difference. Another attack on the atmosphere hypothesis that has been influential was developed by Henle (1962) and this will be discussed next.

Henle on 'rationality'

How rational are people in their reasoning? The atmosphere hypothesis and the ideas of probabilistic inference and illicit conversion suggest major shortfalls from rationality. A contrary view was put forward by Mary Henle (1962), who argued for the essential rationality of everyday thinking. Henle proposed that many apparent instances of illogical thinking involve the implicit introduction of additional premises, the ignoring of some of the given premises and the misinterpretation of still other premises – but, she claimed, the inferences people make are generally rational, given how they have interpreted the premises. Henle illustrated her points with responses given by a sample of graduate students to syllogisms that might be encountered in everyday life. For example:

It's important to talk about things that are in our minds.
We spend so much of our time in the kitchen that household problems are in our minds.
Therefore, it's important to talk about household problems.

Participants were asked to assess the validity of the argument and give their reasons. Henle found that some participants *did not accept the task* as an exercise in pure logic, and did not distinguish logical validity from factual truth. For example, 'No, it's not important to talk about things in our minds unless they worry us'.

Interestingly, this type of response, in which the task is not accepted as a purely logical exercise, is actually fairly typical of people from cultures with little formal education. A number of participants interpreted the premises or the conclusion so that the intended meaning was changed. Participants sometimes ignored entire premises. For example, 'I don't think of household problems so it's not important for me to talk about them'.

Occasionally participants introduced premises that had not been given. For example, 'It's only important to talk about things that really worry us a lot and household problems don't; so it's not important to talk about them.'

Henle (1962) concluded that:

> *when subjects arrive at apparently invalid conclusions, or when they fail to spot a fallacy, they often do so because they have worked with materials different from those intended or because they have undertaken a task different from the one intended. In such cases, if we consider the materials and task as they were actually understood by individual subjects, we fail to find evidence of faulty reasoning. It must be concluded that the presence of error does not constitute evidence that the laws of logic are irrelevant to actual thinking. The data tend, rather, to support the older conception that these laws are widely discernible in the thinking process.*

Henle made a useful point in stressing the effects of the different ways in which participants can interpret task materials and goals. It is easy to assume that people interpret a task exactly as the experimenter intends, but then go on to make extraordinary errors in reasoning. Taking account of possible interpretations may well make people's behaviour more understandable, and may indicate that they have followed logical steps, but based on interpretations different from those intended by the experimenter. Later studies (Begg & Harris, 1982; Ceraso & Provitera, 1971; Newstead & Griggs, 1983) found that many participants misinterpreted traditional premises, but went on to make valid inferences based on the premises as they had understood them. Ceraso and Provitera (1971) examined the role of interpretation by using syllogisms in which the premises were given very clear interpretations. So, instead of simply being told, 'Some As are Bs', participants were told 'Some of the As (but not all) are Bs, but all of the Bs are As'. Another group were given the traditional syllogism statements. People given the clarified premises performed much better than did a traditionally instructed group.

Culture and logic

In the far North all bears are white.
Novaya Zembla is in the far North.
What colour are the bears there?

You may readily deduce that the bears are white in Novaya Zembla. In contrast, Luria (1971), in a study of non-literate peasants in Soviet Central Asia, found that many participants simply did not accept the task as an exercise in decontextualized logic but insisted on tackling it as a real request for solid contextualized real-world information. A typical response was as follows:

But I don't know what kind of bears are there. I have not been there and I don't know. Look, why don't you ask old man X, he was there and he knows. He will tell you.

Greenfield (2005) explains such findings by Luria in terms of a *collectivistic* versus an *individualistic* cultural mindset. The collectivistic mindset is typical of preindustrial societies, which are largely rural and lack formal education. This mindset stresses practical and contextualized knowledge to be used in real social settings against theoretical abstract knowledge to be used in artificial classroom settings. Formal education tends to induce an individualistic mindset in which the existence of different points of view is recognized and formal abstract knowledge of rules and principles (as found in science and mathematics, for example) is valued. The individualistic mindset is typical of industrialized, largely urban and formally educated populations. Although, by some counts, roughly 70 per cent of the world's population are collectivist (Triandis, 1989), Greenfield (2005) points out that both tendencies are present with varying strength in many people – for example, those who have been born into a strongly collectivist group but migrated when young to a big city and received some schooling. Even in highly individualistic societies such as in North America or the United Kingdom, religions generally stress communitarian collectivist values and both tendencies will be present in many people. By using suitable priming methods the less dominant mindset can be evoked – that is, individualism in the case of Asians and collectivism in North Americans (Gardner et al., 1999).

Mental model approaches to syllogisms

A series of studies by Johnson-Laird and his colleagues (Johnson-Laird, 1975; Johnson-Laird & Steedman, 1978) revealed an interesting effect due to the **figure** of the syllogism. (The figure of a syllogism refers to the way the three terms A, B and C are laid out. There are four possible figures – A-B, B-C; B-A, B-C; A-B, C-B; B-A, C-B – and these layouts affect what valid conclusions are preferred.)

> **Four figures of syllogism**
> the four possible layouts of terms, which give four syllogistic figures (i.e., A-B, B-C; B-A, B-C; A-B, C-B; B-A, C-B).

In the experiments, participants had to draw conclusions from syllogistic premises dealing with concrete but uncontroversial matters – for example, 'Some of the parents are scientists; all of the scientists are drivers; therefore . . .?' This particular syllogism, in which the topic-term has not been specified (is it about parents or about drivers?), tended to elicit the conclusion 'Some of the parents are drivers' rather than the equally valid 'Some of the drivers are parents'. While, on the other hand, the premises 'Some of the scientists are parents; all of the drivers are scientists' would tend to elicit the conclusion 'Some of the drivers are parents' rather than the also valid 'Some of the parents are drivers'. Indeed, throughout their experiments, premises of the form 'A-B; B-C' produced a bias towards conclusions of the form 'A-C' (even if 'C-A' conclusions were also valid). This strong effect was dubbed the **figural bias** effect.

> **Figural bias**
> the effect of figure on preferred conclusions.

The atmosphere hypothesis, and the conversion and probabilistic inference hypothesis, do not predict the figural bias effect. In view of this and other problems with the earlier approaches, Johnson-Laird and Steedman (1978) put forward the mental models theory. As we have already outlined this approach in the discussion of propositional reasoning, only a brief recap will be given at this point.

The broad stages proposed by the theory are (1) interpretation of premises; (2) initial heuristic combination of the representations of the two premises; (3) formulation of a conclusion corresponding to the combination of premises; and (4) a logical test (or series of tests) of the initial heuristic combination, which may lead to the conclusion being modified or abandoned. In terms of broad stages, the main novelty over previous approaches is the provision of a final testing stage that can lead back to a changed combination of information in the premises, which in turn may be tested again.

In the mental models approach, the premise representations are assumed to take the form of examples of the items in the premises. So, to represent the premise that 'All the drivers are scientists', participants imagine a few drivers and tag each of them as a scientist by adding a white laboratory coat to each of them. Since the sets of drivers and scientists are not identical, participants should add to the representation a few scientists who are not driving.

Having representations of the individual premises, the next step is to combine them in some way. Johnson-Laird (1975) proposes that there is a heuristic bias towards forming connections that link up all the classes if possible. So, given:

All A are B
Some B are C

these would be combined to yield the invalid conclusion 'Some As are Cs' (and this conclusion is often made).

The mental models theory proposes a combination of premises to yield a tentative conclusion, followed by a logical testing process. Differences in persistence of testing preliminary conclusions would lead to differences in the conclusions finally drawn by different individuals to the same premises. The theory was expressed in the form of a computer program and its performance compared to that of human participants on a set of 64 problems. With some syllogisms the process of testing does not lead to any modifications (hence thoroughness of testing does not matter). Such syllogisms were predicted to be easier than those to which the model would produce a modified conclusion after testing. This prediction was upheld (80.4 per cent correct on predicted 'easy' problems vs. 46.5 per cent correct on others).

An explanation for figural bias is that it arises from the processes of combining premise representations in working memory. That is, with a syllogism of the form A-B, B-C, people encode the first premise and then add on to it a representation of the second premise (A-B, B-C) with a resulting bias towards a conclusion of the form A-C. In the case of B-A, C-B premises, since the middle terms are not adjacent, it would be necessary to store the second premise in working memory first, then encode the first premise to make the combination (C-B, B-A) giving a bias towards C-A conclusions.

Johnson-Laird and Bara (1984) obtained relevant data from an experiment concerning conclusions given to syllogisms that were presented for brief exposures (10 seconds). Even with this short exposure there were clear figural effects; more significantly, however, there were unpredicted effects, due to figure, on the frequency of responses indicating 'no valid conclusion'. The A-B, B-C figure yielded the fewest such responses and the B-A, B-C figure produced the most. With short presentations participants experience difficulty in making combinations of premises in certain figures (such as B-A, B-C, in which reordering of terms in one of the premises is needed to effect premise integration) and thus have a high rate of (incorrect) conclusions that 'no conclusion can be drawn'. It has also been pointed out (Johnson-Laird, 1983; Johnson-Laird & Bara, 1984) that, for certain syllogisms, two or three different combined models of the premises are possible and that all the possible models must be considered before a correct conclusion can be drawn. Johnson-Laird (1983, p. 104) reports data from studies which found that the rate of drawing correct conclusions declined sharply as the number of possible combined models increased from one to three. Johnson-Laird (1983) proposed that these results were due to the load on working memory (see Chapter 6 on short-term memory) occasioned when more than one model must be constructed and evaluated. Using dual task methods, Gilhooly et al. (1993, 1999, 2002) found support for the general notion that syllogisms load working memory, particularly the central executive and phonological loop components of the Baddeley-Hitch working memory model (Baddeley, 2000; also see Chapter 6). A broad range of studies, reviewed by Gilhooly (2005), also supported the view that difficult syllogisms heavily load working memory.

Chapter 6, p176

The mental model theory stresses that people construct mental representations to solve reasoning problems. One such possible mental representation is visual imagery and in Box 14.2 we take a closer look at research that investigated how visual imagery may compensate reasoning abilities in people with dyslexia.

Box 14.2 Research Close Up: Reasoning and dyslexia

Source: Bacon & Handley (2014).

INTRODUCTION

Lots of anecdotal accounts exist which stress that individuals with dyslexia may think and reason in a predominantly visual way, although empirical evidence for this is somewhat mixed (Brunswick et al., 2010). Some studies have shown that individuals with dyslexia often provide very detailed and vivid visual representations, compared with non-dyslexics, when solving reasoning problems (e.g., Bacon & Handley, 2010). Thus Bacon and Handley (2014) set out to explore whether individuals with dyslexia might use visual memory as a compensatory strategy when solving reasoning problems.

© Andrii Kobryn/Shutterstock

EXPERIMENT 1: METHODS AND RESULTS

In the first experiment, a group of dyslexic individuals, as well as a group of non-dyslexic individuals, were asked to perform a visual memory test as well as to solve propositional and syllogistic reasoning tasks. While both groups performed equally well on both the reasoning tasks and the visual memory test, analyses showed that visual memory capacity was more important for the solving of the reasoning tasks for the dyslexic group. Thus, a person with dyslexia performing well on the reasoning task highly correlated with their visual memory performance. For non-dyslexics this association was not found, which may indicate that they did not rely on visual memory to solve the reasoning task to the same degree as did dyslexic individuals.

EXPERIMENT 2: METHODS AND RESULTS

In a follow-up experiment, the researchers wanted to test the results from Experiment 1 even further by constraining the use of visual memory for the participants. While solving the reasoning tasks, the participants were told to also remember a visual pattern, thus limiting their use of visual memory. Results showed that individuals with dyslexia performed worse on both reasoning tasks under high visual memory load than did the individuals without dyslexia. However, when the cognitive load on visual memory was low the dyslexic participants performed as well as the non-dyslexic.

CONCLUSIONS

The results from the study seem to indicate that individuals with dyslexia use visual memory as a compensatory strategy when performing reasoning tasks. Interestingly no support was found for a superior visual memory ability for this group as they performed equally to the non-dyslexic participants on the visual memory test. Also it is reasonable to conclude that for individuals who are not dyslexic, reasoning tasks are not predominantly solved by using visual memory since the non-dyslexic participants did not perform worse under high cognitive visual load. For more on dyslexia, see Chapter 11.

Chapter 11, p416

Evaluation

Mental models theory is continually evolving and has been extended to a wide range of reasoning tasks (Johnson-Laird, 2008; Johnson-Laird & Byrne, 1991). Although it is an impressive exercise in model building, some possible problems have been pointed out. For example, Wetherick and Gilhooly (1990) and Ford (1995) have indicated other possible explanations for figural bias and the number-of-models effect on difficulty.

Wetherick and Gilhooly (1990) argued that figural bias may simply be due to people choosing as the topic of the argument the first term, which is the topic of its premise. So, if we are told 'All the scientists are drivers' and 'All the drivers are golfers' it is natural to take 'Scientists' to be the topic here and to draw a conclusion about scientists, 'All the scientists are golfers'. If the premises were 'Some drivers are golfers' and 'All the scientists are golfers' a conclusion in which 'drivers' was the topic ('Some drivers are scientists') would be more natural. Thus, the figural effect may arise from assumptions made about which term is the topic (scientists or drivers?).

The mental models approach to syllogisms assumes that all participants approach the task in the same way and no explicit mechanisms of change or improvement are provided. However, in any large sample of participants, some will get most syllogisms correct, a few will be at guessing level and the remainder will show the typical variations in item difficulty discussed here and addressed by the mental models approach. Galotti et al. (1986) found that people classed on a pre-test as 'good reasoners' (but who had no training in formal logic) either used or quickly developed shortcut rules that would make laborious explorations of multiple model possibilities unnecessary. For example, better reasoners used the rules that two 'some' premises could only yield no valid conclusion and similarly that two negative premises must give no valid conclusion. Ford (1995), in a very detailed study using concurrent verbal think-aloud and written protocols, found that her participants split into one group who mainly used verbal rules and representations, and another group who used spatial representations like Venn diagrams. Both groups solved at about the same level and showed patterns of difficulty over syllogisms similar to those found by Johnson-Laird and Bara (1984). However, Ford's participants showed no signs of using mental model representations.

Belief bias and dual system theory

As mentioned above, arguments can vary independently in validity and in the truth or believability of the conclusions. Many studies have used abstract materials and so believability is not an issue for those situations. Essentially no participant has prior beliefs about whether or not 'All As are Cs'. However, with real-life materials prior beliefs would be expected to influence judgements of how valid an argument is.

For example, suppose you are given the following syllogism (Kahneman, 2011):

All roses are flowers
Some flowers fade quickly
Therefore, some roses fade quickly.

There is a strong tendency to conclude that this is a valid argument since the conclusion is true. However, if we work just with the premises given, the conclusion does not follow because it may be that there are no roses in the set of flowers that fade quickly. This is an example of **belief bias**, which we will consider next.

> **Belief bias**
> a tendency to accept invalid but believable conclusions and to reject valid but unbelievable conclusions to arguments.

Evans et al. (1983) investigated how the believability of a conclusion and argument validity might interact in affecting the acceptability of arguments as valid or not. In Evans and colleagues' studies, four types of argument, representing all combinations of valid versus invalid and believable versus unbelievable conclusions, were presented and participants had to say whether the conclusion necessarily followed *if the premises were accepted as true*.

Participants were given examples of four types of argument as follows:

Valid argument, believable conclusion (no conflict)
No police dogs are vicious
Some highly trained dogs are vicious
Therefore, some highly trained dogs are not police dogs.

Valid argument, unbelievable conclusion (conflict)
No nutritional things are inexpensive
Some vitamin tablets are inexpensive
Therefore, some vitamin tablets are not nutritional.

Invalid argument, believable conclusion (conflict)
No addictive things are inexpensive
Some cigarettes are inexpensive
Therefore, some addictive things are not cigarettes.

Invalid argument, unbelievable conclusion (no conflict)
No millionaires are hard workers
Some rich people are hard workers
Therefore, some millionaires are not rich people.

Participants indicated whether they accepted the conclusions or not. The results shown in Figure 14.3 indicated that both the validity of the arguments and the believability of conclusions affected how likely people were to accept the conclusion as following from the premises. In addition, the two factors showed an interaction in that the effect of believability was stronger for invalid arguments as against valid arguments.

From the results reported by Evans et al. (1983) presented in Figure 14.3, believability affects both valid

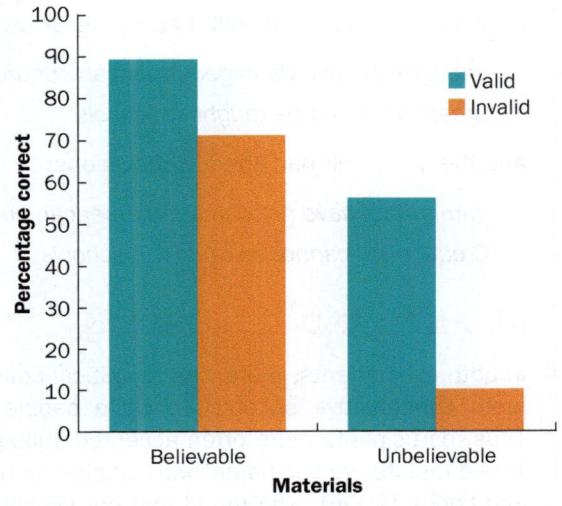

Figure 14.3 Percentage of arguments accepted as function of conclusion's believability and the logical validity of the argument.

Source: Adapted from data in Evans et al. (1983).

and invalid syllogisms, but has a much larger effect on invalid syllogisms such that unbelievable conclusions are much more likely to be correctly rejected for invalid syllogisms than is the case with valid syllogisms. These results support the existence of belief bias in dealing with syllogisms. That is to say, invalid syllogisms with believable conclusions are likely to be accepted as valid, but valid syllogisms with unbelievable conclusions are likely to be rejected as invalid. This indicates that people tend to deal with syllogisms not as purely logical problems for which the believability of conclusions is irrelevant. There is also emerging evidence that ideological belief may bias syllogistic reasoning with real-life content. This is further explored in Box 14.3.

Box 14.3 Research Close Up: Do ideological beliefs affect reasoning?

Source: Calvillo et al. (2019).

© George Sheldon/Shutterstock

INTRODUCTION

The core of political persuasion is to appeal to a person's reasoning ability (Cobb & Kuklinski, 1997). Calvillo et al. (2019) studied whether participants' political ideology affected which conclusions were drawn from politically charged syllogisms. The researcher proposed that participants would be more willing to accept syllogisms as valid if they were consistent with their ideological beliefs.

METHOD

In Experiment 1 the participants consisted of 414 American undergraduates, and in Experiment 2 they consisted of 234 Mechanical Turk workers (people who partake in online surveys/studies for money). Participants were asked to rate their level of political ideology on a scale measuring liberalism/conservatism, as well as to solve 16 political syllogisms, of which half had valid conclusions and half had invalid conclusions. One-half had conservative conclusions:

Immigrants have damaged American culture

Creationism can be taught in schools

And the other half had liberal conclusions:

Immigrants have not damaged American culture

Creationism cannot be taught in schools

RESULTS AND DISCUSSION

In both experiments, there was a political belief bias, such that people high in conservatism accepted more conservative syllogisms, while people high in liberalism accepted more liberal syllogisms. Thus, participants more often accepted syllogisms that were consistent with their ideological beliefs. These results are consistent with studies on motivated political reasoning, such as the study by Taber and Lodge (2006), who found that participants valued arguments that were in favour of their political attitudes as stronger and arguments that were in opposition as weaker.

The belief bias effect has been interpreted in terms of the dual systems or processes approach to thinking (also discussed in relation to decision making in Chapter 13). In this approach (Evans, 2003, 2008), it is proposed that true reasoning is the province of **System 2**, which involves controlled sequential rule-following processes that heavily load working memory. Such processes would enable correct resolution of syllogisms that show belief–validity conflicts. **System 1** thinking processes are rapid, parallel, automatic and reflect prior learning (and so beliefs). This system would produce automatic acceptance of believable conclusions, irrespective of the validity of the argument. It is suggested that both systems are activated in syllogism tasks, but to varying degrees for different individuals and task conditions.

> Chapter 13, p466

> **System 2**
> a hypothetical system that carries out slow, deliberate thinking.
> **System 1**
> a hypothetical system that carries out rapid, intuitive thinking.

Instructions that emphasize the logical nature of the task can reduce belief bias, and opposite instructions can increase the effect (Evans, 2003). Thus, System 2 can override System 1 when the goal requires exact and careful reasoning (Stanovich, 1999). Time pressure (Evans & Curtis-Holmes, 2005) and concurrent working memory load (De Neys, 2006), as well as task difficulty (Brisson et al., 2014), have been found to increase belief bias, and these findings can be explained as due to reduced time and resources limiting the use of System 2 as against System 1.

Neuroscience studies by Goel and colleagues (Goel, 2005; Goel & Dolan, 2003; Goel et al., 2000) using fMRI have found that different brain areas were active when dealing with syllogisms with real-life content (and so prone to belief bias) as against abstract syllogisms of identical logic. Content-based reasoning evoked activity in the left hemisphere temporal system, whereas abstract tasks were associated with activity in the parietal cortex. In syllogism tasks involving belief-validity conflicts, similar to the syllogisms used by Evans et al. (1983), Goel and colleagues found that logically correct judgements involved activity in the right inferior prefrontal cortex, which they suggested is critical in detecting and resolving conflict (System 2), while incorrect judgements were associated with activity in the ventral medial prefrontal cortex, which they argued is associated with intuitive (System 1) responses. These results support the idea of two systems and also suggest a neural basis for the distinction.

In real-life our reasoning is often content-based and not abstract thus we are more likely to be affected in our reasoning in such a way that we stray from the rationalist path. In Box 14.4 we take a closer look at an important field, namely legal reasoning, and how it may be affected by biases and attitudes.

Box 14.4 Practical Application: The psychological model of legal reasoning

The law involves reasoning by jurors and judges to reach definite conclusions, either 'guilty', or 'not guilty' (or additionally 'not proven', if in Scotland). Such reasoning may occasionally be a straightforward application of *modus ponens*. For example, in most jurisdictions there is a law to the effect that if a shop sells alcohol to people below some critical age (18 in UK) then the law has been broken. So, if the owner of a corner shop has definitely sold alcohol to an individual who is 17 years and 11 months old, then it is simple for jurors or a magistrate to apply the 'if . . . then' rule and conclude that the shopkeeper is guilty.

Such simple cases are rare. More commonly, there are many pieces of relevant information of uncertain reliability, some pointing to guilt and some to innocence. How do jurors or appeal court judges reason with such complex material to reach a definite verdict? In legal thinking on this question (Ellsworth, 2005) two schools of thought are:

1 the *rationalist* approach according to which logical reasoning, using rules of deduction, induction and reasoning by analogy leads to conclusions in a one-directional process from evidence to verdict

2 the *realist* approach according to which conclusions emerge from unconscious biases, prejudices and attitudes, and then the conclusions are justified afterwards by selective picking and weighting of evidence (e.g., dismissing all the defence witnesses as unreliable).

Simon (2004) has developed an alternative cognitive model which proposes that jurors seek to form a coherent mental model of the facts in the case such that one verdict is strongly supported and the other possible verdict is only weakly supported. Using a connectionist approach, the idea is that the pieces of evidence are given different weights and are each linked initially more or less strongly to each possible verdict. As evidence comes in and is reflected on, one verdict begins to become more strongly activated and feeds back activation to the pieces of evidence that support it, and so an early tendency to one verdict becomes ever stronger. Thus, reasoning here is not seen as a one-way process from presented information to conclusion but as an *interactive process* where the emerging favoured verdict affects the weights of the pieces of evidence, which in turn strengthen the favoured verdict.

In a study by Simon et al. (2001) participants were shown a story about an investor who had a dispute with a software company. Each statement was initially rated as supporting or not supporting a conclusion that the investor had libelled the company on an electronic forum. The statements were usually rated initially as roughly equally supporting the libel conclusion and the no-libel conclusion. However, when participants were asked to make a definite decision about guilt or not, and after the decision rated the statements again, the ratings polarized so that those who voted guilty rated the statements on the second occasion as strongly supporting the guilty verdict. Those who voted not guilty showed the opposite pattern. Interestingly, when asked to recall how they had originally rated the statements, the participants reported their post-judgement extreme ratings rather than the original middling ratings.

Simon (2004) proposed that in view of the polarizing effect that takes place, advice on legal aspects of cases (e.g., exactly how burglary is defined) should be given before the evidence is heard rather than after, as is the norm. It seems from Simon's results that giving legal advice after the evidence is too late to affect conclusions that have been reached in such a way as to form coherent mental models of the case. Other empirical studies of jurors have also supported the benefits of giving legal advice before the evidence – for example, Lee and Horowitz (1997) found improved recall of relevant information and reduced recall of irrelevant information when jurors were given prior instruction in legal aspects of the case.

It has also been proposed that Simon's coherent mental model might explain why false confessions can have such a detrimental effect on the legal process, since the false confession may affect how individuals in general, and jurors in particular, perceive other pieces of evidence in the case (Kassin, 2017).

INDUCTIVE REASONING: TESTING AND GENERATING HYPOTHESES

In the previous two sections we considered studies of deductive inference from statements (premises) that were to be taken as true. Related tasks arise in inductive reasoning when there is a need to test statements (hypotheses) for truth against external data. Detectives and scientists, for instance, constantly face the inductive problems of generating hypotheses and deciding whether their hypotheses are true or false.

Hypothesis testing assessing hypotheses for truth/falsity against data.
Hypothesis generation deriving possible hypotheses from data for later testing.

Two types of inductive task can be distinguished and these are generally labelled **hypothesis testing** and **hypothesis generation**.

In hypothesis testing, people are required to determine the implications, if any, of some particular observation(s) for the truth of possible generalizations (hypotheses). For example, if we hypothesized that 'All guard dogs in Scotland weigh over 30 kgs', then observations of guard dogs, their weights and geographical locations would bear on the hypothesis just given about guard dogs in Scotland. Note that in this form of reasoning we cannot conclusively prove the hypothesis true, as no matter how many guard dogs are examined in Scotland, a new one might come along that is under 30 kgs. On the other hand, the hypothesis could be shown to be false if a single guard dog weighing less than 30 kgs was discovered.

In hypothesis generation, the person can obtain observations (e.g., weights, colour, barking volume, geographical location) on the objects of interest (e.g., guard dogs) and seek to make a generalization supported by the evidence. Such hypotheses may need further testing and again cannot be conclusively proved but could be disproved.

A possible general approach in hypothesis testing is to follow the **hypothetico-deductive** method. In this technique, implications are deduced from the hypothesis and these implications are then checked against data for truth or falsity. If the implications of the hypothesis turn out to be true, then the hypothesis is supported, otherwise it can be rejected on the grounds that if validly drawn inferences from the hypothesis lead to empirically false conclusions then the hypothesis must be false. Whether the apparently simple prescription embodied in the hypothetico-deductive method is descriptive of behaviour in the face of inductive problems has been the topic of numerous studies, a selection of which will be considered in this chapter. Our review will start with tasks in which people do not have to generate hypotheses, but rather are given some particular hypothesis to test and sources of potentially relevant data. Next, we will discuss a range of more complicated tasks in which people are required to both generate and test their own hypotheses. The hypothesis generating and testing behaviour of scientists in real life will then be considered.

> **Hypothetico-deductive reasoning** a form of inductive reasoning in which a hypothesis is tested by deducing necessary consequences of the hypothesis and determining whether the consequences are true (support the hypothesis) or false (disconfirm or falsify the hypothesis).

Before we turn to these sections, however, we will take a closer look at whether reasoning skills can be improved. Box 14.5 reviews a training programme that was developed to further children's reasoning skills.

Box 14.5 Practical Application: Training in reasoning – Lipman's *Philosophy for Children* programme

An often stated goal of education is to develop thinking skills, including reasoning. Can reasoning be trained even at primary school level? A philosopher, Lipman (1974), decided that the best way to teach children to think was through stories and classroom discussions. He therefore wrote a short children's book called *Harry Stottlemeier's Discovery* (the title is a play on the name Aristotle). The book features Harry and his classmates. Adults occasionally enter in, but the primary philosophical work is the children's. Harry and his friends discover several basic concepts and rules of Aristotelian logic; and they puzzle over questions about the nature of thought, mind, causality, reality, knowledge and belief, right and wrong, and fairness and unfairness.

The story begins with Harry, a thoughtful boy, making a mistake in class one day. He hears his teacher explain that all planets revolve around the sun. Then, lost in a daydream, he misses the explanation about comets, which also revolve around the sun. The teacher asks him, 'What has a long tail, and revolves about the sun once every 70 seven years?' The correct answer is Halley's comet, but since

Harry has not been listening he doesn't know this. Remembering that all planets revolve round the sun, Harry concludes that this too must be a planet. The class laughs when he gives the wrong answer, for they have heard their teacher explain that comets travel round the sun but are not planets.

Harry is saved by the school bell and when walking home wonders to himself why his answer was wrong. He thinks to himself, 'All planets revolve about the sun, but not everything that revolves about the sun is a planet'. Suddenly Harry has an idea: a sentence can't be reversed. 'If you put the last part of a sentence first, it'll no longer be true.' He tries a few examples, 'All oaks are trees, but not all trees are oaks', 'All cucumbers are vegetables, but not all vegetables are cucumbers'. It's true that 'All planets revolve about the sun' but if you turn it round and say that 'All things that revolve about the sun are planets' then it's no longer true. Harry has discovered that 'All X are Y' universal statements cannot necessarily be reversed. In other words he has discovered the 'conversion error' discussed earlier in connection with syllogistic reasoning.

Harry then he meets his friend Lisa. In talking about his discovery she points out that Harry's rule does not always work. The sentence 'No eagles are lions', she says, can be reversed and still be true, 'No lions are eagles'. Logic is more complicated than Harry thinks. However, he and Lisa soon discover a new rule, 'If a true sentence begins with the word *no,* then its reverse is also true. But if it begins with *all,* then its reverse is false'.

In the *Philosophy for Children* programme, children as young as six or seven years of age work with the *Harry Stottlemeier* book and similar materials, coupled with extensive classroom discussions of what they are learning.

Evaluations of the *Philosophy for Children* approach in educational practice have been positive. For example, children who undertook the programme were shown to perform significantly better on follow-up studies than controls, not only in reasoning, but also in maths, reading and creative production (Nickerson et al., 1985). A meta-analysis by Trickey and Topping (2004) synthesized the results from some 10 studies that involved good research practice in the area as follows: measuring outcomes with norm-referenced tests of reading, reasoning and cognitive ability, curriculum measures, measures of self-esteem and pupil behaviour. All 10 studies showed positive outcomes with a mean effect size of 0.43 (about half a standard deviation). Trickey and Topping concluded that *Philosophy for Children* has 'a consistent moderate positive effect . . . on a wide range of outcome measures'. A more recent meta-analysis confirmed earlier results and showed that children who underwent the programme demonstrated highly increased cognitive learning outcomes and increased reasoning skills (Yan et al., 2018).

Testing Hypotheses: The Four-Card Selection Task

Wason (1966, 1968) devised a deceptively simple-looking task to explore hypothetico-deductive reasoning. Because this task involves a mixture of deduction and induction it is often presented within the context of deductive reasoning. However, as Wason saw this task as investigating falsification in assessing hypotheses, it is discussed here with 'induction', which is concerned with establishing the truth or falsity of empirical hypotheses.

Suppose you are given four cards showing:

| E | K | 4 | 7 |

Each card has a letter on one side and a number on the other. Your task is to name the cards that need to be turned over to test the following statement: 'If a card has a vowel on one side, then it has an even number on the other side'. You may find it instructive to pause here and decide on your answer before reading on.

Let us now consider a number of task variants. In each variant, try to decide which of the four cards need to be turned over to test the given rule.

Abstract version: each card has the letter A or B on one side and the number 1 or 2 on the other side. Rule: If a card has a '1' on one side it has an 'A' on the other side.

Concrete version: each card represents a journey and has a destination on one side and a means of transport on the other side. Rule: If a card has 'Manchester' on one side it has 'Train' on the other side.

Drinking rule: each card represents a person in a bar and has the person's age on one side and what he or she is drinking on the other side. Rule: If someone is drinking alcohol they must be 18 or over.

Negative abstract version: each card has the letter A or B on one side and the number 1 or 2 on the other side. Rule: If a card has a '1' on one side it does not have a 'B' on the other side. Cards show:

In all the above cases, the first and fourth card should chosen. Why? See below . . .

On the 'official' intended interpretation of the rule as one of material implication (see the discussion of conditional reasoning above), the most common answers are wrong. To see why they are wrong, and what the correct answer is, let us look at a concrete example. Take the proposed rule or hypothesis, 'Paper burns at 250 degrees C'. If we had a furnace set at 250 degrees C we could test this proposed rule by inserting samples of paper and noting whether they burn or not. A difficulty arises, in that no matter how many different samples of paper conform to the rule there could always be as yet untried papers that would not. Thus, no matter how many 'positives' are recorded, the rule can never be absolutely verified, but it would be falsified if just one sample failed to burn at 250 degrees C. This is a general characteristic of universal hypotheses and the example should cue us to the need to consider potentially falsifying data as well as potentially supporting data in testing rules.

Suppose now that a study was conducted on what sorts of things burn at 250 degrees C and that four cards are available representing four individual experiments. On one side of each card is listed the type of material put into the furnace and, on the other side, whether it burned or not. Which of the four cards below would have to be turned over to test the hypothesis, 'If it is paper, it will burn at 250 degrees C'?

Clearly we must look at the 'Paper' card to see if it burned or not. The 'Plastic' card can be ignored as irrelevant. Surprisingly, perhaps, the 'Burned' card does not need to be turned over. Once we know that the material burned, whether the material was paper or not does not affect the truth of the hypothesis. No information regarding the truth of the hypothesis would be gained by turning over the 'Burned' card and so it should be left untouched. (Paper or Plastic on the other side would both be consistent with the proposed rule.) The 'Did not burn' card should definitely be turned over, since it would be falsifying if 'Paper' were on the other side.

Similarly, in the abstract version – i.e., 'If vowel on one side, then even number on the other side' – the cards showing 'E' and '7' should be examined because they could falsify the rule. The '4' and the 'K' cards may be left unturned since whatever is on their other sides would be consistent with proposed rule. The logic of seeking falsifying evidence was stressed by the influential philosopher of science, Karl Popper (1959). Popper's views were the underlying inspiration behind Wason's four-card task – which can seem rather an arbitrary and highly artificial exercise in logic but is actually rooted in thinking about the very practical question of how science should be done (Wason, 1995).

Basic results

In testing a rule of the form 'if p then q', there are four possible cases that we might find, and these are *p and q, p and not q, not p and q* and *not p and not q*. In logic, only the second case (*p and not q*) is inconsistent with the rule while the remainder are consistent.

When participants are given a conditional rule to test and the opportunity to observe what is paired with cases of p, q, not p and not q in the four-card task, they almost always select the cards showing p and q, rather than the logically correct cards showing p and not q.

One way to describe these results is to say that people are biased towards verification or conformation and so choose the potentially confirming cards (p, q) and ignore the potentially falsifying case (not q). (Note that the p card is potentially falsifying as it might have not q on the reverse side as well as potentially confirming if it has q on the reverse side.) Participants will generally recognize that the not q card falsifies the rule if the not q card is turned over to reveal p, but rarely spontaneously examine it.

Procedural variations

Wason and others examined a number of procedural variables in an attempt to locate the sources of difficulty in this task. For example, in one study (Wason, 1969), the task materials were made strictly binary with only two possible letters and numbers, but this had no effect. Thus the source of the difficulty was not confusion induced by the sheer number of possibilities in the 'vowel–even number' cards.

It was suggested that participants might have been confused by the expression 'the other side of the card' and might have misinterpreted this to mean 'the side face downwards'. Wason and Johnson-Laird (1970) therefore presented participants with cards that had all the information on one side and used masks to hide the appropriate part of the card. Again, no facilitation occurred.

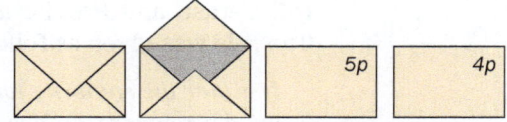

Figure 14.4 Envelopes version of selection task.

Perhaps the apparent 'set' for verification could be broken by instructions that emphasize falsification? However, Wason (1968) found that instructions to pick cards that 'could break the rule' did not enhance performance.

Performance on other reasoning tasks is often improved by concrete material and this is also true for the four-card selection task (e.g., Gilhooly & Falconer, 1974; Wason & Shapiro, 1971). In a very lifelike and concrete example by Johnson-Laird et al. (1972) participants were asked to imagine that they worked in the Post Office, sorting letters, as shown in Figure 14.4.

Their task was to discover whether the following rule had been broken. (This rule was in effect at that time in the UK.)

If a letter is sealed, then it has a 5 penny stamp on it.

Envelopes were provided either sealed or not and bearing either a 4 penny stamp or a 5 penny stamp on their showing side. A parallel abstract condition had the following rule:

If an envelope has a D on one side, then it has a 5 on the other side.

Again, suitable envelopes were provided to test the rule. And 22 out of 24 people tested were correct in the concrete condition, but only 2 out of 24 were correct in the abstract condition.

In sum, it appeared from these early studies that the main facilitating effects on selection task performance were those of using realistic material. Subsequent research reviewed below suggested a range of reasons why concrete materials were helpful in this task.

Interpretation factors

A number of investigators have pointed to ambiguities in the standard four-card task. Typical patterns of performance on the task might be explained in terms of people making interpretations different from that intended, but then going on to reason correctly on their interpretations.

Smalley (1974) distinguished three sources of ambiguity:

1 Is the rule 'reversible' or not? That is, does $p - q$ also mean $q - p$ or not?
2 Does the rule refer to both sides of the card or just to the showing side?
3 Is the task one of verification, falsification or both?

Putting together these ambiguities leads to $(2 \times 2 \times 3) = 12$ possible interpretations of the task. These 12 interpretations logically require certain patterns of card selection. Smalley showed that such interpretations occurred and that his participants' choices were consistent with their interpretations.

Further evidence for the interpretation approach to the four-card task was provided by Bracewell (1974), who gave one group a greatly 'clarified' statement of the task (cf. Ceraso and Provitera's syllogism experiment discussed earlier in this chapter). The rule was given as follows:

> *If either the showing face or the underside face of the card has a J on it then 2 is on the remaining face. This hypothesis should not be interpreted to mean that 2 only occurs with J.*
>
> *Please indicate the card or cards it is necessary to examine in order to see if the above hypothesis is false.*

The success rate with clarified instructions was much higher than that obtained with standard instructions.

The beneficial effects of realistic material could be explained on the 'interpretation' view, to reductions in ambiguity with realistic material. A rule, such as 'If I go to London, I go by car', is unlikely to be interpreted as reversible (i.e., as implying 'If I go by car, I go to London') because the reversed version is implausible. No such plausibility checks would prevent reversal of an abstract rule. In the 'Post Office' variant, the nature of the task – to seek potentially falsifying information – fits the thematic structure and so makes the task less ambiguous.

Matching bias

> **Matching bias**
> in the four-card task, choosing the cards mentioned in the rule.

Evans (1984; Evans & Lynch, 1973; Wason & Evans, 1975) put forward the view that, in the abstract version of the selection task, most people exhibit a **matching bias** in that they simply select the cards showing the symbols mentioned in the rule – that is, the responses match the input and no 'deeper' processing is involved. One main source of evidence for this view is the finding that with a negative form of the rule ('If B on one side, there will not be 3 on the other') the success rate is very high. Most participants select the 'B' card and the '3' card, which is the correct potentially falsifying choice pattern. This arises simply through 'matching'; the participants do not show any special insight into the logic of the task and when re-tested with positive versions of the rule, make the usual errors, as the matching hypothesis predicts.

Memory-cueing (availability) accounts

The rule that Johnson-Laird et al. (1972) used in their 'postal' study was a real-life rule and was well known to their participants at the time of the experiment. However, the rule stopped being used in the United Kingdom many years ago and later studies, using young adults, failed to find facilitating effects of the postal rule condition compared to the abstract condition (Griggs & Cox, 1982). Thus, it is possible that prior experience of specific counter-examples helped performance. People for whom the rule was a real everyday rule would be more likely to think of possible counter-examples from memory than would people for whom the rule was an arbitrary laboratory invention; in other words, falsifying possibilities would be more available to people familiar with the rule in real life.

Griggs and Cox (1982) found a similar effect to that of Johnson-Laird et al.'s 'postal study' in an experiment involving the rule governing the legal drinking age in Florida (where the experiment was conducted). Participants were asked to imagine that they were police officers and they were to ensure that the regulation ('If a person is drinking beer, then the person must be over 19') was being followed. Participants were given four cards that contained information about four people: on one side of each card was the person's age and on the other side, what they were drinking. Face up, the participants saw cards showing '16 years of age', '22 years of age', 'Drinking beer', 'Drinking coke'. The task was to turn over the cards that definitely needed to be turned over to determine whether the rule was being violated. This turned out to be a very easy version of the task and correct choices were made by nearly 75 per cent of participants. As with the postal task, a memory-cueing explanation was suggested.

Pragmatic reasoning schemas

It is a reasonable conclusion from the low levels of performance typical with abstract versions of the conditional-rule testing task, that people do not use formal 'syntactic' rules of logical implication in these tasks. Data outlined in the preceding section raised the possibility of specific memory cueing. A third possibility was developed in Cheng and Holyoak's (1985) notion of pragmatic reasoning schemas. Such schemas are quite abstract rule systems, in that they apply to a wide range of contents, but are not so wide and abstract as syntactic, logical rules. A relevant schema in the context of the four-card problem is the 'permission schema'. The core content of the permission schema is 'If one is to do X, then one must satisfy precondition Y'.

Cheng and Holyoak examined the possible rule of the permission schema in the following study. Participants in Hong Kong and Michigan were instructed in a problem about checking passengers' forms at an airport. The rule to be checked was 'If the form says "ENTERING" on one side, then the other side includes Cholera among the list of diseases'. Four cases corresponding to p, q, not p, and not q were available for examination. Half the participants were given a reason for the 'cholera' rule by being told that the form listed diseases for which the passenger had been inoculated and that a cholera inoculation was needed to protect the entering passengers from the disease. It was expected that this explanation would invoke the 'permission schema' (which matches closely the logic of the conditional). The expectation was justified in that both Hong Kong and Michigan participants showed a marked increase in correct performance when given the rationale for the rule. This result is not consistent with the memory-cueing explanation since participants did not have relevant memories; nor is it consistent with the syntactic rule view, since the logical structure of the task is not affected by the rationale. The result is, however, consistent with the pragmatic reasoning schema approach.

Social contract theory

Cosmides (1989; Tooby & Cosmides, 2009) argued that as a result of evolutionary pressures, people have a number of innate special purpose mechanisms to handle problems that have been critical to survival over many millennia. Specifically, she proposed that special purpose cognitive mechanisms have evolved to detect cheaters. In a **social contract**, individuals agree to take a benefit (e.g., eating deer meat) only if they have paid an agreed cost (e.g., gathered sufficient branches for a cooking fire). Cheats are those who eat the deer meat without having gathered the wood. Thus, possible cheats might be among those who eat the deer meat (they may not have gathered wood) or those who have not gathered wood (they may illicitly eat the meat). Cosmides proposed that humans have evolved so that they possess a 'cheat detecting algorithm' that will focus in on possible cases of cheating.

> **Social contract**
> social contract theory proposes that rules expressing payment of costs for privileges will be easily solved in four-card tasks as the correct choices would uncover cheating.

The relevance of these evolutionary arguments for the four-card task is that versions of the task that fit the social contract pattern produce high rates of correct (falsifying) answers. The 'Drinking Age' problem of Griggs and Cox (1982) and the 'Post Office' problem of Johnson-Laird et al. (1972) are good examples of facilitating problems where a cost has to be paid (in waiting to be old enough or in money) before a benefit can be taken (drinking beer or sending a sealed letter). Cosmides argues that the only reliable facilitations of the four-card task with thematic materials occur when the rule used is a social contract and is understood as such by the participants.

In a series of experiments, Cosmides (1989) set out to test the rival claims of the social contract theory, availability and pragmatic schema approaches. We will first outline the studies comparing social contract and availability explanations.

Problems were devised that concerned unfamiliar social contracts, unfamiliar descriptive rules, familiar descriptive rules and abstract rules. An example of an unfamiliar social contract is 'If a man eats cassava root, then he must have a tattoo on his face'. This rule was framed as a social contract by means of a background story according to which the rule holds among certain Pacific islanders; the cassava root is described as a powerful aphrodisiac only available to married men and only married men are tattooed. In the social contract condition participants are to take on the role of an enforcer of the rule. The four cards indicate on one side whether a man is tattooed or not and on the other side whether he is eating cassava root or molo nuts. The task is to decide whether to turn over cards showing 'Tattooed', 'Not-tattooed', 'Cassava root' or 'Molo nuts'. In the unfamiliar descriptive version the participants are to take on the role of an anthropologist trying to decide whether a proposed descriptive rule that eating cassava roots always goes with being tattooed is being broken. The familiar descriptive problem was a transport and towns problem using places and means of transport familiar to the participants. The abstract version was similar to Wason's original problem. In all cases a 'detective' type of set was induced to encourage participants to look for violations of the rules.

The results of these studies were that participants made a high rate of falsifying (p and not q) choices in the unfamiliar social contract condition ($c.$ 70 per cent), a low rate with unfamiliar descriptive problems ($c.$ 23 per cent) and a medium rate with familiar descriptive problems ($c.$ 42 per cent). The unfamiliar abstract baseline condition yielded $c.$ 27 per cent falsifying responses. Availability of relevant memories cannot explain the high correct rate with the unfamiliar social contract task (although there does seem to be an advantage for familiar descriptive tasks over baseline). Thus, social contracts produced a strong facilitation even when the material was unfamiliar and could not have cued relevant memories.

Further studies by Cosmides (1989) produced more support for social contract theory. In particular, experiments involving so-called 'switched' social contracts produce unusual choices predicted by social contract theory. Consider the cassava root rule. In its normal form this is 'If a man eats cassava root then he must have a tattoo on his face'. In the switched version it is 'If a man has a tattoo on his face then he eats cassava root'. Simply taking the surface logic of the switched rule, a falsifying approach would predict choices of 'Tattoo' and 'Molo nuts'; however, on the social contract interpretation, participants would choose 'Not-tattooed' and 'Cassava root' (more abstractly, the not p and q cards). This prediction arises because it is among the 'Non-tattooed' and the 'Cassava root' eaters that cheats may be found. Participants were tested with the switched social contract, unfamiliar descriptive rules, familiar descriptive rules and abstract descriptive rules. The results indicated a high rate of the not p and q choices for the switched social contract ($c.$ 70 per cent) with a near zero rate of such responses in the other conditions. Thus, social contract theory was again upheld and the data from these experiments cannot be explained in any obvious way by the availability or memory-cuing approach.

An alternative explanation for the ease of processing social contract rules might be found in the pragmatic permission schema approach of Cheng and Holyoak (1985).

Cosmides pointed out that although all social contracts are 'permissions', not all permissions are social contracts, since social contracts always involve costs and benefits while permissions as a class do not always do so. Cosmides argued that permission rules have been facilitating only when they have incorporated costs and benefits and hence have been social contracts. To test this notion, experiments were carried out in which the same rules were framed by means of background stories as either social contracts (in which the actions were taking benefits and the preconditions were costs to be met) or as permissions where the same actions and preconditions were without costs or benefits to the individuals. For example, the Cassava root rule was framed as a social contract as previously, or as a permission in which there was no individual advantage to eating cassava roots or molo nuts and being tattooed was not painful. The permission rule was justified as balancing out the frequency with which the two foods were eaten to conserve food supplies for the group. The outcome was that falsifying choices (p and not q) were more frequent for the social contract version than for the permission version (80 per cent vs. 45 per cent). Switching the rules to 'If a man has a tattoo on his face then he eats cassava root' produced a high rate of not p and q choices in the social contract version compared with the permission version (65 per cent vs. 0 per cent), as predicted by social contract theory.

Overall, Cosmides' evolutionary approach has led to identification of rules that will reliably produce response patterns matching falsification choices (p and not q) or, if switched, will produce choices unlikely to occur in the standard abstract version (not p and q). These findings were replicated by Gigerenzer and Hug (1992).

The research reviewed above on the social contract approach and on the pragmatic reasoning schemas approach has highlighted the facilitating effect of **deontic rules** on four-card selection tasks – that is, use of rules regarding what may or must be done. The research suggests that people do generally have a good grasp of basic deontic rules expressing simple social contracts since their selection task choices are in line with such understanding. This high level of understanding may reflect some evolutionary pressure leading to special purpose mechanisms becoming hard-wired into human brains (Cosmides' proposal), or it may reflect the importance of such practical social knowledge, which might be acquired through general-purpose learning mechanisms during normal development.

> **Deontic rules**
> rules regarding obligations, typically involving terms such as 'should', 'must', 'ought, 'may', and so on.

The work discussed in the next section (Oaksford & Chater, 1994, 2003, 2020) re-addresses the basic issues of inductive reasoning in the four-card selection task and pursues an interpretation of data that leads to a more optimistic conclusion about human rationality than is sometimes drawn (e.g., Cohen, 1981).

The selection task as optimal data selection

Wason's initial studies of the selection task (1966, 1968) were inspired by Popper's (1959) notion that seeking falsification was the rational way to test scientific hypotheses and, by extension, any causal or indicative hypothesis. As we have seen repeatedly, few people spontaneously adopt a falsifying approach to the standard abstract selection task and this aversion to falsification has been seen as a sign of imperfect rationality. However, Oaksford and Chater (1994, 2003, 2020) and Chater and Oaksford (2001) have proposed an alternative normatively based approach. This is an approach in terms of comparative testing of hypotheses to reduce the tester's uncertainty between them and involves the use of a statistical rule known as Bayes' theorem.

In the selection task, a hypothesis is proposed – for example, that 'if a card has p on one side then it has q on the other side'. Among other things, this hypothesis implies that the probability of a card having not q on it given it has a p on it is zero and so the probability of qs must be at least as great as the probability of ps. The alternative hypothesis is that p and q are unrelated (i.e., the null hypothesis), so the probability of not q given p could be greater than zero and the probability of q could be less than the probability of p. Bayes' theorem allows the investigator to revise the probabilities of hypotheses in the light of data that are more or less likely if the hypotheses are true.

Oaksford and Chater show that if the proposed rule and the alternative null hypothesis are viewed as equally likely initially, and the probabilities of ps and qs are seen as fairly low, then the best choices on Bayes' theorem to discriminate between the two hypotheses are the p card, the q card and the not q card, in that order. The not p card would yield no discriminating information. The predicted preference order of card choices, then, is p > q > not q > not p, and this is the order found in a review of 13 papers reporting a total of 34 abstract selection tasks (Oaksford & Chater, 1994).

The optimal data selection model argues that people will home in on rare events as being most informative, and the predictions are based on that assumption. However, in a direct test, Oberauer et al. (2004) gave participants extensive experience of stimuli involving frequent and rare combinations of features, and followed this experience with suitable four-card tasks involving rare and common features. No evidence emerged to show that choices in the four-card task were related to the experienced frequencies, so there are results counter to the optimal data selection model as well as supporting results. A further criticism is that the mechanisms by which selections are made are not specified.

Generating and Testing Hypotheses

In studies of conditional rule testing, such as those discussed earlier, people are given a rule and possible evidence that may or may not support or disconfirm the rule. Usually, in real-life situations we are not given rules to test but must generate possible rules (hypotheses) first, which can then be tested.

The processes of generating and testing self-produced hypotheses have been examined in a number of ways. We will discuss two of the main approaches that have involved the study of (1) Wason's reversed 20 questions task, and (2) performance in simulated research environments.

Wason's reversed 20 questions task

Wason (1960) devised a special task in which people generate over-restrictive hypotheses. Participants were given three numbers, 2, 4, 6, and told that these conformed to a rule that they had to discover. The means of discovery was to be by generating other three-number series that might match the rule or not. The experimenter gave feedback on each triple produced by the participants, who were asked to announce their rule when they were highly confident that it was the correct answer. The correct rule was simply 'numbers in increasing order of magnitude'. As you might expect, people stuck to much more restrictive hypotheses – for example, 'intervals of 2 between increasing numbers', 'arithmetic series'. However, the main interest lay in how the hypotheses were tested. The overwhelming tendency (Wason, 1960) was for people simply to generate series consistent with their particular hypothesis and to keep on doing so until they felt sufficiently confident to announce their hypothesis as correct. Few participants either tried out series that went against their own hypotheses or spontaneously varied their hypotheses. Very little evidence was found for a falsification strategy.

A number of task variations were attempted – to little effect. Even imposing a charge of 12.5 pence for each incorrect rule announcement, although it made participants more cautious about claiming to know the answer, did not affect the bias towards verification.

Tukey (1986) argued that participants in this task do in fact behave in ways that are rational in terms of various alternative philosophies of science. The stress on falsification in many studies of inductive reasoning is derived from Popper's (1959) analysis of scientific method. Tukey points to alternative accounts of scientific inquiry by, for example, Mill (1875/1967), Lakatos (1970), Kuhn (1970) and Bayesian theorists (Hesse, 1975). In Tukey's study it emerged that participants were not always testing particular hypotheses on each trial, but would quite often be examining instances 'at random' or just because they were 'different' in order to gather information that could lead to useful hypotheses. Certainly, people very rarely reported attempting to 'disconfirm' their hypotheses. Attempts to confirm and to simply explore accounted for over half the trials according to the participants' reports. Overall, Tukey's study suggests that an overly narrow view, based on Popperian philosophy of science (Popper, 1959), was initially applied to this task. When alternative approaches to scientific testing were considered, much of the participants' behaviour could be regarded as rational and intelligible rather than irrational and biased.

The reversed 20 questions task, or 2-4-6 task, is intended to represent real-world hypothesis testing. However, in its standard version, the task is not like real-life situations since the hypothesis testing is carried out mainly in the head – that is, the task involves purely internal representations of triples and possible hypotheses. On the other hand, real-world hypothesis testing usually involves using apparatus and instruments that help the person arrive at and test hypotheses. Test results are often represented as graphs and some representations may be more likely than others to help productive hypothesis generation testing (Cheng, 1996; Reinmann, 1999). Vallée-Tourangeau and Krüsi Penney (2005) examined the impact on hypothesis-testing behaviour of a richer external representation of the problem space in a variant of the 2-4-6 task in which sequences involved the digits from 1 to 6. In the study, triples were generated by working with three dice, each of which had six sides as usual. Participants rotated the dice or changed the order of the dice to produce new triples. Control participants carried out the 2-4-6 type of task without dice, but with numbers 1 to 6.

The results (shown in Figure 14.5) indicated that the task was made considerably easier when dice were used to generate the triples for testing as compared with standard paper-and-pencil methods (control group). Only 21 per cent of the control participants announced the correct rule, which is similar to the performance observed in the original Wason (1960) study. In contrast, 66 per cent of the participants with the dice version solved correctly.

The experimental participants produced more triples, which also were of a more varied kind, before announcing their guess than did control participants. It appeared that providing an external, easy to manipulate representation of the space of possible triples made the possible test items salient and easier for participants to generate.

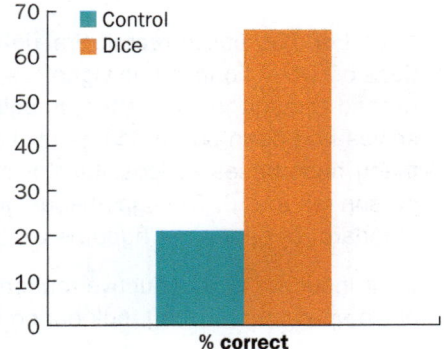

Figure 14.5 Percentage correct in Vallée-Tourangeau and Krüsi Penney's (2005) study of the 2-4-6 task using dice versus controls.

Source: Adapted from Vallée-Tourangeau & Krüsi Penney (2005).

In a follow-up study, participants were given a different way of representing the choice of digits. Instead of dice, which may have cued ideas of randomness and thus have prompted consideration of more possible sequences, participants had to make up their number sequences by choosing from three sets of six-sided counters (hexagons). In each set were six hexagons, one having one dot, one having two dots, one having three dots, and so on up to one having six dots. By choosing hexagons the participants could thus make up sets of numbers to be tested for conformity to the rule or not. This version of the test produced equally beneficial results to the 'dice' version. Thus, it was concluded that it was the ability to manipulate the possibilities externally that was crucial rather than the use of dice themselves. It seems that the external environment in this study helped promote wide testing. It is easier to manipulate possibilities externally in many and varied ways and then observe the results than to manipulate possibilities internally, within working memory. Internal manipulation is probably more liable to effects of habits and 'sets' (see Chapter 12, on problem solving), and leads to less varied possibilities being generated and tested.

Chapter 12, p422

Hypotheses generation is important in many real-life applications and is an important part of a detective's work, which we will take a closer look at in Box 14.6.

Box 14.6 Research Close Up: Does logical reasoning predict police recruits' abilities to generate investigative hypotheses?

Source: Fahsing & Ask (2018).

INTRODUCTION

Abductive reasoning
a strategy by which inferences are drawn regarding the most likely explanation for a set of observations.

Investigating complex crimes is certainly a demanding task, and can have grave consequences for both victims and suspects if not conducted properly. To be able to apply **abductive reasoning**, therefore, is an important reasoning skill for detectives during all parts of the investigation (Fahsing & Ask, 2016). Abductive reasoning is a cognitive process where the best possible explanation is derived from a set of observations. Within a crime investigation, abduction is also important for the generation of possible hypotheses that might explain the evidence or the generation of competing hypotheses that need to be evaluated. In a study by Fahsing and Ask (2018) the authors set out to investigate whether deductive and inductive reasoning ability may predict police recruits' ability to generate investigative hypotheses in criminal cases.

METHOD

A total of 166 police recruit first-year students, with no prior policing experience, were given descriptions of two fictional crime vignettes, which depicted a missing-person case. The participants were told to read through the vignettes, imagine that they had taken place the day before and that they themselves had been put in charge of the investigation. They were then given 30 minutes to generate as many hypotheses as possible for each case – for example, 'the person committed suicide' or 'the person ran away'. The hypotheses generated by the recruits were compared and coded against a 'gold standard' of generated hypotheses by experts within the field of criminal investigation.

Their inductive and deductive reasoning skills were assessed by using their test results from the cognitive aptitude test they took during the recruitment process of the Police University College.

RESULTS AND DISCUSSION

No association was found between the police recruits' deductive and inductive reasoning abilities and their abilities to generate hypotheses in the two crime vignettes. The reason for this may be that deductive and inductive reasoning are qualitatively different from abductive reasoning. Deductive reasoning pertains to generating new knowledge by using rules of formal logic. Inductive reasoning, on the other hand, is about making new predictions from information that has already been given. However, although being more closely related to inductive reasoning, abductive reasoning also allows the reasoner to come up with a hypothesis that is not grounded in already known knowledge – that is, pure guesswork – as long as it is consistent with the observations (Lipton, 2007).

Simulated research environments

Although philosophers of science tend to stress the importance of falsification (Popper, 1959, 2002) and of considering more than one hypothesis at a time (Platt, 1964), the results of Wason and others, discussed above, suggest that naive participants tend neither to consider alternative hypotheses nor to seek out potentially falsifying data. Studies by Mynatt et al. (1977, 1978) sought to investigate such tendencies in complex environments that were intended to simulate real-life research.

In the 1977 study, people saw computer-generated displays on a screen showing various shapes (circles, squares, triangles) of varying degrees of brightness (dim or bright). A particle could be fired across the screen (from a fixed position) in any direction, and it would be stopped when it approached some objects but not others. The overall task was to produce a hypothesis that would account for the behaviour of the particle. The correct answer was that the particle stopped on approaching dim shapes.

At first, participants were allowed to formulate a hypothesis on the basis of the particle's behaviour with one particular configuration of objects (a configuration that favoured adoption of an incorrect hypothesis in terms of object shape). They then chose between pairs of environments; in one they could make observations that would probably confirm the typical wrong hypothesis and in the other they would test alternative hypotheses. Evidence for a **confirmation bias**, involving failure to choose environments allowing tests of alternative hypotheses, was found. However, if participants did obtain explicit falsifying information, they generally used this information to reject incorrect hypotheses. Behaviour in this task was not affected by instructions stressing confirmation or disconfirmation.

> **Confirmation bias**
> in hypothesis testing, a tendency to seek out and attend only to information consistent with the hypothesis, while ignoring falsifying information.

Similar results also emerged from Dunbar's (1993) study of participants attempting to solve a problem in genetics through simulated experiments. The problem was such that there was a typically drawn dominant hypothesis, which most participants started with. Seeking data consistent with the dominant hypothesis led to poor performance, while focusing on discrepancies and difficulties with the initial hypothesis led to more solutions. Box 14.7 takes a further look at how real-life science practices show similar results to those from simulated research experiments.

Box 14.7 Practical Application: Real scientific research environments

Studies of real-life hypothesis testing in the sciences (Chalmers, 1978; Dunbar & Fugelsang, 2005; Mitroff, 1974) are consistent with laboratory studies in that scientists do not seem overly disposed to seek falsifying data or to accept that favoured theories require revision or abandonment in the face of apparently falsifying results.

For example, Galileo ignored much data that was apparently inconsistent with Copernican theory, and protagonists of Newton's theory of gravity did not abandon it in view of the 'misbehaviour' of certain planets.

The typical reaction to observations inconsistent with a favoured theory is to seek an explanation that preserves the theory. In the case of the planet Uranus's orbit, which was not as predicted, a new undiscovered planet was postulated and in due course the theory received spectacular support from the discovery of Neptune in the predicted place. Other anomalies in Newton's theory were never resolved, but the theory was not abandoned.

Mitroff (1974) closely surveyed the attitudes and beliefs about the scientific practice of a group of 43 geologists engaged in the study of lunar geology under the auspices of the Apollo space research programme. These well-established scientists saw their aim as (mainly) confirming, rather than falsifying, hypotheses. The only hypotheses that they were interested in falsifying were the hypotheses of rival scientists! Perhaps, then, the laboratory participants in the Mynatt study discussed above are not untypical in seeking confirmation rather than falsification. Indeed, the relatively high rate of appropriate reactions to falsifying data reported by Mynatt may reflect the artificiality of the environment – for example, participants would probably not doubt their 'instruments' in the way that real scientists might.

Indeed, Fugelsang et al. (2004), in a study of real biological scientists at work, found that unexpected results were nearly always attributed to problems with methods; only if the unexpected results held up on replication did scientists tend to accept them and revise their views accordingly. Similarly, Gorman (1986) has shown in a laboratory task that the possibility of error in feedback 'insulates' hypotheses from rejection.

Mitroff's moon scientists pointed out that 'commitment' was valuable from the point of view of motivating individual scientists. Also, since there would always be scientists with opposing commitments, the 'scientific community' would not be biased as a whole and the rivalry of competing factions would ensure that opposing views would be thoroughly tested by the opposition. Okada and Simon (1997) found that participants who worked in pairs on Dunbar's (1993) genetics problem performed better than single participants, presumably because of mutual critiquing of each other's hypotheses and interpretations of data.

Recently the scientific field of psychology, as well as many other fields like medicine, is going through what has been referred to as the replication crisis, where the results of some well-known studies in psychology have not been possible to replicate (Shrout & Rodgers, 2018). One possible reason why this phenomenon has occurred points to bad scientific practices where the researcher, overly committed to their hypotheses, can't stop searching for confirmatory results and consequently overshoots statistical testing (Wagenmakers et al., 2012). This form of malpractice can lead to false positives results, which do not hold up on replication. To prevent this type of misconduct, pre-registration of studies has been implemented, where the scientist describes their study before it is completed in open databases. By pre-registering their hypotheses, as well as data collection methods and which statistical tests that they plan to perform, the researchers commit publicly to a certain procedure and reduce the risk of false positive results.

Confirmation bias can constitute a serious problem in many real-world applications. Just think about the devastating results a narrow focus on confirmatory hypothesis testing can have in a clinical or forensic setting. Take for example, a physician who only pursues the hypothesis that his patient is having a migraine when he is complaining of terrible headaches and neglects to consider alternative hypotheses, such as a tumour. However, one should not forget that confirmatory hypothesis testing can lead to the correct conclusions and, when it does, may also be praised as an efficient strategy in a, for example, clinical setting (e.g., Norman & Eva, 2010). Before we end this chapter, we will consider a real-world scenario in Box 14.8 where confirmation bias seems to have led a forensic investigation astray, at least temporarily.

> **Box 14.8 When Things Go Wrong: Catching the right perpetrator – the case of the Madrid bombings**

In March 2004, three days before the general elections in Spain, a series of bombs exploded on commuter trains in Madrid. As a consequence, 193 people were killed and approximately 2,000 injured. The attack started a large international investigation and eventually the FBI identified Brandon Mayfield, an American lawyer from Oregon, as the perpetrator. The identification was based on forensic evidence found at the crime scene. Fingerprints lifted from one of the bags containing a detonating device were matched independently to Brandon Mayfield's fingerprints by several independent forensic examiners at the FBI. However, not long after, the Spanish authorities matched the fingerprints from the bag to the real Madrid bomber, an Algerian national by the name of Ouhnane Daoud.

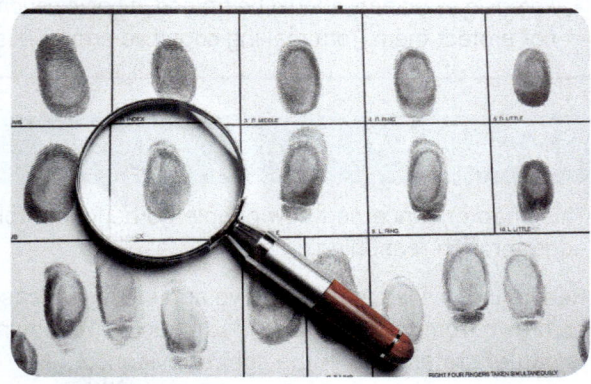
© New Africa/Shutterstock

The FBI forensic laboratories are known for their rigorous training and excellent standards, thus it was quite surprising that so many examiners independently had come to the wrong conclusion concerning the suspect in this high-profile case (Kassin et al., 2013). The internal investigation that followed put forward confirmation bias as one contributing factor for the wrongful identification of Mayfield (OIG, 2006). Now, it is important to remember that in many forensic disciplines it is a human being that performs the main analyses – for example, comparing fingerprints to judge if the patterns are sufficiently similar. What must have become quite evident to you while reading this book is that humans are susceptible to a number of different biases and cognitive errors, and even more alarmingly, we are not necessarily consciously aware of them.

Thus, it should not be very surprising that confirmation bias may affect even very experienced forensic examiners. Confirming this are results from a study by Dror et al. (2006). In the study, the researchers took latent fingerprints from previous cases that had been judged as a match by five experienced forensic examiners and gave them again to the same forensic examiners without telling them that they had already made a match for these in previous cases. Instead, the forensic examiners were given the prints by a colleague and told that the latent fingerprints were actually the erroneously matched prints from the Madrid bombings. The examiners were asked to judge whether there was enough information to make a match or a non-match and, if so, whether they did match or not. Interestingly, only one of the examiners matched the latent fingerprints, thus being consistent with the earlier examination of the fingerprints in the original case. Three of the examiners judged the latent fingerprints to be a non-match and one said that there was insufficient information to perform an analysis. These results are in line with other studies investigating confirmation bias in latent fingerprint identification (e.g., Stevenage & Bennett, 2017).

Some of the suggestions to avoid confirmation bias in forensic investigations that were put forward by Kassin et al. (2013) were as follows:

- *Examination of evidence should be linear.* That is, forensic examiners should document all evidence carefully at the crime scene before comparing it with some specific target. There is always a risk that when a target is presented, the evidence is reassessed in light of the target. If the evidence is processed in isolation from such targets then the influence can be diminished.

- *Blind testing should be conducted.* This means that the examiners should not be exposed to contextual information that is unnecessary for them and might influence their processing of the information. In the case of matching fingerprints, the examiners should not be told that the fingerprints are from

> a suspect, and filler fingerprints might be used since an examiner by default otherwise can conclude that the fingerprints must be from a suspect.
>
> - *Forensic examiners should be trained in basic psychology that is relevant for their work.* Although this will not protect them from making cognitive errors, it is important to be aware of the fact that these occur.

Summary

This chapter concerned how people go beyond information they have been given to derive new knowledge through reasoning.

Reasoning divides into deductive and inductive reasoning. In deductive reasoning true conclusions can be drawn from given statements. Inductive reasoning is concerned with establishing the likely truth or falsity of statements in the light of evidence.

Deductive reasoning splits into propositional reasoning, in which conclusions are drawn from statements involving logical relations such as 'if . . . then', 'and', 'or', and syllogistic reasoning in which conclusions are drawn from statements involving relationships between categories such as 'all', 'some', 'none' and 'some . . . not'.

Conditional inferences (using 'if . . . then' statements) have been found to be prone to the errors of affirming the consequent and denying the antecedent. The *modus ponens* inference is made correctly most of the time but the *modus tollens* inference often proves difficult.

Mental logic approaches explain propositional reasoning in terms of intuitive mental rules that correspond to some of the rules of logic, such as *modus ponens,* but lack others, such as *modus tollens.* Errors are attributed to a lack of appropriate rules or to misinterpretation of task materials – for example, interpreting a conditional as if it were an equivalence. The mental models approach assumes that people tackle reasoning problems by forming mental representations of possible states of the world and drawing inferences from those representations.

Many theories have been put forward for syllogistic reasoning. The atmosphere hypothesis proposes syllogisms are handled by a non-logical process. An alternative proposal for syllogisms is that various 'illogical' processes that have some plausibility may jointly produce many errors. In particular, illicit conversion of premises and probabilistic inference have been proposed. Henle (1962) developed the influential view that people do reason logically, but often misinterpret the premises or the task demands, thus producing errors.

In the mental models approach differences in syllogism difficulty were explained in terms of the number of models required to represent premises and their combinations. Figural bias effects were explained in terms of preferred ways of combining premise representations.

Belief bias effects, as demonstrated in syllogisms, and backed up by neuroscience studies, suggest a role for rapid intuitive thinking drawing on System 1 processes, which could be modified and overridden by executively controlled, slower System 2 processes to overcome biases.

Studies of inductive reasoning have focused on the four-card selection task, which requires hypothetico-deductive reasoning. Typically participants ignore the important potentially falsifying information. Concrete rule content emerged as an important factor in the four-card task, with particularly substantial facilitation for rules in terms of social contracts. Currently, the most likely explanation for such 'content' effects seems to lie in the evocation of reasoning schemas regarding social contracts.

Wason's reversed 20 questions task requires participants to generate their own hypotheses about number sequences and test their hypotheses by making up fresh examples. As in the four-card task, participants tend to ignore potentially falsifying information. However, performance can be improved by allowing participants external aids (such as dice), which make it easier to generate new sequences.

Studies of simulated and real-life scientific discovery indicated that ignoring potentially falsifying information is widespread in real settings as well as in laboratory studies.

 ## Review Questions

1. To what extent are people logical thinkers?
2. What are the roles of System 1 and System 2 processes in reasoning?
3. If we can put men on the moon, how come we can't solve the four-card selection task?
4. How does mental illness affect reasoning?
5. Why are syllogisms difficult?
6. Why might reasoning about social contracts and cheating be relatively easy?
7. Are we biased towards confirming our beliefs?
8. Do scientists really follow Popper's ideas about how to do science?

 ## Discussion Questions

1. In which context do we reason to acquire new knowledge and when do we rely on the reasoning skills of other people, such as experts or friends?
2. Should we trust our own reasoning skills or the skills of proper authorities (for example, researchers within the field) more?
3. In which applied settings, other than those mentioned in the chapter, is reasoning important?

Further Reading

Evans, J. St. B. T., & Frankish, K. (Eds.) (2009). *In two minds*. Oxford University Press.

Evans, J. S. B., & Over, D. E. (2013). Reasoning to and from belief: Deduction and induction are still distinct. *Thinking & Reasoning, 19*(3–4), 267–283.

Johnson-Laird, P. N. (2008). *How we reason*. Oxford University Press.

Oaksford, M., & Chater, N. (Eds.) (2010). *Cognition and conditionals*. Oxford University Press.

Oaksford, M., & Chater, N. (2020). New paradigms in the psychology of reasoning. *Annual Review of Psychology, 71*, 305–330.

Shafir, E., & LeBoeuf, R. A. (2002). Rationality. *Annual Review of Psychology, 53*, 491–517.

Answers to Chapter Problem

Exercise 1.1: 'Which of the following inferences are correct and which are fallacies?'
The answers are as follows:

1. Incorrect (affirming the consequent) **2.** Correct (*modus tollens*)

3. Incorrect (denying the antecedent) **4.** Correct (double negation)

5. Correct (*modus pollens*)

COGNITION AND EMOTION

15

PREVIEW QUESTIONS
INTRODUCTION
WHAT IS AN EMOTION?
! **Box 15.1 When Things Go Wrong:** Emotional processing after frontal lobe injury
CORE EMOTIONS
! **Box 15.2 When Things Go Wrong:** Can those with psychopathic traits recognize emotion in facial expressions?
Box 15.3 Practical Application: Detecting deceit through microexpressions
THE 'CORE' OF EMOTION
THEORIES OF EMOTION AND COGNITION
EARLY THEORIES AND THEIR INFLUENCE
TWO-FACTOR THEORY
AFFECTIVE-PRIMACY: ZAJONC'S THEORY
COGNITIVE PRIMACY: LAZARUS'S THEORY
Box 15.4 Research Close Up: When and why we try to regulate our emotions during our daily life
THE THEORY OF CONSTRUCTED EMOTIONS
THE INFLUENCE OF AFFECT ON COGNITION
AFFECT AND ATTENTION
AFFECT AND PERCEPTION
AFFECT AND MEMORY
Box 15.5 Practical Application: Cognitive behavioural therapy for depression
AFFECT AND DECISION MAKING
Box 15.6 Research Close Up: Do graphic warning labels influence risk perception and quit intentions in smokers?
! **Box 15.7 When Things Go Wrong:** Brain damage and decision making – the role of 'somatic markers' and interoception
SUMMARY
REVIEW QUESTIONS
DISCUSSION QUESTIONS
FURTHER READING

Preview Questions
1. Why is it important for cognitive psychology to consider emotion?
2. What are emotions?
3. What purposes do emotions serve?
4. Is cognition necessary for an emotion to occur?
5. How do different affective states, such as emotion and mood, influence cognition?

INTRODUCTION

In the film *Invasion of the Body Snatchers* (dir. Don Siegel, 1956), a small-town doctor sees several patients who are convinced that their friends and family members have been replaced by imposters. In the movie, the doctor comes to the realization that these patients are not delusional; in fact the members of the community are being replaced by alien doppelgangers. A delusion of this type is seen in a rare disorder called Capgras syndrome (see Box 2.6 in Chapter 2), which demonstrates the importance of emotion to the act of visual recognition.

> Chapter 2, p73

Patients with Capgras believe that their loved ones have been replaced by imposters. D.S. was a 30-year-old man who sustained a serious head injury in a car accident and lay in a coma for three weeks. While he experienced a good recovery from his physical injuries, he became convinced that his father and mother were 'imposters'. When asked about his father, D.S. said: 'He looks exactly like my father, but he really isn't. He's a nice guy, but he isn't my father' (Hirrstein & Ramachandran, 1997, p. 438). D.S.'s ability to discriminate faces was unimpaired, but he showed an abnormal **skin conductance response** to faces, in that the magnitude of his response to familiar faces was not greater than for unfamiliar faces. In such cases, it would seem that while the cognitive processes necessary for overt face recognition are intact, brain damage has altered the connection to emotion, such that a familiar face does not produce the typical emotional response. In the absence of this emotional response, D.S. came to the conclusion that his loved ones had been 'replaced' by imposters.

> **Skin conductance response** or galvanic skin response (GSR) reflects changes in the skin's ability to conduct electricity in the presence of an emotion-eliciting stimulus.

The Capgras delusion illustrates the importance of emotion for cognition: the visual aspects of face recognition may be working effectively, but without the link to emotion, the face seems somehow unfamiliar. As we will see in this chapter, emotion affects many aspects of cognitive processing including perception, attention and memory, and for this reason it is important that cognitive psychology includes emotion as a key aspect of its remit.

WHAT IS AN EMOTION?

Emotion is a fundamental component of human experience, and yet relatively little attention has been given, within psychology, to the scientific study of emotion. Part of the difficulty has been in defining emotion. As Barrett (2006) noted, 'scientists have yet to produce a set of clear and consistent criteria for indicating when an emotion is present and when it is not' (p. 20).

> **Emotion**
> a number of mental states including anger, joy, and disgust.

The term '**emotion**' is used to refer to various mental states that are relatively short-lived and are associated with an eliciting event, be it an environmental trigger (for example, hearing a scream) or a thought (for example, thinking 'Did I leave the oven on?'). They are reactions to a changing and somewhat unpredictable environment, and serve to prompt action. Frijda and Scherer (2009; see also Scherer, 2009) suggest the following four key features of emotion, which distinguish the emotions from other affective states such as mood or temperament:

1 Emotions are bounded episodes elicited when an event occurs that is of relevance to an organism's needs, goals or well-being, where relevance is determined by an

appraisal of the event on a number of criteria, including its novelty, pleasantness or unpleasantness, and its motivational value.
2. Emotions prepare the organism to act so as to deal with an event.
3. Emotions affect most or all bodily systems such that their functioning can be synchronized for an effective response.
4. Emotions establish control precedence over behaviours, so that actions can be prioritized.

Emotions provide us with essential feedback on the execution of our plans relative to our goals, and allow us to detect, and work to reduce, discrepancies between actual and expected outcomes (Bower, 1992). Emotions such as happiness or pride tell us our goals are supported, while sadness and anger signal that our goals are blocked or unfulfilled (see also Frijda 1986; Oatley & Johnson Laird, 1987). As a bounded episode, an emotion has a clear onset – we can pinpoint when the emotion occurred – and a somewhat fuzzy offset – the emotion dissipates over time (Scherer, 2009). Emotions tend to be intense and short-lived, preparing us to act.

By contrast, other affective states, such as mood, are more long-lived. The term 'mood' refers to a more continuous state that is less intense and relatively non-specific compared to emotions – we tend to know the cause of our anger, for example, but will not necessarily know why we are in a bad mood. Moods can be caused by emotions and can be the after-effects of an emotional reaction (Bower, 1992). For example, if you have a disagreement with a friend, you may feel angry, and afterwards remain in a bad mood for some time, even after the initial anger is gone.

The generic term 'affect' refers to the feelings of pleasure or displeasure – a dimension known as valence – as well as the amount of intensity – a dimension known as arousal (Russell, 2003). Mood as well as emotion can therefore be considered different forms of affect or affective state (e.g., Västfjäll et al., 2016), thus we will use the term affect or affective state when referring to both emotions and mood in a broader sense.

Cognitive psychology has been slow to consider emotion, for two main reasons. First, the traditional view of emotions as irrational, and therefore 'in opposition to' rational thought, has pushed emotion to the sidelines of the cognitive agenda. The dominance of the computer metaphor in cognitive psychology (see Chapter 1) is also relevant here. Second, emotion is not easily studied using the traditional methods of cognitive psychology relying, for example, on self-reports from participants. In recent years, however, research on cognitive topics has increasingly considered emotion, as it has become apparent that emotion and cognition are closely connected, and that we cannot fully understand one without consideration of the other. A cognitive psychology that omits consideration of emotion ignores a fundamental aspect of human cognition.

Chapter 1, p2

Amygdala
an almond shaped set of structures located in the medial temporal lobe.
Limbic system
consists of the thalamus, hypothalamus, hippocampus and amygdala, and other structures.
Insula
an area hidden within the folds of the cortex, with connections to the cingulate, amygdala, and orbitofrontal cortex, implicated in aspects of emotion, cognition, and action.

Some of the key areas of the brain involved in emotion are shown in Figure 15.1 (overleaf). Early neuroscientific studies of the brain and emotion suggested that particular regions of the brain might be linked with particular emotions. For example, the **amygdala**, a structure within the **limbic system**, has been linked to fear, the **insula** with disgust, the anterior

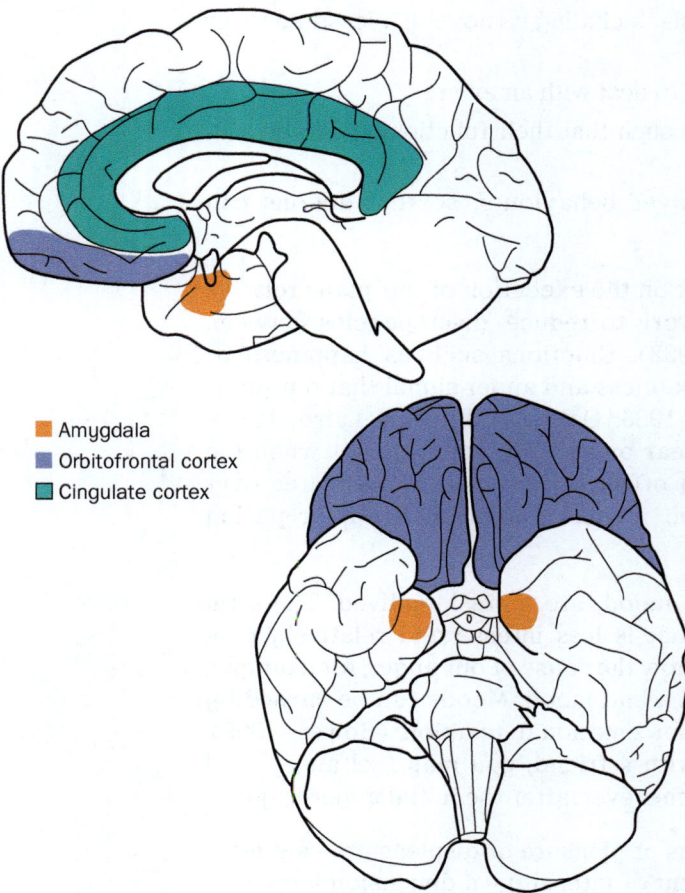

Figure 15.1 Some of the key brain structures involved in emotion.
The figure shows a midsagittal view (top), and a ventral view (bottom) of the human brain.

Source: Adapted from Kringelbach & Rolls (2004).

Default network
a network of brain regions that is active when a person is not focused on the external environment.
Salience network
involved in monitoring the external and internal environments to allow detection of salient stimuli.

cingulate cortex with sadness, and the orbitofrontal cortex with anger. However, the mapping of emotion to brain regions is far more complex than this. While the amygdala is traditionally associated with the fear response, for example, in fact fear activates a number of brain regions in addition to the amygdala, and activation in the amygdala occurs in several emotions other than fear. The amygdala shows increased activity for fear, anger, disgust, happiness and sadness (Lindquist et al., 2012). The amygdala is also linked with arousal, with both positive and negative emotion, while emotional valence (that is, whether it is pleasant or unpleasant) is also linked with the orbitofrontal cortex (see Hamann, 2012; Lindquist & Barrett, 2012). Accounts of emotional processing in the brain are therefore moving away from the locationist approach, which aimed to map discrete emotions to specific brain regions, and instead is focusing on networks of interacting brain regions. Meta-analytic studies point to a number of networks of brain regions, including those associated with the **default network** (medial prefrontal cortex, medial temporal cortex, ventrolateral prefrontal cortex), **salience network** (insular cortex, anterior cingulate cortex, amygdala) and frontoparietal network (ventrolateral prefrontal cortex) (Lindquist & Barrett, 2012; Lindquist et al., 2012). Box 15.1 examines the role of the frontal areas in emotion and the deficits that follow brain injury affecting this region.

! Box 15.1 When Things Go Wrong: Emotional processing after frontal lobe injury

Phineas Gage provides one of the most famous cases of frontal lobe damage ever reported; the case is mentioned, according to MacMillan (2000), in almost 60 per cent of all textbooks of psychology, neuropsychology and the neurosciences. But, as MacMillan points out, we know relatively little about the case beyond the few hundred words written by the attending doctor, John Martyn Harlow, at the time. Gage was a reliable and hard-working railroad foreman who in 1848 suffered an accident while excavating rock, which ▶

sent an iron rod (a so-called tamping iron) through his left eye socket (Figure 15.2). It exited at the top of his head, causing extensive damage to the frontal cortex. After the injury, Gage's temperament and personality underwent considerable changes and his social behaviour was altered. His decision making was compromised and his conduct was in stark contrast to his behaviour before the injury, when he was noted as a reliable and conservative figure. Harlow (1848, pp. 339–340) wrote this account of Gage:

> The equilibrium or balance, so to speak, between his intellectual faculties and animal propensities, seems to have been destroyed. He is fitful, irreverent, indulging at times in the grossest profanity (which was not previously his custom), manifesting but little deference for his fellows, impatient of restraint or advice when it conflicts with his desires, at times pertinaciously obstinate, yet capricious and vacillating, devising many plans of future operations, which are no sooner arranged than they are abandoned in turn for others appearing more feasible.

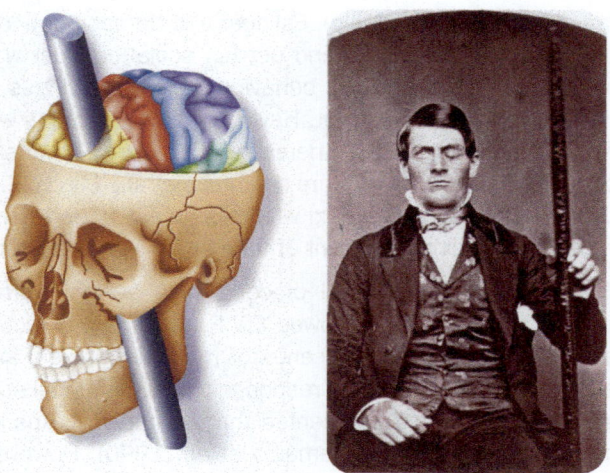

Figure 15.2 Images of Phineas Gage.
Left: a computer reconstruction of Gage's skull. Right: A portrait image of Phineas Gage. This early photograph had been in the possession of two collectors from Maryland, USA, Jack and Beverly Wilgus, for more than 30 years, before it was identified as Gage. It was identified following comparisons of the image with his life mask and the tamping iron, which are held in the Warren Anatomical Museum.

Source: (L) BSIP SA / Alamy Stock Photo; (R) ART Collection / Alamy Stock Photo.

However, some of the facts of Gage's life are at odds with reports of the case. For example, MacMillan (2000) notes that from early in 1851 until a few months before his death in 1860, Gage would appear to have worked as a stagecoach driver, a job that would require a degree of consistency and responsibility that is not generally attributed to him. Did he show recovery of function over time? Or were some of his supposed deficits exaggerated?

There is so much conjecture, fabrication and myth around the Gage case that one cannot be certain how much can be learned from his case about frontal lobe injury and related deficits. Furthermore, Gage's brain was not preserved and so the precise nature of the injury must be inferred from reconstructions and simulations using what is known about the damage to his skull. More recent cases have provided well-documented accounts of frontal lobe injury, and not all result in difficulties of regulating emotion and behaviours (Barrash et al., 2018). However, the extreme nature of Gage's injury means that he is likely to remain the best-known case and to retain an 'odd kind of fame' (MacMillan, 2000) for some time to come.

A more recent well-documented account is that of a man referred to as E.V.R., who was a successful accountant working with a small company. He was married with two children, and was considered to be a responsible and dependable man. At the age of 35 years, E.V.R. was diagnosed with an orbitofrontal meningioma, a type of brain tumour. He had surgery to remove the tumour, which affected the ventromedial frontal areas bilaterally. Eslinger and Damasio (1985) tested E.V.R. eight years after his surgery and noted profound and lasting behavioural changes. E.V.R.'s behavioural issues meant that he was no longer capable of fulfilling his personal and professional responsibilities, yet his intelligence was in the superior range (97–99th percentile). Eslinger and Damasio found that E.V.R. successfully completed formal neuropsychological measures and yet his social conduct was profoundly at odds with this pattern of intact intellect. In contrast to his behaviour before his illness, E.V.R. entered into ill-advised business ventures and was declared bankrupt. Having divorced from his wife of over 17 years, he married a prostitute and was divorced again soon thereafter (Eslinger & Damasio, 1985). He could no longer hold down a job or plan effectively for the future (Damasio et al., 1990). E.V.R. had great difficulty making simple, everyday decisions, such as deciding what restaurant to go to or what clothes to put on in the morning. He would spend an inordinate amount of time going over and over the options, often failing to come to a decision.

E.V.R.'s altered emotional processing is evident from his performance on a skin conductance task. Damasio et al. (1990) showed E.V.R. pictures that would be emotionally arousing (images that typically arouse disgust, such as scenes of mutilated bodies) and neutral pictures. A normal individual shows an elevated skin conductance response to the emotional stimuli, but E.V.R. showed no increase for emotional stimuli. E.V.R. even commented that he had not experienced the kind of feeling he expected, given the content of the images (Damasio et al., 1990). However, when asked to verbally describe the pictures, E.V.R. showed a normal skin conductance response (Damasio et al., 1990), suggesting that the emotional system itself was not the problem. Damasio referred to E.V.R.'s deficit as 'acquired sociopathy' because of the similarity between his emotional reactions post-surgery and those associated with sociopathic disorder.

Some patients, however, show predictably impaired performance on tests of frontal lobe function. Blair and Cipolotti (2000) describe a patient, J.S., who was aggressive, did not follow social norms and was reckless regarding others' safety. J.S. had no psychiatric history or history of aggression before an accident that caused bilateral orbitofrontal brain damage. Yet after his injury, he attacked and wounded a hospital staff member, and was threatening towards staff and other patients. He exhibited some bizarre behaviours, riding around the hospital on a gurney, for example, and throwing furniture. After the injury, J.S. could not keep a job and his behaviour isolated him from friends and family. While he had an average IQ score (verbal IQ 98, performance IQ 92), he showed impairment on some frontal lobe tests.

Like E.V.R., J.S. showed altered skin conductance responses to emotionally arousing pictures. J.S.'s skin conductance responses can be seen in Table 15.1. The range of responses for healthy controls is shown in parentheses. J.S.'s responses were significantly lower than the lowest responding healthy control in each case.

Cases such as these support the notion of a connection between emotional and cognitive processing, particularly in everyday decision making. According to Damasio (1994), people like E.V.R. and J.S., as a result of their injuries, no longer experience the emotional input that normally allows us to effectively weigh up response options and come to an effective decision. Such cases demonstrate the key role of emotion in higher cognition, such as decision making, judgement, problem solving and planning.

Table 15.1 J.S.'s Skin Conductance Responses (SCRs) to Emotionally Arousing Pictures

	J.S.	Healthy controls
Naturalistic expressions:		
Anger	0.058	0.437 (0.250–0.725)
Sadness	0.055	0.421 (0.246–0.790)
Neutral	0.042	0.134 (0.070–0.273)
Objects:		
Threatening	0.062	0.561 (0.245–1.2)
Neutral	0.109	0.251 (0.076–0.5)

Note: SCRs were recorded 1–3 seconds after stimulus onset. The range of responses for healthy controls is shown in parentheses. In contrast to the controls, J.S.'s responses to emotional stimuli are not significantly greater than for the neutral stimuli.

Source: Based on data from Blair & Cipolotti (2000).

The cognitive view of emotions is that they have important immediate and long-term functions that allow us to adapt to a changing environment (Levenson, 1994; Power & Dalgleish, 1997). Before we look at the main cognitive accounts of emotion, let's first consider what makes an emotion.

Core Emotions

Emotions are associated with distinctive facial expressions and gestures. While the display of emotion is to some extent culture-dependent, and emerges through learning and through the acquisition of social conventions called **display rules**, there is evidence for a basic set of motional expressions that is largely consistent across cultures (e.g., see Elfenbein & Ambady, 2002). These arguably correspond to a set of basic or core emotions.

> **Display rules**
> social conventions governing how, when and with whom emotions may be expressed.

Charles Darwin (1872/1998) proposed that there was an innate and universal set of human emotions with associated facial expressions. This proposal was supported by a series of cross-cultural studies in the 1960s. Paul Ekman and colleagues photographed the emotional facial expressions of the South Fore people of New Guinea, an isolated group unfamiliar with Western culture. If facial expressions and gestures are learned within a culture, then we might expect differences across cultural groups; if they have a biological basis, we would expect less cross-cultural variation. Ekman's research supported a set of basic human emotions, associated with particular facial expressions, that are expressed and recognized in a similar way and in the same contexts, across cultures (e.g., Ekman et al., 1969). Ekman identified the basic emotions as anger, disgust, fear, joy, sadness and surprise, although the South Fore people did not seem to make a clear distinction between fear and surprise. Ekman suggested that in their culture, unexpected events were more likely to be negative, so that fear and surprise tended to co-occur. This research supported an innate basis to the facial expressions for anger, disgust, fear, happiness and sadness, which correspond to a set of basic or core human goals, which are consistent cross-culturally (see Power & Dalgleish, 1997).

However, it should be noted that, while a significant proportion of the Fore sample responded in a manner that was consistent with the Western sample, there was considerable variation in recognition of the emotions. For example, while 82 per cent of the Fore sample recognized happiness, 54 per cent recognized fear, with 25 per cent of the sample mistaking fear for anger. Furthermore, the methodology used in such cross-cultural studies of emotion have been criticized by some. For example, Russell (1994) noted that consistency in responses may be inflated by the use of forced-choice formats (but see also Ekman's, 1994, response). While the balance of evidence would support universality in facial expressions, the degree of universality continues to be debated (see Barrett et al., 2019; Prinz, 2004). There are, however, individuals who suffer from poor emotion recognition for facial expression; one such group is people with psychopathic traits and we will explore this issue further in Box 15.2.

> **Box 15.2 When Things Go Wrong: Can those with psychopathic traits recognize emotion in facial expressions?**
>
> Psychopath is term that is often attributed to people who demonstrate callous and manipulative behaviour. Although this rather too casual use of the term is quite unfortunate, it may not come as a surprise that psychopathy actually describes a personality disorder that it associated with affective impairments.

People with a psychopath disorder show a wide range of problematic behaviour and tendencies such as pathological lying, lack of remorse or guilt, shallow affect, lack of empathy, impulsivity and irresponsibility, as well as antisocial behaviour (Hare et al., 2012). It is suggested that approximately 1 per cent of males and 0.5 per cent of females would meet the criteria for psychopathy in the general population, although both genetic as well as environmental factors seem to contribute to the development of psychopathy (Hare et al., 2012). It has been suggested that difficulties in recognizing emotions in other persons may contribute to the development of the disorder (Dawel et al., 2012), while some theorists have suggested that it may be a specific deficit in recognizing fear and sadness, and others suggest a more general deficit for recognizing emotions overall.

Results from a large meta-analysis by Dawel et al. (2012) showed that people reporting psychopathic traits exhibited an impairment in recognizing facial expressions for emotions. Not only did adults as well as adolescents with this traits show deficiency in detecting facial expression of fear and sadness, but also for happiness and surprise, although fear recognition was the poorest. Furthermore, the meta-analysis also showed that they performed less well at recognizing vocal emotional expressions, with deficits in detecting fear, happiness and surprise. It has been suggested that the results are in line with possible impairments in the amygdala, which is important in facial expression recognition.

Other sources support a core set of emotions linked to facial expressions. Blind adults show the same facial emotional expressions as seeing adults, demonstrating that a visual model of facial emotional expressions is not required in order to produce the same expression (Eibl-Eibesfeldt, 1973; Matsumoto & Willingham, 2009). Peleg et al. (2006) showed that adults who were blind from birth showed similar expressions to their family members, suggesting that even the more idiosyncratic aspects of emotional expressions may be inherited. Common facial expressions of emotion are also found in newborn babies, with research suggesting that nature equips the newborn with a 'primal' set of expressions. The primal face of pain, for example, is an expression 'characterized by opening of the mouth, drawing in of the brows, and closing of the eyes' (Schiavenato et al., 2008, p. 460). However, learning also plays a role. For example, infants of depressed mothers, who have reduced facial expressions, show different responses to facial expression than do infants of non-depressed mothers (Field et al., 1998). Of course, facial expressions can be controlled and even faked, so certain aspects of the expression of emotion remain under our control, an issue explored in Box 15.3.

Box 15.3 Practical Application: Detecting deceit through microexpressions

Chapter 10, p324

In Chapter 10, we saw how an analysis of language can help us to detect when someone is lying. Facial expressions present another possible means of detecting deception. Emotions are associated with particular facial expressions. When there is no attempt to conceal an emotion, the whole face is typically involved in producing the expression, which can take between 0.5 and 4 seconds. These macroexpressions can be readily identified. However, we also produce microexpressions, much more fleeting expressions that last less than half a second. These are often associated with attempts to conceal emotion, and it has therefore been suggested that they may be used to detect deception.

Ekman and O'Sullivan (1991) showed a videotape of 10 people who were either lying or telling the truth to a large sample of American participants ($N = 509$), including students, psychiatrists, police, judges, personnel from the Secret Service, FBI, CIA, National Security Agency and the Drug Enforcement Agency. Only the Secret Service personnel performed at an above chance level in identifying liars. The results suggested that, to the trained eye, and under the right viewing conditions, deceptive expressions can be identified. But under normal circumstances, detecting deception is rather tricky. So how easy is it to fake an emotion and are some emotions easier to fake than others?

Porter and ten Brinke (2008) looked for inconsistent emotional expressions and microexpressions in real and deceptive facial expressions. Participants were videotaped as they looked at disgusting, sad, frightening, happy and neutral images; they responded on each occasion with a genuine or deceptive (simulated or masked) expression. The videotape was then analysed frame by frame by two trained coders, and emotional expressions including microexpressions and blink rate were examined.

The analysis showed that masked emotions were associated with more inconsistent expressions and an increased blink rate, compared to real emotions. Happiness was the expression most readily faked, with the negative emotions proving more difficult. Inconsistent **emotional leakage** occurred at some point in all participants. Neutralizing emotions proved more effective than masking them, suggesting that it is easier to appear unemotional rather than having to mask an emotion with a fake emotion. The role of training was apparent in this study: untrained observers proved unable to detect deception.

Emotional leakage
the unintended expression of emotion or a failure to mask an expression.

Might we therefore be able to train people to detect deception from facial expressions? Matsumoto and Hwang (2011) trained participants using a task that embedded full-face microexpressions into a sequence of neutral expressions of the same face. They found that training significantly improved accuracy on the task, an advantage that trained participants retained several weeks later. While the task did not allow a precise replication of real-life microexpressions, it does suggest that, with appropriate training, some people might become skilled lie detectors.

However subsequent studies have questioned the promising results from the Matsumoto and Hwang (2011) study. In another study, by Jordan et al. (2019), participants were trained in recognizing microexpressions in order to detect deception. However this group did not outperform a control group receiving irrelevant training or a group of participants who received no training in lie detection. Thus the utility of focusing on microexpressions in an effort to detect deception remains unproved.

Ekman's (1999) list of the characteristics of the basic emotions is shown in Table 15.2. But which are the core or basic emotions? Ekman et al. (1969) listed six basic emotions: anger, disgust, fear, happiness, sadness and surprise. But this list was subsequently expanded: Ekman(e.g., 1999) lists fear, anger, disgust, sadness and contempt as the 'negative' emotions, and amusement, pride, satisfaction, relief and contentment as 'positive'. Frijda (1986) lists the basic emotions as:

- desire
- joy
- pride
- surprise
- distress
- anger
- aversion
- contempt
- fear
- shame.

Table 15.2 Characteristics that Distinguish the Basic Emotions

1	Distinctive universal signals
2	Distinctive physiology
3	Automatic appraisal, tuned to:
	a distinctive universals in antecedent events
	b distinctive appearance developmentally
4	Presence in other primates
5	Quick onset
6	Brief duration
7	Unbidden occurrence
8	Distinctive thoughts, memories, images
9	Distinctive subjective experience

Source: Based on Ekman (1999).

There is considerable cross-cultural variation in language related to emotion. There are words in English not found in other languages and there are words in other languages not found in English (for a review see Pavlenko, 2014). For example, in German the word 'schadenfreude' refers to a feeling of pleasure derived from someone else's difficulties (several languages have a version of the opposite, such as the Buddhist term 'Mudita'). Polish does not have an exact word for what in English would be called 'disgust' (Wierzbicka, 1986, p. 584). In Japan, 'hagaii' is 'a mood of vulnerable heartache colored by frustration' (Feldman, 2004, p. 269). Tahitians speak of 'musu' (a resistance to the unreasonable demands of parents) and 'mehameha', a sensation that occurs in unusual circumstances of perception. Russell (2005) describes it as the kind of feeling one might have in the presence of a ghost. Lutz (1990, p. 206) notes several types of anger in the Ifaluk people of Micronesia:

> *There is the irritability that often accompanies sickness (tipmochmoch), the anger that builds up slowly in the face of a succession of minor but unwanted happenings (lingeringer), the annoyance that occurs when relatives have failed to live up to their obligations (nguch), and, finally, there is the frustrated anger that occurs in the face of personal misfortunes and slights which one is helpless to overturn (tang). But each of these emotions is sharply distinguished from the anger which is righteous indignation, or justifiable anger (song), and it is only this anger which is morally approved.*

The emerging set of core emotions might therefore have been different if research in the area were dominated by a language other than English.

The 'Core' of Emotion

While facial expressions are important to emotion, there is more to an emotion than a particular facial configuration. Power and Dalgleish (1997) note that emotions are characterized by: certain physiological disturbances; changes in facial expression; and particular gestures, behaviours, thoughts, beliefs and desires. But what is at the 'core' of an emotion? Which of the above conditions is necessary for an emotion? Is it useful to deconstruct emotions – that is, to try to break them down into their constituent and defining features? Is there a sine qua non for emotion?

Clore and Ortony (2000) propose that human emotions are characterized by four components:

1 cognitive
2 motivational-behavioural
3 somatic, and
4 subjective-experiential.

The cognitive component allows us to mentally register the significance of the emotion. This can be conscious or unconscious, and this component is closely associated with **appraisal** and related processes. We will examine appraisal models of emotion later in this chapter. Appraisal models propose that we monitor our environments for information that is of relevance to us – assessing whether something is good or bad, or a threat, and what resources are available to help us deal with it. For example, imagine a young boy is walking home from school when he hears, close behind him, what seems to be a large growling dog. This is potentially a threat, but appraisal allows context, and available resources, to be considered. For example, if this is an unusual event, the boy may feel afraid. But perhaps that dog growls at the boy every time he passes by, in which case the boy might become angry. Perhaps the boy feels sad for the dog, who he knows is locked behind a gate. The emotion he feels depends on his appraisal of the situation. The degree to which cognition is required in order for an emotion to occur remains contentious, and this issue will be discussed shortly, when we look at the theories examining the relationship between emotion and cognition.

> **Appraisal**
> the ways in which people interpret or explain to themselves the meaning of events.

The motivational-behavioural component involves our actions in response to the emotion: do we run away or stay and fight when we encounter a threat? The somatic component involves the activation of the **autonomic nervous system (ANS)** and **central nervous system (CNS)**, and the characteristic physiological responses that occur along with an emotion. The subjective-experiential component involves the actual experience of the emotion for the individual.

> **Autonomic nervous system**
> part of the peripheral nervous system and regulates internal organs.
> **Central nervous system**
> consists of the brain and spinal cord.

The bodily changes that occur with an emotional state are the most apparent component. On the day of an important examination, you may experience a dry mouth, the palms of your hands might feel clammy and you may lose your appetite for food. You may look in the mirror and notice that you are pale. As you enter the examination hall, you may feel your heart racing. William James recognized the importance of this component of an emotion when he wrote in the *Principles of Psychology* (1890, p. 379) that 'emotion dissociated from all bodily feeling is inconceivable'.

Emotions are associated with certain changes in the autonomic nervous system, such as increases or decreases in heart rate, respiration and blood flow (e.g., blushing, pallor), vasodilation (widening of blood vessels), piloerection (hairs standing up on skin), sweating, and urinary and gastrointestinal changes, among others (see Frijda, 1986). These physiological changes prepare the animal for action; for example, the 'fight or flight' response is associated with fear, and the characteristic physiological changes we experience prepare us to fight or flee (see Table 15.3).

It might therefore seem that physiological changes lie at the core of an emotion. However, similar physiological changes can occur without the experience of emotion – for example, when we exercise or take certain drugs. In addition, there is considerable overlap between the physiological states associated with different emotions and there is

Table 15.3 Changes in the Effects of the Autonomic Nervous Systems Associated with Some of the Emotions

Type	Change	ANS-mediated basis	Emotion
Colouration	Reddening	Vasodilation	Anger
	Blushing	Vasodilation	Embarrassment
	Paling	Vasoconstriction	Fear
Moisture and secretions	Sweating and clamminess	Sweat glands	Fear
	Salivation, drooling	Salivary glands	Disgust
	Foaming	Salivary glands	Anger
	Tearing	Lacrimal glands	Sadness
Protrusions	Piloerection	Muscle fibres at base of hair follicles	Fear, anger
	Blood vessels	Vasodilation	Anger
Eyes' appearance	Constriction	Pupils	Anger
	Dilation	Pupils	Fear
	Bulging	Eyelid muscles	Anger, fear
	Twinkling	Lacrimal glands	Happiness

Source: Adapted from Levenson (2004).

debate over whether there is an absolute discriminating factor that can mark one emotion apart from another, physiologically – although, as we will see shortly, neuroscientific approaches are making some progress on this issue.

There is considerable debate over whether an emotional state can be detected based on physiological changes. Ekman reported evidence for distinctive patterns of autonomic nervous system response for anger, fear and disgust (e.g., Ekman et al., 1983; Levenson et al., 1990) but some studies have failed to replicate these patterns. Cacioppo et al. (1993) note that while heart rate is the best available discriminator, 'it too is far from discriminating consistently or fully among the emotions' (p. 125) and therefore 'the cumulative evidence for emotion-specific autonomic patterns remains inconclusive' (p. 132). On the other hand, Rainville et al. (2006) provide evidence for distinct patterns of cardiorespiratory activity associated with the basic emotions. This debate over distinct emotional states has been argued to support the cognitive approach to emotions; if we cannot detect an emotion precisely from somatic changes in the body, then, the argument goes, it must be the cognition that produces the emotion. According to Schachter and Singer (1962) it is only when we evaluate the physiological changes and apply a label to them that we experience a discrete emotion. In other words, cognition is required in order for us to experience a particular emotion. In order to assess whether this is the case, we need to look next at the theoretical accounts of the relationship between emotion and cognition.

THEORIES OF EMOTION AND COGNITION

Theories of the relationship between cognition and emotion basically address a 'chicken and egg' type problem: which comes first? Does emotion come first or does cognition, the way we think about a particular event, bring about the emotion? Various theories on the relationship between emotion and cognition have been proposed to address this question. As Scherer (2000) notes, it is difficult to understand the controversies within current theories without considering their historical roots. We begin with two contrasting early theories on the emotion–cognition connection, which continue to influence the field today: the James-Lange theory and the Cannon-Bard theory. We then examine Schachter's influential two-factor theory, which brought together aspects of James-Lange and Cannon-Bard, before considering proponents and opponents of the appraisal theories, which have occupied the dominant theoretical position in the study of emotion since the 1980s, but which use the term 'appraisal' in a number of different ways (Moors et al., 2013) and vary considerably in their detail. We will end by considering the constructionist view on emotions.

Early Theories and their Influence

James-Lange theory

The James-Lange theory holds that the experience of an emotion follows the physiological changes associated with that state. In other words, an emotion arises from bodily feedback: we feel happy *because* we have smiled; we feel fear *because* we have run away, and so forth. William James (1884) argued that 'our feeling of (physiological) changes as they occur is the emotion' (pp. 189–190). In 1885, Carl Lange proposed a similar account independently, and this view became known as the James-Lange theory. The emotion *is* the perception of bodily changes.

While it seems counter-intuitive that the behaviour *causes* the emotion, there is some evidence for the role of the body in altering emotional state. For example, there is some support for the **facial feedback hypothesis** (Tomkins, 1962, 1963), which states that feedback from the facial muscles can elicit emotion (see Box 15.3). In typical experiments in this area, participants are forced to alter their facial expression and the effect on self-reported emotional state is measured. One of the immediate problems for such studies is this: if participants are faking an expression such as a smile, knowledge of the meaning of that expression, rather that the expression itself, might create the effect. A number of methods have been developed to get around this potential confound. Strack et al. (1988) had participants hold a pen in their mouths in a manner that either inhibited (pursed lips) or engaged (hold with teeth) the muscles for smiling. They found that participants reported more humour in cartoons in the 'smiling' versus 'inhibiting' conditions. Larsen et al. (1992) repeated this procedure with negative emotions, finding higher ratings of sadness following activation of the 'sad' facial muscle configuration. A study by Hennenlotter et al. (2009) made use of their participants' cosmetic use of Botox® injections to investigate what happens when the frown muscles *cannot* be moved. Botox® is a drug made from a toxin produced by the bacterium *Clostridium botulinum*, which is used cosmetically for the temporary reduction of frown lines – it acts by reducing the activity of muscles near the injection site. Hennenlotter and colleagues scanned the brains of 38 women while they imitated either sad or angry facial expressions. Half of the women were tested two weeks after they had had injections to their frown muscles; half of the women had not had the cosmetic procedure. Consistent with previous research, Hennenlotter and colleagues found that imitating an angry or sad expression increased bilateral activity in the amygdala, but in the women who had Botox® injections, angry expressions were associated with reduced activity in the left amygdala. This provides some support for the notion that feedback from muscle activity can influence emotional experience, and concurs with evidence suggesting that expressing an emotion can prolong it. However, it is quite another claim to suggest that such activity is the cause of emotion. It should be noted that the the facial feedback hypothesis has been highly disputed, and a multilab replication of Strack et al.'s (1988) study failed to

> **Facial feedback hypothesis** proposes that feedback from the facial muscles can influence emotional state.

find any support for it (Wagenmakers et al., 2016). However, a large meta-analysis reviewing 136 studies found some support for the hypothesis, although the effect was small and the results rather heterogeneous (Coles et al., 2019). The effect is larger when the facial expression rather seems to initiate an emotional experience than when it only modulates an ongoing experience. Also some types of stimuli, such as imagined scenarios, gave larger effects than others such as pictures.

Evaluation

While bodily changes would seem to play an important role in emotional experience, it does not follow that muscle movement *causes* emotional experience. Taken to an extreme this would suggest that we cannot feel an emotion if we cannot experience the physiological response. If we become paralysed does that mean that we no longer experience emotion? People with spinal cord injuries show minimal effects on emotional processing (Cobos et al., 2004). Similarly, patients who have pure autonomic failure (selective breakdown of neurons, depriving them of bodily feedback) show minor impairments in emotional processing (Heims et al., 2004). People vary considerably in their ability to *detect* visceral changes; the term interoception is used to refer to this ability (Craig, 2002, 2004). For example, some people notice fairly minor changes in heart rate, while others will not notice minor fluctuations. However, it does not follow that people differ in their emotional experiences depending on how readily they detect these inner changes. Furthermore, sometimes our conscious experience of an emotion precedes the bodily changes that occur; for example, you realize you have said something embarrassing, *then* you blush. Sometimes physiological responses similar to emotion occur without emotion (e.g., when we exercise); how is it that, in these cases, the physiological response occurs but does not lead to an emotion? And how do we account for the fact that the same changes can bring about different emotional experiences? These problems suggest that visceral changes alone cannot be enough to produce emotion and that the James-Lange theory provides an incomplete account.

Cannon-Bard Theory

The shortcomings of the James-Lange theory that we have discussed were noted by Walter Cannon (1927), whose challenge to the James-Lange theory focused on the importance of function. First, Cannon argued that the same physiological state can be associated with different emotions; for example, when we feel fear or anger our heart rate increases; the physiological reaction is similar but the emotion varies considerably. Second, he pointed out that the physiological changes that accompany an emotion can occur without an emotional experience. When we exercise, for example, our hearts race, we may perspire, and so on, but we do not feel fear, anger or another emotion, nor do we confuse the physiological reaction with an emotional state. Third, the same bodily changes as occur during emotion occur in different non-emotional states, such as fever, exposure to cold, asphyxia and hypoglycaemia; how is it that this does *not* give rise to an emotion? Fourth, Cannon argued that the conscious experience of emotion occurs quickly, while visceral changes occur slowly, too slowly to be the cause of emotion. He also noted that physiological changes that are characteristic of emotion can be elicited

© Stacey Newman/Shutterstock

artificially using adrenalin, but this does not give rise to an emotion. He ascribed a key role to the thalamus, a position developed by Phillip Bard (1934).

The Cannon-Bard account argues that the emotional experience and the physiological changes arise *concurrently* from the stimulus event; in other words, that the experience of emotion and the bodily changes are independent. An emotion-provoking event leads to signals being sent simultaneously to the cortex (producing the conscious experience of an emotion) and to the autonomic nervous system (producing the physiological changes).

Evaluation

While Cannon and Bard were incorrect in identifying the thalamus as the key region for the production of emotion, the basic idea of separate cortical and subcortical involvement is retained in subsequent theories, including those that propose key involvement of subcortical structures (e.g., LeDoux, 1996; Rolls, 1990). While both early theories have their merits and introduced concepts that have been developed by subsequent accounts, both were ultimately lacking. For a full account of emotion, it became important to consider the role of cognition. In the 1960s, an influential account emerged that takes account of the role of physiology posited by the James-Lange theory, but addresses Cannon's criticism of the need to differentiate between emotion states: Stanley Schachter's two-factor theory (see Figure 15.4).

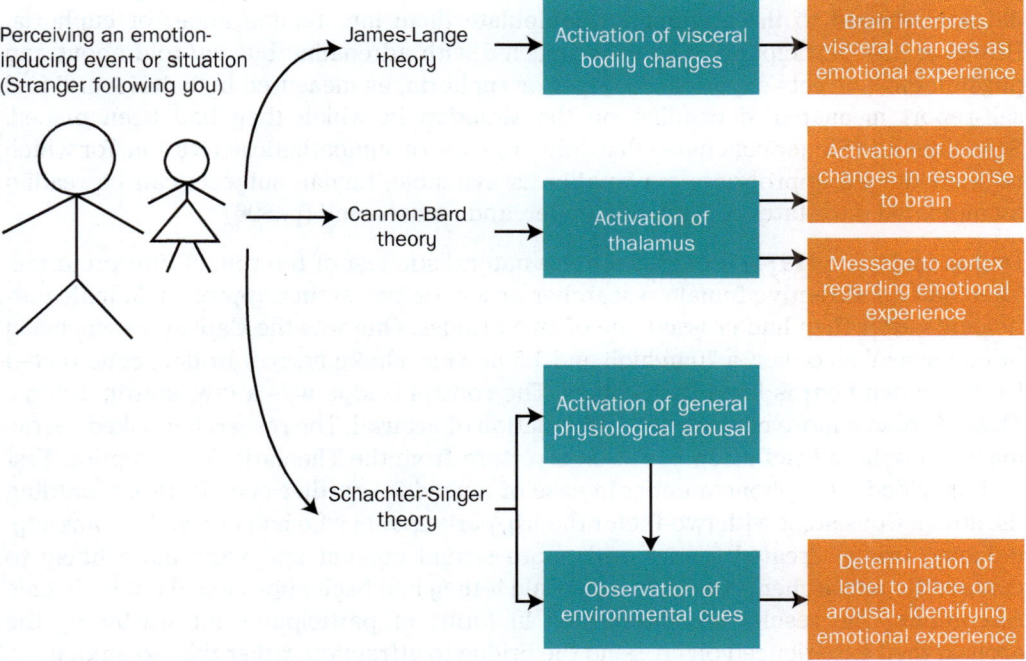

Figure 15.4 Three models of emotion, contrasting the James-Lange, Cannon-Bard and Schachter-Singer accounts.
According to the James-Lange account, activation of bodily (visceral) changes (e.g., heart beating faster, sweating) leads directly to the experience of emotion. The Cannon-Bard account, in contrast, proposed that bodily changes and the experience of emotion occur in parallel. The Schachter-Singer account placed emphasis on the interpretation or appraisal given to the experience, such that bodily changes, along with an evaluation of the environment, provide a label for the arousal, such that different emotions might be elicited, depending on the evaluation applied.

Source: Adapted from Feldman (2004).

Two-Factor Theory

Schachter and Singer's (1962) two-factor theory of emotion proposed, as the name suggests, that two factors create the emotion: physiological arousal and our *interpretation* of it. When we experience arousal, we try to work out the basis for the physiological change. If you are standing outside an examination hall, and you notice that your heart is racing and your mouth is dry, you are likely to interpret the reaction as fear or nervousness. If, however, you are driving home and someone in another car cuts you up, you may interpret the same physical responses as anger. By this account, it is our cognitive interpretation of the initially undifferentiated physiological arousal that produces the emotion; therefore if either arousal or an interpretation is lacking, the emotion will not occur.

In a study investigating this proposal, Schachter and Singer (1962) injected 174 men with adrenaline (epinephrine) or saline and then placed them in social situations designed to provoke 'anger' or 'euphoria'. Having received their injection, half of the participants waited with an angry confederate and half with a 'manic' one. Participants were misinformed as to the nature of the injection; they were told that the study was testing the effects of a vitamin injection called 'suproxin' on vision. Some participants were told to expect some side-effects, such as trembling or palpitations. Other participants were not informed as to any side-effects. They would therefore be unlikely to attribute any arousal to the adrenaline.

Participants injected with adrenaline who were informed as to the physiological effects did not respond to the attempt to manipulate them into feeling anger or euphoria. However, the participants who were injected with adrenaline but *not* told about any physiological effects experienced anger or euphoria, as measured by behavioural and self-report measures, depending on the situation in which they had been placed. Schachter and Singer concluded that, 'given a state of sympathetic activation, for which no immediately appropriate explanation is available, human subjects can be readily manipulated into states of euphoria, anger, and amusement' (p. 396).

Dutton and Aron (1974) provided a more naturalistic test of the role of interpretation. They had an attractive female researcher or a male researcher approach 85 male participants after they had crossed one of two bridges. One was the Capilano suspension bridge near Vancouver, a 70 m high and 1.5 m wide, shaky narrow bridge, constructed from wooden boards lined with cables. The control bridge was a low, sturdy, bridge. This afforded a more naturalistic manipulation of arousal. The researcher asked participants to write a brief story based on a picture from the Thematic Apperception Test and provided a telephone number in case of a need for further clarification regarding the study. Consistent with two-factor theory, participants who had crossed the anxiety-inducing bridge created stories with more sexual content and were more likely to contact the researcher post-study – but only if they had been approached by the female researcher. The results are interpreted in terms of participants misattributing the arousal they experienced on crossing the bridge to attraction rather than to anxiety.

Evaluation

Two-factor theory highlighted the importance of attribution or evaluation and as such paved the way for appraisal theories, but it ascribed a key role to physiological arousal and awareness thereof – by this account, arousal is a necessary condition for an emotional state. Some have argued against this position (e.g., Frijda, 1986; Reisenzein, 1983); awareness of bodily arousal may play a role in the intensity of the emotional experience but it is not the cause of the emotion per se. The theory also suggested that any emotion label could be attached to the physiological state: fear could become attraction or anger, based on the available cognitions. The Schachter and Singer study also had a number of methodological limitations; for example, arousal was artificially induced and participants may have been biased by the instruction, or lack thereof, regarding side-effects. Later studies have only partially reproduced Schachter and Singer's findings, with some data suggesting a negative biasing effect of adrenaline (e.g., Mezzacappa et al., 1999; see also Marshall & Zimbardo, 1979).

While specific aspects of Schachter and Singer's theory have been disputed, the idea that interpretation of physiological state is important has had a lasting influence on appraisal theories of emotion. We turn now to two influential theories that have debated the role of appraisal in emotion, and have asked whether cognition is, in fact, necessary for emotion.

Affective-Primacy: Zajonc's Theory

Robert Zajonc's (1980) affective-primacy (i.e., emotion first) account argues that cognition is not necessary for emotion, and that the two systems can function independently, although he acknowledges that they rarely act independently in everyday life. For Zajonc, 'affect and cognition are separate and partially independent systems . . . although they ordinarily function conjointly, affect could be generated without a prior cognitive process' (1980, p. 117). While cognition can influence emotion at a later stage of processing, the initial emotional response can be unaffected by cognition, according to this view. Zajonc's view is summed up in the subtitle of his 1980 paper: 'preferences need no inferences'. Here, preference, whether or not we like something, is an affective judgement or reaction; essentially it is an emotional response. While cognitive accounts held that affective judgements followed significant information processing, Zajonc argued for the primacy of affect – that is, that an *automatic* affective judgement could be made without cognition (see De Houwer & Hermans, 2010).

> **Mere exposure effect**
> the tendency for people to develop a preference for a stimulus with repeated exposure to it.

The first source of evidence for this account came from the **mere exposure effect** (see Kunst-Wilson & Zajonc, 1980). The mere exposure effect demonstrates that people can develop preferences for stimuli through repeated exposure. Bornstein (1989) reviewed 200 studies of the mere exposure effect, which used a range of stimuli such as nonsense words, ideographs and pictures. The review concluded that, overall, there was evidence that exposure increases liking for the stimulus at moderate repetition and for short or subliminal exposures. In Kunst-Wilson and Zajonc's (1980) study, participants were presented with 10 irregular octagons, each of which was presented five times for 1 millisecond. Following this exposure phase, the participants were subsequently presented with 10 pairs of octagons for 1 second each. One of the pair was an octagon they had seen before and one of the pair was new. The participant was asked which they preferred. While recognition was close to chance (47 per cent), participants showed a statistically significant *preference* for the stimuli to which they had previously been exposed (60 per cent). Of the 24 participants in this experiment, for 17 of them

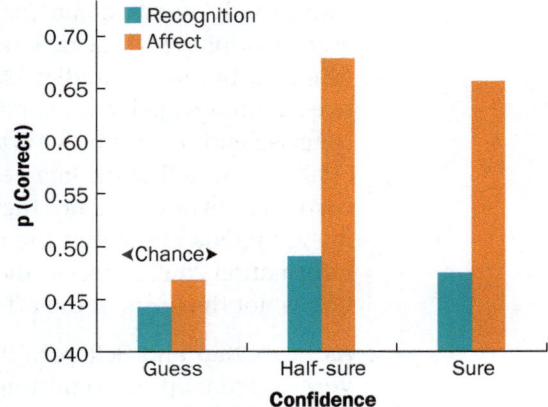

Figure 15.5 The proportion of correct recognition and affective discriminations for responses categorized as guesses, half-sure responses and sure responses.

Source: Kunst-Wilson & Zajonc (1980).

affective judgements discriminated better between old and new stimuli compared to recognition judgements; for four participants, recognition was superior to affective judgements. This may seem to provide support for emotion (here, in the form of an affective preference) in the absence of cognition (since recognition was at chance), however it may be that cognitive processing had occurred.

The research on the mere exposure effect, and the theories that cite it as support for affective primacy, seem to equate cognition with *conscious* cognition or post-perceptual processing (Lazarus, 1995; Leventhal & Scherer, 1987). In a priming study (see Chapter 7), Murphy and Zajonc (1993) presented participants with neutral stimuli that they were not previously familiar with (written Chinese characters), which were preceded by photos of faces showing either positive (happy face) or negative (angry face) emotions. The priming stimuli (faces) were presented for either 4 milliseconds or for 1 second. The participants' task was to assign a rating to the Chinese character that followed the prime. They were to indicate on a 5-point scale whether they thought the character represented a 'good' or a 'bad' concept. For 4-millisecond exposures, the rating assigned to the Chinese character was predicted by the preceding prime; when a happy face came first, the character got a higher liking rating than when an angry face came first. But the effect did not occur when the priming stimulus was presented for 1≈second, presumably because at this duration conscious cognitive processing is possible and we are consciously aware of the prime – its effect on our behaviour can then be moderated. When the faces were clearly visible (consciously perceived), they had no influence on the subsequent ratings. This supports the notion of a fundamental qualitative difference between conscious and unconscious perception, and suggests that our emotions can be affected by unconsciously perceived stimuli. But is this not still cognition?

Evaluation

Other studies have shown low-level cognitive effects that mirror affective responses. Mandler et al. (1987) followed Kunst-Wilson and Zajonc's procedure but included two further conditions. During a testing phase, they had participants make judgements regarding which of the pair of shapes was brighter and which was darker. They confirmed Kunst-Wilson and Zajonc's findings in that recognition was at chance (47 per cent), while preference was significantly higher for pre-exposed stimuli (62 per cent). However, they found that judgements of brightness (60 per cent) and darkness (60 per cent) were also significantly more accurate for pre-exposed stimuli, with no differences between the preference, brightness and darkness conditions. This finding weakens the case for affective primacy, because Mandler et al.'s data show both affective (preference) and cognitive (brightness judgement) effects, while conscious recognition remains at chance level. Neuroscientific research further supports cognitive involvement. Elliott and Dolan (1998) showed that the mere exposure effect is associated with activation in the frontal cortical networks and not the amygdala, and studies of patients with lesions affecting the amygdala show that the mere exposure effect is demonstrated even when visual information cannot access the amygdala (Greve & Bauer, 1990), suggesting that emotion is not the basis of the effect.

As Leventhal and Scherer (1987) pointed out, the debate over the primacy of affect versus primacy of cognition was centred on semantic issues and issues of definition, and 'definitional disputes seldom clarify substantive, theoretical points' (p. 3). The debate dominated research for a considerable period of time, and served to focus attention on the role of cognition in emotion, while also raising the profile of emotion among cognitive researchers (see Schorr, 2001, for a historical overview of the influences on appraisal theories).

Cognitive Primacy: Lazarus's Theory

Richard Lazurus's theory was the first comprehensive **appraisal theory**, of which there are now many variants. What these theories have in common is summed up by Roseman and Smith (2001): 'Whether emotion is generated in response to perceived, remembered, or imagined events, and by automatic or controlled processing, appraisal theories claim that appraisals start the emotion process, initiating the physiological, expressive, behavioural and other changes that comprise the resultant emotional state' (p. 7). Lazarus (1982, 1991) argued that cognitive appraisal is fundamental to emotional experience and that you cannot separate out the cognitive aspect of the emotion. He suggested three types of cognitive appraisal:

> **Appraisal theories** have in common the assertion that emotions result from our interpretations of, or reactions to, events.

1. The primary appraisal is an initial assessment of a situation as being positive, negative or threatening, or irrelevant.
2. The secondary appraisal involves an assessment of the resources we have available to us in dealing with the particular situation.
3. Reappraisal involves continual monitoring of the situation until it is resolved.

Note that Lazarus sees cognition and appraisal as involving both conscious and nonconscious processes. For example, he refers to 'two kinds of appraisal processes – one that operates automatically without awareness or volitional control, and another that is conscious, deliberate, and volitional' (Lazarus, 1991, p. 169). Further versions of this account have attempted to show how the different emotions arise from different patterns of appraisal (e.g., Smith & Lazarus, 1993).

Among the sources of data in support of this approach are studies looking at the effect of the way we think about a stimulus on the emotional experience (e.g., Lazarus & Alfert, 1964; Lazarus et al., 1965; Speisman et al., 1964). Speisman et al. (1964) presented participants with film clips of an anxiety-provoking nature. One clip showed a subincision ritual of the Aboriginal Arunta tribe of north central Australia in which an adolescent boy had a piece of flesh cut from his penis. In another film, a workshop accident is shown; a board caught in a circular saw strikes a worker, who crumbles to the floor in pain. These films were accompanied by one of three soundtracks. The voiceover of the 'denial' soundtrack stated that the workshop film involved actors or that the incision was not painful. In the 'intellectualization' condition, the voiceover encouraged the viewer to take a 'health and safety' perspective for the workshop film, and encouraged an anthropological perspective for the incision film. The final 'trauma' soundtrack focused on the pain and distress depicted. (The background sounds in horror movies are used to similar effect.) A 'no soundtrack' condition was also included. The participants' physiological stress was measured using skin conductance responses.

Those who heard the trauma voiceover had the largest increases in skin conductance (indicating physiological stress), while lowest effects occurred with the intellectualization soundtrack. The denial soundtrack produced a skin conductance increase marginally greater that the intellectualization condition, and those who heard no soundtrack at all produced increases intermediate between those of the threatening condition and the denial condition. Lazarus and colleagues interpreted these data as showing that our appraisals alter the emotional response to the stimulus. By altering the participants' cognitive appraisal of the events, they altered the stress/emotional response. However, attempts to replicate these studies have met with limited success and one would have to question their generalizability to real-life events.

Evaluation

We know that appraisal plays an important role in determining emotion. If you hear a dog growl, what you think about that dog, or about dogs generally, will affect the emotional outcome. If past experience suggests the dog is a threat to you, this will affect your emotional response. On the other hand, if the dog is not a threat, the sound of a growl might merely attract your interest – you may wonder why the dog is growling, whether someone is approaching, for example. Clearly, the appraisal is relevant. However, what is meant by 'appraisal' is rather vague and Lazarus's assertion that appraisal is involved in non-conscious processing and is *always* involved in emotion would have to be questioned. The survival value of a speedy response to a physical threat suggests a 'faster' route, at least on some occasions.

> **Multi-level theories** of emotion propose that both preattentive and conscious cognitive processes are involved in emotion.

It may be that sometimes cognition is involved and sometimes not. The **multi-level theories** (e.g., LeDoux, 1992, 1996) suggest that the Larazus–Zajonc debate is false and that evidence exists to support both views. LeDoux suggests that there are two ways in which an emotion is registered. One is direct, a 'low' route, from the thalamus to the amygdala, and allows very fast responses. This would be important in case of a threat, allowing us to react quickly (e.g., on seeing something move on the ground, which may be a snake). He suggests a second slower route from thalamus via cerebral cortex to amygdala, which allows us to appraise the situation when acting on the emotion.

LeDoux's account highlights a key objection to appraisal theories: it is not the idea of appraisal itself that is problematic but the notion that appraisal is always *cognitive* in nature (see Clore & Ortony, 2008, p. 631). It seems unlikely, however, that any complex emotional experience can occur without cortical involvement.

Subsequent appraisal theories (e.g., Frijda, 1986; Oatley & Johnson Laird, 1987; Ortony et al., 1988; Scherer, 1988) have continued to address the nature of the evaluations that comprise emotions, and make a distinction between undifferentiated physiological responses and fully fledged emotions, suggesting that 'low-level bodily, hormonal, and affective reactions often get the emotional process started, and that cognitive appraisal processes act like a sculptor, shaping general affective reactions into specific emotions' (Clore & Ortony, 2008, p. 629). This, again, suggests that differentiation is needed between initial automatic, low-level or reflexive processes and actual emotional states.

The appraisal theories find support in research that investigates our ability to change how we experience our emotions in our daily life. Which strategies we use and when is the focus of the study in Box 15.4.

Box 15.4 Research Close Up: When and why we try to regulate our emotions during daily life

Source: English et al. (2017).

INTRODUCTION

Every day we regulate how we experience and express our emotions (English et al., 2017). For example, if you feel nervous about giving a speech in front of your class you might use different strategies to try to decrease the anxiety that you are feeling. You may try to distract yourself by shifting your attentional focus to the speech you are giving, instead of focusing on the class that sits in front of you waiting patiently for you to begin. This is an example of down-regulating an emotion and the regulation could also be in the opposite direction – that is, we try to increase a positive emotion.

Several different strategies have been proposed (for a review see Gross, 2014). Some of these are used early in the process of generating the emotions. Thus, they take place before the emotion is fully formed. One such early strategy is distraction, as mentioned above, which helps you to shift focus in a situation. But, you could also try to change the meaning of the situation at hand by cognitive reappraisal. In the example above of giving a speech, you would simple reframe the situation by thinking 'This is a chance for me to practise my presentation skills among friends who know me.' Another emotion regulation strategy, which happens later in the emotion-generative process, is suppression, which is when one actively tries to inhibit one's emotional expression. While early emotion regulation strategies tend to be more efficient in regulating mood than are later strategies, there may be circumstances where these later strategies serve an important purpose. When and why these different strategies are used in everyday life was investigated by English et al. (2017).

In the study, English and colleagues focused on whether certain strategies were selected based on the social context and whether different emotional regulation goals are associated with different strategies. For example, if we do not trust those we are socializing with, we might try to suppress our emotions in order not to become too vulnerable. However, different emotional regulation goals play an important part in which strategies are used. We can divide the regulation goals into two possible main types. Hedonic goals, where the main purpose is to feel more or less positive or negative emotions, and instrumental goals, which in a social setting could be that 'we want to get along' or 'to complete a task'.

METHODS

First-year college students were asked to daily report the most positive event and the most negative in a seven-day diary study. They were also asked to indicate whether other people were involved in this event and how close the relationship was (e.g., family, friend or stranger). The participants were also asked to indicate whether they had tried to influence their emotions, and were asked to rate to what extent they used the strategies cognitive appraisal, suppression and distraction. They also indicated which was the goal of their emotion regulation (hedonic or instrumental).

RESULTS

Emotion regulation strategies were reported for both positive and negative events, but were more commonly used for negative events. Pro-hedonic regulation was the most common regulation, with people trying to decrease negative emotions or increasing positive emotions. However, regulating one's mood was seldom the only goal, and often an instrumental goal was also mentioned, such as 'to avoid conflict' or 'getting work done'.

When it comes to the social context, suppression was used more often when the person was not alone, and it was also used more when instrumental goals were endorsed such as 'avoiding conflict'. Contrary to this, reappraisal was used to the same extent regardless of whether the person was alone or not. But it was used more often for hedonic than for instrumental goals. Distraction as a strategy was reported in equal amounts, regardless of whether the participant was alone or not. Similar to reappraisal, distraction was used more for hedonic than for instrumental goals.

DISCUSSION

This study suggests that emotion regulation strategies vary, depending on social context and which goals are being endorsed (hedonic or instrumental). Interestingly, suppression, which is considered to be a less efficient mood regulation strategy, was often used in situations with non-close persons, suggesting that this strategy is employed when people feel insecure and uncomfortable about expressing their emotions in public.

The Theory of Constructed Emotions

In recent years a constructionist paradigm for studying and understanding emotions has gained in popularity (see Barrett, 2016, 2017; Russell, 2003). The two-factor model, which we address earlier in the chapter, can be seen as an early theory from this paradigm where emotions are viewed as construed by interpreting the arousal and context in which the person is having their experience. The paradigm questions the classical view on emotions put forward by Ekman and colleagues and some of the other earlier theorists. According to the constructionist approach an emotion such as happiness is not a distinct phenomenon; instead, it consists of several highly different instances. As described by Barrett (2016), some instances of happiness can be both pleasant and arousing, such as when you have succeeded in a difficult task, or even unpleasant, such as when you are unable to phone your friend to tell them some happy news. Therefore according to this view, there are no 'natural kinds' of emotions.

In the theory of constructed emotions put forward by Barrett (2017), an emotion is formed when the brain makes meanings of all our sensory input. Thus all information that comes from our bodies – for example, blood rushing, our lungs expanding, and even sounds, sights and smells – is categorized based on past experiences. Instances of emotions are therefore learned within a specific social and cultural context. It should be noted that Barrett stresses that our interpretations of our emotions using past experiences do not cause the emotions, which sets his theory aside from some appraisal theories. The past experiences merely help us to categorize them. Barrett (2016, p. 44) summarizes the theory with the following paragraph:

> *In every waking moment, your brain uses past experience that function as concepts to guide action and give sensations meaning. In this manner your brain models your body in the world. When the concepts involved are emotion concepts, your brain constructs instances of emotion.*

Support of the constructionist view come from neuroscientific studies (e.g., Barrett & Satpute, 2019). Several studies show that the same brain regions are activated across a range of instances of emotions. The results stand in contradiction to the locationist approach, where it is hypothesized that discrete emotions (often referred to as basic emotions) are associated consistently and specifically with increased brain activity in certain brain regions (e.g., Lindquist et al., 2012).

Evaluation

Although some support can be found for the constructionist view from neuroscientific studies, the evidence is not clear-cut, and the scientific claims made by Barrett and colleagues have been challenged by other researchers (e.g., Lench et al., 2013).

The theoretical approaches to the study of cognition and emotion have served to focus attention on the interrelationships between them and the degree to which cognition is involved in emotion, and vice versa. We now turn to this latter issue, namely the influences of affect such as emotion or mood on cognition, or the differences in cognitive processing in the presence of affect.

THE INFLUENCE OF AFFECT ON COGNITION

In the Introduction to this chapter, you read about the case of D.S., a young man who developed the Capgras delusion following a brain injury. This case illustrates the importance of how emotion influences the process of face recognition, and shows how emotional processing works alongside recognition processes to create meaningful experience. Affective states, such as emotions and mood, influence cognition in many ways, and processing of emotional information differs from processing of neutral information. It should be noted that it is often hard to tease from one another the scientific results of influence of affect such as valence and arousal, discrete emotions and moods. Here, we consider some of the ways in which affective states influence the key processes of attention, perception and memory, focusing in particular on memory.

Affect and Attention

Attentional biases are demonstrated when a participant's attention is selectively directed towards a stimulus. One of the most widely used tasks in the study of attentional biases in participants with depression, anxiety or other disorders is the emotional Stroop task. The emotional Stroop task is a variant of the Stroop colour-naming task (see Chapter 11), in which emotional terms take the place of colour terms. In the standard Stroop task, colour terms presented in incongruent colours produce slower response times in a colour naming task than those with congruent colour; for example, it takes longer to respond 'blue' given the word RED written in blue ink, compared to the word BLUE written in blue ink. The effect demonstrates interference from reading in a colour-naming task. In the emotional Stroop task, stimuli are chosen with emotional or threatening content. For example, in a study involving participants with a spider phobia (e.g., Lavy et al., 1993; Watts et al., 1986), words such as 'web' and 'hairy' might feature among the stimuli. In the same way as reading interferes with the task of colour naming in the standard Stroop task, the emotional content of these words will take attention from the primary task, disrupting performance.

> **Attentional bias**
> the tendency for emotional stimuli to capture or draw attention.

> Chapter 11, p374

The effect has been demonstrated in participants with simple phobias, such as spider phobia, but also in generalized anxiety disorder (e.g., Mathews et al., 1995; Mogg et al., 1993), obsessive compulsive disorder (e.g., Foa & McNally, 1986) and post-traumatic stress disorder (e.g., Cassiday et al., 1992). Attentional biases are also evident in those with drug addiction (for an overview see Field et al., 2006). The precise nature of attentional bias in depression continues to be investigated, with conflicting data reported in initial studies in the area (e.g., see MacLeod et al., 1986; Mineka & Sutton, 1992). For example, Mogg et al. (1993) found that anxious participants, but not depressed participants, demonstrated slower colour naming for negative words, supporting a processing bias for negative information in anxiety. On the other hand, Mogg et al. (1995) found that both anxious and depressed participants showed an attentional bias towards negative words, compared to controls. More recently it has become apparent that attentional biases in depression are evident only under specific task conditions, and that depression is associated with deficits in the inhibition of mood-congruent (i.e., negative) material (Joormann et al., 2007).

There are few studies that report emotional Stroop data for non-clinical samples (see Yiend, 2010), but other methods have been used to study the link between emotion and attention in the general population. Lipp and Derakshan (2005) examined attentional bias to fear-relevant animals in undergraduate participants using the attentional probe or dot probe task (MacLeod et al., 1986), with pictures of snakes, spiders, mushrooms and flowers. In the dot probe task, two stimuli, one neutral and one emotional (e.g., threatening), are presented on a computer screen, generally for quite a brief exposure duration. A dot probe is then presented in the location of one or other of the stimuli. Participants have to respond to the probe as quickly as they can by pressing a response key. The response time will be affected by the location where the participant had directed his or her attention when the dot appeared. So, for example, if the participant is anxious, his or her attention will have moved towards the threatening stimulus and away from the neutral one. Responses will then be faster when the probe appears in the location of the threatening stimulus compared to trials where the probe appears in the location of the neutral stimulus. One might predict that stimuli such as pictures of fear-relevant animals would attract attention regardless of a participant's trait or state anxiety; it is important for us to be able to act quickly in the presence of a threat.

Consistent with this, Lipp and Derakshan (2005) found that probes that replaced fear-relevant stimuli (snakes and spiders) were associated with faster responses than those that replaced the non-fear-relevant stimuli. This attentional bias was not correlated with self-reported state or trait anxiety. This type of normal bias towards (potentially) threatening information would seem to have an important survival function, one that may have become maladaptive in those with emotional disorders.

> **Visual search** tasks require an active search of a visual array, usually for a particular object or stimulus feature.

The **visual search** method has also been adapted to study influences of affect on attention. In the typical procedure, a participant has to detect, as quickly as possible, which one of a group of stimuli is discrepant – for example, a number of faces might be shown, with one facial expression different to the rest. Such studies have shown that pre-attentive visual search is faster for emotional information compared to neutral information (see Yiend, 2010, for a useful review). This normal response is also oversensitive in conditions such as anxiety disorders.

Affect and Perception

> Chapter 2, p34

> Chapter 4, p114

Perception and attention are closely related (see Chapters 2 and 4), and it is difficult to tease them apart for the purposes of understanding the influence of affect on perception. However, a number of studies have addressed the influence of affect on perception. Phelps et al. (2006), for example, looked at the effect on early vision. Participants were instructed to look at a fixation point at the centre of a computer screen. A fearful or neutral face appeared briefly (75 milliseconds) on screen. Four stimuli were then presented, one of which was tilted at an angle. Participants simply had to indicate, via button press, the tilt angle (right or left), but the contrast of the stimuli was manipulated. Phelps and colleagues found that when stimuli were preceded by a fearful face, participants could discriminate the orientation at a lower level of contrast than when stimuli were preceded by a neutral face. Presence of an emotional stimulus heightened contrast sensitivity.

In a second experiment, Phelps et al. asked whether emotion interacts with attention so as to affect early vision. This time, the faces were used as attentional pre-cues, presented either peripherally so as to elicit focused attention or distributed so as to spread attention across the display. The results showed that the effect seen in Experiment 1 was magnified when attention was invoked: peripheral cues produced greater contrast sensitivity than the distributed cues. While the sample sizes in this study were rather small, the facilitative effect on early visual processing was clear.

Similarly, it has been shown that affect increases participants' field of view (Schmitz et al., 2009). The influence of affect on perception is therefore seen in even the most basic perceptual processes.

This top-down influence of affect is also evident for other sensory modalities. Siegel and Stefanucci (2011) induced a negative or neutral mood in participants by having them recount a frightening or neutral experience from their past. They were then presented with a series of short, neutral tones (320 and 640 milliseconds) and asked to rate their loudness and duration. Siegel and Stefanucci found that loudness perception was influenced by mood, with participants in a negative mood rating the tones as significantly louder, compared to those in a neutral mood. Consistent with the studies of visual perception, this study suggests a role of affect in heightening auditory perception, a bias that can be exploited to great effect in horror movie soundtracks. Similar effects have been demonstrated for speech perception (e.g., Wang et al., 2009). These data suggest that the influence that affect has on perception may be more pervasive than has traditionally been assumed.

Affect and Memory

Memory was explored in detail in Chapters 6, 7 and 8. How does affect influence memory? Everyday experience would suggest that we are more likely to recall emotionally significant events. But are such memories accurate, or, in some circumstances, might emotions have a detrimental effect on memory? William James wrote that 'an experience may be so exciting emotionally as to almost leave a scar on the cerebral tissue' (1890, p. 670). Memory for emotional events is generally better than for events that do not arouse emotions, with both quantitative and qualitative effects (see Kensinger & Schacter, 2010, for an overview). Intense emotion can have a negative effect on cognition, however.

> Chapter 6, p176
>
> Chapter 7, p218
>
> Chapter 8, p258

Flashbulb memories: effects of emotion

In Chapter 8, you will have read about the idea of a 'flashbulb' memory – that is, a vivid memory for an emotionally significant event that is supposedly called to mind as an exact reproduction of the event, like a 'photographic' memory. Brown and Kulik (1977) argued that a special memory mechanism underlies the vivid experience that is the flashbulb memory. In Chapter 8 we discussed the role of cognitive factors such as rehearsal in the maintenance of flashbulb memories; in this section, we focus on the possible role of emotional factors in flashbulb memories. Events that arouse strong emotions have been studied in order to determine whether a qualitatively distinct kind of memory is involved. For example, participants have been asked about their recollections on hearing about the assassinations of Martin Luther King and President Kennedy (Brown & Kulik, 1977; Winograd & Killinger, 1983), the 11 September 2001 terrorist attacks in the United States (Pezdek, 2003; Talarico & Rubin, 2003), the Hillsborough football stadium disaster in the UK (Wright, 1993; Wright et al., 1998), the resignation of UK prime minister Margaret Thatcher (Conway et al., 1994; Wright et al., 1998) and the assassination of Swedish prime minister Olof Palme (Christianson, 1989). People seem to report much detail of their experience of such public events, but is their memory accurate over time, and is there evidence for a 'flashbulb' effect in memory, with an important role for emotion?

In 1989, 96 football supporters were fatally injured at the Hillsborough stadium in England, during the FA Cup semi-final between Liverpool and Nottingham Forest, as a result of overcrowding of a section of the stands. The disaster received extensive coverage on television and in the other media. Wright (1993) examined 247 participants' memories of the disaster two days, one month and five months after the event occurred. While the event was judged by participants to be of more social and emotional significance over time, their memory for detail of the event faded, and Wright found that memories were reconstructed and open to bias. In this case, it appears that memory was not like a photograph and did not show a 'flashbulb' effect.

Schmolck et al. (2000) examined students' memories of hearing about the verdict in the O.J. Simpson trial in 1995. (This was a highly publicized trial of a well-known former American footballer, O.J. Simpson, who was tried, and acquitted, on two counts of murder following the deaths of his ex-wife and her friend.) Participants' recall was tested three days, 15 months and 32 months after the event. At 15 months, just 50 per cent of recollections were accurate and by 32 months accuracy had fallen to 29 per cent and the number of errors for particular details rose from 11 per cent to 40 per cent, with many participants showing major distortions of memory. The most common error involved source memory; participants tended to misattribute the source of the information. However, Schmolck and colleagues also found that the best predictor of later recall accuracy was the strength of the emotional response of the participant at the time the verdict was announced. Similarly, when Conway et al. (1994) examined people's memories of the resignation of the British prime minister Margaret Thatcher, they found that the greater emotional reaction of UK citizens over non-citizens was associated with accuracy of memory, even when they controlled for knowledge, rehearsal and perceived importance of the event.

This might suggest that emotional and personally experienced events would be associated with better memory. Personal events are very difficult to study, as by their nature they tend to be individualized and it is difficult to determine accuracy in the absence of a means to corroborate the facts. In diary studies, greater emotional intensity is associated with more detailed subsequent recall of the event (Conway, 1995). We do know, however, that memory for personal experiences is open to bias. Experimental tasks have demonstrated that it is relatively easy to implant false memories, for example, and some people in particular are open to suggestion (e.g., Hyman et al., 1995).

The effects of emotions on episodic memory

Emotion affects our memories for events. Furthermore, the timing and nature of the retrieval task has been shown to be crucial, as has been discussed in Chapters 7 and 8. As the delay between the target event and the memory test increases, people become more likely to err (Loftus et al., 1978).

Chapter 7, p218

Chapter 8, p258

When does emotion support memory? Memory for facts would seem to be better when learning is associated with an emotion (Cahill et al., 1995). Emotion-provoking pictures also show a memory advantage, linked to activation of the amygdala. A study by Canli et al. (2000) used fMRI to scan participants' amygdala while they were presented with pictures that were neutral or emotionally negative. After three weeks, participants were given a recognition test and asked to select the pictures they had seen from a set that included pictures they had not seen before. They found increased activation of the amygdala bilaterally for pictures that were rated as more emotionally intense, and memory for these pictures was also better. They found, in particular, that activation of the left amygdala predicted recognition, suggesting an emotion-specific mechanism (see also Hamann et al., 1999). Memory for negative stimuli is generally better than for neutral and even, on some occasions, positive stimuli (Bradley et al., 1992; Ochsner, 2000), consistent with findings from studies of attentional biases (discussed above).

However, on balance, the research suggests that strong negative emotion enhances memory for the central details of an event, but this occurs at the expense of memory for peripheral details, an effect referred to as **tunnel memory** (see Christianson, 1992). This trade-off between central and peripheral aspects of a witnessed event is evident in the weapons-focus effect, a type of object-salience effect that is demonstrated when witnesses focus on a weapon at the expense of other aspects of the crime (e.g., Loftus et al.,

Tunnel memory
the enhancement of memory of central details with reduced memory for peripheral details.

1987; Steblay, 1992). While fewer studies have considered the effect of intense positive emotions it would seem that this tunnel effect of enhanced central details does not apply to the same extent to positive emotions (e.g., Berntsen, 2002).

Therefore the balance of evidence does not support that strong emotions always result in strong unbiased memories for a certain event. However, under many conditions, emotion enhances memory. Levine and Pizarro (2004) provide a useful metaphor – rather than thinking of emotion as writing a record in indelible ink, it is more like a highlighter, increasing the salience of particular aspects of an event in the way a highlighter might be applied during study to a passage of text. They complete the metaphor by suggesting that negative emotion is like a fine highlighter – evidence suggests that it narrows focus so that memory for central aspects of the event might be aided, to the cost of peripheral aspects.

Houston et al. (2013) examined which aspects of memory for an event in an eyewitness scenario would be impaired by emotion. Participants viewed either an emotion-inducing video, which was a crime scenario (a mugging), or a neutral scenario (a conversation). Two staged events were recorded, using the same actors. The results of the first experiment showed that the participants who saw the emotion-inducing video could provide more complete descriptions of the perpetrator of the crime, while participants who saw a neutral scenario produced more complete descriptions of the critical incident overall. The more complete descriptions for participants who saw the emotion-inducing video suggest that their attention was focused on the perpetrator of the crime. However, there was no difference between the two groups with regard to accuracy of the descriptions of the perpetrator.

The results were replicated in a follow-up experiment. However, when asked to pick out the perpetrator from a line-up, those in the emotion condition performed worse than the participants who saw the neutral conditions. Although it should be noted that witnessing a mugging in real life would be a far more shocking event, and might produce different effects on memory.

Mood-congruent memory

There is considerable evidence to suggest a **mood congruency** effect in memory – that is, when we are in a positive mood we more readily recall positive memories, whereas when in a negative mood, negative memories more easily come to mind (Blaney, 1986; Bower, 1981, 1991). This effect is often explained in terms of **network models** of memory such as Bower's associative network theory (Bower, 1981). Specific emotions, such as anger or sadness, like other concepts, are nodes in a network along with emotion-laden memories. When you are in a sad mood, the 'sad' node in the network is activated and, via its connections, activates related memories. In this way emotion is very much tied in with cognition and memory, and imposes a structure on the network of stored relations. Emotions are like other concepts and stored in a semantic network linked to other nodes representing the autonomic responses, behavioural responses, situations that might evoke the emotion, and so on. A related effect is mood-dependent memory; memory for emotionally neutral material is facilitated when the mood state at encoding matches that at retrieval. This is an example of **state-dependent memory**. Mood- and state-dependent memory are discussed in Chapter 8.

> **Mood congruency**
> the tendency to recall events consistent with current mood state.
>
> **Network models**
> of memory treat memories as items related in a network which can affect each other through activation.
>
> **State-dependent memory**
> the facilitation of memory when the mental or physiological state at encoding and retrieval matches.

Chapter 8, p258

Bower (1981) asked participants to keep a diary detailing their moods over a period of one week. A 'happy' or 'sad' mood was then induced (using hypnotic suggestion – a method that is not without its critics) and they were asked to recall events from their diary. A mood congruency effect was noted – if a sad mood had been induced, more sad memories were recalled and if a happy mood was induced more happy memories were recalled. In a similar vein, Eich and Metcalfe (1989) tested the effect of current mood state on learning and subsequent memory. They induced moods in participants by having them listen to classical music that was intended to induce a positive (e.g., Mozart's *Eine kleine Nachtmusik*) or negative (e.g., Barber's *Adagio pour cordes*) mood. Participants were instructed to, at the same time, think of something that made them happy or sad. During the learning phase, 32 triads were presented. Half had the form *category name: category exemplar – target item* (e.g., precious metals: silver – GOLD), and half were of the form *category name: category exemplar – initial letter of target* (e.g., milkshake flavours: chocolate – V). Participants were to generate and state aloud the target item; in the case of 'milkshake flavours: chocolate – V', for example, they were to generate the target 'VANILLA'. On half of the trials, instead of generating the item, it was read aloud by the experimenter and the participants simply repeated it back. Memory was then compared for generated or read items.

Memory was tested two days later, when mood was again induced. Participants initially recalled the items aloud, in any order, with no cues or hints given. They were then presented with a list of the 32 targets along with 32 items that had not been presented during the learning phase. Participants had to respond 'old' or 'new' to indicate items that they had encountered during the learning session two days earlier, or not, respectively. The results are shown in Figure 15.6.

The results showed an effect of mood congruence for both 'read' and 'generate' conditions, with a stronger effect for the 'generate' task. This supported Eich and Metcalfe's assertion that mood-dependent effects in memory are stronger for internal than for external events. Internal events originate from our own mental processes, as opposed to external events, which come to our awareness through the perceptual processes (Eich & Metcalfe, 1989).

Figure 15.6 The effect of matching mood on the recall of read or generated target words.

Source: Based on data from Eich & Metcalfe (1989).

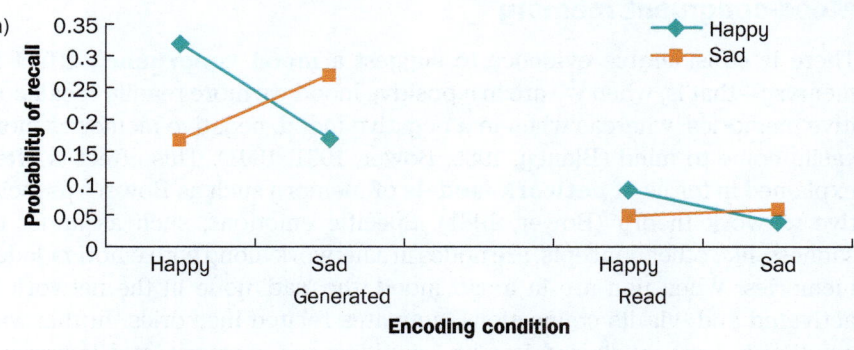
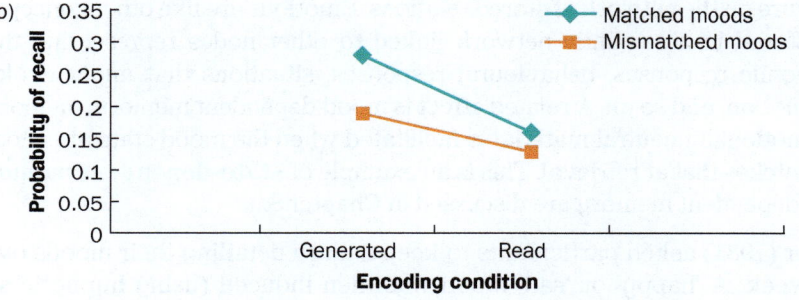

If such effects occur for induced moods, do the findings also apply to clinical mood states? Clark and Teasdale (1982) examined the natural mood states of people who were depressed and found that the recall of negative memories increased during periods of low mood, whereas happier memories were relatively more frequent when a more positive mood state prevailed. Similarly, Burke and Matthews (1992) found that, given neutral cues, anxious participants demonstrated a recall bias towards anxiety-related material compared to non-anxious participants.

Some findings do not fit with an associative network model. Emotion-congruent memory has been shown to be stronger for positive than for negative emotions, and mood-incongruency effects have also been reported. Parrott and Sabini (1990), for example, found that participants in an unhappy mood recalled more positive memories than participants in a happy mood. Such effects are not predicted by classic network or associative theories and have been explained in terms of the influence of motivational factors, by which a number of mood-regulatory processes kick in to reduce or eliminate negative moods. Isen (1985, 1987) suggested that when someone is in a negative mood state, they are motivated to reduce that state and create a more positive mood. Their attention is therefore focused away from the sources of negative mood; this leads to the retrieval of more positive memories and, one assumes, evokes a positive mood in the person, or at least reduces the negative mood. Forgas (1995) proposed the affect infusion model (AIM), which makes the distinction between motivated processing and constructive processing. Motivated processes use 'highly predetermined and directed information search patterns and require little generative, constructive processing' (Forgas, 1995, p. 40). Motivated processing might be used by someone to regulate their moods, and because it accesses previously established goal states it is less susceptible to the effects of current mood. Constructive processing involves a generative processing strategy, using a heuristic or substantive, elaborate, type of processing. According to the model, it is this type of processing that underlies mood-congruency effects. By this account, 'affect is unlikely to influence judgments in a mood-congruent direction during direct access or motivated processing; rather, it should have a mood-congruent effect only when heuristic or substantive processing is used' (Forgas, 1995, p. 40).

The affect infusion model has been applied to studies of **thought congruity**. Thought congruity refers to the influence of mood state on participants' judgements and decision making. In particular, positive moods are associated with more positive or lenient thoughts and judgements. For example, risk taking is greater for those in a happy mood (e.g., Chou et al., 2007). AIM is consistent with findings that thought congruity occurs in some contexts, when judgements demand elaborate cognitive processing, while not in others (Sedikides, 1994). Factors such as thought congruity and state-dependent memory have greatly influenced the cognitive approach to clinical states such as depression (see Box 15.5).

> **Thought congruity**
> the tendency for thoughts and judgements to be consistent with mood state.

 Box 15.5 Practical Application: Cognitive behavioural therapy for depression

The cognitive approach to depression focuses on maladaptive thinking habits, errors, biases and depressogenic (meaning 'depression causing') attributional styles associated with depression (for a review see Rubenstein et al., 2016). Some theories argue that these thinking styles *cause* depression; others see them more as a contributory factor. If such thinking patterns cause or exacerbate depression, then changing these thinking styles should help. This is the basis of cognitive behavioural therapy, or CBT. This approach is associated with the work of Aaron Beck and the rational approach of Albert Ellis. The cognitive approach is summed up by Beck et al. (1979, p. 11) as follows:

> The cognitive model views the other signs and symptoms of depressive syndrome as a consequence of the activation of the negative cognitive patterns. For example, if the patient incorrectly thinks he is being rejected, he will react with the same negative affect that occurs with actual rejection.

By this account, it's not what happens in our lives that is important, it's how we think about or interpret events that is key. Ellis's ABC concept is useful here (e.g., Ellis & Harper, 1975). According to Ellis, when we experience an Activating Event (A), we interpret or think about the event. Our interpretation of the event leads to a Belief (B) about the event in relation to ourselves and to the world. We then experience Emotional Consequences (C) based on the belief. An error occurs when we infer that A (alone) led to C, rather than recognizing that B led to C (see Figure 15.7).

While all of us can demonstrate this kind of maladaptive thinking occasionally, people who are depressed (or those who will become depressed) think like this generally, according to this account. Beck proposed that, in depression, such thinking applies to the self, the immediate world and the future, a pattern known as the depressive cognitive triad. Beck (1967, 1976) developed cognitive therapy (or cognitive behavioural therapy, CBT) as a method of challenging such maladaptive thinking. The purpose of CBT was to challenge cognitive distortions affecting the depressed person's thinking. Butler et al.'s (2006) review of meta-analyses of CBT efficacy concludes that CBT is 'somewhat superior to antidepressants in the treatment of adult depression' (p. 17).

The cognitive distortions described by Beck are negative automatic thoughts that are habitual, involuntary and unconstructive, and create systematic logical errors. Depressive thought is, according to Beck, 'schema driven' (whereby the world is perceived through a depressive schema), but are the thinking patterns of people with depression always distorted and inaccurate? In some (rather limited) circumstances, depressed individuals have been shown to be more accurate than non-depressed individuals. Alloy and Abramson (1979) had participants (a depressed and non-depressed group) rate the degree of control that their responses had over a particular environmental event. On each trial in the task, participants could respond (e.g., press a button) or not respond (e.g., not press). After the response period, a light appeared or did not appear (environmental event). The participants were subsequently asked to rate their control over the outcome (the light coming on). They typically tended to overestimate their control over the outcome in such tasks, a pattern referred to as the outcome-density effect (see Allan, 1993) or illusion of control (see Alloy & Abramson, 1979). Alloy and Abramson found that this effect was absent in depressed individuals, who appeared to have a more accurate view of the effect of their responses on the outcome, a pattern they called 'depressive realism' (e.g., Alloy & Ackerman, 1988).

This is a controversial idea and on the balance of evidence currently available one would have to conclude that depressed individuals show a more realistic view of their chances of success, but only when that view matches the depressive schema with which they are operating. While it is true that depressed individuals have a more accurate view of their own performance and level of control in contingency studies and in chance-determined tasks (Abramson et al., 1978; Klein & Seligman, 1976), it is also the case that depressed individuals *underestimate* the amount of positive feedback (while non-depressed people may overestimate it) in other

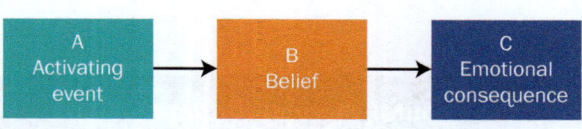

Figure 15.7 Ellis's ABC model.
This proposes that we suffer emotional consequences not directly from an activating event but from our beliefs about the event. For example, an impending examination (A) might be associated with anxiety (C), but because we hold a belief that we will fail (B), it is the fear of failure and not the examination itself that leads to the anxiety.

tasks (see Buchwald, 1977; Moore & Fresco, 2007; Wener & Rehm, 1975). Dunn et al. (2007) showed that depressed participants judged error trials more accurately but correct trials less accurately, for example. Therefore it would seem that the nature of the task is key to the outcome.

There is by now much evidence for the existence of maladaptive thinking styles in depression. However, while much research shows that illogical thoughts are *associated* with depression (e.g., Gara et al., 1993; Haaga et al., 1991), whether such thoughts are the *cause* of depression is less clear. A study suggesting such a causal link showed that younger adults with maladaptive thinking styles were more likely to develop depression than those without (Alloy et al. 2006). Similarly, in a study by Mac Giollabhui et al. (2018), maladaptive thinking styles were associated to onset of depression via increased feelings of hopelessness in youth. This association was increased if the youth experienced a negative life event.

Affect and Decision Making

Considering how often we ask ourselves 'How do I feel about this?' when we make important decisions in real life, it may come as a surprise that research concerning the affective influence on decision making, whether it is emotion or mood, had up until a few decades ago been highly limited. Instead, research within this area was for a long time focused on the cognitive aspects of decision making, such as rational and reason-based processes. However, affective states influence our decisions in many different ways.

We might be influenced by both **integral affect**, which stems from the decision at hand or from the anticipated affect of the decision outcome, and by **incidental affect**, which are affective influences that carry over from another situation or object (Lerner et al., 2015; Loewenstein & Lerner, 2003). For example, when deciding whether to fly or take a train to a location, you might be affected by emotions that will inform your decision. If you enjoy airplane rides the positive emotions you are feeling during the decision will probably influence you to book a flight. However, emotions may also influence us in an anticipatory way. For example, our judgements and decision may be affected by whether we anticipate fear or regret when choosing a certain alternative. This type of emotional influence could be informative but it could also lead to biased decisions. For example, if we feel a fear of flying this might lead us to take the car to a certain destination even though, statistically speaking, the airplane ride is much safer. In addition to this, trying to predict our emotions from a certain decision outcome can be quite difficult and research has found that people are generally quite bad at predicting which emotions they will experience based on certain life outcomes. In a seminal study by Gilbert et al. (1998), assistant professors predicted that they would be much happier during their first five years of receiving tenure (a very sought-after position for an academic). However, the results showed that the professors' happiness levels soon after receiving the tenure decreased to the same levels they had been at before the decision as to tenureship had been made.

> **Integral affect**
> the affect we experience that stems from the actual decision at hand, or might be influenced by the anticipated effects of the decision outcome.
>
> **Incidental affect**
> influences of affect that stem from other sources than the decision at hand, and that may influence our decision making.

Affect that stems from rather irrelevant situations and circumstances may also influence our decisions. These so-called incidental influences of affect, whether they be emotions or moods, that we experience during a decision do not come from the decision at hand but might be connected to another source, such as environmental, personal or even social factors (e.g., Lerner et al., 2015). Consider for example that you are asked to donate to a charity just after you learned that you passed a difficult exam. Your happiness from passing the exam is likely to result in you donating money through a carry-over effect. In a similar manner, if you are in bad mood you might not feel so eager to help a friend. Studies have shown that we are often quite poor at attributing our affective response to the correct source – the judgement or decision at hand – from another source. However, when people are able to recognize the source of their incidental affect they are less willing to let it influence their judgements since they recognize that the affect is uninformative for the current decision (Schwarz, 2000).

> **Affect heuristic** involves substituting feelings (positive or negative) for target attributes in decision problems.

An interesting venue of research has also suggested that we may use an **affect heuristic** by which readily available *feelings* or affective assessments (such as like, attractive, positive vs. dislike, repellent, negative) are substituted for target attributes in order to make quick decisions (Finucane et al., 2003; Slovic et al., 2002). In an example study, Finucane et al. (2000) found that if people were told about the risks of nuclear power (i.e., possible negative effects such as radiation leakage) then their assessment of its possible benefits, such as cheapness, reliability, low carbon emissions and so on, was negatively affected. Conversely, if they were told of the possible benefits of nuclear power first, their assessment of the risks of nuclear power was more positive. Similar results were also found with scenarios involving use of natural gas and food preservatives. These results support the idea of affect-based decision making. Normatively, judgements of risks and of benefits should be independent of each other but Finucane and colleagues argued that people tended to form emotional responses to the initial component to which they were exposed (risks or benefits) and the emotional responses affected the component presented second. In a separate study, Finucane et al. (2000) found that the rated benefits and risks over some 23 technologies (e.g., water fluoridation, mobile phones, microwave ovens) and activities (e.g., surfing, smoking cigarettes, eating beef) were strongly negatively correlated, especially when judgements were made under time pressure versus no time pressure. That is to say, if the risks were rated highly harmful, the benefits were rated low in attractiveness, and vice versa. Very similar findings also emerged from a study of judgements by toxicologists regarding exposures to very small (non-hazardous) quantities of chemicals (Slovic et al., 2002). These findings are consistent with a general tendency to use an overall affective response to each item to guide assessment of risks and benefits such that a positive affective response leads to a low assessment of risk and a high assessment of benefits and the opposite for negative affective responses.

Affective responses to alternatives can be useful in real life and have the benefit of avoiding extended thinking in making decisions. One example is warning labels on cigarette packs, which are further explored in Box 15.6.

 Box 15.6 Research Close Up: Do graphic warning labels influence risk perception and quit intentions in smokers?

Source: Evans et al. (2015).

INTRODUCTION

Since cigarette smoking causes a great many health-related problems, many countries have introduced graphic warning labels on cigarette packs in an effort to decrease public smoking habits. The negative emotions that may be elicited from such warning labels can affect behaviours in many different ways. They may serve as a direct cue, warning people that it is unsafe to smoke via an affect heuristic. It has also been suggested by Peters et al. (2006) that they may serve as spotlight in a two-step process.

First, the affective response of high displeasure when seeing the warning encourages the decision maker to focus on information that is congruent with this feeling, namely risk perception information, which leads to deeper processing of the information. Second, this processed information is used as a guide for judgements and decision. Evans et al. (2015) set up a clinical trial in an effort to better understand the process of how affect from graphic warning labels influences risk perceptions and intentions to quit smoking among smokers.

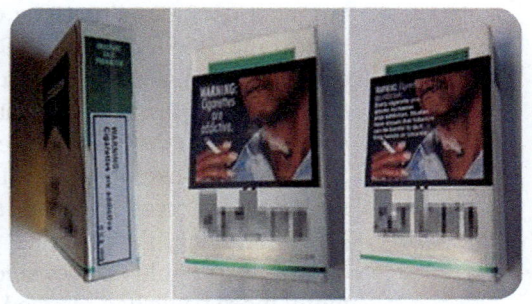

Figure 15.8 The different warning labels used in the experiment.
The first image, on the left, shows the text-only warning label; the second shows the graphical warning label and the last image, on the right, depicts the graphical warning label with elaborated text.

Source: Evans et al. (2015).

METHODS

The sample consisted of 293 adult smokers who had no intention of quitting smoking at the beginning of the experiment. Throughout the experiment, which lasted several weeks, the participants received their own brand of cigarettes but with different warning labels depending on to which condition they were randomized: text-only warning label, a graphic warning label or a graphic warning label that included elaborated text (see Figure 15.8). The participants' smoking behaviours were registered during the trial, and they were also asked to report how much the packaging changed their feelings about smoking and how credible the warnings were. On their final visit to the lab, in order to check their risk perception participants were asked to indicate how likely they believed it was that they would become ill as a consequence of smoking. They also responded to questions concerning their intentions to quit smoking.

RESULTS AND DISCUSSION

Participants who received the packages with graphic images experienced a more negative affect than those who received text-only warnings. This increased negative affect was in turn associated with a higher risk perception and a higher intention to quit smoking. These results are in line with suggestions of there being an affect heuristic, which implies a more direct way in which affective responses influence judgements and decisions.

Results also showed that affect may influence risk perceptions and intentions to quit smoking via a more indirect path, as suggested by Peters et al. (2006), since negative affect was also associated with participants scrutinizing the risks more. This, in turn, led them to find the warning more credible, resulting in increased risk perception and raised intention to quit smoking. Surprisingly, though, the results showed that the participants who received graphical warnings with elaborated text rated the warnings as less credible. The authors suggest that this latter result may be explained by psychological reactance, where long-time smokers found the particular elaborated information given, 'that every smoke increases your addiction', to be slightly overdramatic.

Furthermore, Evans et al. (2015) showed that the graphical warnings led to better memory of the warning labels, which in turn were associated with a higher risk perception. This is line with earlier research, which found an increase in memory performance for negatively valenced information.

Going with the decision that feels right is a low-effort way of deciding, which is probably most useful in situations where learning which choices are good and which bad is important. Bechara et al. (1997) used the Iowa Gambling Task and presented people with four decks of cards on a table. They were then asked to choose cards over many trials and, depending on what a card said, either won or lost money. Gradually, it emerged that two decks were usually good and two usually bad. It took people about 25 trials to consciously report this. However, after about 13 trials, skin conductance recordings showed electrical spikes associated with fear responses when they reached for a bad deck. Participants' choices of the good decks rose after the 13th trial even though they could not consciously report which decks were good and which bad until many more trials had elapsed. Damasio (1994) labels emotional responses such as feelings of fear 'somatic markers'. Interestingly, inability to use affective cues or somatic markers in decision making appears to have a marked negative effect on quality of decisions (Damasio, 1994); this is explored in Box 15.7.

> **Box 15.7 When Things Go Wrong: Brain damage and decision making – the role of 'somatic markers' and interoception**
>
> The importance of affect in decision making was underlined in studies by Damasio (1994) of patients with damage to the ventromedial frontal cortices of the brain. Such patients can undertake abstract reasoning tasks as well as persons without this lesion but have impaired emotional reactions coupled with poor ability in making risky decisions. Damasio proposed that, normally, risky decision options evoke 'somatic markers' – that is, affective responses that warn people of danger and so deter risky decisions. However, these cues are not available to patients with damage to the ventromedial frontal cortices. In a gambling situation, participants could select cards from any one of four decks. On the back of each card was a statement as to whether the card had won or cost the participants money. Normal persons without the lesion and patients with brain damage outside the prefrontal cortices soon learned to avoid decks with attractive payoffs but also with catastrophic losses. However, patients with prefrontal cortical damage did not come to learn appropriate anticipatory responses and did not avoid the high-risk decks, even after extensive learning opportunities. The normal persons without the lesion and control patients showed learned skin conductance responses indicating fear reactions to the 'bad' decks after about 13 trials. However, the patients with prefrontal cortical damage did not show skin conductance responses and, without the affective 'warning signals', learned much more slowly and continued to make bad choices even after consciously reporting which decks were good and which bad. It seems that lack of somatic markers or affective responses in the prefrontal cortex brain-damaged group led to impaired decision making under conditions of risk that would normally evoke an affective heuristic.
>
> Supportive results for the somatic marker hypothesis came from a subsequent study using the Iowa Gambling Task. Dunn et al. (2010) recorded bodily changes just before choices were made from either the good or bad decks of cards. The recorded changes differed between good and bad decks, and participants whose bodily responses differed more prior to good and bad deck choices made better decisions. Furthermore, participants who were more accurate at monitoring their bodily responses – that is, had superior **interoception** (indicated by ability to count heartbeats) – performed better at the gambling task.
>
> **Interoception** sensitivity to internal bodily stimuli.
>
> In a study of interoception and risky monetary decision making, Sokol-Hessner et al. (2015), similarly to Dunn et al. (2010), found that interoceptive ability was positively correlated with loss aversion. In a real-life setting, Kandasamy et al. (2016) found that interoceptive ability in a sample of financial traders in the City of London predicted

▶ their profitability ($r = .52$) and how long they kept their jobs in the financial markets ($r = .59$). It seems that signals from the body ('gut feelings') contribute to market success.

In conclusion, it seems that impaired sensitivity to somatic markers due to brain damage impairs risky decision making, as reported by Damasio (1994), but also that greater sensitivity to somatic markers, as indexed by better interoceptive ability, aids successful risky decision making.

Summary

In this chapter, we have seen that emotional and cognitive processing are closely connected, and that the study of emotion is of central relevance to our understanding of cognitive functioning. Emotion is a fundamental component of human experience. The term 'emotion' refers to various mental states that have an object (they are 'about something') and a valence (they are pleasant or unpleasant), and that are associated with characteristic physiological changes, facial expressions, thoughts and behaviours. While cognitive psychology has traditionally omitted the study of emotion from its key concerns, data from neuroscientific studies and other sources is showing that emotion is of central importance and must be considered if we are to fully understand cognition.

The cognitive view of emotions is that they have important short- and long-term functions that allow us to adapt in an unpredictable environment. There is evidence for a core set of emotions linked to particular facial expressions that are produced and recognized cross-culturally, and that would not seem to depend on learning. This view has been partly challenged by the constructionist view of emotions.

Various theories on the relationship between emotion and cognition have been considered in this chapter. These theories address whether, or the extent to which, cognition is required in order for an emotion to occur.

We also looked at the influence of affect, such as mood, and emotions on cognition, such as attention, perception, memory and decision making.

Emotional stimuli tend to capture and draw attention to themselves in what is referred to as attentional bias. Fearful stimuli have been found to facilitate visual processing and negative mood seems to heighten auditory perception.

Research suggests that emotional memories are better remembered than neutral. In particular, negative emotions seem to enhance the memory for central details. There also seems to exist a mood-congruence effect in memory – here we remember positive memories better when in a positive mood, and vice versa. There is also an emotional state-dependent memory effect where memory is facilitated when the emotional state of the encoding matches the retrieval.

Both integral and incidental affect can influence our judgements and decisions. Integral affects are emotions that stem from the decision at hand or emotions that are anticipated to arise from the decision outcome. Incidental affect can be both emotions and mood that one experiences but that do not stem from the decision at hand, and may even be the result of a carry-over effect from another situation.

Affective information may be used as an heuristic, by which readily available feelings or affective assessments (such as like, attractive, positive vs. dislike, repellent, negative) are substituted for target attributes in order to make quick decisions.

Review Questions

1. Which are the predominant emotion theories and what constitutes them?
2. Is cognition required for an emotional response?
3. In what ways do affective states such as emotions and mood influence cognition?
4. Do affective states help or hinder memory?

Discussion Questions

1. Which theoretical account of the relationship between emotion and cognition best accounts for the evidence?
2. What criticism can be aimed at the research investigating the ways affective states influence memory?
3. If you were to conduct a study of your own that aimed to investigate the impact of specific emotions on cognition, how would you ensure that you are actually measuring the emotions experienced?

Further Reading

Kensinger, E. A., & Ford, J. H. (2020). Retrieval of emotional events from memory. *Annual Review of Psychology, 71,* 251–272.

Kensinger, E. A., & Schacter, D. L. (2010). Memory and emotion. In M. Lewis, J. M. Haviland-Jones, & L. Barrett (Eds.), *Handbook of emotion*. Guilford Press.

Lerner, J. S., Li, Y., Valdesolo, P., & Kassam, K. S. (2015). Emotion and decision making. *Annual Review of Psychology, 66,* 799–823.

MacMillan, M. (2000). *An odd kind of fame: Stories of Phineas Gage*. MIT Press.

Porter, S., & ten Brinke, L. (2008). Reading between the lies: Identifying concealed and falsified emotions in universal facial expressions. *Psychological Science, 19,* 508–514.

Yiend, J. (2010). The effects of emotion on attention: A review of attentional processing of emotional information. *Cognition and Emotion, 24*(1), 3–47.

Glossary

Abductive reasoning a strategy by which inferences are drawn regarding the most likely explanation for a set of observations.

Access consciousness includes representations that are broadcast for use in reasoning and control of action and can be reported.

Acquired dyslexia reading difficulties following brain injury.

Action slips involve an action being completed when it was not intended.

Ad hoc categories are categories formed of items that meet a given goal, e.g. the category of 'items to take on a picnic' is ad hoc.

Adversary problems problems in which the solver has to deal with a rational opponent as in board games.

Affect heuristic involves substituting feelings (positive or negative) for target attributes in decision problems.

Afterimage occurs when vision of an object remains after presentation has ceased–for example, after staring at a bright light.

Agency ability of an entity, biological or physical, to independently act upon the world to create change in order to achieve goals

Agrammatism a pattern of syntactic deficit affecting speech production following brain injury.

Agraphia the inability to produce written words as the result of a brain injury.

Alexia the inability to understand written words as the result of a brain injury.

Algorithm a problem solving method that is guaranteed to solve but may do so only with high mental load.

Allophones are phonetic variants of the same phoneme.

Alphabetic scripts represent the phonemes or sounds in a language.

Ambidextrous ambidextrous individuals show a reduced hand preference, and are typically able to use their right and left hands with equal ease.

Ambient intelligence an environment that senses our presence using advanced sensors and computing technology in a way that allows the environment to respond to the needs of people.

Amnesia a pattern of memory loss affecting elements of long-term memory, while short-term memory remains intact.

Amnesic syndrome a pattern of memory loss characterized by impaired long-term memory and spared short-term memory.

Amodal representations are representations that are abstract and do not involve any sensory codes.

Amygdala is an almond shaped set of structures located in the medial temporal lobe.

Anarthria a disorder affecting the motor function underlying speech.

Anomic aphasia a word finding disorder.

Anterograde amnesia impairment of memory for events that occurred after the onset of amnesia.

Aphasia the term given to a group of language disorders that occur following brain injury.

Appraisal to the ways in which people interpret or explain to themselves the meaning of events.

Appraisal theories have in common the assertion that emotions result from our interpretations of, or reactions to, events.

Apraxia is a neurological condition typically resulting from brain damage where a person loses the ability to perform activities that they are physically able and willing to do.

Arcuate fasciculus the band of fibres connecting Broca's and Wernicke's areas.

Areas of interest in eye tracking research these provide detailed quantitative data on eye fixations and durations related to key sentence elements.

Articulatory suppression the interference that occurs when participants are required to repeat (non-relevant) verbal material while engaged in a primary task drawing on the same modality.

Artificial intelligence the attempt to program computers to carry out complex tasks such as medical diagnosis, planning and using natural language.

Aspirated aspirated consonants are pronounced with a small puff of air, depending on their position in a word.

Association a linkage between mental contents such that activation of one content activates linked content, e.g. table → chair.

Associative chain theory is a behaviourist theory that explains how sequences of action arise from linking together associations between individual action components.

Atmosphere effect is a tendency to draw conclusions in syllogisms that are over influenced by the form of the premises rather than the logic of the argument.

Attention system a framework of the human brain containing three different systems for alerting, orienting and the executive function.

Attentional bias the tendency for emotional stimuli to capture or draw attention.

Autobiographical memories episodic memories for personally experienced events in a person's life.

Autonoetic ('self-knowing') consciousness allows humans to use memory to relive past events and imagine ourselves in the future, from a self-perspective. It is a distinctive aspect of episodic memory.

Autonoetic memories memories that are associated with a sense of self-awareness and that are relived during recollection.

Autonomic nervous system is part of the peripheral nervous system and regulates internal organs.

Availability heuristic involves judging frequency or probability of events by how easy it is to bring the events to mind.

Axiom a statement that is taken to be self-evident as true, it serves as a starting point for further reasoning. In Integrated Information Theory (IIT) axioms describe regularities in conscious experience.

Backwards propagation a way of modifying weights on the links between units in a connectionist network, in response to errors, to obtain the desired output.

Basal ganglia are a group of neurons in the base of the forebrain that are connected to cortex and involved in action selection. Disorders of the basal ganglia are related to movement disorders such as Parkinson's disease.

Base rate of an event is the overall probability of the event in a population; so, the base rate of 'engineers' in the UK is the probability that a randomly selected person in the UK will be an engineer.

Basic level categories are categories formed of items that are highly similar and at an intermediate level in a concept hierarchy.

Basilar membrane a stiff structural element located in the inner ear, which contains specialized fluids as well as the hair cells that are key in transducing sound energy into neural impulses.

Belief bias a tendency to accept invalid but believable conclusions and to reject valid but unbelievable conclusions to arguments.

Binding problem describes the issue that although perception works via analysis of separate perceptual features our subjective experience has all these features bound together.

Binocular rivalry arises when different images are presented simultaneously to the two eyes and results in experiencing seeing one image and then the other alternately.

Blindsight a phenomenon typically arising from brain damage to visual cortex where afflicted individuals report that they do not see certain visual targets, but when asked to report properties of these targets they do so better than chance.

Bottom up stimulus-driven processing of incoming sensory information that produces increasingly elaborate and meaningful representations of the input.

Bound morpheme is a morpheme that cannot form a word on its own, but forms a word when attached to a free morpheme.

Brainstem the region in the posterior part of the brain that serves to connect the cortex to the spinal cord. Its functions include basic physiological processes, as well as the communication of sensory and motor information between brain and body.

Brainstorming stimulating the production of unusual ideas, by stressing quantity as against quality and deferment of evaluation of ideas.

Breadth first search searching a state-action space by generating all possible states from each intermediate state.

Broca's aphasia an acquired language disorder characterized by non-fluent speech, reduced speech output and problems with grammar processing.

Broca's area an area located in the left temporal lobe, damage to which is associated with aphasia (speech deficits).

Glossary

Brodmann areas developed in 1909 by Korbinian Brodmann, a German neurologist, who divided the brain into approximately 50 regions distinguished by the structural properties of the neuronal architecture.

Capture errors involve a failure to override a routine set of actions; a routine or well-practised action is performed when another action was intended.

Categorical perception is the perception of stimuli on a sensory continuum as falling into distinct categories.

Categorical syllogism a deductive problem where one determines which inferences follow from the assumptions of category membership.

Categorization a mnemonic strategy involving the grouping of items into familiar categories.

Category exemplar tasks tasks where participants are given category names one by one and are asked to generate exemplars for each. Some categories will have been encountered during an earlier stage.

Causality the relationship between cause and effect; the way in which one process or state produces another process or state.

Central executive the component of working memory proposed to control and coordinate the activity of the other components, including the phonological loop and the visuo-spatial sketchpad.

Central nervous system consists of the brain and spinal cord.

Central processing unit (CPU) in computing, the central processing unit is the part of a computer that controls operations and executes commands.

Central sulcus a major anatomical landmark on the brain that forms the boundary between parietal cortex and frontal cortex.

Cerebellum brain structure located behind and underneath the larger cerebrum. Although traditionally known for its contribution to producing movement, it is also important for cognitive function.

Change blindness the phenomenon where substantial differences between two nearly identical scenes are not noticed when presented sequentially.

Choking the occurrence of inferior performance despite striving and incentives for superior performance.

Chunking a strategy to improve memory by grouping smaller units together into a larger unit, or 'chunk'.

Clause a part of a sentence containing a subject and verb.

Closed-class words, such as articles, conjunctions, prepositions, remain stable over time and are not added to.

Co-articulation the tendency for a speech sound to be influenced by sounds preceding or following it.

Coarticulation effects the modification that occurs to any given speech sound due to the sounds that occur before or after it in the speech chain.

Cocktail party problem describes how we successfully focus on one speaker in a background of noise and other conversations.

Cognitive lockup a type of cognitive error that results from the human tendency to detect and deal with faults sequentially.

Cognitive psychology the scientific study of how people and animals process information.

Cognitive sandwich describes the view that perception and action are like slices of bread that surround cognition as the filling of a sandwich.

Common coding is a theory of perception and action production which holds that both production and perception share certain representations of actions in the world.

Communication any means by which information is shared.

Computational-Representational Understanding of Mind (CRUM) the general hypothesis that the mind has mental representations that are acted upon by mental computational processes.

Computer metaphor in cognitive psychology, an analogy drawn between human cognitive processing and information processing in a computer, which provides a tool for thinking about how the mind operates.

Concepts are mental representations of classes of items such as 'cats', 'even numbers', and so on.

Conduction aphasia when the patient has a specific difficulty affecting the repetition of speech.

Cones special neurons in the retina that are sensitive to different-coloured light, and densely packed to resolve fine image detail.

Confabulation the tendency for patients with memory, frontal lobe or other deficits to fill in gaps in their recollection with fabricated details; these can be plausible or fantastical in nature, the former type presenting a challenge for testing.

Confirmation bias, in hypothesis testing, is a tendency to seek out and attend only to information consistent with the hypothesis while ignoring falsifying information.

Conjunction fallacy is the mistaken belief that the conjunction of two events (A and B) is more likely than either one of A or B.

Connectionism an approach to cognition in terms of networks of simple neuron-like units that pass activation and inhibition through receptor, hidden and output units.

Consequentialism the view that decisions between options are based on the expected results or consequences of selecting each option.

Consonantal scripts represent the consonants of the language.

Conspecifics members of the same species.

Content words words that provide meaning to the sentence; these contrast with function words, which do the grammatical work of the sentence.

Context effects occur if memory is better when the external environment at testing is the same as at learning.

Continuity editing a film-making technique to produce a smooth continuous experience across changes in camera shot.

Contralateral relating to the opposite side of the body.

Corpus a collection or database of linguistic data, often nowadays held in electronic form.

Corpus callosum the thick band of nerve fibres that connects the left and right cerebral hemispheres.

Creative in the 'standard definition', this denotes a product novel to the producer of the product and valuable in some way; an alternative definition is that the product is novel and is intended to meet a goal (without necessarily succeeding in meeting a goal).

Creative synthesis task a task in which participants have to combine presented shapes to make novel interesting combinations.

Critical incident analysis is gaining information about naturalistic decision making by analysing detailed recalls of recent important decisions.

Crossed aphasia language dysfunction following right hemisphere damage in a right-handed individual.

Cued recall when a hint or cue is given to task participants to aid recall.

Decay a process by which information is lost from STM over time.

Decision making is the cognitive process of choosing between alternative possible actions.

Declarative or explicit memory involves conscious recollection of memories such as events, facts, people and places.

Deductive reasoning is drawing logically necessary conclusions from given information.

Deep network a connectionist network with multiple layers of hidden units between the input and output units.

Default mode network (DMN) a network of brain regions that is active when a person is not focused on the external environment.

Deficient processing the view that massed repetitions lead to deficient processing of the second presentation.

Degrees of freedom of a joint are the number of ways it can move. For example, the shoulder has three (up-down, forward-backward, rotate along axis of bone).

Deliberate practice practice activity specifically designed to improve aspects of performance.

Deliberation a process by which decision makers consider their options, representing the options and outcomes as well as evaluating them.

Demand characteristics the aspects of a research study that convey the hypotheses or aims to the participants and may thereby shape performance.

Deontic rules are rules regarding obligations and typically involve terms such as 'should', 'must', 'ought, 'may' and so on.

Deontological approach the view that decisions affecting others (i.e., moral or ethical decisions) should be based on principles irrespective of consequences.

Depictive representation theory in a depictive representation, each part of the representation corresponds to a part of the represented object, as in a photograph.

Depth first search searching a state-action space by generating one state only from each intermediate state.

Derivational morphemes create new words with new meaning when added to a stem.

Descriptive approaches aim to describe how decisions are actually taken as against how they should be made. Psychologists focus on the descriptive approach.

Descriptive Experience Sampling (DES) a method of obtaining descriptions of inner experience, including thoughts, feelings, perceptions, sensations, by cuing self reports with randomly spaced beeps.

Detour problems problems in which the hill climbing method does not work well, as the solver has to move away from the goal at some stage.

Developmental dyslexia a prevalent and persistent neurodevelopmental disorder that affects the learning of reading and writing.

Dichotic listening task a task where differing stimuli are presented to each ear.

Dictator Game a game in which one player, the Dictator, decides on a split of a money amount with a second player who has to accept the Dictator-decided split.

Digit span the number of digits that can be held in memory and is used as a measure of STM.

Direct object in a sentence is the receiver of an action denoted by the verb.

Direct perception also termed event perception and ecological perception, this refers to the bottom-up process by which objects and their function are recognized.

Directed forgetting (DF) memory impairment brought about by instructions to forget some items.

Discourse multi-sentence speech and includes dialogue, conversation and narrative.

Disfluency a hesitation or disruption to the normal fluency of speech. By contrast, the term 'dysfluency' is used to refer to an abnormal disruption to fluency, such as following brain damage. The use of the prefix 'dys-' signals 'abnormal'.

Displacement a process by which information coming into STM causes information already held there to be lost.

Display rules are social conventions governing how, when and with whom emotions may be expressed.

Distributed attention is reminiscent of preattentive vision and allows rapid statistical analysis of the entire scene.

Dizygotic dizygotic, or fraternal, twins develop from two separate eggs and are not genetically identical.

Dorsal stream the visual pathway from occipital cortex to parietal cortex that is involved in locating and guiding how to use an object.

Dorsolateral prefrontal cortex the dorsolateral prefrontal cortex (DLPFC) is a brain region in the frontal cortex that has been implicated in cognition for functions such as working memory, executive function and metacognition.

Double dissociation arises when, following brain injury, some people do well on one task, 'A', and poorly on a second task, 'B', while others with different brain injuries show the opposite pattern. In such cases the two tasks are said to be doubly dissociated.

Double dissociation of function contrasting patterns of deficit in two patients or patient groups; provides evidence for functionally independent systems.

Down syndrome or trisomy 21, is a genetic disorder characterized by the presence of a third copy of chromosome 21 and associated with mild to moderate intellectual disability.

Dual coding hypothesis proposes that concrete words can be encoded both verbally and by means of images representing their meaning; in contrast, abstract words can only be coded verbally. Dual coding is one explanation of why concrete words are easier to remember.

Dual-task paradigm arises when one measures performance on two tasks independently and together. If performance when performed independently and together is equal, then the two tasks do not compete for resources.

Dynamical systems approach to motor control emphasizes interaction between the body and the environment and uses special mathematics that describe how a system's behaviour changes over time.

Dysexecutive syndrome a range of deficits reflecting problems with executive function and control, and often associated with injury to the frontal areas of the brain.

Early selection when the filter for attention occurs early in the stream of information processing.

Echoic memory sensory memory specific to auditory stimuli.

Ecological validity the degree to which the results of a laboratory study can be applied to a real life situation.

Elaborative interrogation a learning technique where the learner prompts her- or himself to generate explanations for facts.

Elaborative rehearsal organizes the information so that it can be integrated into LTM.

Electrocortical stimulation of the surface of the cortex allows a surgeon to locate, and avoid damage to, brain regions associated with a particular cognitive function.

Electroencephalography (EEG) a functional brain imaging method showing waves of electrical activity from scalp recorders.

Elimination by aspects (EBA) a decision procedure for multi-attribute choices that considers attributes of alternatives in order of importance, eliminating alternatives that do not meet a minimum value on each attribute as the process continues.

Embodied view of cognition holds that cognition is about the experiences arising from a perceptual system tightly linked to an action system rather than the manipulations of abstract representations.

Emotion a number of mental states including anger, joy, and disgust.

Emotional leakage the unintended expression of emotion or a failure to mask an expression.

Empiricism the philosophical school which holds that all knowledge comes from experience.

Encoding the function by which information is coded in a form that allows it to be stored in memory.

Encoding specificity principle if the context at recall is similar to the context at encoding then memory will be enhanced.

Encoding variability encoding varies with the context at the study period.

Endowment effect is a tendency to over-value a possessed object and to require more money to sell it than to buy it in the first place.

Episodic buffer the component of working memory proposed for the temporary storage of information integrated from the phonological loop, the visuo-spatial sketchpad and long-term memory into single structures or episodes.

Episodic memory memory for events, experiences and episodes.

Equilibrium point hypothesis is a theory of motor control that emphasizes how the problem of control can be simplified by taking into account muscle properties.

Essentialism the view that all members of a given category share some key property.

Event-related potentials (ERP) a functional brain imaging method recording electrical activity during repeated stimulus presentations.

Exemplar theories propose that categories are represented purely by stored examples or instances and each example is linked to the category name.

Expected value is the long-term average value of a repeated decision which is determined by the probability and size of the outcome. So if the chance of winning £100 in a gamble is 0.5, then the expected value is £50.

Expertise the accumulated high level knowledge that allows outstanding performance in complex problem areas.

External attention deals primarily with sensory events external to the body.

Eye tracking involves the measurement of people's eye movements while reading or inspecting a visual scene.

Facial feedback hypothesis proposes that feedback from the facial muscles can influence emotional state.

False memories inaccurate recollections of events that did not occur, or distortions of events that did occur.

Family resemblance is the tendency for members of a category to be similar to each other but without having any one characteristic in common to all of them.

Feedforward feedforward processing describes a bottom-up process where lower levels of a network progressively stimulate higher levels of the network.

Feeling of warmth rating is a rating of how close the solver feels to problem solution, taken at intervals during the solving process.

Feeling-of-knowing a subjective sense of knowing that we know a word; an example of metamemory—our knowledge about the contents of our memories.

Field perspective when a person recalls a memory from a first-person perspective. They are experiencing the event.

Field study the collection of raw data outside of the laboratory in a natural environment.

Figural bias is the effect of figure on preferred conclusions.

Firing rates a term from neurophysiology where the activity of a single cell or group of cells is recorded. A high firing rate indicates great activity of the cell due to sensitivity to the incoming information.

Fixation occurs when the eye settles briefly on a region of interest in a visual scene.

Flashbulb memory a vivid memory of a dramatic event and of the circumstances in which the event was experienced or heard about.

Fluent aphasia is when the patient's speech is fluent, but not meaningful.

Foreign accent syndrome describes a rare condition, resulting from brain injury, whereby an individual produces phonetic and prosodic errors in their speech, such that it sounds non-native like.

Forgetting processes leading to a loss of ability to retrieve previously learned information.

Forward models are used to predict the relationship between actions and their consequences. Given a motor command the forward model predicts the resulting behaviour of the body and the world.

Four figures of syllogism are the four possible layouts of terms which give four syllogistic figures, i.e. A-B, B-C; B-A, B-C; A-B, C-B; B-A, C-B.

Framing effects arise when irrelevant features of a situation affect the decisions that are made.

Free morpheme is a morpheme that can stand alone as a word.

Free recall when participants in a task recall the information in any order, without hints or clues to recall.

Frontal eye fields found in the frontal cortex and involved with the generation and control of eye movements.

Function words provide grammatical structure that shows how content words relate to each other within a sentence.

Functional fixity a difficulty in thinking of a novel use for a familiar object.

Functional imaging functional imaging methods detect brain activity.

Functional integration the way in which brain regions communicate and act together.

Functional Magnetic Resonance Imaging (fMRI) a method of imaging brain activity that uses oxygenation levels of blood flow, and has good temporal and spatial resolution.

Functional reference the use by animals of a specific call to stand for a specific object or threat.

Galvanic skin response the electrical characteristics of the skin are known to change due to the activity of sweat glands, which can be linked to psychological arousal. This measure of galvanic skin response is often taken as an indication of emotional response.

Garden path sentence a grammatically correct but ambiguous sentence that biases the reader's initial parsing.

Geneplore a model for creative thinking which stresses the role of a generative and exploratory phase.

Generalizability the degree to which results are broadly applicable to a wide range of situations.

Generic Parts Technique a method of overcoming functional fixity by analysing objects into parts and sub-parts.

Geons the elements of a set of volumetric primitives or shapes that can be recognized from any viewpoint, proposed by Biederman in his recognition by components (RBC) theory.

Glia support cells of the nervous system that take part in tissue repair and in the formation of myelin.

Global aphasia is an acquired language disorder involving extreme impairment of language function.

Global workspace theory proposes that consciousness requires interactions across a broad range of brain areas.

Glutamate an excitatory neurotransmitter that acts on both central and peripheral divisions of the nervous system and plays a key role in sensory processing.

Goal-subgoal space a representation of how an overall problem goal can be broken down into subgoals and sub-subgoals.

Grapheme is the written representation of a phoneme.

Grapheme–colour synaesthesia one of the more common types of synaesthesia in which a written letter or number is spontaneously associated with a colour.

Grapheme-to-phoneme conversion (GPC) route this route allows us to sound out words based on letter–sound correspondences.

Haptic perception the combination of abilities that allow us to represent the material characteristics of objects and surfaces for recognition.

Head turn preference procedure (or the preferential looking paradigm) a method used to examine infants' and toddlers' sensitivity to changes in visual and auditory stimuli.

Hedonic calculus a utilitarian proposal that an option be assessed in terms of the overall balance of pleasure as against pain that would result from choosing that option. The option having the greatest excess of pleasure over pain should be chosen on this view.

Heuristic a problem solving method that often finds a low-effort solution but is not guaranteed to solve.

High amplitude sucking paradigm a method used to study young infants up to 4 months old by reinforcing non-nutritive sucking responses with sound stimuli.

Hippocampus a small curved formation in the brain involved in the formation of new memories and in processing spatial information.

Homesign a gestural language system that emerges through use by linguistically isolated deaf persons.

Homographs are words with the same spelling, but more than one meaning and pronunciation.

Homologous in biology means to have the corresponding position, structure and possibly function. It is common to consider across species what anatomical parts are homologous. For brain regions this is important for using data obtained in say monkeys to predict relations in human brain.

Human factors the multidisciplinary study of the interplay between human capabilities and failings and interactions with technology, machines and other aspects of the physical environment.

Hyperthymesia 'hypermemory' or highly superior autobiographical memory (HSAM), evident in some individuals.

Hypothesis generation is deriving possible hypotheses from data for later testing.

Hypothesis testing is assessing hypotheses for truth/falsity against data.

Hypothetico-deductive reasoning is a form of inductive reasoning in which a hypothesis is tested by deducing necessary consequences of the hypothesis and determining whether the consequences are true (supporting the hypothesis) or false (disconfirming or falsifying the hypothesis).

Iconic store the sensory memory store for visual stimuli.

Ideomotor theory relates how thinking about the results of an action can give rise to producing the action.

Ill-defined problem a problem in which starting conditions, or actions available or goals are not completely specified.

Illusionism the view that consciousness is an introspective illusion caused by introspection creating the misrepresentation that experiences have special properties.

Imagery is the mental representation of sensory properties of objects– experienced as like perceiving the object but with less vividness than in reality.

Imagination inflation the strengthening of a false memory through repeated retrieval.

Inattentional blindness the failure to notice a clearly visible target due to attention being diverted from the target.

Incidental affect influences of affect that stem from other sources than the decision at hand, and that may influence our decision making.

Incidental learning learning that takes place without any intention to learn.

Incubation a period in which a problem is set aside; it may be 'immediate', directly after presentation, or 'delayed', after a period of conscious work.

Indirect object in a sentence states to or for whom (or what) the action of the verb affected.

Inductive reasoning is the process of inferring probable conclusions from given information.

Inference rule a rule for reaching a conclusion given a particular pattern of propositions–for example, *modus ponens* (from the Latin for 'mode of affirming'), which states that, given 'If p then q' and 'not q', we can infer 'not p'.

Inflectional morpheme serves a grammatical function, changing the case or tense of a word for example.

Information processing approach a metaphor for understanding mental activity, based on computing.

Inner scribe the component of the visuo-spatial sketchpad, within working memory, that allows spatial processing.

Inner speech the subjective experience of hearing our thoughts, as if 'spoken' by an inner voice, when reading silently for example.

Insight a restructuring of a problem that makes the solution obvious and understandable.

Insula is an area hidden within the folds of the cortex, with connections to the cingulate, amygdala, and orbitofrontal cortex, implicated in aspects of emotion, cognition, and action.

Interacting affect the affect we experience that stems from the actual decision at hand, or might be influenced by the anticipated effects of the decision outcome.

Interactive activation is a term used to describe the pattern of network activity generated by excitatory and inhibitory interactions of feature detectors and object representations.

Interference occurs when remembering is disrupted by related memories.

Internal attention deals primarily with our internally generated thoughts, desires and motivations.

Internal representations mental representations of external objects and events.

Interoception sensitivity to internal bodily stimuli.

Intrusions involuntary mental pictures with very detailed sensory impressions of the witnessed event, such as sights, sounds, feelings and bodily sensations.

Intrusive memories persistent unwanted memories (e.g., of traumatic events) that frequently come to mind.

Invariance is the principle that choices between alternatives should not be affected by how the options are described.

Invariance problem reflects the variation in the production of speech sounds across speech contexts.

Invariants in vision, these are properties of the three-dimensional object being viewed that can be derived from any two-dimensional image of the object.

Inverse problem in vision is where there are more than one interpretation of the 3D world given the 2D image information.

Involuntary memories the unintentional recollection of past personal experiences.

Isotropic fractionator method a method of dissolving brain tissue into a liquid form, preserving the nuclei of the neurons, which can then be counted in a sample and the count scaled up for a whole-brain estimate of numbers of neurons.

Knowledge-lean problems problems such as puzzles that do not require specialist knowledge.

Knowledge-rich problems problems that require extensive specialist knowledge.

Language production a number of processes by which we convert a thought into language output, in the form of speech, sign language or writing.

Late closure attaches incoming material to the phrase that is currently being processed.

Late selection when the filter for attention occurs late in the stream of information processing. Thus the filter eliminates some information that has already been processed.

Lateral thinking a set of techniques developed by E. de Bono for solving problems creatively by using indirect approaches to find novel solutions.

Lateralization of function the asymmetric representation of cognitive function in the cerebral hemispheres of humans and higher primates.

Law of Mass Action states that the efficiency of any complex function of the cortical areas of the brain is reduced proportionately to the amount of damage the cortex as a whole has suffered but not to damage of any particular cortical area.

Leading questions questions that suggest or prompt a particular answer, and that can skew or bias the information provided, particularly in the context of witness questioning.

'Leaky' rationality the view that the process of deciding on a chosen option can affect the utility or satisfaction that the decision maker obtains from the chosen option.

Learning processes of acquiring information for mental storage and later use.

Lemma an uninflected word from which inflected words can then be derived.

Lemma is an abstract word form that contains syntactic and semantic information about the word.

Levels of processing a theory that better learning results from deeper semantic processing, which produces stronger, more elaborated memory traces than superficial-level processing.

Lexeme is the basic lexical unit that gives the word's morpho-phonological properties.

Lexical access is the process by which we access stored knowledge about words.

Lexical bias tendency for phonological speech errors to result in real words.

Lexical decision task a task where participants are presented with a letter string and must decide whether or not it is a word.

Lexical or direct route to reading involves the selection of a word from the lexicon.

Lexicographic strategies a class of decision procedures that consider attributes in a fixed order–e.g., elimination by aspects (EBA).

Likelihood principle states that the preferred organization of a perceptual object or event will be the one that is most likely.

Limbic system consists of the thalamus, hypothalamus, hippocampus and amygdala, and other structures.

Linguistic determinism the proposal that language determines thought.

Linguistic relativity the proposal that language affects thought.

Linguistic universals are linguistic features said to be found in all languages.

Load theory how the amount of processing an unattended stimulus will receive depends upon how difficult it is to process the attended target.

Localist representation is where a single unit represents a particular concept.

Localization the view that specific mental functions are tied to specific brain areas; this also appears as the modularity hypothesis and may be contrasted with the distributed view, that functions are realized by joint action of many areas.

Logographic scripts represent morphemes or the units of meaning of words.

Long-term depression (LTD) the long-lasting reduction in the effectiveness of the signal transmission between two neurons.

Long-term memory the system where information is held for longer periods, and can be accessed when needed.

Long-term potentiation (LTP) the long-lasting improvement in signal transmission between two neurons that results from stimulating them at the same time.

Loss aversion is a key idea of prospect theory that there is a greater dislike of losing utility than liking for gaining the same degree of utility.

Magnetic resonance imaging (MRI) a high-definition method for structural imaging using strong magnetic fields.

Maintenance rehearsal retains information in STM.

Masking reduced perception of a visual stimulus when another stimulus is presented in spatial or temporal proximity to it.

Matching bias, in the four-card task, is choosing the cards mentioned in the rule.

McGurk effect a perceptual illusion that illustrates the interplay of visual and auditory processing in speech perception.

Memory trace a mental representation of stored information.

Mental lexicon our store of knowledge about words and their uses.

Mental maps mental representations of a spatial layout.

Mental models approach is the view that people tackle logical reasoning problems by forming mental representations of possible states of the world and draw inferences from those representations.

Mental operations inner actions manipulating mental representations.

Mental representations inner representations such as an image or a verbal concept of some external reality.

Mere exposure effect the tendency for people to develop a preference for a stimulus with repeated exposure to it.

Meta-analysis examination of a set of independent studies on the same topic done to provide a view of the what is revealed by the overall results.

Metacognition awareness of one's own thoughts and cognitive processes.

Metamemory the ability to monitor and control the content of memory. It allows us to know whether we know something.

Method of interacting images a mnemonic strategy in which vivid and bizarre images are formed of the items to be recalled, interacting in some way.

Method of loci is a mnemonic strategy in which a familiar route is imagined and images of the items to be recalled are linked to landmarks on the route.

Minimal attachment introduces new items into the phrase structure using as few syntactic nodes as possible.

Minimal pair a pair of words in a language that differ in just one sound.

Mirror neurons are neurons with the special property that they represent both the sensory aspects of perceiving actions as well as motor aspects of how to produce the action.

Mnemonic a learning device used to aid memory.

Modularity the view that cognition involves many separate independent modules or processors specialized for different types of processing.

Monozygotic monozygotic twins are identical twins that develop from a single zygote and share all of their genes.

Mood congruency the tendency to recall events consistent with current mood state.

Mood-dependent memory effect means that memory is better when mood at learning is reinstated at testing.

Morphemes are the meaning units of language.

Morphology is the level of linguistic analysis concerned with morphemes and their role within words.

Motor primitives are the basis set of elemental movements that serve as building blocks for an animal's repertoire of movements.

Motor system includes the components of the central and peripheral nervous systems along with the muscles, joints and bones that enable movement.

Multi-attribute decision problem is a decision task in which the alternatives vary in many dimensions or aspects.

Multi-attribute utility theory (MAUT) a procedure in which the utilities of the attributes of an option are aggregated to produce an overall utility for an option having many attributes.

Multi-level theories of emotion propose that both preattentive and conscious cognitive processes are involved in emotion.

Naturalistic decision making making real-life decisions in the field.

Negative recency effect the tendency for recall of items from the end of a list to be poorer than for those from the start or middle of the list in a final, cumulative recall task.

Neologisms in aphasia, neologisms are non-words that are produced in place of intended word targets and, if excessive, constitute what is referred to as jargon aphasia.

Network models of memory treat memories as items related in a network which can affect each other through activation.

Neural correlates of consciousness (NCC) defined by Christof Koch as the minimal set of neuronal events and mechanisms jointly sufficient for a specific conscious percept.

Neuroeconomics is the study of neural processes underlying economic decisions.

Neurolinguistics is the study of the relationship of brain function to language processing.

Neurological homunculus a representation of the areas of cortex involved in sensory and motor functions by a model human figure (Latin: homunculus = little man) in which the body parts are scaled to reflect the size of the cortical areas that involve those parts. Thus, hands and fingers of the homunculus are much larger than the trunk. The homunculus can be sensory or motor, and although both are similar they are not identical.

Neurons the basic units of the nervous system, principally consisting of a cell, axon and dendrites.

Neuropsychology the study of psychological effects of brain damage and disease.

noetic memory memory for facts.

Non-adversary problems problems in which the solver is dealing with inert problem materials with no rational opponent.

Non-declarative or implicit memory memory that is not accessed consciously and that we are not able to report verbally. It includes memory which benefits from previous experience but without our awareness of that experience.

Non-fluent aphasia is when the patient's speech output is reduced, laboured, or absent.

Non-plan internal errors occur when the intrusion is external to the planned content of the utterance.

Non-rapid eye movement (NREM) sleep non-rapid eye movement (NREM) sleep has three stages, including the deep sleep you need to feel refreshed in the morning. During NREM sleep, muscles relax, dreaming is rare and brain waves have distinct characteristics.

Non-semantic reading a pattern of reading deficit whereby the patient can read an irregular word (which cannot be sounded out) and yet cannot access its meaning.

Normative approaches attempt to establish ideal ways of deciding that will give the best decision possible. Economists have tended to develop normative models.

Nudge colloquially, a nudge is a gentle push; in the field of behaviour engineering it is the concept of unconsciously promoting one path of behaviour while not being restrictive about the availability or reward of other paths of behaviour.

Object of a sentence is the word or words that receives the action, or is acted on, by the subject of the sentence.

Observer perspective when a person remembers a memory from a third-person perspective. They are observing the event from the outside.

Omission bias the tendency to judge harms resulting from inactions (omissions) as less harmful or culpable than the same harms resulting from actions (commissions).

Onomatopoeia words that sound like the thing to which they refer–for example, the bird name 'cuckoo' or the 'beep' of a car horn.

Onset of a word is the initial phoneme or phonemes. The time follows the onset.

Opaque or orthographically deep languages are those where the relationship between letters and sounds is more complex.

Open-class words are content words such as nouns, verbs and adjectives. New words can be added to this class of words.

Operational definition a description involving the actions, procedures or processes that can be used to evidence how a phenomenon is observed and measured.

Opportunity costs the loss of potential gains from one alternative when another alternative is chosen.

Optimal control theory of motor control provides a framework for implementing principles that produce movements that optimally satisfy some criterion.

Orthographic relates to orthography, which refers to the conventions used to represent a language in a writing system.

Over-extension a normal pattern of error in language development whereby children use the same word for a wider class of objects than is appropriate, for example using the term 'bird' for all flying things.

Paired associates learning a memory task in which participants are presented with pairs of items (typically, words) at study and on test are given the first word and asked to recall the second word in each pair.

Parallel processing is the ability to divide the process of solving a problem into multiple parts and to work simultaneously on each part.

Paraphasias speech errors in aphasia whereby unintended phonemes, syllables or words are output.

Parapraxes are slips of the tongue or other actions originally thought to reflect unconscious motives.

Parkinson's Disease is a progressive degenerative neurological disorder characterized by a distinctive pattern of motor and cognitive dysfunction.

Parsing is the process by which we assign a syntactic structure to a sentence.

Pegword method is a mnemonic strategy in which to be recalled items are linked by imagery to an already learned sequence list of imagable words.

Perception our sensory experience of the world.

Perceptual learning a type of learning that occurs at a low level of processing and includes the development of enhanced sensory processing abilities.

Permastore involves the long-term retention of content that has been acquired and relearned over a period of time, even if rarely used thereafter.

Perseveration the inappropriate repetition of an action.

Perseverative errors involve the inappropriate repetition of a previous response when that response is no longer appropriate.

Persistent vegetative state a clinical condition involving 'wakefulness without awareness'–patients may open their eyes, move spontaneously, exhibit sleep and waking cycles, but be unresponsive to external stimulation and are assumed to lack any awareness.

Phenomenal consciousness includes the experiential properties of sensations, feelings and perceptions.

Phenomenology the view that the study of immediate experience should be the basis of psychology.

Phoneme the smallest meaningful sound unit within a language.

Phoneme restoration effect describes the tendency to hear a complete word even when a phoneme has been removed from the input.

Phones are the basic speech sounds.

Phonetics is the study of speech sounds.

Phonological dyslexia affects non-word reading, but real words can be read.

Phonological loop the component of working memory proposed for the temporary storage and manipulation of sound or phonological information. It comprises a short-term phonological store for auditory memory traces and an articulatory rehearsal component to reactivate memory traces.

Phonological similarity effect the finding that recall is poorer for an ordered list of verbal items when the items sound alike, compared to performance on lists of items that do not sound alike.

Phonology the system of sounds in language.

Phonotactic constraints describe the language-specific sound groupings that occur in a language.

Phonotactic rules stipulate which combinations of sounds are 'permitted' in a language.

Phrase a group of words referring to a particular idea.

Phrase structure tree is a graphic representation of the syntactic structure of a sentence.

Phrenology an early form of localization that attempted, unsuccessfully, to link psychological functions to bumps in the skull taken to reflect growth of the brain in specific areas.

Place model a model of sound perception where the perceived pitch of a sound is determined by the location (place) on the basilar membrane that is stimulated.

Point electrical stimulation a technique for directly stimulating points on the cortex exposed during surgery using a thin electrode and low-voltage current; body movements and verbal reports are combined with records of electrode placements to provide maps of cortical involvement with different experiences and body movements.

Positron emission tomography (PET) a functional imaging method that uses positron emissions from radioactive glucose to indicate areas of increased blood flow in the brain.

Postulate suggested as true to form the basis for further reasoning. In Integrated Information Theory (IIT), properties required of a conscious physical substrate are called postulates, since the existence of the physical substrate is itself only postulated.

Pragmatics the understanding of the communicative functions of language and the conventions that govern language use.

Preattentive visual processes can simultaneously analyse the entire scene and detect the presence of unique features.

Predictive coding principle for encoding sensory information wherein the perceptual input is compared to the expected perceptual input, and this difference between expectation and input is what is encoded.

Preference reversal when an original preference switches–for example, as the decision maker moves closer in time to the choice alternatives being delivered.

Premises are statements assumed to be true from which conclusions are drawn.

Primacy effect enhanced recall of items at the start of a list compared to those in the middle.

Primary memory the term introduced by William James (1890) to describe memory 'belonging to the rearward portion of the present space of time', now referred to as short-term memory.

Prime name for the stimulus used to affect subsequent response in an experiment.

Priming an implicit memory effect whereby exposure to a stimulus affects a subsequent response.

Proactive interference occurs when previous learning impairs later learning.

Probabilistic classification learning involves learning a set of associations that cannot readily be memorized; information from across many trials must be used to complete the task.

Probabilistic functionalism theory of perception (developed by Egon Brunswik) as involving the use of cues from the environment that can probabilistically predict some feature of the environment.

Problem a situation in which you have a goal but do not know how to achieve it.

Problem space an abstract representation of possible states of a problem.

Procedural memory a type of non-declarative memory involving memory for how to perform skills and actions.

Productivity of language the ability to generate novel utterances.

Progress monitoring theory theory that, during problem solving, people track progress to the goal and switch approach if insufficient progress is detected.

Progressive deepening searching a state-action space by using depth first search to a limited depth, When depth limit is reached, search backs up to start and repeats, avoiding previously explored branches and so on until the whole space has been searched up to the initial depth limit. If a solution is not found, increase depth limit, and repeat until the goal is reached.

Proper nouns names for specific people and places, typically written with a capital letter, such as Ken, Sandra and London.

Propositional reasoning is reasoning about statements connected by logical relations such as 'and' 'or', 'not', 'if'.

Proprioception the sense of how our limbs are positioned in space.

Prosody the rhythm, intonation and stress patterns in speech.

Prospect theory is a decision theory stressing relative gains and losses.

Prospection the capacity to represent the future.

Prospective memory allows us to remember to perform certain actions. It has been described as the ability to 'remember to remember'.

Prototype is an ideal example that best represents a category.

Psycholinguistics is the branch of study concerned with the mental processes underlying language comprehension and production.

Psychological distance the subjective experience of how close or far something or someone is from the self in the here and now.

Psychophysics a branch of psychology that examines the relationship between physical properties of stimuli and the resulting sensations and psychological events produced by these stimuli.

Pulses involve intentions that are time-locked.

Pure word deafness is a deficit affecting the ability to recognize speech sounds, while comprehension of non-speech sounds remains intact.

Pure word meaning deafness when the patient can repeat back the word, but cannot understand it.

Qualia qualities of experience, most typically perceptual experience.

Rapid eye movement (REM) sleep during REM sleep the eyes move rapidly from side to side behind closed eyelids. Brain wave activity becomes closer to that seen in wakefulness, dreaming often occurs, and arm and leg muscles become temporarily paralysed.

Rate model a model of sound perception where the perceived pitch of a sound is determined by the way the basilar membrane encodes the frequencies contained in the sound.

Re-enactment is the partial repetition of the internal processes involved in previous perceptions or actions.

Reasoning is the cognitive process of deriving new information from old information.

Recency effect the tendency, given a list of items to remember, to recall those from the end of the list more readily than items from the middle.

Receptive field the receptive field of a neuron indicates the physical space that stimulates the neuron. In vision it is the region of visual field to which that neuron is sensitive if stimulated with light.

Recognition when a task participant must verify if an item is a target.

Recognition primed decision is expert knowledge based decision making in which cues in the situation are recognized as indicating particular actions.

Recollection the act of recalling something to mind.

Reconsolidation the process by which old memories become destabilized during retrieval and therefore susceptible to modifications.

Recurrent networks are a type of artificial neural network with connections between units arranged so to obtain a cycle of activation. This design allows a temporal context to be designed into the computation.

Recurrent processing within a network, involves computations that occur in a cyclical fashion.

Recursion the ability to extend sentences infinitely by embedding phrases within sentences.

Reflexive self-referential.

Rehearsal a set of processes by which we can act on currently active information.

Repetition priming the finding that repeated exposure to a word leads to faster responses in a lexical decision task.

Repetition suppression used in fMRI experiments; with repeated presentation of the same stimulus there is a decrease in activity that is not seen when stimulation is varied.

Representativeness increases with the realism and naturalness of the study's materials and tasks.

Representativeness heuristic involves judging frequency or probability of an event or object by how representative or typical it is of its category.

Restructuring changing how one represents a problem.

Retrieval the function by which information is recollected as needed.

Retrieval-induced forgetting (RIF) an impaired ability to recall some items caused by earlier retrieval of related items.

Retroactive interference occurs when later learning impairs memory for earlier learning.

Retrograde amnesia impairment of memory for events that occurred before the onset of amnesia.

Retrograde facilitation the beneficial effect on memory that can be the result of a period of sleep or inactivity following a study period, or even the result of taking certain drugs.

Ribot's Law (1881) Ribot's Law of retrograde amnesia states that recently formed memories are more susceptible to impairment than are older memories.

Right ear advantage for speech sounds refers to the finding that language sounds are processed more efficiently when presented to the right ear compared to the left.

Rime the remaining syllable that follows the onset in a word.

Risk A decision involves risk if there is a probability that one of the options could lead to negative outcomes for the decision maker.

Risk aversion is avoiding risky choices even when a higher expected value than riskless alternatives.

Risk seeking is a preference for risky choices even when riskless alternatives of higher value are available.

Riskless decisions involve choices where the outcomes of the choices are known with certainty.

Rods special neurons in the periphery of the retina that are effective in low levels of light and to sense motion.

Saccades are fast movements of the eye made when reading or scanning an image.

Sacrifice dilemmas problems in which decisions are required about whether to cause the deaths of one or more people to save the lives of a greater number of people.

saliance 'network' involved in monitoring the external and internal environments to allow detection of salient stimuli.

Sapir–Whorf hypothesis the proposal that language affects thought and, in a strong form, that the way we think is determined by the language we use.

Satisficing a decision procedure for multi-attribute choices that sets minimum acceptable levels for each attribute and selects the first alternative that meets or satisfies those requirements.

Savings is a way of assessing forgetting by comparing trials needed for relearning as against trials required for original learning. If fewer trials are needed for relearning then savings have been demonstrated.

Schema a framework that represents a plan or a theory, supporting the organization of knowledge.

Schwa an unstressed neutral vowel sound found in many English words.

Secondary memory the term introduced by William James (1890) to refer to memory proper, which we now think of as long-term memory; for James it was '*the knowledge of an event, or fact,* of which meantime we have not been thinking,*with the additional consciousness that we have thought or experienced it before*' (p. 649).

Self-concept the beliefs a person holds about themselves regarding behaviours, traits and abilities.

Self-continuity the view of oneself as being the same person over time.

Self-efficacy a person's sense of their own competence to complete a certain task or achieve a goal.

Semantic dementia a progressive neurological disorder exhibiting gradual impairment of semantic memory functions.

Semantic memory memory for facts and knowledge about the world.

Semantic priming the finding that responses to a target word are faster when it is preceded by a semantically associated word, the 'prime'.

Semantics is the study of meaning.

Sensation entails the processes by which physical properties are converted to neural signals.

Sensory memory a temporary sensory register that allows input from the sensory modalities to be prolonged.

Sentence verification tasks these tasks present a sentence frame with a target word, and the participant must decide if the word fits in the frame.

Sentences can be thought of as a linguistic representation of a complete thought, and in writing is marked with an end point punctuation mark such as a full stop, question mark or exclamation point.

Serial position curve used to plot recall of a word list such that performance is examined as a function of a word's position in a list.

Set a tendency to persist with one approach to a problem.

Shadowing a technique that involves repeating back an auditorily presented message.

Short-term memory the store where information is temporarily held in an accessible state.

Simulation involves programming computers to solve problems in a similar way to humans.

Single-attribute decision problems involve alternatives that vary in only one dimension.

Skin conductance or galvanic skin response (GSR) reflects changes in the skin's ability to conduct electricity in the presence of an emotion-eliciting stimulus.

Slang describes an informal pattern of speech that is considered to be 'non-standard'.

Slips of the ear occur when we misperceive a word or phrase in speech.

Social cognition the ways in which people make sense of themselves and of others in order to function effectively in a social world.

Social contract theory proposes that rules expressing payment of costs for privileges will be easily solved in 4 card tasks as the correct choices would uncover cheating.

Social Judgement Theory (SJT) an approach to modelling complex judgements as linear equations combining cue values to reach an overall judgement.

Somatic perception of the body through touch and sensing the orientation of limbs in space.

Somatoperception perception related to the body itself, including the location of the body in space, the body's relationship to contact with external objects, and the perception of internal states of the body.

Sound-symbolism the idea that the sounds of words can themselves carry meaning.

Spacing effect occurs when material studied on many separate occasions is better learned than material studied in one continuous session even if total study times are equal.

Spandrel something that occurs as a by-product of the evolution of some other characteristic, rather than being a direct product of adaptive selection.

Specific language impairment (SLI) a specific learning disability wherein language development lags behind cognitive development without explanation.

Speech perception is the process by which we convert a stream of speech into individual words and sentences.

Split brain a set of disorders resulting from disconnection of the cerebral hemispheres by partial or complete severing of the corpus callosum.

Spoonerisms a type of speech error in which sound components of words are transposed during their utterance, resulting in a humorous error.

Spotlight the metaphor of attention where we can think of attention as a spotlight that illuminates locations of interest.

State-action space a representation of how problems can be transformed from starting state through intermediate states to the goal.

State-dependent memory effect occurs if memory is better when internal physiological conditions at learning are reinstated at testing.

State-dependent memory the facilitation of memory when the mental or physiological state at encoding and retrieval matches.

Status quo bias is a tendency to prefer the current state of affairs.

Steps intentions that have a wider time frame in which they can occur.

Stimulus onset asynchrony the time between the onset of a stimulus and the presentation of a mask.

Storage the function by which information is retained in memory.

Strategies systematic ways to carry out a cognitive task such as solving a problem.

Stroop task used to demonstrate the Stroop effect, whereby the naming of colours shows interference when the colour of the word and meaning of the word are incongruent.

Structural imaging structural imaging methods show brain anatomy.

Subject of a sentence is the word or words that gives what the sentence is about or performs the action.

Subjective probability how likely a person believes an outcome to be irrespective of the objective probability.

Subliminal perception the case where a stimulus is presented below threshold (e.g., too fast or too dim) but its effects on behaviour can still be measured.

Surface dyslexia is characterized by a deficit in the reading of irregular words, while the reading of regular words is spared.

Syllabic scripts use a symbol to represent each syllable.

Syllogistic reasoning is reasoning about groups/sets using statements connected by logical relations of 'some', 'none', 'all' and 'some not'.

Synaesthesia an uncommon condition where stimulation of one perceptual modality results in experiencing a percept in a typically unrelated modality (e.g., tasting a sound).

Synaesthete a person with synaesthesia.

Synectics a set of methods developed by G. M. Prince and W. J. J. Gordon in the 1950s for combining different apparently irrelevant concepts to produce creative solutions.

Syntax the rules governing the ways words can be combined to create meaningful sentences.

System 1 a hypothetical system that carries out rapid, intuitive thinking.

System 2 a hypothetical system that carries out slow, deliberate thinking.

Talent having a talent for a particular activity means having pre-existing capacities and abilities relevant to acquiring skill in that activity–often assumed to be innate.

Telegraphic speech a pattern of speech characterized by reduction to basic content words; the term derives from the days when the sending of telegrams required payment per word, which led to the sending of short, efficient messages.

Temporal discounting the decline in subjective value (utility) of an outcome with a time delay to its being received.

The Wada test is a pre-surgical test of hemispheric dominance involving the selective anaesthesizing of the left and right hemispheres.

Think/no-think (TNT) a memory manipulation in which participants are instructed not to retrieve a memory even when a strong cue is present.

Thinking a process of mental exploration of possible actions and states of the world.

Thought congruity is the tendency for thoughts and judgements to be consistent with mood state.

Thought experiment use imagined situations to work out the implications of a theory.

Tip-of-the-tongue a temporary inability to access a known word.

Tonal languages use changes in tone to alter the meaning of the word.

Tonotopic map where the auditory processing of different tones is arranged in an orderly layout in cortex.

Top down or conceptually driven processes reflect the influence of higher-order cognitive processes such as thoughts, beliefs and expectations.

Torque is a measure from physics that measures rotational force such as when muscles apply a force for a limb to rotate about a joint centre.

Transcranial direct current stimulation (tDCS) a non-invasive method of stimulating the brain by passing a weak direct current through the brain.

Transcranial magnetic stimulation (TMS) a non-invasive method of temporarily exciting or inhibiting cortical areas by means of magnetic stimulation.

Transparent or shallow orthography uses a one-to-one correspondence between the letters and sounds.

Tunnel memory the enhancement of memory of central details with reduced memory for peripheral details.

Two-system view is that there are two modes of thought, System 1 and System 2.

Typicality is the extent to which an object is representative of a category.

Ultimatum Game a bargaining game in which one player decides a split of money with a second player–if the second player does not accept the split, both get no money.

Unconscious Thought Effect (UTE) the beneficial effect on decision making of setting the decision aside immediately after the choice information is presented.

Utilitarianism a theory of choice whereby choosers act so as to maximize their happiness or utility.

Utility is the subjective value of an option.

Utilization behaviour dysfunctional automatic reaching for and use of objects in the environment.

Valid arguments are those in which the conclusions must be true if the premises are true.

Vection the perception of one's body moving in space due to visual stimulation.

Ventral stream the visual pathway from occipital cortex to temporal cortex that is involved in recognition of the object being viewed.

Verbal learning the area of experimental psychology concerned with how we learn and remember language-based items such as word lists.

Vestibular sensation the sense of balance and orientation in space.

Viewpoint invariant relationship any aspect of an object that is preserved no matter the direction from which we view the object.

Virtual reality (VR) a three-dimensional environment created by a computer that can be presented to an observer, typically through special display equipment such as a head mounted display.

Visual cache the component of the visuo-spatial sketchpad, within working memory, that stores visual information.

Visual field the total area within which objects can be seen in central or peripheral vision; as such, each eye receives input from right and left visual fields to create binocular vision.

Visual search tasks require an active search of a visual array, usually for a particular object or stimulus feature.

Visuo-spatial processing is the mental manipulation of visual or spatial information.

Visuo-spatial sketchpad the component of working memory proposed for the temporary storage and manipulation of visual and spatial information.

Voicing is when speech sounds are produced while the vocal cords are vibrating.

Water maze a usually a circular container of milky water in which there is a submerged platform to which rats learn to swim from any starting point.

Wechsler Memory Scale a widely used neurocognitive assessment that measures visual memory, auditory memory and working memory.

Well-defined problem a problem in which starting conditions, actions available and goals are all completely specified.

Wernicke–Geschwind model a simplified model of language function used as the basis for classifying aphasia disorders.

Wernicke's aphasia a fluent aphasia, characterized by fluent but meaningless output and repetition errors.

Wernicke's area a brain area in the lower posterior left Sylvian fissure that plays an important role in language comprehension and the production of meaningful speech.

William's syndrome a neurodevelopmental disorder with a number of distinctive features, including a fractionation of linguistic and non-linguistic cognition.

Wisconsin Card Sorting Test a standardized neuropsychological test that assesses set-shifting, an aspect of executive functioning that allows us to change cognitive strategy as the demands of a task require.

Word the smallest unit of grammar that can be meaningfully produced on its own; it can consist of one or more morphemes.

Word length effect the recall advantage for shorter words compared to longer words when immediate serial recall is tested.

Word naming tasks require participants to name a word, while response time is measured.

Word superiority effect the finding that a target letter within a letter string is detected more readily when the string forms a word.

Working memory the system in which information is held and manipulated in order to perform a task.

Φ in Integrated Information Theory (IIT), the quantity Φ provides a measure of the amount of consciousness in a system defined by its conceptual structure. The quantity Φ^{max} is the intrinsic irreducibility of the entire conceptual structure.

References

A

Abdellaoui, M., Bleichrodt, H., & Kammoun, H. (2013). Do financial professionals behave according to prospect theory? An experimental study. *Theory and Decision, 74,* 411–429.

Aboitiz, F., Ossandón, T., Zamorano, F., Palma, B., & Carrasco, X. (2014). Irrelevant stimulus processing in ADHD: Catecholamine dynamics and attentional networks. *Frontiers in Psychology, 5,* 183.

Abrams, R. A., Davoli, C. C., Du, F., Knapp III, W. H., & Paull, D. (2008). Altered vision near the hands. *Cognition, 107*(3), 1035–1047.

Abramson, L. Y., Seligman, M. E. P., & Teasdale, J. (1978). Learned helplessness in humans: Critique and reformulation. *Journal of Abnormal Psychology, 87,* 49–74.

Acar, S., & Sen, S. (2013). A multi-level meta-analysis of the relationship between creativity and schizotypy. *Psychology of Aesthetics, Creativity and the Arts, 7,* 214–228.

Adams, I. L., Lust, J. M., Wilson, P. H., & Steenbergen, B. (2014). Compromised motor control in children with DCD: A deficit in the internal model? A systematic review. *Neuroscience & Biobehavioral Reviews, 47,* 225–244.

Adams, J. W., & Hitch, G. J. (1998). Children's mental arithmetic and working memory. In C. Donlan (Ed.), *The Development of Mathematical Skills* (pp. 153–173). Psychology Press.

Adelson, B. (1981). Problem solving and the development of abstract categories in programming languages. *Memory and Cognition, 9,* 422–433.

Aglioti, S., De Souza, J. F., & Goodale, M. A. (1995). Size-contrast illusions deceive the eye but not the hand. *Current Biology, 5,* 679–685.

Aguilar, P., Brussino, S., & Fernandez-Dols, J.-M. (2013). Psychological distance increases uncompromising consequentialism. *Journal of Experimental Social Psychology, 49,* 449–452.

Ahn, W., Kim, N. S., Lassaline, M. E., & Dennis, M. (2000). Causal status as a determinant of feature centrality. *Cognitive Psychology, 41,* 361–416.

Aitchison, J. (1996). *The Seeds of Speech: Language Origin and Evolution.* Cambridge University Press.

Akata, Z., Hendricks, L. A., Alaniz, S., & Darrell, T. (2018). Generating post-hoc rationales of deep visual classification decisions. In *Explainable and Interpretable Models in Computer Vision and Machine Learning* (pp. 135–154). Springer.

Akhand, O., Balcer, L. J., & Galetta, S. L. (2019). Assessment of vision in concussion. *Current Opinion in Neurology, 32*(1), 68–74.

Akyürek, E. G., & Hommel, B. (2005). Short-term memory and the attentional blink: Capacity versus content. *Memory & Cognition, 33*(4), 654–663.

Alais, D., & Burr, D. (2004). The ventriloquist effect results from near-optimal bimodal integration. *Current Biology, 14*(3), 257–262.

Alber, J., Della Sala, S., & Dewar, M. (2014). Minimizing interference with early consolidation boosts 7-day retention in amnesic patients. *Neuropsychology, 28*(5), 667–675.

Alberini, C. M., & LeDoux, J. E. (2013). Memory reconsolidation. *Current Biology, 23*(17), R746–R750.

Albert, M. L., & Bear, D. (1974). Time to understand: A case study of word deafness with reference to the role of time in auditory comprehension, *Brain, 97,* 373–384.

Albonico, A., & Barton, J. (2019). Progress in perceptual research: The case of prosopagnosia. *F1000 Research, 8.*

Albright, T. D. (2017). Why eyewitnesses fail. *Proceedings of the National Academy of Sciences, 114*(30), 7758–7764.

Alea, N., & Bluck, S. (2003). Why are you telling me that? A conceptual model of the social function of autobiographical memory. *Memory, 11*(2), 165–178.

Aleksander, I. (2017). Machine consciousness. In S. Schneider & M. Velmans (Eds.), *The Blackwell Companion to Consciousness* (pp. 93–105). John Wiley & Sons.

Allan, L. G. (1993). Human contingency judgments: Rule based or associative? *Psychological Bulletin, 114,* 435–448.

Allendorfer, J. B., Hernando, K. A., Hossain, S., Nenert, R., Holland, S. K., & Szaflarski, J. P. (2016). Arcuate fasciculus asymmetry has a hand in language function but not handedness. *Human Brain Mapping, 37,* 3297–3309.

Allison, T., Ginter, H., McCarthy, G., Nobre, A. C., Puce, A., Luby, M., & Spencer, D. D. (1994). Face recognition in human extrastriate cortex. *Journal of Neurophysiology, 71*(2), 821–825.

Allison, T., Puce, A., & McCarthy, G. (2000). Social perception from visual cues: Role of the STS region. *Trends in Cognitive Science, 4,* 267–278.

Alloy, L. B., & Abramson, L. Y. (1979). Judgment of contingency in depressed and nondepressed students: Sadder but wiser? *Journal of Experimental Psychology: General, 108,* 441–485.

Alloy, L. B., Abramson, L. Y., Whitehouse, W. G., Hogan, M. E., Panzarella, C., & Rose, D. T. (2006). Prospective incidence of first onsets and recurrences of depression in individuals at high and low cognitive risk for depression. *Journal of Abnormal Psychology, 115*(1), 145.

Alloy, L. B., & Ackerman, L. Y. (1988). Depressive realism: Four theoretical perspectives. In L. B. Alloy (Ed.), *Cognitive Processes in Depression* (pp. 223–265). Guilford Press.

Allport, D. A. (1980). Attention and performance. In G. Claxton (Ed.), *International Library of Psychology.* Routledge and Kegan Paul.

Allport, D. A. (1983). Language and cognition. In R. Harris (Ed.), *Approaches to Language.* Pergamon Press.

Allport, D. A., & Funnell, E. (1981). Components of the mental lexicon. *Philosophical Transactions of the Royal Society of London, B295,* 397–410.

Altmann, C. F., Uesaki, M., Ono, K., Matsuhashi, M., Mima, T., & Fukuyama, H. (2014). Categorical speech perception during active discrimination of consonants and vowels. *Neuropsychologia, 64,* 13–23.

Altmann, G. T. M. (1998). Ambiguity in sentence processing. *Trends in Cognitive Sciences, 2,* 146–152.

Amalberti, R. (2001). The paradoxes of almost totally safe transportation systems. *Safety Science, 37*(2–3), 109–126.

Amano, T., Sandel, B., Eager, H., Bulteau, E., Svenning, J.-C., Dalsgaard, B., Rahbek, C., Davies, R. G., & Sutherland, W. J. (2014). Global distribution and drivers of language extinction risk. *Proceedings of the Royal Society B: Biological Sciences, 281,* 20141574.

American Psychiatric Association (2013). *Diagnostic and Statistical Manual of Mental Disorders* (5th ed.). American Psychiatric Publishing.

Amlung, M., Petker, T., Jackson, J., Balodis, I., & MacKillop, J. (2016). Steep discounting of delayed monetary and food rewards in obesity: A meta-analysis. *Psychological Medicine, 46,* 2423–2434.

Anbarci, N., Arin, K. P., Kuhlenkasper, T., & Zenker, C. (2018). Revisiting loss aversion: Evidence from professional tennis. *Journal of Economic Behavior & Organization, 153,* 1–18.

Andersen, R. A., & Buneo, C. A. (2002). Intentional maps in posterior parietal cortex. *Annual Review of Neuroscience, 25*(1), 189–220.

Anderson, J. R. (2004). *Cognitive Psychology and its Implications* (6th ed.). Worth.

Anderson, M. C. (2003). Rethinking interference theory: Executive control and the mechanisms of forgetting. *Journal of Memory and Learning, 49,* 415–445.

Anderson, M. C. (2005). The role of inhibitory control in forgetting unwanted memories: A consideration of three methods. In C. MacLeod & B. Uttl (Eds.), *Dynamic Cognitive Processes.* Springer Verlag.

Anderson, M. C., & Bell, T. A. (2001). Forgetting our facts: The role of inhibitory processes in the loss of propositional knowledge. *Journal of Experimental Psychology: General, 130,* 544–570.

Anderson, M. C., & Green, C. (2001). Suppressing unwanted memories by executive control. *Nature, 410,* 366–369.

Anderson, M. C., Bjork, R. A., & Bjork, E. L. (1994). Remembering can cause forgetting: Retrieval dynamics in long term memory. *Journal of Experimental Psychology: Learning, Memory and Cognition, 20,* 1063–1087.

Anderson, M. C., & Neely, J. H. (1996). Interference and inhibition in memory retrieval. In E. L. Bjork & R. A. Bjork (Eds.), *Memory.* Academic Press.

Anderson, M. C., Ochsner, K. N., Cooper, J., Robertson, E., Gabrieli, S. W., Glover, G. H., & Gabrieli, J. D. E. (2004). Neural systems underlying the suppression of unwanted memories. *Science, 303,* 232–235.

Andics, A., McQueen, J. M., Petersson, K. M., Gal, V., Rudas, G., & Vidnyanszky, Z. (2010). Neural mechanisms for voice recognition. *Neuroimage, 52*(4), 1528–1540.

Andoh, J., Milde, C., Tsao, J. W., & Flor, H. (2018). Cortical plasticity as a basis of phantom limb pain: Fact or fiction? *Neuroscience, 387,* 85–91.

Andreetta, S., Cantagallo, A., & Marini, A. (2012). Narrative discourse in anomic aphasia. *Neuropsychologia, 50*(8), 1787–1793.

Andreetta, S., & Marini, A. (2015). The effect of lexical deficits on narrative disturbances in fluent aphasia. *Aphasiology, 6*(3), 705–723.

Anguera, J. A., & Gazzaley, A. (2015). Video games, cognitive exercises, and the enhancement of cognitive abilities. *Current Opinion in Behavioral Sciences, 4,* 160–165.

Anzai, Y., & Simon, H. A. (1979). The theory of learning by doing. *Psychological Review, 86,* 124–140.

Anzellotti, F., Onofrj, V., Maruotti, V., Ricciardi, L., Franciotti, R., Bonanni, L., Thomas, A., & Onofrj, M. (2011). Autoscopic phenomena: Case report and review of literature. *Behavioral and Brain Functions, 7*(1), 2.

Applegate, D. L., Bixby, R. M., Chvatal, V., & Cook, W. J. (2006). *The Travelling Salesman Problem.* Princeton University Press.

Ardila, A. (2010). A proposed reinterpretation and reclassification of aphasic syndromes. *Aphasiology, 24*(3), 363–394.

Ardila, A. (2020). A cross-linguistic comparison of category verbal fluency test (ANIMALS): A systematic review. *Archives of Clinical Neuropsychology, 35*(2), 213–225.

Ardila, A., Bernal, B., & Rosselli, M. (2016). How extended is Wernicke's area? Meta-analytic connectivity study of BA20 and integrative proposal. *Neuroscience Journal,* 4962562.

Armstrong, K. M., Fitzgerald, J. K., & Moore, T. (2006). Changes in visual receptive fields with microstimulation of frontal cortex. *Neuron, 50*(5), 791–798.

Arning, L., Stock, A.-K., Kloster, E., Epplen, J. T., & Beste, C. (2014). NPY2-receptor variation modulates iconic memory processes. *European Neuropsychopharmacology, 24*(8), 1298–1302.

Asaly-Zetawi, M., & Lipka, O. (2019). Note-Taking Skill Among Bilingual Students inAcademia: Literacy, Language and Cognitive Examination. *Frontiers in Psychology, 10,* 870.

Asaridou, S. S., Demir-Lira, Ö. E., Goldin-Meadow, S., Levine, S. C., & Small, S. L. (2020). Language development and brain reorganization in a child born without the left hemisphere. *Cortex, 127,* 290–312.

Atchley, P., & Andersen, G. J. (1995). Discrimination of speed distributions – sensitivity to statistical properties. *Vision Research, 35*(22), 3131–3144.

Atkeson, C. G., Hale, J. G., Pollick, F. E., Riley, M., Kotosaka, S., Schaal, S., Shibata, T., Tevatia, G., Ude, A., Vijayakumar, S., Kawato, E., & Kawato, M. (2000). Using humanoid robots to study human behavior. *IEEE Intelligent Systems and their Applications, 15*(4), 46–55.

Atkinson, A. P., & Adolphs, R. (2011). The neuropsychology of face perception: Beyond simple dissociations and functional selectivity. *Philosophical Transactions of the Royal Society B – Biological Sciences, 366* (1571), 1726–1738.

Atkinson, Q. (2011). Phonemic diversity supports a serial founder effect model of language expansion from Africa. *Science, 332,* 346–349.

Atkinson, R. C., & Shiffrin, R. M. (1968). Human memory: A proposed system and its control processes. In K. W. Spence & J. T. Spence (Eds.), *The Psychology of Learning and Motivation* (Vol. 2, pp. 89–195). Academic Press.

Atwood, M. E., & Polson, P. G. (1976). A process model for water jug problems. *Cognitive Psychology, 8,* 191–216.

Atwood, M. E., Masson, M. E. J., & Polson, P. G. (1980). Further exploration with a process model for water jug problems. *Memory & Cognition, 8,* 182–192.

Autin, F., & Croizet, J. (2012). Improving working memory efficiency by reframing metacognitive interpretation of task difficulty. *Journal of Experimental Psychology: General, 141*(4), 610–618.

Auvray, M., & Deroy, O. (2015). How do synesthetes experience the world? In M. Matthen (Ed.), *Oxford Handbook of Philosophy of Perception* (pp. 640–658). Oxford University Press.

Averbach, E. A., & Coriell, A. S. (1961). Short-term memory in vision. *Bell Systems Technical Journal, 40,* 309–328.

Averell, L., & Heathcote, A. (2011). The form of the forgetting curve and the fate of memories. *Journal of Mathematical Psychology, 55*(1), 25–35.

Awh, E., Jonides, J., & Reuter-Lorenz, P. A. (1998). Rehearsal in spatial working memory. *Journal of Experimental Psychology: Human Perception and Performance, 24*(3), 780–790.

Awh, E., & Jonides, J. (2001). Overlapping mechanisms of attention and spatial working memory. *Trends in Cognitive Sciences, 5*(3), 119–126.

Awh, E., & Pashler, H. (2000). Evidence for split attentional foci. *Journal of Experimental Psychology: Human Perception and Performance, 26*(2), 834–846.

Awh, E., Vogel, E. K., & Oh, S. H. (2006). Interactions between attention and working memory. *Neuroscience, 139*(1), 201–208.

Ayotte, J., Peretz, I., & Hyde, K. (2002). Congenital amusia – A group study of adults afflicted with a music-specific disorder. *Brain, 125,* 238–251.

Ayotte, J., Peretz, I., Rousseau, I., Bard, C., & Bojanowski, M. (2000). Patterns of music agnosia associated with middle cerebral artery infarcts. *Brain, 123,* 1926–1938.

Ayton, P., Onkal, D., & McReynolds, L. (2011). Effects of ignorance and information on judgments and decisions. *Judgment and Decision Making, 6,* 381–391.

B

Baars, B. J. (1988). *A Cognitive Theory of Consciousness.* Cambridge University Press.

Baars, B. J. (1997). *In the Theater of Consciousness: The Workspace of the Mind.* Oxford University Press.

Baars, B. J. (2002). The conscious access hypothesis: Origins and recent evidence. *Trends in Cognitive Sciences, 6*(1), 47–52.

Baars, B. J., & Motley, M. T. (1974). Spoonerisms: Experimental elicitation of human speech errors. Journal Supplement Abstract Service. *Catalog of Selected Documents in Psychology.*

Baas, M., Nijstad, B. A., Boot, N. C., & De Dreu, C. K. W. (2016). Mad genius revisited: Vulnerability to psychopathology, bio-behavioral approach-avoidance, and creativity. *Psychological Bulletin, 142,* 668–692.

Baayen, R. H., Piepenbrock, R., & Gulikers, L. (1995). The CELEX Lexical Database (Release 2) [CD-ROM]. University of Pennsylvania.

Bachiller, P., Bustos, P., & Manso, L. J. (2008). Attentional selection for action in mobile robots. In J. Aramburo & A. Ramirez-Trevino (Eds.), *Advances in Robotics, Automation and Control.* InTech.

Bachorowski, J. A., & Owren, M. J. (1999). Acoustic correlates of talker sex and individual talker identity are present in a short vowel segment produced in running speech. *Journal of the Acoustical Society of America, 106*(2), 1054–1063.

Bacon, A. M., & Handley, S. (2010). Dyslexia, reasoning and the importance of visual-spatial processes. In *Dyslexia and Creativity: Investigations from Differing Perspectives* (pp. 25–49). Nova Science Publishers.

Bacon, A. M., & Handley, S. J. (2014). Reasoning and dyslexia: Is visual memory a compensatory resource? *Dyslexia, 20*(4), 330–345.

Badcock, P. B., Friston, K. J., & Ramstead, M. J. (2019). The hierarchically mechanistic mind: A free-energy formulation of the human psyche. *Physics of Life Reviews, 31,* 104–121.

Baddeley, A. (1993). Holy war or wholly unnecessary? Some thoughts on the 'conflict' between laboratory studies and everyday memory. In G. M. Davies & R. H. Logie (Eds.), *Memory in Everyday Life.* Elsevier Science Publishers.

Baddeley, A. (2012). Working memory: Theories, models, and controversies. *Annual Review of Psychology, 63*(1), 1–29.

Baddeley, A. (2019). *Working Memories: Postmen, Divers and the Cognitive Revolution* (Chapter 7). Routledge.

Baddeley, A. C., & Lieberman, K. (1980). Spatial working memory. In R. S. Nickerson (Ed.), *Attention and Performance* (Vol. 8, pp. 521–539). Erlbaum.

Baddeley, A. D. (1984). The fractionation of human memory. *Psychological Medicine, 14,* 259–264.

Baddeley, A. D. (1986). *Working Memory.* Oxford University Press.

Baddeley, A. D. (1992a). Consciousness and working memory. *Consciousness and Cognition, 1,* 3–6.

Baddeley, A. D. (1992b). Working memory. *Science, 255,* 556–559.

Baddeley, A. D. (1992). Working memory. *Science, 255,* 556–559.

Baddeley, A. D. (1996a). Exploring the central executive. *Quarterly Journal of Experimental Psychology, 49A,* 5–28.

Baddeley, A. D. (1996a). The fractionation of working memory. *Proceedings of the National Academy of Sciences of the United States of America, 93,* 13468–13472.

Baddeley, A. D. (1996b). Exploring the central executive. *Quarterly Journal of Experimental Psychology: Human Experimental Psychology, 49*(A), 5–28.

Baddeley, A. D. (1999). *Essentials of Human Memory.* Hove: Psychology Press.

Baddeley, A. D. (2000). The episodic buffer: A new component of working memory? *Trends in Cognitive Sciences, 4*, 417–423.

Baddeley, A. D. (2003). Working memory: Looking back and looking forward. *Nature Reviews Neuroscience, 4*(10), 829–839.

Baddeley, A. D. (2004). The psychology of memory. In A. D. Baddeley, M. D. Kopelman, & B. A. Wilson (Eds.), *The Essential Handbook of Memory Disorders for Clinicians* (pp. 1–13). Wiley.

Baddeley, A. D. (2007). *Working Memory, Thought and Action.* Oxford University Press.

Baddeley, A. D. (2009). Working memory. In A. D. Baddeley, M. W. Eysenck, & M. C. Anderson (Eds.), *Memory.* Psychology Press.

Baddeley, A. D., & Andrade, J. (2000). Working memory and the vividness of imagery. *Journal of Experimental Psychology: General, 129*, 126–145.

Baddeley, A. D., Chincotta, D. M., & Adlam, A. (2001). Working memory and the control of action: Evidence from task switching. *Journal of Experimental Psychology: General, 130*, 641–657.

Baddeley, A. D., Grant, S., Wight, E., & Thompson, N. (1975). Imagery and visual working memory. In P. M. Rabbitt and S. Dornic (Eds.), *Attention and Performance*, Vol. V. Academic Press.

Baddeley, A. D., & Hitch, G. (1974). Working memory. In G. H. Bower (Ed.), *The Psychology of Learning and Motivation: Advances in Research and Theory* (Vol. 8, pp. 47–89). Academic Press.

Baddeley, A. D., & Hitch, G. J. (2017). Is the levels of processing effect language-limited? *Journal of Memory and Language, 92*, 1–13.

Baddeley, A. D., & Hitch, G. J. (2019). The phonological loop as a buffer store: An update. *Cortex, 112*, 91–106.

Baddeley, A. D., Lewis, V. J., & Vallar, G. (1984). Exploring the articulatory loop. *Quarterly Journal of Experimental Psychology, 36*, 233–252.

Baddeley, A. D., & Logie, R. H. (1999). Working memory: The multiple component model. In A. Miyake & P. Shah (Eds.), *Models of Working Memory: Mechanisms of Active Maintenance and Executive Control* (pp. 28–61). Cambridge University Press.

Baddeley, A. D., & Longman, D. J. A. (1978). The influence of length and frequency of training session on the rate of learning to type. *Ergonomics, 21*(8), 627–635.

Baddeley, A. D., Papagno, C., & Vallar, G. (1988). When long-term learning depends on short-term storage. *Journal of Memory and Language, 27*, 586–595.

Baddeley, A., Thomson, N., & Buchanan, M. (1975). Word length and the structure of short-term memory. *Journal of Verbal Learning & Verbal Behavior, 14*, 575–589.

Baddeley, A. D., & Warrington, E. K. (1970). Amnesia and the distinction between long- and short-term memory. *Journal of Verbal Learning & Verbal Behavior, 9*(2), 176–189.

Baddeley, A. D., & Warrington, E. K. (1973). Memory coding and amnesia. *Neuropsychologia, 11*, 159–165.

Baddeley, A. D., & Wilson, B. A. (1985). Phonological coding and short-term memory in patients without speech. *Journal of Memory and Language, 24*, 490–502.

Baddeley, A. D., & Wilson, B. A. (1988). Frontal amnesia and the dysexecutive syndrome. *Brain and Cognition, 7*, 212–30.

Baek, J., & Chong, S. C. (2020). Distributed attention model of perceptual averaging. *Attention, Perception, & Psychophysics, 82*(1), 63–79.

Baese-Berk, M. (2018). Perceptual learning for native and non-native speech. *Psychology of Learning and Motivation, 68*, 1–29.

Bahrick, H. P. (1983). The cognitive map of a city: Fifty years of learning and memory. In G. H. Bower (Ed.), *The Psychology of Learning and Motivation, 17.* Academic Press.

Bahrick, H. P., Bahrick, P. O., & Wittlinger, R. P. (1975). Fifty years of memory for names and faces: A cross-sectional approach. *Journal of Experimental Psychology: General, 104*, 54–75.

Bahrick, H. P. D. (1984). Fifty years of language attrition: Implications for programmatic research. *Modern Language Journal, 68*, 105–118.

Bahrick, H. P., Hall, L. K., & Berger, S. A. (1996). Accuracy and distortion in memory for high school grades. *Psychological Science, 7*, 265–271.

Ballard, I. C., Kim, B., Liatsis, A., Aydogan, G., Cohen, J. D., & McClure, S. M. (2017). More is meaningful: The magnitude effect in intertemporal choice depends on self-control. *Psychological Science, 28*, 1443–1454.

Balota, D. A., & Chumbley, J. I. (1984). Are lexical decisions a good measure of lexical access? The role of word frequency in the neglected decision stage. *Journal of Experimental Psychology: Human Perception and Performance, 10*, 340–357.

Banaji, M. R., & Crowder, R. (1989). The bankruptcy of everyday memory. *American Psychologist, 44*, 1185–1193.

Banbury, S. P., & Berry, D. C. (2005). Office noise and employee concentration: Identifying causes of disruption and potential improvements. *Ergonomics, 48*(1), 25–37.

Banbury, S. P., Macken, W. J., Tremblay, S., & Jones, D. M. (2001). Auditory distraction and short-term memory: Phenomena and practical implications. *Human Factors, 43*(1), 12–29.

Banks, M. I., Krause, B. M., Endemann, C. M., Campbell, D. I., Kovach, C. K., Dyken, M. E., Kawasaki, H., & Nourski, K. V. (2020). Cortical functional connectivity indexes arousal state during sleep and anesthesia. *Neuro Image, 211*, 116627.

Banks, W. P. (2002). On timing relations between brain and world. *Consciousness and Cognition, 11*, 141–143.

Bard, E. G., Shillcock, R. C., & Altmann, G. T. M. (1988). The recognition of words after their acoustic offsets in spontaneous speech: Effects of subsequent context. *Perception & Psychophysics, 44*, 395–408.

Bard, P. (1934). Emotion. I. The neuro-humoral basis of emotional reactions. In C. Murchison (Ed.), *A Handbook of General Experimental Psychology.* Clark University.

Bargh, J. A. (2016). Awareness of the prime versus awareness of its influence: Implications for the real-world scope of unconscious higher mental processes. *Current Opinion in Psychology, 12*, 49–52.

Baron, J. (1994). Nonconsequentialist decisions. *Behavioral and Brain Sciences, 17*, 1–42.

Baron, J., & Jurney, J. (1993). Norms against voting for coerced reform. *Journal of Personality and Social Psychology, 64*, 347–355.

Baron, J., & Ritov, I. (1993). Intuitions about penalties and compensation in the context of tort law. *Journal of Risk and Uncertainty, 7*, 17–33.

Baron-Cohen, S. (1997). *Mindblindness: An Essay on Autism and Theory of Mind.* MIT Press.

Baronchelli, A., Ferrer-i-Cancho, R., Pastor-Satorras, R., Chater, N., & Christiansen, M. H. (2013). Networks in cognitive science. *Trends in Cognitive Sciences, 17*, 348–360.

Barrash, J., Stuss, D. T., Aksan, N., Anderson, S. W., Jones, R. D., Manzel, K., & Tranel, D. (2018). 'Frontal lobe syndrome'? Subtypes of acquired personality disturbances in patients with focal brain damage. *Cortex, 106*, 65–80.

Barrett, D. (2015). Dreams: Thinking in a different biochemical state. In M. Kramer & M. Glucksman (Eds.), *Dream Research: Contributions to Clinical Practice* (pp. 80–94). Routledge.

Barrett, H. C., & Kurzban, R. (2006). Modularity in cognition: Framing the debate. *Psychological Review, 113*, 628–647.

Barrett, L. F. (2006). Solving the emotion paradox: Categorization and the experience of emotion. *Personality and Social Psychology Review, 10*, 20–46.

Barrett, L. F. (2016). Navigating the science of emotion. In *Emotion Measurement* (pp. 31–63). Woodhead Publishing.

Barrett, L. F. (2017). *How Emotions Are Made: The Secret Life of the Brain.* Houghton Mifflin Harcourt.

Barrett, L. F., Adolphs, R., Marsella, S., Martinez, A. M., & Pollak, S. D. (2019). Emotional expressions reconsidered: Challenges to inferring emotion from human facial movements. *Psychological Science in the Public Interest, 20*(1), 1–68.

Barrett, L. F., & Satpute, A. B. (2019). Historical pitfalls and new directions in the neuroscience of emotion. *Neuroscience Letters, 693*, 9–18.

Barsalou, L. W. (1983). Ad hoc categories. *Memory and Cognition, 11*, 211–227.

Barsalou, L. W. (1985). Ideals, central tendency, and frequency of instantiation as determinants of graded structure in categories. *Journal of Experimental Psychology: Learning, Memory and Cognition, 11*, 629–654.

Barsalou, L. W. (1999). Perceptual symbol systems. *Behavioral and Brain Sciences, 22*(4), 577–660.

Barsalou, L. W. (2003). Situated simulation in the human conceptual system. *Language and Cognitive Processes, 18*, 513–562.

Barsalou, L. W. (2008). Grounded cognition. *Annual Review of Psychology, 59*, 617–645.

Barshi, I., & Farris, C. (2016). *Misunderstandings in ATC Communication: Language, Cognition, and Experimental Methodology.* Routledge.

Bartha, L., & Benke, T. (2003). Acute conduction aphasia: An analysis of 20 cases. *Brain and Language, 85*, 93–108.

Bartlett, F. C. (1932). *Remembering: A Study in Experimental and Social Psychology.* Cambridge University Press.

Bartlett, L., Martin, A., Neil, A. L., Memish, K., Otahal, P., Kilpatrick, M., & Sanderson, K. (2019). A systematic review and meta-analysis of workplace mindfulness training randomized controlled trials. *Journal of Occupational Health Psychology, 24*(1), 108.

Bartolomeo, P. (2002). The relationship between visual perception and visual mental imagery: A re-appraisal of the neuropsychological evidence. *Cortex, 38,* 357–378.

Bartolomeo, P. (2008). The neural correlates of visual mental imagery: An ongoing debate. *Cortex, 44,* 107–108.

Bartolozzi, C., Natale, L., Nori, F., & Metta, G. (2016). Robots with a sense of touch. *Nature Materials, 15*(9), 921.

Barton, J. J., & Corrow, S. L. (2016). The problem of being bad at faces. *Neuropsychologia, 89,* 119–124.

Barton, M. E., & Komatsu, L. K. (1989). Defining features of natural kinds and artifacts. *Journal of Psycholinguistic Research, 18,* 433–447.

Basden, B. H., & Basden, D. R. (1996). Directed forgetting: Further comparisons of the item and list methods. *Memory, 4,* 633–653.

Basden, B. H., Basden, D. R., & Gargano, G. J. (1993). Directed forgetting in implicit and explicit memory tests: A comparison of methods. *Journal of Experimental Psychology: Learning, 19,* 603–616.

Bassetti, C., Vella, S., Donati, F., Wielepp, P., & Weder, B. (2000). SPECT during sleepwalking. *Lancet, 356* (9228), 484–485.

Basso, A., Spinnler, H., Vallar, G., & Zanobio, E. (1982). Left hemisphere damage and selective impairment of auditory verbal short-term memory: A case study. *Neuropsychologia, 20,* 263–274.

Basu Mallick, D., Magnotti, J. F., & Beauchamp, M. S. (2015). Variability and stability in the McGurk effect: Contributions of participants, stimuli, time, and response type. *Psychonomic Bulletin & Review, 22,* 1299–1307.

Bateman, L., Jones, C., & Jomeen, J. (2017). A narrative synthesis of women's out-of-body experiences during childbirth. *Journal of Midwifery & Women's Health, 62*(4), 442–451.

Batouli, S. A. H., Hasani, N., Gheisari, S., Behzad, E., & Oghabian, M. A. (2016). Evaluation of the factors influencing brain language laterality in presurgical planning. *Physica Medica, 32*(10), 1201–1209.

Bauer, R. M. (1984). Autonomic recognition of names and faces in prosopagnosia: A neuropsychological application of the guilty knowledge test. *Neuropsychologia, 22*(4), 457–469.

Bauman, C. W., McGraw, A. P., Bartels, D. M., & Warren, C. (2014). Revisiting external validity: Concerns about trolley problems and other sacrificial dilemmas in moral psychology. *Social and Personality Psychology Compass, 8/9,* 536–544.

Baumann, O., & Belin, P. (2010). Perceptual scaling of voice identity: Common dimensions for different vowels and speakers. *Psychological Research-Psychologische Forschung, 74*(1), 110–120.

Bavelas, J., Gerwing, J., Sutton, C., & Prevost, D. (2008). Gesturing on the telephone: Independent effects of dialogue and visibility. *Journal of Memory and Language, 58*(2), 495–520.

Bayer, J. B., & Campbell, S. W. (2012). Texting while driving on automatic: Considering the frequency-independent side of habit. *Computers in Human Behavior, 28*(6), 2083–2090.

Bayley, P. J., Frascino, J. C., & Squire, L. R. (2005). Robust habit learning in the absence of awareness and independent of the medial temporal lobe, *Nature, 436,* 550–553.

Beaman, C. P. (2010). Working memory and working attention: What could possibly evolve? *Current Anthropology, 51,* s1, s27–s38.

Bear, A., Kagan, A., & Rand, D. G. (2017). Co-evolution of cooperation and cognition: The impact of imperfect deliberation and context-sensitive intuition. *Proceedings in Biological Science, 284,* 20162326.

Beardsworth, T., & Buckner, T. (1981). The ability to recognize oneself from a video recording of one's movements without seeing one's body. *Bulletin of the Psychonomic Society, 18*(1), 19–22.

Beattie, G. (1982) Turn-taking and interruption in political interviews: Margaret Thatcher and Jim Callaghan compared and contrasted. *Semiotica, 39*(1/2), 93–114.

Beauchamp, M. S., & Martin, A. (2007). Grounding object concepts in perception and action: Evidence from fMRI studies of tools. *Cortex, 43*(3), 461–468.

Beauvois, M. F., & Derouesné, J. (1979). Phonological alexia: Three dissociations. *Journal of Neurology, Neurosurgery, & Psychiatry 42,* 1115–1124.

Bechara, A., Damasio, H., Tranel, D., & Damasio, A. R. (1997). Deciding advantageously before knowing the advantageous strategy. *Science, 275*(5304), 1293–1295.

Beck, A. (1967). *Cognitive Therapy and the Emotional Disorders*. Meridian.

Beck, A. (1976). *Cognitive Therapy and the Emotional Disorders*. Meridian.

Beck Lidén, C., Krüger, O., Schwarz, L., Erb, M., Kardatzki, B., Scheffler, K., & Ethofer, T. (2016). Neurobiology of knowledge and misperception of lyrics. *NeuroImage, 134,* 12–21.

Beck, A. T. (1991). Cognitive therapy: A 30-year retrospective. *American Psychologist, 46,* 368–375.

Beck, A. T., Rush, A. J., Shaw, B. F., & Emery, G. (1979). *Cognitive Therapy of Depression*. Guilford.

Beck, C., Kardatzki, B., & Ethofer, T. (2014). Mondegreens and Soramimi as a method to induce misperceptions of speech content–influence of familiarity, wittiness, and language competence. *PLOS One, 9,* e84667.

Begg, I. & Harris, G. (1982). On the interpretation of syllogisms. *Journal of Verbal Learning and Verbal Behaviour, 21,* 595–620.

Begg, I., & Denny, J. P. (1969). Empirical reconciliation of atmosphere and conversion interpretations of syllogistic reasoning errors. *Journal of Experimental Psychology, 81*(2), 351.

Beilock, S. (2010). *Choke: What the Secrets of the Brain Reveal About Getting it Right When You Have to.* Simon and Schuster.

Belin, P., Fecteau, S., & Bedard, C. (2004). Thinking the voice: Neural correlates of voice perception. *Trends in Cognitive Sciences, 8*(3), 129–135.

Belin, P., Zatorre, R. J., Lafaille, P., Ahad, P., & Pike, B. (2000). Voice-selective areas in human auditory cortex. *Nature, 403* (6767), 309–312.

Belletier, C., Normand, A., Camos, V., Barrouillet, P., & Huguet, P. (2019). Choking under experimenter's presence: Impact on proactive control and practical consequences for psychological science. *Cognition, 189,* 60–64.

Bellugi, U., & Wang, P. (1996). Williams syndrome: From cognition to brain to gene. In *Encyclopedia of Neuroscience* (pp. 1–5). Elsevier.

Bentham, J. (1789). *The Principles of Morals and Legislation.*

Bentin, S., McCarthy, G., & Wood, C. C. (1985). Event related potentials, lexical decision and semantic priming. *Electroencephalography and Clinical Neurophysiology, 60,* 343–355.

Berent, I., Steriade, D., Lennertz, T., & Vaknin, V. (2007). What we know about what we have never heard: Evidence from perceptual illusions. *Cognition, 104,* 591–630.

Berlin, L. (2007). Radiologic errors and malpractice: A blurry distinction. *American Journal of Roentgenology, 189*(3), 517–522.

Berlin, L. (2007a). Accuracy of diagnostic procedures: Has it improved over the past five decades? *American Journal of Roentgenology, 188*(5), 1173–1178.

Berlin, L. (2007b). Radiologic errors and malpractice: A blurry distinction. *American Journal of Roentgenology, 189*(3), 517–522.

Berlin, L. (2014). Radiologic errors, past, present and future. *Diagnosis, 1*(1), 79–84.

Berndt, R. A., & Caramazza, A. (1980). A redefinition of the syndrome of Broca's aphasia: Implications for a neuropsychological model of language. *Applied Psycholinguistics, 1,* 225–278.

Bernoulli, D. (1954). Exposition of a new theory on the measurement of risk. *Econometrica, 22,* 23–26. (Translation of Bernoulli, D. (1738). Specimen theoriae novae de mensura sortis. *Papers of the Imperial Academy of Science of St. Petersburg, 5,* 175–192.)

Bernstein, N. A. (1967). *The Co-ordination and Regulation of Movements*. Pergamon.

Berntsen, D. (2002). Tunnel memories for autobiographical events: Central details are remembered more frequently from shocking than from happy experiences. *Memory & Cognition, 30*(7), 1010–1020.

Berntsen, D. (2012). Spontaneous recollections: Involuntary autobiographical memories are a basic mode of remembering. In D. Berntsen & D. C. Rubin (Eds.), *Understanding Autobiographical Memory: Theories and Approaches* (pp. 290–310). Cambridge University Press.

Bertelson, P., & Radeau, M. (1981). Cross-modal bias and perceptual fusion with auditory-visual spatial discordance. *Perception & Psychophysics, 29*(6), 578–584.

Berube, S., Nonnemacher, J., Demsky, C., Glenn, S., Saxena, S., Wright, A., Tippett, D. C., & Hillis, A. E. (2019). Stealing cookies in the twenty-first century: Measures of spoken narrative in healthy versus speakers with aphasia. *American Journal of Speech-Language Pathology, 28*(1S), 321–329.

Best, C. T. (1988). The emergence of cerebral asymmetries in early human development: A literature review and a neuroembryological model. In D. L.

Molfese & S. J. Segalowitz (Eds.), *Brain Lateralization in Children: Developmental Implications* (pp. 5–34). Guilford Press.

Beste, C., Saft, C., Güntürkün, O., & Falkenstein, M. (2008). Increased cognitive functioning in symptomatic Huntington's disease as revealed by behavioural and event-related potential indices of auditory sensory memory and attention. *Journal of Neuroscience, 28*, 11695–11702.

Bever, T. G. (1970). The cognitive basis for linguistics structures. In J. R. Hayes (Ed.), *Cognition and the Development of Language*. Wiley.

Bhat, N. A., Sharma, V., & Kumar, D. (2018). Prospective memory in obsessive compulsive disorder. *Psychiatry Research, 261*, 124–131.

Bhatia, S., & Stewart, N. (2018). Naturalistic multiattribute choice. *Cognition, 179*, 71–88.

Bialystok, E., Shenfield, T., & Codd, J. (2000). Languages, scripts, and the environment: Factors in developing concepts of print. *Developmental Psychology, 36*(1), 66–76.

Bickerton, D. (2014). *More Than Nature Needs: Language, Mind, and Evolution*. Harvard University Press.

Bidelman, G. M., Moreno, S., & Alain, C. (2013). Tracing the emergence of categorical speech perception in the human auditory system. *Neuroimage, 79*, 201–212.

Biederman, I. (1987a). Recognition-by-components – A theory of human image understanding. *Psychological Review, 94*(2), 115–147.

Biederman, I. (1987b). Recognition-by-components: A theory of human image understanding. *Psychological Review, 94*(2), 115–147.

Biederman, I., & Gerhardstein, P. C. (1995). Viewpoint-dependent mechanisms in visual object recognition – Reply to Tarr and Bulthoff (1995). *Journal of Experimental Psychology – Human Perception and Performance, 21*(6), 1506–1514.

Biederman, I., Rabinowitz, J. C., Glass, A. L., & Stacy, E. W., Jr. (1974). On the information extracted from a glance at a scene. *Journal of Experimental Psychology, 103*(3), 597–600.

Biggs, J. B., Kember, D., & Leung, D. Y. P. (2001). The revised two factor study process questionnaire: R-SPQ-2F. *British Journal of Educational Psychology, 71*, 133–149.

Billard, A. G., Calinon, S., & Dillmann, R. (2016). Learning from humans. In *Springer Handbook of Robotics* (pp. 1995–2014). Springer.

Binder, J. R. (2015). The Wernicke area: Modern evidence and a reinterpretation. *Neurology, 85*(24), 2170–2175.

Binder, J. R. (2017). Current controversies on Wernicke's area and its role in language. *Current Neurology and Neuroscience Reports, 17*(8), 58.

Binder, J. R., Frost, J. A., Hammeke, T. A., Bellgowan, P. S. F., Springer, J. A., Kaufman, J. N., & Possing, E. T. (2000). Human temporal lobe activation by speech and nonspeech sounds. *Cerebral Cortex, 10*(5), 512–528.

Binford, T. O. (1981). Inferring surfaces from images. *Artificial Intelligence, 17*(1–3), 205–244.

Biotteau, M., Chaix, Y., Blais, M., Tallet, J., Péran, P., & Albaret, J. M. (2016). Neural signature of DCD: A critical review of MRI neuroimaging studies. *Frontiers in Neurology, 7*, 227.

Birnbaum, I. M., Parker, E. S., Hartley, J. T., & Noble, E. P. (1978). Alcohol and memory: Retrieval processes. *Journal of Verbal Learning and Verbal Behavior, 17*, 325–35.

Bish, C. L., Blanck, H. M., Serdula, M. K., Marcus, M., Kohl III, H. W., & Khan, L. K. (2005). Diet and physical activity behaviors among Americans trying to lose weight: 2000 Behavioral Risk Factor Surveillance System. *Obesity Research, 13*(3), 596–607.

Bisley, J. W., & Mirpour, K. (2019). The neural instantiation of a priority map. *Current Opinion in Psychology, 29*, 108–112.

Bisoglio, J., Michaels, T. I., Mervis, J. E., & Ashinoff, B. K. (2014). Cognitive enhancement through action video game training: Great expectations require greater evidence. *Frontiers in Psychology, 5*, 136.

Bjork, R. A. (1970). Positive forgetting: The non-interference of items intentionally forgotten. *Journal of Verbal Learning and Verbal Behavior, 9*, 255–268.

Bjork, R. A. (1972). Theoretical implications of directed forgetting. In A. W. Melton & E. Martin (Eds.), *Coding Processes in Human Memory* (pp. 217–235). Winston & Sons.

Bjork, R. A., Bjork, E. L., & Anderson, M. C. (1998). Varieties of goal directed forgetting. In J. M. Golding & C. M. MacLeod (Eds.), *Intentional Forgetting: Interdisciplinary Approaches*. Erlbaum.

Bläsing, B., Puttke, M., & Schack, T. (2018). *The Neurocognition of Dance: Mind, Movement and Motor Skills*. Routledge.

Blair, R. J., & Cipolotti, L. (2000). Impaired social response reversal: A case of 'acquired sociopathy'. *Brain, 123*, 1122–1141.

Blakemore, S. J., Wolpert, D. M., & Frith, C. D. (2002). Abnormalities in the awareness of action. *Trends in Cognitive Sciences, 6*(6), 237–242.

Blaney, P. H. (1986). Affect and memory: A review. *Psychological Bulletin, 99*, 229–246.

Blanke, O., & Arzy, S. (2005). The out-of-body experience: Disturbed self-processing at the temporo-parietal junction. *The Neuroscientist, 11*(1), 16–24.

Blanke, O., Landis, T., Spinelli, L., & Seeck, M. (2004). Out-of-body experience and autoscopy of neurological origin. *Brain, 127*(2), 243–258.

Blanke, O., Ortigue, S., Landis, T., & Seeck, M. (2002). Stimulating illusory own-body perceptions. *Nature, 419*(6904), 269–270.

Blanke, O., Slater, M., & Serino, A. (2015). Behavioral, neural, and computational principles of bodily self-consciousness. *Neuron, 88*(1), 145–166.

Blanken, G., Dittmann, J., & Wallesch, C.-W. (2002). Parallel or serial activation of word forms in speech production? Neurolinguistic evidence from an aphasic patient. *Neuroscience Letters, 325*, 72–74.

Bliss, J. C., Crane, H. D., Mansfield, P. K., & Townsend, J. T. (1966). Information available in brief tactile presentations. *Perception and Psychophysics, 1*, 273–283.

Block, N. (1995). On a confusion about a function of consciousness. *Behavioral and Brain Sciences, 18*(2), 227–247.

Bloom, K. L., & Shuell, J. T. (1981). Effects of massed and distributed practice on the learning and retention of second language vocabulary. *Journal of Educational Research, 74*, 245–248.

Bluck, S. (2003). Autobiographical memory: Exploring its functions in everyday life. *Memory, 11*(2), 113–123.

Bluck, S. (2017). Remember and review of forget and let go? Views from a functional approach to autobiographical memory. *International Journal of Reminiscence and Life Review, 4*(1), 3–7.

Bobak, A. K., Hancock, P. J., & Bate, S. (2016). Super recognisers in action: Evidence from face matching and face memory tasks. *Applied Cognitive Psychology, 30*(1), 81–91.

Bock, J. K. (1986). Syntactic persistence in language production. *Cognitive Psychology, 18*, 355–387.

Bock, K., & Levelt, W. J. M. (1994). Language production: Grammatical encoding. In M. A. Gernsbacher (Ed.), *Handbook of Psycholinguistics* (pp. 945–984). Academic Press.

Boden, M. (2004). *The Creative Mind: Myths and Mechanisms* (2nd ed.). Routledge.

Boly, M., Massimini, M., Tsuchiya, N., Postle, B. R., Koch, C., & Tononi, G. (2017). Are the neural correlates of consciousness in the front or in the back of the cerebral cortex? Clinical and neuroimaging evidence. *Journal of Neuroscience, 37*(40), 9603–9613.

Bond, Z. S., & Garnes, S. (1980). Misperception of fluent speech. In R. Cole (Ed.), *Perception and Production of Fluent Speech* (pp. 115–132). Erlbaum.

Bongaerts, T., Planken, B., & Schils, E. (1995). Can late starters attain a native accent in a foreign language: A test of the critical period hypothesis. In D. Singleton & Z. Lengyel (Eds.), *The Age Factor in Second Language Acquisition* (pp. 30–50). Multilingual Matters.

Bonhannon, J. N., III (1988). Flashbulb memories for the Space Shuttle disaster: A tale of two theories. *Cognition, 29*, 179–196.

Bonhomme, V., Staquet, C., Montupil, J., Defresne, A., Kirsch, M., Martial, C., Vanhaudenhuyse, A., Chatelle, C., Larroque, S. K., Raimondo, F., Demertzi, A., Bodart, O., Laureys, S., & Gosseries, O. (2019). General anesthesia: A probe to explore consciousness. *Frontiers in Systems Neuroscience, 13*, 36.

Bonnefon, J. F., & Hilton, D. J. (2002). The suppression of *modus ponens* as a case of pragmatic preconditional reasoning. *Thinking & Reasoning, 8*(1), 21–40.

Boomer, D. S., & Laver, J. D. M. (1968). Slips of the tongue. *British Journal of Disorders of Communication, 3*(1), 1–12.

Borghi, A. M. (2005). Object concepts and action. In D. Pecher & R. A. Zwaan (Eds.), *Grounding Cognition: The Role of Perception and Action in Memory, Language, and Thinking*. Cambridge University Press.

Born, J., Rasch, B., & Gais, S. (2006). Sleep to remember. *Neuroscientist, 12*, 410–424.

Bornstein, M. H. (1989). *Maternal Responsiveness: Characteristics and Consequences*. Jossey-Bass.

Boroditsky, L. (2001). Does language shape thought? Mandarin and English speakers' conceptions of time. *Cognitive Psychology, 43*, 1–22.

Boroditsky, L. (2012). How the languages we speak shape the ways we think: The FAQs. In M. J. Spivey, K. McRae, & M. F. Joanisse (Eds.), *Cambridge Handbooks in*

Psychology. The Cambridge Handbook of Psycholinguistics (pp. 615–632). Cambridge University Press.

Boroditsky, L., & Ramscar, M. (2002). The roles of body and mind in abstract thought. *Psychological Science, 13,* 185–188.

Bose, A., & Buchanan, L. (2007). A cognitive and psycholinguistic investigation of neologisms. *Aphasiology, 21,* 726–738.

Botvinick, M. M. (2008). Hierarchical models of behavior and prefrontal function. *Trends in Cognitive Sciences, 12*(5), 201–208.

Botvinick, M., & Cohen, J. (1998). Rubber hands 'feel' touch that eyes see. *Nature, 391* (6669), 756–756.

Botvinick, M. M., & Plaut, D. C. (2002). Representing task context: Proposals based on a connectionist model of action. *Psychological Research, 66*(4), 298–311.

Bouchard, T. J. Jr., & Hare, M. (1970). Size, performance and potential in brainstorming groups. *Journal of Applied Psychology, 54,* 51–55.

Bourdin, P., Barberia, I., Oliva, R., & Slater, M. (2017). A virtual out-of-body experience reduces fear of death. *PLOS One, 12*(1), e0169343.

Bousefield, W. A. (1953). The occurrence of clustering in recall of randomly arranged associates. *Journal of General Psychology, 49,* 229–240.

Bouvier, S. E., & Engel, S. A. (2006). Behavioral deficits and cortical damage loci in cerebral achromatopsia. *Cerebral Cortex, 16*(2), 183–191.

Bowden, E. M., & Grunewald, K. (2018). Whose insight is it anyway? In F. Vallee-Tourangeau (Ed.), *Insight: On The Origins of New Ideas* (pp. 28–50). Routledge.

Bowden, E. M., & Jung-Beeman, M. (2003). Aha! Insight experience correlates with solution activation in the right hemisphere. *Psychonomic Bulletin Review, 10,* 730–737.

Bower, G. H. (1970). Imagery as a relational organizer in associative learning. *Journal of Verbal Learning and Verbal Behavior, 9,* 529–533.

Bower, G. H. (1981). Mood and memory. *American Psychologist, 36,* 129–148.

Bower, G. H. (1991). Mood congruity of social judgements. In J. P. Forgas (Ed.), *Emotion and Social Judgements* (pp. 31–53). Pergamon.

Bower, G. H. (1992). How might emotions affect learning? In F. A. Christianson (Ed.), *The Handbook of Emotion and Memory: Research and Theory* (pp. 3–32). Lawrence Erlbaum.

Bower, G. H., & Clark, M. C. (1969). Narrative stories as mediators for serial learning. *Psychonomic Science, 14,* 181–182.

Bower, G. H., Clark, M. C., Lesgold, A. M., & Winzenz, D. (1969). Hierarchical retrieval schemes in recall of categorised word lists. *Journal of Verbal Learning and Verbal Behavior, 8,* 323–343.

Bower, G. H., & Karlin, M. B. (1974). Depth of processing pictures of faces and recognition memory. *Journal of Experimental Psychology, 103,* 751–757.

Boye, M., Gunturkun, O., & Vauclair, J. (2005). Right ear advantage for conspecific calls in adults and subadults, but not infants, California sea lions (*Zalophus californianus*): Hemispheric specialization for communication? *European Journal of Neuroscience, 21,* 1727–1732.

Bracewell, R. J. (1974). *Interpretation Factors in The Four Card Selection Task.* Paper presented at the Selection Task Conference, Trento, Italy, 17–19 April.

Bradley, M. M., Greenwald, M. K., Petry, M. C., & Lang, P.J. (1992). Remembering pictures: Pleasure and arousal in memory. *Journal of Experimental Psychology: Learning, Memory, and Cognition, 18,* 379–390.

Brady, A. P. (2017). Error and discrepancy in radiology: Inevitable or avoidable? *Insights into Imaging, 8*(1), 171–182.

Braine, M. D. S., Reiser, B. J., & Rumain, B. (1984). Some empirical justification for a theory of natural propositional logic. In G. H. Bower (Ed.), *The Psychology of Learning and Motivation.* Vol. 18. Academic Press.

Bramham, C. R., & Srebo, B. (1989). Synaptic plasticity in the hippocampus is modulated by behavioral state. *Brain Research, 493,* 74–86.

Braun, A. R., Balkin, T. J., Wesensten, N. J., Carson, R. E., Varga, M., Baldwin, P., Selbie, S., Belenky, G., & Herscovitch, P. (1997). Regional cerebral blood flow throughout the sleep–wake cycle: An (H_2O)-O^{15} PET study. *Brain, 120,* 1173–1197.

Braun, N., Debener, S., Spychala, N., Bongartz, E., Sörös, P., Müller, H. H., & Philipsen, A. (2018). The senses of agency and ownership: A review. *Frontiers in Psychology, 9,* 535.

Brázdil, M., Marecek, R., Urbánek, T., Kašpárek, T., Mikl, M., Rektor, I., & Zeman, A. (2012). Unveiling the mystery of déjà vu: The structural anatomy of déjà vu. *Cortex, 48*(9), 1240–1243.

Bredart, S., Brennen, T., & Valentine, T. (2002). *The Cognitive Psychology of Proper Names.* Taylor & Francis.

Bregman, A. S. (1990). *Auditory Scene Analysis: The Perceptual Organization of Sound.* MIT Press.

Breiman, L., Friedman, J. H., Olshen, R. A., & Stone, C. J. (1993). *Classification and Regression Trees.* Chapman Hall.

Brener, R. (1940). An experimental investigation of memory span. *Journal of Educational Psychology, 26,* 467–483.

Brenner, E., & Smeets, J. B. J. (1996). Size illusion influences how we lift but not how we grasp an object. *Experimental Brain Research, 111*(3), 473–476.

Brewer, W. F. (1996). What is recollective memory? In D. C. Rubin (Ed.), *Remembering Our Past: Studies in Autobiographical Memory* (pp. 19–66). Cambridge University Press.

Brewer, W. F. (1999). Bartlett's concept of the schema and its impact on theories of knowledge representation in contemporary cognitive psychology. In A. Saito (Ed.), *Bartlett, Culture and Cognition.* (pp. 69–89). Psychology Press.

Brewer, W. F., & Treyens, J. C. (1981). Role of schemata in memory for places. *Cognitive Psychology, 13,* 207–230.

Brewin, C. R. (2001). Memory processes in post-traumatic stress disorder. *International Review of Psychiatry, 13*(3), 159–163.

Brewin, C. R., Gregory, J. D., Lipton, M., & Burgess, N. (2010). Intrusive images in psychological disorders: Characteristics, neural mechanisms, and treatment implications. *Psychological Review, 117*(1), 210–232.

Brigham, J. C. (2002). Face identification: Basic processes and developmental changes. In M. L. Eisen, J. A. Quas, & G. S. Goodman (Eds.), *Memory and Suggestibility in the Forensic Interview* (pp. 115–140). Erlbaum.

Brigham, J. C., Bennett, L. B., Meissner, C. A., & Mitchell, T. L. (2007). *The Influence of Race on Eyewitness Memory.* Lawrence Erlbaum.

Briner, S. W., Joss, L. M., & Virtue, S. (2011). Hemispheric processing of sarcastic text. *Journal of Neurolinguistics, 24*(4), 466–475.

Brisson, J., de Chantal, P. L., Forgues, H. L., & Markovits, H. (2014). Belief bias is stronger when reasoning is more difficult. *Thinking & Reasoning, 20*(3), 385–403.

Broadbent, D. E. (1958). *Perception and Communication.* Pergamon.

Broadbent, D. E. (1971). *Decision and Stress.* Academic Press.

Broadbent, D. E. (1975). The magic number seven after fifteen years. In A. Kennedy & A. Wilkes (Eds.), *Studies in Long-Term Memory* (pp. 3–18). John Wiley & Sons.

Broadbent, D. E. (1981). Task combination and selective intake of information. *Acta Psychologica, 50*(3), 253–290.

Broadbent, D. E., & Broadbent, M. H. P. (1987). From detection to identification: Response to multiple targets in rapid serial visual presentation. *Perception & Psychophysics, 42*(2), 105–113.

Broca, P. (1861). Remarques sur le siege de la faculte du langage articule. suivies d'une observation d'aphenie. *Bulletin et Memoires de la Societe Anatomique de Paris, 2,* 330–357.

Brooks, L. R. (1967). The suppression of visualization by reading. *Quarterly Journal of Experimental Psychology, 19,* 289–299.

Brooks, L. R. (1968). Spatial and verbal components of the act of recall. *Canadian Journal of Psychology, 22,* 349–368.

Brouwer, H., Fitz, H., & Hoeks, J. C. J. (2012). Getting real about semantic illusions: Rethinking the functional role of the P600 in language comprehension. *Brain Research, 1446,* 127–143.

Brown, A. S. (1991). A review of the tip-of-the-tongue experience. *Psychological Bulletin, 109,* 204–223.

Brown, A. S. (2002). Consolidation theory and retrograde amnesia in humans. *Psychonomic Bulletin & Review, 9,* 403–425.

Brown, A. S. (2003). A review of the déjà vu experience. *Psychological Bulletin, 129,* 394–413.

Brown, A. S. (2004a). The déjà vu illusion. *Current Directions in Psychological Science, 13,* 256–259.

Brown, A. S. (2004b). *The Déjà Vu Experience.* Psychology Press.

Brown, A. S., & Marsh, E. J. (2010). Digging into déjà vu: Recent research findings on possible mechanisms. In B. H. Ross (Ed.), *The Psychology of Learning and Motivation,* Vol. 53 (pp. 33–62). Academic Press.

Brown, A. S., Burrows, C. N., & Caderao, K. C. (2013). Partial word knowledge in the absence of recall. *Memory & Cognition, 41*(7), 967–977.

Brown, C. M., & Hagoort, P. (1993). The processing nature of the N400: Evidence from masked priming. *Journal of Cognitive Neuroscience, 5*, 34–44.

Brown, G. D. A. (1984). A frequency count of 190,000 words in the London-Lund Corpus of English Conversation. *Behavioural Research Methods Instrumentation and Computers, 16*(6), 502–532.

Brown, J. (1981). *Jargonaphasia*. Academic Press.

Brown, K. F., Kroll, J. S., Hudson, M. J., Ramsay, M., Green, J., Vincent, C. A., Fraser, G., & Sevdalis, N. (2010). Omission bias and vaccine rejection by parents of healthy children: Implications for the influenza A/H1N1 vaccination programme. *Vaccine, 28*, 4181–4185.

Brown, L. & Jones, P. E. (2014). *Bringing Back the Child: Language Development After Extreme Deprivation*. Cambridge Scholars Publishing.

Brown, R. M., & Robertson, E. M. (2007). Off-line processing: reciprocal interactions between declarative and procedural memories. *Journal of Neuroscience, 27*(39), 10468–10475.

Brown, R., & Kulik, J. (1977). Flashbulb memories. *Cognition, 5*, 73–99.

Brown, R., & McNeill, D. (1966). The 'tip of the tongue phenomenon'. *Journal of Verbal Learning and Verbal Behavior, 5*, 325–337.

Brown, R., Lau, H., & LeDoux, J. E. (2019). Understanding the higher-order approach to consciousness. *Trends in Cognitive Sciences, 23*(9), 754–768.

Bruce, K. R., & Pihl, R. O. (1997). Forget 'drinking to forget': Enhanced consolidation of emotionally charged memory by alcohol. *Experimental Clinical Psychopharmacology, 5*, 242–250.

Bruce, V., & Young, A. (1986). Understanding face recognition. *British Journal of Psychology, 77*, 305–327.

Bruno, M. A., Walker, E. A., & Abujudeh, H. H. (2015). Understanding and confronting our mistakes: The epidemiology of error in radiology and strategies for error reduction. *Radiographics, 35*(6), 1668–1676.

Bruno, N. (2001). When does action resist visual illusions? *Trends in Cognitive Sciences, 5*(9), 379–382.

Bruns, P. (2019). The ventriloquist illusion as a tool to study multisensory processing: An update. *Frontiers in Integrative Neuroscience, 13*, 51.

Brunswik, E. (1943). Organismic achievement and environmental probability. *Psychological Review, 50*, 255–272.

Brunswik, E. (1955). In defense of probabilistic functionalism: A reply. *Psychological Review, 55*, 236–242.

Brunswick, N., Martin, G. N., & Marzano, L. (2010). Visuospatial superiority in developmental dyslexia: Myth or reality? *Learning and Individual Differences, 20*(5), 421–426.

Bryant, R. A., O'Donnell, M. L., Creamer, M., McFarlane, A. C., & Silove, D. (2011). Posttraumatic intrusive symptoms across psychiatric disorders. *Journal of Psychiatric Research, 45*, 842–847.

Brysbaert, M. (2019). How many words do we read per minute? A review and meta-analysis of reading rate. *Journal of Memory and Language, 109*, 104047.

Brysbaert, M., Stevens, M., Mandera, P., & Keuleers, E. (2016). How many words do we know? Practical estimates of vocabulary size dependent on word definition, the degree of language input and the participant's age. *Frontiers in Psychology, 7*, 1116.

Buccino, G., Vogt, S., Ritzl, A., Fink, G. R., Zilles, K., Freund, H.-J., & Rizzolatti, G. (2004). Neural circuits underlying imitation learning of hand actions: An event-related fMRI study. *Neuron, 42*(2), 323–334.

Buchwald, A. M. (1977). Depressive mood and estimates of reinforcement frequency. *Journal of Abnormal Psychology, 86*(4), 443.

Buckingham, H. W. (1981). Explanations for the concept of apraxia of speech. In M. T. Sarno (Ed.), *Acquired Aphasia* (pp. 271–302). Academic Press.

Buckner, R. L., Andrews-Hanna, J. R., & Schacter, D. L. (2008). The brain's default network: Anatomy, function and relevance to disease. *Annals of the New York Academy of Science, 1124*, 1–38.

Budson, A. E., & Price, B. H. (2005). Current concepts – memory dysfunction. *New England Journal of Medicine, 352*(7), 692–699.

Bugelski, B. R., Kidd, E., & Segmen, J. (1968). Image as a mediator in one-trial paired associate learning. *Journal of Experimental Psychology, 76*, 69–73.

Bulevich, J. B., Roediger, H. L., Balota, D. A., & Butler, A. C. (2006). Failures to find suppression of episodic memories in the think/no-think paradigm. *Memory & Cognition, 34*, 1569–1577.

Bulley, A., & Schacter, D. L. (2020). Deliberating trade-offs with the future. *Nature: Human Behaviour, 4*, 238–247.

Bulley, A., Miloyan, B., Pepper, G. V., Gullo, M. J., Henry, J. D., & Suddendorf, T. (2019). Cuing both positive and negative episodic foresight reduces delay discounting but does not affect risk-taking. *Quarterly Journal of Experimental Psychology, 72*, 1998–2017.

Bülthoff, H., Wallraven, C., & Giese, M. A. (2016). Perceptual robotics. In *Springer Handbook of Robotics* (pp. 2095–2113). Springer.

Bundick, T., & Spinella, M. (2000). Subjective experience, involuntary movement, and posterior alien hand syndrome. *Journal of Neurology, Neurosurgery & Psychiatry, 68*(1), 83–85.

Buonomano, D. V., & Karmarkar, U. R. (2002). How do we tell time? *Neuroscientist, 8*, 42–51.

Buratti, S., MacLeod, S., & Allwood, C. M. (2014). The effects of question format and co-witness peer discussion on the confidence accuracy of children's testimonies. *Social Influence, 9*(3), 189–205.

Burgess, N., & Hitch, G. J. (2005). Computational models of working memory: Putting long-term memory into context. *Trends in Cognitive Science, 9*, 535–541.

Burgess, P. W., Dumontheil, I., Gilbert, S. J., Okuda, J., Schölvinck, M. L., & Simons, J. S. (2007). On the role of rostral prefrontal cortex (area 10) in prospective memory. In M. Kliegel, M. A. McDaniel, & G. O. Einsten (Eds.), *Prospective Memory: Cognitive, Neuroscience, Developmental and Applied Perspectives*. Erlbaum.

Burgoyne, A. P., Sala, G., Gobet, F., Macnamara, B. N., Campitelli, G., & Hambrick, D. Z. (2016). The relationship between cognitive ability and chess skill: A comprehensive meta-analysis. *Intelligence, 59*, 72–83.

Burke, M., & Matthews, A. (1992). Autobiographical memory and clinical anxiety. *Cognition and Emotion, 6*, 23–35.

Burnett, G., Large, D. R. & Salanitri, D. (2019). How will drivers interact with vehicles of the future? Royal Automobile Club Foundation for Motoring Report.

Busby, L. P., Courtier, J. L., & Glastonbury, C. M. (2018). Bias in radiology: The how and why of misses and misinterpretations. *Radiographics, 38*(1), 236–247.

Buser, D., Sterchi, Y., & Schwaninger, A. (2020). Why stop after 20 minutes? Breaks and target prevalence in a 60-minute X-ray baggage screening task. *International Journal of Industrial Ergonomics, 76*, 102897.

Butler, A. C. (2010). Repeated testing produces superior transfer of learning relative to repeated studying. *Journal of Experimental Psychology: Learning, Memory, and Cognition, 36*(5), 1118–1133. https://doi.org/10.1037/a0019902

Butler, S. (2019). Crumbs! Judge deems brownie a cake and free from VAT charges. *Guardian*, 16 January.

Butters, N. (1984). Alcoholic Korsakoffs syndrome: An update. *Seminars in Neurology, 4*, 226–244.

Butterworth, B. (1980). Evidence from pauses in speech. In B. Butterworth (Ed.), *Language Production, Volume 1: Speech and Talk* (pp. 155–176). Academic Press.

Byrd, D., & Mintz, T. H. (2010). *Discovering Speech, Words, and Mind*. Wiley.

Byrne, R. M. J. (1989). Suppressing valid inferences with conditionals. *Cognition, 31*, 61–83.

Byrne, R. W., & Russon, A. E. (1998). Learning by imitation: A hierarchical approach. *Behavioral and Brain Sciences, 21*(5), 667–684.

C

Cacioppo, J. T., Klein, D. J., Berntson, G. G., & Hatfield, E. (1993). The psychophysiology of emotion. In R. Lewis & J. M. Haviland (Eds.), *The Handbook of Emotion* (pp. 119–142). Guilford Press.

Cahill, L., Babinsky, R. Markowitch, H. J., & McGaugh, J. L. (1995). The amygdala and emotional memory. *Nature, 377*, 295–296.

Calder, A. J., & Young, A. W. (2005). Understanding the recognition of facial identity and facial expression. *Nature Reviews Neuroscience, 6*(8), 641–651.

Calvillo, D. P., Swan, A. B., & Rutchick, A. M. (2019). Ideological belief bias with political syllogisms. *Thinking & Reasoning*, 1–20.

Calvo-Merino, B., Grèzes, J., Glaser, D. E., Passingham, R. E., & Haggard, P. (2006). Seeing or doing? Influence of visual and motor familiarity in action observation. *Current Biology, 16*(19), 1905–1910.

Camerer, C. (2013). Goals, methods and progress in neuroeconomics. *Annual Review of Economics, 5*, 16.1–16.31.

Camilleri, A. R., & Newell, B. R. (2013). Mind the gap? Description, experience, and the continuum of uncertainty in risky choice. In *Decision Making: Neural and Behavioural Approaches – Progress in Brain Research*. Elsevier.

Campbell, D. T. (1960). Blind variation and selective retention in creative thought as in other knowledge processes. *Psychological Review, 67*, 380–400.

Campitelli, G., & Gobet, F. (2004). Adaptive expert decision making: Skilled chess players search more and deeper. *Journal of the International Computer Games Association, 27,* 209–216.

Campitelli, G., & Gobet, F. (2011). Deliberate practice: Necessary but not sufficient. *Current Directions in Psychological Science, 20,* 280–285.

Campos-Magdaleno, M., Leiva, D., Pereiro, A. X., Lojo-Seoane, C., Mallo, S. C., Nieto-Vieites, A., Juncos-Rabadán, O., & Facal, D. (2020). Longitudinal patterns of the tip-of-the-tongue phenomenon in people with subjective cognitive complaints and mild cognitive impairment. *Frontiers in Psychology, 11.*

Canli, T., Zhao, Z., Brewer, J., Gabrieli, J. D. E., & Cahill, L. (2000). Activation in the human amygdala associates event-related arousal with later memory for individual emotional experience. *Journal of Neuroscience, 20,* RC99, 1–5.

Cannon, W. B. (1927). The James-Lange theory of emotions. *American Journal of Psychology, 39,* 115–124.

Caño, A., Rapp, B., Costa, A., & Juncadella, M. (2008). Deafness for the meanings of number words. *Neuropsychologia, 46*(1), 63–81.

Caplan, D. (1987). *Neurolinguistics and Linguistic Aphasiology.* Cambridge University Press.

Caplan, D., & Hildebrandt, N. (1988). *Disorders of Syntactic Comprehension.* The MIT Press.

Caplan, D. & Waters, G.S. (1999). Verbal working memory and sentence comprehension. *Behav Brain Sci., 22*(1):77-94.

Caramazza, A., Anzellotti, S., Strnad, L., & Lingnau, A. (2014). Embodied cognition and mirror neurons: A critical assessment. *Annual Review of Neuroscience, 37,* 1–15.

Carey, D. P. (2001). Do action systems resist visual illusions? *Trends in Cognitive Sciences, 5*(3), 109–113.

Carota, F., Moseley, R., & Pulvermuller, F. (2012). Body-part-specific representations of semantic noun categories. *Journal of Cognitive Neuroscience, 24,* 1492–1509.

Carpenter, P. A., & Just, M. A. (1983). What your eyes do while your mind is reading. In K. Rayner (Ed.), *Eye Movements in Reading: Perceptual and Language Processes.* Academic Press.

Carpenter, S. K., Cepeda, N. J., Rohrer, D., Kang, S. H., & Pashler, H. (2012). Using spacing to enhance diverse forms of learning: Review of recent research and implications for instruction. *Educational Psychology Review, 24*(3), 369–378.

Carr, T. H., Davidson, B. J., & Hawkins, H. L. (1978). Perceptual flexibility in word recognition: Strategies affect orthographic computation but not lexical access. *Journal of Experimental Psychology: Human Perception and Performance, 4,* 674–690.

Carramazza, A., & Zurif, E. (1976). Dissociations of algorithmic and heuristic processes in sentence comprehension: Evidence from aphasia. *Brain and Language, 3,* 572–582.

Carson, S. H. (2019). Creativity and mental illness. In J. C. Kaufman & R. J. Sternberg (Eds.), *The Cambridge Handbook of Creativity.* Cambridge University Press.

Carson, S. H., Peterson, J. B., & Higgins, D. M. (2005). Reliability, validity and factor structure of the creative achievement questionnaire. *Creativity Research Journal, 17,* 37–50.

Caspers, S., Zilles, K., Laird, A. R., & Eickhoff, S. B. (2010). ALE meta-analysis of action observation and imitation in the human brain. *Neuroimage, 50*(3), 1148–1167.

Casscells, W., Schoenberger, A., & Grayboys, T. (1978). Interpretation by physicians of clinical laboratory results. *New England Journal of Medicine, 299,* 999–1000.

Cassiday, K. L., McNally, R. J., & Zeitlin, S. B. (1992). Cognitive processing of trauma cues in rape victims with posttraumatic stress disorder. *Cognitive Therapy and Research, 16,* 28395.

Castel, A. D., Pratt, J., & Drummond, E. (2005). The effects of action video game experience on the time course of inhibition of return and the efficiency of visual search. *Acta Psychologica, 119*(2), 217–230.

Catani, M. (2017). A little man of some importance. *Brain, 140,* 3055–3061.

Cattaneo, L., Sandrini, M., & Schwarzbach, J. (2010). State-dependent TMS reveals a hierarchical representation of observed acts in the temporal, parietal, and premotor cortices. *Cerebral Cortex, 20*(9), 2252–2258.

Cattell, J. M. (1888). 'Psychometrische untersuchungen'. *Philosophische Studien, 4,* 241–250.

Cavanaugh, M. R., Barbot, A., Carrasco, M., & Huxlin, K. R. (2019). Feature-based attention potentiates recovery of fine direction discrimination in cortically blind patients. *Neuropsychologia, 128,* 315–324.

Ceraso, J., & Provitera, A. (1971). Sources of error in syllogistic reasoning. *Cognitive Psychology, 2,* 400–410.

Chadwick, A. C., Heywood, C. A., Smithson, H. E., & Kentridge, R. W. (2019). Translucence perception is not dependent on cortical areas critical for processing colour or texture. *Neuropsychologia, 128,* 209–214.

Chalmers, A. F. (1978). *What is this Thing Called Science?* Open University Press.

Chalmers, D. (2017). The hard problem of consciousness. In S. Schneider & M. Velmans (Eds.), *The Blackwell Companion to Consciousness* (2nd ed.) (pp. 32–42). John Wiley & Sons Ltd.

Chalmers, D. J. (1995). Facing up to the problem of consciousness. *Journal of Consciousness Studies, 2*(3), 200–219.

Chalmers, D. J. (1996). *The Conscious Mind: In Search of a Fundamental Theory.* Oxford University Press.

Chambers, D., & Reisberg, D. (1985). Can mental images be ambiguous? *Journal of Experimental Psychology: Human Perception and Performance, 11,* 317–328.

Chambers, D., & Reisberg, D. (1992). What an image depicts depends on what an image means. *Cognitive Psychology, 24,* 145–174.

Chan, D. (2017). The AI that has nothing to learn from humans. *The Atlantic,* 20 October.

Chan, J. C., & LaPaglia, J. A. (2013). Impairing existing declarative memory in humans by disrupting reconsolidation. *Proceedings of the National Academy of Sciences, 110*(23), 9309–9313.

Chapman, C. E. (1994). Active versus passive touch – Factors influencing the transmission of somatosensory signals to primary somatosensory cortex. *Canadian Journal of Physiology and Pharmacology, 72*(5), 558–570.

Chapman, G. B., & Winquist, J. R. (1998). The magnitude effect: Temporal discount effects and restaurant tips. *Psychonomic Bulletin and Review, 5,* 119–123.

Chapman, L. J., & Chapman, A. P. (1959). Atmosphere effect re-examined. *Journal of Experimental Psychology, 58,* 220–226.

Charness, N. (1989). Expertise in chess and bridge. In D. Klahr & K. Kotovsky (Eds.), *Complex Information Processing: The Impact of H.A. Simon.* Lawrence Erlbaum.

Chartrand, J.-P., Peretz, I., & Belin, P. (2008). Auditory recognition expertise and domain specificity. *Brain Research, 1220,* 191–198.

Chase, W. G., & Simon, H. A. (1973). Perception in chess. *Cognitive Psychology, 4,* 55–81.

Chater, N., & Oaksford, M. (2001). Human rationality and the psychology of reasoning. where do we go from here? *British Journal of Psychology, 92,* 193–216.

Chen, B., Ma, H., Qin, L. Y., Gao, F., Chan, K. M., Law, S. W., & Liao, W. H. (2016). Recent developments and challenges of lower extremity exoskeletons. *Journal of Orthopaedic Translation, 5,* 26–37.

Chen, L., & Vroomen, J. (2013). Intersensory binding across space and time: A tutorial review. *Attention, Perception, & Psychophysics, 75*(5), 790–811.

Chen, X. J., Wang, Y., Liu, L. L., Cui, J. F., Gan, M. Y., Shum, D. H., & Chan, R. C. (2015). The effect of implementation intention on prospective memory: A systematic and meta-analytic review. *Psychiatry Research, 226*(1), 14–22.

Chen, Y., Fu, S., Iversen, S. D., Smith, S. M., & Matthews, P. M. (2002). Testing for dual brain processing routes in reading: A direct contrast of Chinese character and pinyin reading using fMRI. *Journal of Cognitive Neuroscience, 14*(7), 1088–1098.

Cheney, D. L., & Seyfarth, R. M. (2005). Constraints and preadaptations in the earliest stages of language evolution. *Linguistic Review, 22,* 135–159.

Cheng, P. C.-H. (1996). Scientific discovery with law encoding diagrams. *Creativity Research Journal, 9,* 145–162.

Cheng, P. W., & Holyoak, K. J. (1985). Pragmatic reasoning schemas. *Cognitive Psychology, 17,* 391–416.

Cherry, E. C. (1953). Some experiments on the recognition of speech, with one and with two ears. *Journal of the Acoustical Society of America, 25*(5), 975–979.

Chevalier, P., Kompatsiari, K., Ciardo, F., & Wykowska, A. (2020). Examining joint attention with the use of humanoid robots: A new approach to study fundamental mechanisms of social cognition. *Psychonomic Bulletin & Review, 27,* 217–236.

Chi, M. T. H., Glaser, R., & Rees, E. (1982). Expertise in problem solving. In R. J. Sternberg (Ed.), *Advances in the Psychology of Human Intelligence,* Vol. 1. Lawrence Erlbaum.

Chiel, H. J., & Beer, R. D. (1997). The brain has a body: Adaptive behavior emerges from interactions of nervous system, body and environment. *Trends in Neurosciences, 20*(12), 553–557.

Chomsky, N. (1957). *Syntactic Structures*. Mouton.

Chomsky, N. (1965). *Aspects of the Theory of Syntax*. The MIT Press.

Chomsky, N. (1980). *Rules and Representations*. Blackwell.

Chomsky, N. (1986). *Knowledge of Language: Its Nature, Origin, and Use*. Greenwood Publishing Group.

Chong, S. C., & Treisman, A. (2003). Representation of statistical properties. *Vision Research, 43*(4), 393–404.

Chopin, A., Bediou, B., & Bavelier, D. (2019). Altering perception: The case of action video gaming. *Current Opinion in Psychology, 29*, 168–173.

Chou, K. L., Lee, T. M. C., & Ho, A. H. Y. (2007). Does mood state change risk taking tendency in older adults. *Psychology and Aging, 22*, 310–318.

Chou, K. L., Lee, T., & Ho, A. H. (2007). Does mood state change risk taking tendency in older adults? *Psychology and Aging, 22*(2), 310.

Chow, M., Macnamara, B. N., & Conway, A. R. A. (2016). Phonological similarity in working memory span tasks. *Memory & Cognition, 44*, 937.

Christensen, J. F., Gaigg, S. B., & Calvo-Merino, B. (2018). I can feel my heartbeat: Dancers have increased interoceptive accuracy. *Psychophysiology, 55*(4), e13008.

Christensen, J. F., Gomila, A., Gaigg, S. B., Sivarajah, N., & Calvo-Merino, B. (2016). Dance expertise modulates behavioral and psychophysiological responses to affective body movement. *Journal of Experimental Psychology: Human Perception and Performance, 42*(8), 1139.

Christensen, J. F., Nadal, M., Cela-Conde, C. J., & Gomila, A. (2014). A norming study and library of 203 dance movements. *Perception, 43*(2–3), 178–206.

Christianson, S. A. (1989). Flashbulb memories: Special but not so special. *Memory and Cognition, 17*, 435–443.

Christianson, S. A. (1992). Emotional stress and eyewitness memory: A critical review. *Psychological Bulletin, 112*, 284–309.

Christoff, K., Cosmelli, D., Legrand, D., & Thompson, E. (2011). Specifying the self for cognitive neuroscience. *Trends in Cognitive Sciences, 15*(3), 104–112.

Christoff, K., Gordon, A., & Smith, R. (2008). The role of spontaneous thought in human cognition. In O. Vartanian & D. R. Mandel(Eds.), *Neuroscience of Decision Making*. Psychology Press.

Chu, B. (2017). What is nudge theory and why should we care?, *The Independent*, 9 October.

Chubb, C., Nam, J. H., Bindman, D. R., & Sperling, G. (2007). The three dimensions of human visual sensitivity to first-order contrast statistics. *Vision Research, 47*(17), 2237–2248.

Chun, M. M. (2011). Visual working memory as visual attention sustained internally over time. *Neuropsychologia, 49*(6), 1407–1409.

Chun, M. M., Golomb, J. D., & Turk-Browne, N. B. (2011). A taxonomy of external and internal attention. *Annual Review of Psychology, 62*, 73–101.

Cichy, R. M., Khosla, A., Pantazis, D., Torralba, A., & Oliva, A. (2016). Comparison of deep neural networks to spatio-temporal cortical dynamics of human visual object recognition reveals hierarchical correspondence. *Scientific Reports, 6*, 27755.

Cienki, A., & Müller, C. (2008). Metaphor, gesture, and thought. In R. W. Gibbs (Ed.), *The Cambridge Handbook of Metaphor and Thought* (pp. 483–501). Cambridge University Press.

Ciesielski, B. G., Armstrong, T., Zald, D. H., & Olatunji, B. O. (2010). Emotion modulation of visual attention: categorical and temporal characteristics. *PLOS One, 5*(11).

Clahsen, H., & Almazan, M. (1998). Syntax and morphology in children with William's syndrome. *Cognition, 68*, 167–198.

Clancy, S. A., & McNally, R. J. (2005/2006). Who needs repression? Normal memory processes can explain 'forgetting' of childhood sexual abuse. *Scientific Review of Mental Health Practice, 4*(2), 66–73.

Clark, A. (1997). *Being There: Putting Brain, Body, and World Together Again*. MIT Press.

Clark, D. M., & Teasdale, J. D. (1982). Diurnal variation in clinical depression and accessibility of memories of positive and negative experiences. *Journal of Abnormal Psychology, 91*, 87–95.

Clark, E. V. (2003). *First Language Acquisition*. Cambridge University Press.

Clark, H. H., & Clark, E. V. (1977). *Psychology and Language: An Introduction to Psycholinguistics*. Harcourt Brace Jovanovich.

Clark, H. H., & Fox Tree, J. E. (2002). Using uh and um in spontaneous speaking. *Cognition, 84*, 73–111.

Clark, J. J., & Yuille, A. L. (1990). *Data Fusion for Sensory Information Processing Systems*. Kluwer Academic.

Cleary, A. M. (2019). The biasing nature of the tip-of-the-tongue experience: When decisions bask in the glow of the tip-of-the-tongue state. *Journal of Experimental Psychology: General, 148*(7), 1178–1191.

Clerkin, E. M., Hart, E., Rehg, J. M., Yu, C., & Smith, L. B. (2017). Real-world visual statistics and infants' first-learned object names. *Philosophical Transactions of the Royal Statistical Society B, 372* (1711), 20160055.

Clifton, C., Jr., Staub, A., & Rayner, K. (2007). Eye movements in reading words and sentences. In R. Van Gompel, M. Fisher, W. Murray, & R. L. Hill (Eds.), *Eye Movement Research: A Window on Mind and Brain* (pp. 341–372). Elsevier.

Clore, G. L., & Ortony, A. (2000). Cognition in emotion: Always, sometimes, or never? In L. Nadel, R. Lane, & G. L. Ahern (Eds.), *The Cognitive Neuroscience of Emotion*. Oxford University Press.

Clore, G. L., & Ortony, A. (2008). Appraisal theories: How cognition shapes affect into emotion. In M. Lewis, J. M. Haviland-Jones, & L. F. Barrett (Eds.), *Handbook of Emotions* (pp. 628–642). The Guilford Press.

Clough, S., & Gordon, J. K. (2020). Fluent or nonfluent? Part A. Underlying contributors to categorical classifications of fluency in aphasia. *Aphasiology, 34*(5), 515–539.

Cobb, M. D., & Kuklinski, J. H. (1997). Changing minds: Political arguments and political persuasion. *American Journal of Political Science*, 88–121.

Cobos, P., Sánchez, M., Pérez, N., & Vila, J. (2004). Effects of spinal cord injuries on the subjective component of emotions. *Cognition and Emotion, 18*, 281–287.

Coderre, E., Filippi, C., Newhouse, P., & Dumas, J. (2008). The Stroop effect in kana and kanji scripts in native Japanese speakers: An fMRI study. *Brain and Language, 107*, 124–132.

Coenen, A. M. L., & Van Luijtelaar, E. L. J. M. (1997). Effects of benzodiazepines, sleep and sleep deprivation on vigilance and memory. *Acta Neurologica Belgica, 97*, 123–129.

Cohen, A. L., & Hicks, J. L. (2017). Implementation intentions. In *Prospective Memory* (pp. 81–97). Springer.

Cohen, B., Dai, M., Yakushin, S. B., & Cho, C. (2019). The neural basis of motion sickness. *Journal of Neurophysiology, 121*(3), 973–982.

Cohen, G., & Faulkner, D. (1986). Memory for proper names: Age differences in retrieval. *British Journal of Developmental Psychology, 4*, 187–197.

Cohen, L. J. (1981). Can human irrationality be experimentally demonstrated? *Behavioral and Brain Sciences, 4*, 317–331.

Cohen, M. A., Cavanagh, P., Chun, M. M., & Nakayama, K. (2012). The attentional requirements of consciousness. *Trends in Cognitive Sciences, 16*(8), 411–417.

Cohen, N. J., & Squire, L. R. (1981). Retrograde amnesia and remote memory impairment. *Neuropsychologia, 19*, 337–356.

Cohen, R. A. (2014). *The Neuropsychology of Attention*. Springer.

Colchester, A., Kingsley, D., Lasserson, D., Kendall, B., Bello, F., Rush, C., Stevens, T. G., Goodman, G., Heilpern, G., Stanhope, N., & Kopelman, M. D. (2001). Structural MRI volumetric analysis in patients with organic amnesia: 1. Methods and comparative findings across diagnostic groups. *Journal of Neurology & Psychiatry, 71*, 13–22.

Coles, N. A., Larsen, J. T., & Lench, H. C. (2019). A meta-analysis of the facial feedback literature: Effects of facial feedback on emotional experience are small and variable. *Psychological Bulletin, 145*(6), 610–651.

Colle, H. A., & Welsh, A. (1976). Acoustic masking in primary memory. *Journal of Verbal Learning and Verbal Behavior, 15*, 17–32.

Collins, A. M., & Loftus, E. F. (1975). A spreading-activation theory of semantic processing. *Psychological Review, 82*, 407–428.

Coltheart, M., Rastle, K., Perry, C., Langdon, R., & Ziegler, J. (2001). DRC: A dual route cascaded model of visual word recognition and reading aloud. *Psychological Review, 108*, 204–256.

Comrie, B. (1989). *Language Universals and Linguistic Typology*. Blackwell.

Comrie, B. (2005). Writing systems. In M. Haspelmath, M. S. Dryer, D. Gil, & B. Comrie (Eds.), *The World Atlas of Language Structures* (pp. 568–571). Oxford University Press.

Connor, S. (2000). *Dumbstruck: A Cultural History of Ventriloquism*. Oxford University Press.

Connors, E., Miller, N., Lundregan, T., & McEwan, T. (1996). *Convicted by Juries, Exonerated by Science: Case Studies* in the Use of DNA Evidence to Establish Innocence After Trial: National Institute of Justice.

Conrad, R. (1964). Acoustic confusions in immediate memory. *British Journal of Psychology, 55*, 75–84.

Constable, A., Stackhouse, J., & Wells, B. (1997). Developmental word-finding difficulties and phonological processing: The case of the missing handcuffs. *Applied Psycholinguistics, 18*, 507–536.

Conway, M. A. (1992). A structural model of autobiographical memory. In M. A. Conway, H. Spinnler, & W. A. Wagenaar (Eds.), *Theoretical Perspectives on Autobiographical Memory* (pp. 167–194). Kluwer Academic Publishers.

Conway, M. A. (1995). *Flashbulb Memories*. Erlbaum.

Conway, M. A. (2005). Memory and the self. *Journal of Memory and Language, 53*(4), 594–628.

Conway, M. A. (2009). Episodic memories. *Neuropsychologia, 47*(11), 2305–2313.

Conway, M. A., Anderson, S. J., Larsen, S. F., Donnelly, C. M., McDaniel, M. A., McClelland, A. G. R., Rawles, R. E., & Logie, R. H. (1994). The formation of flashbulb memories. *Memory and Cognition, 22*, 326–343.

Conway, M. A., Cohen, G., & Stanhope, N. (1992). Very long-term memory for knowledge acquired at school and university. *Applied Cognitive Psychology, 6*, 467–482.

Cooke, S. F., & Bliss, T. V. (2006). Plasticity in the human central nervous system. *Brain, 129*, 1659–1673.

Cooney, J. W., & Gazzaniga, M. S. (2003). Neurological disorders and the structure of human consciousness. *Trends in Cognitive Sciences, 7*(4), 161–165.

Cooper, S. A., Joshi, A. C., Seenan, P. J., Hadley, D. M., Muir, K. W., Leigh, R. J., & Metcalfe, R. A. (2012). Akinetopsia: Acute presentation and evidence for persisting defects in motion vision. *Journal of Neurology, Neurosurgery, and Psychiatry, 83*(2), 229–230.

Cooper, R. P., Schwartz, M. F., Yule, P., & Shallice, T. (2005). The simulation of action disorganisation in complex activities of daily living. *Cognitive Neuropsychology, 22*(8), 959–1004.

Cooper, R. P., & Shallice, T. (2000). Contention scheduling and the control of routine activities. *Cognitive Neuropsychology, 17*, 297–338.

Copeland, D. E., & Radvansky, G. A. (2001). Phonological similarity in working memory. *Memory and Cognition, 29*, 774–776.

Corballis, M. C. (1994). Split decisions: Problems in the interpretation of results from commissurotomized subjects. *Behavioral Brain Research, 64* (1–2), 163–172.

Corballis, M. C. (2003). From mouth to hand gesture: Speech and the evolution of right handedness. *Behavioral & Brain Sciences, 26*, 199–260.

Corballis, M. C. (2017). Language evolution: A changing perspective. *Trends in Cognitive Sciences, 27*, 229–236.

Corbetta, M., & Shulman, G. L. (2002). Control of goal-directed and stimulus-driven attention in the brain. *Nature Reviews Neuroscience, 3*(3), 201–215.

Corkin, S. (2002). 'What's new with the amnesic patient H.M.?' *Nature Reviews Neuroscience, 3*(2), 153–160.

Cornell, T. L., Fromkin, V. A., & Mauner, G. (1993). A linguistic approach to language processing in Broca's aphasia: A paradox resolved. *Current Directions in Psychological Science, 2*, 47–52.

Coslett, H. B. (1991). Read but not write 'idea': Evidence for a third reading mechanism. *Brain and Language, 40*, 425–443.

Cosmides, L. (1989). The logic of social exchange: Has natural selection shaped how humans reason? Studies with the Wason selection task. *Cognition, 31*, 187–276.

Cosmides, L., & Tooby, J. (1996). Are humans good intuitive statisticians after all? Rethinking some conclusions from the literature on judgment under uncertainty. *Cognition, 58*, 1–73.

Costa, A., Foucart, A., Hayakawa, S., Aparici, M., Apesteguia, J., Heafner, J., & Keysar, B. (2014). Your morals depend on language. *PLOS One, 9*(4), e94842. doi: 10.1371/journal.pone.0094842.

Cowan, N. (1984). On short and long auditory stores. *Psychological Bulletin, 96*, 341–370.

Cowan, N. (1988). Evolving conceptions of memory storage, selective attention, and their mutual constraints within the human information processing system. *Psychological Bulletin, 104*, 163–191.

Cowan, N. (1995a). *Attention and Memory: An Integrated Framework*. Oxford University Press.

Cowan, N. (1995b). Verbal working memory: A view with a room. *American Journal of Psychology, 108*, 123–155.

Cowan, N. (1998). Visual and auditory working memory capacity. *Trends in Cognitive Sciences, 2*, 77–78.

Cowan, N. (1999). An embedded-processes model of working memory. In A. Miyake & P. Shah (Eds.), *Models of Working Memory: Mechanisms of Active Maintenance and Executive Control*. Cambridge University Press.

Cowan, N. (2001). The magical number 4 in short-term memory: A reconsideration of mental storage capacity. *Behavioral and Brain Sciences, 24*, 87–185.

Cowan, N. (2008). Sensory memory. In H. L. Roediger, III (Ed.) & J. Byrne (Vol. Ed.), *Cognitive Psychology of Memory: Vol. 2. Learning and Memory: A Comprehensive Reference* (pp. 23–32). Elsevier.

Cowan, N. (2009). Sensory and immediate memory. In W. P. Banks (Ed.), *Encyclopedia of Consciousness* (pp. 327–339). Academic Press.

Cowan, N. (2010). Multiple concurrent thoughts: The meaning and developmental neuropsychology of working memory. *Developmental Neuropsychology, 35*(5), 447–474.

Cowan, N. (2010a). The magical mystery four: How is working memory capacity limited, and why? *Current Directions in Psychological Science, 19*, 51–57.

Cowan, N. (2015). George Miller's magical number of immediate memory in retrospect: Observations on the faltering progression of science. *Psychological Review, 122*(3), 536–541.

Cowan, N., Beshin, N., & Della Sala, S. (2004). Verbal recall in amnesiacs under conditions of diminished retroactive interference. *Brain, 27*, 825–834.

Cowan, N., Morey, C. C., & Chen, Z. (2007). The legend of the magical number seven. In S. Della Sala (Ed.), *Tall Tales About the Mind and Brain: Separating Fact From Fiction* (pp. 45–59). Oxford University Press.

Craig, A. D. (2002). How do you feel? Interoception: The sense of the physiological condition of the body. *Nature Reviews Neuroscience, 3*, 655–666.

Craig, A. D. (2003). Interoception: The sense of the physiological condition of the body. *Current Opinion in Neurobiology, 13*(4), 500–505.

Craig, A. D. (2004). Human feelings: Why are some more aware than others? *Trends in Cognitive Sciences, 8*, 239–241.

Craig, A. D. (2009). How do you feel – now? The anterior insula and human awareness. *Nature Reviews Neuroscience, 10*(1), 59.

Craig, M., Della Sala, S., & Dewar, M. (2014). Autobiographical thinking interferes with episodic memory consolidation. *PLOS One, 9*(4), e93915. doi: 10.1371/journal.pone.0093915.

Craik, F. I. M. (1970). The fate of primary memory items in free recall. *Journal of Verbal Learning and Verbal Behavior, 9*, 143–148.

Craik, F. I. M. (1986). A functional account of age differences in memory. In F. Klix & H. Hagendorf (Eds.), *Human Memory and Cognitive Capabilities: Mechanisms and Performances* (pp. 409–422). Elsevier Science Publishers, North-Holland.

Craik, F. I. M. (2002). Levels of processing: Past, present . . . and future. *Memory, 10*, 305–318.

Craik, F. I. M., & Lockhart, R. S. (1972). Levels of processing: A framework for memory research. *Journal of Verbal Learning and Verbal Behavior, 11*, 671–684.

Craik, F. I. M., & Tulving, E. (1975). Depth of processing and the retention of words in episodic memory. *Journal of Experimental Psychology: General, 104*, 268–294.

Cranford, E. A., & Moss, J. (2012). Is insight always the same? A protocol analysis of insight in compound remote associate problems. *Journal of Problem Solving, 4*, 128–153.

Creanza, N., Ruhlen, M., Pemberton, T. J., Rosenberg, N. A., Feldman, M. W., & Ramachandran, S. (2015). A comparison of worldwide phonemic and genetic variation in human populations. *Proceedings of the National Academy of Sciences (PNAS), 112*, 1265–1272.

Crick, F. (1994). *The Astonishing Hypothesis: The Scientific Search for The Soul*. Scribner.

Crick, F. (1995). *The Astonishing Hypothesis: The Scientific Search for the Soul*. Touchstone.

Crick, F., & Koch, C. (2003). A framework for consciousness. *Nature Neuroscience, 6*(2), 119–126.

Critchley, H. D., Wiens, S., Rotshtein, P., Öhman, A., & Dolan, R. J. (2004). Neural systems supporting interoceptive awareness. *Nature Neuroscience, 7*(2), 189–195.

Croskerry, P. (2009). Clinical cognition and diagnostic error: Applications of a dual process model of reasoning. *Advances in Health Sciences Education, 14*(1), 27–35.

Cross, E. S., Hamilton, A. F. D. C., & Grafton, S. T. (2006). Building a motor simulation de novo: Observation of dance by dancers. *Neuroimage, 31*(3), 1257–1267.

Cross, E. S., Hortensius, R., & Wykowska, A. (2019). From social brains to social robots: Applying neurocognitive insights to human–robot interaction. *Philosophical Transactions of the Royal Society, B, 374*, 20180024.

Crosson, B., & Warren, R. L. (1981). Dichotic ear preference for C-V-C words in Wernicke's and Broca's aphasias. *Cortex, 17*(2), 249–258.

Crowder, R. G. (1976). *Principles of Learning and Memory*. Erlbaum.

Crozier, W. E., Luke, T. J., & Strange, D. (2020). Taking the bait: Interrogation questions about hypothetical evidence may inflate perceptions of guilt. *Psychology, Crime & Law*, 1–24.

Cruse, D., Chennu, S., Chatell, C., Bekinschtein, T. A., Fernandez-Espejo, D., Pickard, J. D., Laureys, S., & Owen, A. M. (2011). Bedside detection of awareness in the vegetative state: A cohort study. *The Lancet*, September, online issue, http://dx.doi.org/10.1016/S0140-6736(11)61224-5.

Crystal, D. (1997). *The Cambridge Encyclopaedia of Language* (2nd ed.). Cambridge University Press.

Crystal, D. (2000). *Language Death*. Cambridge University Press.

Cuetos, F., & Mitchell, D. C. (1988). Cross-linguistic differences in parsing: Restrictions on the use of the Late Closure strategy in Spanish. *Cognition, 30*, 73–105.

Cummings, L. (2019). Describing the Cookie Theft picture: Sources of breakdown in Alzheimer's dementia. *Pragmatics and Society, 10*(2), 153–176.

Curtiss, S. (1977). *Genie: A Psycholinguistic Study of a Modern-Day 'Wild Child'*. Academic Press.

Curtiss, S. (1981). Dissociations between language and cognition: Cases and implications. *Journal of Autism and Developmental Disorders, 2*, 15–30.

Cushing, S. (1994). *Fatal Words: Communication Clashes and Aircraft Crashes*. University of Chicago Press.

Cuskley, C., Simner, J. and Kirby, S. (2017) Phonological and orthographic influences in the bouba-kiki effect. *Psychological Research, 81*(1), 119–130.

Custers, E. J., & ten Cate, O. T. (2011). Very long-term retention of basic science knowledge in doctors after graduation. *Medical Education, 45*(4), 422–430.

Custers, R., & Aarts, H. (2010). The unconscious will: How the pursuit of goals operates outside of conscious awareness. *Science, 329* (5987), 47–50.

Cutler, A., & Butterfield, S. (1992). Rhythmic cues to speech segmentation: Evidence from juncture misperception. *Journal of Memory and Language, 31*, 218–236.

Cutler, A., & Carter, D. M. (1987). The predominance of strong initial syllables in the English vocabulary. *Computer Speech, & Language, 2*, 133–142.

Cutler, A., Dahan, D., & van Donselaar, W. (1997). Prosody in the comprehension of spoken language: A literature review. *Language and Speech, 40*, 141–210.

Cutler, A., Mehler, J., Norris, D. G., & Segui, J. (1986). The syllable's differing role in the segmentation of French and English. *Journal of Memory and Language, 25*, 385–400.

Cutler, A., Mehler, J., Norris, D. G., & Segui, J. (1992). The monolingual nature of speech segmentation by bilinguals. *Cognitive Psychology, 24*, 381–410.

Cutler, A., & Norris, D. (1979). Monitoring sentence comprehension. In W. E. Cooper & E. T. C. Walker (Ed.), *Sentence Processing: Psycholinguistic Studies Presented to Merill Garrett* (pp. 113–134). Erlbaum.

Cutler, A., & Norris, D. G. (1988). The role of strong syllables in segmentation for lexical access. *Journal of Experimental Psychology: Human Perception and Performance, 14*, 113–121.

Cutler, V., & Paddock, S. (2009). Use of threat image projection (TIP) to enhance security performance. In *43rd Annual 2009 International Carnahan Conference on Security Technology* (pp. 46–51). IEEE, October.

Cutting, J. E. (2016). Narrative theory and the dynamics of popular movies. *Psychonomic Bulletin & Review, 23*(6), 1713-1743.

Cutting, J. E., DeLong, J. E., & Nothelfer, C. E. (2010). Attention and the evolution of Hollywood film. *Psychological Science, 21*(3), 432–439.

Cutting, J. E., & Kozlowski, L. T. (1977). Recognizing friends by their walk: Gait perception without familiarity cues. *Bulletin of the Psychonomic Society, 9*(5), 353–356.

Cuttler, C., & Graf, P. (2007). Sub-clinical compulsive checkers' prospective memory is impaired. *Journal of Anxiety Disorders, 21*, 338–352.

Cytowic, R. E. (2003). *The Man Who Tasted Shapes* (MIT Press edition with new Afterword). MIT Press.

D

D'Angelo, M. C., & Humphreys, K. R. (2015). Tip-of-the-tongue states reoccur because of implicit learning, but resolving them helps. *Cognition, 142*, 166–190.

D'Souza H., Karmiloff-Smith, A. (2017). Neurodevelopmental disorders. *WIREs Cognitive Science, 8*(1–2), e1398.

Dahan, D. (2010). The time course of interpretation in speech comprehension. *Current Directions in Psychological Science, 19*(2), 121–126.

Dakin, S. C., & Watt, R. J. (1997). The computation of orientation statistics from visual texture. *Vision Research, 37*(22), 3181–3192.

Dalrymple-Alford, E. C., & Budayr, B. (1966). Examination of some aspects of the Stroop Color-Word Test. *Perceptual and Motor Skills, 23*, 1211–1214.

Damasio, A. (1994). *Descartes' Error: Emotion, Reason and the Human Brain*. G. P. Putnam.

Damasio, A. R., Tranel, D., & Damasio, H. (1990). Individuals with sociopathic behavior caused by frontal damage fail to respond autonomically to social stimuli. *Behavioural Brain Research, 41*, 81–94.

Damasio, A., Tranel, D., & Damasio, H. (1992). Verbs but not nouns: Damage to left temporal cortices impairs access to nouns but not verbs, *Society for Neuroscience Abstracts, 18*, 387.

Danek, A. H. (2018). Magic tricks, sudden re-structuring, and the Aha! experience: A new model of nonmonotonic problem solving. In F. Vallee-Tourangeau (Ed.), *Insight: On the Origins of New Ideas* (pp. 51–78). Routledge.

Danek, A. H., Fraps, T., von Muller, A., Grothe, B., & Ollinger, M. (2014). Working wonders? Investigating insight with magic tricks. *Cognition, 130*, 174–185.

Daniel, T. A., & Camp, A. L. (2020). Emojis affect processing fluency on social media. *Psychology of Popular Media, 9*(2), 208–213.

Daniels, P. T., & Share, D. L. (2018). Writing system variation and its consequences for reading and dyslexia. *Scientific Studies of Reading, 22*(1), 101–116.

Danquah, A. N., Farrell, M. J., & O'Boyle, D. J. (2008). Biases in the subjective timing of perceptual events: Libet *et al.* (1983) revisited. *Consciousness and Cognition, 17*, 616–627.

Dantzig, G., Fulkerson, R., & Johnson, S. (1954). Solution of a large-scale travelling-salesman problem. *Journal of the Operations Research Society of America, 2*, 393–410.

Darwin, C. (1998). *The Expression of the Emotions in Man and Animals* (3rd ed.) Oxford University Press. (First published 1872.)

Darwin, C. J., Turvey, M. T., & Crowder, R. G. (1972). An auditory analogue of the Sperling partial report procedure: Evidence for brief auditory store. *Cognitive Psychology, 3*, 255–267.

Davies, M. L., Harries, P. A., Gilhooly, K. J., Gilhooly, M. L. M., & Cairns, D. (2013). Detection and prevention of financial abuse against elders. *Journal of Financial Crime, 21*, 84–89.

Dawel, A., O'Kearney, R., McKone, E., & Palermo, R. (2012). Not just fear and sadness: Meta-analytic evidence of pervasive emotion recognition deficits for facial and vocal expressions in psychopathy. *Neuroscience & Biobehavioral Reviews, 36*(10), 2288–2304.

Dayan, E., Casile, A., Levit-Binnun, N., Giese, M. A., Hendler, T., & Flash, T. (2007). Neural representations of kinematic laws of motion: Evidence for action-perception coupling. *Proceedings of the National Academy of Sciences of the United States of America, 104*(51), 20582–20587.

de Bono, E. (1967). *The Use of Lateral Thinking*. Jonathan Cape.

de Bono, E. (2015). *Lateral Thinking: Creativity Step by Step*. Harper Colophon.

De Gelder, B., Vroomen, J., Pourtois, G., & Weiskrantz, L. (1999). Non-conscious recognition of affect in the absence of striate cortex. *Neuroreport, 10*(18), 3759–3763.

De Groot, A. D. (1965). *Thought and Choice in Chess*. Mouton.

De Groot, A. M. B., & Van Hell, J. G. (2005). The learning of foreign language vocabulary. In J. F. Kroll & A. M. B. de Groot (Eds.), *Handbook of Bilingualism: Psycholinguistic Approaches* (pp. 9–29). Oxford University Press.

de Haan, E. H. F., Fabri, M., Dijkerman, H. C., Foschi, N., Lattanzi, S., & Pinto, Y. (2020). Unified tactile detection and localisation in split-brain patients. *Cortex, 124*, 217–223.

De Houwer, J., & Hermans, D. (2010). Do feelings have a mind of their own? In J. De Houwer & D. Hermans (Eds.), *Cognition and*

Emotion: Reviews of Current Research and Theories (pp. 38–65). Psychology Press.

de Leeuw, E. (2019). Native speech plasticity in the German-English late bilingual Stefanie Graf: A longitudinal study over four decades. *Journal of Phonetics, 73,* 24–39.

de Lira, J. O., Minett, T. S. C., Ferreira Bertolucci, P. H., & Ortiz, K. Z. (2014). Analysis of word number and content in discourse of patients with mild to moderate Alzheimer's disease. *Dementia & Neuropsychologia, 8*(3), 260–265.

De Neys, W. (2006). Automatic-heuristic and executive-analytic processing in reasoning: Chronometric and task considerations. *Quarterly Journal of Experimental Psychology, 59,* 1070–1110.

de Ruiter, J. P. (2000). The production of gesture and speech. In D. McNeill (Ed.), *Language and Gesture* (pp. 284–311). Cambridge University Press.

De Ruiter, J. P., Mitterer, H., & Enfield, N. J. (2006). Projecting the end of a speaker's turn: A cognitive cornerstone of conversation. *Language, 82,* 515–535.

de Villiers Scheepers, M. J., & Maree, L. (2015). Fostering team creativity in higher education settings. *e-Journal of Business Education & Scholarship of Teaching, 9,* 70–86.

De Vito, D., & Fenske, M. J. (2017). Suppressing memories of words and familiar objects results in their affective devaluation: Evidence from think/no-think tasks. *Cognition, 162,* 1–11.

de Vries, M. H., Barth, A. C. R., Maiworm, S., Knecht, S., Zwitserlood, P., & Flöel, A. (2010). Electrical stimulation of Broca's area enhances implicit learning of an artificial grammar. *Journal of Cognitive Neuroscience, 22,* 2427–2436.

Debray, S. B. E., & Demeestere, J. (2018). Alien hand syndrome. *Neurology, 91*(11), 527.

Defeyter, M. A., & German, T. B. (2003). Acquiring an understanding of design: Evidence from children's insight problem solving. *Cognition, 89,* 133–155.

Deffenbacher, K. A., Bornstein, B. H., Penroad, S. A., & McGorty, E. K. (2004). A meta-analytic review of the effects of high stress on eyewitness memory. *Law and Human Behavior, 28,* 687–706.

Degand, L., & van Bergen, G. (2016). Discourse markers as turn-transition devices: Evidence from speech and instant messaging. *Discourse Processes, 55,* 47–71.

Dehaene, S., Kerszberg, M., & Changeux, J. P. (1998). A neuronal model of a global workspace in effortful cognitive tasks. *Proceedings of the National Academy of Sciences, 95*(24), 14529–14534.

Dehaene, S., Lau, H., & Kouider, S. (2017). What is consciousness, and could machines have it? *Science, 358*(6362), 486–492.

Dekhtyar, M., Kiran, S., & Gray, T. (2020). Is bilingualism protective for adults with aphasia? *Neuropsychologia, 1392,* March, 107355.

Dell, G. S. (1986). A spreading activation theory of retrieval in sentence production. *Psychological Review, 93,* 283–321.

Dell, G. S. (1995). Speaking and misspeaking. In L. Gleitman & M. Liberman (Eds.), *Invitation to Cognitive Science, Part I: Language.* MIT Press.

Dell, G. S., Burger, L. K., & Svec, W. R. (1997). Language production and serial order: A functional analysis and a model. *Psychological Review, 104,* 123–147.

Dell, G. S., & O' Seaghdha, P. G. (1991). Mediated and convergent lexical priming in language production: A comment on Levelt et al. *Psychological Review, 98,* 604–614.

Dell, G. S., & Reich, P. A. (1981). Stages in sentence production: An analysis of speech error data. *Journal of Verbal Learning & Verbal Behavior, 20,* 611–629.

Della Sala, S., Gray, C., Baddeley, A. D., Allamano, N., & Wilson, L. (1999). Pattern span: A tool for unwelding visuo-spatial memory. *Neuropsychologia, 37,* 1189–1199.

Delogu, F., Brouwer, H., & Crocker, M. W. (2019). Event-related potentials index lexical retrieval (N400) and integration (P600) during language comprehension. *Brain and Cognition, 135,* 103569.

Demartsev, V., Strandburg-Peshkin, A., Ruffner, M., & Manser, M. (2018). Vocal turn-taking in meerkat group calling sessions. *Current Biology, 28*(22), 3661–3666.

Demertzi, A., Tagliazucchi, E., Dehaene, S., Deco, G., Barttfeld, P., Raimondo, F., Martial, C., Fernandez-Espejo, D., Rohaut, B., Voss, H., Schiff, N., Owen, A., Laureys, S., Naccache, L., & Sitt, J. (2019). Human consciousness is supported by dynamic complex patterns of brain signal coordination: Distinct brain patterns sustain conscious states. *Science Advances, 5*(2), eaat7603.

Deng, J., Dong, W., Socher, R., Li, L. J., Li, K.,& Fei-Fei, L. (2009). Image Net: A large-scale hierarchical imagedatabase. In *2009 IEEE Conference on Computer Vision and Pattern Recognition* (pp. 248–255), June. IEEE.

Dennett, D. C. (1991). *Consciousness Explained.* Little, Brown & Company.

DePaulo, B. M., Lindsay, J. J., Malone, B. E., Muhlenbruck, L., Charlton, K., & Cooper, H. (2003) Cues to deception. *Psychological Bulletin, 129,* 74–118.

DeRosa, D. M., Smith, C. L., & Hantula, D. A. (2007). The medium matters: Mining the long promised merit of group interaction in creative idea generation tasks in a meta-analysis of the electronic group brainstorming literature. *Computers in Human Behavior, 23,* 1549–1581.

Derraugh, L. S., Neath, I., Surprenant, A. M., Beaudry, O., & Saint-Aubin, J. (2017). The effect of lexical factors on recall from working memory: Generalizing the neighborhood size effect. *Canadian Journal of Experimental Psychology, 71*(1), 23–31.

Deutsch, J. A., & Deutsch, D. (1963). Attention: Some theoretical considerations. *Psychological Review, 70*(1), 80–90.

Dewaele, J. M. (2009). The cognitive perspective: The age factor. In K. Knapp & B. Seidlhofer (Eds.), *Handbook of Foreign Language Communication and Learning* (pp. 279–306). Mouton De Gruyter.

Dewar, M., Alber, J., Butler, C., Cowan, N., & Della Sala, S. (2012). Brief wakeful restingboosts new memories over the long term. *Psychological Science, 23,* 955–960.

Dewar, M., Alber, J., Cowan, N., & Della Sala, S. (2014). Boosting long-term memory via wakeful rest: Intentional rehearsal is not necessary, consolidation is sufficient. *PLOS One, 9*(10), e109542.

Dewar, M. T., Cowan, N., & Della Sala, S. (2007). Forgetting due to retroactive interference: A fusion of Muller and Pilzecker's (1900) early insights into forgetting and recent research on anterograde amnesia. *Cortex, 43,* 616–634.

Dewar, M., Della Sala, S., Beschin, N., & Cowan, N. (2010). Profound retroactive interference in anterograde amnesia. What interferes? *Neuropsychology, 24,* 357.

Dewar, M., Fernandez Garcia, Y., Cowan, N., & Della Sala, S. (2009). Delaying interference enhances memory consolidation in amnesic patients. *Neuropsychology, 23,* 627–634.

Dhami, M. K. (2003). Psychological models of professional decision making. *Psychological Science, 14,* 175–180.

Dhami, M. K., & Ayton, P. (2001). Bailing and jailing the fast and frugal way. *Journal of Behavioral Decision Making, 14,* 141–168.

Dhami, M. K., & Belton, I. (2011). On getting inside the judge's mind. *Translational Issues in Psychological Science, 3,* 214–226.

Dhami, M. K., & Mumpower, J. L. (2018). Kenneth R. Hammond's contributions to the study of judgment and decision making. *Judgment and Decision Making, 13,* 1–22.

Di Lollo, V. (2018). Attention is a sterile concept; iterative reentry is a fertile substitute. *Consciousness and Cognition, 64,* 45–49.

Diedrichsen, J., Shadmehr, R., & Ivry, R. B. (2010). The coordination of movement: Optimal feedback control and beyond. *Trends in Cognitive Sciences, 14*(1), 31–39.

Dijiksterhuis, A., & Meurs, T. (2006). Where creativity resides: The generative power of unconscious thought. *Consciousness and Cognition, 15,* 135–146.

Dijiksterhuis, A., & Nordgren, L. F. (2006). A theory of unconscious thought. *Perspectives on Psychological Science, 1,* 95–109.

Dijkstra, A. (2005). Bilingual visual word recognition and lexical access. In J. F. Kroll & A. De Groot (Eds.), *Handbook of Bilingualism: Psycholinguistic Approaches* (pp. 178–201). Oxford University Press.

Dijksterhuis, A., Bos, M. W., Nordgren, L. F., & Van Baaren, R. B. (2006). On making the right choice: The deliberation-without-attention effect. *Science, 311,* 1005–1007.

Dijkstra, N., Bosch, S. E., & van Gerven, M. A. J. (2019). Shared neural mechanisms of visual perception and imagery. *Trends in Cognitive Sciences, 23,* 423–434.

Dillon, P. C., Graham, W. K., & Aidells, A. L. (1972). Brainstorming on a 'hot' problem: Effects of training and practice on individual and group performance. *Journal of Applied Psychology, 56,* 487–490.

Dingli, S. (2008). Thinking outside the box: Edward de Bono's lateral thinking. In T. Rickards, M. A. Runco, & S. Moger (Eds.), *The Routledge Companion to Creativity* (pp. 338–350). Routledge.

Dipellegrino, G., Fadiga, L., Fogassi, L., Gallese, V., & Rizzolatti, G. (1992). Understanding motor events: A neurophysiological study. *Experimental Brain Research, 91*(1), 176–180.

Dismukes, R. K. (2012). Prospective memory in workplace and everyday situations. *Current Directions in*

Psychological Science, 21(4), 215–220.

Dismukes, R. K., Berman, B. A., & Loukopoulos, L. (2007). *The Limits of Expertise: Rethinking Pilot Error and the Causes of Airline Accidents*. Routledge.

Dittrich, W. H. (1993). Action categories and the perception of biological motion. *Perception, 22*(1), 15–22.

Dittrich, W. H., Troscianko, T., Lea, S. E. G., & Morgan, D. (1996). Perception of emotion from dynamic point-light displays represented in dance. *Perception, 25*(6), 727–38.

Dixon, M. L., De La Vega, A., Mills, C., Andrews-Hanna, J., Spreng, R. N., Cole, M. W., & Christoff, K. (2018). Heterogeneity within the frontoparietal control network and its relationship to the default and dorsal attention networks. *Proceedings of the National Academy of Sciences, 115*(7), E1598–E1607.

Dlugaiczyk, J., Gensberger, K. D., & Straka, H. (2019). Galvanic vestibular stimulation: From basic concepts to clinical applications. *Journal of Neurophysiology, 121*(6), 2237–2255.

Dobbs, D. (2005). Fact or phrenology? *Scientific American Mind, 16,* 24–31.

Dobie, T. G. (2019). *Motion Sickness: A Motion Adaptation Syndrome* (Vol. 6). Springer.

Dodds, R. A., Ward, T. B., & Smith, S. M. (2012). A review of the experimental literature on incubation in problem solving and creativity. In M. A. Runco (Ed.), *Creativity Research Handbook* (Vol. 3). Hampton Press.

Dominik, T., Dostál, D., Zielina, M., Šmahaj, J., Sedláčková, Z., & Procházka, R. (2017). Libet's experiment: Questioning the validity of measuring the urge to move. *Consciousness and Cognition, 49,* 255–263.

Donald, M. (1991). *Origins of the Modern Mind: Three Stages in the Evolution of Culture and Cognition*. Harvard University Press.

Donald, T. W. (1999). Preconditions for the evolution of protolanguages. In M. C. Corballis & I. Lea (Eds.), *The Descent of Mind* (pp. 355–365). Oxford University Press.

Donaldson, H. H. (1895). *The Growth of the Brain*. Scribner.

Downing, P. E. (2000). Interactions between visual working memory and selective attention. *Psychological Science, 11*(6), 467–473.

Doyle, A. C. (1887). A study in scarlet. *Beeton's Christmas Annual 1887*. Ward Lock.

Dresner, E., & Herring, S. C. (2010). Functions of the nonverbal in CMC: Emoticons and illocutionary force. *Communication Theory, 20*(3), 249–268.

Drews, F. A., Pasupathi, M., & Strayer, D. L. (2008). Passenger and cell phone conversations in simulated driving. *Journal of Experimental Psychology: Applied, 14*(4), 392–400.

Driver, J. (1996). Enhancement of selective listening by illusory mislocation of speech sounds due to lip-reading. *Nature, 381* (6577), 66–68.

Dronkers, N. F. (1996). A new brain region for coordinating speech articulation. *Nature, 384,* 159–161.

Dronkers, N. F., & Larsen, J. (2001). Neuroanatomy of the classical syndromes of aphasia. In R. S. Berndt (Ed.), *Handbook of Neuropsychology, Vol. 3* (pp. 19–30). Elsevier.

Dronkers, N. F., Plaisant, O., Iba-Zizen, M. T., & Cabanis, E. A. (2007). Paul Broca's historic cases: High resolution MR imaging of the brains of Leborgne and Lelong. *Brain, 130,* 1432–1441.

Dronkers, N. F., Wilkins, D. P., Van Valin, R. D., Redfern, B. B., & Jaeger, J. J. (2004). Lesion analysis of the brain areas involved in language comprehension. *Cognition, 92,* 145–177.

Dror, I., Charlton, D., & Péron, A. (2006). Contextual information renders experts vulnerable to making erroneous identifications. *Forensic Science International, 156*(1), 74–78.

Dry, M., Lee, M. D., Vickers, D., & Hughes, P. (2006). Human performance on visually presented travelling salesperson problems with varying numbers of nodes. *Journal of Problem Solving, 1,* 20–32.

Dryer, M. S. (2005). Order of subject, object, and verb. In M. Haspelmath, M. S. Dryer, D. Gil, & B. Comrie (Eds.), *The World Atlas of Language Structures*. Oxford University Press.

Duchaine, B., & Yovel, G. (2015). A revised neural framework for face processing. *Annual Review of Vision Science, 1,* 393–416.

Dudai, Y. (2004). The neurobiology of consolidation, or, how stable is the engram? *Annual Review of Psychology, 55,* 51–86.

Dunbar, K. (1993). Concept discovery in a scientific domain. *Cognitive Science, 17,* 397–434.

Dunbar, K., & Fugelsang, J. (2005). Scientific thinking and reasoning. In K. J. Holyoak & R. G. Morrison (Eds.), *The Cambridge Handbook of Thinking and Reasoning*. Cambridge University Press.

Duncan, J. (1984). Selective attention and the organization of visual information. *Journal of Experimental Psychology: General, 113*(4), 501–517.

Duncker, K. (1945). On problem solving. *Psychological Monographs, 58,* 1–113.

Dunlosky, J., Rawson, K. A., Marsh, E. J., Nathan, M. J., & Willingham, D. T. (2013). Improving students' learning with effective learning techniques: Promising directions from cognitive and educational psychology. *Psychological Science in the Public Interest, 14*(1), 4–58.

Dunn, B. D., Dalgleish, T., Lawrence, A. D., & Ogilvie, A. D. (2007). The accuracy of self-monitoring and its relationship to self-focused attention in dysphoria and clinical depression. *Journal of Abnormal Psychology, 116,* 1–15.

Dunn, B. D., Galton, H. C., Morgan, R., Evans, D., Oliver, C., Meyer, M., Cusack, R., Lawrence, A. D., & Dalgleish, T. (2010). Listening to your heart: How interoception shapes emotion experience and intuitive decision making. *Psychological Science, 21,* 1835–1844.

Dunnette, M. D., Campbell, J., & Jaastad, K. (1963). The effects of group participation on brainstorming effectiveness for two industrial samples. *Journal of Applied Psychology, 47,* 10–37.

Durgin, F. H., Baird, J. A., Greenburg, M., Russell, R., Shaughnessy, K., & Waymouth, S. (2009). Who is being deceived? The experimental demands of wearing a backpack. *Psychonomic Bulletin & Review, 16*(5), 964–969.

Durgin, F. H., Klein, B., Spiegel, A., Strawser, C. J., & Williams, M. (2012). The social psychology of perception experiments: Hills, backpacks, glucose and the problem of generalizability. *Journal of Experimental Psychology: Human Perception and Performance, 38,* 1582–1595.

Dutton, D. G., & Aron, A. P. (1974). Some evidence for heightened sexual attraction under conditions of high anxiety. *Journal of Personality and Social Psychology, 30,* 510–517.

E

Easton, R. D., & Moran, P. W. (1978). A quantitative confirmation of visual capture of curvature. *Journal of General & Psychology, 98* (1st half), 105–112.

Ebbinghaus, H. (1885). *Memory: A Contribution to Experimental Psychology.* Trans. H. A. Ruger & C. E. Bussenius (1913). Originally published in New York by Teachers College, Columbia University.

Eckstein, M. P. (2011). Visual search: A retrospective. *Journal of Vision, 11,* 14.

Edwards, A., Elwyn, G. J., Covey, E., M., & Pill, R. (2001). Presenting risk information: A review of the effects of 'framing' and other manipulations on patient outcomes. *Journal of Health Communication, 6,* 61–82.

Edwards, T., Kingston, K., Hardy, L., & Gould, D. (2002). A qualitative analysis of catastrophic performances and the associated thoughts, feelings, and emotions. *Sport Psychologist, 16*(1), 1–19.

Efron, R. (1970a). Effects of stimulus duration on perceptual onset and offset latencies. *Perception & Psychophysics, 8,* 231–234.

Efron, R. (1970b). The minimum duration of a perception. *Neuropsychologia, 8,* 57–63.

Efron, R. (1970c). The relationship between the duration of a stimulus and the duration of a perception. *Neuropsychologia, 8,* 37–55.

Egly, R., Driver, J., & Rafal, R. D. (1994). Shifting visual attention between objects and locations: Evidence from normal and parietal lesion subjects. *Journal of Experimental Psychology – General, 123*(2), 161–177.

Ehrlich, S. F., & Rayner, K. (1981). Contextual effects on word perception and eye movements during reading. *Journal of Verbal Learning and Verbal Behaviour, 20,* 641–655.

Eibl-Eibesfeldt, I. (1973). The expressive behaviour of the deaf-and-blind born. In M. von Cranach & I. Vine (Eds.), *Social Communication and Movement*. Academic Press.

Eich, E. (1995). Searching for mood dependent memory. *Psychological Science, 6,* 67–75.

Eich, E., & Metcalfe, J. (1989). Mood dependent memory for internal versus external events. *Journal of Experimental Psychology: Learning Memory and Cognition, 15,* 443–455.

Eich, J. E. (1980). The cue-dependent nature of state-dependent retention. *Memory and Cognition, 8,* 157–173.

Eichenbaum, H. (2011). *The Cognitive Neuroscience of Memory: An Introduction*. Oxford University Press.

Eimas, P. D., & Corbit, J. D. (1973). Selective adaptation of linguistic feature detectors. *Cognitive Psychology, 4*, 99–109.

Eimas, P. D., Siqueland, E. R., Jusczyk, P. W., & Vogorito, J. (1971). Speech perception in infants. *Science, 171*, 303–306.

Einstein, O., & McDaniel, M. (2005). Prospective memory: Multiple retrieval processes. *Current Directions in Psychological Science, 14*, 286–290.

Einstein, O., McDaniel, M., Thomas, R., Mayfield, S., Shank, H., Morrisette, N., & Breneiser, J. (2005). Multiple processes in prospective memory retrieval: Factors determining monitoring versus spontaneous retrieval. *Journal of Experimental Psychology, 134*, 327–342.

Ekman, P. (1994). Strong evidence for universals in facial expressions: A reply to Russell's mistaken critique. *Psychological Bulletin, 115*(2), 268–287.

Ekman, P. (1999). Basic emotions. In T. Dalgleish & M. Power (Eds.), *Handbook of Cognition and Emotion*. John Wiley & Sons.

Ekman, P., Levenson, R. W., & Friesen, W. V. (1983). Autonomic nervous system activity distinguishes among emotions. *Science, 221*, 1208–1210.

Ekman, P., & O'Sullivan, M. (1991). Who can catch a liar? *American Psychologist, 46*, 913–920.

Ekman, P., Sorenson, E. R., & Friesen, W. V. (1969). Pan-cultural elements in facial displays of emotion. *Science, 164*, 86–88.

Ekroll, V., Sayim, B., & Wagemans, J. (2013). Against Better Knowledge: The Magical Force of A modal Volume Completion. I-Perception, 4(8), 511–515. doi: 10.1068/i0622sas

Ekstrand, B. R. (1972). To sleep, perchance to dream (about why we forget). In C. P. Duncan, L. Sechrest, & A. W. Melton (Eds.), *Human Memory: Festschrift for Benton J. Underwood*. Appleton Century Crofts.

Elder, R. S., & Krishna, A. (2012). The 'visual depiction effect' in advertising: Facilitating embodied mental simulation through product orientation. *Journal of Consumer Research, 36*, 988–1003.

Elfenbein, H. A., & Ambady, N. (2002). Is there an in group advantage in emotion recognition? *Psychological Bulletin, 128*(2), 243–249.

Ellenbogen, J. M., Hulbert, J. C., Stickgold, R., Dinges, D. F., & Thompson-Schill, S. L. (2006). Interfering with theories of sleep and memory: Sleep, declarative memory, and associative interference. *Current Biology, 16*, 1290–1294.

Elliot, R., Newman, A. L., Longe, O. A., & Deakin, J. F. (2003). Differential response patterns in the striatum and orbitofrontal cortex to financial reward in humans: A parametric functional magnetic resonance imaging study. *Journal of Neuroscience, 23*, 303–307.

Elliott, D., Helsen, W. F., & Chua, R. (2001). A century later: Woodworth's (1899) two-component model of goal-directed aiming. *Psychological Bulletin, 127*(3), 342–357.

Elliott, R., & Dolan, R. J. (1998). The medial prefrontal cortex in depression. In D. Ebert & K. P. Ebmeier (Eds.), *New Models for Depression*. Karger.

Ellis, A., & Harper, R. A. (1975). *A New Guide to Rational Living*. Prentice-Hall.

Ellis, A. W., Miller, D., & Sin, G. (1983). Wernicke's aphasia and normal language processing: A case study in cognitive neuropsychology. *Cognition, 15*, 111–144.

Ellis, A., & Young, A. (1988) *Human Cognitive Neuropsychology*. Lawrence Erlbaum Associates Ltd.

Ellis, A. W., & Young, A. W. (1996). *Human Cognitive Neuropsychology: A Textbook with Readings*. Psychology Press.

Ellis, C., & Urban, S. (2016) Age and aphasia: A review of presence, type, recovery and clinical outcomes. *Topics in Stroke Rehabilitation, 23*(6), 430–439.

Ellis, H. D., & Lewis, M. B. (2001). Capgras delusion: A window on face recognition. *Trends in Cognitive Sciences, 5*(4), 149–156.

Ellis, H. D., Luaute, J. P., & Retterstol, N. (1994). Delusional misidentification syndromes. *Psychopathology, 27*(3-5), 117–120.

Ellis, J. A., & Cohen, G. (2008). Memory for intentions, actions and plans. In G. Cohen, & M. A. Conway (Eds.), *Memory in the Real World* (3rd ed.). (pp. 141–172). Psychology Press.

Ellis, N. C., & Hennelly, R. A. (1980). A bilingual word-length effect: Implications for intelligence testing and the relative ease of mental calculation in Welsh and English. *British Journal of Psychology, 71*, 289–318.

Ellsworth, P. C. (2005). Legal reasoning. In K. J. Holyoak & R. G. Morrison (Eds.), *The Cambridge Handbook of Thinking and Reasoning*. Cambridge University Press.

Elman, J. L. (1990). Finding structure in time. *Cognitive Science, 14*(2), 179–211.

Elman, J. L., & McClelland, J. L. (1988). Cognitive penetration of the mechanisms of perception: Compensation for coarticulation of lexically restored phonemes. *Journal of Memory and Language, 27*, 143–165.

Elsey, J. W., Van Ast, V. A., & Kindt, M. (2018). Human memory reconsolidation: A guiding framework and critical review of the evidence. *Psychological Bulletin, 144*(8), 797–848.

Emmorey, K. (2015). The neurobiology of sign language. In A. W. Toga (Ed.), *Brain Mapping: An Encyclopedic Reference, vol. 3* (pp. 475-479). Academic Press, Elsevier.

Engel, C. (2011). Dictator games: A meta study. *Experimental Economics, 14*, 583–610.

Engelhardt, P. E. (2020). Developmental dyslexia: Where do we go from here? *Brain Sciences, 10*(3), 151.

Engle, R. W. (2002). Working memory capacity as executive attention. *Current Directions in Psychological Science, 11*, 19–23.

Engle, R. W., & Conway, A. R. A. (1998). Working memory and comprehension. In R. H. Logie & K. J. Gilhooly (Eds.), *Working Memory and Thinking*. Psychology Press.

Engle, R. W., & Oransky, N. (1999). The evolution from short-term to working memory: Multi-store to dynamic models of temporary storage. In R. Sternberg (Ed.), *The Nature of Human Cognition*. MIT Press.

English, T., Lee, I. A., John, O. P., & Gross, J. J. (2017). Emotion regulation strategy selection in daily life: The role of social context and goals. *Motivation and Emotion, 41*(2), 230–242.

Enoch, D. (2013). On analogies, disanalogies, and moral philosophy: A comment on John Mikhails's Elements of Moral Cognition. *Jerusalem Review of Legal Studies, 8*, 1–25.

Entwistle, N. (1987). *Understanding Classroom Learning*. Hodder & Stoughton.

Erdelyi, M. H. (1974). A new look at the New Look: Perceptual defense and vigilance. *Psychological Review, 81*, 1–25.

Ericsson, K. A. (1999). Creative expertise as superior reproducible performance: Innovative and flexible aspects of expert performance. *Psychological Inquiry, 10*, 329–333.

Ericsson, K. A. (2003). Exceptional memorizers: Made, not born. *Trends in Cognitive Sciences, 7*, 233–235.

Ericsson, K. A., & Chase, W. G. (1982). Exceptional memory. *American Scientist, 70*, 607–615.

Ericsson, K. A., Cheng, X., Pan, Y., Ku, Y., Ge, Y., & Hu, Y. (2017). Memory skills mediating superior memory in a world-class memorist. *Memory, 25*, 1294–1302.

Ericsson, K. A., Delaney, P. F., Weaver, G., & Mahadevan, R. (2004). Uncovering the structure of a memorist's superior 'basic' memory capacity. *Cognitive Psychology, 49*(3), 191–237.

Ericsson, K. A., & Kintsch, W. (1995). Long-term working memory. *Psychological Review, 102*, 211–245.

Ericsson, K. A., Krampe, R. T., & Tesch-Rohmer, C. (1993). The role of deliberate practice. *Psychological Review, 100*, 363–406.

Ericsson, K. A., & Simon, H. A. (1993). *Protocol Analysis: Verbal Reports as Data*. MIT Press.

Eriksen, C. W., & St. James, J. D. (1986). Visual-attention within and around the field of focal attention: A zoom lens model. *Perception & Psychophysics, 40*(4), 225–240.

Eriksen, C. W., & Yeh, Y. Y. (1985). Allocation of attention in the visual field. *Journal of Experimental Psychology: Human Perception and Performance, 11*(5), 583–597.

Erman, L. D., & Lesser, V. R. (1980). The HEARSAY-II speech understanding system: A tutorial. In W. Lea (Ed.), *Trends in Speech Recognition*. Prentice-Hall.

Ernst, M. O., & Banks, M. S. (2002). Humans integrate visual and haptic information in a statistically optimal fashion. *Nature, 415*(6870), 429–433.

Eslinger, P. J., & Damasio, A. R. (1981). Age and type of aphasia in patients with stroke. *Journal of Neurology, Neurosurgery, and Psychiatry, 44*(5), 377–381.

Eslinger, P. J., & Damasio, A. R. (1985). Severe disturbance of higher cognition after bilateral frontal lobe ablation: Patient EVR. *Neurology, 35*, 1731–1741.

Estes, W. K. (1972). An associative basis for coding and organization in memory. In A. W. Melton & E. Martin (Eds.), *Coding Processes in Human Memory*. V. H. Winston, & Sons.

Estival, D., Farris, C., & Molesworth, B. (2016). *Aviation English: A Lingua Franca for Pilots and Air Traffic Controllers*. Routledge.

Etchell, A., Adhikari, A., Weinberg, L. S., Choo, A. L., Garnett, E. O., Chow, H. M., & Chang, S.-E. (2018). A systematic literature review of sex differences in childhood language and brain development. *Neuropsychologia, 114*, 19–31.

Evans, A. T., Peters, E., Strasser, A. A., Emery, L. F., Sheerin, K. M., & Romer, D. (2015). Graphic warning labels elicit affective and thoughtful responses from smokers:

Results of a randomized clinical trial. *PLOS One, 10*(12).

Evans, J. St. B. T. (1977). Linguistic factors in reasoning. *Quarterly Journal of Experimental Psychology, 29*, 297–306.

Evans, J. St. B. T. (1984). Heuristic and analytic processes in reasoning. *British Journal of Psychology, 75*, 451–458.

Evans, J. St. B. T. (2003). In two minds: Dual process accounts of reasoning. *Trends in Cognitive Sciences, 7*, 454–459.

Evans, J. St. B. T. (2008). Dual processing accounts of reasoning, judgment, and social cognition. *Annual Review of Psychology, 59*, 255–278.

Evans, J. St. B. T., Barston, J. L., & Pollard, P. (1983). On the conflict between logic and belief in syllogistic reasoning. *Memory & Cognition, 11*, 295–306.

Evans, J. St. B. T., & Curtis-Holmes, J. (2005). Rapid responding increases belief bias: Evidence for the dual process theory of reasoning. *Thinking & Reasoning, 11*, 382–389.

Evans, J. St. B. T., & Lynch, J. S. (1973). Matching bias in the selection task. *British Journal of Psychology, 64*, 391–397.

Evans, N., & Levinson, S. C. (2009). The myth of language universals: Language diversity and its importance for cognitive science. *Behavioral and Brain Sciences, 32*(5), 429–492.

Everitt, B. J., & Robbins, T. W. (2016). Drug addiction: updating actions to habits to compulsions ten years on. *Annual Review of Psychology, 67*, 23–50.

Eysenck, M. W. (1978). Levels of processing: Critique. *British Journal of Psychology, 69*, 157–169.

F

Fahsing, I. A., & Ask, K. (2016) The making of an expert detective: The role of experience in English and Norwegian police officers' investigative decision making. *Psychology, Crime & Law, 22*(3), 1–44.

Fahsing, I. A., & Ask, K. (2018). In search of indicators of detective aptitude: Police recruits' logical reasoning and ability to generate investigative hypotheses. *Journal of Police and Criminal Psychology, 33*(1), 21–34.

Farah, M. J. (1990). *Visual Agnosia: Disorders of Object Recognition and What They Tell us About Normal Vision*. MIT Press.

Farah, M. J., & Hammond, K. M. (1988). Mental rotation and orientation-invariant object recognition: Dissociable processes. *Cognition, 29*, 29–46.

Farah, M. J., Hammond, K. M., Levine, D. N., & Calvanio, R. (1988a). Electrophysiological evidence for a shared representational medium for visual images and visual percepts. *Journal of Experimental Psychology: General, 117*, 248–257.

Farah, M. J., Hammond, K. M., Levine, D. N., & Calvanio, R. (1988b). Visual and spatial mental imagery: Dissociable systems of representation. *Cognitive Psychology, 20*, 439–462.

Farrell, S., Oberauer, K., Greaves, M., Pasiecznik, K., Lewandowsky, S., & Jarrold, C. (2016). A test of interference versus decay in working memory: Varying distraction within lists in a complex span task. *Journal of Memory and Language, 90*, 66–87.

Farrer, C., & Frith, C. D. (2002). Experiencing oneself vs. another person as being the cause of an action: The neural correlates of the experience of agency. *Neuroimage, 15*(3), 596–603.

Fasolo, B., McClelland, G. H., & Lange, K. A. (2005). The effect of site design and interattribute correlations on interactive web-based decisions. In C. P. Haugtved, K. Machleit, & R. Yalch (Eds.), *Online consumer psychology: Understanding and influencing behaviour in the virtual world* (pp. 325–344). Lawrence Erlbaum.

Fawcett, J. M., Russell, E. J., Peace, K. A., & Christie, J. (2013). Of guns and geese: A meta-analytic review of the 'weapon focus' literature. *Psychology, Crime & Law, 19*(1), 35–66.

Federenko, E., & Blank, I. A. (2020). Broca's area is not a natural kind. *Trends in Cognitive Sciences, 24*(4), 270–284.

Feinberg, T. E., & Farah, M. J. (2004). The agnosias. In W. G. Bradley (Ed.), *Neurology in Clinical Practice: Principles of Diagnosis and Management*. Taylor & Francis.

Feinberg, T. E., Schindler, R. J., Flanagan, N. G., & Haber, L. D. (1992). Two alien hand syndromes. *Neurology, 42*(1), 19–19.

Feldman, A. G. (1966). Functional tuning of nervous system with control of movement or maintenance of a steady posture. 2. Controllable parameters of muscles. *Biophysics-USSR, 11*(3), 565.

Feldman, A. G. (1986). Once more on the equilibrium-point hypothesis lambda-model for motor control. *Journal of Motor Behavior, 18*(1), 17–54.

Feldman, A. G., & Latash, M. L. (2005). Testing hypotheses and the advancement of science: Recent attempts to falsify the equilibrium point hypothesis. *Experimental Brain Research, 161*(1), 91–103.

Feldman, B. (2016). The Trolley Problem is the internet's most philosophical meme. *New York*, 9 August.

Feldman, R. S. (2004). *Understanding Psychology* (7th ed.). McGraw-Hill.

Ferguson, K. A., & Cardin, J. A. (2020). Mechanisms underlying gain modulation in the cortex. *Nature Reviews Neuroscience*, 1–13.

Fermin, A. S., Sakagami, M., Kiyonari, T., Li, Y., Matsumoto, Y., & Yamagishi, T. (2016). Representation of economic preferences in the structure and function of the amygdala and prefrontal cortex. *Scientific Reports, 6*, 20982.

Fernandez-Duque, D., & Johnson, M. L. (2002). Cause and effect theories of attention: The role of conceptual metaphors. *Review of General Psychology, 6*(2), 153–165.

Ferreira, F. (2003). Prosody. In L. Nadel (Ed.), *Encyclopedia of Cognitive Science* (pp. 762–768). Macmillan Reference Ltd.

Ferreira, F., Christianson, K., & Hollingworth, A. (2001). Misinterpretations of garden-path sentences: Implications for models of sentence processing and reanalysis. *Journal of Psycholinguistic Research, 30*, 3–20.

Ferri, S., Kolster, H., Jastorff, J., & Orban, G. A. (2013). The overlap of the EBA and the MT/V5 cluster. *NeuroImage, 66*, 412–425.

Ferris, C. F., Kulkarni, P., Sullivan, J. M., Harder, J. A., Messenger, T. L., & Febo, M. (2005). Pup suckling is more rewarding than cocaine: Evidence from functional magnetic resonance imaging and three-dimensional computational analysis. *Journal of Neuroscience, 25*, 149–156.

Fiebelkorn, I. C., & Kastner, S. (2020). Functional specialization in the attention network. *Annual Review of Psychology, 71*, 221–249.

Fiedler, K. (1988). The dependence of the conjunction fallacy on subtle linguistic factors. *Psychological Research, 50*, 123–129.

Field, J. (2003). *Psycholinguistics: A Resource Book for Students*. Routledge.

Field, M., Mogg, K., & Bradley, B. P. (2006). Attention to drug-related cues in drug abuse and addiction: component processes. In R. Wiers & A. Stacy (Eds.), *Handbook of Implicit Cognition and Addiction*. Sage.

Field, T., Pickens, J., Fox, N. A., Gonzalez, J., & Nawrocki, T. (1998). Facial expression and EEG responses to happy and sad face/voices by 3-month-old infants of depressed mothers. *British Journal of Developmental Psychology, 16*, 486–494.

Fillmore, M. T., Kelly, T. H., Rush, C. R., & Hays, L. (2001). Retrograde facilitation of memory by triazolam: Effects on automatic processes. *Psychopharmacology, 158*, 314–321.

Finke, R. A. (1989). *Principles of Mental Imagery*. MIT Press.

Finke, R. A., Ward, T. B., & Smith, S. M. (1992). *Creative Cognition: Theory, Research, Applications*. MIT Press.

Finucane, M. L., Alhakami, A., Slovic, P., & Johnson, S. M. (2000). The affect heuristic in judgments of risks and benefits. *Journal of Behavioral Decision Making, 13*, 1–17.

Finucane, M. L., Peters, E., & Slovic, P. (2003). Judgment and decision making: The dance of affect and reason. In S. L. Schneider & J. Shanteau (Eds.), *Emerging Perspectives on Judgment and Decision Research*. Cambridge University Press.

Fisher, R. P., & Geiselman, R. E. (2018). Investigative interviewing. In V. B. Van Hasselt & M. Bourke (Eds.), *Handbook of Behavioral Criminology: Contemporary Strategies and Issues* (pp. 451–465). Springer.

Fisher, R. P., & Schreiber, N. (2017). Interview protocols to improve eyewitness memory. In *The Handbook of Eyewitness Psychology: Volume I* (pp. 53–80). Psychology Press.

Fisk, J. E., & Pidgeon, N. (1996). Component probabilities and the conjunction fallacy: Resolving signed summation and the low component model in a contingent approach. *Acta Psychologica, 94*, 1–20.

Fiske, S. T. (2010). Venus and Mars or down to Earth: Stereotypes and realities of gender differences. *Perspectives on Psychological Science, 5*(6), 688–692.

Fitzgerald, R. J., Price, H. L., & Valentine, T. (2018). Eyewitness identification: Live, photo, and video lineups. *Psychology, Public Policy, and Law, 24*(3), 307–325.

Fitzpatrick, P., Harada, K., Kemp, C. C., Matsumoto, Y., Yokoi, K., & Yoshida, E. (2016). Humanoids. In *Springer Handbook of Robotics* (pp. 1789–1818). Springer.

Fivush, R. (2011). The development of autobiographical memory. *Annual Review of Psychology, 62*, 559–582.

Flach, R., Knoblich, G., & Prinz, W. (2004). Recognizing one's own clapping: The role of temporal cues. *Psychological Research – Psychologische Forschung, 69*(1–2), 147–156.

Flash, T., & Handzel, A. A. (2007). Affine differential geometry analysis of human arm movements. *Biological Cybernetics, 96*(6), 577–601.

Flash, T., & Hochner, B. (2005). Motor primitives in vertebrates and invertebrates. *Current Opinion in Neurobiology, 15*(6), 660–666.

Flash, T., & Hogan, N. (1985). The coordination of arm movements: An experimentally confirmed mathematical-model. *Journal of Neuroscience, 5*(7), 1688–1703.

Flavell, J. H. (1979). Metacognition and cognitive monitoring: A new area of cognitive–developmental inquiry. *American Psychologist, 34*(10), 906–911.

Fleck, J. I., & Weisberg, R. W. (2004). The use of verbal protocols as data: An analysis of insight in the candle problem. *Memory and Cognition, 32*, 990–1006.

Fleming, L. (2017). Phoneme inventory size and the transition from monoplanar to dually patterned speech. *Journal of Language Evolution, 2*(1), 52–66.

Fleming, R. W., & Storrs, K. R. (2019). Learning to see stuff. *Current Opinion in Behavioral Sciences, 30*, 100–108.

Foa, E. B., & McNally, R. J. (1986). Sensitivity to feared stimuli in obsessive-compulsives: A dichotic listening analysis. *Cognitive Therapy and Research, 10*, 477–485.

Fodor, J. A. (1983). *The Modularity of Mind: An Essay on Faculty Psychology*. MIT Press.

Fodor, J. A. (1998). *Concepts: Where Cognitive Science Went Wrong*. Clarendon Press.

Fodor, J. A. (1999). Let your brain alone. *London Review of Books, 21*, 19.

Foer, J. (2011). Secrets of a mind-gamer. *New York Times*, 15 February.

Foer, J. (2012). *Moonwalking with Einstein: The Art and Science of Remembering Everything*. Penguin Books.

Fogassi, L., Ferrari, P. F., Gesierich, B., Rozzi, S., Chersi, F., & Rizzolatti, G. (2005). Parietal lobe: From action organization to intention understanding. *Science, 308*(5722), 662–667.

Foot, P. (1967). The problem of abortion and the doctrine of the double effect. *Oxford Review, 5*, 1–5.

Ford, M. (1995). Two modes of mental representation and problem solution in syllogistic reasoning. *Cognition, 54*, 1–71.

Forgas, J. P. (1995). Mood and judgment: The Affect Infusion Model (AIM). *Psychological Bulletin, 117*, 39–66.

Forslund, H. B., Torgerson, J. S., Sjöström, L., & Lindroos, A. K. (2005). Snacking frequency in relation to energy intake and food choices in obese men and women compared to a reference population. *International Journal of Obesity, 29*(6), 711–719.

Forster, K. I. (1979). Levels of processing and the structure of the language processor. In W. E. Cooper & E. Walker (Eds.), *Sentence Processing: Psycholinguistic essays presented to Merrill Garrett*. Erlbaum.

Forster, K. I. (1989). Basic issues in lexical processing. In W. Marslen-Wilson (Ed.), *Lexical Representation and Process* (pp. 75–107). The MIT Press.

Forster, K. I., & Davis, C. (1984). Repetition priming and frequency attenuation in lexical access. *Journal of Experimental Psychology: Learning, Memory, and Cognition, 10*, 680–698.

Foss, D. J. (1969). Decision processes during sentence comprehension: Effects of lexical item difficulty and position upon reaction times. *Journal of Verbal Learning and Verbal Behavior, 8*, 457–462.

Foss, D. J. (1970). Some effects of ambiguity upon sentence comprehension. *Journal of Verbal Learning and Verbal Behavior, 9*, 699–706.

Foster, D. H., & Gilson, S. J. (2002). Recognizing novel three-dimensional objects by summing signals from parts and views. *Proceedings of the Royal Society of London Series B – Biological Sciences, 269*(1503), 1939–1947.

Fougnie, D., & Marois, R. (2006). Distinct capacity limits for attention and working memory: Evidence from attentive tracking and visual working memory paradigms. *Psychological Science, 17*(6), 526–534.

Foulsham, T., Walker, E., & Kingstone, A. (2011). The where, what and when of gaze allocation in the lab and the natural environment. *Vision Research, 51*(17), 1920–1931.

Fox Tree, J. E. (1995). The effects of false starts and repetitions on the processing of subsequent words in spontaneous speech. *Journal of Memory and Language, 34*, 709–738.

Fox Tree, J. E. (2001). Listeners' uses of um and uh in speech comprehension. *Memory & Cognition, 29*, 320–326.

Franconeri, S. L., Alvarez, G. A., & Enns, J. T. (2007). How many locations can be selected at once? *Journal of Experimental Psychology: Human Perception and Performance, 33*(5), 1003–1012.

Frankish, K. (2016). Illusionism as a theory of consciousness. *Journal of Consciousness Studies, 23*(11–12), 11–39.

Franklin, S., Howard, D., & Patterson, K. (1994). Abstract word meaning deafness. *Cognitive Neuropsychology, 11*, 1–34.

Franz, V. H. (2001). Action does not resist visual illusions. *Trends in Cognitive Sciences, 5*(11), 457–459.

Frauenfelder, U. H., Scholen, M., & Content, A. (2001). Bottom-up inhibition in lexical selection: Phonological mismatch effects in spoken word recognition, *Language and Cognitive Processes, 16*, 583–607.

Frazier, L. (1979). *On Comprehending Sentences: Syntactic Parsing Strategies*. Indiana University Linguistics Club.

Frazier, L. (1987). Sentence processing. In M. Coltheart (Ed.), *Attention and Performance, Volume 12: The Psychology of Reading* (pp. 559–586). Erlbaum.

Frazier, L. (1989). Against lexical generation of syntax. In W. D. Marslen-Wilson (Ed.), *Lexical Representation and Process*. The MIT Press.

Frederick, S., Lee, L., & Baskin, E. (2014). The limits of attraction. *Journal of Marketing Research, 51*, 487–507.

Freud, S. (1900/1976). *The Interpretation of Dreams*. Hogarth.

Freud, S. (1914). The psychopathology of everyday life (A. A. Brill, Trans.). T. Fisher Unwin. (Original work published 1901.)

Freud, S. (1922). *Introductory Lectures on Psycho-Analysis*. George Allen, & Unwin.

Frijda, N. H. (1986). *The Emotions*. Cambridge University Press.

Frijda, N. H., & Scherer, K. R. (2009). Emotion definition (psychological perspectives). In D. Sander & K. R. Scherer (Eds.), *Oxford Companion to Emotion and the Affective Sciences* (pp. 142–143). Oxford University Press.

Friston, K. (2018). Does predictive coding have a future? *Nature Neuroscience, 21*(8), 1019.

Frith, C. (2012). Explaining delusions of control: The comparator model 20 years on. *Consciousness and Cognition, 21*(1), 52–54.

Frith, C. D., & Frith, U. (1999). Interacting minds: A biological basis. *Science, 286*(5445), 1692–1695.

Frith, U., & Frith, C. D. (2003). Development and neurophysiology of mentalizing. *Philosophical Transactions of the Royal Society B-Biological Sciences, 358*(1431), 459–473.

Fromkin, V. (1971). The non-anomalous nature of anomalous utterances. *Language, 51*, 696–719.

Fromkin, V. (Ed.) (1973). *Speech Errors as Linguistic Evidence*. Mouton.

Fromkin, V., Krashen, S., Curtiss, S., Rigler, D., & Rigler, M. (1974). The development of language in Genie: A case of language acquisition beyond the 'critical period'. *Brain and Language, 1*, 81–107.

Fromkin, V., Rodman, R., & Hyams, N. M. (2003). *An Introduction to Language*. Thomson/Heinle.

Fromkin, V., Rodman, R., & Hyams, N. (2010). *An Introduction to Language* (9th ed.). Wadsworth Cengage Learning.

Fromkin, V., Rodman, R., & Hyams, N. (2018). *An introduction to language* (11th ed.). Cengage Learning.

Frost, R., Katz, L., & Bentin, S. (1987). Strategies for visual word recognition and orthographical depth: A multilingual comparison. *Journal of Experimental Psychology: Human Perception and Performance, 13*, 104–115.

Fugelsang, J., Stein, C., Green, A., & Dunbar, K. (2004). Theory and data interactions of the scientific mind: Evidence from the molecular and the cognitive laboratory. *Canadian Journal of Experimental Psychology, 58*, 132–141.

Funnell, E. (1983). Phonological processes in reading: New evidence form acquired dyslexia. *British Journal of Psychology, 74*, 159–180.

Fusser, F., Linden, D. E. J., Rahm, B., Hampel, H., Haenschel, C., & Mayer, J. S. (2011). Common capacity-limited neural mechanisms of selective attention and spatial working memory encoding. *European Journal of Neuroscience, 34*(5), 827–838.

G

Gage, N. M., & Baars, B. J. (2018). Language and thought. In N. M. Gage & B. J. Baars (Eds.), *Fundamentals of Cognitive Neuroscience* (2nd ed.) (pp. 185–214). Academic Press.

Gagnepain, P., Henson, R. N., & Anderson, M. C. (2014). Suppressing unwanted memories reduces their unconscious influence via targeted cortical inhibition. *Proceedings of the National Academy of Sciences, 111*(13), 1310–1319.

Gainotti, G. (2000). What the locus of brain lesion tells us about the nature of the cognitive defect underlying category-specific disorders: A review. *Cortex, 36,* 539–559.

Galaverna, F., Bueno, A. M., Morra, C. A., Roca, M., & Torralva, T. (2016). Analysis of errors in verbal fluency tasks inpatients with chronic schizophrenia. *European Journal of Psychiatry, 30*(4), 305–320.

Galifret, Y. (2006). Visual persistence and cinema? *C.R. Biologies, 329,* 369–385.

Gallace, A., Auvray, M., Tan, H. Z., & Spence, C. (2006). Visual transients impair the detection of tactile changes: A novel case of crossmodal change blindness? *Neuroscience Letters, 398,* 280–285.

Gallace, A., & Spence, C. (2014). *In Touch with the Future: The Sense of Touch From Cognitive Neuroscience to Virtual Reality.* Oxford University Press.

Gallace, A., Tan, H. Z., Haggard, P., & Spence, C. (2008). Short term memory for tactile stimuli, *Brain Research, 1190,* 132–142.

Gallace, A., Tan, H. Z., & Spence, C. (2006). The failure to detect tactile change: A tactile analogue of visual change blindness. *Psychonomic Bulletin & Review, 13,* 300–303.

Gallagher, M., & Ferrè, E. R. (2018). Cybersickness: A multisensory integration perspective. *Multisensory Research, 31*(7), 645–674.

Gallagher, S. (2012). Multiple aspects in the sense of agency. *New Ideas in Psychology, 30*(1), 15–31.

Gallagher, S. (2017). *Enactivist Interventions: Rethinking the Mind.* Oxford University Press.

Gallese, V., Fadiga, L., Fogassi, L., & Rizzolatti, G. (1996). Action recognition in the premotor cortex. *Brain, 119,* 593–609.

Gallese, V., Gernsbacher, M. A., Heyes, C., Hickok, G., & Iacoboni, M. (2011). Mirror neuron forum. *Perspectives on Psychological Science, 6*(4), 369–407.

Galotti, K. M. (2007). Decision structuring in important real-life choices. *Psychological Science, 18,* 320–325.

Galotti, K. M., Baron, J., & Sabini, J. P. (1986). Individual differences in syllogistic reasoning: Deduction rules or mental models? *Journal of Experimental Psychology: General, 115,* 16–25.

Gandour, J., Ponglorpisit, S., Khunadorn, F., & Dechongkit, S. (1992). Lexical tones in Thai after unilateral brain damage. *Brain and Language, 43,* 275–307.

Gangemi, A., Mancini, F., & Johnson-Laird, P. N. (2013). Models and cognitive change in psychopathology. *Journal of Cognitive Psychology, 25*(2), 157–164.

Ganis, G., Thompson, W. L., & Kosslyn, S. (2004). Brain areas underlying visual mental imagery and visual perception: An fMRI study. *Cognitive Brain Research, 20,* 226–241.

Gara, M. A., Woolfolk, R. L., Cohen, B. D., Goldston, R. B., Allen, L. A., & Novalany, J. (1993). Perception of self and other in major depression. *Journal of Abnormal Psychology, 102,* 93–100.

Gardner, W. L., Gabriel, S., & Lee, A. (1999). 'I' value freedom, but 'we' value relationships: Self-construal priming mimics cultural differences in judgment. *Psychological Science, 10,* 321–326.

Garnham, A., Shillock, R. C., Brown, G. D., Mill, A. I. D., & Culter, A. (1981). Slips of the tongue in the London-Lund Corpus of spontaneous conversation. In G. Brown & A. Cutler (Eds.), *Slips of the Tongue and Language Production* (pp. 251–263). Mouton.

Garrett, B. L. (2011). *Convicting the Innocent: Where Criminal Prosecutions Go Wrong.* Harvard University Press.

Garrett, M. F. (1975). The analysis of sentence production. In G. Bower (Ed.) *The Psychology of Learning and Motivation* (volume 9, pp. 133–177). Academic Press.

Garrett, M. F. (1980). Levels of processing in sentence production. In B. Butterworth (Ed.), *Language Production, Volume 1: Speech and Talk* (pp. 177–220). Academic Press.

Garrett, M. F. (1982). Production of speech: Observations from normal and pathological language use. In A. W. Ellis (Ed.), *Normality and Pathology in Cognitive Function* (pp. 19–76). Academic Press.

Garrett, M. F. (1992). Disorders of lexical selection. *Cognition, 42,* 143–180.

Gaskell, M. G., & Marslen-Wilson, W. D. (1997). Integrating form and meaning: A distributed model of speech perception. *Language and Cognitive Processes, 12,* 613–656.

Gassert, R., & Dietz, V. (2018). Rehabilitation robots for the treatment of sensorimotor deficits: A neurophysiological perspective. *Journal of Neuroengineering and Rehabilitation, 15*(1), 46.

Gathercole, S. E., & Baddeley A. D. (1993). *Working Memory and Language.* Psychology Press.

Gathercole, S. E., & Baddeley, A. D. (1989). Evaluation of the role of phonological STM in the development of vocabulary in children: A longitudinal study. *Journal of Memory & Language, 28,* 200–213.

Gathercole, S. E., & Baddeley, A. D. (1990). Phonological memory deficits in language disordered children: Is there a causal connection? *Journal of Memory and Language, 29,* 336–360.

Gathercole, S. E., Hitch, G. J., Service, E., & Martin, A. J. (1997). Short-term memory and long-term learning in children. *Developmental Psychology, 33,* 966–979.

Gauthier, I., Tarr, M. J., Moylan, J., Skudlarski, P., Gore, J. C., & Anderson, A. W. (2000). The fusiform 'face area' is part of a network that processes faces at the individual level. *Journal of Cognitive Neuroscience, 12*(3), 495–504.

Gavansk, I., & Roskos-Ewoldsen, D. (1991). Representativeness and conjoint probability. *Journal of Personality and Social Psychology, 61,* 181–192.

Gazzaley, A., & Nobre, A. C. (2012). Top-down modulation: Bridging selective attention and working memory. *Trends in Cognitive Sciences, 16*(2), 129–135.

Gazzaniga, M. (1980). The role of language for conscious experience: Observations from split-brain man. *Progress in Brain Research, 54,* 689–696.

Gazzaniga, M. S. (1981). 1981 Nobel Prize for physiology or medicine. *Science, 214*(4520), 517–518.

Gazzaniga, M. S. (1983). Right hemisphere language following brain bisection: A 20-year perspective. *American Psychologist, 38*(5), 525–537.

Gazzaniga, M. S. (2005). Forty-five years of split-brain research and still going strong. *Nature Reviews Neuroscience, 6*(8), 653–659.

Gazzaniga, M. S., Bogen, J. E., & Sperry, R. W. (1965). Observations on visual perception after disconnexion of the cerebral hemispheres in man. *Brain, 88*(2), 221–236.

Gazzaniga, M. S., Mangun, G., & Ivry, R. (Eds.) (1998). *Cognitive Neuroscience: The Biology of the Mind.* W. W. Norton & Co.

Gazzaniga, M. S., & Sperry, R. W. (1967). Language after section of the cerebral commissures. *Brain, 90,* 131–148.

Gebhard, J. W., & Mowbray, G. H. (1959). On discriminating the rate of visual flicker and auditory flutter. *American Journal of Psychology, 72*(4), 521–529.

Geiselman, R. E., Fisher, R. P., Firstenberg, I., Hutton, L. A., Sullivan, S. J., Avetissian, I. V., & Prosk, A. L. (1984). Enhancement of eyewitness memory: An empirical evaluation of the cognitive interview. *Journal of Police Science & Administration, 12,* 74–80.

Geisler, W. S., & Kersten, D. (2002). Illusions, perception and Bayes. *Nature Neuroscience, 5*(6), 508–510.

Gell-Mann, M., & Ruhlen, M. (2011). The origin and evolution of word order. *Proceedings of the National Academy of Sciences, 108*(42), 17290–17295.

Gelman, S. A., & Wellman, H. (1991). Insides and essences: Early understandings of the non-obvious. *Cognition, 38,* 213–244.

Gentner, T. Q., Fenn, K. M., Margoliash, D., & Nusbaum, H. C. (2006). Recursive syntactic pattern learning by songbirds. *Nature, 440,* 1204–1207.

Gentry, S. V., Gauthier, A., Ehrstrom, B. L. E., Wortley, D., Lilienthal, A., Car, L. T., Dauwels-Okutsu, S., Nikolaou, C. K., Zary, N., Campbell, J., & Car, J. (2019). Serious gaming and gamification education in health professions: Systematic review. *Journal of Medical Internet Research, 21*(3), e12994.

George, A. M., Brown, P. M., Scholz, B., Scott-Parker, B., & Rickwood, D. (2018). 'I need to skip a song because it sucks': Exploring mobile phone use while driving among young adults. *Transportation Research Part F: Traffic Psychology and Behaviour, 58,* 382–391.

George, M. S., & Aston-Jones, G. (2010). Noninvasive techniques for probing neurocircuitry and treating illness: Vagus nerve stimulation (VNS), transcranial magnetic stimulation (TMS) and transcranial direct current stimulation (tDCS). *Neuropsychopharmacology: Official Publication of the American College of Neuropsychopharmacology [online], 35*(1), 301–316. Available at: http://www.pubmedcentral.nih.gov/articlerender.fcgi?artid=3055429&tool=pmcentrez&rendertype=abstract Direct source: http://www.nature.com/npp/journal/v35/n1/full/npp200987a.html.

Gepshtein, S., Seydell, A., & Trommershauser, J. (2007). Optimality of human movement under natural variations of visual-motor uncertainty. *Journal of Vision, 7*(5).

Gerbella, M., Caruana, F., & Rizzolatti, G. (2019). Pathways for smiling, disgust and fear recognition in blindsight patients. *Neuropsychologia, 128,* 6–13.

German, T. B., & Barrett, H. C. (2005). Functional fixity in a technologically sparse culture. *Psychological Science, 16,* 1–5.

Gertel, V. H., Zhang, H., & Diaz, M. T. (2020). Stronger right hemisphere functional connectivity supports executive aspects of language in older adults. *Brain and Language, 206,* July, 104771.

Geskin, J., & Behrmann, M. (2018). Congenital prosopagnosia without object agnosia? A literature review. *Cognitive Neuropsychology, 35*(1–2), 4–54.

Gfeller, K., Christ, A., Witt, S., & Mehr, M. (2003). The effects of familiarity and complexity on appraisal of complex songs by cochlear implant recipients and normal hearing adults. *Journal of Music Therapy, 40*(2), 78–112.

Gibson, J. J. (1962). Observations on active touch. *Psychological Review, 69*(6), 477–491.

Gibson, J. J. (1979). *The Ecological Approach to Visual Perception.* Houghton Mifflin.

Giese, M. A., & Poggio, T. (2003). Neural mechanisms for the recognition of biological movements. *Nature Reviews Neuroscience, 4*(3), 179–192.

Gigerenzer, G. (1993). The bounded rationality of probabilistic mental models. In K. I. Manktelow & D. E. Over (Eds.), *Rationality: Psychological and Philosophical perspectives.* Routledge.

Gigerenzer, G. (2007). *Gut Feelings.* Allen Lane.

Gigerenzer, G., & Hug, K. (1992). Domain specific reasoning: Social contracts, cheating, and perspective change. *Cognition, 43,* 127–171.

Gigerenzer, G., Todd, P. M., & ABC Research Group (1999). *Simple Heuristics That Make us Smart.* Oxford University Press.

Gilbert, D. T., Pinel, E. C., Wilson, T. D., Blumberg, S. J., & Wheatley, T. P. (1998). Immune neglect: A source of durability bias in affective forecasting. *Journal of Personality and Social Psychology, 75*(3), 617–638.

Gilhooly, K. J. (2005). Working memory and strategies in reasoning. In M. J. Roberts & E. J. Newton (Eds.), *Methods of Thought: Individual Differences in Reasoning Strategies.* Psychology Press.

Gilhooly, K. J., & Falconer, W. (1974). Concrete and abstract terms and relations in testing a rule. *Quarterly Journal of Experimental Psychology, 26,* 355–359.

Gilhooly, K. J., Fioratou, E., Anthony, S., & Wynn, V. (2007). Divergent thinking: Strategies and executive involvement in generating novel uses for familar objects. *British Journal of Psychology, 98,* 611–625.

Gilhooly, K. J., Georgiou, G. J., Sirota, M., & Paphiti-Galeano, A. (2015). Incubation and suppression processes in creative problem solving. *Thinking and Reasoning, 21,* 147–164.

Gilhooly, K. J., Georgiou, G., Garrison, J., Reston, J., & Sirota, M. (2012). Don't wait to incubate: Immediate versus delayed incubation in divergent thinking. *Memory & Cognition, 40*(6), 966–975.

Gilhooly, K. J., Logie, R. H., & Wynn, V. (1999). Syllogistic reasoning tasks, working memory and skill. *European Journal of Cognitive Psychology, 11,* 473–498.

Gilhooly, K. J., Logie, R. H., & Wynn, V. (2002). Syllogistic reasoning tasks and working memory: Evidence from sequential presentation of premises. *Current Psychology, 21,* 111–120.

Gilhooly, K. J., Logie, R. H., Wetherick, N. E., & Wynn, V. (1993). Working memory and strategies in syllogistic reasoning tasks. *Memory and Cognition, 21,* 115–124.

Gilhooly, K. J., & Murphy, P. (2005). Differentiating insight from non-insight problems. *Thinking and Reasoning, 11,* 279–302.

Gilhooly, K. J., Phillips, L. H., Wynn, V. E., Logie, R. H., & Della Sala, S. (1999). Planning processes and age in the five-disc Tower of London task. *Thinking and Reasoning, 5,* 339–361.

Gilhooly, K. J., & Webb, M. E. (2018). Working memory and insight problem solving. In F. Vallee-Tourangeau (Ed.), *Insight: On the Origin of New Ideas* (pp. 105–109). Routledge.

Gilhooly, K. J., Wynn, V. E., Phillips, L. H., Logie, R. H., & Della Sala, S. (2002). Visuo-spatial and verbal working memory in the five-disc Tower of London task. *Thinking and Reasoning, 8,* 165–178.

Gladwell, M. (2009). *Outliers: The Story of Success.* Penguin Books.

Gladwell, M. (2013). Complexity and the ten-year-rule. *The New Yorker,* 21 August.

Glancy, G. D., Bradford, J. M., & Fedak, L. (2002). A comparison of R. v. Stone with R. v. Parks: Two cases of automatism. *Journal of the American Academy of Psychiatry and the Law, 30*(4), 541–547.

Glanzer, M., & Razel, M. (1974). The size of the unit in short-term storage. *Journal of Verbal Learning & Verbal Behavior, 12,* 114–131.

Glaze, J. A. (1928). The association value of nonsense syllables. *Journal of Genetic Psychology, 35,* 255–269.

Glenberg, A. M. (1977). Influences of retrieval process on the spacing effect in free recall. *Journal of Experimental Psychology: Human Learning and Memory, 3,* 282–294.

Glenberg, A. M., & Kaschak, M. P. (2004). The body's contribution to language. *The Psychology of Learning and Motivation, 45,* 93–126.

Glover, S. (2004). Separate visual representations in the planning and control of action. *Behavioral and Brain Sciences, 27,* 3–78.

Glucksberg, S., & Cowan, G. N. (1970). Memory for nonattended auditory material. *Cognitive Psychology, 1,* 149–156.

Gobet, F. (2019). *The Psychology of Chess.* Routledge.

Gobet, F., Chassy, P., & Bilalic, M. (2011). *Foundations of Cognitive Psychology.* McGraw-Hill Education.

Gobet, F., & Ereku, M. H. (2014). Checkmate to deliberate practice: The case of Magnus Carlsen. *Frontiers in Psychology, 5,* 1–3.

Gobet, F., & Simon, H. A. (1996). Recall of rapidly presented random chess positions is a function of skill. *Psychonomic Bulletin & Review, 3,* 159–163.

Gobet, F., & Waters, A. J. (2003). The role of constraints in expert memory. *Journal of Experimental Psychology: Learning, Memory and Cognition, 29,* 1082–1094.

Godden, D. R., & Baddeley, A. D. (1975). Context-dependent memory in two natural environments: On land and underwater. *British Journal of Psychology, 66,* 325–332.

Godden, D. R., & Baddeley, A. D. (1980). When does context influence recognition memory? *British Journal of Psychology, 71,* 99–104.

Goel, V. (2005). Cognitive neuroscience of deductive reasoning. In K. J. Holyoak & R. G. Morrison (Eds.), *The Cambridge Handbook of Thinking and Reasoning.* Cambridge University Press.

Goel, V., Buchelm, C., Rith, C., & Olan, J. (2000). Dissociation of mechanisms underlying syllogistic reasoning. *Neuroimage, 12,* 504–514.

Goel, V., & Dolan, R. J. (2003). Reciprocal neural response within lateral and ventral medial prefrontal cortex during hot and cold reasoning. *Neuroimage, 20*(4), 2314–2321.

Goel, V., Vartanian, O., Bartolo, A., Hakim, L., Ferraro, A. M., Isella, V., Appollonio, I., Drei, S., & Nichelli, P. (2013). Lesions to right prefrontal cortex impair real-world planning through premature commitments. *Neuropsychologia, 51,* 713–724.

Goh, W. D., & Lu, S. H. X. (2012). Testing the myth of encoding-retrieval match. *Memory & Cognition, 40,* 28–39.

Goldberg, R. F., Perfetti, C. F., & Schneider, W. (2006). Perceptual knowledge retrieval activates sensory brain regions. *Journal of Neuroscience, 26,* 4917–4921.

Goldenberg, O., Larson, J. J., & Wiley, J. (2013). Goal instructions, response format and idea generation in groups. *Small Group Research, 44,* 227–256.

Goldin-Meadow, S. (1982). The resilience of recursion: A study of a communication system developed without a conventional language model. In E. Wanner & L. R. Gleitman (Eds.), *Language Acquisition: The State of the Art.* Cambridge University Press.

Goldin-Meadow, S. (2003). *Hearing Gesture: How Our Hands Help us Think.* Belknap Press of Harvard University Press.

Goldin-Meadow, S., & Mylander, C. (1990). The role of parental input in the development of a morphological system. *Journal of Child Language, 17,* 527–563.

Goldin-Meadow, S., Nusbaum, H., Kelly, S. D., & Wagner, S. (2001). Explaining math: Gesturing lightens the load. *Psychological Science, 12*(6), 516–522.

Goldinger, S. D., Papesh, M. H., Barnhart, A. S., Hansen, W. A., & Hout, M. C. (2016). The poverty of embodied cognition. *Psychonomic Bulletin & Review, 23*(4), 959–978.

Goldman-Eisler, F. (1968). *Psycholinguistics: Experiments in Spontaneous Speech.* Academic Press.

Goldman-Rakic, P. S. (1992). Working memory and the mind. *Scientific American, 267,* 110–117.

Goldstein, D. G., & Gigerenzer, G. (2002). Models of ecological rationality: The recognition heuristic. *Psychological Review, 109,* 75–90.

Gollan, T. H., & Acenas, L. R. (2004). What is a TOT? Cognate and translation effects on tip-of-the-tongue states in Spanish-English and Tagalog-English bilinguals. *Journal of Experimental Psychology: Learning, Memory, and Cognition, 30*(1), 246–269.

Gollwitzer, P. M. (1999). Implementation intentions: Strong effects of simple plans. *American Psychologist, 54*(7), 493–503.

Golmohammadi, R., Darvishi, E., Faradmal, J., Poorolajal, J., & Aliabadi, M. (2020). Attention and short-term memory during occupational noise exposure considering task difficulty. *Applied Acoustics, 158.*

Gomila, T., & Calvo, P. (2008). Directions for an embodied cognitive science: Toward an integrated approach. In P. Calvo & T. Gomila (Eds.), *Handbook of Cognitive science: An Embodied*

Approach (pp. 1–25). Elsevier Science.

Gonzalez, J., Barros-Loscertales, A., Pulvermuller, F., Meseguer, V., & Sanjuan, A. (2006). Reading cinnamon activates olfactory brain regions. *Neuroimage, 32,* 906–912.

Goodale, M. A., & Milner, A. D. (1992). Separate visual pathways for perception and action. *Trends in Neurosciences, 15*(1), 20–25.

Goodglass, H. (1993). *Understanding Aphasia.* Academic Press.

Goodglass, H., & Geschwind, N. (1976). Language disorders (aphasia). In E. C. Carterette & M. P. Friedman (Eds.), *Handbook of Perception, Volume vii: Language and Speech.* Academic Press.

Goodglass, H., & Kaplan, E. (1983). *The Assessment of Aphasia and Related Disorders.* Lea & Febiger.

Goodglass, H., in collaboration with Kaplan, E., & Barresi, B. (2001) *Boston Diagnostic Aphasia Examination* (3rd ed.) [kit]. PRO-ED.

Goodrich, M. A., & Schultz, A. C. (2007). Human–robot interaction: A survey. *Foundations and Trends in Human–Computer Interaction, 1*(3), 203–275.

Gordon, W. J. J. (1961). *Synectics: The Development of Creative Capacity.* Harper & Row.

Gordon, W. J. J. (1981). *The New Art of the Possible: The Basic Course in Synectics.* Porpoise Books.

Gorgey, A. S. (2018). Robotic exoskeletons: The current pros and cons. *World Journal of Orthopedics, 9*(9), 112.

Gorman, M. E. (1986). How the possibility of error affects falsification on a task that models scientific problem solving. *British Journal of Psychology, 77,* 85–96.

Gosavi, R. S., & Hubbard, E. M. (2019). A colorful advantage in iconic memory. *Cognition, 187,* 32–37.

Goswami, U. (2002). Phonology, reading development, and dyslexia: Across-linguistic perspective. *Annals of Dyslexia, 52,* 139–163.

Gottfredson, L. S. (1997). Why g matters? The complexities of everyday life. *Intelligence, 24,* 79–132.

Goudeau, S., & Croizet, J. C. (2017). Hidden advantages and disadvantages of social class: How classroom settings reproducesocial inequality by staging unfair comparison. *Psychological Science, 28,* 162–170.

Goulden, R., Nation, P., & Read, J. (1990). How large can a receptive vocabulary be? *Applied Linguistics, 11,* 341–363.

Grabner, R. H., Stern, E., & Neubauer, A. (2007). Individual differences in chess expertise: A psychometric investigation. *Acta Psychologica, 124,* 398–420.

Graf, P., & Grondin, S. (2008). Time perception and time-based prospective memory. In J. Glicksohn & M. S. Myslobodsky (Eds.), *Timing the Future: The Case for a Time-Based Prospective Memory* (pp. 1–24). World Scientific.

Graf, P., & Schacter, D. L. (1985). Implicit and explicit memory for new associations in normal and amnesic subjects. *Journal of Experimental Psychology: Learning, Memory, and Cognition, 11,* 501–518.

Graf, P., & Schacter, D. L. (1987). Selective effects of interference on implicit and explicit memory for new associations. *Journal of Experimental Psychology: Learning, Memory, and Cognition, 13,* 45–53.

Graf, P., Squire, L. R., & Mandler, G. (1984). The information that amnesic patients do not forget. *Journal of Experimental Psychology: Learning, Memory, and Cognition, 10,* 164–178.

Graff-Radford, J., Rubin, M. N., Jones, D. T., Aksamit, A. J., Ahlskog, J. E., Knopman, D. S., Petersen, R. C., Boeve, B. F., & Josephs, K. A. (2013). The alien limb phenomenon. *Journal of Neurology, 260*(7), 1880–1888.

Grafton, S. T., Fadiga, L., Arbib, M. A., & Rizzolatti, G. (1997). Premotor cortex activation during observation and naming of familiar tools. *Neuroimage, 6*(4), 231–236.

Granhag, P. A., Ask, K., & Giolla, E. M. (2014). Eyewitness recall: An overview of estimator-based research. In D. S. Lindsay & T. J. Perfect (Eds.), *The SAGE Handbook of Applied Memory* (pp. 541–558). SAGE Publications.

Granhag, P. A., Strömwall, L. A., & Billings, J. F. (2003). 'I'll never forget the sinking ferry!' How social influence makes false memories surface. In M. Vanderhallen, G. Vervaeke, P. J. van Koppen, & J. Goethals (Eds.), *Much ado About Crime. Chapters on Psychology and law* (pp. 129–140). Politeia.

Graven, T., & Desebrock, C. (2018). Bouba or kiki with and without vision: Shape–audio regularities and mental images. *Acta Psychologica, 188,* 200–212.

Graziano, M. S. (2013). *Consciousness and the Social Brain.* Oxford University Press.

Graziano, M. S. (2016). Consciousness engineered. *Journal of Consciousness Studies, 23* (11–12), 98–115.

Graziano, M. S., Guterstam, A., Bio, B. J., & Wilterson, A. I. (2019). Toward a standard model of consciousness: Reconciling the attention schema, global workspace, higher-order thought, and illusionist theories. *Cognitive Neuropsychology,* 1–18.

Graziano, M. S., & Kastner, S. (2011). Human consciousness and its relationship to social neuroscience: A novel hypothesis. *Cognitive Neuroscience, 2*(2), 98–113.

Graziano, M. S., & Webb, T. W. (2014). A mechanistic theory of consciousness. *International Journal of Machine Consciousness, 6*(2), 163–176.

Green, A. J. K., & Gilhooly, K. J. (1990). Individual differences and effective learning procedures: The case of statistical computing. *International Journal of Man-Machine Studies, 33,* 97–119.

Green, C. S., & Bavelier, D. (2003). Action video game modifies visual selective attention. *Nature, 423*(6939), 534–537.

Green, C. S., & Bavelier, D. (2006a). Effect of action video games on the spatial distribution of visuospatial attention. *Journal of Experimental Psychology: Human Perception and Performance, 32*(6), 1465–1478.

Green, C. S., & Bavelier, D. (2006b). Enumeration versus multiple object tracking: The case of action video game players. *Cognition, 101*(1), 217–245.

Green, C. S., & Bavelier, D. (2007). Action-video-game experience alters the spatial resolution of vision. *Psychological Science, 18*(1), 88–94.

Green, K. P., Kuhl, P. K., Meltzoff, A. N., & Stevens, E. B. (1991). Integrating speech information across talkers, gender, and sensory modality: Female faces and male voices in the McGurk effect. *Perception & Psychophysics, 50,* 524–536.

Greenberg, D. L. (2007). Comment on 'Detecting awareness in the vegetative state'. *Science, 315,* 1221b.

Greenberg, J. H. (1963). Some universals of grammar with particular reference to the order of meaningful elements. In J. H. Greenberg, *Universals of Language* (pp. 58–90). MIT Press.

Greenberg, J. H. (Ed.) (1978). *Universals of Human Language.* Stanford University Press.

Greene, J. D., Sommerville, R. B., Nystrom, L. E., Darley, J. M., & Cohen, J. D. (2001). An fMRI investigation of emotional engagement in moral judgment. *Science, 293,* 2105–2108.

Greene, R. L. (1989). Spacing effects in memory: Evidence for a two process account. *Journal of Experimental Psychology: Learning, Memory and Cognition, 15,* 371–377.

Greenfield, P. M. (2005). Paradigms of cultural thought. In K. J. Holyoak & R. G. Morrison (Eds.), *The Cambridge Handbook of Thinking and Reasoning.* Cambridge University Press.

Greenfield, P. M., DeWinstanley, P., Kilpatrick, H., & Kaye, D. (1994). Action video games and informal education: Effects on strategies for dividing visual attention. *Journal of Applied Developmental Psychology, 15*(1), 105–123.

Greve, K. W., & Bauer, R. M. (1990). Implicit learning of new faces in prosopagnosia: An application of the mere-exposure paradigm. *Neuropsychologia, 28,* 1035–1041.

Grice, H. P. (1957). Meaning. *Philosophical Review, 66*(3).

Grice, H. P. (1975). Logic and conversation. In P. Cole & J. Morgan (Eds.), *Syntax and Semantics, Volume 3: Speech Acts* (pp. 41–58). Academic Press.

Griggs, R. A., & Cox, J. R. (1982). The elusive thematic-materials effect in Wason's selection task. *British Journal of Psychology, 73,* 407–420.

Grill-Spector, K., Weiner, K. S., Gomez, J., Stigliani, A., & Natu, V. S. (2018). The functional neuroanatomy of face perception: From brain measurements to deep neural networks. *Interface Focus, 8*(4), 20180013.

Grill-Spector, K., Weiner, K. S., Kay, K., & Gomez, J. (2017). The functional neuroanatomy of human face perception. *Annual Review of Vision Science, 3,* 167–196.

Grodner, D., Gibson, E., & Watson, D. (2005). The influence of contextual contrast on syntactic processing: Evidence for strong-interaction in sentence comprehension, *Cognition, 95,* 275–296.

Grodzinsky, Y., & Santi, A. (2008). The battle for Broca's region. *Trends in Cognitive Sciences, 12*(12), 474–480.

Groome, D., Dewart, H., Esgate, A., Gurney, K., Kemp, R., & Towell, N. (1999). *An Introduction to Cognitive Psychology: Processes and Disorders.* Psychology Press.

Grosjean, F. (1980). Spoken word recognition processes and the gating paradigm. *Perception and Psychophysics, 28,* 267–283.

Grosjean, F. (1985). The recognition of words after their acoustic offset: Evidence and implications. *Perception and Psychophysics, 38,* 299–310.

Grosjean, F. (2008). *Studying Bilinguals.* Oxford University Press.

Grosjean, F., & Gee, J. (1987). Prosodic structure and spoken word recognition. *Cognition, 25,* 135–155.

Gross, J. J. (2014). *Handbook of Emotion Regulation* (2nd ed.). Guilford Press.

Gross, M., Smith, A. P., Graveline, Y., Beaty, R., Schooler, J., & Seli, P. (2020). Comparing the phenomenological qualities of stimulus-independent thought, stimulus-dependent thought and dreams using experience sampling. *PsyArXiv,* 27 April.

Gross, R. G., & Grossman, M. (2008). Update on apraxia. *Current Neurology and Neuroscience Reports, 8*(6), 490–496.

Grossenbacher, P. G., & Lovelace, C. T. (2001). Mechanisms of synesthesia: Cognitive and physiological constraints. *Trends in Cognitive Sciences, 5*(1), 36–41.

Grossman, E. D., & Blake, R. (2002). Brain areas active during visual perception of biological motion. *Neuron, 35*(6), 1167–1175.

Grueter, M., Grueter, T., Bell, V., Horst, J., Laskowski, W., Sperling, K., Halligan, P. W., Ellis, H. D., & Kennerknecht, I. (2007). Hereditary prosopagnosia: The first case series. *Cortex, 43*(6), 734–749.

Grüter, T., Grüter, M., & Carbon, C. C. (2008). Neural and genetic foundations of face recognition and prosopagnosia. *Journal of Neuropsychology, 2,* 79–97.

Guclu, U., & van Gerven, M. A. J. (2015). Deep neural networks reveal a gradient in the complexity of neural representations across the ventral stream. *Journal of Neuroscience, 35*(27), 10005–10014.

Gudjonsson, G. H. (2018). *The Psychology of False Confessions: Forty Years of Science and Practice.* John Wiley & Sons Ltd.

Guitard, D., Saint-Aubin, J., Tehan, G., & Tolan, A. (2018). Does neighborhood size really cause the word length effect? *Memory & Cognition, 46*(2), 244–260.

Gunnars, T., & Bruck J. N. (2020). Visual perception. In J. Vonk & T. Shackelford (Eds.), *Encyclopedia of Animal Cognition and Behavior.* Springer.

Gunning, D., & Aha, D. W. (2019). DARPA's Explainable Artificial Intelligence Program. *AI Magazine, 40*(2), 44–58.

Gunns, R. E., Johnston, L., & Hudson, S. M. (2002). Victim selection and kinematics: A point-light investigation of vulnerability to attack. *Journal of Nonverbal Behavior, 26,* 129–158.

Gurney, D. J., Pine, K. J., & Wiseman, R. (2013). The gestural misinformation effect: Skewing eyewitness testimony through gesture. *American Journal of Psychology, 126,* 301–314.

Guthrie, L. G., Vallee-Tourangeau, F., Vallee-Tourangeau, G., & Howard, C. (2015). Learning and interactivity in solving a transformation problem. *Memory and Cognition, 43,* 723–735.

H

Haaga, D. A., Dyck, M. J., & Ernst, D. (1991). Empirical status of cognitive theory of depression. *Psychological Bulletin, 110,* 215–236.

Haber, R. N., & Standing, L. G. (1969). Direct measures of short-term visual storage. *Quarterly Journal of Experimental Psychology, 21,* 43–54.

Hacking, I. (1975). *The Emergence of Probability: A Philosophical Study of Early Ideas About Probability, Induction and Statistical Inference.* Cambridge University Press.

Hadzibeganovic, T., van den Noort, M., Bosch, P., Perc, M., van Kralingen, R., Mondt, K., & Coltheart, M. (2010). Cross-linguistic neuroimaging and dyslexia: A critical view. *Cortex, 46,* 1312–1316.

Haggard, P. (2001). The psychology of action. *British Journal of Psychology, 92,* 113–128.

Haggard, P. (2005). Conscious intention and motor cognition. *Trends in Cognitive Sciences, 9*(6), 290–295.

Haggard, P. (2017). Sense of agency in the human brain. *Nature Reviews Neuroscience, 18*(4), 196.

Haggard, P. (2019). The neurocognitive bases of human volition. *Annual Review of Psychology, 70,* 9–28.

Haggard, P., Clark, S., & Kalogeras, J. (2002). Voluntary action and conscious awareness. *Nature Neuroscience, 5*(4), 382–385.

Haggard, P., & Eimer, M. (1999). On the relation between brain potentials and the awareness of voluntary movements. *Experimental Brain Research, 126*(1), 128–133.

Hagoort, P., & Brown, C. M. (2000). ERP effects of listening to speech compared to reading: The P600/SPS to syntactic violations in spoken sentences and rapid serial visual presentation. *Neuropsychologia, 38,* 1531–1549.

Haken, H., Kelso, J. A. S., & Bunz, H. (1985). A theoretical model of phase transitions in human hand movements. *Biological Cybernetics, 51*(5), 347–356.

Hakim, N., Adam, K. C., Gunseli, E., Awh, E., & Vogel, E. K. (2019). Dissecting the neural focus of attention reveals distinct processes for spatial attention and object-based storage in visual working memory. *Psychological Science, 30*(4), 526–540.

Hall, D., & Riddoch, J. (2010). Word meaning deafness: Spelling words that are not understood. *Cognitive Neuropsychology, 14,* 1131–1164.

Hall, T. (1970). *Carl Friedrich Gauss: A Biography.* MIT Press.

Hamamé, C. M., Vidal, J. R., Ossandón, T., Jerbi, K., Dalal, S. S., Minotti, L., Bertrand, O., Kahane, P., & Lachaux, J.-P. (2012). Reading the mind's eye: Online detection of visuo-spatial working memory and visual imagery in the inferior temporal lobe. *NeuroImage, 59*(1), 872–879.

Hamann, S. B. (2012). Mapping discrete and dimensional emotions onto the brain: Controversies and consensus, *Trends in Cognitive Neurosciences, 16,* 458–466.

Hamann, S. B., Ely, T., Grafton, S., & Kilts, C. (1999). Amygdala activity related to enhanced memory for pleasant and aversive stimuli, *Nature Neuroscience, 2,* 289–293.

Hambrick, D. Z., Oswald, F. L., Altmann, M., Meinz, E. J., Gobet, F., & Campitelli, G. (2014). Deliberate practice: Is that all it takes to become an expert? *Intelligence, 45,* 34–45.

Hammond, K. R. (1996). *Human Judgment and Social Policy: Irreducible Uncertainty, Inevitable Error, Unavoidable Injustice.* Oxford University Press.

Hammond, K. R. (2001). Expansion of Egon Brunswik's psychology, 1955–1995. In K. R. Hammond & T. R. Stewart (Eds.), *The Essential Brunswik* (pp. 464–480). Oxford University Press.

Hampton, J. A. (1979). Polymorphous concepts in semantic memory. *Journal of Verbal Learning and Verbal Behavior, 18,* 441–461.

Hampton, J. A. (1981). An investigation of the nature of abstract concepts. *Memory and Cognition, 9,* 149–156.

Hampton, J. A., Aina, B., Andersson, J. M., Mirza, H. Z., & Parmar, S. (2012). The Rumsfeld effect: The unknown unknown. *Journal of Experimental Psychology: Learning, Memory and Cognition, 38,* 340–355.

Hancock, P. J. B., Bruce, V., & Burton, A. M. (2000). Recognition of unfamiliar faces. *Trends in Cognitive Sciences, 4*(9), 330–337.

Handzel, A., & Flash, T. (1999). Geometric methods in the study of human motor control. *Cognitive Studies, 6,* 1–13.

Hanley, J. R., & Young, A. W. (2019). ELD revisited: A second look at a neuropsychological impairment of working memory affecting retention of visuo-spatial material. *Cortex, 112,* 172–179.

Hanley, J. R., Young, A. W., & Pearson, N. (1991). Impairment of the visuo-spatial sketch pad. *Quarterly Journal of Experimental Psychology, 43A,* 101–125.

Hansen, P. G., & Jespersen, A. M. (2013). Nudge and the manipulation of choice: A framework for the responsible use of the nudge approach to behaviour change in public policy. *European Journal of Risk Regulation, 4*(1), 3–28.

Hardcastle, W. J., & Hewlett N. (Eds.) (1999). *Coarticulation.* Cambridge University Press.

Hardt, O., Nader, K., & Nadel, L. (2013). Decay happens: The role of active forgetting in memory. *Trends in Cognitive Sciences, 17*(3), 111–120.

Hardwick, R. M., Caspers, S., Eickhoff, S. B., & Swinnen, S. P. (2018). Neural correlates of action: Comparing meta-analyses of imagery, observation, and execution. *Neuroscience & Biobehavioral Reviews, 94,* 31–44.

Hare, R. D., Neumann, C. S., & Widiger, T. A. (2012). Psychopathy. In T. A. Widiger (Ed.), *The Oxford Handbook of Personality Disorders* (pp. 478–504). Oxford library of psychology. Oxford University Press.

Harley, T. A. (1995). *The Psychology of Language.* Psychology Press.

Harley, T. A. (2006). Speech errors: Psycholinguistic approach. In K. Brown (Ed.), *Encyclopedia of Language & Linguistics* (2nd ed.) (pp. 739–745). Elsevier.

Harley, T. A. (2008). *The Psychology of Language* (3rd ed.). Psychology Press.

Harley, T. A. (2010). *Talking the Talk: Language, Psychology and Science.* Psychology Press.

Harlow, J. M. (1848). Passage of an iron rod through the head. *Boston Medical and Surgical Journal, 39,* 389–393. (Republished in *Journal of Neuropsychiatry and Clinical Neuroscience, 11,* 281–283.)

Harpainter, M., Sim, E.-J., Trumpp, N. M., Ulrich, M., & Kiefer, M. (2019). The grounding of abstract concepts in the motor and visual system: An fMRI study. *Cortex, 124,* 1–22.

Harrington, J., Palethorpe, S., & Watson, C. I. (2000a). Does the Queen still speak the Queen's English?, *Nature, 407,* 927–928.

Harrington, J., Palethorpe, S., & Watson, C. I. (2000b). Monophthongal vowel changes received pronunciation: An acoustic analysis of the Queen's Christmas broadcasts. *Journal of the International Phonetic Association, 30,* 63–78.

Harris, C. M., & Wolpert, D. M. (1998). Signal-dependent noise determines motor planning. *Nature, 394*(6695), 780–784.

Harris, L. M., Vaccaro, L., Jones, M. K., & Boots, G. M. (2010). Evidence of impaired event-based prospective memory in clinical obsessive-compulsive checking. *Behaviour Change, 27*(2), 84–92.

Harris. M., & Coltheart, M. (1986). *Language Processing in Children and Adults: An Introduction.* Routledge.

Harvey, S. (2014). Creative synthesis: Exploring the process of extraordinary group creativity. *Academy of Management Review, 39,* 324–343.

Hashash, M., Zeid, M. A., & Moacdieh, N. (2019). Social media browsing while driving: Effects on driver performance and attention allocation. *Transportation Research Part F: Traffic Psychology and Behaviour, 63,* 67–82.

Haugeland, J. (1998). *Having Thought: Essays in the Metaphysics of Mind.* Harvard University Press.

Haukioja, J., Nyquist, M., & Jylkka, J. (2020). Reports from Twin Earth: Both deep structure and appearance determine the reference of natural kind terms. *Mind and Language,* in press. https://doi.org/10.1111/mila.12278

Hauser, M. D. (2006). *Moral Minds: How Nature Designed our Universal Sense of Right and Wrong.* Ecco/HarperCollins.

Hawthorne, K., Järvikivi, J., & Tucker, B. V. (2018). Finding word boundaries in Indian English-accented speech. *Journal of Phonetics, 66,* 145–160.

Haxby, J. V., Hoffman, E. A., & Gobbini, M. I. (2000). The distributed human neural system for face perception. *Trends in Cognitive Sciences, 4*(6), 223–233.

Hay, J. C., Pick, H. L., & Ikeda, K. (1965). Visual capture produced by prism spectacles. *Psychonomic Science, 2*(8), 215–216.

Hayati, A. M., & Shariatifar, S. (2009). Mapping strategies. *Journal of College Reading and Learning, 39*(2), 53–67.

Haynes, J. D., & Rees, G. (2005). Predicting the orientation of invisible stimuli from activity in human primary visual cortex. *Nature Neuroscience, 8*(5), 686–691.

Hayward, W. G. (2003). After the viewpoint debate: Where next in object recognition? *Trends in Cognitive Sciences, 7*(10), 425–427.

Head, H., & Holmes, G. (1911). Sensory disturbances from cerebral lesions. *Brain, 34,* 102–254.

Heavey, C. L., & Hurlburt, R. T. (2008). The phenomena of inner experience. *Consciousness and Cognition, 17,* 798–810.

Heavey, C. L., Hurlburt, R. T., & Lefforge, N. L. (2010). Descriptive experience sampling: A method for exploring momentary inner experience. *Qualitative Research in Psychology, 7,* 345–368.

Hebb, D. O. (1949). *The Organization of Behavior: A Neuropsychological Theory.* Wiley.

Heeger, D. J., & Zemlianova, K. O. (2020). Dynamic normalization. *bioRxiv,* 30 May. doi: https://doi.org/10.1101/2020.03.22.002634.

Heider, F., & Simmel, M. (1944). An experimental study of apparent behavior. *American Journal of Psychology, 57,* 243–259.

Heims, H. C., Critchley, H. D., Dolan, R., Mathias, C. J., & Cipolotti, L. (2004). Social and motivational functioning is not critically dependent on feedback of autonomic responses: Neuropsychological evidence from patients with pure autonomic failure. *Neuropsychologia, 42,* 1979–1988.

Heiser, M., Iacoboni, M., Maeda, F., Marcus, J., & Mazziotta, J. C. (2003). The essential role of Broca's area in imitation. *European Journal of Neuroscience, 17*(5), 1123–1128.

Hellawell, S. J., & Brewin, C. R. A. (2002). Comparison of flashbacks and ordinary autobiographical memories of trauma: Cognitive resources and behavioural observations. *Behaviour Research and Therapy, 40,* 1143–1156.

Helmholtz, H. V. (1898). *Vortrage und Reden,* Vol. 1. Vieweg.

Helmholtz, H. V., & Southall, J. P. C. (1962). *Helmholtz's Treatise on Physiological Optics.* Dover Publications.

Hemmerich, W. A., Shahal, A., & Hecht, H. (2019). Predictors of visually induced motion sickness in women. *Displays, 58,* 27–32.

Hemphill, R. E., & Stengel, E. J. (1940). A study on pure word-deafness. *Journal of Neurology and Psychiatry, 3*(3), 251–262.

Henderson, J. M., & Hollingworth, A. (1999). The role of fixation position in detecting scene changes across saccades. *Psychological Science, 10*(5), 438–443.

Henderson, L. (1972). Spatial and verbal codes and the capacity of STM. *Quarterly Journal of Experimental Psychology, 24,* 485–495.

Henle, M. (1962). On the relation between logic and thinking. *Psychological Review, 69,* 366–378.

Hennenlotter, A., Dresel, C., Castrop, F., Ceballos Baumann, A., Wohlschlager, A., & Haslinger, B. (2009). The link between facial feedback and neural activity within central circuitries of emotion: New insights from botulinum toxin-induced denervation of frown muscles. *Cerebral Cortex, 19*(3), 537–542.

Henry, J. D., Crawford, J.R., & Phillips, L. H. (2004). Verbal fluency performance in dementia of the Alzheimer's type: A meta-analysis. *Neuropsychologia, 42,* 1212–1222.

Herculano-Houzel, S. (2009). The human brain in numbers: A linearly scaled up primate brain. *Frontiers in Human Neuroscience, 3,* Article 31.

Herculano-Houzel, S. (2016). *The Human Advantage: A New Understanding of How Our Brain Became Remarkable.* MIT Press.

Herman, L. M., Richards, D.G., & Wolz, J. P. (1984). Comprehension of sentences by bottlenosed dolphins. *Cognition, 16,* 129–219.

Herrera, E., Cuetos, F., & Ribacoba, R. (2012) Verbal fluency in Parkinson's disease patients on/off dopamine medication. *Neuropsychologia, 50*(14), 3636–3640.

Hertel, P. T., & Calcaterra, G. (2005). Intentional forgetting benefits from thought substitution. *Psychonomic Bulletin & Review, 12,* 484–489.

Hertwig, R., & Erev, I. (2009). The description–experience gap in risky choice. *Trends in Cognitive Science, 13,* 517–523.

Hesse, M. (1975). Bayesian methods and the initial probabilities of theories. In G. Maxwell & R. M. Anderson, Jr. (Eds.), *Induction, Probability and Confirmation.* University of Minnesota Press.

Heyes, C. (2011). Automatic imitation. *Psychological Bulletin, 137*(3), 463–483.

Hickok, G., & Hauser, M. (2010). (Mis)understanding mirror neurons. *Current Biology, 20*(14), R593–594.

Hicks, J. L., & Starns, J. J. (2004). Retrieval-induced forgetting occurs in tests of item recognition. *Psychonomic Bulletin & Review, 11,* 125–130.

Higuchi, S., Holle, H., Roberts, N., Eickhoff, S. B., & Vogt, S. (2012). Imitation and observational learning of hand actions: Prefrontal involvement and connectivity. *Neuroimage, 59*(2), 1668–1683.

Hilts, P. J. (1995). *Memory's Ghost: The Nature of Memory and the Strange Tale of Mr. M.* Simon & Schuster.

Hinrichs, J. V., Ghoneim, M. M., & Mewaldt, S. P. (1984). Diazepam and memory: Retrograde facilitation produced by interference reduction. *Psychopharmacology, 84,* 158–162.

Hintzman, D. L. (1974). Theoretical implications of the spacing effect. In R. L. Solso (Ed.), *Theories in Cognitive Psychology: The Loyola Symposium.* Lawrence Erlbaum.

Hirstein, W., & Ramachandran, V. S. (1997). Capgras syndrome: A novel probe for understanding the neural representation of the identity and familiarity of persons. *Proceedings of The Royal Society, Biological Sciences, 264* (1380), 437–444.

Hirstein, W., & Sifferd, K. (2011). The legal self: Executive processes and legal theory. *Consciousness and Cognition, 20*(1), 156–171.

Hiscock, M. (1988). Behavioral asymmetries in normal children. In D. L. Molfese & S. J. Segalowitz (Eds.), *Brain Lateralization in Children: Developmental Implications* (pp. 85–169). Guilford.

Hitch, G. J., & Fergusen, J. (1991). Prospective memory for future intentions. *European Journal of Cognitive Psychology, 3,* 285–295.

Ho, C., Reed, N., & Spence, C. (2007). Multisensory in-car warning signals for collision avoidance. *Human Factors, 49*(6), 1107–1114.

Hockett, C. F. (1960). The origin of speech. *Scientific American, 203,* 88–96.

Hodge, F. S., Colton, R. H., & Kelley, R. T. (2001). Vocal intensity characteristics in normal and elderly speakers. *Journal of Voice, 15,* 503–511.

Hofer, F., & Schwaninger, A. (2005). Using threat image projection data for assessing individual screener performance. *WIT Transactions on the Built Environment, 82.*

Hoff, E. (2005). *Language Development* (3rd ed.). Wadsworth.

Hoffman, B. (2010). 'I think I can, but I'm afraid to try': The role of self-efficacy beliefs and mathematics anxiety in mathematics problem-solving efficiency. *Learning and Individual Differences, 20* (3), 276–283.

Hoffman, B., & Schraw, G. (2009). The influence of self-efficacy and working memory capacity on problem-solving efficiency. *Learning and Individual Differences, 19,* 91–100.

Hoffrage, U., Hafenbradl, S., & Marewski, J. N. (2018). The fast-and-frugal heuristics program. In L.

J. Ball & V. A. Thompson (Eds.), *The Routledge International Handbook of Thinking and Reasoning* (pp. 325–345). Routledge.

Hohne, E.A. & Jusczyk, P. W. (1994). Two-month-old infants' sensitivity to allophonic differences. *Perception & Psychophysics, 56*(6), 613–623.

Holcomb, P. J. (1988). Automatic and attentional processing: An event-related brain potential analysis of semantic priming. *Brain and Language, 35,* 66–85.

Holcomb, P. J. (1993). Semantic priming and stimulus degradation: Implications for the role of the N400 in language processing. *Psychophysiology, 30,* 47–61.

Holding, D. (1970). Guessing behaviour and the Sperling store. *Quarterly Journal of Experimental Psychology, 22,* 248–256.

Holding, D. H. (1979). The evaluation of chess positions. *Simulation and Games, 10,* 207–221.

Holding, D. H. (1985). *The Psychology of Chess.* Lawrence Erlbaum.

Holding, D. H., & Reynolds, J. R. (1982). Recall or evaluation of chess positions as determinants of chess skill. *Memory and Cognition, 10,* 237–242.

Holmlund, T. B., Cheng, J., Foltz, P. W., Cohen, A. S., & Elvevåg, B. (2019). Updating verbal fluency analysis for the 21st century: Applications for psychiatry. *Psychiatry Research, 273,* 767–769.

Holt, N., Bremner, A., Sutherland, A., Vliek, M., Passer, M., & Smith, R. (2012). *Psychology: The Science of Mind and Behaviour.* McGraw-Hill Education.

Holt, N., Bremner, A., Sutherland, A., Vliek, M., Passer, M., & Smith, R. (2019). *Psychology: The Science of Mind and Behaviour.* McGraw-Hill Education.

Holtgraves, T. (2012). The role of the right hemisphere in speech act comprehension. *Brain and Language, 121*(1), 58–64.

Holtzer, R., Jacobs, S., & Demetriou, E. (2020). Intraindividual variability in verbal fluency performance is moderated by and predictive of mild cognitive impairments. *Neuropsychology, 34*(1), 31–42.

Home Office (2010). *Code of Practice for the Identification of Persons by Police Officers.* Police and Criminal Evidence Act (PACE) 1984. Code D.

Hommel, B. (2019). Theory of Event Coding (TEC) V2. 0: Representing and controlling perception and action. *Attention, Perception, & Psychophysics, 81*(7), 2139–2154.

Hommel, B., Chapman, C. S., Cisek, P., Neyedli, H. F., Song, J. H., & Welsh, T. N. (2019). No one knows what attention is. *Attention, Perception, & Psychophysics, 81*(7), 2288–2303.

Hommel, B., Musseler, J., Aschersleben, G., & Prinz, W. (2001). The Theory of Event Coding (TEC): A framework for perception and action planning. *Behavioral and Brain Sciences, 24*(5), 849–878.

Hoosain, R. (1984). Experiments on digit span in the Chinese and English languages. In H. S. R. Kao & R. Hoosain (Eds.), *Psychological studies of the Chinese language* (pp. 23–28). Chinese Language Society.

Hoosain, R., & Salili, F. (1988). Language differences, working memory and mathematical ability. In M.M. Gruneberg, PE. Morris, & R.N. Sykes (Eds.), *Practical Aspects of Memory: Current Research and Issues,* Vol.2, pp.512-517. London: Wiley.

Hopkins, B. (2017). Study of child development: An interdisciplinary enterprise. In B. Hopkins, E. Geangu, & S. Linkenauger (Eds.), *The Cambridge Encyclopedia of Child Development* (pp. 1–16). Cambridge University Press.

Hostetter, A. B., & Alibali, M. W. (2008). Visible embodiment: Gestures as simulated action. *Psychonomic Bulletin & Review, 15*(3), 495–514.

Hostetter, A. B., & Alibali, M. W. (2019). Gesture as simulated action: Revisiting the framework. *Psychonomic Bulletin & Review, 26*(3), 721–752.

Houston, K. A., Clifford, B. R., Phillips, L. H., & Memon, A. (2013). The emotional eyewitness: The effects of emotion on specific aspects of eyewitness recall and recognition performance. *Emotion, 13,* 118–128.

Howard, L. A., & Tipper, S. P. (1997). Hand deviations away from visual cues: Indirect evidence for inhibition. *Experimental Brain Research, 113*(1), 144–152.

Howard, R. W. (2012). Longitudinal effects of different types of practice on the development of chess expertise. *Applied Cognitive Psychology, 26,* 359–369.

http://advocatusatheist.blogspot.com/2011/10/trolley-problem-thought.html

https://www.youtube.com/watch?v=68MiW2KK1us

https://www.youtube.com/watch?v=Bd5iEke6UlE

Hu, Y., Ericsson, K. A., Yang, D., & Lu, C. (2009). Superior self paced memorization of digits in spite of a normal digit span: The structure of a memorist's skill. *Journal of Experimental Psychology: Learning, Memory and Cognition, 35,* 1426–1442.

Huang, Y., Su, L., & Ma, Q. (2020). The Stroop effect: An activation likelihood estimation meta-analysis in healthy young adults. *Neuroscience Letters, 716,* 134683.

Hubal, R., Mitroff, S. R., Cain, M. S., Scott, B., & DeWitt, R. (2010). *Simulating a Vigilance Task: Extensible Technology for Baggage Security Assessment and Training.* Paper presented at the Technologies for Homeland Security (HST), 2010 IEEE International Conference.

Hubbard, E. M., & Ramachandran, V. S. (2005). Neurocognitive mechanisms of synesthesia. *Neuron, 48*(3), 509–520.

Hubbard, T. L., & Favretto, A. (2003). Naïve impetus and Michotte's 'tool effect': Evidence from representational momentum. *Psychological Research, 67*(2), 134–152.

Hubel, D. H., & Wiesel, T. N. (1959). Receptive fields of single neurones in the cat's striate cortex. *Journal of Physiology, 148*(3), 574–591.

Hubel, D. H., & Wiesel, T. N. (1962). Receptive fields, binocular interaction and functional architecture in the cat's visual cortex. *Journal of Physiology, 160,* 106–154.

Huber, R. A., Wicki, M. L., & Bernauer, T. (2019). Public support for environmental policy depends on beliefs concerning effectiveness, intrusiveness and fairness. *Environmental Politics, 29*(4), 649–673.

Huddleston, R., & Pullum, G. K. (2002). *The Cambridge Grammar of the English Language.* Cambridge University Press.

Hugdahl, K. (2011). Fifty years of dichotic listening research – Still going and going and . . . *Brain and Cognition, 76*(2), 211–213.

Hugdahl, K., & Westerhausen, R. (2016). Speech processing asymmetry revealed by dichotic listening and functional brain imaging. *Neuropsychologia, 93,* 466–481.

Hull, C. L. (1933). The meaningfulness of 320 selected nonsense syllables. *American Journal of Psychology, 45*(4), 730–734.

Hull, R., & Vaid, J. (2007). Bilingual language lateralization: A meta-analytic tale of two hemispheres. *Neuropsychologia, 45*(9), 1987–2008.

Hulleman, J., & Olivers, C. N. (2017). The impending demise of the item in visual search. *Behavioral and Brain Sciences, 40,* 1–69.

Hulme, C., Thomson, N., Muir, C., & Lawrence, A. (1984). Speech rate and the development of short-term memory. *Journal of Experimental Child Psychology, 38,* 241–253.

Humphrey, N. (2002). *The Uses of Consciousness the Mind Made Flesh: Essays From the Frontiers of Psychology and Evolution* (pp. 65–85). Oxford University Press.

Humphreys, G. W., & Forde, E. M. E. (1998). Disordered action schema and action disorganisation syndrome. *Cognitive Neuropsychology, 15*(6–8), 771–811.

Humphreys, G. W., & Riddoch, M. J. (1987). *To See But Not to See: A Case Study of Visual Agnosia.* Erlbaum.

Huppert, D., Benson, J., & Brandt, T. (2017). A historical view of motion sickness – A plague at sea and on land, also with military impact. *Frontiers in Neurology, 8,* 114.

Hurlburt, R. T., Alderson-Day, B., Fernyhough, C. P., & Kuhn, S. (2017). Can inner experience be apprehended in high fidelity? Examining brain activation and experience from multiple perspectives. *Frontiers in Psychology, 8,* 43.

Hurlburt, R. T., & Heavey, C. L. (2001). Telling what we know: Describing inner experience. *Trends in Cognitive Sciences, 5,* 400–403.

Hurley, S. L. (1998). *Consciousness in Action.* Harvard University Press.

Huxley, T. H. (1896). *Methods and Results: Collected Essays* (Vol. 1). Appleton.

Huybregts, M. A. C. (2017). Phonemic clicks and the mapping asymmetry: How language emerged and speech developed. *Neuroscience & Biobehavioral Reviews, 81,* Part B, 279–294.

Hyde, J. S. (2005). The gender similarities hypothesis. *American Psychologist, 60,* 581–592.

Hyde, J. S. (2016). Sex and cognition: Gender and cognitive functions. *Current Opinion in Neurobiology, 38,* 53–56.

Hygge, S. (2003). Classroom experiments on the effects of difference noise sources and sound levels on long-term recall and recognition in children. *Applied Cognitive Psychology, 17,* 895–914.

Hyman, I. E., Husband, T. H., & Billings, F. J. (1995). False memories of childhood experiences. *Applied Cognitive Psychology, 9,* 181–197.

Hyman, I. E., Jr., & Pentland, J. (1996). The role of mental imagery in the creation of false childhood memories. *Journal of Memory and Language, 35,* 101–117.

Hymes, D. (1972). On communicative competence. In J. B. Pride & J. Homes (Eds.), *Sociolinguistics*. Penguin.

I

Imai, M., Kanero, J., & Masuda, T. (2016). The relation between language, culture, and thought. *Current Opinion in Psychology, 8*, 70–77.

Ingram, J. (2007). *Neurolinguistics*. Cambridge University Press.

Innocence Project (2020) Eyewitness misidentification. Innocence Project website: https://www.innocenceproject.org/causes/eyewitness-misidentification

Inokuchi, E., & Kamio, Y. (2013). Qualitative analyses of verbal fluency in adolescents and young adults with high functioning autism spectrum disorder. *Research in Autism Spectrum Disorders, 7*, 1403–1410.

Intons-Peterson, M. J. (1983). Imagery paradigms: How vulnerable are they to experimenter expectations. *Journal of Experimental Psychology: Human Perception and Performance, 9*, 394–412.

Intraub, H. (1997). The representation of visual scenes. *Trends in Cognitive Sciences, 1*, 217–221.

Intraub, H., Gottesman, C. V., & Bills, A. (1998). Effects of perceiving and imagining scenes on memory for pictures. *Journal of Experimental Psychology: Learning, Memory, and Cognition, 24*, 186–201.

Intraub, H., Gottesman, C. V., Willey, E. V., & Zuk, I. J. (1996). Boundary extension for briefly glimpsed photographs: Do common perceptual processes result in unexpected memory distortions? *Journal of Memory and Language, 35*, 118–134.

Irwin, H. J. (1985). *Flight of Mind: A Psychological Study of the Out-of-Body Experience*. Scarecrow Press.

Isarida, T., & Isarida, T. K. (2014). Environmental context-dependent memory. *Advances in Experimental Psychology Research*, 115–151.

Isen, A. M. (1985). The asymmetry of happiness and sadness in effects on memory in normal college students. *Journal of Experimental Psychology: General, 114*, 388–391.

Isen, A. M. (1987). Positive affect, cognitive processes, and social behavior. In *Advances in Experimental Social Psychology* (Vol. 20, pp. 203–253). Academic Press.

Itti, L. (2015). New eye-tracking techniques may revolutionize mental health screening. *Neuron, 88*(3), 442–444.

Itti, L., & Koch, C. (2001). Computational modelling of visual attention. *Nature Reviews Neuroscience, 2*(3), 194–203.

Iverson, P., Kuhl, P. K., Akahane-Yamada, R., Diesch, E., Tohkurae, Y., Kettermann, A., & Siebert, C. (2003). A perceptual interference account of acquisition difficulties for non-native phonemes. *Cognition, 87*, B47–B57.

Iyengar, S. S., Wells, R. E., & Schwartz, B. (2006). Doing better but feeling worse: Looking for the 'best' job undermines satisfaction. *Psychological Science, 17*, 143–150.

J

Jackson, F. (1982). Epiphenomenal qualia. *Philosophical Quarterly, 32*(127), 127–136.

Jackson, M. I., & Ferencz, J. (2008). Charles Bonnet syndrome: Visual loss and hallucinations. *Canadian Medical Association Journal, 181*, 175–176.

Jacobs, D. W. (2003). What makes viewpoint-invariant properties perceptually salient? *Journal of the Optical Society of America A – Optics Image Science and Vision, 20*(7), 1304–1320.

Jacobs, N., & Garnham, A. (2007). The role of conversational hand gestures in a narrative task. *Journal of Memory and Language, 56*(2), 291–303.

Jacobson, J. Z., & Dodwell, P. C. (1979). Saccadic eye movements during reading. *Brain and Language, 8*(3), 303–314.

Jalbert, A., Neath, I., Bireta, T. J., & Surprenant, A. M. (2011). When does length cause the word length effect? *Journal of Experimental Psychology: Learning, Memory, and Cognition, 37*(2), 338–353.

James, K. H. (2017). The importance of handwriting experience on the development of the literate brain. *Current Directions in Psychological Science, 26*(6), 502–508.

James, L. E., Schmank, C. J., Castro, N., & Buchanan, T. W. (2018). Tip of the tongue states increase under evaluative observation. *Journal of Psycholinguistic Research, 47*(1), 169–178.

James, W. (1884). What is an emotion? *Mind, 9*, 188–205.

James, W. (1890). *Principles of Psychology*. Henry Holt & Co.

James, W. (1890). *The Principles of Psychology* (Vol. 1). Henry Holt and Company.

James, W. (1890). *The Principles of Psychology* (2 vols.). Henry Holt.

Jamison, K. (1993). *Touched With Fire: Manic-Depressive Illness and the Artistic Temperament*. Free Press/Macmillan.

Jarosz, A. F., Colflesh, G. H., & Wiley, J. (2012). Uncorking the muse: Alcohol intoxication facilitates creative problem solving. *Consciousness and Cognition, 21*, 487–493.

Jastorff, J., & Orban, G. A. (2009). Human functional magnetic resonance imaging reveals separation and integration of shape and motion cues in biological motion processing. *Journal of Neuroscience, 29*(22), 7315–7329.

Jastrow, J. (1899). The mind's eye. *Popular Science Monthly, 54*, 299–312.

Jay, T. B., & Danks, J. H. (1977). Ordering of taboo adjectives. *Bulletin of the Psychonomic Society, 9*, 405–408.

Jazayeri, M., & Shadlen, M. N. (2010). Temporal context calibrates interval timing. *Nature Neuroscience, 13*(8), 1020–U1152.

Jeannerod, M. (1984). The timing of natural prehension movements. *Journal of Motor Behavior, 16*(3), 235–254.

Jeannerod, M., Arbib, M. A., Rizzolatti, G., & Sakata, H. (1995). Grasping objects: The cortical mechanisms of visuomotor transformation. *Trends in Neurosciences, 18*(7), 314–320.

Jeffries, R., Polson, P. G., Razran, L., & Attwood, M. E. (1977). A process model for missionaries–cannibals and other river crossing problems. *Cognitive Psychology, 9*, 412–420.

Jelinek, L., Moritz, S., Heeren, D., & Naber, D. (2006). Everyday memory functioning in obsessive-compulsive disorder. *Journal of the International Neuropsychological Society, 12*, 746–749.

Jenkins, J. G., & Dallenbach, K. M. (1924). Obliviscence during sleep and waking. *American Journal of Psychology, 35*, 605–612.

Jipp, M. (2016). Reaction times to consecutive automation failures: A function of working memory and sustained attention. *Human Factors, 58*(8), 1248–1261.

Johansson, G. (1973). Visual-perception of biological motion and a model for its analysis. *Perception & Psychophysics, 14*(2), 201–211.

Johnson, E. J., & Goldstein, D. (2003). Do defaults save lives? *Science, 302*, 1338–1339.

Johnson, K., & Shiffrar, M. (2013). People watching: Social, perceptual and neuropsychological studies of body. *Perception*. Oxford University Press.

Johnson-Laird, P. N. (1975). Models of deduction. In R. C. Falmagne (Ed.), *Reasoning: Representation and Process* (pp. 7–54). Lawrence Erlbaum.

Johnson-Laird, P. N. (1983). *Mental Models*. Cambridge University Press.

Johnson-Laird, P. N. (1999). Deductive reasoning. *Annual Review of Psychology, 50*, 109–135.

Johnson-Laird, P. N. (2008). *How We Reason*. Oxford University Press, USA.

Johnson-Laird, P. N., & Bara, B. G. (1984). Syllogistic inference. *Cognition, 16*, 1–61.

Johnson-Laird, P. N., & Byrne, R. M. J. (1991). *Deduction*. Lawrence Erlbaum.

Johnson-Laird, P. N., Byrne, R. M. J., & Schaeken, W. (1992). Propositional reasoning by model. *Psychological Review, 90*, 418–439.

Johnson-Laird, P. N., Byrne, R. M. J., & Schaeken, W. (1994). Why models rather than rules give a better account of propositional reasoning: A reply to Bonatti and to O'Brien, Braine and Yang. *Psychological Review, 101*, 734–739.

Johnson-Laird, P. N., Legrenzi, P., & Legrenzi, M. S. (1972). Reasoning and a sense of reality. *British Journal of Psychology, 63*, 395–400.

Johnson-Laird, P. N., Mancini, J. L., & Gangemi, A. (2006). A hyper-emotion theory of psychological illnesses. *Psychological Review, 113*, 822–841.

Johnson-Laird, P. N., & Steedman, M. (1978). The psychology of syllogisms. *Cognitive Psychology, 10*, 64–99.

Johnston, R. A., & Edmonds, A. J. (2009). Familiar and unfamiliar face recognition: A review. *Memory, 17*(5), 577–596.

Jones, D. M., & Macken, W. J. (1993). Irrelevant tones produce an irrelevant speech effect: Implications for phonological coding in working memory. *Journal of Experimental Psychology: Learning, Memory, and Cognition, 19*(2), 369–381.

Jones Leonard, B., McNaughton, B. L., & Barnes, C. A. (1987). Suppression of hippocampal synaptic activity during slow-wave sleep. *Brain Research, 425*, 174–177.

Jones, G. (2003). Testing two theories of insight. *Journal of Experimental Psychology: Learning, Memory and Cognition, 29*, 1017–1027.

Jones, G. V. (1983). On double dissociation of function. *Neuropsychologia, 21*(4), 397–400.

Jones, P. (1995). Contradictions and unanswered questions in the Genie case: A fresh look at the linguistic evidence. *Language & Communication, 15*(3), 261–280.

Jonides, J., Smith, E. E., Koeppe, R. A., Awh, E., Minoshima, S., & Mintun, M. A. (1993). Spatial working memory in humans as revealed by PET. *Nature, 363*, 623–625.

Joormann, J., Yoon, K. L., & Zetsche, U. (2007). Cognitive inhibition in depression. *Applied and Preventive Psychology, 12*, 128–139.

Jordan, M. I. (1986). *Serial Order: A Parallel Distributed Approach*. Institute for Cognitive Science, University of California, San Diego.

Jordan, M. I. (1997). Serial order: A parallel distributed processing approach. In J. W. Donahoe & V. Packard Dorsel (Eds.), *Neural-Network Models of Cognition* (pp. 471–495). Elsevier Science.

Jordan, M. I., & Rumelhart, D. E. (1992). Forward models: Supervised learning with a distal teacher. *Cognitive Science, 16*(3), 307–354.

Jordan, S., Brimbal, L., Wallace, D. B., Kassin, S. M., Hartwig, M., & Street, C. N. (2019). A test of the micro-expressions training tool: Does it improve lie detection *Journal of Investigative Psychology and Offender Profiling, 16*(3), 222–235.

Jost, A. (1897). Die assoziations festigkeit in ihrer abhangigkeit von der verteilung der wiederholungen. *Zeitschrift fur Psychologie, 14*, 436–472.

Ju, Y.-J., & Lien, Y.-W. (2018). Who is prone to wander and when? Examining an integrative effect of working memory capacity and mindfulness trait on mind wandering under different task loads. *Consciousness and Cognition, 63*, 1–10.

Jung-Beeman, M., Bowden, E. M., Haberman, J., Frymiare, J. L., Arambel-Liu, S., Greenblatt, R., Reber, P. J., & Kounios, J. (2004). Neural activity when people solve verbal problems with insight. *PLOS Biology, 2*, 0500–0510.

Jusczyk, P. W., & Aslin, R. N. (1995). Infants' detection of speech patterns of words in fluent speech. *Cognitive Psychology, 29*, 1–23.

Jusczyk, P. W., Houston, D. M., & Newsome, M. (1999). The beginnings of word segmentation in English learning infants. *Cognitive Psychology, 39*, 159–207.

Juslin, P. N., & Laukka, P. (2003). Communication of emotions in vocal expression and music performance: Different channels, same code? *Psychological Bulletin, 129*(5), 770–814.

Jutzeler, C. R., Curt, A., & Kramer, J. L. K. (2015). Relationship between chronic pain and brain reorganization after deafferentation: a systematic review of functional MRI findings. *NeuroImage: Clinical, 9*, 599–606.

K

Kadosh, R. (2013). Using transcranial electrical stimulation to enhance cognitive functions in the typical and atypical brain. *Translational Neuroscience, 4*, 20–33.

Kadosh, R., Soskik, S., Iuculano, T., Kanai, R., & Walsh, V. (2010). Modulating neuronal activity produces specific and long lasting changes in numerical competence. *Current Biology, 20*, 2016–2020.

Kahn Jr, C. E. (2017). From images to actions: Opportunities for artificial intelligence in radiology. *Radiology, 285*(3), 719–720.

Kahneman, D. (1973). *Attention and Effort*. Prentice-Hall.

Kahneman, D. (2003). A perspective on judgment and choice: Mapping bounded rationality. *American Psychologist, 58*, 697–720.

Kahneman, D. (2011). *Thinking, Fast and Slow*. Allen Lane.

Kahneman, D., Knetsch, J. L., & Thaler, R. H. (1990). Experimental tests of the endowment effect and the Coase theorem. *Journal of Political Economy, 98*, 1325–1348.

Kahneman, D., & Tversky, A. (1979). Prospect theory: An analysis of decision under risk. *Econometrica, 47*, 263–291.

Kahneman, D., & Tversky, A. (1984). Choices, values and frames. *American Psychologist, 39*, 341–350.

Kalat, J. W. (2007). *Biological Psychology*. Cengage Learning.

Kalenine, S., Buxbaum, L. J., & Coslett, H. B. (2010). Critical brain regions for action recognition: Lesion symptom mapping in left hemisphere stroke. *Brain, 133*(11), 3269–3280.

Kaminski, J., Call, J., & Fischer, J. (2004). Word learning in a domestic dog: Evidence for 'fast mapping'. *Science, 304*(5677), 1682–1683.

Kaminski, J., Tempelmann, S., Call, J., & Tomasello, M. (2009). Domestic dogs comprehend human communication with iconic signs. *Developmental Science, 12*(6), 831–837.

Kandasamy, N., Garfinkel, S. N., Page, L., Critchley, H. D., Gurnell, M., & Coates, J. M. (2016). Interoceptive ability predicts survival on a London trading floor. *Scientific Reports, 6*, 32986.

Kandel, E. R. (2004). The molecular biology of memory storage: A dialog between genes and synapses. *Bioscience Reports, 24*(4–5), 475–522.

Kandel, E. R., & Schwartz, J. H. (1985). *Principles of Neural Science* (2nd ed.). Elsevier.

Kandel, E., Schwartz, J., & Jessell, T. (2000). *Principles of Neural Science*. McGraw-Hill Education.

Kane, M. J., Brown, L. H., McVay, J. C., Silvia, P. J., Myin-Germeys, I., & Kwapil, T. R. (2007). For whom the mind wanders, and when: An experience-sampling study of working memory and executive control in daily life. *Psychological Science, 18*, 614–621.

Kane, M. J., Gross, G. M., Chun, C. A., Smeekens, B. A., Meier, M. E., Silvia, P. J., & Kwapil, T. R. (2017). For whom the mind wanders, and when, varies across laboratory and daily-life settings. *Psychological Science, 28*(9), 1271–1289.

Kanwisher, N., McDermott, J., & Chun, M. M. (1997). The fusiform face area: A module in human extrastriate cortex specialized for face perception. *Journal of Neuroscience, 17*(11), 4302–4311.

Kar, K., Kubilius, J., Schmidt, K., Issa, E. B., & DiCarlo, J. J. (2019). Evidence that recurrent circuits are critical to the ventral stream's execution of core object recognition behavior. *Nature Neuroscience, 22*(6), 974.

Kardas-Nelson, M. (2019). Despite high rates of vaccination, pertussis cases are on the rise. Is a new vaccination strategy needed? *British Medical Journal, 366*, 14460.

Kassin, S. M. (2017). False confessions: How can psychology so basic be so counterintuitive? *American Psychologist, 72*(9), 951–964.

Kassin, S. M., Dror, I. E., & Kukucka, J. (2013). The forensic confirmation bias: Problems, perspectives, and proposed solutions. *Journal of Applied Research in Memory and Cognition, 2*(1), 42–52.

Katayama, M., & Kawato, M. (1993). Virtual trajectory and stiffness ellipse during multijoint arm movement predicted by neural inverse models. *Biological Cybernetics, 69*(5–6), 353–362.

Kaufman, D. M., & Milstein, M. J. (2013). Visual disturbances. In *Kaufman's Clinical Neurology for Psychiatrists* (pp. 261–285). Elsevier.

Kaufman, E., Reips, U.-D., & Wittmann, W. W. (2013). A critical meta-analysis of lens model studies in human judgment and decision-making. *PLOS One, 8*, e83528.

Kawato, M. (1999). Internal models for motor control and trajectory planning. *Current Opinion in Neurobiology, 9*(6), 718–727.

Kawato, M., & Gomi, H. (1992). A computational model of 4 regions of the cerebellum based on feedback-error learning. *Biological Cybernetics, 68*(2), 95–103.

Kaye, L.K., Malone, S. A., & Wall, H. J. (2017). Emojis: Insights, affordances, and possibilities for psychological science. *Trends in Cognitive Sciences, 21*(2), 66–68.

Kazi, S., Demetriou, A., Spanoudis, G., Zhang, X. K., & Wang, Y. (2012). Mind–culture interactions: How writingmolds mental fluidity in early development. *Intelligence, 40*(6), 622–637.

Keator, L. M., Sheppard, S. M., Faria, A. V., Kim, K., Saxena, S., Wright, A., & Hillis, A. E. (2019). Cookie Theft picture description: Linguistic and neural correlates. *Conference Abstract: Academy of Aphasia 56th Annual Meeting*. doi: 10.3389/conf.fnhum.2018.228.00097

Keefe, J. M., Sy, J. L., Tong, F., & Zald, D. H. (2019). The emotional attentional blink is robust to divided attention. *Attention, Perception, & Psychophysics, 81*(1), 205–216.

Keither, M. (2005). Repetition priming modulates category-related effects on event-related potentials: Further evidence for multiple cortical semantic systems. *Journal of Cognitive Neuroscience, 17*, 199–211.

Kejic, M., McClelland, J., Bartholdy, S., Chamali, R., Campbell, I. C., & Schmidt, U. (2020). Bad things come to those who do not wait: Temporal discounting is associated with compulsive overeating, eating disorder psychopathology and food addiction. *Frontiers in Psychiatry, 10*, 978.

Kelly, S., Byrne, K., & Holler, J. (2011). Raising the ante of communication: Evidence for enhanced gesture use in high stakes situations. *Information, 2*, 579–593.

Kelso, J. A. S. (1984). Phase-transitions and critical-behavior in human bimanual coordination. *American Journal of Physiology, 246*(6), 1000–1004.

Kelso, J. A. S. (1995). *Dynamic patterns: The Self-Organization of Brain and Behavior*. MIT Press.

Kemp, S., Wilkinson, K., Caswell, H., Reynders, H., & Baker, G. (2008). The base rate of Wada test failure. *Epilepsy & Behaviour, 13*, 630–633.

Kendon, A. (2004). *Gesture: Visible Action as Utterance*. Cambridge University Press.

Kenealy, P. M. (1997). Mood-state-dependent retrieval: The effects of induced mood on memory reconsidered. *Quarterly Journal of Experimental Psychology, 50A*, 290–317.

Kennet, Y. (2018). Investigating creativity from a semantic network perspective. In Z. Kapoula (Ed.),

Exploring Transdisciplinarity in Art and Sciences (pp. 49–75). Springer International Publishing AG.

Kensinger, E. A., & Schacter, D. L. (2010). Memory and emotion. In M. Lewis, J. M. Haviland-Jones, & L. Barrett (Eds.), *Handbook of Emotion*. Guilford Press.

Kensinger, E. A., Ullman, M. T., & Corkin, S. (2001). Bilateral medial temporal lobe damage does not affect lexical or grammatical processing: Evidence from amnesic patient H.M. *Hippocampus, 11*, 347–360.

Kentridge, R. W., Heywood, C. A., & Weiskrantz, L. (1999). Attention without awareness in blindsight. *Proceedings of the Royal Society of London Series B – Biological Sciences, 266* (1430), 1805–1811.

Keogh, R., & Pearson, J. (2011). Mental imagery and visual working memory. *PLOS One, 6*, e29211.

Keogh, R., & Pearson, J. (2014). The sensory strength of voluntary visual imagery predicts visual working memory capacity. *Journal of Vision, 14*, 7.

Kerkman, J. N., Daffertshofer, A., Gollo, L. L., Breakspear, M., & Boonstra, T. W. (2018). Network structure of the human musculoskeletal system shapes neural interactions on multiple time scales. *Science Advances, 4*(6), eaat0497.

Kerr, D. S., & Murthy, U. S. (2004). Divergent and convergent idea generation in teams: A comparison of computer-mediated and face-to-face communication. *Group Decision and Negotiation, 13*, 381–399.

Kessler, K., & Braithwaite, J. J. (2016). Deliberate and spontaneous sensations of disembodiment: Capacity or flaw? *Cognitive Neuropsychiatry, 21*(5), 412–428.

Keys, D. J., & Schwartz, B. (2007). 'Leaky' rationality: How research on behavioral decision making challenges normative standards of rationality. *Perspectives on Psychological Science, 2*, 162–180.

Khalighinejad, N., Brann, E., Dorgham, A., & Haggard, P. (2019). Dissociating cognitive and motoric precursors of human self-initiated action. *Journal of Cognitive Neuroscience, 31*(5), 754–767.

Kietzman, P. M., & Visscher, P. K. (2015). The anti-waggle dance: Use of the stop signal as negative feedback. *Frontiers in Ecology and Evolution, 3*, 14.

Kilian-Hütten, N., Formisano, E., & Vroomen, J. (2017). Multisensory integration in speech processing: Neural mechanisms of cross-modal aftereffects. In *Neural Mechanisms of Language* (pp. 105–127). Springer.

Kilner, J. M. (2011). More than one pathway to action understanding. *Trends in Cognitive Sciences, 15*(8), 352–357.

Kilner, J. M., & Lemon, R. N. (2013). What we know currently about mirror neurons. *Current Biology, 23*(23), R1057–R1062.

Kilner, J. M., Neal, A., Weiskopf, N., Friston, K. J., & Frith, C. D. (2009). Evidence of mirror neurons in human inferior frontal gyrus. *Journal of Neuroscience, 29*(32), 10153–10159.

Kim, D., Stephens, J. D. W., & Pitt, M. A. (2012). How does context play a part in splitting words apart? Production and perception of word boundaries in casual speech. *Journal of Memory and Language, 66*(4), 509–529.

Kim, Y. W., & Mansfield, L. T. (2014). Fool me twice: Delayed diagnoses in radiology with emphasis on perpetuated errors. *American Journal of Roentgenology, 202*(3), 465–470.

Kimura, D. (1961). Cerebral dominance and the perception of verbal stimuli. *Canadian Journal of Psychology, 15*, 166–170.

Kimura, D. (1967). Functional asymmetry of the brain in dichotic listening. *Cortex, 3*, 163–178.

Kingdom, F. A. A., & Prins, N. (2016). *Psychophysics: A Practical Introduction*. Academic Press.

Kingston, J. A., & Lyddy, F. (2013). Self-efficacy and short-term memory capacity as predictors of proportional reasoning. *Learning and Individual Differences, 26*, 185–190.

Kinukawa, T., Takeuchi, N., Sugiyama, S., Nishihara, M., Nishiwaki, K., & Inui, K. (2019). Properties of echoic memory revealed by auditory-evoked magnetic fields. *Nature Scientific Reports, 9*, 12260.

Kirchner, H., & Thorpe, S. J. (2006). Ultra-rapid object detection with saccadic eye movements: Visual processing speed revisited. *Vision Research, 46*(11), 1762–1776.

Kita, S., & Ozyurek, A. (2003). What does cross-linguistic variation in semantic coordination of speech and gesture reveal? Evidence for an interface representation of spatial thinking and speaking. *Journal of Memory and Language, 48*(1), 16–32.

Kiyonaga, A., & Egner, T. (2013). Working memory as internal attention: Toward an integrative account of internal and external selection processes. *Psychonomic Bulletin & Review, 20*(2), 228–242.

Klatzky, R. L. (1980). *Human Memory: Structures and Processes* (2nd ed.). Freeman.

Klatzky, R. L., Lederman, S. J., & Metzger, V. A. (1985). Identifying objects by touch – An expert system. *Perception & Psychophysics, 37*(4), 299–302.

Klatzky, R. L., Pellegrino, J. W., McCloskey, B. P., & Doherty, S. (1989). Can you squeeze a tomato? The role of motor representations in semantic sensibility judgments. *Journal of Memory and Language, 28*, 56–77.

Klauer, S. G., Dingus, T. A., Neale, V. L., Sudweeks, J. D., & Ramsey, D. J. (2006). *The Impact of Driver Inattention on Near-Crash/Crash Risk: An Analysis Using the 100-car Naturalistic Driving Study Data*. National Highway Traffic Safety Administration.

Klein, D. C., & Seligman, M. E. P. (1976). Reversal of performance deficits and perceptual deficits in learned helplessness and depression. *Journal of Abnormal Psychology, 85*, 11–26.

Klein, G. (2015). Reflections on applications of naturalistic decision making. *Journal of Occupational and Organizational Psychology, 88*, 382–386.

Klein, G., Calderwood, R., & Clinton-Cirocco, A. (2010). Rapid decision making on the fire ground: The original study plus a postscript. *Journal of Cognitive Engineering and Decision Making, 4*, 186–209.

Klein, G., Wolf, S., Militello, L., & Zsambok, C. (1995). Characteristics of skilled option generation in chess. *Organizational Behavior and Human Decision Processes, 62*, 63–69.

Klein, R. (1988). Inhibitory tagging system facilitates visual search. *Nature, 334* (6181), 430–431.

Klein, R. M. (2000). Inhibition of return. *Trends in Cognitive Sciences, 4*(4), 138–147.

Klein, S. B., & Loftus, J. (2002). Memory and temporal experience: The effects of episodic memory loss on an amnesic patient's ability to remember the past and imagine the future. *Social Cognition, 20*, 353–379.

Klein, W., & Perdue, C. (1997). The basic variety (or: couldn't natural languages be much simpler?). *Second Language Research, 13*(4), 301–347.

Kleinschmidt, D. F., & Jaeger, T. F. (2015). Robust speech perception: Recognize the familiar, generalize to the similar, and adapt to the novel. *Psychological Review, 122*(2), 148–203.

Klenk, M. (2019). The influence of situational factors in sacrificial dilemmas on utilitarian moral judgments. *SSRN*, 64pp. Available at: https://ssrn.com/abstract=3501289.

Kljajevic, V., & Erramuzpe, A. (2018). Proper name retrieval and structural integrity of cerebral cortex in midlife: A cross-sectional study. *Brain and Cognition, 120*, 26–33.

Knight, A., Underhill, P. A., Mortenson, H. M., & Zhivotovsky, L. A. (2003). African Y chromosome and mtDNA divergence provides insight into the history of click languages. *Current Biology, 13*, 464–473.

Knoblich, G., & Flach, R. (2003). Action identity: Evidence from self-recognition, prediction, and coordination. *Consciousness and Cognition, 12*(4), 620–632.

Knoblich, G., Ohlsson, S., Haider, H., & Rhenius, D. (1999). Constraint relaxation and chunk decomposition in insight problem solving. *Journal of Experimental Psychology: Learning, Memory and Cognition, 25*, 1534–1556.

Knowlton, B., Squire, L., & Gluck, M. (1994). Probabilistic classification learning in amnesia. *Learning and Memory, 1*, 106–120.

Ko, S. J., Judd, C. M., & Blair, I. V. (2006). What the voice reveals: Within- and between-category stereotyping on the basis of voice. *Personality and Social Psychology Bulletin, 32*(6), 806–819.

Koch, C. (2004). *The Quest for Consciousness: A Neurobiological Approach*. Roberts and Co.

Koch, C., & Ullman, S. (1985). Shifts in selective visual attention: Towards the underlying neural circuitry. *Human Neurobiology, 4*(4), 219–227.

Koechlin, E. (2008). The cognitive architecture of the human lateral prefrontal cortex. In P. Haggard, Y. Rossetti, & M. Kawato (Eds.), *Attention and Performance XXII: Sensorimotor Foundations of Higher Cognition*. Oxford University Press.

Koehler, K., & Eckstein, M. P. (2017). Beyond scene gist: Objects guide search more than scene background. *Journal of Perception and Performance, 43*(6), 1177.

Kohler, E., Keysers, C., Umilta, M. A., Fogassi, L., Gallese, V., & Rizzolatti, G. (2002). Hearing sounds, understanding actions: Action representation in mirror neurons. *Science, 297*(5582), 846–848.

Kohler, W. (1925). *The Mentality of Apes*. Harcourt Brace.

Kok, E. M., Jarodzka, H., de Bruin, A. B., BinAmir, H. A.,

Robben, S. G., & van Merriënboer, J. J. (2016). Systematic viewing in radiology: Seeing more, missing less? *Advances in Health Sciences Education, 21*(1), 189–205.

Kolers, P. A., & Roediger, H. L. (1984). Procedures of mind. *Journal of Verbal Learning and Verbal Behavior, 23*, 425–449.

Koleva, K., Mon-Williams, M., & Klepousniotou, E. (2019). Right hemisphere involvement for pun processing: Effects of idiom decomposition. *Journal of Neurolinguistics, 51*, 165–183.

Kolk, H. (2007). Variability is the hallmark of aphasic behaviour: Grammatical behaviour is no exception. *Brain and Language, 101*, 99–102.

Komatsu, L.K. (1992). Recent views on conceptual structure. *Psychological Bulletin, 112*, 500–526.

Kondziella, D., Friberg, C. K., Frokjaer, V. G., Fabricius, M., & Moller, K. (2016). Preserved consciousness in vegetative and minimal conscious states: Systematic review and meta-analysis. *Journal of Neurology, Neurosurgery and Psychiatry, 87*, 485–492.

Konen, C. S., Behrmann, M., Nishimura, M., & Kastner, S. (2011). The functional neuroanatomy of object agnosia: A case study. *Neuron, 71*(1), 49–60.

Kong, J., Gollub, R. L., Webb, J. M., Vangel, M. G., & Kwong, K. (2007). Test-retest study of fMRI signal change evoked by electro-acupuncture stimulation. *NeuroImage, 34*, 1171–1181.

Koohestani, A., Nahavandi, D., Asadi, H., Kebria, P. M., Khosravi, A., Alizadehsani, R., & Nahavandi, S. (2019). A knowledge discovery in motion sickness: A comprehensive literature review. *IEEE Access, 7*, 85755–85770.

Kopelman, M. D., Lasserson, D., Kingsley, D., Bello, F., Rush, C., Stanhope, N., Stevens, T., Goodman, G., Heilpern, G., Kendall, B., & Colchester, A. (2001). Structural MRI volumetric analysis in patients with organic amnesia, 2: Correlations with anterograde memory and executive tests in 40 patients. *Journal of Neurology, Neurosurgery and Psychiatry, 71*, 23–28.

Kopelman, M. D., Thomson, A., Guerrini, I., & Marshall, E. J. (2009). The Korsakoff syndrome: Clinical aspects, psychology and treatment. *Alcohol and Alcoholism, 44*(2), 148–154.

Kording, K. P. (2007). Decision theory: What 'should' the nervous system do? *Science, 318*(5850), 606–610.

Körding, K. P., Beierholm, U., Ma, W. J., Quartz, S., Tenenbaum, J. B., & Shams, L. (2007). Causal inference in multisensory perception. *PLoS one, 2*(9), e943.

Kording, K. P., & Wolpert, D. M. (2006). Bayesian decision theory in sensorimotor control. *Trends in Cognitive Sciences, 10*(7), 319–326.

Koriat, A. (2007). Metacognition and consciousness. In P. D. Zelazo, M. Moscovich, & E. Thompson (Eds.), *The Cambridge Handbook of Consciousness* (pp. 289–325). Cambridge University Press.

Koriat, A., & Goldsmith, M. (1996). Memory metaphors and the real life/laboratory controversy: Correspondence versus storehouse conceptions of memory. *Behavioral and Brain Sciences, 19*, 167–187.

Kosslyn, S. M. (1973). Scanning visual images: Some structural implications. *Perception and Psychophysics, 14*, 90–94.

Kosslyn, S. M., Ball, T. M., & Reiser, B. J. (1978). Visual images preserve metric spatial information: Evidence from studies of image scanning. *Journal of Experimental Psychology: Human Perception and Performance, 4*, 56–60.

Kosslyn, S. M., & Thompson, W. L. (2003). When is early visual cortex activated during visual mental imagery? *Psychological Bulletin, 129*, 723–746.

Kosslyn, S. M., Thompson, W. L., Kim, I. J., & Alpert, N. M. (1995). Topographical representations of mental images in primary visual cortex. *Nature, 378*, 496–498.

Kouider, S., & Faivre, N. (2017). Conscious and unconscious perception. In Schneider, S., & Velmans, M. (Eds.), *The Blackwell Companion to Consciousness* (pp. 551–561). John Wiley & Sons.

Kounios, J., & Beeman, M. (2014). The cognitive neuroscience of insight. *Annual Review of Psychology, 65*, 71–93.

Kozlowski, L. T., & Cutting, J. E. (1977). Recognizing sex of a walker from a dynamic point-light display. *Perception & Psychophysics, 21*(6), 575–580.

Krafnick, A. J., & Evans, T. M. (2019). Neurobiological sex differences in developmental dyslexia. *Frontiers in Psychology, 9*, 2669.

Kramer, A. F., & Hahn, S. (1995). Splitting the beam: Distribution of attention over noncontiguous regions of the visual field. *Psychological Science, 6*(6), 381–386.

Kramer, M. R., Porfido, C. L., & Mitroff, S. R. (2019). Evaluation of strategies to train visual search performance in professional populations. *Current Opinion in Psychology, 29*, 113–118.

Krasne, S., Hillman, J. D., Kellman, P. J., & Drake, T. A. (2013). Applying perceptual and adaptive learning techniques for teaching introductory histopathology. *Journal of Pathology Informatics, 4*.

Krasovskaya, S., & MacInnes, W. J. (2019). Salience models: A computational cognitive neuroscience review. *Vision, 3*(4), 56.

Krauss, M. (1992). The world's languages in crisis. *Language, 68*, 1–42.

Krauss, R. M., Chen, Y., & Gottesman, R. F. (2000). Lexical gestures and lexical access: A process model. In D. McNeill (Ed.), *Language and Gesture* (pp. 261–283). Cambridge University Press.

Krieber, M., Bartl-Pokorny, K. D., Pokorny, F. B., Einspieler, C., Langmann, A., Körner, C., Falck-Ytter, T., & Marschik, P. B. (2016). The relation between reading skills and eye movement patterns in adolescent readers: Evidence from a regular orthography. *PLOS One, 11*(1), e0145934.

Kringelbach, M. L., & Rolls, E. T. (2004), The functional neuroanatomy of the human orbitofrontal cortex: Evidence from neuroimaging and neuropsychology, *Progress in Neurobiology, 72*, 341–372.

Kristjánsson, T., Thornton, I. M., Chetverikov, A., & Kristjánsson, Á. (2020). Dynamics of visual attention revealed in foraging tasks. *Cognition, 194*, 104032.

Krizhevsky, A., Sutskever, I., & Hinton, G. E. (2012). ImageNet classification with deep convolutional neural networks. In *Advances in Neural Information Processing Systems, 25*(2), 1097–1105.

Kroes, M. C., Tendolkar, I., Van Wingen, G. A., Van Waarde, J. A., Strange, B. A., & Fernández, G. (2014). An electroconvulsive therapy procedure impairs reconsolidation of episodic memories in humans. *Nature Neuroscience, 17*(2), 204–206.

Kroll, J. F., & Dussias, P. E. (2004). The comprehension of words and sentences in two languages. In T. Bhatia & W. Ritchie (Eds.), *The Handbook of Bilingualism*. Blackwell.

Kroos, C., Herath, D. C., & Stelarc (2011). From robot arm to intentional agent: The Articulated Head. In S. Goto (Ed.), *Advances in Robotics, Automation and Control* (pp. 215–240). InTech.

Kucera, H., & Francis, W. N. (1967). *Computational Analysis of Present-Day American English*. Brown University Press.

Kuffler, D. P. (2018). Origins of phantom limb pain. *Molecular Neurobiology, 55*(1), 60–69.

Kuhl, P. K. (1993). Early linguistic experience and phonetic perception: Implications for theories of developmental speech perception. *Journal of Phonetics, 21*, 125–139.

Kuhl, P. K., & Miller, J. D. (1978). Speech perception by the chinchilla: Identification functions for synthetic VOT stimuli. *Journal of the Acoustical Society of America, 63*, 905–917.

Kuhn, G., & Tatler, B. W. (2005). Magic and fixation: Now you don't see it, now you do. *Perception, 34*(9), 1155–1161.

Kuhn, G., Amlani, A. A., & Rensink, R. A. (2008). Towards a science of magic. *Trends in Cognitive Sciences, 12*(9), 349–354.

Kuhn, G., Caffaratti, H. A., Teszka, R., & Rensink, R. A. (2014). A psychologically-based taxonomy of misdirection. *Frontiers in Psychology, 5*, 1392.

Kuhn, T. (1970). *The Structure of Scientific Revolutions* (2nd ed.). University of Chicago Press.

Kunst-Wilson, W. R., & Zajonc, R. B. (1980). Affective discrimination of stimuli that cannot be recognized. *Science, 207*(4430), 557–558.

Kusumi, T. (2006). Human metacognition and the déjà vu phenomenon. In K. Fujita & S. Itakura (Eds.), *Diversity of Cognition: Evolution, Development, Domestication, and Pathology*. Kyoto University Press.

Kutas, M., & Hillyard, S. A. (1980). Reading senseless sentences: Brain potentials reflect semantic incongruity. *Science, 207*, 203–205.

Kuzmina, E., Goral, M., Norvik, M., & Weekes, B. S. (2019). What influences language impairment in bilingual aphasia? A meta-analytic review. *Frontiers in Psychology, 10*, 445.

Kvavilashvili, L. (1987). Remembering intention as adistinct form of memory. *British Journal of Psychology, 78*, 507–518.

Kvavilashvili, L., & Ellis, J. (2004). Ecological validity and twenty years of real life/laboratory controversy in memory research: A critical (and historical) review. *History and Philosophy of Psychology, 6*, 59–80.

Kwan, M. H., & Cutler, A. (2020). Universals of listening: Equivalent prosodic entrainment in tone and non-tone languages. *Cognition, 202,* 104311.

Kyaga, S., Lichtenstein, P., Boman, M., Hultman, C., Langstrom, N., & Landen, M. (2011). Creativity and mental disorder: Family study of 300,000 people with severe mental disorder. *British Journal of Psychiatry, 199,* 373–379.

Kyritsis, M., Gulliver, S. R., Feredoes, E., & Din, S. U. (2018). Human behaviour in the Euclidean travelling salesperson problem: Computational modelling of heuristics and figural effects. *Cognitive Systems Research, 52,* 387–399.

L

Laberge, D. (1983). Spatial extent of attention to letters and words. *Journal of Experimental Psychology: Human Perception and Performance, 9*(3), 371–379.

Laberge, D., & Brown, V. R. (1987). Comparison of moving-spotlight and gradient models of attention. *Bulletin of the Psychonomic Society, 25*(5), 349–349.

Lacquaniti, F., Terzuolo, C., & Viviani, P. (1983). The law relating the kinematic and figural aspects of drawing movements. *Acta Psychologica, 54*(1–3), 115–130.

Ladefoged, P. (1993). *A Course in Phonetics.* (3rd ed.). Harcourt Brace Jovanovich.

Laeng, B., & Sulutvedt, U. (2014). The eye pupil adjusts to imaginary light. *Psychonomic Science, 25,* 188–197.

Lakatos, I. (1970). Falsification and the methodology of scientific research programmes. In I. Lakatos & A. Musgrave (Eds.), *Criticism and the Growth of Knowledge.* Cambridge University Press.

Lakoff, G., & Johnson, M. (2008). *Metaphors We Live By.* University of Chicago Press.

Lamberty, G. J., Beckwith, B. E., & Petros, T. V. (1990). Posttrial treatment with ethanol enhances recall of prose narratives. *Physiology and Behavior, 48,* 653–58.

Lambon Ralph, M. A. (2014). Neurocognitive insights on conceptual knowledge and its breakdown. *Philosophical Transactions of the Royal Society B, 369,* 20120392. http://dx.doi.org/10.1098/rstb.2012.0392

Lamme, V. A. (2010). How neuroscience will change our view on consciousness. *Cognitive Neuroscience, 1*(3), 204–220.

Lamme, V. A. F. (2003). Why visual attention and awareness are different. *Trends in Cognitive Sciences, 7*(1), 12–18.

Lamme, V. A. F., & Roelfsema, P. R. (2000). The distinct modes of vision offered by feed forward and recurrent processing. *Trends in Neurosciences, 23*(11), 571–579.

Lamont, P., Henderson, J. M., & Smith, T. J. (2010). Where science and magic meet: The illusion of a 'science of magic'. *Review of General Psychology, 14*(1), 16–21.

Lamont, P., and Wiseman, R. (1999). *Magic in Theory.* Hermetic Press.

Lander, K., Bruce, V., & Bindemann, M. (2018). Use-inspired basic research on individual differences in face identification: Implications for criminal investigation and security. *Cognitive Research: Principles and Implications, 3*(1), 26.

Landy, D., & Goldstone, R. L. (2007). How abstract is symbolic thought? *Journal of Experimental Psychology – Learning Memory and Cognition, 33*(4), 720–733.

Landy, M. S., Maloney, L. T., Johnston, E. B., & Young, M. (1995). Measurement and modeling of depth cue combination – in defense of weak fusion. *Vision Research, 35*(3), 389–412.

Lang, P. J., Bradley, M. M., & Cuthbert, B. N. (1998). Emotion, motivation, and anxiety: Brain mechanisms and psychophysiology. *Biological Psychiatry, 44*(12), 1248–1263.

Lange, C. (1885). *Om Sindsbevægelser. Et Psyko-Fysiologisk Studie* [On emotions. A psycho-physiological study]. Lund. Also published in German (1887, 1910), French (1895, 1902) and English(1922). Danish edition reprinted in 1985, edited by O. Rafaelsen and published by Jansssenpharma.

Lange, J., & Lappe, M. (2006). A model of biological motion perception from configural form cues. *Journal of Neuroscience, 26*(11), 2894–2906.

Langer, A., Feingold-Polak, R., Mueller, O., Kellmeyer, P., & Levy-Tzedek, S. (2019). Trust in socially assistive robots: Considerations for use in rehabilitation. *Neuroscience & Biobehavioral Reviews, 104,* 231–239.

Langton, S. R. H., Law, A. S., Burton, A. M., & Schweinberger, S. R. (2008). Attention capture by faces. Cognition, 107, 330–342.

Large, A. M., Bediou, B., Cekic, S., Hart, Y., Bavelier, D., & Green, C. S. (2019). Cognitive and behavioral correlates of achievement in a complex multi-player video game. *Media and Communication, 7*(4), 198–212.

Larkin, J. H. (1978). Problem solving in physics: Structure, process and learning. In J. M. Scandura & C. J. Brainerd (Eds.), *Structural/Process Models of Complex Human Behavior.* Sijthoff & Noordhoff.

Larsen, J. D., & Baddeley, A. (2003). Disruption of verbal STM by irrelevant speech, articulatory suppression, and manual tapping: Do they have a common source? *Quarterly Journal of Experimental Psychology. A: Human Experimental Psychology, 56*(8), 1249–1268.

Larsen, R. J., Kasimatis, M., & Frey, K. (1992). Facilitating the furrowed brow: An unobtrusive test of the facial feedback hypothesis applied to unpleasant affect. *Cognition and Emotion, 6,* 321–338.

Lashley, K. (1929). *Brain Mechanisms and Intelligence.* University of Chicago Press.

Lashley, K. S. (1951). The problem of serial order in behavior. In L. A. Jeffress (Ed.), *Cerebral Mechanisms in Behavior.* Wiley.

Latash, M., & Zatsiorsky, V. (2001). *Classics in Movement Science.* Human Kinetics.

Latinus, M., & Belin, P. (2011). Human voice perception. *Current Biology, 21*(4), R143–R145.

Lau, H., & Brown, R. (2019). The emperor's new phenomenology? The empirical case for conscious experiences without first-order representations. In A. Pautz & D. Stoljar (Eds.), *Blockheads!: Essays on Ned Block's Philosophy of Mind and Consciousness* (pp. 171–197). MIT Press.

Lau, H. C., & Passingham, R. E. (2006). Relative blindsight in normal observers and the neural correlate of visual consciousness. *Proceedings of the National Academy of Sciences, 103*(49), 18763–18768.

Lau, H., & Rosenthal, D. (2011). Empirical support for higher-order theories of conscious awareness. *Trends in Cognitive Sciences, 15*(8), 365–373.

Laurienti, P. J., Burdette, J. H., Maldjian, J. A., & Wallace, M. T. (2006). Enhanced multisensory integration in older adults. *Neurobiology of Aging, 27*(8), 1155–1163.

Lavie, N. (1995). Perceptual load as a necessary condition for selective attention. *Journal of Experimental Psychology: Human Perception and Performance, 21*(3), 451–468.

Lavie, N. (2005). Distracted and confused? Selective attention under load. *Trends in Cognitive Sciences, 9*(2), 75–82.

Lavy, E., van den Hout, M. A., & Arntz, A. (1993). Attentional bias and facilitated escape: A pictorial test. *Advances of Behaviour Research and Therapy, 15,* 279–289.

Laws, K. R., Leeson, V. C., & McKenna, P. J. (2006). Domain specific deficits in schizophrenia. *Cognitive Neuropsychiatry, 11,* 537–556.

Lawson, R., Fernandes, A. M., Albuquerque, P. B., & Lacey, S. (2015). Remembering touch: Using interference tasks to study tactile and haptic memory. In P. Jolicoeur, C. Lefebvre, & J. Martinez-Trujillo (Eds.), *Mechanisms of Sensory Working Memory* (pp. 239–259). Academic Press.

Lazarus, R. S. (1982). Thoughts on the relations between emotion and cognition. *American Psychologist, 37,* 1019–1024.

Lazarus, R. S. (1991). *Emotion and Adaptation.* Oxford University Press.

Lazarus, R. S. (1995). Vexing research problems inherent in cognitive-mediational theories of emotion – and some solutions. *Psychological Inquiry, 6,* 183–196.

Lazarus, R. S., & Alfert, E. (1964). The short-circuiting of threat by experimentally altering cognitive appraisal, *Journal of Abnormal and Social Psychology, 69,* 195–205.

Lazarus, R. S., Opton, E. M., Nomikos, M. S., & Rankin, N. O. (1965). The principle of short-circuiting of threat: Further evidence. *Journal of Personality, 33,* 622–635.

Le Brun. Y., & Leleux, C. (1986). Central communication disorders in deaf signers. In J. Nespolous, P. Perrott, & A. R. Lecours (Eds.), *The Biological Foundation of Gestures: Motor and Semiotic Aspects* (pp. 255–269). Erlbaum.

Le Doux, J. E. (1992). Brain mechanisms of emotion and emotional learning. *Current Opinion in Neurobiology, 2*(2), 191–197.

Le Doux, J. E. (1996). *The Emotional Brain.* Simon & Schuster.

Lea, S. E. G., & Dittrich, W. H. (2000). What do birds see in moving video images? In J. Fagot (Ed.), *Picture Perception in Animals.* Psychology Press.

Lederman, S. J., & Klatzky, R. L. (1986). Hand movements: A window into haptic object recognition.

Lederman, S. J., & Klatzky, R. L. (1987). Hand movements: A window into haptic object recognition. *Cognitive Psychology, 19*(3), 342–368.

Lederman, S. J., & Klatzky, R. L. (2009). Haptic perception: A tutorial. *Attention Perception & Psychophysics, 71*(7), 1439–1459.

Lee, C. S., Nagy, P. G., Weaver, S. J., & Newman-Toker, D. E. (2013). Cognitive and system factors contributing to diagnostic errors in radiology. *American Journal of Roentgenology, 201*(3), 611–617.

Lee, J. L., Nader, K., & Schiller, D. (2017). An update on memory reconsolidation updating. *Trends in Cognitive Sciences, 21*(7), 531–545.

Lee, L. F., & Horowitz, I. A. (1997). Enhancing juror competence in a complex trial. *Applied Cognitive Psychology, 11*, 305–314.

Lee, S. H., Kwan, A. C., Zhang, S., Phoumthipphavong, V., Flannery, J. G., Masmanidis, S. C., Taniguchi, H., Huang, Z. J., Zhang, F., Boyden, E. S., Deisseroth, K., & Dan, Y. (2012). Activation of specific interneurons improves V1 feature selectivity and visual perception. *Nature, 488*(7411), 379–383.

Lee, S. H., Kravitz, D. J., & Baker, C. I. (2012). Disentangling visual imagery and perception of real-world objects. *Neuroimage, 59*, 4064–4073.

Legrenzi, P., Girotto, V., & Johnson-Laird, P. N. (2003). Models of consistency. *Psychological Science, 14*, 131–137.

Legrenzi, P., & Umilta, C. (2011). *Neuromania: On the Limits of Brain Science.* Oxford University Press.

Lehrer, J. (2008). The eureka hunt: Why do good ideas come to us when they do? *The New Yorker,* 28 July, 40–45.

Lemon, R. N., & Edgley, S. A. (2010). Life without a cerebellum. *Brain, 133*(3), 652–654.

Lench, H. C., Bench, S. W., & Flores, S. A. (2013). Searching for evidence, not a war: Reply to Lindquist, Siegel, Quigley, and Barrett (2013). *Psychological Bulletin, 139*(1), 264–268.

Lenneberg, E. H. (1967). *Biological Foundations of Language.* Wiley.

Leopold, D. A., & Logothetis, N. K. (1996). Activity changes in early visual cortex reflect monkeys' percepts during binocular rivalry. *Nature, 379*(6565), 549–553.

Lerner, J. S., Li, Y., Valdesolo, P., & Kassam, K. S. (2015). Emotion and decision making. *Annual Review of Psychology, 66*, 799–823.

Levelt, W. J. M. (1989). *Speaking: From Intention to Articulation.* ACL-MIT Press series in natural-language processing. The MIT Press.

Levelt, W. J. M. (1992). Accessing words in speech production: Stages, processes and representations. *Cognition, 42*, 1–22.

Levelt, W. J. M. (2001). Spoken word production: A theory of lexical access. *Proceedings of the National Academy of Sciences, 98*(23), 13464–13513.

Levelt, W. J. M., Roelofs, A. P. A., & Meyer, A. S. (1999). A theory of lexical access in speech production. *Behavioral and Brain Sciences, 22*(1), 1–37.

Levelt, W. J. M., Schriefers, H., Vorberg, D., Meyer, A. S., Pechmann, T., & Havinga, J. (1991). The time course of lexical access in speech production: A study of picture naming. *Psychological Review, 98*(1), 122–142.

Levenson, R. W. (1994). Human emotions: A functional view. In P. Ekman & R. J. Davidson (Eds.), *The Nature of Emotion: Fundamental Questions* (pp. 123–126). Oxford University Press.

Levenson, R. W. (2004). Blood, sweat, and fears: The autonomic architecture of emotion. In P. Ekman, J. J. Campos, R. J. Davidson, & F. B. M. de Waal (Eds.), *Emotions Inside Out.* New York Academy of Sciences.

Levenson, R. W., Ekman, P., & Friesen, W. V. (1990). Voluntary facial action generates emotion-specific autonomic nervous system activity. *Psychophysiology, 27*, 363–384.

Leventhal, H., & Scherer, K. R. (1987). The relationship of emotion to cognition: A functional approach to semantic controversy. *Cognition and Emotion, 1*, 3–28.

Levin, D. T., & Simons, D. J. (1997). Failure to detect changes to attended objects in motion pictures. *Psychonomic Bulletin, & Review, 4*(4), 501–506.

Levin, D. T., & Simons, D. J. (2000). Perceiving stability in a changing world: Combining shots and integrating views in motion pictures and the real world. *Media Psychology, 2*(4), 357–380.

Levine, L. J., & Pizarro, D. A. (2004). Emotion and memory research: A grumpy overview. *Social Cognition, 22*, 530–554.

Levinson, S. C. (2016). Turn-taking in human communication: Origins and implications for language processing. *Trends in Cognitive Science, 20*(1), 6–14.

Levy, R. (2008). Expectation-based syntactic comprehension. *Cognition, 106*, 1126–1177.

Lewis-Peacock, J. A., Drysdale, A. T., Oberauer, K., & Postle, B. R. (2012). Neural evidence for a distinction between short-term memory and the focus of attention. *Journal of Cognitive Neuroscience, 24*, 61–79.

Li, D., Vlisides, P. E., Kelz, M. B., Avidan, M. S., & Mashour, G. A. (2019). Dynamic cortical connectivity during general anesthesia in healthy volunteers. *Anesthesiology: The Journal of the American Society of Anesthesiologists, 130*(6), 870–884.

Li, X. B., & Basso, M. A. (2008). Preparing to move increases the sensitivity of superior colliculus neurons. *Journal of Neuroscience, 28*(17), 4561–4577.

Liberal Democrat History Group (2019). *Liberal Thinkers.* Liberal Democrat History Group.

Liberman, A. (2009). The etymology of 'brain' and cognates. *Nordic Journal of English Studies, 8*, 45–59.

Liberman, A. M., Harris, K. S., Hoffman, H. S., & Griffith, B. C. (1957). The discrimination of speech sounds within and across phoneme boundaries. *Journal of Experimental Psychology, 54*, 358–368.

Libet, B. (1985). Unconscious cerebral initiative and the role of conscious will in voluntary action. *Behavioral and Brain Sciences, 8*(4), 529–539.

Libet, B. (2002). The timing of mental events: Libet's experimental findings and their implications. *Consciousness and Cognition, 11*, 291–299.

Libet, B., Gleason, C. A., Wright, E. W., & Pearl, D. (1983). Time of unconscious intention to act in relation to onset of cerebral activity (readiness-potential): The unconscious initiation of a freely voluntary act. *Brain, 106*, 623–642.

Lichtenstein, S., Slovic, P., Fischhoff, B., Layman, M., & Coombes, B. (1978). Judged frequency of lethal events. *Journal of Experimental Psychology: Human Learning and Memory, 4*, 551–578.

Limb, C. J., & Roy, A. T. (2014). Technological, biological, and acoustical constraints to music perception in cochlear implant users. *Hearing Research, 308*, 13–26.

Lindquist, K. A., & Barrett, L. F. (2012). A functional architecture of the human brain: Insights from emotion. *Trends in Cognitive Sciences, 16*, 533–540.

Lindquist, K. A., Wager, T. D., Kober, H., Bliss-Moreau, E., & Barrett, L. F. (2012). The brain basis of emotion: A meta-analytic review. *Behavioral and Brain Sciences, 35*(3), 121–143.

Lindsay, R. C. L., Mansour, J. K., Bertrand, N. K., & Whaley, E. I. (2011). Face recognition in eyewitness memory: Face perception and recognition in eyewitness memory. In A. Calder, G. Rhodes, M. Johnson, J. Haxby, & J. Keane (Eds.), *The Handbook of Face Perception.* Oxford University Press.

Lindsay, R. C. L., & Wells, G. L. (1985). Improving eyewitness identifications from lineups: Simultaneous versus sequential lineup presentation. *Journal of Applied Psychology, 70*(3), 556–564.

Lindstrom, M. (2011). You love your iPhone, literally. *New York Times,* 30 September.

Linell, P. (2015). Mishearings are occasioned by contextual assumptions and situational affordances. *Language & Communication, 40*, 24–37.

Linn, L. (1954). Psychological implications of the 'activating system.' *American Journal of Psychiatry, 110*, 61–65.

Linton, M. (1978). Real-world memory after six years: An in vivo study of very long-term memory. In M. M. Gruneberg, P. E. Morris, & R. N. Sykes (Eds.), *Practical Aspects of Memory* (pp. 69–76). Academic Press.

Lipman, M. (1974). *Harry Stottlemeier's Discovery.* Institute for the Advancement of Philosophy for Children.

Lipnicki, D. M., & Byrne, D. G. (2005). Thinking on your back: Solving anagrams faster when supine than when standing. *Brain Research: Cognitive Brain Research, 24*, 719–722.

Lipp, O. V., & Derakshan, N. (2005). Attentional bias to pictures of fear relevant animals in a dot probe task. *Emotion, 5*(3), 365–369.

Lipshitz, R., Klein, G., Orasanu, J., & Salas, E. (2001). Taking stock of naturalistic decision making. *Journal of Behavioral Decision Making, 14*, 331–352.

Lipton, P. (2007). Alien abduction: Inference to the best explanation and the management of testimony. *Episteme, 4*(3), 238–251.

Lisman, S. A. (1974). Alcoholic 'blackout': State dependent learning? *Archive of General Psychiatry, 30*, 46–53.

Lister, R. G., Eckardt, M. J., & Weingartner, H. (1987). Ethanol intoxication and memory: Recent developments and new directions. In M. Galanter (Ed.), *Recent*

Developments in Alcoholism, Vol. 5. Plenum.

Littlemore, J. (2009). *Applying Cognitive Linguistics to Second Language Learning and Teaching*. Palgrave Macmillan.

Liu, L., & Jaeger, T. F. (2018). Inferring causes during speech perception. *Cognition, 174*, 55–70.

Liversedge, S. P., & Findlay, J. M. (2000). Saccadic eye movements and cognition. *Trends in Cognitive Sciences, 4*, 6–14.

Locke, J. (1690/2004). *An Essay Concerning Human Understanding*. Penguin.

Lockwood, G., & Dingemanse, M. (2015). Iconicity in the lab: A review of behavioral, developmental, and neuroimaging research into sound-symbolism. *Frontiers in Psychology, 6*, 1246.

Loewenstein, G. (1987). Anticipation and the valuation of delayed consumption. *Economic Journal, 97*, 666–684.

Loewenstein, G., & Lerner, J. S. (2003). The role of affect in decision making. *Handbook of Affective Science, 619*(642), 3.

Loftus, E. F. (1975). Leading questions and the eyewitness report. *Cognitive Psychology, 7*, 560–572.

Loftus, E. F. (1980). *Memory*. Addison-Wesley.

Loftus, E. F. (1993). The reality of repressed memories. *American Psychologist, 48*, 518–537.

Loftus, E. F. (1994). The repressed memory controversy. *American Psychologist, 49*(5), 443–445.

Loftus, E. F. (1997). Creating false memories. *Scientific American, 277*, 70–75.

Loftus, E. F. (2019). Eyewitness testimony. *Applied Cognitive Psychology, 33*(4), 498–503.

Loftus, E. F., Loftus, G. R., & Messo, J. (1987). Some facts about weapon focus. *Law and Human Behavior, 11*, 55–62.

Loftus, G. R. & Loftus, E. F. (1976). *Human Memory: The Processing of Information*. Routledge.

Loftus, E. F., Miller, D. G., & Burns, H. J. (1978). Semantic integration of verbal information into a visual memory. *Human Learning and Memory, 4*, 19–31.

Loftus, E. F., & Palmer, J. C. (1974). Reconstruction of automobile destruction: An example of the interaction between language and memory. *Journal of Verbal Learning and Verbal Behavior, 13*(5), 585–589.

Loftus, E. F., & Zanni, G. (1975). Eyewitness testimony: The influence of the wording of a question. *Bulletin of Psychonomic Society, 5*, 86–88.

Logan, G. D. (2004). Cumulative progress in formal theories of attention. *Annual Review of Psychology, 55*, 207–234.

Logie, R. H. (1995). *Visuo-Spatial Working Memory*. Lawrence Erlbaum.

Logie, R. H. (2016). Retiring the central executive. *Quarterly Journal of Experimental Psychology, 69*(10), 2093–2109.

Logie, R.H. (2016) Retiring the central executive, *The Quarterly Journal of Experimental Psychology*, 69:10, 2093-2109.

Logie, R. H. (2019). Converging sources of evidence and theory integration in working memory: A commentary on Morey, Rhodes, and Cowan (2019). *Cortex, 112*, 162–171.

Logie, R. H., & Cowan, N. (2015). Perspectives on working memory: introduction to the special issue. *Memory & Cognition, 43*(3), 315–324.

Logie, R. H., & D'Esposito, M. (2007). Working memory in the brain. *Cortex, 43*(1), 1–4.

Logie, R. H., Gilhooly, K. J., & Wynn, V. (1994). Counting on working memory in arithmetic problem solving. *Memory & Cognition, 22*, 395–410.

Logie, R. H., Pernet, C. R., Buonocore, A., & Della Sala, S. (2011). Low and high imagers activate networks differentially in mental rotation. *Neuropsychologia, 49*, 3071–3077.

Logothetis, N. K. (1998). Single units and conscious vision. *Philosophical Transactions of the Royal Society B – Biological Sciences, 353* (1377), 1801–1818.

Logothetis, N. K., & Sheinberg, D. L. (1996). Visual object recognition. *Annual Review of Neuroscience, 19*, 577–621.

Longo, M. R., Azanon, E., & Haggard, P. (2010). More than skin deep: Body representation beyond primary somatosensory cortex. *Neuropsychologia, 48*(3), 655–668.

Longo, M. R., Long, C., & Haggard, P. (2012). Mapping the invisible hand: A body model of a phantom limb. *Psychological Science, 23*(7), 740–742.

Looi, V., Gfeller, K., & Driscoll, V. D. (2012). Music appreciation and training for cochlear implant recipients: A review. In *Seminars in Hearing* (Vol. 33, No. 04, November, pp. 307–334). Thieme Medical Publishers.

Looney, V., & Meier, R. P. (2014). Genie's middle-finger points and signs: A case study. *Gesture, 14*(1), 97–107.

López, E., Steiner, A. J., Hardy, D. J., IsHak, W. W., & Anderson, W. B. (2016). Discrepancies between bilinguals' performance on the Spanish and English versions of the WAIS Digit Span task: Cross-cultural implications. *Applied Neuropsychology: Adult, 23*(5), 343–352.

Loschky, L. C., Larson, A. M., Smith, T. J., & Magliano, J. P. (2020). The scene perception and event comprehension theory (SPECT) applied to visual narratives. *Topics in Cognitive Science, 12*(1), 311–351.

Louie, J. F., & Mouloua, M. (2019). Predicting distracted driving: The role of individual difference in working memory. *Applied Ergonomics, 74*, 154–161.

Loula, F., Prasad, S., Harber, K., & Shiffrar, M. (2005). Recognizing people from their movement. *Journal of Experimental Psychology – Human Perception and Performance, 31*(1), 210–220.

Lowet, E., Gomes, B., Srinivasan, K., Zhou, H., Schafer, R. J., & Desimone, R. (2018). Enhanced neural processing by covert attention only during microsaccades directed toward the attended stimulus. *Neuron, 99*(1), 207–214.

Lu, C., & Tang, X. (2015). Surpassing human-level face verification performance on LFW with Gaussian Face. *Twenty-ninth AAAI Conference on Artificial Intelligence*. March.

Luchins, A. W. (1942). Mechanization in problem solving: The effect of Einstellung. *Psychological Monographs, 54*.

Luke, T. J., Crozier, W. E., & Strange, D. (2017). Memory errors in police interviews: The bait question as a source of misinformation. *Journal of Applied Research in Memory and Cognition, 6*(3), 260–273.

Lung, C. T., & Dominowski, R. L. (1985). Effects of strategy instructions and practice on nine-dot problem solving. *Journal of Experimental Psychology: Learning, Memory and Cognition, 11*, 804–811.

Lunke, K., & Meier, B. (2018). New insights into mechanisms of enhanced synaesthetic memory: Benefitsare synaesthesia-type-specific. *PLoS ONE, 13*(9), e0203055.

Luria, A. R. (1968). *The Mind of the Mnemonist*. Basic Books.

Luria, A. R. (1971). Towards the problem of the historical nature of psychological processes. *International Journal of Psychology, 6*, 259–272.

Lutz, C. (1990). Morality, domination and understandings of 'justifiable anger' among the Ifaluk. In G. Semin & K. Gergen (Eds.), *Everyday Understanding* (pp. 204–226). Sage.

Luzzatti, C., Vecchi, T., Agazzi, D., Cesa-Bianchi, M., & Vergani, C. (1998). A neurological dissociation between preserved visual and impaired spatial processing in mental imagery. *Cortex, 34*(3), 461–469.

Lyddy, F., Farina, F., Hanney, J., Farrell, L., & Kelly O'Neill, N. (2014). An analysis of language in university students' text messages. *Journal of Computer-Mediated Communication, 19*(3), 546–561.

M

Mac Giollabhui, N., Hamilton, J. L., Nielsen, J., Connolly, S. L., Stange, J. P., Varga, S., Burdette, E., Olino, T. M., Abramson, L. Y., & Alloy, L. B. (2018). Negative cognitive style interacts with negative life events to predict first onset of a major depressive episode in adolescence via hopelessness. *Journal of Abnormal Psychology, 127*(1), 1–11.

Macaluso, E., Noppeney, U., Talsma, D., Vercillo, T., Hartcher-O'Brien, J., & Adam, R. (2016). The curious incident of attention in multisensory integration: Bottom-up vs. top-down. *Multisensory Research, 29*(6–7), 557–583.

MacCabe, J. H., Sarasian, A., Almquvist, C., Lichtenstein, H., Larsson, H., & Kyaga, S. (2018). Artistic creativity and risk for schizophrenia, bipolar disorder and unipolar depression: A Swedish population based case control study and sib-pair analysis. *British Journal of Psychiatry*. doi:10.1192/bjp.2018.23

MacFarland, D. (1999). *Animal Behaviour*. Longman.

Macfarlane, D. A. (1930). The role of kinesthesis in maze learning. *University of California Publications in Psychology, 4*, 277–305.

MacGregor, J. N., Chronicle, E. P., & Ormerod, T. C. (2006). A comparison of heuristic and human performance on open versions of the travelling salesperson problem. *Journal of Problem Solving, 1*, 33–43.

MacGregor, J. N., & Chu, Y. (2011). Human performance on the travelling salesman and related problems: A review. *Journal of Problem Solving, 3*, 1–29.

MacGregor, J. N., & Ormerod, T. (1996). Human performance on the travelling salesman problem.

Perception and Psychophysics, 58, 527–539.

MacGregor, J. N., Ormerod, T. C., & Chronicle, E. P. (2001). Information processing and insight: A process model of performance on the nine-dot and related problems. *Journal of Experimental Psychology: Learning, Memory and Cognition, 27,* 176–201.

Mack, A., & Rock, I. (1998). *Inattentional Blindness.* MIT Press.

MacKay, D. G. (1987). *The Organization of Perception and Action: A Theory for Language and Other Cognitive Skills.* Springer-Verlag.

Macknik, S. L., King, M., Randi, J., Robbins, A., Thompson, J., & Martinez-Conde, S. (2008). Attention and awareness in stage magic: Turning tricks into research. *Nature Reviews Neuroscience, 9*(11), 871–879.

Maclay, H., & Osgood, C. E. (1959). Hesitation phenomena in spontaneous English speech. *Word, 15,* 19–44.

MacLeod, C. M. (1991). Half a century of research on the Stroop effect: An integrative review. *Psychological Bulletin, 109*(2), 163–203.

MacLeod, C. M., & MacDonald, P. A. (2000). Inter-dimensional interference in the Stroop effect: Uncovering the cognitive and neural anatomy of attention. *Trends in Cognitive Sciences, 4,* 383–391.

MacLeod, C., Mathews, A., & Tata, P. (1986). Attentional bias in emotional disorders. *Journal of Abnormal Psychology, 95*(1), 15–20.

MacLin, O. H., MacLin, M. K., & Malpass, R. S. (2001). Race, arousal, attention, exposure, and delay: An examination of factors moderating face recognition. *Psychology, Public Policy, and Law, 7*(1), 134–152.

MacMillan, M. (2000). *An Odd Kind of Fame: Stories of Phineas Gage.* The MIT Press.

Macnamara, B. N., & Maitra, M. (2019). The role of deliberate practice in expert performance: Revisiting Ericsson, Krampe & Tesch-Rohmer (1993). *Royal Society Open Science, 6.*

MacNeilage, P. F. (1999). Whatever happened to articulate speech? In M. C. Corballis & S. E. G. Lea (Eds.), *The Descent of Mind: Psychological Perspectives on Hominid Evolution* (pp. 116–137). Oxford University Press.

Maddieson, I. M. (1984). *Patterns of Sounds.* Cambridge University Press.

Maffei, C., Capasso, R., Cazzolli, G., Colosimo, C., Dell'Acqua, F.,

Piludu, F., Catani, M., & Miceli, G. (2017). Pure word deafness following left temporal damage: Behavioral and neuroanatomical evidence from a new case. *Cortex, 97,* 240–254.

Magnussen, S., Melinder, A., Stridbeck, U., & Raja, A. Q. (2010). Beliefs about factors affecting the reliability of eyewitness testimony: A comparison of judges, jurors and the general public. *Applied Cognitive Psychology: The Official Journal of the Society for Applied Research in Memory and Cognition, 24*(1), 122–133.

Maguire, E. A., Valentine, E. R., Wilding, J. M., & Kapur, N. (2003). Routes to remembering: The brains behind superior memory. *Nature Neuroscience, 6,* 90–95.

Maier, N. R. F. (1931). Reasoning in humans II: The solution of a problem and its appearance in consciousness. *Journal of Comparative Psychology, 12,* 181–194.

Malmberg, K. J., Raaijmakers, J. G. W., & Shiffrin, R. M. (2019). 50years of research sparked by Atkinson and Shiffrin (1968). *Memory & Cognition, 47*(4), 561–574.

Malt, B. C. (1990). Features and beliefs in the mental representation of categories. *Journal of Memory and Language, 29,* 289–315.

Malt, B. C. (1994). Water is not H_2O. *Cognitive Psychology, 27,* 41–70.

Malt, B. C., & Smith, E. E. (1982). The role of familiarity in determining typicality. *Memory & Cognition, 10,* 69–75.

Mamassian, P., & Landy, M. S. (2010). It's that time again. *Nature Neuroscience, 13*(8), 914–916.

Mamassian, P., Landy, M. S., & Maloney, L. T. (2002). Bayesian modelling of visual perception. In R. P. N. Rao, B. A. Olshausen, & M. S. Lewicki (Eds.), *Probabilistic Models of the Brain: Perception and Neural Function.* MIT Press.

Mandich, A., & Polatajko, H. J. (2003). Developmental coordination disorder: Mechanisms, measurement and management. *Human Movement Science, 22* (4–5).

Mandler, G. (1967). Organization and memory. In K. W. Spence & J. T. Spence (Eds.), *The Psychology of Learning and Motivation* (Vol. 1, pp. 327–372). New York: Academic Press.

Mandler, G., & Pearlstone, Z. (1966). Free and constrained concept learning and subsequent recall. *Journal of Verbal Learning and Verbal Behavior, 5,* 126–131.

Mandler, G., Nakamura, Y., & Shebo-Van Zandt, B. J. (1987). Nonspecific effects of exposure on

stimuli that cannot be recognized. *Journal of Experimental Psychology: Learning, Memory & Cognition, 13,* 646–648.

Mann, R. E., Cho-Young, J., & Vogel-Sprott, M. (1984). Retrograde enhancement by alcohol of delayed free recall performance. *Pharmacology and Biochemistry of Behavior, 20,* 639–642.

Mann, S., Vrij, A., & Bull, R. (2004). Detecting true lies: Police officers' ability to detect suspects' lies. *Journal of Applied Psychology, 89,* 137–149.

Manns, J. R., Hopkins, R. O., & Squire, L. R. (2003). Semantic memory and the human hippocampus. *Neuron, 38,* 127–133.

Manzi, A., Martinez, S., & Durmysheva, Y. (2017). Cognitive correlates of lecture note taking: Handwriting speed and attention. *North American Journal of Psychology, 19*(1), 195–217.

Mapelli, D., & Behrmann, M. (1997). The role of color in object recognition: Evidence from visual agnosia. *Neurocase, 3,* 237–247.

Marcus, S. L., & Rips, L. J. (1979). Conditional reasoning. *Journal of Verbal Learning and Verbal Behaviour, 18,* 199–233.

Marek, S., & Dosenbach, N. U. (2018). The frontoparietal network: Function, electrophysiology, and importance of individual precision mapping. *Dialogues in Clinical Neuroscience, 20*(2), 133.

Marinsek, N. L., Gazzaniga, M. S., & Miller, M. B. (2016) Split-brain, split-mind. In S. Laureys, O. Gosseries, & G. Tononi (Eds.), *The Neurology of Consciousness* (2nd ed.) (pp. 271–279). Academic Press.

Markovits, H. (1988). Conditional reasoning, empirical evidence on a concrete task. *Quarterly Journal of Experimental Psychology, 45A,* 133–148.

Markowitsch, H. J., & Staniloiu, A. (2012). Amnesic disorders. *The Lancet, 380*(9851), 1429–1440.

Marr, D. (1982). *Vision: A Computational Investigation Into the Human Representation and Processing of Visual Information.* W. H. Freeman.

Marsh, R. L., Hicks, J. L., & Landau, J. D. (1998). An investigation of everyday prospective memory. *Memory & Cognition, 24,* 633–643.

Marshall, G. D., & Zimbardo, P. G. (1979). Affective consequences of inadequately explained physiological arousal. *Journal of Personality and Social Psychology, 37,* 970–988.

Marshall, J. C., & Newcombe, F. (1973). Patterns of paralexia: A

psycholinguistic approach. *Journal of Psycholinguistic Research, 2,* 175–199.

Marslen-Wilson, W. (1987). Functional parallelism in spoken word-recognition. *Cognition, 25,* 71–102.

Marslen-Wilson, W. D. (1990). Activation, competition, and frequency in lexical access. In G. T. M. Altmann (Ed.), *Cognitive Models of Speech Processing: Psycholinguistics and Computational Perspectives* (pp. 148–172). The MIT Press.

Marslen-Wilson, W. D., & Tyler, L. K. (1980). The temporal structure of spoken language understanding. *Cognition, 8,* 1–71.

Martin, A., & Caramazza, A. (2003). Neuropsychological and neuroimaging perspectives on conceptual knowledge: An introduction. *Cognitive Neuropsychology, 20,* 195–212.

Martin, A., Kronbichler, M., & Richlan, F. (2016). Dyslexic brain activation abnormalities in deep and shallow orthographies: A meta-analysis of 28 functional neuroimaging studies. *Human Brain Mapping, 37*(7), 2676–2699.

Martinez-Trujillo, J. C., & Treue, S. (2004). Feature-based attention increases the selectivity of population responses in primate visual cortex. *Current Biology, 14*(9), 744–751.

Marupaka, N., Iyer, L., & Minai, A. A. (2013). Connectivity and thought: The influence of semantic network structure in a neurodynamical model of thinking. *Neural Networks, 32,* 147–158.

Mashour, G. A. (2018). Highways of the brain, traffic of the mind. *Anesthesiology: The Journal of the American Society of Anesthesiologists, 129*(5), 869–871.

Mashour, G. A., Roelfsema, P., Changeux, J. P., & Dehaene, S. (2020). Conscious processing and the global neuronal workspace hypothesis. *Neuron, 105*(5), 776–798.

Mason, O., & Claridge, G. (2006). The Oxford–Liverpool Inventory of Feelings and Experiences (O-LIFE): Further description and extended norms. *Schizophrenia Research, 82,* 203–211.

Massaro, D. W. (1975). Backward recognition masking. *Journal of the Acoustical Society of America, 58*(5), 1059–1065.

Massaro, D. W. (1976). Perceptual processing in dichotic listening. *Journal of Experimental Psychology: Human Learning and Memory, 2,* 331–339.

Massaro, D. W. (1994). Psychological aspects of speech perception: Implications for research and theory. In M. Gemsbacher (Ed.), *Handbook of Psycholinguistics* (pp. 219–263). Academic Press.

Massaro, D. W. (2001). Speech perception. In N. J. Smelser & P. B. Baltes (Eds.), *International Encyclopedia of the Social & Behavioral Sciences*. Elsevier.

Massaro, D. W., & Cohen, M. (1983). Phonological context in speech perception. *Perception and Psychophysics, 34,* 338–348.

Mast, F. W., & Kosslyn, S. (2002). Visual mental images can be ambiguous: Insights from insights from individual differences in spatial transformation abilities. *Cognition, 81,* 57–70.

Masters, R. S. W. (1992). Knowledge, knerves and know-how: The role of explicit versus implicit knowledge in the breakdown of a complex motor skill under pressure. *British Journal of Psychology, 83,* 343–358.

Mataró, M., Jurado, M. Á., García-Sánchez, C., Barraquer, L., Costa-Jussà, F. R., & Junqué, C. (2001). Long-term effects of bilateral frontal brain lesion: 60 years after injury with an iron bar. *Archives of Neurology, 58*(7), 1139–1142.

Matchock, R. L., Levine, M. E., Gianaros, P. J., & Stern, R. M. (2008). Susceptibility to nausea and motion sickness as a function of the menstrual cycle. *Women's Health Issues, 18*(4), 328–335.

Matheson, H.E., & Barsalou, L. (2018). Embodiment and grounding in cognitive neuroscience. In S. L. Thompson-Schill (Ed.), *Stevens' Handbook of Experimental Psychology and Cognitive Neuroscience*, Vol. 3. John Wiley & Sons.

Mathews, A., Mogg, K., Kentish, J., & Eysenck, M., (1995). Effect of psychological treatment on cognitive bias in generalized anxiety disorder. *Behaviour Research and Therapy, 33*(3), 293–303.

Matsumoto, D., & Hwang, H. (2011). Evidence for training the ability to read micro expressions of emotion. *Motivation and Emotion, 35*(2), 181–191.

Matsumoto, D., & Willingham, B. (2009). Spontaneous facial expressions of emotion of congenitally and noncongenitally blind individuals. *Journal of Personality and Social Psychology, 96,* 1–10.

Mattar, A. A. G., & Gribble, P. L. (2005). Motor learning by observing. *Neuron, 46*(1), 153–160.

Mattys, S.L., Baddeley, A., & Trenkic, D. (2018). Is the superior verbal memory span of Mandarin speakers due to faster rehearsal? *Memory & Cognition, 46,* 361–369.

Mattys, S. L., Melhorn, J. F., & White, L. (2007). Effects of syntactic expectations on speech segmentation. *Journal of Experimental Psychology: Human Perception and Performance, 33,* 960–977.

Maule, J., & Villejoubert, G. (2007). What lies beneath: Reframing framing effects. *Thinking and Reasoning, 13,* 25–44.

Mayberry, E. J., Sage, K., & Lambon Ralph, M. A. (2011). At the edge of semantic space: The breakdown of coherent concepts in semantic dementia is constrained by typicality and severity but not modality. *Journal of Cognitive Neuroscience, 23,* 2240–2251.

Mayberry, R. I., Davenport, T., Roth, A., & Halgren, E. (2018). Neurolinguistic processing when the brain matures without language. *Cortex, 99,* 390–403.

Mayer, E., & Rossion, B. (2007). Prosopagnosia. In O. Godefroy & J. Bogousslavsky (Eds.), *The Behavioral and Cognitive Neurology of Stroke* (pp. 315–334). Cambridge University Press.

Mazzoni, G., & Mamon, A., (2003). Imagination can create false memories. *Psychological Science, 14,* pp. 186–8.

Mazzoni, G., Scoboria, A., & Harvey, L. (2010). Nonbelieved memories. *Psychological Science, 21*(9), 1334–1340.

McAdams, C. J., & Maunsell, J. H. R. (1999). Effects of attention on orientation-tuning functions of single neurons in macaque cortical area V4. *Journal of Neuroscience, 19*(1), 431–441.

McAleer, P., Todorov, A., & Belin, P. (2014). How do you say 'Hello'? Personality impressions from brief novel voices. *PLoS ONE, 9*(3), e90779.

McCaffrey, T. (2012). Innovation relies on the obscure: A key to overcoming the classic problem of functional fixedness. *Psychological Science, 23*(3), 215–218.

McCall, R., McGee, F., Mirnig, A., Meschtscherjakov, A., Louveton, N., Engel, T., & Tscheligi, M. (2019). A taxonomy of autonomous vehicle handover situations. *Transportation Research Part A: Policy and Practice, 124,* 507–522.

McCarley, J. S., Kramer, A. F., Wickens, C. D., Vidoni, E. D., & Boot, W. R. (2004). Visual skills in airport-security screening. *Psychological Science, 15*(5), 302–306.

McCausland, S., Kingston, J., & Lyddy, F. (2015) Processing costs when reading short message service shortcuts: An eye-tracking study. *Writing Systems Research, 7*(1), 97–107.

McClelland, J. L., Mirman, D., & Holt, L. L. (2006). Are there interactive processes in speech perception? *Trends in Cognitive Sciences, 10,* 363–369.

McClelland, J. L., & Rumelhart, D. E. (1981). An interactive activation model of context effects in letter perception. 1. An account of basic findings. *Psychological Review, 88*(5), 375–407.

McCloskey, M. E., & Glucksberg, S. (1978). Natural categories: Well defined or fuzzy sets? *Memory and Cognition, 6,* 462–472.

McClure, S. M., Laibson, D. I., Loewenstein, G., & Cohen, J. D. (2004). Separate neural systems value immediate and delayed monetary rewards. *Science, 306,* 503–507.

McClure, S. M., Li, J., Tomlin, D., Cypert, K. S., Latane, M. M., & Montague, P. R. (2003). Neural correlates of behavioral preference for culturally familiar drinks. *Neuron, 44,* 379–387.

McCormick, P. A., & Klein, R. (1990). The spatial distribution of attention during covert visual orienting. *Acta Psychologica, 75*(3), 225–242.

McCoy, A. N., Crowley, J. C., Haghighian, G., Dean, H. L., & Platt, M. L. (2003). Saccade reward signals in posterior cingulate cortex. *Neuron, 40,* 1031–1040.

McDermott, H. J. (2004). Music perception with cochlear implants: A review. *Trends in Amplification, 8*(2), 49–82.

McGeoch, J. A., & McDonald, W. T. (1931). Meaningful relation and retroactive inhibition. *American Journal of Psychology, 43,* 579–588.

McGeoch, J. A., & Nolen, M. E. (1933). Studies in retroactive inhibition. IV. Temporal point of interpolation and degree of retroactive inhibition. *Journal of Comparative Psychology, 15,* 407–417.

McGurk, H., & MacDonald, J. (1976). Hearing lips and seeing voices. *Nature, 264* (5588), 746–748.

McHugo, M., Olatunji, B. O., & Zald, D. H. (2013). The emotional attentional blink: What we know so far. *Frontiers in Human Neuroscience, 7,* 151.

McIsaac, H. K., & Eich, E. (2004). Vantage point in traumatic memory. *Psychological Science, 15*(4), 248–253.

McKay, L. S., Simmons, D. R., McAleer, P., Marjoram, D., Piggot, J., & Pollick, F. E. (2012). Do distinct atypical cortical networks process biological motion information in adults with autism spectrum disorders? *Neuroimage, 59,* 1524–1533.

McKelvie, S. J. (2019). Classical introspectionism revisited: Implications of research on visual imagery for the functions of pristine inner experience as apprehended by Descriptive Experience Sampling. *Current Psychology,* February.

McManus, I. C., Richards, P., Winder, B. C., & Sproston, K. A. (1998). Clinical experience, performance in final examinations, and learning style in medical students: A prospective study. *British Medical Journal, 316,* 345–350.

McNally, R. J., & Geraerts, E. (2009). A new solution to the recovered memory debate. *Perspectives on Psychological Science, 4*(2), 126–134.

McNeill, D. (1992). *Hand and Mind: What Gestures Reveal About Thought.* University of Chicago Press.

McNeill, D. (2005). *Gesture and Thought.* University of Chicago Press.

McNeill, D., & Duncan, S. D. (2000). Growth points in thinking-for-speaking. In D. McNeill (Ed.), *Language and Gesture* (pp. 141–161). Cambridge University Press.

McQueen, J. M., Norris, D., & Cutler, A. (1994). Competition in spoken word recognition: Spotting words in other words. *Journal of Experimental Psychology: Learning, Memory, and Cognition, 20,* 621–638.

McQueen, J. M., Otake, T., & Cutler, A. (2001). Rhythmic cues and possible-word constraints in Japanese speech segmentation. *Journal of Memory and Language, 45,* 103–132.

McWilliams, L., Bellhouse, S., Yorke, J., Lloyd, K., & Armitage, C. J. (2019). Beyond 'planning': A meta-analysis of implementation intentions to support smoking cessation. *Health Psychology, 38*(12), 1059.

Meadow, A., Parnes, S. J., & Reese, H. (1959). Influence of brainstorming instruction and problem sequence on a creative problem solving test. *Journal of Applied Psychology, 43,* 413–416.

Medin, D. L. (1989). Concepts and conceptual structure. *American Psychologist, 44,* 1469–1481.

Medin, D. L., & Ortony, A. (1989). Psychological essentialism. In S. Vosniadou & A. Ortony (Eds.),

Similarity and Analogical Reasoning. Cambridge University Press.

Meers, R., Nuttall, H. E., & Vogt, S. (2020). Motor imagery alone drives corticospinal excitability during concurrent action observation and motor imagery. *Cortex, 126*, 322.

Megherbi, H., Elbro, C., Oakhill, J., Segui, J., & New, B. (2018). The emergence of automaticity in reading: Effects of orthographic depth and word decoding ability on an adjusted Stroop measure. *Journal of Experimental Child Psychology, 166*, 652–663.

Mei, N., Flinker, A., Zhu, M., Cai, Q., & Tian, X. (2020). Lateralization in the dichotic listening of tones is influenced by the content of speech. *Neuropsychologia, 140*, 107389.

Meissner, C. A., & Brigham, J. C. (2001). Thirty years of investigating the own-race bias in memory for faces: A meta-analytic review. *Psychology, Public Policy, and Law, 7*(1), 3–35.

Mekki, M., Delgado, A. D., Fry, A., Putrino, D., & Huang, V. (2018). Robotic rehabilitation and spinal cord injury: A narrative review. *Neurotherapeutics, 15*(3), 604–617.

Melnick, M. D., Tadin, D., & Huxlin, K. R. (2016). Relearning to see in cortical blindness. *The Neuroscientist, 22*(2), 199–212.

Melzack, R. (1990). Phantom limbs and the concept of a neuromatrix. *Trends in Neurosciences, 13*(3), 88–92.

Melzack, R. (1992). Phantom limbs. *Scientific American, 266*(4), 120–126.

Memon, A., Meissner, C. A., & Fraser, J. (2010). The cognitive interview: A meta-analytic review and study space analysis of the past 25 years. *Psychology, Public Policy and Law, 16*(4), 340–372.

Mendes, M., Schwaninger, A., & Michel, S. (2011). Does the Application of Virtually Merged Images Influence the Effectiveness of Computer-Based Training in X-Ray Screening? Paper presented at the Security Technology (ICCST), 2011 IEEE International Carnahan Conference.

Mendes, S. (writer). (1999). *American Beauty*: Dreamworks SKG.

Menon, V. (2010). Large scale brain networks in cognition: Emerging principles. In O. Sporn (Ed.), *Analysis and Function of Large Scale Brain Networks* (pp. 43–54). Society for Neuroscience.

Merikle, P. M., & Daneman, M. (1998). Psychological investigations of unconscious perception. *Journal of Consciousness Studies, 5*(1), 5–18.

Meringer, R., & Mayer, K. (1895). *Versprechen und Verlesen: Eine Psychologisch-Linguistiche Studie* (Mistakes in speech and reading: A psychological and linguistic study). Gùschense Verlagsbuchhandlung.

Metcalfe, J., & Dunlosky, J. (2008). Metamemory. In H. L. Roediger, III (Ed.), *Cognitive Psychology of Memory. Vol. 2 of Learning and Memory: A Comprehensive Reference* (pp. 349–362). Elsevier.

Metcalfe, J., & Weibe, D. (1987). Intuition in insight and non-insight problem solving. *Memory and Cognition, 15*, 238–246.

Metzinger, T. K. (2018). Why is virtual reality interesting for philosophers? *Frontiers in Robotics and AI, 5*, 101.

Meyer, D. E., & Schvaneveldt, R. W. (1971). Facilitation in recognizing pairs of words: Evidence of a dependence between retrieval operations. *Journal of Experimental Psychology, 90*, 227–234.

Mezzacappa, E. S., Katkin, E., & Palmer, S. N. (1999). Epinephrine, arousal, and emotion: A new look at two-factor theory. *Cognition and Emotion, 13*(2), 181–199.

Michotte, A. É. (1946). *La Perception De La Causalité*. Institut supérieur de philosophie.

Michotte, A. É. (1963). *The Perception of Causality*. New York: Basic Books.

Michotte, A. É., Thinès, G., Costall, A., & Butterworth, G. (1990). *Michotte's Experimental Phenomenology of Perception*. Lawrence Erlbaum.

Milgram, S. (1967). The small world problem. *Psychology Today, 2*, 60–67.

Mill, J. S. (1875/1967). *A System of Logic*. Longman.

Miller, G. A. (1956). The magical number seven, plus or minus two. *The Psychological Review, 63*, 81–97.

Miller, G. A. (1962). *Psychology: The Science of Mental life*. Hutchinson.

Miller, G. A. (1968). The Psycholinguists. In *The Psychology of Communication: Seven Essays*. Penguin.

Miller, G. A., Galanter, E., & Pribram, K. H. (1960). *Plans and the Structure of Behavior*. Holt, Rinehart, & Winston.

Miller, J. L., & Jusczyk, P. W. (1989). Seeking the neurobiological bases of speech perception. *Cognition, 33*, 111–137.

Miller, J., Shepherdson, P., & Trevena, J. (2011). Effects of clock monitoring on electroencephalographic activity: Is unconscious movement initiation an artifact of the clock? *Psychological Science, 22*(1), 103–109.

Miller, N., Lowit, A., & O'Sullivan, H. (2006). What makes acquired foreign accent syndrome foreign? *Journal of Neurolinguistics, 19*, 385–409.

Milner, B. (1963). Effects of different brain lesions on card sorting. *Archives of Neurology, 9*, 100–110.

Milner, B., Corkin, S., & Teuber, H. L. (1968). Further analysis of the hippocampal amnesic syndrome: 14-year follow-up study of HM. *Neuropsychologia, 6*(3), 215–234.

Minami, H., & Dallenbach, K. M. (1946). The effects of activity upon learning and retention in the cockroach. Periplaneta Americana. *American Journal of Psychology, 59*, 1–58.

Mineka, S., & Sutton, S. K. (1992). Cognitive biases and the emotional disorders, *Psychological Science 3*, 65–69.

Miozzo, M., & Caramazza, A. (1997). On knowing the auxiliary of a verb that cannot be named: Evidence for the independence of grammatical and phonological aspects of lexical knowledge. *Journal of Cognitive Neuroscience, 9*, 160–166.

Mirpour, K., Bolandnazar, Z., & Bisley, J. W. (2019). Neurons in FEF keep track of items that have been previously fixated in free viewing visual search. *Journal of Neuroscience, 39*(11), 2114–2124.

Mitchell, D. B. (2006). Nonconscious priming after 17 years: Invulnerable implicit memory? *Psychological Science, 17*(11), 925–929.

Mitchell, D. B., Kelly, C. L., & Brown, A. S. (2018). Replication and extension of long-term implicit memory: Perceptual priming but conceptual cessation. *Consciousness and Cognition, 58*, 1–9.

Mitroff, I. I. (1974). *The Subjective Side of Science*. Elsevier.

Mittelstädt, J. M., Wacker, J., & Stelling, D. (2019). Emotional and cognitive modulation of cybersickness: The role of pain catastrophizing and body awareness. *Human Factors, 61*(2), 322–336.

Miyake, A., & Shah, P. (Eds.). (1999). *Models of Working Memory: Mechanisms of Active Maintenance and Executive Control*. Cambridge University Press.

Moen, I. (2004). Monrad-Krohn's foreign accent syndrome case. In C. Code, Y. Joanette, A. Roch Lecours, & C.-W. Wallesch (Eds.), *Classic Cases in Neuropsychology* (pp. 146–157). Psychology Press.

Mogg, K., Bradley, B. P., & Williams, R. (1995). Attentional bias in anxiety and depression: The role of awareness. *British Journal of Clinical Psychology, 34*, 17–36.

Mogg, K., Bradley, B. P., Williams, R., & Mathews, A. (1993). Subliminal processing of emotional information in anxiety and depression. *Journal of Abnormal Psychology, 102*, 304–311.

Moher, J., Anderson, B. A., & Song, J. H. (2015). Dissociable effects of salience on attention and goal-directed action. *Current Biology, 25*(15), 2040–2046.

Molesworth, B. R. C., Burgess, M., & Koh, S. (2017). The relationship between noise and mode of delivery on recognition memory and working memory. *Applied Acoustics, 116*, 329–336.

Molfese, D. L., & Betz, J. C. (1988). Electrophysiological indices of the early development of lateralization for language and cognition and their implications for predicting later development. In D. L. Molfese & S. J. Segalowitz (Eds.), *Brain Lateralization in Children* (pp. 171–190). Guilford Press.

Molfese, V. J., Molfese, D. L., & Parsons, C. (1983). Hemispheric processing of phonological information. In S. J. Segalowitz (Ed.), *Language Functions and Brain Organization*. Elsevier.

Monrad-Krohn, G. H. (1947). Dysprosody or altered 'melody of language'. *Brain, 70*, 405–415.

Montero-Melis, G., van Paridon, J., Ostarek, M., & Bylund, E. (2019). Does the motor system functionally contribute to keeping words in working memory? A pre-registered replication of Shebani and Pulvermuller (2013). *PsyArXiV, 11*, October. 10.31234/osf.io/pqf8k

Monti, M. M., Vanhaudenhuyse, A., Coleman, M. R., Bolu, M., Pickard, J. D., Tshibanda, J.-F. L., Owen, A. N., & Laureys, S. (2010). Willful modulation of brain activity and communication in disorders of consciousness. *New England Journal of Medicine, 362*, 579–589.

Moody, T. (1994). Conversations with zombies. *Journal of Consciousness Studies, 1*, 196–200.

Moore, M. T., & Fresco, D. M. (2007). Depressive realism and attributional style: Implications for individuals at risk for depression. *Behavior Therapy, 38*, 144–154.

Moore, T., & Armstrong, K. M. (2003). Selective gating of visual signals by microstimulation of frontal cortex. *Nature, 421*(6921), 370–373.

Moore, T., & Fallah, M. (2001). Control of eye movements and spatial attention. *Proceedings of the National Academy of Sciences, 98*(3), 1273–1276.

Mooren, N., Krans, J., Näring, G., & van Minnen, A. (2019). Vantage perspective in analogue trauma memories: An experimental study. *Cognition and Emotion, 33*(6), 1261–1270.

Moors, A., Ellsworth, P. C., Scherer, K. R., & Frijda, N. H. (2013). Appraisal theories of emotion: State of the art and future development. *Emotion Review, 5*, 119–124.

Moran, A. (2012). *Sports and Exercise Psychology: A Critical Introduction.* 2nd ed. Hove: Psychology Press.

Moran, J., & Desimone, R. (1985). Selective attention gates visual processing in the extrastriate Cortex. *Science, 229* (4715), 782–784.

Moran, S., & McCloy, D. (eds.) (2019). PHOIBLE 2.0. Jena: Max Planck Institute for the Science of Human History. Available online at http://phoible.org (accessed 2 July 2020).

Moray, N. (1959). Attention in dichotic-listening: Affective cues and the influence of instructions. *Quarterly Journal of Experimental Psychology, 11*(1), 56–60.

Moray, N., Bates, A., & Barnett, T. (1965). Experiments on the four-eared man. *Journal of the Acoustical Society of America, 38*, 196–206.

Moray, N., & Rotenberg, I. (1989) Fault management in process control: Eye movements and action. *Ergonomics, 32*(11), 1319–1342.

Moreton, R., Pike, G., & Havard, C. (2019). A task- and role-based perspective on super-recognizers: Commentary on 'Super-recognizers: From the laboratory to the world and back again'. *British Journal of Psychology, 110*, 486–488.

Moritz, S., Jacobsen, D., Willenborg, B., Jelinek, L., & Fricke, S. (2006). A check on the memory deficit hypothesis of obsessive-compulsive checking. *European Archives of Psychiatry and Clinical Neuroscience, 256*, 82–86.

Morris, P. E. (1992). Theories of memory. In M. M. Gruneberg & P. E. Morris (Eds.), *Aspects of Memory: The Practical Aspects.* Routledge.

Morrison, J. B., & Tversky, B. (1997). Body schemas. *Proceedings of the Meetings of the Cognitive Science Society* (pp. 525–529). Mahwah, NJ: Erlbaum.

Morton, J. (1970). A functional model of memory. In D. A. Norman (Ed.), *Models of Human Memory.* Academic Press.

Morton, J. (1979). Word recognition. In J. Morton & J. C. Marshall (Eds.), *Psycholinguistics, Volume 2: Structures and Processes.* Paul Elek.

Morton, J., & Patterson, K. E. (1980). A new attempt at an interpretation or an attempt at a new interpretation. In M. Coltheart, K. E. Patterson, & J. C. Marshall (Eds.), *Deep Dyslexia* (pp. 91–118). Routledge & Kegan Paul.

Morton, N., & Morris, R. G. (1995). Image transformation dissociated from visuospatial working memory. *Cognitive Neuropsychology, 12*, 767–791.

Moseley, C. (2007). *Encyclopedia of the World's Endangered Languages.* Routledge.

Most, S. B., Smith, S. D., Cooter, A. B., Levy, B. N., & Zald, D. H. (2007). The naked truth: Positive, arousing distractors impair rapid target perception. *Cognition and Emotion, 21*(5), 964–981.

Moxley, J. H., Ericsson, K. A., Charness, N., & Krampe, R. T. (2012). The role of intuition and deliberative thinking in experts' superior tactical decision making. *Cognition, 124*, 72–78.

Moyer, R. S. (1973). Comparing objects in memory: Evidence suggesting and internal psychophysics. *Perception and Psychophysics, 13*, 180–184.

Mrazek, M. D., Smallwood, J., & Schooler, J. W. (2012). Mindfulness and mind-wandering: Finding convergence through opposing constructs. *Emotion, 12*(3), 442–448.

Mueller, K. D., Koscik, R. L., LaRue, A., Clark, L. R., Hermann, B., Johnson, S. C., & Sager, M. A. (2015). Verbal fluency and early memory decline: Results from the Wisconsin Registry for Alzheimer's Prevention. *Archives of Clinical Neuropsychology, 30*(5), 448–457.

Mueller, C. W., Lisman, S. A., & Spear, N. E. (1983). Alcohol enhancement of human memory: Tests of consolidation and interference hypotheses. *Psychopharmacology, 80*, 226–230.

Mueller, P. A., & Oppenheimer, D. M. (2014). The pen is mightier than the keyboard: Advantages of longhand over laptop note taking. *Psychological Science, 25*(6), 1159–1168.

Mukamel, R., Ekstrom, A. D., Kaplan, J., Iacoboni, M., & Fried, I. (2010). Single-neuron responses in humans during execution and observation of actions. *Current Biology, 20*(8), 750–756.

Muller, G. E., & Pilzecker, A. (1900). Experimentelle Beitrage zur Lehre vom Gedachtnis [Experimental contributions to the science of memory]. *Zeitschrift fur Psychologie. Erganzungsb and, 1*, 1–300.

Murdoch, B. E. (2009). *Acquired Speech and Language Disorders.* John Wiley & Sons.

Murphy, G. L. (2004). *The Big Book of Concepts.* MIT Press.

Murphy, G. L., & Medin, D. (1985). The role of theories in conceptual coherence. *Psychological Review, 92*, 289–316.

Murphy, G., & Greene, C. M. (2016). Perceptual load affects eyewitness accuracy and susceptibility to leading questions. *Frontiers in Psychology, 7*, 1322.

Murphy, S. T., & Zajonc, R. B. (1993). Affect, cognition, and awareness: Affective priming with optimal and suboptimal stimulus exposures. *Journal of Personality & Social Psychology, 64*(5), 723–739.

Murray, A., & Jones, D. M. (2002). Articulatory complexity at item boundaries in serial recall: The case of Welsh and English digit span. *Journal of Experimental Psychology: Learning, Memory and Cognition, 28*, 594–598.

Murray, D. J. (1965). Vocalization-at-presentation and immediate recall, with varying presentation-rates. *Quarterly Journal of Experimental Psychology, 17*, 41–56.

Murray, D. J. (1988). *A History of Western Psychology* (2nd ed.). Prentice Hall.

Münsterberg, H. (1916). *The photoplay: A Psychological Study.* D. Appleton & Co.

Mynatt, C. R., Doherty, M. E., & Tweney, R. D. (1977). Confirmation bias in a simulated research environment: An experimental study of scientific inference. *Quarterly Journal of Experimental Psychology, 29*, 85–95.

Mynatt, C. R., Doherty, M. E., & Tweney, R. D. (1978). Consequences of confirmation and disconfirmation in a simulated research environment. *Quarterly Journal of Experimental Psychology, 30*, 395–406.

N

Naccache, L., Blandin, E., & Dehaene, S. (2002). Unconscious masked priming depends on temporal attention. *Psychological Science, 13*(5), 416–424.

Nachev, P., & Husain, M. (2007). Comment on 'Detecting awareness in the vegetative state'. *Science, 315*, 1221a.

Nagy, W. E., & Anderson, R. C. (1984). How many words are there in printed English? *Reading Research Quarterly, 19*, 304–330.

Nairne, J. S. (2002). The myth of the encoding-retrieval match. *Memory, 10*, 389–395.

Nairne, J. S. (2010). Adaptive memory: Evolutionary constraints on remembering. *Psychology of Learning & Motivation, 53*, 1–32.

National Institute of Justice (US). Technical Working Group for Eyewitness Evidence (1999). *Eyewitness Evidence: A Guide for Law Enforcement.* US Department of Justice, Office of Justice Programs, National Institute of Justice.

National Safety Council (2010). *Understanding the Distracted Brain: Why Driving While Using Hands-Free Cell Phones is Risky Behavior.* NSC White Paper.

Navarrete, E., Pastore, M., Valentini, R., & Peressotti, F. (2015). First learned words are not forgotten: Age-of-acquisition effects in the tip-of-the-tongue experience. *Memory & Cognition, 43*(7), 1085–1103.

Naveh-Benjamin, M., & Ayres, T. J. (1986). Digit span, reading rate, and linguistic relativity. *Quarterly Journal of Experimental Psychology, 38A*, 739–751.

Navon, D. (1984). Resources: A theoretical soup stone. *Psychological Review, 91*(2), 216–234.

Navon, D., & Miller, J. (2002). Queuing or sharing? A critical evaluation of the single-bottleneck notion. *Cognitive Psychology, 44*(3), 193–251.

Nee, D. E., Wager, T. D., & Jonides, J. (2007). Interference resolution: Insights from a meta-analysis of neuroimaging tasks. *Cognitive, Affective & Behavioral Neuroscience, 7*, 1–17.

Neisser, U. (1967). *Cognitive Psychology.* Prentice-Hall.

Neisser, U. (1976). *Cognition and Reality: Principles and Implications of Cognitive Psychology.* W. H. Freeman.

Neisser, U. (1978). Memory: What are the important questions? In M. M. Gruneberg, P. E. Morris, & R. N. Sykes (Eds.), *Practical Aspects of Memory.* Academic Press.

Neisser, U. (1981). John Dean's memory: A case study. *Cognition, 9*(1), 1–22.

Neisser, U. (1982). Snapshots or benchmarks? In U. Neisser (Ed.), *Memory Observed: Remembering in Natural Contexts.* W.H. Freeman.

Neisser, U. (1988). Time present and time past. In M. M. Gruneberg, P. E. Morris, & R. N. Sykes (Eds.), *Practical Aspects of Memory: Current Research and Issues* (vol. 2). Wiley.

Neisser, U., & Becklen, R. (1975). Selective looking: Attending to visually specified events. *Cognitive Psychology, 7*(4), 480–494.

Nelson, K. (1993). The psychological and social origins of

autobiographical memory. *Psychological Science, 4*(1), 7–14.

Nelson, T. O., & Narens, L. (1990). Metamemory: A theoretical framework and new findings. *The Psychology of Learning and Motivation, 26*, 125–141.

Nenkov, G. Y., Morrin, M., Ward, A., Schwartz, B., & Hulland, J. (2008). A short form of the Maximisation Scale: Factor structure, reliability and validity studies. *Judgment & Decision Making, 5*, 371–388.

Nermend, K., & Łatuszyńska, M. (Eds.) (2017). *Neuroeconomic and Behavioral Aspects of Decision Making*. Springer International Publishing, AG.

Neuschatz, J. S., Lampinen, J. M., Preston, E. L., Hawkins, E. R., & Toglia, M. P. (2002). The effect of memory schemata on memory and the phenomenological experience of naturalistic situations. *Applied Cognitive Psychology: The Official Journal of the Society for Applied Research in Memory and Cognition, 16*(6), 687–708.

Newell, A. (1980). Physical symbol systems. *Cognitive Science, 4*, 135–183.

Newell, A., Shaw, J. C., & Simon, H. A. (1958). Elements of a theory of human problem solving. *Psychological Review, 65*, 151–166.

Newell, B. R. (2015). Decision making under risk: Beyond Kahneman and Tversky's (1979) prospect theory. In M.W. Eysenck & D. Groome (Eds.), *Cognitive Psychology: Revisiting the Classic Studies* (pp. 162–175). Sage.

Newell, B. R., Lagnado, D. A., & Shanks, D. (2007). *Straight Choices: The Psychology of Decision Making*. Psychology Press.

Newell, B. R., & Shanks, D. R. (2014). Unconscious influence on decision making: A critical review. *Behavioral and Brain Sciences, 37*, 1–61.

Newstead, S. E., & Griggs, R. A. (1983). Drawing inferences from quantified statements: A study of the square of opposition. *Journal of Verbal Learning and Verbal Behaviour, 22*, 535–546.

Newtson, D. (1973). Attribution and unit of perception of ongoing behavior. *Journal of Personality and Social Psychology, 28*(1), 28–38.

Nickerson, R. S., Perkins, D. N., & Smith, E. E. (1985). *The Teaching of Thinking*. Lawrence Erlbaum.

Nigro, G., & Neisser, U. (1983). Point of view in personal memories. *Cognitive Psychology, 15*(4), 467–482.

Nijboer, M., Borst, J. P., van Rijn, H., & Taatgen, N. A. (2016). Driving and multitasking: The good, the bad, and the dangerous. *Frontiersin Psychology, 7*, 1718.

Nijboer, M., Borst, JP., van Rijn, H. & Taatgen, NA. (2016) Driving and Multitasking: The Good, the Bad, and the Dangerous. *Front. Psychol.* 7:1718. doi: 10.3389/fpsyg.2016.01718

Nijdam, M. J., Baas, M. A. M., Olff, M., & Gersons, B. P. R. (2013). Hotspots in trauma memories and their relationship to successful trauma-focused psychotherapy: A pilot study. *Journal of Traumatic Stress, 26*, 38–44.

Nijstad, B. A., Stroebe, W., & Lodewijkx, H. F. N. (2003). Production blocking and idea generation: Does blocking interfere with cognitive processes? *Journal of Experimental Social Psychology, 39*, 531–548.

Noë, A. (2004). *Action in Perception*. MIT Press.

Noe, C., & Fischer-Baum, S. (2020). Early lexical influences on sublexical processing in speech perception: Evidence from electrophysiology. *Cognition, 197*, 104162.

Noel, J. P., Ishizawa, Y., Patel, S. R., Eskandar, E. N., & Wallace, M. T. (2019). Leveraging nonhuman primate multisensory neurons and circuits in assessing consciousness theory. *Journal of Neuroscience, 39*(38), 7485–7500.

Nolan, V. (2003). Whatever happened to Synectics? *Creativity and Innovation Management, 12*, 24–27.

Nooteboom, S. (2010). Monitoring for speech errors has different functions in inner and overt speech. In M. Everaert, T. Lentz, H. De Mulder, & O. Nilsen (Eds.), *The Linguistic Enterprise: From Knowledge of Language to Knowledge in Linguistics* (pp. 231–234). John Benjamins.

Nooteboom, S. G., & Quené, H. (2008). Self-monitoring and feedback: A new attempt to find the main cause of lexical bias in phonological speech errors. *Journal of Memory and Language, 58*, 837–861.

Nooteboom, S. G., & Quené, H. (2017). Self-monitoring for speech errors: Two-stage detection and repair with and without auditory feedback. *Journal of Memory and Language, 95*, pp. 19–35.

Nooteboom, S. G., & Quené, H. (2020). Repairing speech errors: Competition as a source of repairs. *Journal of Memory and Language, 111*, 104069.

Norman, D. A. (1981). Categorization of action slips. *Psychological Review, 88*, 1–15.

Norman, D. A. (Ed.) (1970). *Models of Human Memory*. Academic Press.

Norman, D. A., & Bobrow, D. G. (1975). Data-limited and resource-limited processes. *Cognitive Psychology, 7*(1), 44–64.

Norman, D. A., & Shallice, T. (1986). Attention to action. Willed and automatic control of behaviour. In R. J. Davidson, G. E. Schwartz, & D. Shapiro (Eds.), *Consciousness and Self-Regulation*. Plenum Press.

Norman, E., Pfuhl, G., Sæle, R. G., Svartdal, F., Låg, T., & Dahl, T. I. (2019). Metacognition in psychology. *Review of General Psychology, 23*(4), 403–424.

Norman, G. R., & Eva, K. W. (2010). Diagnostic error and clinical reasoning. *Medical Education, 44*(1), 94–100.

Norris, D., Butterfield, S., Hall, J., & Page, M. P. A. (2018). Phonological recoding under articulatory suppression. *Memory & Cognition, 46*, 173–180.

Norris, D., McQueen, J. M., & Cutler, A. (2000). Merging information in speech recognition: Feedback is never necessary. *Behavioral & Brain Sciences, 23*, 299–370.

Nozari, N., Dell, G. S., & Schwartz, M. F. (2011). Is comprehension necessary for error detection? A conflict-based account of monitoring in speech production. *Cognitive Psychology, 63*(1), 1–33.

NTSB (2016). Collision between a car operating with automated vehicle control systems and a tractor-semitrailer truck. https://www.ntsb.gov/investigations/Accident Reports/Reports/HAR1702.pdf

Núñez, R. (2004). Do real numbers really move? Language, thought, and gesture: The embodied cognitive foundations of mathematics. *Embodied Artificial Intelligence, 3139*, 54–73.

Núñez, R., Allen, M., Gao, R., Rigoli, C. M., Relaford-Doyle, J., & Semenuks, A. (2019). What happened to cognitive science? *Nature Human Behaviour, 3*(8), 782–791.

Nutt, P. C. (1984). Types of organizational decision processes. *Administrative Sciences Quarterly, 29*, 414–450.

Nutt, P. C. (2005). Search during decision making. *European Journal of Operational Research, 160*, 851–876.

O

O'Brien, D. P., Braine, M. D. S., & Yang, Y. (1994). Propositional reasoning by mental models? Simple to refute in principle and in practice. *Psychological Review*, 101, 701–704.

O'Connell, D., & Kowal, S. (2004). The history of research on the filled pause as evidence of the written language bias in linguistics (Linell, 1982). *Journal of Psycholinguistic Research, 33*, 459–474.

O'Craven, K. M., Downing, P. E., & Kanwisher, N. (1999). fMRI evidence for objects as the units of attentional selection. *Nature, 401* (6753), 584–587.

O'Hara, K. P., & Payne, S. J. (1998). The effects of operator implementation cost on planfulness of problem solving and learning. *Cognitive Psychology, 35*, 34–70.

O'Keefe, J. (2014). Spatial cells in the hippocampal formation. *Nobel Lecture*, 7 December. Nobel Prize website: www.nobelprize.org

O'Regan, J. K. (1979). Saccades size control in reading: Evidence for the linguistic control hypothesis. *Perception and Psychophysics, 25*, 501–509.

O'Rourke, T. B., & Holcomb, P. J. (2002). Electrophysiological evidence for the efficiency of spoken word processing. *Biological Psychology, 60*(2–3), 121–150.

O'Sullivan, J. A., Herrero, J., Smith, E., Schevon, C., McKhann, G. M., Sheth, S. A., Mehta, A. D., & Mesgarani, N. (2019). Hierarchical encoding of attended auditory objects in multi-talker speech perception. *Neuron, 104*(6), 1195–1209.

O'Sullivan, J. A., Shamma, S. A., & Lalor, E. C. (2015). Evidence for neural computations of temporal coherence in an auditory scene and their enhancement during active listening. *Journal of Neuroscience, 35*(18), 7256–7263.

Oaksford, M., & Chater, N. (1994). A rational analysis of the selection task as optimal data selection. *Psychological Review, 101*, 608–631.

Oaksford, M., & Chater, N. (2003). Optimal data selection: Revision, review and re-evaluation. *Psychonomic Bulletin & Review, 10*, 289–318.

Oaksford, M., & Chater, N. (2020). New paradigms in the psychology of reasoning. *Annual Review of Psychology, 71*, 305–330.

Oatley, K., & Johnson-Laird, P. N. (1987). Towards a cognitive theory of emotions. *Cognition and Emotion, 1*, 29–50.

Oberauer, K. (2002). Access to information in working memory: Exploring the focus of attention. *Journal of Experimental Psychology: Learning, Memory, and Cognition, 28*, 411–421.

Oberauer, K. (2019). Is rehearsal an effective maintenance strategy for working memory? *Trends in Cognitive Sciences, 23*(9), 798–809.

Oberauer, K. (2019a). Working memory and attention: A conceptual analysis and review. *Journal of Cognition, 2*(1), 36.

Oberauer, K., Weidenfeld, A., & Hornig, R. (2004). Logical reasoning and probabilities: A comprehensive test of Oaksford and Chater (2001). *Psychonomic Bulletin & Review, 11,* 521–527.

Obler, L. K., & Gjerlow, K. (1999). *Language and The Brain.* Cambridge University Press.

Ochsner, K. N. (2000). Are affective events richly recollected or simply familiar? The experience and process of recognizing feelings past. *Journal of Experimental Psychology: General, 129,* 242–261.

Odegaard, B., Knight, R. T., & Lau, H. (2017). Should a few null findings falsify prefrontal theories of conscious perception? *Journal of Neuroscience, 37*(40), 9593–9602.

Oesch, N., & Dunbar, R. I. M. (2017). The emergence of recursion in human language: Mentalising predicts recursive syntax task performance. *Journal of Neurolinguistics, 43,* Part B, 95–106.

Ohlsson, S. (1992). Information processing explanations of insight and related phenomena. In M. T. Keane & K. J. Gilhooly (Eds.), *Advances in the Psychology of Thinking.* Harvester-Wheatsheaf.

Ohlsson, S. (2018). The dialectic between routine and creative cognition. In F. Vallee-Tourangeau (Ed.), *Insight: On the Origins of New Ideas* (pp. 8–27). Routledge.

Ohshiro, T., Angelaki, D. E., & DeAngelis, G. C. (2011). A normalization model of multisensory integration. *Nature Neuroscience, 14*(6), 775.

OIG (2006). A review of the FBI's handling of the Brandon Mayfield case. *Office of the Inspector General, Oversight & Review Division, US Department of Justice.*

Oizumi, M., Albantakis, L., & Tononi, G. (2014). From the phenomenology to the mechanisms of consciousness: Integrated information theory 3.0. *PLOS Computational Biology, 10*(5), e1003588.

Okada, T., & Simon, H. A. (1997). Collaborative discovery in a scientific domain. *Cognitive Science, 21,* 109–141.

Olds, J. (1956). Pleasure centers in the brain. *Scientific American, 195,* 105–117.

Oliva, A., & Torralba, A. (2001). Modeling the shape of the scene: A holistic representation of the spatial envelope. *International Journal of Computer Vision, 42*(3), 145–175.

Oliver, A. (2018). Your money and your life: Risk attitudes over gains and losses. *Journal of Risk and Uncertainty, 57,* 29–50.

Oliver, N., Calvard, T., & Potočnik, K. (2017). Cognition, technology, and organizational limits: Lessons from the Air France 447 disaster. *Organization Science, 28*(4), 597–780.

Olivers, C. N. L., & Nieuwenhuis, S. (2006). The beneficial effects of additional task load, positive affect, and instruction on the attentional blink. *Journal of Experimental Psychology: Human Perception and Performance, 32,* 364–379.

Ollinger, M., Jones, G., Faber A. H., & Knoblich, G. (2013). Cognitive mechanisms of insight: The role of heuristics and representational change in solving the eight-coin problem. *Journal of Experimental Psychology: Learning, Memory and Cognition, 39,* 931–939.

Ollinger, M., Jones, G., & Knoblich, G. (2014). The dynamics of search, impasse, and representational change provide a coherent explanation of difficulty in the nine-dot problem. *Psychological Research, 78,* 266–275.

Olson, J. A., Demacheva, I., & Raz, A. (2015). Explanations of a magic trick across the life span. *Frontiers in Psychology, 6,* 219.

Olson, R., Keenan, J., Byrne, B., & Samuelsson, S. (2019). Etiology of developmental dyslexia. In L. Verhoeven, C. Perfetti, & K. Pugh (Eds.), *Developmental Dyslexia Across Languages and Writing Systems* (pp. 391–412). Cambridge University Press.

Oppenheim, G. M., & Dell, G. S. (2010). Motor movement matters: The flexible abstractness of inner speech. *Memory & Cognition, 38,* 1147–1160.

Ormerod, T. C., MacGregor, J. N., & Chronicle, E. P. (2002). Dynamics and constraints in insight problem solving. *Journal of Experimental Psychology: Learning, Memory and Cognition, 28,* 791–799.

Ortmann, A., Gigerenzer, G., Borges, B., & Goldsten, D. G. (2008). The recognition heuristic: A fast and frugal way to investment choice? In C. R. Plott & V. L. Smith (Eds.), *Handbook of Experimental Economics Results.* Elsevier/North Holland.

Ortony, A., Clore, G. L., & Collins, A. (1988). *The Cognitive Structure of Emotions.* Cambridge University Press.

Oruc, I., Balas, B., & Landy, M. S. (2019). Face perception: A brief journey through recent discoveries and current directions. *Vision Research, 157,* 1–9.

Osborn, A. F. (1958). *Applied Imagination.* Scribners.

Ost, J., Vrij, A., Costall, A., & Bull, R. (2002). Crashing memories and reality monitoring: Distinguishing between perceptions, imaginations and 'false memories'. *Applied Cognitive Psychology, 16,* 125–134.

Ostarek, M., & Huettig, F. (2019). Six challenges for embodiment research. *Current Directions in Psychological Science, 28*(6), 593–599.

Osterhout, L., & Holcomb, P. J. (1992). Event related potentials elicited by syntactic anomaly. *Journal of Memory and Language, 31,* 785–806.

Osterhout, L., McLaughlin, J., & Bersick, M. (1997). Event-related brain potentials and human language. *Trends in Cognitive Sciences, 1,* 203–209.

Ostry, D. J., & Feldman, A. G. (2003). A critical evaluation of the force control hypothesis in motor control. *Experimental Brain Research, 153*(3), 275–288.

Otgaar, H., Howe, M. L., Patihis, L., Merckelbach, H., Lynn, S. J., Lilienfeld, S. O., & Loftus, E. F. (2019). The return of the repressed: The persistent and problematic claims of long-forgotten trauma. *Perspectives on Psychological Science, 14*(6), 1072–1095.

Otsuka-Hirota, N., Yamamoto, H., Miyashita, K., & Nagatsuka, K. (2014). Invisibility of moving objects: A core symptom of motion blindness. *BMJ Case Reports.*

Oviedo-Trespalacios, O., Haque, M., King, M., & Washington, S. (2016). Understanding the impacts of mobile phone distraction on driving performance: A systematic review. *Transportation Research Part C: Emerging Technologies, 72,* 360–380.

Owen, A. M. (2019). The search for consciousness. *Neuron, 102*(3), 526–528.

Owen, A. M., Coleman, M. R., Boly, M. Davis, M. H., Laureys, S., Jolles, D., & Pickard, J. D. (2007). Response to comments on 'Detecting awareness in the vegetative state'. *Science, 315,* 1221c.

Owen, A. M., Coleman, M. R., Boly, M., Davis, M. H., Laureys, S., Jolles, D., & Pickard, J. D. (2006). Detecting awareness in the vegetative state. *Science, 313,* 1402.

P

Page, M. P. A. (2006). What can't functional neuroimaging tell the cognitive psychologist? *Cortex, 42,* 428–443.

Paivio, A. (1965). Abstractness, imagery, and meaningfulness in paired associates learning. *Journal of Verbal Learning and Verbal Behaviour, 4,* 32–38.

Paivio, A. (1969). Mental imagery in associative learning and memory. *Psychological Review, 76,* 241–263.

Paivio, A. (1971). *Imagery and Verbal Processes.* Holt, Rinehart & Winston.

Paivio, A. (1975). Perceptual comparisons through the mind's eye. *Memory and Cognition, 3,* 635–647.

Paivio, A. (1983). The empirical case for dual coding. In J. C. Yuille (Ed.), *Imagery, Memory and Cognition* (pp. 307–322). Erlbaum.

Papies, E. K., Best, M., Gelibter, E., & Barsalou, L. (2017). The role of simulations in consumer experiences and behavior: Insights from the Grounded Cognition Theory of Desire. *Journal of the Association for Consumer Research, 2*(4), 402–418.

Papies, E. K., Potjes, I., Keesman, M., Schwinghammer, S., & Van Koningsbruggen, G. M. (2014). Using health primes to reduce unhealthy snack purchases among overweight consumers in a grocery store. *International Journal of Obesity, 38*(4), 597–602.

Park, H. D., & Blanke, O. (2019). Coupling inner and outer body for self-consciousness. *Trends in Cognitive Sciences, 23*(5), 377–388.

Parker, E. S., Birnbaum, I. M., Weingartner, H., Hartley, J. T., Stillman, R. C., & Wyatt, R. J. (1980). Retrograde enhancement of human memory with alcohol. *Psychopharmacology, 69,* 219–222.

Parker, E. S., Cahill, L., & McGaugh, J. L. (2006). A case of unusual autobiographical remembering. *Neurocase, 12*(1), 35–49

Parker, E. S., Morihisa, J. M., Wyatt, R. J., Schwartz, B. L., Weingartner, H., & Stillman, R. C. (1981). The alcohol facilitation effect on memory: A dose-response study. *Psychopharmacology, 74,* 88–92.

Parker-Jones, O., Alfaro-Almagro, F., & Jbabdi, S. (2018). An empirical 21st century evaluation of phrenology. *Cortex, 106,* 26–35.

Parkin, A. (2000). *Essentials of Cognitive Psychology.* Psychology Press.

Parkin, A. J. (1997). *Memory and Amnesia: An Introduction* (2nd ed.). Blackwell.

Parkin, A. J., & Leng, N. R. C. (1993). *Neuropsychology of the Amnesic Syndrome.* Erlbaum.

Parnes, S. J., & Meadow, A. (1963). Development of individual creative talent. In C. W. Taylor & F. Barron (Eds.), *Scientific Creativity: Its Recognition and Development.* J. Wiley.

Parr, T., & Friston, K. J. (2019). Attention or salience? *Current Opinion in Psychology, 29,* 1–5.

Parrott, W. G., & J. Sabini, J. (1990). Mood and memory under natural conditions: Evidence for mood incongruent recall. *Journal of Personality and Social Psychology, 59,* 321–336.

Paton, W., Bain, S. A., Gozna, L., Gilchrist, E., Heim, D., Gardner, E., Cairns, D., McGranaghan, P., & Fischer, R. (2018). The combined effects of questioning technique and interviewer manner on false confessions. *Journal of Investigative Psychology and Offender Profiling, 15*(3), 335–349.

Patterson, K. E., Marshall, J. C., & Coltheart, M. (Eds.) (1985). *Surface Dyslexia*. Erlbaum.

Paulesu, E., Harrison, J. E., Baron-Cohen, S., Watson, J. D. G., Goldstein, L., Heather, J., Frackowiak, R. S. J. & Frith, C. D. (1995). The physiology of coloured hearing: A PET activation study of colour–word synaesthesia. *Brain, 118,* 661–676.

Paulesu, E., McCrory, E. Fazio, F. Menoncello, L., Brunswick, N., Cappa, S. F., & Frith, U. (2000). A cultural effect on brain function. *Nature Neuroscience, 3*(1), 91–96.

Pavlas, D., Rosen, M. A., Fiore, S. M., & Salas, E. (2008). *Using Visual Attention Video Games and Traditional Interventions to Improve Baggage Screening.* Paper presented at the Proceedings of the Human Factors and Ergonomics Society Annual Meeting 2008.

Pavlenko, A. (2014). *The Bilingual Mind: And What it Tells us About Language and Thought.* Cambridge University Press.

Payne, J. (1976). Task complexity and contingent processing in decision making: An information search and protocol analysis. *Organizational Behavior and Human Performance, 16,* 366–387.

Payne, J. W., Bettman, J. R., & Johnson, E. J. (1988). Adaptive strategy selection in decision making. *Journal of Experimental Psychology: Learning, Memory and Cognition, 14,* 534–552.

Payne, J. W., Bettman, J. R., & Johnson, E. J. (1993). *The Adaptive Decision Maker.* Cambridge University Press.

Pearson, J., Naselaris, T., Holmes, E. A., & Kosslyn, S. M. (2015). Mental imagery: Functional mechanisms and clinical applications. *Trends in Cognitive Sciences, 19,* 590–602.

Peelen, M. V., Wiggett, A. J., & Downing, P. E. (2006). Patterns of fMRI activity dissociate overlapping functional brain areas that respond to biological motion. *Neuron, 49*(6), 815–822.

Peiffer-Smadja, N., & Cohen, L. (2019). The cerebral bases of the bouba–kiki effect. *NeuroImage, 186,* 679–689.

Peinkhofer, C., Dreier, J. P., & Kondziella, D. (2019). Semiology and mechanisms of near-death experiences. *Current Neurology and Neuroscience Reports, 19*(9), 62.

Peirce, C. S., & Jastrow, J. (1884). On small differences of sensation. *Memoirs of the National Academy of Sciences, 3*(1), 73–83.

Peleg, G., Katzir, G., Peleg, O., Kamara, M., Brodsky, L., Hel-Or, H., Keren, D., & Nevo, E. (2006). Hereditary family signature of facial expression. *Proceedings from the National Academy of Sciences, 103,* 15921–15926.

Penfield, W., & Boldrey, E. (1937). Somatic motor and sensory representation in the cerebral cortex of man as studied by electrical stimulation. *Brain, 60,* 389–440.

Penfield, W. & Rasmussen, T. L. (1950). *The Cerebral Cortex of Man: A Clinical Study of Localisation of Function.* Macmillan.

Pentland, A. (2007). Social signal processing. *Signal Processing Magazine, 24*(4), 108–111.

Perea, M., Acha, J., & Carreiras, M. (2009). Eye movements when reading text messaging (txt msgng). *Quarterly Journal of Experimental Psychology, 62,* 1560–1567.

Pereira, A., Altgassen, M., Atchison, L., de Mendonça, A., & Ellis, J. (2018). Sustaining prospective memory functioning in amnestic mild cognitive impairment: A lifespan approach to the critical role of encoding. *Neuropsychology, 32*(5), 634–644.

Pereira, A., de Mendonça, A., Silva, D., Guerreiro, M., Freeman, J., &Ellis, J. (2015). Enhancing prospective memory in mild cognitive impairment: The role of enactment. *Journal of Clinical and Experimental Neuropsychology, 37,* 863–877.

Perry, C. J., & Fallah, M. (2017). Effector-based attention systems. *Annals of the New York Academy of Sciences, 1396*(1), 56–69.

Pessoa, L. (2019). Embracing integration and complexity: Placing emotion within a science of brain and behaviour. *Cognition and Emotion, 33*(1), 55–60.

Peters, E., Lipkus, I., & Diefenbach, M. A. (2006). The functions of affect in health communications and in the construction of health preferences. *Journal of Communication, 56,* S140–S162.

Peterson, L. R., & Johnson, S. T. (1971). Some effects of minimizing articulation on short-term memory. *Journal of Verbal Learning and Verbal Behavior, 10,* 346–354.

Petersen, M. R., Beecher, M. D., Zoloth, S. R., Moody, D. B., & Stebbins, W. C. (1978). Neural lateralization of species-specific vocalizations by Japanese macaques (*Macaca fuscata*). *Science, 202,* 324–327.

Peterson, R. L., & Pennington, B. F. (2015). Developmental dyslexia. *Annual Review of Clinical Psychology, 11*(1), 283–307.

Petersen, S. E., & Posner, M. I. (2012). The attention system of the human brain: 20 years after. *Annual Review of Neuroscience, 35,* 73–89.

Petersen, S. E., & Sporns, O. (2015). Brain networks and cognitive architectures. *Neuron, 88,* 207–219.

Pezdek, K. (2003). Event memory and autobiographical memory for the events of September 11, 2001. *Applied Cognitive Psychology, 17,* 1033–1045.

Phelps, E. A., Ling, S., & Carrasco, M. (2006). Emotion facilitates perception and potentiates the perceptual benefit of attention. *Psychological Science, 17,* 292–299.

Philbeck, J. W., & Witt, J. K. (2015). Action-specific influences on perception and post perceptual processes: Present controversies and future directions. *Psychological Bulletin, 141*(6), 1120–1144.

Phillips, F., Natter, M. B., & Egan, E. J. (2015). Magically deceptive biological motion: The French drop sleight. *Frontiers in Psychology, 6,* 371.

Phillips, J. K., Klein, G., & Sieck, W. R. (2004). Expertise in judgment and decision making: A case for training intuitive decision skills. In D. J. Koehler & N. Harvey (Eds.), *Blackwell Handbook of Judgment and Decision Making.* Blackwell Publishing.

Phillips, M. R., McAuliff, B. D., Kovera, M. B., & Cutler, B. L. (1999). Double-blind photoarray administration as a safeguard against investigator bias. *Journal of Applied Psychology, 84*(6), 940–951.

Phillips, P. J., & O'Toole, A. J. (2014). Comparison of human and computer performance across face recognition experiments. *Image and Vision Computing, 32*(1), 74–85.

Phillips, P. J., Yates, A. N., Hu, Y., Hahn, C. A., Noyes, E., Jackson, K., Cavazos, J. G., Jeckeln, G., Ranjan, R., Sankaranarayanan, S., Chen, J.-C., Castillo, C. D., Chellappa, R., White, D., & O'Toole, A. J. (2018). Face recognition accuracy of forensic examiners, superrecognizers, and face recognition algorithms. *Proceedings of the National Academy of Sciences, 115*(24), 6171–6176.

Pijlaarsdam, G., Van den Bergh, H., & Couzijn, M. (Eds.) (1996). *Theories, Models and Methodology in Writing.* Amsterdam University Press.

Pillemer, D. B. (1992). Remembering personal circumstances: A functional analysis. In E. Winograd & U. Neisser (Eds.), *Affect and Accuracy in Recall: Studies of 'Flashbulb' Memories* (pp. 236–264). Cambridge University Press.

Pillemer, D. B. (2003). Directive functions of autobiographical memory: The guiding power of the specific episode. *Memory, 11*(2), 193–202.

Pilley, J. W. (2013). Border collie comprehends sentences containing a prepositional object, verb, and direct object. *Learning & Motivation, 44*(4), 229–240.

Pillutla, M. M., & Murningham, J. K. (1996). Unfairness, anger and spite: Emotional rejections of ultimatum offers. *Organizational Behavior and Human Decision Processes, 68,* 208.

Pinker, S. (1994). *The Language Instinct.* Penguin.

Pinker, S. (1997). Foreword. In D. McGuinness (Ed.), *Why Our Children Can't Read and What We Can Do About It* (pp. ix–x). Free Press.

Pisoni, D. B., Kronenberger, W. G., Harris, M. S., & Moberly, A. C. (2017). Three challenges for future research on cochlear implants. *World Journal of Otorhinolaryngology – Head and Neck Surgery, 3*(4), 240–254.

Pitchert, D., & Katsikopoulos, K. V. (2008). Green defaults: Information presentation and pro-environmental behavior. *Journal of Environmental Psychology, 28,* 63–73.

Pizlo, Z. (2001). Perception viewed as an inverse problem. *Vision Research, 41*(24), 3145–3161.

Pizlo, Z., & Zheng, L. (2005). Solving combinatorial problems: The 15-puzzle. *Memory and Cognition, 33,* 1069–1084.

Plaisier, M. A., Tiest, W. M. B., & Kappers, A. M. L. (2008). Haptic pop-out in a hand sweep. *Acta Psychologica, 128*(2), 368–377.

Planton, S., Jucla, M., Roux, F.-E.,& Démonet, J.-F. (2013). The 'handwriting brain': A meta-analysis of neuroimaging studies of motor versusorthographic processes. *Cortex, 49*(10), 2772–2787.

Platt, J. R. (1964). Strong inference. *Science, 146,* 347–353.

Plaut, D. C., McClelland, J. L., Seidenberg, M. S., & Patterson, K. (1996). Understanding normal and impaired word reading: Computational principles in quasi-regular domains. *Psychological Review, 103*, 56–115.

Plazzi, G., Vetrugno, R., Provini, F., & Montagna, P. (2005). Sleepwalking and other ambulatory behaviours during sleep. *Neurological Sciences, 26*, S193–S198.

Plihal, W., & Born, J. (1997). Effects of early and late nocturnal sleep on declarative and procedural memory. *Journal of Cognitive Neuroscience, 9*, 534–47.

Plihal, W., & Born, J. (1999). Effects of early and late nocturnal sleep on priming and spatial memory. *Psychophysiology, 36*, 571–582.

Plummer, C., Kleinitz, A., Vroomen, P., & Watts, R. (2007). Of Roman chariots and goats in overcoats: The syndrome of Charles Bonnet. *Journal of Clinical Neuroscience, 14*, 709–714.

Pobric, G., Jefferies, E., & Lambon Ralph, M. A. (2010). Category-specific versus category-general semantic impairment induced by transcranial magnetic stimulation. *Current Biology, 20*, 964–968.

Pockett, S., & Miller, A. (2007). The rotating spot method of timing subjective events. *Consciousness and Cognition, 16*, 241–254.

Poincaré, H. (1908). *Science Et Methode*. Flammarion.

Poincaré, H. (1910). Mathematical creation. *The Monist, 20*, 321–333.

Poincaré, H. (1929). *The Foundations of Science*. Science House.

Poizner, H., Bellugi, U., & Iragui, V. (1984). Apraxia and aphasia for a visual-gestural language. *American Journal of Physiology, 246*, R868–R883.

Polczyńska, M. M., Japardi, K., & Bookheimer, S. Y. (2017). Lateralizing language function with pre-operative functional magnetic resonance imaging in early proficient bilingual patients. *Brain and Language, 170*, July, 1–11.

Poldrack, R. A. (2006). Can cognitive processes be inferred from neuroimaging data? *Trends in Cognitive Science, 19*, 59–63.

Politis, I., Brewster, S., & Pollick, F. (2019). Using multimodal displays to signify critical handovers of control to distracted autonomous car drivers. *International Journal of Mobile Human Computer Interaction, 9*(3), 1–16.

Pollack, I., & Pickett, J. M. (1964). The unintelligibility of excerpts from conversations. *Language & Speech, 6*, 165–171.

Pollatos, O., Herbert, B. M., Matthias, E., & Schandry, R. (2007). Heart rate response after emotional picture presentation is modulated by interoceptive awareness. *International Journal of Psychophysiology, 63*(1), 117–124.

Pollick, F. E., Kay, J. W., Heim, K., & Stringer, R. (2005). Gender recognition from point-light walkers. *Journal of Experimental Psychology-Human Perception and Performance, 31*(6), 1247–1265.

Pollick, F. E., Paterson, H. M., Bruderlin, A., & Sanford, A. J. (2001). Perceiving affect from arm movement. *Cognition, 82*(2), B51–B61.

Pollick, F. E., & Sapiro, G. (1997). Constant affine velocity predicts the 1/3 power law of planar motion perception and generation. *Vision Research, 37*(3), 347–353.

Pomerantz, J. R., & Kubovy, M. (1986). Theoretical approaches to perceptual organization: Simplicity and likelihood principles. In K. R. Boff, L. Kaufman, & J. P. Thomas (Eds.), *Handbook of Perception and Human Performance: Volume H. Cognitive Processes and Performance* (pp. 36.31–36.46). Wiley.

Pomerleau, D. A. (1990). Neural network based autonomous navigation. In C. Thorpe (Ed.), *Vision and Navigation: The CMU Navlab* (pp. 83–92). Kluwer Press.

Ponsot, E., Burred, J. J., Belin, P., & Aucouturier, J. J. (2018). Cracking the social code of speech prosody using reverse correlation. *Proceedings of the National Academy of Sciences, 115*(15), 3972–3977.

Popper, K. (2002). *Popper: The Logic of Scientific Discovery*. Routledge Classics.

Popper, K. R. (1959). *The Logic of Scientific Discovery*. Hutchinson.

Porter, S., & Ten Brinke, L. (2008). Reading between the lies: Identifying concealed and falsified emotions in universal facial expressions. *Psychological Science, 19*, 508–514.

Posner, M. I. (1980). Orienting of attention. *Quarterly Journal of Experimental Psychology, 32*, 3–25.

Posner, M. I. (1982). Cumulative development of attentional theory. *American Psychologist, 37*(2), 168–179.

Posner, M. I., & Cohen, Y. (1984). Components of visual orienting. In H. Bouma & D. Bouwhuis (Eds.), *Attention and Performance vol. X* (pp. 531–556). Erlbaum.

Posner, M. I., & Keele, S. W. (1970). Retention of abstract ideas. *Journal of Experimental Psychology, 77*, 353–363.

Posner, M. I., & Petersen, S. E. (1990). The attention system of the human brain. *Annual Review of Neuroscience, 13*, 25–42.

Postman, L., Stark, K., & Henschel, D. M. (1969). Conditions of recovery after unlearning. *Journal of Experimental Psychology, 82*, 1–24.

Potter, J. M. (1980). What was the matter with Dr. Spooner? In V. Fromkin (Ed.), *Errors in Linguistic Performance: Slips of the Tongue, Ear, Pen, and Hand* (pp. 13–34). Academic Press.

Potter, M. C., & Levy, E. I. (1969). Recognition memory for a rapid sequence of pictures. *Journal of Experimental Psychology, 81*(1), 10–15.

Pouw, W., Harrison, S. J., & Dixon, J. A. (2019). Gesture–speech physics: The biomechanical basis for the emergence of gesture–speech synchrony. *Journal of Experimental Psychology: General, 149*(2), 391–404

Power, M., & Dalgleish, T. (1997). *Cognition and Emotion: From Order to Disorder*. Psychology Press.

Power, R. A., Steinberg, S., Bjornsdottir, G., Reitveld, C. A., Abdellaoui, A., Nivard, M. M., Johannesson, M., Galesloot, T. E., Hottenga, J. J., Willemsen, G., Cesarini, D., Benjamin, D. J., Magnusson, P. K., Ullén, F., Tiemeier, H., Hofman, A., van Rooij, F. J., Walters, G. B., Sigurdsson, E., . . . Stefansson, K. (2015). Polygenic risk scores for schizophrenia and bipolar disorder predict creativity. *Nature Neuroscience, 18*, 953–955.

Prasad, S., Loula, F., & Shiffrar, M. (2005). The visual analysis of actions performed by the self and others. *Journal of Cognitive Neuroscience*, 249–249.

Pratt, J., & Abrams, R. A. (1994). Action-centered inhibition: Effects of distractors on movement planning and execution. *Human Movement Science, 13*(2), 245–254.

Price, T., Wadewitz, P., Cheney, D., Seyfarth, R., Hammerschmidt, K., & Fischer, J. (2015). Vervets revisited: A quantitative analysis of alarm call structure and context specificity. *Scientific Reports, 5*, 13220.

Prinz, J. (2004). Which emotions are basic? In D. Evans & P. Cruse (Eds.), *Emotion, Evolution and Rationality* (pp. 69–88). Oxford University Press.

Prinz, W. (1997). Perception and action planning. *European Journal of Cognitive Psychology, 9*(2), 129–154.

Proffitt, D. R. (2006). Embodied perception and the economy of action. *Perspectives on Psychological Science, 1*(2), 110–122.

Proverbio, A. M., Raso, G., & Zani, A. (2018). Electrophysiological indexes of incongruent audio visual phonemic processing: Unraveling the McGurk effect. *Neuroscience, 385*, 215–226.

Provini, F., Tinuper, P., Bisulli, F., & Lugaresi, E. (2011). Arousal disorders. *Sleep Medicine, 12*, S22–S26.

Pugh, K., & Verhoeven, L. (2018) Introduction to this Special Issue: Dyslexia across languages and writing systems. *Scientific Studies of Reading, 22*(1), 1–6.

Pulvermuller, F. (2013). Semantic embodiment, disembodiment or misembodiment? In search of meaning in modules and neuron circuits. *Brain and Language, 127*, 86–103.

Putnam, H. (1975). The meaning of 'meaning'. In *Philosophical Papers Vol. 2, Mind, Language and Reality*. Cambridge University Press.

Pyers, J. E., Gollan, T. H., & Emmorey, K. (2009). Bimodal bilinguals reveal the source of tip-of-the-tongue states. *Cognition, 112*(2), 323–329.

Pylyshyn, Z. W. (1973). What the mind's eye tells the mind's brain: A critique of mental imagery. *Psychological Bulletin, 80*, 1–24.

Pylyshyn, Z. W. (1981). The imagery debate: Analogue media versus tacit knowledge. *Psychological Review, 88*, 16–45.

Pylyshyn, Z. W. (1984). *Computation and Cognition*. MIT Press.

Pylyshyn, Z. W. (2002). Mental imagery: In search of a theory. *Behavioral and Brain Sciences, 5*, 157–238.

Q

Qin, L., Li, Z. R., Chen, Z., Bill, M. A., & Noyce, D. A. (2019). Understanding driver distractions in fatal crashes: An exploratory empirical analysis. *Journal of Safety Research, 69*, 23–31.

Qiu, J., Luo, Y., Wang, Q., Zhang, F., & Zhang, Q. (2006). Brain mechanism of Stroop interference effect in Chinese characters. *Brain Research, 1072*(1), 186–193.

Quesque, F., & Brass, M. (2019). The role of the temporoparietal junction in self–other distinction. *Brain Topography, 32*(3), 1–13.

R

Racine, E., Nguyen, V., Saigle, V., & Dubljevic, V. (2017). Media portrayal of a landmark

Racsmány, M., Demeter, G., Csigó, K., Harsányi, A., & Németh, A. (2011). An experimental study of prospective memory in obsessive-compulsive disorder. *Journal of Clinical and Experimental Neuropsychology, 33*(1), 85–91.

Radek, L., Kallionpää, R. E., Karvonen, M., Scheinin, A., Maksimow, A., Långsjö, J., Kaisti, K., Vahlberg, T., Revonsuo, A., Scheinin, H., & Valli, K. (2018). Dreaming and awareness during dexmedetomidine- and propofol-induced unresponsiveness. *British Journal of Anaesthesia, 121*(1), 260–269.

Radvansky, G. (2006). *Human Memory*. Pearson.

Raibert, M. H. (1986). *Legged Robots That Balance*. MIT Press.

Raichle, M. E., & Snyder, A. Z. (2007). A default model of brain function: A brief history of an evolving idea. *NeuroImage, 37*, 1083–1090.

Rainville, P., Bechara, A., Naqvi, N. H., & Damasio, A. R. (2006). Basic emotions are associated with distinct patterns of cardiorespiratory activity. *International Journal of Psychophysiology, 6*.

Ramachandran, V. S., Chunharas, C., & Marcus, Z. (2019). Constructing calendars in the brain. *Neurocase*, 1–11

Ramachandran, V. S., & Hirstein, W. (1998). The perception of phantom limbs – The D. O. Hebb lecture. *Brain, 121*, 1603–1630.

Ramachandran, V. S., & Hubbard, E. M. (2001). Synaesthesia: A window into perception, thought and language. *Journal of Consciousness Studies, 8*(12), 3–34.

Ramon, M., Bobak, A. K., & White, D. (2019). Super-recognizers: From the lab to the world and back again. *British Journal of Psychology, 110*, 461–479.

Rand, D. G., Peysakhovitch, A., Kraft-Todd, G. T., Newman, G. E., Wurzbacher, O., Nowak, M., & Greene, J. D. (2014). Social heuristics shape intuitive cooperation. *Nature Communications, 5*, 3677.

Rao, R. P. N., & Ballard, D. H. (1999). Predictive coding in the visual cortex: A functional interpretation of some extra-classical receptive-field effects. *Nature Neuroscience, 2*(1), 79.

Rao, R. P. N., Zelinsky, G. J., Hayhoe, M. M., & Ballard, D. H. (2002). Eye movements in iconic visual search. *Vision Research, 42*(11), 1447–1463.

Rapp, B., & Goldrick, M. (2000). Discreteness and interactivity in spoken word production. *Psychological Review, 107*, 460–499.

Räsänen, O., Doyle, G., & Frank, M.C. (2018). Pre-linguistic segmentation of speech into syllable-like units, *Cognition, 171*, 130–150.

Raschle, N. M., Chang, M., & Gaab, N. (2011). Structural brain alterations associated with dyslexia predate reading onset. *NeuroImage, 57*(3), 742–749.

Rasmussen A.S., & Berntsen, D. (2011). The unpredictable past: Spontaneously retrieved autobiographical memories outnumber autobiographical memories retrieved strategically. *Consciousness and Cognition, 20*, 1842–1846.

Rasmussen, T., & Milner, B. (1977). The role of early left-brain injury in determining lateralization of cerebral speech functions. *Annals of the New York Academy of Sciences, 299*, 355–369.

Rasmussen, A. S., Ramsgaard, S. B., & Berntsen, D. (2015). Frequency and functions of involuntary and voluntary autobiographical memories across the day. *Psychology of Consciousness: Theory, Research, and Practice, 2*(2), 185.

Ratcliff, R., & McKoon, G. (1986). More on the distinction between episodic and semantic memories. *Journal of Experimental Psychology: Learning, Memory, and Cognition, 12*, 312–313.

Ratneshwar, S., Barsalou, L. W., Pechmann, C., & Moore, M. (2001). Goal-derived categories: Roles of personal and situational goals in category representation. *Journal of Consumer Psychology, 10*, 147–157.

Rauschecker, J. P. (2018) Where did language come from? Precursor mechanisms in nonhuman primates. *Current Opinion in Behavioral Sciences, 21*, 195–204.

Rauss, K., & Pourtois, G. (2013). What is bottom-up and what is top-down in predictive coding? *Frontiers in Psychology, 4*, 276.

Ray, S. B., Mishra, M. V., & Srinivasan, N. (2020). Attentional blink with emotional faces depends on emotional expressions: A relative positive valence advantage. *Cognition and Emotion*, 5 March, 1–20.

Raymond, J. E., Shapiro, K. L., & Arnell, K. M. (1992). Temporary suppression of visual processing in an RSVP task: An attentional blink? *Journal of Experimental Psychology: Human Perception and Performance, 18*(3), 849.

Rayner, K. (1998). Eye movements in reading and information processing: Twenty years of research. *Psychological Bulletin, 124*, 372–422.

Rayner, K. (2009). Eye movements in Reading: Models and data. *Journal of Eye Movement Research, 2*(5), 1–10.

Rayner, K., & Clifton, C., Jr. (2002). Language processing. In D. Medin (Vol. Ed.), *Stevens Handbook of Experimental Psychology* (3rd ed.). *Volume 2: Memory and Cognitive Processes* (pp. 261–316). John Wiley & Sons.

Rayner, K., & Duffy, S. A. (1988). On-line comprehension processes and eye movements in reading. In M. Daneman, G. E. MacKinnon, & T. G. Waller (Eds.), *Reading Research: Advances in Theory and Practice* (Vol. 6). Academic Press.

Rayner, K., & McConkie, G. W. (1976). What guides a reader's eye movements? *Vision Research, 16*, 829–837.

Rayner, K., Pollatsek, A., & Reichle, E. D. (2003). Eye movements in reading: Models and data. *Behavioral and Brain Sciences, 26*, 507–526.

Rayner, K., Schotter, E. R., Masson, M. E., Potter, M. C., & Treiman, R. (2016). So much to read, so little time: How do we read, and can speed reading help? *Psychological Science in the Public Interest, 17*(1), 4–34.

Rea, C. P., & Modigliani, V. (1985). The effect of expanded v. massed practice on the retention of multiplication facts and spelling lists. *Human Learning, 4*, 11–18.

Read, D., Olivola, C. Y., & Hardisty, D. J. (2017). The value of nothing: Asymmetric attention to opportunity costs drives intertemporal decision making. *Management Science, 63*, 4277–4297.

Reardon, S. (2019). Rival theories face off over brain's source of consciousness. *Science, 366*, 293–293.

Reason, J. (1979). Actions not as planned: The price of automatization. In G. Underwood & R. Stevens (Eds.), *Aspects of Consciousness* (pp. 67–89). Academic Press.

Reason, J. (1990). *Human Error*. Cambridge University Press.

Reason, J. (2000). The Freudian slip revisited. *The Psychologist, 13*(12), 10–11.

Reason, J. T. (1978). Motion sickness adaptation: A neural mismatch model. *Journal of the Royal Society of Medicine, 71*(11), 819–829.

Rebenitsch, L., & Owen, C. (2016). Review on cybersickness in applications and visual displays. *Virtual Reality, 20*(2), 101–125.

Recanzone, G. H. (2003). Auditory influences on visual temporal rate perception. *Journal of Neurophysiology, 89*(2), 1078–1093.

Recanzone, G. H. (2009). Interactions of auditory and visual stimuli in space and time. *Hearing Research, 258* (1–2), 89–99.

Reed, C. L., Grubb, J. D., & Steele, C. (2006). Hands up: Attentional prioritization of space near the hand. *Journal of Experimental Psychology: Human Perception and Performance, 32*(1), 166–177.

Reed, S. K. (1972). Pattern recognition and categorization. *Cognitive Psychology, 3*, 382–407.

Reed, S. K., & Friedman, M. P. (1973). Perceptual and conceptual categorization. *Memory & Cognition, 1*, 157–163.

Reggev, N., Zuckerman, M., & Maril, A. (2011). Are all judgments created equal? An fMRI study of semantic and episodic metamemory predictions. *Neuropsychologia, 49*, 1332–1342.

Reicher, G. M. (1969). Perceptual recognition as a function of meaningfulness of the stimulus material. *Journal of Experimental Psychology, 81*, 274–280.

Reilly, R. G. (1999). A case study of transient dyslexia. *Brain and Language, 70*(3), 336–346.

Reingold, E. M., & Merikle, P. M. (1988). Using direct and indirect measures to study perception without awareness. *Perception & Psychophysics, 44*(6), 563–575.

Reinmann, P. (1999). The role of external representations in distributed problem solving. *Learning and Instruction, 9*, 411–418.

Reisenzein, R. (1983). The Schachter theory of emotion: Two decades later *Psychological Bulletin, 94*, 239–264.

Reitman, W. R. (1976). Skilled perception in Go: Deducing memory structures from inter-response times. *Cognitive Psychology, 8*, 336–356.

Renoult, L., Davidson, P. S. R., Palombo, D. J., Moscovitch, M., & Levine, B. (2012). Personal semantics: At the crossroads of semantic and episodic memory. *Trends in Cognitive Sciences, 16*, 550–558.

Rensink, R. A. (2002). Change detection. *Annual Review of Psychology, 53*, 245–277.

Rensink, R. A., O'Regan, J. K., & Clark, J. J. (1997). To see or not to see: The need for attention to perceive changes in scenes. *Psychological Science, 8*(5), 368–373.

Rescorla, M. (2020). The computational theory of mind. In E. N. Zalta (Ed.), *The Stanford Encyclopedia of Philosophy* (spring 2020 edition). https://plato.stanford.

edu/archives/spr2020/entries/computational-mind/

Reubold, U., & Harrington, J. (2017). The influence of age on estimating sound change acoustically from longitudinal data. In S. E. Wagner & I. Buchstaller (Eds.), *Panel Studies of Language Variation and Change* (pp. 129–152). Routledge.

Reverberi, C., Toraldo, A., D'Agostino, S., & Skrap, M. (2005). Better without lateral frontal cortex. Insight problems solved by frontal patients. *Brain, 128*, 2882–2890.

Reynolds, J. H., & Desimone, R. (2003). Interacting roles of attention and visual salience in V4. *Neuron, 37*(5), 853–863.

Reynolds, J. H., & Heeger, D. J. (2009). The normalization model of attention. *Neuron, 61*(2), 168–185.

Ribot, T. R. (1882). *Diseases of Memory*. Appleton & Co.

Richards, B. A., Lillicrap, T. P., Beaudoin, P., Bengio, Y., Bogacz, R., Christensen, A., Clopath, C., Costa, R. P., de Berker, A., Ganguli, S., Gillon, C. J., Hafner, D., Kepecs, A., Kriegeskorte, N., Latham, P., Lindsay, G. W., Miller, K. D., Naud, R., Pack, C. C., ... Gillon, C. J. (2019). A deep learning framework for neuroscience. *Nature Neuroscience, 22*(11), 1761–1770.

Richardson, J. T. E., & Baddeley, A. D. (1975). The effect of articulatory suppression in free recall. *Journal of Verbal Learning and Verbal Behavior, 14*(6), 623–629.

Richlan, F. (2020). The functional neuroanatomy of developmental dyslexia across languages and writing systems. *Frontiers in Psychology, 11*, 155.

Richmond, L. L., Gold, D. A., & Zacks, J. M. (2017). Event perception: Translations and applications. *Journal of Applied Research in Memory and Cognition, 6*(2), 111–120.

Richmond, L. L., & Zacks, J. M. (2017). Constructing experience: Event models from perception to action. *Trends in Cognitive Sciences, 21*(12), 962–980.

Rindal, E. J., DeFranco, R. M., Rich, P. R., & Zaragoza, M. S. (2016). Does reactivating a witnessed memory increase its susceptibility to impairment by subsequent misinformation? *Journal of Experimental Psychology: Learning, Memory, and Cognition, 42*(10), 1544–1558.

Riordan, M. A. (2017). The communicative role of non-face emojis: Affect and disambiguation. *Computers in Human Behavior, 76*, 75–86.

Rips, L. J. (1989). Similarity, typicality and categorisation. In F. C. Keil & R. A. Wilson (Eds.), *Explanation and Cognition*. MIT Press.

Rips, L. J., & Collins, A. (1993). Categories and resemblance. *Journal of Experimental Psychology: General, 122*, 468–486.

Ritov, I., & Baron, J. (1990). Reluctance to vaccinate: Omission bias and ambiguity. *Journal of Behavioral Decision Making, 3*, 263–277.

Rizzolatti, G., Fadiga, L., Fogassi, L., & Gallese, V. (1996). Premotor cortex and the recognition of motor actions. *Cognitive Brain Research, 3*, 131–141.

Rizzolatti, G., Fogassi, L., & Gallese, V. (2001). Neurophysiological mechanisms underlying the understanding and imitation of action. *Nature Reviews Neuroscience, 2*(9), 661–670.

Rizzolatti, G., Riggio, L., Dascola, I., & Umiltá, C. (1987). Reorienting attention across the horizontal and vertical meridians: Evidence in favor of a premotor theory of attention. *Neuropsychologia, 25*(1), 31–40.

Rizzolatti, G., Riggio, L., & Sheliga, B. M. (1994). Space and selective attention. *Attention and Performance XV, 15*, 231–265.

Rizzolatti, G., & Sinigaglia, C. (2010). The functional role of the parieto-frontal mirror circuit: Interpretations and misinterpretations. *Nature Reviews Neuroscience, 11*(4), 264–274.

Rizzolatti, G., & Sinigaglia, C. (2016). The mirror mechanism: A basic principle of brain function. *Nature Reviews Neuroscience, 17*, 757–765. https://doi.org/10.1038/nrn.2016.135.

Robertson, D. & Bindemann, M. (2019). Consolidation, wider reflection, and policy: Response to 'Super-recognisers: From the lab to the world and back again'. *British Journal of Psychology, 110*, 489–491.

Roberson, D., Davidoff, J., & Braisby, N. (1999). Similarity and categorisation: Neuropsychological evidence for a dissociation in explicit categorisation tasks. *Cognition, 71*, 1–42.

Robertson, D. J., Noyes, E., Dowsett, A. J., Jenkins, R., & Burton, A. M. (2016). Face recognition by metropolitan police super-recognisers. *PLoS ONE, 11*(2), e0150036.

Robinaugh, D. J., & McNally, R. J. (2010). Autobiographical memory for shame or guilt provoking events: Association with psychological symptoms. *Behaviour Research and Therapy, 48*(7), 646–652.

Robinson, Z., Maley, C. J., & Piccinini, G. (2015). Is consciousness a spandrel? *Journal of the American Philosophical Association, 1*(2), 365–383.

Robson, J. G. (1980). Neural images: The physiological basis of spatial vision. In C. S. Harris (Ed.), *Visual Coding and Adaptability*. Lawrence Erlbaum.

Robus, C. M., Hand, C. J., Filik, R., & Pitchford, M. (2020). Investigating effects of emoji on neutral narrative text: Evidence from eye movements and perceived emotional valence. *Computers in Human Behavior, 109*, 106361.

Roediger III, H. L., Putnam, A. L., & Smith, M. A. (2011). Ten benefits of testing and their applications to educational practice. In *Psychology of Learning and Motivation* (Vol. 55, pp. 1–36). Academic Press.

Roediger III, H. L., & Pyc, M. A. (2012). Inexpensive techniques to improve education: Applying cognitive psychology to enhance educational practice. *Journal of Applied Research in Memory and Cognition, 1*(4), 242–248.

Roediger III, H. L., Zaromb, F. M., & Lin, W. (2017). A typology of memory terms. In R. Menzel (Ed.), *Learning Theory and Behavior*, Vol. 1 of Byrne, J. H. (Ed.), *Learning and Memory: A Comprehensive Reference* (2nd ed.) (pp. 7–19). Academic Press.

Roediger, H. L., Bergman, E. T., & Meade, M. L. (2000). Repeated reproduction from memory. In A. Saito (Ed.), *Bartlett, Cognition and Culture* (pp. 115–134). Routledge.

Roediger, H. L., & Guynn, M. J. (1996). Retrieval processes. In E. L. Bjork & R. A. Bjork (Eds.), *Memory*. Academic Press.

Roediger, H. L., & Karpicke, J. D. (2006a). Test-enhanced learning: Taking memory tests improves long term retention. *Psychological Science, 17*, 249–255.

Roediger, H. L., & Karpicke, J. D. (2006b). The power of testing memory: Basic research and implications for educational practice. *Perspectives on Psychological Science, 1*, 181–201.

Roediger, H. L., Marsh, E. J., & Lee, S. C. (2002). Varieties of memory. In D. L. Medin & H. Pashler (Eds.), *Stevens' Handbook of Experimental Psychology*, 3rd ed., Vol. 2: *Memory and Cognitive Processes* (pp. 1–41). John Wiley & Sons.

Roediger, H. L., Weldon, M. S., & Challis, B. H. (1989). Explaining dissociations between implicit and explicit measures of retention: A processing account. In H. L. Roediger & F. I. M. Craik (Eds.), *Varieties of Memory and Consciousness: Essays in Honour of Endel Tulving* (pp. 3–14). Erlbaum.

Roesch, M. R., & Olson, C. R. (2004). Neuronal activity related to reward value and motivation in primate frontal cortex. *Science, 304*, 307.

Rogers, T. T., Lambon Ralph, M. A., Garrard, P., Bozeat, S., McClelland, J. L., Hodges, J. R., & Patterson, K. (2004). Structure and deterioration of semantic memory: A neuropsychological and computational investigation. *Psychological Review, 111*, 205–235.

Roland, P. E., & Friberg, L. (1985). Localization of cortical areas activated by thinking. *Journal of Neurophysiology, 53*, 1219–1243.

Rolls, E. T. (1990). A theory of emotion, and its application to understanding the neural basis of emotion. *Cognition and Emotion, 4*, 161–190.

Rosch, E. (1973). On the internal structure of perceptual and semantic categories. In T. E. Moore (Ed.), *Cognitive Development and the Acquisition of Language* (pp. 111–144). Academic Press.

Rosch, E. (1975). Cognitive representations of semantic categories. *Journal of Experimental Psychology: General, 104*, 192–233.

Rosch, E. (1978). Principles of categorization. In E. Rosch & B. B. Lloyd (Eds.), *Cognition and Categorization*. Lawrence Erlbaum.

Rosch, E., & Mervis, C. B. (1975). Family resemblance: Studies in the internal structure of categories. *Cognitive Psychology, 7*, 573–605.

Rosch, E., Mervis, C. B., Gray, W. D., Johnson, D. M., & Boyes-Braem, P. (1976). Basic objects in natural categories. *Cognitive Psychology, 8*, 382–439.

Roseman, I. J., & Smith, C. A. (2001). Appraisal theory. In K. Scherer, A. Schorr, & T. Johnstone (Eds.), *Appraisal Processes in Emotion: Theory, Methods, Research*. Oxford University Press.

Rosenbaum, D. A. (2005). The Cinderella of psychology: The neglect of motor control in the science of mental life and behavior. *American Psychologist, 60*(4), 308–317.

Rosenbaum, D. A. (2006). *Human Motor Control*. Academic Press/Elsevier.

Rosenbaum, D. A., & Feghhi, I. (2019). The time for action is at hand. *Attention, Perception, & Psychophysics, 81*(7), 2123–2138.

Rosenbaum, D. A., Meulenbroek, R. J., Vaughan, J., & Jansen, C. (2001). Posture-based motion planning: Applications to grasping. *Psychological Review, 108*(4), 709–734.

Rosenblum, L. D., Gordon, M. S., & Jarquin, L. (2000). Echolocating distance by moving and stationary listeners. *Ecological Psychology, 12*(3), 181–206.

Rosenthal, D. (2000). Consciousness, content, and metacognitive judgments. *Consciousness and Cognition, 9*(2), 203–214.

Rosenthal, D. (2019). Consciousness and confidence. *Neuropsychologia, 128,* 255–265.

Roskies, A. L. (2010). How does neuroscience affect our conception of volition? *Annual Review of Neuroscience, 33,* 109–130.

Ross, B. H., & Landauer, T. K. (1978). Memory for at least one of two items: Test and failure of several theories of spacing effects. *Journal of Verbal Learning and Verbal Behavior, 17,* 669–680.

Ross, J., & Lawrence, K. A. (1968). Some observations on memory artifice. *Psychonomic Science, 13,* 107–108.

Ross, T. P., O'Connor, S., Holmes, G., Fuller, B., & Henrich, M. (2019). The reliability and validity of the action fluency test in healthy college students. *Archives of Clinical Neuropsychology, 34*(7), 1175–1191.

Rossion, B., Gauthier, I., Tarr, M. J., Despland, P., Bruyer, R., Linotte, S., et al. (2000). The N170 occipito-temporal component is delayed and enhanced to inverted faces but not to inverted objects: An electrophysiological account of face-specific processes in the human brain. *Neuroreport, 11*(1), 69–74.

Roth, A. E. (1995). Bargaining experiments. In J. H. Kagel & A. E. Roth (Eds.), *Handbook of Experimental Economics.* Princeton University Press.

Roth, W. M. (2000). From gesture to scientific language. *Journal of Pragmatics, 32*(11), 1683–1714.

Rothen, N., Meier, B., & Ward, J. (2012). Enhanced memory ability: Insights from synaesthesia. *Neuroscience and Biobehavioral Reviews, 36*(8), 1952–1963.

Rothen, N., Seth, A. K., & Ward, J. (2018). Synesthesia improves sensory memory, when perceptual awareness is high. *Vision Research, 153,* 1–6.

Rouault, M., & Koechlin, E. (2018). Prefrontal function and cognitive control: From action to language. *Current Opinion in Behavioral Sciences, 21,* 106–111.

Rounis, E., Maniscalco, B., Rothwell, J. C., Passingham, R. E., & Lau, H. (2010). Theta-burst transcranial magnetic stimulation to the prefrontal cortex impairs metacognitive visual awareness. *Cognitive Neuroscience, 1*(3), 165–175.

Rouw, R., & Scholte, H. S. (2007). Increased structural connectivity in grapheme-color synesthesia. *Nature Neuroscience, 10*(6), 792.

Rowe, J. B., Owen, A. M., Johnsrude, I. S., & Passingham, R. E. (2001). Imaging the mental components of a planning task. *Neuropsychologia, 39,* 315–327.

Rubenstein, L. M., Freed, R. D., Shapero, B. G., Fauber, R. L., & Alloy, L. B. (2016). Cognitive attributions in depression: Bridging the gap between research and clinical practice. *Journal of Psychotherapy Integration, 26*(2), 103.

Rubin, D. C., & Wenzel, A. E. (1996). One hundred years of forgetting: A quantitative description of retention. *Psychological Bulletin, 103,* 734–760.

Ruggeri, K., Alí, S., Berge, M. L., Bertoldo, G., Bjørndal, L. D., Cortijos-Bernabeu, A., Davison, C., Demić, E., Esteban-Serna, C., Friedemann, M., Gibson, S.P., Jarke, H., Karakasheva, R., Khorrami, P. R., Kveder, J., Andersen, T. L., Lofthus, I. S., McGill, L., Nieto, A. E., . . . Folke, T. (2020). Replicating patterns of prospect theory for decision under risk. *Nature Human Behaviour, 4,* 622–633.

Ruiz Garate, V., Parri, A., Yan, T., Munih, M., Molino Lova, R., Vitiello, N., & Ronsse, R. (2017). Experimental validation of motor primitive-based control for leg exoskeletons during continuous multi-locomotion tasks. *Frontiers in Neurorobotics, 11,* 15.

Rumain, B., Connell, J., & Braine, M. D. (1983). Conversational comprehension processes are responsible for reasoning fallacies in children as well as adults: *If* is not the biconditional. *Developmental Psychology, 19*(4), 471.

Rumelhart, D. E., & McClelland, J. L. (1982). An interactive activation model of context effects in letter perception. 2. The contextual enhancement effect and some tests and extensions of the model. *Psychological Review, 89*(1), 60–94.

Rumelhart, D. E., & Norman, D. A. (1982). Simulating a skilled typist: A study of skilled cognitive-motor performance. *Cognitive Science, 6*(1), 1–36.

Runco, M. A., & Jaeger, G. J. (2012). The standard definition of creativity. *Creativity Research Journal, 24,* 92–96.

Rung, J. M., Peck, S., Hinnenkamp, J. E., Preston, E., & Madden, G. J. (2019). Changing delay discounting and impulsive choice: Implications for addictions, prevention, and human health. *Perspectives in Behavior Science, 42,* 397–417.

Russell, A., Penny, L., & Pemberton, C. (1995). Speaking fundamental frequency changes over time in women: A longitudinal study. *Journal of Speech, Language, and Hearing Research, 38,* 101–109.

Russell, J. A. (1994). Is there universal recognition of emotion from facial expression? A review of the cross-cultural studies. *Psychological Bulletin, 115*(1), 102–141.

Russell, J. A. (2003). Core affect and the psychological construction of emotion. *Psychological Review, 110*(1), 145–172.

Russell, J. A. (2005). Emotion in human consciousness is built on core affect. *Journal of Consciousness Studies, 12,* 26–42.

Russell, R., Duchaine, B., & Nakayama, K. (2009). Super-recognizers: People with extraordinary face recognition ability. *Psychonomic Bulletin & Review, 16*(2), 252–257.

Rylander, G. (1939). *Personality Changes After Operations on the Frontal Lobes.* E. Munksgaard.

Ryle, G. (1949). *The Concept of Mind.* University of Chicago Press.

Rymer, R. (1992). A silent childhood. *New Yorker,* 13 & 20 April.

S

Saberi, K., & Perrott, D. R. (1999). Cognitive restoration of reversed speech. *Nature, 398,* 760.

Sack, A. T., & Schuhmann, T. (2012). Hemispheric differences within the fronto-parietal network dynamics underlying spatial imagery. *Frontiers in Psychology, 28*(3), 214.

Sacks, H., Schegloff, E., & Jefferson, G. (1974). A simplest systematics for the organization of turn-taking for conversation. *Language, 50*(4), 696–735.

Sacks, O. (2007). A neurologist's notebook: The abyss. *Music and Amnesia. New Yorker,* 24 September.

Sacks, O. W. (1997). *The Island of the Colorblind.* New York: A. A. Knopf.

Sadler-Smith, E. (2015). Wallas' four-stage model of the creative process: More than meets the eye? *Creativity Research Journal, 27,* 342–352.

Saffran, E. M., & Marin, O. S. M. (1975). Immediate memory for word lists and sentences in a patient with deficient auditory short-term memory. *Brain and Language, 2,* 420–433.

Sahraie, A., Trevethan, C. T., MacLeod, M. J., Murray, A. D., Olson, J. A., & Weiskrantz, L. (2006). Increased sensitivity after repeated stimulation of residual spatial channels in blindsight. *Proceedings of the National Academy of Sciences of the United States of America, 103*(40), 14971–14976.

Sakreida, K., Higuchi, S., DiDio, C., Ziessler, M., Turgeon, M., Roberts, N., & Vogt, S. (2018). Cognitive control structures in the imitation learning of sequences and rhythms: A fMRI study. *Cerebral Cortex, 28,* 907–923.

Sala, G., & Gobet, F. (2017). Experts' memory superiority for domain-specific random material generalizes across fields of expertise: A meta-analysis. *Memory and Cognition, 45,* 183–193.

Salame, P., & Baddeley, A. D. (1986). Phonological factors in STM: Similarity and the unattended speech effect. *Bulletin of the Psychonomic Society, 24,* 263–265.

Salthouse, T. A. (1990). Working memory as a processing resource in cognitive aging. *Developmental Review, 10,* 101–124.

Salvi, C., Beeman, M., Bikson, M., McKinley, R., & Grafman, J. (2020). TDCS to the right anterior temporal lobe facilitates insight problem solving. *Scientific Reports, 10.* https://doi.org/10.1038/s41598-020-57724-1

Sampietro, A. (2019). Emoji and rapport management in Spanish WhatsApp chats. *Journal of Pragmatics, 143,* 109–120.

Samson, D., & Pillon, A. (2003). A case of impaired knowledge for fruit and vegetables. *Cognitive Neuropsychology, 20,* 373–400.

Samuel, A. G. (1997). Lexical activation produces potent phonemic percepts. *Cognitive Psychology, 32,* 97–127.

Samuel, A. G., & Kat, D. (2003). Inhibition of return: A graphical meta-analysis of its time course and an empirical test of its temporal and spatial properties. *Psychonomic Bulletin & Review, 10*(4), 897–906.

Samuelson, W., & Zeckhauser, R. (1988). Status quo bias in decision making. *Journal of Risk and Uncertainty, 1,* 7–59.

Sanders, R. D., Gaskell, A., Raz, A., Winders, J., Stevanovic, A., Rossaint, R., Boncyk, C., Defresne, A., Tran, G., Tasbihgou, S., Meier, S., Vlisides,

P. E., Fardous, H., Hess, A., Bauer, R. M., Absalom, A., Mashour, G. A., Bonhomme, V., Coburn, M., & Sleigh, J. (2017). Incidence of connected consciousness after tracheal intubation: A prospective, international, multicenter cohort study of the isolated forearm technique. *Anesthesiology: The Journal of the American Society of Anesthesiologists*, 126(2), 214–222.

Sanders, R. D., Tononi, G., Laureys, S., & Sleigh, J. W. (2012). Unresponsiveness ≠ unconsciousness. *Anesthesiology: The Journal of the American Society of Anesthesiologists*, 116(4), 946–959.

Sanfey, A. G., Rilling, J. K., Aronson, J. A., Nystrom, L. E., & Cohen, J. D. (2003). The neural basis of economic decision-making in the ultimatum game. *Science*, 300, 1755–1758.

Sanford, P., Lawson, A. L., King, A. N., & Major, M. (2020). Libet's intention reports are invalid: A replication of Dominik et al. (2017). *Consciousness and Cognition*, 77, 102836.

Santhouse, A. M., Howard, R. J., & Fffytche, D. H. (2000). Visual hallucinatory syndromes and the anatomy of the visual brain. *Brain*, 123, 2055–2064.

Sarkamo, T., Tervaniemi, M., Soinila, S., Autti, T., Silvennoinen, H. M., Laine, M. et al. (2009). Cognitive deficits associated with acquired amusia after stroke: A neuropsychological follow-up study. *Neuropsychologia*, 47(12), 2642–2651.

Sarva, H., Deik, A., & Severt, W. L. (2014). Pathophysiology and treatment of alien hand syndrome. *Tremor and Other Hyperkinetic Movements*, 4.

Satel, J., Wilson, N. R., & Klein, R. M. (2019). What neuroscientific studies tell us about inhibition of return. *Vision*, 3(4), 58.

Satin, G. E., & Fisher, R. P. (2019). Investigative utility of the cognitive interview: Describing and finding perpetrators. *Law and Human Behavior*, 43(5), 491–506.

Sato, M. (2020). The neurobiology of sex differences during language processing in healthy adults: A systematic review and a meta-analysis. *Neuropsychologia*, 14016, March, 107404.

Saunders, J., & MacLeod, M. D. (2006). Can inhibition resolve retrieval competition through the control of spreading activation? *Memory & Cognition*, 34, 307–322.

Savage-Rumbaugh, S., Shanker, S. G., & Talbot, J. (1998) *Apes, Language and the Human Mind*. Oxford University Press.

Scarborough, D. L., Cortese, C., & Scarborough, H. S. (1977). Frequency and repetition effects in lexical memory. *Journal of Experimental Psychology: Human Perception and Performance*, 3, 1–17.

Scepkowski, L. A., & Cronin-Golomb, A. (2003). The alien hand: Cases, categorizations, and anatomical correlates. *Behavioral and Cognitive Neuroscience Reviews*, 2(4), 261–277.

Schaal, S., Mohajerian, P., & Ijspeert, A. (2007). Dynamics systems vs. optimal control – A unifying view. *Computational Neuroscience: Theoretical Insights into Brain Function*, 165, 425–445.

Schachter, S., Rauscher, F., Christenfeld, N., & Tyson Crone, K. (1994). The vocabularies of academia. *Psychological Science*, 5(1), 37–41.

Schachter, S., & Singer, J. E. (1962). Cognitive, social and physiological determinants of emotional state. *Psychological Review*, 69, 379–399.

Schachter, S., Christenfeld, N. J. S., Ravina, B., & Bilous, F. R. (1991). Speech disfluency and the structure of knowledge. *Journal of Personality and Social Psychology*, 60, 362–367.

Schacter, D. L. (1987). Implicit memory: History and current status. *Journal of Experimental Psychology: Learning, Memory, and Cognition*, 13(3), 501–518.

Schacter, D. L. (1999). The seven sins of memory. *American Psychologist*, 54(3), 182–203.

Schacter, D. L. (2013). Memory: sins and virtues. *Annals of the New York Academy of Sciences*, 1303(1).

Schacter, D. L., & Addis, D. R. (2007). The cognitive neuroscience of constructive memory: Remembering the past and imagining the future. *Philosophical Transactions of the Royal Society B: Biological Sciences*, 362(1481), 773–786.

Schacter, D. L., Wagner, A. D., & Buckner, R. L. (2000). Memory systems of 1999. In E. Tulving & F. I. M. Craik (Eds.), *Oxford Handbook of Memory* (pp. 627–643). Oxford University Press.

Schaeken, W., Vandierendonck, A., Schroyens, W., d'Ydewalle, G., & Klauer, K. C. (2013). The mental models theory of relational reasoning: Premises' relevance, conclusions' phrasing and cognitive economy. In *The Mental Models Theory of Reasoning* (pp. 149–170). Psychology Press.

Schenkman, B. N., & Nilsson, M. E. (2010). Human echolocation: Blind and sighted persons' ability to detect sounds recorded in the presence of a reflecting object. *Perception*, 39(4), 483–501.

Scherer, K. R. (1988). Criteria for emotion-antecedent appraisal: A review, in V. Hamilton, G. H. Bower, & N. H. Frijda (Eds.), *Cognitive Perspectives on Emotion and Motivation* (pp. 89–126). Kluwer.

Scherer, K. R. (2000). Psychological models of emotion. In J. Borod (Ed.), *The Neuropsychology of Emotion* (pp. 137–162). Oxford University Press.

Scherer, K. R. (2009). Emotions are emergent processes: They require a dynamic computational architecture. *Philosophical Transactions of the Royal Society B: Biological Sciences*, 364 (1535), 3459–3474.

Schiavenato, M., Byers, J. F., Scovanner, P., McMahon, J. M., Xia, Y., Lu, N., & He, H. (2008). Neonatal pain facial expression: Evaluating the primal face of pain. *Pain*, 138(2), 460–471.

Schilling, M. A. (2005). A 'small world' network model of cognitive insight. *Creativity Research Journal*, 17, 131–154.

Schirmer-Mokwa, K. L., Fard, P. R., Zamorano, A. M., Finkel, S., Birbaumer, N., & Kleber, B. A. (2015). Evidence for enhanced interoceptive accuracy in professional musicians. *Frontiers in Behavioral Neuroscience*, 9, 349.

Schlickum, M. K., Hedman, L., Enochsson, L., Kjellin, A., & Fellander-Tsai, L. (2009). Systematic video game training in surgical novices improves performance in virtual reality endoscopic surgical simulators: A prospective randomized study. *World Journal of Surgery*, 33(11), 2360–2367.

Schlittmeier, S. J., Feil, A., Liebl, A., & Hellbrück, J. R. (2015). The impact of roadtraffic noise on cognitive performance in attention-based tasks depends onnoise level even within moderate-level ranges. *Noise & Health*, 17(76), 148–157.

Schlittmeier, S. J., & Hellbrück, J. (2009). Background music as noise abatement in open-plan offices: A laboratory study on performance effects and subjective preferences. *Applied Cognitive Psychology*, 23(5), 684–697.

Schlottmann, A., Ray, E. D., Mitchell, A., & Demetriou, N. (2006). Perceived physical and social causality in animated motions: Spontaneous reports and ratings. *Acta Psychologica*, 123(1–2), 112–143.

Schmader, T. (2010). Stereotype threat deconstructed. *Current Directions in Psychological Science*, 19(1), 14–18.

Schmidt, R. C., Carello, C., & Turvey, M. T. (1990). Phase-transitions and critical fluctuations in the visual coordination of rhythmic movements between people. *Journal of Experimental Psychology – Human Perception and Performance*, 16(2), 227–247.

Schmitz, T. W., De Rosa, E., & Anderson, A. K. (2009). Opposing influences of affective state valence on visual cortical encoding. *Journal of Neuroscience*, 29, 7199–7207.

Schmolck, H., Buffalo, E. A., & Squire, L. R. (2000). Memory distortions develop over time: Recollections of the O. J. Simpson trial verdict after 15 and 32 months. *Psychological Science*, 11, 39–45.

Schneider, S. (2017). Daniel Dennett on the nature of consciousness. In Schneider, S., & Velmans, M. (Eds.), *The Blackwell Companion to Consciousness* (pp. 314–326). John Wiley & Sons.

Schneider, W., & Shiffrin, R. M. (1977). Controlled and automatic human information processing: I. Detection, search, and attention. *Psychological Review*, 84, 1–66.

Schnyder, U., Ehlers, A., Elbert, T., Foa, E. B., Gersons, B. P., Resick, P. A., Sahpiro, F., & Cloitre, M. (2015). Psychotherapies for PTSD: What do they have in common? *European Journal of Psychotraumatology*, 6(1), 28186.

Scholl, B. J., & Tremoulet, P. D. (2000). Perceptual causality and animacy. *Trends in Cognitive Sciences*, 4(8), 299–309.

Schorr, A. (2001). Subjective measurements in appraisal research: Present state and future perspectives. In K. R. Scherer, A. Schorr, & T. Johnstone (Eds.), *Appraisal Processes in Emotion: Theory, Methods, Research. Series in Affective Science*. Oxford University Press.

Schraagen, J. M. (2018). Naturalistic decision making. In L. J. Ball & V. A. Thompson (Eds.), *The Routledge International Handbook of Thinking and Reasoning* (pp. 487–501). Routledge.

Schroyens, W. (2010). A critical review of thinking about what is true, possible, and irrelevant in reasoning from from or reasoning about conditional propositions. *Journal of Cognitive Psychology*, 325, 2016–2021.

Schultz, J., & Bülthoff, H. H. (2013). Parametric animacy percept evoked by a single moving dot mimicking natural stimuli. *Journal of Vision*, 13(4), 15–15.

Schulze, C., & Newell, B. R. (2018). Decision making under risk: An experience-based perspective. In L. J. Ball & V. A. Thompson (Eds.), *The Routledge International*

Handbook of Thinking and Reasoning (pp. 502–522). Routledge.

Schurger, A., Sitt, J. D., & Dehaene, S. (2012). An accumulator model for spontaneous neural activity prior to self-initiated movement. *Proceedings of the National Academy of Sciences, 109*(42), E2904–E2913.

Schwabe, L., Nader, K., & Pruessner, J. C. (2014). Reconsolidation of human memory: Brain mechanisms and clinical relevance. *Biological Psychiatry, 76*(4), 274–280.

Schwartz, B. (2004). *The Paradox of Choice: Why More is Less*. Ecco Press.

Schwartz, B., Ward, A., Montessero, J., Lyubomirsky, S., White, K., & Lehman, D. R. (2002). Maximizing versus satisficing: Happiness is a matter of choice. *Journal of Personality and Social Psychology, 83*, 1178–1197.

Schwartz, M. F. (2006). The cognitive neuropsychology of everyday action and planning. *Cognitive Neuropsychology, 23*(1), 202–221.

Schwartz, M. F., Reed, E. S., Montgomery, M., Palmer, C., & Mayer, N. H. (1991). The quantitative description of action disorganization after brain-damage: A case study. *Cognitive Neuropsychology, 8*(5), 381–414.

Schwarz, N. (2000). Emotion, cognition, and decision making. *Cognition & Emotion, 14*(4), 433–440.

Sciutti, A., & Sandini, G. (2017). Interacting with robots to investigate the bases of social interaction. *IEEE Transactions on Neural Systems and Rehabilitation Engineering, 25*(12), 2295–2304.

Scoboria, A., Boucher, C., & Mazzoni, G. (2015). Reasons for withdrawing belief in vivid autobiographical memories. *Memory, 23*(4), 545–562.

Scoboria, A., Jackson, D. L., Talarico, J., Hanczakowski, M., Wysman, L., & Mazzoni, G. (2014). The role of belief in occurrence within autobiographical memory. *Journal of Experimental Psychology: General, 143*(3), 1242–1258.

Scorsese, M. (Writer). (1976). *Taxi Driver*. USA: Columbia Films.

Scott, S. H. (2004). Optimal feedback control and the neural basis of volitional motor control. *Nature Reviews Neuroscience, 5*(7), 534–546.

Scott, S. H., Clegg, F., Rudge, P., & Burgess, P. (2006). Foreign accent syndrome, speech rhythm and the functional neuroanatomy of speech production. *Journal of Neurolinguistics, 19*, 370–384.

Scoville, W. B., & Milner, B. (1957). Loss of recent memory after bilateral hippocampal lesions. *Journal of Neurology, Neurosurgery, & Psychiatry, 20*(1), 11–21.

Searle, J. (2013). Theory of mind and Darwin's legacy. *Proceedings of the National Academy of Sciences, 110*, 10343–10348.

Sedikides, C. (1994). Incongruent effects of sad mood on self-conception valence: It's a matter of time. *European Journal of Social Psychology, 24*, 161–172.

Seidenberg, M. (2017). *Language at the Speed of Sight: How We Read, Why so Many Can't, and What Can be Done About It*. Hachette Book Group, Inc., Basic Books.

Seidenberg, M. S., & McClelland, J. L. (1989). A distributed, developmental model of word recognition and naming. *Psychological Review, 96*, 523–568.

Seifert, C. M., Meyer, D. E., Davidson, N., Patalano, A. L., & Yaniv, I. (1995). Demystification of cognitive insight: Opportunistic assimilation and the prepared mind perspective. In R. J. Sternberg & J. E. Davidson (Eds.), *The Nature of Insight*. MIT Press.

Selfridge, O. G. (1958). *Pandemonium: A Paradigm for Learning*. Paper presented at the Proceedings of the Symposium on the Mechanisation of Thought Processes, London.

Seli, P., Kane, M. J., Smallwood, J., Schacter, D. L., Maillet, D., Schooler, J. W., & Smilek, D. (2018). Mind-wandering as a natural kind: A family-resemblances view. *Trends in Cognitive Sciences, 22*(6), 479–490.

Sells, S. B. (1936). The atmosphere effect: An experimental study of reasoning. *Archives of Psychology, 29*, 3–72.

Sells, S. B., & Koob, H. F. (1937). A classroom demonstration of 'atmosphere effect' in reasoning. *Journal of Educational Psychology, 72*, 197–200.

Senft, E., Lemaignan, S., Baxter, P. E., Bartlett, M., & Belpaeme, T. (2019). Teaching robots social autonomy from in situ human guidance. *Science Robotics, 4*(35).

Serences, J. T. (2008). Value-based modulations in human visual cortex. *Neuron, 60*(6), 1169-1181.

Service, E. (1992). Phonology, working memory, and foreign language learning. *Quarterly Journal of Experimental Psychology, 45A*, 21–50.

Seyfarth, R. M., Cheney, D. L., & Marler, P. (1980). Monkey responses to three different alarm calls: Evidence of predator classification and semantic communication. *Science, 210*, 801–803.

Seymour, P. H. K., Aro, M., & Erskine, J. M. (2003). Foundation literacy acquisition in European orthographies. *British Journal of Psychology, 94*, 143–174.

Shadmehr, R., & Krakauer, J. W. (2008). A computational neuroanatomy for motor control. *Experimental Brain Research, 185*(3), 359–381.

Shaffer, D. M., McManama, E., Swank, C., & Durgin, F. H. (2013). Sugar and space? Not the case: Effects of low blood glucose on slant estimation are mediated by beliefs. *i-Perception, 4*, 147–155.

Shah, P., Hall, R., Catmur, C., & Bird, G. (2016). Alexithymia, not autism, is associated with impaired interoception. *Cortex, 81*, 215–220.

Shah, P., & Miyake, A. (1996). The separability of working memory resources for spatial thinking and language processing: An individual differences approach. *Journal of Experimental Psychology: General, 125*, 4–27.

Shahin, A. J. (2019). Neural evidence accounting for interindividual variability of the McGurk illusion. *Neuroscience Letters, 707*, 134322.

Shallice, T. (1979). Neuropsychological research and the fractionation of memory systems. In L.-G. Nillson (Ed.), *Perspectives on Memory Research* (pp. 257–277). Erlbaum.

Shallice, T. (1982). Specific impairments of planning. *Philosophical Transactions of the Royal Society of London, B, 298*, 199–209.

Shallice, T. (2002). Fractionation of the supervisory system. In D. T. Stuss & R. Knight (Eds.), *Principles of Frontal Lobe Functions*. Oxford University Press.

Shallice, T., & Burgess, P. W. (1991). Deficits in strategy application after frontal lobe damage in man, *Brain, 114*, 727–741.

Shallice, T., & Butterworth, B. (1977). Short-term memory impairment and spontaneous speech. *Neuropsychologia, 15*, 729–735.

Shallice, T., & Papagno, C. (2019). Impairments of auditory-verbal short-term memory: Do selective deficits of the input phonological buffer exist? *Cortex, 112*, 107–121.

Shallice, T., & Warrington, E. K. (1970). Independent functioning of verbal memory stores: A neuropsychological study. *Quarterly Journal of Experimental Psychology, 22*, 261–273.

Shallice, T., & Warrington, E. K. (1974). The dissociation between long-term retention of meaningful sounds and verbal material. *Neuropsychologia, 12*, 553–555.

Shams, L., & Beierholm, U. R. (2010). Causal inference in perception. *Trends in Cognitive Sciences, 14*(9), 425-432.

Shanks, D. R. (2017). Regressive research: The pitfalls of post hoc data selection in the study of unconscious mental processes. *Psychonomic Bulletin & Review, 24*(3), 752–775.

Shankweiler, D., & Studdert-Kennedy, M. (1967). Identification of consonants and vowels presented to the left and right ears. *Quarterly Journal of Experimental Psychology, 19*, 59–63.

Shapiro, L. (2007). The embodied cognition research programme. *Philosophy Compass, 2*(2), 338–346.

Shapiro, L. (2019). *Embodied Cognition*. Routledge.

Share, D. (2008). On the Anglocentricities of current reading research and practice: The perils of overreliance on an 'outlier' orthography. *Psychological Bulletin, 134*(4), 584–615.

Shea, C. H., Kovacs, A. J., & Panzer, S. (2011). The coding and inter-manual transfer of movement sequences. *Frontiers in Psychology, 2*, 52.

Shebani, Z., & Pulvermuller, F. (2013). Moving hands and feet specifically impairs working memory for arm- and leg-related action words. *Cortex, 49*, 222–231.

Sheen, M., Kemp, S., & Rubin, D. C. (2001). Twins dispute memory ownership: A new false memory phenomenon. *Memory & Cognition, 29*, 779–788.

Shepard, R. N., & Metzler, J. (1971). Mental rotation of three-dimensional objects. *Science, 171*, 701–703.

Sheppard, J. P., Raposo, D., & Churchland, A. K. (2013). Dynamic weighting of multisensory stimuli shapes decision-making in rats and humans. *Journal of Vision, 13*, 1–19.

Shergill, S. S., Samson, G., Bays, P. M., Frith, C. D., & Wolpert, D. M. (2005). Evidence for sensory prediction deficits in schizophrenia. *American Journal of Psychiatry, 162*(12), 2384–2386.

Sheridan, T. B. (2016). Human–robot interaction: status and challenges. *Human Factors, 58*(4), 525–532.

Shiell, M. M., Hausfeld, L., & Formisano, E. (2018). Activity in human auditory cortex represents spatial separation between concurrent sounds. *Journal of Neuroscience, 38*(21), 4977–4984.

Shimamura, A. P. (1992), Organic amnesia. In L. R. Squire (Ed.), *Encyclopedia of Learning and Memory* (pp. 30–35). Macmillan.

Shin, Y. K., Proctor, R. W., & Capaldi, E. J. (2010). A review of contemporary ideomotor theory. *Psychological Bulletin, 136*(6), 943–974.

Shin, Y. S., Shin, N. Y., Jang, J. H., Shim, G., Park, H. Y., Shin, M. S., & Kwon, J. S. (2016). Erratum: Corrigendum to 'Switching strategy underlies phonemic verbal fluency impairment in obsessive-compulsive disorder' (*Journal of Obsessive-Compulsive and Related Disorders* (2012), *1*(4), 221–227), *Journal of Obsessive-Compulsive and Related Disorders, 10*. Available at: https://doi.org/10.1016/j.jocrd.2016.07.003

Shipley, T. (1964). Auditory flutter-driving of visual flicker. *Science, 145*(3638), 1328–1330.

Shipley, T. F. (2008). An invitation to an event. In T. F. Shipley & J. M. Zacks (Eds.), *Understanding Events: From Perception to Action*. Oxford University Press.

Shrout, P. E., & Rodgers, J. L. (2018). Psychology, science, and knowledge construction: Broadening perspectives from the replication crisis. *Annual Review of Psychology, 69*, 487–510.

Siciliano, B., & Khatib, O. (2019). Humanoid robots: Historical perspective, overview, and scope. In A. Goswami & P. Vadakkepat (Eds.), *Humanoid Robotics: A Reference* (pp. 3–8). Springer.

Siegel, E. H., & Stefanucci, J. K. (2011). A little bit louder now: Negative affect increases perceived loudness. *Emotion, 11*, 1006–1011.

Silk, T. J., Bellgrove, M. A., Wrafter, P., Mattingley, J. B., & Cunnington, R. (2010). Spatial working memory and spatial attention rely on common neural processes in the intraparietal sulcus. *Neuroimage, 53*(2), 718–724.

Silver, D., Schrittwieser, J., Simonyan, K., Antonoglou, I., Huang, A., Guez, A., Hubert, T., Baker, L., Lai, M., Bolton, A., Chen, Y., Lillicrap, T., Hui, F., Sifre, L., van den Driessche, G., Graepel, T., & Hassabis, D. (2017). Mastering the game of Go without human knowledge. *Nature, 550*, 354–359.

Silveri, M. C., Brita, A. C., Liperoti, R., Piludu, F., & Colosimo, C. (2018). What is semantic in semantic dementia? The decay of knowledge of physical entities but not of verbs, numbers and body parts. *Aphasiology, 32*, 989–1009.

Simmons, W. K., & Barsalou, L. W. (2003). The similarity-in-topography principle: Reconciling theories of conceptual deficits. *Cognitive Neuropsychology, 20*, 451–486.

Simner, J. (2012). Defining synaesthesia. *British Journal of Psychology, 103*(1), 1–15.

Simner, J., Mulvenna, C., Sagiv, N., Tsakanikos, E., Witherby, S. A., Fraser, C., Scott, K., & Ward, J. (2006). Synaesthesia: The prevalence of a typical cross-modal experiences. *Perception, 35*, 1024–1033.

Simon, A. (2004). A third view of the black box: Cognitive coherence in legal decision making. *University of Chicago Law Review, 71*, 511–586.

Simon, A., Pham, L. B., Quang, A., & Holyoak, K. J. (2001). The emergence of coherence over the course of decision making. *Journal of Experimental Psychology: Learning, Memory, and Cognition, 27*, 1250–1260.

Simons, D. J., & Chabris, C. F. (1999). Gorillas in our midst: Sustained in attentional blindness for dynamic events. *Perception, 28*(9), 1059–1074.

Simon, H. A. (1956). Rational choice and the structure of environments. *Psychological Review, 63*, 129–138.

Simon, H. A. (1966). Scientific discovery and the psychology of problem solving. In R. G. Colodny (Ed.), *Mind and Cosmos: Essays in Contemporary Science and Philosophy*. University of Pittsburgh Press.

Simon, H. A. (1978). Rationality as process and product of thought. *American Economic Association, 68*, 1–16.

Simon, H. A., & Chase, W. G. (1973). Skill in chess. *American Scientist, 61*, 394–403.

Simons, D. J., & Chabris, C. F. (1999). Gorillas in our midst: Sustained inattentional blindness for dynamic events. *Perception, 28*(9), 1059–1074.

Simonton, D. K. (1995). Foresight in insight? A Darwinian answer. In R. J. Sternberg & J. E. Davidson (Eds.), *The Nature of Insight* (pp. 465–494). MIT Press.

Simonton, D. K. (2003). Scientific creativity as constrained stochastic behavior: The integration of product, person and process perspectives. *Psychological Bulletin, 129*, 475–494.

Simonton, D. K. (2013). What is a creative idea? Little-c versus Big-C creativity. In J. Chan & K. Thomas (Eds.), *Handbook of Research on Creativity* (pp. 69–83). Edward Elgar.

Simonton, D. K. (2018). Creative ideas and the creative process: Good news and bad news for the neuroscience of creativity. In R. E. Jung & O. Vartanian (Eds.), *The Cambridge Handbook of the Neuroscience of Creativity* (pp. 9–18). Cambridge University Press.

Singleton, D. (2001). Age and second language acquisition. *Annual Review of Applied Linguistics, 21*, 77–89.

Sinha, P., Balas, B., Ostrovsky, Y., & Russell, R. (2006). Face recognition by humans: Nineteen results all computer vision researchers should know about. *Proceedings of the IEEE, 94*(11), 1948–1962.

Sio, U. N., & Ormerod, T. (2012). Does incubation enhance problem solving? A meta-analytic review. *Psychological Bulletin, 135*, 94–120.

Sivak, M. (1996). The information that drivers use: Is it indeed 90% visual? *Perception, 25*(9), 1081–1089.

Skaggs, E. B. (1925). Further studies in retroactive inhibition. *Psychological Monographs*. (Whole No. 161), *34*, 1–60.

Skaggs, E. B. (1933). A discussion on the temporal point of interpolation and degree of retroactive inhibition. *Journal of Comparative Psychology, 16*, 411–414.

Skinner, B. F. (1938). *The Behavior of Organisms*. Appleton.

Slattery, T. J., Sturt, P., Christianson, K., Yoshida, M., & Ferreira, F. (2013). Lingering misinterpretations of garden path sentences arise from competing syntactic representations. *Language, 69*(2), 104–120.

Sleigh, J., Warnaby, C., & Tracey, I. (2018). General anaesthesia as fragmentation of selfhood: Insights from electroencephalography and neuroimaging. *British Journal of Anaesthesia, 121*(1), 233–240.

Slobin, D. I. (1966). Grammatical transformations and sentence comprehension in childhood and adulthood. *Journal of Verbal Learning and Verbal Behavior, 5*, 219–227.

Sloman, S. A. (1996). The empirical case for two systems of reasoning. *Psychological Bulletin, 119*, 3–22.

Slovic, P., Finucane, M., Peters, E., & MacGregor, D. G. (2002). The affect heuristic. In T. Gilovich, D. Griffin, & D. Kahneman (Eds.), *Heuristics and Biases*. Cambridge University Press.

Smalley, N. S. (1974). Evaluating a rule against possible instances. *British Journal of Psychology, 65*, 293–304.

Smeets, J. B., van der Kooij, K., & Brenner, E. (2019). A review of grasping as the movements of digits in space. *Journal of Neurophysiology, 122*(4), 1578–1597.

Smith, C. A., & Lazarus, R. S. (1993). Appraisal components, core relational themes, and the emotions. *Cognition and Emotion, 7*, 233–296.

Smith, D. T., & Schenk, T. (2012). The premotor theory of attention: Time to move on? *Neuropsychologia, 50*(6), 1104–1114.

Smith, E. E., Langston, C. & Nisbett, R. (1992). The case for rules in reasoning. *Cognitive Science, 16*, 1–40.

Smith, L., & Gilhooly, K. (2006). Regression versus fast and frugal models of decision making: The case of prescribing for depression. *Applied Cognitive Psychology, 20*, 265–274.

Smith, S. M., Brown, H. O., Toman, J. E. P., & Goodman, L. S. (1947). The lack of cerebral effects of D-tubocurarine chloride, *Anesthesiology, 8*, 1–14.

Smith, S. M., & Vela, E. (2001). Environmental context-dependent memory: A review and meta-analysis. *Psychonomic Bulletin & Review, 8*(2), 203–220.

Smith, T. J. (2010). Film (cinema) perception. In E. B. Goldstein (Ed.), *Encyclopedia of Perception*. Los Angeles: Sage.

Smith, T. J. (2015). The role of audience participation and task relevance on change detection during a card trick. *Frontiers in Psychology, 6*, 13.

Smith, T. J., & Henderson, J. M. (2008). Edit blindness: The relationship between attention and global change blindness in dynamic scenes. *Journal of Eye Movement Research, 2*, 1–17.

Smyth, M. M. (1996). Interference with rehearsal in spatial working memory in the absence of eye movements. *Quarterly Journal of Experimental Psychology Section A: Human Experimental Psychology, 49*(4), 940–949.

Smyth, M. M., & Pelky, P. L. (1992). Short-term retention of spatial information. *British Journal of Psychology, 83*, 359–374.

Snook, B., Dhami, M. K., & Kavanagh, J. (2011). Simply criminal: Predicting burglars' occupancy decisions with a simple heuristic. *Law and Human Behavior, 35*, 316–326.

Sohlberg, M. M., & Mateer, C. A. (2017). *Cognitive Rehabilitation: An Integrative Neuropsychological Approach*. Guilford Publications.

Sokol-Hessner, P., Hartley, C. A., Hamilton, J. R., & Phelps, E. A. (2015). Interoceptive ability predicts aversion to losses. *Cognition and Emotion, 29*(4), 695–701.

Solomon, K. O., & Barsalou, L. W. (2001). Representing properties locally. *Cognitive Psychology, 43,* 129–169.

Solomon, K. O., & Barsalou, L. W. (2004). Perceptual simulation in property verification. *Memory and Cognition, 32,* 244–259.

Sörqvist, P. (2010). Effects of aircraft noise and speech on prose memory: What role for working memory capacity? *Journal of Environmental Psychology, 30*(1), 112–118.

Sotiropoulos, A., & Hanley, J. R. (2017) Developmental surface and phonological dyslexia in both Greek and English. *Cognition, 168,* 205–216.

Soto, D., Heinke, D., Humphreys, G. W., & Blanco, M. J. (2005). Early, involuntary top-down guidance of attention from working memory. *Journal of Experimental Psychology: Human Perception and Performance, 31*(2), 248–261.

Sousa, D. A. (2014) *How the Brain Learns to Read.* Corwin Press.

Souza, A.S. & Oberauer, K. (2018). Does articulatory rehearsal help immediate serial recall? *Cognitive Psychology, 107,* 1–21.

Speisman, J. C., Lazarus, R. S., Mordkoff, A., & Davison, L. (1964). Experimental reduction of stress based on ego-defense theory. *Journal of Abnormal and Social Psychology, 68*(4), 367–380.

Spencer, L., & Hanley, J. R. (2003). The effects of orthographic consistency on reading development and phonological awareness: Evidence from children learning to read in Wales. *British Journal of Psychology, 94,* 1–28.

Sperduti, M., Delaveau, P., Fossati, P., & Nadel, J. (2011). Different brain structures related to self-and external-agency attribution: A brief review and meta-analysis. *Brain Structure and Function, 216*(2), 151–157.

Sperling, G. (1960). The information available in brief visual presentations. *Psychology Monographs, 74,* 1–29.

Sperry, R. W. (1952). Neurology and the mind–body problem. *American Scientist, 40*(2).

Sperry, R. W. (1974). Lateral specialization in the surgically separated hemispheres. In F. Schmitt & F. Worden (Eds.), *Neurosciences Third Study Program* (pp. 1–12). The MIT Press.

Spiers, H. J., Maguire, E. A., & Burgess, N. (2001). Hippocampal amnesia. *Neurocase, 7,* 357–382.

Spitzer, H., Desimone, R., & Moran, J. (1988). Increased attention enhances both behavioral and neuronal performance. *Science, 240*(4850), 338–340.

Spranca, M., Minsk, E., & Baron, J. (1991). Omission and commission in judgment and choice. *Journal of Experimental Psychology, 27,* 76–105.

Spreen, O., & Strauss, E. (1998). *A Compendium of Neuropsychological Tests: Administration, Norms, and Commentary* (2nd ed.). Oxford University Press.

Spreng, R. N., Sepulcre, J., Turner, G. R., Stevens, W. D., & Schacter, D. L. (2013). Intrinsic architecture underlying the relations among the default, dorsal attention, and frontoparietal control networks of the human brain. *Journal of Cognitive Neuroscience, 25*(1), 74–86.

Spreng, R. N., Stevens, W. D., Chamberlain, J. P., Gilmore, A. W., & Schacter, D. L. (2010). Default network activity, coupled with the frontoparietal control network, supports goal-directed cognition. *Neuroimage, 53*(1), 303–317.

Springer, S. P., & Deutsch, G. (1981). *Left brain, Right Brain.* W. H. Freeman.

Sprugnoli, G., Rossi, S., Emmendorfer, A., Rossi, A., Liew, S.-L., Tatti, E., di Lorenzo, G., Pascual-Leone, A., & Santarnecchi, E. (2017). Neural correlates of Eureka moment. *Intelligence, 62,* 99–118.

Squire, L. R. (1986). The neuropsychology of memory dysfunction and its assessment. In I. Grant & K. Adams (Eds.), *Neuropsychological Assessment of Neuropsychiatric Disorders* (pp. 268–299). Oxford University Press.

Squire, L. R. (1987). *Memory and Brain.* Oxford University Press.

Squire, L. R. (1992). Declarative and nondeclarative memory: Multiple brain systems supporting learning and memory. *Journal of Cognitive Neuroscience, 4,* 232–243.

Squire, L. R. (1993). The organization of declarative and nondeclarative memory. In T. Ono, L. R. Squire, M. Raichle, D. Perrett, & M. Fukuda (Eds.), *Brain Mechanisms of Perception and Memory: From Neuron to Behavior* (pp. 219–227). Oxford University Press.

Squire, L. R. (2004). Memory systems of the brain: A brief history and current perspective. *Neurobiology of Learning and Memory, 82,* 171–177.

Squire, L. R. (Ed.). (2008). *The Encyclopedia of Neuroscience.* Elsevier.

Squire, L. R. (2009). The legacy of patient H.M. for neuroscience. *Neuron, 61,* 6–9.

Squire, L. R., Clark, R. E., & Knowlton, B. J. (2001). Retrograde amnesia. *Hippocampus, 11,* 50–55.

Squire, L. R., & Dede, A. J. (2015). Conscious and unconscious memory systems. *Cold Spring Harbor Perspectives in Biology, 7*(3), a021667.

Squire, L. R., & Moore, R. Y. (1979). Dorsal thalamic lesion in a noted case of chronic memory dysfunction. *Annals of Neurology, 6,* 503–506.

Squire, L. R., & Slater, P. C. (1978). Anterograde and retrograde memory impairment in chronic amnesia. *Neuropsychologia, 16,* 313–322.

Squire, L. R., Stark, C. E. L., & Clark, R. E. (2004). The medialtemporal lobe. *Annual Review of Neuroscience, 27,* 279–306.

Squire, L. R., & Zola, S. M. (1996). Structure and function of declarative and nondeclarative memory systems. *Proceedings of the National Academy of Sciences of the United States of America, 93,* 13515–13522.

Stanovich, K. E. (1999). *Who is rational? Studies of Individual Differences in Reasoning.* Erlbaum.

Stanovich, K. E., & West, R. F. (2000). Individual differences in reasoning: Implications for the rationality debate. *Behavioral and Brain Sciences, 23,* 645–665.

Staubli, U., Rogers, G., & Lynch, G. (1994). Facilitation of glutamate receptors enhances memory. *Proceedings of the National Academy of Sciences of the United States of America, 91*(2), 777–781.

Steblay, N. K. (2018). All is not as it seems: Avoidable pitfalls in the interpretation of lineup field data. *Psychology, Public Policy, and Law, 24*(3), 292–306.

Steblay, N. M. (1992). A meta-analytic review of the weapon focus effect. *Law and Human Behavior, 16,* 413–24.

Steele, C. M., & Aronson, J. (1995). Stereotype threat and the intellectual test performance of African Americans. *Journal of Personality and Social Psychology, 69,* 797–811.

Stein, M. B., Forde, D. R., Anderson, G., & Walker, J. R. (1997). Obsessive-compulsive disorder in the community: An epidemiologic survey with clinical reappraisal. *American Journal of Psychiatry, 154,* 1120–1126.

Stein, T., Utz, V., & Van Opstal, F. (2020). Unconscious semantic priming from pictures under backward masking and continuous flash suppression. *Consciousness and Cognition, 78,* 102864.

Stemberger, J. P. (1985). An interactive activation model of language production. In A. W. Ellis (Ed.), *Progress in the Psychology of Language* (pp. 143–186). Erlbaum.

Sternad, D., Dean, W., & Schaal, S. (2000). Interaction of rhythmic and discrete pattern generators in single-joint movements. *Human Movement Science, 19,* 627–664.

Stevenage, S., & Bennett, A. (2017). A biased opinion: Demonstration of cognitive bias on a fingerprint matching task through knowledge of DNA test results. *Forensic Science International, 276,* 93–106.

Stewart, L., von Kriegstein, K., Warren, J. D., & Griffiths, T. D. (2006). Music and the brain: Disorders of musical listening. *Brain, 129,* 2533–2553.

Stigler, J. W., Lee, S. Y., & Stevenson, H. W. (1986). Digit memory in Chinese and English: Evidence for a temporally limited store. *Cognition, 23,* 1–20.

Stivers, T., Enfield, N. J., Brown, P., Englert, C., Hayashi, M., Heinemann, T., Hoymann, G., Rossano, F., de Ruiter, J. P., Yoon, K.-E., & Levinson, S. C. (2009). Universals and cultural variation in turn-taking in conversation. *Proceedings of the National Academy of Sciences of the United States of America, 106,* 10587–10592.

Stock, A., & Stock, C. (2004). A short history of ideo-motor action. *Psychological Research – Psychologische Forschung, 68*(2–3), 176–188.

Storms, G. (2004). Exemplar models in the study of natural language concepts. *Psychology of Learning and Motivation, 42,* 1–39.

Storms, G., De Boeck, P., & Rus, W. (2000). Prototype and exemplar-based information in natural language categories. *Journal of Memory and Language, 42,* 51–73.

Strack, F., Martin, L., & Stepper, S. (1988). Inhibiting and facilitating conditions of the human smile: A nonobtrusive test of the facial feedback hypothesis. *Journal of Personality and Social Psychology, 54,* 768–777.

Strayer, D. L., & Johnston, W. A. (2001). Driven to distraction: Dual task studies of simulated driving and conversing on a cellular phone. *PsychologicalScience, 12*(6), 462–466.

Strick, M., Dijksterhuis, A., Bos, M. W., Sjoersma, A., Van Baaren, R. B., & Nordgren, L. F. (2011). A meta-analysis on unconscious thought effects. *Social Cognition, 29,* 738–762.

Stroop, J. R. (1935). Studies of interference in serial verbal reactions. *Journal of Experimental Psychology, 18,* 643–662.

Studdert-Kennedy, M. (1974). The perception of speech. In T. A. Sebeok (Ed.), *Current Trends in Linguistics, vol. 12: Linguistics and Adjacent Arts and Sciences.* Mouton.

Studdert-Kennedy, M. (1975). Dichotic studies: Two questions. *Brain and Language, 2,* 123–130.

Suddendorf, T., & Corballis, M. C. (2008). Episodic memory and mental time travel. In E. Dere, J. P. Huston, & A. Easton (Eds.), *Handbook of Episodic Memory Research,* Vol. 18 (pp. 31–42). Elsevier.

Sugase, Y., Yamane, S., Ueno, S., & Kawano, K. (1999). Global and fine information coded by single neurons in the temporal visual cortex. *Nature, 400*(6747), 869–873.

Sunderland, A., Harris, J. E., & Baddeley, A. D. (1983). Do laboratory tests predict everyday memory? *Journal of Verbal Learning and Verbal Behaviour, 22,* 341–357.

Sunstein, C.R. (2015). The ethics of nudging. *Yale Journal on Regulation, 32,* 413–450.

Sussman, E. S., Horváth, J., Winkler, I., & Orr, M. (2007). The role of attention in the formation of auditory streams. *Perception & Psychophysics, 69*(1), 136-152.

Sutherland, S. (1998). Book reviews: Feature selection. *Nature, 392,* 350.

Suzuki, K., Mito, G., Kawamoto, H., Hasegawa, Y., & Sankai, Y. (2007). Intention-based walking support for paraplegia patients with Robot Suit HAL. *Advanced Robotics, 21*(12), 1441–1469.

Sweetser, E. E. (1998). Regular metaphoricity in gesture: Bodily-based models of speech interaction. In B. Caron (Ed.), *Actes du 16e Congres International des Linguists.* Elsevier.

Swinnen, S. P. (2002). Intermanual coordination: From behavioural principles to neural-network interactions. *Nature Reviews Neuroscience, 3*(5), 350–361.

Swinney, D. (1979). Lexical access during sentence comprehension: (Re) consideration of context effects. *Journal of Verbal Learning and Verbal Behavior, 18,* 645–659.

Syeda-Mahmood, T. (2018). Role of big data and machine learning in diagnostic decision support in radiology. *Journal of the American College of Radiology, 15*(3), 569–576.

Symonds, C. (1953). Aphasia. *Journal of Neurology and Psychiatry, 16*(1), 1–6.

Szaflarski, J. P., Rajagopal, A., Altaye, M., Byars, A. W., Jacola, L., Schmithorst, V. J., Schapiro, M. B., Plante, E., & Holland, S. K. (2012). Left-handedness and language lateralization in children. *Brain Research, 1433,* 85–97.

T

Taber, C. S., & Lodge, M. (2006). Motivated skepticism in the evaluation of political beliefs. *American Journal of Political Science, 50*(3), 755–769.

Taft, M., & Hambly, G. (1986). Exploring the cohort model of spoken word recognition. *Cognition, 22,* 259–282.

Talarico, J. M., & Rubin, D. C. (2003). Confidence, not consistency, characterizes flashbulb memories. *Psychological Science, 14,* 455–461.

Tambovtsev, Y., & Martindale, C. (2007). Phoneme frequencies follow a yule distribution. *SKASE Journal of Theoretical Linguistics, 4*(2), 1–11.

Tan K, Dong S, Li X, Liu X, Wang C, Li J, & Nieh, J.C. (2016) Honey Bee Inhibitory Signaling Is Tuned to Threat Severity and Can Act as a Colony Alarm Signal. *PLoS Biol* 14(3): e1002423.

Tanaka, Y., Tiest, W. M. B., Kappers, A. M., & Sano, A. (2014). Contact force and scanning velocity during active roughness perception. *PloS one, 9*(3), e93363.

Tang, R., & Braver, T. S. (2020). Towards an individual differences perspective in mindfulness training research: Theoretical and empirical considerations. *Frontiers in Psychology, 11,* 19 May.

Taplin, J. E. (1971). Reasoning with conditional sentences. *Journal of Verbal Learning and Verbal Behaviour, 10,* 219–225.

Taraban, R., & McClelland, J. L. (1988). Constituent attachment and thematic role assignment in sentence processing: Influences of content-based expectations. *Journal of Memory & Language, 27,* 597–632.

Tarr, M. J., & Bulthoff, H. H. (1995). Is human object recognition better described by geon structural descriptions or by multiple views? Comment on Biederman and Gerhardstein (1993). *Journal of Experimental Psychology – Human Perception and Performance, 21*(6), 1494–1505.

Tarr, M. J., & Bulthoff, H. H. (1998). Image-based object recognition in man, monkey and machine. *Cognition, 67* (1–2), 1–20.

Tatler, B. W., & Kuhn, G. (2007). Don't look now: The magic of misdirection. In *Eye Movements* (pp. 697–714). Elsevier.

Tatler, B. W., Wade, N. J., Kwan, H., Findlay, J. M., & Velichkovsky, B. M. (2010). Yarbus, eye movements, and vision. *1*(1), 7–27.

Taylor, D. W., Berry, P. C., & Block, C. H. (1958). Does group participating when using brainstorming facilitate or inhibit creative thinking? *Administrative Science Quarterly, 3,* 23–47.

Tentori, K., Crupi, V., & Russo, S. (2013). On the determinants of the conjunction fallacy: Probability versus inductive confirmation. *Journal of Experimental Psychology: General, 142,* 235–255.

Teuber, H.-L. (1955). Physiological psychology. *Annual Review of Psychology, 6,* 267–296.

Teubner-Rhodes, S. E., Mishler, A., Corbett, R., Andreu, L., Sanz-Torrent, M., Trueswell, J. C., & Novick, J. M. (2016). The effects of bilingualism on conflict monitoring, cognitive control, and garden-path recovery. *Cognition, 150,* 213–231.

Thagard, P. (2005). *Mind: Introduction to Cognitive Science.* MIT Press.

Thaler, R. (1980). Towards a positive theory of consumer choice. *Journal of Economic Behavior and Organization, 1,* 39–60.

Thaler, R. H., & Benartzi, S. (2004). Save more tomorrow: Using behavioral economics to increase employee saving. *Journal of Political Economy, 112*(S1), 164–187.

Thaler, R. H., & Sunstein, C. R. (2009). *Nudge: Improving Decisions About Health, Wealth, and Happiness.* Penguin.

Theocharopoulou, F., Cocks, N., Pring, T., & Dipper, L. T. (2015). TOT phenomena: Gesture production in younger and older adults. *Psychology and Aging, 30*(2), 245–252.

Thomas, J. C. Jr. (1974). An analysis of behavior in the Hobbits–Orcs problem. *Cognitive Psychology, 6,* 257–269.

Thompson, C. P., Cowan, T. M., & Frieman, J. (1993). *Memory Search by a Memorist.* Lawrence Erlbaum Associates, Inc.

Thompson, D., Mackenzie, I.G., Leuthold, H., & Filik, R. (2016). Emotional responses to irony and emoticons in written language: Evidence from EDA and facial EMG. *Psychophysiology, 53*(7), 1054–1062.

Thompson, J. C., & Baccus, W. (2012). Form and motion make independent contributions to the response to biological motion in occipitotemporal cortex. *NeuroImage, 59,* 625–634.

Thompson, K. G., Biscoe, K. L., & Sato, T. R. (2005). Neuronal basis of covert spatial attention in the frontal eye field. *Journal of Neuroscience, 25*(41), 9479–9487.

Thompson, R. G., Moulin, C. J. A., Conway, M. A., & Jones, R. W. (2004). Persistent déjà vu: A disorder of memory. *International Journal of Geriatric Psychiatry, 19,* 906–907.

Thomson, D. M., & Tulving, E. (1970). Associative encoding and retrieval: Weak and strong cues. *Journal of Experimental Psychology, 86,* 255–262.

Thomson, J. J. (1976). Killing, letting die, and the Trolley Problem. *The Monist, 59,* 204–217.

Thorndike, E. L. (1898). *Animal Intelligence.* Macmillan.

Thorndike, E. L., & Lorge, I. (1944). *The Teacher's Word Book of 30,000 Words.* Teachers College, Columbia University.

Thorpe, S., Fize, D., & Marlot, C. (1996). Speed of processing in the human visual system. *Nature, 381* (6582), 520–522.

Thothathiri, M., & Snedeker, J. (2008). Give and take: Syntactic priming during spoken language comprehension. *Cognition, 108*(1), 51–68.

Thurlow, C. (2003). Generation txt? The sociolinguistics of young people's text-messaging. *Discourse Analysis Online, 1*(1), 30.

Tipper, S. P., Driver, J., & Weaver, B. (1991). Object-centered inhibition of return of visual-attention. *Quarterly Journal of Experimental Psychology Section A: Human Experimental Psychology, 43*(2), 289–298.

Tipper, S. P., Lortie, C., & Baylis, G. C. (1992). Selective reaching: Evidence for action-centered attention. *Journal of Experimental Psychology: Human Perception and Performance, 18*(4), 891–905.

Tobia, K. P., Newman, G. E., & Knobe, J. (2020). Water is and is not H_2O. *Mind and Language, 35*(2), 183–208.

Tobler, P. N., Fiorillo, C. D., & Schultz, W. (2005). Adaptive coding of reward value by dopamine neurons. *Science, 307* (5715), 1642–1645.

Tolkien, J. R. R. (1966). *The Hobbit* (3rd ed.). Allen & Unwin.

Tollestrup, P. A., Turtle, J. W., & Yuille, J. C. (1994). Actual victims and witnesses to robbery and fraud: An archival analysis. In D. F. Ross, J. D. Reed & M. P. Taylor (Eds.), *Adult Eyewitness Testimony: Current Trends and Developments.* Wiley.

Tolman, E. C. (1948). Cognitive maps in animals and man. *Psychological Review, 55*, 189–208.

Tomkins, S. S. (1962). *Affect, Imagery, Consciousness. Volume 1: The Positive Affects*. New York: Springer.

Tomkins, S. S. (1963). *Affect, Imagery, Consciousness. Volume 2: The Negative Affects*. Springer.

Tononi, G. (2008). Consciousness as integrated information: A provisional manifesto. *The Biological Bulletin, 215*(3), 216–242.

Tononi, G. (2017). The integrated information theory of consciousness: An outline. In S. Schneider & M. Velmans (Eds.), *The Blackwell Companion to Consciousness* (pp. 243–256). John Wiley & Sons.

Tononi, G., Boly, M., Massimini, M., & Koch, C. (2016). Integrated information theory: From consciousness to its physical substrate. *Nature Reviews Neuroscience, 17*(7), 450–461.

Tononi, G., & Koch, C. (2008). The neural correlates of consciousness: An update. *Year in Cognitive Neuroscience 2008*(1124), 239–261.

Tooby, J., & Cosmides, L. (2009). Conceptual foundations of evolutionary psychology. In A. Rosenberg & R. Arp (Eds.), *Philosophy of Biology*. John Wiley & Sons Inc.

Torppa, R., & Huotilainen, M. (2019). Why and how music can be used to rehabilitate and develop speech and language skills in hearing-impaired children. *Hearing Research, 380*, 108–122.

Torralba, A., Oliva, A., Castelhano, M. S., & Henderson, J. M. (2006). Contextual guidance of eye movements and attention in real-world scenes: The role of global features in object search. *Psychological Review, 113*(4), 766–786.

Torralva, T., Laffaye, T., Báez, S., Gleichgerrcht, E., Bruno, D., Chade, A., Ibañez, A., Manes, F., Gershanik, O., & Roca, M. (2015). Verbal fluency as a rapid screening test for cognitive impairment in early Parkinson's disease. *Journal of Neuropsychiatry and Clinical Neurosciences, 27*(3), 244–247.

Towse, J. N., & Hitch, G. J. (2007). Variation in working memory due to normal development. In A. R. A. Conway, C. Jarrold, M. J. Kane, A. Miyake & J. N. Towse (Eds.), *Variation in Working Memory* (pp. 109–133). Oxford University Press.

Travers, E., Khalighinejad, N., Schurger, A., & Haggard, P. (2020). Do readiness potentials happen all the time? *NeuroImage, 206*, 116286.

Treiman, R., Clifton, C., Jr., Meyer, A. S., & Wurm, L. H. (2003). Language comprehension and production. In A. F. Healy & R. W. Proctor (Eds.), *Experimental Psychology. Volume 4* (pp. 527–547). Wiley.

Treisman, A. (1964). Monitoring and storage of irrelevant messages in selective attention. *Journal of Verbal Learning and Verbal Behavior, 3*, 449–459.

Treisman, A. M. (2006). How the deployment of attention determines what we see. *Visual Cognition, 14*(4–8), 411–443.

Treisman, A. M., & Gelade, G. (1980). A feature-integration theory of attention. *Cognitive Psychology, 12*(1), 97–136.

Treisman, A. M., & Schmidt, H. (1982). Illusory conjunctions in the perception of objects. *Cognitive Psychology, 14*(1), 107–141.

Tremblay, L. & Schultz, W. (1999). Relative reward preference in primate orbitofrontal cortex. *Nature, 398*, 704.

Tremblay, P., & Dick, A. S. (2016). Broca and Wernicke are dead, or moving past the classic model of language neurobiology. *Brain and Language, 162*, 60–71.

Tremoliere, B., De Neys, W., & Bonnefon, J.-F. (2018). Reasoning and moral judgment: A common experimental toolbox. In L. J. Ball & V. A. Thompson (Eds.), *The Routledge International Handbook of Thinking and Reasoning* (pp. 575–589). Routledge.

Tremoulet, P. D., & Feldman, J. (2000). Perception of animacy from the motion of a single object. *Perception, 29*(8), 943–951.

Trevena, J., & Miller, J. (2010). Brain preparation before a voluntary action: Evidence against unconscious movement initiation. *Consciousness and Cognition, 19*(1), 447–456.

Triandis, H. (1989). Cross-cultural studies of individualism and collectivism. *Nebraska Symposium on Motivation, 37*, 41–133.

Trickey, S., & Topping, K. J. (2004). Philosophy for children: A systematic review. *Research Papers in Education, 19*, 363–278.

Trojano, L., Crisci, C., Lanzillo, B., Elefante, R., & Caruso, G. (1993). How many alien hand syndromes? Follow up of a case. *Neurology, 43*(12), 2710–2710.

Troje, N. F. (2002). Decomposing biological motion: A framework for analysis and synthesis of human gait patterns. *Journal of Vision, 2*(5), 371–387.

Trommershauser, J., Landy, M. S., & Maloney, L. T. (2006). Humans rapidly estimate expected gain in movement planning. *Psychological Science, 17*(11), 981–988.

Trueswell, J. C. (1996). The role of lexical frequency in syntactic ambiguity resolution. *Journal of Memory and Language, 35*, 566–585.

Tucker, M., & Ellis, R. (1998). On the relations between seen objects and components of potential actions. *Journal of Experimental Psychology-Human Perception and Performance, 24*(3), 830–846.

Tuckey, M., & Brewer, N. (2003). How schemas affect eyewitness memory over repeated retrieval attempts. *Applied Cognitive Psychology, 17*, 785–800.

Tuffiash, M., Roring, R. W., & Ericsson, K. A. (2007). Expert performance in Scrabble: Implications for the study of the structure and acquisition of complex skills. *Journal of Experimental Psychology: Applied, 13*, 124–134.

Tukey, D. D. (1986). A philosophical and empirical analysis of subject's modes of inquiry in Wason's 2-4-6 task. *Quarterly Journal of Experimental Psychology, 38A*, 5–34.

Tulving, E. (1972). Episodic and semantic memory. In E. Tulving & W. Donaldson (Eds.), *Organisation of Memory* (pp. 381–403). Academic Press.

Tulving, E. (1983). *Elements of Episodic Memory*. Oxford University Press.

Tulving, E. (1985). Memory and consciousness. *Canadian Psychologist, 25*, 1–12.

Tulving, E. (1999). Study of memory: processes and systems. In J. K. Foster & M. Jelicic (Eds.), *Memory: Systems, Process, or Function?* (pp. 11–30). Oxford University Press.

Tulving, E. (2002). Episodic memory: From mind to brain. *Annual Review of Psychology, 53*, 1–25.

Tulving, E. (2004). Episodic memory: From mind to brain. *Revue Neurologique, 160*, S9–S23.

Tulving, E. (2007). 'Are there 256 different kinds of memory?'. In J. S. Nairne (Ed.), *The Foundations of Remembering: Essays in Honor of Henry L. Roediger, III* (pp. 39–52). Psychology Press.

Tulving, E., Schacter, D. L., & Stark, H. A. (1982). Priming effects in word-fragment completion are independent of recognition memory. *Journal of Experimental Psychology: Learning, Memory, and Cognition, 8*(4), 336–342.

Turing, A. M. (1950). Computing machinery and intelligence. *Mind, 59*, 433–460.

Turvey, M. T. (1990). Coordination. *American Psychologist, 45*(8), 938–953.

Tversky, A. (1972). Elimination by aspects: A theory of choice. *Psychological Review, 79*, 281–299.

Tversky, A., & Kahneman, D. (1974). Judgment under uncertainty: Heuristics and biases. *Science, 125*, 1124–1131.

Tversky, A., & Kahneman, D. (1981). The framing of decisions and the psychology of choice. *Science, 211*, 453–458.

Tversky, A., & Kahneman, D. (1983). Extensional vs. intuitive reasoning: The conjunction fallacy in probability judgment. *Psychological Review, 90*, 293–315.

Tversky, A., & Kahneman, D. (1992). Advances in prospect theory: Cumulative representation of uncertainty. *Journal of Risk and Uncertainty, 5*, 297–323.

Tversky, B. (2011). Visualizing thought. *Topics in Cognitive Science, 3*(3), 499–535.

Twomey, T., Price, C. J., Waters, D., & MacSweeney, M. (2020). The impact of early language exposure on the neural system supporting language in deaf and hearing adults. *NeuroImage, 209*, 116411.

U

Ucros, C. G. (1989). Mood state-dependent memory: A meta-analysis. *Cognition & Emotion, 3*, 139–167.

Ullman, S., Vidal-Naquet, M., & Sali, E. (2002). Visual features of intermediate complexity and their use in classification. *Nature Neuroscience, 5*(7), 682–687.

Uman, M. A. (1986). *All About Lightning*. Dover Publications.

Underwood, B. J. (1957). Interference and forgetting. *Psychological Review, 64*, 49–60.

Ungerleider, L. G., & Mishkin, M. (1982). Two cortical visual systems. In D. Ingle, M. A. Goodale, & R. J. W. Mansfield (Eds.), *Analysis of Visual Behavior* (pp. 549–586). MIT Press.

United Biscuits (UK) Ltd. No. 2 (LON/91/160).

Uno, Y., Kawato, M., & Suzuki, R. (1989). Formation and control of optimal trajectory in human multijoint arm movement – Minimum torque-change model. *Biological Cybernetics, 61*(2), 89–101.

Unsworth, N., & Robison, M. K. (2019). Working memory capacity and sustained attention: A cognitive-energetic perspective. *Journal of Experimental Psychology: Learning, Memory, and Cognition, 18*, 562–573.

V

Vaid, J., & Gupta, A. (2002). Exploring word recognition in a semi-alphabetic script: The case of

Devanagari. *Brain and Language, 81*, 679–690.

Vaidya, C. J., Gabrieli, J. D. E., Keane, M. M., & Monti, L. A. (1995). Perceptual and conceptual memory processes in globalamnesia. *Neuropsychology, 9*, 580–591.

Valentine, T., & Maras, K. (2011). The effect of cross-examination on the accuracy of adult eyewitness testimony. *Applied Cognitive Psychology, 25*(4), 554–561.

Vallacich, J. S., Dennis, A. R., & Connolly, T. (1994). Idea generation in computer based groups: A new ending to an old story. *Organisational Behavior and Decision Processes, 7*, 448–467.

Vallar, G. (2019). A 'purest' impairment of verbal short-term memory. The case of PV and the phonological short-term store. In S. MacPherson & S. Della Sala (Eds.), *Cases of Amnesia: Contributions to Understanding Memory and the Brain* (pp. 261–291). Routledge.

Vallée-Tourangeau, F., & Krüsi Penney, A. (2005). The impact of external representation in a rule discovery task. *European Journal of Cognitive Psychology, 17*, 820–834.

van Kerkoerle, T., Self, M. & Roelfsema, P. (2017). Layer-specificity in the effects of attention and working memory on activity in primary visual cortex. *Nature Communications, 8*, 13804.

Van Meter, P., & Garner, J. (2005). The promise and practice of learner-generated drawing: Literature review and synthesis. *Educational Psychology Review, 17*(4), 285–325.

Van Petten, C., Coulson, S., Rubin, S., Plante, E., & Parks, M. (1999). Timecourse of word identification and semantic integration in spoken language. *Journal of Experimental Psychology: Learning, Memory, and Cognition, 25*, 394–417.

Van Rooij, T., Roederer, M., Wareham, T., Van Rooij, I., McLeod, H. L., & Marsh, S. (2015). Fast and frugal trees: Translating population based pharmacogenomics to medication prioritization. *Personalized Medicine, 12*, 117–128.

Van Rullen, R., & Thorpe, S. J. (2001). Is it a bird? Is it a plane? Ultra-rapid visual categorisation of natural and artifactual objects. *Perception, 30*(6), 655–668.

Van Vugt, B., Dagnino, B., Vartak, D., Safaai, H., Panzeri, S., Dehaene, S., & Roelfsema, P. R. (2018). The threshold for conscious report: Signal loss and response bias in visual and frontal cortex. *Science, 360*(6388), 537–542.

Vangeneugden, J., Pollick, F., & Vogels, R. (2009). Functional differentiation of macaque visual temporal cortical neurons using a parametric action space. *Cerebral Cortex, 19*(3), 593–611.

Vanlancker, D. R., Kreiman, J., & Cummings, J. (1989). Voice perception deficits: Neuroanatomical correlates of phonagnosia. *Journal of Clinical and Experimental Neuropsychology, 11*(5), 665–674.

Vannucci, M. & Chiorri, C. (2018). Individual differences inself-consciousness and mind wandering: Further evidence for a dissociation between spontaneous and deliberate mind wandering. *Personality and Individual Differences, 121*, 57–61.

Varley, R. (2014). Reason without much language. *Language Sciences, 46*, 232–244.

Västfjäll, D., Slovic, P., Burns, W. J., Erlandsson, A., Koppel, L., Asutay, E., & Tinghög, G. (2016). The arithmetic of emotion: Integration of incidental and integral affect in judgments and decisions. *Frontiers in Psychology, 7*, 325.

Veale, R., Hafed, Z. M., & Yoshida, M. (2017). How is visual salience computed in the brain? Insights from behaviour, neurobiology and modelling. *Philosophical Transactions of the Royal Society B: Biological Sciences, 372* (1714), 20160113.

Vecera, S. P., & Farah, M. J. (1994). Does visual attention select objects or locations? *Journal of Experimental Psychology: General, 123*(2), 146.

Veldre, A., Reichle, E. D., Wong, R., & Andrews, S. (2020). The effect of contextual plausibility on word skipping during reading. *Cognition, 197*, 104184.

Veling, H., & Van Knippenberg, A. (2004). Remembering can cause inhibition: Retrieval induced inhibition as a cue independent process. *Journal of Experimental Psychology: Learning, Memory, & Cognition, 30*, 315–318.

Velmans, M. (2009). *Understanding Consciousness* (2nd ed.). Routledge/Psychology Press.

Vera, A. H., & Simon, H. A. (1993). Situated action: A symbolic interpretation. *Cognitive Science, 17*, 7–48.

Verbaarschot, C., Farquhar, J., & Haselager, P. (2019). Free Wally: Where motor intentions meet reason and consequence. *Neuropsychologia, 133*, 107156.

Vernon, D., Hofsten, C. von, & Fadiga, L. (2010). *A roadmap for Cognitive Development in Humanoid Robots.* http://dx.doi.org/10.1007/978-3-642-16904-5 (MIT access only).

Vertes, R. P., & Eastman, K. E. (2000). The case against memory consolidation in REM sleep. *Behavioral and Brain Sciences*, 867–876.

Vieten, C., Wahbeh, H., Cahn, B. R., MacLean, K., Estrada, M., Mills, P., Murphy, M., Shapiro, S., Radin, D., Josipovic, Z., Presti, D. E., Sapiro, M., Bays, J. C., Russell, P., Vago, D., Travis, F., Walsh, R., & Delorme, A. (2018). Future directions in meditation research: Recommendations for expanding the field of contemplative science. *PLOS One, 13*(11).

Vigliocco, G., Antonini, T., & Garrett, M. F. (1997). Grammatical gender is on the tip of Italian tongues. *Psychological Science, 8*, 314–317.

Vignando, M., Aiello, M., Rinaldi, A., Cattaruzza, T., Mazzon, G., Manganotti, P., Eleopra, R., & Rumiati, R. I. (2019). Food knowledge depends upon the integrity of both sensory and functional properties: A VBM, TBSS and DTI tractography study. *Scientific Reports, 9*, 7439.

Vinciarelli, A., Pantic, M., & Bourlard, H. (2009). Social signal processing: Survey of an emerging domain. *Image and Vision Computing, 27*(12), 1743–1759.

Vinding, M. C., Jensen, M., & Overgaard, M. (2014). Distinct electrophysiological potentials for intention in action and prior intention for action. *Cortex, 50*, 86–99.

Vitevitch, M. S., Siew, C. S. Q., Castro, N., Goldstein, R., Gharst J. A., Kumar, J. J., & Boos, E. B. (2015). Speech error and tip of the tongue diary for mobile devices. *Frontiers in Psychology, 6*, 1190.

Viviani, P., & Cenzato, M. (1985). Segmentation and coupling in complex movements. *Journal of Experimental Psychology – Human Perception and Performance, 11*(6), 828–845.

Viviani, P., & Stucchi, N. (1992). Biological movements look uniform: Evidence of motor-perceptual interactions. *Journal of Experimental Psychology – Human Perception and Performance, 18*(3), 603–623.

Vlisides, P. E., Li, D., Zierau, M., Lapointe, A. P., Ip, K. I., McKinney, A. M., & Mashour, G. A. (2019). Dynamic cortical connectivity during general anesthesia in surgical patients. *Anesthesiology: The Journal of the American Society of Anesthesiologists, 130*(6), 885–897.

Voelker, R. (2019). Eye-tracking test approved to help diagnose concussion. *Jama, 321*(7), 638–638.

Vogt, S. (1995). On relations between perceiving, imagining and performing in the learning of cyclical movement sequences. *British Journal of Psychology, 86*, 191–216.

Vogt, S., Buccino, G., Wohlschlager, A. M., Canessa, N., Shah, N. J., Zilles, K., Eickhoff, S. B., Freund, H.-J., Rizzolatti, G., & Fink, G. R. (2007). Prefrontal involvement in imitation learning of hand actions: Effects of practice and expertise. *Neuroimage, 37*(4), 1371–1383.

Vogt, S., Di Rienzo, F., Collet, C., Collins, A., & Guillot, A. (2013). Multiple roles of motor imagery during action observation. *Frontiers in Human Neuroscience, 7*, 807.

Vogt, S., & Thomaschke, R. (2007). From visuo-motor interactions to imitation learning: Behavioural and brain imaging studies. *Journal of Sports Sciences, 25*(5), 497–517.

Volz, L. J., & Gazzaniga, M. S. (2017). Interaction in isolation: 50years of insights from split-brain research, *Brain, 140*(7), 2051–2060.

von Bartheld, C. S., Bahney, J., & Herculano-Houzel, S. (2016). The search for true numbers of neurons and glial cells in the human brain: A review of 150 years of cell counting. *Journal of Comparative Neurology, 524*, 3865–3895.

Von Frisch, K. (1962). Dialects in the language of the bees. *Scientific American, 207*, 79–87.

Voss, M. J., Zukosky, M., & Wang, R. F. (2018). A newapproach to differentiate states of mind wandering: Effects of working memory capacity. *Cognition, 179*, 202–212.

Vossel, S., Geng, J. J., & Fink, G. R. (2014). Dorsal and ventral attention systems: Distinct neural circuits but collaborative roles. *The Neuroscientist, 20*(2), 150–159.

Vrecko, S. (2010). Neuroscience, power and culture: An introduction. *History of the Human Sciences, 23*, 1–10.

Vrij, A. (2004). Why professionals fail to catch liars and how they can improve. *Legal and Criminological Psychology, 9*, 159–181.

Vrij, A., Edward, K., & Bull, R. (2001) People's insight into their own behaviour and speech content while lying. *British Journal of Psychology, 92*, 373–389.

Vrij, A., & Fisher, R. (2016). Which lie detection tools are ready for use in the criminal justice system? *Journal of Applied Research in Memory and Cognition, 5*(3), 302–307.

Vrij, A., & Mann, S. (2001). Telling and detecting lies in a high-stake situation: The case of a convicted murderer. *Applied Cognitive Psychology, 15*, 187–203.

Vul, E., Harris, C., Winklielan, P., & Pashler, H. (2009). Puzzlingly high correlations in fMRI studies of emotion, personality, and social cognition. *Perspectives on Psychological Science, 4*, 274–290.

W

Wacewicz, S., & Żywiczyński, P. (2015). Language evolution: Why Hockett's design features are a non-starter. *Biosemiotics, 8*(1), 29–46.

Wade, M. G., & Kazeck, M. (2018). Developmental coordination disorder and its cause: The road less travelled. *Human Movement Science, 57*, 489–500.

Wagenmakers, E.-J., Beek, T., Dijkhoff, L., Gronau, Q. F., Acosta, A., Adams, R. B., Jr., Albohn, D. N., Allard, E. S., Benning, S. D., Blouin-Hudon, E.-M., Bulnes, L. C., Caldwell, T. L., Calin-Jageman, R. J., Capaldi, C. A., Carfagno, N. S., Chasten, K. T., Cleeremans, A., Connell, L., & DeCicco, J. M., & Zwaan, R. A. (2016). Registered replication report: Strack, Martin, & Stepper (1988). *Perspectives on Psychological Science, 11*, 917–928.

Wagenmakers, E. J., Wetzels, R., Borsboom, D., van der Maas, H. L., & Kievit, R. A. (2012). An agenda for purely confirmatory research. *Perspectives on Psychological Science, 7*(6), 632–638.

Waite, S. A., Grigorian, A., Alexander, R. G., Macknik, S. L., Carrasco, M., Heeger, D., & Martinez-Conde, S. (2019). Analysis of perceptual expertise in radiology: Current knowledge and a new perspective. *Frontiers in Human Neuroscience, 13*, 213.

Walen, A. (2016). Retributive justice. In E. N. Zalta (Ed.), *The Stanford Encyclopedia of Philosophy Archive* (Winter 2016 ed.). Available at: https://plato.stanford.edu/archives/win2016/entries/justice-retributive/.

Wall, A., Borg, J., & Palmcrantz, S. (2015). Clinical application of the Hybrid Assistive Limb (HAL) for gait training: A systematic review. *Frontiers in Systems Neuroscience, 9*, 48.

Wallas, G. (1926). *The Art of Thought*. Jonathan Cape.

Wallentin, M. (2009). Putative sex differences in verbal abilities and language cortex: A critical review. *Brain & Language, 108*, 175–183.

Walther, J. B., & D'Addario, K. P. (2001). The impacts of emoticons on message interpretation incomputer-mediated communication. *Social Science Computer Review, 19*(3), 324–347.

Wammes, J. D., Meade, M. E., & Fernandes, M. A. (2017). Learning terms and definitions: Drawing and the role of elaborative encoding. *Acta Psychologica, 179*, 104–113.

Wang, J., Nicol, T., Skoe, E., Sams, M., & Kraus, N. (2009). Emotion modulates early auditory response to speech. *Journal of Cognitive Neuroscience, 21*(11), 2121–2128.

Wang, S., Jiang, M., Duchesne, X. M., Laugeson, E. A., Kennedy, D. P., Adolphs, R., & Zhao, Q. (2015). Atypical visual saliency in autism spectrum disorder quantified through model-based eye tracking. *Neuron, 88*(3), 604–616.

Ward, A. F., & Wegner, D. M. (2013). Mind-blanking: When the mind goes away. *Frontiers in Psychology, 4*, 650.

Ward, G. (2001). A critique of the working memory model. In J. Andrade (Ed.), *Working Memory in Perspective* (pp. 219–239). Psychology Press.

Ward, G., & Allport, A. (1997). Planning and problem-solving using the 5-disc Tower of London task. *Quarterly Journal of Experimental Psychology, 50*, 49–78.

Ward, J. E. (2006). *The Student's Guide to Cognitive neuroscience*. Psychology Press.

Ward, J. (2008). *The Frog Who Croaked Blue: Synesthesia and the Mixing of the Senses*. Routledge.

Ward, J. (2015). *The Student's Guide to Cognitive Neuroscience* (3rd ed.) (pp. 82–83). Psychology Press.

Ward, J., Thompson-Lake, D., Ely, R., & Kaminski, F. (2008). Synaesthesia, creativity and art: Whatis the link? *British Journal of Psychology, 99*, 127–141.

Warren, D., Welch, R., & McCarthy, T. (1981). The role of visual-auditory 'compellingness' in the ventriloquism effect: Implications for transitivity among the spatial senses. *Perception & Psychophysics, 30*, 557–564.

Warren, R. M., & Obusek, C. J. (1971). Speech perception and phonemic restorations. *Perception & Psychophysics, 9*, 358–362.

Warren, R. M., & Warren, R. P. (1970). Auditory illusions and confusions. *Scientific American, 223*, 30–36.

Warrington, E. K., Logue, V., & Pratt, R. T. (1972). The anatomical localisation of selective impairment of auditory verbal short-term memory. *Neuropsychologia, 9*, 377–387.

Warrington, E. K., & McCarthy, R. (1983). Category specific access dysphasia. *Brain, 106*, 859–878.

Warrington, E. K., & Shallice, T. (1969). The selective impairment of auditory verbal short-term memory. *Brain, 92*, 885–896.

Warrington, E. K., & Shallice, T. (1972). Neuropsychological evidence of visual storage in short-term memory tasks. *Quarterly Journal of Experimental Psychology, 24*, 30–40.

Warrington, E. K., & Shallice, T. (1984). Category specific semantic impairments. *Brain, 107*, 829–853.

Was, C. A., & Woltz, D. J. (2007). Re-examining the relationship between working memory and comprehension: The role of available long-term memory. *Journal of Memory and Language, 56*, 86–102.

Waskan, J. (2018). Robot consciousness. In R. J. Gennaro (Ed.), *The Routledge Handbook of Consciousness* (pp. 408–419). Routledge.

Wason, P. C. (1960). On the failure to eliminate hypotheses in a conceptual task. *Quarterly Journal of Experimental Psychology, 12*, 129–140.

Wason, P. C. (1966). Reasoning. In B. M. Foss (Ed.), *New Horizons in Psychology*. Penguin.

Wason, P. C. (1968). Reasoning about a rule. *Quarterly Journal of Experimental Psychology, 20*, 273–281.

Wason, P. C. (1969). Regression in reasoning? *British Journal of Psychology, 60*, 471–480.

Wason, P. C. (1995). Creativity in research. In S. E. Newstead & J. St. B. T. Evans (Eds.), *Perspectives on Thinking and Reasoning: Essays in Honour of Peter Wason*. Lawrence Erlbaum Associates Ltd.

Wason, P. C., & Evans, J. St. B. T. (1975). Dual processes in reasoning? *Cognition, 3*, 141–154.

Wason, P. C., & Johnson-Laird, P. N. (1970). A conflict between selecting and evaluating information in an inferential task. *British Journal of Psychology, 61*, 509–515.

Wason, P. C., & Johnson-Laird, P. N. (1972). *Psychology of Reasoning: Structure and Content*. Batsford.

Wason, P. C., & Shapiro, D. (1971). Natural and contrived experience in a reasoning problem. *Quarterly Journal of Experimental Psychology, 23*, 63–71.

Wassermann, E. (2013). Transcranial brain stimulation. Behavioral Neurology Unit, National Institute of Neurological Disorders and Stroke, National Institutes of Health, United States Department of Health and Human Services. Archived from the original available at: http://intra.ninds.nih.gov/Research.asp?People_ID=196 (accessed 29 October 2013).

Watson, J. B. (1913). Psychology as the behaviorist views it. *Psychological Review, 20*, 158–177.

Watts, F. N., McKenna, F. P., Sharrock, R., & Trezise, L. (1986). Colour naming of phobia-related words. *British Journal of Psychology, 77*, 97–108.

Waugh, N. C., & Norman, D. A. (1965). Primary memory. *Psychological Review, 72*, 89–104.

Weatherholtz, K., & Jaeger, T. F. (2016). Speech perception and generalization across talkers and accents. *Linguistics: Oxford Research Encyclopedias*.

Weaver, C. A. III (1993). Do you need a 'flash' to form a flashbulb memory? *Journal of Experimental Psychology: General, 122*, 39–46.

Webb, C. E., & Dennis, N. A. (2019). Memory for the usual: The influence of schemas on memory for non-schematic information in younger and older adults. *Cognitive Neuropsychology*, 1–17.

Weech, S., & Troje, N. F. (2017). Vection latency is reduced by bone-conducted vibration and noisy galvanic vestibular stimulation. *Multisensory Research, 30*(1), 65–90.

Wegner, D. M. (2003). The mind's best trick: How we experience conscious will. *Trends in Cognitive Sciences, 7*(2), 65–69.

Wegner, D. M., & Wheatley, T. (1999). Apparent mental causation: Sources of the experience of will. *American Psychologist, 54*(7), 480–492.

Weiner, K. S., & Grill-Spector, K. (2012). The improbable simplicity of the fusiform face area. *Trends in Cognitive Sciences, 16*(5), 251–254.

Weingartner, H. J., Sirocco, K., Curran, V., & Wolkowitz, O. (1995). Memory facilitation following the administration of the benzodiazepine triazolam. *Experimental Clinical Psychopharmacology, 3*, 298–303.

Weisberg, R. W. (1994). Genius and madnesss? A quasi-experimental test of the hypothesis that manic depression increases creativity. *Psychological Science, 5*, 361–367.

Weisberg, R. W. (1995). Prolegomena to theories of insight in problem solving: Definition of terms and a taxonomy of problems. In R. J. Sternberg & J. E. Davidson (Eds.), *The Nature of Insight* (pp. 157–196). MIT Press.

Weisberg, R. W. (2006). *Creativity: Understanding Innovation in Problem Solving, Science, Invention and the Arts*. J. Wiley.

Weisberg, R. W. (2018). Insight, problem solving and creativity: An integration of findings. In F. Vallee-Tourangeau (Ed.), *Insight: On the Origins of New Ideas* (pp. 191–215). Routledge.

Weisberg, R. W. (2018a). Reflections on a personal journey

studying the psychology of creativity. In R. J. Sternberg & J. Kaufmann (Eds.), *The Nature of Human Creativity* (pp. 351–373). Cambridge University Press.

Weisberg, R. W., & Alba, J. W. (1981). An examination of the alleged role of 'fixation' in the solution of several 'insight' problems. *Journal of Experimental Psychology: General, 110*, 169–192.

Weiskrantz, L., Warrington, E. K., Sanders, M. D., & Marshall, J. (1974). Visual capacity in the hemianopic field following a restricted occipital ablation. *Brain, 97*(1), 709–728.

Weissman, B., & Tanner, D. (2018). A strong wink between verbal and emoji-based irony: How the brainprocesses ironic emojis during language comprehension. *PLOS One, 13*(8), e0201727.

Welch, G. B., & Burnett, C. T. (1924). Is primacy a factor in association-formation. *American Journal of Psychology, 35*, 396–401.

Welch, R. B., Duttonhurt, L. D., & Warren, D. H. (1986). Contributions of audition and vision to temporal rate perception. *Perception & Psychophysics, 39*(4), 294–300.

Welch, R. B., & Warren, D. H. (1980). Immediate perceptual response to intersensory discrepancy. *Psychological Bulletin, 88*(3), 638–667.

Wells, G. L., & Loftus, E. F. (2003). Eyewitness memory for people and events. In A. M. Goldstein (Ed.), *Handbook of Psychology*. Vol. 11, *Forensic Psychology* (pp. 149–160). John Wiley.

Wells, G. L., & Turtle, J. W. (1986). Eyewitness identification: The importance of lineup models. *Psychological Bulletin, 99*(3), 320–329.

Wells, H. G. (1908). *First and Last Things*. London.

Wen, W., & Haggard, P. (2020). Prediction error and regularity detection underlie two dissociable mechanisms for computing the sense of agency. *Cognition, 195*, 104074.

Wener, A. E., & Rehm, L. (1975). Depressive affect: A test of behavioral hypotheses. *Journal of Abnormal Psychology, 84*, 221–227.

Wenke, D., Fleming, S. M., & Haggard, P. (2010). Subliminal priming of actions influences sense of control over effects of action. *Cognition, 115*(1), 26–38.

Wernicke, C. (1874). *Der Aphasische Symtomemcomplex.* M. Cohn und Weigert.

Wertheimer, M. (1945). *Productive Thinking.* Harper & Row.

Wetherick, N. E., & Gilhooly, K. J. (1990). Syllogistic reasoning: Effects of premise order. In K. Gilhooly, M. T. G. Keane, R. Logie, & G. Erdos (Eds.), *Lines of Thought: Reflections in the Psychology of Thinking*, Vol. 1. John Wiley.

Weylman, S. T., Brownell, H. H., & Gardner, H. (1988). 'It's what you mean, not what you say': Pragmatic language use in brain-damaged patients. In F. Plum (Ed.), *Language, Communication, and the Brain* (pp. 229–243). Raven Press.

Whaley, C. P. (1978). Word-nonword classification time. *Journal of Verbal Learning and Verbal Behavior, 17*, 143–154.

Wheaton, L. A., & Hallett, M. (2007). Ideomotor apraxia: A review. *Journal of the Neurological Sciences, 260* (1–2), 1–10.

Wheeldon, L. R., & Levelt, W. J. M. (1995). Monitoring the time course of phonological encoding. *Journal of Memory and Language, 34*(3), 311–334.

Wheeler, D. D. (1970). Processes in word recognition. *Cognitive Psychology, 1*, 59–85.

Whelan, C. W., Wagstaff, G. F., & Wheatcroft, J. M. (2014). High-stakes lies: Verbal and nonverbal cues to deception in public appeals for help with missing or murdered relatives. *Psychiatry, Psychology and Law, 21*(4), 523–537.

Whitaker, H. (1982). Levels of impairment in disorders of speech. In R. Malatesha & L. Hartlage (Eds.), *Neuropsychology and Cognition – Volume 1: Proceedings of the NATO Advanced Study Institute on Neuropsychology and Cognition.* Martinus Nijhoff Publishers.

White, A. (2004). What happened? Alcohol, memory blackouts and the brain. http://pubs.niaaa.nih.gov/publications/arh27-2/186-196.htm.

Whorf, B. L. (1956). *Language, Thought, and Reality: Selected Writings.* Technology Press of Massachusetts Institute of Technology.

Whorf, B. L. (1956). *Language, thought, and reality: Selected writings of Benjamin Lee Whorf* (Ed. J. B. Carroll) (pp. 51–56). The MIT Press.

Wick, F. A., Alaoui Soce, A., Garg, S., Grace, R. C., & Wolfe, J. M. (2019). Perception in dynamic scenes: What is your Heider capacity?. *Journal of Experimental Psychology: General, 148*(2), 252.

Wickelgren, W. (1974). *How to Solve Problems*. W.H. Freeman.

Wickelgren, W. A. (1969). Context-sensitive coding associative memory and serial order in (speech) behavior. *Psychological Review, 76*(1), 1–15.

Wickens, C. D. (1991). Processing resources and attention. In D. Damos (Ed.), *Multiple Task Performance* (pp. 3–34). Taylor & Francis.

Wickens, C. D. (2002). Multiple resources and performance prediction. *Theoretical Issues in Ergonomic Science, 3*, 159–177.

Wierda, S. M., Van Rijn, H., Taatgen, N. A., & Martens, S. (2010). Distracting the mind improves performance: An ERP study. *PLOS One, 5*(11).

Wierzbicka, A. (1986). Human emotions: Universal or culture-specific? *American Anthropologist, 88*(3), 584–594.

Wilkins, A. J., & Baddeley, A. D. (1978). Remembering to recall in everyday life: An approach to absentmindedness. In M. M. Gruneberg, P. E. Morris, & R. N. Sykes (Eds.), *Practical Aspects of Memory*. Academic Press.

Wilkins, M. (1928). The effect of changed material on ability to do formal syllogistic reasoning. *Archives of Psychology, 16*, 83.

Williams, H. L., Conway, M. A., & Cohen, G. (2008). Autobiographical memory. In G. Cohen & M. A. Conway (Eds.), *Memory in the Real World* (3rd ed.) (pp. 21–90). Psychology Press.

Williams, J. J., & Lombrozo, T. (2010). The role of explanation in discovery and generalization: Evidence from category learning. *Cognitive Science, 34*(5), 776–806.

Williams, J. J., & Lombrozo, T. (2013). Explanation and prior knowledge interact to guide learning. *Cognitive Psychology, 66*, 55–84.

Williams, J. J., Lombrozo, T., & Rehder, B. (2013). The hazards of explanation: Overgeneralization in the face of exceptions. *Journal of Experimental Psychology: General, 142*, 1006–1014.

Williford, T., & Maunsell, J. H. (2006). Effects of spatial attention on contrast response functions in macaque area V4. *Journal of Neurophysiology, 96*(1), 40–54.

Willingham, D. (2002). Allocating student study time. *American Educator*, Summer. www.aft.org/newspubs/periodicals/ac/summer2002

Wills, J. A., Hackel, L., Feldmanhall, O., Parnamets, P., & Van Bavel, J. J. (2020). The social neuroscience of cooperation. In D. Poeppel, M. Gazzaniga, & G. R. Mangun (Eds.), *The Cognitive Neurosciences* (6th ed.). MIT Press.

Wilson, A. D., & Golonka, S. (2013). Embodied cognition is not what you think it is. *Frontiers in Psychology, 4*, 58.

Wilson, B. S. (2015). Getting a decent (but sparse) signal to the brain for users of cochlear implants. *Hearing Research, 322*, 24–38.

Wilson, M. (2002). Six views of embodied cognition. *Psychonomic Bulletin & Review, 9*(4), 625–636.

Wilson, S. H., Greer, J. F., & Johnson, R. M. (1973). Synectics, a creative problem solving technique for the gifted. *Gifted Child Quarterly, 17*, 260–267.

Winawer, J., Huk, A. C., & Boroditsky, L. (2010). A motion aftereffect from visual imagery of motion. *Cognition, 114*, 276–284.

Winkler, R. (2005). The need for speed. *New York Times*, 13 November.

Winograd, E. (1988). Some observations on prospective remembering. In M. M. Gruneberg, P. E. Morris, & R. N. Sykes (Eds.), *Practical Aspects of Memory: Current Research and Issues* (pp. 348–353). Wiley.

Winograd, E., & Killinger, W. A. (1983). Relating age at encoding in early childhood to adult recall: Development of flashbulb memories. *Journal of Experimental Psychology General, 112*, 413–422.

Wirth, M., Rahman, R. A., Kuenecke, J., Koenig, T., Horn, H., Sommer, W., & Dierks, T. (2011). Effects of transcranial direct current stimulation (tDCS) on behaviour and electrophysiology of language production. *Neuropsychologia, 49*(14), 3989–3998.

Wit, J. K., Kemmerer, D., Linkenauger, L., & Culham, J. (2010). A functional role for motor simulation in identifying tools. *Psychological Science Online First,* published on 16 July. doi:10.1177/0956797610378307

Wittgenstein, L. (1953). *Philosophical Investigations.* Basil Blackwell.

Wixted, J. T. (2004). The psychology and neuroscience of forgetting. *Annual Review of Psychology, 55*, 235–269.

Wixted, J. T. (2010). The role of retroactive interference and consolidation in everyday forgetting. In S. Della Sala (Ed.), *Forgetting*. Psychology Press.

Wixted, J. T., & Wells, G. L. (2017). The relationship between eyewitness confidence and identification accuracy: A new synthesis. *Psychological Science in the Public Interest, 18*(1), 10–65.

Woike, J. K., Hoffrage, U., & Martignon, L. (2017). Integrating and testing natural frequencies, Naive Bayes and fast-and-frugal trees. *Decision, 4*, 234–260.

Wolfe, J. M. (1994). Guided Search 2.0: A revised model of visual search. *Psychonomic Bulletin & Review, 1*(2), 202–238.

Wolfe, J. M., Horowitz, T. S., & Kenner, N. M. (2005). Rare items often missed in visual searches. *Nature, 435*(7041), 439–440.

Wolfe, J. M., Võ, M. L. H., Evans, K. K., & Greene, M. R. (2011). Visual search in scenes involves selective and nonselective pathways. *Trends in Cognitive Sciences, 15*(2), 77–84.

Wolman, D. (2012). A tale of two halves. *Nature, 483*, 260–263.

Wolpert, D. M., & Ghahramani, Z. (2000). Computational principles of movement neuroscience. *Nature Neuroscience, 3*(11), 1212–1217.

Wolpert, D. M., & Kawato, M. (1998). Multiple paired forward and inverse models for motor control. *Neural Networks, 11*(7–8), 1317–1329.

Wolpert, D. M., Shergill, S. S., Bays, P. M., & Frith, C. D. (2003). Two eyes for an eye: The neuroscience of force escalation. *Science, 301* (5630), 187.

Woodman, G. F., & Vogel, E. K. (2008). Selective storage and maintenance of an object's features in visual working memory. *Psychonomic Bulletin & Review, 15*(1), 223–229.

Woods, A. J., Philbeck, J. W., & Danoff, J. V. (2009). The various perceptions of distance: An alternative view of how effort affects distance judgments. *Journal of Experimental Psychology: Human Perception, & Performance, 35*, 1104–1117.

Woods, A. T., & Newell, F. N. (2004). Visual, haptic and cross-modal recognition of objects and scenes. *Journal of Physiology – Paris, 98*(1–3), 147–159.

Woodworth, R. S. (1899). The accuracy of voluntary movement. *Psychological Review, 3* (Suppl. 13), 1–119.

Woodworth, R. S., & Sells, S. B. (1935). An atmosphere effect in formal syllogistic reasoning. *Journal of Experimental Psychology, 18*(4), 451–460.

Worthington, A. (2016). Treatments and technologies in the rehabilitation of apraxia and action disorganisation syndrome: A review. *Neuro Rehabilitation, 39*(1), 163–174.

Worthington, A. (2017). Emerging technologies for the rehabilitation of executive dysfunction and action disorganisation. *Austin Journal of Clinical Neurology, 4*(4), 1116.

Wright, B., & Garrett, M. (1984). Lexical decision in sentences: Effects of syntactic structure. *Memory & Cognition, 12*(1), 31–45.

Wright, D. B. (1993). Recall of the Hillsborough disaster over time: systematic biases of 'flashbulb' memories. *Applied Cognitive Psychology, 7*, 129–138.

Wright, D. B., Gaskell, G. D., & O'Muircheartaigh, C. A. (1998). Flashbulb memory assumptions: Using national surveys to explore cognitive phenomena. *British Journal of Psychology, 36*, 443–456.

Wright, S. (1954). The death of Lady Mondegreen. *Harper's Magazine, 209*(1254), 48–51.

Wundt, W. (1899) Zur Kritik tachistosckopisher Versuche. *Phil. Stud., 15*, 287–317.

Wurtz, R. H. (2009). Recounting the impact of Hubel and Wiesel. *Journal of Physiology, 587*(12), 2817–2823.

Y

Yan, S., Walters, L. M., Wang, Z., & Wang, C. C. (2018). Meta-analysis of the effectiveness of philosophy for children programs on students' cognitive outcomes. *Analytic Teaching and Philosophical Praxis, 39*(1), 13–33.

Yang, T. X., Peng, Z. W., Wang, Y., Geng, F. L., Miao, G. D., Shum, D. H., Cheung, E. F., & Chan, R. C. (2015). The nature of prospective memory deficit in patients with obsessive-compulsive disorder. *Psychiatry Research, 230*(2), 479–486.

Yarbus, A. L. (1967). *Eye Movements and Vision*. Plenum Press.

Yaroush, R., Sullivan, M. J., & Ekstrand, B. R. (1971). Effect of sleep on memory: II. Differential effect of the first and second half of the night. *Journal of Experimental Psychology, 88*(3), 361.

Yeung, P., Ho, C. S., Chan, D. W., & Chung, K. K. (2019). Writing motivation and performance in Chinese children. *Reading and Writing: An Interdisciplinary Journal, 33*, 427–449.

Yiend, J. (2010). The effects of emotion on attention: A review of attentional processing of emotional information. *Cognition and Emotion, 24*(1), 3–47.

Young, A. W., & Burton, A. M. (2018). Are we face experts? *Trends in Cognitive Sciences, 22*(2), 100–110.

Young, A. W., & Noyes, E. (2019). We need to talk about super-recognizers: Invited commentary on: Ramon, M., Bobak, A. K., & White, D., Super recognizers: From the lab to the world and back again. *British Journal of Psychology, 110*, 492–494.

Young, A. W., & Ellis, H. D. (1989). *Handbook of Research on Face Processing*. North Holland.

Z

Zacks, J. M., Speer, N. K., Swallow, K. M., Braver, T. S., & Reynolds, J. R. (2007). Event perception: A mind–brain perspective. *Psychological Bulletin, 133*(2), 273–293.

Zacks, J. M., & Tversky, B. (2001). Event structure in perception and conception. *Psychological Bulletin, 127*(1), 3–21.

Zajac, R., Westera, N., & Kaladelfos, A. (2018). The 'good old days' of courtroom questioning: Changes in the format of child cross-examination questions over 60years. *Child Maltreatment, 23*(2), 186–195.

Zajonc, R. B. (1980). Feeling and thinking: Preferences need no inferences. *American Psychologist, 35*(2), 151–175.

Zakay, D. (1985). Post-decisional confidence and conflict experienced in a choice process. *Acta Psychologica, 58*, 75–80.

Zambaldi, C. F., Cantilino, A., Farias, J. A., Moraes, G. P., & Botelho Sougey, E. (2011). Dissociative experience during childbirth. *Journal of Psychosomatic Obstetrics & Gynecology, 32*(4), 204–209.

Zatorre, R. J., Halpern, A. R., Perry, D. W., Meyer, E., & Evans, A. C. (1996). Hearing in the mind's ear: A PET investigation of musical imagery and perception. *Journal of Cognitive Neuroscience, 8*, 29–46.

Zeki, S. (1991). Cerebral akinetopsia (visual-motion blindness) – A review. *Brain, 114*, 811–824.

Zeman, A. (2006). What do we mean by 'conscious' and 'aware'? *Neuropsychological Rehabilitation, 16*(4), 356–376.

Zerilli-Zavgorodni, T., & Bisighini, S. (2014). Charles Bonnet syndrome: Comprehensive review providing an optometric approach to diagnosis and management. *Optometry and Visual Performance, 2*, 26–38.

Zhang, L. L., Wang, J. Q., Qi, R. R., Pan, L. L., Li, M., & Cai, Y. L. (2016). Motion sickness: Current knowledge and recent advance. *CNS Neuroscience & Therapeutics, 22*(1), 15–24.

Zhao, B., Gherri, E., & Della Sala, S. (2019). Age effects in mental rotation are due to the use of a different strategy. *Aging, Neuropsychology and Cognition*. doi: 10.1080/13825585.2019.1632255

Zihl, J., & Heywood, C. A. (2015). The contribution of LM to the neuroscience of movement vision. *Frontiers in Integrative Neuroscience, 9*, 6.

Zito, G. A., Wiest, R., & Aybek, S. (2020). Neural correlates of sense of agency in motor control: A neuroimaging meta-analysis. *PLoS One, 15*(6), e0234321.

Zola, D. (1984). Redundancy and word perception during reading. *Perception and Psychophysics, 36*, 277–284.

Zwicker, J. G., Missiuna, C., Harris, S. R., & Boyd, L. A. (2012). Developmental coordination disorder: A review and update. *European Journal of Paediatric Neurology, 16*(6), 573–581.

Name Index

A

Abdellaoui, M., Bleichrodt, H., & Kammoun, H. 472
Aboitiz, F., Ossandón, T., Zamorano, F., Palma, B., & Carrasco, X. 120
Abrams, R. A., Davoli, C. C., Du, F., Knapp III, W. H., & Paull, D. 142
Acar, S., & Sen, S. 462, 578
Adams, I. L., Lust, J. M., Wilson, P. H., & Steenbergen, B. 100
Adams, J. W., & Hitch, G. J. 203
Adelson, B. 450
Aglioti, S., De Souza, J. F., & Goodale, M. A. 47
Aguilar, P., Brussino, S., & Fernandez-Dols, J.-M. 497
Ahn, W., Kim, N. S., Lassaline, M. E., & Dennis, M. 304
Air France 193
Aitchison, J. 331
Akata, Z., Hendricks, L. A., Alaniz, S., & Darrell, T. 67
Akhand, O., Balcer, L. J., & Galetta, S. L. 70
Akyürek, E. G., & Hommel, B. 137
Alais, D., & Burr, D. 59
Alber, J., Della Sala, S., & Dewar, M. 279
Alberini, C. M., & LeDoux, J. E. 279
Albert, M. L., & Bear, D. 404
Albonico, A., & Barton, J. 76
Albright, T. D. 76
Alea, N., & Bluck, S. 243
Aleksander, I. 167
AlexNet 67
Allan, L. G. 578
Allison, T., Ginter, H., McCarthy, G., Nobre, A. C., Puce, A., Luby, M., & Spencer, D. D. 74
Allison, T., Puce, A., & McCarthy, G. 80
Alloy, L. B., & Abramson, L. Y. 578
Alloy, L. B., & Ackerman, L. Y. 578
Alloy, L. B., Abramson, L. Y., Whitehouse, W. G., Hogan, M. E., Panzarella, C., & Rose, D. T. 579
Allport, D. A. 125, 369
Allport, D. A., & Funnell, E. 369
Alpha Go Zero (Google Deep Mind Project) 16–17
Altmann, C. F., Uesaki, M., Ono, K., Matsuhashi, M., Mima, T., & Fukuyama, H. 384
Altmann, G. T. M. 400, 402–3
Amalberti, R. 193
Amano, T., Sandel, B., Eager, H., Bulteau, E., Svenning, J.-C., Dalsgaard, B. et al. 330, 331
American Academy of Neurology 30
American Beauty (Sam Mendes film) 72
Amlung, M., Petker, T., Jackson, J., Balodis, I., & MacKillop, J. 474–5
Anbarci, N., Arin, K. P., Kuhlenkasper, T., & Zenker, C. 472
Andersen, R. A., & Buneo, C. A. 142
Anderson, J. R. 15
Anderson, M. C. 279, 280
Anderson, M. C., & Bell, T. A. 281
Anderson, M. C., & Green, C. 280, 282
Anderson, M. C., & Neely, J. H. 270
Anderson, M. C., Bjork, R. A., & Bjork, E. L. 280
Anderson, M. C., Ochsner, K. N., Cooper, J., Robertson, E., Gabrieli, S. W., Glover, G. H., & Gabrieli, J. D. E. 282
Andics, A., McQueen, J. M., Petersson, K. M., Gal, V., Rudas, G., & Vidnyanszky, Z. 78
Andoh, J., Milde, C., Tsao, J. W., & Flor, H. 57
Andreetta, S., & Marini, A. 369
Andreetta, S., Cantagallo, A., & Marini, A. 369
Anguera, J. A., & Gazzaley, A. 127
Anzai, Y., & Simon, H. A. 435
Anzellotti, F., Onofrj, V., Maruotti, V., Ricciardi, L., Franciotti, R., Bonanni, L., Thomas, A., & Onofrj, M. 171
Apollo 13 mission 426–7
Applegate, D. L., Bixby, R. M., Chvatal, V., & Cook, W. J. 438
Applied Imagination (Osborn, A.) 458
Ardila, A. 362, 370
Ardila, A., Bernal, B., & Rosselli, M. 365, 370
Aristotle 6, 531
Armstrong, K. M., Fitzgerald, J. K., & Moore, T. 142
Arning, L., Stock, A.-K., Kloster, E., Epplen, J. T., & Beste, C. 179
Articulated Head project 117–18
Arunta tribe in central Australia 567
Asaly-Zetawi, M., & Lipka, O. 371
Atchley, P., & Andersen, G. J. 131
Atkeson, C. G., Hale, J. G., Pollick, F. E., Riley, M., Kotosaka, S., Schaal, S. et al. 88
Atkinson, A. P., & Adolphs, R. 75
Atkinson, R. C., & Shiffrin, R. M. 179, 187–8, 192, 198, 226
Atwood, M. E., & Polson, P. G. 433
Atwood, M. E., Masson, M. E. J., & Polson, P. G. 433
Autin, F., & Croizet, J. 214–16
Auvray, M., & Deroy, O. 182
Averbach, E. A., & Coriell, A. S. 181
Averell, L., & Heathcote, A. 269
Awh, E., & Jonides, J. 140–1
Awh, E., & Pashler, H. 126
Awh, E., Jonides, J., & Reuter-Lorenz, P. A. 140–41
Awh, E., Vogel, E. K., & Oh, S. H. 139, 140
Ayotte, J., Peretz, I., & Hyde, K. 53
Ayotte, J., Peretz, I., Rousseau, I., Bard, C., & Bojanowski, M. 53
Ayton, P., Onkal, D., & McReynolds, L. 491

B

Baars, B. J. 155, 162, 166, 214
Baars, B. J., & Motley, M. T. 348
Baas, M., Nijstad, B. A., Boot, N. C., & De Dreu, C. K. W. 461
Baayen, R. H., Piepenbrock, R., & Gulikers, L. 396
Bachiller, P., Bustos, P., & Manso, L. J. 117
Bachorowski, J. A., & Owren, M. J. 78
Bacon, A. M., & Handley, S. 525–6
Badcock, P. B., Friston, K. J., & Ramstead, M. J. 108
Baddeley, A. C., & Lieberman, K. 140, 204
Baddeley, A. D. 4–5, 15, 263, 268, 283–4
 long-term memory 227, 228, 256, 525
 sensory, short-term and working memory 196, 197–9, 202, 203, 206, 207, 210–11, 212–14
Baddeley, A. D., & Andrade, J. 313
Baddeley, A. D., & Hitch, G. J. 192, 195, 196, 198, 202, 203, 205–6, 262
Baddeley, A. D., & Logie, R. H. 206
Baddeley, A. D., & Longman, D. J. A. 267
Baddeley, A. D., & Warrington, E. K. 190
Baddeley, A. D., & Wilson, B. 198, 207
Baddeley, A. D., Chincotta, D. M., & Adlam, A. 203
Baddeley, A. D., Grant, S., Wight, E., & Thompson, N. 199, 200, 204–5
Baddeley, A. D., Papagno, C., & Vallar, G. 202

Baek, J., & Chong, S. C. 131
Baese-Berk, M. 379
Bahrick, H. P. 252–3, 269
Bahrick, H. P., Bahrick, P. O., & Wittlinger, R. P. 252–3
Bahrick, H. P., Hall, L. K., & Berger, S. A. 245–6
Ballard, I. C., Kim, B., Liatsis, A., Aydogan, G., Cohen, J. D., & McClure, S. M. 474
Balota, D. A., & Chumbley, J. I. 396
Banaji, M. R., & Crowder, R. 283–4
Banbury, S. P., & Berry, D. C. 201
Banbury, S. P., Macken, W. J., Tremblay, S., & Jones, D. M. 201
Banks, M. I., Krause, B. M., Endemann, C. M., Campbell, D. I., Kovach, C. K., Dyken, M. E. et al. 156
Banks, W. P. 170
Barber, Samuel 576
Bard, E. G., Shillcock, R. C., & Altmann, G. T. M. 393
Bard, Phillip 563
Bargh, J. A. 158
Baron, J. 494
Baron, J., & Jurney, J. 495, 496
Baron, J., & Ritov, I. 495
Baron-Cohen, S. 155
Baronchelli, A., Ferrer-i-Cancho, R., Pastor-Satorras, R., Chater, N., & Christiansen, M. H. 311
Barrash, J., Stuss, D. T., Aksan, N., Anderson, S. W., Jones, R. D., Manzel, K., & Tranel, D. 553
Barrett, H. C., & Kurzban, R. 22
Barrett, L. F. 11, 550, 570
Barrett, L. F., & Satpute, A. B. 570
Barrett, L. F., Adolphs, R., Marsella, S., Martinez, A. M., & Pollak, S. D. 555
Barsalou, Lawrence W. 12, 43, 107, 301, 304, 308, 309, 312
Barshi, I., & Farris, C. 399
Bartha, L., & Benke, T. 368
Bartlett, F. C. 232–3, 235–6, 286, 287, 388
Bartlett, L., Martin, A., Neil, A. L., Memish, K., Otahal, P., Kilpatrick, M., & Sanderson, K. 155
Bartolomeo, P. 321
Bartolozzi, C., Natale, L., Nori, F., & Metta, G. 67
Barton, J. J., & Corrow, S. L. 76
Barton, M. E., & Komatsu, L. K. 305–6
Basden, B. H., & Basden, D. R. 281
Basden, B. H., Basden, D. R., & Gargano, G. J. 281
Bassetti, C., Vella, S., Donati, F., Wielepp, P., & Weder, B. 154
Basso, A., Spinnler, H., Vallar, G., & Zanobio, E. 191
Basu Mallick, D., Magnotti, J. F., & Beauchamp, M. S. 390
Bateman, L., Jones, C., & Jomeen, J. 171
Bauer, R. M. 73
Bauman, C. W., McGraw, A. P., Bartels, D. M., & Warren, C. 497
Baumann, O., & Belin, P. 78
Bavelas, J., Gerwing, J., Sutton, C., & Prevost, D. 330
Bayer, J. B., & Campbell, S. W. 197
Bayesian Decision Theory 41, 92
Bayley, P. J., Frascino, J. C., & Squire, L. R. 229
Beaman, C. P. 195
Bear, A., Kagan, A., & Rand, D. G. 506
Beardsworth, T., & Buckner, T. 102
Beattie, G. 341
Beauchamp, M. S., & Martin, A. 108

Name Index

Beauvois, M. F., & Derouesné, J. 417
Bechara, A., Damasio, H., Tranel, D., & Damasio, A. R. 582
Beck, A. T., Rush, A. J., Shaw, B. F., & Emery, G. 578
Beck, Aaron 517–18, 578
Beck, C., Kardatzki, B., & Ethofer, T. 382
Beck Lidén, C., Krüger, O., Schwarz, L., Erb, M., Kardatzki, B., Scheffler, K., & Ethofer, T. 382
Begg, I., & Denny, J. P. 521
Begg, I. & Harris, G. 522
Beilock, S. 97
Belin, P., Fecteau, S., & Bedard, C. 78
Belin, P., Zatorre, R. J., Lafaille, P., Ahad, P., & Pike, B. 78
Belletier, C., Normand, A., Camos, V., Barrouillet, P., & Huguet, P. 97
Bellugi, U., & Wang, P. 329
Bentham, Jeremy 493
Berent, I., Steriade, D., Lennertz, T., & Vaknin, V. 382
Berlin, L. 129
Berndt, R. A., & Caramazza, A. 403
Bernoulli, D. 471
Bernstein, Nikolai 84–5
Berntsen, D. 244, 575
Bertelson, P., & Radeau, M. 58
Best, C. T. 363
Beste, C., Saft, C., Gunturkun, O., & Falkenstein, M. 179
Bever, T. G. 402–3
Bhat, N. A., Sharma, V., & Kumar, D. 240
Bhatia, S., & Stewart, N. 487
Białystok, E., Shenfield, T., & Codd, J. 371
Bidelman, G. M., Moreno, S., & Alain, C. 384
Biederman, I. 64, 65
Biederman, I., & Gerhardstein, P. C. 66
Biederman, I., Rabinowitz, J. C., Glass, A. L., & Stacy, E. W., Jr. 131
Biggs, J. B., Kember, D., & Leung, D. Y. P. 288
Billard, A. G., Calinon, S., & Dillmann, R. 37
Binder, J. R. 370
Binder, J. R., Frost, J. A., Hammeke, T. A., Bellgowan, P. S. F., Springer, J. A. et al. 78
Binford, T. O. 63, 64
Biotteau, M., Chaix, Y., Blais, M., Tallet, J., Péran, P., & Albaret, J. M. 100
Birnbaum, I. M., Parker, E. S., Hartley, J. T., & Noble, E. P. 277
Bish, C. L., Blanck, H. M., Serdula, M. K., Marcus, M., Kohl III, H. W., & Khan, L. K. 159, 160
Bisley, J. W., & Mirpour, K. 133
Bisoglio, J., Michaels, T. I., Mervis, J. E., & Ashinoff, B. K. 127
Bjork, R. A. 187, 281
Bjork, R. A., Bjork, E. L., & Anderson, M. C. 280–81
Blair, R. J., & Cipolotti, L. 554
Blakemore, S. J., Wolpert, D. M., & Frith, C. D. 110, 169
Blaney, P. H. 575
Blanke, O., & Arzy, S. 171
Blanke, O., Landis, T., Spinelli, L., & Seeck, M. 171
Blanke, O., Ortigue, S., Landis, T., & Seeck, M. 171
Blanke, O., Slater, M., & Serino, A. 168, 172
Bläsing, B., Puttke, M., & Schack, T. 105
Bliss, J. C., Crane, H. D., Mansfield, P. K., & Townsend, J. T. 186
Block, N. 155
Bloom, K. L., & Shuell, J. T. 267
Bluck, S. 243, 280
Boas, Franz 235
Bobak, A. K., Hancock, P. J., & Bate, S. 77
Bock, J. K. 397
Boden, M. 452

Boly, M., Massimini, M., Tsuchiya, N., Postle, B. R., Koch, C., & Tononi, G. 166
Bond, Z. S., & Garnes, S. 383
Bonhannon, J. N. III 285
Bonhomme, V., Staquet, C., Montupil, J., Defresne, A., Kirsch, M., Martial, C., Vanhaudenhuyse, A. et al. 156
Bonnefon, J. F., & Hilton, D. J. 514
Borghi, A. M. 107, 108
Born, J., Rasch, B., & Gais, S. 275
Bornstein, M. H. 565
Boroditsky, L. 329, 331
Boroditsky, L., & Ramscar, M. 309
Bose, A., & Buchanan, L. 368
Boston Diagnostic Aphasia Examination 366
Boston Dynamics 85–6
Botox® 561
Botvinick, M., & Cohen, J. 110
Botvinick, M. M. 95
Botvinick, M. M., & Plaut, D. C. 95
Bouchard, T. J. Jr., & Hare, M. 458
Bourdin, P., Barberia, I., Oliva, R., & Slater, M. 172
Bousfield, W. A. 263
Bouvier, S. E., & Engel, S. A. 49
Bowden, E. M., & Grunewald, K. 440
Bowden, E. M., & Jung-Beeman, M. 441
Bower, G. H. 264, 266, 551, 575–6
Bower, G. H., & Clark, M. C. 7
Bower, G. H., & Karlin, M. B. 263
Bower, G. H., Clark, M. C., Lesgold, A. M., & Winzenz, D. 263
Boye, M., Gunturkun, O., & Vauclair, J. 385
Bracewell, R. J. 535–6
Bradley, M. M., Greenwald, M. K., Petry, M. C., & Lang, P.J. 574
Brady, A. P. 129
Braine, David 514–15
Braine, M. D. S., Reiser, B. J., & Rumain, B. 514–15, 516
Bramham, C. R., & Srebo, B. 275
Braun, A. R., Balkin, T. J., Wesensten, N. J., Carson, R. E., Varga, M., Baldwin, P. et al. 154
Braun, N., Debener, S., Spychala, N., Bongartz, E., Sörös, P., Müller, H. H., & Philipsen, A. 110
Brázdil, M., Marecek, R., Urbánek, T., Kaspárek, T., Mikl, M., Rektor, I., & Zeman, A. 249
Bregman, A. S. 71
Breiman, L., Friedman, J. H., Olshen, R. A., & Stone, C. J. 492
Brener, R. 210
Brenner, E., & Smeets, J. B. J. 47
Brewer, W. F. 236, 241
Brewer, W. F., & Treyens, J. C. 233–5
Brewin, C. R., Gregory, J. D., Lipton, M., & Burgess, N. 244
Brigham, J. C. 77
Brigham, J. C., Bennett, L. B., Meissner, C. A., & Mitchell, T. L. 77
Brisson, J., de Chantal, P. L., Forgues, H. L., & Markovits, H. 529
Broadbent, D. E. 121, 126, 128, 167, 187, 188
Broadbent, D. E., & Broadbent, M. H. P. 133
Broca, Paul 20, 21, 365–7
Brodmann, Korbinian 55
Brooks, L. R. 203–5, 313
Brouwer, H., Fitz, H., & Hoeks, J. C. J. 418
Brown, A. S. 248–9, 276, 280
Brown, A. S., & Marsh, E. J. 249
Brown, C. M., & Hagoort, P. 418
Brown, G. D. A. 396
Brown, J. 386
Brown, K. F., Kroll, J. S., Hudson, M. J., Ramsay, M., Green, J., Vincent, C. A., Fraser, G., & Sevdalis, N. 494–5
Brown, L. & Jones, P. E. 326
Brown, R., & Kulik, J. 284, 573

Brown, R., & McNeill, D. 349
Brown, R., Lau, H., & LeDoux, J. E. 173
Brown, R. M., & Robertson, E.M. 232
Bruce, K. R., & Pihl, R. O. 276, 277
Bruce, V., & Young, A. 74
Bruno, M. A., Walker, E. A., & Abujudeh, H. H. 129
Bruno, N. 47
Bruns, P. 58
Brunswick, N., Martin, G. N., & Marzano, L. 525
Brunswik, Egon 501
Bryant, R. A., O'Donnell, M. L., Creamer, M., McFarlane, A. C., & Silove, D. 244
Brysbaert, M. 404–5, 413
Brysbaert, M., Stevens, M., Mandera, P., & Keuleers, E. 376
Buccino, G., Vogt, S., Ritzl, A., Fink, G. R., Zilles, K., Freund, H.-J., & Rizzolatti, G. 104, 105
Buchwald, A. M. 579
Buckingham, H. W. 366
Buckner, R. L., Andrews-Hanna, J. R., & Schacter, D. L. 31
Buddha 213
Budson, A. E., & Price, B. H. 225
Bugelski, B. R., Kidd, E., & Segmen, J. 264
Bulevich, J. B., Roediger, H. L., Balota, D. A., & Butler, A. C. 282
Bulley, A., & Schacter, D. L. 473
Bulley, A., Milojan, B., Pepper, G. V., Gullo, M. J., Henry, J. D., & Suddendorf, T. 473–4
Bundick, T., & Spinella, M. 111
Buonomano, D. V., & Karmarkar, U. R. 378
Burgess, N., & Hitch, G. J. 214
Burgess, P. W., Dumontheil, I., Gilbert, S. J., Okuda, J., Schölvinck, M. L., & Simons, J. S. 212
Burgoyne, A. P., Sala, G., Gobet, F., Macnamara, B. N., Campitelli, G., & Hambrick, D. Z. 450
Burke, M., & Matthews, A. 577
Burnett, G., Large, D. R. & Salanitri, D. 61
Busby, L. P., Courtier, J. L., & Glastonbury, C. M. 130
Buser, D., Sterchi, Y., & Schwaninger, A. 127
Bush, George W. 285
Butler, A. C. 289
Butler, S. 298
Butters, N. 224
Butterworth, B. 344
Byrd, D., & Mintz, T. H. 379
Byrne, R. W., & Russon, A. E. 104

C

Cacioppo, J. T., Klein, D. J., Berntson, G. G., & Hatfield, E. 560
Cahill, L., Babinsky, R. Markowitch, H. J., & McGaugh, J. L. 574
Calder, A. J., & Young, A. W. 74
Calvillo, D. P., Swan, A. B., & Rutchick, A. M. 528
Calvo-Merino, B., Grèzes, J., Glaser, D. E., Passingham, R. E., & Haggard, P. 105
Camerer, C. 504
Campbell, Donald T. 457
Campitelli, G., & Gobet, F. 448, 449, 452
Campos-Magdaleno, M., Leiva, D., Pereiro, A. X., Lojo-Seoane, C., Mallo, S. C. et al. 348
Canli, T., Zhao, Z., Brewer, J., Gabrieli, J. D. E., & Cahill, L. 574
Cannon, Walter 562–3
Caplan, D. 364
Caplan, D., & Hildebrandt, N. 370
Caplan, D. & Waters, G.S. 202, 370
Caramazza, A., Anzellotti, S., Strnad, L., & Lingnau, A. 104
Carey, D. P. 47
Carlsen, Magnus 449
Carota, F., Moseley, R., & Pulvermuller, F. 309
Carpenter, P. A., & Just, M. A. 413

Name Index

Carpenter, S. K., Cepeda, N. J., Rohrer, D., Kang, S. H., & Pashler, H. 267
Carr, T. H., Davidson, B. J., & Hawkins, H. L. 410
Carramazza, A., & Zurif, E. 401–2
Carson, S. H. 462
Carson, S. H., Peterson, J. B., & Higgins, D. M. 462
Caspers, S., Zilles, K., Laird, A. R., & Eickhoff, S. B. 104
Casscells, W., Schoenberger, A., & Grayboys, T. 482–3
Cassiday, K. L., McNally, R. J., & Zeitlin, S. B. 571
Castel, A. D., Pratt, J., & Drummond, E. 127
Catani, M. 24
Cattaneo, L., Sandrini, M., & Schwarzbach, J. 104
Cattell, J. M. 396
Cavanaugh, M. R., Barbot, A., Carrasco, M., & Huxlin, K. R. 162, 167
Ceraso, J., & Provitera, A. 522, 536
Chadwick, A. C., Heywood, C. A., Smithson, H. E., & Kentridge, R. W. 49
Chalmers, A. F. 152
Chalmers, D. J. 543
Chambers, D., & Reisberg, D. 318–19
Chan, J. C., & LaPaglia, J. A. 279–80
Chao Lu 7
Chapman, C. E. 68
Chapman, G. B., & Winquist, J. R. 473
Chapman, L. J., & Chapman, A. P. 520–21
Charles Bonnet syndrome 312, 319–20
Charness, N. 450, 451
Chartrand, J.-P., Peretz, I., & Belin, P. 28
Chase, W. G., & Simon, H. A. 450
Chater, N., & Oaksford, M. 539
Chen, M., Ma, H., Qin, L. Y., Gao, F., Chan, K. M., Law, S. W., & Liao, W. H. 85
Chen, L., & Vroomen, J. 58
Chen, X. J., Wang, Y., Liu, L. L., Cui, J. F., Gan, M. Y., Shum, D. H., & Chan, R. C. 238
Chen, Y., Fu, S., Iversen, S. D., Smith, S. M., & Matthews, P. M. 406, 407
Cheney, D. L., & Seyfarth, R. M. 334
Cheng, P. C. H. 541
Cheng, P. W., & Holyoak, K. J. 537, 538
Cherry, E. C. 121
Chevalier, P., Kompatsiari, K., Ciardo, F., & Wykowska, A. 117
Chi, M. T. H., Glaser, R., & Rees, E. 451
Chiel, H. J., & Beer, R. D. 108
Chomsky, Noam 340, 401
Chong, S. C., & Treisman, A. 131
Chopin, A., Bediou, B., & Bavelier, D. 127
Chou, K. L., Lee, T. M. C., & Ho, A. H. Y. 162, 577
Chow, M., Macnamara, B. N., & Conway, A. R. A. 202
Christensen, J. F., Gaigg, S. B., & Calvo-Merino, B. 107
Christensen, J. F., Gomila, A., Gaigg, S. B., Sivarajah, N., & Calvo-Merino, B. 105–7
Christensen, J. F., Nadal, M., Cela-Conde, C. J., & Gomila, A. 106
Christianson, S. A. 573, 574
Christoff, K., Cosmelli, D., Legrand, D., & Thompson, E. 168
Christoff, K., Gordon, A., & Smith, R. 208
Chu, B. 489
Chubb, C., Nam, J. H., Bindman, D. R., & Sperling, G. 131
Chun, M. M. 139
Chun, M. M., Golomb, J. D., & Turk-Browne, N. B. 118–19, 126
CIA (Central Intelligence Agency) 557
Cichy, R. M., Khosla, A., Pantazis, D., Torralba, A., & Oliva, A. 67
Cienki, A., & Müller, C. 109
Ciesielski, B. G., Armstrong, T., Zald, D. H., & Olatunji, B. O. 134

Clahsen, H., & Almazan, M. 329
Clancy, S. A., & McNally, R. J. 283
Clark, A. 44, 108
Clark, D. M., & Teasdale, J. D. 577
Clark, E. V. 376
Clark, H. H., & Clark, E. V. 351
Clark, H. H., & Fox Tree, J. E. 343
Clark, J. J., & Yuille, A. L. 59
Clerkin, E. M., Hart, E., Rehg, J. M., Yu, C., & Smith, L. B. 301
Clifton, C., Jr., Staub, A., & Rayner, K. 412, 413
Clooney, George 479
Clore, G. L., & Ortony, A. 559, 568
Clough, S., & Gordon, J. K. 370
Cobb, M. D., & Kuklinski, J. H. 528
Cobos, P., Sánchez, M., Pérez, N., & Vila, J. 562
Coderre, E., Filippi, C., Newhouse, P., & Dumas, J. 412
Coenen, A. M. L., & Van Luijtelaar, E. L. J. M. 277
Cohen, A. L., & Hicks, J. L. 238
Cohen, B., Dai, M., Yakushin, S. B., & Cho, C. 59
Cohen, D., & Faulkner, D. 348
Cohen, L. J. 126
Cohen, M. A., Cavanagh, P., Chun, M. M., & Nakayama, K. 168
Cohen, N. J., & Squire, L. R. 227
Cohen, R. A. 539
Colchester, A., Kingsley, D., Lasserson, D., Kendall, B., Bello, F., Rush, C., Stevens, T. G. et al. 224
Coles, N. A., Larsen, J. T., & Lench, H. C. 562
Colle, H. A., & Welsh, A. 200
Collins, A. M., & Loftus, E. F. 311
Coltheart, M., Rastle, K., Perry, C., Langdon, R., & Ziegler, J. 415–16
Comrie, B. 330, 405, 406
Connor, S. 58
Connors, J., Miller, N., Lundregan, T., & McEwan, T. 77
Conrad, R. 202
Consciousness and Cognition 170
Constable, A., Stackhouse, J., & Wells, B. 369
Conway, M. A. 241, 243, 574
Conway, M. A., Anderson, S. J., Larsen, S. F., Donnelly, C. M., McDaniel, M. A. et al. 573, 574
Conway, M. A., Cohen, G., & Stanhope, N. 252
Cooke, T., & Bliss, T. V. 274
Cooney, J. W., & Gazzaniga, M. S. 160
Cooper, R. P., & Shallice, T. 95, 96, 97–8, 206
Cooper, R. P., Schwartz, M. F., Yule, P., & Shallice, T. 99
Cooper, S. A., Joshi, A. C., Seenan, P. J., Hadley, D. M., Muir, K. W., Leigh, R. J., & Metcalfe, R. A. 49
Copeland, D. E., & Radvansky, G. A. 202
Copernican Heliocentric Theory 6, 543–4
Corballis, M. C. 161, 330
Corbetta, M., & Shulman, G. L. 119–20
Corkin, S. 220, 221, 222, 223
Coslett, H. B. 417
Cosmides, L. 537, 538–9
Cosmides, L., & Tooby, J. 482–3
Costa, A., Foucart, A., Hayakawa, S., Aparici, M., Apesteguia, J., Heafner, J., & Keysar, B. 497–9
Cotton, Ronald 286
Cowan, N. 178, 179, 180, 186, 188, 190, 194, 195–6, 213, 214
Cowan, N., Beshin, N., & Della Sala, S. 278
Cowan, N., Morey, C. C., & Chen, Z. 188
Craig, A. D. 107, 111, 562
Craig, M., Della Sala, S., & Dewar, M. 272
Craik, F. I. M. 190, 238, 263
Craik, F. I. M., & Lockhart, R. S. 261
Craik, F. I. M., & Tulving, E. 261–3
Cranford, E. A., & Moss, J. 442
Crick, F., & Koch, C. 162

Crick, Francis 18, 152, 162
Critchley, H. D., Wiens, S., Rotshtein, P., Öhman, A., & Dolan, R. J. 107
Croskerry, P. 129
Cross, E. S., Hamilton, A. F. D. C., & Grafton, S. T. 105
Cross, E. S., Hortensius, R., & Wykowska, A. 117
Crosson, B., & Warren, R. L. 386
Crowder, R. G. 267
Crozier, W. E., Luke, T. J., & Strange, D. 390
Cruse, D., Chennu, S., Chatell, C., Bekinschtein, T. A., Fernandez-Espejo, D. et al. 30
Crystal, D. 331, 339
Cuetos, F., & Mitchell, D. C. 402
Curtiss, S. 326
Curtiss-Yamada Comprehensive Language Evaluation (CYCLE-R) 403
Cushing, S. 399–400
Custers, E. J., & ten Cate, O. T. 252
Custers, R., & Aarts, H. 159
Cutler, A., & Butterfield, S. 383
Cutler, A., & Carter, D. M. 380
Cutler, A., & Norris, D. 380, 391
Cutler, A., Dahan, D., & van Donselaar, W. 380, 383
Cutler, A., Mehler, J., Norris, D. G., & Segui, J. 383
Cutler, V., & Paddock, S. 127
Cutting, J. E. 145
Cutting, J. E., & Kozlowski, L. T. 78
Cutting, J. E., DeLong, J. E., & Nothelfer, C. E. 145
Cuttler, C., & Graf, P. 239–40
Cyberdene Robot Suit HAL (Hybrid Assistive Limb) 86
Cytowic, R. E. 57

D

Dahan, D. 393
Dakin, S. C., & Watt, R. J. 131
Dalrymple-Alford, E. C., & Budayr, B. 411
Damasio, A. 212, 554, 582, 583
Damasio, A. R., Tranel, D., & Damasio, H. 554
Damasio, A., Tranel, D., & Damasio, H. 212
Danek, A. H. 440, 446
Danek, A. H., Fraps, T., von Muller, A., Grothe, B., & Ollinger, M. 446–7
Daniel, T. A., & Camp, A. L. 414
Daniels, P. T., & Share, D. L. 410
Danquah, A. N., Farrell, M. J., & O'Boyle, D. J. 170
Daoud, Ouhnane 545
Darwin, C. J., Turvey, M. T., & Crowder, R. G. 184
Darwin, Charles 453, 555
Davies, M. L., Harries, P. A., Gilhooly, K. J., Gilhooly, M. L. M., & Cairns, D. 502–4
Dawel, A., O'Kearney, R., McKone, E., & Palermo, R. 556
Dax, Marc 365
Dayan, E., Casile, A., Levit-Binnun, N., Giese, M. A., Hendler, T., & Flash, T. 102
De Bono, Edward 459–60
De Gelder, B., Vroomen, J., Pourtois, G., & Weiskrantz, L. 162
De Groot, A. D. 450, 451
De Groot, A. M. B., & Van Hell, J. G. 7
De Houwer, J., & Hermans, D. 565
De Leeuw, E. 377
De Neys, W. 529
De Ruiter, J. P. 108
De Villiers Scheepers, M. J., & Maree, L. 459
De Vito, D., & Fenske, M. J. 282
De Vries, M. H., Barth, A. C. R., Maiworm, S., Knecht, S., Zwitserlood, P., & Flöel, A. 364
Dean, John 245
Debray, S. B. E., & Demeestere, J. 111
Defeyter, M. A., & German, T. B. 429
Deffenbacher, K. A., Bornstein, B. H., Penrod, S. A., & McGorty, E. K. 286

Dehaene, S., Kerszberg, M., & Changeux, J. P. 165
Dehaene, S., Lau, H., & Kouider, S. 167
Dekhtyar, M., Kiran, S., & Gray, T. 370
Dell, G. S. 355–7
Della Sala, S., Gray, C., Baddeley, A. D., Allamano, N., & Wilson, L. 204
Delogu, F., Brouwer, H., & Crocker, M. W. 418
Demartsev, V., Strandburg- Peshkin, A., Ruffner, M., & Manser, M. 341
Demertzi, A., Tagliazucchi, E., Dehaene, S., Deco, G., Barttfeld, P., Raimondo, F. et al. 163–5
Deng, J., Dong, W., Socher, R., Li, L. J., Li, K.,& Fei-Fei, L. 67
Dennett, D. C. 157
DePaulo, B. M., Lindsay, J. J., Malone, B. E., Muhlenbruck, L., Charlton, K., & Cooper, H. 344
Depp, Johnny 479
DeRosa, D. M., Smith, C. L., & Hantula, D. A. 459
Derraugh, L. S., Neath, I., Surprenant, A. M., Beaudry, O., & Saint-Aubin, J. 199
Deutsch, J. A., & Deutsch, D. 121
Dewar, M., Alber, J., Butler, C., Cowan, N., & Della Sala, S. 272
Dewar, M., Alber, J., Cowan, N., & Della Sala, S. 272–3
Dewar, M., Della Sala, S., Beschin, N., & Cowan, N. 279
Dewar, M., Fernandez Garcia, Y., Cowan, N., & Della Sala, S. 278
Dewar, M. T., Cowan, N., & Della Sala, S. 279
Dhami, M. K. 492, 502
Dhami, M. K., & Ayton, P. 492
Dhami, M. K., & Belton, I. 492
Dhami, M. K., & Mumpower, J. L. 501
Di Lollo, V. 126
Princess Diana, death of 284, 285
Dictator Game 505–6
Diedrichsen, J., Shadmehr, R., & Ivry, R. B. 88
Dijksterhuis, A., & Meurs, T. 455–6
Dijksterhuis, A., & Nordgren, L. F. 455
Dijksterhuis, A., Bos, M. W., Nordgren, L. F., & Van Baaren, R. B. 489–91
Dijkstra, A. 398
Dijkstra, N., Bosch, S. E., & van Gerven, M. A. J. 320–21
Dillon, P. C., Graham, W. K., & Aidells, A. L. 458
Dingli, S. 460
Dipellegrino, G., Fadiga, L., Fogassi, L., Gallese, V., & Rizzolatti, G. 103
Dismukes, R. K. 237, 238
Dismukes, R. K., Berman, B. A., & Loukopoulos, L. 193
Dittrich, W. H. 78
Dittrich, W. H., Troscianko, T., Lea, S. E. G., & Morgan, D. 78
Dixon, M. L., De La Vega, A., Mills, C., Andrews- Hanna, J., Spreng, R. N., Cole, M. W., & Christoff, K. 120
Dlugaiczyk, J., Gensberger, K. D., & Straka, H. 60
Dobbs, D. 30
Dobie, T. G. 60
Dodds, R. A., Ward, T. B., & Smith, S. M. 454–5
Dominik, T., Dostál, D., Zielina, M., Šmahaj, J., Sedláčková, Z., & Procházka, R. 170
Donald, M. 213
Donald, T. W. 327
Donaldson, H. H. 19
Downing, P. E. 140
Doyle, A. Conan 260, 510
Dresner, E., & Herring, S. C. 414
Drews, F. A., Pasupathi, M., & Strayer, D. L. 196
Driver, J. 58
Dronkers, N. F. 370
Dronkers, N. F., Plaisant, O., Iba-Zizen, M. T., & Cabanis, E. A. 365

Dronkers, N. F., Wilkins, D. P., Van Valin, R. D., Redfern, B. B., & Jaeger, J. J. 403
Dror, I., Charlton, D., & Péron, A. 545
Drug Enforcement Agency (US) 557
Dry, M., Lee, M. D., Vickers, D., & Hughes, P. 438
Dryer, M. S. 340
Duchaine, B., & Yovel, G. 75
Dudai, Y. 278
Dunbar, K. 543, 544
Dunbar, K., & Fugelsang, J. 543
Duncan, J. 124
Duncker, K. 427, 428
Dunlosky, J., Rawson, K. A., Marsh, E. J., Nathan, M. J., & Willingham, D. T. 289
Dunn, B. D., Dalgleish, T., Lawrence, A. D., & Ogilvie, A. D. 579
Dunn, B. D., Galton, H. C., Morgan, R., Evans, D., Oliver, C., Meyer, M. et al. 582
Dunnette, M. D., Campbell, J., & Jaastad, K. 458
Durgin, F. H., Baird, J. A., Greenburg, M., Russell, R., Shaughnessy, K., & Waymouth, S. 44
Durgin, F. H., Klein, B., Spiegel, A., Strawser, C. J., & Williams, M. 44
Dutton, D. G., & Aron, A. P. 564

E

Eastern Airlines 193
Easton, R. D., & Moran, P. W. 58
Ebbinghaus, Hermann 226, 267, 268–9, 284
Eckstein, M. P. 128
Edwards, A., Elwyn, G. J., Covey, E., M., & Pill, R. 477
Edwards, T., Kingston, K., Hardy, L., & Gould, D. 97
Efron, R. 185
Egly, R., Driver, J., & Rafal, R. D. 123
Ehrlich, S. F., & Rayner, K. 413
Eibl-Eibesfeldt, I. 556
Eich, E. 266
Eich, E., & Metcalfe, J. 576
Eichenbaum, H. 222
Eimas, P. D., & Corbit, J. D. 384
Eimas, P. D., Siqueland, E. R., Jusczyk, P. W., & Vogorito, J. 384
Einstein, Albert 6
Einstein, O., & McDaniel, M. 237
Einstein, O., McDaniel, M., Thomas, R., Mayfield, S., Shank, H., Morrisette, N., & Breneiser, J. 237
Ekman, P. 555, 557, 558, 570
Ekman, P., & O'Sullivan, M. 344, 557
Ekman, P., Levenson, R. W., & Friesen, W. V. 560
Ekman, P., Sorenson, E. R., & Friesen, W. V. 555, 557
Ekstrand, B. R. 275
Elder, R. S., & Krishna, A. 308
Elfenbein, H. A., & Ambady, N. 555
Queen Elizabeth II 377
Ellenbogen, J. M., Hulbert, J. C., Stickgold, R., Dinges, D. F., & Thompson-Schill, S. L. 275
Elliot, R., Newman, A. L., Longe, O. A., & Deakin, J. F. 504
Elliott, D., Helsen, W. F., & Chua, R. 84
Ellis, A., & Harper, R. A. 578
Ellis, A. W., & Young, A, W. 387, 404
Ellis, C., & Urban, S. 369
Ellis, H. D., & Lewis, M. B. 73
Ellis, H. D., Luaute, J. P., & Retterstol, N. 73
Ellis, J. A. 238
Ellis, J., & Cohen, G. 237
Ellis, N. C., & Hennelly, R. A. 200
Ellsworth, P. C. 529–30
Elman, J. L. 95
Elsey, J. W., Van Ast, V. A., & Kindt, M. 279, 280
Emmorey, K. 365
Engel, C. 506

Engelhardt, P. E. 410
Engle, R. W. 195
Engle, R. W., & Conway, A. R. A. 202
English, T., Lee, I. A., John, O. P., & Gross, J. J. 568–9
English Football Association 491
Enoch, D. 497
Entwhistle, N. 288
Erdelyi, M. H. 157
Ericsson, K. A. 8, 448–9
Ericsson, K. A., & Simon, H. A. 427
Ericsson, K. A., and Chase, W, G. 265
Ericsson, K. A., and Kintsch, W. 210, 214
Ericsson, K. A., Cheng, X., Pan, Y., Ku, Y., Ge, Y., & Hu, Y. 7–8
Ericsson, K. A., Delaney, P. F., Weaver, G., & Mahadevan, R. 265
Ericsson, K. A., Krampe, R. T., & Tesch-Rohmer, C. 448–9, 450
Eriksen, C. W., & St. James, J. D. 123
Eriksen, C. W., & Yeh, Y. Y. 123, 126
Erman, L. D., & Lesser, V. R. 393
Ernst, M. O., and Banks, M. S. 59
Eslinger, P. J., & Damasio, A. R. 211–12, 369, 553–4
Estes, W. K. 95
Estival, D., Farris, C., & Molesworth, B. 399, 400
MS *Estonia* ferry disaster 285
Evans, A. T., Peters, E., Strasser, A. A., Emery, L. F., Sheerin, K. M., & Romer, D. 580–81
Evans, J. St. B. T. 488, 513, 529, 536
Evans, J. St. B. T., & Curtis-Holmes, J. 529
Evans, J. St. B. T., & Lynch, J. S. 536
Evans, J. St. B. T., Barston, J. L., & Pollard, P. 527–8, 529
Evans, N., & Levinson, S. C. 331
Everitt, B. J., & Robbins, T. W. 230
Eysenck, M. W. 263, 268

F

Fahsing, I. A., & Ask, K. 542–3
Farah, M. J. 69
Farah, M. J., & Hammond, K. M. 205
Farah, M. J., Hammond, K. M., Levine, D. N., & Calvanio, R. 205, 319
Farrell, S., Oberauer, K., Greaves, M., Pasiecznik, K., Lewandowsky, S., & Jarrold, C. 213
Farrer, C., & Frith, C. D. 111
Fasolo, B., McClelland, G. H., & Lange, K. A. 486
Fawcett, J. M., Russell, E. J., Peace, K. A., & Christie, J. 286
FBI (Federal Bureau of Investigation) 545, 557
Fechner, Gustav 158
Federenko, E., & Blank, I. A. 365
Feinberg, T. E., & Farah, M. J. 387
Feinberg, T. E., Schindler, R. J., Flanagan, N. G., & Haber, L. D. 111
Feldman, A. G. 86, 558, 563
Feldman, A. G., & Latash, M. L. 86
Feng Wang, World Memory Champion 8
Ferguson, K. A., & Cardin, J. A. 139
Fermat, Pierre de 469
Fermin, A. S., Sakagami, M., Kiyonari, T., Li, Y., Matsumoto, Y., & Yamagishi, T. 506
Fernandez-Duque, D., & Johnson, M. L. 126
Ferreira, F. 377
Ferreira, F., Christianson, K., & Hollingworth, A. 403
Ferri, S., Kolster, H., Jastorff, J., & Orban, G. A. 80
Ferris, C. F., Kulkarni, P., Sullivan, J. M., Harder, J. A., Messenger, T. L., & Febo, M. 28
Fiebelkorn, I. C., & Kastner, S. 142
Fiedler, K. 480
Field, J. 330, 384, 412
Field, M., Mogg, K., & Bradley, B. P. 571

Field, T., Pickens, J., Fox, N. A., Gonzalez, J., & Nawrocki, T. 556
Fillmore, M. T., Kelly, T. H., Rush, C. R., & Hays, L. 277
Finke, R. A. 314
Finke, R. A., Ward, T. B., & Smith, S. M. 456, 457
Finucane, M. L., Alhakami, A., Slovic, P., & Johnson, S. M. 580
Finucane, M. L., Peters, E., & Slovic, P. 580
Fisher, R. P., & Schreiber, N. 287
Fisher, Ron 287
Fisk, J. E., & Pidgeon, N. 481
Fiske, S. T. 360
Fitzgerald, R. J., Price, H. L., & Valentine, T. 76
Fitzpatrick, P., Harada, K., Kemp, C. C., Matsumoto, Y., Yokoi, K., & Yoshida, E. 88
Fivush, R. 243
Flach, R., Knoblich, G., & Prinz, W. 102
Flash, T., & Handzel, A. A. 102
Flash, T., & Hochner, B. 104
Flash, T., & Hogan, N. 88
Flavell, J. H. 172
Fleck, J. I., & Weisberg, R. W. 442
Fleming, R. W., & Storrs, K. R. 39
Foa, E. B., & McNally, R. J. 571
Fodor, J. A. 17, 22, 301
Foer, Joshua 6
Fogassi, L., Ferrari, P. F., Gesierich, B., Rozzi, S., Chersi, F., & Rizzolatti, G. 103
Foot, Phillipa 496–7
Footbridge Problem 496–9
Ford, M. 526
Forgas, J. P. 577
Forslund, H. B., Torgerson, J. S., Sjöström, L., & Lindroos, A. K. 159
Forster, K. I. 395
Forster, K. I., & Davis, C. 397
Foss, D. J. 397
Foster, D. H., & Gilson, S. J. 66
Fougnie, D., & Marois, R. 140
Foulsham, T., Walker, E., & Kingstone, A. 70
Fox Tree, J. E. 343, 344
Franconeri, S. L., Alvarez, G. A., & Enns, J. T. 126
Frankish, K. 157
Franz, V. H. 47
Frauenfelder, U. H., Scholen, M., & Content, A. 392
Frazier, L. 402–3
Frederick, S., Lee, L., & Baskin, E. 487
Freud, Sigmund 282, 346
Frijda, N. H. 551, 557, 559, 564, 568
Frijda, N. H., and Scherer, K. R. 550–51
Friston, K. 41
Frith, C. 92
Frith, C. D., & Frith, U. 73, 155
Fromkin, V. 346–7
Fromkin, V., Krashen, S., Curtiss, S., Rigler, D., & Rigler, M. 326
Frost, R., Katz, L., & Bentin, S. 406
Fugelsang, J., Stein, C., Green, A., & Dunbar, K. 544
Fusser, F., Linden, D. E. J., Rahm, B., Hampel, H., Haenschel, C., & Mayer, J. S. 140

G

Gage, N. M., & Baers, B. J. 329
Gage, Phineas 23, 212, 552–3
Gainotti, G. 306
Galaverna, F., Bueno, A. M., Morra, C. A., Roca, M., & Torralva, T. 362
Galifret, Y. 181
Galileo 543–4
Gall, Franz Joseph 21–2
Gallace, A., & Spence, C. 187
Gallace, A., Auvray, M., Tan, H. Z., & Spence, C. 187

Gallace, A., Tan, H. Z., Haggard, P., & Spence, C. 186–7
Gallagher, M., & Ferrè, E. R. 60
Gallagher, S. 108, 110
Gallese, V., Fadiga, L., Fogassi, L., & Rizzolatti, G. 103
Gallese, V., Gernsbacher, M. A., Heyes, C., Hickok, G., & Iacoboni, M. 104
Galotti, K. M. 501
Galotti, K. M., Baron, J., & Sabini, J. P. 526
Gandour, J., Ponglorpisit, S., Khunadorn, F., & Dechongkit, S. 364
Ganis, G., Thompson, W. L., & Kosslyn, S. 319
Gara, M. A., Woolfolk, R. L., Cohen, B. D., Goldston, R. B., Allen, L. A., & Novalany, J. 579
Gardner, W. L., Gabriel, S., & Lee, A. 523
Garrett, B. L. 286
Garrett, M. F. 346, 347, 351–2
Gaskell, M. G., & Marslen-Wilson, W. D. 391
Gassert, R., & Dietz, V. 85
Gathercole, S. E., & Baddeley, A. D. 202, 205
Gathercole, S. E., Hitch, G. J., Service, E., & Martin, A. J. 202
Gauss, Carl Friedrich 426
Gauthier, I., Tarr, M. J., Moylan, J., Skudlarski, P., Gore, J. C., & Anderson, A. W. 75
Gavanski, I., and Roskos-Ewoldsen, D. 481
Gazzaley, A., & Nobre, A. C. 139
Gazzaniga, M. S. 161
Gazzaniga, M. S., Bogen, J. E., & Sperry, R. W. 161
Gebhard, J. W., & Mowbray, G. H. 58
Geiselman, Ed 287
Geiselman, R., Fisher, R. P., Firstenberg, I., Hutton, L. A., Sullivan, S. J., Avetissian, I. V., & Prosk, A. L. 287–8
Geisler, W. S., & Kersten, D. 41
Gell-Mann, M., & Ruhlen, M. 340
Gelman, S. A. and Wellman, H. 305
Gentner, T. Q., Fenn, K. M., Margoliash, D., & Nusbaum, H. C. 341
Gentry, S. V., Gauthier, A., Ehrstrom, B. L. E., Wortley, D., Lilienthal, A., Car, L. T., Dauwels-Okutsu, S. et al. 127
George, A. M., Brown, P. M., Scholz, B., Scott-Parker, B., & Rickwood, D. 197
George, M. S., & Aston-Jones, G. 27
Gepshtein, S., Seydell, A., & Trommershauser, J. 92
Gerbella, M., Caruana, F., & Rizzolatti, G. 162
German, T. B., & Barrett, H. C. 429
Geskin, J., & Behrmann, M. 76
Gestalt psychologists 36–7
Gfeller, K., Christ, A., Witt, S., & Mehr, M. 55
Gibson, J. J. 42, 68, 72, 87
Giese, M. A., & Poggio, T. 80
Gigerenzer, G. 483, 488, 489, 491, 492–3, 494, 499, 502
Gigerenzer, G., and Hug, K. 539
Gigerenzer, G., Todd, P. M., & ABC Research Group 480, 491–2
Gilbert, D. T., Pinel, E. C., Wilson, T. D., Blumberg, S. J., & Wheatley, T. P. 579
Gilhooly, K. J. 525
Gilhooly, K. J., & Falconer, W. 535
Gilhooly, K. J., & Murphy, P. 440
Gilhooly, K. J., and Webb, M. E. 441
Gilhooly, K. J., Fioratou, E., Anthony, S., & Wynn, V. 308
Gilhooly, K. J., Georgiou, G., Garrison, J., Reston, J., & Sirota, M. 455, 456
Gilhooly, K. J., Georgiou, G. J., Sirota, M., & Paphiti-Galeano, A. 455
Gilhooly, K. J., Logie, R. H., & Wynn, V. 435, 525
Gilhooly, K. J., Logie, R. H., Wetherick, N. E., & Wynn, V. 525
Gilhooly, K. J., Phillips, L. H., Wynn, V. E., Logie, R. H., & Della Sala, S. 435, 525

Gladwell, Malcolm 448
Glancy, G. D., Bradford, J. M., & Fedak, L. 154
Glanzer, M., and Razel, M. 189
Glaze, J. A. 268
Glenberg, A. M. 267
Glenberg, A. M., and Kaschak, M. P. 308
Glover, S. 47
Glucksberg, S., and Cowan, G. N. 185
Gobet, F., and Ereku, M. H. 449
Gobet, F., and Simon, H. A. 451
Gobet, F., and Waters, A. J. 451
Gobet, F., Chassy, P., & Bilalic, M. 65
Gobet, Fernand 450, 451, 452
Godden, D. R., and Baddeley, A. D. 266
Goel, V. 529
Goel, V., & Dolan, R. J. 529
Goel, V., Buchelm, C., Rith, C., & Olan, J. 529
Goel, V., Vartanian, O., Bartolo, A., Hakim, L., Ferraro, A. M., Isella, V. et al. 438–9
Goh, W. D., & Lu, S. H. X. 268
Goldberg, R. F., Perfetti, C. F., & Schneider, W. 309
Goldenberg, O., Larson, J. J., & Wiley, J. 458
Goldin-Meadow, S. 108, 341
Goldin-Meadow, S., Nusbaum, H., Kelly, S. D., & Wagner, S. 110
Goldinger, S. D., Papesh, M. H., Barnhart, A. S., Hansen, W. A., & Hout, M. C. 44
Goldman-Eisler, F. 344
Goldstein, D. G., and Gigerenzer, G. 491
Gollan, T. H., & Acenas, L. R. 349
Gollwitzer, P. M. 238
Golmohammadi, R., Darvishi, E., Faradmal, J., Poorolajal, J., & Aliabadi, M. 201
Gomila, T., & Calvo, P. 43, 44
Gonzalez, J., Barros-Loscertales, A., Pulvermuller, F., Meseguer, V., & Sanjuan, A. 309
Goodale, M. A., and Milner, A. D. 47
Goodglass, H. 367, 403
Goodglass, H., & Kaplan, E. 386
Goodglass, H., and Geschwind, N. 367
Goodrich, M. A., & Schultz, A. C. 37
Google Deep Mind Project 16–17
Google Scholar 490
Gordon, W. J. J. 459
Gorgey, A. S. 86
Gorman, M. E. 544
Gosavi, R. S., and Hubbard, E. M. 183
Goswami, U. 408
Gottfredson, L. S. 450
Goudeau, S., & Croizet, J. C. 216
Grabner, R. H., Stern, E., & Neubauer, A. 450
Graf, P., & Grondin, S. 238
Graf, P., & Schacter, D. L. 227
Graf, P., Squire, L. R., & Mandler, G. 230
Graff-Radford, J., Rubin, M. N., Jones, D. T., Aksamit, A. J., Ahlskog, J. E. et al. 111
Grafton, S. T., Fadiga, L., Arbib, M. A., & Rizzolatti, G. 108
Granhag, P. A., Ask, K., & Giolla, E. M. 285
Gravitation, Universal Law of 6
Graziano, M. S. 168
Graziano, M. S., & Kastner, S. 168
Graziano, M. S., & Webb, T. W. 167
Graziano, M. S., Guterstam, A., Bio, B. J., & Wilterson, A. L. 168
Green, A. J. K., & Gilhooly, K. J. 284
Green, C. S., & Bavelier, D. 127
Green, K. P., Kuhl, P. K., Meltzoff, A. N., & Stevens, E. B. 390
Greenberg, D. L. 29
Greenberg, J. H. 382
Greene, J. D., Sommerville, R. B., Nystrom, L. E., Darley, J. M., & Cohen, J. D. 497
Greene, R. L. 267
Greenfield, P. M. 523

Greenfield, P. M., DeWinstanley, P., Kilpatrick, H., & Kaye, D. 127
Greve, K. W., & Bauer, R. M. 566
Grice, H. P. 342
Griggs, R. A., & Cox, J. R. 536–7
Grill-Spector, K., Weiner, K. S., Gomez, J., Stigliani, A., & Natu, V. S. 75
Grill-Spector, K., Weiner, K. S., Kay, K., & Gomez, J. 74
Grodner, D., Gibson, E., & Watson, D. 403
Grosjean, F. 392
Grosjean, F., & Gee, J. 377, 391, 394
Gross, J. J. 569
Gross, M., Smith, A. P., Graveline, Y., Beaty, R., Schooler, J., & Seli, P. 10–11
Gross, R. G., & Grossman, M. 99
Grossenbacher, P. G., & Lovelace, C. T. 58
Grossman, E. D., & Blake, R. 80
Grueter, M., Grueter, T., Bell, V., Horst, J., Laskowski, W., Sperling, K., Halligan, P. W. et al. 76
Guclu, U., & van Gerven, M. A. J. 67
Gudjonsson, G. H. 390
Guitard, D., Saint-Aubin, J., Tehan, G., & Tolan, A. 199
Gunnars, T., & Bruck, J. N. 49
Gunning, D., & Aha, 2019, D. W. 67
Gunns, R. E., Johnston, L., & Hudson, S. M. 78
Gurney, D. J., Pine, K. J., & Wiseman, R. 287
Guthrie, L. G., Vallee- Tourangeau, F., Vallee-Tourangeau, G., & Howard, C. 434

H

Haaga, D. A., Dyck, M. J., & Ernst, D. 579
Haber, R. N., & Standing, L. G. 182
Hacking, I. 469
Hadzibeganovic, T., van den Noort, M., Bosch, P., Perc, M., van Kralingen, R., Mondt, K., & Coltheart, M. 409–10
Haggard, P. 101, 110, 169, 170
Haggard, P., & Eimer, M. 170
Haggard, P., Clark, S., & Kalogeras, J. 110
Haken, H., Kelso, J. A. S., & Bunz, H. 87
Hakim, N., Adam, K. C., Gunseli, E., Awh, E., & Vogel, E. K. 140
Hall, D., & Riddoch, J. 387
Hall, T. 426
Hamamé, C. M., Vidal, J. R., Ossandón, T., Jerbi, K., Dalal, S. S., Minotti, L. et al. 203
Hamann, S. B. 552
Hamann, S. B., Ely, T., Grafton, S., & Kilts, C. 574
Hambrick, D. Z., Oswald, F. L., Altmann, M., Meinz, E. J., Gobet, F., & Campitelli, G. 449
Hammond, K. R. 501
Hampton, J. A. 301, 303
Hampton, J. A., Aina, B., Andersson, J. M., Mirza, H. Z., & Parmar, S. 250–52
Hancock, P. J. B., Bruce, V., & Burton, A. M. 74
Handzel, A., & Flash, T. 102
Hanley, J. R., & Young, A. W. 203, 204
Hanley, J. R., Young, A. W., & Pearson, N. 203, 204
Hansen, P. G., & Jespersen, A. M. 159
Hardcastle, W. J., & Hewlett, N. 378
Hardt, O., Nader, K., & Nadel, L. 275
Hardwick, R. M., Caspers, S., Eickhoff, S. B., & Swinnen, S. P. 104
Hare, R. D., Neumann, C. S., & Widiger, T. A. 556
Harley, T. A. 398, 417
Harlow, H. M. 23, 212, 552–3
Harpainter, M., Sim, E.-J., Trumpp, N. M., Ulrich, M., & Kiefer, M. 309
Harrington, J., Palethorpe, S., & Watson, C. I. 377
Harris, C. M., & Wolpert, D. M. 88
Harris, L. M., Vaccaro, L., Jones, M. K., & Boots, G. M. 240
Harris, M., & Coltheart, M. 405
Harvard Medical School 482–3
Harvey, S. 459
Hashash, M., Zeid, M. A., & Moacdieh, N. 197
Haugeland, J. 44
Haukioja, J., Nyquist, M., & Jyllka, J. 307
Hauser, M. D. 497
Hawthorne, K., Järvikivi, J., & Tucker, B. V. 380
Haxby, J. V., Hoffman, E. A., & Gobbini, M. I. 74–5
Hay, J. C., Pick, H. L., & Ikeda, K. 58
Hayati, A. M., & Shariatifar, S. 290
Haynes, J. D., & Rees, G. 162
Hayward, W. G. 66
Head, H., & Holmes, G. 57
Heavey, C. L., and Hurlburt, R. T. 9
Heavey, C. L., Hurlburt, R. T., & Lefforge, N. L. 9
Hebb, D. O. 187
Heeger, D. J., & Zemlianova, K. O. 139
Heider, F., & Simmel, M. 72
Heiser, M., Iacoboni, M., Maeda, F., Marcus, J., & Mazziotta, J. C. 104
Hellawell, S. J., & Brewin, C. R. A. 244
Helmholtz, H. V., & Southall, J. P. C. 41
Helmholtz, Herman 453–4
Hemmerich, W. A., Shahal, A., & Hecht, H. 60
Hemphill, R. E., and Stengel, E. J. 386
Henderson, J. M., & Hollingworth, A. 70
Henderson, L. 188
Henle, Mary 521–2
Hennenlotter, A., Dresel, C., Castrop, F., Ceballos Baumann, A., Wohlschlager, A., & Haslinger, B. 561
Henry, J. D., Crawford, J.R., & Phillips, L. H. 361
Herculano-Houzel, Suzana 19–20
Herman, L. M., Richards, D.G., & Wolz, J. P. 400
Herrera, E., Cuetos, F., & Ribacoba, R. 362
Hertel, P. T., and Calcaterra, G. 282
Hesse, M. 541
Heyes, C. 102
Hickok, G., & Hauser, M. 104
Hicks, J. L., & Starns, J. J. 281
Higuchi, S., Holle, H., Roberts, N., Eickhoff, S. B., & Vogt, S. 104, 105
Hillsborough football stadium disaster (UK) 573
Hilts, P. J. 222
Hindu Arabic representation system 42–3
Hinrichs, J. V., Ghoneim, M. M., & Mewaldt, S. P. 277
Hintzman, D. L. 267
Hippocrates 18
Hirrstein, W., & Ramachandran, V. S. 550
Hirstein, W., & Sifferd, 2011, K. 154
Hirstein, W., and Ramachandran, V. S. 73
Hiscock, M. 363
Hitch, G. J., and Ferguson, J. 239
H1N1 influenza A 494–5
Ho, C., Reed, N., & Spence, C. 61
Hockett, Charles 332–4
Hodge, F. S., Colton, R. H., & Kelley, R. T. 377
Hofer, F., & Schwaninger, A. 127
Hoffman, B. 214
Hoffman, B., & Schraw, G. 214
Hoffrage, U., Hafenbradl, S., & Marewski, J. N. 491
Holcomb, P. J. 418
Holding, D. H. 182, 448, 452
Holding, D. H., & Reynolds, J. R. 451
Holmlund, T. B., Cheng, J., Foltz, P. W., Cohen, A. S., & Elvevåg, B. 362
Holt, N., Bremner, A., Sutherland, A., Vliek, M., Passer, M., & Smith, R. 19, 48, 52, 54, 57
Holtzer, R., Jacobs, S., & Demetriou, E. 361
Hommel, B. 101
Hommel, B., Chapman, C. S., Cisek, P., Neyedli, H. F. et al. 126, 142
Hommel, B., Musseler, J., Aschersleben, G., & Prinz, W. 101
Honda, Asimo from 37
Hoosain, R. 200
Hoosain, R., & Salili, F. 200
Hopkins, B. 213
Hostetter, A. B., and Alibali, M. W. 109
Houston, K. A., Clifford, B. R., Phillips, L. H., & Memon, A. 575
Howard, L. A., & Tipper, S. P. 142
Howard, R. W. 448
Hu, Y., Ericsson, K. A., Yang, D., & Lu, C. 7
Huang, Y., Su, L., & Ma, Q. 412
Hubal, R., Mitroff, S. R., Cain, M. S., Scott, B., & DeWitt, R. 127
Hubbard, E. M., & Ramachandran, V. S. 57
Hubbard, T. L., & Favretto, A. 71
Hubel, D. H., & Wiesel, T. N. 49–51
Huber, R. A., Wicki, M. L., & Bernauer, T. 495–6
Huddleston, R., & Pullum, G. K. 331
Hugdahl, K. 385
Hugdahl, K., & Westerhausen, R. 385
Hull, C. L. 268
Hull, R., & Vaid, J. 361
Hulleman, J., & Olivers, C. N. 132
Hulme, C., Thomson, N., Muir, C., & Lawrence, A. 200
Hume, David 8
Humphrey, N. 155
Humphreys, G. W., & Forde, E,. M. E. 98
Humphreys, G. W., & Riddoch, M. J. 69
Huppert, D., Benson, J., & Brandt, T. 59
Hurlburt, R. T., & Heavey, C. L. 9
Hurlburt, R. T., Alderson- Day, B., Fernyhough, C. P., & Kuhn, S. 9
Hurley, S. L. 44
Huxley, T.H. 157
Huybregts, M. A. C. 332
Hyde, J. S. 360
Hygge, S. 201
Hyman, I. E., Husband, T. H., & Billings, F. J. 574
Hyman, I. E., Jr., & Pentland, J. 246
Hymes, D. 341

I

Ifaluk people of Micronesia 558
Imai, M., Kanero, J., & Masuda, T. 329
Innocence Project 77
Inokuchi, E., & Kamio, Y. 362
Intons-Peterson, M. J. 317
Intraub, H. 210, 211
Invasion of the Body Snatchers (Don Siegel film) 550
Iowa Gambling Task 582
Irwin, H. J. 171
Isarida, T., & Isarida, T. K. 266
Isen, A. M. 577
Itti, L. 70
Itti, L., & Koch, C. 70, 132

J

Jackson, F. 153
Jackson, M. L. & Ferencz, J. 320
Jacobs, D. W. 64
Jacobs, N., & Garnham, A. 330
Jacobson, J. Z., & Dodwell, P. C. 413
Jaffa Cakes 297–8, 299
Jalbert, A., Neath, I., Bireta, T. J., & Surprenant, A. M. 199
James, K. H. 371
James, William 101, 178, 187, 195, 206
  cognition and emotion 559, 561, 573
  attention 116, 120–21
  language production 327, 348
Jamison, K. 461
Jarosz, A. F., Colflesh, G. H., & Wiley, J. 442

Name Index

Jastorff, J., & Orban, G.A. 80
Jastrow, J. 318
Jay, T. B., & Danks, J. H. 343
Jazayeri, M., & Shadlen, M. N. 41
Jeannerod, M. 93
Jeannerod, M., Arbib, M. A., Rizzolatti, G., & Sakata, H. 93
Jeffries, R., Polson, P. G., Razran, L., & Attwood, M. E. 433
Jelinek, L., Moritz, S., Heeren, D., & Naber, D. 240
Jenkins, J. G., and Dallenbach, K. M. 271, 275
Jipp, M. 193
Johansson, Gunnar 79
Johnson, E. J., and Goldstein, D. 489
Johnson, K., & Shiffrar, M. 78
Johnson-Laird, P. N. 515, 516, 523–5, 526
Johnson-Laird, P. N., & Byrne, R. M. J. 515, 526
Johnson-Laird, P. N., & Steedman, M. 515, 523
Johnson-Laird, P. N., and Bara, B. G. 524, 526
Johnson-Laird, P. N., Byrne, R. M. J., & Schaeken, W. 515, 516, 517
Johnson-Laird, P. N., Legrenzi, P., & Legrenzi, M. S. 535, 536, 537
Johnson-Laird, P. N., Mancini, J. L., & Gangemi, A. 517–18
Johnston, R. A., & Edmonds, A. J. 74
Jones, D. M. and Macken, W. J. 201
Jones, G. 447
Jones, G. V. 326
Jones, P. 191
Jones Leonard, B., McNaughton, B. L., & Barnes, C. A. 275
Jonides, J., Smith, E. E., Koeppe, R. A., Awh, E., Minoshima, S., & Mintun, M. A. 205
Joormann, J., Yoon, K. L., & Zetsche, U. 571
Jordan, M. I. 95
Jordan, M. I., & Rumelhart, D. E. 88
Jost, A. 267
Journal of Experimental Psychology 411
Ju, Y.-J., & Lien, Y.-W. 210
Jung-Beeman, M., Bowden, E. M., Haberman, J., Frymiare, J. L., Arambel-Liu, S. et al 440, 442
Jusczyk, P. W. 382
Jusczyk, P. W., and Aslin, R. N. 382
Jusczyk, P. W., Houston, D. M., & Newsome, M. 381
Juslin, P. N., & Laukka, P. 78
Jutzeler, C. R., Curt, A., & Kramer, J. L. K. 57

K

Kadosh, R. 24
Kadosh, R., Soskik, S., Iuculano, T., Kanai, R., & Walsh, V. 24
Kahn Jr., C. E. 130
Kahneman, D. 122, 126, 128, 471, 488, 527
Kahneman, D., and Tversky, A. 469, 470–71, 475–6, 499
Kahneman, D., Knetsch, J. L., & Thaler, R. H. 472
Kalat, J. W. 222
Kalenine, S., Buxbaum, L. J., & Coslett, H. B. 104
Kaminski, J., Call, J., & Fischer, J. 400
Kaminski, J., Tempelmann, S., Call, J., & Tomasello, M. 400
Kandasamy, N., Garfinkel, S. N., Page, L., Critchley, H. D., Gurnell, M., & Coates, J. M. 582–3
Kandel, E. R. 274
Kandel, E. R., and Schwartz, J. H. 19
Kandel, E., Schwartz, J., & Jessell, T. 52, 57
Kane, M. J., Brown, L. H., McVay, J. C., Silvia, P. J., Myin-Germeys, I., & Kwapil, T. R. 208–9
Kane, M. J., Gross, G. M., Chun, C. A., Smeekens, B. A., Meier, M. E., Silvia, P. J., & Kwapil, T. R. 207–10
Kanwisher, N., McDermott, J., & Chun, M. M. 74, 75

Kar, K., Kubilius, J., Schmidt, K., Issa, E. B., & DiCarlo, J. J. 67
Kardas-Nelson, M. 495
Kassin, S. M. 390, 530
Kassin, S. M., Dror, I. E., & Kukucka, J. 545–6
Katayama, M., & Kawato, M. 87
Kaufman, D. M., & Milstein, M. J. 320
Kaufman, E., Reips, U.-D., & Wittmann, W. W. 502
Kawato, M. 87, 88
Kawato, M., & Gomi, H. 87
Kaye, L.K., Malone, S. A., & Wall, H. J. 414
Kazi, S., Demetriou, A., Spanoudis, G., Zhang, X. K., & Wang, Y. 371
Keefe, J. M., Sy, J. L., Tong, F., & Zald, D. H. 134–7
Keither, M. 309
Kejic, M., McClelland, J., Bartholdy, S., Chamali, R., Campbell, I. C., & Schmidt, U. 474–5
Kelly, S., Byrne, K., & Holler, J. 109
Kelso, J. A. S. 87
Kendon, A. 108
Kenealy, P. M. 267
Kennedy, John F. 573
  assassination of 284
Kennet, Y. 311
Kensinger, E. A., & Schacter, D. L. 573
Kensinger, E. A., Ullman, M. T., & Corkin, S. 221
Kentridge, R. W., Heywood, C. A., & Weiskrantz, L. 162
Keogh, R., and Pearson, J. 314
Kerkman, J. N., Daffertshofer, A., Gollo, L. L., Breakspear, M., & Boonstra, T. W. 108
Kerr, D. S., & Murphy, U. S. 458, 459
Kessler, K., & Braithwaite, J. J. 171
Keys, D. J., and Schwartz, B. 486, 487
Khalighinejad, N., Brann, E., Dorgham, A., & Haggard, P. 170
Kietzman, P. M., & Visscher, P. K. 336
Kilian-Hütten, N., Formisano, E., & Vroomen, J. 60
Kilner, J. M. 104
Kilner, J. M., & Lemon, R. N. 104
Kilner, J. M., Neal, A., Weiskopf, N., Friston, K. J., & Frith, C. D. 104
Kim, D., Stephens, J. D. W., & Pitt, M. A. 382
Kim, Y. W., & Mansfield, L. T. 129, 130
Kimura, D. 363, 385
King, Martin Luther 573
Kingdom, F. A. A., & Prins, N. 158
Kingston, J. A., & Lyddy, F. 214
Kinukawa, T., Takeuchi, N., Sugiyama, S., Nishihara, M., Nishiwaki, K., & Inui, K. 185
Kirchner, H., & Thorpe, S. J. 69
Kita, S., & Ozyurek, A. 108
Kiyonaga, A., & Egner, T. 140
Klatzky, R. L. 194
Klatzky, R. L., Lederman, S. J., & Metzger, V. A. 67
Klatzky, R. L., Pellegrino, J. W., McCloskey, B. P., & Doherty, S. 308
Klauer, S. G., Dingus, T. A., Neale, V. L., Sudweeks, J. D., & Ramsey, D. J. 60
Klein, D. C., & Seligman, M. E. P. 578
Klein, G. 132
Klein, G., Calderwood, R., & Clinton-Cirocco, A. 500, 502
Klein, G., Wolf, S., Militello, L., & Zsambok, C. 500, 502
Klein, R. M. 499–500, 501
Klein, S. B., & Loftus, J. 237
Kleinschmidt, D. F., & Jaeger, T. F. 378
Klenk, M. 499
Kljajevic, V., & Erramuzpe, A. 349–50
Knight, A., Underhill, P. A., Mortensen, H. M., & Zhivotovsky, L. A. 332
Knoblich, G., & Flach, R. 102
Knoblich, G., Ohlsson, S., Haider, H., & Rhenius, D. 443
Knowlton, B., Squire, L., & Gluck, M. 229

Ko, S. J., Judd, C. M., & Blair, I. V. 78
Koch, C., and Ullman, S. 132
Koch, Christof 155, 162
Koechlin, E. 98
Koehler, K., & Eckstein, M. P. 132
Kohler, E., Keysers, C., Umilta, M. A., Fogassi, L., Gallese, V., & Rizzolatti, G. 103
Kohler, W. 427
Kok, E. M., Jarodzka, H., de Bruin, A. B., BinAmir, H. A., Robben, S. G., & van Merriënboer, J. J. 130
Kolers, P. A., & Roediger, H. L. 231
Kolk, H. 370
Komatsu, L. K. 301
Kondziella, D., Friberg, C. K., Frokjaer, V. G., Fabricius, M., & Moller, K. 30
Konen, C. S., Behrmann, M., Nishimura, M., & Kastner, S. 68
Kong, J., Gollub, R. L., Webb, J. M., Vangel, M. G., & Kwong, K. 27
Koohestani, A., Nahavandi, D., Asadi, H., Kebria, P. M., Khosravi, A., Alizadehsani, R., & Nahavandi, S. 60
Kopelman, M. D., Lasserson, D., Kingsley, D., Bello, F., Rush, C., Stanhope, N., Stevens, T., Goodman, G. et al. 224
Kopelman, M. D., Thomson, A., Guerrini, I., & Marshall, E. J. 224
Kording, K. P. 92
Kording, K. P., & Wolpert, D. M. 92
Koriat, A. 172
Koriat, A., & Goldsmith, M. 283–4
Kosslyn, S. M. 314, 319
Kosslyn, S. M., and Thompson, W. I. 320
Kosslyn, S. M., Ball, T. M., & Reiser, B. J. 314–15, 317
Kosslyn, S. M., Thompson, W. L., Kim, I. J., & Alpert, N. M. 319
Kouider, S., & Faivre, N. 158
Kounios, J., & Beeman, M. 441
Kozlowski, L. T., & Cutting, J. E. 78
Krafnick, A. J., & Evans, T. M. 407
Kramer, A. F., & Hahn, S. 126
Kramer, M. R., Porfido, C. L., & Mitroff, S. R. 127
Krasne, S., Hillman, J. D., Kellman, P. J., & Drake, T. A. 130
Krasovskaya, S., & MacInnes, W. J. 132
Krauss, M. 330–31
Krauss, R. M., Chen, Y., & Gottesman, R. F. 108
Krieber, M., Bartl-Pokorny, K. D., Pokorny, F. B., Einspieler, C., Langmann, A. et al. 413
Kringelbach, M. L., & Rolls, E. T. 552
Kristjánsson, T., Thornton, I. M., Chetverikov, A., & Kristjánsson, Á. 132
Krizhevsky, A., Sutskever, I., & Hinton, G. E. 67
Kroes, M. C., Tendolkar, I., Van Wingen, G. A., Van Waarde, J. A., Strange, B. A., & Fernández, G. 279
Kroll, J. F., & Dussias, P. E. 398
Kroos, C., Herath, D. C., & Stelarc 117
Kucera, H., & Francis, W. N. 396
Kuffler, D. P. 57
Kuhl, P. K. 385
Kuhl, P. K., & Miller, J. D. 384
Kuhn, G., & Tatler, B. W. 147
Kuhn, G., Amlani, A. A., & Rensink, R. A. 147
Kuhn, G., Caffaratti, H. A., Teszka, R., & Rensink, R. A. 147
Kuhn, T. 541
Kulpe, Oswald 9
Kunst-Wilson, W. R., & Zajonc, R. B. 565, 566
Kusumi, T. 249
Kutas, M., and Hillyard, S. A. 363, 418
Kuzmina, E., Goral, M., Norvik, M., & Weekes, B. S. 370
Kvavilashvili, L. 239

Name Index

Kvavilashvili, L., & Ellis, J. 283–4
Kwan, M. H., & Cutler, A. 377
Kyaga, S., Lichtenstein, P., Boman, M., Hultman, C., Langstrom, N., & Landen, M. 461–2
Kyritsis, M., Gulliver, S. R., Feredoes, E., & Din, S. U. 437, 438

L

Laberge, D. 122
Laberge, D., & Brown, V. R. 122
Lacquaniti, F., Terzuolo, C., & Viviani, P. 102
Ladefoged, P. 331
Laeng, B., and Sulutvedt, U. 318
Lakatos, I. 541
Lakoff, G., and Johnson, M. 108
Lamberty, G. J., Beckwith, B. E., & Petros, T. V. 277
Lambon Ralph, M. A. 312
Lamme, V. A. 137, 165, 167
Lamme, V. A., & Roelfsema, P. R. 137
Lamont, P., & Wiseman, R. 148
Lamont, P., Henderson, J. M., & Smith, T. J. 147
Lander, K., Bruce, V., & Bindemann, M. 77
Landy, D., & Goldstone, R. L. 110
Landy, M. S., Maloney, L. T., Johnston, E. B., & Young, M. 59
Lang, P. J., Bradley, M. M., & Cuthbert, B. N. 106
Lange, Carl 561
Lange, J., and Lappe, M. 80
Langer, A., Feingold-Polak, R., Mueller, O., Kellmeyer, P., & Levy-Tzedek, S. 38
Langton, S. R. H., Law, A. S., Burton, A. M., & Schweinberger, S. R. 137
Large, A. M., Bediou, B., Cekic, S., Hart, Y., Bavelier, D., & Green, C. S. 127
Larkin, J. H. 451
Larsen, J. D., & Baddeley, A. D. 200
Larsen, R. J., Kasimatis, M., & Frey, K. 561
Lashley, K. S. 23, 93–4, 220
Latash, M., & Zatsiorsky, V. 84
Latinus, M., & Belin, P. 78, 79
Lau, H., & Brown, R. 173
Lau, H., & Rosenthal, D. 173
Lau, H. C., & Passingham, R. E. 173
Laurienti, P. J., Burdette, J. H., Maldjian, J. A., & Wallace, M. T. 61
Lavie, N. 122
Lavy, E., van den Hout, M. A., & Arntz, A. 571
Laws, K. R., Leeson, V. C., & McKenna, P. J. 306
Lawson, R., Fernandes, A. M., Albuquerque, P. B., & Lacey, S. 198
Lazarus, R. S., & Alfert, E. 567
Lazarus, R. S., Opton, E. M., Nomikos, M. S., & Rankin, N. O. 567
Lazarus, Richard S. 566, 567, 568
Le Brun, Y., & Leleux, C. 365
Le Doux, J. E. 563, 568
Lea, S. E. G., & Dittrich, W. H. 182
Lederman, S. J., & Klatzky, R. L. 67–8
Lee, C. S., Nagy, P. G., Weaver, S. J., & Newman-Toker, D. E. 129, 130
Lee, J. L., Nader, K., & Schiller, D. 279
Lee, L. F., and Horowitz, L. A. 530
Lee, S.-H., Kravitz, D. J., & Baker, C. I. 320
Lee, S. H., Kwan, A. C., Zhang, S., Phoumthipphavong, V., Flannery, J. G. et al. 139
Legrenzi, P., & Umilta, C. 26
Legrenzi, P., Girotto, V., & Johnson-Laird, P. N. 516
Lehrer, J. 426
Lemon, R. N., & Edgly, S. A. 166
Lench, H. C., Bench, S. W., & Flores, S. A. 570
Lenneberg. E. H. 327
Leopold, D. A., & Logothetis, N. K. 162
Lerner, J. S., Li, Y., Valdesolo, P., & Kassam, K. S. 579, 580

Levelt, W. J. M. 343, 350, 352–5, 377
Levenson, R. W. 555, 560
Levenson, R. W., Ekman, P., & Friesen, W. V. 560
Leventhal, H., & Scherer, K. R. 566
Levin, D. T., and Simons, D. J. 145
Levine, L. J., and Pizarro, D. A. 575
Levinson, S. C. 342
Levy, R. 395
Lewis-Peacock, J. A., Drysdale, A. T., Oberauer, K., & Postle, B. R. 214
Li, D., Vlisides, P. E., Kelz, M. B., Avidan, M. S., & Mashour, G. A. 156
Li, X. B., & Basso, M. A. 138
Liberal Democrat History Group 493
Liberman, A. 17
Liberman, A. M., Harris, K. S., Hoffman, H. S., & Griffith, B. C. 384
Libet, B. 170
Libet, B., Gleason, C. A., Wright, E. W., & Pearl, D. 169, 170
Lichtenstein, S., Slovic, P., Fischhoff, B., Layman, M., & Coombes, B. 478
Limb, C. J., & Roy, A. T. 55
Lindquist, K. A., & Barrett, L. F. 552
Lindquist, K. A., Wager, T. D., Kober, H., Bliss-Moreau, E., & Barrett, L. F. 552, 570
Lindsay, R. C. L., & Wells, G. L. 77
Lindsay, R. C. L., Mansour, J. K., Bertrand, N. K., & Whaley, E. I. 76
Lindstrom., M. 27
Linell, P. 383
Linn, L. 249
Lipman, M. 531–2
Lipnicki, D. M., and Byrne, D. G. 28
Lipp, O. V., and Derakshan, N. 571–2
Lipshitz, R., Klein, G., Orasanu, J., & Salas, E. 499
Lipton, P. 543
Lister, R. G., Eckardt, M. J., & Weingartner, H. 277
Littlemore, J. 109
Liu, J., & Jaeger, T. F. 378
Liversedge, S. P., & Findlay, J. M. 413
Locke, John 8
Lockwood, G., & Dingemanse, M. 332
Loewenstein, G. 473
Loewenstein, G., & Lerner, J. S. 579
Loftus, E. F. 76, 224, 282, 285
Loftus, E. F., and Palmer, J. C. 286, 329, 388–90
Loftus, E. F., and Zanni, D. 286
Loftus, E. F., Loftus, G. R., & Messo, J. 574–5
Loftus, E. F., Miller, D. G., & Burns, H. J. 574
Loftus, G. R., & Loftus, E. F. 184
Logan, G. D. 126
Logie, R. H. 191, 203, 213
Logie, R. H., & Cowan, N. 214
Logie, R. H., & D'Esposito, M. 214
Logie, R. H., Gilhooly, K. J., & Wynn, V. 203
Logie, R. H., Pernet, C. R., Buonocore, A., & Della Sala, S. 317
Logothetis, N. K. 162, 163
Logothetis, N. K., & Sheinberg, D. L. 66
London Metropolitan Police 77
London transport system, July 2005 attacks on 284
Longo, M. R., Azanon, E., & Haggard, P. 57
Longo, M. R., Long, C., & Haggard, P. 57
Looi, V., Gfeller, K., & Driscoll, V. D. 55
Looney, V., & Maier, R. P. 326
López, E., Steiner, A. J., Hardy, D. J., IsHak, W. W., & Anderson, W. B. 200
Loschky, L. C., Larson, A. M., Smith, T. J., & Magliano, J. P. 146
Louie, J. F., & Mouloua, M. 196
Loula, F., Prasad, S., Harber, K., & Shiffrar, M. 102
Lowet, E., Gomes, B., Srinivasan, K., Zhou, H., Schafer, R. J., & Desimone, R. 142
Lu, C., & Tang, X. 74
Luchins, A. W. 428

Luke, T. J., Crozier, W. E., & Strange, D. 390
Lullin, Charles 319–20
Lung, C. T., & Dominowski, R. L. 444
Lunke, K., & Meier, B. 182, 184
Luria, A. R. 182, 264–5, 522–3
Lutz, C. 558
Luzzatti, C., Vecchi, T., Agazzi, D., Cesa-Bianchi, M., & Vergani, C. 205
Lyddy, F., Farina, F., Hanney, J., Farrell, L., & Kelly O'Neill, N. 414

M

Mac Giollabhui, N., Hamilton, J. L., Nielsen, J., Connolly, S. L., Stange, J. P., Varga, S., Burdette, E. et al. 579
McAdams, C. J., & Maunsell, J. H. R. 138
McAleer, P., Todorov, A., & Belin, P. 78
Macaluso, E., Noppeney, U., Talsma, D., Vercillo, T., Hartcher-O'Brien, J., & Adam, R. 59
MacCabe, J. H., Sarasian, A., Almquvist, C., Lichtenstein, H., Larsson, H., & Kyaga, S. 461
McCaffrey, T. 460
McCall, R., McGee, F., Mirnig, A., Meschtscherjakov, A., Louveton, N., Engel, T., & Tscheligi, M. 61
McCarley, J. S., Kramer, A. F., Wickens, C. D., Vidoni, E. D., & Boot, W. R. 127
McCausland, S., Kingston, J., & Lyddy, F. 414
McClelland, J. L., & Rumelhart, D. E. 95
McClelland, J. L., and Elman, J. L. 391, 393, 394
McClelland, J. L., Mirman, D., & Holt, L. L. 394
McCloskey, M. E., & Glucksberg, S. 298, 299
McClure, S. M., Laibson, D. I., Loewenstein, G., & Cohen, J. D. 505
McClure, S. M., Li, J., Tomlin, D., Cypert, K. S., Latane, M. M., & Montague, P. R. 504
McCormick, P. A., & Klein, R. 126
McCoy, A. N., Crowley, J. C., Haghighian, G., Dean, H. L., & Platt, M. L. 504
McDermott, H. J. 55
MacFarland, D. 330
Macfarlane, D. A. 14
McGeoch, J. A., & Nolen, E. 279
McGeoch, J. A., and McDonald, W. T. 269–70
MacGregor, J. N., & Chu, Y. 438
MacGregor, J. N., & Ormerod, T. 438
MacGregor, J. N., Chronicle, E. P., & Ormerod, T. C. 438
MacGregor, J. N., Ormerod, T. C., & Chronicle, E. P. 433, 443, 444–5
McGurk, H., & MacDonald, J. 58, 390
McHugo, M., Olatunji, B. O., & Zald, D. H. 134
McIsaac, H. K., & Eich, E. 243
Mack, A., & Rock, I. 143–4, 167
McKay, L. S., Simmons, D. R., McAleer, P., Marjoram, D., Piggot, J., & Pollick, F. E. 80
McKelvie, S. J. 9
Macknik, S. L., King, M., Randi, J., Robbins, A., Thompson, J., & Martinez-Conde, S. 147
Maclay, H., & Osgood, C. E. 343
MacLeod, C. M. 411–12
MacLeod, C. M., & MacDonald, P. A. 411
MacLeod, C., Mathews, A., & Tata, P. 571
MacLin, O. H., MacLin, M. K., & Malpass, R. S. 77
McManus, I. C., Richards, P., Winder, B. C., & Sproston, K. A. 288
MacMillan, M. 212, 552–3
McNally, R. J., and Geraerts, E. 283
Macnamara, B. N., and Maitra, M. 449–50
MacNeilage. P. F. 327, 331
McNeill, D. 108, 330
McNeill, D., & Duncan, S. D. 108
McQueen, J. M., & Cutler, A. 377
McQueen, J. M., Norris, D., & Cutler, A. 380
McQueen, J. M., Otake, T., & Cutler, A. 383

McWilliams, L., Bellhouse, S., Yorke, J., Lloyd, K., & Armitage, C. J. 238
Maddieson, I. M. 338
Maffei, C., Capasso, R., Cazzolli, G., Colosimo, C., Dell'Acqua, F., Piludu, F., Catani, M., & Miceli, G. 386–7
Magnussen, S., Melinder, A., Stridbeck, U., & Raja, A. Q. 286
Maguire, E. A., Valentine, E. R., Wilding, J. M., & Kapur, N. 8, 265
Mahadevan, Rajan 265
Maier, N. E. F. 428
Malmberg, K. J., Raaijmakers, J. G. W., & Shiffrin, R. M. 214
Malt, B. C. 307
Malt, B. C., & Smith, E. E. 302
Mamassian, P., & Landy, M. S. 41
Mamassian, P., Landy, M. S., & Maloney, L. T. 41
Manchester United 491
Mandich, A., & Polatajko, H. J. 100
Mandler, G. 188
Mandler, G., and Pearlstone, Z. 263
Mandler, G., Nakamura, Y., & Shebo-Van Zandt, B. J. 566
Mann, R. E., Cho-Young, J., & Vogel-Sprott, M. 277
Mann, S., Vrij, A., & Bull, R. 345
Mann Gulch, Montana, forest fire at 426
Manns, J. R., Hopkins, R. O., & Squire, L. R. 276
Mapelli, D., & Behrmann, M. 66
Marcus, S. L., and Rips, L. J. 513
Marek, S., & Dosenbach, N. U. 120
Markovits, H. 513
Markowitsch, H. J., & Staniloiu, A. 224
Marr, David 42–3, 72, 155
Marsh, R. L., Hicks, J. L., & Landau, J. D. 237
Marshall, G. D., & Zimbardo, P. G. 565
Marshall, J. C., & Newcombe, F. 417
Marslen-Wilson, W. 392
Marslen-Wilson, W. D., & Tyler, L. K. 378, 391, 393
Martin, A., and Caramazza, A. 306
Martin, A., Kronbichler, M., & Richlan, F. 408, 409
Martinez-Trujillo, J. C., & Treue, S. 138
Marupaka, N., Iyer, L., & Minai, A. A. 311
Marx, Groucho 400
Mashour, G. A. 156
Mashour, G. A., Roelfsema, P., Changeux, J. P., & Dehaene, S. 165
Mason, O., & Claridge, G. 462
Massaro, D. W. 185, 186, 378, 385
Massaro, D. W., & Cohen, M. 384, 390
Masters, R. S. W. 97
Mataró, M., Jurado, M. Á., García-Sánchez, C., Barraquer, L., Costa-Jussà, F. R., & Junqué, C. 212
Matchock, R. L., Levine, M. E., Gianaros, P. J., & Stern, R. M. 60
Matheson, H. E., & Barsalou, L. 308
Mathews, A., Mogg, K., Kentish, J., & Eysenck, M. 571
Matsumoto, D., & Willingham, B. 556
Matsumoto, D., and Hwang, H. 557
Mattar, A. A. G., & Gribble, P. L. 105
Mattys, S. L., Melhorn, J. F., & White, L. 382
Mattys, S.L., Baddeley, A., & Trenkic, D. 199, 200
Maule, J., & Villejoubert, G. 477
Mayberry, E. J., Sage, K., & Lambon Ralph, M. A. 312
Mayberry, R. I., Davenport, T., Roth, A., & Halgren, E. 326, 361
Mayer, E., & Rossion, B. 76
Mayfield, Brandon 545
Mazzoni, G., & Mamon, A. 246
Mazzoni, G., Scoboria, A., & Harvey, L. 248
Meadow, A., Parnes, S. J., & Reese, H. 458
Medin, D. L. 305
Medin, D. L., & Ortony, A. 305

Meers, R., Nuttall, H. E., & Vogt, S. 104
Megherbi, H., Elbro, C., Oakhill, J., Segui, J., & New, B. 412
Mei, N., Flinker, A., Zhu, M., Cai, Q., & Tian, X. 385
Meissner, C. A., & Brigham, J. C. 77
Mekki, M., Delgado, A. D., Fry, A., Putrino, D., & Huang, V. 86
Melnick, M. D., Tadin, D., & Huxlin, K. R. 162
Melzack, R. 57
Memon, A., Meissner, C. A., & Fraser, J. 288
Memory: A Contribution to Experimental Psychology (Ebbinghaus, H.) 267
Mendes, M., Schwaninger, A., & Michel, S. 127
Menon, V. 31
Merikle, P. M., & Daneman, M. 158
Metcalfe, J., & Dunlosky, J. 250
Metcalfe, J., & Weibe, D. 440, 441
Metzinger, T. K. 172
Meyer, D. E., & Schvaneveldt, R. W. 397, 410
Mezzacappa, E. S., Katkin, E., & Palmer, S. N. 565
Michotte, Albert Éduard 71–2
Milgram, S. 311
Mill, John Stuart 8, 541
Miller, G. A. 9, 188, 401
Miller, G. A., Galanter, E., & Pribram, K. H. 94, 192, 195
Miller, J. L., & Jusczyk, P. W. 378
Miller, J., Shepherdson, P., & Trevena, J. 170
Miller, N., Lowit, A., & O'Sullivan, H. 381
Milner, B. 207
Milner, B., Corkin, S., & Teuber, H. L. 220, 222, 223, 224
Minami, H., & Dallenbach, K. M. 271–2, 278
Mirpour, K., Bolandnazar, Z., & Bisley, J. W. 133
Mitchell, D. B. 231
Mitchell, D. B., Kelly, C. L., & Brown, A. S. 231
Mitroff, I. I. 543–4
Mittelstädt, J. M., Wacker, J., & Stelling, D. 60
Miyake, A., and Shah, P. 194–5
Moen, I. 381
Mogg, K., Bradley, B. P., & Williams, R. 571
Mogg, K., Bradley, B. P., Williams, R., & Mathews, A. 571
Moher, J., Anderson, B. A., & Song, J. H. 142
Molaison, Henry Gustav ('H.M.') 220–23
Molesworth, B. R. C., Burgess, M., & Koh, S. 201
Molfese, D. L., & Betz, J. C. 363
Molfese, V. J., Molfese, D. L., & Parsons, C. 384, 385
Monrad-Krohn, G. H. 381
Montero-Melis, G., van Paridon, J., Ostarek, M., & Bylund, E. 311
Monti, M. M., Vanhaudenhuyse, A., Coleman, M. R., Bolu, M., Pickard, J. D. et al. 29
Moody, T. 157
Moonwalking with Einstein (Foer, J.) 6
Moore, M. T., & Fresco, D. M. 579
Moore, T., & Armstrong, K. M. 142
Moore, T., & Fallah, M. 142
Mooren, N., Krans, J., Näring, G., & van Minnen, A. 242–3
Moran, J. 229
Moran, J., & Desimone, R. 138
Moran, S., and McCloy, D. 336
Moray, N. 121
Moray, N., and Rotenberg, I. 192–3
Moray, N., Bates, A., & Barnett, T. 184
Moreton, R., Pike, G., & Havard, C. 77
Moritz, S., Jacobsen, D., Willenborg, B., Jelinek, L., & Fricke, S. 240
Morris, P. E. 237, 238
Morrison, J. B., & Tversky, B. 308
Morton, J. 395
Morton, J., & Patterson, K. E. 395
Morton, N., and Morris, R. G. 205

Moseley, C. 330
Mosso, Angelo 26
Most, S. B., Smith, S. D., Cooter, A. B., Levy, B. N., & Zald, D. H. 134
Moxley, J. H., Ericcsson, K. A., Charness, N., & Krampe, R. T. 500
Moyer, R. S. 314
Mozart, Wolfgang Amadeus 576
Mrazek, M. D., Smallwood, J., & Schooler, J. W. 210
Mueller, C. W., Lisman, S. A., & Spear, N. E. 277
Mueller, K. D., Koscik, R. L., LaRue, A., Clark, L. R., Hermann, B., Johnson, S. C., & Sager, M. A. 361
Mueller, P. A., & Oppenheimer, D. M. 371
Mukamel, R., Ekstrom, A. D., Kaplan, J., Iacoboni, M., & Fried, I. 104
Muller, G. E., and Pilzecker, A. 279
Murdoch, B. E. 365
Murphy, G. L. 304
Murphy, G. L., & Greene, C. M. 390
Murphy, G. L., & Medin, D. 304
Murphy, S. T., and Zajonc, R. B. 566
Murray, A., & Jones, D. M. 200
Murray, D. J. 6, 200
Music Academy of West Berlin 449
Mynatt, C. R., Doherty, M. E., & Tweney, R. D. 543, 544

N

Naccache, L., Blandin, E., & Dehaene, S. 167
Nachev, P., & Husain, M. 29
Nagy, W. E., & Anderson, R. C. 339
Nairne, J. S. 268
National Safety Council 146
National Security Agency (US) 557
Naveh-Benjamin, M., & Ayres, T. J. 200
Navon, D. 125
Navon, D., & Miller, J. 125
Necker cube 318
Neisser, U., & Becklen, R. 144–5
Neisser, Ulric 72, 180, 185, 187, 245, 283–4, 285, 287
Nelson, K. 243
Nelson, T. O., and Narens, L. 172
Nenkov, G. Y., Morrin, M., Ward, A., Schwartz, B., & Hulland, J. 487
Nermend, K., & Latuszynska, M. 504
Neuschatz, J. S., Lampinen, J. M., Preston, E. L., Hawkins, E. R., & Toglia, M. P. 235
Newell, A. 307
Newell, A., Shaw, J. C., & Simon, H. A. 15
Newell, B. R. 475–6
Newell, B. R., & Shanks, D. R. 491
Newell, B. R., Lagnado, D. A., & Shanks, D. 473
Newstead, S. E., & Griggs, R. A. 522
Newton, Sir Isaac 543–4
Newtson, D. 72
Nickerson, R. S., Perkins, D. N., & Smith, E. E. 532
Nigro, G., & Neisser, U. 241
Nijboer, M., Borst, JP., van Rijn, H., & Taatgen, NA. 196–7
Nijdam, M. J., Baas, M. A. M., Olff, M., & Gersons, B. P. R. 245
Nijstad, B. A., Stroebe, W., & Lodewijkx, H. F. N. 459
Nixon, Richard 245
Noë, A. 44
Noe, C., & Fischer-Baum, S. 395
Noel, J. P., Ishizawa, Y., Patel, S. R., Eskandar, E. N., & Wallace, M. T. 167
Nolan, V. 459
Nooteboom, S. G., & Quené, H. 347
Norman, D. A. 187, 346
Norman, D. A., and Bobrow, D. G. 124
Norman, D. A., and Shallice, T. 206
Norman, E., Pfuhl, G., Sæle, R. G., Svartdal, F., Låg, T., & Dahl, T. I. 172

O

Norman, G. R., & Eva, K. W. 544
Norris, D., Butterfield, S., Hall, J., & Page, M. P. A. 200
Norris, D., McQueen, J. M., & Cutler, A. 395
NTSB (National Transportation Safety Board) 61
Nutt, P. C. 500

Oaksford, M., & Chater, N. 539–40
Oatley, K., & Johnson Laird, P. N. 551, 568
Oberauer, K. 140, 196, 199, 213
Oberauer, K., Weidenfeld, A., & Hornig, R. 540
Obler, L. K., & Gjerlow, K. 369
O'Brien, D. P., Braine, M. D. S., & Yang, Y. 517
Ochsner, K. N. 574
O'Craven, K. M., Downing, P. E., & Kanwisher, N. 124
Odegaard, B., Knight, R. T., & Lau, H. 166
Oesch, N., & Dunbar, R. I. M. 341
O'Hara, K. P., and Payne, S. J. 436
Ohlsson, S. 443, 455
Ohshiro, T., Angelaki, D. E., & DeAngelis, G. C. 139
OIG (Oversight Inspector General, US) 545
Oizumi, M., Albantakis, L., & Tononi, G. 166
Okada, T., and Simon, H. A. 544
Olds, J. 504
Oliva, A., & Torralba, A. 131
Oliver, A. 472
Oliver, N., Calvard, T., & Potoc¢nik, K. 193
Olivers, C. N. L., & Nieuwenhuis, S. 135, 137
Ollinger, M., Jones, G., & Knoblich, G. 444
Ollinger, M., Jones, G., & Faber A. H., & Knoblich, G. 444
Olson, J. A., Demacheva, I., & Raz, A. 146
Olson, R., Keenan, J., Byrne, B., & Samuelsson, S. 407
Oppenheim, G. M., and Dell, G. S. 11–12
O'Regan, J. K. 413
Ormerod, T. C., MacGregor, J. N., & Chronicle, E. P. 445
O'Rourke, T. B., and Holcomb, P. J. 392
Ortmann, A., Gigerenzer, G., Borges, B., & Goldsten, D. G. 492
Ortony, A., Clore, G. L., & Collins, A. 568
Oruc, I., Balas, B., & Landy, M. S. 74
Osborn, Alex 458
Ost, J., Vrij, A., Costall, A., & Bull, R. 285
Ostarek, M., & Huettig, F. 44
Osterhout, L., & Holcomb, P. J. 363, 418
Osterhout, L., McLaughlin, J., & Bersick, M. 384, 418
Ostry, D. J., & Feldman, A. G. 87
O'Sullivan, J. A., Shamma, S. A., & Lalor, E. C. 71
O'Sullivan, J., Herrero, J., Smith, E., Schevon, C., McKhann, G. M., Sheth, S. A. et al. 71
Otgaar, H., Howe, M. L., Patihis, L., Merckelbach, H., Lynn, S. J., Lilienfeld, S. O., & Loftus, E. F. 282–3
Otsuka-Hirota, N., Yamamoto, H., Miyashita, K., & Nagatsuka, K. 49
Outliers (Gladwell. M.) 448
Oviedo-Trespalacios, O., Haque, M., King, M., & Washington, S. 196
Owen, A. M. 30
Owen, A. M., Coleman, M. R., Boly, M. Davis. H., Laureys, S., Jolles, D., & Pickard, J. D. 29–30
Owen, A. M., Coleman, M. R., Boly, M., Davis. H., Laureys, S., Jolles, D., & Pickard, J. D. 29–30

P

Page, M. P. A. 17
Paivio, A. 263–4, 314–15
Palme, Olof 573
Papies, E. K., Best, M., Gelibter, E., & Barsalou, L. 308
Papies, E. K., Potjes, I., Keesman, M., Schwinghammer, S., & Van Koningsbruggen, G. M. 159–60
Park, H. D., & Blanke, O. 155
Parker, E. S., Birnbaum, I. M., Weingartner, H., Hartley, J. T., Stillman, R. C., & Wyatt, R. J. 277
Parker, E. S., Cahill, L., & McGaugh, J. L. 182, 265
Parker, E. S., Morihisa, J. M., Wyatt, R. J., Schwartz, B. L., Weingartner, H., & Stillman, R. C. 277
Parker-Jones, O., Alfaro- Almagro, F., & Jbabdi, S. 22
Parkin, A. J. 189, 223
Parnes, S. J., & Meadow, A. 458
Parr, T., & Friston, K. J. 138
Parrott, W. G., and Sabini, J. 577
Pascal, Blaise 469
Paton, W., Bain, S. A., Gozna, L., Gilchrist, E., Heim, D., Gardner, E., Cairns, D., McGranaghan, P., & Fischer, R. 390
Patterson, K. E., Marshall, J. C., & Coltheart, M. 417
Paulesu, E., Harrison, J. E., Baron-Cohen, S., Watson, J. D. G., Goldstein, L., Heather, J. et al. 183
Paulesu, E., McCrory, E. Fazio, F. Menoncello, L., Brunswick, N., Cappa, S. F., & Frith, U. 407
Pavlas, D., Rosen, M. A., Fiore, S. M., & Salas, E. 127
Pavlenko, A. 558
Payne, J. 484–5, 486
Payne, J. W., Bettman, J. R., & Johnson, E. J. 485
Pearson, J., Naselaris, T., Holmes, E. A., & Kosslyn, S. M. 318
Peelen, M. V., Wigget, A. J., & Downing, P. E. 80
Peinkhofer, C., Dreier, J. P., & Kondziella, D. 171
Peleg, G., Katzir, G., Peleg, O., Kamara, M., Brodsky, L., Hel-Or, H., Keren, D., & Nevo, E. 556
Penfield, W., & Rasmussen, T. L. 25
Penfield, W., and Boldrey, E. 24
Penfield, Wilder 23–6
Pentland, A. 72
Perea, M., Acha, J., & Carreiras, M. 414
Pereira, A., Altgassen, M., Atchison, L., de Mendonça, A., & Ellis, J. 238
Pereira, A., de Mendonça, A., Silva, D., Guerreiro, M., Freeman, J., & Ellis, J. 238
Perry, C. J., & Fallah, M. 142
Pessoa, L. 134
Peters, E., Lipkus, I., & Diefenbach, M. A. 581
Petersen, M. R., Beecher, M. D., Zoloth, S. R., Moody, D. B., & Stebbins, W. C. 385
Petersen, S. E., & Posner, M. I. 119
Petersen, S. E., & Sporns, O. 30
Peterson, L. R., & Johnson, S. T. 200
Peterson, R. L., & Pennington, B. F. 407, 408–9
Pezdek, K. 285, 573
Phelps, E. A., Ling, S., & Carrasco, M. 572
Philbeck, J. W., & Witt, J. K. 44
Phillips, F., Natter, M. B., & Egan, E. J. 147
Phillips, J. K., Klein, G., & Sieck, W. R. 499
Phillips, M. R., McAuliff, B. D., Kovera, M. B., & Cutler, B. L. 77
Phillips, P. J., & O'Toole, A. J. 74
Phillips, P. J., Yates, A. N., Hu, Y., Hahn, C. A., Noyes, E., Jackson, K., Cavazos, J. G., Jeckeln, G., Ranjan, R. et al. 74, 77
Pijlaarsdam, G., Van den Bergh, H., & Couzijn, M. 371
Pilemer, D. B. 243–4
Pilley, J. W. 400
Pillutla, M. M., & Murningham, J. K. 505
Pinker, S. 377, 378, 382, 405
Pisoni, D. B., Kronenberger, W. G., Harris, M. S., & Moberly, A. C. 54
Pitchert, D., & Katsikopoulos, K. V. 489
Pizlo, Z. 39
Pizlo, Z., and Zheng, L. 436
Plaisier, M. A., Tiest, W. M. B., & Kappers, A. M. L. 67
Planton, S., Jucla, M., Roux, F.-E.,& Démonet, J.-F. 371
Plato 6
Platt, J. R. 543
Plaut, D. C., McClelland, J. L., Seidenberg, M. S., & Patterson, K. 416
Plazzi, G., Vetrugno, R., Provini, F., & Montagna, P. 154
Plihal, W., & Born, J. 276
Plummer, C., Kleinitz, A., Vroomen, P., & Watts, R. 312, 320
Pobric, G., Jefferies, E., & Lambon Ralph, M. A. 312
Pockett, S., & Miller, A. 170
Poincaré, Henri 453, 455, 456–7
Poizner, H., Bellugi, U., & Iragui, V. 365
Poldrack, R. A. 28–9
Police and Criminal Evidence Act (UK, 1984) 76
Politis, I., Brewster, S., & Pollick, F. 61
Pollack, L., and Pickett, J. M. 380
Pollatos, O., Herbert, B. M., Matthias, E., & Schandry, R. 107
Pollick, F. E., & Sapiro, G. 102
Pollick, F. E., Kay, J. W., Heim, K., & Stringer, R. 78
Pollick, F. E., Paterson, H. M., Bruderlin, A., & Sanford, A. J. 78
Pomerantz, J. R., & Kubovy, M. 41, 64
Pomerleau, D. A. 17
Ponsot, E., Burred, J. J., Belin, P., & Aucouturier, J. J. 78
Popper, Karl 534, 539, 541, 543
Porter, S., & ten Brinke, L. 557
Posner, M. I. 126
Posner, M. I., & Cohen, Y. 132
Posner, M. I., & Keele, S. W. 300
Posner, M. I., & Petersen, S. E. 119
Postman, L., Stark, K., & Henschel, D. M. 270
Potter, M. C., & Levy, E. I. 69
Pouw, W., Harrison, S. J., & Dixon, J. A. 108
Power, M., & Dalgleish, T. 555, 558
Power, R. A., Steinberg, S., Bjornsdottir, G., Reitveld, C. A., Abdellaoui, A., Nivard, M. M., Johannesson, M. et al. 461–2
Powerhouse Museum in Sydney 117
Prasad, S., Loula, F., & Shiffrar, M. 102
Pratt, J., & Abrams, R. A. 142
The Principles of Psychology (James, W.) 101, 116, 178, 559
Prinz, J. 101, 555
Procter & Gamble 436–8
Proffitt, D. R. 44
Proverbio, A. M., Raso, G., & Zani, A. 390
Provini, F., Tinuper, P., Bisulli, F., & Lugaresi, E. 154
The Psychopathology of Everyday Life (Freud, S.) 346
Pugh, K., & Verhoeven, L. 410
Pulvermuller, F. 309
Putnam, Hilary 307
Pylyshyn, Z. W. 307, 317–18, 319

Q

Qin, L., Li, Z. R., Chen, Z., Bill, M. A., & Noyce, D. A. 146
Qiu, J., Luo, Y., Wang, Q., Zhang, F., & Zhang, Q. 412
Quesque, F., & Brass, M. 111

R

Racine, E., Nguyen, V., Saigle, V., & Dubljevic, V. 170
Racsmány, M., Demeter, G., Csigó, K., Harsányi, A., & Németh, A. 240
Radek, L., Kallionpää, R. E., Karvonen, M., Scheinin, A., Maksimow, A., Långsjö, J. et al. 156
Radvansky, G. 210
Raibert, M. H. 85
Raichle, M. E., & Snyder, A. Z. 31
Rainville, P., Bechara, A., Naqvi, N. H., & Damasio, A. R. 560
Ramachandran, V. S., & Hirstein, W. 57
Ramachandran, V. S., and Hubbard, E. M. 333
Ramachandran, V. S., Chunharas, C., & Marcus, Z. 58
Ramon, M., Bobak, A. K., & White, D. 77
Rand, D. G., Peysakhovitch, A., Kraft-Todd, G. T., Newman, G. E., Wurzbacher, O., Nowak, M., & Greene, J. D. 506
Rao, R. P., & Ballard, D. H. 41
Rao, R. P. N., Zelinsky, G. J., Hayhoe, M. M., & Ballard, D. H. 70
Rapp, B., & Goldrick, M. 347
Räsänen, O., Doyle, G., & Frank, M. C. 380, 382
Raschle, N. M., Chang, M., & Gaab, N. 408
Rasmussen, A. S., & Berntsen, D. 244
Rasmussen, A. S., Ramsgaard, S. B., & Berntsen, D. 244
Rasmussen, T., and Milner, B. 360
Ratcliff, R., & McKoon, G. 228
Ratneshwar, S., Barsalou, L. W., Pechmann, C., & Moore, M. 302–3
Rauschecker, J. P. 330
Rauss, K., & Pourtois, G. 41
Ray, S. B., Mishra, M. V., & Srinivasan, N. 137
Raymond, J. E., Shapiro, K. L., & Arnell, K. M. 133–4
Rayner, K. 412
Rayner, K., & Clifton, C. Jr. 410
Rayner, K., & Duffy, S. A. 413
Rayner, K., & McConkie, G. W. 413
Rayner, K., Pollatsek, A., & Reichle, E. D. 396
Rayner, K., Schotter, E. R., Masson, M. E., Potter, M. C., & Treiman, R. 404–5
Rea, C. P., & Modigliani, B. 267
Read, D., Olivola, C. Y., & Hardisty, D. J. 474
Reardon, S. 167
Reason, J. 59, 98, 346
Rebenitsch, L., & Owen, C. 59
Recanzone, G. H. 58
Reed, C. L., Grubb, J. D., & Steele, C. 142
Reed, S. K. 300, 303
Reed, S. K., & Friedman, M. P. 300
Reggev, N., Zuckerman, M., & Maril, A. 250
Reicher, G. M. 410
Reilly, R. G. 417
Reingold, E. M., & Merikle, P. M. 158
Reinmann, R. 541
Reisenzein, R. 564
Reitman, W. R. 450
Renoult, L., Davidson, P. S. R., Palombo, D. J., Moscovitch, M., & Levine, B. 254
Rensink, R. A. 143, 167
Rensink, R. A., O'Regan, J. K., & Clark, J. J. 143, 167
Rescorla, M. 429
Reubold, U., & Harrington, J. 377
Reverberi, C., Toraldo, A., D'Agostino, S., & Skrap, M. 442
Reynolds, J. H., & Desimone, R. 138
Reynolds, J. H., and Heeger, D. J. 138–9
Ribot, T. R. 276

Richards, B. A., Lillicrap, T. P., Beaudoin, P., Bengio, Y., Bogacz, R., Christensen, A., Clopath, C., Costa, R. P. et al. 67
Richardson, J. T. E., & Baddeley, A. D. 202
Richlan, F. 408
Richmond, L. L., & Zacks, J. M. 72
Richmond, L. L., Gold, D. A., & Zacks, J. M. 72
Rindal, E. J., DeFranco, R. M., Rich, P. R., & Zaragoza, M. S. 280
Riordan, M. A. 414
Rips, L. J. 304
Rips, L. J., & Collins, A. 302, 304
Ritov, L., & Baron, J. 494
Rizzolatti, G., & Sinigaglia, C. 103, 104
Rizzolatti, G., Fadiga, L., Fogassi, L., & Gallese, V. 103
Rizzolatti, G., Fogassi, L., & Gallese, V. 103
Rizzolatti, G., Riggio, L., & Sheliga, B. M. 142
Rizzolatti, G., Riggio, L., Dascola, I., & Umiltá, C. 142
Roberson, D., Davidoff, J., & Braisby, N. 304
Robertson, D. J., & Bindemann, M. 77
Robertson, D. J., Noyes, E., Dowsett, A. J., Jenkins, R., & Burton, A. M. 77
Robinaugh, D. J., & McNally, R. J. 243
Robinson, Z., Maley, C. J., & Piccinini, G. 157
Robson, J. G. 138
Robus, C. M., Hand, C. J., Filik, R., & Pitchford, M. 413–15
Roediger, H. L., & Guynn, M. J. 266
Roediger, H. L., and Karpicke, J. D. 289
Roediger, H. L., Bergman, E. T., & Meade, M. L. 236
Roediger, H. L., Marsh, E. J., & Lee, S. C. 226
Roediger, H. L., Weldon, M. S., & Challis, B. H. 230
Roediger III, H. L., & Pyc, M. A. 289
Roediger III, H. L., Putnam, A. L., & Smith, M. A. 288
Roediger III, H. L., Zaromb, F. M., & Lin, W. 179
Roesch, M. R., & Olson, C. R. 504
Rogers, T. T., Lambon Ralph, M. A., Garrard, P., Bozeat, S., McClelland, J. L., Hodges, J. R., & Patterson, K. 312
Roland, P. E., and Friberg, L. 319
Rolls, E. T. 563
Roman representation system 43
Rosch, E. 63, 299, 303, 479
Rosch, E., & Mervis, C. B. 299, 303
Rosch, E., Mervis, C. B., Gray, W. D., Johnson, D. M., & Boyes-Braem, P. 299, 300–301
Roseman, I. J., and Smith C. 567
Rosenbaum, D. A. 14, 93
Rosenbaum, D. A., & Feghhi, I. 93
Rosenbaum, D. A., Meulenbroek, R. J., Vaughan, J., & Jansen, C. 93
Rosenblum, L. D., Gordon, M. S., & Jarquin, L. 71
Rosenthal, D. M. 172–3
Roskies, A. L. 169
Ross, B. H., & Landauer, T. K. 267
Ross, J., and Lawrence, K. A. 264
Ross, T. P., O'Connor, S., Holmes, G., Fuller, B., & Henrich, M. 362
Roth, A. E. 109
Roth, W. M. 505
Rothen, N., Meier, B.,& Ward, J. 183
Rothen, N., Seth, A. K., & Ward, J. 183
Rouault, M., & Koechlin, E. 98
Rounis, E., Maniscalco, B., Rothwell, J. C., Passingham, R. E., & Lau, H. 173
Rouw, R., & Scholte, H. S. 58
Rowe, J. B., Owen, A. M., Johnsrude, I. S., & Passingham, R. E. 435
Royal College of Physicians 30
Rubenstein, L. M., Freed, R. D., Shapero, B. G., Fauber, R. L., & Alloy, L. B. 577
Rubin, D. C., & Wenzel, A. E. 269

Ruggeri, K., Alí, S., Berge, M. L., Bertoldo, G., Bjørndal, L. D., Cortijos-Bernabeu, A., Davison, C., Demic', E. et al. 476
Ruiz Garate, V., Parri, A., Yan, T., Munih, M., Molino Lova, R., Vitiello, N., & Ronsse, R. 86
Rumain, B., Connell, J., & Braine, M. D. 513
Rumelhart, D. E., & McClelland, J. L. 15–16, 95
Rumelhart, D. E., & Norman, D. A. 89
Rumsfeld, Donald 250
Runco, M. A., & Jaeger, G. J. 452
Rung, J. M., Peck, S., Hinnenkamp, J. E., Preston, E., & Madden, G. J. 474
Russell, A., Penny, L., & Pemberton, C. 377
Russell, J. A. 551, 555, 558
Russell, R., Duchaine, B., & Nakayama, K. 74, 77
Rylander, G. 207
Ryle, G. 226–7
Rymer, R. 326

S

Saberi, K., and Perrott, D. R. 388
Sack, A. T., & Schuhmann, T. 205
Sacks, O. W. 49, 224, 229
Sadler-Smith, E. 454
Saffran, E. M., & Marin, O. S. M. 191
Sahraie, A., Trevethan, C. T., MacLeod, M. J., Murray, A. D., Olson, J. A., & Weiskrantz, L. 161
Sakreida, K., Higuchi, S., DiDio, C., Ziessler, M., Turgeon, M., Roberts, N., & Vogt, S. 104
Sala, G., and Gobet, F. 451
Salame, P., & Baddeley, A. D. 200
Salthouse, T. A. 196
Salvi, C., Beeman, M., Bikson, M., McKinley, R., & Grafman, J. 441
Sampietro, A. 414
Samson, D., & Pillon, A. 306
Samuel, A. G. 388
Samuel, A. G., & Kat, D. 132
Samuelson, W., and Zeckhauser, R. 472
Sanders, R. D., Gaskell, A., Raz, A., Winders, J., Stevanovic, A., Rossaint, R., Boncyk, C., Defresne, A. et al. 156
Sanders, R. D., Tononi, G., Laureys, S., & Sleigh, J. W. 156
Sanfey, A. G., Rilling, J. K., Aronson, J. A., Nystrom, L. E., & Cohen, J. D. 505
Sanford, P., Lawson, A. L., King, A. N., & Major, M. 170
Santhouse, A. M., Howard, R. J., & Fffytche, D. H. 312, 320
Sarkamo, T., Tervaniemi, M., Soinila, S., Autti, T., Silvennoinen, H. M., Laine, M. et al. 53
Sarva, H., Deik, A., & Severt, W. L. 111
Satel, J., Wilson, N. R., & Klein, R. M. 132
Satin, G. E., & Fisher, R. P. 288
Sato, M. 361
Saunders, J., & MacLeod, M. D. 281
Savage-Rumbaugh, S., Shanker, S. G., & Talbot, J. 400
Scarborough, D. L., Cortese, C., & Scarborough, H. S. 397
Scepkowski, L. A., & Cronin-Golomb, A. 111
Schaal, S., Mohajerian, P., & Ijspeert, A. 88
Schachter, S., and Singer, J. E. 560, 564–5
Schacter, D. L. 227, 254
Schacter, D. L., & Addis, D. R. 239
Schacter, D. L., Wagner, A. D., & Buckner, R. L. 226
Schaeken, W., Vandierendonck, A., Schroyens, W., d'Ydewalle, G., & Klauer, K. C. 515
Schenkman, B. N., & Nilsson, M. E. 71
Scherer, K. R. 550–51, 560, 568
Schiavenato, M., Byers, J. F., Scovanner, P., McMahon, J. M., Xia, Y., Lu, N., & He, H. 556
Schilling, M. A. 311

Schirmer-Mokwa, K. L., Fard, P. R., Zamorano, A. M., Finkel, S., Birbaumer, N., & Kleber, B. A. 107
Schlickum, M. K., Hedman, L., Enochsson, L., Kjellin, A., & Fellander-Tsai, L. 127
Schlittmeier, S. J., and Hellbrück, J. 201
Schlittmeier, S. J., Feil, A., Liebl, A., & Hellbrück, J. R. 201
Schlottmann, A., Ray, E. D., Mitchell, A., & Demetriou, N. 72
Schmader, T. 216
Schmidt, R. C., Carello, C., & Turvey, M. T. 87
Schmitz, T. W., De Rosa, E., & Anderson, A. K. 572
Schmolck, H., Buffalo, E. A., & Squire, L. R. 574
Schneider, S. 157
Schneider, W., & Shiffrin, R. M. 206
Schnyder, U., Ehlers, A., Elbert, T., Foa, E. B., Gersons, B. P., Resick, P. A., Sahpiro, F., & Cloitre, M. 245
Scholl, B. J., & Tremoulet, P. D. 72
Schorr, A. 566
Schraagen, J. M. 499
Schroyens, W. 513
Schultz, J., & Bülthoff, H. H. 72
Schulze, C., & Newell, B. R. 476
Schurger, A., Sitt, J. D., & Dehaene, S. 170
Schwabe, L., Nader, K., & Pruessner, J. C. 280
Schwartz, B. 98
Schwartz, B., Ward, A., Montessero, J., Lyubomirsky, S., White, K., & Lehman, D. R. 98
Schwartz, M. F. 486–7
Schwarz, N. 580
Sciutti, A., & Sandini, G. 38, 72
Scoboria, A., Boucher, C., & Mazzoni, G. 247–8
Scoboria, A., Jackson, D. L., Talarico, J., Hanczakowski, M., Wysman, L., & Mazzoni, G. 247
Scott, S., Clegg, F., Rudge, P., & Burgess, P. 381
Scott, S. H. 88
Scoville, W. B., & Milner, B. 220–22, 276, 278
Scoville, William Beecher 221
Searle, J. 170
Secret Service (US) 557
Sedikides, C. 577
Segner, Johann Andreas 180
Seidenberg, M. 413
Seidenberg, M. S., and McClelland, J. L. 416
Seifert, C. M., Meyer, D. E., Davidson, N., Patalano, A. L., & Yaniv, I. 455
Selfridge, O. G. 62
Seli, P., Kane, M. J., Smallwood, J., Schacter, D. L., Maillet, D., Schooler, J. W., & Smilek, D. 210
Sells, S. B., & Koob, H. F. 520
Senft, E., Lemaignan, S., Baxter, P. E., Bartlett, M., & Belpaeme, T. 38, 72
Service, E. 202
Seyfarth, R. M., Cheney, D. L., & Marler, P. 334–5
Seymour, P. H. K., Aro, M., & Erskine, J. M. 406
Shadmehr, R., & Krakauer, J. W. 92
Shaffer, D. M., McManama, E., Swank, C., & Durgin, F. H. 44
Shah, P., and Miyake, A. 207
Shah, P., Hall, R., Catmur, C., & Bird, G. 107
Shallice, T. 191, 206, 435
Shallice, T., & Butterworth, B. 191
Shallice, T., & Warrington, E. K. 191
Shallice, T., and Burgess, P. W. 212
Shallice, T., and Papagno, C. 191
Shams, L., & Beierholm, U. R. 59
Shanks, D. R. 158
Shankweiler, D., and Studdert-Kennedy, M. 385
Shapiro, L. 44, 108
Share, D. 410
Shea, C. H., Kovacs, A. J., & Panzer, S. 105
Shebani, Z., & Pulvermuller, F. 310–11

Sheen, M., Kemp, S., & Rubin, D. C. 246–7
Shepard, R. N., & Metzler, J. 315–17
Sheppard, J. P., Raposo, D., & Churchland, A. K. 60
Shergill, S. S., Samson, G., Bays, P. M., Frith, C. D., & Wolpert, D. M. 92
Sheridan, T. B. 37
Shiell, M. M., Hausfeld, L., & Formisano, E. 71
Shimamura, A. P. 222
Shin, Y. K., Proctor, R. W., & Capaldi, E. J. 101
Shin, Y. S., Shin, N. Y., Jang, J. H., Shim, G., Park, H. Y., Shin, M. S., & Kwon, J. S. 362
Shipley, T. F. 58, 72
Shrout, P. E., & Rodgers, J. L. 544
Siciliano, B., & Khatib, O. 37
Siegel, Don 550
Siegel, E. F., and Stefanucci, J. K. 572–3
Silk, T. J., Bellgrove, M. A., Wrafter, P., Mattingley, J. B., & Cunnington, R. 140
Silver, D., Schrittwieser, J., Simonyan, K., Antonoglou, I., Huang, A., Guez, A., Hubert, T., Baker, L., Lai, M. et al. 16
Silver Blaze (Doyle, A.C.) 510
Silveri, M. C., Brita, A. C., Liperoti, R., Piludu, F., & Colosimo, C. 306
Simmons, W. K., and Barsalou, L. W. 308
Simner, J. 57
Simner, J., Mulvenna, C., Sagiv, N., Tsakanikos, E., Witherby, S. A., Fraser, C., Scott, K., & Ward, J. 182
Simon, A., Pham, L. B., Quang, A., & Holyoak, K. J. 530
Simon, H. A., and Chase, W. G. 448
Simon, Herbert A. 456, 484, 530
Simons, D. J., & Chabris, C. F. 145
Simons, Dan 144–5
Simonton, D. K. 453, 457
Simpson, O.J. 574
Sinha, P., Balas, B., Ostrovsky, Y., & Russell, R. 74
Sio, U. N., and Ormerod, T. 455
Sivak, M. 60
Skaggs, E. B. 279
Skinner, B.F. 12, 14
Slattery, T. J., Sturt, P., Christianson, K., Yoshida, M., & Ferreira, F. 403
Sleigh, J., Warnaby, C., & Tracey, I. 156
Slobin, D. I. 401
Sloman, S. A. 488
Slovic, P., Finucane, M., Peters, E., & MacGregor, D. G. 580
Smalley, N. S. 535
Smeets, J. B., van der Kooij, K., & Brenner, E. 93
Smith, C. A., & Lazarus, R. S. 567
Smith, D. T., & Schenk, T. 142
Smith, E. E., Langston, C. & Nisbett, R. 298
Smith, L., and Gilhooly, K. 492
Smith, S. M., & Vela, E. 266
Smith, S. M., Brown, H. O., Toman, J. E. P., & Goodman, L. S. 11
Smith, T. J., and Henderson, J. M. 145–6
Smith, Tim 145, 147
Smyth, M. M. 140
Smyth, M. M., & Pelky, P. L. 140
Snook, B., Dhami, M. K., & Kavanagh, J. 492
Sohlberg, M. M., & Mateer, C. A. 99
Sokol-Hessner, P., Hartley, C. A., Hamilton, J. R., & Phelps, E. A. 582
Solomon, K. O., and Barsalou, L. W. 308
Sony, Aibo from 37
Sotiropoulos, A., & Hanley, J. R. 409
Soto, D., Heinke, D., Humphreys, G. W., & Blanco, M. J. 140
Sousa, D. A. 407
Speisman, J. C., Lazarus, R. S., Mordkoff, A., & Davison, L. 567
Spencer, L., & Hanley, J. R. 406

Sperduti, M., Delaveau, P., Fossati, P., & Nadel, J. 111
Sperling, G. 180–82, 183, 184, 185, 186, 188
Sperry, R. W. 152, 161, 359
Spiers, H. J., Maguire, E. A., & Burgess, N. 227
Spitzer, H., Desimone, R., & Moran, J. 138
Spranca, M., Minsk, E., & Baron, J. 495
Spreng, R. N., Sepulcre, J., Turner, G. R., Stevens, W. D., & Schacter, D. L. 120
Spreng, R. N., Stevens, W. D., Chamberlain, J. P., Gilmore, A. W., & Schacter, D. L. 120
Springer, S. P., & Deutsch, G. 357, 363
Sprugnoli, G., Rossi, S., Emmendorfer, A., Rossi, A., Liew, S.-L., Tatti, E. et al. 441
Squire, L. R. 190, 220, 221, 228, 230, 231, 282
Squire, L. R., & Dede, A. J. 227
Squire, L. R., & Moore, R. Y. 224
Squire, L. R., & Slater, P. C. 224
Squire, L. R., and Zola, S. M. 229, 230
Squire, L. R., Clark, R. E., & Knowlton, B. J. 276
Squire, L. R., Stark, C. E. L., & Clark, R. E. 226
Stanovich, K. E. 510, 529
Stanovich, K. E., and West, R. F. 488
Staubli, U., Rogers, G., & Lynch, G. 179
Steblay, N. K. 77, 575
Steele, C. M., & Aronson, J. 216
Stein, M. B., Forde, D. R., Anderson, G., & Walker, J. R. 239
Stein, T., Utz, V., & Van Opstal, F. 158
Sternad, D., Dean, W., & Schaal, S. 93
Stevenage, S., & Bennett, A. 545
Stewart, L., von Kriegstein, K., Warren, J. D., & Griffiths, T. D. 53
Stigler, J. W., Lee, S. Y., & Stevenson, H. W. 200
Stivers, T., Enfield, N. J., Brown, P., Englert, C., Hayashi, M., Heinemann, T. et al. 341–2
Stock, A., & Stock, C. 101
Storms, G. 303
Storms, G., De Boeck, P., & Rus, W. 303
Strack, F., Martin, L., & Stepper, S. 561–2
Strayer, D. L., and Johnston, W. A. 196
Strick, M., Dijksterhuis, A., Bos, M. W., Sjoersma, A., Van Baaren, R. B., & Nordgren, L. F. 491
Stroop, J. R. 411–12
Studdert-Kennedy, M. 384
Suddendorf, T., & Corballis, M. C. 237
Sugase, Y., Yamane, S., Ueno, S., & Kawano, K. 40
Sunderland, A., Harris, J. E., & Baddeley, A. D. 254–6
Sunstein, C. R. 488
Sussman, E. S., Horváth, J., Winkler, I., & Orr, M. 71
Sutherland, S. 126
Suzuki, K., Mito, G., Kawamoto, H., Hasegawa, Y., & Sankai, Y. 86
Sweetser, E. E. 109
Swinnen, S. P. 87
Swinney, D. 398
Sydney Opera House 203
Syeda-Mahmood, T. 130
Symonds, C. 386

T

Taber, C. S., and Lodge, M. 528
Taft, M., & Hambly, G. 392
Talarico, J. M., & Rubin, D. C. 573
Tambovtsev, Y., and Martindale, C. 337
Tanaka, Y., Tiest, W. M. B., Kappers, A. M., & Sano, A. 67
Tang, R., & Braver, T. S. 155
Taplin, J. E. 513
Taraban, R., & McClelland, J. L. 403
Tarr, M.. J., & Bulthoff, H. H. 64, 66
Tatler, B. W., & Kuhn, G. 147

Name Index

Tatler, B. W., Wade, N. J., Kwan, H., Findlay, J. M., & Velichkovsky, B. M. 70
Taylor, D. W., Berry, P. C., & Block, C. H. 458
Technical Working Group for Eyewitness Evidence (US) 76
Tenerife, Los Rodeos airport on 399–400
Tentori, K., Crupi, V., & Russo, S. 481–2
Teuber, H. L. 190–91
Teubner-Rhodes, S. E., Mishler, A., Corbett, R., Andreu, L., Sanz-Torrent, M., Trueswell, J. C., & Novick, J. M. 403
Thagard, P. 429
Thaler, R. 472
Thaler, R. H., & Sunstein, C. R. 159, 488
Thaler, R. H., and Benartzi, S. 489
Thatcher, Margaret 573, 574
The Lord of the Rings (Tolkien, J.R.R.) 432
Thomas, J. C., Jr. 432–3
Thompson, C. P., Cowan, T. M., & Frieman, J. 265
Thompson, D., Mackenzie, I.G., Leuthold, H., & Filik, R. 414
Thompson, J. C., & Baccus, W. 80
Thompson, Jennifer 286
Thompson, K. G., Biscoe, K. L., & Sato, T. R. 142
Thompson, R. G., Moulin, C. J. A., Conway, M. A., & Jones, R. W. 248
Thomson, D. M., & Tulving, E. 266
Thomson, Judith 496–7
Thorndike, E. L., & Lorge, L. 396
Thorndike, Edward 11
Thorpe, S., Fize, D., & Marlot, C. 69
Thothathiri, M., and Snedeker, J. 397
Thurlow, C. 414
Tipper, S. P., Driver, J., & Weaver, B. 132
Tipper, S. P., Lortie, C., & Baylis, G. C. 142
Titchener, Edward 9
Tobia, K. P., Newman, G. E., & Knobe, J. 307
Tobler, P. N., Fiorillo, C. D., & Schultz, W. 504
Tolkien, J.R.R. 432
Tollestrup, P. A., Turtle, J. W., & Yuille, J. C. 286
Tolman, Edward C. 12–14
Tomkins, S. S. 561
Tononi, G. 166
Tononi, G., & Koch, C. 162
Tononi, G., Boly, M., Massimini, M., & Koch, C. 166, 167
Tooby, J., & Cosmides, L. 537
Torppa, R., & Huotilainen, M. 55
Torralba, A., Oliva, A., Castelhano, M. S., & Henderson, J. M. 70
Torralva, T., Laffaye, T., Báez, S., Gleichgerrcht, E., Bruno, D., Chade, A., Ibañez, A. et al. 362
Towse, J. N., and Hitch, G. J. 196
Transplant Dilemma 496–9
Travers, E., Khalighinejad, N., Schurger, A., & Haggard, P. 170
Treiman, R., Clifton, C., Jr., Meyer, A. S., & Wurm, L. H. 391
Treisman, A. M. 121, 131, 185
Treisman, A. M., & Schmidt, H. 128–9
Treisman, A. M., and Gelade, G. 128, 130
Tremblay, L., & Schulz, W. 504
Tremblay, P., & Dick, A. S. 370
Tremoliere, B., De Neys, W., & Bonnefon, J.-F. 499
Tremoulet, P. D., & Feldman, J. 72
Trevena, J., & Miller, J. 170
Triandis, H. 523
Trickey, S., and Topping, K. J. 532
Trojano, L., Crisci, C., Lanzillo, B., Elefante, R., & Caruso, G. 111
Troje, N. F. 78
Trolley Problem 496–9
Trommershauser, J., Landy, M. S., & Maloney, L. T. 92
Trueswell, J. C. 403

Trump, Donald 311
Tucker, M., and Ellis, R. 107–8
Tuckey, M., & Brewer, N. 235
Tuffiash, M., Roring, R. W., & Ericsson, K. A. 449
Tukey, D. D. 541
Tulving, E., Schacter, D. L., & Stark, H. A. 230
Tulving, Endel 226, 227, 228, 229, 232, 237, 249, 287
Turing, A. M. 17
Turvey, M. T. 87
Tversky, A. 110, 484
Tversky, A., & Kahneman, D. 471, 476–7, 478–81, 488, 493
Twomey, T., Price, C. J., Waters, D., & MacSweeney, M. 327

U

Ucros, C. G. 267
UK Postcodes 4–5
Ullman, S., Vidal-Naquet, M., & Sali, E. 66
Ultimatum Game 505–6
Uman, M. A. 182
Underwood, B. J. 270
Ungerleider, L. G., & Mishkin, M. 47
United Biscuits 297–8
Uno, Y., Kawato, M., & Suzuki, R. 88
Unsworth, N., and Robison, M. K. 194

V

Vaid, J., & Gupta, A. 405
Vaidya, C. J., Gabrieli, J. D. E., Keane, M. M., & Monti, L. A. 230
Valentine, T., & Maras, K. 390
Vallacich, J. S., Dennis, A. R., & Connolly, T. 459
Vallar, G. 191
Vallée-Tourangeau, F., and Krüsi Penney, A. 541
Van Gogh, Vincent 453
Van Kerkoerle, T., Self, M. & Roelfsema, P. 182
Van Meter, P., & Garner, J. 290
Van Petten, C., Coulson, S., Rubin, S., Plante, E., & Parks, M. 392
Van Rooij, T., Roederer, M., Wareham, T., Van Rooij, I., McLeod, H. L., & Marsh, S. 492
Van Rullen, R., & Thorpe, S. J. 69
Van Vugt, B., Dagnino, B., Vartak, D., Safaai, H., Panzeri, S., Dehaene, S., & Roelfsema, P. R. 166
Vangeneugden, J., Pollick, F., & Vogels, R. 80
Vanlancker, D. R., Kreiman, J., & Cummings, J. 53, 78
Vannucci, M., & Chiorri, C. 210
Varley, R. 329
Veale, R., Hafed, Z. M., & Yoshida, M. 70
Vecera, S. P., & Farah, M. J. 124
Veldre, A., Reichle, E. D., Wong, R., & Andrews, S. 413
Veling, H., & Van Knippenberg, A. 281
Velmans, M. 344
Vera, A. H., & Simon, H. A. 307
Verbaarschot, C., Farquhar, J., & Haselager, P. 170
Vernon, D., Hofsten, C. von, & Fadiga, L. 37
Vertes, R. P., & Eastman, K. E. 276
Vieten, C., Wahbeh, H., Cahn, B. R., MacLean, K., Estrada, M., Mills, P., Murphy, M., Shapiro, S., Radin, D. et al. 155
Vignando, M., Aiello, M., Rinaldi, A., Cattarruzza, T., Mazzon, G., Manganotti, P., Eleopra, R., & Rumiati, R. I. 307
Vincennes (USN) 499
Vinciarelli, A., Pantic, M., & Bourlard, H. 72
Vinding, M. C., Jensen, M., & Overgaard, M. 170
Vision (Marr, D.) 42
Vitevitch, M. S., Siew, C. S. Q., Castro, N., Goldstein, R., Gharst J. A., Kumar, J. J., & Boos, E. B. 348

Viviani, P., & Cenzato, M. 102
Viviani, P., & Stucchi, N. 102
Vlisides, P. E., Li, D., Zierau, M., Lapointe, A. P., Ip, K. I., McKinney, A. M., & Mashour, G. A. 156
Voelker, R. 70
Vogt, S. 105
Vogt, S., & Thomaschke, R. 102
Vogt, S., Buccino, G., Wohlschlager, A. M., Canessa, N., Shah, N. J. et al. 104–5
Vogt, S., Di Rienzo, F., Collet, C., Collins, A., & Guillot, A. 104
Von Bartheld, C. S., Bahney, J., & Herculano-Houzel, S. 19
Von Frisch, K. 336
Voss, M. J., Zukosky, M., & Wang, R. F. 210
Vossel, S., Geng, J. J., & Fink, G. R. 120
Vrecko, S. 27
Vrij, A., & Fisher, R. 344
Vul, E., Harris, C., Winklielan, P., & Pashler, H. 27

W

Wade, M. G., & Kazek, M. 100
Wagenmakers, E.-J., Beek, T., Dijkhoff, L., Gronau, Q. F., Acosta, A., Adams, R. B., Jr., Albohn, D. N., Allard, E. et al. 562
Wagenmakers, E. J., Wetzels, R., Borsboom, D., van der Maas, H. L., & Kievit, R. A. 544
Waite, S. A., Grigorian, A., Alexander, R. G., Macknik, S. L., Carrasco, M., Heeger, D., & Martinez-Conde, S. 129
Walen, A. 495
Wall, A., Borg, J., & Palmcrantz, S. 86
Wallas, G. 454–5
Wallentin, M. 360–61
Walther, J. B., & D'Addario, K. P. 414
Wammes, J. D., Meade, M. E., & Fernandes, M. A. 290–91
Wang, J., Nicol, T., Skoe, E., Sams, M., & Kraus, N. 573
Wang, S., Jiang, M., Duchesne, X. M., Laugeson, E. A., Kennedy, D. P., Adolphs, R., & Zhao, Q. 70
Ward, A. F., & Wegner, E. M. 165
Ward, G. 213
Ward, G., & Allport, A. 435
Ward, J. 20, 21, 57
Ward, J. E. 435
Ward, J., Thompson-Lake, D., Ely, R., & Kaminski, F. 183
Warren, D., Welch, R., & McCarthy, T. 58
Warren, R. M., and Obusek, C. J. 388
Warren, R. M., and Warren, R. P. 387
Warren Anatomical Museum 553
Warrington, E. K., and McCarthy, R. 306
Warrington, E. K., and Shallice, T. 191, 306–7
Warrington, E. K., Logue, V., & Pratt, R. T. 191
Was, C. A., & Woltz, D. J. 202
Waskan, J. 167
Wason, P. C. 532–5, 539
  reversed 20 questions task 540–42
Wason, P. C., & Evans, J. St. B. T. 536
Wason, P. C., & Shapiro, D. 535
Wason, P. C., and Johnson-Laird, P. N. 521, 535
Wassermann, E. 27
Watson, John B. 11–12
Watts, F. N., McKenna, F. P., Sharrock, R., & Trezise, L. 571
Waugh, N. C., & Norman, D. A. 187
Wearing, Clive 224
Weatherholtz, K., & Jaeger, T. F. 378
Weaver, C. A. III 285
Webb, C. E., & Dennis, N. A. 235
Weech, S., and Troje, N. F. 60
Wegner, D. M. 169
Wegner, D. M., & Wheatley, T. 169
Weiner, K. S., and Grill-Spector, K. 75

Name Index

Weingartner, H. J., Sirocco, K., Curran, V., & Wolkowitz, O. 277
Weisberg, R. W. 440, 442, 452, 461
Weisberg, R. W., & Alba, J. W. 444
Weiskrantz, L., Warrington, E. K., Sanders, M. D., & Marshall, J. 161
Weissmann, B., & Tanner, D. 414
Welch, G. B., & Burnett, C. T. 189
Welch, R. B., & Warren, D. H. 58
Welch, R. B., Duttonhurt, L. D., & Warren, D. H. 58
Wells, G. L., & Loftus, E. F. 252
Wells, G. L., and Turtle, J. W. 77
Wells, H.G. 297
Wen, W., & Haggard, P. 169
Wener, A. E., & Rehm, L. 579
Wenke, D., Fleming, S. M., & Haggard, P. 110
Wernicke, Carl 311–12, 358–9, 367–8, 386
Wertheimer, M. 426
Wetherick, N. E., and Gilhooly, K. J. 526
Whaley, C. P. 396
Wheaton, L. A., & Hallett, M. 99
Wheeler, D. D. 410
Whelan, C. W., Wagstaff, G. F., & Wheatcroft, J. M. 345
Whitaker, H. 380
White, A. 277
Whorf, B. L. 388, 398
Wick, F. A., Alaoui Soce, A., Garg, S., Grace, R. C., & Wolfe, J. M. 72
Wickelgren, W. A. 93, 433
Wickens, C. D. 124–5
Wierda, S. M., Van Rijn, H., Taatgen, N. A., & Martens, S. 135
Wierzbicka, A. 558
Wilkins, A. J., and Baddeley, A. D. 239
Wilkins, M. 519, 521
Williams, H. L., Conway, M. A., & Cohen, G. 241
Williams, J. J., & Lombrozo, T. 289, 305
Williams, J. J., Lombrozo, T., & Rehder, B. 305
Williford, T., & Maunsell, J. H. 138
Willingham, D. 267
Wills, J. A., Hackel, L., Feldmanhall, O., Parnamets, P., & Van Bavel, J. J. 506
Wilson, A. D., & Golonka, S. 43
Wilson, B. S. 44, 54
Wilson, S. H., Greer, J. F., & Johnson, R. M. 459
Winawer, J., Huk, A. C., & Boroditsky, L. 318
Winkler, R. 181
Winograd, E. 237
Winograd, E., & Killinger, W. A. 573
Wirth, M., Rahman, R. A., Kuenecke, J., Koenig, T., Horn, H., Sommer, W., & Dierks, T. 364
Wit, J. K., Kemmerer, D., Linkenauger, L., & Culham, J. 308
Wittgenstein, Ludwig 299
Wixted, J. T. 272, 275
Wixted, J. T., & Wells, G. L. 286
Woike, J. K., Hoffrage, U., & Martignon, L. 492
Wolfe, J. M. 130
Wolfe, J. M., Horowitz, T. S., & Kenner, N. M. 132
Wolfe, J. M., Võ, M. L. H., Evans, K. K., & Greene, M. R. 130, 131
Wolpert, D. M., & Ghahramani, Z. 88
Wolpert, D. M., & Kawato, M. 88
Wolpert, D. M., Shergill, S. S., Bays, P. M., & Frith, C. D. 90–92
Wolpert, Daniel 90–92
Woodman, G. F., & Vogel, E. K. 124
Woods, A. J., Philbeck, J. W., & Danoff, J. V. 44
Woods, A. T., & Newell, F. N. 67
Woodworth, R. S. 84, 88
Woodworth, R. S., and Sells, S. 520
World Trade Center, September 11 attacks on 284, 285
Worthington, A. 99
Wright, B., and Garrett, M. 397
Wright, D. B. 382, 573
Wright, D. B., Gaskell, G. D., & O'Muircheartaigh, C. A. 573
Wright, S. 483
Wundt, Wilhelm 8–9, 260
Wurtz, R. H. 49

Y

Yan, S., Walters, L. M., Wang, Z., & Wang, C. C. 532
Yang, T. X., Peng, Z. W., Wang, Y., Geng, F. L., Miao, G. D., Shum, D. H., Cheung, E. F., & Chan, R. C. 240
Yarbus, A. L. 70
Yaroush, R., Sullivan, M. J., & Ekstrand, B. R. 275
Yeung, P., Ho, C. S., Chan, D. W., &Chung, K. K. 371
Yiend, J. 571, 572
Young, A., & Ellis, H. D. 73
Young, A. W., & Burton, A. M. 77
Young, A. W., & Noyes, E. 77
YouTube 24

Z

Zacks, J. M., & Tversky, B. 72
Zacks, J. M., Speer, N. K., Swallow, K. M., Braver, T. S., & Reynolds, J. R. 72
Zajac, R., Westera, N., & Kaladelfos, A. 390
Zajonc, Robert B. 565–6, 568
Zakey, D. 485
Zambaldi, C. F., Cantilino, A., Farias, J. A., Moraes, G. P., & Botelho Sougey, E. 171
Zatorre, R. J., Halpern, A. R., Perry, D. W., Meyer, E., & Evans, A. C. 319
Zeki, S. 49
Zeman, A. 152
Zerilli-Zavgorodni, T., & Bisighini, S. 312, 320
Zhang, L. L., Wang, J. Q., Qi, R. R., Pan, L. L., Li, M., & Cai, Y. L. 59
Zhao, B., Gherri, E., & Della Sala, S. 317
Zihl, J., & Heywood, C. A. 49
Zito, G. A., Wiest, R., & Aybek, S. 171
Zola, D. 410
Zwicker, J. G., Missiuna, C., Harris, S. R., & Boyd, L. A. 100

Subject Index

A

Abductive reasoning 542
Access consciousness 155–6
Acquired dyslexia 416
Action disorganization syndrome, cognitive rehabilitation for 99–100
Action observation
  mirror mechanisms and 103–5
    evaluation of 105
Action planning, brain structure for 98
Action production
  brain damage and 97–100
  hierarchical models of 94–7
Action representation
  common codes for action perception and production 101–3
  evaluation of 101–3
  historical perspectives 100–101
  perception and 100–111
  theories of 100–105
Action sequences 93–5
  hierarchical representation of an action sequence 95
Action slips 237
Adaptive toolbox 491–9
Adversary problems 425
Affect 551
  influence of cognition of 570–82
Affect heuristic 580
Affect infusion model (AIM) 577
Affective-primacy 565–6
Afterimage 144
Agency
  attention and 118
  motor cognition and 110–11
  volition, consciousness and 168–70
Agrammatism 401–2
Agraphia 364
Alexia 364
Algorithms 432
Alien hand syndrome 111
Allophones 337
Alpha Go Zero program 16–17
Alphabetic scripts 405
Ambidextrous individuals 360
Ambient intelligence 99–100
Ambiguity of images 318–19
Amnesia 190
  memory and 220, 223–5
  when things go wrong 278–9
Amnesic syndrome
  long-term memory and 223
  sensory, short-term and working memory and 190
Amodal representations 308
  grounded representations vs 307–09
    evaluation of 307–09
Amygdala
  cognitive psychology 18, 19
  emotion and cognition 551–2
Anarthria 364
Anderson's ACT-R model 15
Anomia 403–4
Anomic aphasia 368–9
Anterograde amnesia 223
Aphasia
  evidence from 364–70
  individual differences in 369–70
  language production and 343, 364

sensory, short-term and working memory and 191
Appraisal 559
Appraisal theory 567
Apraxia
  cognitive rehabilitation for action disorganization syndrome and 99–100
  language production and 364
  motor cognition and 98–9
Areas of interest (AoIs) 414–15
Arenate fasciculus 358, 368
Articulated Head project 117–18
Artificial intelligence (AI) 15
Aspirated consonants 336–7
Associationism 8
Associative chain theory 93
Attention 115–49
  affect and 571–2
  afterimage 144
  agency 118
  Articulated Head project 117–18
  attention system of human brain 119–20
  attentional biases 571
  attentional blink 133–7
    emotion perception, use in examination of 134–7
  attentional mechanisms
    in controlling actions 142
    in perception and working memory 137–41
  attentional resources, interactions of 125
  binding problem 129
  bottom-up processing 120
  brain, attention system of 119–20
  brainstem 119
  central processing unit (CPU) 122
  change blindness 143
  cocktail party problem 121
  concentration and 116
  consciousness and 116, 167–8
  continuity editing 145–6
  controlling actions, attentional mechanisms in 142
  default mode network (DFM) 120
  discussion questions 149
  distributed attention 131–2
  dual-task paradigm 124
  early selection 121
  executive system 120
  external attention 118–19
  failures of 143–8
  feature integration theory (FIT) 128, 130
  feedforward 137–8
  filter theory of 121–2, 126
  focalization and 116
  frontal eye fields (FEFs) 120, 142
  further reading 149
  guided search, schematic of 131
  heuristics 129
  inattentional blindness 143–4
  inferior frontal gyrus (IFG) 120
  inhibition of return 132–3
  internal attention 118–19
  James' *Principles of Psychology* on 116
  late selection 121
  load theory 122
  middle frontal gyrus (MFG) 120
  neural mechanism of attention in primary visual cortex 137–9
  Normalization Model of 138–9
  objects, attachment to 123–4

orienting system 119–20
perception, attentional mechanisms in 137–41
perceptual learning 130
practical applications
  movies, attention and continuity editing in 145–6
  robot attention 116–18
  video game play in enhancing cognition and attention 127
preattentive visual processes 128
preview questions 115
primary visual cortex, neural mechanism of attention in 137–9
receptive field 138
recurrent processing 138
research close ups
  dual task, use in examination of attention and working memory 140–41
  emotion perception, use of attention blink for examination of 134–7
resource theory of 122–6
review questions 149
saliency maps 132–3
spatial information, maintenance of 140
spotlight of 122–3, 124
summary 148
taxonomy of 118–19
theories of 120–26
  evaluation of 126
top-down processing 120
ventral attention network (VAN) 120
visual attention 128–37
visual search 128–32
  evaluation of 132
when things go wrong
  magic, attention, misdirection and 146–8
  medical images, errors in interpretation of 129–30
working memory, attentional mechanisms in 137–41
zoom model of 123
Attentional Schema Theory (AST) 168
Auditory system 51–5
  damage to, effects of 53
  primary auditory cortex, pathways into 52
  secondary auditory cortex 53
Autobiographical memory 241–9
  reasons for choice to withdraw 247–8
Autonoetic ('self-knowing') consciousness 232
Autonoetic ('self-knowing') memories 241
Autonomic nervous system (ANS) 559
  emotions and 559–60
Availability heuristic 478–9
Axioms 166

B

Background noise, understanding effects of 201
Backwards propagation 16
'Bad things come to those who do not wait ..' 474–5
Barriers to insight 428–9
Basal ganglia 92
Base rates, decision making and 482–3
Basilar membrane 51–3
Bayesian Decision Theory 41
Behaviourism 11–14
Binding problem 129
Binocular rivalry 162, 163
Biological motion, social perception of 78–80
  evaluation of 80

Subject Index

Blind variation and selective retention model of information processing 456–7
Blindsight 161–2
Body and perception 43–4
Bottom-up processing
    attention 120
    language comprehension 391
Bound morphemes 338
Bower's associative network theory 575–6
Brain
    attention system of 119–20
    brain areas involved in long-term memory 225
    brain basics 18–20
    brain imaging 25–31
    brain stem 19
    brainstem 119
    concepts in the, hub-and-spoke model 311–12
    consciousness and 160–73
    cortex, point stimulation map of 24
    language comprehension and 403–4
    stimulation methods 23–5
    stocking of, Sherlock Holmes on 260
    structures involved in emotion 552
    surgery on, memory impairment following 220–23
Brain damage
    action production and 97–100
    decision making and 582–3
    sources of 21
Brain networks, consciousness and 163–5
Brainstorming 458–61
    evaluation of 460–61
Breadth first search 431–2
Broca's aphasia 401–2, 403
    language production and 365–7
Broca's area 19, 20–21
    language production and 358, 365
Brodmann areas 55

C

Cakes vs biscuits, distinction between 397–8
Canon-Bard theory 562–3
    evaluation of 563
Capgras delusion 550
Capgras syndrome 73
Cases
    case against consciousness 157
    'E.V.R.', case of 211–12
    'H.M.', case of 220–23
Categorical perception 383–5
Categorical syllogisms 518–19
Category exemplar tasks 230
Category-specific deficits and pathologies 306–7
Causal Bayesian inference 59
Causality 59
Central executive network 31
Central nervous system (CNS) 559
Central processing unit (CPU) 122
Central suicus 55
Cerebellum 18, 19
    motor cognition and 92
Change blindness
    attention and 143
    consciousness and 167
    sensory, short-term and working memory and 187
Charles Bonnet syndrome 319–20
Choking 97
Chunking 188
Clauses in language production 344, 351
Closed-class words 396
Co-articulation
    language comprehension and 378–9
    language production and 337

motor cognition and 94
Cochlear implants 54–5
Cocktail party problem 121
Cognition, language and 328–9
Cognitive interview 287–8
Cognitive lockup 192
    working memory, attention and human error 192–4
Cognitive maps 12–14
Cognitive neuropsychology 20–23
Cognitive neuroscience 18–31
Cognitive-primacy 567–8
Cognitive psychology 3–32
    Alpha Go Zero program 16–17
    amygdala 18, 19
    Anderson's ACT-R model 15
    artificial intelligence 15
    associationism 8
    backwards propagation 16
    behaviourism 11–14
    brain basics 18–20
    brain damage, sources of 21
    brain imaging 25–31
    brain stem 19
    brain stimulation methods 23–5
    Broca's area 19, 20–21
    central executive network 31
    cerebellum 18, 19
    cognitive neuropsychology 20–23
    cognitive neuroscience 18–31
    cognitive psychology 4–5
    computerized axial tomography (CAT) scans 25
    connectionism 15–16, 17
    connectionist network 16
    Copernican Heliocentric Theory 6
    corpus callosum 18
    cortex, point stimulation map of 24
    deep networks 16–17
    default mode network (DMN) 31
    Descriptive Experience Sampling (DES) 9
    discussion questions 32
    double dissociation 23
    electroencephalography (EEG) 25–6, 30
    empiricism 8
    event-related potentials (ERP) 25–6
    frontal lobe 19
    functional imaging 25
    functional integration, networks and 30–31
    functional level of analysis 17
    functional magnetic resonance imaging (fMRI) 26–8, 29, 30
    further reading 32
    glia 19
    Google Deep Mind Project 16
    hippocampus 13, 18, 19
    historical perspective 6–17
    hypothalamus 19
    imaging studies, cognitive processes and 28–9
    information processing
        cognitive revolution of 14–17
        information processing approach 14
    internal representations 15
    introspectionism 8–10
    isotropic fractionator method 20
    keyword method of memory training 7
    Law of Mass Action 23
    localized functions 21
    locations in brain, terms for 18
    magnetic resonance imaging (MRI) 25
    mental operations 15
    mental representations 4
    mnemonics 6
    modularity 22
    navigation, connectionist network for 17
    networks and functional integration 30–31

neurological homunculus 24
neurons 18–19
    schematic outline of a neuron 20
neuropsychology 20, 21
occipital lobe 19
parietal lobe 19
persistent vegetative states 29–30
phenomenology 8
phrenological map 22
phrenology 21–2
pituitary gland 19
point electrical stimulation 23–4
positron emission tomography (PET) 26
practical applications
    memory training 6–8
    UK postcode and cognitive psychology 4–5
preview questions 3
primary auditory cortex 19
primary motor cortex 19, 25
primary visual cortex 19
research close ups
    cognitive maps 12–14
    waking and dreaming thoughts, experience sampling of qualities of 10–11
review questions 32
salience network 31
as scientific endeavour, youthfulness of 5
Self-Observation 9
simulation 15
somatosensory cortex 19
spatial learning strategies 9
spinal cord 19
story mnemonic, memory training and 7
strategies 14–15
structural imaging 25
summary 31–2
temporal lobe 19
thalamus 19
transcranial direct current stimulation (tDCS) 23, 24, 27
transcranial magnetic stimulation (TMS) 23, 24, 27
Universal Law of Gravitation 6
water maze 13–14
Wernicke's area 19
when things go wrong
    neuroscientific methods to detect awareness in 'vegetative states' 29–30
    'vegetative states,' neuroscientific methods to detect awareness in 29–30
X-ray computed tomography 25
Cognitive robotics and human-robot interaction 37–8
Cognitive sandwich 100
Cohort model of speech perception 391–3
    evaluation of 393
Common coding 101–2
    interference problem for 102
Communication 330
    language and 330–43
Complex actions, production of 93–100
Compound Remote Associate (CRAT) items 441
Compulsions, prospective memory deficit and 239–40
Computational-Representational Understanding of Mind (CRUM) 429
Computational theory of perception 42
Computations, achievement of 43
Computer metaphor of memory 187
Computerized axial tomography (CAT) scans 25
Concentration and attention 116
Concepts and imagery 295–323
    ambiguity of images 318–19
    amodal representations 308

Subject Index

Concepts and imagery—*Cont.*
  grounded representations vs 307–09
    evaluation of 307–09
  brain, concepts in the, hub-and-spoke model 311–12
  concepts 296
  conceptual representation, theories of 296–312
  connected concepts, network models 311
  consciousness, complexity of 152
  definitional approach 297–8
  depictive representation theory 317–18
  discussion questions 323
  essentialism 305–7
  exemplar-based approaches 303–4
    evaluation of 304
  family resemblance 299–300
  further reading 323
  grounded representations vs amodal representations 307–09
    evaluation of 309
  grounded theory, simulation and 308–9
  hub-and-spoke model 311–12
  image scanning and comparing 314–18
  imagery 296
    concepts and 312–21
    critical views of research and theory on 317–18
    neuropsychology/neuroscience of 319–21
    processing of, evaluation of 321
    visuo-spatial processing and 313–14
  knowledge-based approaches 304–5
    evaluation of 305
  long-term knowledge, basis of 296
  network models 311
  practical application
    cakes vs biscuits 397–8
    goal-derived ad hoc categories, consumer goods and 302–3
  preview questions 295
  prototype approaches 299–302
    ad hoc categories 301
    basic level categories 301
    categories of prototypes, levels of 300–301
    evaluation of 301–2
    introduction to prototypes 299–300
  re-enactment 308
  research close ups
    mental rotation 315–17
    testing grounded theory of concepts using dual task methods in working memory for action words 310–11
  review questions 323
  semantic dementia 312
  simulation 308
  summary 321–2
  theory-based approaches 304–5
    evaluation of 305
  thought experiments 307
  transcranial magnetic stimulation (TMS) 312
  typicality 299
  when things go wrong
    category-specific deficits and pathologies 306–7
    spontaneous vivid imagery - Charles Bonnet syndrome 319–20
Conceptually-driven speech production 327
Conduction aphasia 368
Cones, perception and 46
Confabulation 359–60
Confirmation bias 543
Conjunction fallacy, explanations of 479–80, 481–2
Connected concepts, network models and 311
Connectionism 15–16, 17
Connectionist network 16
Conscious, cognition, affective primacy and 566
Consciousness 151–75

access consciousness 155–6
agency, volition and consciousness 168–70
attention, consciousness and 167–8
attention and 116
Attentional Schema Theory (AST) 168
axioms 166
binocular rivalry 162, 163
blindsight 161–2
brain and 160–73
case against 157
change blindness 167
concept of, complexity of 152
default mode network (DMN) 164
discussion questions 175
dorsolateral prefrontal cortex (DLPFC) 173
electroencephalography (EEG) 152, 169
feedforward processing 165
feeling-of-knowing 172
field studies 159
forward model 169
functions of 155–60
further reading 175
Global Neuronal Workspace (GNW) Hypothesis 165, 166–7
global workspace approaches 162–7
global workspace theory 155
higher-order theories of 173
I quantity 166
illusionism 157
implicit memory 156
inattentional blindness 167
Integrated Information Theory (IIT) 166–7
interoceptive signals 155
'Mary's Room' experiment 153
metacognition 172–3
neural correlates of consciousness (NCC) 162
neuropsychology 161–2
non-declarative memory 156
non-rapid eye movement (NREM) sleep 154
nudges 158
operational definition of 152
phenomenal consciousness 155–6
postulates 166
practical application, general anaesthesia, effects on consciousness of 156
preview questions 151
primes 158
psychophysics 158
qualia 153
rapid eye movement (REM) sleep 154
recurrent brain activity 165
Recurrent Processing Theory 165
reflexive connections 155
research close ups
  brain networks and consciousness 163–5
  supraliminal primes, promotion of healthy eating with 159–60
review questions 174
salience network 164
self-awareness and integration 155–6
spandrel 157
split-brain 161
subliminal perception 157
summary 174
supraliminal stimuli 158–9
transcranial magnetic stimulation (TMS) 173
unconscious processing 157–9
understanding consciousness, problem of 152–3
volition and 169–70
  evaluation of 169–70
when things go wrong
  law and sleepwalking 154
  out-of-body experience 171–2
  sleepwalking and the law 154
Consequentialism 493
Consolidation 278–9

Consonantal scripts 405
Conspecifics 385
  language production and 334
Constructed emotions, theory of 570
  evaluation of 570
Content words, language production and 326, 338
Context
  context effects on visual word recognition 410
  role in language comprehension 387–90
Continuity editing 145–6
Contralateral connections 385
Controlling actions, attentional mechanisms in 142
Copernican Heliocentric Theory 6
Core emotions 555–8
'Core' of emotions 558–60
Corpus, language production and 347–8
Corpus callosum 18
Cowan's embedded processes model 195–6
Creative Achievement Questionnaire (CAQ) 461–2
Creative problem solving 452–62
Creative processes, information processing theory of 456–7
Creative synthesis task 457
Creativity and psychopathology 461–2
Critical incident analysis 500
Cross-cultural variation in language related to emotion 558
Cross-language manifestation of dyslexia 407–10
Crossed aphasia 364
Cued recall 227
Cybersickness 59–60

D

Dance expertise, use in study of action representation 105–7
Decay 188
Deception, use of speech cues in detection of deception 344–5
Decision making 467–507
  adaptive toolbox 491–9
  affect and 579–82
  availability heuristic 478–9
  base rates 482–3
  conjunction fallacy, explanations of 479–80, 481–2
  consequentialism 493
  critical incident analysis 500
  decision making 468
  deliberation 473
  deontological approach 493
  descriptive approaches to 468
  Dictator Game 505–6
  discussion questions 507
  elimination by aspects (EBA) 484
  endowment effect 472
  expected value theory 469–71
  fast-and-frugal heuristics 491–9
  framing 476
  framing and prospect theory 476–7
  further reading 507
  hedonic calculus 493
  heuristics
    consequentialism and 493–9
    evaluation of 492–3
  heuristicsrecognition heuristic 491
  invariance 476
  'leaky' rationality 486–7
  lexicographic strategies 485
  loss aversion 471–2
  metacognition 473
  multi-attribute alternatives, decision processes for 483–7
  multi-attribute decision models, testing of 484–7
  multi-attribute decision problem 468–9

Subject Index

multi-attribute utility theory (MAUT) 483–4, 500–501
naturalistic choices? 487
naturalistic decision making 499–504
neuroeconomics 504
neuroscience approaches to 504–6
normative approaches to 468
omission bias 494–5
opportunity costs 474
practical applications
    financial abuse of elderly people, application of SJT to detection of 502–4
    resisting effective but coerced policies 496
    two-system theory and 'nudge' 488–9
preference reversal 473
preview questions 467
probabilistic functionalism 501
probability judgements 477–83
prospect theory 471, 472
prospection 473
psychological distance 497
punishment and 495
real-life choices 500–504
    evaluation of 502
real-world loss aversion 472
recognition heuristic 491
recognition primed decision making 500
representativeness heuristic 478, 479–80
    conjunction fallacy in 479–80
research close ups
    morals and language 498–9
    unconscious thought effect (UTE) on decisions 490–91
resistance to coerced reform 495–6
review questions 507
risk 468
risk aversion 470
risk seeking 471
risklessness 468
sacrifice dilemmas 496–9
satisficing 484
selective probability and prospect theory 475–7
single attribute alternatives 468–9
social heuristics perspective 506
Social Judgement Theory (SJT), real-life choices and 501–4
status quo bias 472
subjective probabilities 471
summary 506–7
temporal discounting and utility 472–4
two-system approaches to 487–91
    systems 1 and 2 488
Ultimatum Game 505
unconscious thought and 489–91
utilitarianism 493
    deontological rules vs 496–9
utility 471
    prospect theory and 471–4
    when things go wrong, 'bad things come to those who do not wait ..' 474–5
Declarative memory 232–56
    evaluation of 253–4
Deductive reasoning 511–30
Deductive tasks 511
Deep networks 16–17
Default mode network (DMN) 31, 120
    consciousness and 164
Default network 552
Definitional approach 297–8
Degrees of freedom 85
Deliberate practice 448–9
Deliberation 473
Demand characteristics 246
Deontic rules 539
Deontological approach to decision making 493
Depictive representation theory 317–18

Depression, cognitive behavioural therapy (CBT) for 577–9
Depth first search 431
Derivational morphemes 338
Descriptive approaches to decision making 468
Descriptive Experience Sampling (DES) 9
Detour problems 438
Developmental dyslexia 407–8
Dichotic listening 385
Dichotic listening tasks 363
Dictator Game 505–6
Digit span 188
Direct objects 338
Direct perception 42
Direct route 416
Discourse 341–3
    implicit rules of 342
Discussion questions
    attention 149
    cognitive psychology 32
    concepts and imagery 323
    consciousness 175
    decision making 507
    emotion and cognition 584
    language comprehension 419
    language production 372
    learning and forgetting 293
    long-term memory 257
    motor cognition 113
    perception 81
    problem solving 463
    reasoning 547
    sensory, short-term and working memory 217
Disfluency 343–4
Displacement 188
Display rules 555
Distributed attention 131–2
Dizygotic twins 407–8
Dorsal stream, perception and 46
Dorsolateral prefrontal cortex (DLPFC) 173
Double dissociation 23
    perception and 73
Double dissociation of function 190–92, 416–17
    evaluation of 192
Down syndrome 329
Drawing and learning terms (and their definitions) 290–91
Dual route model of reading 415–16
Dual task, use in examination of attention and working memory 140–41
Dual-task paradigm, attention and 124
Dynamical systems theory 87–8
Dyslexia
    cross-language manifestation of 407–10
    developmental dyslexia 407–8
    phonological dyslexia 417
    reasoning and 525–6

E

Ear, slips of the 382–3
Early selection, attention and 121
Echoic memory 184–6
    evaluation of 185–6
Ecological validity 284
Effective studying 288–90, 291
Eight- and fifteen-puzzle 436
Elaborative interrogation 289
Elaborative rehearsal 188
Electroencephalography (EEG) 25–6, 30
    consciousness and 152, 169
Electrophysiological data 417–18
Electrrocortical stimulation 358
Elimination by aspects (EBA) 484
Embodied cognition 107–10
Embodied view of cognition 43–4

embodied cognition, claims of 44
Emotion 550–60
    components of, Clore and Ortony's view 559
    facial expressions, psychopathic traits and recognition of emotion in 555–6
    perception of, use of attention blink for examination of 134–7
Emotion and cognition 549–84
    affect 551
        influence of cognition of 570–82
    affect heuristic 580
    affect infusion model (AIM) 577
    affective-primacy 565–6
    amygdala 551–2
    appraisal 559
    appraisal theory 567
    attention, affect and 571–2
    attentional biases 571
    autonomic nervous system (ANS) 559
        emotions and 559–60
    basic emotions, characteristics of 558
    Bower's associative network theory 575–6
    brain structures involved in emotion 552
    Canon-Bard theory 562–3
        evaluation of 563
    Capgras delusion 550
    central nervous system (CNS) 559
    cognitive-primacy 567–8
    components of emotion, Clore and Ortony's view 559
    conscious, cognition, affective primacy and 566
    constructed emotions, theory of 570
        evaluation of 570
    core emotions 555–8
    'core' of emotions 558–60
    cross-cultural variation in language related to emotion 558
    decision making, affect and 579–82
    default network 552
    discussion questions 584
    display rules 555
    early theories and influence 561–3
    emotion 550–60
    emotion-congruent memory, strength of 577
    emotional leakage 557
    emotional states, detection through physiological changes 560
    episodic memory, effects of emotions on 574–5
    facial feedback hypothesis 561
    flashbulb memories 573–4
    Frijda's list of basic emotions 557
    further reading 584
    incidental affect 579
    insula 551–2
    integral affect 579
    interoception 582–3
    James-Lange theory 561–2, 563
        evaluation of 562
    Lazarus's theory 567–8
        evaluation of 568
    limbic system 551–2
    memory, affect and 573–7
    mere exposure effect 565
    mood, effect of matching on recall of target words 576
    mood-congruent memory 575–7
    multi-level theories 568
    network models 575
    perception, affect and 572–3
    practical applications
        depression, cognitive behavioural therapy (CBT) for 577–9
        microexpressions, detection of deceit through 556–7
    research close ups

Subject Index

Emotion and cognition—*Cont.*
   graphic warning labels, influence on smokers 580–81
   regulation of emotions in daily life 568–9
  review questions 584
  salience network 552
  Schachter-Singer two factor theory 563, 564–5
   evaluation of 564–5
  skin conductance responses (SCRs) 550
   to emotionally arousing pictures 554
  state-dependent memory 575
  summary 583
  theories of emotion and cognition 560–70
  thought congruity 577
  tunnel memory 574–5
  two-factor theory 564–5
  visual search 572
  when things go wrong
   brain damage and decision making 582–3
   emotional processing after frontal lobe injury 552–4
   facial expressions, psychopathic traits and recognition of emotion in 555–6
   frontal lobe injury, emotional processing after 552–4
   psychopathic traits, facial expressions and 555–6
   somatic markers, interoception and 582–3
  Zajonc's theory 565–6
   evaluation of 566
Empiricism 8
Encoding 178
Endowment effect 472
Episodic memory 227, 232–7
  effects of emotions on 574–5
  semantic memory and, key differences between 228
Equilibrium point hypothesis 86–7
Essentialism 305–7
Event-related potential (ERP) 25–6
  language comprehension and 392, 417–18
  language production and 363
Everyday memory 283–91
  evaluation of 291
  measurement of 254–6
Executive system, attention and 120
Exemplar-based approaches 303–4
  evaluation of 304
Expected value theory 469–71
Expert problem solving 448–52
Expertise 448
  expertise acquisition 448–50
  expertise research, evaluation of 452
  nature of 450–52
Explicit memory 226
External attention 118–19
Extrastriate body area (EBA) 80
Eye movements 412–13
Eye tracking 396
Eyewitness testimony 285–7, 291

F

Faces, social perception of 74–7
Facial expressions, psychopathic traits and recognition of emotion in 555–6
Facial feedback hypothesis 561
Failures of attention 143–8
False memories 246–7
Family resemblance 299–300
Fast-and-frugal heuristics 491–9
Fatal distraction, working memory and driving performance 196–7
Feature integration theory (FIT) 128, 130
Feedforward 137–8
Feedforward processing 165

Feeling-of-knowing 172
  language production and 348
'Feeling the warmth' 440
Field perspective on long-term memory 241
Field studies of consciousness 159
Fifteen-puzzle 436
Filter theory of attention 121–2, 126
Financial abuse of elderly people, application of SJT to detection of 502–4
Firing rates 53
Fixation 412
Flashbulb memories
  emotion, cognition and 573–4
  learning and forgetting 284–5, 291
Fluent aphasia 367
Focalization and attention 116
Force escalation, tit-for-tat and 90–92
Foreign accent syndrome 380
Forensics, eyewitness testimony and super recognizers 76–7
Forgetting 260, 268–83
  alcohol, effects of 276–7
  benzodiazepines, effects of 276–7
  consolidation 271–9
  consolidation, neuroscience accounts of sleep effects on 275–6
  decay, consolidation and 271–9
  directed forgetting (DF) 281
  effects of sleep on memory 275
  evaluation of 283
  functional approaches to 280–82
  interference 269–70
  intrusive memories 280
  long-term depression (LTD) 273–4
  long-term potentiation (LTP) 273–4
  memory, effects of sleep on 275
  neurophysiological mechanism of learning and 273–5
  paired associates learning paradigm 270
  proactive interference 269
  reconsolidation of memories 279–80
  research close up, long-term memory, wakeful rest and improvement of 272–3
  research close up, wakeful rest and improvement of long-term memory 272–3
  retrieval-induced forgetting (RIF) 280–81
  retroactive interference 269, 287
  retrograde amnesia 276
  retrograde facilitation 275, 277
  savings 268–9
  think/no-think (TNT) 281–2
  when things go wrong
   amnesia 278–9
   consolidation 278–9
   recovered memory controversy 282–3
   retrograde interference 278–9
Forward models
  consciousness 169
  motor cognition 88–9
Four card selection task 532–40
Framing 476
  prospect theory and 476–7
Free morphemes 338
Free recall 227
Frequency effects 396
Frijda's list of basic emotions 557
Frontal eye fields (FEFs) 120, 142
Frontal lobe 19
Frontal lobe injury, emotional processing after 552–4
Function, double dissociation of 190–92
Function words 339
Functional fixity 427–8
Functional imaging 25
Functional integration, networks and 30–31
Functional level of analysis 17

Functional Magnetic Resonance Imaging (fMRI) 26–8, 29, 30
  language comprehension and 408
Functional reference 334
Functions of consciousness 155–60
Fundamental concepts of perception 38–44
Further reading
  attention 149
  cognitive psychology 32
  concepts and imagery 323
  consciousness 175
  decision making 507
  emotion and cognition 584
  language comprehension 420
  language production 373
  learning and forgetting 293
  long-term memory 257
  motor cognition 113
  perception 81
  problem solving 463
  reasoning 547
  sensory, short-term and working memory 217
Fusiform face area (FFA) 75

G

Galvanic skin response (GSR) 106
Garden path sentences 402
Geneplore model of information processing 457
General anaesthesia, effects on consciousness of 156
Generalizability 284
Generalizations 370
Generic Parts Technique 460–61
Gestalt approach to problem solving 426–9
  evaluation of 429
Gestalt laws of perceptual organization 37
Gesture 108–10
Glia 19
Global aphasia 365
Global Neuronal Workspace (GNW) Hypothesis 165, 166–7
Global workspace approaches 162–7
Global workspace theory 155
Glutamate 179
Goal-derived ad hoc categories, consumer goods and 302–3
Goal-subgoal space 430, 434–6
Google Deep Mind Project 16
Grapheme 406
Grapheme-colour synaesthesia 183
Grapheme-to-phoneme conversion (GPC) route 416–17
Graphic warning labels, influence on smokers 580–81
Grounded representations vs amodal representations 307–09
  evaluation of 309
Grounded theory
  of concepts, testing of 310–11
  simulation and 308–9
Guided search, schematic of 131

H

Habit learning 229–30
Haptic and tactile memory 186–7
Head turn preference procedure 381–2
Hedonic calculus 493
Herimholtz on creative thinking 453–4
Hesitation 343–4
Heuristics
  attention and 129
  consequentialism and 493–9
  in decision making, evaluation of 492–3
  heuristic method of problem solving 432

Subject Index

Hierarchical models of action production 94–7
High amplitude sucking paradigm 384
Higher-order theories of consciousness 173
Hippocampus 13, 18, 19
Historical perspectives
    cognitive psychology 6–17
    problem solving 425–39
Hockett's design features for language 333
Homesign 340
Homographs 397
Homologous brain regions 104
Hub-and-spoke model 311–12
Human factors in language comprehension 398
Human memory, susceptibility of 245–9
Human movement, point-light display of 79
Human perceptual systems 44–61
Hyperthymesia 182
Hypothalamus 19
Hypothesis generation 530–31
    and testing 530–46
Hypothesis testing 530–31
    four card selection task 532–40
        abstract version 533, 534
        basic results 534
        concrete version 533
        drinking rule 533
        interpretation factors 535–6
        matching bias 536
        money-cueing (availability) accounts 536–7
        negative abstract version 533
        pragmatic reasoning schemas 537
        procedural variations 534–5
        selection task as optimal data selection 539–40
        social contract theory 537–9
Hypothetico-deductive method 531

I

Iconic memory 180–82
    evaluation of 182
Idea strength and activation, fresh look at 456
Ideological beliefs and reasoning 528
Ideomotor theory 100–101
Ill defined problems 425
Illusionism 157
Illusions, perceptual inaccuracies and 36
Image scanning and comparing 314–18
Imagery 296
    concepts and 312–21
    critical views of research and theory on 317–18
    neuropsychology/neuroscience of 319–21
    processing of, evaluation of 321
    visuo-spatial processing and 313–14
Images and shapes 39
Imagination inflation 246
Imaging studies, cognitive processes and 28–9
Impasse-insight sequence 442
Implicit memory 226
    consciousness and 156
Inattentional blindness 143–4
    consciousness and 167
Incidental affect 579
Increasing idea production 457–61
Incubation 454–5
    research on 454–6
    working of 455–6
Indirect objects 338
Inductive reasoning 530–46
Inductive tasks 511
Infections, amnesia and 224
Inferior frontal gyrus (IFG) 120
Inflectional morphemes 338
Information flows, bottom-up and top-down processing 40–41
    evaluation of 40–41

Information loss 39
Information processing, cognitive revolution of 14–17
Information processing approach 14
    perception and 42–4
    problem solving and 429–38
    evaluation of 438
Information processing theories
    creative processes 456–7
    insight and 443–8
Inhibition of return 132–3
Insight 426
    barriers to 428–9
    'insight problems' and insight solving processes 440
    insight revisited 439–48
    non-insight problem solving and, comparison of 440–42
    non-insight problem solving vs neuroscience approach to 440–41
    working memory in 441–2
Insula 551–2
Integral affect 579
Integrated Information Theory (IIT) 166–7
Interactive activation 95
Intermittent conscious work 455
Internal attention 118–19
Internal representations 15
Interoception 582–3
Interoceptive signals 155
Interviewing eyewitnesses 286–7
Introspectionism 8–10
Intrusions 242
Invariance 476
Invariance problem 378–9
Invariants 42
Inverse problem 85
Investigative hypotheses, logical reasoning and generation of 542–3
Involuntary memories 244
Involuntary traumatic recollections, experiences of 244–5
I quantity 166
Isotropic fractionator method 20

J

James-Lange theory 561–2, 563
    evaluation of 562
James' *Principles of Psychology*
    action representation, perception and 101
    attention 116
    emotion 559
    sensory, short-term and working memory 178

K

Keyword method of memory training 7
Kiki-bouba stimuli 333
Knowledge
    acquisition of, process of 260–61
    do we know what we don't know? 250–52
Knowledge-based approaches 304–5
    evaluation of 305
Knowledge leanness 425
Knowledge richness 425
    knowledge-rich (or expert) problem solving 448–52

L

Language
    ambiguity in, accident prevention and 399–400
    components of 336–43
    exposure to 326–7
    relationship to behaviour 94

Language comprehension 375–420
    acquired dyslexia 416
    agrammatism 401–2
    alphabetic scripts 405
    anomia 403–4
    areas of interest (AoIs) 414–15
    bottom-up processing 391
    brain and 403–4
    Broca's aphasia 401–2, 403
    categorical perception 383–5
    closed-class words 396
    co-articulation 378–9
    cohort model of speech perception 391–3
        evaluation of 393
    consonantal scripts 405
    conspecifics 385
    context
        context effects on visual word recognition 410
        role of 387–90
    contralateral connections 385
    cues to word boundaries 381–2
    developmental dyslexia 407–8
    dichotic listening 385
    direct route 416
    discussion questions 419
    dizygotic twins 407–8
    double dissociation of function 416–17
    dual route model of reading 415–16
    ear, slips of the 382–3
    electrophysiological data 417–18
    event-related potential (ERP) 392, 417–18
    eye movements 412–13
    eye tracking 396
    fixation 412
    foreign accent syndrome 380
    frequency effects 396
    functional Magnetic Resonance Imaging (fMRI) 408
    further reading 420
    garden path sentences 402
    grapheme 406
    grapheme-to-phoneme conversion (GPC) route 416–17
    head turn preference procedure 381–2
    high amplitude sucking paradigm 384
    homographs 397
    human factors 398
    invariance problem 378–9
    late closure 402–3
    lemmas 376
    lexical access 395–8
    lexical ambiguity 397–400
    lexical decision task 392, 396
    lexical route 416
    lexicon 376, 395
    linguistic determinism 388
    linguistic relativity 388, 398
    localist representation 393–4
    logographic scripts 405
    McGurk effect 390
    mental lexicon 376
    minimal attachment 402
    monozygotic twins 407–8
    neologisms 386, 403–4
    neurophysioligy of speech comprehension 403–4
    neuropsychology of reading 416–17
    non-semantic reading 416
    onset 382
    opaque languages 406
    open-class words 396
    orthographically deep languages 406
    paraphasias 386, 403–4
    parsing 401
    phoneme restoration effect 387

Subject Index

Language comprehension—Cont.
  phonemes 376
  phonological dyslexia 417
  phonotactic constraints 382
  phrase structure tree 402
  practical applications
    language ambiguity and accident prevention 399–400
    leading questions, effect on memory of 388–90
  preview questions 375
  priming 396
  priming effects 396–7
  prosody 377
  psycholinguistics 401
  pure word deafness 386, 404
  pure word meaning deafness 387, 404
  reading 404–18
    dual route model of 415–16
    neuropsychology of 416–17
  repetition priming 397
  research close up
    reading sentences containing emoji 413–15
    Stroop effect 411–12
  review questions 419
  right ear advantage for speech sounds 385
  rime 382
  saccades 412
  schemas 388–9
  schwa 380
  segmentation of speech 379–81
  semantic priming 396–7
  sentence verification tasks 396, 401
  sentences, understanding meaning in 395–403
  shallow orthography 406
  slips of the ear 382–3
  speech comprehension 376–7
  speech perception 376
  speech perception, models of 391–5
  speech sounds, right ear advantage for 385
  summary 419
  surface dyslexia 417
  syllabic scripts 405
  syntactic context 397
  syntax and semantics 400–403
  top-down influences 387–90
  top-down processing 383, 391
  trace model of speech perception 393–5
    architecture of 394
    evaluation of 394–5
  transparent orthography 406
  understanding speech 377–87
  understanding words and sentences 395–403
  visual cues 390
  visual word recognition, context effects on 410
  voicing 384
  Wernicke's aphasia 402, 403
  Wernicke's area 403
  when things go wrong
    cross-language manifestation of dyslexia 407–10
    dyslexia, cross-language manifestation of 407–10
    language comprehension in aphasia 386–7
  word boundaries, cues to 381–2
  word naming tasks 396
  word superiority effect 410
  words, understanding meaning in 395–403
  writing systems 405–7
Language production 325–72
  agraphia 364
  alexia 364
  allophones 337
  ambidextrous individuals 360
  anarthria 364
  anomic aphasia 368–9

aphasia 343, 364
  evidence from 364–70
  individual differences in 369–70
apraxia 364
arenate fasciculus 358, 368
aspirated consonants 336–7
bound morphemes 338
Broca's aphasia 365–7
Broca's area 358, 365
clauses 344, 351
co-articulation 337
cognition, language and 328–9
communication 330
communication, language and 330–43
components of language 336–43
conceptually-driven speech production 327
conduction aphasia 368
confabulation 359–60
conspecifics 334
content words 326, 338
corpus 347–8
crossed aphasia 364
derivational morphemes 338
dichotic listening tasks 363
direct objects 338
discourse 341–3
  implicit rules of 342
discussion questions 372
disfluency 343–4
Down syndrome 329
electrocortical stimulation 358
event-related potentials (ERPs) 363
feeling-of-knowing 348
fluent aphasia 367
free morphemes 338
function words 339
functional reference 334
further reading 373
generalizations 370
global aphasia 365
hesitation 343–4
Hockett's design features for language 333
homesign 340
indirect objects 338
inflectional morphemes 338
kiki-bouba stimuli 333
language, exposure to 326–7
language production 327
language universals 330–36
lateralization of function 357–60
leading questions 329
left-hemisphere, language and 360–70
lemma 339, 351
lexeme 351
lexical bias 347
lexical categories 332
lexicon 339
linguistic analysis, levels of 327
linguistic determinism 329
linguistic relativity 329
linguistic universals 331
magnetic resonance imaging (MRI) 349–50
mental lexicon 331, 339
metacognition 348
minimal pairs 337–8
morphemes 338–9
morphology 338
neologisms 367
neurolinguistics 357
neuropsychological cases, evaluation of data from 370
neuroscience of 357–60
non-fluent aphasia 366
non-fluent disorders 365–6
non-plan internal errors 352
non-verbal communication 330

object 340
onomatopoeia 332
orthography 370–71
over-extension 326
paraphasias 367–8
parapraxes 346
Parkinson's disease 361–2
pauses 343–4
phonemes 336–8
phones 336
phonetics 336
phonology 336
phonotactic rules 337
phrases 340
practical applications
  deception, use of speech cues in detection of deception 344–5
  lecture notes, typed or handwritten? 370–71
  speech cues, use in detection of deception 344–5
pragmatics 341
preservative errors 362
preview questions 325
productivity of language 340
proper nouns 348
prosody 364
recursion 340
research close ups
  proper name retrieval in youth and mid-life 349–50
  symbolic communication in non-human animals 334–5
  vervet monkey alarm calls 334–5
review questions 372
Sapir-Whorf hypothesis 329
schemas 341
semantic memory 339
semantics, lexicon and 339
sentences 340
slang 340
slips of the tongue 346–8
social cognition 327
sound-symbolism 332
specific language impairment (SLI) 329, 369
speech errors 343–50
  types of, examples of 346
speech production
  conceptually-driven 327
  Dell's model 355–7
  Dell's model, evaluation of 355–7
  Garrett's model 351–2
  Garrett's model, evaluation of 352
  interactive theories of 355–7
  Leveit's model 352–5
  Leveit's model, evaluation of 354–5
  modular theories of 351–5
  theories of 350–57
split brain 359–60
Spoonerisms 347
subject 340
summary 372
syntax 326, 338, 339–41
telegraphic speech 366–7
tip-of-the-tongue (TOT) effects 339
tip-of-the-tongue (TOT) state 348–50
tonal languages 331
transcranial magnetic stimulation (TMS) 363–4
typical population, evidence from 363–4
visual field 357
Wada test 360
Wernicke-Gerschwind model 358
Wernicke's aphasia 367–8
Wernicke's area 358
when things go wrong
  split brain 359–60
  verbal fluency tasks in clinical settings 361–3

Subject Index

William's syndrome 328–9
words 339
written language 330
Late selection, attention and 121
Lateral thinking 459
Lateralization of function 357–60
Law and sleepwalking 154
Law of Mass Action 23
Lazarus's theory 567–8
    evaluation of 568
Leading questions 329
    effect on memory of 388–90
'Leaky' rationality 486–7
Learning 260, 261–8
    categorization 263
    context-dependent retrieval 266–7
    context effects 266
    deficient processing 267
    dual-coding hypothesis 264
    encoding specificity principle 266
    encoding variability 267
    evaluation of 267–8
    incidental learning 261
    interacting images, method of 263–4
    levels of processing 261–3
    loci, method of 263–4
    memory trace 261
    method of interacting images 263–4
    method of loci 263–4
    mnemonics 263–4
    mood-dependent memory effect 266–7
    neurophysiological mechanism of
        forgetting and 273–5
    paired associates learning paradigm 270
    pegword method 263–4
    practical applications
        exceptionally good memories - nature of
            nurture? 264–5
        nature of nurture, exceptionally good
            memories and? 264–5
    processing levels 261–3
    research close up, levels of processing 261–2
    spaced vs massed trials 267
    spacing effect 267
    state-dependent learning effect 266–7
Learning and forgetting 259–93
    brain stocking, Sherlock Holmes on 260
    discussion questions 293
    ecological validity 284
    effective studying 288–90, 291
    elaborative interrogation 289
    everyday memory 283–91
        evaluation of 291
    eyewitness testimony 285–7, 291
    flashbulb memories 284–5, 291
    forgetting 260, 268–83
        alcohol, effects of 276–7
        benzodiazepines, effects of 276–7
        consolidation 271–9
        consolidation, neuroscience accounts of
            sleep effects on 275–6
        decay, consolidation and 271–9
        directed forgetting (DF) 281
        effects of sleep on memory 275
        evaluation of 283
        functional approaches to 280–82
        interference 269–70
        intrusive memories 280
        long-term depression (LTD) 273–4
        long-term potentiation (LTP) 273–4
        memory, effects of sleep on 275
        neurophysiological mechanism of
            learning and 273–5
        paired associates learning paradigm 270
        proactive interference 269
        reconsolidation of memories 279–80

research close ups
    long-term memory, wakeful rest and
        improvement of 272–3
    wakeful rest and improvement of long-
        term memory 272–3
retrieval-induced forgetting (RIF) 280–81
retroactive interference 269, 287
retrograde amnesia 276
retrograde facilitation 275, 277
savings 268–9
think/no-think (TNT) 281–2
when things go wrong
    amnesia 278–9
    consolidation 278–9
    recovered memory controversy 282–3
    retrograde interference 278–9
further reading 293
generalizability 284
interviewing eyewitnesses 286–7
knowledge acquisition, process of 260–61
practical application, cognitive interview 287–8
preview questions 259
real-world memory 283–91
    evaluation of 283–91
representativeness 284
research close ups
    drawing and learning terms (and their
        definitions) 290–91
    learning terms (and their definitions),
        drawing and 290–91
review questions 292–3
studying, effectiveness in 288–90, 291
summary 291–2
Learning terms (and their definitions), drawing
    and 290–91
Lecture notes, typed or handwritten? 370–71
Left-hemisphere, language and 360–70
Lemmas 339, 351
    language comprehension and 376
Lexeme 351
Lexical access 395–8
Lexical ambiguity 397–400
Lexical bias 347
Lexical categories 332
Lexical decision task 392, 396
Lexical route to language comprehension 416
Lexicographic strategies in decision making 485
Lexicon 376, 395
    language production and 339
Life-or-death problem solving 426–7
Likelihood principle 41–2
Limbic system 551–2
Linguistic analysis, levels of 327
Linguistic determinism 388
    language production and 329
Linguistic relativity 388, 398
    language production and 329
Linguistic universals 331
Lipman's *Philosophy for Children*
    programme 531–2
Load theory 122
Localist representation, language
    comprehension and 393–4
Localized functions 21
Locations in brain, terms for 18
Logical reasoning and generation of investigative
    hypotheses 542–3
Logographic scripts 405
Long-term knowledge, basis of 296
Long-term memory 219–57
    action slips 237
    amnesia, memory and 220, 223–5
    amnesic syndrome 223
    anterograde amnesia 223
    autobiographical memory 241–9
    autonoetic ('self-knowing') consciousness 232

autonoetic ('self-knowing') memories 241
belief in memory, reasons for choice to
    withdraw 248
brain areas involved in 225
brain surgery, memory impairment
    following 220–23
category exemplar tasks 230
cued recall 227
declarative memory 232–56
    evaluation 253–4
demand characteristics 246
discussion questions 257
episodic and semantic memory, key differences
    between 228
episodic memory 227, 232–7
explicit memory 226
false memories 246–7
field perspective 241
free recall 227
further reading 257
habit learning 229–30
human memory, susceptibility of 245–9
imagination inflation 246
implicit memory 226
infections, amnesia and 224
intrusions 242
involuntary memories 244
memory as (re)constructive process 232–7
metamemory 250
multiple memory systems model 226–8
noetic memories 241
non-declarative memory 228–32
    evaluation 231–2
observer perspective 241
permastore 252
personal past experiences, memories of 243–4
practical applications
    everyday memory, measurement of 254–6
    measurement of everyday memory 254–6
    prospective memory, improvement of 238
preview questions 219
priming 230
probabilistic classification learning 229
procedural memory 229
prospective memory, imagining future events
    and 237–40
pulses 238
recognition 227
repetition priming 230
research close ups
    autobiographical memories, reasons for
        choice to withdraw 247–8
    compulsions, prospective memory deficit
        and checking 239–40
    do we know what we don't know? 250–52
    knowing what we don't know? 250–52
    prospective memory deficit, checking
        compulsions and 239–40
    remembering traumatic events 242–3
    schemas, role on memory of 233–5
    traumatic events, memories of 242–3
retrograde amnesia 224
review questions 257
Ribot's Law (1881) 222
self-concept 243
self-continuity 243
'self-knowing' consciousness 232
semantic and episodic memory, key differences
    between 228
semantic memory 227, 249–54
sensory, short-term and working
    memory and 178
skill learning 229
steps 238
structure of 226–8
summary 256

Subject Index

Long-term memory—*Cont.*
   susceptibility of human memory 245–9
   verbal learning 226
   Wechsler Memory Scale 222
   when things go wrong
      case of 'H.M.' 220–23
        involuntary traumatic recollections, experiences of 244–5
        post-traumatic stress disorder (PTSD), suffering from 244–5
   word stem completion task 231
Loss aversion 471–2

M

Machines to help us move, design of 85–6
Madrid bombings and catching the right perpetrator 545–6
Magic, attention, misdirection and 146–8
Magic tricks, insight generation and 446–7
Magnetic resonance imaging (MRI) 25
   language production and 349–50
Maintenance rehearsal 188
'Mary's Room' experiment 153
Masking 186
McGurk effect 390
Measurement of everyday memory 254–6
Medical images, errors in interpretation of 129–30
Memory
   affect and 573–7
   belief in, reasons for choice to withdraw 248
   memory training 6–8
   modal model of memory 187
   mood-congruent memory 575–7
   as (re)constructive process 232–7
   see also Long-term memory; Sensory, short-term and working memory
Mental illness and reasoning 517–18
Mental lexicon 376
   language production and 331, 339
Mental operations 15
Mental representations 4
Mental rotation 315–17
Mere exposure effect 565
Meta-analysis 111
Metacognition
   consciousness and 172–3
   decision making and 473
   language production and 348
   motor cognition and 99
Metamemory 250
Microexpressions, detection of deceit through 556–7
Middle frontal gyrus (MFG) 120
Mind wandering, working memory and 207–10
Minimal attachment 402
Minimal pairs 337–8
Mirror mechanisms and action observation 103–5
Mirror neuron system (MNS) 104–5
Mirror neurons 103
Mnemonics 6
Modal model of memory 187
Modality appropriate hypothesis 58–9
Modularity 22
Monozygotic twins 407–8
Mood, effect of matching on recall of target words 576
Mood-congruent memory 575–7
Morals and language 498–9
Morphemes 338–9
Morphology 338
Motion sickness 59–60
Motor cognition 83–113
   action observation
      mirror mechanisms and 103–5
        evaluation of 105

action planning, brain structure for 98
action production
   brain damage and 97–100
   hierarchical models of 94–7
action representation
   common codes for action perception and production 101–3
   evaluation of 101–3
   historical perspectives 100–101
   perception and 100–111
   theories of 100–105
action sequences 93–5
   hierarchical representation of an action sequence 95
agency 110–11
ambient intelligence 99–100
apraxia 98–9
associative chain theory 93
basal ganglia 92
brain damage and action production 97–100
cerebellum 92
choking 97
co-articulation 94
cognitive sandwich 100
common coding 101–2
   interference problem for 102
complex actions, production of 93–100
degrees of freedom 85
discussion questions 113
dynamical systems theory 87–8
embodied cognition 107–10
equilibrium point hypothesis 86–7
forward models 88–9
further reading 113
galvanic skin response (GSR) 106
gesture 108–10
hierarchical models of action production 94–7
homologous brain regions 104
ideomotor theory 100–101
interactive activation 95
inverse problem 85
language, relationship to behaviour 94
meta-analysis 111
metacognition 99
mirror mechanisms and action observation 103–5
mirror neuron system (MNS) 104–5
mirror neurons 103
motor control 84–93
   evaluation of theories of 92–3
motor primitives 104–5
motor system 84
movement planning, theories of 86–93
optimal control theory 88, 89–90, 92
   illustration of 89–90
parallel processing 94–5
practical applications
   cognitive rehabilitation for apraxia and action disorganization syndrome 99–100
   design of machines to help us move 85–6
preview questions 83
production of complex actions 93–100
recurrent networks 95–6
repetition suppression 104
research close ups
   dance expertise, use in study of action representation 105–7
   force escalation, tit-for-tat and 90–92
   tit-for-tat and force escalation 90–92
review questions 112
speech production 94
summary 112
test-operate-test-exit (TOTE) unit 94–5
torque 88
when things go wrong, alien hand syndrome 111

Movies, attention and continuity editing in 145–6
Multi-attribute alternatives, decision processes for 483–7
Multi-attribute decision models, testing of 484–7
Multi-attribute decision problem 468–9
Multi-attribute utility theory (MAUT) 483–4, 500–501
Multi-level theories in emotion and cognition 568
Multiple memory systems model 226–8
Multisensory integration 57–61
   evaluation of 60
Multisensory warning signals for handover between autonomous and manual driving 60–61

N

Naturalistic choice 487
Naturalistic decision making 499–504
Navigation, connectionist network for 17
Negative recency effect 190
Neologisms 386, 403–4
   language production and 367
Network models
   concepts and imagery 311
   emotion and cognition 575
Networks and functional integration 30–31
Neural correlates of consciousness (NCC) 162
Neural mechanism of attention in primary visual cortex 137–9
Neuroeconomics 504
Neurolinguistics 357
Neurological homunculus 24
Neurons 18–19
   schematic outline of a neuron 20
Neurophysiology of speech comprehension 403–4
Neuropsychology
   cognitive psychology and 20, 21
   consciousness and 161–2
   neuropsychological cases, evaluation of data from 370
   of reading 416–17
Neuroscience
   detection of awareness in 'vegetative states' 29–30
   of language production 357–60
Neuroscience approach to
   decision making 504–6
   insight vs non-insight problem solving 440–41
Noetic memories 241
Non-adversary problems 425
Non-declarative memory
   consciousness and 156
   long-term memory and 228–32
   evaluation 231–2
Non-fluent aphasia 366
Non-fluent disorders 365–6
Non-plan internal errors 352
Non-rapid eye movement (NREM) sleep 154
Non-semantic reading 416
Non-verbal communication 330
Normalization Model of attention 138–9
Normative approaches to decision making 468
Nudges, consciousness and 158

O

Objects
   attachment to, attention and 123–4
   language production and 340
   recognition of, perception and 63–9
Observer perspective 241
Occipital lobe 19
Omission bias 494–5
Onomatopoeia 332
Onset 382
Opaque languages 406

Open-class words 396
Operational definition of 152
Opportunity costs 474
Optimal control theory 88, 89–90, 92
    illustration of 89–90
Orienting system, attention and 119–20
Orthography 370–71
    orthographically deep languages 406
Out-of-body experience 171–2
Over-extension 326

P

Pandemonium model 62–3
Parallel processing 94–5
Paraphasias 367–8
    language comprehension and 386, 403–4
Parapraxes 346
Parietal lobe 19
Parkinson's disease 361–2
Parsing 401
Pauses 343–4
Perception 35–81
    affect and 572–3
    attentional mechanisms in 137–41
    auditory system 51–5
        damage to, effects of 53
        primary auditory cortex, pathways into 52
        secondary auditory cortex 53
    basilar membrane 51–3
    Bayesian Decision Theory 41
    biological motion, social perception of 78–80
        evaluation of 80
    body and 43–4
    Brodmann areas 55
    causal Bayesian inference 59
    causality 59
    central suicus 55
    computational theory 42
    computations, achievement of 43
    cones 46
    direct perception 42
    discussion questions 81
    dorsal stream 46
    double dissociation 73
    embodied view of cognition 43–4
        embodied cognition, claims of 44
    extrastriate body area (EBA) 80
    faces, social perception of 74–7
    firing rates 53
    fundamental concepts 38–44
    further reading 81
    fusiform face area (FFA) 75
    Gestalt laws of perceptual organization 37
    human movement, point-light display of 79
    human perceptual systems 44–61
    illusions, perceptual inaccuracies and 36
    images and shapes 39
    information flows, bottom-up and top-down processing 40–41
        evaluation of 40–41
    information loss 39
    information processing approach 42–4
    invariants 42
    likelihood principle 41–2
    modality appropriate hypothesis 58–9
    multisensory integration 57–61
        evaluation of 60
    objects, recognition of 63–9
    Pandemonium model 62–3
    perception 36
    perceptual learning, attention and 130
    perceptual organization, likelihood principle 41–2
    perceptual representation, from physical world to 38–9
    perceptual systems, basic organization of 46
    place model 53
    practical applications
        cochlear implants 54–5
        cognitive robotics and human-robot interaction 37–8
        forensics, eyewitness testimony and super recognizers 76–7
        multisensory warning signals, autonomous and manual driving and 60–61
        super recognizers 77
    predictive coding 41
    preview questions 35
    primary sensory areas in human brain 45
    principles and theories of 39–43
    proprioception 45
    prosody 78
    rate model 53
    recognition 62–72
        events, recognition of 71–2
        face recognition, neural model of 75
        geons 64–5
            geon properties and objects composed of geons 65
        haptic perception 67–8
        learning features for 66
        objects, recognition of
            evaluation of 67
        recognition by components (RBC) approach 64, 66
        scenes, recognition of 69–71
        schema 72
        somatoperceptive object recognition 67–8
        viewpoint invariant relationship 64
        visual agnosia 68–9
        visual stimuli, contour deletion and 65
    representation, choice of 42–3
    research close up, primary visual cortex, discovery of feature detectors in 49–51
    review questions 81
    rods 46
    sensation 36
    social perception 72–80
    somatic 36
    somatoperception 47
    somatoperception system 55–7
        primary somatosensory system, pathways into 56
    summary 80
    synaesthesia 57–8
    tonotopic map 53
    vection 60
    ventral stream 46
    ventriloquism 58
    vestibular sensation 45
    virtual reality (VR) 59
    visual illusions 36
    visual object recognition 63–6
    visual system 46–51
        evaluation of 47–9
        primary visual cortex, pathways from eye into 48
        primary visual cortex, pathways out of 49
    voice-sensitive brain regions 79
    voices, social perception of 78
    when things go wrong
        Capgras syndrome 73
        cybersickness 59–60
        motion sickness 59–60
Permastore 252
Persistent vegetative states 29–30
Personal accounts of creative problem solving 453–4
Personal past experiences, memories of 243–4
Phenomenal consciousness 155–6
Phenomenology 8
Phoneme restoration effect 387
Phonemes 376
    language production and 336–8
Phones 336
Phonetics 336
Phonological dyslexia 417
Phonology 336
Phonotactic constraints 382
Phonotactic rules 337
Phrases 340
    phrase structure tree 402
Phrenology 21–2
    phrenological map 22
Pituitary gland 19
Place model 53
Poincaré on creative thinking 453
Point electrical stimulation 23–4
Positron emission tomography (PET) 26
Post-traumatic stress disorder (PTSD), suffering from 244–5
Postulates 166
Practical applications
    application of SJT to detection of financial abuse of elderly people 502–4
    background noise, understanding effects of 201
    cakes vs biscuits 397–8
    cochlear implants 54–5
    cognitive interview 287–8
    cognitive lockup - working memory, attention and human error 192–4
    cognitive rehabilitation for apraxia and action disorganization syndrome 99–100
    cognitive robotics and human-robot interaction 37–8
    deception, use of speech cues in detection of deception 344–5
    depression, cognitive behavioural therapy (CBT) for 577–9
    design of machines to help us move 85–6
    everyday memory, measurement of 254–6
    fatal distraction - working memory and driving performance 196–7
    financial abuse of elderly people, application of SJT to detection of 502–4
    forensics, eyewitness testimony and super recognizers 76–7
    general anaesthesia, effects on consciousness of 156
    Generic Parts Technique 460–61
    goal-derived ad hoc categories, consumer goods and 302–3
    language ambiguity and accident prevention 399–400
    leading questions, effect on memory of 388–90
    lecture notes, typed or handwritten? 370–71
    life-or-death problem solving 426–7
    Lipman's *Philosophy for Children* programme 531–2
    measurement of everyday memory 254–6
    memory training 6–8
    microexpressions, detection of deceit through 556–7
    movies, attention and continuity editing in 145–6
    multisensory warning signals for handover between autonomous and manual driving 60–61
    prospective memory, improvement of 238
    psychological model for legal reasoning 529–30
    real scientific research environments 543–4
    resisting effective but coerced policies 496
    robot attention 116–18
    speech cues, use in detection of deception 344–5
    super recognizers 77
    training in reasoning 531–2

Subject Index

Practical applications—*Cont.*
   two-system theory and 'nudge' 488–9
   UK postcode and cognitive psychology 4–5
   video game play in enhancing cognition and attention 127
Pragmatics 341
Preattentive visual processes 128
Predictive coding 41
Preference reversal 473
Premises 511
Preservative errors 362
Preview questions
   attention 115
   cognitive psychology 3
   concepts and imagery 295
   consciousness 151
   decision making 467
   language comprehension 375
   language production 325
   learning and forgetting 259
   long-term memory 219
   motor cognition 83
   perception 35
   problem solving 423
   reasoning 509
   sensory, short-term and working memory 177
Primacy effect 189
Primary auditory cortex 19
Primary memory 178
Primary motor cortex 19, 25
Primary sensory areas in human brain 45
Primary visual cortex 19
   discovery of feature detectors in 49–51
   neural mechanism of attention in 137–9
Primes, consciousness and 158
Priming 396
   long-term memory 230
Priming effects 396–7
Principles and theories of perception 39–43
Probabilistic functionalism 501
Probability judgements 477–83
Probablistic classification learning 229
Problem situations 424
Problem solving 423–64
   adversary problems 425
   algorithm 432
   barriers to insight 428–9
   blind variation and selective retention model of information processing 456–7
   brainstorming 458–61
      evaluation of 460–61
   breadth first search 431–2
   Compound Remote Associate (CRAT) items 441
   Computational-Representational Understanding of Mind (CRUM) 429
   creative 452
   Creative Achievement Questionnaire (CAQ) 461–2
   creative problem solving 452–62
   creative processes, information processing theory of 456–7
   creative synthesis task 457
   deliberate practice 448–9
   depth first search 431
   detour problems 438
   discussion questions 463
   eight- and fifteen-puzzle 436
   expert problem solving 448–52
   expertise 448
      expertise acquisition 448–50
      expertise research, evaluation of 452
      nature of 450–52
   'feeling the warmth' 440
   fifteen-puzzle 436
   fresh look at idea strength and activation 456
   functional fixity 427–8

further reading 463
Geneplore model of information processing 457
Gestalt approach 426–9
   evaluation of 429
goal-subgoal space 430, 434–6
Herimholtz on creative thinking 453–4
heuristic method 432
history and background 425–39
ill defined problems 425
impasse-insight sequence 442
increasing idea production 457–61
incubation 454–5
   incubation research 454–6
   working of 455–6
information processing approach 429–38
   evaluation of 438
information processing theories of insight 443–8
information processing theory of creative processes 456–7
insight 426
   barriers to 428–9
   'insight problems' and insight solving processes 440
   insight revisited 439–48
   insight vs non-insight problem solving, neuroscience approach to 440–41
   insight vs non-insight problem solving, working memory in 441–2
   and non-insight problem solving, comparison of 440–42
intermittent conscious work 455
knowledge leanness 425
knowledge-rich (or expert) problem solving 448–52
knowledge richness 425
lateral thinking 459
neuroscience approach to insight vs non-insight problem solving 440–41
non-adversary problems 425
personal accounts of creative problem solving 453–4
Poincaré on creative thinking 453
practical applications
   Generic Parts Technique 460–61
   life-or-death problem solving 426–7
preview questions 423
problem situations 424
problem space 430
problems and problem types 424–5
progress monitoring theory 444–8
progressive deepening 432
representational change 443–4
research close ups
   magic tricks, insight generation and 446–7
   travelling salesperspn problems 436–8
restructuring 426
review questions 463
river crossing problems, interactivity and 433–4
set tendency 427–8
Simon model of information processing 456
state-action space 430–33
summary 462–3
synectics 459
talent 449
thinking 424
Tower of London tasks 435
transcranial direct current stimulation (TDCS) 441
unconscious work 455–6
Wallas's stage analysis 454
well defined problems 425
when things go wrong
   creativity and psychopathology 461–2
   psychopathology and creativity 461–2

   right prefrontal cortex damage and real-world planning 438–9
   working memory in insight vs non-insight problem solving 441–2
Problems *see* When things go wrong
Procedural memory 229
Production of complex actions 93–100
Productivity of language 340
Progress monitoring theory 444–8
Progressive deepening 432
Proper name retrieval in youth and mid-life 349–50
Proper nouns 348
Propositional reasoning 511–18
   basic results 513
   correct and false inferences 512
   evaluation of mental models vs mental logic 516–17
   inference rule 512
   mental logic approaches 514–15
   mental models 515–16
   suppression effects 513–14
Propriception 45
Prosody 364
   language comprehension and 377
   perception and 78
Prospect theory 471, 472
   framing and 476–7
   selective probability and 475–7
   utility and 471–4
Prospection 473
Prospective memory
   imagining future events and 237–40
   improvement of 238
   prospective memory deficit, checking compulsions and 239–40
Prototype approaches 299–302
   ad hoc categories 301
   basic level categories 301
   categories of prototypes, levels of 300–301
   evaluation of 301–2
   introduction to prototypes 299–300
Psycholinguistics 401
Psychological distance 497
Psychological model for legal reasoning 529–30
Psychopathology
   creativity and 461–2
   psychopathic traits, facial expressions and 555–6
Psychophysics 158
Pulses 238
Punishment and decision making 495
Pure word deafness 386, 404
Pure word meaning deafness 387, 404

Q

Qualia 153

R

Rapid eye movement (REM) sleep 154
Rate model of perception 53
Reading 404–18
   dual route model of 415–16
   neuropsychology of 416–17
   sentences containing emoji 413–15
Reading suggestions *see* Further reading
Real-life choices 500–504
   evaluation of 502
Real scientific research environments 543–4
Real-world loss aversion 472
Real-world memory 283–91
   evaluation of 283–91
Reasoning 509–47
   abductive reasoning 542
   categorical syllogisms 518–19

Subject Index

confirmation bias 543
deductive reasoning 511–30
deductive tasks 511
deontic rules 539
discussion questions 547
four card selection task 532–40
further reading 547
hypothesis generation 530–31
hypothesis generation and testing 530–46
hypothesis testing 530–31
hypothesis testing, four card selection task 532–40
   abstract version 533, 534
   basic results 534
   concrete version 533
   drinking rule 533
   interpretation factors 535–6
   matching bias 536
   money-cueing (availability) accounts 536–7
   negative abstract version 533
   pragmatic reasoning schemas 537
   procedural variations 534–5
   selection task as optimal data selection 539–40
   social contract theory 537–9
hypothetico-deductive method 531
inductive reasoning 530–46
inductive tasks 511
practical applications
   Lipman's *Philosophy for Children* programme 531–2
   psychological model for legal reasoning 529–30
   real scientific research environments 543–4
   training in reasoning 531–2
premises 511
preview questions 509
propositional reasoning 511–18
   basic results 513
   correct and false inferences 512
   evaluation of mental models vs mental logic 516–17
   inference rule 512
   mental logic approaches 514–15
   mental models 515–16
   suppression effects 513–14
reasoning process, example of 510
research close ups
   dyslexia and reasoning 525–6
   ideological beliefs and reasoning 528
   investigative hypotheses, logical reasoning and generation of 542–3
   logical reasoning and generation of investigative hypotheses 542–3
review questions 547
simulated research environments 543–4
summary 546–7
syllogistic reasoning 511, 518–30
   atmosphere effect 519, 520
   basic findings from studies of 519
   belief bias and dual system theory 526–9
   categorical syllogisms 518–19
   conversion errors vs atmosphere 520–21
   culture and logic 522–3
   dual system theory, systems 1 and 2 529
   figural bias 523
   four figures of syllogism 523
   Henle on 'rationality' 521–2
   illicit conversion 520–21
   mental model approaches to syllogisms 523–6
   mental model approaches to syllogisms, evaluation of 526
   probabilistic interference 520–21
Wason's reversed 20 questions task 540–42
when things go wrong

Madrid bombings and catching the right perpetrator 545–6
mental illness and reasoning 517–18
Recency effect 188–9
Receptive field, attention and 138
Recognition
long-term memory and 227
perception and 62–72
   events, recognition of 71–2
   face recognition, neural model of 75
   geons 64–5
      geon properties and objects composed of geons 65
   haptic perception 67–8
   learning features for 66
   objects, recognition of
      evaluation of 67
   recognition by components (RBC) approach 64, 66
   scenes, recognition of 69–71
   schema 72
   somatoperceptive object recognition 67–8
   viewpoint invariant relationship 64
   visual agnosia 68–9
   visual stimuli, contour deletion and 65
recognition heuristic 491
recognition primed decision making 500
Recollection 178
Recovered memory controversy 282–3
Recurrent brain activity 165
Recurrent networks 95–6
Recurrent processing 138
Recurrent processing theory 165
Recursion 340
Re-enactment 308
Reflexive connections 155
Regulation of emotions in daily life 568–9
Rehearsal 187–8
Remembering traumatic events 242–3
Repetition priming 397
long-term memory and 230
Repetition suppression, motor cognition and 104
Representation, choice of 42–3
Representational change 443–4
Representativeness 284
Representativeness heuristic 478, 479–80
conjunction fallacy in 479–80
Research close ups
autobiographical memories, reasons for choice to withdraw 247–8
brain networks and consciousness 163–5
cognitive maps 12–14
compulsions, prospective memory deficit and checking 239–40
dance expertise, use in study of action representation 105–7
do we know what we don't know? 250–52
drawing and learning terms (and their definitions) 290–91
dual task, use in examination of attention and working memory 140–41
dyslexia and reasoning 525–6
emotion perception, use of attention blink for examination of 134–7
force escalation, tit-for-tat and 90–92
graphic warning labels, influence on smokers 580–81
ideological beliefs and reasoning 528
investigative hypotheses, logical reasoning and generation of 542–3
knowing what we don't know? 250–52
learning terms (and their definitions), drawing and 290–91
logical reasoning and generation of investigative hypotheses 542–3
magic tricks, insight generation and 446–7

mental rotation 315–17
morals and language 498–9
primary visual cortex, discovery of feature detectors in 49–51
proper name retrieval in youth and mid-life 349–50
prospective memory deficit, checking compulsions and 239–40
reading sentences containing emoji 413–15
regulation of emotions in daily life 568–9
remembering traumatic events 242–3
schemas, role on memory of 233–5
self-efficacy and working memory 214–16
Stroop effect 411–12
supraliminal primes, promotion of healthy eating with 159–60
symbolic communication in non-human animals 334–5
testing grounded theory of concepts using dual task methods in working memory for action words 310–11
tit-for-tat and force escalation 90–92
traumatic events, memories of 242–3
travelling salesperspn problems 436–8
unconscious thought effect (UTE) on decisions 490–91
vervet monkey alarm calls 334–5
waking and dreaming thoughts, experience sampling of qualities of 10–11
working memory and mind wandering 207–10
Resistance to coerced reform 495–6
Resisting effective but coerced policies 496
Resource theory of attention 122–6
Restructuring, problem solving and 426
Retrieval of memory 178
Retrograde amnesia 224
Retrograde interference 278–9
Review questions
attention 149
cognitive psychology 32
concepts and imagery 323
consciousness 174
decision making 507
emotion and cognition 584
language comprehension 419
language production 372
learning and forgetting 292–3
long-term memory 257
motor cognition 112
perception 81
problem solving 463
reasoning 547
sensory, short-term and working memory 217
Ribot's Law (1881) 222
Right ear advantage for speech sounds 385
Right prefrontal cortex damage and real-world planning 438–9
Rime, language comprehension and 382
Risk 468
Risk aversion 470
Risk seeking 471
Risklessness 468
River crossing problems, interactivity and 433–4
Robot attention 116–18
Rods, perception and 46

S

Saccades 412
Sacrifice dilemmas 496–9
Salience maps 132–3
Salience network 31
   consciousness and 164
   emotion, cognition and 552
Sapir-Whorf hypothesis 329
Satisficing 484

Subject Index

Schachter-Singer two factor theory 563, 564–5
   evaluation of 564–5
Schemas 388–9
   language production and 341
   role in memory of 233–5
Schwa 380
Secondary memory 178
Segmentation of speech 379–81
Selective probability and prospect theory 475–7
Self-awareness and integration 155–6
Self-concept 243
Self-continuity 243
Self-efficacy and working memory 214–16
'Self-knowing' consciousness 232
Self-observation 9
Semantic and episodic memory, key differences between 228
Semantic dementia 312
Semantic memory 339
   long-term memory and 227, 249–54
Semantic priming 396–7
Semantics, lexicon and 339
Sensation, perception and 36
Sensory, short-term and working memory 177–217
   amnesia 190
   amnesic syndrome 190
   aphasia 191
   change blindness 187
   chunking 188
   cognitive lockup 192
   computer metaphor 187
   Cowan's embedded processes model 195–6
   decay 188
   digit span 188
   discussion questions 217
   displacement 188
   double dissociation of function 190–92
      evaluation of 192
   echoic memory 184–6
      evaluation of 185–6
   elaborative rehearsal 188
   encoding 178
   function, double dissociation of 190–92
   further reading 217
   glutamate 179
   grapheme-colour synaesthesia 183
   haptic and tactile memory 186–7
   hyperthymesia 182
   iconic memory 180–82
      evaluation of 182
   James' *Principles of Psychology* 178
   long-term memory (LTM) 178
   maintenance rehearsal 188
   masking 186
   mind wandering, working memory and 207–10
   modal model of memory 187
   negative recency effect 190
   practical applications
      background noise, understanding effects of 201
      cognitive lockup - working memory, attention and human error 192–4
      fatal distraction - working memory and driving performance 196–7
   preview questions 177
   primacy effect 189
   primary memory 178
   recency effect 188–9
   recollection 178
   rehearsal 187–8
   research close ups
      self-efficacy and working memory 214–16
      working memory and mind wandering 207–10
   retrieval 178
   review questions 217

secondary memory 178
sensory memory 178, 179–87
serial position curve 189
shadowing 185
short-term memory (STM) 178, 187–92
stimulus onset asynchrony 186
storage 178
summary 216–17
synaesthesia 182
synaesthete 182
three-stage model of memory 179
top-down influence on memory 179
when things go wrong
   case of 'E.V.R.' 211–12
   synaesthesia and sensory memory 182–4
working memory (WM) 178, 192, 194–216
   Baddeley's working memory model 197–214
      anarthria 198–9
      articulatory suppression, effects of 200
      capture errors 206
      central executive 197–8, 205–7
      coarticulation effects 200
      dysexecutive syndrome 207
      episodic buffer 198, 210–11
      evaluation of 212–14
      inner scribe 203
      inner speech 199
      irrelevant speech effect 200–201
      perseveration 207
      phonological loop 198–203
      phonological loop, functions of 202–3
      phonological similarity effect 202
      rehearsal 199
      schemas 206
      self-efficacy 214
      Stroop task 206–7
      utilization behaviour 207
      visual cache 203
      visuo-spatial sketchpad (VSSP) 198, 203–4, 205–6, 210
      Wisconsin Card Sorting Test 207
      word length effect 199–200
   cognitive lockup and 192–4
   driving performance and 196–7
   self-efficacy and 214–16
Sensory memory 178, 179–87
Sentence verification tasks 396, 401
Sentences
   language production and 340
   understanding meaning in 395–403
Serial position curve 189
Set tendency 427–8
Shadowing 185
Shallow orthography 406
Short-term memory (STM) 178, 187–92
Simon model of information processing 456
Simulated research environments 543–4
Simulation 15
   concepts and imagery 308
Single attribute alternatives 468–9
Skill learning 229
Skin conductance responses (SCRs) 550
   to emotionally arousing pictures 554
Slang 340
Sleepwalking and the law 154
Slips of the ear 382–3
Slips of the tongue 346–8
Social cognition 327
Social heuristics perspective 506
Social Judgement Theory (SJT), real-life choices and 501–4
Social perception 72–80
Somatic markers, interoception and 582–3
Somatic perception 36
Somatoperception 47
Somatoperception system 55–7

primary somatosensory system, pathways into 56
Somatosensory cortex 19
Sound-symbolism 332
Spandrel 157
Spatial information, maintenance of 140
Spatial learning strategies 9
Specific language impairment (SLI) 329, 369
Speech comprehension 376–7
Speech cues, use in detection of deception 344–5
Speech errors 343–50
   types of, examples of 346
Speech perception 376
   models of 391–5
Speech production
   conceptually-driven 327
   Dell's model 355–7
   Dell's model, evaluation of 355–7
   Garrett's model 351–2
   Garrett's model, evaluation of 352
   interactive theories of 355–7
   Levelt's model 352–5
   Levelt's model, evaluation of 354–5
   modular theories of 351–5
   Motor cognition 94
   theories of 350–57
Speech sounds, right ear advantage for 385
Spinal cord 19
Split-brain
   consciousness and 161
   language production and 359–60
Spontaneous vivid imagery, Charles Bonnet syndrome 319–20
Spoonerisms 347
Spotlight of attention 122–3, 124
State-action space 430–33
State-dependent memory 575
Status quo bias 472
Steps in long-term memory 238
Stimulus onset asynchrony 186
Storage, memory and 178
Story mnemonic, memory training and 7
Strategies 14–15
Stroop effect 411–12
Structural imaging 25
Structure of long-term memory 226–8
Studying, effectiveness in 288–90, 291
Subject, language production and 340
Subjective probabilities 471
Subliminal perception 157
Summaries
   attention 148
   cognitive psychology 31–2
   concepts and imagery 321–2
   consciousness 174
   decision making 506–7
   emotion and cognition 583
   language comprehension 419
   language production 372
   learning and forgetting 291–2
   long-term memory 256
   motor cognition 112
   perception 80
   problem solving 462–3
   reasoning 546–7
   sensory, short-term and working memory 216–17
Super recognizers 77
Supraliminal primes, promotion of healthy eating with 159–60
Supraliminal stimuli 158–9
Surface dyslexia 417
Susceptibility of human memory 245–9
Syllabic scripts 405
Symbolic communication in non-human animals 334–5

Subject Index

Synaesthesia
  perception and 57–8
  sensory memory and 182–4
Synaesthete 182
Synectics 459
Syntactic context 397
Syntax
  language production and 326, 338, 339–41
  semantics and 400–403

T

Talent, problem solving and 449
Taxonomy of attention 118–19
Telegraphic speech 366–7
Temporal discounting and utility 472–4
Temporal lobe 19
Test-operate-test-exit (TOTE) unit 94–5
Testing grounded theory of concepts 310–11
Thalamus 19
Theories
  action representation, theories of 100–105
  appraisal theory 567
  associative chain theory 93
  of attention 120–26
    evaluation of 126
  attentional schema theory (AST) 168
  Bayesian decision theory 41
  Bower's associative network theory 575–6
  Canon-Bard theory 562–3
    evaluation of 563
  computational theory of perception 42
  Copernican heliocentric theory 6
  creative processes, information processing theory of 456–7
  depictive representation theory 317–18
  dynamical systems theory 87–8
  of emotion and cognition 560–70
  expected value theory 469–71
  feature integration theory (FIT) 128, 130
  filter theory of attention 121–2, 126
  global workspace theory 155
  grounded theory
    of concepts, testing of 310–11
    simulation and 308–9
  higher-order theories of consciousness 173
  ideomotor theory 100–101
  information processing theories
    creative processes 456–7
    insight and 443–8
  Integrated Information Theory (IIT) 166–7
  James-Lange theory 561–2, 563
    evaluation of 562
  Lazarus's theory 567–8
    evaluation of 568
  load theory 122
  multi-attribute utility theory (MAUT) 483–4, 500–501
  multi-level theories in emotion and cognition 568
  optimal control theory 88, 89–90, 92
    illustration of 89–90
  principles and theories of perception 39–43
  progress monitoring theory 444–8
  recurrent processing theory 165
  resource theory of attention 122–6
  Schachter-Singer two factor theory 563, 564–5
    evaluation of 564–5
  selective probability and prospect theory 475–7
  social contract theory 537–9
  social judgement theory (SJT), real-life choices and 501–4
  speech production
    interactive theories of 355–7
    modular theories of 351–5
  two-factor theory of emotion and cognition 564–5
  two-system theory and 'nudge' 488–9
  Zajonc's theory 565–6
    evaluation of 566
  see also Prospect theory
Theory-based approaches 304–5
  evaluation of 305
Thinking, problem solving and 424
Thought congruity 577
Thought experiments 307
Three-stage model of memory 179
Tip-of-the-tongue (TOT) effects 339
Tip-of-the-tongue (TOT) state 348–50
Tit-for-tat and force escalation 90–92
Tonal languages 331
Tonotopic map 53
Top-down influence
  on language comprehension 387–90
  on memory 179
Top-down processing
  attention 120
  language comprehension 383, 391
Torque 88
Tower of London tasks 435
Trace model of speech perception 393–5
  architecture of 394
  evaluation of 394–5
Training in reasoning 531–2
Transcranial direct current stimulation (tDCS) 23, 24, 27
  insight vs non-insight problem solving, neuroscience approach to 441
Transcranial magnetic stimulation (TMS) 23, 24, 27
  concepts and imagery 312
  consciousness and 173
  language production and 363–4
Transparent orthography 406
Traumatic events, memories of 242–3
Travelling salesperspn problems 436–8
Tunnel memory 574–5
Two-factor theory of emotion and cognition 564–5
Two-system approaches to decision making 487–91
  systems 1 and 2 488
  two-system theory and 'nudge' 488–9
Typicality 299
  typical populations, evidence from 363–4

U

UK postcode and cognitive psychology 4–5
Ultimatum Game 505
Unconscious processing 157–9
Unconscious thought and decision making 489–91
Unconscious thought effect (UTE) on decisions 490–91
Unconscious work, problem solving and 455–6
Understanding consciousness, problem of 152–3
Understanding speech 377–87
Understanding words and sentences 395–403
Universal Law of Gravitation 6
Utilitarianism 493
  deontological rules vs 496–9
Utility
  decision making and 471
  prospect theory and 471–4
  temporal discounting and 472–4

V

Vection, perception and 60
'Vegatative states,' neuroscientific methods to detect awareness in 29–30
Ventral attention network (VAN) 120
Ventral stream, perception and 46
Ventriloquism 58
Verbal fluency tasks in clinical settings 361–3
Verbal learning 226
Vervet monkey alarm calls 334–5
Vestibular sensation 45
Video game play in enhancing cognition and attention 127
Virtual reality (VR) 59
Visual attention 128–37
Visual cues 390
Visual field, language production and 357
Visual illusions, perception and 36
Visual object recognition 63–6
Visual search 128–32
  emotion, cognition and 572
  evaluation of 132
Visual system 46–51
  evaluation of 47–9
  primary visual cortex, pathways from eye into 48
  primary visual cortex, pathways out of 49
Visual word recognition, context effects on 410
Voice-sensitive brain regions 79
Voices, social perception of 78
Voicing 384
Volition and consciousness 169–70
  evaluation of 169–70

W

Wada test 360
Waking and dreaming thoughts, experience sampling of qualities of 10–11
Wallas's stage analysis 454
Wason's reversed 20 questions task 540–42
Water maze 13–14
Wechsler Memory Scale 222
Well defined problems 425
Wernicke-Gerschwind model of language production 358
Wernicke's aphasia
  language comprehension and 402, 403
  language production and 367–8
Wernicke's area 19
  language comprehension and 403
  language production and 358
When things go wrong
  alien hand syndrome 111
  amnesia 278–9
  'bad things come to those who do not wait ..' 474–5
  brain damage and decision making 582–3
  Capgras syndrome 73
  case of 'E.V.R.' 211–12
  case of 'H.M.' 220–23
  category-specific deficits and pathologies 306–7
  consolidation 278–9
  creativity and psychopathology 461–2
  cross-language manifestation of dyslexia 407–10
  cybersickness 59–60
  dyslexia, cross-language manifestation of 407–10
  emotional processing after frontal lobe injury 552–4
  facial expressions, psychopathic traits and recognition of emotion in 555–6
  frontal lobe injury, emotional processing after 552–4
  involuntary traumatic recollections, experiences of 244–5
  language comprehension in aphasia 386–7
  law and sleepwalking 154
  Madrid bombings and catching the right perpetrator 545–6

When things go wrong—*Cont.*
  magic, attention, misdirection and 146–8
  medical images, errors in interpretation of 129–30
  mental illness and reasoning 517–18
  motion sickness 59–60
  neuroscientific methods to detect awareness in 'vegetative states' 29–30
  out-of-body experience 171–2
  post-traumatic stress disorder (PTSD), suffering from 244–5
  psychopathic traits, facial expressions and 555–6
  psychopathology and creativity 461–2
  recovered memory controversy 282–3
  retrograde interference 278–9
  right prefrontal cortex damage and real-world planning 438–9
  sleepwalking and the law 154
  somatic markers, interoception and 582–3
  split brain 359–60
  spontaneous vivid imagery - Charles Bonnet syndrome 319–20
  synaesthesia and sensory memory 182–4
  'vegetative states,' neuroscientific methods to detect awareness in 29–30
  verbal fluency tasks in clinical settings 361–3
William's syndrome 328–9

Words
  closed-class words 396
  content words, language production and 326, 338
  language production and 339
  understanding meaning in 395–403
  word boundaries, cues to 381–2
  word naming tasks 396
  word stem completion task 231
  word superiority effect 410
Working memory (WM) 178, 192, 194–216
  attentional mechanisms in 137–41
  Baddeley's working memory model 197–214
    anarthria 198–9
    articulatory suppression, effects of 200
    capture errors 206
    central executive 197–8, 205–7
    coarticulation effects 200
    dysexecutive syndrome 207
    episodic buffer 198, 210–11
    evaluation of 212–14
    inner scribe 203
    inner speech 199
    irrelevant speech effect 200–201
    perseveration 207
    phonological loop 198–203
    phonological loop, functions of 202–3
    phonological similarity effect 202
    rehearsal 199
    schemas 206
    self-efficacy 214
    Stroop task 206–7
    utilization behaviour 207
    visual cache 203
    visuo-spatial sketchpad (VSSP) 198, 203–4, 205–6, 210
    Wisconsin Card Sorting Test 207
    word length effect 199–200
  cognitive lockup and 192–4
  driving performance and 196–7
  in insight vs non-insight problem solving 441–2
  mind wandering and 207–10
  self-efficacy and 214–16
Writing systems 405–7
Written language 330

X

X-ray computed tomography 25

Z

Zajonc's theory 565–6
  evaluation of 566
Zoom model of attention 123